Pocket Dictionary

Korean – English
English – Korean

Berlitz Publishing
Union, NJ · Munich · Singapore

Original edition edited by the Langenscheidt Editorial Staff

Compiled by LEXUS Ltd.

Neither the presence nor the absence of a designation
that any entered word constitutes a trademark should be regarded
as affecting the legal status of any trademark.

Berlitz Publishing
95 Progress Street
Union, NJ 07083
USA

Printed in Germany
ISBN 981-246-541-3

04 05 06 07 08 5. 4. 3. 2. 1.

Preface

Here is a new dictionary of English and Korean, a tool with some 40,000 references for those who work with the English and Korean languages at beginner's or intermediate level.

Focusing on modern usage, the dictionary offers coverage of everyday language, including vocabulary from areas such as computers and business.

The Korean in this dictionary is written both in Korean script and in a romanized pronunciation system - a specially modified version of McCune-Reischauer.

The two sides of this dictionary, the English-Korean and the Korean-English, are quite different in structure and purpose. The English-Korean is designed for productive usage, for self-expression in Korean. The Korean-English is a decoding dictionary, a dictionary to enable the native speaker of English to understand Korean.

Clarity of presentation has been a major objective. The editors have provided the means to enable you, the user of the dictionary, to get straight to the translation that fits a particular context of use. Is the *mouse* you need for your computer, for example, the same in Korean as the *mouse* you don't want in the house? Is *flimsy* referring to furniture the same in Korean as *flimsy* referring to an excuse? The English-Korean dictionary is rich in sense distinctions like this – and in translation options tied to specific, identified senses.

Grammatical or function words are treated in some detail, on both the English-Korean and the Korean-English sides. And a large number of idiomatic phrases are given to show how the two languages correspond in context.

All in all, this is a book full of information, which will, we hope, become a valuable part of your language toolkit.

Contents

How to use the dictionary

To get the most out of your dictionary you should understand how and where to find the information you need. Whether you are yourself writing a text in Korean or wanting to understand a text in Korean, the following pages should help.

1. How and where do I find a word?

1.1 English headwords. The English word list is arranged in alphabetical order.

Sometimes you might want to look up terms made up of two separate words, for example **antivirus program**, or hyphenated words, for example **absent-minded**. These words are treated as though they were a single word and their alphabetical ordering reflects this. Compound words like **bookseller**, **bookstall**, **bookstore** are also listed in alphabetical order.

The only exception to this strict alphabetical ordering is made for English phrasal verbs - words like ♦**go off**, ♦**go out**, ♦**go up**. These are positioned directly after their main verb (in this case **go**), rather than being scattered around in alphabetical positions.

1.2 Korean headwords. The Korean word list is arranged in English alphabetical order by being sorted on the romanization system. The Hangul romanization chart on pages 15-19 will help with this.

You will need to remember the following special points about the alphabetical ordering of the Hangul romanization system:

i)   ŏ and ŭ are each treated as separate vowels and are listed before o and u respectively

ii) words starting with ch' are listed after words starting with ch

iii) words starting with k' are listed after words starting with k

iv) words starting with p' are listed after words starting with p

v)   words starting with t' are listed after words starting with t

vi) when an apostrophe occurs within a word it is handled as coming after z, so, for example, a typical sequence is:

choripsshigŭi 조립식의 prefabricated
chorip tanwi 조립 단위 module
chorip'ada 조립하다 assemble, set up

vii) romanization can change according to the position of a Korean letter in a word. So, for example, the *p* in

ip 입 mouth

will become a *b* in

ibŭl tamulda 입을 다물다 clam up, keep silent

This means that some phrases in an entry may have a romanization that differs from the main headword. And some compound words may be listed at some distance from the headword.

The chart on pages 15-19 shows which letters are liable to these changes.

viii) Some commonly used phrases or expressions are entered in their alphabetical position rather than under the main term from which they are derived. For example:

majayo! 맞아요! that's it!, that's right!

will be found under maj... and not under

mat-tta 맞다 be right

ix) Some roman letters (including: b, d, g, j, r,) are not used to start words in the romanization system used in this dictionary. However, important suffixes or infixes may begin with some of these letters. These suffixes and infixes have been listed in a block at the end of the preceding letter of the roman alphabet. For example:

...dŏrado ...더라도 even though

is listed in a block at the end of letter C (since there is no letter D).

1.3 Running heads. If you are looking for an English or a Korean word you can use the **running heads** printed in bold in the top corner of each page. The running head on the left tells you the *first* headword on the left-hand page and the one on the right tells you the *last* headword on the right-hand page.

2. Swung dashes

2.1 A swung dash (~) replaces the entire headword when the headword is repeated within an entry:

> **sly** kyohwarhan 교활한; *on the ~* nam mollae saltchak 남 몰래 살짝

Here *on the ~* means *on the sly*.

2.2 When a headword changes form in an entry, for example if it is put in the past tense or in the plural, then the past tense or plural ending is added to the swung dash - but only if the rest of the word doesn't change:

> **fluster** *v/t* tanghwanghage hada 당황하게 하다; *get ~ed* tanghwanghada 당황하다

But:

> **horrify**: *I was horrified* ch'unggyŏktchŏgiŏssŏyo 충격적이었어요
>
> ◆**come back** toraoda 돌아오다; *it came back to me* tashi saenggangnassŏ 다시 생각났어

2.3 Headwords made up of two, or sometimes three, words are replaced by a single swung dash:

> ◆**hold on** *v/i* (*wait*) kidarida 기다리다; TELEC kkŭntchiank'o it-tta 끊지않고 있다; *now ~ a minute!* chamkkanman kidaryŏ poseyo! 잠깐만 기다려 보세요!
>
> ◆**come in on**: *~ a deal* kŏraee ch'amgahada 거래에 참가하다

3. What do the different typefaces mean?

3.1 All Korean and English headwords and the Arabic numerals differentiating English parts of speech appear in **bold**:

> **alcoholic 1** *n* alk'o-ol chungdoktcha 알코올 중독자 **2** *adj* alk'o-olssŏng-ŭi 알코올성의

3.2 *italics* are used for:

a) abbreviated grammatical labels: *adj, adv, v/i, v/t* etc

b) all the indicating words which are the signposts pointing to the correct translation for your needs

> **mailbox** (*in street*) uch'et'ong 우체통; (*of house*) up'yŏnham 우편함; COMPUT meilbakssŭ 메일박스

Thai 1 *adj* T'aegugŭi 태국의 **2** *n* (*person*) T'aegugin 태국인; (*language*) T'aegugŏ 태국어

serve 1 *n* (*in tennis*) sŏbŭ 서브 **2** *v/t food, meal* naeda 내다; *person, guests* shijungdŭlda 시중들다; *customer in shop* moshida 모시다; *one's country, the people* pongsahada 봉사하다

hwamulsshil 화물실 hold (*on ship, plane*)

yŏbo 여보 honey (*form of address to husband*)

3.3 All phrases (examples and idioms) are given in **secondary bold italics**:

ch'aegim 책임 responsibility; accountability; *...e ch'aegimi it-tta* ...에 책임이 있다 be responsible for

knowledge chishik 지식; *to the best of my ~* naega algo itkkironŭn 내가 알고 있기로는; *have a good ~ of* ...e chŏngt'onghada ...에 정통하다

3.4 Normal typeface is used for the translations.

3.5 If a translation is given in italics, and not in the normal typeface, this means that the translation is more of an *explanation* in the other language and that an explanation has to be given because there is no real equivalent:

walk-up *n* ellibeit'ŏga ŏmnŭn ap'at'ŭ 엘리베이터가 없는 아파트

kkakttugi 깍두기 *spicy, pickled white radish*

4. What do the various symbols and abbreviations tell you?

4.1 A solid black lozenge is used to indicate a phrasal verb:

♦ *auction* **off** kyŏngmaehada 경매하다

4.2 A white lozenge ◊ is used to divide up longer entries into more easily digested chunks of related bits of text:

a, an ◊ (*no equivalent in Korean*): *a book about Korea* Han-guge kwanhan ch'aek 한국에 관한 책; *he bought a car* kŭnŭn ch'arŭl sassŏyo 그는 차를 샀어요 ◊ (*with a measure word*) hanaŭi 하나의, han 한; *a cup of coffee* k'ŏp'i han chan 커피 한 잔; *five men and a woman* tasŏt namjawa han yŏja 다섯 남자와 한 여자 ◊ (*per*) han 한; *$50 a ride* han pŏne 50tallŏ 한 번에 50달러; *$15 a head* han saram tang 15tallŏ 한 사람 당 15달러

It is also used, in the Korean-English dictionary, to split translations within an entry when the part of speech of each translation is different:

kŭndae 근대 modern times ◊ modern

kŏmsa 검사 examination (*of patient*); prosecutor ◊ exploratory

4.3 The abbreviation F tells you that the word or phrase is used colloquially rather than in formal contexts. The abbreviation V warns you that a word or phrase is vulgar or taboo. Be careful how you use these words. The abbreviation H means that the word is used to make yourself humble before the person you are speaking to.

4.4 A colon before an English or Korean word or phrase means that usage is restricted to this specific example (at least as far as this dictionary's choice of vocabulary is concerned):

accord: *of one's own* ~ chabaltchŏgŭro 자발적으로

shisok 시속: *shisok 150mairŭi sokttoro* 시속 150마일의 속도로 at a speed of 150 mph

4.5 The letters X and Y are used to indicate insertion points for other words if you are building a complete sentence in Korean, for example:

glue 1 *n* p'ul 풀 **2** *v/t* p'ullo puch'ida 풀로 붙이다; *~ X to Y* Xŭl / rŭl Ye p'ullo puch'ida X을 / 를 Y에 풀로 붙이다

Suspension points (...) are used in a similar way:

◆ **major in** ...ŭl/rŭl chŏn-gonghada ...을 / 를 전공하다

5. Does the dictionary deal with grammar too?

5.1 All English headwords are given a part of speech label, unless, in normal modern English, the headword is only used as one part of speech and so no confusion or ambiguity is possible. In these cases no part of speech label is needed.

abolish p'yejihada 폐지하다

lastly majimagŭro 마지막으로

But:

glory *n* yŏnggwang 영광 (*n* given because 'glory' could be a verb)

own[1] *v/t* soyuhada 소유하다 (*v/t* given because 'own' is also an adjective)

5.2 Korean headwords are not given part of speech labels. Where their English translations are of more than one part of speech, these are separated by a white lozenge. For example:

>**Sŏyang** 서양 the West ◊ Western

5.3 Where a Korean word has a grammatical function, this is illustrated:

>**...nŭn** ...는 (*forms adjectives*): ***nurŏputtchiannŭn***
>눌어붙지 않는 nonstick

>**...rŭl** ...를 *object particle*

>**...get...** ...겠... shall (*indicates future tense, intention, or supposition*)

5.4 Particles

Particles such as **...rŭl** ...를, **...ŭl** ...을 or **...e** ...에 are included with translations in the English-Korean half of the dictionary:

>**correspond** ... **~ to** ...e haedanghada ...에 해당하다

>♦**count on** ...ege kidaeda ...에게 기대다

>**infer**: **~ X from Y** Yesŏ Xŭl / rŭl ch'uronhada Y에서
>X을 / 를 추론하다

This shows you the ending that is needed when you are building a sentence in Korean.

Some particle endings have more than one version. For example, **ŭl** is used after consonants and **rŭl** after vowels.

These particles are mostly omitted on the Korean-English side of the dictionary.

6. hada 하다

In the English-Korean dictionary an appropriate form of the verb **hada** 하다 'to do' is used to mark the insertion point for any verb that would be used in a real sentence. For example:

>**when...** 2 *conj* ...hal ttae ...할 때

>**about** ... **be ~ to ...** mak ...haryŏgo hada 막 ...하려고
>하다

can[1] ◊ (*ability*) ...hal su it-tta ...할 수 있다

These forms are used to show a general structure, which, in a particular example, may become, say:

> ***can you hear me?*** nae marŭl tŭrŭl su issŏyo? 내 말을 들을 수 있어요?

In the Korean-English part of the dictionary, the verb **hada** is removed in such cases and only the element which would be common to any verbal insertion is left:

> **ttae** ... *-l ttae* -ㄹ때 when

> **su** 수: *...l su it-tta* ...ㄹ 수 있다 can; *...l su ŏptta* ...ㄹ 수 없다 cannot

7. English adjectives and Korean descriptive verbs

In general the English-Korean dictionary will give an adjectival form that corresponds to an English adjective. For example:

> **pretty** yeppŭn 예쁜

In Korean these adjectives are formed from "descriptive verbs". The form of the descriptive verb that corresponds to an English adjective is made by adding **n** ㄴ to the verb stem:

> **yeppŭ** 예쁘 + ㄴ = 예쁜 pretty

Where in English "is pretty" is formed from the verb "be" + the adjective "pretty", in Korean it is formed by the single descriptive verb **yeppŭda** 예쁘다 be pretty.

> **that little girl is wearing a very pretty hat**
> chŏ chagŭn yŏja aiga aju yeppŭn mojarŭl ssŏssŏyo
> 저 작은 여자 아이가 아주 예쁜 모자를 썼어요

> **those flowers are really pretty**
> 저꽃이 참 예뻐요
> chŏ kkoch'i ch'am yeppŏyo

Korean personal pronouns

As a result of Confucian cultural influence on Korean society and language, personal pronouns and the way in which they are used in Korean reflect a concern for relative seniority and status. There is a large variety of forms of pronouns. The following table provides a basic outline (but is not exhaustive).

	I	you	she / he
plain	na / nae 나 / 내	nŏ / ne 너 / 네	i / kŭ / chŏ saram 이 / 그 / 저 사람
humble	chŏ / che 저 / 제		
honorific		sŏnsaeng(nim) 선생(님); tangshin 당신	i- / kŭ- / chŏ-bun 이 / 그 / 저분

	we	you	they
plain	uri 우리	nŏhŭi(dŭl) 너희(들)	i / kŭ / chŏ saramdŭl 이 / 그 / 저 사람들
humble	chŏhŭi(dŭl) 저희(들)		
honorific		sŏnsaeng(nim)dŭl 선생(님)들	i- / kŭ- / chŏ-bundŭl 이 / 그 / 저분들

I

When referring to oneself before equals and juniors the plain form **na** 나 may be used (**nae** 내 with the subject particle **ka** 가). When speaking to an older person or someone in seniority, the humble term **chŏ** 저 is used (**che** 제 with the subject particle **ka** 가).

You (singular)

The term **nŏ** 너 (**ne** 네 with the subject particle **ka** 가) may only be used by adults to young children, by older siblings to younger siblings or between intimate friends.

Although **tangshin** 당신 is considered a respectful form of you, its use is somewhat restricted and it should definitely not be used when speaking to older people. Koreans generally avoid using *you* when speaking to people with whom they are not familiar and address each other with appropriate titles such as **sŏnsaengnim** 선생님 (sir, a polite form), **ajŏsshi** 아저씨 (used to address men), **ajumma** 아줌마 (used to address women), **samonim** 사모님 (madam, a polite form), and so on. Actual job titles can also be used as a form of address together with the honorific ending **nim** 님. For instance you could address some-one as 'doctor, taxi-driver, professor, manager etc'.

She / he

These forms are not really simple pronouns but a combination of the demonstrative forms **i** 이 (this), **kŭ** 그 (that), and **chŏ** 저 (that over there) and the words **saram** 사람 (person) and **pun** 분 (*respectful* person). The terms **i** 이, **kŭ** 그, and **chŏ** 저 may also be used with other words such as **yŏja** 여자 (woman), **agasshi** 아가씨 (young lady), **ajŏsshi** 아저씨 (uncle) and so on to form alternative equivalents to *she/he* in English. They may also be used with the word **kŏt** 것 (thing) to form the de-monstrative pronouns *this*, *that*, and *that over there*. The terms **kŭnŭn** 그는 and **kŭnyŏnŭn** 그녀는 are also used in written Korean to indicate *he* and *she* respectively.

We

Korean also uses **uri** 우리 and derivatives where English uses *I* or *my* etc:

> **uri abŏji** 우리 아버지 my father (literally: our father)

This reflects the tendency for Koreans to emphasize the group over the individual.

You (plural)

The same as *you* (singular) with the addition of the plural suffix **-dŭl** 들. The same restrictions on usage also apply.

They

The same as *she/he* with the addition of the plural suffix **-dul** 들.

Finally, it is important to remember that, in Korean, the subject of a sentence is often omitted, providing that context removes any ambiguity.

Here are some examples of the use and omission of personal pronouns in Korean:

ŏdi kaseyo?
어디가세요
where are you going? (*you* omitted)

hak-kkyo-e kassŏyo
학교에 갔어요
I / he / she / we / they went to school (subject omitted)

ajŏsshi, naeil Sŏure kaseyo?
아저씨, 내일 서울에 가세요?
are you going to Seoul tomorrow? (ajŏsshi used in place of *you*)

nega haenni?
네가 했니?
did you do it? (adult to a child; *it* omitted)

kŭbuni osyŏssŏyo
그분이 오셨어요
he came (use of the honorific form, showing respect)

kwajangnim, k'ŏp'i han chan hashigessŏyo?
과장님, 커피 한 잔 하시겠어요?
would you like a cup of coffee? (kwajangnim is a common title for a department manager)

The pronunciation of Korean

Vowels

ㅏ	a	as in c*a*t
		longer as in f*a*ther when coming at the end of a word or when coming before a syllable that starts with a vowel or a *y* (eg: **ch'uk'ayŏn** 축하연)
ㅓ	ŏ	a short *o* sound as in f*au*lt or the British pronunciation of n*o*t
ㅗ	o	a longer *o* sound as in *o*we
ㅜ	u	as in d*o*
―	ŭ	a short sound as in heav*e*n
ㅣ	i	a short *i* as in t*i*n
		longer as in s*ee* when coming at the end of a word or when coming before a syllable starting with a vowel or a *y* (eg: **p'iano** 피아노)
ㅐ	ae	as in b*ear* or h*air*y but without any *r* sound
ㅔ	e	as in *e*delweiss
ㅑ	ya	as in *ya*m
		as in *ya*rd but without the *r* sound when it comes at the end of a word or before a vowel or before the letter *h*
ㅕ	yŏ	as in *Yo*rk but without the *r* sound
ㅛ	yo	as in *yo*del
ㅠ	yu	as in *you*
ㅒ	yae	as in *yea*h
ㅖ	ye	as in *Ya*le
ㅘ	wa	as in abatt*oir*
ㅙ	wae	as in *whe*re

ㅚ	oe	as in *way* but sometimes shorter as in *whe*n
ㅝ	wŏ	as in *wa*sh
ㅞ	we	as in *way*
ㅟ	wi	as in *wi*nd
		longer as in *wee* when coming at the end of a word or when coming before a syllable that starts with a vowel or a *y* (eg: **kwiyŏun** 귀여운)
ㅢ	ŭi	officially pronounced uh-ee; but Koreans often say this as in Y*a*le

Consonants

ㄱ at the start and the end of a word	k	강 kang 시작 shijak	between a *k* and a *g*
vowel + ㄱ + vowel	g	가구 kagu	
ㄴ, ㄹ, ㅁ, ㅇ + ㄱ + vowel	g	설계도 sŏlgyedo	
ㄴ	n	나 na	
ㄷ at the start and the end of a word	t	달 tal 곧 kot	between a *t* and a *d*
vowel + ㄷ + vowel	d	바둑 paduk	
ㄴ, ㄹ, ㅁ, ㅇ + ㄷ + vowel	d	날다 nalda	
ㄹ at the start of a word	l	라디오 ladio	for loan words, it is between an *l* and an *r*; we have used an *l*
at the end of a word	l	달 tal	
vowel + ㄹ + vowel	r	사랑 sarang	
ㄹ + consonant	l	물건 mulgŏn	
ㅁ	m	밤 pam	

→

ㅂ	at the start and the end of a word	p	보리 pori 밥 pap	between a *p* and a *b*
	vowel + ㅂ + vowel	b	아버지 abŏji	
	ㄴ, ㄹ, ㅁ, ㅇ + ㅂ + vowel	b	담배 tambae	
ㅅ		s	상표 sangp'yo	as in *s*aint
	ㅅ + ㅣ, ㅒ, ㅑ, ㅕ, ㅛ, ㅠ, ㅖ, ㅟ	sh	신 shin 섀시 shyaeshi 쉬다 shwida	
	at the end of a word	t	것 kŏt	
ㅇ	at the start of a word	silent	아버지 abŏji	a filler letter
	at the end of a word	ng	자랑 charang	as in you*ng*
ㅈ	at the start of a word	ch	자유 chayu	as in *j*ade but between a *ch* and a *j*
	at the end of a word	t	낮 nat	
	vowel + ㅈ + vowel	j	자주 chaju	
	ㄴ, ㄹ, ㅁ, ㅇ + ㅈ + vowel	j	반지 panji	
ㅊ		ch'	차 ch'a	as in *ch*urch but pronounced more strongly
	at the end of a word	t	닻 tat	
ㅋ		k'	코 k'o	as in *k*ing, but pronounced more strongly
	at the end of a word	k	부엌 puŏk	as in coo*k*

→

ㅌ		t'	타다 t'ada	as in *t*errace, but pronounced more strongly
	at the end of a word	t	논밭 nonbat	as in fla*t*
ㅍ		p'	파란 p'aran	as in *p*opstar, but pronounced more strongly
	at the end of a word	p	입 ip	as in hi*p*
ㅎ	at the start of a word	h	하늘 hanŭl	as in *h*ello

The four consonants ch', k', t' and p' (known as aspirated consonants) are pronounced with a stronger puff of breath than their basic equivalents (ch, k, t and p). If you hold your palm in front of your face when speaking these consonants you should be able to feel your breath.

Double consonants

These are also known as 'tense consonants'. They are pronounced with more force than their single equivalents.

ㄲ	kk	깨다 kkaeda	as in book *k*eeper
ㄸ	tt	때 ttae	as in hit *t*en
ㅃ	pp	빠른 (pparŭn)	as in top *p*eople
ㅆ	ss	쌀 (ssal)	as in those *s*ongs
ㅉ	tch	짜르다 (tcharŭda)	as in that *j*udge

General notes on the pronunciation system

Double vowels are each given their full value. So, for example, **p'yeam** is pronounced 'p'yay-am' and **uul** is pronounced 'oo-ool'.

g is always as in *g*ive, not as in *g*in
s is always as in loo*s*e, not as in lo*s*e

There is no stress in Korean, so give equal weight to all syllables.

What is written and what is said

There are many combinations of Korean consonants or of

vowels plus consonants that, taken together, create a sound that is not reflected in the actual Korean script. So, for example, in:

관점 **kwantchŏm** point of view
the letter ㅈ (ch/j) is actually pronounced ㅉ (tch)

맞다 **mat-tta** be right
the letter ㄷ (t) is actually pronounced ㄸ (tt)

고압선용 철탑 **koapssŏnnyong ch'ŏlt'ap** electricity pylon
the letter 용 (yong) is actually pronounced 농 (nyong)

학교 **hak-kkyo** school
the letter ㄱ (k/g) is actually pronounced ㄲ (kk)

괴롭히다 **koerop'ida** trouble
the letter ㅂ (p/b) is actually pronounced ㅍ (p')

괜찮다 **kwaench'ant'a** be OK, be alright
the letters 찮 (ch'an) and 다 (ta) are actually pronounced ch'ant'a

The romanization system used in this dictionary reflects this feature of Korean pronunciation.

Abbreviations

adj	adjective	MIL	military
adv	adverb	MOT	motoring
ANAT	anatomy	MUS	music
BIO	biology	*n*	noun
BOT	botany	NAUT	nautical
Br	British English	*pej*	pejorative
CHEM	chemistry	PHOT	photography
COM	commerce, business	PHYS	physics
		POL	politics
COMPUT	computers, IT term	*prep*	preposition
conj	conjunction	*pron*	pronoun
EDU	education	PSYCH	psychology
ELEC	electricity, electronics	RAD	radio
		RAIL	railroad
euph	euphemistic	REL	religion
F	familiar, colloquial	s.o.	someone
fig	figurative	SP	sports
FIN	financial	sth	something
fml	formal usage	TECH	technology
GRAM	grammar	TELEC	telecommunications
H	humble, showing humility to the listener	THEA	theatre
		TV	television
		V	vulgar
hum	humorous	*v/i*	intransitive verb
interj	interjection	*v/t*	transitive verb
LAW	law	→	see
MATH	mathematics	®	registered trademark
MED	medicine		

A

aak 아악 court music
aböji 아버지 father
ach'i 아치 arch
ach'im 아침 morning; breakfast;
 ach'ime 아침에 in the morning;
 ach'imŭl mŏktta 아침을 먹다 have
 breakfast
ach'ŏm 아첨 flattery
ach'ŏmhada 아첨하다 flatter, butter
 up
ach'ŏmhanŭn 아첨하는 flattering
ach'ŏmkkun 아첨꾼 flatterer;
 yesman
adamhan 아담한 compact; small
adongbok 아동복 children's clothes
adŭl 아들 son; boy
aech'ŏroun 애처로운 pathetic;
 touching
aedo 애도 condolences
aeguk-kka 애국가 national anthem
aeguksshim 애국심 patriotism
aeguktcha 애국자 patriot
aeguktchŏgin 애국적인 patriotic
aehoga 애호가 fan; devotee;
 connoisseur; *ch'a aehoga* 차
 애호가 avid tea drinker
aehohada 애호하다 be fond of
aein 애인 lover; sweetheart;
 boyfriend; girlfriend
aejijungjihada 애지중지하다 pamper
aejŏng 애정 affection, fondness
aejŏng-i innŭn 애정이 있는 loving
aek 액 fluid
aekch'e 액체 liquid
aekkŭlk'e hanŭn 애끓게 하는
 heartbreaking
aekssellŏreit'ŏ 액셀러레이터 gas,
 accelerator
aekssellŏreit'ŏ p'edal 액셀러레이터
 페달 gas pedal, accelerator
aektchŏng p'yoshi changch'i 액정
 표시 장치 LCD, liquid crystal
 display
aelbŏm 앨범 (photograph) album

aemaehan 애매한 evasive
aemaemohohan 애매모호한
 ambiguous; noncommittal
aemp'ŭ 앰프 amplifier
aemu 애무 caress
aemuhada 애무하다 caress; kiss; pet
aengk'ŏ 앵커 anchor man
aengmusae 앵무새 parrot
aengmyŏnkka 액면가 face value
aengmyŏn kŭmaek 액면 금액
 denomination FIN
aenimeishyŏn 애니메이션 animation
aep'ŭt'ŏ shyeibŭ loshyŏn 애프터
 셰이브 로션 aftershave
aep'ŭt'ŏ sŏbisŭ 애프터 서비스 after
 sales service
aerosahang 애로사항 bottleneck;
 logjam
aesŏk'ada 애석하다 be regrettable;
 ...dani aesŏk'agunyo ...다니
 애석하군요 it's a pity that ...
aessŭda 애쓰다 make an effort;
 *kŭnyŏnŭn ihaeharyŏgo aessŏt-
 tta* 그녀는 이해하려고 애썼다 she
 was struggling to understand; *...gi
 wihae mopsshi aessŭda* ...기 위해
 몹시 애쓰다 take great pains to ...
aet'age parada 애타게 바라다 long
 for; *muŏt hanŭn kŏsŭl aet'age
 parada* 무엇 하는 것을 애타게
 바라다 be longing to do sth
aet'ajŏgin 애타적인 altruistic
aet'onghan 애통한 tragic *voice*
aewandongmul 애완동물 pet
 (*animal*)
aeyong 애용 patronage, custom
agami 아가미 gill
agasshi 아가씨 ma'am; miss
 (*unmarried woman*)
agi 아기 baby
agŏ 악어 alligator; crocodile
agŭi 악의 ill will; malice
agŭiga ŏmnŭn 악의가 없는
 inoffensive

agüi innŭn 악의 있는 malevolent; malicious

agüi-ŏmnŭn kŏjinmal 악의없는 거짓말 white lie

agun 악운 bad luck; devil's own luck

agyong 악용 abuse

ahop 아홉 nine

ahop pŏntchaeŭi 아홉 번째의 ninth

ahŭn 아흔 ninety

ahŭn pŏntchaeŭi 아흔 번째의 nintieth

ai 아이 child, kid

aiemep'ŭ 아이엠에프 IMF

aik'on 아이콘 icon COMPUT

aik'yu 아이큐 IQ

Aillaendŭ 아일랜드 Ireland ◊ Irish

airainŏ 아이라이너 eyeliner

airisŭ 아이리스 iris BOT

airŏni 아이러니 irony

aishyaedou 아이섀도우 eyeshadow

aishyop'inghada 아이쇼핑하다 go window-shopping

aisŭ hak'i 아이스 하키 (ice) hockey

aisŭ k'eik'ŭ 아이스 케이크 Popsicle®, ice lolly

aisŭ k'ŏp'i 아이스 커피 iced coffee

aisŭ k'ŭrim 아이스 크림 ice cream

aisŭ k'ŭrim kage 아이스 크림 가게 ice-cream parlor

aisŭ pakssŭ 아이스 박스 icebox, refrigerator

ajaeng 아쟁 (seven-stringed) zither

ajang-ajang kŏt-tta 아장아장 걷다 toddle

...ajida ...아지다 become ..., get ...

ajik 아직 yet, so far; *kŭ saramŭn yŏgi wassŏyo? – ajik* 그 사람은 여기 왔어요? – 아직 is he here yet? – not yet

ajiktto 아직도 still, even now

ajirang-i 아지랑이 haze

ajŏsshi 아저씨 uncle (*friendly form of address for men who are not actually related*)

aju 아주 extremely, very; completely

aju chohŭn 아주 좋은 amazing, excellent

aju manŭn 아주 많은 a huge amount of

ajumma 아줌마 aunt (*friendly form of address for women who are not actually related*)

ajumoni 아주머니 *polite form of* **ajumma**

ak 악 evil; vice

akch'wi 악취 stench

akdan 악단 band, group

akkaptta 아깝다 be regrettable

akkida 아끼다 stint on, be mean with; hold dear; *noryŏgŭl akkiji ant'a* 노력을 아끼지 않다 be unstinting in one's efforts

ak-kki 악기 (musical) instrument

ak-kkiŭi ŭmŭl match'uda 악기의 음을 맞추다 tune up

akkyŏ ssŭda 아껴 쓰다 stretch, eke out

akppo 악보 sheet music, score

akssent'ŭ 악센트 accent, stress

akssŏng-ŭi 악성의 malignant *tumor*

akssu 악수 handshake

akssuhada 악수하다 shake hands

aktchang 악장 movement MUS

aktchŏn kot'u 악전 고투 struggle, hard time

akttang 악당 villain, scoundrel

ak'ada 악하다 be evil; be immoral

ak'wa 악화 decline, worsening

ak'wadoeda 악화되다 deteriorate; decline, get worse (*of health*)

ak'washik'ida 악화시키다 aggravate

al 알 egg

alda 알다 know; understand, see; appreciate, acknowledge; be aware of; *naega algo itkkironŭn* 내가 알고 있기로는 to the best of my knowledge; *naega al pa anida* 내가 알 바 아니다 for all I care; *naega alkke mwŏya!* 내가 알게 뭐야! I don't give a damn!; *naega anŭn han* 내가 아는 한 as far as I know; *naega anŭn paronŭn* 내가 아는 바로는 for all I know

algaeng-i 알갱이 grain (*of rice*); *chagŭn algaeng-i* 작은 알갱이 granule

algi shwiun 알기 쉬운 clear, lucid

alk'o-ol 알코올 alcohol

alk'o-ol chungdoktcha 알코올 중독자 alcoholic

alk'o-olssŏng-ŭi 알코올성의 alcoholic

alk'oori ŏmnŭn 알코올이 없는 nonalcoholic

allak 안락 comfort

allak'an 안락한 comfortable

allakssa 안락사 euthanasia

allakssa shik'ida 안락사 시키다 put away, put down *animal*

allak ŭija 안락 의자 armchair

allanggŏrinŭn 알랑거리는 slimy, smarmy

allerŭgi 알레르기 allergy; *...e allerŭgi panŭng-i it-tta* ...에 알레르기 반응이 있다 be allergic to

allibai 알리바이 alibi

allida 알리다 inform

allim 알림 announcement

alluminyum 알루미늄 aluminum

allyak 알약 tablet

allyŏjida 알려지다 break, become known

allyŏjin 알려진 noted

allyŏjuda 알려주다 inform; *Xege Yrŭl allyŏjuda* X에게 Y를 알려주다 inform X of Y

allyŏjum 알려줌 hint

almajŭn 알맞은 proper, fitting

almat-tta 알맞다 be proper, be fitting

almomŭi 알몸의 nude

alp'abesŭi 알파벳의 alphabetical

alp'abet 알파벳 alphabet

am 암 cancer

ama 아마 probably; perhaps

amach'uŏ 아마추어 layman; amateur

amado 아마도 perhaps, maybe; probably; presumably

amch'o 암초 reef

amdamhan 암담한 dark, grim

Amerik'a 아메리카 America ◊ American

Amerik'a Haptchungguk 아메리카 합중국 United States (of America)

Amerik'ain 아메리카인 American

amgihada 암기하다 memorize

amho 암호 password

amhŭk 암흑 darkness, blackness

amhŭk-kka 암흑가 underworld (*criminal*)

Amit'abul 아미타불 Amitabha Buddha

amk'ae 암캐 bitch (*dog*)

amk'ŏt 암컷 female (*animal, plant*)

ammal 암말 mare

ammŏri 앞머리 fringe (*hair*)

ammun 앞문 front door

amnae 암내 body odor

amnyang 암양 ewe

amnyŏgŭl kahada 압력을 가하다 pressure, force

amnyŏk 압력 pressure

amnyŏk tanch'e 압력 단체 pressure group, lobby

amnyu 압류 seizure, impounding

amnyuhada 압류하다 seize, impound

amnyuri 앞유리: (*chadongch'a*) *amnyuri* (자동차) 앞유리 windshield

amondŭ 아몬드 almond

amp'yosang 암표상 scalper

amsae 암새 hen (*of bird*)

amsal 암살 assassination

amsalbŏm 암살범 assassin

amsalttan 암살단 hit squad

amsan 암산 mental arithmetic

amsarhada 암살하다 assassinate

amshi 암시 pointer; hint

amshihada 암시하다 imply; point to; indicate

amshijang 암시장 black market

amso 암소 cow

amssasŭm 암사슴 doe

amt'ak 암닭 hen (*of chicken*)

amt'waeji 암퇘지 sow

amu 아무 any; none; anyone; so-and-so; *amu ch'yok'ollitto* 아무 쵸콜릿도 (+ *negative verb*) none of the chocolate; *amu kŏktchŏng ŏmnŭn* 아무 걱정 없는 carefree

amudo 아무도 (+ *negative verb*) nobody

amu ...do 아무 ...도 (+ *negative verb*) any ...at all; *amu saenggaktto ŏpsshi* 아무 생각도 없이 without any thought at all; *kŭnŭn amu yŏngojado ŏptta* 그는 아무 연고지도 없다 he doesn't have any family

amugae 아무개 so-and-so; any person

amugaemunja 아무개문자 wildcard character COMPUT

amu kŏt 아무 것 (+ *negative verb*) nothing, not any

amu kot 아무 곳 anywhere

amuri 아무리: *amuri k'ŭda* / *puyuhada hadŏrado* 아무리 크다 / 부유하다 하더라도 however big / rich they are

amurŏk'e 아무렇게 in whatever way

amurŏk'ena hanŭn 아무렇게나 하는 offhand

amurŏn 아무런 any; *amurŏn chuŭirŭl haji ant'a* 아무런 주의를 하지 않다 not take any notice of

amu ttae 아무 때 any time; *chŏnŭn amu ttaerado chossŭmnida* 저는 아무 때라도 좋습니다 any time is alright with me

amut'ŭn 아무튼 anyway

an 안 inside; *...(ŭ)ro anŭl taeda* ...(으)로 안을 대다 line with; insulate with

an... 안 ... (*negating particle*): *wae hak-kkyoe anwassŏyo?* 왜 학교에 안왔어요? why didn't you come to school?

anae 아내 wife

anaewŏn 안내원 tour operator

anallogŭ 아날로그 analog

ana ollida 안아 올리다 scoop up

anaunsŏ 아나운서 announcer

anbu 안부 (kind) regards; *Minaege anbu chŏnhae chuseyo* 민아에게 안부 전해주세요 give my regards to Mina

ando 안도 relief; *andoŭi hansumŭl shwida* 안도의 한숨을 쉬다 heave a sigh of relief

andwaetkkunyo! 안됐군요! what a pity!; *kŭ yŏjaga andwaetkkunyo* 그 여자가 안됐군요 I feel sorry for her

...ane ...안에 in; *tu shigan ane* 두 시간 안에 in two hours (from now)

anemone 아네모네 snowdrop

...anesŏ ...안에(서) in

an-gae 안개 fog

an-gae kkin 안개 낀 foggy; misty

anggap'ŭmŭl hada 앙갚음을 하다 pay back, get even with

angk'orŭ 앙코르 encore

angma 악마 devil, demon

angmong 악몽 nightmare

angmulda 악물다 clench

angmyŏng nop'ŭn 악명 높은 infamous, notorious

an-gwa ŭisa 안과 의사 ophthalmologist

an-gyŏng 안경 glasses

an-gyŏngsang 안경상 optician

anida 아니다 be not; no; *igŏshi anira chŏgŏt* 이것이 아니라 저것 not this one, that one; *usŭl iri anida* 웃을 일이 아니다 it's not funny

anihage nak-kkwanjŏgin saeng-gak 안이하게 낙관적인 생각 wishful thinking

anikkoun saram 아니꼬운 사람 creep, jerk

anin 아닌 no

anio 아니오 no

anjang 안장 saddle

anjŏlbujŏl mot'ada 안절부절 못하다 be in a flap; get the jitters; fidget

anjŏlbujŏl mot'anŭn 안절부절 못하는 jittery; uptight

anjŏn 안전 safety

anjŏnbelt'ŭ 안전벨트 safety belt

anjŏngdoeda 안정되다 stabilize, steady, become stable

anjŏngdoen 안정된 stable, balanced

anjŏngshik'ida 안정시키다 stabilize, steady, make stable

anjŏngssŏng 안정성 stability

anjŏn-gun 안전군 security forces

anjŏng yoppŏp 안정 요법 rest cure

anjŏnhada 안전하다 be safe; be secure

anjŏnhage 안전하게 safely

anjŏnhage hada 안전하게 하다 secure, make safe

anjŏnhaji anŭn 안전하지 않은 unsafe

anjŏnhan 안전한 safe, secure

anjŏn helmet 안전 헬멧 crash helmet

anjŏnp'in 안전핀 safety pin

anjŏnssŏng 안전성 safety, security

anjŏnŭl saenggak'anŭn 안전을 생각하는 safety-conscious

anjŏn usŏn 안전 우선 safety first

ankkam 안감 lining

anma 안마 massage

anmadang 안마당 courtyard

anmahada 안마하다 massage

anmasa 안마사 masseur; masseuse

anmogi nop'ŭn 안목이 높은

discerning
anmu 안무 choreography
anmuga 안무가 choreographer
annae 안내 directions, guidance
annaech'aektcha 안내책자 handbook
annaehada 안내하다 direct, guide
annaeja 안내자 guide; usher
annaesŏ 안내서 guide(book)
annae tesŭk'ŭ 안내 데스크 reception desk
annaewŏn 안내원 courier
annyŏng 안녕 hello, hi; goodbye, so long
annyŏnghaseyo 안녕하세요 good morning; good afternoon; good evening
annyŏnghi chumushipsshiyo 안녕히 주무십시요 good night
annyŏnghi chumusyŏssŏyo 안녕히 주무셨어요 good morning (on waking up)
annyŏnghi kaseyo 안녕히 가세요 goodbye (polite, to person leaving)
annyŏnghi kyeseyo 안녕히 계세요 goodbye (polite, to person staying)
anppang 안방 master bedroom; living room
ansaek 안색 coloring, complexion
anshikch'ŏ 안식처 haven
anshim 안심 peace of mind; relief
anshimhada 안심하다 feel easy; feel safe
anshimhanŭn 안심하는 secure
anshimshik'ida 안심시키다 reassure
anshingnyŏn 안식년 sabbatical
ansŏng match'umŭi 안성 맞춤의 tailor-made fig
antchŏgŭro 안쪽으로 inward
antchoge(sŏ) 안쪽에(서) in back, out the back
antchok 안쪽 inside, nearside
antchok kil 안쪽 길 inside lane
antchuin 안주인 hostess
antchumŏni 안주머니 inside pocket
antta 안다 hug
antta 앉다 sit, sit down; settle, alight
anttŭl 안뜰 courtyard, quadrangle
ant'a 않다 be not; do not; ...e ikssuk'aji ant'a ...에 익숙하지 않다 not be familiar with

ant'ena 안테나 antenna
anŭi 안의 internal
anŭk'an 아늑한 cozy, snug
anŭn ch'e hanŭn saram 아는 체 하는 사람 know-it-all
anŭro 안으로 inside, indoors ◊ into
ap 앞 front
apch'ukttoen 압축된 compact
apch'uk'ada 압축하다 compress; condense
appa 아빠 dad, pop
appak'ada 압박하다 oppress
appubun 앞부분 opening, beginning
app'in 압핀 thumbtack
ap sŏn 앞 선 advanced
apssŏ kada 앞서 가다 lead the way, lead
apssŭng 압승 landslide victory
apssuhada 압수하다 confiscate
aptchang sŏda 앞장 서다 lead on, go ahead
aptchehada 압제하다 tyrannize
aptchŏng 압정 tack
...aptchoge(sŏ) ...앞쪽에(서) before; in front of, at the front of
aptchogŭi 앞쪽의 front
aptchul 앞줄 front row
aptchwasŏk sŭnggaek 앞좌석 승객 front seat passenger
apttodanghada 압도당하다 dazzle; overwhelm
apttohada 압도하다 dominate; overwhelm
apttohanŭn 압도하는 devastating
apttwiro 앞뒤로 back and forth, to and fro
ap'ahada 아파하다 be in pain; ap'asŏ momŭl kuburida 아파서 몸을 구부리다 double up in pain; ap'ayo? 아파요? is it sore?; momi ap'ayo? 몸이 아파요? are you ill?
ap'at'ŭ 아파트 apartment
ap'at'ŭ tanji 아파트 단지 apartment block
ap'e 앞에 be ahead of
ap'e(sŏ) 앞에(서) in front; at the front
ap'i poiji annŭn 앞이 보이지 않는 blind corner
ap'ŭda 아프다 ache, hurt

Ap'ŭganisŭt'an 아프가니스탄
 Afghanistan ◊ Afghan
ap'ŭi 앞의 preceding
ap'ŭm 아픔 ache, pain; discomfort
ap'ŭn 아픈 sick; painful, sore
Ap'ŭrik'a 아프리카 Africa ◊
 African
Ap'ŭrik'a saram 아프리카 사람
 African
ap'ŭro 앞으로 forward; onward
arabia suttcha 아라비아 숫자 digit;
 Arabic numbers
Arabin 아랍인 Arab
Arabŏ 아랍어 Arabic (*language*)
araboda 알아보다 check; check out;
 recognize, identify
arabol su innŭn 알아볼 수 있는
 recognizable; discernible
arach'aeda 알아채다 notice; take
 note of; detect; sense; spot
arach'arida 알아차리다 perceive;
 become aware of; interpret
arae 아래 the lower part ◊ under,
 below
araech'ŭng-ŭi 아래층의 downstairs
araech'ung-e(sŏ) 아래층에(서)
 downstairs
...araee(sŏ) ...아래에(서) below,
 under; lower than
araetchogŭro 아래쪽으로 down,
 downward

araet saram 아랫 사람 subordinate
araet-tchoge(sŏ) 아랫쪽에(서)
 below
arae-ŭi 아래의 subordinate
aranaeda 알아내다 find out;
 identify
ara nuwŏ it-tta 앓아 누워 있다 be
 confined to one's bed
ara tŭt-tta 알아 듣다 catch, hear
Arŭhent'ina 아르헨티나 Argentina
 ◊ Argentinian
arŭmdaptta 아름답다 be beautiful
arŭmdaum 아름다움 beauty
arŭmdaun 아름다운 beautiful, lovely;
 fond *memories*
arŭn-gŏrida 아른거리다 shimmer
aryak 알약 pill
Ashia 아시아 Asia ◊ Asian
Ashiain 아시아인 Asian
asŭp'alt'ŭ 아스팔트 asphalt,
 pavement
asŭp'aragŏsŭ 아스파라거스
 asparagus
asŭp'irin 아스피린 aspirin
asurajang 아수라장 pandemonium
ausŏng 아우성 outcry
...aya handa ...아야 한다 have to,
 must; be bound to
...ayaman hada ...아야만 하다 have
 (got) to; should, must
ayŏn 아연 zinc

CH

cha 자 ruler
chaa 자아 self; ego
chabach'aeda 잡아채다 snatch; pull away
chabadangginŭn kori 잡아당기는 고리 ring-pull
chabaek 자백 confession
chabaek'ada 자백하다 confess
chabaltchŏgin 자발적인 spontaneous; voluntary
chabaltchŏgŭro 자발적으로 of one's own accord
chabamŏktta 잡아먹다 prey on, feed on; absorb
chabang 자방 ovary (of plant, flower)
chaba ppoptta 잡아 뽑다 pull up plant
chaba tanggida 잡아 당기다 pull; tug, haul
chaba t'ada 잡아 타다 catch bus etc
chabi 자비 mercy
chabiroun 자비로운 merciful
chabon 자본 capital, money
chabon chŭngga 자본 증가 capital growth
chabon-ga 자본가 capitalist
chabonjuŭi 자본주의 capitalism
chabonjuŭija 자본주의자 capitalist, believer in capitalism
chabonjuŭijŏk 자본주의적 capitalist
chabushim 자부심 ego, self-esteem
chach'aek 자책 remorse
chach'i 자치 autonomy
chach'wi 자취 mark, trace
chach'wi-rŭl kamch'uda 자취를 감추다 disappear, run away
chada 자다 sleep; drop (of wind)
chadong 자동 automatic movement; intransitivity ◊ automatic
chadong chŏmmyŏl changch'i 자동 점멸 장치 flasher, direction indicator
chadong chojong changch'i 자동

조종 장치 autopilot
chadongch'a 자동차 automobile; motor vehicle
chadongch'a haengnyŏl 자동차 행렬 motorcade
chadongch'a sanŏp 자동차 산업 automobile industry
chadongch'a suriso 자동차 수리소 garage (for repairs)
chadonghwa 자동화 automation
chadonghwahada 자동화하다 automate
chadongkigye 자동기계 automatic
chadong ondo chojŏl changch'i 자동 온도 조절 장치 thermostat
chadong p'anmaegi 자동 판매기 vending machine
chadongsa 자동사 intransitive verb
chadong sohwa changch'i 자동 소화 장치 sprinkler
chadong taech'e 자동 대체 banker's order
chadong-ŭngdapkki 자동응답기 answerphone
chadong-ŭro 자동으로 automatically
chadu 자두 plum
chae 재 ash; ashes
chaebaech'ihada 재배치하다 relocate
chaebaeyŏrhada 재배열하다 rearrange
chaebal 재발 relapse
chaebangmun 재방문 follow-up visit
chaebangsong 재방송 repeat, rerun
chaebarhada 재발하다 recur
chaebarhanŭn 재발하는 recurrent
chaebŏl 재벌 conglomerate
chaebongsa 재봉사 tailor
chaebongt'ŭl 재봉틀 sewing machine
chaebongt'ŭllo paktta 재봉틀로 박다 machine
chaech'aegi 재채기 sneeze
chaech'aegihada 재채기하다 sneeze

chaech'ep'ohada 재체포하다
recapture

chaech'i 재치 tact; wit; witticism

chaech'i innŭn 재치 있는 tactful;
quickwitted; witty

chaech'i innŭn mal 재치 있는 말
quip

chaech'i ŏmnŭn 재치 없는 tactless

chaech'ŏng 재청 encore

chaech'ok'ada 재촉하다 hurry up

chaeda 재다 take *temperature*

chaedan 재단 foundation,
organization

chaegae 재개 renewal

chaegaebarhada 재개발하다
redevelop

chaegaehada 재개하다 renew,
resume

chaegaejanghada 재개장하다
reopen

chaegal 재갈 gag; *chaegarŭl mullida* 재갈을 물리다 gag

chaegŏmt'o 재검토 review (*of
situation*)

chaegŏmt'ohada 재검토하다 review
situation

chaegŏnhada 재건하다 reconstruct

chaegŏrae 재거래 repeat business

chaego chŏngni seil 재고 정리 세일
clearance sale

chaegohada 재고하다 reconsider

chaego josa 재고 조사 stocktaking

chaegŭro mirŏ ollida 잭으로 밀어
올리다 jack up

chaegyoyuk kwajŏng 재교육 과정
refresher course

chaehae 재해 disaster

chaehae chiyŏk 재해 지역 disaster
area

Chaehŏnjŏl 재헌절 Constitution Day

chaehoe 재회 reunion

chaehoehada 재회하다 reunite

chaehonhada 재혼하다 remarry

chaehyŏnhada 재현하다 reproduce;
reconstruct *crime*; return (*of doubts
etc*)

chaeil kyop'o 재일 교포 Korean
resident in Japan

chaemi kyop'o 재미 교포 Korean
resident in the USA

chaejalgŏrida 재잘거리다 yap

chaejin 재진 follow-up visit

chaejŏng 재정 finance ◊ financial

chaejŏngga 재정가 financier

chaejŏngnihada 재정리하다
readjust; reschedule; rearrange

chaejŏgŭnghada 재적응하다
readjust (*to conditions*)

chaejŭ 재즈 jazz

chaeju nŏmkki 재주 넘기
somersault

chaeju nŏmtta 재주 넘다 somersault

chaejurŭl purida 재주를 부리다
juggle; deal with

chaek 잭 jack (*for car, in cards*)

chaek'it 재킷 jacket

chaem 잼 conserve; jelly

chaemi 재미 fun, amusement

chaemiinnŭn 재미있는 amusing,
entertaining; interesting

chaemiinnŭn saram 재미있는 사람
clown, joker

chaemi ŏmnŭn 재미없는
uninteresting

chaemiro 재미로 for fun, for kicks

chaemok 재목 lumber

Chaemubu 재무부 Ministry of
Finance

Chaemujanggwan 재무장관
Secretary of the Treasury

chaemujanghada 재무장하다 rearm

chaemul 재물 worldly goods

Chaemusŏng 재무성 Treasury
Department

chaengban 쟁반 tray

chaenggi 쟁기 plow

chaengtchŏm 쟁점 issue, matter

chaeng-ŭi 쟁의 dispute

chaenŭng 재능 flair, talent

chaenŭng-innŭn 재능있는 talented

chaeŏjida 재어지다 measure

chaeppalli 재빨리 quickly, swiftly

chaepparŭge tolda 재빠르게 돌다
spin around

chaepparŭn 재빠른 agile, nimble

chaepssage umjigida 잽싸게
움직이다 move quickly, zap along

chaep'an 재판 judgment LAW;
reprint; *Xŭl/rŭl chaep'ane kŏlda*
X을/를 재판에 걸다 take X to court

chaep'anhada 재판하다 judge; try
LAW; reprint

chaep'ojanghada 재포장하다
resurface
chaep'yŏnsŏng 재편성
reorganization
chaep'yŏnsŏnghada 재편성하다
reorganize
chaeryang 재량 discretion; *tang-shinŭi chaeryang-ŭro* 당신의 재량으로 at your discretion
chaeryo 재료 ingredient; material
chaesaeng 재생 replay, playback; reproduction
chaesaeng iyong 재생 이용
recycling
chaesaeng iyonghada 재생 이용하다 recycle
chaesaengshik 재생식
reproduction; breeding
chaesaengshik'ada 재생식하다
reproduce; breed
chaesaengshik'anŭn 재생식하는
reproductive
chaesan 재산 means; possessions; assets
chaesangyŏnghada 재상영하다
rerun
chaesan kwalli sangt'aee noyŏ it-tta 재산 관리 상태에 놓여 있다 be in receivership
chaesayonghada 재사용하다 reuse
chaesayong-i kanŭnghan 재사용이 가능한 reusable
chaeshihap 재시합 replay
chaeshihap'ada 재시합하다 replay
chaesuŏmnŭn saram 재수없는 사람
jinx (*person*)
chaesuŏpkkun! 재수없군! hard luck!
chaettŏri 재떨이 ashtray
chaet'onghap'ada 재통합하다
reunite
chaet'ujahada 재투자하다 reinvest, plow back
chaewŏjuda 재워주다 put up
chaewŏn 재원 financial resources
chaga chejak yŏnghwa 자가 제작 영화 home movie
chagae 자개 mother-of-pearl
chagae changshik 자개 장식
mother-of-pearl inlay
chagajida 작아지다 grow smaller; *chŏmjŏm chagajida* 점점 작아지다

dwindle
chagal 자갈 gravel; shingle; pebble; gravestone
chagayong unjŏnsa 자가용 운전사
chauffeur
chagi 자기 china (*pottery*); honey, darling; magnetism ◊ magnetic
chagi chabon 자기 자본 equity capital
chagi chashin 자기 자신 oneself
chagi chungshimŭi 자기 중심의
egocentric
chagi kŭrŭt 자기 그릇 china (*material*)
chagi manjok 자기 만족
complacency
chagi manjoktchŏgin 자기 만족적인
complacent
chagi maŭmdaerohada 자기 마음대로 하다 have one's (own) way
chagi pang-ŏ 자기 방어 self-defense
chagi ponwiŭi 자기 본위의 self-centered
chagi pulsshin 자기 불신 self-doubt
chagi sŏnjŏn-ga 자기 선전가
exhibitionist
chagi suyang 자기 수양 self-discipline
chagiya! 자기야! darling!
chagŏp inbu 작업 인부 workman
chagŏp kongjŏngdo 작업 공정도
flowchart
chagŏpsshil 작업실 studio
chagŏptchang 작업장 workshop
chagŏpttae 작업대 work bench
chagŏp yŏn-gu 작업 연구 work study
chagŭk 자극 spur, incentive
chagŭk'ada 자극하다 rouse, stimulate; spur on; arouse
chagŭk'anŭn 자극하는 provocative; controversial; pungent
chagŭktchŏgin 자극적인 electric *atmosphere*; stimulating; provocative, alluring; sharp *taste*
chagŭm 자금 fund
chagŭmahan 자그마한 diminutive; insignificant
chagŭm chiwŏnŭl hada 자금 지원을 하다 finance

chagŭm pujogŭro pullihan 자금 부족으로 불리한 underfunded

chagŭmsŏng 자금성 forbidden city

chagŭmŭl taeda 자금을 대다 bankroll

chagŭn 작은 little, small; low

chaguk 자국 mark, trace; one's own country; *chagugŭl naeda* 자국을 내다 mark, stain; *nullŏ tchigŭn chaguk* 눌러 찍은 자국 imprint

chagŭmnong 자급농 subsistence farmer

chagung 자궁 uterus, womb

chagung chŏkch'ulssul 자궁 적출술 hysterectomy

chagungam kŏmsa 자궁암 검사 cervical smear

chagungnada 자국나다 mark, become stained

chagyŏgi innŭn 자격이 있는 eligible

chagyŏgi ŏmnŭn 자격이 없는 ineligible; unqualified

chagyŏgŭl chuda 자격을 주다 entitle, qualify

chagyŏgŭl ŏt-tta 자격을 얻다 qualify

chagyŏk 자격 qualification; *...l chagyŏgi it-tta* ...ㄹ 자격이 있다 be qualified to ...; *tongdŭnghan / tarŭn chagyŏgida* 동등한 / 다른 자격이다 be on the same / a different footing

chagyŏktchŭng 자격증 certificate

chagyŏktchŭng-i innŭn 자격증이 있는 qualified

chagyong 작용 action; operation; function

chahoesa 자회사 subsidiary; wholly owned subsidiary

chainhada 자인하다 acknowledge, admit; *choerŭl chainhada* 죄를 자인하다 incriminate oneself

chainhanŭn 자인하는 self-confessed

chajangga 자장가 lullaby

chaje 자제 self-control

chajehada 자제하다 control oneself, restrain oneself

chajehanŭn 자제하는 lowkey

chajilgurehan changshin-gu 자질구레한 장신구 knick-knacks; trinket

chajinhaesŏ hada 자진해서 하다 volunteer

chajŏng 자정 midnight; *chajŏng-e* 자정에 at midnight

chajŏn-gŏ 자전거 bicycle

chajŏn-gŏ haendŭl 자전거 핸들 handlebars

chajŏn-gŏrŭl t'ada 자전거를 타다 bike; pedal

chajonshim 자존심 pride, self-respect

chajŭn 잦은 frequent

chaju 자주 often

chaju ch'at-tta 자주 찾다 frequent, visit

chaju onŭn 자주 오는 frequent

chajuppich'ŭi 자주빛의 purple

chak-kka 작가 writer; scriptwriter; author

chak-kkak'ada 착각하다 mistake, confuse

chak-kkok 작곡 composition

chak-kkok-kka 작곡가 composer

chak-kkok'ada 작곡하다 compose

chakppyŏl insa 작별 인사 parting greeting; *nuguege chakppyŏl insarŭl hada* 누구에게 작별 인사를 하다 say goodbye to s.o.

chakp'um 작품 work (*literary, artistic*)

chakssa chak-kkok-kka 작사 작곡가 songwriter

chakssaga 작사가 lyricist

chakssal 작살 harpoon

chakssihada 작시하다 rhyme

chakssŏnghada 작성하다 draw up, write; *ch'ogorŭl chakssŏnghada* 초고를 작성하다 draft

chaktchŏnghada 작정하다 decide, determine; *muŏsŭl haryŏgo chaktchŏnghada* 무엇을 하려고 작정하다 be intent on doing sth; *X hanŭn kŏsŭl chaktchŏnghada* X 하는 것을 작정하다 set out to do X

chaktchŏng-ida 작정이다 intend; *muŏsŭl hal chaktchŏng-ida* 무엇을 할 작정이다 intend to do sth

chaktchŏn kiji 작전 기지 base MIL

chaktta 작다 be small, be little

chakttonghada 작동하다 go, function; perform; engage, kick in

chakttong pullyang 작동 불량 malfunction

chakŭktche 자극제 stimulant

chak'uji 자쿠지 jacuzzi, whirlpool

chal 잘 well; nicely

chal allyŏjin 잘 알려진 well-known

chal anŭn 잘 아는 familiar

chal arajunŭn 잘 알아주는 sympathetic, understanding

chal cha 잘 자 good night (*informal*)

chal hada 잘 하다 do well; *na-ege marŭl chal haet-tta* 내게 말을 잘 했다 good thing you told me

chal igŭn 잘 익은 well-done *food*

chal ihaehada 잘 이해하다 sympathize with

chal ijŏbŏrinŭn 잘 잊어버리는 forgetful

chal it-tta 잘 있다 be well

chaljalmot 잘잘못 right and wrong

chal kakkuŏjin 잘 가꾸어진 in good condition

chal kŏnjodoen 잘 건조된 seasoned *wood*

challabŏrida 잘라버리다 slash

challanaeda 잘라내다 cut off

challan ch'ŏk'anŭn 잘난 척하는 pretentious

challanoŭn ppang 잘라놓은 빵 sliced bread

chal mandŭrŏjin 잘 만들어진 well-made

chal minnŭn 잘 믿는 credulous

chalmot 잘못 error; wrong ◊ wrongly; badly; *nŏŭi/naŭi chalmoshida* 너의/나의 잘못이다 it's your/my fault

chalmot chidodoen 잘못 지도된 misguided

chalmot chun 잘못 준 misplaced

chalmot ch'ŏltchahada 잘못 철자하다 misspell

chalmot haesŏk'ada 잘못 해석하다 misinterpret, misconstrue

chalmot iltta 잘못 읽다 misread

chalmot kŏllin chŏnhwa 잘못 걸린 전화 wrong number

chalmot kyesanhada 잘못 계산하다 miscalculate

chalmot match'uda 잘못 맞추다 mismatch

chalmot p'andanhada 잘못 판단하다 misjudge

chalmot saenggak'ada 잘못 생각하다 be under a misapprehension

chalmot sayonghada 잘못 사용하다 misuse

chalmot taruda 잘못 다루다 mishandle

chalmot-ttoeda 잘못되다 go wrong; *mwŏga chalmot twaennayo?* 뭐가 잘못 됐나요? is something wrong?

chalmot-ttoen 잘못된 wrong; unfortunate

chalmot-ttoen haesŏk 잘못된 해석 misinterpretation

chalmot-ttoen inswae 잘못된 인쇄 misprint

chalmot-ttoen unyŏng 잘못된 운영 mismanagement

chalmot unyŏnghada 잘못 운영하다 mismanage

chal nan ch'ehanŭn 잘 난 체하는 smug

chal padadŭrida 잘 받아들이다 be receptive to

chal saenggin 잘 생긴 good-looking

chal sagwida 잘 사귀다 cultivate *person*

chal salp'yŏboda 잘 살펴보다 study, examine

chal songnŭn 잘 속는 gullible

chal sonjildoen 잘 손질된 well groomed

chal tadŭmŏjin 잘 다듬어진 polished, accomplished

chal toeda 잘 되다 work, succeed; work out, be successful

chal tolbonŭn 잘 돌보는 caring

chal tolbwajunŭn 잘 돌봐주는 obliging

chal tolda 잘 돌다 negotiate

chal towajunŭn 잘 도와주는 supportive

chal ttaragada 잘 따라가다 stick to

cham 잠 sleep

chamae toshi 자매 도시 twin town

chamagŭl talda 자막을 달다 subtitle

chamak 자막 subtitle

chaman 자만 conceit

chamanhanŭn 자만하는 conceited

chamanshim 자만심 vanity
chambok'ada 잠복하다 lurk
chamdŭlda 잠들다 fall asleep
chamgida 잠기다 fasten
chamgŭda 잠그다 fasten; lock; turn off *faucet*
chamhaengssŏng-ŭi 잠행성의 insidious
chami kkaeda 잠이 깨다 wake (up)
chami tŭlda 잠이 들다 drop off; go to sleep
chamjaehada 잠재하다 lurk
chamjaejŏgin 잠재적인 potential, possible
chamjaejŏgŭro 잠재적으로 potentially
chamjaeryŏk 잠재력 potential, possibilities
chamjarie tŭlda 잠자리에 들다 go to bed
chamkkan 잠깐 a bit, a while
chamkkanmanyo 잠깐만요 just a second
chamkkan tong-anŭi 잠깐 동안의 fleeting
cham mot irunŭn 잠 못 이루는 sleepless
chamot 잠옷 pajamas; nightshirt; nightdress
chamot paji 잠옷 바지 pajama pants
chamot wit-ttori 잠옷 윗도리 pajama jacket
chamshi antta 잠시 앉다 perch, sit
chamshi chungdandoem 잠시 중단됨 lull, break
chamshidong-an 잠시동안 briefly
chamshi hu 잠시 후 a little later; *nanŭn chamshi hue kŏgi toch'ak'al kŏmnida* 나는 잠시 후에 거기 도착할 겁니다 I'll be there in a bit
chamshi mŏmum 잠시 머뭄 stopover
chamshi mŏmurŭda 잠시 머무르다 stop over
chamshinham 참신함 novelty
chamshi tong-an 잠시 동안 for a while, for a moment
chamsu 잠수 dive (*underwater*)
chamsubu 잠수부 diver, frogman
chamsuhada 잠수하다 dive,

submerge; go diving
chamsuham 잠수함 submarine
chamulssoe 자물쇠 bolt; lock
chamulssoe chejogong 자물쇠 제조공 locksmith
chamulssoeŭi pŏnho 자물쇠의 번호 combination (*of safe*)
chamyŏnghan 자명한 self-evident
chamyŏngjong shigye 자명종 시계 alarm clock
chan 잔 cup; tumbler; *... han chan* ...한 잔 a drink of; a glass of; a cup of
chanaegŭl ch'ogwahanŭn inch'ul 잔액을 초과하는 인출 overdraft
chanaekppoda tŏ inch'urhada 잔액보다 더 인출하다 have an overdraft; *...esŏ chanaekppoda tŏ inch'ulshik'ida* ...에서 잔액보다 더 인출시키다 overdraw
chanch'itssang 잔칫상 spread, meal
chandi 잔디 lawn; (piece of) turf
chandibat 잔디밭 turf, grass
chandi kkangnŭn kigye 잔디 깎는 기계 lawn mower
chandon 잔돈 change, loose change
chang 장 chief, head; sheet (*of paper*); chapter; scene (*in theater*); exposure (*on film*); copy; ice rink ◊ *countword for paper and thin flat objects*
chang-ae 장애 problem; disorder MED; hitch; hindrance; obstacle; burden
chang-aemul 장애물 stumbling-block; blockage; hurdle SP
chang-aemul kyŏnggi 장애물 경기 steeplechase (*athletics*)
chang-aemul kyŏngju 장애물 경주 hurdles
chang-aemul kyŏngjuja 장애물 경주자 hurdler
chang-aemul kyŏngjuma 장애물 경주마 jumper (*horse*)
chang-aemul ttwiŏnŏmkki 장애물 뛰어넘기 show jumping
chang-aeŏpsshi 장애없이 without a hitch
chang-ak'ada 장악하다 take over; *muŏsŭl chang-ak'ada* 무엇을 장악하다 tighten one's grip on sth

changbi 장비 equipment, plant; kit

changboda 장보다 do one's shopping

changbu 장부 accounts book; (real) man; *changburŭl sogida* 장부를 속이다 fiddle the accounts

changch'i 장치 apparatus, equipment; device; system

changgap 장갑 glove

changgapch'a 장갑차 armored vehicle

changgi 장기 Korean chess

changgijŏgin 장기적인 long-range; *changgijŏgŭro* 장기적으로 in the long term

changgiŭi 장기의 long-term

changgŏriŭi 장거리의 long-distance

changgo 장고 hourglass drum

changgun 장군 general MIL; checkmate

changgunp'ul 장군풀 rhubarb

changgwan 장관 minister, secretary; spectacle

changgwan-ŭi 장관의 ministerial

changgyo 장교 officer MIL

changhak-kkŭm 장학금 grant, scholarship

changhwa 장화 boot

chang-in 장인 craftsman; father-in-law

chang-in ŏrŭn 장인 어른 father-in-law

changjŏng 장정 binding; epic journey

changjŏngbon 장정본 hardback (*book*)

changjŏnhada 장전하다 load *gun*

changjo 장조 major MUS

changjogŭi paltchŏnŭl hada 장족의 발전을 하다 make great strides

changk'waehan 장쾌한 stirring

changma 장마 the rains

changmach'ŏl 장마철 rainy season

changmi 장미 rose

changmun 작문 composition, essay

changmyŏn 장면 scene

changnaesŏng ŏmnŭn chigŏp 장래성 없는 직업 dead-end job

changnaeŭi hŭimang 장래의 희망 expectations

changnan 장난 prank; *nuguege*

changnanjirŭl hada 누구에게 장난질을 하다 play a trick on s.o.; *chitkkujŭn changnan* 짓궂은 장난 practical joke

changnanch'ida 장난치다 fool around

changnankkam 장난감 toy

changnankkurŏgi 장난꾸러기 little rascal, cheeky child

Changno Kyohoe 장로 교회 Presbyterian Church

changnong 장롱 chest, box

changnyeshik 장례식 funeral

changnyŏhan 장려한 magnificent

changnyŏn ŏnjen-ga 작년 언젠가 sometime last year

chang-ŏ 장어 eel

chan-go 잔고 balance

chan-go chohoe 잔고 조회 bank statement

chan-goran 잔고란 debit

chan-gorane kiip'ada 잔고란에 기입하다 debit

chang pon mulgŏn 장 본 물건 shopping, purchases

changp'a 장파 long wave

changp'yŏn yŏnghwa 장편 영화 movie; feature

changsahada 장사하다 trade, do business

changshik 장식 decoration, decor

changshik-kka 장식가 painter

changshiktchang 장식장 cabinet

changshik'ada 장식하다 embellish, adorn

changshingnyong-ŭi 장식용의 ornamental

changshin-gu 장신구 accessory

changso 장소 place, spot; site; venue; room, space; *...ŭl/rŭl wihan changsoga ŏptta* ...을/를 위한 장소가 없다 there's no room for

changsshik 장식 décor

changsshikp'um 장식품 ornament

changsshik'ada 장식하다 decorate

changtchŏm 장점 merit, strength

changttae nop'i ttwigi 장대 높이 뛰기 polevault

changt'ip'usŭ 장티푸스 typhoid

chang-ŭisa 장의사 mortician

chanhae 잔해 wreck, wreckage

chaninhada 잔인하다 be cruel

chaninhage 잔인하게 brutally

chaninham 잔인함 cruelty; brutality; ferocity

chanmorae 잔모래 grit (for roads)

chansorihada 잔소리하다 go on at, nag

chansorihanǔn 잔소리하는 nagging

chanttǔk mǒktta 잔뜩 먹다 eat one's fill

chanyǒgǔm 잔여금 balance, remainder

chanyǒmul 잔여물 residue

chaoesǒn 자외선 ultraviolet rays

chapch'o 잡초 weed

chapkki 잡기 catch

chap-ppi 잡비 incidental expenses

chapssǒk 잡석 rubble

chaptchi 잡지 magazine, journal

chaptchong 잡종 hybrid

chaptchonggyǒn 잡종견 mongrel

chaptta 잡다 catch; seize; hold

chapttahan kǒttǔl 잡다한 것들 odds and ends, little jobs

chapttam 잡담 chat, small talk

chapttamhada 잡담하다 chat, gossip

chapttongsani 잡동사니 odds and ends; paraphernalia

chap'an 자판 dial, face

chap'an-gi 자판기 vending machine

chap'ojagishig-ǔi haengdong 자포자기식의 행동 an act of desperation

chap'yetchǔng-ǔi 자폐증의 autistic

charada 자라다 grow; *chal charada* 잘 자라다 flourish

charak 자락 patch (of fog)

charanada 자라나다 grow up

charang 자랑 pride

charanghada 자랑하다 boast

charang kǒri 자랑 거리 boast

charangsǔrǒpkke 자랑스럽게 proudly

charangsǔrǒptta 자랑스럽다 be proud

charangsǔrǒun 자랑스러운 proud

charhada 잘하다 be good at

charhan hǔngjǒng 잘한 흥정 bargain, good deal

chari 자리 place, seat; floor mat

charijaptta 자리잡다 settle down, calm down (in lifestyle)

charirǔl mandǔlda 자리를 만들다 move up, make room

charǒ kada 자러 가다 go to bed

charǔda 자르다 carve; cut

charǔgi 자르기 cut; carve *meat*

charu 자루 hilt; shaft ◊ *countword for pencils, brushes, pens, chalk, scissors, rifles etc*

charyo 자료 materials; data

chasal 자살 suicide

chasan 자산 asset

chasan sodǔksse 자산 소득세 capital gains tax

chasarhada 자살하다 commit suicide

chase 자세 position, posture

chasehada 자세하다 be detailed

chasehage 자세하게 in detail

chasehan chosa 철저한 조사 investigation, probe

chasehan naeyong 자세한 내용 detail

chasehi chosahada 자세히 조사하다 scrutinize, probe

chasehi poda 자세히 보다 peer; study, pore over

chashik 자식 offspring

chashin 자신 self-confidence; *chashinǔl ǒktchehal su ǒpkke toeda* 자신을 억제할 수 없게 되다 lose control of oneself, get angry, get upset

chashin innǔn 자신 있는 self-confident, self-assured

chashini nǒmch'yǒboinǔn 자신이 넘쳐보이는 flamboyant

chasǒjǒn 자서전 autobiography

chasǒk 자석 magnet

chasǒn 자선 charity; philanthropy

chasǒn-ga 자선가 philanthropist

chasǒnshimi manǔn 자선심이 많은 charitable

chasǒn tanch'e 자선 단체 charity (organization)

chasǒnǔi 자선의 charitable

chason 자손 descendant

chasonida 자손이다 be descended from

chasu 자수 embroidery

chasusǒnggahan saram 자수성가한 사람 self-made man

chattchip 찻집 tearoom
chattchujŏnja 찻주전자 teapot
chat'aek kŭnmu 자택 근무 work from home
chaŭishigi kanghan 자의식이 강한 self-conscious
chaŭm 자음 consonant
chawihada 자위하다 masturbate
chawŏn 자원 resource
chawŏn ipttaehada 자원 입대하다 enlist
chawŏnja 자원자 volunteer
chawŏn kogal 자원 고갈 a drain on resources
chawŏn pohoronja 자원 보호론자 conservationist
chayŏn 자연 nature
chayŏng-ŭi 자영의 self-employed
chayŏn kwahak 자연 과학 natural science
chayŏn kwahaktcha 자연 과학자 natural scientist
chayŏn pohogu 자연 보호구 nature reserve
chayŏnsa 자연사 natural death
chayŏn shikp'um 자연 식품 whole food
chayŏnsŭrŏpkke 자연스럽게 naturally
chayŏntchŏgin 자연적인 natural *death*
chayŏnŭi 자연의 natural *resources etc*
chayu 자유 freedom, liberty
chayujuŭiŭi 자유주의의 liberal
chayu kyeyagŭi 자유 계약의 freelance
chayuro 자유로 at liberty
chayurowajin 자유로와진 emancipated, liberated
chayu shijang kyŏngje 자유 시장 경제 free market economy
chayuŭi 자유의 free, at liberty
chayuŭi yŏshinsang 자유의 여신상 Statue of Liberty
che 제 my; *kŭ sŭt'eik'ŭnŭn che kŏshimnida* 그 스테이크는 제 것입니다 the steak is for me
chean 제안 approach, arrival; motion, proposal; suggestion
cheanhada 제안하다 advance,

propose, suggest; hold out, offer
cheap'ada 제압하다 restrain
chebal 제발 please, kindly
chebang 제방 river bank
chebi 제비 swallow
chebikkot 제비꽃 violet
chebinghada 제빙하다 de-ice
chebingje 제빙제 de-icer
chebi ppopkki 제비 뽑기 raffle, draw
chebirŭl ppoptta 제비를 뽑다 draw
chebok 제복 uniform
chebyŏng 제병 wafer
chech'oje 제초제 weedkiller
chech'uran 제출안 submission
chech'urhada 제출하다 bring in, introduce; hand in; send in; submit, lodge; *chŭnggŏrŭl chech'urhada* 증거를 제출하다 produce evidence
chedae 제대 discharge (*from the army*)
chedaero 제대로 properly
chedan 제단 altar
chedop'an 제도판 drawing board
chegihada 제기하다 raise, bring up *question*
chegirŏl 제기랄 damn!
chegŏ 제거 removal, elimination
chegŏhada 제거하다 eliminate, root out
chegong 제공 offer
chegonghada 제공하다 offer, provide; *chinael kosŭl chegong-hada* 지낼 곳을 제공하다 accommodate
chegop 제곱 square MATH
chegopkkŭn 제곱근 square root
chegugŭi 제국의 imperial
cheguk 제국 empire
cheguryŏk 제구력 control
chegwajŏm 제과점 confectioner's
chehada 제하다 allow; calculate
chehan 제한 restriction; qualification
chehandoen 제한된 confined *space*; qualified, limited
chehan-guyŏk 제한구역 restricted area
chehanhada 제한하다 confine, restrict; qualify
chehan pŏmwi 제한 범위 parameter

chehan shigan 제한 시간 time limit

che himŭro kkuryŏnagada 제 힘으로 꾸려나가다 fend for oneself

che himŭro ŏdŭn 제 힘으로 얻은 well-earned

cheil 제일 best

cheil choahanŭn 제일 좋아하는 favorite

cheja 제자 disciple

chejae 제재 sanction, penalty

chejak 제작 production

chejaktcha 제작자 producer

chejak'ada 제작하다 produce

chejarie tollyŏnot'a 제자리에 돌려놓다 put back, replace

chejŏnghada 제정하다 enact *law*; legislate

chejŏngshin 제정신 sanity

chejŏngshinŭi 제정신의 sane, lucid

chejŏngshinŭl ilt'a 제정신을 잃다 go insane; be beside oneself

chejohada 제조하다 manufacture

chejoŏp 제조업 manufacture; manufacturing

chejoŏptcha 제조업자 manufacturer

chel 젤 gel

chemŏt-ttaeroin 제멋대로인 wanton; wayward

chemok 제목 title, name; ...(*i*)*ranŭn chemogŭi* ...(이)라는 제목의 entitled, called; *chagŭn chemok* 작은 제목 subheading

chemot-ttaero nolda 제멋대로 놀다 run wild

chemoyongp'um 제모용품 hair remover

chemul 제물 sacrifice

chemyŏngshik'ida 제명시키다 drop

chenjang! 젠장! damn it!

cheŏ 제어 control

cheŏban 제어반 control panel

cheŏhada 제어하다 bring under control

cheoehada 제외하다 eliminate, rule out; exclude, leave out

cheoehago 제외하고 aside from, except for; excluding

cheoeshik'ida 제외시키다 leave out; *chŏnŭn i iresŏ cheoeshik'yŏ chushipssshio* 저는 이 일에서 제외시켜 주십시오 leave me out of this

cheppang-ŏptcha 제빵업자 baker

chep'um 제품 product; goods; wares

chero sŏngjang 제로 성장 zero growth

chesa 제사 ancestral rite

Chesam Segye 제3 세계 Third World

cheshigane 제시간에 promptly, on time; *cheshigan ane hada* 제시간 안에 하다 make it, get there on time

cheshihada 제시 하다 put in *request*

chesŏlgi 제설기 snowplow

chet'ŭ enjin 제트 엔진 jet engine

chet'ŭgi 제트기 jet

cheŭi 제의 proposition

cheŭihada 제의하다 make overtures to

chewang chŏlgae 제왕 절개 Cesarean section

cheyagŭi 제약의 pharmaceutical

cheyak 제약 pharmaceuticals

chiap 지압 acupressure massage

chibae 지배 control; domination

chibaehada 지배하다 control, be in control of; dominate

chibaehanŭn 지배하는 ruling

chibaein 지배인 manager

chibaejŏgin 지배적인 domineering

chibaejŏk ikkwŏn 지배적 이권 controlling interest

chibang 지방 region; province; fat (*on meat*) ◊ regional; local

chibang chach'i 지방 자치 local government

chibang-i manŭn 지방이 많은 fatty

chibang kŏmsa 지방 검사 DA, district attorney

chibang punkkwŏnhwa hada 지방 분권화 하다 decentralize

chibang saram 지방 사람 local; inhabitant

chibang t'ŭkssanmul 지방 특산물 local produce

chiban il 집안 일 chore; housework

chibe 집에 home, at home

chibesŏ mandŭn 집에서 만든 homemade

chibŏdŭlda 집어들다 hold

chibŏmnŭn 집없는 homeless

chibŏ nŏt'a 집어 넣다 get in; store;

fit in

chibŏ tŭlda 집어 들다 pick up

chibu 지부 branch, chapter

chibul 지불 payment, settlement

chibul nŭngnyŏgi innŭn 지불 능력이 있는 solvent

chibul ponggŭp ch'ongaek 지불 봉급 총액 payroll

chibul pullŭng-ŭi 지불 불능의 insolvent

chibung 지붕 roof

chibung kkokttaegi 지붕 꼭대기 ridge (*of roof*)

chiburhada 지불하다 pay, pay up, settle

chiburin 지불인 payer

chibyohan 집요한 persistent

chich'e 지체 delay, holdup

chich'ehada 지체하다 delay, wait

chich'eshik'ida 지체시키다 detain, delay

chich'ida 지치다 tire, flag

chich'ige hada 지치게 하다 tire, wear out, exhaust

chich'ige hanŭn 지치게 하는 tiring, exhausting, wearing

chich'il chul morŭnŭn 지칠 줄 모르는 tireless, inexhaustible

chich'im 지침 pointer; guidelines

chich'in 지친 run-down, worn out, pooped

chich'ul 지출 expenditure

chida 지다 lose; get a beating; go down (*of sun*); be out (*of sun, flower*)

chidae 지대 zone

chido 지도 map; leadership

chidoch'aek 지도책 atlas

chidoja 지도자 leader; mastermind

chidoja sŏn-gŏ hoeŭi 지도자 선거 회의 leadership contest

chidok'ada 지독하다 be vicious; be terrible; be tough

chidok'age 지독하게 terribly, atrociously; viciously

chidoryŏk 지도력 leadership skills

chigagi innŭn 지각이 있는 conscious, aware

chigak 지각 awareness; insight

chigak'ada 지각하다 be delayed

chigap 지갑 billfold, pocketbook

chigech'a 지게차 forklift truck

chigŏptchŏgin 직업적인 professional

chigŏp 직업 employment; job; profession; trade

chigŏp annaeso 직업 안내소 employment agency

chigŏp manjokto 직업 만족도 job satisfaction

chigŏpssang-ŭi 직업상의 vocational

chigohan 지고한 lofty, high

chigo it-tta 지고 있다 be behind

chigŭjaegŭhyŏng 지그재그형 zigzag

chigŭjaegŭro umjigida 지그재그로 움직이다 zigzag

chigŭjaegŭshigŭi 지그재그식의 erratic

chigŭlgŏrida 지글거리다 sizzle

chigŭm 지금 now, currently, at present; *paro chigŭm* 바로 지금 right now

chigŭmbut'ŏ 지금부터 from now on

chigŭmkkaji 지금까지 ever; yet; so far

chigŭmtchŭm 지금쯤 by now

chigŭmŭi 지금의 current

chigŭmŭn 지금은 at the moment

chigŭp'ada 지급하다 issue

chigu 지구 earth; globe

chigubon 지구본 globe

chiguin 지구인 inhabitant of earth

chiguryŏk 지구력 endurance

chigwŏn 직원 attendant; staff; personnel

chigyŏng 지경 boundary; verge; ...ㄹ 지경이다 *...l chigyŏng-ida* be on the verge of

chigyŏwŏhada 지겨워하다 loathe

chiha 지하 underground

chiha ch'anggo 지하 창고 vault, cellar

chihach'ŏl 지하철 subway RAIL

chihach'ŭng 지하층 basement

chihado 지하도 underpass

chihaesŏ 지하에서 underground

chihashil 지하실 cellar, basement

chihasumyŏn 지하 수면 waterline

chiha undong 지하 운동 underground activities

chihwihada 지휘하다 conduct MUS

chihwija 지휘자 conductor

chihye 지혜 wisdom

chihyŏng 지형 terrain
chijang-ŭl pat-tta 지장을 받다 suffer
chiji 지지 support, backing
chijida 지지다 fry
chijihada 지지하다 support; endorse; confirm, stand by
chijija 지지자 supporter, follower; following
chijil 지질 geology (of area) ◊ geological
chijin 지진 earthquake
chijinhak 지진학 seismology
chijirhak 지질학 geology (subject)
chijirhaktcha 지질학자 geologist
chijirhaktchŏk 지질학적 geological
chijŏbunhada 지저분하다 be messy; be filthy
chijŏbunham 지저분함 disorder, untidiness
chijŏgwida 지저귀다 chirp; twitter
chijŏk'ada 지적하다 point out
chijŏm 지점 branch
chijŏmjang 지점장 branch manager; *ŭnhaeng chijŏmjang* 은행 지점장 bank manager
chijŏnghada 지정하다 designate
chiju 지주 land owner
chik kangha 직 강하 plummet
chik-kkagŭro 직각으로 at right-angles to
chik-kkak 직각 right-angle
chik-kkwan 직관 intuition
chik-kkyŏng 직경 diameter
chikssagak'yŏng 직사각형 rectangle
chikssa kŏriesŏ 직사 거리에서 at point-blank range
chiktchang-e it-tta 직장에 있다 be at work
chiktchŏp 직접 in person, personally
chiktchŏptchŏgin 직접적인 direct
chiktchŏptchogŭro 직접적으로 firsthand ◊ at first hand
chik'aeng pihaenggi 직행 비행기 through flight
chik'aeng-ŭi 직행의 direct, nonstop
chik'aeng-ŭro 직행으로 nonstop
chik'aeng yŏlch'a 직행 열차 through train
chik'am 직함 title, form of address
chik'ang 직항 direct flight
chik'ida 지키다 defend; keep to;

guard; keep *promise*
chik'yŏboda 지켜보다 watch; monitor; keep an eye on, look after
chil 질 vagina
chilbyŏng 질병 disease
chilch'aek'ada 질책하다 rebuke
chilch'ŏk'an 질척한 slimey
chilgin 질긴 stout; tough
chilgŏp'age hada 질겁하게 하다 appall
chiljil kkŭlda 질질 끌다 drag on
chillajŭn 닳낮은 mediocre
chillida 질리다 be fed up with
chillin 질린 fed up
chillo 진로 path
chillyobi 진료비 fee
chillyo kwajŏng 진료 과정 course of treatment
chillyoso 진료소 clinic; infirmary
chilmŏjida 짊어지다 hump; shoulder *burden*
chilmun 질문 question
chilmunhada 질문하다 ask; question
chilmunsŏ 질문서 questionnaire
chilso 질소 nitrogen
chilsshik 질식 suffocation
chilsshik shik'ida 질식 시키다 smother; suffocate
chiltchu 질주 sprint
chiltchuhada 질주하다 race, sprint; tear; gallop
chilt'u 질투 jealousy
chilt'uhada 질투하다 be jealous; be jealous of
chilt'uhanŭn 질투하는 jealous
chilt'ushim 질투심 jealousy
chim 짐 load, burden; belongings; *chim kkurida* 짐 꾸리다 pack
chimjak'ada 짐작하다 suspect
chimmach'a 짐마차 cart
chimsŭng 짐승 beast
chimun 지문 fingerprint
chimyŏng subaedoen 지명 수배된 wanted
chin 진 gin; resin
chinach'ida 지나치다 exceed, overdo
chinach'ige 지나치게 overly; unduly
chinach'ige pohohada 지나치게 보호하다 overprotect
chinach'ige sŏlch'inŭn 지나치게 설치는 hyperactive

chinach'in 지나친 drastic, excessive, undue

chinach'yŏ kada 지나쳐 가다 turn away

chinaeda 지내다 celebrate; get along, progress; *yojŭm musŭn irŭl hamyŏ chinaeshimnikka?* 요즘 무슨 일을 하며 지내십니까? what are you up to these days?

chinagada 지나가다 pass; pass by, go by; get on; *ttwiŏsŏ / kŏrŏsŏ chinagada* 뛰어서 / 걸어서 지나가다 run / walk past

chinan myŏch'il 지난 며칠 the past few days

chinan pŏne 지난 번에 last time

chinap 진압 repression

chinap'ada 진압하다 suppress, put down

chinasŏ 지나서 beyond; past, by

chinbo 진보 advance

chinbohada 진보하다 advance, progress

chinbojŏgin 진보적인 progressive

chinbuhan 진부한 trite; corny; stale *news*; ready-made *solution*

chinch'arhada 진찰하다 examine

chinch'ŏkttoeda 진척되다 get on, make progress

chinch'ul 진출 penetration

chinch'urhada 진출하다 penetrate; *uri t'imŭn chun-gyŏlssŭngjŏne chinch'urhaet-tta* 우리 팀은 준결승전에 진출했다 our team has gotten through to the semi-final

chinch'wijŏgin 진취적인 enterprising, dynamic, go-ahead

chinch'wijŏk kisang 진취적 기상 enterprise, initiative

chindansŏ 진단서 medical certificate

chindo 진도 rate

chindoga nagada 진도가 나가다 progress

chindong 진동 vibration

chindonghada 진동하다 pulsate; rock

ching 징 gong

chingbyŏng 징병 draft MIL

chingbyŏnghada 징병하다 draft MIL

chingbyŏng kip'ija 징병 기피자 draft dodger

chinggyehada 징계하다 discipline

chinggyeŭi 징계의 disciplinary

chin-gihan 진기한 rare

chingjip-ppyŏng 징집병 draftee

chingmul 직물 fabric, textile; texture

chingmu naeyong sŏlmyŏngsŏ 직무 내용 설명서 job description

chingmurŏp 직물업 textile business; textiles

chingmyŏnhada 직면하다 face

chingnŭng 직능 function

chingnyu 직류 direct current

chin-gong 진공 vacuum

chin-gong ch'ŏngsogi 진공 청소기 vacuum cleaner

chin-gonggwan 진공관 vacuum flask

chin-gongp'ojang-ŭi 진공포장의 vacuum-packed

chingse 징세 taxation

chingsuhada 징수하다 levy

chinhaeng 진행 progress

chinhaeng chung-ida 진행 중이다 be under way

chinhaengdoeda 진행되다 proceed; progress; come along

chinhaenghada 진행하다 advance, go on; front TV

chinhaenghanŭn 진행하는 progressive

chinhan 진한 dark; deep *color*; strong *tea etc*

chinhongsaegŭi 진홍색의 crimson

chinhŭk 진흙 clay; mud

chinhŭkt'usŏng-iŭi 진흙투성이의 muddy

chinhwa 진화 evolution

chinhwahada 진화하다 evolve

chinida 지니다 assume

chinigo tanida 지니고 다니다 carry around

chinimno 진입로 access road

chinji 진지 position

chinjihage 진지하게 in earnest; *nugurŭl chinjihage saenggak'ada* 누구를 진지하게 생각하다 take s.o. seriously

chinjihan 진지한 earnest, serious

chinjŏlmŏri nanŭn 진절머리 나는 disgusting, repulsive

chinjŏng 진정 lull

chinjŏngdoeda 진정되다 quieten down

chinjŏngje 진정제 sedative, tranquilizer

chinjŏngshik'ida 진정시키다 control; pacify; soothe; defuse; keep down *costs*

chinjŏngŭro 진정으로 seriously

chinjŏ piŏ 진저 비어 gingerbeer

chinju 진주 pearl

chinmi 진미 delicacy

chinp'um 진품 rarity

chinshil 진실 truth

chinshillo 진실로 truly; sincerely

chinshimiya 진심이야 I'm serious

chinshimŭi 진심의 whole-hearted

chinshimŭro 진심으로 sincerely

chinshirhada 진실하다 be truthful, be sincere

chinshirŭl iptchŭnghada 진실을 입증하다 vindicate

chinsu 진수 launch

chinsuhada 진수하다 launch

chinsul 진술 statement

chinsushik 진수식 launch ceremony

chinsusŏn 진수선 launch

chintcha 진짜 the real thing ◊ authentic, genuine; original; real; truthful

chint'ang surŭl mashida 진탕 술을 마시다 go on a bender

chint'oeyangnan 진퇴양난 dilemma; deadlock

chint'ongje 진통제 painkiller

chint'onik 진토닉 gin and tonic

chinŭng 지능 intelligence, brains

chinŭrŏmi 지느러미 fin

chinwŏnji 진원지 epicenter

chinyŏl 진열 display; *chinyŏldoen* 진열된 in the window

chinyŏltchang 진열장 display cabinet

chinyŏltttae 진열대 stall

chinyŏrhada 진열하다 display, lay out

chiŏnaen iyagi 지어낸 이야기 story

chiok 지옥 hell

chip 집 home; house; collection (*of writings*); straw

chipch'ak'ada 집착하다 cling to

chipkke 집게 tongs

chipkkebal 집게발 pincers

chipkke sonkkarak 집게 손가락 forefinger, index finger

chipkkwŏnhanŭn 집권하는 in power

chipkkyŏltchi 집결지 rendez-vous

chipp'iltcha 집필자 author

chipsaram 집사람 wife

chipsshi 집시 gipsy

chiptchŏk hoero 집적 회로 integrated circuit

chiptchung 집중 concentration

chiptchunghada 집중하다 concentrate

chiptchungjŏgin 집중적인 intensive

chiptchung kangjwa 집중 강좌 crash course

chiptchung kyŏrŭihada 집중 결의하다 centralize

chiptchung k'osŭ 집중 코스 intensive course

chiptchung sagyŏk 집중 사격 burst

chiptchungshik'ida 집중시키다 concentrate

chiptchuso 집주소 home address

chipttan 집단 circle, set, group

chipttanjŏgin 집단적인 collective

chipttan p'ok'aeng-ŭl kahada 집단 폭행을 가하다 lynch

chipttŭri 집들이 housewarming

chip'aeng yuye 집행 유예 probation; reprieve

chip'ang-i 지팡이 walking stick

chip'ap 집합 set MATH

chip'atchang 집하장 terminal

chip'apch'e 집합체 complex

chip'ŏ 지퍼 zipper

chip'ŏrŭl chamgŭda 지퍼를 잠그다 zip up

chip'ŏrŭl yŏlda 지퍼를 열다 unzip

chip'oe 집회 congregation REL

chip'ŭch'a 지프차 jeep

chip'ye 지폐 (bank) bill

chip'yŏngsŏn 지평선 horizon

chip'yo 지표 barometer *fig*

chirado 지라도: ...*l chirado* ...ㄹ 지라도 while; although; even though

chire 지레 lever

chirhwan 질환 condition MED

chiri 지리 geography

chirijŏk 지리적 geographical

chirimyŏllŏrhan 지리멸렬한 scrappy
chiroe 지뢰 mine
chiroepat 지뢰밭 minefield
chiroe t'amsaeksssŏn 지뢰 탐색선 minesweeper
chirŭi 질의 vaginal
chirŭmkkil 지름길 short cut
chiruhada 지루하다 be tedious; drag
chiruhaejida 지루해지다 be bored
chiruhaesŏ mich'ilkkŏt kat'ŭn 지루해서 미칠것 같은 deadly, boring
chiruhan 지루한 boring, dull
chiryu 지류 tributary
chisa 지사 governor
chisang 지상 the ground ◊ ground; earthly, terrestrial
chisang kŭnmuwŏn 지상 근무원 ground crew; ground staff
chisang kwanje 지상 관제 ground control
chishigi innŭn 지식이 있는 knowledgeable
chishigin 지식인 intellectual
chishiginŭi 지식인의 intellectual, highbrow
chishihada 지시하다 instruct
chishik 지식 knowledge, learning
chishi sahang 지시 사항 instruction
chisŏng 지성 intellect
chisŏng-in 지성인 intellectual
chisok 지속 persistence
chisok kigan 지속 기간 duration
chisoktchŏgin 지속적인 enduring; persistent
chisokttoeda 지속되다 last
chisok'ada 지속하다 persist; maintain; sustain
chitchŏgin 지적인 intellectual
chitchŏgŭro 지적으로 mentally
chitkkujŭn 짓궂은 mischievous
chit-tta 짖다 bark
chit'aenghada 지탱하다 bear, hold, support
chit'ŭm 짙음 depth
chit'ŭn 짙은 thick
chiuda 지우다 erase, delete; scrap; remove; blot out *memory*
chiugae 지우개 eraser
chiwi 지위 position; status, standing
chiwŏn 지원 application; backup
chiwŏnhada 지원하다 apply for

chiwŏnsŏ 지원서 application form
chiyŏgŭi 지역의 regional
chiyŏk 지역 area; region; district; quarter
chiyŏk pŏnho 지역 번호 area code
chiyŏnshik'ida 지연시키다 stall
chŏ 저 I; me; mine; that
chŏ araee 저 아래에 down there
chŏbŏduda 접어두다 put aside; *chinan irŭn kŭnyang chŏbŏduja* 지난 일은 그냥 접어두자 let bygones be bygones
chŏbŏ nŏt'a 접어 넣다 tuck in
chŏbŭn chari 접은 자리 fold
chŏch'eontchŭng 저체온증 hypothermia
chŏch'uk ŭnhaeng 저축 은행 savings bank
chŏch'uk'ada 저축하다 save
chŏdang 저당 mortgage
chŏdang chap'ida 저당 잡히다 mortgage; pawn
chŏgiap 저기압 depression, low
chŏgiap chidae 저기압 지대 low-pressure area
chŏgi araetchoge 저기 아래쪽에 down there
chŏgŏdo 적어도 at least
chŏgŏduda 적어두다 note down
chŏgŏsŭn muŏshimnikka? 저것은 무엇입니까? what is that?
chŏgŏt 저것 that one
chŏgoesŏnŭi 적외선의 infra-red
chŏgori 저고리 short jacket
chŏgŭmhada 저금하다 put aside, save
chŏgŭn 적은 small; slight; a small number of
chŏgŭnghada 적응하다 adapt, acclimatize
chŏgŭngnyŏgi innŭn 적응력이 있는 adaptable
chŏgŭngshik'igi 적응시키기 conditioning
chŏgŭng-ŭl mot'anŭn 적응을 못하는 maladjusted
chŏgyŏkppyŏng 저격병 sniper
chŏgyongdoeda 적용되다 apply; apply to
chŏgyonghada 적용하다 apply
chŏhadoeda 저하되다 slip, decline

chŏhang 저항 resistance
chŏhanghada 저항하다 resist
chŏhangnyŏgi innŭn 저항력이 있는
resistant
chŏjak-kkwŏn 저작권 copyright
chŏjang 저장 store, stock
chŏjanghada 저장하다 store;
preserve; save COMPUT
chŏjangshikp'um 저장식품
preserves
chŏjang t'aengk'ŭ 저장 탱크 tank
chŏjangt'ong 저장통 bin
chŏji 저지 jersey; lowlands
chŏjibang-ŭi 저지방의 low-fat
chŏjihada 저지하다 save
chŏjil 저질 mediocrity
chŏjŏllo 저절로 by itself
chŏjo 저조 low
chŏjul tchada 젖을 짜다 milk
chŏjul tteda 젖을 떼다 wean
chŏjŭn 젖은 soggy
chŏju 저주 curse
chŏjuhada 저주하다 curse
chŏk 적 enemy; adversary
chŏkch'urŭi 적출의 legitimate
chŏk-kkŭktchŏgin 적극적인 positive
chŏkkkŭk p'anmae 적극 판매
hardsell
chŏkppŏbŭi 적법의 legitimate
chŏksshida 적시다 soak
Chŏksshiptcha 적십자 Red Cross
chŏksshiŭi 적시의 timely
chŏkssŏng 적성 aptitude
chŏktaeshim 적대심 antagonism
chŏktcha 적자 deficit
chŏktchaehada 적재하다 load; carry
chŏktchaehan 적재한 laden
chŏktchaga nada 적자가 나다 in the
red
chŏktcha saengjon 적자 생존
survival of the fittest
chŏktchŏrhan 적절한 appropriate;
right; pertinent
chŏktta 적다 take notes
chŏkttaejŏgin 적대적인 hostile
chŏkttaeshim 적대심 hostility
chŏkttanghada 적당하다 be suitable;
be adequate
chŏkttanghage 적당하게
moderately; in moderation
chŏkttanghan 적당한 adequate;
moderate; reasonable; decent;
suitable
chŏkttanghi hada 적당히 하다
moderate
chŏktto 적도 equator
chŏk'alloriŭi 저칼로리의 low-calorie
chŏk'ap'ada 적합하다 be suited for,
be cut out for
chŏk'ap'age 적합하게 properly
chŏk'ap'an 적합한 morally fit
chŏk'apssŏng 적합성 compatibility
chŏl 절 clause; passage; verse; bow,
obeisance; Buddhist temple
chŏlbak'an 절박한 imminent
chŏlbyŏk 절벽 cliff
chŏlch'a 절차 procedure
chŏlch'wisŏn 절취선 perforations
chŏlgae 절개 incision
chŏlgyohada 절교하다 drop
chŏllŭmbariŭi 절름발이의 lame
chŏllŭmgŏrida 절름거리다 hobble
chŏllyak 전략 strategy
chŏllyaktchŏgin 전략적인 strategic
chŏllye ŏmnŭn 전례 없는 unheard-
of, unprecedented
chŏllyŏm 전렴 commitment
chŏllyu 전류 current ELEC
chŏlmang 절망 despair
chŏlmanghada 절망하다 despair;
chŏlmanghayŏ 절망하여 in despair
chŏlmangjŏgin 절망적인 desperate
chŏlmtta 젊다 be young
chŏlmŭn 젊은 young, youthful
chŏlmŭni 젊은이 youth, youngster,
young man
chŏlmyohan 절묘한 exquisite
chŏlp'andoen 절판된 out of print
chŏlsshirhan 절실한 pressing
chŏltchŏng 절정 climax; high point;
summit; height
chŏltchŏng-e tarhada 절정에 달하다
culminate in
chŏlttae absolutely; *chŏlttae andoemnida!* 절대 안됩니다! absolutely
not!
chŏlttaejŏgin 절대적인 absolute;
*chŏlttaero amuegedo iyagi-
haesŏnŭn andoemnida* 절대로
아무에게도 이야기해서는 안됩니다
on no account must you tell
anybody

chŏlttanhada 절단하다 sever; amputate

chŏlttotchoe 절도죄 larceny

chŏlttuk-kkŏrim 절뚝거림 limp

chŏm 점 dot; spot; mole; *mŏnji han chŏm ŏmnŭn* 먼지 한 점 없는 spotless

chŏmaek 점액 mucus

chŏmanje 점안제 drops

chŏmch'ajŏgin 점차적인 gradual

chŏmch'ajŏgŭro 점차적으로 gradually

chŏmch'ajŏgŭro ŏpssŏjida 점차적으로 없어지다 peter out

chŏmgŏm 점검 inspection

chŏmgŏmhada 점검하다 check; inspect; vet

chŏmho 점호 roll call

chŏmhwa changch'i 점화 장치 ignition

chŏmhwahada 점화하다 set off *explosion*

chŏmhwajŏn 점화전 spark plug

chŏmhwa p'ullŏgŭ 점화 플러그 (spark) plug

chŏmida 저미다 mince

chŏmjaeng-i 점쟁이 fortune-teller

chŏmjanch'i mot'an 점잖지 못한 indecent

chŏmjanŭn 점잖은 gentle

chŏmjŏk 점적 drip

chŏmjŏm 점점 by degrees, gradually; *chŏmjŏm tŏ manŭn hakssaengdŭl / shigan* 점점 더 많은 학생들 / 시간 more and more students / time; *chŏmjŏm ch'uwŏjida / tŏwŏjida* 점점 추워지다 / 더워지다 be getting colder / warmer; *chŏmjŏm sarajida* 점점 사라지다 die away; fade away; slowly disappear

chŏm kŭlkkol 점 글꼴 bitmap font

chŏmnŭn 접는 folding

chŏmnyŏng 점령 capture; occupation

chŏmnyŏnghada 점령하다 capture; occupy

chŏmp'ŏ 점퍼 jumper COMPUT

chŏmp'o 점포 booth

chŏmshim 점심 lunch

chŏmshimshigan 점심시간 lunch break, lunchtime

chŏmsŏn 점선 dotted line

chŏmsŏngga 점성가 astrologer

chŏmsŏng komu 점성 고무 gum

chŏmsŏngsul 점성술 astrology; horoscope

chŏmsŏni tchik'in 점선이 찍힌 perforated

chŏmsu 점수 point

chŏmtcha 점자 braille

chŏmwŏn 점원 assistant; clerk

chŏmyŏnghan 저명한 distinguished, eminent

chŏn 전 pancake (*Korean-style*)

chŏn(ŭi) 전(의) preceding; front; former ◊ before; ago

chŏnaegŭl naeda 전액을 내다 pay in full

chŏnap 전압 voltage

chŏnbanjŏgin 전반적인 overall

chŏnbŏnŭi 전번의 last

chŏnbo 전보 telegram

chŏnbok 전복 overthrow

chŏnbokshik'ida 전복시키다 bring down, topple

chŏnbok'ada 전복하다 overthrow, overturn

chŏnbu 전부 in all; all of it; altogether

chŏnbuin 전부인 ex-wife

chŏnbuŭi 전부의 complete

chŏn chong-ŏbwŏn 전 종업원 workforce

chŏnch'a 전차 streetcar

chŏnch'ae 전채 appetizer, hors d'oeuvre

chŏnch'e 전체 whole; *Miguk chŏnch'e* 미국 전체 the whole of the United States

chŏnch'ejŏgin 전체적인 general

chŏnch'ejŏgŭro 전체적으로 throughout

chŏnch'ejuŭi 전체주의 totalitarianism

chŏnch'ejuŭiŭi 전체주의의 totalitarian

chŏnch'eŭi 전체의 entire; overall; total

chŏnch'isa 전치사 preposition

chŏndaehada 전대하다 sublet

chŏndal sudan 전달 수단 vehicle

(for information)

chŏndan 전단 leaflet

chŏndangp'o 전당포 pawnshop

chŏndangp'o chuin 전당포 주인 pawnbroker

chŏndarhada 전달하다 communicate; deliver

chŏndoga ch'angch'anghan 전도가 창창한 promising

chŏndohada 전도하다 conduct ELEC; evangelize

chŏndŭnggat 전등갓 lampshade

...chŏne ...전에 before ◊ previously; *3il chŏne* 3일 전에 3 days ago; *...gi chŏne* ...기 전에 before ...ing

chŏn-gaehada 전개하다 develop, pan out

chŏng-aek 정액 semen, sperm

chŏngbaksshik'ida 정박시키다 moor

chŏngbaktchang 정박장 berth, moorings

chŏngbandaeŭi 정반대의 diametrically opposed

chŏngbidoeda 정비되다 be in good order

chŏngbigong 정비공 fitter

chŏngbiwŏn 정비원 ground staff

chŏngbo 정보 information, data, intelligence

chŏngbo chegongja 정보 제공자 informant, source

chŏngboga manŭn 정보가 많은 informative

chŏngbok 정복 conquest; mastery

chŏngbo kigwan 정보 기관 intelligence service

chŏngbo kisul 정보 기술 IT, information technology

chŏngboktcha 정복자 conqueror

chŏngbo kwahak 정보 과학 information science

chŏngbo kwahaktcha 정보 과학자 information scientist

chŏngbok'ada 정복하다 conquer

chŏngbu 정부 government; mistress; *chŏngbu kyugyŏge ttarŭda* 정부 규격에 따르다 conform to government standards

chŏngch'aek 정책 policy

chŏngch'ahada 정차하다 call at

chŏngch'ak'ada 정착하다 settle; settle down

chŏngch'al 정찰 reconnaissance

chŏngch'i 정치 politics

chŏngch'iga 정치가 politician, statesman

chŏngch'i hŏn-gŭm 정치 헌금 political donation

chŏngch'ijŏgin 정치적인 political

chŏngch'ijŏk mangmyŏng-ŭl shinch'ŏnghada 정치적 망명을 신청하다 seek political asylum

chŏngch'ŏo 정처 fixed place; *chŏngch'ŏŏpsshi pangnanghada* 정처없이 방랑하다 drift

chŏngdang 정당 party

chŏngdanghage 정당하게 justifiably; justly

chŏngdanghan 정당한 legitimate; above board

chŏngdanghwa 정당화 justification

chŏngdanghwahada 정당화하다 justify

chŏngdanghwa hal su innŭn 정당화할 수 있는 justifiable

chŏngdang kangnyŏng 정당 강령 party platform

chŏngdo 정도 degree; *50 chŏngdo* 50정도 50 or so, about 50; *i chŏngdoro k'ŭda / noptta* 이 정도로 크다 / 높다 this big / high; *i chŏngdo sokttomyŏn* 이 정도 속도면 at this rate

chŏngdondoen 정돈된 straight, tidy

chŏngdonhada 정돈하다 clear up, tidy

chŏngdorŭl ttŏrŏttŭrida 정도를 떨어뜨리다 downgrade

chŏnggage 정각에 on time

chŏnggak tu shie 정각 두 시에 at two o'clock prompt

chŏnggang-i 정강이 shin

chŏnggi hanggongp'yŏn 정기 항공편 scheduled flight

chŏnggi iptchangkkwŏn 정기 입장권 season ticket

chŏnggijŏgŭro 정기적으로 periodically

chŏnggijŏn 정기전 fixture

chŏnggi kanhaengmul 정기 간행물 periodical

chŏnggi kudok 정기 구독 subscription

chŏnggi kudoktcha 정기 구독자 subscriber

chŏnggi kudok'ada 정기 구독하다 subscribe to

chŏnggisŏn 정기선 liner

chŏnggi sŭngch'akkwŏn 정기 승차권 season ticket

chŏnggŏjang 정거장 depot RAIL

chŏnggwansa 정관사 definite article

chŏnggyohage hada 정교하게 하다 refine

chŏnggyohan 정교한 sophisticated; fine *print*

chŏnggyosujik 정교수직 chair

chŏnggyuŭi wich'ie 정규의 위치에 onside

chŏnghada 정하다 set, fix

chŏnghaptchŏgin 정합적인 coherent

chŏnghwahada 정화하다 purify

chŏnghwak 정확 accuracy, precision

chŏnghwak'ada 정확하다 be right

chŏnghwak'age 정확하게 precisely

chŏnghwak'an 정확한 accurate; definite; exact

chŏnghwak'i 정확히 exactly; punctually, on the dot

chŏnghwak'i aranaeda 정확히 알아내다 pinpoint

chŏnghyŏng oekkwaŭi 정형 외과의 orthopedic

chŏn-gi 전기 electricity, power; biography

chŏn-gi ch'ŏngsogi 전기 청소기 hoover

chŏn-giga t'onghago innŭn 전기가 통하고 있는 live *wire*

chŏn-gi kisa 전기 기사 electrician

chŏn-gi papssot 전기 밥솥 (electric) rice cooker

chŏn-girŭl t'onghage hada 전기를 통하게 하다 electrify

chŏn-gisŏn 전기선 power line

chŏn-gisŏnyong komut'eip'ŭ 전기선용 고무테입 friction tape

chŏn-gi somoga chŏgŭn shiganŭi 전기 소모가 적은 시간의 off-peak electricity

chŏn-gi tamnyo 전기 담요 electric

blanket

chŏngit-tchul 전깃줄 wire

chŏn-giŭi 전기의 electric, electrical

chŏn-gi ŭija 전기 의자 electric chair

chŏngja 정자 sperm

chŏngja ŭnhaeng 정자 은행 sperm bank

chŏngje 정제 tablet

chŏngjehada 정제하다 refine

chŏngje sŏlt'ang 정제 설탕 confectioners' sugar

chŏngjeso 정제소 refinery

chŏngji 정지 halt; suspension

chŏngjihan 정지한 stationary

chŏngjik 정직 honesty, integrity

chŏngjik'ada 정직하다 be on the level

chŏngjik'an 정직한 honest

chŏngji pŏt'ŭn 정지 버튼 off switch

chŏngjishik'ida 정지시키다 suspend; *chiburŭl chŏngjishik'ida* 지불을 정지시키다 stop a check

chŏngjŏn 정전 power cut, power outage

chŏngjŏn-gi 정전기 static ELEC

chŏngjong 정종 distilled rice wine

chŏngjunghage 정중하게 respectfully

chŏngjunghan 정중한 courteous; deferential; gallant

chŏngkka 정가 net COM

chŏngkkwŏn 정권 regime

chŏngk'ŭ p'udŭ 정크 푸드 junk food

chŏngmaek 정맥 vein

chŏngmaeng-naeŭi 정맥내의 intravenous

chŏngmal 정말 truth; fact ◊ truly, really; quite; very

chŏngmallo 정말로 actually; really; sure enough

chŏngmil chosahada 정밀 조사하다 investigate in detail

chŏngmil kŏmsahada 정밀 검사하다 overhaul

chŏngmil kŏmt'ohada 정밀 검토하다 overhaul

chŏngmun 정문 front entrance

chŏngmyŏn 정면 façade

chŏngmyŏnch'ungdorŭi 정면충돌의 head-on

chŏngnarahan 적나라한 naked *truth*,

aggression; stark

chŏngnyŏgŭl tahada 정력을 다하다 burn oneself out

chŏngnyŏltchŏgin 정열적인 passionate

chŏngnyŏn 정년 retirement age

chŏngnyujang 정류장 (bus) depot; (bus) shelter; (bus) stop

chŏngnyu ktchŏm 정육점 butcher's

chŏngnyuktchŏm chuin 정육점 주인 butcher

chŏng-ŏri 정어리 sardine

chŏng-o 정오 midday

chŏn-gongdae 천공대 drilling rig

chŏn-gonghada 전공하다 specialize; specialize in; major in

chŏngsa 정사 love affair

chŏngsang 정상 norm; peak, summit; tip; pinnacle ◊ normal; *chŏngsang-e orŭda* 정상에 오르다 get to the top

chŏngsanghwahada 정상화하다 normalize

chŏngsang sangt'ae 정상 상태 normality

chŏngsang-ŭro 정상으로 normally

chŏngshigŭi 정식의 proper, real

chŏngshik 정식 set meal

chŏngshin 정신 mind; soul, spirit ◊ psycho-, mental; *chŏngshini mŏnghada* 정신이 멍하다 my mind's a blank

chŏngshinbunsŏk 정신분석 psychoanalysis

chŏngshin chang-aega innŭn 정신 장애가 있는 mentally handicapped

chŏngshin ch'angnane kŏllin 정신 착란에 걸린 demented

chŏngshin ch'angnanŭi 정신 착란의 delirious

chŏngshin ch'arige hada 정신 차리게 하다 bring around

chŏngshini mŏnghan 정신이 멍한 dazed

chŏngshini nagada 정신이 나가다 be out of one's mind

chŏngshin isang 정신 이상 insanity

chŏngshin isang-ŭi 정신 이상의 disturbed

chŏngshin kamŭng 정신 감응 telepathy

chŏngshin kamŭng-ŭi 정신 감응의 telepathic

chŏngshinkkwaŭi 정신과의 psychiatric

chŏngshinkkwa ŭisa 정신과 의사 psychiatrist

chŏngshinŏpsshi chikkŏrida 정신없이 지껄이다 rave on mindlessly

chŏngshin pagyaktcha 정신박약자 imbecile

chŏngshinppyŏng 정신병 mental illness

chŏngshinppyŏng-i innŭn 정신병이 있는 mentally ill

chŏngshinppyŏngja 정신병자 psychopath

chŏngshinppyŏng-ŭi 정신병의 mental, crazy

chŏngshinppyŏng-wŏn 정신병원 asylum, mental hospital

chŏngshin punsŏk 정신 분석 psychoanalysis

chŏngshin punsŏk haktcha 정신 분석 학자 psychoanalyst

chŏngshin punsŏk'ada 정신 분석하다 psychoanalyse

chŏngshin punyŏltchŭng 정신 분열증 schizophrenia

chŏngshin punyŏltchŭng hwanja 정신 분열증 환자 schizophrenic patient

chŏngshin punyŏltchŭng-ŭi 정신 분열증의 schizophrenic

chŏngshin sangt'ae 정신 상태 mental state

chŏngshintchŏgin 정신적인 spiritual; platonic

chŏngshintchŏk chang-aega innŭn 정신적 장애가 있는 mentally handicapped

chŏngshintchŏk hakttae 정신적 학대 mental cruelty

chŏngshinŭi 정신의 mental

chŏngshinŭihak 정신의학 psychiatry

chŏngsŏnhan 정선한 select, exclusive

chŏngt'ong 정통 familiarity

chŏngt'onghada 정통하다 know; have a good knowledge of; master; be a master of

chŏng-ŭi 정의 justice; definition
chŏng-ŭirŭl naerida 정의를 내리다 define
chŏn-gŭk 전극 electrode
chŏn-gu 전구 light bulb
chŏn-gun 전군 the forces MIL
chŏng-wŏn 정원 garden
chŏng-wŏnnyong kawi 정원용 가위 clippers
chŏng-wŏnsa 정원사 gardener
chŏng-ye 정예 elite
chŏng-yeŭi 정예의 elite
chŏn-gyŏng 전경 foreground
chŏnhada 전하다 pass on, relay
chŏnhaejuda 전해주다 pass, hand
chŏnhanŭn mal 전하는 말 message
chŏnhuŭi 전후의 postwar
chŏnhwa 전화 telephone; phone call; *chŏnhwarŭl ssŏdo toemnikka?* 전화를 써도 됩니까 can I use the phone?
chŏnhwabŏnhobu 전화번호부 phone book
chŏnhwahada 전화하다 phone, call
chŏnhwa kŏlda 전화 걸다 phone
chŏnhwa kyohwan-guk 전화 교환국 telephone exchange
chŏnhwan 전환 change; changeover; conversion
chŏnhwanjŏm 전환점 turning point
chŏnhwa pŏnho 전화 번호 telephone number
chŏnhwa pŏnhobu 전화 번호부 telephone directory
chŏnhwa p'anmae 전화 판매 telesales
chŏnhwarŭl hada 전화를 하다 make a telephone call
chŏnhwarŭl kkŭnt'a 전화를 끊다 hang up
chŏnhwarŭl kŏlda 전화를 걸다 call; telephone; dial
chŏnhwarŭl pat-tta 전화를 받다 answer the telephone
chŏnhyang 전향 convert
chŏnhyangshik'ida 전향시키다 convert *person*
chŏnhyŏ 전혀 entirely, completely, utterly; *chŏnhyŏ ...ji ant'a* 전혀 ...지 않다 be anything but; do anything but; *chŏnhyŏ kwanshimi*

ŏpssŏ 전혀 관심이 없어 I couldn't care less
chŏnhyŏng 전형 stereotype
chŏnhyŏngjŏgin 전형적인 typical
chŏnimja 전임자 predecessor
chŏnja 전자 the former; electron ◊ electronic
chŏnja chep'um 전자 제품 electrical appliance
chŏnja chŏngbo ch'ŏri 전자 정보 처리 EDP, electronic data processing
chŏnjaeng 전쟁 war; warfare
chŏnjaeng chŏnŭi 전쟁 전의 prewar
chŏnjaeng p'oro 전쟁 포로 prisoner of war
chŏnjaengt'ŏ 전쟁터 battlefield, battleground
chŏnjaeng-ŭi ch'amsa 전쟁의 참사 horrors of war
chŏnja keship'an 전자 게시판 bulletin board
chŏnja konghak 전자 공학 electronics
chŏnja k'adŭ 전자 카드 smart card
chŏnja orak 전자 오락 electronic game
chŏnjarenji 전자렌지 microwave
chŏnja sanŏp 전자 산업 electronics industry
chŏnja up'yŏn 전자 우편 electronic mail
chŏnje chŏngch'i 전제 정치 tyranny
chŏnjejokkŏn 전제조건 prerequisite
chŏnji 전지 battery
chŏnjin 전진 advance
chŏnjinhada 전진하다 advance; move on
chŏnjip 전집 collected works
chŏnjugok 전주곡 prelude
chŏnkkwa 전과 criminal record
chŏnmang 전망 prospects
chŏnmang-i chŏun chijŏm 전망이 좋은 지점 vantage point
chŏnmŏgi twaeji 젖먹이 돼지 sucking pig
chŏnmun 전문 specialty
chŏnmun chishik 전문 지식 expertise
chŏnmun-ga 전문가 expert, specialist

chŏnmun-gaŭi ch'unggo 전문가의 충고 expert advice

chŏnmunindaptchi anŭn 전문인답지 않은 unprofessional

chŏnmunjik chongsaja 전문직 종사자 professional

chŏnmunjŏgin 전문적인 professional

chŏnmunjŏguro 전문적으로 professionally

chŏnmun kisul 전문 기술 expertise

chŏnmunsŏng 전문성 technicality, technical nature

chŏnmunŭi 전문의 technical

chŏnmunŭro hada 전문으로 하다 specialize; specialize in

chŏnmun yong-ŏ 전문 용어 terminology, jargon

chŏnmyŏlshik'ida 전멸시키다 exterminate, wipe out

chŏnmyŏnjŏgin 전면적인 sweeping

chŏnnamp'yŏn 전남편 ex-husband

chŏnnamu 전나무 fir

Chŏnnŭngja 전능자 the Almighty

chŏnnŭn pae 젓는 배 rowboat

chŏnnyŏm 전념 dedication

chŏnnyŏmhada 전념하다 dedicate oneself to; keep one's mind on; concentrate

chŏnnyŏmhanŭn 전념하는 single-minded, dedicated

chŏnsa 전사 warrior, fighter

chŏnsanhwahada 전산화하다 computerize

chŏnsegi 전세기 charter flight

chŏnsegŭm 전세금 deposit money for a lease on an apartment

chŏnsegyeŭi 전세계의 global

chŏnse naeda 전세 내다 charter

chŏnse not'a 전세 놓다 lease an apartment on a deposit basis

chŏnshi 전시 display; exhibition; wartime

chŏnshiganjero 전시간제로 full time

chŏnshiganjeŭi 전시간제의 full-time

chŏnshihada 전시하다 display, show, exhibit

chŏnshindaeŭi 전신대의 full-length

chŏnshinju 전신주 telegraph pole

chŏnshin mach'wi 전신 마취 general anesthetic

chŏnship'um 전시품 exhibit

chŏnsŏl 전설 legend

chŏnsŏljŏgin 전설적인 legendary

chŏnsŏn 전선 front MIL, (*of weather*); cord; cable

chŏnsŏnggi 전성기 heyday

chŏnsonghada 전송하다 export COMPUT

chŏnsongnyŏguro hada 전속력으로 하다 flat out

chŏnsul 전술 tactics

chŏnsultchŏgin 전술적인 tactical

chŏntchŏk 전적 complete, whole; *chŏntchŏguro matsŭmnida* 전적으로 맞습니다 that's absolutely right

chŏnt'ong 전통 tradition

chŏnt'ongjŏgin 전통적인 traditional, conventional

chŏnt'ongjŏguro 전통적으로 traditionally

chŏnt'u 전투 battle; combat; hostilities

chŏnt'ugi 전투기 fighter (*airplane*)

chŏnŭi 전의 former

chŏnŭnghan 전능한 retarded

chŏnya 전야 eve

chŏnyŏge 저녁에 in the evening

chŏnyŏk 전역 evening; all parts; *Hanguk chŏnyŏgŭl yŏhaenghada* 한국 전역을 여행하다 travel all over Korea

chŏnyŏk shikssa 저녁 식사 supper

chŏnyŏm 전염 transmission

chŏnyŏmdoenŭn 전염되는 contagious

chŏnyŏmppyŏng 전염병 plague

chŏnyŏmshik'ida 전염시키다 transmit *disease*

chŏnyŏmssŏng-ŭi 전염성의 infectious

chŏnyul 전율 thrill

chŏŏgada 저어가다 row

chŏpch'aktche 접착제 adhesive

chŏpch'ak'ada 접착하다 bond, stick

chŏpch'ok 접촉 contact; touch

chŏpch'ok yŏng-yŏk 접촉 영역 interface

chŏpch'ok'ada 접촉하다 approach, contact; touch

chŏpkkŭn 접근 access

chŏpkkŭnhada 접근하다 access

chŏpkkŭn pangbŏp 접근 방법 approach

chŏppuchi'gi 접붙이기 graft BOT

chŏpssi 접시 plate

chŏpssogŭl kkŭnt'a 접속을 끊다 go off-line

chŏpssokssa 접속사 conjunction GRAM

chŏpssoksshik'ida 접속시키다 connect

chŏpssu kyewŏn 접수 계원 desk clerk

chŏpssok'ada 접속하다 interface; connect with; go on-line to

chŏpssuwŏn 접수원 receptionist

chŏptchi 접지 ground ELEC

chŏptchihada 접지하다 ground ELEC

chŏptta 접다 fold; fold up; turn down

chŏpttusa 접두사 prefix

chŏp'ae it-tta 접해 있다 border

chŏp'ida 접히다 fold up

chŏp'yŏnŭro 저편으로 beyond

chŏrhoehada 철회하다 retrograde

chŏrida 절이다 marinate; pickle

chŏrim 저림 pins and needles

chŏrŏn! 저런! good heavens!

chŏryak 절약 economy; saving

chŏryakpun 절약분 saving

chŏryak undong 절약 운동 economy drive

chŏryak'ada 절약하다 economize; economize on, save

chŏryak'anŭn 절약하는 economical, thrifty

chŏryak'yŏng 절약형 economy size

chŏryŏn 절연 insulation

chŏryŏnhada 절연하다 insulate; sever

chŏsok'an 저속한 vulgar

chŏsŭng 저승 underworld

chŏsuji 저수지 reservoir

chŏtkkarak 젓가락 chopsticks

chŏtkkasŭm 젖가슴 bosom, breast

chŏtkkoktchi 젖꼭지 nipple; teat

chŏt-tta 젖다 get wet

chŏt-tta 젓다 paddle

chŏt'aek 저택 mansion

chŏŭi 저의 ㅐ my

chŏŭm poepkkessŭmnida 처음 뵙겠습니다 how do you do (*formal greeting used on first meeting*)

chŏŭmŭi 저음의 deep; bass

chŏul 저울 scales

chŏ wie 저 위에 over there

cho 조 trillion; millet; article, clause; dynasty; tune; air

choahada 좋아하다 like, be fond of; *muŏt hanŭn kŏsŭl choahada* 무엇 하는 것을 좋아하다 like to do sth; *Xŭl/rŭl Ypoda tŏ choahada* X을/를 Y보다 더 좋아하다 prefer X to Y

choajida 좋아지다 pick up, improve; *nŏn uni choassŏ* 넌 운이 좋았어 you were lucky

choayo 좋아요 right, OK

chobashimhada 조바심하다 be on tenterhooks

chobŭn 좁은 narrow

chobŭn kil 좁은 길 lane

chobumo 조부모 grandparents

choch'a 조차 even, into the bargain; *choch'a ant'a* 조차 않다 not even

choch'ado 조차도 even; *naŭi abŏji choch'ado* 나의 아버지 조차도 even my father

choch'i 조치 step, measure

choch'wirŭl ch'wihada 조치를 취하다 take action

choe 죄 sin; guilt; responsibility

choe chit-tta 죄 짓다 sin

choe chiŭn 죄 지은 guilty

choech'aek-kkam 죄책감 guilt; *...e taehae choech'aek-kkamŭl nŭkkida* ...에 대해 죄책감을 느끼다 feel bad about, feel guilty about

choein 죄인 sinner

choemsoe 죔쇠 clamp

choemsoero choeda 죔쇠로 죄다 clamp

choeoehada 제외하다 rule out

choerŭl ssŭiuda 죄를 씌우다 incriminate

choesonghamnida 죄송합니다 excuse me; I beg your pardon

choesu 죄수 prisoner

choesu hosongch'a 죄수 호송차 patrol wagon

chogaek 조객 mourner

chogak 조각 bit; piece; slice; fragment; shred; lump; carving, sculpture; *p'ai/ppang han chogak*

파이/빵 한 조각 a piece of pie/bread

chogak-kka 조각가 sculptor

chogak kŭrim match'ugi 조각 그림 맞추기 jigsaw (puzzle)

chogak naeda 조각 내다 shred

chogakp'um 조각품 sculpture

chogamdok 조감독 assistant director

chogangnada 조각나다 splinter

choging 조깅 jog; jogging

chogingbok 조깅복 jogging suit

choginghada 조깅하다 go for a run, jog

choging shyujŭ 조깅 슈즈 jogger

chogok 조곡 suite MUS

chogŭm 조금 a bit, a little; a bit of; just a couple ◊ any ◊ some; slightly; *ppang/p'odoju chogŭm* 빵/포도주 조금 a little bread/wine

chogŭmaham 조그마함 modesty

chogŭmahan 조그마한 tiny; modest

chogŭmdo 조금도 (not) at all, in the least, in the slightest; *chogŭmdo animnida* 조금도 아닙니다 not in the slightest

chogŭmsshik 조금씩 little by little

chogŭmsshik tonŭl naeda 조금씩 돈을 내다 chip in

chogŭmŭi 조금의 a few

chogŭmŭn 조금은 little

chohabe kaip'aji anŭn 조합에 가입하지 않은 non-union

chohang 조항 article, clause, section; provision

chohap 조합 association; union; partnership

chohoe 조회 reference

chohoehada 조회하다 refer to

chohwa 조화 harmony; reconciliation

chohwadoen 조화된 harmonious

chohwashik'ida 조화시키다 harmonize; reconcile

chohyŏngjŏgin 조형적인 figurative

choida 조이다 tie

chojak 조작 mockery; fabrication

chojak'ada 조작하다 manufacture; fix; manipulate

chojanghada 조장하다 further *cause*

chojap'an 조잡한 crude

chojeshil 조제실 dispensary

chojik 조직 organization; system; organ ANAT; tissue

chojiktcha 조직자 organizer

chojiktchŏgin 조직적인 systematic

chojik'ada 조직하다 organize

chojŏng chohwa 조정 조화 coordination

chojŏng chohwashik'ida 조정 조화시키다 coordinate

chojŏnghada 조정하다 set, adjust

chojŏrhada 조절하다 tune up

chojong 조종 operation; manipulation; aviation

chojong changch'i 조종 장치 controls

chojonghada 조종하다 operate; manipulate; steer; pilot

chojonghanŭn 조종하는 manipulative

chojongsa 조종사 pilot

chojongshil 조종실 cockpit; flight deck

chokki 조끼 vest

chokkŏn 조건 condition, requirement; *...ranŭn chokkŏnŭro* ...라는 조건으로 on condition that

chokkŏnbuŭi 조건부의 conditional

chokkŏnppŏp 조건법 conditional

chokpo 족보 genealogy book

choktchang 족장 chief

choktchebi 족제비 weasel

choktchipkke 족집게 tweezers

chok'a 조카 nephew

chok'attal 조카딸 niece

chok'ŏ 조커 joker

chol 졸 pawn

cholda 졸다 doze, snooze

cholgi 졸기 doze, snooze

chollamaeda 졸라매다 fasten tightly; *hŏrittirŭl chollamaeda* 허리띠를 졸라매다 tighten one's belt *fig*

chollida 졸리다 be sleepy

chollin 졸린 sleepy

choltchak 졸작 trash

chom 좀 some; something; *chom hashigessŏyo?* 좀 하시겠어요? would you like some?

chomajomahage hanŭn 조마조마하게 하는 nerve-racking

choman-gan 조만간 sooner or later

chomirhada 조밀하다 be dense; *in-*

guga chomirhan 인구가 조밀한 densely populated

chomiryo 조미료 seasoning; flavoring

chommŏgŭm 좀먹음 erosion *fig*

chommŏktta 좀먹다 erode *fig*

chomttoduktchil 좀도둑질 pilfering

Chomultchu 조물주 the Creator

chomyŏng 조명 lighting

chomyŏnghada 조명하다 illuminate, light

chomyŏngt'an 조명탄 flare

chonan 조난 disaster; accident

chonan sangt'aeŭi 조난 상태의 in distress

chonan shinho 조난 신호 distress signal

chong 종 species; bell

chong-ari 종아리 calf

chongbŏm 종범 accessory LAW

chongdalsae 종달새 lark

chonggi 종기 boil

chonggyo 종교 religion

chonggyojŏgin 종교적인 religious; sacred

chonghap pohŏm 종합 보험 comprehensive insurance

chong-i 종이 paper; *chong-i han chang* 종이 한 장 a piece of paper

chong-i kabang 종이 가방 paper bag

chong-ik'ŏp 종이컵 paper cup

chong-i mukkŭm 종이 묶음 pad

chong-ip'yojiŭi yŏmkkap'an ch'aek 종이표지의 염가판 책 paperback

chong-iro mandŭn 종이로 만든 (made of) paper

chong-i ullida 종이 울리다 chime

chongma 종마 stallion

chongnyang 종양 growth, tumor

chongnyohada 종료하다 log off; shut down

chongnyonaeda 종료내다 shut down

chongnyu 종류 kind, sort; *chŏgŏsŭn ŏttŏn chongnyuŭi kaeimnikka?* 저것은 어떤 종류의 개입니까? what kind of dog is that?; *oman chongnyuŭi saram* 오만 종류의 사람 all kinds of people

chongŏbwŏn 종업원 worker

chongŏbwŏn ch'ongsu 종업원 총수 payroll

chongp'a 종파 denomination

chongsahada 종사하다 practice

chongtchŏm 종점 terminus

chong-ŭl ch'yŏsŏ pullŏjuseyo 종을 쳐서 불러주세요 please ring for attention

chon-gyŏng 존경 respect

chon-gyŏnghada 존경하다 respect, have a great regard for

chon-gyŏnghanŭn sŏnsaengnim-kke 존경하는 선생님께 Dear Sir

chonham 존함 name

chonjae 존재 being, existence

chonjaehada 존재하다 exist

chonjaerŭl mit-tta 존재를 믿다 believe in

chonjunghada 존중하다 respect

chonŏm 존엄 dignity

choŏn 조언 advice; hint; pointer; *nuguŭi choŏnŭl padadŭrida* 누구의 조언을 받아들이다 take s.o.'s advice

choŏnhada 조언하다 advise

choŏp tanch'uk'ada 조업 단축하다 be on short time

chopch'ok'aji ank'o chinaeda 접촉하지 않고 지내다 be out of touch

choptta 좁다 be narrow

chop'ap pubun 접합 부분 joint

chorangmal 조랑말 pony

choribnyongp'um 조립용품 kit

choribŏp 조리법 recipe

choribŭi 조립의 modular

choriga sŏnŭn 조리가 서는 coherent

chorip 조립 assembly

chorip kongjang 조립 공장 assembly plant

choripsshigŭi 조립식의 prefabricated

chorip tanwi 조립 단위 module

chorip'ada 조립하다 assemble, set up

chorŏp 졸업 graduation

chorŏpssaeng 졸업생 graduate

chorŏp'ada 졸업하다 graduate

chorong 조롱 mockery; taunt

choronghada 조롱하다 ridicule; *hyungnaenaemyŏ choronghada* 흉내내며 조롱하다 mock chorŭda 조르다 press for; badger; pester

choryŏktcha 조력자 mentor

choryu 조류 current; tide; birds, fowls

choryu poho kuyŏk 조류 보호 구역 bird sanctuary

choryuŭi naejang 조류의 내장 giblets

chosa 조사 investigation; scrutiny; survey

chosadan 조사단 panel

chosahada 조사하다 examine, investigate; survey

chosang 조상 ancestor; ancestry

chosang sungbae 조상 숭배 ancestral worship

chosanwŏn 조산원 midwife

chose 조세 tax; taxes; taxation

choseŭi 조세의 fiscal

choshim 조심 caution

choshimhada 조심하다 take care; guard against; beware of; *kyedanŭl choshimhaseyo!* 계단을 조심하세요! mind the step!

choshimsŏng innŭn 조심성 있는 guarded, careful

choshimsŏng ŏmnŭn 조심성 없는 careless

choshimsŭrŏpkke 조심스럽게 carefully

choshimsŭrŏun 조심스러운 cautious

chosŏkp'a 조석파 tidal wave

Chosŏn Minjujuŭi Inmin Konghwaguk 조선 민주주의 인민 공화국 Democratic People's Republic of Korea, DPRK

chosŏnso 조선소 dockyard

choso 조소 ridicule

chosu 조수 assistant; tide

chosuga 조숙아 premature baby

chosuk'an 조숙한 precocious

chot 촛 ∨ prick

chot'a 좋다 be good; *...do chot'a* ...해도 좋다 may

choŭn 좋은 good; *choŭn shiganŭl ponaeda* 좋은 시간을 보내다 have a good time

choyak 조약 treaty

choyonghada 조용하다 be quiet

choyonghaejida 조용해지다 quieten

down, settle down

choyonghage 조용하게 in silence

choyonghage hada 조용하게 하다 quieten down

choyongham 조용함 hush

choyonghan 조용한 quiet; silent

choyonghi! 조용히! hush!, silence!

choyonghi hada 조용히 하다 be quiet, shut up; *chom choyonghi hae!* 좀 조용히 해! just be quiet!

choyurhada 조율하다 tune

chŭbi manŭn 즙이 많은 juicy

chŭk 즉 namely

chŭk-kkaktchŏgin 즉각적인 speedy, prompt; instant

chŭksshi 즉시 instantly; on the spot, straight away

chŭksshiro 즉시로 immediately

chŭksshiŭi 즉시의 immediate

chŭkssŏgesŏ chit-tta 즉석에서 짓다 improvise, wing it

chŭkssŏgesŏ mandŭlda 즉석에서 만들다 improvize

chŭkssŏgŭi 즉석의 off the cuff

chŭkssŏk shikp'um 즉석 식품 fast food

chŭk'ŭ 즈크 canvas

chŭk'ŭng-ŭro hada 즉흥으로 하다 improvize

chŭlgida 즐기다 enjoy; relish

chŭlgŏpkke chinaeda 즐겁게 지내다 enjoy oneself

chŭlgŏpkke hada 즐겁게 하다 entertain; *urinŭn chŏngmal chŭlgŏpkke ponaessŏyo* 우리는 정말 즐겁게 보냈어요 we had a lovely time

chŭlgŏptta 즐겁다 be delightful, be pleasant

chŭlgŏum 즐거움 enjoyment; amusement

chŭlgŏun 즐거운 enjoyable; pleasing

chŭlgŏun Sŏngt'ani toegirŭl paramnida! 즐거운 성탄이 되기를 바랍니다! Merry Christmas!

chŭngbalshik'ida 증발시키다 vaporize

chŭngbarhada 증발하다 evaporate

chŭngga 증가 increase

chŭnggahada 증가하다 increase

chŭnggahanŭn 증가하는 increasing

chŭnggashik'ida 증가시키다 increase, step up

chŭnggi 증기 vapor

chŭnggŏ 증거 evidence, proof

chŭnggŏrŭl taeda 증거를 대다 substantiate

chŭnghu 증후 symptom; ...ŭi chŭnghurŭl poida ...의 증후를 보이다 be symptomatic of

chŭng-in 증인 witness

chŭng-insŏk 증인석 witness stand

chŭng-inŭro sŏmyŏnghada 증인으로 서명하다 witness

chŭng-inŭro sŏmyŏngham 증인으로 서명함 witness

chŭng-inŭro sŏnsŏhada 증인으로 선서하다 swear in as a witness

chŭngjŏnghada 증정하다 present

chŭngjobu 증조부 great-grandfather

chŭngjomo 증조모 great-grandmother

chŭngkkwŏn kŏraeso 증권 거래소 stock exchange

chŭngkkwŏn shijang 증권 시장 stock market

chŭngkkwŏn shijang punggoe 증권 시장 붕괴 stockmarket crash

chŭngmyŏnghada 증명하다 prove; validate, verify

chŭngmyŏngsŏ 증명서 certificate; ID

chŭng-ŏn 증언 evidence

chŭng-ŏnhada 증언하다 testify, give evidence

chŭng-o 증오 hatred, animosity

chŭngp'ok'ada 증폭하다 amplify

chŭngsangŭl poida 증상을 보이다 be sickening for

chŭngsŏ 증서 diploma

chŭngson 증손 great-grandchild

chŭng-wŏn-gun 증원군 reinforcements

chu 주 note; province, state; week; Lord

chubang 주방 kitchen

chubangjang 주방장 chef

chubangyong seje 주방용 세제 dishwashing liquid

chubu 주부 housewife

chubyŏn 주변 perimeter

chubyŏn changch'i 주변 장치 peripheral COMPUT

chuch'a 주차 parking

chuch'a changso 주차 장소 parking place

chuch'adae 주차대 rack

chuch'agŭmji 주차금지 no parking

chuch'ahada 주차하다 park

chuch'ajang 주차장 parking lot

chuch'a wiban tansogwŏn 주차 위반 단속원 traffic warden

chuch'a wiban ttaktchi 주차 위반 딱지 parking ticket

chuch'a yogŭmgi 주차 요금기 parking meter

chuch'eŭishik 주체의식 sense of independence and sovereignty; kungmin chuch'eŭishik 국민 주체의식 sense of national identity

chuch'iŭi 주치의 family doctor

chuda 주다 give; assign; allow; give away

chudang 주당 weekly rate

chudo 주도 initiative

chudoen 주된 main

chudohada 주도하다 lead the way

chudojŏgin 주도적인 leading

chudokkwŏn 주도권 supremacy

chudoro 주도로 main road

chudung-i 주둥이 muzzle, snout; spout

chudun-gun 주둔군 garrison

chugan 주간 weekly

chugan kongnyŏn 주간 공연 matinée (of play)

chugan kosok toro 주간 고속 도로 interstate

chugan sangnyŏng 주간 상영 matinée (of movie)

chuga toeŏ it-tta 주가 되어 있다 predominate

chugida 죽이다 kill; deaden

chugijŏgin 주기적인 periodic

chugŏganŭn 죽어가는 dying

chugŏŭi 주거의 residential

chugŭl unmyŏng 죽을 운명 mortality

chugŭm 죽음 death

chugŭn 죽은 dead

chugŭndŭshi choyonghan 죽은듯이 조용한 deadly quiet

chugŭnkkae 주근깨 freckle

chugŭn saram 죽은 사람 the deceased

chugŭp 주급 weekly payment

chugwanjŏgin 주관적인 subjective

chugyŏ ŏpssaeda 죽여 없애다 eliminate, kill

chugyo 주교 bishop

chuhaeng 주행 run, drive

chuhaeng anjŏngssŏng 주행 안정성 road holding

chuhaeng kŏrigye 주행 거리계 odometer

Chuhan Migun 주한 미군 American Military Forces in Korea

chuhongsaek 주홍색 scarlet

chuhwangsaek 주황색 orange (*color*)

chuhyŏng 주형 cast, mold

chuin 주인 host; landlord; owner, master; mistress

chuin ŏmnŭn 주인 없는 stray (*dog*)

chuip 주입 injection; transfusion

chuipkku 주입구 inlet

chuip'ada 주입하다 infuse; instil; indoctrinate; pump; *konggirŭl chuip'ada* 공기를 주입하다 inflate; pump up

chujang 주장 case, argument; claim, assertion; allegation; team captain

chujanghada 주장하다 argue; claim, insist, maintain; *chagirŭl chujang-hada* 자기를 주장하다 assert oneself

chujangdoen 주장된 alleged

chuje 주제 motif; topic

chujega 주제가 theme song

chujenŏmun 주제넘은 uncalled-for

chujŏhada 주저하다 waver

chujŏhanŭn 주저하는 tentative

chujŏnja 주전자 kettle; jug; teapot; coffee pot

chujohada 주조하다 cast *metal*

chujo kongjang 주조 공장 foundry

chuju 주주 shareholder, stockholder

chujung-e 주중에 midweek

Chu Kidomun 주 기도문 Lord's Prayer

chuktta 죽다 die; *algo ship'ŏ chuk-kket-tta* 알고 싶어 죽겠다 I'm dying to know; *amŭro chuktta* 암으로 죽다 die of cancer

chuk'ŭ pakssŭ 주크 박스 jukebox

chul 줄 column, line; file; strap; string; *chul chiŏ* 줄 지어 in single file; *han churŭi kyedan* 한 줄의 계단 flight (of stairs); *churŭl ch'ida* 줄을 치다 rope off; *churŭl sŏda* 줄을 서다 stand in line

chulda 줄다 decrease, diminish

chuldambaerŭl p'iuda 줄담배를 피우다 chain smoke

chuldambaerŭl p'iunŭn saram 줄담배를 피우는 사람 chain smoker

chulgi 줄기 stalk, stem; trunk; wisp

chulgot 줄곧 all the time; *chulgot irhayŏ* 줄곧 일하여 on the go

chulja 줄자 tape measure

chuljabŭn 줄잡은 conservative

chullŏmkki chul 줄넘기 줄 skipping rope

chullŏmkkihada 줄넘기하다 skip

chulmunŭi 줄무늬 stripe

chulmunŭi ŏlluk 줄무늬 얼룩 streak

chulmunŭi-ŭi 줄무늬의 striped

chul sŏda 줄 서다 line up

chult'agi chul 줄타기 줄 high wire

chumal 주말 weekend; *chumare* 주말에 on the weekend

chumnenjŭ 줌렌즈 zoom lens

chumnenjŭro match'uda 줌렌즈로 맞추다 zoom in on

chumŏk 주먹 fist

chumŏk k'oŭi 주먹코의 snub-nosed

chumŏktchil 주먹질 punch, thump

chumŏni 주머니 pouch, bag; pocket

chumŏnik'al 주머니칼 pocketknife

chumoja 주모자 ringleader

chumok 주목 attention, notice; *mut saramŭi chumogŭl pat-tta* 뭇 사람의 주목을 받다 be in the limelight

chumok'ada 주목하다 pay attention

chumok'ae chushipsshio 주목해 주십시오 your attention please

chumok'al manhan 주목할 만한 remarkable; notable; noticeable

chumun 주문 order; magic spell; *chumune match'uda* 주문에 맞추다 fill an order

chumunhada 주문하다 order

chunbi 준비 preparation

chunbidoen 준비된 ready; *muŏsŭl hal chunbiga toeŏ it-tta* 무엇을 할

준비가 되어 있다 be prepared to do sth, be willing to do sth

chunbihada 준비하다 arrange, fix; prepare; get ready

chunbihaesŏ 준비해서 in preparation for

chunbihanŭn tan-gye-esŏ 준비하는 단계에서 at the planning stage

chunbi undong-ŭl hada 준비 운동을 하다 warmup

chung 중 Buddhist monk; middle ◊ among; out of; in ◊ while; *yŏl kae chung han kae* 열 개 중 한 개 one in ten; *...ŭi chung-ang-esŏ* ...의 중앙에서 in the middle of; *...chung-e* ...중에 in the middle of

chung-ang 중앙 center ◊ central

chung-ang anjŏn changch'i 중앙 안전 장치 central locking

chung-ang chamgŭm changch'i 중앙 잠금 장치 central heating

chung-ang ch'ŏri changch'i 중앙 처리 장치 CPU, central processing unit

chung-ang pullidae 중앙 분리대 median strip

chung-ang ŭnhaeng-ŭi kibon kŭmni 중앙 은행의 기본 금리 base rate

chungbokdoeda 중복되다 overlap

chungch'ŭnghyŏng-ŭi ap'at'ŭ 중층형의 아파트 duplex (apartment)

chungch'ujŏgin 중추적인 spinal

chungdaehada 중대하다 be important; *...ranŭn kŏsŭn kŭk'i chungdaehamnida* ...라는 것은 극히 중대합니다 it is vital that

chungdaehan 중대한 significant, momentous; great; grave

chungdan 중단 disruption, interruption; pause

chungdanhada 중단하다 interrupt; cease; pause; cut out; *chamshi chungdanhada* 잠시 중단하다 take a break

chungdan ŏmnŭn 중단 없는 non-stop

chungdan ŏpsshi 중단 없이 non-stop

chungdanshik'ida 중단시키다 cease; pause; disrupt, interrupt; disconnect

chungdo-e 중도에 midway

chungdogida 중독이다 be addicted to

chungdok 중독 addiction

chungdokssŏng-ida 중독성이다 be addictive

chungdoktcha 중독자 addict

Chungdong 중동 Middle East ◊ Middle Eastern

chungdop'a 중도파 center group, center party

chungdŭng kyoyuk 중등 교육 secondary education

chunggae 중개 mediation; *...saiŭi chunggae yŏk'arŭl hada* ...사이의 중개 역할을 하다 bridge *fig*

chunggaehada 중개하다 mediate

chunggaeja 중개자 go-between

chunggaeŏp 중개업 agency

chunggaeŏptcha 중개업자 broker

chunggan chijŏmŭi 중간 지점의 halfway

chunggane 중간에 halfway

chunggan hyushik 중간 휴식 half time

chunggan irŭm 중간 이름 middle name

chunggankkŭp 중간급 middleweight

chunggan k'ŭgi 중간 크기 medium size

chunggansaegŭi 중간색의 neutral *color*

chunggan sang-in 중간 상인 middleman

chungganŭi 중간의 middle; medium; intermediate

chunggoro 중고로 secondhand

chunggoŭi 중고의 secondhand

Chunggug-ŏ 중국어 Chinese (*language*)

Chungguk 중국 China ◊ Chinese

Chungguk pont'o 중국 본토 mainland China

Chungguk pukkyŏngŏ 중국 북경어 Mandarin (*language*)

Chungguk saram 중국 사람 Chinese (*person*)

chunggyehada 중계하다 relay

chunggyein 중계인 contact

chunghan 중한 heavy

chunghon 중혼 bigamy

chunghwahada 중화하다 counteract

chunghwanjashil 중환자실 intensive care (unit)

chung-ida 중이다: *kŭgŏsŭn kŏmt'o / chosa chung-ida* 그것은 검토 / 조사 중이다 it is under review / investigation

chungjae 중재 intervention; mediation; arbitration

chungjaehada 중재하다 intervene; intercede; arbitrate, mediate

chungjaein 중재인 mediator, intermediary

chungji 중지 cessation

chungjihada 중지하다 discontinue; abort

chungjishik'ida 중지시키다 break up

chungjoe 중죄 felony

chungmae kyŏrhon 중매 결혼 arranged marriage

chungnibŭi 중립의 neutral

chungnip 중립 neutrality; *chungnibe* 중립에 in neutral

chungnipssŏng 중립성 neutrality

chungniptchŏgin 중립적인 nonaligned

chungnip wich'i 중립 위치 neutral

chungnyang ch'ogwaŭi 중량 초과의 overweight

chungnyŏk 중력 gravity

chungnyŏn 중년 middle age ◊ middle-aged

chungnyohada 중요하다 matter, be important

chungnyohan 중요한 important

chungnyong 중용 moderation

chungnyosŏng 중요성 importance

chung-ŏlgŏrida 중얼거리다 mumble, mutter

chungp'a 중파 medium wave

chungsa 중사 sergeant

chungsanch'ŭng 중산층 middle classes

chungsang 중상 slander

chungsanghada 중상하다 slander

chungsang moryak 중상 모략 smear campaign

chungsanmo 중산모 top hat

Chungse 중세 Middle Ages ◊ medieval

chungshimbue innŭn 중심부에 있는 central

chungshimdae 중심대 crossbar

chungshimga 중심가 main street

chungshimji 중심지 center (*region*)

chungshimjŏk 중심적 central; *mu-ŏse chungshimjŏgida* 무엇에 중심적이다 be central to sth

chungshimŭi 중심의 central

chungshimŭl tuda 중심을 두다 center on

chungso kiŏp 중소 기업 small and medium industry

chungt'ae 중태 serious condition MED

chungt'ae-esŏ pŏsŏnan 중태에서 벗어난 out of danger MED

chungt'oehada 중퇴하다 drop out

chungt'oeja 중퇴자 dropout

chung-wi 중위 (first) lieutenant

chun-gyŏlssŭng 준결승 semifinal

chung-yohada 중요하다 be important

chung-yohan 중요한 important, crucial

chung-yo insa 중요 인사 very important person

chung-yo shinch'e kigwan 중요 신체 기관 vital organs

chunim 주님 Lord (Jesus)

chunjun-gyŏlssŭng 준준결승 quarter-final

chunjun-gyŏlssŭng chinch'ultcha 준준결승 진출자 quarter-finalist

chun kunsajŏgin 준 군사적인 paramilitary

chun kunsayowŏn 준 군사요원 paramilitary

chunŏmhan 준엄한 austere

chunsŏrhada 준설하다 dredge

chunsuja 준수자 conformist

chun ŭiryo hwalttong chongsaja 준 의료 활동 종사자 paramedic

chuŏ 주어 subject GRAM

chup'asu 주파수 frequency

chu(rib)ŭi 주(립)의 state, provincial

churi chida 줄이 지다 be streaked with

churida 줄이다 reduce; turn down *volume, heating*; cut down, cut down on; cut short; shorten; narrow

churin irŭm 줄인 이름 diminutive

churŏdŭlda 줄어들다 go down; die down; shrink

churŏdŭrŏ it-tta 줄어들어 있다 be down (of numbers, amount)

churo 주로 mainly

churŭm 주름 pleat; crease; wrinkle

churŭm changshik 주름 장식 ruffle

churŭm chegŏsul 주름 제거술 facelift

churŭmjida 주름지다 wrinkle

churŭmjige hada 주름지게 하다 wrinkle

churyehada 주례하다 marry

churyŏssŭda 줄여쓰다 abbreviate

churyu p'anmaejŏm 주류 판매점 liquor store

chusa 주사 injection

chusagi 주사기 syringe

chusahada 주사하다 inject

chusa panŭl 주사 바늘 hypodermic needle

chusawi 주사위 dice

chushik 주식 stock, share

chushik chungmae-in 주식 중매인 stockbroker

chushik hoesa 주식 회사 stock company

chushik shijang 주식 시장 (stock) market

chusŏk 주석 gloss, explanation; tin

chuso 주소 address

chusorok 주소록 address book; mailing list

chusorŭl ssŭda 주소를 쓰다 address letter

chuso sŏngmyŏngnok 주소 성명록 directory

chut'aek 주택 housing

chut'aek sajŏng 주택 사정 housing conditions

chut'aek tanji 주택 단지 housing project

chuŭi 주의 attention; warning; notice

chuŭi chuda 주의 주다 tick off

chuŭigip'ŭn 주의깊은 attentive, watchful

chuŭihada 주의하다 pay attention, take notice of

chuŭi kipkke saenggak'ada 주의 깊게 생각하다 mull over

chuŭirŭl kiurida 주의를 기울이다 pay attention

chuŭirŭl kkŭlda 주의를 끌다 draw attention

chuŭirŭl tollida 주의를 돌리다 sidetrack

chuŭishik'ida 주의시키다 caution

chuwi 주위 perimeter, periphery ◊ around; **chuwie** 주위에 around, in the area

chuwiŭi 주위의 surrounding

chuwŏ moŭda 주워 모으다 gather up

chuwŏ ollida 주워 올리다 pick up

chuya p'yŏngbunshi 주야 평분시 equinox

chuyŏnhada 주연하다 star

chuyŏnŭro hada 주연으로 하다 feature; star

chuyohan 주요한 main, major; predominant

chuyo shikp'um 주요 식품 staple food

chuyoshikttan 주요식단 staple diet

chuyu p'ŏmp'ŭ 주유 펌프 gas pump

chuyuso 주유소 gas station

chwach'ŭk haendŭl unjŏn 좌측 핸들 운전 left-hand drive

chwach'ugŭi 좌측의 port; left-hand

chwadamhoe 좌담회 talk show

chwagol shin-gyŏngt'ong 좌골 신경통 sciatica

chwaigŭi 좌익의 left-wing

chwaik 좌익 left wing ◊ left-wing

chwajŏl 좌절 frustration; setback; discouragement

chwajŏlsshik'ida 좌절시키다 frustrate; defeat; foil, thwart

chwajŏrhada 좌절하다 collapse; go to pieces; get discouraged

chwaumyŏng 좌우명 motto

chwayak 좌약 suppository

chwi 쥐 mouse; rat

chwikkori 쥐꼬리 rat tail

chwikkorimanhan 쥐꼬리만한 derisory, paltry

chyusŭ 쥬스 juice

CH'

ch'a 차 vehicle; car; tea; *ch'aro teryǒjuda* 차로 데려다주다 drive, take by car; *ch'arǔl t'ago kabǒrida* 차를 타고 가버리다 drive away

ch'abǒrida 차버리다 ditch, jilt

ch'abunhan 차분한 placid, serene; imperturbable

ch'abyǒl 차별 discrimination

ch'abyǒrhada 차별하다 differentiate between; discriminate against

ch'ach'a 차차 by degrees

ch'ach'ang 차창 car window; bus window; train window

ch'ach'e 차체 bodywork

ch'ach'e kongjang 차체 공장 body shop

ch'ach'uk 차축 axle

ch'ada 차다 be filled, be packed; be satisfied; expire; kick; reject

ch'adanhada 차단하다 block out; exclude

ch'ado 차도 driveway

ch'adorǔl poida 차도를 보이다 make progress (*in health*)

ch'ado tchogǔi 차도 쪽의 offside MOT

ch'ae 채 bat ◊ *countword for buildings*

ch'aegim 책임 responsibility; accountability; *...e ch'aegimi it-tta* ...에 책임이 있다 be responsible for; *ch'aegimǔl chida* 책임을 지다 be held accountable for, answer for; *ch'aegimǔl chǒn-gahada* 책임을 전가하다 pass the buck

ch'aegimi innǔn 책임이 있는 responsible

ch'aegimi mugǒun 책임이 무거운 responsible *job*

ch'aegimja 책임자 person in charge; *ch'aegimjarǔl mannal su issǔlkkayo?* 책임자를 만날 수 있을까요? can I see the manager?

ch'aegim pohǒm 책임 보험 liability insurance

ch'aegurhada 채굴하다 mine for

ch'aegwangch'ang 채광창 skylight

ch'aegwǒnja 채권자 creditor

ch'aek 책 book

ch'aek-kkabang 책가방 school bag

ch'aekkwǒn 채권 bond

ch'aekssang 책상 desk

ch'aektchang 책장 bookcase

ch'aek k'ǒbǒ 책 커버 dust jacket

ch'aemp'iǒn 챔피언 champion

ch'aemuja 채무자 debtor

ch'aeng 챙 visor

ch'aenggyǒduda 챙겨두다 set aside

ch'aengnyak 책략 maneuver

ch'aenǒl 채널 channel

ch'aeshigǔi 채식의 vegetarian

ch'aeshiktchuǔija 채식주의자 vegetarian

ch'aesǒktchang 채석장 quarry

ch'aetchiktchil 채찍질 beating; whip

ch'aetchiktchirhada 채찍질하다 whip, beat

ch'aet'aek 채택 choice, selection; adoption

ch'aet'aek'hada 채택하다 select, choose; adopt

ch'aeuda 채우다 complete, fill out; do up, fasten; fill; chill

ch'aewǒ nǒt'a 채워 넣다 stuff

ch'agaptta 차갑다 be cold; be coldhearted

ch'agaun 차가운 cold; cool

ch'age hada 차게 하다 chill

ch'agi 차기 kick

ch'ago 차고 (parking) garage

ch'agwandan 차관단 consortium

ch'agyonghada 착용하다 put on; wear; *anjǒnbelt'ǔrǔl ch'agyonghashio* 안전벨트를 착용하시오 fasten your seatbelt

ch'ai 차이 difference; *amurǒn ch'aiga ǒptta* 아무런 차이가 없다 it

doesn't make any difference

ch'ajaboda 찾아보다 look; look up;
look out for

ch'ajabogi 찾아보기 index

ch'ajagada 찾아가다 pay a visit to

ch'ajanaeda 찾아내다 dig out; dig up

ch'ajang 차장 conductor (*on train*)

ch'aja tanida 찾아 다니다 scour,
search

ch'ajihada 차지하다 occupy, take up

ch'ajŭngnanŭn kŏt 짜증나는 것
irritation

ch'akch'wi 착취 exploitation

ch'akch'wihada 착취하다 exploit;
tonŭl ch'akch'wihada 돈을
착취하다 bleed, drain *fig*

ch'ak-kkak 착각 delusion

ch'ak-kkak'ada 착각하다 mistake;
*nŏn sŭsŭro ch'ak-kkak'ago innŭn
kŏya* 넌 스스로 착각하고 있는 거야
you're deluding yourself

ch'akssaek 착색 stain (*for wood*)

ch'akssaek'ada 착색하다 stain *wood*

ch'aksshi 착시 optical illusion

ch'aksshirhan saenghwarŭl hada
착실한 생활을 하다 go straight

ch'akssŏk'ayŏ chushipsshio
착석하여 주십시오 please take a seat

ch'akssuhada 착수하다 start,
commence; mount; launch; *chinjihage ch'akssuhada* 진지하게
착수하다 start in earnest; knuckle
down

ch'aktchap'an 착잡한 complex;
*nanŭn kŭege ch'aktchap'an
shimjŏng-ŭl kajigo it-tta* 나는
그에게 착잡한 심정을 가지고 있다 I
have mixed feelings about him

ch'ak'an ch'ŏk'anŭn saram 착한
척하는 사람 goody-goody

ch'algwasang 찰과상 graze

ch'alk'ak'anŭn soriga nada
찰칵하는 소리가 나다 click

ch'alssak ch'ida 찰싹 치다 swat

ch'alssak ttaerida 찰싹 때리다 slap,
cuff

ch'alssak ttaerim 찰싹 때림 blow,
cuff

ch'am 참 truth ◊ true ◊ truly; what!

ch'amara! 참아라! just be patient!

ch'amch'i 참치 tuna

ch'amga 참가 participation

ch'amgahada 참가하다 enter;
participate; play in; *kŏrae
ch'amgahada* 거래에 참가하다
come in on a deal

ch'amgaja 참가자 entrant,
participant; entry

ch'amgashik'ida 참가시키다 enter

ch'amgohada 참고하다 consult

ch'amgo tosŏ 참고 도서 reference
book

ch'am-gyŏn chal hanŭn saram 참견
잘 하는 사람 busybody

ch'amgyŏnhada 참견하다 poke
one's nose into

ch'amgyŏnhagi choahanŭn
참견하기 좋아하는 nosy

ch'amho 참호 trench

ch'a mŏlmi 차 멀미 car sickness

ch'amp'ae 참패 thashing, massacre
SP

ch'amp'aeshik'ida 참패시키다
thrash SP

ch'amsae 참새 sparrow

ch'amshinhan 참신한 refreshing;
gratifying

ch'amsŏk 참석 attendance

ch'amsŏktcha 참석자 turnout

ch'amsŏk'ada 참석하다 attend, be
present; *chamkkan ch'amsŏk'ada*
잠깐 참석하다 put in an appearance

ch'amsŏn 참선 meditation
(*Buddhism*)

ch'amsŏnhada 참선하다 meditate
(*Buddhism*)

ch'amtta 참다 contain, repress;
contain oneself; stand, tolerate;
stomach

ch'amŭlssŏng 참을성 patience

ch'amŭlssŏng innŭn 참을성 있는
patient

ch'amŭlssŏng itkke 참을성 있게
patiently

ch'amŭlssŏng ŏmnŭn 참을성 없는
impatient

ch'amŭl su innŭn 참을 수 있는
tolerable

ch'amŭl su ŏmnŭn 참을 수 없는
intolerable

ch'amŭro 참으로 vitally

ch'amyŏhada 참여하다 take part in

ch'anban yangnon 찬반 양론 the pros and cons

ch'angbaek 창백 pallor

ch'angbaek'an 창백한 pale, pasty

ch'anggo 창고 depot, warehouse; storehouse; stockroom; ... *ch'anggo-e nŏ-ŏ pogwanhada* ... 창고에 넣어 보관하다 put in storage

ch'anggu 창구 wicket, window

ch'angja 창자 bowels, gut

ch'angjaktcha 창작자 author

ch'angjo 창조 creation

ch'angjohada 창조하다 create

ch'angjoja 창조자 creator

ch'angjojŏgin 창조적인 creative

ch'angjomul 창조물 creation, work

ch'angmun 창문 window

ch'angmunŭl yŏrŏ chushigessŭmnikka? 창문을 열어 주시겠습니까? would you mind opening the window?

ch'angnyŏ 창녀 prostitute, hooker

ch'angnyuk 착륙 landing, touchdown

ch'angnyuk changch'i 착륙 장치 undercarriage, landing gear

ch'angnyukshik'ida 착륙시키다 land

ch'angnyuk'ada 착륙하다 land, touch down

ch'angshija 창시자 originator

ch'angsŏltcha 창설자 creator, founder

ch'angt'ŏk 창턱 windowsill

ch'ang-ŭijŏgin 창의적인 inventive

ch'ang-yuri 창유리 pane, windowpane

ch'anmija 찬미자 admirer

ch'annip 찻잎 tea leaf

ch'ansa 찬사 compliment

ch'ansahada 찬사하다 compliment, pay a compliment

ch'ansahanŭn 찬사하는 complimentary

ch'ansŏnghada 찬성하다 approve; approve of; be in favor of

ch'ansongga 찬송가 hymn

ch'antchang 찬장 cupboard (*in kitchen*); sideboard

ch'a pongji 차 봉지 teabag

ch'apssal 찹쌀 glutinous rice, sticky rice

ch'ap'okttŭng 차폭등 sidelight

ch'arida 차리다 prepare *meal*; set up *shop*; dress up; keep; collect *one's senses*; take care; preserve; *ch'arin kŏn optchiman mani tŭseyo* 차린 건 없지만 많이 드세요 please help yourself

ch'aryang 차량 railroad car, carriage

ch'aryang kujo hoesa 차량 구조 회사 wrecking company

ch'aryang kyŏninso 차량 견인소 pound (*for cars*)

ch'aryang tŭngnok pŏnho 등록 번호 license plate number

ch'arye 차례 turn, act; *nŏŭi ch'arye* 너의 차례 over to you; *ch'arye ch'aryero* 차례 차례로 in turns; *che ch'aryeimnida* 제 차례입니다 it's my turn; *tangshin ch'aryeyeyo* 당신 차례예요 it's your turn

ch'aryŏ ipta 차려 입다 dress up; *mŏttchige ch'aryŏ ipta* 멋지게 차려 입다 get dolled up

ch'aryŏnaeda 차려내다 serve up

ch'a sech'ŏk 차 세척 car wash

ch'asŏn 차선 (*traffic*) lane

ch'atchan 찻잔 teacup

ch'atkki himdŭn 찾기 힘든 elusive

ch'atssutkkarak 찻숟가락 teaspoon

ch'attchan set'ŭ 찻잔 세트 tea service, tea set

ch'attchŏmja 차점자 runner-up

ch'at-tta 찾다 find; look for; search for *place*

ch'ayang 차양 awning

ch'ayongja 차용자 tenant

ch'e 체 sieve, strainer; pretense

ch'ege 체계 system

ch'egejŏguro 체계적으로 systematically

ch'egyŏk 체격 physique, build

ch'ehada 체하다 pretend

ch'ehŏm 체험 experience

ch'ehyŏng 체형 corporal punishment

ch'ein 체인 chain

ch'einjŏm 체인점 chain (*of stores*)

ch'eisŏ 체이서 chaser

ch'ejil 체질 constitution

ch'ejo 체조 gymnastics

ch'ejobok 체조복 leotard

ch'ejung kwadaŭi 체중 과다의 overweight

ch'ejung midarŭi 체중 미달의 underweight

ch'ejung-ŭl nŭrida 체중을 늘이다 put on weight

Ch'ek'o 체코 Czech

Ch'ek'o konghwaguk 체코 공화국 Czech Republic

Ch'ek'oŏ 체코어 Czech (language)

Ch'ek'o saram 체코 사람 Czech (person)

ch'ek'ŭaut'ada 체크아웃하다 check out

ch'ek'ŭinhada 체크인하다 check in

ch'ek'ŭ munŭi 체크 무늬 check pattern

ch'ek'ŭ munŭiŭi 체크 무늬의 checked

ch'ek'ŭp'oint'ŭ 체크포인트 checkpoint

ch'ello 첼로 cello

ch'emyŏnŭl ch'arinŭn 체면을 차리는 image-conscious

ch'emyŏnŭl ilt'a 체면을 잃다 lose face; be in the doghouse

ch'emyŏnŭl sonsangshik'ida 체면을 손상시키다 degrade; chagiŭi ch'emyŏnŭl sonsangshik'ida 자기의 체면을 손상시키다 compromise oneself

ch'emyŏnŭl sonsangshik'inŭn 체면을 손상시키는 degrading

ch'enae 체내 inside the body; ch'enaee(sŏ) 체내에(서) internally; ch'enae pangsanŭng punp'o sajin 체내 방사능 분포 사진 scan MED

ch'enap 체납 delinquency

ch'enyŏmhanŭn 체념하는 resigned

ch'eŏ lip'ŭt'ŭ 체어 리프트 chair lift

ch'ep'o 체포 arrest

ch'ep'ohada 체포하다 arrest, pick up

ch'ero ch'ida 체로 치다 sift

ch'eryŏginnŭn 체력있는 athletic

ch'eryŏk 체력 stamina

ch'eryu 체류 residence, stay

ch'esŭ 체스 chess

ch'esŭp'an 체스판 chessboard

ch'eyuk 체육 gym, gymnastics

ch'eyuk-kkwan 체육관 gym, gymnasium

ch'eyuk kyosa 체육 교사 gymnast

ch'ia 치아 teeth ◊ dental

ch'ia kŏmsa 치아 검사 dental checkup

ch'ida 치다 hit, knock; buffet; count, include; strike (of clock); crash (of thunder); draw curtain; pitch tent; take exam

ch'igi 치기 slap, blow

ch'igwan 치관 crown

ch'ijanghada 치장하다 preen oneself

ch'ijil 치질 piles

ch'ijŭ 치즈 cheese

ch'ijŭbŏgŏ 치즈버거 cheeseburger

ch'ijŭk'eik 치즈케익 cheesecake

ch'ikkwa 치과 dental clinic

ch'ikkwa ŭisa 치과 의사 dentist

ch'ik'yŏ ollagan 치켜 올라간 slanting

ch'il 칠 seven; paint; varnish; laquer; ch'il chu-ŭi 칠 주의 wet paint

ch'ilgi 칠기 lacquerware

ch'ilmyŏnjo 칠면조 turkey

ch'ilp'an 칠판 blackboard

ch'ilsship 칠십 seventy

ch'im 침 saliva; acupuncture

ch'ima 치마 skirt

ch'imbŏm 침범 invasion; intrusion

ch'imbŏmhada 침범하다 invade; intrude

ch'imch'ak 침착 calm, composure; poise

ch'imch'ak'ada 침착하다 keep one's cool

ch'imch'ak'age hae! 침착하게 해! steady on!

ch'imch'ak'age it-tta 침착하게 있다 keep calm; keep one's wits about one

ch'imch'ak'am 침착함 presence of mind

ch'imch'ak'an 침착한 calm, composed; poised; unflappable

ch'imch'ehada 침체하다 stagnate

ch'imch'ehan 침체한 stagnant

ch'imdae 침대 bed

ch'imdaebo 침대보 bedspread

ch'imdaech'a 침대차 sleeping car

ch'imdaech'atkkan 침대찻간

couchette
ch'imdaek'an 침대칸 berth
ch'imdaeppo 침대보 cover, blanket
ch'imgu 침구 bedclothes
ch'imha 침하 subsidence
ch'imhaehada 침해하다 encroach on
rights
ch'imip 침입 break-in, raid
ch'imiptcha 침입자 intruder, raider
ch'imip'ada 침입하다 encroach on;
trepass; infiltrate; break in; raid
ch'imjönmul 침전물 sediment
ch'immugŭl chik'ida 침묵을 지키다
stay silent
ch'immuk 침묵 silence
ch'immukshik'ida 침묵시키다
silence
ch'imnyak 침략 invasion
ch'imnyak'ada 침략하다 invade
ch'imnyŏpssu 침엽수 conifer
ch'imp'anji 침판지 chimpanzee
ch'imshik 침식 erosion
ch'imshik'ada 침식하다 erode
ch'imshil 침실 bedroom
ch'imsul 침술 acupuncture
ch'imt'u 침투 penetration
ch'imŭl hŭllida 침을 흘리다 dribble
ch'imŭl paet-tta 침을 뱉다 spit
ch'imurhae it-tta 침울해 있다 be
gloomy, feel down
ch'imurhage nŭkkida 침울하게
느끼다 be feeling low
ch'imurhan 침울한 melancholy;
dismal; sullen; somber
ch'imyŏngjŏgin 치명적인 fatal,
lethal; devastating, shattering
ch'imyŏngsang-ŭi 치명상의 fatally
injured
ch'inaehanŭn 친애하는 dear
ch'inbumo 친부모 biological parents
ch'inch'ŏgi toenŭn 친척이 되는
related
ch'inch'ŏk 친척 relative, relation
ch'ingch'an 칭찬 praise
ch'ingch'anhada 칭찬하다 praise;
pay a compliment
ch'ingch'anhal manhan 칭찬할 만한
creditable; praiseworthy
ch'ingho 칭호 form of address
ch'ing-ŏlgŏrida 칭얼거리다 whine,
complain

ch'ingsong 칭송 applause, praise
ch'ingsonghada 칭송하다 applaud,
praise
ch'in-gŭnhan 친근한 familiar,
friendly
ch'in-gu 친구 friend, buddy
ch'in-guga toeda 친구가 되다 make
friends
ch'in-gyo moim 친교 모임 get-
together
ch'inhada 친하다 be close;
Xwa / kwa ch'inhage toeda X와 / 과
친하게 되다 be friendly with X, be
friends with X
ch'inhan 친한 friendly; close
ch'inhwan-gyŏngjŏgin 친환경적인
environmentally friendly
ch'inhwan-gyŏng sech'ŏktche
친환경 세척제 biological detergent
ch'injŏl 친절 kindness
ch'injŏrhada 친절하다 be kind
ch'injŏrhage 친절하게 kindly;
nuguege ch'injŏrhage hada
누구에게 친절하게 하다 do s.o. a
good turn
ch'injŏrhan 친절한 kind
ch'inmogŭi 친목의 social
ch'insuk'am 친숙함 intimacy
ch'insuk'an 친숙한 intimate
ch'iŏ nŏmŏttŭrida 치어 넘어뜨리다
knock over; run over
ch'iŏridŏ 치어리더 cheerleader
ch'ip 칩 chip
ch'irhada 칠하다 paint
ch'irhŭk 칠흑 pitch black
ch'irŭda 치르다 pay; take
examination; undergo; hold
ceremony
ch'irwŏl 칠월 July
ch'iryo 치료 cure; treatment; therapy
ch'iryo chŏnmun-ga 치료 전문가
therapist
ch'iryohada 치료하다 treat; cure
ch'iryoŭi 치료의 therapeutic
ch'isŏk 치석 plaque
ch'isot-tta 치솟다 rocket, soar, shoot
up
ch'issu 치수 size; measurements
ch'issurŭl chaeda 치수를 재다
measure
ch'itssol 칫솔 toothbrush

ch'it'ong 치통 toothache
ch'iuda 치우다 brush; clear; remove; put away
ch'iyak 치약 toothpaste
ch'iyŏl kyojŏnggi 치열 교정기 brace
ch'iyŏrhan 치열한 cut-throat
ch'iyok 치욕 a disgrace; *ch'iyoktchŏgin iriyeyo* 치욕적인 일이에요 it's a disgrace
ch'iyokssŭrŏpkke 불명예스럽게 disgracefully, shamefully
ch'ŏbanghada 처방하다 prescribe
ch'ŏbangjŏn 처방전 prescription
ch'ŏbŏl 처벌 punishment; penalty
ch'ŏbŏrhada 처벌하다 punish; penalize
ch'ŏbun 처분 disposal
ch'ŏbunhada 처분하다 dispose of; part with
ch'ŏhada 처하다 run into
ch'ŏhyŏng 처형 sister-in-law (*wife's elder sister*)
ch'ŏje 처제 sister-in-law (*wife's younger sister*)
ch'ŏjida 저지다 hang down; *ch'uk ch'ŏjida* 축 처지다 sag (*of ceiling, rope*)
ch'ŏk 척 *countword for boats*
ch'ŏkch'u 척추 spine
ch'ŏkch'u chiapssa 척추 지압사 chiropractor
ch'ŏkch'udongmul 척추동물 vertebrate
ch'ŏkch'ugol 척추골 vertebra
ch'ŏkch'uŭi 척추의 spinal
ch'ŏktto 척도 yardstick, criterion
ch'ŏk'ada 척하다 pretend, play-act
ch'ŏl 철 season, period
ch'ŏlgap sang-ŏ aljŏt 철갑 상어 알젓 caviar
ch'ŏlgongso 철공소 ironworks
ch'ŏlgŭn k'onk'ŭrit'ŭ 철근 콘크리트 reinforced concrete
ch'ŏlk'ŏdŏnghanŭn sori 철커덩하는 소리 clang
ch'ŏlk'ŏdŏnghanŭn soriga nada 철커덩하는 소리가 나다 clang
ch'ŏlmang 철망 wire netting
ch'ŏlmul 철물 hardware
ch'ŏlmultchŏm 철물점 hardware store

ch'ŏlssa 철사 wire
ch'ŏlssŏk ttaerida 철썩 때리다 whack
ch'ŏlssu 철수 withdrawal
ch'ŏlssuhada 철수하다 withdraw (*of troops*)
ch'ŏlssushik'ida 철수시키다 withdraw *troops*
ch'ŏltcha 철자 spelling
ch'ŏltchahada 철자하다 spell
ch'ŏltcha hwagin 철자 확인 spellcheck
ch'ŏltcha hwagin togu 철자 확인 도구 spellchecker
ch'ŏltchŏhage 철저하게 thoroughly
ch'ŏltchŏhan 철저한 thorough; exhaustive
ch'ŏltchŏhi chosahada 철저히 조사하다 look through
ch'ŏltto 철도 rail; railroad; track
ch'ŏma 처마 eaves
ch'ŏmbusŏ 첨부서 covering letter
ch'ŏmdan kisul 첨단 기술 high technology, high tech
ch'ŏmdanŭi 첨단의 leading-edge
ch'ŏmgaje 첨가제 (food) additive
ch'ŏn 천 cloth; thousand
ch'ŏ-nam 처남 brother-in-law (*wife's younger brother*)
ch'ŏnbak'an 천박한 shallow, superficial; small-minded
ch'ŏnch'amanbyŏrijiyo 천차만별이지요 it varies
ch'ŏnch'ŏnhi 천천히 slowly
ch'ŏnch'ung 촌충 tapeworm
ch'ŏndung 천둥 thunder
ch'ŏngbaji 청바지 jeans
ch'ŏngbu sarinja 청부 살인자 hitman
ch'ŏngch'ŏnbyŏngnyŏk-kkwa kach'i 청천벽력과 같이 like a bolt from the blue
ch'ŏngch'un-gi 청춘기 youth (*age*)
ch'ŏngch'wihada 청취하다 tune in to
ch'ŏngch'wija 청취자 listener; audience (*of radio program*)
ch'ŏngdong 청동 bronze
ch'ŏngdongsaek 청동색 bronze
ch'ŏnggak chang-ae 청각 장애 deafness

ch'ŏngganghada 청강하다 audit
ch'ŏnggangsaeng 청강생 auditor
ch'ŏnggu 청구 claim
ch'ŏngguhada 청구하다 charge; claim
ch'ŏnggusŏ 청구서 bill
ch'ŏnggyŏl 청결 purity
ch'ŏnggyodo 청교도 puritan
ch'ŏnghada 청하다 request
ch'ŏnghon 청혼 proposal
ch'ŏnghonhada 청혼하다 propose
ch'ŏngja 청자 celadon ware
ch'ŏngjin-gii 청진기 stethoscope
ch'ŏngjinhada 청진하다 sound
ch'ŏngjung 청중 audience
ch'ŏngnokssaek 청록색 turquoise
ch'ŏngnyang ŭmnyo 청량 음료 soft drink
ch'ŏngnyŏk 청력 hearing
ch'ŏng-ŏ 청어 herring
ch'ŏn-gonggi 천공기 drill
ch'ŏngsajin 청사진 blueprint
ch'ŏngsan 청산 settlement; liquidation
ch'ŏngsanhada 청산하다 go into liquidation; settle; write off
ch'ŏngsobu 청소부 cleaner
ch'ŏngsohada 청소하다 clean; clean up; rub down; *kkaekkŭt'age ch'ŏngsohada* 깨끗하게 청소하다 clean out *room, closet*
ch'ŏngsohanŭn ajumma 청소하는 아줌마 cleaning woman
ch'ŏngsokkwa 청소과 sanitation department
ch'ŏngsonyŏn 청소년 adolescents, juveniles ◊ juvenile, adolescent
ch'ŏngsonyŏn pihaeng 청소년 비행 youthful misdemeanors
ch'ŏnguk 천국 heaven
Ch'ŏng-wadae 청와대 The Blue House (*South Korean President's residence*)
ch'ŏng-wŏnsŏ 청원서 petition
ch'ŏnhamujŏgŭi 천하무적의 unbeaten
ch'ŏnhan 천한 humble, menial
ch'ŏnjae 천재 genius
ch'ŏnjaejibyŏn 천재지변 catastrophe, disaster
ch'ŏnjang 천장 ceiling

ch'ŏnjang-ŭi nop'i 천장의 높이 headroom
Ch'ŏnji ch'angjo 천지 창조 Creation REL
ch'ŏnjinhan 천진한 childlike; disarming
Ch'ŏnjugyo 천주교 Roman Catholicism
Ch'ŏnjugyo shinja 천주교 신자 Catholic
Ch'ŏnjugyoŭi 천주교의 Catholic
ch'ŏnmagŭl ch'ida 천막을 치다 camp
ch'ŏnmak 천막 tent
ch'ŏnmaneyo 천만에요 you're welcome
ch'ŏnmunhak 천문학 astronomy
ch'ŏnmunhaktcha 천문학자 astronomer
ch'ŏnmunhaktchŏgin 천문학적인 astronomical
ch'ŏnnyŏn 천년 millennium
ch'ŏn pŏntchaeŭi 천 번째의 thousandth
ch'ŏn pŏnŭi 천 번의 thousandth
ch'ŏnshik 천식 asthma
ch'ŏnsŏng 천성 nature, disposition
ch'ŏntchogak 천조각 pad, wad
ch'ŏnyŏ 처녀 virgin (*female*)
ch'ŏnyŏ hanghae 처녀 항해 maiden voyage
ch'ŏnyŏndu 천연두 smallpox
ch'ŏnyŏn kassŭ 천연 가스 natural gas
ch'ŏrhada 철하다 file
ch'ŏrhak 철학 philosophy
ch'ŏrhaktcha 철학자 philosopher
ch'ŏrhatchŏgin 철학적인 philosophical
ch'ŏrhoehada 철회하다 pull out; withdraw; backpedal; dispense with, waive
ch'ŏrihada 처리하다 take care of, deal with; cope with; cope; process; transact
ch'ŏrŏm 처럼 as, like
chŏryak'ada 절약하다 economize
ch'ŏshinhada 처신하다 conduct oneself
ch'ŏt 첫 first; *...ŭi ch'ŏtchaenare* ...의 첫째날에 on the 1st of ...

ch'ŏt-tchaero 첫째로 in the first place

ch'ŏtwŏlgŭp 첫 월급 starting salary

ch'ŏŭm 처음 start

ch'ŏŭmbut'ŏ 처음부터 initially; from the start

ch'ŏŭmbut'ŏ shijak'ada 처음부터 시작하다 start from scratch

ch'ŏŭmenŭn 처음에는 originally, at first

ch'ŏŭmŭi 처음의 first

ch'ŏŭmŭro 처음으로 first; the first time

ch'o 초 candle; excerpt; second; draft; vinegar; beginning, early part ◊ ultra-; *yuwŏl ch'oe* 유월 초에 in early June

ch'oboja 초보자 beginner

ch'och'im 초침 second hand (*on clock*)

ch'odae 초대 invitation

ch'odaehada 초대하다 invite

ch'odŭnghak-kkyo 초등학교 elementary school, infant school

ch'odŭnghak-kkyo kyosa 초등학교 교사 elementary teacher

ch'oe-agŭi sangt'ae-enŭn 최악의 상태에는 if the worst comes to worst

ch'oe-ak 최악 the worst

ch'oech'ŏmdan 최첨단 frontier

ch'oech'ŏmdanŭi 최첨단의 state-of-the-art

ch'oech'oŭi 최초의 original; initial

ch'oedae 최대 maximum; *...ŭl ch'oedaehan hwaryonghayŏ kkŭrŏnaeda* ...을 최대한 활용하여 끌어내다 make the most of

ch'oedaehanŭi 최대한의 utmost

ch'oedaehanŭro 최대한으로 at the outside

ch'oedaehanŭro iyonghada 최대한으로 이용하다 make the best of

ch'oedaehwahada 최대화하다 maximize

ch'oedae saengsannyŏk 최대 생산력 capacity

ch'oedae sobiryang 최대 소비량 peak consumption

ch'oedaeŭi 최대의 maximum

ch'oego 최고 the best

ch'oegoch'i 최고치 peak

ch'oegoch'ie tarhada 최고치에 달하다 peak

ch'oegogŭbŭi 최고급의 first-rate

ch'oego hando 최고 한도 ceiling, limit

ch'oego kyŏngnyŏngja 최고 경영자 CEO, Chief Executive Officer

ch'oego p'umjil pojŭng kigan 최고 품질 보증 기간 best before date

ch'oego saryŏnggwan 최고 사령관 commander-in-chief

ch'oego suwi 최고 수위 high water

ch'oegoŭi 최고의 best; top; terrific

ch'oegoŭmbuŭi 최고음부의 treble

ch'oegowiŭi 최고위의 supreme

ch'oegŭn 최근 newly

ch'oegŭne 최근에 recently; lately

ch'oegŭnŭi 최근의 recent; latest

ch'oehu t'ongch'ŏp 최후 통첩 ultimatum

ch'oehuŭi kyŏng-ŭi 최후의 경의 last respects; *nuguege ch'oehuŭi kyŏng-ŭirŭl p'yohada* 누구에게 최후의 경의를 표하다 pay one's last respects to s.o.

ch'oejŏgŭi 최적의 optimum

ch'oejŏk 최적 optimum

ch'oejŏng-ŭi 최종의 final

ch'oejŏ ponggŭp 최저 봉급 minimum wage

ch'oejŏ saenghwal sujun 최저 생활 수준 subsistence level

ch'oejŏŭi 최저의 rock-bottom

ch'oejong 최종 the last; the end ◊ final

ch'oejong kyŏlkwa 최종 결과 end result

ch'oejong myŏngdan 최종 명단 shortlist

ch'oejong sayongja 최종 사용자 end-user

ch'oejongsuro 최종수로 at the last count

ch'oemyŏnsul 최면술 hypnosis

ch'oemyŏnsurŭl kŏlda 최면술을 걸다 hypnotize

ch'oemyŏn yoppŏp 최면 요법 hypnotherapy

ch'oerugasŭ 최루가스 tear gas

ch'oesang-ŭi 최상의 top, best; ultimate

ch'oeshin chŏngborŭl chuda 최신 정보를 주다 update

ch'oeshinŭi 최신의 latest; up-to-date

ch'oeshin yuhaeng-ŭi 최신 유행의 trendy

ch'oesŏnŭl tahada 최선을 다하다 do one's best

ch'oeso 최소 minimum

ch'oesohanŭi 최소한의 minimum

ch'oesohwahada 최소화하다 minimize

ch'oesoryang 최소량 least

ch'oesoŭi 최소의 minimal

ch'oeusŏn sahang 최우선 사항 priority

ch'ogangdaeguk 초강대국 superpower

ch'ogi 초기 infancy

ch'ogiŭi 초기의 early, first

ch'ogo 초고 draft

ch'ogosok yŏlch'a 초고속 열차 bullet train

ch'ogwahada 초과하다 exceed; overrun time

ch'ogwahanŭn 초과하는 in excess of

ch'ogwa kŭnmu 초과 근무 overtime

ch'ogwa suhamul 초과 수하물 excess baggage

ch'ogwa yogŭm 초과 요금 excess fare

ch'ohyŏndaejŏgin 초현대적인 futuristic

ch'o ilkki 초 읽기 countdown

ch'oinjŏgin 초인적인 enormous

ch'oinjong 초인종 doorbell

ch'ojayŏnjŏgin 초자연적인 supernatural

ch'ojŏnyŏge 초저녁에 at nightfall

ch'ojohaehada 초조해하다 panic, flap

ch'ojohan 초조한 edgy

ch'ok-kkam 촉감 (sense of) touch

ch'okppak'an 촉박한 tight (of time)

ch'okssu 촉수 tentacle

ch'oktchin 촉진 boost

ch'oktchinhada 촉진하다 promote, foster

ch'oktchinje 촉진제 catalyst

ch'oktchinshik'ida 촉진시키다 boost

ch'ok'ollit 초콜릿 chocolate

ch'ok'ollit k'eik 초콜릿 케익 chocolate cake, brownie

ch'ok'ŭ 초크 choke

ch'ong 총 gun

ch'ong-aek 총액 total amount of money

ch'ong-al 총알 bullet; shotgun pellet

ch'ongbiyong 총비용 capital expenditure

ch'ongch'e 총체 the whole, all

ch'ongch'ong kŏrŭmŭro kada 총총 걸음으로 가다 trot

ch'onggak 총각 bachelor

ch'onggak p'at'i 총각 파티 stag party

ch'onggi hyudaeja 총기 휴대자 gunman

ch'onggye 총계 total; sum; gross

ch'onghoe 총회 general meeting

ch'ongkyŏlssan 총결산 bottom line

ch'ongmae k'ŏnbŏt'ŏ 총매 컨버터 catalytic converter

ch'ongmyŏngham 총명함 intelligence, brightness

ch'ongmyŏnghan 총명한 intelligent, bright

ch'ongsang 총상 gunshot wound

ch'ongsarhada 총살하다 shoot dead

ch'ongsŏn-gŏ 총선거 general election

ch'ongssori 총소리 gunshot

ch'ongŭk 촌극 sketch THEA

ch'onssŭrŏun 촌스러운 provincial, parochial

ch'onsŭrŏpkke hwaryŏhan 촌스럽게 화려한 gaudy

ch'onsŭrŏun 촌스러운 dowdy

ch'oraehada 초래하다 bring, create; incur

ch'orahan 초라한 humble

ch'osanghwa 초상화 portrait

ch'oshimja 초심자 novice

ch'osohyŏng 초소형 miniature, midget

ch'ossŭngttal 초승달 new moon

ch'otchŏm 초점 focus; ch'otchŏmi mat-tta / mat-tchi ant'a 초점이 맞다 / 맞지 않다 be in focus / out of focus; ch'otchŏmŭl match'uda 초점을 맞추다 focus on

ch'ot-ttae 촛대 candlestick
ch'oŭmp'a 초음파 ultrasound
ch'oŭmsok 초음속 supersonic speed
◊ supersonic
ch'owŏltchŏgin 초월적인
transcendental
ch'owŏn 초원 meadow
ch'oyŏn 초연 première
ch'oyŏnhan 초연한 aloof, remote
ch'ŭktchŏng 측정 measurement,
reading
ch'ŭktchŏnghada 측정하다 gauge
ch'ŭktchŏngppŏp 측정법 system (of
measurement)
ch'ŭng 층 layer; floor; tier; deck
ch'ŭnggye 층계 the stairs
ch'ŭnggyech'am 층계참 landing
ch'ubang 추방 exile; expulsion
ch'ubanghada 추방하다 exile;
t'up'yoe ŭihae ch'ubanghada
투표에 의해 추방하다 vote out
ch'ubangja 추방자 exile
ch'ubun 추분 the autumnal equinox
ch'uch'ŏn 추천 recommendation,
endorsement
ch'uch'ŏnhada 추천하다
recommend, endorse
ch'uch'ŏnsŏ 추천서 reference
ch'uch'ŏntchang 추천장 testimonial
ch'uch'ŭk 추측 guess; conjecture;
speculation
ch'uch'ŭk'ada 추측하다 expect;
gather; speculate; guess
ch'uch'ul 추출 extraction
ch'udohada 추도하다 mourn
ch'uga 추가 addition, supplement ◊
additional, extra
ch'uga-aek 추가액 supplement FIN
ch'ugahada 추가하다 add
ch'uga hangmok 추가 항목 add-on
ch'uganp'an 추간판 slipped disc
ch'ugaro 추가로 in addition
ch'uga yogŭm 추가 요금 extra
charge
ch'ugu 추구 search; pursuit
ch'uguhada 추구하다 pursue; search
for; seek
ch'ugyŏk 추격 chase
ch'uhu t'ongjiga issŭl ttaekkaji
추후 통지가 있을 때까지 until
further notice

ch'ujap'an 추잡한 lewd
ch'ujinhada 추진하다 propel, drive;
go ahead with; set things in motion
ch'ujinnyŏk 추진력 driving force
ch'ujŏk 추적 pursuit
ch'ujŏktcha 추적자 pursuer
ch'ujŏk'ada 추적하다 pursue; stalk;
trace
ch'ujŏng 추정 presumption
ch'ujŏngdoeda 추정되다 be
presumed; *muŏshi ...ttaemunŭro
ch'ujŏngdoeda* 무엇이 ...때문으로
추정되다 attribute sth to ...
ch'ujŏnghada 추정하다 presume
ch'ukch'ŏk 축척 scale
ch'ukch'ŏk tomyŏn 축척 도면 scale
drawing
ch'ukch'uk'age hada 축축하게 하다
dampen, moisten
ch'ukch'uk'an 축축한 damp, moist
ch'uk-kka 축가 carol
ch'uk-kku 축구 soccer
ch'uk-kku sŏnsu 축구 선수 soccer
player
ch'uk-kkugong 축구공 football, ball
ch'ukppok'ada 축복하다 bless
ch'ukssohada 축소하다 cut back
ch'uktche 축제 carnival; festival;
feast
ch'uktcheŭi 축제의 festive
ch'uk'a 축하 congratulations
ch'uk'ahada 축하하다 celebrate;
congratulate
ch'uk'a haengsa 축하 행사
festivities
ch'uk'ahamnida 축하합니다
congratulations on
ch'uk'ayŏn 축하연 celebration
ch'ulbal 출발 departure; starting;
start; *choŭn/nappŭn ch'ulbarŭl
hada* 좋은/나쁜 출발을 하다 get off
to a good/bad start; *sae ch'ulbal* 새
출발 a new departure
ch'ulbal shigak 출발 시각 departure
time
ch'ulbal shigan 출발 시간 flight time
ch'ulbaltchŏm 출발점 starting point;
threshold
ch'ulbarhada 출발하다 leave, go;
depart; set off
ch'ulgŭnhada 출근하다 go to work

ch'ulgu 출구 exit

ch'ullabwŏn 출납원 cashier

ch'ullyŏk 출력 output

ch'ullyŏk'ada 출력하다 output

ch'ulmahada 출마하다 run, stand; *taet'ongnyŏnge ch'ulmahada* 대통령에 출마하다 run for President

ch'ulp'an 출판 publication

ch'ulp'andoeda 출판되다 be published, be out

ch'ulp'anhada 출판하다 publish

ch'ulp'anŏp 출판업 publishing

ch'ulp'anŏptcha 출판업자 publisher (*person*)

ch'ulp'ansa 출판사 publisher (*company*)

ch'ulsan hyuga 출산 휴가 maternity leave

ch'ulssaeng chŏnŭi 출생 전의 prenatal

ch'ulssaeng chŭngmyŏngsŏ 출생 증명서 birth certificate

ch'ulssaengguk 출생국 native country

ch'ulssaengji 출생지 birthplace

ch'ulssaengnyul 출생률 birthrate

ch'ulssaeng-ŭi 출생의 native

ch'ulssan 출산 birth

ch'ulssan chŏnŭi 출산 전의 antenatal

ch'ulssanhada 출산하다 bear *child*

ch'ulsshihada 출시하다 appear, come out; bring out; release

ch'ulsshinida 출신이다 originate, come from

ch'ulsshin sŏngbun 출신 성분 background

ch'ulssŏk 출석 attendance

ch'ulchang 출장 business trip

ch'ulchŏnhada 출전하다 compete; go in for, enter

ch'ulttongshik'ida 출동시키다 call out

ch'ulttu 출두 appearance (*in court*)

ch'ulttuhada 출두하다 appear (*in court*); report

ch'ult'oegŭn shigan 출퇴근 시간 rush hour

ch'ult'oegŭn shigan kirok-kkye 출퇴근 시간 기록계 time clock

ch'um 춤 dance

ch'umch'uda 춤추다 dance

ch'unbun 춘분 the spring equinox

ch'ungbunhada 충분하다 be sufficient; be satisfactory; *kŭgŏllo ch'ungbunhamnida* 그걸로 충분합니다 that should be enough

ch'ungbunhage 충분하게 sufficiently

ch'ungbunhan 충분한 enough

ch'ungbunhan yang 충분한 양 enough

ch'ungbunhi 충분히 duly; enough

ch'ungch'i 충치 cavity

ch'ungch'iga saenggida 충치가 생기다 decay (*of teeth*)

ch'ungdol 충돌 collision; crash; conflict; impact

ch'ungdolshik'ida 충돌시키다 crash

ch'ungdong 충동 urge; impulse; *ch'ungdongjŏgŭro muŏsŭl hada* 충동적으로 무엇을 하다 do sth on an impulse

ch'ungdongjŏgin 충동적인 impulsive

ch'ungdong kumae 충동 구매 impulse buy

ch'ungdongtchŏgŭro 충동적으로 on the spur of the moment

ch'ungdorhada 충돌하다 crash; collide with, hit; clash; be at odds with

ch'unggo 충고 used, secondhand; advice; warning

ch'unggohada 충고하다 advise *caution etc*

ch'unggo han madi 충고 한 마디 piece of advice

ch'unggyŏgesŏ pŏsŏnaji mot'ada 충격에서 벗어나지 못하다 be in shock

ch'unggyŏgŭl pat-tta 충격을 받다 be shocked; be flabbergasted

ch'unggyŏk 충격 blow, shock

ch'unggyŏktchŏgin 충격적인 shocking, horrifying

ch'unghyŏldoen 충혈된 bloodshot

ch'ungjŏnhada 충전하다 charge *battery*

ch'ungjokshik'ida 충족시키다 meet, satisfy

ch'ungmanhada 충만하다 be full, be

filled; *hwalgiga ch'ungmanhan*
활기가 충만한 exuberant
ch'ungmyŏn 측면 side
ch'ungnongtchŭng 축농증 sinusitis
ch'ungshil 충실 fidelity, faithfulness
ch'ungshimŭro 충심으로 heartily,
cordially
ch'ungshirhada 충실하다 stick by;
be faithful, be loyal; *sangdaeege
ch'ungshirhada* 상대에게 충실하다
be faithful to one's partner
ch'ungshirhan 충실한 faithful,
staunch
ch'ungsŏngshim 충성심 sense of
loyalty; *kiŏbe taehan
ch'ungsŏngshim* 기업에 대한
충성심 sense of corporate loyalty
ch'ungsŏngsŭrŏun 충성스러운 loyal
ch'ungsu 충수 appendix
ch'ungsuyŏm 충수염 appendicitis
ch'uŏk 추억 memory
ch'up'a 추파 leer
ch'urak 추락 crash, fall
ch'urak'ada 추락하다 crash
ch'urhanghada 출항하다 sail, depart
ch'urhyŏl 출혈 bleeding; hemorrhage
ch'urhyŏn 출현 arrival, appearance
ch'urhyŏrhada 출혈하다 bleed;
hemorrhage
ch'urimmun 출입문 door; entrance;
exit
ch'urimul 추리물 whodunnit
ch'urip 출입 access
ch'uripkku 출입구 doorway
ch'urip kŭmji 출입 금지 off limits; no
trespassing
Ch'urip Kwalliguk 출입 관리국
Immigration Bureau
ch'urip'ang kŭmji 출입항 금지 ban,
embargo
ch'uron 추론 deduction, conclusion;
line of reasoning
ch'uronhada 추론하다 deduce; infer
ch'uryŏn 출연 appearance (*on TV
etc*)
ch'uryŏnaeda 추려내다 remove,
weed out
ch'uryŏnhada 출연하다 appear (*on
TV etc*)

ch'uryŏnjin 출연진 cast (*of play*)
ch'usangjŏgin 추상적인 abstract
ch'ushin 추신 PS, postscript
Ch'usŏk 추석 Harvest Festival
ch'usu 추수 harvest
Ch'usu Kamsajŏl 추수 감사절
Thanksgiving (Day)
ch'uun 추운 cold; freezing
ch'uwi 추위 cold; *chŏnŭn mopsshi
ch'uwŏyo* 저는 몹시 추워요 I'm
freezing cold
ch'uwŏrhada 추월하다 pass MOT
ch'waryŏng 촬영 photography
ch'waryŏnghada 촬영하다 film,
shoot
ch'waryŏngjangso 촬영장소 set (*for
movie*)
ch'waryŏng kisa 촬영 기사
cameraman
ch'wich'im shigan 취침 시간
bedtime
ch'widŭk'ada 취득하다 take
ch'wigŭp 취급 treatment
ch'wigŭp chuŭi 취급 주의 handle
with care!
ch'wihada 취하다 get drunk
ch'wihan 취한 high, loaded, stoned
ch'wihyang 취향 taste
ch'wiimshigŭl kŏhaenghada
취임식을 거행하다 inaugurate
ch'wiji akttan 취주 악단 brass
band
ch'wijung-ŭi 취중의 drunken
ch'wimi 취미 pastime, hobby
ch'wiso 취소 cancellation;
withdrawal
ch'wisohada 취소하다 cancel;
withdraw; tear up
ch'yat'ŭ 챠트 chart, map

...dago hani ...다고 하니 that
...dani ...다니 that
...dŏrado ...더라도 even though
...do ...도 as well, also
...do ŏptta ...도 없다 without any ...
at all
...dorok ...도록 so that, in order to;
till; as ... as possible
...dŭshi ...듯이 like, as; as if

E

...e ...에 in; at; on; for; *...e ch'aegimi it-tta* ...에 책임이 있다 be responsible for
...eda(ga) ...에다(가) at; in; on
...ege ...에게 to (*a person*)
...egesŏ ...에게서 from (*a person*)
Eijŭ 에이즈 Aids
Eijŭ yangsŏng panŭng 에이즈 양성 반응 HIV-positive
eksŭsedae 엑스세대 (X-세대) generation X (*Korea's contemporary youth without the same values and sense of purpose as their parents*)
ellibeit'ŏ 엘리베이터 elevator
emt'i 엠티 MT, Membership Training (*for college freshmen*)
en 엔 yen FIN
enamel 에나멜 enamel
enamel kajuk 에나멜 가죽 patent leather
enjin 엔진 engine, motor
enjin ttukkŏng 엔진 뚜껑 hood MOT
enŏji 에너지 energy, power

enŏjirŭl chŏryak'anŭn 에너지를 절약하는 energy-saving
ensedae 엔세대 (N-세대) networking generation (*via internet and cell phone*)
ent'ŏ k'i 엔터 키 enter key
eŏk'on 에어콘 air-conditioning
eŏrobik 에어로빅 aerobics
ep'isodŭ 에피소드 episode
ep'it'aijyŏ 에피타이져 appetizer, starter
erŏ 에러 error COMPUT
erŏ mesiji 에러 메시지 error message
...esŏ ...에서 in; at; on; from
...esŏbut'ŏ ...에서부터 from ... onward
esŭk'ŏlleitŏ 에스컬레이터 escalator
ewŏssada 에워싸다 encircle

...ga ...가 *subject particle* → **...ka** ...가
...get... ...겠... shall (*indicates future tense, intention or supposition*)
...gi ...기 위해 in order to
...go ...고 and

H

habanshin mabihwanja 하반신
마비환자 paraplegic
habŭidoen 합의된 concerted
habŭihada 합의하다 agree, agree on
habu chojik 하부 조직 infrastructure
habu kujo 하부 구조 infrastructure
(*of organisation*)
hach'anŭn 하찮은 insignificant
hach'ŏnghada 하청하다 subcontract
hach'ŏng-ŏptcha 하청업자
subcontractor
hada 하다 ◊ do; make; play; put on ◊
(*makes nouns into verbs*): *saranghada* 사랑하다 love ◊ *...ge hada*
...게 하다 make; let; *nugurŭl
haengbok'age hada* 누구를
행복하게 하다 make s.o. happy
hadan 하단 bottom, lower part;
hwamyŏnŭi hadane 화면의 하단에
at the bottom of the screen
hadŭ k'ap'i 하드 카피 hard copy
hadŭ tisŭk'ŭ 하드 디스크 hard disk
hadŭweŏ 하드웨어 hardware
hae 해 harm; *haerŭl ip'ida* ...에 해를
입히다 be to the detriment of
haeansŏn 해안선 coastline; waterline
haebalgodo 해발고도 altitude
haebang 해방 emancipation,
liberation
haebanghada 해방하다 emancipate,
liberate
haeboda 해보다 try
haebuhak 해부학 anatomy
haebyŏn 해변 beach; *haebyŏne*
해변에 at the seaside
Haebyŏngdae 해병대 Marine Corps
haebyŏnkka 해변가 seaside
haebyŏn lijot'ŭ 해변 리조트 seaside
resort
haech'ehada 해체하다 break up;
take down
haech'ibaek 해치백 hatchback
haech'ida 해치다 harm, impair
haech'iuda 해치우다 finish off *task*;

kill, do away with
haech'o 해초 seaweed
haech'ung 해충 vermin
haedanghada 해당하다 correspond
to
haedap 해답 answer, solution
haedo 해도 chart
haedoktche 해독제 antidote
haedok'ada 해독하다 decode
haego 해고 dismissal
haegohada 해고하다 fire; lay off
haegol 해골 skeleton; skull
haegoshik'ida 해고시키다 dismiss
haegŭi 핵의 nuclear
haegŭm 해금 two-stringed fiddle
haegun 해군 navy; marine
haegun taejang 해군 대장 admiral
haegun kiji 해군 기지 naval base
haegyŏl 해결 fix, solution; resolution
(*of problem*)
haegyŏlch'aek 해결책 solution
haegyŏrhada 해결하다 settle, sort
out, clear up; work out, crack, solve
haegyŏrhal su innŭn 해결할 수 있는
solvable
haegyŏri kollanhan 해결이 곤란한
difficult, knotty *problem*
haehak 해학 humor
haehyŏp 해협 strait
haejil muryŏp 해질 무렵 sunset,
dusk; *haejin hue* 해진 후에 after
sunset
haejŏkp'an 해적판 pirated version
haek 핵 nucleus ◊ nuclear
haek enŏji 핵 에너지 nuclear energy
haek konggyŏk'ada 핵 공격하다
make a nuclear strike
haek mugi 핵 무기 nuclear weapons
haek mullihak 핵 물리학 nuclear
physics
haek punnyŏl 핵 분열 nuclear
fission
haek p'yegimul 핵 폐기물 nuclear
waste

haeksshim 핵심 core; heart, nub

haeksshimbu 핵심부 heart, center

haeksshimch'ǔng 핵심층 hard core

haeksshimjǒgin 핵심적인 essential, key

haekssǔregi 핵쓰레기 atomic waste

haek'ǒ 해커 hacker

haelssuk'an 핼쑥한 ghastly

haem ham

haema 해마 walrus

haembǒgǒ 햄버거 hamburger

haemsǔt'ǒ 햄스터 hamster

haemyǒnghada 해명하다 explain, shed light on

haenaeda 해내다 beat; argue down; succeed; accomplish; *chal hae-naeda* 잘 해내다 do well

haenagada 해나가다 carry on

haendǔbaek 핸드백 purse, pocket book, *Br* handbag

haendǔl 핸들 (steering) wheel

haendǔp'on 핸드폰 cell phone

haeng 행 for, bound for; *Sǒurhaeng pihaenggi* 서울행 비행기 a plane bound for Seoul

haengbok 행복 happiness, well-being

haengbok'ada 행복하다 be happy

haengbok'age 행복하게 happily

haengbok'an 행복한 happy

haengdong 행동 act, deed; behavior

haengdonghada 행동하다 act, behave

haengdong pangch'im 행동 방침 course of action

haenggǔllaidǒ 행글라이더 hang glider

haenghada 행하다 render

haengjin 행진 march, procession

haengjinhada 행진하다 march, parade

haengjǒng 행정 administration

haengjǒnggwan 행정관 administrator

haengjǒng kuyǒk 행정 구역 precinct, district

haengjǒng samu 행정 사무 civil service

haengju 행주 dishcloth

haengnakkaek 행락객 vacationist

haengno 행로 course

haengnyǒl 행렬 procession

haengsa 행사 event; function; events; observance

haengsa wiwǒn 행사 위원 marshal

haengsǒng 행성 planet

haeng-un 행운 good fortune; *haeng-uni itkkirǔl!* 행운이 있기를! all the best!

haeng-unǔl kajyǒonǔn 행운을 가져오는 lucky

haeng-unǔl pilda 행운을 빌다 wish good luck

haeng-wi 행위 conduct; deed

haeoe 해외 abroad

haeoe kyop'o 해외 교포 overseas Koreans

haep'ari 해파리 jellyfish

haeri 해리 nautical mile

haeroun 해로운 harmful, damaging

haesam 해삼 sea cucumber, sea slug

haesan 해산 childbirth; confinement

haesangdo 해상도 resolution (*of monitor*)

haesang kyot'ong 해상 교통 shipping

haesanhada 해산하다 give birth; disperse *crowd*; dissolve *assembly*

haesanmul 해산물 seafood

haeshigye 해시계 sundial

haesǒk 해석 interpretation

haesǒk'ada 해석하다 interpret

haesǒl 해설 commentary

haesǒltcha 해설자 commentator

haetppit 햇빛 sunshine

haetppyǒch'e t'ada 햇볕에 타다 tan, go brown

haetppyǒch'e t'aeuda 햇볕에 태우다 get a suntan

haetppyǒch'ǔl tchoeda 햇볕을 쬐다 sunbathe

haetppyǒt'e(sǒ) 햇볕에(서) in the sun

haeunhoesa 해운회사 shipping company

haeyang 해양 ocean, sea

hagang 하강 fall, descent

haganghada 하강하다 descend

hagǔp 하급 low class

hagu 하구 estuary

hagwi 학위 degree

hagwirǔl ttada 학위를 따다

graduate, get one's degree
hagwŏn 학원 academy; institute
hahyang shiseŭi shijang 하향
시세의 시장 bear market
haip'ai 하이파이 hi-fi
haip'ŏt'ekssŭt'ŭ 하이퍼텍스트
hypertext
hairait'ŭ 하이라이트 highlight
hak 학 crane (*bird*)
hak-kki 학기 semester
hak-kkŭp 학급 class
hak-kkwa 학과 department
hak-kkyo 학교 school
hak-kkyo sŏnsaengnim 학교 선생님
schoolteacher
hak-kkujŏgin 학구적인 academic
hakppi 학비 tuition fee
hakppu 학부 faculty
hakssaeng 학생 pupil, student
hakssaeng kunsa kyoryŏndan 학생
군사 교련단 cadet corps
hakssaeng undong 학생 운동
student movement
hakssal 학살 slaughter
hakssaltcha 학살자 killer, murderer
hakssarhada 학살하다 slaughter
hakssŭp 학습 learning
hakssŭp kokssŏn 학습 곡선
learning curve
haktcha 학자 scholar
haktchang 학장 dean
hakttae 학대 abuse; maltreatment
hakttaehada 학대하다 abuse;
maltreat
hakttong 학동 schoolchildren
hak'oe 학회 institute
hal il ŏmnŭn 할 일 없는 unoccupied
halkkamalkka saenggak'ada
할까말까 생각하다 think about
doing
halkki 핥기 lick
halk'wida 할퀴다 claw; scratch
halk'wigi 할퀴기 scratch
hal marŭl irŭn 할 말을 잃은
speechless
halmŏni 할머니 grandmother, granny
hal su ŏpsshi ... 할 수 없이 ... have
to ..., be compelled to ...
haltta 핥다 lick
halttanghada 할당하다 assign;
commit

halt'amŏktta 핥아먹다 lap up, drink
hama 하마 hippopotamus
hamburo manjida 함부로 만지다
tamper with
hamburo taruda 함부로 다루다
mishandle
hamch'uk 함축 implication
hamch'uktchŏgin 함축적인 implicit
hamdae 함대 fleet
hamjŏng 함정 pitfall; trap; *nugurŭl
hamjŏng-e ppattŭrida* 누구를
함정에 빠뜨리다 set a trap for s.o.;
hamjŏng-e ppajida 함정에 빠지다
be trapped
hamkke 함께 with, along with ◊
together
hamkke hada 함께 하다 share
feelings
hamkke nanuda 함께 나누다 share;
hamkke ssŭda 함께 쓰다 share
room etc
hamnihwahada 합리화하다
rationalize
hamnijŏgin 합리적인 rational
hamnisŏng 합리성 rationality
hamnyuhada 합류하다 join
hamonik'a 하모니카 harmonica,
mouthorgan
hamppak chŏt-tta 함빡 젖다 be wet
through
han 한 limit; *...nŭn han* ...는 한 so
long as
hana 하나 one; single; *hananŭn ...,
namŏjinŭn ...* 하나는 ..., 나머지는 ...
one ..., the others ...
hanaga toen 하나가 된 united
hanasshik 하나씩 one by one
hanbam chung-e 한밤 중에 in the
middle of the night
hanbŏn 한번 one time, once
hanbŏn tŏ 한번 더 once more
hanbok 한복 Korean costume
hanch'ang ttaeida 한창 때이다 be in
one's prime
hando 한도 limit; *muŏsŭl handoro
chŏnghada* 무엇을 한도로 정하다
draw the line at sth
handoga ŏmnŭn 한도가 없는 open-
ended
...handokkajinŭn ...한도까지는 to
such an extent that

hangahan ttaee 한가한 때에 in an idle moment

hang-ari 항아리 storage jar

han-gaunde 한가운데 center, middle

han-gaundero tuda 한가운데로 두다 center, put in the center

hangbok 항복 surrender

hangbok'ada 항복하다 surrender, capitulate, give in

hangbyŏnhada 항변하다 plead; *yujoe / mujoerŭl hangbyŏnhada* 유죄 / 무죄를 항변하다 plead guilty / not guilty

hangch'e 항체 antibody

hanggong 항공 aviation, flight

hanggongbonghamnyŏpssŏ 항공봉함엽서 air letter

hanggonggi 항공기 aircraft

hanggonghak 항공학 aeronautics

hanggong kyot'ong 항공 교통 air traffic

hanggong kyot'ong kwanje 항공 교통 관제 air-traffic control

hanggong kyot'ong kwanjewŏn 항공 교통 관제원 air-traffic controller

hanggongmoham 항공모함 aircraft carrier

hanggongp'yŏn 항공편 flight

hanggongp'yŏn pŏnho 항공편 번호 flight number

hanggongp'yŏnŭro 항공편으로 by air

hanggongsa 항공사 airline

hanggongsajin 항공사진 aerial photograph

hanggong-ujugonghak 항공우주공학 aerospace industry

hanggong unsonghada 항공 운송하다 fly; send by air

hanggong-up'yŏnŭro 항공우편으로 by airmail

hanggu 항구 harbor; port

hanggudoshi 항구도시 seaport

hanghae 항해 voyage, sea journey

hanghaehada 항해하다 navigate; sail

hanghaesa 항해사 navigator; mate

hanghaesul 항해술 navigation

han-gi 한기 chill

han-gil 한길 mainroad

hangmok 항목 item

hangmokppyŏl kwanggo 항목별 광고 classified advertisement

Hangmu 학무 Crane Dance

hangmun 학문 scholarship

hangnoesŏ pŏsŏnada 항로에서 벗어나다 stray off course

hangnyŏn 학년 academic year; form, class

han-gŏrŭm naedidida 한걸음 내디디다 take a step

hangsaeng multchil 항생 물질 antibiotic

hangsang 항상 always; *tang-shinŭn / kŭnŭn hangsang kŭrŏch'ana!* 당신은 / 그는 항상 그렇잖아! that's typical of you / him!

hangso 항소 appeal LAW

hangsohada 항소하다 appeal LAW

hangssok kŏri 항속 거리 range

hang-ŭi 항의 protest; uproar

hang-ŭihada 항의하다 protest

han-gŭl 한글 hangul, Korean script

Han-gugŏ 한국어 Korean (*language*)

Han-guk 한국 (South) Korea ◊ (South) Korean

Han-guk-kkye 한국계 Korean descent

Han-guk Pangsong Kongsa 한국 방송 공사 Korean Broadcasting System, KBS

Han-guk saram 한국 사람 (South) Korean

Han-gukssan 한국산 made in Korea

han-gye 한계 limit, limitation; *han-gyee irŭda* 한계에 이르다 reach one's limit

han-gyerŭl chŏnghada 한계를 정하다 delimit

hangyŏul 한겨울 midwinter

hanjŏngdoen 한정된 restricted

hanjŏnghada 한정하다 limit

hankkŏbone 한꺼번에 in one, at once

han kyŏure 한 겨울에 in the depths of winter

han myŏng kŏnnŏ 한 명 건너 every other person

hannaeng chŏnsŏn 한랭 전선 cold front

hannyŏrŭm 한여름 midsummer

hanŏmnŭn 한없는 unlimited

han pamtchung-e 한 밤중에 in the middle of the night

han p'an taegyŏl 한 판 대결 showdown

hanp'yŏnŭronŭn ..., tarŭn hanp'yŏnŭronŭn 한편으로는..., 다른 한편으로는 on the one hand ..., on the other hand

hansanhan ttae 한산한 때 offpeak

hanshi 한시 hanshi (*poem in Chinese characters*)

hanshimhan 한심한 pitiful

hansum 한숨 sigh

hansum chada 한숨 자다 take a nap

hansum chit-tta 한숨 짓다 sigh

hantcha 한자 Chinese character

hantchoguro kiurŏjin 한쪽으로 기울어진 lop-sided

hanttae(e) 한때(에) once, formerly; *hanttae nanŭn kŭrŭl choahaessŏt-tta / arassŏt-tta* 한때 나는 그를 좋아했었다 / 알았었다 I used to like / know him

hant'anhada 한탄하다 deplore

hant'anhal 한탄할 deplorable

hant'ŏk naeda 한턱 내다 pick up the tab; treat

hanŭisa 한의사 Chinese herbal medicine practitioner

hanŭiwŏn 한의원 Chinese medicine clinic

hanŭl 하늘 sky; *hanŭl wie* 하늘 위에 up in the sky; *hanŭl nopkke* 하늘 높게 high in the sky

Hanŭnim 하느님 God

hanyak 한약 Chinese herbal medicine

hanyakppang 한약방 Chinese herbal pharmacy

Hanyang 한양 Hanyang (*Choson name for Seoul*)

hanyŏ 하녀 maid (*servant*)

hapch'ang 합창 chorus, refrain

hapch'angdan 합창단 choir, chorus

hapch'ida 합치다 combine; merge

hapch'yŏjida 합쳐지다 join, meet

Hapkkido 합기도 Hapkido (*martial art*)

hapkkŭm 합금 alloy

hapkkye 합계 total

hapkkyehada 합계하다 add up

hapkkyŏktchŏm 합격점 pass mark

hapkkyŏk'ada 합격하다 pass *examination*

hap-ppŏp 합법 legality

hap-ppŏp t'ujaeng 합법 투쟁 work-to-rule

hap-ppŏptchŏgin 합법적인 lawful, legal

hap-ppŏp'wahada 합법화하다 legalize

hap-ppyŏng 합병 merger

hap-ppyŏnghada 합병하다 amalgamate, merge; annex; unite

hap-ppyŏngtchŭng 합병증 complications MED

happ'an 합판 plywood

hapssŏng 합성 synthesis; composition

hapssŏngmul 합성물 compound

haptcha hoesa 합자 회사 joint-stock company

haptchak t'uja 합작 투자 joint venture

hapttanghada 합당하다 be appropriate; *kŭnŭn hapttanghan taeurŭl padat-tta* 그는 합당한 대우를 받았다 he got what he deserved

hap'ŭ 하프 harp

hap'um 하품 yawn

hap'umhada 하품하다 yawn

harabŏji 할아버지 grandfather, grandad

harak 하락 fall, drop

harak'ada 하락하다 fall, drop

harin 할인 discount

harinhada 할인하다 discount; *ishibul harinhayŏ* 20불 할인하여 $20 discount

harinkka(gyŏk) 할인가(격) bargain price

harinkkwŏn 할인권 discount voucher

harin p'anmae 할인 판매 sale

harirŏmnŭn 할릴없는 unavoidable

haru 하루 day; *harue sebŏnŭi hanggongp'yŏn* 하루에 세번의 항공편 three flights a day

haru chong-il 하루 종일 all day

haru kŏnnŏ 하루 건너 every other day

haruppamŭl chinaeda 하룻밤을 지내다 stay overnight

haru shwida 하루 쉬다 take a day off

haryŏgo momburimch'ida 하려고 몸부림치다 struggle to do

haryŏgo noryŏk'ada 하려고 노력하다 strive to do

hasan 하산 descent

hasu 하수 sewage

hasu ch'ŏrijang 하수 처리장 sewage plant

hasugu 하수구 drain

hasugwan 하수관 sewer

hasuk 하숙 board and lodging

hasukssaeng 하숙생 boarder

hasuktchip 하숙집 boarding house

hasuk'ada 하숙하다 board with

hat ch'ok'ollit 핫 초콜릿 hot chocolate

hattogŭ 핫도그 hot dog

hat'ŭ 하트 hearts

hawi 하위 low rank

Hawŏn 하원 House of Representatives

hayan 하얀 white

hayan saek 하얀 색 white

hayat'a 하얗다 be white

hayŏt'ŭn 하여튼 anyhow

hearil su ŏmnŭn 헤아릴 수 없는 impenetrable; inestimable

hebikküp 헤비급 heavyweight

hech'yŏnagada 헤쳐나가다 wriggle out of

heding 헤딩 header (*in soccer*)

hedŭp'on 헤드폰 earphones

hedŭrait'ŭ 헤드라이트 headlamp, headlight

hellik'opt'ŏ 헬리콥터 helicopter, chopper

hellik'opt'ŏ nalgae 헬리콥터 날개 rotor blade

helmet 헬멧 helmet

helssŭ k'ŭllŏp 헬스 클럽 fitness center, health club

hemaeda 헤매다 stray

hengguda 헹구다 rinse

heŏdŭraiŏ 헤어드라이어 hairdryer

heŏjida 헤어지다 break up, part

heŏsŭp'ŭrei 헤어스프레이 (hair) lacquer

heroin 헤로인 heroin

hiashinsŭ 히아신스 hyacinth

hiiing! 히이잉! neigh!

him 힘 energy; might; power; strength; impetus

himch'an 힘찬 forceful

himdŭlda 힘들다 be difficult; be arduous

himdŭn 힘든 difficult; strenuous

himdŭnŭn 힘드는 painstaking, laborious

himgyŏun 힘겨운 heavy, profuse

himinnŭn 힘있는 mighty; firm

himŏmnŭn 힘없는 weak, feeble

himssen 힘센 strong

himtchul 힘줄 tendon

himŭl ppaeda 힘을 빼다 relax

hinghinggŏrida 힝힝거리다 neigh

hint'ŭ 힌트 hint

hisŭt'eri 히스테리 hysteria, hysterics

hisŭt'erisŏng-ŭi 히스테리성의 hysterical

hit'ŭ 히트 hit MUS

hit'ŭgok sunwi 히트곡 순위 the charts

hŏbihada 허비하다 fritter away, waste

hŏbŭ 허브 herb

hŏbŭ ch'a 허브 차 herbal tea

hŏga 허가 permission, approval

hŏgabat-tta 허가받다 receive permission

hŏgahada 허가하다 clear, authorize; grant; *ipkkugŭl hŏgahada* 입국을 허가하다 admit to a country; *tŭrŏonŭn kŏsŭl hŏgahada* 들어오는 것을 허가하다 admit, allow in

hŏga pat-tta 허가 받다 be licensed; be authorized

hŏgasŏ 허가서 permit

hŏgatchŭng 허가증 license, permit

hŏgu 허구 fabrication; fiction; lie

hŏhwangdoen iyagi 허황된 이야기 farfetched story

hŏksshin-ga 혁신가 innovator

hŏlda 헐다 demolish

hŏlgŏpkke 헐겁게 loosely

hŏlgŏun 헐거운 loose

hŏlkkap 헐값 dirt-cheap price

hŏllanshik'ida 혼란시키다 confuse

hŏllŏnghan 헐렁한 baggy; roomy; floppy

hŏlttŏgida 힐떡이다 be winded

hŏlttŏk-kkŏrida 힐떡거리다 gasp, puff

hŏlttŭnnŭn 힐뜨는 disparaging

hŏlttŭt-tta 힐뜻다 slander; malign

hŏmak'an 험악한 forbidding; inclement; unsavory

hŏmdam 험담 gossip

hŏmhan pawi 험한 바위 crag

hŏmulda 허물다 pull down

hŏmurŏjida 허물어지다 disintegrate

hŏmurŏjin 허물어진 dilapidated

hŏmurŏmnŭn 허물없는 candid, frank; familiar

hŏnbyŏng 헌병 MP, military police

Hŏnggari 헝가리 Hungary ◊ Hungarian

hŏnggŏp(tchogak) 헝겊(조각) patch

hŏnggŏp'ŭl taeda 헝겊을 대다 patch

hŏngk'ŭrŏjige hada 헝클어지게 하다 ruffle

hŏngk'ŭrŏjin 헝클어진 disheveled

hŏnhyŏltcha 헌혈자 blood donor

hŏnppŏp 헌법 constitution

hŏnppŏpssang-ŭi 헌법상의 constitutional

hŏnshiltchŏgŭro 현실적으로 in practice

hŏnshin 헌신 commitment, devotion; donation

hŏnshinjŏgida 헌신적이다 be devoted to

hŏnshinjŏgin 헌신적인 devoted

hŏp'ung 허풍 tall story; hot air

hŏp'ungjang-i 허풍장이 show-off

hŏp'ung-ŭl ttŏlda 허풍을 떨다 exaggerate; boast, brag, talk big

hŏrak 허락 permission

hŏrak'ada 허락하다 allow, permit

hŏri 허리 waist

hŏrirŭl p'yŏda 허리를 펴다 straighten up

hŏrisŏn 허리선 waistline

hŏritti 허리띠 belt

hŏrŏppajin 헐어빠진 dilapidated

hŏrŭmhan 허름한 run-down

hŏse 허세 bravado

hŏshigŏmnŭn 허식없는 unpretentious

hŏshik 허식 affectation

hŏshim t'anhoe 허심 탄회 candor

hŏshimt'anhoehada 허심탄회하다 be open-minded

hŏsuabi 허수아비 scarecrow

hŏsuk'ihan 허스키한 husky voice

hŏtchŏm 허점 blind spot; loophole

hŏtkkallida 헛갈리다 mix up, confuse

hŏtkkan 헛간 barn

hŏtkkich'imhada 헛기침하다 clear one's throat

hŏtppae purŭm 헛배 부름 wind, flatulence; gas

hŏtssomunŭl p'ŏttŭrinŭn saram 헛소문을 퍼뜨리는 사람 scaremonger

hŏtssorihada 헛소리하다 rave; ramble

hŏtssugo 헛수고 vain effort; *küdŭrŭi noryŏgŭn hŏtssugoro torakat-tta* 그들의 노력은 헛수고로 돌아갔다 their efforts were in vain

hŏt-ttidida 헛디디다 lose one's footing, stumble

hŏt-ttoege 헛되게 in vain

hŏt-ttoen 헛된 vain

hŏt'ŭn sori 허튼 소리 nonsense, hokum

hŏyak 허약 infirmity

hŏyak'ada 허약하다 be frail

hŏyak'an 허약한 infirm; delicate; puny

hŏyŏngshim 허영심 vanity; *hŏyŏng-shimi manŭn* 허영심이 많은 vain

hŏyongdoel su innŭn 허용될 수 있는 permissible

hŏyong pŏmwi 허용 범위 latitude

ho 호 issue, edition

hobak 호박 pumpkin; amber

hobŏk'ŭrap'ŭt'ŭ 호버크라프트 hovercraft

hoch'ik'isŭ 호치키스 stapler

hoch'ik'isŭ al 호치키스 알 staple

hoch'ik'isŭro tchiktta 호치키스로 찍다 staple

hoch'ulgi 호출기 pager, bleeper

hoch'ul shigan 호출 시간 access time

hoch'urhada 호출하다 summon;

page, bleep

hodoege kkujit-tta 호되게 꾸짖다
scold severely, chew out

hodohada 호도하다 gloss over,
whitewash

hodu 호두 walnut

hodu kkanŭn kigu 호두 까는 기구
nutcracker

hoe 회 round, heat; raw fish

hoebanjugŭl parŭda 회반죽을
바르다 plaster

hoebanjuk 회반죽 plaster; mortar

hoebi 회비 fee

hoebok 회복 recovery

hoebok-kki 회복기 convalescence

hoeboktoeda 회복되다 revive,
recover

hoebok'ada 회복하다 rebuild;
recover; *kŭŭi hoebogŭn sunjorowat-tta* 그의 회복은 순조로왔다
he has made a good recovery; *kŏn-
gang-ŭl hoebok'ada* 건강을
회복하다 convalesce

hoebok'al su ŏmnŭn 회복할 수 없는
incurable

hoegohae pomyŏn 회고해 보면 in
retrospect

hoegojŏn 회고전 retrospective

hoegorok 회고록 memoirs

hoegwisŏn 회귀선 tropics

hoegye 회계 accounts

hoegyejangbu 회계장부 accounts
book; *hoegyejangburŭl chŏngnihada* 회계장부를 정리하다 do the
books; *hoegye kyŏlssanhada* 회계
결산하다 balance the books

hoegyesa 회계사 accountant

hoegye tamdangja 회계 담당자
treasurer

hoegye yŏndo 회계 연도 fiscal year,
financial year

hoehwa 회화 conversation; picture

hoehwa chakp'um 회화 작품
painting

hoejin 회진 round

hoejŏn 회전 revolution, rotation,
turn, rev

hoejŏnhada 회전하다 turn, rotate,
swivel

hoejŏn mongma 회전 목마 carousel

hoejŏnmun 회전문 revolving door

hoejŏnshik kŏnjogi 회전식 건조기
tumble-dryer

hoejŏnshik'ida 회전시키다 spin;
swing, turn

hoejung chŏndŭng 회중 전등
flashlight

hoek 획 stroke (*in writing*)

hoekch'aek'ada 획책하다 plot

hoek-kkijŏgin 획기적인 epoch-
making

hoekttŭk'ada 획득하다 acquire,
obtain

hoengdan 횡단 crossing

hoengdan podo 횡단 보도
crosswalk

hoenggyŏngmak 횡격막 diaphragm
ANAT

hoengjae 횡재 windfall

hoengnyŏng 횡령 embezzlement

hoengnyŏnghada 횡령하다
embezzle

hoengp'orŭl purinŭn 횡포를 부리는
dictatorial

hoengsŏlsusŏl 횡설수설 gibberish;
rambling

hoe-oribaram 회오리바람 whirlwind,
tornado

hoep'i 회피 evasion

hoep'ihada 회피하다 evade

hoero 회로 circuit

hoero ch'adan-gi 회로 차단기
circuit breaker

hoero kyegip'an 회로 계기판 circuit
board

hoesa 회사 business, company, firm;
hoesa piyong-ŭro 회사 비용으로
at the company's expense

hoesa chibunŭl sadŭrida 회사
지분을 사들이다 buy out *company*

hoesa ch'a 회사 차 company car

hoesaek 회색 gray

hoesang 회상 reminiscence

hoesanghada 회상하다 recollect

hoesapŏp 회사법 company law

hoesonghada 회송하다 forward
letter

hoessu 횟수 frequency

hoeŭi 회의 meeting, conference;
assembly; council; *kŭnŭn hoeŭi
chung-ida* 그는 회의 중이다 he's in
a meeting

hoeŭijŏgin 회의적인 skeptical
hoeŭiron 회의론 skepticism
hoeŭironja 회의론자 skeptic
hoeŭishil 회의실 conference room
hoewŏn 회원 member; membership
hoewŏn su 회원 수 membership, number of members
hoewŏntchŭng 회원증 membership card
hoeyujŏgin 회유적인 conciliatory
hogak 호각 whistle
hogami kanŭn 호감이 가는 likable, amiable
hogamŭl kajida 호감을 가지다 be well disposed toward
hogishim 호기심 curiosity; *hogishimesŏ* 호기심에서 out of curiosity
hogishim manŭn 호기심 많은 curious, inquisitive
hogishimŭl chagŭk'anŭn 호기심을 자극하는 intriguing
hogŭn 혹은 or
hohŭp 호흡 breathing
hohŭp kollan 호흡 곤란 breathlessness
hohwandoeji annŭn 호환되지 않는 incompatible
hohwanhal su innŭn 호환할 수 있는 compatible
hohwan pulganŭng 호환 불가능 incompatibility
hohwansŏng 호환성 compatibility
hohwaroptta 호화롭다 be luxurious
hohwaroun 호화로운 de luxe
hoil 호일 foil
hojŏ 호저 porcupine
hojŏk 호적 census registration; census register
hojŏkssurŭl mannada 호적수를 만나다 meet one's match
hojŏn 호전 improvement, upturn
hojŏnjŏgin 호전적인 belligerent
hojŏnshik'ida 호전시키다 turn around
Hoju 호주 Australia ◊ Australian
Hojuin 호주인 Australian
hojumŏni 호주머니 pocket
hok 혹 bump, lump; hump
hokp'yŏnghada 혹평하다 criticize severely

hoksshi 혹시: *hoksshi kŭga ttŏnassŭltchi morŭgessŭmnida* 혹시 그가 떠났을지 모르겠습니다 I don't know whether he has left
hokttok'an 혹독한 brutal
hol 홀 hall
hollan 혼란 confusion, muddle; unrest; turmoil
hollanhada 혼란하다 be confused; be chaotic
hollanshik'ida 혼란시키다 confuse
hollansŭrŏpda 혼란스럽다 be topsy-turvy
hollansŭrŏun 혼란스러운 shaken; topsy-turvy
hollansŭrŏwŏ hada 혼란스러워 하다 be mixed up
hollo 홀로 by itself
hollograem 홀로그램 hologram
hollye 혼례 marriage
holssu 홀수 odd number
holssusŏn 홀수선 waterline
holtchak-kkŏrida 홀짝거리다 sip
holtchuk'an 홀쭉한 sunken
holttak panhada 홀딱 반하다 be infatuated with, have a crush on
holttak pŏsŭn 홀딱 벗은 stark naked
holttak ppajida 홀딱 빠지다 dote on
hom 홈 rut
homil 호밀 rye
homil ppang 호밀 빵 rye bread
hom kyŏnggi 홈 경기 home match
hom kyŏnggijang-esŏ 홈 경기장에서 at home SP
homo 호모 fag *pej*
homp'eiji 홈페이지 home page
homt'ong 홈통 gutter (*on roof*)
hondonghada 혼동하다 confuse
hongbo 홍보 PR, public relations
hongch'a 홍차 black tea
hongch'ae 홍채 iris (*of eye*)
hongdŭngga 홍등가 red light district
honghap 홍합 mussel
hong-igin-gan 홍익인간 devotion to the welfare of mankind
hongjo 홍조 blush
hongjorŭl ttin 홍조를 띤 rosy
Hong Kilttong 홍 길동 Hong Kil-tong (*Korean Robin Hood*)
Hongk'ong 홍콩 Hong Kong
hongnyŏk 홍역 measles

hongsu 홍수 flood

hon-gyo 혼교 promiscuity

honhammul 혼합물 concoction, mixture

honhap 혼합 blend, mixture; hybrid; solution

honhap'ada 혼합하다 blend

honja 혼자 alone; on my/her etc own

honjap 혼잡 congestion

honjap'ada 혼잡하다 be congested; be disordered

honjasŏ 혼자서 single-handedly; by oneself; *honjasŏ ŏtchŏl su ŏmnŭn* 혼자서 어쩔 수 없는 alone and helpless

honjŏn(ŭi) 혼전(의) premarital

honsŏn 혼선 interference

honsu sangt'ae 혼수 상태 coma; trance; *honsu sangt'aee ppajida* 혼수 상태에 빠지다 go into a trance; lapse into a coma

hop 홉 hop BOT

horabi 홀아비 widower

horanggashinamu 호랑가시나무 holly

horang-i 호랑이 tiger

horihorihan 호리호리한 lanky

horŭmon 호르몬 hormone

hosohada 호소하다 appeal for; complain of

hosonghada 호송하다 convoy

hosŭ 호스 hose

hosŭt'essŭ 호스테스 hostess, escort

hosu 호수 lake

hot'el 호텔 hotel; *hot'ere muktta* 호텔에 묵다 stay in a hotel

hot'el chong-ŏbwŏn 호텔 종업원 maid

hot'ong-ŭl ch'ida 호통을 치다 bawl out

hoŭi 호의 favor; goodwill; *nuguege hoŭirŭl pep'ulda* 누구에게 호의를 베풀다 do s.o. a favor

hoŭijŏgin 호의적인 favorable

hoŭng 호응 response

howihada 호위하다 escort, convoy

hŭbip 흡입 suction

hŭbipkki 흡입기 inhaler

hŭbip'ada 흡입하다 inhale

hŭbyŏn 흡연 smoking

hŭbyŏnja 흡연자 smoker

hŭbyŏnshil 흡연실 smoking compartment

hŭgin 흑인 black, negro

hŭibak'an 희박한 thin, rare; sparse; *in-guga hŭibak'an* 인구가 희박한 sparsely populated

hŭida 희다 white ◊ be white

hŭigok 희곡 drama

hŭigŭk 희극 comedy

hŭimang 희망 hope

hŭimang-e ch'an 희망에 찬 hopeful

hŭimanghada 희망하다 hope

hŭimang-ŭl irŭn 희망을 잃은 hopeless

hŭimihaejida 희미해지다 fade

hŭimihan 희미한 faint

hŭimihan pit 희미한 빛 glimmer

hŭisa 회사 donation

hŭisaeng 희생 cost; sacrifice; death toll; victim

hŭisaenghada 희생하다 make sacrifices; sacrifice

hŭisaengja 희생자 victim

hŭisaengshikida 희생시키다 victimize

hŭisaengnyang 희생양 scapegoat

hŭisahada 회사하다 donate

hŭi-yŏmŏlgŏn 희여멀건 wishy-washy

hŭk 흙 soil, earth

hŭktcharo 흑자로 in the black FIN

hŭlkkŭt poda 흘끗 보다 catch sight of, catch a glimpse of

hŭllida 흘리다 shed *blood, sweat, tears*; spill *water*

hŭm 흠 blemish, flaw; blot; groove; nick, cut

hŭmjabŭlde ŏmnŭn 흠잡을데 없는 faultless

hŭmjaptta 흠잡다 find fault with

hŭmnaeda 흠내다 blemish

hŭmŏmnŭn 흠없는 flawless

hŭmppŏk chŏjŭn 흠뻑 젖은 dripping, soaking wet

hŭmppŏk chŏksshida 흠뻑 적시다 drench

hŭmppŏk chŏt-tta 흠뻑 젖다 get drenched

hŭmtchibŏmnŭn 흠집없는 unscathed

hŭndŭlda 흔들다 shake; swing; wave; wiggle; undermine; *Xŭl/rŭl toege hŭndŭlda* ×을/를 되게 흔들다 give X a good shake

hŭndŭlgŏrida 흔들거리다 rock; roll; sway; swing; wag

hŭndŭlgŏrinŭn 흔들거리는 shaky

hŭndŭllida 흔들리다 shake; vibrate; tremble

hŭndŭl ŭija 흔들 의자 rocking chair

hŭngbun 흥분 excitement, kick, thrill; stimulation

hŭngbundoeda 흥분되다 be excited

hŭngbunhada 흥분하다 get excited; *nŏmu hŭngbunhaji maseyo!* 너무 흥분하지 마세요! don't get excited!, take it easy!

hŭngbunshik'ida 흥분시키다 excite

hŭngbunshik'inŭn 흥분시키는 exciting

hŭngch'ŏngmangch'ŏng shyop'ing-ŭl hada 흥청망청 쇼핑을 하다 go on a shopping spree

hŭngjŏnghada 흥정하다 bargain

hŭngmijinjinhan 흥미진진한 very interesting

hŭngmi kkŭlda 흥미 끌다 intrigue

hŭngmirŭl irŭk'ige hada 흥미를 일으키게 하다 interest; arouse interest

hŭngmirŭl kajida 흥미를 가지다 take an interest in

hŭngmirŭl todunŭn 흥미를 돋우는 compelling

hŭnhaji anŭn 흔하지 않은 uncommon

hŭnjŏk 흔적 trace; trail; vestige

hŭnŭjŏk-kkŏrinŭn 흐느적거리는 limping

hŭnŭkkim 흐느낌 sob

hŭnŭkkyŏ ulda 흐느껴 울다 sob

hŭpssuhada 흡수하다 absorb

hŭpssussŏng-ŭi 흡수성의 absorbent

hŭrida 흐리다 be cloudy

hŭrige hada 흐리게 하다 blur; dim

hŭrim 흐림 blur

hŭrin 흐린 cloudy; misty; overcast

hŭrit'aejida 흐릿해지다 blur

hŭrit'an 흐릿한 dim; fuzzy; vague; glazed

hŭrŭda 흐르다 run, flow; stream

hŭrŭm 흐름 current; flow

hŭrŭnŭn 흐르는 flowing; runny

hŭryŏjida 흐려지다 mist over

hŭryŏjin 흐려진 misty; *ont'ong hŭryŏjida* 온통 흐려지다 cloud over

hŭt'ŏjida 흩어지다 disperse, scatter

hŭt'ŏjin 흩어진 scattered

hŭt'ŭrŏjin 흐트러진 disheveled

huban 후반 second half

hubida 후비다 dig up; grub; *k'orŭl hubida* 코를 후비다 pick one's nose

hubo 후보 nominee

huboja 후보자 candidate

hubo sŏnsu 후보 선수 reserve SP

hubul 후불 deferred payment; *nanŭn hubullo chigŭppannŭnda* 나는 후불로 지급받는다 I'm paid in arrears

huch'ŏnssŏng myŏnnyŏk kyŏlp'iptchŭng 후천성 면역 결핍증 Aids, acquired immune deficiency syndrome

huch'u 후추 pepper

hudae 후대 posterity

hudu 후두 larynx

hududuk ttŏrŏjida 후두둑 떨어지다 patter

hududuk'anŭn sori 후두둑하는 소리 patter, pattering sound

huduyŏm 후두염 laryngitis

hue 후에: *...n(ŭn) hue* ...ㄴ(은) 후에 since; after

hugak 후각 sense of smell

hugi 후기 epilog

hugyŏnin 후견인 guardian

huhoe 후회 penitence

huhoehada 후회하다 regret; repent

huhoesŭrŏpkkedo 후회스럽게도 regretfully, sadly

huim(ja) 후임(자) successor

huimjaga toeda 후임자가 되다 succeed *person*

huja 후자 the latter

hujin 후진 reverse (gear)

hujinhada 후진하다 reverse, back

hujinshik'ida 후진시키다 reverse, back

huk p'unggim 훅 풍김 whiff

hullyŏn 훈련 drill, exercise; training

hullyŏnhada 훈련하다 practice, drill; train

hullyŏn kyehoek 훈련 계획 training scheme

hullyŏnsa 훈련사 trainer

hullyŏnshik'ida 훈련시키다 train

hullyunghada 훌륭하다 be magnificent; be worthy; admirable; be noble; be great

hullyunghage 훌륭하게 wonderfully, beautifully

hullyunghan 훌륭한 brilliant, fine; masterly; respectable

hultchŏk-kkŏrida 훌쩍거리다 sniffling, snivelling

hultchŏk ttwida 훌쩍 뛰다 leap

hultta 훑다 thresh; strip; remove

hult'ŏboda 훑어보다 skim through *book*; look over *person*

humch'ida 훔치다 steal

humi 후미 inlet

humijin kot 후미진 곳 cove

hunjang-ŭl suyŏhada 훈장을 수여하다 decorate, award a medal

hunjehada 훈제하다 smoke *ham etc*

hunje soegogi 훈제 쇠고기 pastrami

huraip'aen 후라이팬 frying pan

Hurench'ihurai 후렌치후라이 French fries

huryŏch'ida 후려치다 punch

huryŏm 후렴 refrain MUS

hushik 후식 dessert

hut'ŏptchigŭnhada 후텁지근하다 be sultry (*of weather*)

hut'oe 후퇴 setback; retreat

hut'oehada 후퇴하다 retreat; pull out

huwi 후위 back SP

huwŏn 후원 sponsorship, patronage

huwŏnhada 후원하다 back (up), support; sponsor

huwŏnja 후원자 supporter; sponsor; backer; patron

hwanada 화나다 get angry

hwa 화 anger, annoyance

hwabun 화분 pollen; flowerpot

hwabunnyang 화분량 pollen count

hwabyŏng 화병 vase; hypochondria

hwach'a 화차 wagon

hwach'anghada 화창하다 be bright, be sunny

hwach'anghan nalssi 화창한 날씨 Indian summer

hwadan 화단 flowerbed

hwadŏk 화덕 furnace

hwaek sugŭrida 홱 수그리다 duck

hwaek tanggida 홱 당기다 yank, jerk

hwaetppul 횃불 torch (*with flame*)

hwaet-ttae 횃대 perch

hwaet-ttaee antta 횃대에앉다 perch

hwaga 화가 painter, drawer

hwaga ch'isot-tta 화가 치솟다 flareup

hwaga nada 화가 나다 get angry, get worked up

hwaga nan 화가 난 angry, sore

hwagang-am 화강암 granite

hwagin 확인 inspection; confirmation; identification; OK COMPUT

hwaginhada 확인하다 check; confirm; identify; check for; query

hwaginhae tuda 확인해 두다 keep a check on

hwahae 화해 reconciliation; settlement

hwahaehada 화해하다 make up; be reconciled

hwahaeshik'ida 화해시키다 reconcile

hwahak 화학 chemistry

hwahak chep'um 화학 제품 chemical

hwahaktcha 화학자 chemist

hwahaktchŏn 화학전 chemical warfare

hwahak yoppŏp 화학 요법 chemotherapy

hwahwan 화환 garland, wreath

hwail 화일 file COMPUT

hwail maenijŏ 화일 매니저 file manager

hwajae 화재 fire, blaze

hwajae kyŏngbogi 화재 경보기 fire alarm

hwajae p'inan changch'i 화재 피난 장치 fire escape

hwajang 화장 cremation; make-up; beauty care

hwajangdae 화장대 dressing table

hwajanghada 화장하다 cremate; put on make-up

hwajangjang 화장장 crematorium

hwajangji 화장지 tissue; toilet paper

hwajangp'um 화장품 make-up;

cosmetics

hwajangshil 화장실 restroom, bathroom; toilet

hwaje 화제 topic

hwajerŭl pakkŭda 화제를 바꾸다 change the subject

hwak ch'isosŭm 확 치솟음 blaze

hwak-kkohan 확고한 strong, definite, determined, firm

hwakkobudonghan 확고부동한 unswerving

hwaksshilssŏng 확실성 certainty; inevitability

hwaksshin 확신 certainty; confidence

hwaksshine ch'an 확신에 찬 assured

hwaksshinhada 확신하다 be positive; firmly believe; *Xŭl/rŭl hwaksshinhaji mot'ada* X을/를 확신하지 못하다 be uncertain about X

hwaksshinhanŭn 확신하는 certain, sure

hwaksshinshik'ida 확신시키다 convince

hwaksshirhada 확실하다 be certain, be definite

hwaksshirhage 확실하게 reliably

hwaksshirhan 확실한 marked, definite

hwaksshirhi 확실히 certainly definitely; decidedly; doubtless

hwakssŏnggi 확성기 loudspeaker

hwaktae 확대 zoom in

hwaktchang 확장 expansion; extension

hwaktchanghada 확장하다 expand; diversify

hwaktchang k'adŭ 확장카드 expansion card COMPUT

hwaktchŏngdoeda 확정되다 be finalized

hwaktchŏng kŭmaek 확정 금액 sum insured

hwaktchŭng 확증 confirmation

hwaktchŭnghada 확증하다 confirm

hwakttae chŏgyonghada 확대 적용하다 stretch *rules*

hwakttaehada 확대하다 blow up, enlarge; magnify; escalate

hwak t'ŭin 확 트인 panoramic

hwal 활 bow MUS

hwalbarhada 활발하다 be lively, be brisk

hwalgangno 활강로 chute

hwalgang sŭk'i 활강 스키 downhill skiing

hwalgi 활기 vigor, energy

hwalgi ch'an 활기 찬 lively

hwalgirŭl purŏnŏt'a 활기를 불어넣다 enliven

hwalgonghada 활공하다 glide

hwallyŏk 활력 drive, energy; vitality

hwalsŏng 활성 active COMPUT

hwaltcha 활자 moveable type

hwaltchak p'in 활짝 핀 in full bloom

hwaltchak ut-tta 활짝 웃다 beam, smile

hwaltchuro 활주로 runway, tarmac

hwalttong 활동 activity, action

hwalttongga 활동가 activist

hwalttong hoewŏn 활동 회원 active member

hwalttongjŏgin 활동적인 active; energetic, dynamic

hwamul 화물 freight; shipment, consignment

hwamulch'a 화물차 freight car; truck

hwamul pihaenggi 화물 비행기 freight plane

hwamulsŏn 화물선 freighter

hwamulsshil 화물실 hold (*on ship, plane*)

hwamul unbanttae 화물 운반대 pallet

hwamul unsongnyo 화물 운송료 freight (costs)

hwamul yŏlch'a 화물 열차 freight train

hwamyŏn 화면 screen; *hwamyŏn-sang-e* 화면상에 on screen

hwamyŏne p'yoshihada 화면에 표시하다 display

hwamyŏn pohogi 화면 보호기 screen saver

hwanada 화나다 be annoyed; get annoyed, blow up

hwanaege hada 화내게 하다 anger

hwanan 화난 exasperated

hwanbul 환불 refund, rebate

hwanbul pulgaŭi 환불 불가의

hwanburhada

nonreturnable *deposit*

hwanburhada 환불하다 refund

hwandae 환대 hospitality

hwandaehanŭn 환대하는 hospitable

hwandŭnggi p'illŭm k'arusel 환등기 필름 카루셀 carousel (*for slides*)

hwan-gap 환갑 sixtieth birthday (*61ˢᵗ birthday in the West, since Koreans are one year old at birth*)

hwangdal 황달 jaundice

hwangdodae 황도대 zodiac

hwangdodaeŭi shibi kung 황도대의 십이 궁 12 signs of the zodiac

hwanggalssaek 황갈색 buff (*color*)

hwanggŭmshiganttae 황금시간대 prime time

hwanggŭp'i 황급히 in double-quick time

Hwangha 황하 Yellow River

Hwanghae 황해 Yellow Sea

hwanghol 황홀 ecstasy

hwanghorhan 황홀한 ecstatic

hwan-gich'ang 환기창 vent, ventilation window

hwan-gi changch'i 환기 장치 ventilator; ventilation

hwan-gigaeng 환기갱 ventilation shaft

hwan-gihada 환기하다 ventilate

hwan-gishik'ida 환기시키다 air *room*; challenge; evoke

hwangje 황제 emperor

hwangmuji 황무지 desert; wilderness

hwangnyanghan 황량한 bleak, desolate; godforsaken

hwangp'ye chiyŏk 황폐 지역 wasteland

hwangp'yehaejida 황폐해지다 ravaged by war

hwangp'yehan 황폐한 desolate, inhospitable

hwangsae 황새 stork

hwangsaek shinho-e 황색 신호에 at amber (*of traffic light*)

hwangso 황소 bull, ox

hwangsonghada 황송하다 be indebted, be obliged; *kŭnŭn hwangsonghagedo na-ege marŭl kŏrŏssŏ* 그가 황송하게도 내게 말을 걸었어 he condescended to speak to me

hwan-gyŏng 환경 conditions; surroundings; environment

hwan-gyŏngboho 환경보호 environmental protection

hwan-gyŏngbohoronja 환경보호론자 environmentalist

Hwan-gyŏngch'ŏng 환경처 Department of the Interior

hwan-gyŏng-oyŏm 환경오염 environmental pollution

hwanhada 환하다 be bright; be open

hwanhage 환하게 brightly

hwanhan 환한 bright, broad *smile*

hwanhi pinnanŭn 환히 빛나는 radiant

hwanho 환호 cheer; cheering; jubilation

hwanhohada 환호하다 cheer

hwanhohanŭn 환호하는 jubilant

hwanhoŭi sori 환호의 소리 hurray

hwanhŭi 환희 joy, delight; rapture

hwanja 환자 patient

hwanjŏnhada 환전하다 exchange

hwanmyŏl 환멸 disillusionment

hwannyul 환율 exchange rate

hwanŏŭm 환어음 bill of exchange

hwanp'unggi 환풍기 ventilation fan

hwansaeng 환생 reincarnation

hwansan 환산 conversion

hwansang 환상 fantasy

hwansangjŏgin 환상적인 fantastic

hwansanhada 환산하다 convert

hwansanp'yo 환산표 conversion table

hwanyŏng 환영 reception, welcome; vision; illusion

hwanyŏnghada 환영하다 welcome

hwanyŏng pannŭn 환영 받는 welcome

Hwaŏmgyŏng 화엄경 Flower Garland Sutra

hwap'urihada 화풀이하다 take it out on

hwarang 화랑 gallery

Hwarangdo 화랑도 Youth Corps

hwarŭl ch'amtta 화를 참다 keep one's temper

hwarŭl naeda 화를 내다 lose one's temper; vent one's anger

hwaryŏhada 화려하다 be sumptuous

hwaryŏhage changshik'an 화려하게

장식한 ornate
hwaryŏham 화려함 splendor
hwaryonghada 활용하다 put to
practical use, utilize
hwaryongshik'ida 활용시키다
conjugate
hwasal 화살 arrow
hwasalp'yo kŭlsoe 화살표 글쇠
arrow key COMPUT
hwasan 화산 volcano
hwasang 화상 burn (*injury*)
hwasang hoeŭi 화상 회의 video
conference
hwashin 화신 embodiment
hwasŏk 화석 fossil
hwasŏng 화성 harmony
Hwasshi 화씨 Fahrenheit
hwayak 화약 gunpowder
hwayoil 화요일 Tuesday
hwesonhada 훼손하다 mutilate;
defame
hwibaryu 휘발유 gasoline, gas
hwich'ŏnggŏrida 휘청거리다 stagger
hwida 휘다 bend, warp
hwidurŭda 휘두르다 brandish; wield;
flick
hwigalgyŏ ssŭda 휘갈겨 쓰다 scrawl
hwigehada 휘게하다 warp
hwigi shwiun 휘기 쉬운 pliable
hwijang 휘장 drapery
hwijŏnnŭn kigu 휘젓는 기구 whisk
hwijŏt-tta 휘젓다 stir; whisk
hwik kkŭjibŏnaeda 휙 끄집어내다
pull out, whip out
hwilch'ŏ 휠체어 wheelchair
hwin 휜 bent
hwip'aram 휘파람 whistle
hwip'aramŭl pulda 휘파람을 불다
whistle
hwŏlsshin kŭ chŏne 훨씬 그 전에
long before then
hwŏnhada 훤하다 be broad; be
extensive; be well versed in; ...*ŭl*/*rŭl*
hwŏnhi alda ...을/를 훤히 알다
have at one's fingertips
hwŏnhi t'ŭin 훤히 트인 open and
bright
hyŏmnyŏktcha 협력자 co-worker,
collaborator (*on a project*)
hyŏng 형 elder brother
hyŏnshiljŏgin 현실적인 realistic

hyang 향 incense
hyanggi 향기 aroma, scent; bouquet
hyangginanŭn 향기나는 fragrant
hyanghada 향하다 face
hyanghayŏ 향하여 to; toward; facing
hyangsang 향상 improvement
hyangsangdoeda 향상되다 get
better
hyangsanghada 향상하다 improve,
progress
hyangsangshik'ida 향상시키다
improve, upgrade
hyangsu 향수 perfume; nostalgia
hyangsuppyŏng-ul alt'a 향수병을
앓다 be homesick
hyang-yŏn 향연 banquet, dinner
hyesŏng 혜성 comet
hyet'aekpat-tchi mot'an 혜택받지
못한 underprivileged
hyŏ 혀 tongue
hyŏbŭihada 협의하다 confer
hyŏksshin 혁신 innovation
hyŏksshinhanŭn hoesa 혁신하는
회사 innovative company
hyŏksshinjŏgin 혁신적인 innovative
hyŏlgi 혈기 blood
hyŏlgu 혈구 corpuscle
hyŏlgwan 혈관 blood vessel
hyŏlgwan ishik 혈관 이식 bypass
MED
hyŏllyu 혈류 bloodstream
hyŏlssaegi anjohŭn 혈색이 안좋은
sickly
hyŏltchŏntchŭng 혈전증 thrombosis
hyŏlt'ong 혈통 blood; pedigree
hyŏlt'ong-i punmyŏnghan 혈통이
분명한 pedigree
hyŏmnyŏk kwan-gye 협력 관계
partnership
hyŏmnyŏktcha 협력자 collaborator
(*on a project*)
hyŏmnyŏktchŏgin 협력적인
cooperative
hyŏmnyŏk 협력 cooperation
hyŏmnyŏk'ada 협력하다 cooperate;
collaborate; ... *wa*/*kwa*
hyŏmnyŏk'ayŏ ...와/과 협력하여 in
association with
hyŏmo 혐오 disgust
hyŏmogamŭl irŭk'ida 혐오감을
일으키다 disgust

hyŏmohada 혐오하다 detest
hyŏmosŭrŏun 혐오스러운 disgusting
hyŏmŭi 혐의 charge LAW
hyŏmŭija 혐의자 suspect
hyŏmŭirŭl pannŭn 혐의를 받는
suspected
hyŏn 현 chord
hyŏnak-kki 현악기 stringed
instrument
hyŏnak-kki yŏnjuja 현악기 연주자
string player; strings
hyŏnch'ang 현창 porthole
Hyŏnch'ung-il 현충일 Memorial Day
hyŏndae 현대 modern times ◊
modern
hyŏndaehwa 현대화 modernization
hyŏndaehwahada 현대화하다
modernize
hyŏndaejŏgin 현대적인 modern
hyŏndaejŏgŭro pakkuda 현대적으로
바꾸다 modernize
hyŏndaeŭi 현대의 contemporary
hyŏngbu 형부 brother-in-law
(*woman's elder sister's husband*)
hyŏnggwang 형광 fluorescence
hyŏnggwangp'en 형광펜 highlighter
hyŏnggwang-ŭi 형광의 fluorescent
hyŏn-gitchŭng 현기증 giddiness;
vertigo
hyŏn-gitchŭng-i nada 현기증이 나다
feel dizzy
hyŏngje chamae 형제 자매 brothers
and sisters
hyŏngmyŏng 혁명 revolution
hyŏngmyŏngga 혁명가
revolutionary
hyŏngmyŏngjŏgin 혁명적인
revolutionary *ideas*
hyŏngmyŏng-ŭi 혁명의
revolutionary *spirit*
hyŏngmyŏng-ŭl irŭk'ida 혁명을
일으키다 revolutionize
hyŏng-ŏnhal su ŏmnŭn 형언할 수
없는 indescribable
hyŏngp'yŏnŏmnŭn 형편없는
wretched, pathetic; useless;
disreputable
hyŏngp'yŏnŏpsshi 형편없이
dreadfully; poorly
hyŏngsa 형사 detective; criminal
case

hyŏngsang 형상 figure
hyŏngsasang-ŭi 형사상의 criminal
hyŏngshik 형식 format, make-up;
formality
hyŏngshiktchŏgin 형식적인 formal;
perfunctory
hyŏngshiktchŏgŭro 형식적으로
formally
hyŏngsŏng 형성 formation
hyŏngsŏnghanŭn 형성하는
formative
hyŏngsŏngshik'ida 형성시키다 mold
hyŏngsu 형수 sister-in-law (*elder
brother's wife*)
hyŏngt'ae 형태 form
hyŏn-gŭm 현금 cash; *kŭ chariesŏ
hyŏn-gŭmŭro* 그 자리에서
현금으로 cash down
hyŏn-gŭm harin 현금 할인 cash
discount
hyŏn-gŭm inch'ulgi 현금 인출기
cash machine, ATM
hyŏn-gŭmŭro naeda 현금으로 내다
pay (in) cash
hyŏn-gŭmŭro pakkuda 현금으로
바꾸다 cash *check*
hyŏn-gŭm yuch'urip 현금 유출입
cash flow
hyŏn-gwan 현관 entrance, porch
hyŏng-yongsa 형용사 adjective
hyŏnhaengbŏmŭro 현행범으로 in
the very act
hyŏnhaktchŏgin 현학적인 pedantic
hyŏnjae 현재 the present
hyŏnjaehyŏng 현재형 present GRAM
hyŏnjaeronŭn 현재로는 presently, at
the moment
hyŏnjaeŭi 현재의 current, present;
going
hyŏnjang 현장 scene; *hyŏnjang-
e(sŏ)* 현장에(서) on the scene; on
the spot; on site
hyŏnji shigan 현지 시간 local time
hyŏnjŏhan 현저한 remarkable,
striking
hyŏnjonhanŭn 현존하는 existing
hyŏnmigyŏng 현미경 microscope
hyŏnmyŏnghada 현명하다 be wise
hyŏnmyŏng-hage 현명하게 wisely
hyŏnmyŏnghan 현명한 clever;
sensible; wise; advisable

hyŏnsang 현상 phenomenon; development (*of film*)
hyŏnsanghada 현상하다 develop *film*
hyŏnshil 현실 reality
hyŏnshiltchŏgin 현실적인 realistic
hyŏnshiltchuŭi 현실주의 realism
hyŏnshiltchuŭija 현실주의자 realist
hyŏnsugyo 현수교 suspension bridge
hyŏpkkok 협곡 gorge
hyŏp-ppak 협박 threat, intimidation
hyŏp-ppak p'yŏnji 협박 편지 threatening letter
hyŏp-ppak'ada 협박하다 intimidate, threaten
hyŏpssang 협상 negotiation
hyŏpssangga 협상가 negotiator
hyŏpssanghada 협상하다 negotiate
hyŏpsshimtchŭng 협심증 angina
hyŏptchugok 협주곡 concerto
hyŏpttong 협동 collaboration, cooperation
hyŏpttong chagŏp 협동 작업 teamwork
hyŏpttong chohap 협동 조합 cooperative COM
hyŏpttonghada 협동하다 pull together
hyŏraek kŏmsa 혈액 검사 blood test
hyŏraek saemp'ŭl 혈액 샘플 blood sample
hyŏraek ŭnhaeng 혈액 은행 blood bank
hyŏraek'yŏng 혈액형 blood group
hyŏrap 혈압 blood pressure
hyo 효 filial piety (*Confucian*)
hyokkwaga ŏmnŭn 효과가 없는 ineffective
hyokkwajŏgin 효과적인 effective
hyokkwarŭl churida 효과를 줄이다 counter the effect of
hyomo 효모 yeast
hyoryŏgi innŭn 효력이 있는 effective
hyoryŏgŭl nat'anaeda 효력을 나타내다 take effect
hyoyul 효율 efficiency
hyoyultchŏgin 효율적인 efficient
hyoyurhwa 효율화 rationalization
hyoyurhwahada 효율화하다 rationalize

hyudaep'um pogwanso 휴대품 보관소 checkroom
hyudaeyong-(ŭi) 휴대용(의) portable
hyudaeyong ŭija 휴대용 의자 deckchair
hyuga 휴가 vacation; leave
hyugarŭl kat-tta 휴가를 갖다 take a holiday
hyuga yŏhaenggaek 휴가 여행객 vacationer
hyuge shigan 휴게 시간 intermission, interval
hyugeshil 휴게실 lobby
hyugeso 휴게소 service area
hyuhoe 휴회 recess
hyuhwasan 휴화산 dormant volcano
hyuil 휴일 holiday
hyuji 휴지 toilet paper; waste paper
hyujit'ong 휴지통 wastepaper basket
hyujŏn 휴전 cease-fire; truce; armistice
hyujŏngdoeda 휴정되다 adjourn
hyujŏnsŏn 휴전선 ceasefire line
hyung-ak 흉악 atrocity
hyung-akppŏm 흉악범 thug
hyung-akssŏng 흉악성 enormity
hyung-ak'an 흉악한 hideous
hyunghada 흉하다 be hideous; be unlucky
hyunghan 흉한 ugly
hyungmul 흉물 monstrosity
hyungnae 흉내 impersonation take-off
hyungnaenaeda 흉내내다 imitate, take off, mimic; simulate
hyungnaenaegi 흉내내기 impression, take off
hyungp'ohan 흉포한 ferocious
hyungt'ŏ 흉터 scar; *hyungt'ŏrŭl namgida* 흉터를 남기다 leave a scar
hyushik 휴식 rest, respite; *kabyŏun hyushik shigan* 가벼운 휴식 시간 coffee break
hyushikch'ŏ 휴식처 resting place; lounge
hyushik-kki 휴식기 break
hyuyangji 휴양지 resort

...i ...이 (*subject particle*): ***...i it-tta***
...이 있다 there is/are

i 이 two ◊ tooth; louse; profit; interest
FIN; reason; person ◊ this

ibalssa 이발사 barber

ibanja 입안자 draftsman

ibe taego punŭn pubun 입에 대고
부는 부분 mouthpiece

ibi ttak pŏrŏjin 입이 딱 벌어진
open-mouthed; wide-mouthed

ibŏboda 입어보다 try on

ibul tamulda 입을 다물다 clam up,
keep silent

ibŭl ttak pŏlligo paraboda 입을 딱
벌리고 바라보다 gape

ibul 이불 coverlet

ibunppŏp 이분법 dichotomy

ibwŏnhada 입원하다 go into hospital

ibwŏn hwanja 입원 환자 in-patient

ibyang 입양 adoption

ibyang-a 입양아 foster child

ibyanghada 입양하다 adopt

ibyŏl 이별 farewell; parting

ich'ajŏgŭro chung-yohan
이차적으로 중요한 of secondary
importance

ich'ie matkke 이치에 맞게
reasonably

ich'ŭng ch'imdae 이층 침대 bunk
beds

ich'yŏjida 잊혀지다 fall into oblivion

ida 이다 be; ***nanŭn hakssaeng-
iyeyo*** 나는 학생이에요 I am a
student

idan kiŏ 이단 기어 second gear

ideollogi 이데올로기 ideology

idojŏdo anin kyŏng-u 이도저도 아닌
경우 a borderline case

idong 이동 shift; transfer; mobility

idong chŏnhwa 이동 전화 cell
phone

idonghada 이동하다 travel around;
change direction

idong-i kanŭnghan 이동이 가능한
mobile

idong musŏn chŏnhwa 이동 무선
전화 cellular phone

idongssŏng 이동성 mobility

idŭgi toeda 이득이되다 be profitable,
pay off

idŭngsŏgŭi 이등석의 second class

Idu 이두 Idu (*Silla-Choson writing
system*)

iga ŏmnŭn 이가 없는 toothless

iga ppajida 이가 빠지다 be chipped

igida 이기다 win; beat; win out; mix

igijŏgin 이기적인 selfish

igŏt 이것 this ◊ this one

igŏttŭl 이것들 these

igŭllu 이글루 igloo

igŭn 익은 ripe

igŭnishyŏn k'i 이그니션 키 ignition
key

iguktchŏgin 이국적인 exotic

igyŏn 이견 different opinion;
difference (of opinion)

igyŏnaeda 이겨내다 get over,
overcome, surmount

igyodo 이교도 heathen

iha 이하 not exceeding, less than;
under; below; the following; ***...iharo***
...이하로 below

ihae 이해 understanding

ihaeganŭn 이해가는 meaningful

ihaehada 이해하다 understand

ihaengjŏng ssaik'ŭrŭi 이행정
싸이클의 two-stroke

ihaeryŏk 이해력 understanding,
comprehension

ihaeshik'ida 이해시키다 make
understand; get through

ihaeshimnŭnnŭn 이해심있는
understanding *person*

ihangnyŏn 이학년 sophomore

ihasŏnnyŏm 이하선염 mumps

ihon 이혼 divorce

ihonhada 이혼하다 divorce, get
divorced

ihonhan 이혼한 divorced
ihonnam 이혼남 divorcee (*man*)
ihonnyŏ 이혼녀 divorcee (*woman*)
ihuro 이후로 since; *chinan chu ihuro* 지난 주 이후로 since last week
iigi andoenŭn 이익이 안되는 uneconomic
iigi ŏmnŭn 이익이 없는 unprofitable
iigi toeda 이익이 되다 benefit
iigŭl naeda 이익을 내다 yield a profit
iigŭl ŏt-tta 이익을 얻다 get a profit; benefit
iigŭl poda 이익을 보다 make a profit
iik 이익 benefit; profit, return
iinyong pang 이인용 방 double room
ija 이자 interest
ijayul 이자율 interest rate
ije 이제 now; no longer, not any more; *ije kŭmanhae!* 이제 그만해! I've had enough!, stop!
ijel 이젤 easel
ijiltchŏgin 이질적인 alien
ijinppŏp 이진법 binary system
Ijipt'ŭ 이집트 Egypt ◊ Egyptian
ijŏbŏrida 잊어버리다 forget, lose sight of (*sg*)
ijŏbŏrigo tŭgo kada 잊어버리고 두고 가다 leave behind, forget
ijŏk haeng-wija 이적 행위자 collaborator *pej*
ijŏk'ada 이적하다 transfer
ijŏne 이전에 before; formerly
ijŏngp'yo 이정표 milestone
ijŏnhada 이전하다 relocate
ijŏnŭi 이전의 ex-; previous, prior
ijŭl su ŏmnŭn 잊을 수 없는 unforgettable
iju 이주 migration; emigration; immigration
ijuhada 이주하다 migrate; immigrate
ijuja 이주자 settler, immigrant
ijung chuch'ashik'ida 이중 주차시키다 double park
ijungch'ang 이중창 duo
ijung in-gyŏkja 이중 인격자 two-faced person
ijung inkkyŏk 이중 인격 split personality
ijungju 이중주 duet

ijung kuktchŏk 이중 국적을 dual nationality
ijungt'ŏk 이중턱 double chin
ijung-ŭi 이중의 dual
ijung yuri 이중 유리 double glazing
iju nodongja 이주 노동자 migrant worker
ikki 이끼 moss
ikki kkin 이끼 낀 mossy
ikkŭlda 이끌다 head, lead; steer
ikkŭlgo kada 이끌고 가다 lead up to
ikssahada 익사하다 be drowned
ikssalburida 익살부리다 joke
ikssashik'ida 익사시키다 drown
ikssuk'aejida 익숙해지다 familiarize oneself with, get used to
ikssuk'aji anŭn 익숙하지 않은 unfamiliar; *...e ikssuk'aji ant'a* ...에 익숙하지 않다 be unfamiliar with, be unaccustomed to
iktta 익다 get used to; get cooked; ripen
ikttŏn kot 읽던 곳 place (*in a book*)
ik'ida 익히다 familiarize; cook
il 일 affair; business; job; pursuit; work; things; *ne irina haera!* 네 일이나 해라! mind your own business!
ilbangjŏgin 일방적인 one-sided, unilateral
ilbang t'onghaengno 일방 통행로 one-way street
ilbanhwa 일반화 generalization
ilbanhwahada 일반화하다 generalize
ilbanin 일반인 civilian
ilbanjŏgin 일반적인 general
ilbanjŏgŭro 일반적으로 generally, in general
ilban sabyŏng 일반 사병 the ranks
ilbŏlle 일벌레 workaholic
ilbo 일보 a step; *ilbo chiktchŏne it-tta* 일보 직전에 있다 be on the verge of
Ilbon 일본 Japan ◊ Japanese
Ilbonŏ 일본어 Japanese (*language*)
Ilbon saram 일본 사람 Japanese
ilbubun 일부분 one part, a portion
ilburŏ 일부러 deliberately
ilbu saramdŭl 일부 사람들 some people
ilch'erŭl p'ohamhayŏ 일체를

포함하여 all inclusive

ilch'i 일치 agreement, consensus; match, correspondence

ilch'ihada 일치하다 agree, match, correspond; agree with

ilch'ihanŭn 일치하는 corresponding, matching; coinciding

ilch'ishik'ida 일치시키다 agree; reconcile

ilch'ŭng 일층 first floor

ilch'ul 일출 sunrise

ilda 일다 brew, get up

ilgan shinmun 일간 신문 daily paper

ilgi 일기 diary

ilgido 일기도 weather chart

ilgi yebo 일기 예보 weather forecast

ilgop 일곱 seven

ilgop pŏntchaeŭi 일곱번째의 seventh

ilgŭl kŏri 읽을 거리 reading matter

ilgŭl su innŭn 읽을 수 있는 readable

ilgwa 일과 routine

ilgwal 일괄 package

ilgwaljŏgŭro ch'wigŭp'ada 일괄적으로 취급하다 lump together

ilgwangnyogŭl hada 일광욕을 하다 sunbathe

ilgwanjagŏp yŏl 일관작업 열 assembly line

ilgwansŏng 일관성 consistency

ilgwansŏng innŭn 일관성 있는 consistent

il hoebun 일 회분 installment, episode

iljikssŏnŭro 일직선으로 in a straight line

ilkkaewŏjuda 일깨워주다 remind

ilkke hada 잃게 하다 cost; cause the loss of

ilkki ŏryŏun 읽기 어려운 illegible; unreadable; *ilkki shwiun* 읽기 쉬운 legible; easy to read

illanssŏng ssangdung-i 일란성 쌍둥이 identical twins

illyŏk 인력 manpower

illyŏnbŏnho 일련번호 serial number

illyŏne 일년에 in a year, per annum

illyŏne han ponŭi 일년에 한 번의 annual

illyu 인류 human race; humanity; man

illyunch'a 일륜차 wheelbarrow; monocycle

illyuŭi 일류의 first-rate

ilmol 일몰 sunset

ilmyŏn 일면 front page

ilmyŏn kisa 일면 기사 front page news

ilsangjŏgin 일상적인 everyday

ilshijŏk yŏn-gi 일시적 연기 reprieve

ilssang 일상 everyday

ilssangbok 일상복 clothes for everyday wear

ilssangjŏgin 일상적인 routine

ilssangjŏgŭro 일상적으로 as a matter of routine, routinely

ilssang-yong-ŏ 일상용어 vernacular

ilssanhwat'anso 일산화탄소 carbon monoxide

ilssappyŏng 일사병 sunstroke

ilsshibul 일시불 lump sum

ilsshijŏgin 일시적인 temporary, casual

ilsshijŏgŭro 일시적으로 temporarily

ilsshijŏk chŭngga 일시적 증가 temporary increase, bulge

ilsshijŏk pyŏndong 일시적 변동 temporary fluctuation, blip

ilsshijŏk taeyuhaeng 일시적 대유행 passing fad, craze

ilsshik 일식 eclipse of the sun

ilsshirŭl chŏnghada 일시를 정하다 fix a time

ilsohada 일소하다 clean up

ilsson 일손 hand, worker

iltchesagyŏk 일제 사격 volley

iltchi 일지 diary; logbook

...iltchido morŭnda ...일지도 모른다 may, might

iltchigin 일찍인 early

iltchik 일찍 early

iltchŏne 일전에 the other day

iltchŏng 일정 agenda; schedule

iltchŏng-aek 일정액 flat rate

iltchŏngch'i anŭn 일정치 않은 unsettled

iltchŏnghada 일정하다 be regular

iltchŏnghaji anŭn 일정하지 않은 erratic

iltchŏnghan 일정한 particular, specific; regular, uniform

iltchŏng-i kkwak ch'ada 일정이 꽉 차다 booked up

iltchŏng kigan 일정 기간 stint

iltchŏngsang 일정상 on the agenda

iltta 읽다 read

ilttŭngshil 일등실 first class
cabin/compartment

ilt'a 잃다 lose

ima 이마 forehead, brow

imbak'an 임박한 pending, impending

imdae 임대 lease

imdae chadongch'a 임대 자동차
rental car

imdaehada 임대하다 lease, rent

imdae kyeyaksŏ 임대 계약서 rental
agreement

imdaeryo 임대료 rent

imdaeyong 임대용 for rent

imeil 이메일 e-mail

imeil chuso 이메일 주소 e-mail
address

imeillo ponaeda 이메일로 보내다 e-
mail, send by e-mail

imeirŭl ponaeda 이메일을 보내다 e-
mail, send an e-mail to

imgŭm tonggyŏl 임금 동결 wage
freeze

imhak 임학 forestry

imi 이미 already

imiji 이미지 image

imin 이민 emigrant

Imin-guk 이민국 Immigration

iminhada 이민하다 emigrate

imjaga pakkwida 임자가 바뀌다
change hands

immagae 입마개 muzzle

immasŭl tashida 입맛을 다시다 lick
one's lips

immu 임무 task, brief; assignment;
duty

immyŏng 임명 appointment; posting

immyŏnghada 임명하다 appoint,
nominate

immyŏngja 임명자 appointee

imnyŏk 입력 input; enter, return

imnyŏkshik'ida 입력시키다 enter
COMPUT; **k'ŏmp'yut'ŏe imnyŏksshik'yŏ not'a** 컴퓨터에
입력시켜 놓다 put sth on computer

imnyŏk tanja 입력 단자 input port

imnyŏk'ada 입력하다 enter, key in

imo 이모 aunt (*mother's sister*)

imobu 이모부 uncle (*mother's sister's
husband*)

imsanbok 임산복 maternity dress

imsang-ŭi 임상의 clinical

imshi chigwŏn 임시 직원 temporary
employee, temp

imshi chŏjangso 임시 저장소 buffer
COMPUT

imshijigŭro irhada 임시직으로
일하다 work on a temporary basis,
temp

imshijŏgin 임시적인 temporary,
provisional

imshin 임신 conception; pregnancy

imshinbu 임신부 expectant mother

imshinhada 임신하다 conceive; be
pregnant

imshinhan 임신한 pregnant

imshinjung-ida 임신 중이다 be
expecting

imshi pyŏnt'ong 임시 변통 stopgap

imshi sudan 임시 수단 makeshift

imshiŭi 임시의 temporary, acting

imun 이문 margin

...inae-e ...이내에 within

inboisŭ 인보이스 invoice

inbun 인분 (human) feces; portion

Inch'e Myŏnyŏk Kyŏlp'ip Pairŏsŭ
인체 면역 결핍 바이러스 HIV

inch'i 인치 inch

inch'ing taemyŏngsa 인칭 대명사
personal pronoun

inch'ŏk 인척 in-laws

inch'ul 인출 withdrawal

inch'urhada 인출하다 withdraw

indae 인대 ligament

Indian 인디안 (American) Indian

indo 인도 footpath, sidewalk;
surrender; India ◊ Indian

Indoch'aina 인도차이나 Indochina ◊
Indochinese

indohada 인도하다 lead, take;
extradite; usher in

Indoin 인도인 Indian (*person*)

indojuŭi 인도주의 humanism;
humanitarianism

Indoneshia 인도네시아 Indonesia ◊
Indonesian

Indoneshiain 인도네시아인
Indonesian (*person*)

in-gan 인간 human (being)

in-ganjŏgin 인간적인 human,

humane

in-ganssŏng 인간성 humanity, humaneness

in-gan ssŭregi 인간 쓰레기 lowlife

in-girŭl ŏt-tta 인기를 얻다 catch on

ingkko 잉꼬 budgerigar

ingk'ŭ 잉크 ink

ingk'ŭ chet p'ŭrint'ŏ 잉크 젯 프린터 inkjet (printer)

ingmyŏng tong-ŏptcha 익명 동업자 silent partner

ingmyŏng-ŭi 익명의 anonymous

in-gong 인공 man-made

in-gong hohŭpkki 인공 호흡기 respirator

in-gongjinŭng 인공지능 artificial intelligence

in-gongjŏgin 인공적인 artificial

in-gong-wisŏng 인공위성 satellite

in-gong-wisŏng chŏpsshi 인공위성 접시 satellite dish

in-gu 인구 population

in-gu miltto 인구 밀도 population density

ing-yŏ 잉여 surplus

inhaesŏ 인해서: *kŭgŏsŭ(ro) in-haesŏ* 그것으로 인해서 so, for that reason

inhwa 인화 print

inhwassŏng(-ŭi) 인화성(의) inflammable

inhyŏng 인형 doll

inishyŏl 이니셜 initial

inishyŏllo ssŭda 이니셜로 쓰다 initial

injae sŭk'aut'ŭ tamdangja 인재 스카우트 담당자 headhunter *fig*

inji 인지 perception

...inji ...인지 if; whether; *...inji anidŭnji kane* ...인지 아니든지 간에 whether or not; *...inji ...inji* ...인지 ...인지 whether ... or ...

injil 인질 hostage

injilbŏm 인질범 hostage taker

injillo chap'ida 인질로 잡히다 be taken hostage

injŏgi kkŭnk'in 인적이 끊긴 deserted

injŏng 인정 acknowledgment

injŏnghada 인정하다 admit; approve of

injŏng-i manŭn 인정이 많은

philanthropic; benevolent

injŏng-innŭn 인정있는 humane

injŏng ŏmnŭn 인정 없는 inhuman

injŏp'an 인접한 adjacent

injong 인종 race

injong ch'abyŏl p'yeji 인종 차별 폐지 abolish racial discrimination, desegregate

injong ch'abyŏltchŏgin 인종 차별적인 racist

injong ch'abyŏltchuŭi 인종 차별주의 racism

injong ch'abyŏltchuŭija 인종 차별주의자 racist

injong p'yŏngdŭng 인종 평등 racial equality

injoŭi 인조의 artificial

inkki 인기 popularity

inkkiinnŭn 인기있는 fashionable, popular

inkki-it-tta 인기있다 be popular

inkkiŏmnŭn 인기없는 unpopular

inkkirŭl ŏt-tta 인기를 얻다 become popular, take off

ink'yubeit'ŏ 인큐베이터 incubator

inmom 잇몸 gum (*in mouth*)

inmul 인물 character

inp'ŭlle(ishyŏn) 인플레(이션) inflation

inp'ŭlleishyŏnŭl yubarhanŭn 인플레이션을 유발하는 inflationary

inp'yŏnŭro 인편으로 by hand

insa 인사 greeting, bow

insaek'ada 인색하다 be miserly

insaek'an 인색한 mean, stingy; miserly; grudging

insaeng 인생 life

insaeng-ŭl chŭlgida 인생을 즐기다 enjoy life

insahada 인사하다 greet; bow

insakkwa 인사과 personnel; human resources

insam 인삼 ginseng

insang 인상 raise, rise; image, reputation; impression; *nuguege choŭn/nappŭn insangŭl chuda* 누구에게 좋은/나쁜 인상을 주다 make a good/bad impression on s.o.; *...(ŭ)n insangŭl pat-tta* ...(으)ㄴ 인상을 받다 I get the impression that

insangjŏgin 인상적인 impressive; imposing, striking

insa pulssŏng 인사 불성 stupor

insa tamdang pujang 인사 담당 부장 personnel manager

inshik 인식 awareness

inshim chot'a 인심 좋다 be generous

inshim choŭn 인심 좋은 generous, good-hearted

inshyullin 인슐린 insulin

insŭt'ŏnt'ŭ k'ŏp'i 인스턴트 커피 instant coffee

insŭt'ŏnt'ŭ shikp'um 인스턴트 식품 convenience food

insu 인수 takeover; factor MATH

insuhada 인수하다 take over

inswae 인쇄 print

inswaegi 인쇄기 printing press

inswaehada 인쇄하다 printout

inswaemul 인쇄물 printed matter

inswaeŏptcha 인쇄업자 printer (person)

int'elli 인텔리 egghead; the intelligentsia

int'eriŏ tijain 인테리어 디자인 interior design

int'eriŏ tijainŏ 인테리어 디자이너 interior designer

int'ŏbyu 인터뷰 interview

int'ŏbyuhada 인터뷰하다 interview

int'ŏbyuhanŭn saram 인터뷰하는 사람 interviewer

int'ŏch'einji 인터체인지 interchange

int'ŏk'ŏm 인터컴 intercom

Int'ŏnesŭl tullŏboda 인터넷을 둘러보다 surf the Net

Int'ŏnet 인터넷 Internet; *Int'ŏnet sangesŏ* 인터넷 상에서 on the Internet

int'ŏpeisŭ 인터페이스 interface

inwijŏgin 인위적인 artificial, insincere

inyŏmjŏgin 이념적인 ideological

inyong 인용 quotation; extract

inyonghada 인용하다 quote; *chakkkaŭi kŭrŭl inyonghada* 작가의 글을 인용하다 quote from an author

inyongmun 인용문 quote (*from author*)

inyong puho 인용 부호 quotation marks

iŏp'on 이어폰 earphones

...iŏsŏ ...이어서 next to

...ioe-e ...이외에 besides, except for

ip 잎 leaf; blade; foliage

ip 입 mouth; *han ip* 한 입 a bite, a mouthful; *nanŭn surŭl ibe taeji anssŭmnida* 나는 술을 입에 대지 않습니다 I never touch alcohol, I don't drink

ipch'al 입찰 tender; bid

ipch'arhada 입찰하다 bid

ipch'ullyŏk k'odŭ 입출력 코드 access code

ipch'ullyŏk'ada 입출력하다 access

ipkkimŭl pulda 입김을 불다 blow

ipkku 입구 entrance, entry

ipkkuk 입국 arrivals (*at airport*); entry (*to country*)

ipkkuk hŏga 입국 허가 admission (*to country*)

ipkkukpija 입국비자 entry visa

i ppajin chaguk 이 빠진 자국 chip (*in cup etc*)

ip ppakkŭro naeda 입 밖으로 내다 let out *gasp, scream etc*

ip-ppangch'e 입방체 cube

ip-ppang-ŭi 입방의 cubic

ip-ppang yongjŏk 입방 용적 cubic volume

ip-ppang yongnyang 입방 용량 cubic capacity

ip-ppŏp 입법 legislation

ip-ppŏp-ppu 입법부 legislature

ipssahada 입사하다 join

ipssanghan 입상한 prizewinning

ipsshim choŭn 입심 좋은 glib, voluble

ipssŏk 입석 standing room

ipssuhada 입수하다 pick up

ipssul 입술 lip

iptchang 입장 entrance; stance; situation

iptchang hŏga 입장 허가 admission

iptchang kŭmji 입장 금지 no admittance

iptchangnyo 입장료 entrance fee

iptchŭng 입증 verification

iptchŭnghada 입증하다 establish, prove

iptta 입다 wear; put on

ipttaehada 입대하다 enlist

ip'agŭl hŏgahada 입학을 허가하다 admit to school

ip'akkŭm 입학금 fee

ip'ak tŭngnogŭl hada 입학 등록을 하다 register (*for school, university*)

ip'ak tŭngnok 입학 등록 registration (*at school, university*)

ip'ak wŏnsŏ 입학 원서 application form (*for school, university*)

ip'oehada 입회하다 join

ip'oe hŏga 입회 허가 admission

ip'oein 입회인 observer

ip'oerŭl hŏgahada 입회를 허가하다 admit to an organization

ip'ubo 입후보 candidacy

iraero 이래로 since

Irak'ŭ 이라크 Iraq ◊ Iraqi

Iran 이란 Iran ◊ Iranian

irhada 일하다 work

irhoe 일회 one time, once

irhoe pogyongnyang 일회 복용량 a dose

irhoeyong 일회용 disposable, throw-away

irhŭn 일흔 seventy

irhŭn pŏntchaeŭi 일흔 번째의 seventieth

irijŏri kŏnilda 이리저리 거닐다 stroll around

iri kkŭnnada 일이 끝나다 get off (work)

irŏbŏrin 잃어버린 missing

irŏktchŏrŏk 이럭저럭 somehow or other; **irŏktchŏrŏk ...haenaeda** 이럭저럭 ...해내다 manage to ... one way or another; **irŏktchŏrŏk saenghwarhada** 이럭저럭 생활하다 scrape a living, get by somehow

irŏk'e 이렇게 this way

irŏn 이런 like this; **irŏn shigŭro irŏnat-tta** 이런 식으로 일어났다 it happened like this; **irŏn, irŏn!** 이런, 이런! well, well!; **irŏn, sesange!** 이런, 세상에! (oh) dear!, dear me!

irŏna antta 일어나 앉다 sit up

irŏnada 일어나다 happen; come about; get up, rise

irŏnal kŏt kattchi anŭn 일어날 것 같지 않은 improbable; dim *prospects*

irŏsŏda 일어서다 stand (up), rise

iron 이론 theory

iron mullihak 이론 물리학 theoretical physics

ironsang-ŭro 이론상으로 in theory

irŭda 이르다 come to; reach; carry (*of sound*); range; **chŏgŏsŭn ch'ilman wŏne irŭnda** 저것은 70000원에 이른다 that comes to 70,000 won

irŭge 이르게 early

irŭk'ida 일으키다 cause; generate, stir up; cast *doubt*

irŭl shik'ida 일을 시키다 make work

irŭm 이름 name; first name

irŭmppunin 이름뿐인 nominal

irŭmp'yo 이름표 nametag

irŭmŭl chit-tta 이름을 짓다 name; **Yŭi irŭmŭl ttasŏ Xŭi irŭmŭl chit-tta** Y의 이름을 따서 X의 이름을 짓다 name X for Y

irŭn 이른 early

irŭn 잃은 lost

iruŏjida 이루어지다 be formed; **iruŏjyŏ it-tta** 이루어져 있다 consist of

irwŏl 일월 January

irwŏn 일원 member

irwŏnida 일원이다 belong to, be a member of

irye 이레 exception

iryejŏgin 이례적인 exceptional

iryejŏgŭro 이례적으로 exceptionally

iryŏkssŏ 이력서 résumé

iryoil 일요일 Sunday

iryongp'um 일용품 daily necessity; daily necessities

iryu 이류 inferiority

iryuk 이륙 takeoff, liftoff

iryuk'ada 이륙하다 take off (*of airplane*)

iryu(ŭi) 이류(의) second-rate; inferior

isa 이사 director; move

isa chŏnmun ŏpch'e 이사 전문 업체 movers

isahada 이사하다 move house, move away

isahoe 이사회 board (of directors)

isa hoeŭi 이사 회의 board meeting

isa hoeŭishil 이사 회의실 board room

isahŭl 이사흘 couple of days

isak 이삭 ear (*of grain*)

isanagada 이사나가다 move out

isang 이상 not less than, more than ◊ ideal ◊ strangeness; **10,000 isang-ŭro** 10,000 이상으로 upward of 10,000; **ch'a-e muŏshin-ga isang-i it-tta** 차에 무엇인가 이상이 있다 there is something wrong with the car

isanghada 이상하다 be strange

isanghage 이상하게 curiously, strangely

isanghagedo 이상하게도 curiously enough

isangjŏgin 이상적인 ideal

isangjuŭijŏgin 이상주의적인 idealistic

isanhwat'anso 이산화탄소 greenhouse gas

isaoda 이사오다 move in

isatchim unsong-ŏptcha 이삿짐 운송업자 movers

isattchim t'ŭrŏk 이삿짐 트럭 movers' van

ishik chojik 이식 조직 graft

ishik susul 이식 수술 transplant

ishik'ada 이식하다 transplant

iship 이십 twenty

isŏ 이서 endorsement

isŏhada 이서하다 endorse

isŏng 이성 the opposite sex; reason

isŏng-aeŭi 이성애의 heterosexual

issŭl su ŏmnŭn 있을 수 없는 unacceptable

issŭm 있음 presence

issushigae 이쑤시개 toothpick

isŭk'eip'ŭ 이스케이프 escape COMPUT

isŭl 이슬 dew

isŭlbi 이슬비 drizzle

isŭlbiga naerida 이슬비가 내리다 drizzle

Isŭllamgyo 이슬람교 Islam (religion)

Isŭllam kuk-kka 이슬람 국가 Islam, Islamic world

Isŭllam minjok 이슬람 민족 Islam (people)

Isŭrael 이스라엘 Israel ◊ Israeli

Isŭraerin 이스라엘인 Israeli

itchŏm 이점 advantage; perk; plus

itchoguro 이쪽으로 this way

itta 잇다 join; inherit; knit together; preserve

it-tta 있다 be; exist; stay; be located; have, possess; **...i/ga issŭmnikka?** ...이/가 있습니까? do you have ...?; **... it-tta** ...있다 there is/are ◊ (forms continuous present of action verbs): **...go it-tta** ...고 있다 ...ing; **nŏnŭn irŭl chinach'ige hago it-tta** 너는 일을 지나치게 하고 있다 you're overdoing things

it-tta 잊다 forget; get over

it-ttarŭda 잇따르다 follow one after another; **...ŭl/rŭl it-ttara** ...을/를 잇따라 one after another

it-ttarŭn 잇따른 successive

it'ajŏgin 이타적인 altruistic

it'al 이탈 departure

It'allia 이탈리아 Italy ◊ Italian

It'alliain 이탈리아인 Italian

It'alliaŏ 이탈리아어 Italian (language)

it'ŭlmada 이틀마다 every other day

iŭirŭl chegihada 이의를 제기하다 raise an objection, object

iŭirŭl shinch'ŏnghada 이의를 신청하다 take exception, object

iŭmp'yo 이음표 hyphen

iŭn chari 이은 자리 join

iut 이웃 neighborhood; neighbor

iut saram 이웃 사람 neighbor

iut'ada 이웃하다 border on

iwŏl 이월 February

iyagi 이야기 story, tale

iyagihada 이야기하다 tell, narrate

iyagihagi 이야기하기 narration

iyagishigŭi 이야기식의 narrative

iyong 이용 use

iyonghada 이용하다 use, draw on; take advantage of; manipulate

iyu 이유 cause; reason; **amu iyu ŏpsshi** 아무 이유 없이 for nothing, for no reason

---

-ja -자 (suffix for persons): **tokch'angja** 독창자 soloist; **tong-ŏptcha** 동업자 partner

...jamaja ...자 마자 as soon as

K

...ka ...가 (*subject particle*): *kŭ che-ŭiga maŭme tŭmnikka?* 그 제의가 마음에 듭니까? does that offer interest you?
kaap'ada 가압하다 push, pressure
kabal 가발 wig
kabang 가방 bag
kabŏrida 가버리다 go off, leave
kabyŏn 가변 variableness ◊ variable
kabyŏpkke 가볍게 lightly
kabyŏpkke hada 가볍게 하다 lighten
kabyŏptta 가볍다 be light; be slight; be frivolous
kabyŏum 가벼움 lightness
kabyŏun 가벼운 light; airy; dismissive
kach'aŏmnŭn 가차없는 ruthless
kach'i 가치 value, worth, merit
kach'i anŭn 같지 않은 unlike
kach'i chada 같이 자다 sleep with; have sex with
kach'iga it-tta 가치가 있다 be worth; merit; count, be important
kach'iga ŏmnŭn 가치가 없는 worthless
kach'iga orŭda 가치가 오르다 rise in value
kach'iga ttŏrŏjida 가치가 떨어지다 fall in value; depreciate
kach'i hada 같이 하다 join in
kach'i harak 가치 하락 depreciation
kach'i itkke yŏgida 가치 있게 여기다 value, prize
kach'iŏmnŭn 가치없는 worthless
kach'i oda 같이 오다 come along, come too
kach'i put'ŏit-tta 같이 붙어있다 be stuck together
kach'irŭl ttŏrŏttŭrida 가치를 떨어뜨리다 detract from; run down
kach'ŏbun sodŭk 가처분 소득 disposable income
kach'uk 가축 domestic animal; livestock
kach'uk uri 가축 우리 corral
kada 가다 go (*toward listener*); come; get along (*come to party etc*); proceed (*of people*); *yŏgŭro kanŭn kire issŏyo* 역으로 가는 길에 있어요 it's on the way to the station
kadak 가닥 strip, strand
kadonghaji mot'age hada 가동하지 못하게 하다 immobilize
kadŭk ch'ada 가득 차다 fill up (*of place*) ◊ full up
kadŭk ch'aeuda 가득 채우다 fill up, top up
kadŭk ch'ait-tta 가득 차있다 be bristling with; be crammed with
kadŭk ch'an 가득 찬 full
kadŭk'an 가득한 full of
kaduda 가두다 lock in
kae 개 dog ◊ *general countword*
kaeam 개암 hazelnut
kaeamnamu 개암나무 hazel (tree)
kaebal 개발 development
kaebaldosangguk 개발도상국 developing country
kaebaltcha 개발자 developer
kaebangdoen 개방된 open *market, society*
kaebarhada 개발하다 develop
kaebarhayŏ iyonghada 개발하여 이용하다 exploit, make use of
kaebyŏltchŏgŭro 개별적으로 individually
kae chul 개 줄 leash
kaech'arhada 개찰하다 punch *ticket*
kaech'ŏk'ada 개척하다 pioneer
Kaech'ŏnjŏl 개천절 National Foundation Day
kaech'uk'ada 개축하다 rebuild
kaeda 개다 clear, clear up (*of weather*); fold
kaegae 개개 individually, one by one
kaegaeŭi 개개의 individual, separate
kaegŭ 개그 gag, joke

kaegulgaegul ulda 개굴개굴 울다 croak (*of frog*)

kaeguri 개구리 frog

kaegwanhada 개관하다 inaugurate

kaehoeshik 개회식 opening ceremony

kaehwahada 개화하다 civilize

kaehyŏk 개혁 reform

kaehyŏk undong 개혁 운동 crusade (*for reform*)

kaehyŏk'ada 개혁하다 reform

kaein 개인 individual ◊ individual, personal

kaeinbisŏ 개인 비서 PA, personal assistant

kaein hwagin pŏnho 개인 확인 번호 PIN, personal identification number

kaeinjuŭi 개인주의 individualism

kaeinjuŭija 개인주의자 individualist

kaein kyosa 개인 교사 (private) tutor

kaein kyosŭp 개인 교습 (private) tuition

kaeintchŏgin 개인적인 personal, private

kaeinŭi 개인의 individual; personal

kaeinyong k'ŏmp'yut'ŏ 개인용 컴퓨터 PC, personal computer

kaeinyong sŭt'ereo 개인용 스테레오 personal stereo

kaejip 개집 kennel

kaejŏng 개정 sitting (*of court*); reform

kaejŏng chungim 개정 중임 session (*of parliament*)

kaejo 개조 conversion; renovation

kaejohada 개조하다 convert; renovate

kaekch'a 객차 car (*of a train*)

kaekkwanjŏgin 객관적인 objective

kaeksshil 객실 cabin

kaekssil tamdangja 객실 담당자 room clerk

kaekwan 개관 survey

kaek'owŏnsung-i 개코원숭이 baboon

kaemi 개미 ant

kae mok-kkŏri 개 목걸이 (dog) collar

kaemyŏnghada 개명하다 rename

kaenbŏsŭ 캔버스 canvas (*for painting*)

kaeng 갱 gang; pit, coal mine

kaengshin 갱신 renewal

kaengshinhada 갱신하다 renew

kaenyŏm 개념 concept

kaeŏp'ada 개업하다 set up (*in business*)

kaesaekki ∨ 개새끼 son of a bitch, bastard

kaeshi 개시 initiation

kaeshihada 개시하다 initiate

Kaeshin-gyo 개신교 Protestantism

kaeŭich'i ank'o 개의치 않고 regardless of

kaeul 개울 stream

kaeyo 개요 outline; syllabus

kage 가게 store

kage chuin 가게 주인 storekeeper

kagi shwiun 가기 쉬운 accessible

kagonghada 가공하다 process *food, raw materials*

kagonghaji anŭn 가공하지 않은 raw *sugar, iron*

kagu 가구 furniture

kagu han chŏm 가구 한 점 a piece of furniture

kagurŭl tŭryŏ not'a 가구를 들여 놓다 furnish

kagyanggakssaek 각양각색 medley, mixture, assortment

kagye 가계 descent, ancestry; housekeeping (*money*)

kagyebu 가계부 housekeeping book

kagyŏgi orŭda 가격이 오르다 appreciate, increase in value

kagyŏgi pissan 가격이 비싼 expensive

kagyŏgŭl maegida 가격을 매기다 price

kagyŏgŭl naerida 가격을 내리다 mark down, reduce the price of

kagyŏgŭl ollida 가격을 올리다 mark up *price*

kagyŏk 가격 cost; price

kagyŏk harin kyŏngjaeng 가격 할인 경쟁 price war

kagyŏk insang 가격 인상 price rise; mark-up

kahada 가하다 inflict

kahok 가혹 severity

kahok'an 가혹한 harsh; oppressive

kaijrŏ oda

kaijrŏ oda 가지러 오다 come for; collect

kaip'ada 가입하다 join, become a member

kajami 가자미 turbot

kajang 가장 most, very ◊ wage earner; masquerade

kajang chal naganŭn sangp'yo 가장 잘 나가는 상표 brand leader

kajang chari 가장 자리 edge

kajanghada 가장하다 act; put on; pretend

kajangjari 가장자리 edge; rim; brim; brink; verge

kajang mudobok 가장 무도복 fancy dress

kajang mudohoe 가장 무도회 fancy-dress party

kaji 가지 branch; twig; eggplant

kajida 가지다 own, have; hold; *iriro kŭgŏsŭl kajyŏda chullaeyo?* 이리로 그것을 가져다 줄래요? bring it here, will you?

kajigakssaegŭi 가지각색의 miscellaneous

kajigakssaek 가지각색 assortment

kajigo it-tta 가지고 있다 have got

kajigo kada 가지고 가다 take, remove

kajigo nolda 가지고 놀다 toy with

kajirŏ kada 가지러 가다 collect, call for

kajirŏnhi kkot-tta 가지런히 꽂다 put neatly; fix neatly; arrange

kajirŭl ch'ida (가지를) 치다 prune *branch*

kajŏng 가정 assumption; home

kajŏngnyong k'ŏmp'yut'ŏ 가정용 컴퓨터 home computer

kajŏng kyosa 가정 교사 home tutor

kajŏng kyoyuk 가정 교육 upbringing; home education

kajŏngbu 가정부 housekeeper

kajŏnghada 가정하다 assume, suppose

kajŏngjŏgin 가정적인 homeloving, homely

kajŏngnyong-i anin 가정용이 아닌 not designed for use in the home

kajŏnjep'um 가전제품 (household) appliance

kajok 가족 family; household

kajok kyehoek 가족 계획 family planning

kajoktchŏgin 가족적인 paternalistic

kajoktchuŭi 가족주의 paternalism

kajuk 가죽 hide, skin (*of animal*); leather

kajuk kkŭn 가죽 끈 lead, leash; (leather) strap

kajyŏoda 가져오다 bring; get, fetch; earn

kak 각 each, every, all; angle

kakkai 가까이 near ◊ about, approximately

kakkaie 가까이에 at hand, to hand ◊ near; *ŭnhaeng kakkaie* 은행 가까이에 near the bank

kakkaie(sŏ) 가까이에(서) locally

kakkai hagi shwiun 가까이 하기 쉬운 approachable

kakkai kaji mot'age hada 가까이 가지 못하게 하다 prevent from going near, keep away

kakkai tagagada 가까이 다가가다 approach, draw near

kakkai tagaoda 가까이 다가오다 draw near (*of time*)

kakkaihagi ŏryŏun 가까이하기 어려운 unapproachable

kakkapkke 가깝게 close, near

kakkaptta 가깝다 be close, be near

kakkasŭro 가까스로 scarcely, barely; hardly

kakkasŭro ppajyŏnagada 가까스로 빠져나가다 have a narrow escape (*from arrest*)

kakkasŭro saranamtta 가까스로 살아남다 have a narrow escape (*from death*)

kakkaun 가까운 close, near

kak-kkage 각각에 each

kak-kkagŭi 각각의 each, respective

kak-kkak 각각 each

kak-kki 각기 respectively

kak-kkwang 각광 footlights

kakkŭm 가끔 occasionally, sometimes

kakppon 각본 screenplay

kakssaek 각색 adaptation

kaktcha 각자 each other

kaktchu 각주 footnote

kalbi 갈비 spare ribs, barbecued ribs

kalbippyŏ 갈비뼈 rib

kalbitchim 갈비찜 steamed (beef) ribs

kalbi t'ang 갈비탕 beef rib soup

kalda 갈다 change, replace; grind; sharpen; plow

kalga mŏktta 갉아 먹다 nibble

kalgigalgi tchit-tta 갈기갈기 찢다 tear up

kalgo tadŭmtta 갈고 다듬다 polish up

kalgori 갈고리 hook

kalgyŏ ssŭda 갈겨 쓰다 scribble

kalgyŏ ssŭgi 갈겨 쓰기 scribble

kal kiri mŏlda 갈 길이 멀다 it's a long way off

kalk'wi 갈퀴 rake

kallajida 갈라지다 branch off; diverge

kallajin t'ŭm 갈라진 틈 crevice

kallyak 간략 simplicity; brevity; *kallyak'i p'yŏnjirŭl ssŭda* 간략히 편지를 쓰다 drop a line

kallyakhada 간략하다 be simple; be brief

kalmaegi 갈매기 gull; seagull

kalmang 갈망 craving, longing

kalmanghada 갈망하다 crave, long for

kalp'i 갈피 point, sense; *nae maŭmi kalp'irŭl mot-tchamnŭnda* 내 마음이 갈피를 못잡는다 my mind is in a whirl

kalsaek 갈색 brown

kalssurok tŏ 갈수록 더 increasingly

kaltchŭng 갈증 thirst

kaltta 갉다 gnaw

kalttae 갈대 reed

kama 가마 kiln

kamang 가망 chance, possibility

kamang-innŭn 가망있는 hopeful, promising

kamang ŏmnŭn 가망 없는 hopeless, useless

kamangsŏng 가망성 probability

kamanhaejuda 감안해주다 make allowances

kamanhi 가만히 still; *kamanhi issŏ!* 가만히 있어! keep still!

kamanittchi mot'anŭn 가만있지 못하는 restless

kambang 감방 cell (*for prisoner*)

kamchwŏjin 감춰진 hidden

kamch'altcha 감찰자 inspector (*in factory*)

kamch'o 감초 licorice

kamch'ok 감촉 feeling; touch; *shilk'ŭwa / myŏn-gwa kat'ŭn kamch'ogida* 실크와 / 면과 같은 감촉이다 it feels like silk / cotton

kamch'uda 감추다 conceal, cover up; withhold

kamdanghada 감당하다 control

kamdanghal su innŭn / ŏmnŭn 감당할 수 있는 / 없는 controllable / uncontrollable

kamdok 감독 director (*of movie*); direction (*of movie*)

kamdoktcha 감독자 supervisor

kamdok'ada 감독하다 direct *movie*; supervise

kamdongjŏgin 감동적인 emotional, poignant

kamdongshik'ida 감동시키다 move, touch (*emotionally*)

kamdongshik'inŭn 감동시키는 touching

kamgaginnŭn 감각있는 tasteful

kamgagŏmnŭn 감각없는 numb

kamgak 감각 sensation; sense (*sight, touch, smell etc*)

kamgaktchŏgin 감각적인 sensuous

kamgi 감기 cold, chill (*illness*)

kamgida 감기다 close; wind round

kamgie kŏllida 감기에 걸리다 catch a cold

kamgin 감긴 closed

kamgŭm 감금 captivity, confinement; detention

kamgŭmhada 감금하다 confine, imprison

kamgyŏk'ada 감격하다 be thrilled

kamgyŏk'age hanŭn 감격하게 하는 thrilling

kamhaenghae popsshida 감행해 봅시다 let's risk it

kamhi 감히 daringly; *nega kamhi ŏttŏk'e!* 네가 감히 어떻게! how dare you!

kamhihada 감히 하다 dare; *kunŭn kamhi hal su ŏpssŏssŏyo* 그는

감히 할 수 없었어요 he didn't dare

kamhyŏnghada 감형하다 commute *death sentence*

kamja 감자 potato

kamja ch'ip 감자 칩 potato chip

kamja t'wigim 감자 튀김 French fries; fried potatoes

kamji 감지 perception (*through senses*)

kamjihada 감지하다 perceive (*with senses*)

kamjilnage hanŭn 감질나게 하는 tantalizing

kamjŏng 감정 emotion; valuation

kamjŏngga 감정가 connoisseur

kamjŏng-i sanghagi shwiun 감정이 상하기 쉬운 sensitive

kamjŏngjŏgin 감정적인 emotional

kamjŏng-ŭi p'okppal 감정의 폭발 outburst of emotion

kamjŏng-ŭl ŏngnurŭji mot'ada 감정을 억누르지 못하다 be unable to control one's emotions, be overcome by emotion

kamjŏnsashik'ida 감전사시키다 electrocute

kammiroun 감미로운 mellow

kammiryo 감미료 sweetener (*for drink*)

kammyŏng 감명 deep impression; *nuguege / muŏse kammyŏng pat-tta* 누구에게 / 무엇에 감명 받다 be impressed by s.o. / sth

kammyŏng chuda 감명 주다 make an impression

Kamni Kyohoe 감리 교회 Methodist Church

kamok 감옥 prison

kamsa 감사 gratitude; thanks; audit

kamsagwan 감사관 auditor

kamsahada 감사하다 be grateful for; thank; audit

kamsahagedo 감사하게도 thankfully

kamsahal chul morŭnŭn 감사할 줄 모르는 ungrateful

kamsahamnida 감사합니다 thank you (*polite*)

kamsahanŭn 감사하는 thankful

kamsang 감상 sentimentality, sentiment

kamsangjŏgin 감상적인 sentimental

kamshihada 감시하다 monitor, watch; spy on; picket

kamso 감소 decrease, decline

kamsohada 감소하다 decline, decrease

kamsok'ada 감속하다 decelerate, slow down

kamsuhada 감수하다 reconcile oneself

kamsusŏng-i kanghan 감수성이 강한 susceptible

kamsusŏng-i yeminhan 감수성이 예민한 impressionable

kamtta 감다 wind, wind up *clock*; close

kamt'an 감탄 admiration

kamt'anhada 감탄하다 admire

kamum 가뭄 drought

kamwŏn 감원 lay-off, staff cut

kamwŏndoeda 감원되다 be laid off

kamwŏnhada 감원하다 lay off

kamwŏnshik'ida 감원시키다 lay off

kamyŏm 감염 infection

kamyŏmdoeda 감염되다 become infected

kamyŏmdoen 감염된 infected

kamyŏmshik'ida 감염시키다 infect

kamyŏn 가면 mask

ka-myŏng 가명 pseudonym

kan 간 liver (*food*)

kanan 가난 poverty

kananhada 가난하다 be poor

kananhan 가난한 poor, deprived

kanbu 간부 executive

kanch'ŏk'ada 간척하다 reclaim

kanch'ŏnghada 간청하다 implore, plead with

kanch'ŏp 간첩 secret agent, spy

kang 강 river

kang-aji 강아지 puppy, pup; whelp

kangbak kwannyŏm 강박 관념 obsession; compulsion

kangbak kwannyŏme sarojap'in 강박 관념에 사로잡힌 obsessive; compulsive

Kangbuk 강북 Kangbuk (*Seoul, north of the Han river*)

kangbyŏn 강변 riverside

kangch'ŏl 강철 steel

kangdo 강도 intensity; burglar; burglary

kangdojil 강도질 robbery
kangdojirhada 강도질하다 burglarize
kangdo(rŭl) tanghada 강도(를) 당하다 be robbed
kangdŭngshik'ida 강등시키다 downgrade
kanggan 강간 rape
kangganbŏm 강간범 rapist
kangganhada 강간하다 rape
kanggŏnhan 강건한 virile
kanggyŏnghan 강경한 strong, firm
kanggyŏngnonja 강경론자 hardliner, hawk *fig*
kanghada 강하다 be strong
kanghaejida 강해지다 strengthen; harden (*of attitude*); intensify
kanghage 강하게 strongly
kangham 강함 strength, intensity
kanghan 강한 intense, strong, high
Kanghwado 강화도 Kanghwa Island
kanghwahada 강화하다 reinforce; tighten *control*, *security*
kangjangje 강장제 tonic
kangje 강제 force
kangjejŏgin 강제적인 forced
kangjero 강제로 by force; *Xŭl/rŭl kangjero Yhadorok mandŭlda* X을/를 강제로 Y하도록 만들다 force X to do Y
kangjo 강조 emphasis, accent
kangjohada 강조하다 emphasize; highlight
Kangnam 강남 Kangnam (*Seoul, south of the Han river*)
kangnyŏk shilsshihada 강력 실시하다 forcibly carry out, enforce
kangnyŏk'ada 강력하다 be powerful
kangnyŏk'age 강력하게 violently, very strongly
kangnyŏk'an 강력한 powerful, strong; intense
kangnyŏk'i 강력히 strongly
kangnyŏn 강연 talk, lecture
kangnyŏrham 강렬함 violence (*of gale*)
kangnyŏrhan 강렬한 strong, violent
kang-ŏgwi 강 어귀 river mouth
kangppadak 강바닥 riverbed
kangp'an 강판 grater
kangp'ung 강풍 gale

kangsa 강사 lecturer; instructor
kangse 강세 strength; stress, emphasis; *tallŏ kangse* 달러 강세 a run on the dollar
kangse chusik shijang 강세 주식 시장 bull market
kangtchŏm 강점 strong point
kangt'a 강타 blow, punch
kangt'ahada 강타하다 smash, bang
kangt'al 강탈 extortion
kangt'arhada 강탈하다 rob
kang-ŭi 강의 lecture
kang-ŭihada 강의하다 give a lecture, lecture
kang-ŭishil 강의실 lecture hall
kang-u 강우 rainfall
kan-gyŏk 간격 space
kan-gyŏrhage 간결하게 briefly
kan-gyŏrhan 간결한 brief, succinct
kan-gyŏrhi hada 간결히 하다 shorten, trim
kangyohada 강요하다 coerce, force; press, urge; insist on
kanho 간호 care (*of sick person*)
kanho ŏmmu 간호 업무 nursing
kanhosa 간호사 nurse
kanho shilssŭpssaeng 간호 실습생 student nurse
kani ch'imdae 간이 침대 cot
kani maejŏm 간이 매점 kiosk
kani shikttang 간이 식당 snack bar
kanjang 간장 soy sauce; liver ANAT
kanjilppyŏng 간질병 epilepsy
kanjilppyŏng hwanja 간질병 환자 epileptic (*person*)
kanjirida 간질이다 tickle
kanjirŏp'ida 간지럽히다 tickle
kanjirŭi paltchak 간질의 발작 epileptic fit
kanjŏppi 간접비 overhead FIN
kanjŏptchŏgin 간접적인 indirect
kanjŏptchŏguro 간접적으로 indirectly
kanjŏrhada 간절하다 be eager, be earnest
kanjŏrhan 간절한 eager
kanjŏrhi 간절히 eagerly
kan kogi 간 고기 ground meat
kanjuhada 간주하다 deem, consider
kannan 갓난 newborn
kannyŏm 간염 hepatitis

kanp'ahanŭn

kanp'ahanŭn 간파하는 penetrating
kanp'an 간판 notice; signboard (*outside shop, on building*); front, cover organization
kansahae poinŭn 간사해 보이는 shifty-looking *person*
kansahan 간사한 shifty, deceitful
kanshik 간식 snack
kanshinhi 간신히 barely, only just
kansŏndoro 간선도로 arterial road
kansŏp 간섭 interference
kansŏp'ada 간섭하다 interfere
kansu 간수 guard
kansuhada 간수하다 store, keep
kanttanhada 간단하다 be simple; be brief
kanttanhage 간단하게 simply
kanttanham 간단함 simplicity
kanttanhan 간단한 simple, straightforward
kanttanhi 간단히 plainly, simply
kant'ong 간통 adultery; *kant'ongŭl tanghada* 간통을 당하다 commit adultery
kant'ŏng kwan-gye 간통 관계 adulterous relationship; adultery
kanŭlda 가늘다 be thin
kanŭn 가는 thin; fine
kanŭnghada 가능하다 be possible
kanŭnghage hada 가능하게 하다 allow, enable
kanŭnghan 가능한 possible; *kanŭnghan han ppalli* 가능한 한 빨리 as soon as possible; *kanŭnghan kajang tchalbŭn / pparŭn...* 가능한 가장 짧은 / 빠른... the shortest / quickest possible
kanŭngssŏng 가능성 possibility; likelihood; *kanŭngssŏng-i kŏŭi hŭibak'an* 가능성이 거의 희박한 just remotely possible
kanŭn kire 가는 길에: *...ro kanŭn kire* ...로 가는 길에 on the way
kanŭrŏjida 가늘어지다 get thin
kanyalp'ŭn 가냘픈 slender, slight
kap 갑 pack (*of cigarettes*)
kap 값 price
kapkkangnyu 갑각류 shellfish
kap pissan 값 비싼 expensive
kapp'an 갑판 deck NAUT

kapssangsŏn 갑상선 thyroid (gland)
kapsshi pissan 값이 비싼 expensive
kapsshi ssan 값이 싼 inexpensive, cheap
kapssŭl naerida 값을 내리다 knock down, reduce the price of
kaptchagi 갑자기 suddenly, all of a sudden
kaptchakssŭrŏn 갑작스런 sudden, unexpected; abrupt
kaptta 갚다 repay
kap'arŭn 가파른 steep
karaanch'ida 가라앉히다 calm down; sink
kara-anjŭn 가라앉은 subdued
karaantta 가라앉다 go down; subside, settle; cool (down); sink; go under
karaibŭl ot 가라입을 옷 a change of clothes
karaiptta 가라입다 change *clothes*, get changed
karak 가락 tune; pitch; tone
karaok'e 가라오케 karaoke
karat'ada 갈아타다 change *train etc*
karat'agi 갈아타기 change (*in travel*)
karida 가리다 shade; veil *face, eyes*
karik'ida 가리키다 indicate, point at
karoch'aeda 가로채다 intercept
karodŭng 가로등 streetlight
karo panghyang-ŭro 가로 방향으로 landscape *print*
karŭch'ida 가르치다 teach; instruct; coach
karŭdsa 가르다 mark out, set apart
karŭma 가르마 part (*in hair*)
karŭmarŭl t'ada 가르마를 타다 part one's hair
karu 가루 powder
karubinu 가루 비누 washing powder
karyŏnaeda 가려내다 sort out
karyŏptta 가렵다 itch
karyŏum 가려움 itch
kasa 가사 lyrics; housekeeping
kasang 가상 imagination
kasang hyŏnshil 가상 현실 virtual reality
kasang konggan 가상 공간 cyberspace
kashi 가시 thorn; spine; splinter; fish bone

kashi ch'ŏlssa 가시 철사 barbed wire

kashige hada 가시게 하다 rinse away *taste*

kasŏkppang 가석방 parole

kasŏl 가설 temporary construction; hypothesis

kasŏl hwaltchuro 가설 활주로 temporary landing strip

kasŏrhada 가설하다 build; suppose

kasok 가속 acceleration

kasokshik'ida 가속시키다 accelerate

kasok'ada 가속하다 accelerate

kasoktto 가속도 rate of acceleration

kassŭ t'aengk'ŭ 가스탱크 gasometer; gas works

kasŭ 가스 gas (*for cooking*)

kasŭk'et 가스켓 gasket

kasŭm 가슴 chest, bust

kasŭmari 가슴앓이 heartburn

kasŭmi mani p'ain 가슴이 많이 파인 low-cut

kasŭmi pinyaka'n 가슴이 빈약한 flat-chested

kasŭmŭl tŭrŏnaen 가슴을 드러낸 bare-chested

kasŭpkki 가습기 humidifier

kasu 가수 singer

kat 갓 traditional horsehair hat

katcha 가짜 fake

katch'uda 갖추다 possess; have in stock

katch'i 같이 as, like; together with

katch'uŏ chuda 갖추어 주다 equip

katkko nolda 갖고 놀다 mess around with

kat-tta 같다 be the same; be equal; be like; come to MATH; be on a par with; it appears that; *...kŏt kat-tta* ...것 같다 it seems like

kat'a poida 같아 보이다 seem like

kat'ŏ 가터 garter

kat'ŭn 같은 like, such as ◊ same; equal; identical; *...wa / kwa kat'ŭn kŏt* ...와 / 과 같은 것 something like; *kat'ŭn nop'iŭi* 같은 높이의 flush, level

kaŭl 가을 fall, autumn

kaun 가운 gown

kaunde 가운데 middle ◊ among, amongst

kawi 가위 scissors

kawiro charŭda 가위로 자르다 cut with scissors, clip, trim

Kaya 가야 Kaya (*Ancient Kingdom*)

kayagŭm 가야금 Kaya zither

kayŏnssŏng-ŭi 가연성의 flammable

kayongssŏng-ŭi 가용성의 soluble

ke 게 crab

kedaga 게다가 besides, moreover

kegŏlssŭrŏpkke 게걸스럽게 ravenously

kegŏlssŭrŏptta 게걸스럽다 be ravenous

kegŏlssŭrŏun 게걸스러운 ravenous

keim 게임 game (*in tennis*)

keim sent'ŏ 게임 센터 amusement arcade

kerilla 게릴라 guerrilla

keshi 게시 notice, bulletin

keshihada 게시하다 post, put up *notice*

keship'an 게시판 bulletin board

...ket ...겠... shall (*indicates future tense, intention or supposition*)

keŭllihada 게을리하다 shirk

keŭrŭda 게으르다 be lazy

keŭrŭm 게으름 indolence

keŭrŭmbaeng-i 게으름뱅이 layabout

keŭrŭn 게으른 lazy

keyangdoeda 게양되다 fly (*of flag*)

ki 기 era; flag; energy

kia 기아 starvation

kiapkkye 기압계 barometer

kiban 기반 basis, footing

kibarhan 기발한 extraordinary, striking

kibarhan saenggak 기발한 생각 inspiration

kibok 기복 ups and downs

kibonjŏgin 기본적인 basic, fundamental

kibonjŏgŭro 기본적으로 basically

kibonkap 기본값 default COMPUT

kibonŭi 기본의 rudimentary, basic

kibsŭ 깁스 plaster cast

kibu 기부 contribution; donation

kibugŭm mojip 기부금 모집 collection (*in church*)

kibuhada 기부하다 contribute, donate

kibuja 기부자 contributor, donor

kibun 기분 mood, frame of mind; *kibun chŏnhwan* 기분 전환 diversion, recreation; *kibun chŏnhwanŭro* 기분 전환으로 for a change; *onŭl kibuni ŏttŏseyo?* 오늘 기분이 어떠세요? how are you feeling today?

kibunjoŭn 기분좋은 agreeable, pleasant

kibun p'ulda 기분 풀다 lighten up

kibun sanghagehada 기분 상하게하다 upset, offend

kibun sanghan 기분 상한 upset; *kibuni chot'a / nappŭda* 기분이 좋다 / 나쁘다 be in a good / bad mood; *kibuni chot'a / p'uri chugŏit-tta* 기분이 좋다 / 풀이 죽어있다 be in good / poor spirits; *kibuni karaantta* 기분이 가라앉다 weigh down (*with worries*); *kibuni nappŭn* 기분이 나쁜 bad-tempered, moody

kibunŭl todunŭn 기분을 돋우는 exhilarating

kich'a 기차 train

kich'ayŏk 기차역 railroad station

kich'e 기체 gas (*oxygen etc*)

kich'eŭi 기체의 pneumatic

kich'im 기침 cough

kich'imhada 기침하다 cough

kich'im sorirŭl naeda 기침 소리를 내다 cough (*to get attention*)

kich'im shirŏp 기침 시럽 cough syrup

kich'im yak 기침 약 cough medicine

kich'o 기초 basis; foundations (*of building*) ◊ basic, fundamental

kich'obut'ŏ hada 기초부터 하다 get down to basics

kich'o chagŏp 기초 작업 groundwork

kich'ohada 기초하다 rest on, be based on

kich'ojŏgin 기초적인 basic

kich'oŭi 기초의 rudimentary

kida 기다 crawl

kidae 기대 expectation, hope

kidaeda 기대다 count on, rely on; lean; balance; recline, lie back

kidaedoenŭn 기대되는 prospective

kidaehada 기대하다 expect; look forward to; bank on

kidaeŏ not'a 기대어 놓다 prop; lean

kidarida 기다리다 wait for; wait, hang on

kido 기도 prayer

kidohada 기도하다 pray

Kidok-kkyo 기독교 Christianity ◊ Christian

Kidok-kkyo Ch'ŏngnyŏnhoe 기독교 청년회 YMCA

Kidok-kkyo Pangsong 기독교 방송 Christian Broadcasting System, CBS

Kidok-kkyo shinja 기독교 신자 Christian (*person*)

kidung 기둥 column; pole; stilts; supports

kiga kkŏkkin 기가 꺾인 demoralized

kiga mak'inŭn 기가 막히는 staggering, astonishing

kigabait'ŭ 기가바이트 gigabyte

kigan 기간 period, spell, term

kigan shisŏl 기간 시설 infrastructure (*of society*)

kigo 기고 contribution (*to magazine*)

kigoga 기고가 columnist

kigohada 기고하다 contribute (*to magazine, newspaper*)

kigŭn 기근 famine

kigu 기구 organization; balloon (*for flight*)

kigwan 기관 institution; machinery (*governmental*)

kigwanch'ong 기관총 machine gun

kigwanjiyŏm 기관지염 bronchitis

kigwansa 기관사 driver; engineer (*of train*)

kigwan tanch'ong 기관 단총 submachine gun

kigye 기계 appliance, machine ◊ mechanical

kigye changch'i 기계 장치 mechanism

kigyegong 기계공 mechanic

kigyehwahada 기계화하다 mechanize

kigyejŏgin 기계적인 mechanical

kigyejŏgŭro 기계적으로 mechanically

kigyeryu 기계류 machinery, machines

kigyŏlssu 기결수 convict

kigyo 기교 trick, knack; technique

kihahak 기하학 geometry

kihahaktchŏk 기하학적 geometric(al)

kihan mallyo 기한 만료 expiry

kiho 기호 symbol, character; choice; preference

kihoe 기회 chance, opportunity; *kihoerŭl chuda* 기회를 주다 give a break, give an opportunity; *muŏsŭl hal kihoerŭl kajida* 무엇을 할 기회를 가지다 get to do sth

kihonja 기혼자 married person

kihon namsŏng 기혼 남성 married man

kihon yŏsŏng 기혼 여성 married woman

kihu 기후 climate

kihyŏng 기형 deformity; freak

kiil 기일 term, condition

kiinhada 기인하다 result from

kiip'ada 기입하다 enter, write down; fill in, fill out

kija 기자 reporter, journalist

kijahoegyŏn 기자회견 press conference

kijang 기장 captain (*of aircraft*)

kijil 기질 disposition, nature

kijinmaektchinhan 기진맥진한 dog-tired

kijŏgwi 기저귀 diaper

kijŏk 기적 miracle

kijŏkkach'i 기적같이 miraculously

kijŏktchŏgin 기적적인 miraculous

kijŏlsshik'ida 기절시키다 stun (*with a blow*)

kijŏrhada 기절하다 pass out, faint

kijo yŏnsŏl 기조 연설 keynote speech

kijŭng 기증 donate

kijŭnghada 기증하다 donate

kijun 기준 standard

kijunggi 기중기 crane; hoist

kikkŏi 기꺼이 gladly, willingly, with pleasure; *kikkŏi ...hada* 기꺼이 ...하다 be willing to do

kikkŏi padadŭrida 기꺼이 받아들이다 welcome

kikkwŏn 기권 abstention

kikkwŏnhada 기권하다 abstain

kil 길 route; road; avenue; path;

fathom NAUT; *kirŭl ilt'a* 길을 잃다 stray, wander away; get lost

kil annaerŭl hada 길 안내를 하다 navigate

kilda 길다 be long

kildŭryöjin 길들여진 tame

kilge 길게 at length

kilge nŭllida 길게 늘리다 lengthen; pad *speech*

kilge pomyŏn 길게 보면 in the long run

kilkka 길가 roadside

kilmot'ung-i 길모퉁이 corner

kiltŭrida 길들이다 domesticate

kim 김 steam; laver, edible seaweed

kimch'i 김치 kimchee (*spicy pickled cabbage*)

kimi 기미 sign, indication; streak, touch

kimil 기밀 secrecy ◊ secret

kimi sŏrida 김이 서리다 mist up, steam up

kimirŭi 기밀의 classified, confidential

kimppajin 김빠진 bland; flat *beer*

kimppap 김밥 rice rolled in edible seaweed

kimyoham 기묘함 peculiarity, strangeness

kimyohan 기묘한 peculiar; quaint

kin 긴 long, lengthy

kinbak-kkam 긴박감 tension

kin-gŭp 긴급 urgency

kinjang 긴장 tension, strain

kinjangdoeda 긴장되다 tense up; be tense

kinjangdoen 긴장된 tense *muscle*; keyed up

kinjangdoenŭn 긴장되는 tense *moment*

kinjanghan 긴장한 tense *voice, person*

kinjang-ŭl p'ulda 긴장을 풀다 relax, unwind

kinjang-ŭro ttakttak'aejin 긴장으로 딱딱해진 uptight, inhibited

kinjang wanhwa 긴장 완화 détente

kin kŏt'ot 긴 겉옷 gown

kin somaeŭi 긴 소매의 long-sleeved

kinŭng 기능 craft, trade; function

kinŭngk'i 기능키 function key

COMPUT

kinŭng tanwi 기능 단위 unit

kinŭng-ŭl hada 기능을 하다 function as

kinyŏm 기념 commemoration ◊ memorial

kinyŏmbi 기념비 memorial, monument

kinyŏmhada 기념하다 commemorate, mark

kinyŏmil 기념일 (wedding) anniversary

kinyŏmmul 기념물 memento

kinyŏmp'um 기념품 souvenir

kinyŏm tongsang 기념 동상 monument

kinyŏmŭro 기념으로 in commemoration of

kiŏ 기어 gear

kiŏ chŏnhwan changch'i 기어 전환 장치 gear shift

kiŏk 기억 memory

kiŏk yongnyang 기억 용량 storage capacity

kiŏk'ada 기억하다 remember; store COMPUT; *muŏsŭl kiŏk'ago it-tta* 무엇을 기억하고 있다 bear sth in mind

kiŏngnyŏk 기억력 memory

kiŏp 기업 corporation ◊ business *ethics, style etc*

kiŏpkka 기업가 entrepreneur

kipkke 깊게 deeply

kipkke hada 깊게 하다 deepen

kippŏhada 기뻐하다 be delighted

kippŏhanŭn 기뻐하는 delighted; gleeful

kippŏnalttwida 기뻐날뛰다 exult

kiptta 깊다 be deep

kippŭda 기쁘다 be glad

kippŭge 기쁘게 happily, gladly; pleasantly

kippŭge hada 기쁘게 하다 please

kippŭm 기쁨 joy, delight

kippŭn 기쁜 pleased, glad

kip'i 깊이 depth ◊ deeply, soundly

kip'i chamdŭn 깊이 잠든 fast asleep

kip'ŏgada 깊어가다 draw on, advance

kip'oga saenggida 기포가 생기다 blister (*of paint*)

kip'o sujun-gi 기포 수준기 spirit level

kip'ŭm 깊음 depth

kip'ŭn 깊은 deep, profound

kip'um 기품 nobility; elegance

kip'um innŭn 기품 있는 distinguished, dignified

kip'yoso 기표소 polling booth

kiri 길이 length

kirin 기린 giraffe

kirogŭl kkaenŭn 기록을 깨는 record-breaking

kirok 기록 memo; archives; writing (*script*); *muŏshi kirogŭl namgida* 무엇의 기록을 남기다 keep track of sth

kirok munsŏ 기록 문서 record (*written document*)

kirok poyuja 기록 보유자 record holder

kirŭda 기르다 keep; grow; breed

kirŭl kkŏktta 기를 꺾다 daunt, deter, dishearten

kirŭl kkŏngnŭn 기를 꺾는 demoralizing

kirŭm 기름 oil

kirŭmch'irŭl hada 기름칠을 하다 oil

kirŭmgi kkin 기름기 낀 lank, greasy *hair*

kirŭmkki manŭn 기름기 많은 oily, greasy

kirŭmt'ong 기름통 sump

kiryagi p'ungbuhan 기략이 풍부한 resourceful

kiryak 기략 resources

kisa 기사 article (*in newspaper*); engineer; (machine) operator

kisadojŏgin 기사도적인 chivalrous

kisaek 기색 tinge

kisaeng 기생 kisaeng (*traditional female entertainer*)

kisaengch'unggat'ŭn saram 기생충같은 사람 parasite

kisaeng tongshingmul 기생 동식물 parasite

kisa kŏri 기사 거리 copy (*written material*)

kisang 기상 original idea; weather

kisanghak 기상학 meteorology

kisang yebo 기상 예보 weather forecast

kisang yebowŏn 기상 예보원 weatherman

kisŏngbok 기성복 off the peg, ready-to-wear

kiso 기소 prosecution

kisohada 기소하다 prosecute

kisojach'ŭk 기소자측 prosecution

kisŭk 기슭 slope (*of mountain*)

kisu 기수 rider, jockey

kisuk hak-kkyo 기숙 학교 boarding school

kisukssa 기숙사 dormitory

kisul 기술 skill; technique

kisultcha 기술자 technician

kisultchŏgin 기술적인 technical

kisultchŏgŭro 기술적으로 technically

kit 깃 collar

kitchŏm 기점 starting point

kitppal 깃발 flag

kit'a 기타 the rest; and so on; guitar

kit'adŭngdŭng 기타 등등 and so on, et cetera

kit'a yŏnjuga 기타 연주가 guitarist

kit'ŏl 깃털 feather; plumage

kit'ong 기통 cylinder (*in engine*)

kiulda 기울다 slant; tilt; swing (*of public opinion*)

kiulgi 기울기 slope (*of handwriting*)

kiun 기운 energy; vigor; vapor

kiuni nada 기운이 나다 cheer up

kiunŭl naege hada 기운을 내게 하다 cheer up

kiurida 기울이다 devote; tilt; *kwi kiurida* 귀 기울이다 prick up one's ears

kiwŏn 기원 origin

kiyŏ 기여 contribution (*to discussion*)

kiyŏhada 기여하다 contribute (*to discussion*)

kkach'ibal 까치발 bracket (*for shelf*)

kkadaroptta 까다롭다 be difficult; be strict; be picky

kkadaroun 까다로운 fussy, picky; tricky

kkaeda 깨다 break *record*; rouse

kkaedarŭm 깨달음 realization; understanding; enlightenment

kkaedat-tta 깨닫다 realize; *Xŭl/rŭl kkaedatchi mot'ada* X을/를 깨닫지 못하다 be unconscious of X

kkaejida 깨지다 break; shatter

kkaejin 깨진 broken

kkaek-kkaek-kkŏrida 꽥꽥거리다 squeal

kkaekkŭshi 깨끗이 completely, clean

kkaekkŭt'ada 깨끗하다 be clean; be pure; be chaste

kkaekkŭt'age hada 깨끗하게 하다 clean

kkaekkŭt'an 깨끗한 clean; pure; tidy, neat

kkaengkkaenggŏrida 깽깽거리다 yelp

kkaennip 깻잎 (pickled) sesame leaf

kkaeŏinnŭn 깨어있는 awake

kkaeŏjida 깨어지다 break up (*of ice*)

kkaeŏjigi shiun 깨어지기 쉬운 breakable

kkaettŭrida 깨뜨리다 break; break off *relationship*; terminate

kkaeuch'ida 깨우치다 educate; make realize

kkaeuda 깨우다 wake

kkaji 까지 until; by; no later than; to; up to; *1989nyŏnkkaji* 1989년까지 until 1989; *hot'elkkaji* 호 텔까지 as far as the hotel

kkakkabŏrida 깎아버리다 shave off *beard*

kkakkanaeda 깍아내다 shave off *from piece of wood*

kkakka tadŭmtta 깎아다듬다 whittle

kkaktta 깎다 cut; trim; shear; shave; sharpen; peel; cut *price*; haggle

kkakttugi 깍두기 spicy, pickled white radish

kkalboda 깔보다 criticize, knock

kkalda 깔다 pave

kkalgae 깔개 rug

kkamagwi 까마귀 crow; raven

kkamppagida 깜박이다 flicker, glimmer

kkamppakkŏrida 깜박거리다 twinkle; blink

kkamtchak nollada 깜짝 놀라다 be astonished; *Xŭl/rŭl kkamtchak nollage hada* X을/를 깜짝 놀라게 하다 give X a fright

kkangch'unggŏrimyŏ ttwiŏdanida 깡충거리며 뛰어다니다 skip around

kkangmarŭn 깡마른 skinny

kkangp'ae 깡패 bully; hoodlum,

gangster

kkangt'ong 깡통 can (*for food*)

kkangt'ong ttagae 깡통 따개 can opener

kkich'ida 끼치다 cause; *namege p'yerŭl kkich'ida* 남에게 폐를 끼치다 make a nuisance of oneself, cause trouble; *kŏktchŏng-ŭl kkich'ida* 걱정을 끼치다 affect; concern

kkida 끼이다 be wedged; be caught between

kkilkkil ut-tta 낄낄 웃다 giggle

kkik'anŭn sori 끽하는 소리 screech

kkingkkangjok 낑깡족 *orenjijok* wannabes

kkingkkinggŏrida 낑낑거리다 whimper, whine

kkiŏ nŏt'a 끼어 넣다 squeeze in

kkiuda 끼우다 slot in

kkiwŏjida 끼워지다 slot in

kkiwŏnŏtki 끼워넣기 open; retrieve COMPUT

kkiwŏ nŏt'a 끼워 넣다 put, insert; tuck

kkŏjida 꺼지다 blow out, go out (*of candle*); collapse; vanish

kkŏjin 꺼진 dead *battery, engine*

kkŏjyŏ it-tta 꺼져 있다 be out (*of light, fire*)

kkŏjyŏ pŏrida 꺼져 버리다 buzz off; go out (*of fire*); *kkŏjyŏ (pŏryŏ)!* 꺼져 (버려)! beat it!, get lost!

kkŏk-kkŏk-kkŏrinŭn sori 꺽꺽거리는 소리 squawk

kkŏkkŏnaeda 꺾어내다 break off *piece of chocolate etc*

kkŏktta 꺾다 destroy; break off; pluck; dash

kkŏm 껌 chewing gum

kkŏnaeda 꺼내다 take out (*from bag, pocket etc*); *...e taehan marŭl kkŏnaeda* ...에 대한 말을 꺼내다 drag in

kkŏptchil 껍질 shell; peel; husk; skin

kkŏrida 꺼리다 shun

kkŏrimch'ik'ada 꺼림칙 하다 feel uncomfortable about

kkobak 꼬박 whole

kkobulgŏrinŭn 꼬불거리는 curly

kkoch'ikkoch'i k'aeda 꼬치꼬치

캐다 poke around

kkoch'i p'ida 꽃이 피다 flower

kkoda 꼬다 twist; *tarirŭl kkoda* 다리를 꼬다 cross one's legs

kkoe 꾀 wile, strategem

kkoeda 꾀다 entice; persuade

kkoehada 꾀하다 engineer, contrive

kkoim 꼬임 kink, twist

kkoji 꽂이 rack

kkojiptta 꼬집다 pinch

kkok 꼭 surely; firmly, tightly; exactly

kkoktchi 꼭지 stem; tap, faucet; nipple; handle

kkokttaegi 꼭대기 top, crest

kkokttugaksshi 꼭두각시 puppet

kkolsanaum 꼴사나움 clumsiness

kkoma 꼬마 the little ones; urchin

kkomkkomhan 꼼꼼한 thorough; scrupulous

kkomtchagank'o innŭn 꼼짝않고 있는 stand stock-still

kkomtchak'ada 꼼짝하다 budge, stir; *kŏgisŏ kkomtchaktto hajima!* 거기서 꼼짝도 하지마! stay right there!

kkongch'o 꽁초 stub

kkonnip 꽃잎 petal

kkori 꼬리 tail; *ne kkori pol man-haguna!* 네 꼬리 볼 만하구나! what a sight you are!

kkorip'yo 꼬리표 tag, label

kkorip'yorŭl puch'ida 꼬리표를 붙이다 label, stick a label on

kkorŭrŭkkŏrida 꼬르륵거리다 rumble

kkoshyŏsŏ ŏdŏnaeda 꼬셔서 얻어내다 wheedle

kkot 꽃 flower; blossom

kkotchangsu 꽃장수 florist

kkot hantabal 꽃 한 다발 a bunch of flowers

kkotkkoji 꽃꽂이 arrangement (*of flowers*)

kkotkkot'an 꼿꼿한 straight (*erect, not bent*)

kkotppyŏng 꽃병 vase

kkot-tta 꽂다 attach; pin

kkot-ttabal 꽃다발 bouquet

kkŭch'ŭl maet-tta 끝을 맺다 wind up, finish

kkŭda 끄다 blow out; switch off; be

off; stall

kkŭdŏgim 끄덕임 nod

kkŭdŏmnŭn 끝없는 endless, never-ending

kkŭjibŏ naeda 끄집어 내다 mention, drag up

kkŭl 끌 chisel

kkŭlda 끌다 pull; haul; tow; drag; move slowly; attract; spin out, prolong; appeal to, be attractive to

kkŭlgi 끌기 tow; drag COMPUT

kkŭllida 끌리다 trail, lag behind; be dragged; be attracted to; *...e(ge) maŭmi kkŭllida* ...에(게) 마음이 끌리다 be attached to; *nuguege maŭmi kkŭllida* 누구에게 마음이 끌리다 be attracted to s.o.

kkŭlt'a 끓다 boil

kkŭmtchigi 끔찍이 terribly; exceedingly; kindly

kkŭmtchik'ada 끔찍하다 be hideous

kkŭmtchik'an 끔찍한 hideous, terrible

kkŭn 끈 band (*material*); lace (*for shoe*); tie, bond; string; strap (*of shoe, dress, bra*)

kkŭndŏktchige toep'urihada 끈덕지게 되풀이하다 persist in

kkŭndŏktchige toep'urihanŭn 끈덕지게 되풀이하는 persistent

kkŭn-gi 끈기 perseverance, persistence

kkŭnimŏmnŭn 끊임없는 continuous, incessant

kkŭnimŏpsshi 끊임없이 incessantly, forever

kkŭnimŏpsshi kyesok'aesŏ 끊임없이 계속해서 on and on, endlessly

kkŭnjilgin 끈질긴 dogged; high-powered *salesman*; nagging *pain*

kkŭnjŏk-kkŏrinŭn 끈적거리는 sticky; tacky; gooey

kkŭnjŏk-kkŭnjŏk'an 끈적끈적한 tacky; gooey

kkŭnmach'ida 끝마치다 finish off *drink, meal, work etc*

kkŭnmaejŭm 끝맺음 finish (*of product*)

kkŭnmat 끝맛 aftertaste (*from food, drink*)

kkŭnnada 끝나다 end, finish; result in; *ije ta kkŭnnat-tta* 이제 다 끝났다 it's all over now

kkŭnnaeda 끝내다 finish, conclude; *ta kkŭnnaebŏrida* 다 끝내버리다 finish up

kkŭnnaeji anŭn 끝내지 않은 unfinished

kkŭnŏjida 끊어지다 break; blow *fuse*; break off with; be interrupted; run out

kkŭnŏjin 끊어진 dead

kkŭntchiank'o it-tta 끊지않고 있다 hold on TELEC

kkŭntchimalgo kidariseyo 끊지말고 기다리세요 hold the line

kkŭnt'a 끊다 give up, kick; disconnect, cut off; hang up TELEC

kkŭnŭl maeda 끈을 매다 strap on; put on *watch, holster*; lace up

kkŭnŭm 끊음 withdrawal (*from drugs*)

kkŭrida 끓이다 boil, brew

kkŭrŏ antta 끌어 안다 snuggle up to

kkŭrŏjuda 끌어주다 give a tow

kkŭrŏ nŏmch'ida 끓어 넘치다 boil over

kkŭrŏ ollida 끌어 올리다 boost; push up; connect; hitch up; hoist; pull up

kkŭrŏ tanggida 끌어 당기다 pull; drag; retract *undercarriage*

kkŭrŏ tŭrida 끌어 들이다 drag

kkŭt 끝 end, bottom (*of street*); edge; point; nozzle ◊ exit COMPUT; *yŏnghwarŭl kkŭtkkaji poda* 영화를 끝까지 보다 watch a movie to the end

kkŭttchangnaeda 끝장내다 put an end to, end

kkŭt'ŭro 끝으로 in conclusion

kkubŏk-kkubŏk cholda 꾸벅꾸벅 졸다 doze off

kkubulkkuburhan 꾸불꾸불한 winding *road*

kkujit-tta 꾸짖다 scold

kkujunhada 꾸준하다 be persistent; persevere, plug away

kkujunhan 꾸준한 unrelenting

kkuk ch'amtta 꾹 참다 stifle

kkul

kkul 꿀 honey

kkulkkŏk-kkulkkŏk mashida
꿀꺽꿀꺽 마시다 gulp down

kkulkkulgŏrida 꿀꿀거리다 grunt

kkum 꿈 dream; ambition

kkumgat'ŭn 꿈같은 dreamlike,
dream

kkumida 꾸미다 embellish;
embroider; exaggerate; make up
story; decorate

kkumijianŭn 꾸미지 않은
unadorned, undecorated, plain;
austere

kkumin iyagi 꾸민 이야기 fiction

kkumin kŏt 꾸민 것 make-believe,
pretense

kkumkkuda 꿈꾸다 dream

kkumkkyŏlgat'ŭn 꿈결같은 dreamy
voice, look

kkumt'ŭlgŏrimyŏ naagada
꿈틀거리며 나아가다 wriggle (*along
the ground*)

kkumŭl kkuda 꿈을 꾸다 dream

kkumuldaenŭn 꾸물대는 slow

kkumulgŏrida 꾸물거리다 dawdle,
move slowly

kkumyŏjin il 꾸며진 일 set-up,
frame-up

kkumyŏnaen iyagi 꾸며낸 이야기
yarn, story

kkurida 꾸리다 bundle up

kkurŏmi 꾸러미 bundle

kkurŏmiro ssada 꾸러미로 싸다
parcel up

kkuryŏgada 꾸려가다 manage
money

kkuryŏnagada 꾸려나가다 manage,
get by (*financially*)

kkwae 꽤 quite, fairly

kkwaek-kkwaek ulda 꽥꽥 울다
quack

kkwaenggwari 꽹과리 small gong
(*made of brass*)

kkwak 꽉 hard; fast; full; compact;
packed

kkwak chaptta 꽉 잡다 grip, clutch

kkwak choenŭn 꽉 죄는 skimpy

kkwak chwida 꽉 쥐다 clasp,
squeeze; clench

kkwak ch'ada 꽉 차다 be jam-packed

kkwak ch'ait-tta 꽉 차있다 be

jammed (*of roads*)

kkwak ch'an 꽉 찬 completely full

kkwak kkiida 꽉 끼이다 squeeze in

kkwak tŭrŏch'an 꽉 들어찬
chockfull, crowded

kkwemaeda 꿰매다 sew; stitch; darn

kkwemaeŏ talda 꿰매어 달다 sew
on

kkyŏantta 껴안다 clasp (*to oneself*)

kŏaegŭi sanggŭm 거액의 상금
jackpot

kŏaegŭi sanggŭmŭl t'ada 거액의
상금을 타다 hit the jackpot

kŏbe chillida 겁에 질리다 be
terrified

kŏbe chillin 겁에 질린 panic-stricken

kŏbi manŭn 겁이 많은 easily
frightened; spineless; cowardly

kŏbŭl mŏgŭn 겁을 먹은 fearful;
cowardly, chicken

kŏbŭl mŏk-kko mullŏsŏda 겁을
먹고 물러서다 chicken out

kŏbuhada 거부하다 veto; reject;
refuse

kŏbuk 거북 turtle; tortoise

kŏbukkwŏn 거부권 right of veto

kŏbukssŏn 거북선 turtle ship (*first
armored warship*)

kŏbuk'aehada 거북해하다 feel
awkward

kŏbuk'an 거북한 awkward,
embarrassing

kŏch'ida 걷히다 lift, clear (*of fog*)

kŏch'ilda 거칠다 be rough

kŏch'ilge taehada 거칠게 대하다
manhandle; treat roughly

kŏch'in 거친 rough; coarse; rugged

kŏch'yŏsŏ 거쳐서 by way of, via

kŏdaehada 거대하다 be enormous

kŏdaeham 거대함 enormity

kŏdaehan 거대한 enormous, huge

kŏdŏollida 걷어올리다 roll up *sleeves*

kŏdŭrŭm p'iunŭn 거드름 피우는
pompous

kŏgidaga 거기다가 moreover

kŏin 거인 giant

Kŏjedo 거제도 Koje Island

kŏji 거지 beggar

kŏjinmal 거짓말 lie

kŏjinmarhada 거짓말하다 lie, tell a
lie

kŏjit 거짓 pretense

kŏjitmaljaeng-i 거짓말쟁이 liar

kŏjŏ ŏt-tta 거저 얻다 cadge, bum

kŏjŏrhada 거절하다 deny; reject; refuse

kŏjŭ 거즈 gauze

kŏjuhada 거주하다 inhabit; reside

kŏju hŏga 거주 허가 residence permit

kŏjuja 거주자 inhabitant; resident

kŏjuji 거주지 residence (*house etc*)

kŏkkuro 거꾸로 upside down; back to front

kŏkkuro hada 거꾸로 하다 reverse

kŏkkuro toen 거꾸로 된 inverse *order*; reverse

kŏktchŏng 걱정 concern, worry, anxiety

kŏktchŏngdoenŭn 걱정되는 worrying

kŏktchŏnghada 걱정하다 worry; be worried, be concerned

kŏktchŏnghanŭn 걱정하는 concerned, anxious

kŏktchŏngshik'ida 걱정시키다 worry, trouble

kŏktchŏngsŭrŏn 걱정스런 worried

kŏktchŏngsŭrŏptta 걱정스럽다 be worried

kŏlch'ida 걸치다 extend, range; span; throw on *clothes*

kŏlda 걸다 hang; stake; be on (*of brake*)

kŏlle 걸레 cloth; tramp (*woman*)

kŏllejirhada 걸레질하다 mop; swab; wipe

kŏllida 걸리다 catch *illness*; take *time*

kŏllŏnaeda 걸러내다 strain; sift

kŏllyŏ nŏmŏjida 걸려 넘어지다 trip, stumble; trip over, stumble over

kŏllyŏonŭn 걸려오는 incoming *phonecall*

kŏlssang 걸상 stool

kŏlssoe 걸쇠 clasp; latch

kŏlsŭk'aut'ŭ 걸스카우트 girl scout

kŏltchuk'age hada 걸쭉하게 하다 thicken

kŏltchuk'an 걸쭉한 thick

kŏm 검 sword

kŏman 거만 arrogance

kŏmanhada 거만하다 be arrogant

kŏmanhan 거만한 arrogant, stuck-up

kŏmch'algwan 검찰관 public prosecutor

kŏmda 검다 be black; be dark

kŏmgŏ 검거 round-up (*of suspects, criminals*)

kŏmgŏhada 검거하다 round up *suspects, criminals*

kŏmi 거미 spider

kŏmijul 거미줄 cobweb

kŏmjŏngsaek 검정색 black

kŏmmanŭn 겁많은 timid

kŏmmŏgŭn 겁먹은 timid

kŏmmŏktta 겁먹다 be afraid, be scared; get cold feet; be overawed

kŏmmunso 검문소 checkpoint

kŏmnada 겁나다 be frightened; be frightened of

kŏmnage hada 겁나게 하다 terrify

kŏmnage hanŭn 겁나게 하는 terrifying

kŏmnanŭn 겁나는 frightening, unnerving

kŏmnyŏk 검역 quarantine (*for animals*)

kŏmp'yowŏn 검표원 inspector (*on buses*)

kŏmp'yut'ŏ chulp'an 컴퓨터 출판 desktop publishing

k'ŏmp'yut'ŏ ch'ŏriga kanŭnghan 컴퓨터 처리가 가능한 machine-readable

k'ŏmp'yut'ŏŭi sohyŏng ch'ŏrigi 컴퓨터의 소형 처리기 microprocessor

kŏmsa 검사 examination (*of patient*); prosecutor ◊ exploratory

kŏmsaek'ada 검색하다 navigate

kŏmshi 검시 post-mortem

kŏmshigwan 검시관 coroner

kŏmt'ohada 검토하다 go over, check; take stock; consider

kŏmŭn 검은 black

kŏmul 거물 tycoon, big shot

kŏmun-go 거문고 zither

kŏmusŭrehan 거무스레한 swarthy

kŏmusŭrŭmhan 거무스름한 dark, somber

kŏmyŏl chedo 검열 제도 censorship

kŏmyŏrhada 검열하다 censor

kŏnbae 건배! cheers!

kŏnbaehada 건배하다 toast
(*drinking*); **nugurŭl wihae
kŏnbaehajago hada** 누구를 위해
건배하자고 하다 propose a toast to
s.o.

kŏnban 건반 keyboard (*of piano*)

kŏnbangjida 건방지다 be forward, be
impertinent

kŏnbangjige kulda 건방지게 굴다
get smart with, be cheeky with

kŏnbangjin 건방진 forward,
impertinent, insolent

kŏnch'o 건초 hay

kŏnch'oyŏl 건초열 hay fever

kŏnch'ugŏp 건축업 builder
(*company*); building trade

kŏnch'ugŏptcha 건축업자 builder
(*person*)

kŏnch'uk 건축 building

kŏnch'uk'ak 건축학 architecture
(*subject*)

kŏnch'ungmul 건축물 construction,
structure

kŏnch'ungnyangshik 건축양식
architecture (*style*)

kŏndal 건달 rogue, good-for-nothing

kŏndubaktchillo 곤두박질로
headlong

kŏn-gang 건강 health; **tangshinŭi
kŏn-gang-ŭl wihae!** 당신의 건강을
위해! your health!

kŏn-gang chindan 건강 진단 checkup MED

kŏn-gang-e chŏun 건강에 좋은
healthy, wholesome

kŏn-ganghada 건강하다 be healthy

kŏn-ganghan 건강한 fit, healthy

kŏn-gang munje 건강 문제 medical
problem

kŏn-gang sangt'ae 건강 상태
condition, state of health

kŏn-gang shikp'um 건강 식품
health food

kŏn-gang shikp'umjŏm 건강 식품점
health food store

kŏnjanghan 건장한 burly

kŏnjŏnhada 건전하다 be wholesome,
be healthy

kŏnjŏnhan 건전한 wholesome,
healthy; sound

kŏnjogi 건조기 drier; dry season

kŏnjohada 건조하다 be dry, be arid

kŏnjohan 건조한 dry

kŏnmosŭp 겉모습 exterior, façade

kŏnmul 건물 building

kŏnmul chosawŏn 건물 조사원
surveyor

kŏnnejuda 건네주다 hand over, give

kŏnnŏ 건너 over, across

kŏnnŏda 건너다 cross, go across

kŏnnŏgada 건너가다 cross, go across

kŏnnŏ p'yŏn 건너 편 across, on the
other side of

kŏnnŏsŏ 건너서 across

kŏnp'odo 건포도 raisin; currant

kŏnsŏl 건설 construction

kŏnsŏltchŏgin 건설적인 constructive

kŏnsŏrŏp 건설업 construction
industry

kŏptchaeng-i 겁쟁이 chicken,
coward

kŏptchuda 겁주다 frighten

kŏptchuŏ tchoch'anaeda 겁주어
쫓아내다 scare away

kŏp'um 거품 bubble; foam; froth

kŏp'umnanŭn 거품나는 effervescent

kŏrae 거래 deal; dealing; dealings;
business; transaction

kŏraehada 거래하다 deal with; deal
in; bank with

kŏraerŭl maedŭp chit-tta 거래를
매듭 짓다 clinch a deal

kŏri 거리 distance; street; **kŏrie(sŏ)**
거리에(서) in the street

kŏri 걸이 rack

kŏrikkimŏpsshi marhada
거리낌없이 말하다 speak out

kŏrirŭl tuda 거리를 두다 distance
oneself

kŏrŏdanida 걸어다니다 walk around

kŏrŏgada 걸어가다 walk away

kŏrŏmaeda 걸어매다 hitch (onto)

kŏrŏ nŏmŏttŭrida 걸어 넘어뜨리다
trip up

kŏrŏsŏ 걸어서 on foot

kŏrŏsŏ kada 걸어서 가다 walk, go
on foot

kŏrŏsŏ kŏnnŏda 걸어서 건너다 walk
across

kŏrŭda 거르다 filter

kŏrŭm 걸음 step, pace; **kŏrŭmi
nŭrida / pparŭda** 걸음이

느리다 /빠르다 be a slow/fast walker
kŏsehada 거세하다 neuter *animal*
kŏsehan hwangso 거세한 황소 steer (*animal*)
kŏshida 것이다: *...l kŏshida* ...ㄹ 것이다, shall, will
kŏshiktchŭng 거식증 anorexia
kŏshiktchŭng-ŭl alt'a 거식증을 앓다 be anorexic
kŏshil 거실 living room
kŏsŭllida 거슬리다 grate; jar on
kŏsŭllinŭn 거슬리는 harsh, abrasive
kŏsŭllŏ ollagada 거슬러 올라가다 go back, date back
kŏt 것 thing ◊ (*forms equivalent of relative clause*): *kŭ sarami naeil olgŏsŭl arayo* 그 사람이 내일 올것을 알아요 I know that he will come tomorrow; *nae ch'in-guga ŏjae pyŏngwŏne ibwŏnhan kŏsŭl tŭŏssŏyo* 내 친구가 어제 병원에 입원한 것을 들었어요 I heard that my friend went into the hospital yesterday; *chibe iltchik kanŭn kŏsi natkk'essŏyo* 집에 일찍 가는 것이 낫겠어요 it'd be better to go home early ◊ (*forms equivalent of noun form in ...ing*): *suhagŭl konbuhanŭn kŏsi shiptchi anayo* 수학을 공부하는 것이 쉽지 않아요 studying math is not easy
kŏtch'ire 걷치레 pose, pretense
kŏtkki 걷기 walking
kŏt-tta 걷다 walk
kŏt'ŭronŭn 겉으로는 outwardly, externally
kŏŭi 거의 almost; *kŏŭi kat-tta* 거의 같다 be almost like, verge on; *kŏŭi ŏptta* 거의 없다 scarcely any; *kŏŭi ta* 거의 다 all but, nearly all
kŏul 거울 mirror
kŏwi 거위 goose
kŏyŏk'ada 거역하다 disobey
...ko ...고 and
koa 고아 orphan
koanhada 고안하다 devise
koanmul 고안물 gimmick
koap 고압 high voltage; high pressure ◊ high-voltage; high-pressure
koap kkassŭ 고압 가스 propellant
koapssŏnnyong ch'ŏlt'ap 고압선용

철탑 (electricity) pylon
koawŏn 고아원 orphanage
kobaek 고백 confession
kobaek'ada 고백하다 confess
kobal 고발 accusation
kobarhada 고발하다 charge, accuse
koch'arhada 고찰하다 look at, consider
koch'e 고체 solid mass
koch'ida 고치다 correct; repair
koch'ŭng piltting 고층 빌딩 high-rise building
koch'u 고추 red pepper; chilli
koch'ugaru 고추가루 chilli (pepper) powder
koch'ujang 고추장 red pepper paste
kodae 고대 antiquity ◊ ancient
kodaehada 고대하다 be anxious for
kodo 고도 altitude
kodok 고독 solitude
kodok'ada 고독하다 be solitary; lonely
kodok'an 고독한 solitary
kodong 고동 beat (*of heart*)
kodongch'ida 고동치다 pulsate (*of heart, blood*)
kodo pulp'ohwa multchil 고도 불포화 물질 polyunsaturate
kodŭn 곧은 straight (*not curly*)
kodŭnghak-kkyo 고등학교 high school
kodŭnghakssaeng 고등학생 high school student
Kodŭng Pŏbwŏn 고등 법원 Supreme Court
kodŭrŭm 고드름 icicle
koemul 괴물 monster
koemulgat'ŭn 괴물같은 monstrous, frightening
koengjanghada 굉장하다 be awesome
koengjanghage 굉장하게 very, terrifically
koengjanghan 굉장한 awesome; terrific; tremendous
koengjanghi 굉장히 greatly; beautifully; tremendously
koeng-ŭm 굉음 boom (*noise*)
koeŏ innŭn 괴어 있는 stagnant
koeroe chŏngbu 괴뢰 정부 puppet government

koerop'ida 괴롭히다 trouble; torment

koerop'im 괴롭힘 harassment

koetcha 괴짜 crank, eccentric

kogaek 고객 customer, client

kogaek kwalli 고객 관리 customer relations

kogaerŭl chŏt-tta 고개를 젓다 shake one's head

kogaerŭl kkŭdŏgida 고개를 끄덕이다 nod one's head

kogi 고기 meat

kogiap 고기압 high pressure (*weather*)

kogohak 고고학 archeology

kogohaktcha 고고학자 archeologist

kogŭl 고글 goggles (*for skiing*)

kogŭp 고급 high class ◊ high-class

kogŭp chaptchi 고급 잡지 glossy (*magazine*)

koguk 고국 home; native country; *koguge kada* 고국에 가다 go home

Koguryŏ 고구려 Koguryo (*Ancient Kingdom*)

kogwihan 고귀한 noble

kogye 곡예 acrobatics

kogyesa 곡예사 acrobat

kogyeyong kŭne 곡예용 그네 trapeze

kogyŏrhan 고결한 virtuous

kohae 고해 confession

kohaehada 고해하다 confess

kohaeshil 고해실 confessional

kohae shinbu 고해 신부 confessor

koham 고함 roar, bellow

koham chirŭda 고함 지르다 yell, cry out

kohamch'ida 고함치다 roar, bellow

kohamch'yŏ purŭda 고함쳐 부르다 yell

kohwan 고환 testicle

kohyang 고향 home; roots

kohyŏrap 고혈압 hypertension

koin 고인 the dead, the deceased; ancient people

koindol 고인돌 dolmen

kojajiljaeng-i 고자질쟁이 telltale

kojajirhada 고자질하다 tell tales, snitch

kojang 고장 breakdown; crash (*of computer*)

kojang suri 고장 수리 troubleshooting

kojang-i nada 고장이 나다 play up; break down; crash COMPUT

kojang-i ŏmnŭn 고장이 없는 trouble-free

kojangna it-tta 고장나 있다 be down, not be working

kojangnan 고장난 out of order, not working

kojibi ssen 고집이 센 stubborn, obstinate

kojip 고집 obstinacy

kojip'ada 고집하다 be stubborn; stand by, adhere to

kojishik'an 고지식한 conservative; straight

kojŏn 고전 classic

kojŏngdoeda 고정되다 be fixed

kojŏngdoen 고정된 fixed *part*, *exchange rate*

kojŏnghada 고정하다 fasten, fix; *umjigiji ank'e kojŏnghada* 움직이지 않게 고정하다 set *broken limb*

kojŏngshik'ida 고정시키다 fix; attach; stabilize; strap in; *muŏsŭl chejarie kojŏngshik'ida* 무엇을 제자리에 고정시키다 lock sth in position

Kojosŏn 고조선 Old Choson (*Ancient Kingdom*)

kojup'a 고주파 high-frequency

kokka toro 고가 도로 overpass (*for car*)

kokkurajida 고꾸라지다 fall head over heels

kokssŏn 곡선 curve

koktcho 곡조 tune

koktchoga arŭmdaun 곡조가 아름다운 melodious

kol 골 goal, target

kolbanppyŏ 골반뼈 pelvis

kolch'i ap'ŭn 골치 아픈 troublesome

kolch'itkkŏri 골칫거리 bother, headache

kolch'o 골초 heavy smoker

kolden 골덴 corduroy

kolden paji 골덴 바지 corduroy pants, cords

kolk'ip'ŏ 골키퍼 goalkeeper

kollan 곤란 hardship; embarrassment
kollanaeda 골라내다 pick on; select
kollanhada 곤란하다 be arduous; be awkward
kolmok 골목 alley
kolmok-kkil 골목길 side street
kolmu 골무 thimble
kolp'anji 골판지 corrugated cardboard
kolp'ŭ 골프 golf
kolp'ŭjang 골프장 golf course; golf club
kolp'ŭ k'ŭllŏp 골프 클럽 golf club (*instrument*)
koltcha 골자 core
koltchagi 골짜기 valley
koltchitkkŏri 골칫거리 pest, nuisance
kolttae 골대 goalpost
kolttongp'um 골동품 antique
kolttongp'um sang-in 골동품 상인 antique dealer
kom 곰 bear (*animal*)
komak 고막 eardrum
komapkkedo 고맙게도 thankfully
komapkke yŏginŭn 고맙게 여기는 grateful
komapssŭmnida 고맙습니다 thank you (*polite*)
komaptta 고맙다 thank
komawŏ 고마워 thanks
kombo chaguk 곰보 자국 spot (*caused by measles etc*)
komgomhi saenggak'ada 곰곰히 생각하다 reflect; brood; ponder
komin 고민 distress
komindoenŭn 고민되는 vexed
kominhada 고민하다 worry, fret
kominhage hada 고민하게 하다 concern, worry
komo 고모 aunt (*own, sister of father*)
komobu 고모부 uncle (*father's sister's husband*)
komp'ang-i 곰팡이 mold, mildew
komp'ang-i p'in 곰팡이 핀 moldy
komp'angnae nanŭn 곰팡내 나는 musty
komtta 곪다 go septic
komu 고무 rubber
komu chŏtkkoktchi 고무 젖꼭지 pacifier (*for baby*)

komujul 고무줄 elastic
komul 고물 junk
komul sujipsso 고물 수집소 junkyard
komun 고문 adviser; torture
komunhada 고문하다 torture
komu paendŭ 고무 밴드 rubber band
komu pot'ŭ 고무 보트 inflatable boat
komyŏng-ŭro changshik'ada 고명으로 장식하다 garnish
konbong 곤봉 club, stick
konch'ung 곤충 insect
kong 공 ball (*tennis, golf etc*); zero
kongbaek 공백 blank; empty space; gap
kongbŏm 공범 accomplice
Kongboch'ŏ 공보처 Ministry of Information
kongbu 공부 study, learning
kongbuhada 공부하다 study, learn
kongch'aek 공책 notebook
kongch'ŏga 공처가 henpecked husband
kongch'ŏn 공천 nomination
kongch'ŏnhada 공천하다 nominate
kongch'ŏnja 공천자 nominee; nomination
kongdan 공단 satin
kongdong 공동 cooperation ◊ joint, common
kongdong chŏja 공동 저자 collaborator (*in writing book etc*)
kongdong chŏngnipkkŭm 공동 적립금 kitty, common fund
kongdongch'e 공동체 community
kongdonggigŭm 공동기금 pool, kitty, common fund
kongdong ikkwŏnŭro hada 공동 이권으로 하다 pool, combine, merge
kongdong kujwa 공동 구좌 joint account
kongdong soyuja 공동 소유자 part owner
kongdong-ŭro chŏjak'ada 공동으로 저작하다 collaborate (*on book etc*)
kongdong-ŭro irhada 공동으로 일하다 collaborate, work together
kongdong yŏn-guhada 공동 연구하다 collaborate (*in research*)

kongdŭrin 공들인 elaborate
konggaehada 공개하다 unveil *plans*
konggaejŏgin 공개적인 public
konggaejŏguro 공개적으로 publicly
konggae maeip 공개 매입 takeover bid
konggal 공갈 blackmail
konggal ch'ida 공갈 치다 blackmail
konggal ch'inŭn saram 공갈 치는 사람 blackmailer
konggan 공간 space, room
konggi 공기 air; bowl, dish (*for rice*)
konggiga ant'onghanŭn 공기가 안통하는 airtight
konggiga shinsŏnhan 공기가 신선한 airy *room*
konggi tŭril 공기 드릴 pneumatic drill
konggo 공고 notice, announcement
konggohada 공고하다 notify
konggong 공공 public
konggong kigwan 공공 기관 institute (*special home*)
konggong pumun 공공 부문 public sector
konggŭbwŏn 공급원 supplier
konggŭp 공급 supply, provision
konggŭpkkwa suyo 공급과 수요 supply and demand
konggŭp'um 공급품 supplies
konggŭp'ada 공급하다 supply, provide
konggun 공군 air force
konggun kiji 공군 기지 airbase
konggyŏk 공격 offensive, aggression MIL
konggyŏktchŏgin 공격적인 aggressive
konggyŏk'ada 공격하다 attack, go on the offensive
konghak 공학 engineering
konghang 공항 airport
konghang t'ŏminŏl 공항 터미널 air terminal
konghŏ 공허 vacuum *fig*
konghŏham 공허함 emptiness; vanity (*of hopes*)
konghŏhan 공허한 hollow *words*
konghŏn 공헌 contribution (*of time, effort*)
konghŏnhada 공헌하다 contribute

(*with time*)
Konghwadang chijija 공화당 지지자 Republican
Konghwadang-wŏn 공화당원 Republican, member of the Republican party
konghwaguk 공화국 republic
kong-ik saŏp 공익 사업 public utilities
kong-in hoegyesa 공인 회계사 certified public accountant
Kongja 공자 Confucius
kongjakssae 공작새 peacock
kongjang 공장 plant; factory; mill
kongjangjang 공장장 foreman
kongje 공제 deduction (*from salary*)
kongjŏ 공저 collaboration (*on book etc*)
kongjŏnghada 공정하다 be fair, be just
kongjŏnghage 공정하게 fairly, justly
kongjŏnghan 공정한 fair, just
kongjŏnhada 공전하다 idle (*of engine*); orbit
kongjon 공존 coexistence
kongjonhada 공존하다 coexist
kongjŭng 공증 notarization
kongjŭng-in 공증인 notary
kongjung 공중 public; air; midair; *kongjung-esŏ* 공중에서 in midair
kongjung chŏnhwa 공중 전화 pay phone
kongjung chŏnhwa pakssŭ 공중 전화 박스 phone booth
kongjung napch'i 공중 납치 hijack
kongjung napch'ibŏm 공중 납치범 hijacker
kongjung napch'ihada 공중 납치하다 hijack
kongjung pihaenghada 공중 비행하다 fly past (in formation)
kongju 공주 princess
kongmin p'yŏngdŭngkkwŏn 공민 평등권 civil rights
kongmohada 공모하다 conspire with, be in cahoots with
kongmul 곡물 cereal (*grain*)
kongmuwŏn 공무원 civil servant, government official
kongnip hak-kkyo 공립 학교 public school

kongno 공로 credit, honor; *Xe tae-han kongnorŭl injŏngpat-tta* X에 대한 공로를 인정받다 get the credit for X

kongnyŏnhada 공연하다 perform, stage; co-star; be futile

kongnyong 공룡 dinosaur

kong-ŏp 공업 manufacturing

kong-ŏpttanji 공업 단지 industrial estate

kongp'an 공판 trial; *kongp'an chung* 공판 중 on trial

kongp'o 공포 horror, terror

kongp'otchŭng 공포증 phobia

kongp'o yŏnghwa 공포 영화 horror movie

kongp'yŏngham 공평함 detachment, objectivity

kongp'yŏnghan 공평한 detached, objective

kongp'yohada 공표하다 declare, state; issue *warning*

kongsa 공사 construction; public and private affairs; minister; *kongsa chung* 공사 중 under construction

kongsajang 공사장 building site, construction site

kongsajang inbu 공사장 인부 construction worker

Kongsandang 공산당 Communist Party

Kongsandang-ŭi 공산당의 Communist

kongsang-e chamgida 공상에 잠기다 daydream

kongsang kwahak sosŏl 공상 과학 소설 science fiction

kongsang kwahak sosŏl chaptchi 공상 과학 소설 잡지 science fiction fanzine

Kongsanjuŭi 공산주의 Communism ◊ Communist

Kongsanjuŭija 공산주의자 Communist

Kongsanjuŭiŭi 공산주의의 Communist

kongshihada 공시하다 post, show *profits*

kongshik 공식 formula; formality ◊ formal, official

kongshiktchŏgin 공식적인 state, ceremonial

kongshiktchŏguro 공식적으로 officially, strictly speaking; *kongshiktchŏguro allida* 공식적으로 알리다 officially announce

kongshik'wadoen 공식화된 official, confirmed

kongsŏgin 공석인 vacant

kongsŏk 공석 vacancy

kongsonhada 공손하다 be polite

kongsonhage 공손하게 politely

kongsonhan 공손한 polite

kongsshik pangmun 공식 방문 state visit

kongtcharo 공짜로 for nothing, for free

kongtchŏgin 공적인 official; *kongtchŏgin changso-e(sŏ)* 공적인 장소에(서) in public

kongtchŏguro 공적으로 formally

kongt'eip'ŭ 공테이프 blank tape

kongt'ong 공통 common *language etc*

kongt'onghada 공통하다 be common

kongt'ong-ŭro 공통으로 in common; *muŏsŭl nuguwa kongt'ong-ŭro kajigo it-tta* 무엇을 누구와 공통으로 가지고 있다 have sth in common with s.o.

kong-wŏn 공원 park

kong-ye 공예 craft

kong-yŏn 공연 performance

kon-gyŏng 곤경 impasse; mess; plight

kon-gyŏng-e ch'ŏhada 곤경에 처하다 be in a jam

kon-gyŏng-e ch'ŏhae it-tta 곤경에 처해 있다 be in a fix

kon-gyŏng-esŏ kuhaenaeda 곤경에서 구해내다 bail out *fig*

kong-yŏnhada 공연하다 perform

kong-yŏnja 공연자 performer

koppi 고삐 rein

kopssem 곱셈 multiplication

kopssŭlgŏrida 곱슬거리다 curl

kopssŭlgŏrim 곱슬거림 curl

kopssŭlgŏrinŭn 곱슬거리는 curly; frizzy

kopssŭlgopssŭrhan 곱슬곱슬한 fuzzy

koptta 곱다 be fine; be fair; be pretty; be gentle

kop'ada 곱하다 multiply

kop'umkkyŏgŭi 고품격의 upmarket

kora ttŏrŏjida 곯아 떨어지다 crash out, fall asleep

korae 고래 whale

koraegorae sorich'ida 고래고래 소리치다 rant and rave

koraejabi 고래잡이 whaling

korhamsŏk 골함석 corrugated iron

kori 고리 catch (locking device); hook; link; loop

korilla 고릴라 gorilla

korip 고립 isolation

koripsshik'ida 고립시키다 cut off, isolate

koripttoen 고립된 lonely, isolated

korŭda 고르다 pick and choose; plump for

korŭge 고르게 evenly, regularly

korŭji ank'e 고르지 않게 unevenly

korŭji anŭn 고르지 않은 uneven

korŭm 고름 pus

korŭn 고른 even, regular

koryŏ 고려 consideration, thoughtfulness, concern; Koryo (Kingdom)

koryŏhada 고려하다 allow for; make allowances; take on board; consider

koryŏhaji ank'o 고려하지 않고 with no regard for

koryŏhal sahang 고려할 사항 consideration, factor

kosaeng 고생 hardship; toil

kosaenghada 고생하다 suffer, be in pain

kosang 고상 elegance

kosanghan 고상한 elegant

kosŏngnŭng 고성능 high performance

kosŏngnŭng-ŭi 고성능의 high-powered

kosogŭro kamtta 고속으로 감다 fast forward

kosohada 고소하다 sue

kosohaehada 고소해하다 gloat; gloat over

kosok ch'asŏn 고속 차선 fast lane

kosok ellibeit'ŏ 고속 엘리베이터 express elevator

kosok kamkki 고속 감기 fast forward

kosok kiŏ 고속 기어 high (gear)

kosokttoro 고속도로 freeway, highway, expressway

kosok yŏlch'a 고속 열차 high-speed train

kosŭmdoch'i 고슴도치 hedgehog

kosu 고수 drummer

kosuhada 고수하다 hold on to belief; stick to story, opinion

kot 곧 soon, in a minute

kot 곳 joint; place; patch; ...nŭn kot ...는 곳 where

kotpparo 곧바로 straight; straight away

kot-tchang 곧장 straight; directly, immediately

kot-tchang tallyŏgada 곧장 달려가다 run directly to; make a beeline for

kot'ong 고통 suffering; distress; agony

kot'ongsŭrŏun 고통스러운 painful; agonizing

koŭiga anin 고의가 아닌 unintentional

koŭijŏgin 고의적인 deliberate

koŭijŏgŭro 고의적으로 deliberately

koŭmŭi 고음의 high-pitched

koun 고운 fine

kowi insa 고위 인사 dignitary

kowi kogwanŭi 고위 관의 high-level

kowŏn 고원 plateau

koyak'ada 고약하다 be foul; be bad

koyak'an 고약한 ugly; vicious; foul; bad; koyak'an naemsaega nada 고약한 냄새가 나다 stink, have a foul smell

koyang-i 고양이 cat

koyo 고요 peace; quietness; silence

koyohada 고요하다 be calm

koyohaejida 고요해지다 calm down

koyohan 고요한 still, calm, quiet

koyongdoeda 고용되다 be employed, be on the payroll

koyongdoen 고용된 in the pay of

koyonghada 고용하다 employ, hire

koyong-in 고용인 employee; servant

koyongju 고용주 employer

kŭ 그 the ◊ he; *kŭ sŭsŭro* 그 스스로 by himself

kŭbakke 그밖에 everyone else

kŭbakkŭi tarŭn kŏsŭn? 그밖의 다른 것은? anything else?

kŭbu 급우 school friend

kŭbyŏ 급여 allowance (*money*)

kŭ chashin 그 자신 himself

kŭ chik'ue 그 직후에 whereupon

kŭ chŏne paro 그 전에 바로 shortly before that

kŭ chŏngdo 그 정도 thereabouts

kŭ chŏngdo-ŭi 그 정도의 such a ◊ to that extent

kŭ chŏnjue 그 전주에 the week before

kŭ chŏnnal 그 전날 the day before

kŭ chŏnnare 그 전날에 the day before

kŭch'ida 그치다 stop

kŭdŭl 그들 them; they; those

kŭdŭl chashin 그들 자신 themselves

kŭdŭl sŭsŭro 그들 스스로 by themselves

kŭdŭrŭi 그들의 their; those

kŭdŭrŭi kŏt 그들의 것 theirs

kŭgŏllo twaessŏyo 그걸로 됐어요 alright, that's enough!

kŭgŏsŭi 그것의 its

kŭgŏsŭl 그것을 it (*as object*)

kŭgŏsŭn 그것은 it (*as subject*)

kŭgŏt chach'e 그것 자체 itself

kŭgŏttŭl 그것들 they; those (*things*)

kŭgŏt tul ta 그것 둘 다 both of them (*things*)

kŭgŏttŭrŭi 그것들의 those

kŭgot malgo 그곳 말고 not there

kŭgup'a 극우파 right-wing extremism

kŭ hu chulgot 그 후 줄곧 ever since

kŭ hue 그 후에 subsequently; later, afterward

kŭ ihue 그 이후에 after that

kŭjŏkke 그저께 the day before yesterday

kŭjŏ kŭrŏn 그저 그런 satisfactory; so so, average

kŭk 극 pole

kŭkch'anŭi p'yŏng 극찬의 평 rave review

kŭ kose 그 곳에 there

kŭk'i chagŭn 극히 작은 microscopic, minute

kŭk'i chungdaehan 극히 중대한 vitally important

kŭk'wa 극화 dramatization

kŭk'wahada 극화하다 dramatize

kŭk'yŏng 극형 capital punishment

kŭkppi 극비 top secret

kŭkppiŭi 극비의 classified

kŭkppok'ada 극복하다 conquer, overcome

kŭksshimhan 극심한 acute, extreme

kŭksso chŏnja konghak 극소 전자 공학 microelectronics

kŭkssoryang 극소량 iota, grain

kŭktchak-kka 극작가 dramatist

kŭktchang 극장 theater

kŭktchang annaewŏn 극장 안내원 usherette, attendant

kŭktchi 극지 pole ◊ polar

kŭktchŏgin 극적인 dramatic; rousing

kŭktchŏgin sanghwang 극적인 상황 drama, excitement

kŭktta 긁다 scrape; scratch

kŭkttan 극단 extreme; theater company

kŭkttanjŏgin 극단적인 extreme; immoderate

kŭktto 극도 extreme

Kŭkttong 극동 Far East ◊ Far Eastern

kŭkttoŭi p'iro 극도의 피로 exhaustion

kŭlja 글자 character (*in typography*)

kŭlkki 긁기 scratch

kŭlkkol 글꼴 font

kŭlk'in chaguk 긁힌 자국 scrape; scratch

kŭllaidŏ 글라이더 glider

kŭlsseyo 글쎄요 I'm not sure

kŭlsshi 글씨 handwriting

kŭl ssŭgi 글 쓰기 writing

kŭltcha 글자 letter (*of alphabet*)

kŭltchach'e 글자체 script; font

kŭltcha kŭdaero 글자 그대로 literally, to the letter

kŭltcha match'ugi nori 글자 맞추기 놀이 crossword

kŭm 금 gold; break, fracture

kŭmaek 금액 amount

kŭmanduda 그만두다 stop, quit; drop; drop out

kŭmanhan kach'iga it-tta 그만한 가치가 있다 be good value

kŭmbak 금박 gilt

kŭmbal mŏri yŏja 금발 머리 여자 blonde

kŭmbang 금방 directly, immediately

kŭmbung-ŏ 금붕어 goldfish

kŭmdan hyŏnsang 금단 현상 withdrawal symptoms

kŭmgage hada 금가게 하다 crack, fracture

Kŭmgang 금강 Kum River

Kŭmganggyŏng 금강경 Diamond Sutra

kŭmgi 금기 taboo

kŭmgo 금고 safe

kŭmgoe 금괴 gold ingot

kŭmhada 금하다 bar, forbid, ban

kŭmhonshik 금혼식 golden wedding anniversary

kŭmi kada 금이 가다 crack; split up

kŭmi kan 금이 간 cracked

kŭmji 금지 ban, prohibition; *kŭmnyŏn kŭmji* 금연 금지 no smoking

kŭmjidoeda 금지되다 be forbidden

kŭmjidoen 금지된 forbidden

kŭmjihada 금지하다 forbid, ban

kŭmjiryŏng 금지령 prohibition

kŭmjŏn tŭngnok-kki 금전 등록기 cash register

Kŭmjuppŏp 금주법 Prohibition

kŭmnyoil 금요일 Friday

kŭmnyu 급류 torrent; rapids

kŭmnyung 금융 finance; funding ◊ financial; monetary

kŭmnyung shijang 금융 시장 money market

kŭmsegongsa 금세공사 goldsmith

kŭmshi ch'omunida 금시 초문이다 that's news to me

kŭmshik 금식 fast (*not eating*)

kŭmsok 금속 metal

kŭmsokssŏng-ŭi 금속성의 metallic

kŭmul 그물 mesh, net

kŭmyŏn 금연 no smoking

kŭmyoktchŏgin 금욕적인 austere

kŭnbon 근본 root; source; origin

kŭnbonjŏgin 근본적인 basic, fundamental

kŭnbonjŏguro 근본적으로 radically

kŭnch'in 근친 next of kin

kŭnch'insanggan 근친상간 incest

kŭnch'ŏ 근처 vicinity; ...*ŭi kŭnch'ŏe(sŏ)* ...의 근처에(서) in the vicinity of; *kŭnch'ŏe it-tta* 근처에 있다 be around

kŭndae 근대 modern times ◊ modern

kŭndaeŭi 근대의 modern

kŭndaehwa 근대화 modernization

kŭne 그네 swing

kŭngjŏngjŏgin 긍정적인 positive

kŭn-gŏ 근거 basis, foundation; ground, reason

kŭn-gŏga toeda 근거가 되다 underlie

kŭn-gŏji 근거지 stronghold

kŭn-gŏjirŭl tugo it-tta ...에 근거지를 두고 있다 be based in

kŭn-gŏ ŏmnŭn 근거 없는 groundless, unfounded

kŭn-gyo 근교 environs; suburbs ◊ suburban

kŭnjŏng tchoktchi 근정 쪽지 compliments slip

kŭnjŏp 근접 proximity

kŭnjŏrhada 근절하다 stamp out, eradicate

kŭnmuhada 근무하다 serve

kŭnmu shigan 근무 시간 work hours; work day

kŭnmyŏnhan 근면한 industrious

kŭnŏmhan 근엄한 grave

kŭnsahan 근사한 gorgeous; neat, terrific

kŭnshian 근시안 myopia

kŭnshianjŏgin 근시안적인 shortsighted *fig*; short-term

kŭnshianŭi 근시안의 shortsighted; myopic

kŭnshimhada 근심하다 worry about, have on one's mind

kŭnŭl 그늘 shade; *kŭnŭre(sŏ)* 그늘에(서) in the shade

kŭnŭljige hada 그늘지게 하다 eclipse *fig*

kŭnŭljin 그늘진 shady

kŭnŭn 그는 he

kŭnwŏn 근원 origin; source; root

kŭnwŏnjŏgin 근원적인 underlying

kŭnyang 그냥 as it is; just; ***kŭnyang
nongdamiyeyo*** 그냥 농담이예요 I
was just kidding
kŭnyŏ 그녀 she
kŭnyŏ chashin 그녀 자신 herself
kŭnyŏrŭl 그녀를 her (*object*)
kŭnyŏ sŭsŭro 그녀 스스로 by herself
kŭnyŏŭi 그녀의 her
kŭnyŏŭi kŏt 그녀의 것 hers
kŭnyuk 근육 muscle ◊ muscular
kŭnyuk chŭnggangje 근육 증강제
anabolic steroid
kŭpkkangha 급강하 dive; sudden
drop
kŭpkkanghahada 급강하하다 dive;
drop suddenly
kŭpssangssŭng 급상승 jump; surge;
sudden increase
kŭpssangssŭnghada 급상승하다
jump; increase
kŭpssok naengdong naengjanggo
급속 냉동 냉장고 deep freeze (*with
fast freeze capability*)
kŭpssok'ada 급속하다 be rapid, be
fast
kŭpssok'i orŭda 급속히 오르다 rise
rapidly, spiral
kŭpssŭp 급습 raid
kŭpssŭp'ada 급습하다 raid
kŭpssugwan 급수관 water pipe
kŭptchinjŏgin 급진적인 radical
kŭptchinjuŭi 급진주의 radicalism
kŭptchinjuŭija 급진주의자 radical
(*person*)
kŭptchŭng 급증 explosion
kŭp'ada 급하다 be urgent; be
impatient; be sudden
kŭp'aeng 급행 express; haste ◊
express; hasty; ***kŭp'aeng
yŏlch'a / pŏssŭ*** 급행 열차/버스
express train/bus
kŭp'an 급한 urgent; hasty, rash
kŭp'i kada 급히 가다 dash; rush;
zoom
kŭraedo 그래도 nevertheless, still,
even so
kŭraem 그램 gram
kŭraendŭ p'iano 그랜드 피아노
grand piano
kŭraengk'uch'uk 크랭크축
crankshaft

kŭraenyudang 그래뉴당 granulated
sugar
kŭraep'ik 그래픽 graphic
kŭraep'ik k'adŭ 그래픽카드 graphics
card COMPUT
kŭraep'ikssŭ 그래픽스 graphics
kŭraesŏ 그래서 and; so that; that's
why; ***kŭraesŏ?*** 그래서? so what?
kŭraeyaman hada 그래야만 하다
must do, have to do
kŭraeyo 그래요 indeed, really; yes
kŭreihaundŭ 그레이하운드
grayhound
kŭreip'ŭp'ŭrut'ŭ 그레이프프루트
grapefruit
kŭreip'ŭp'ŭrut'ŭ chusŭ
그레이프프루트 주스 grapefruit juice
kŭri 그리 so ◊ there; that direction;
kŭri manch'i anŭn saram 그리
많지 않은 사람 not so many people
kŭrida 그리다 draw; paint
kŭrigo 그리고 and
kŭrigo nasŏ 그리고 나서 then, after
that
kŭrim 그림 drawing; picture;
illustration
kŭrimch'aek 그림책 picture book
kŭrimgwa kat'ŭn 그림과 같은
picturesque
kŭrimja 그림자 shadow
kŭrim kŭrigi 그림 그리기 painting
kŭrim put 그림 붓 paintbrush
kŭrimŭl kŭrida 그림을 그리다 draw
kŭrimyŏpssŏ 그림엽서 (picture)
postcard
Kŭrisŭ 그리스 Greece ◊ Greek
Kŭrisŭdo 그리스도 Christ
Kŭrisŭŏ 그리스어 Greek (*language*)
kŭriwŏhada 그리워하다 miss
kŭrŏch'i anŭmyŏn 그렇지 않으면
otherwise
kŭrŏch'i anŭn kŏt kat'ayo 그렇지
않은 것 같아요 I guess not
kŭrŏch'iman 그렇지만 but
kŭrŏgil paramnida 그러길 바랍니다
I hope so
kŭrŏktchŏrŏk hada 그럭저럭 하다
get by, just manage; ***yŏrŭi ŏpsshi
kŭrŏktchŏrŏk hada*** 열의 없이
그럭저럭 하다 plod along, plod on
kŭrŏk'e 그렇게 such; so; ***kŭrŏk'e***

haseyo 그렇게 하세요 do it like that; go ahead; **kŭrŏk'e manch'i anŭn** 그렇게 많지 않은 not so much; **kŭrok'e mani?** 그렇게 많이? as much as that?; **kŭrŏl kŏyeyo** 그럴 거예요 I expect so

kŭrŏlttŭt'an 그럴듯한 probable; plausible

kŭrŏmedo pulguhago 그럼에도 불구하고 nevertheless, nonetheless

kŭrŏmŭro 그러므로 therefore

kŭrŏmyŏnsŏdo 그러면서도 at the same time, however

kŭrŏn 그런 such, of that kind; **kŭrŏn kŏt kat'ayo** 그런 것 같아요 it looks that way, I guess so; **kŭrŏn kyŏng-ue** 그런 경우에 in that case; **kŭrŏn sanghwang-esŏnŭn** 그런 상황에서는 under those circumstances; **kŭrŏnŭn kwajŏng-e** 그러는 과정에 in the process

kŭrŏna 그러나 however; whereas; but

kŭrŏnde 그런데 but; and yet; by the way

kŭrŏt'a 그렇다 be that way; be so; be true

kŭrŏt'a hadŏrado 그렇다 하더라도 even so, but then (again)

kŭrŏt'amyŏn 그렇다면 then (deducing); if so

kŭrŏt'ŏrado 그렇더라도 though

kŭrol suyŏng 크롤 수영 crawl (in swimming)

kŭrosŏ 그로서 as such, in that capacity

kŭrŭl 그를 him

kŭrŭl ssŭda 글을 쓰다 write

kŭrŭrŏnggŏrida 그르렁거리다 purr

kŭrŭt 그릇 bowl, dish ◊ countword for cooked rice

kŭrŭttoen 그릇된 false

kŭrup 그룹 group

kŭrut'ŏgi 그루터기 stump

kŭ saie 그 사이에 in the meantime, meanwhile

kŭsŭllida 그슬리다 scorch

kŭsŭllin 그슬린 scorched; charred

kŭ tangshienŭn 그 당시에는 in those days

kŭ taŭmnal 그 다음날 the day after, the next day

kŭ taŭmŭi 그 다음의 following

kŭ ttae 그 때 then, at that time

kŭ ttaeenŭn 그 때에는 by then

kŭt-tta 긋다 strike

kŭŭi 그의 his

kŭŭi kŏt 그의 것 his

kŭŭllida 그을리다 singe

kŭŭrŭm 그을음 soot

kŭ yŏja 그 여자 she

ku 구 nine; sphere; district (part of a city)

kuaehada 구애하다 make a pass at

kubich'im 굽이침 swell

kubijida 굽이지다 wind, coil

kubunhada 구분하다 sort

kuburida 구부리다 bend, bend down

kuburigi shwiun 구부리기 쉬운 flexible

kuburŏjida 구부러지다 curve; buckle

kuburŏjin 구부러진 crooked

kubyŏl 구별 distinction; differentiation

kubyŏrhada 구별하다 tell; mark out; differentiate; **olk'o kŭrŭmŭl kubyŏrhada** 옳고 그름을 구별하다 know right from wrong

kuch'ehwadoeda 구체화되다 form, take shape, develop

kuch'ehwahada 구체화하다 embody, crystallize

kuch'ejŏgin 구체적인 concrete, specific; definite

kuch'ida 굳히다 cement; harden

kuch'ŏng 구청 district office

kuch'uk'am 구축함 destroyer NAUT

kuch'urhada 구출하다 extricate; release; free

kudŏbŏrin 굳어버린 confirmed, inveterate

kudŏgi 구더기 maggot

kudŏjida 굳어지다 solidify

kudu 구두 shoe

kudusoe 구두쇠 miser

kudu susŏntchip 구두 수선집 heel bar, shoe repairer

kudutppŏp 구두법 punctuation

kuduttchŏm 구두점 punctuation mark

kuduttchŏmŭl tchiktta 구두점을

찍다 punctuate
kugae 구개 palate ANAT
kugang 구강 mouth ◊ oral MED
kugida 구기다 crease, crumple
kugimsal 구김살 crease
Kugŏ 국어 Korean language
kugŏrhada 구걸하다 beg; cadge
kugoe ch'ubang 국외 추방
deportation
kugoero ch'ubanghada 국외로
추방하다 deport
kugŭn 구근 bulb BOT
kugŭpch'a 구급차 ambulance
kugŭp sangja 구급 상자 first aid kit
kugyŏjida 구겨지다 crease; ruffle
kugyŏng 구경 sightseeing; aperture;
caliber
kugyŏnghada 구경하다 see; watch;
see the sights
kugyŏnghwahada 국영화하다
nationalize
kugyŏngkkun 구경꾼 onlooker
kuhada 구하다 save, rescue; find,
come by
kuhoek 구획 block, section
kuibi kanŭnghan 구입이 가능한
obtainable
kuiyong yŏnggye 구이용 영계
broiler (*chicken*)
kujebullŭng-in saram 구제불능인
사람 hopeless case, disaster area
kujech'aek 구제책 remedy
kujik'ada 구직하다 be seeking
employment
kujo 구조 set-up; structure; rescue;
salvation
kujo chojŏng 구조 조정 structural
alteration; shake-up
kujoch'a 구조차 wrecker, recovery
vehicle
kujodae 구조대 rescue party
kujohada 구조하다 rescue, salvage
kujowŏn 구조원 lifeguard
kujwa 구좌 account
kujwa pŏnho 구좌 번호 account
number
kuk 국 soup
kuk kŭrŭt 국 그릇 soup bowl
kukch'ae 국채 national debt
kukki 국기 (national) flag
kuk-kka 국가 state, nation; national

anthem
Kuk-kka Poanppŏp 국가 보안법
National Security Law
kuk-kkaŭi 국가의 national
kuk-kkyŏng 국경 border
kukko 국고 national treasury
kukkun 국군 armed forces
kukppang 국방 national defense
kukppangbi yesan 국방비 예산
defense budget
Kukppangbu 국방부 Department of
Defense
Kukppangbuhanggwan 국방부 장관
Defense Secretary
kukppu mach'wi 국부 마취 local
anesthetic
Kukssech'ŏng 국세청 Internal
Revenue (Service)
kukssu 국수 noodles
kuktcha 국자 ladle; scoop
kuktche 국제 international
kuktchejŏgin 국제적인 international
kuktchejŏgŭro 국제적으로
internationally
kuktche kyŏrhon 국제 결혼
international marriage, mixed
marriage
Kuktche Sabŏp Chaep'anso 국제
사법 재판소 International Court of
Justice
kuktche suji 국제 수지 balance of
payments
Kuktche T'onghwa Kigŭm 국제
통화 기금 IMF, International
Monetary Fund
Kuktche Yŏnhap 국제 연합 United
Nations
kuktchŏk 국적 nationality
Kuk'oe 국회 Congress; Parliament;
National Assembly
kuk'oeŭi 국회의 congressional
kuk'oe ŭisadang 국회 의사당
parliamentary buildings
kuk'oe ŭiwŏn 국회 의원 member of
Congress
kuk'oe wiwŏn 국회 위원
congressman
kuk'wa 국화 chrysanthemum
kul 굴 oyster; tunnel; burrow
kulbok'ada 굴복하다 surrender, give
in; knuckle under; succumb

kulch'ak changch'i 굴착 장치 (oil) rig

kulch'ak-kki 굴착기 excavator

kulgok 굴곡 twist, bend

kulgŭn kŭlsshich'e 굵은 글씨체 bold *print*

kulkko t'ak'an mokssori 굵고 탁한 목소리 gruff voice

kullida 굴리다 run

kullim 군림 reign

kullimhada 군림하다 reign

kullŏ ttŏrŏjida 굴러 떨어지다 tumble

kullyŏ nŏmŏttŭrida 굴려 넘어뜨리다 roll over

kulttuk 굴뚝 chimney, smokestack; funnel

kultt'uksae 굴뚝새 wren

kumae 구매 purchase

kumaehada 구매하다 buy, purchase

kumaeja 구매자 buyer

kumaesŏrŭl ponaeda 구매서를 보내다 invoice

kumie mat-tta 구미에 맞다 cater for, meet the needs of

kumjurida 굶주리다 starve

kumŏng 구멍 hole; pit; puncture

kumŏng magae 구멍 마개 stopper

kumŏng naeda 구멍 내다 drill; make a hole

kumŏng ttult'a 구멍 뚫다 puncture; punch a hole in

kumyŏng 구명 lifesaving

kumyŏng chokki 구명 조끼 life jacket

kumyŏngjŏng 구명정 lifeboat

kumyŏng tti 구명 띠 life belt

kun 군 the military, army; county; Mr; Lord

kunae 구내 premises; yard

kunae shikttang 구내 식당 canteen (*on the premises*)

kunbi 군비 arms, weapons

kunbongmuhada 군복무하다 do military service

kun chudunji 군 주둔지 garrison

kunch'im hŭllida 군침 흘리다 slobber, drool

kunch'im tolge hanŭn 군침 돌게 하는 mouthwatering

kundae 군대 troops; the services

kundan 군단 corps

kungdung-i 궁둥이 hip; posterior; buttocks

kunggŭktchŏgin 궁극적인 final

kunggŭktchŏgŭro 궁극적으로 eventually

kunggŭmhada 궁금하다 wonder; be anxious about

kunggwŏl 궁궐 palace

kunggwŏlgat'ŭn 궁궐같은 palatial

kunghada 궁하다 be in want; *toni kunghan* 돈이 궁한 hard up, broke

kun-gi 군기 colors

kungji 궁지 predicament; *kungjie moranŏt'a* 궁지에 몰아넣다 drive into a corner

kungmin 국민 national, citizen; the people

kungmin ch'ongsaengsan 국민 총생산 GNP, gross national product

kungmin t'up'yo 국민 투표 referendum

Kungmubu Changgwan 국무부 장관 Secretary of State

Kungmuch'ongni 국무총리 Prime Minister

kungmul 국물 broth

Kungmusŏng 국무성 State Department

kungnae 국내 domestic

kungnae ch'ongsaengsan 국내 총생산 GDP, gross domestic product

kungnaesŏn pihaenggi 국내선 비행기 domestic flight

kungnaewoeesŏ 국내외에서 at home and abroad

kungnip kong-wŏn 국립 공원 national park

kun-goguma 군고구마 baked sweet potato

kunham 군함 warship

kunin 군인 soldier; serviceman

kunju 군주 monarch

kunjung 군중 crowd, crush

kunppŏp hoeŭi 군법 회의 court martial

kunsa 군사 military affairs ◊ military

kunsal 군살 flab

kunsaryŏk 군사력 military capability

kunsashisŏl 군사시설 military

installation
kunyonggi 군용기 warplane
kupssülgörinün 굽슬거리는 wavy
kuptta 굽다 bake; roast; broil
kup'il su ömnün 굽힐 수 없는 inflexible
kurhaji ank'o haenaeda 굴하지 않고 해내다 carry on undaunted
kuri 구리 copper
kuröngt'öng-i 구렁텅이 abyss
kurüda 구르다 roll
kurüm 구름 cloud
kurüng 구릉 hill ◊ hilly
kuryök 굴욕 humiliation
kuryogül chuda 굴욕을 주다 humiliate
kuryokkamül katkkehada 굴욕감을 갖게하다 feel humiliated
kuryoktchögin 굴욕적인 humiliating
kuryu chung 구류 중 in custody
kuryu chung-ida 구류 중이다 be in custody; be on remand
kuryushik'ida 구류시키다 remand in custody
kusaek 구색 selection, assortment
kusang 구상 framework
Kusegun 구세군 Salvation Army
Kuseju 구세주 Lord of Salvation, Savior
kushik 구식 old-fashioned
kuship 구십 ninety
kusöge(sö) 구석에(서) in the corner
kusöguro molda 구석으로 몰다 corner, drive into a corner
kusök 구석 corner
kusöng 구성 composition, make-up; plot
kusöngdoeda 구성되다 comprise
kusöngdoeö it-tta 구성되어 있다 be composed of
kusönghada 구성하다 compose, constitute, make up, form
kusöng yoso 구성 요소 component, constituent
kusok'ada 구속하다 tie down, restrict; intern
kusongnyögi innün 구속력이 있는 binding
kusül 구슬 beads
kusüllida 구슬리다 coax
kusülp'ün 구슬픈 plaintive

kusülp'ün sori 구슬픈 소리 wail
kusülp'ün sorirül naeda 구슬픈 소리를 내다 wail
kusul 구술 oral statement ◊ oral *exam*
kusurhada 구술하다 dictate
kut 굿 shaman rite of exorcism
kutkke kyölsshimhada 굳게 결심하다 make a firm decision, put one's foot down, be firm
kut-tta 굳다 harden
kut'a 구타 beating
kut'ahada 구타하다 beat up
kut'o 구토 vomit
kuün 구운 baked; roasted
kuwöjida 구워지다 be roasted
kuwöl 구월 September
kuwön 구원 salvation
kuwönhada 구원하다 redeem
Kuyak Söngsö 구약 성서 Old Testament
kuyök 구역 territory
kuyöktchil nanün 구역질 나는 disgusting, sick
kwa 과 section, department; faculty; lesson ◊ with ◊ and; as, like
kwabansu 과반수 majority
kwabansuida 과반수이다 be in the majority
kwabu 과부 widow
kwabugat'ün shinse 과부같은 신세 grass widow
kwabuhahada 과부하하다 overload
kwadae p'yöngkkadoen 과대 평가된 overrated
kwadae p'yöngkkahada 과대 평가하다 overestimate
kwadae sönjön 과대 선전 hype
kwadahage chibuldoen 과다하게 지불된 overpaid
kwadahan 과다한 excessive
kwadogi 과도기 transitional period
kwadojögin 과도적인 transitional
kwaench'ant'a 괜찮다 be OK, be alright; *kwaench'anayo* 괜찮아요 it's not bad; that's alright; *anio, kwaench'ansümnida* 아니오. 괜찮습니다 no, I don't mind; *tambaerül p'iwödo kwaench'ank'essümnikka?* 담배를

피워도 괜찮겠습니까? do you mind if I smoke?

kwaench'anŭn 괜찮은 acceptable

kwaench'anŭn chŏngdoŭi 괜찮은 정도의 decent, acceptable

kwagamhan 과감한 drastic

kwagamhi haeboda 과감히 해보다 venture boldly

kwagŏ 과거 past; civil service examination (*formerly*)

kwagŏe 과거에 in the past

kwagŏ punsa 과거 분사 past participle

kwagŏ shije 과거 시제 past tense

kwagyŏngnonja 과격론자 extremist

kwahak 과학 science

kwahak kisul 과학 기술 technology

kwahak kisul kongp'otchŭng 과학 기술 공포증 technophobia

kwahak kisulsang-ŭi 과학 기술상의 technological

Kwahak-kkisulch'ŏ 과학기술처 Ministry of Science and Technology

kwahaktcha 과학자 scientist

kwahaktchŏgin 과학적인 scientific

kwail 과일 fruit

kwail chyussŭ 과일 쥬스 fruit juice

kwail saellŏdŭ 과일 샐러드 fruit salad

kwaing pogyong 과잉 복용 overdose

kwaing pohohada 과잉 보호하다 overprotect

kwajang 과장 exaggeration; department manager

kwajangdoeda 과장되다 be over the top, be exaggerated

kwajangdoen 과장된 exaggerated; melodramatic, theatrical

kwajanghada 과장하다 exaggerate

kwajanghan sŏnjŏn 과장한 선전 hype

kwajanghayŏ p'yohyŏnhada 과장하여 표현하다 dramatize, exaggerate

kwajaryu 과자류 confectionery

kwaje 과제 project

kwajŏng 과정 process

kwajunghan 과중한 stiff

kwak 곽 carton; holder; tub

kwallamgaek 관람객 visitor (*at exhibition*)

kwallamsŏk 관람석 stand; booth (*at exhibition*)

kwalli 관리 administration; management; mandarin

kwalliin 관리인 administrator; manager; caretaker

kwallija 관리자 administrator; manager

kwalliŭi 관리의 managerial

kwallyŏn 관련 connection, link; involvement; *...wa / kwa kwallyŏn-hayŏ* ...와/과 관련하여 in connection with

kwallyŏndoeda 관련되다 be connected with, be involved in; be relevant; be related

kwallyŏndoen 관련된 related; relevant

kwallyŏni innŭn 관련이 있는 related

kwallyŏni it-tta 관련이 있다 be related to; be relevant to

kwallyŏni ŏmnŭn 관련이 없는 irrelevant

kwallyŏnshik'ida 관련시키다 bring in, involve; connect, link

kwallyŏnssŏng 관련성 relevance

kwallyo 관료 bureaucrat

kwallyoje 관료제 bureaucracy

kwallyojŏgin 관료적인 bureaucratic

kwallyojuŭi 관료주의 bureaucracy, red tape

kwalmok'al manhan 괄목할 만한 spectacular

kwaminhan 과민한 hypersensitive

kwamok 과목 subject (*branch of learning*)

kwan 관 casket, coffin; pipe; tube; crown; mansion

kwanak-kki 관악기 wind instrument

kwanch'al 관찰 observation

kwanch'allyŏgi yerihan 관찰력이 예리한 observant

kwanch'altcha 관찰자 observer

kwanch'arhada 관찰하다 observe

kwanch'ŏng 관청 office, position

kwanch'ŭksso 관측소 observatory

kwandaehada 관대하다 be generous

kwandaehan 관대한 generous; broadminded; lenient; soft; permissive

-kwang -광 enthusiast, fan; craze, mania; *yŏnghwagwang / chaejŭgwang* 영화광 / 재즈광 movie / jazz freak
kwan-gae 관개 irrigation
kwan-gaehada 관개하다 irrigate
kwan-gaek 관객 spectator
kwan-gaeyong suro 관개용 수로 irrigation canal
kwangbŏmwihan 광범위한 extensive, wide
Kwangboktchŏl 광복절 Liberation Day
kwangbu 광부 miner
kwangch'ŏnsu 광천수 mineral water
kwangch'ŭng 광층 seam (*of ore*)
kwangdaeppyŏ 광대뼈 cheekbone
kwanggagŭi 광각의 wide-angle
kwanggo 광고 advertisement, advert, commercial; advertising
kwanggohada 광고하다 advertise; publicize
kwanggoju 광고주 advertiser
kwanggo munan 광고 문안 advertising copy, text
kwanggo-ŏp 광고업 advertising
kwanggo pangsong 광고 방송 commercial break
kwanggop'an 광고판 billboard
kwanggo p'osŭt'ŏ 광고 포스터 bill, poster
kwanggo taehaengsa 광고 대행사 advertising agency
kwanggyŏng 광경 sight, spectacle
kwanggyŏnppyŏng 광견병 rabies
kwanghwarhan 광활한 vast
kwangjang 광장 square, plaza
kwangkki 광기 madness, insanity
kwangmul 광물 mineral
kwangnaeda 광내다 polish
kwangnŭng 관능 sensuality
kwangnŭngtchŏgin 관능적인 sensual
kwangnyŏn 광년 light year
kwang-ŏp 광업 mining
kwangp'ok'aejida 광폭해지다 go berserk
kwangsan 광산 mine
kwangshinja 광신자 fanatic
kwangshinjŏgin 광신적인 fanatical
kwangsŏk 광석 ore

kwangsŏmnyu 광섬유 fiber optics
kwangsŏmnyuŭi 광섬유의 fiber optic
kwangt'aegi ŏmnŭn 광택이 없는 matt
kwangt'aek nanŭn 광택 나는 glossy
kwangt'aek p'eint'ŭ 광택 페인트 gloss paint
kwangt'aektche 광택제 polish
kwan-gwang 관광 tour; sightseeing
kwan-gwang annaeso 관광 안내소 tourist (information) office
kwan-gwanggaek 관광객 visitor, tourist
kwan-gwanghada 관광하다 tour; go sightseeing
kwan-gwang-ŏp 관광업 tourism
kwan-gwang-ŏptcha 관광업자 tour operator
kwan-gwang yŏhaeng 관광 여행 sightseeing tour
kwan-gye 관계 connection, relationship
kwan-gyedoeda 관계되다 get involved with
kwan-gyedoenŭn 관계되는 concerned, involved
kwan-gyega kkŭnnada 관계가 끝나다 be through, be finished
kwan-gyehada 관계하다 involve, concern; get mixed up with
kwan-gyeŏmnŭn 관계없는 unrelated
kwan-gyeŏpsshi 관계없이 irrespective of
kwan-gyerŭl kkŭnt'a 관계를 끊다 dissociate oneself from
kwanhada 관하다 be related to; *...e kwanhaesŏ* ...에 관해서 with regard to; *i chŏme kwanhaesŏnŭn* 이 점에 관해서는 in this regard; *...e kwanhan* ...에 관한 about, concerning; *...e kwanhayŏ* ...에 관하여 concerning; *muŏse kwanhan kŏshimnikka?* 무엇에 관한 것입니까? what's it about?
kwanhae tŭt-tta 관해 듣다 hear about
kwanjanori 관자놀이 temple ANAT
kwanjet'ap 관제탑 control tower
kwanjŏl 관절 joint ANAT
kwanjŏllyŏm 관절염 arthritis

kwanjung 관중 crowd, audience
kwanjungsŏk 관중석 auditorium
kwanmok 관목 bush, shrub; shrubbery
kwanmun 관문 gateway
kwannŭngjŏgin 관능적인 erotic; tasty; sexy; sultry
kwannŭngjuŭi 관능주의 eroticism
kwanyong 관용 forgiveness; clemency
kwansa 관사 article
kwanse 관세 customs; duty, tariff
Kwanseguk 관세국 Customs and Tariff Bureau
kwanshim 관심 interest
kwanshimi innŭn 관심이 있는 interested
kwanshimsa 관심사 concern, business
kwanshimŭl kajida 관심을 가지다 care; care about; have an interest in
kwansŭp 관습 custom, convention; institution
kwansŭppŏp 관습법 unwritten law
kwansŭptchŏgin 관습적인 customary; unwritten
kwantchŏm 관점 position, point of view; *chŏrŏhan kwantchŏmesŏ* 저러한 관점에서 from that point of view, in that respect
kwant'onghada 관통하다 pierce, penetrate
kwanŭro ponaeda 관으로 보내다 pipe
kwanyŏgŭi hanbokp'an 관녁의 한복판 bull's-eye
kwanyŏgŭl match'uda 관녁을 맞추다 hit the bull's-eye
kwanyŏhada 관여하다 concern oneself with
kwanyŏk 관녁 target
kwanyong 관용 tolerance
kwanyong innŭn 관용 있는 tolerant
kwanyongjŏgin 관용적인 idiomatic
kwanyong-ŏ 관용어 idiom
kwarho 괄호 bracket; parenthesis
kwaro 과로 overwork
kwarohada 과로하다 overwork
kwaroshik'ida 과로시키다 overwork s.o.
kwase 과세 taxation

kwashi 과시 demonstration, display
kwashihada 과시하다 parade, flaunt, show off
kwashihanŭn 과시하는 ostentatious
kwashil 과실 malpractice
kwasok 과속 speeding
kwasok pŏlgŭm 과속 벌금 speeding fine
kwasok'ada 과속하다 speed, drive too quickly
kwaso p'yŏngkkahada 과소 평가하다 minimize; undervalue; underestimate
kwasuwŏn 과수원 orchard
kwayuk 과육 pulp
kwedo 궤도 orbit
kweyang 궤양 ulcer
kwi 귀 ear
kwiari 귀앓이 earache
kwich'ank'e hada 귀찮게 하다 bother, disturb
kwich'ank'e kulda 귀찮게 굴다 pester
kwich'ant'a 귀찮다 be a nuisance; *irŏk'e kwich'anŭl suga!* 이렇게 귀찮을 수가! what a nuisance!
kwich'anŭn 귀찮은 tiresome, annoying
kwich'ŏng-i ttŏrŏjil ttŭt'an 귀청이 떨어질 듯한 deafening, ear-piercing
kwie kösŭllinŭn 귀에 거슬리는 grating; strident; harsh
kwiga 귀가 homecoming
kwigahada 귀가하다 return home
kwiga kire 귀가 길에 homeward (*to own country*)
kwiga mŏn 귀가 먼 hard of hearing
kwigori 귀고리 earring
kwiguk kire 귀국 길에 homeward (*to own country*)
kwihwahada 귀화하다 become naturalized
kwihwan 귀환 return
kwiji 귀지 earwax
kwijok 귀족 aristocrat; nobility
kwijunghada 귀중하다 be precious
kwijunghan 귀중한 precious, valuable
kwijungp'um 귀중품 valuables
kwimŏgŭn 귀먹은 deaf
kwimŏk-kke hada 귀먹게 하다

deafen
kwiri 귀리 oats
kwirŭl tchonggŭt seuda 귀를 쫑긋 세우다 prick up one's ears
kwishin 귀신 ghost
kwishin-gat'ŭn 귀신같은 ghostly
kwitturami 귀뚜라미 cricket (*insect*)
kwiyŏpta 귀엽다 be cute, be lovable
kwiyŏun 귀여운 cute, pretty
kwŏlli 권리 right, claim; title
kwŏllyŏk 권력 power, authority
kwŏllyŏk chipttan 권력 집단 the Establishment
kwŏn 권 bloc ◊ *countword for books*
kwŏnch'ong 권총 pistol, revolver
kwŏnch'ongjip 권총집 holster
kwŏnhada 권하다 offer
kwŏnhan puyŏ 권한 부여 mandate, authority
kwŏnhanŭl chuda 권한을 주다 authorize
kwŏnjwa-esŏ ttŏrŏjida 권좌에서 떨어지다 fall from power
kwŏnt'ae 권태 boredom
kwŏnt'u 권투 boxing
kwŏnt'uhada 권투하다 box SP
kwŏnt'u shihap 권투 시합 boxing match
kwŏnt'u sŏnsu 권투 선수 boxer
kwŏnwi 권위 authority
kwŏnwiinnŭn 권위있는 authoritative, definitive
kwŏnwijaida 권위자이다 be an authority
kwŏnyanggi 권양기 winch, windlass
kwŏnyuhada 권유하다 canvass; drum up
-kye -계: *chaejŭgye / mayak-kkye* 재즈계 / 마약계 jazz scene / drugs scene; *k'ŏmpyut'ŏgye / yŏngŭk-kkye* 컴퓨터계 / 연극계 the world of computers / the world of the theater
kye 계 credit union; loan club
kyebu 계부 stepfather
kyedan 계단 stair, step
kyedanshik pat 계단식 밭 terraced field
kyeganŭro 계간으로 quarterly
kyegi 계기 gauge
kyegip'an 계기판 dashboard
kyegŏlssŭre mŏktta 게걸스레 먹다

wolf (down)
kyegŭp 계급 class, rank; stripe
kyegŭp chojik 계급 조직 hierarchy
kyegŭp t'ujaeng 계급 투쟁 class warfare
kyehoek 계획 plan; project; strategy
kyehoektchŏgin 계획적인 premeditated
kyehoektchŏgin p'agoe 계획적인 파괴 sabotage
kyehoektchŏgŭro 계획적으로 systematically
kyehoektchŏgŭro p'agoehada 계획적으로 파괴하다 sabotage
kyehoek'ada 계획하다 plan, propose
kyejibae 계집애 little girl; chick, babe
kyejip 계집 female *pej*
kyejŏl 계절 season
kyeju kyŏnggi 계주 경기 relay
kyemo 계모 stepmother
kyemongdoen 계몽된 enlightened, liberal
kyemonghada 계몽하다 enlighten
kyeŏmnyŏng 계엄령 martial law
kyep'i 계피 cinnamon
kyeran 계란 egg
kyeran hurai 계란 후라이 fried egg
kyeryak 계략 plot, conspiracy
kyeryanggi 계량기 meter
kyesan 계산 sum; calculation
kyesandae 계산대 checkout; counter; cash desk
kyesan-gi 계산기 calculator
kyesanhada 계산하다 count, calculate
kyesanjŏgin 계산적인 calculating
kyesansŏ 계산서 bill, check
kyesansŏro ch'ŏngguhada 계산서로 청구하다 bill, invoice
kyesanŭl hal su innŭn 계산을 할 수 있는 numerate
kyesok irŏn sangt'aeramyŏn 계속 이런 상태라면 at this rate; if things go on like this
kyesok ... it-tta 계속 ... 있다 remain, stay
kyesok kajigo it-tta 계속 가지고 있다 hold on to, keep
kyesok myŏt shigan tong-an 계속 몇 시간 동안 for hours on end
kyesok namait-tta 계속 남아있다

hold out
kyesok noryŏk'ada 계속 노력하다
keep (on) trying
kyesok panbok'aesŏ 계속 반복해서
over and over again
kyesok panghaehada 계속 방해하다
keep (on) interrupting
kyesok salda 계속 살다 live on
kyesok seda 계속 세다 keep count
of
kyesok shich'ŏnghada 계속
시청하다 follow *TV series*, *news*
kyesoktchŏgin 계속적인 continual
kyesok ttŏdŭrŏdaeda 계속
떠들어대다 go on about
kyesokttoeda 계속되다 continue
kyesokttoenŭn 계속되는 constant,
continuous
kyesok yŏllak'ada 계속 연락하다
keep up with, stay in touch with
kyesok yujihada 계속 유지하다
retain
kyesok'ada 계속하다 continue, carry
on; pursue; *kyesok kŏt-tta / iyagi
hada* 계속 걷다 / 이야기 하다
walk / talk on; *kyesok ibwŏnhae
itkke hada* 계속 입원해 있게 하다
keep in the hospital
kyesok'aesŏ 계속해서 in succession;
perpetually; persistently; continually
kyesok'aesŏ hada 계속해서 하다
persevere
kyesok'aesŏ irŏnada 계속해서
일어나다 follow, dog
kyesŭng 계승 succession (*to the
throne*)
kyesŭnghada 계승하다 succeed (*to
the throne*)
kyesu 계수 sister-in-law (*younger
brother's wife*)
kyeyak 계약 contract, agreement;
deal
kyeyak-kkŭm 계약금 down payment,
deposit
kyeyakssang-ŭi 계약상의
contractual
kyeyaktcha 계약자 contractor
kyeyak wiban 계약 위반 breach of
contract
kyŏdŭrang-i 겨드랑이 armpit
kyŏgillo 격일로 on alternate days

kyŏja 겨자 mustard
kyŏk'an 격한 heated
kyŏkppyŏn 격변 upheaval; revulsion
kyŏkp'ahada 격파하다 whip, defeat
kyŏksshimhan 격심한 vigorous
kyŏktcha 격자 grid
kyŏktta 겪다 go through, experience
kyŏkt'oehada 격퇴하다 repel
kyŏl 결 texture
kyŏlbaek 결백 innocence; purity
kyŏlbaek'an 결백한 innocent; pure
kyŏlbyŏl 결별 separation
kyŏlgŭn 결근 absence
kyŏlgŭnhan 결근한 absent
kyŏlguk 결국 after all, in the end;
*kyŏlguk pyŏng-wŏn shinserŭl
chida* 결국 병원 신세를 지다 wind
up in the hospital
kyŏlkkwa 결과 consequence, result;
outcome
kyŏlk'o 결코 surely, assuredly
kyŏllon 결론 conclusion; decision;
kyŏllone irŭda 결론에 이르다 come
to a decision
kyŏllonŭl naerida 결론을 내리다
conclude, deduce
kyŏlmal 결말 ending; conclusion;
upshot
kyŏlmangnyŏm 결막염 conjunctivitis
kyŏlmarŭl chit-tta 결말을 짓다 wind
up; tie up the loose ends
kyŏlp'ip 결핍 lack, deficiency
kyŏlp'ipttoeda 결핍되다 be deficient
in
kyŏlssandoeda 결산되다 balance
kyŏlsshim 결심 determination,
resolution
kyŏlsshimhada 결심하다 decide
kyŏlsshimhan 결심한 determined
kyŏlssŏk 결석 absence
kyŏlssŏk'ada 결석하다 be absent
kyŏlssŏk'an 결석한 absent
kyŏlsok 결속 solidarity
kyŏlssŭng 결승 final
kyŏlssŭngjŏm 결승점 winning post,
finish
kyŏlssŭngjŏn 결승전 finals; decider
SP
kyŏlssŭngjŏn ch'ultchŏn sŏnsu
결승전 출전 선수 finalist
kyŏlssŭngsŏn 결승선 finishing line

kyŏltchang 결장 colon ANAT
kyŏltchŏm 결점 defect, shortcoming
kyŏltchŏm innŭn 결점 있는 faulty
kyŏltchŏmi innŭn 결점이 있는 defective, faulty
kyŏltchŏng 결정 decision; *kyŏltchŏng-ŭl hada* 결정을 하다 make a decision; *kyŏltchŏng-ŭl naerida* 결정을 내리다 decide, settle
kyŏltchŏngdoeji anŭn 결정되지 않은 unsettled, undecided
kyŏltchŏnghada 결정하다 decide, determine
kyŏltchŏnghaji mot'ada 결정하지 못하다 be undecided about; be unable to decide
kyŏltchŏngjŏgin 결정적인 conclusive; critical, crucial; definitive
kyŏltchŏngjŏgin kömt'o 결정적인 검토 acid test
kyŏltchŏngjŏk shigi 결정적 시기 decisive moment
kyŏlttanssŏng-i ŏmnŭn 결단성이 없는 indecisive
kyŏmja 겸자 forceps
kyŏmson 겸손 humility, modesty
kyŏmsonhada 겸손하다 be humble, be modest
kyŏmsonhan 겸손한 modest, unassuming
kyŏnbon 견본 sample, specimen
kyŏndida 견디다 endure, wear, last; cope; do without; resist
kyŏndil su innŭn 견딜 수 있는 bearable
kyŏndil su ŏmnŭn 견딜 수 없는 unbearable
kyŏndiŏnaeda 견디어내다 withstand
...kyŏng ...경 around, about; *idal malgyŏng* 이달 말경 around the end of this month
kyŏngapkkol 견갑골 shoulder blade
kyŏngbi 경비 expenses
kyŏngbirŭl chŏlgamhanŭn 경비를 절감하는 cost-conscious
kyŏngbiwŏn 경비원 security guard; bouncer
kyŏngbŏmtchoe 경범죄 misdemeanor

kyŏngbogi 경보기 alarm
kyŏngboŭm 경보음 alert; signal
kyŏngch'al 경찰 police; cop; *kyŏngch'are ch'asuhada* 경찰에 자수하다 give oneself up to the police
kyŏngch'algwan 경찰관 policeman; marshal
kyŏngch'al kuk-kka 경찰 국가 police state
kyŏngch'al kuktchang 경찰 국장 superintendent
kyŏngch'al sarin chŏndam pusŏ 경찰 살인 전담 부서 homicide (department)
kyŏngch'alsŏ 경찰서 police station
kyŏngch'i 경치 landscape; view
kyŏngch'ŏp 경첩 hinge
kyŏngdo 경도 longitude
kyŏnggam sayu 경감 사유 mitigating circumstances
kyŏnggi 경기 game; meet; fight; play; business; things; times
kyŏnggi ch'amgaja 경기 참가자 participant, entrant SP
kyŏnggi ch'imch'e 경기 침체 (economic) downturn
kyŏnggiga p'okttŭnghada 경기가 폭등하다 boom COM
kyŏnggija 경기자 player
kyŏnggijang 경기장 playing field; stadium
kyŏnggi kirok 경기 기록 record SP
kyŏnggi p'okttŭng 경기 폭등 boom
kyŏnggŏnhan 경건한 pious, devout
kyŏnggo 경고 alarm, warning
kyŏnggohada 경고하다 warn, alert; raise the alarm
kyŏnggwa 경과 passage (*of time*)
kyŏnggwahada 경과하다 elapse
kyŏnggwan 경관 officer; sights
kyŏnggye 경계 boundary, limit
kyŏnggyehada 경계하다 be on one's guard against, look out for
kyŏnggyehanŭn 경계하는 alert
kyŏnggyesŏn 경계선 boundary, border
kyŏnghŏm 경험 experience
kyŏnghŏminnŭn 경험있는 experienced
kyŏnghŏmi ŏmnŭn 경험이 없는

inexperienced

kyŏnghŏmŭl ssahŭn 경험을 쌓은
seasoned *traveler etc*

kyŏnghohada 경호하다 escort, act as
bodyguard to

kyŏnghowŏn 경호원 bodyguard

kyŏnghyang 경향 tendency; trend

kyŏnghyang-i it-tta 경향이 있다
tend toward; *...nŭn kyŏnghyang-i
it-tta* ...는 경향이 있다 be liable to

kyŏngjaeng 경쟁 contest; rivalry;
competition

kyŏngjaenghada 경쟁하다 compete;
rival

kyŏngjaengja 경쟁자 competitor,
rival; competitors; the competition

kyŏngjaengjŏgin 경쟁적인
competitive *person*

kyŏngjaengnyŏk innŭn 경쟁력 있는
competitive *bid*

kyŏngjaeng sangdae 경쟁 상대
competitor

kyŏngjak 경작 cultivation

kyŏngjak'ada 경작하다 plow, till;
cultivate

kyŏngje 경제 economy

kyŏngje chaptchi 경제 잡지
financial magazine

kyŏngje chejae 경제 제재 economic
sanctions

kyŏngjehak 경제학 economics

kyŏngjehaktcha 경제학자 economist

kyŏngjejŏgin 경제적인 economical,
cheap

kyŏngjejŏgŭro 경제적으로
economically

kyŏngjejŏk ch'ŭngmyŏn 경제적
측면 economics; financial aspects

kyŏngjeŭi 경제의 economic

kyŏngjŏgŭl ullida 경적을 울리다
hoot, sound one's horn

kyŏngjŏk 경적 horn

kyŏngjŏn 경전 holy scriptures, holy
book

kyŏngju 경주 race; racing

kyŏngjuch'a 경주차 racing car

kyŏngjuhada 경주하다 race, run

kyŏngjuja 경주자 runner, athlete;
racing driver

kyŏngjujang 경주장 racetrack

kyŏngju k'osŭ 경주 코스 racecourse

kyŏngjuma 경주마 racehorse

kyŏngma 경마 horse race; the races

kyŏngmae 경매 auction

kyŏngmaehada 경매하다 auction

kyŏngmyŏl 경멸 contempt, scorn

kyŏngmyŏrhada 경멸하다 despise;
scorn

kyŏngmyŏrhal manhan 경멸할 만한
contemptible

kyŏngmyŏrhanŭn 경멸하는
derogatory; scornful

kyŏngmyŏrŏ 경멸어 pejorative

kyŏngnapkko 격납고 hangar

kyŏngnihayŏ 격리 하여 in isolation

kyŏngni pyŏngdong 격리 병동
isolation ward

kyŏngnishik'ida 격리시키다 isolate

kyŏngno 격노 rage, fury

kyŏngnohada 격노하다 rage, be in a
rage

kyŏngnohanŭn 격노하는 furious

kyŏngno shik'ida 격노 시키다
infuriate

kyŏngnye 경례 salute; bow

kyŏngnyehada 경례하다 salute; bow

kyŏngnyerŭl pat-tta 경례를 받다
take the salute

kyŏngnyŏ 격려 boost,
encouragement

kyŏngnyŏhada 격려하다 encourage,
incite

kyŏngnyŏk 경력 career, profession;
experience

kyŏngnyŏl 격렬 intensity

kyŏngnyŏn 경련 convulsion; twitch

kyŏngnyŏng 경영 management (*of
big company*)

kyŏngnyŏnghada 경영하다 manage
big company

kyŏngnyŏnghak 경영학 business
studies; management studies

kyŏngnyŏnghak sŏkssa 경영학
석사 Master's in Business
Administration, MBA

kyŏngnyŏng-in 경영인 manager,
executive; proprietor

kyŏngnyŏngja 경영자 manager (*of
company*)

kyŏngnyŏngjin 경영진 management,
managers

kyŏngnyŏngju 경영주 manager

(*owner*)

kyŏngnyŏngkkwŏn maemae 경영권 매매 management buyout

kyŏngnyŏng sangdamja 경영 상담자 management consultant

kyŏngnyŏng taehagwŏn 경영 대학원 business school

kyŏngnyŏngt'im 경영팀 management team

kyŏngnyŏni ilda 경련이 일다 twitch; jerk

kyŏng-nyŏnŭi 격년의 biennial

kyŏngnyŏrhada 격렬하다 be violent

kyŏngnyŏrhaejida 격렬해지다 intensify

kyŏngnyŏrhage 격렬하게 furiously, violently; with a vengeance

kyŏngnyŏrham 격렬함 violence

kyŏngnyŏrhan 격렬한 drastic *change*; stormy; turbulent; violent

kyŏngnyŏ yŏnsŏl 격려 연설 pep talk

kyŏngnyuhayŏ 경유하여 via

kyŏngŏnhan 경건한 reverent

kyŏn-gohan 견고한 solid, strong

kyŏngsa 경사 slant; slope

kyŏngsado 경사도 gradient

kyŏngsajida 경사지다 slope; descend

kyŏngsa-myŏn 경사면 side (*of mountain*)

kyŏngshihada 경시하다 downplay

kyŏngŭirŭl p'yohada 경의를 표하다 show respect to

kyŏng-u 경우 case, instance

kyŏn-gwa 견과 nut

kyŏng-wi 경위 inspector

kyŏngyŏng kwalli 경영 관리 running (*of business*)

kyŏnhae 견해 view, opinion

kyŏninhada 견인하다 tow away

kyŏninnyong patchul 견인용 밧줄 towrope

kyŏnje 견제 restraint, brake

kyŏnjŏk 견적 estimate; quotation

kyŏnjŏk'ada 견적하다 quote

kyŏnnunjil 곁눈질 leer

kyŏnnunjirhada 곁눈질하다 look away; sneak a glance at

kyŏnsonhan 겸손한 humble

kyŏnsŭp 견습 probation

kyŏnsŭp kigan 견습 기간 trial

period, probation period

kyŏnsŭp kwajŏng 견습 과정 training course

kyŏnsŭpsaeng 견습생 apprentice; trainee

kyŏnuda 겨누다 point

kyŏnyang 겨냥 aim

kyŏnyanghada 겨냥하다 aim (at); measure

kyŏpch'ida 겹치다 clash

kyŏrhaek 결핵 tuberculosis

kyŏrhamŭl koch'ida 결함을 고치다 debug

kyŏrhap 결합 combination

kyŏrhap'ada 결합하다 combine, unite

kyŏrhon 결혼 marriage (*institution*)

kyŏrhon chŭngmyŏngsŏ 결혼 증명서 marriage certificate

kyŏrhon kinyŏmil 결혼 기념일 wedding anniversary

kyŏrhon panji 결혼 반지 wedding ring

kyŏrhon saenghwal 결혼 생활 married life; marriage

kyŏrhon sangdamwŏn 결혼 상담원 marriage counselor

kyŏrhon yego 결혼 예고 banns

kyŏrhonhada 결혼하다 marry, get married

kyŏrhonhan 결혼한 married

kyŏrhonshik 결혼식 marriage, wedding

kyŏrhonshingnal 결혼식날 wedding day

kyŏrhonŭi 결혼의 marital

kyŏron chŏnŭi 결혼 전의 prenuptial

kyŏruda 겨루다 play *opponent*; fight, contest

kyŏryŏnham 결연함 resolution, determination

kyŏtssoe 곁쇠 skeleton key

kyŏt'e(sŏ) 곁에(서) beside, next to

kyŏu 겨우 barely, only just

kyŏul 겨울 winter

kyŏul kat'ŭn 겨울같은 wintry

kyŏul sŭp'och'ŭ 겨울 스포츠 winter sports

kyobok 교복 uniform

kyobok sang-ŭi 교복 상의 tunic

kyoch'a 교차 intersection

kyoch'ahada 교차하다 intersect, cross

kyoch'ajŏm 교차점 junction

kyoch'ak sangt'ae 교착 상태 deadlock

kyoch'aro 교차로 cross street

kyoch'ehada 교체하다 alternate

kyodae 교대 shift; turn; *kyodaero hada* 교대로 하다 take turns in doing, do in rotation; *ch'arŭl kyodaero unjŏnhada* 차를 교대로 운전하다 take turns at the wheel

kyodaehada 교대하다 relieve, take over from

kyodae kŭnmu 교대 근무 shift work

kyodogwan 교도관 guard

kyodoso 교도소 jail, penitentiary

kyodosojang 교도소장 prison warden

kyogu mokssa 교구 목사 vicar

kyogu mokssagwan 교구 목사관 vicarage

kyohoe 교회 church

kyohun 교훈 moral, message; school motto

kyohwan 교환 exchange, flow

kyohwang 교황 pope

kyohwanhada 교환하다 exchange, trade; *muŏtkkwa muŏsŭl kyohwanhada* 무엇과 무엇을 교환하다 trade sth for sth

kyohwan kanŭng t'onghwa 교환 가능 통화 hard currency

kyohwansu 교환수 operator TELEC

kyohwanŭro 교환으로 in exchange; in exchange for

kyohwarham 교활함 cunning

kyohwarhan 교활한 crafty, cunning, sly; devious

kyohyanggok 교향곡 symphony

kyojang 교장 principal (*of school*)

kyoje 교제 contact

kyojehada 교제하다 associate with; keep company

kyojigwŏn 교직원 faculty, teaching staff

kyojik 교직 teaching (*profession*)

kyojŏn 교전 battle; war; hostilities

kyojŏn chung-ida 교전 중이다 be at war

kyojŏng 교정 manipulation

kyojŏnghada 교정하다 manipulate; 교정하다 correct *proofs*

kyojŏngswae 교정쇄 proof (*of book*)

kyokkwa kwajŏng 교과 과정 course (*series of lessons*); curriculum

kyokkwasŏ 교과서 textbook

kyomushil 교무실 staffroom

kyomyohada 교묘하다 be crafty; be clever; *kyomyohage shiganŭl kkŭlda* 교묘하게 시간을 끌다 stall, play for time

kyomyohan 교묘한 sneaky, crafty

kyomyohi hoep'ihada 교묘히 회피하다 evade, dodge *responsibility*

kyomyohi umjigida 교묘히 움직이다 maneuver

kyo-oe 교외 suburb

kyop'yŏn 교편 pointer

kyori 교리 dogma

kyoryu 교류 alternating current

kyosa 교사 teacher; academic; teachers; staff

kyosaeng 교생 student teacher

kyosa hullyŏn 교사 훈련 teacher training

kyosarhada 교살하다 strangle

kyoshil 교실 classroom

kyoshin 교신 contact

kyoshinhada 교신하다 contact

kyosŏp 교섭 approach; advance; proposal

kyosu 교수 professor

kyosudae 교수대 gallows

kyosuhyŏng-e ch'ŏhada 교수형에 처하다 string up, hang

kyot'ong 교통 traffic

Kyot'ongbu 교통부 Department of Transportation

kyot'ong ch'ejŭng 교통 체증 traffic jam

kyot'ong honjap 교통 혼잡 jam ; traffic congestion

kyot'ongmang chŏngch'e 교통망 정체 gridlock

kyot'ong p'yojip'an 교통 표지판 signpost

Kyot'ong Pŏpkkyu 교통 법규 Highway Code, rules of the road

kyot'ong shinho 교통 신호 traffic sign

kyct'ong sudan 교통 수단 means of transportation

kyot'ong sun-gyŏng 교통 순경 traffic cop; traffic police

kyoyang-i ŏmnŭn 교양이 없는 lowbrow

kyoyuge kwanhan 교육에 관한 educational

kyoyuk 교육 education; training

kyoyukpat-tta 교육받다 be educated; receive one's training

kyoyukpadŭn 교육받은 educated

kyoyukpat-tchi mot'an 교육받지 못한 uneducated

Kyoyukppu 교육부 Department of Education

kyoyukshik'ida 교육시키다 train

kyoyuk shilssŭpssaeng 교육 실습생 student teacher

kyoyuktchŏgin 교육적인 educational, instructive, informative

kyoyuk'ada 교육하다 educate

kyuch'igŭl ttarŭda 규칙을 따르다 follow the rules, toe the line

kyuch'ik 규칙 rule, regulation

kyuch'iktchŏgin 규칙적인 regular

kyugyŏk'wahada 규격화하다 standardize

kyujehada 규제하다 regulate

kyuje yangmul 규제 약물 controlled substance

kyujŏng 규정 stipulation, condition

kyujŏnghada 규정하다 stipulate, provide for

kyul 귤 mandarin orange

kyumo 규모 size, scale

kyumoga chulda 규모가 줄다 downsize

kyumorŭl churida 규모를 줄이다 downsize

kyundŭnghage 균등하게 equally; *kyundŭnghage nanuda* 균등하게 나누다 share out equally

kyunhyŏng 균형 balance, equilibrium; *kyunhyŏng-ŭl chaptta* 균형을 잡다 balance

kyunhyŏng chap'in 균형 잡힌 balanced, well-balanced

kyunyŏl 균열 rift

kyuyul 규율 discipline

K'

k'adŭ 카드 card
k'adŭk'i 카드키 cardkey
k'adŭshik saegin 카드식 색인 card index
k'aeda 캐다 nose about
k'aedi 캐디 caddie
k'aemp'ing 캠핑 camping
k'aemp'ŭ 캠프 camp
K'aenada 캐나다 Canada ◊ Canadian
k'aengk'aeng chit-tta 캥캥 짖다 yap
k'aep 캡 cap
k'aepsshyul 캡슐 capsule
k'ajino 카지노 casino
k'akt'eil 칵테일 cocktail
k'al 칼 knife
k'allal 칼날 blade
k'alla sajin 칼라 사진 color photograph
k'alla t'ellebijŏn 칼라 텔레비젼 color TV
k'allaro toen 칼라로 된 (in) color
k'allori 칼로리 calorie
k'alshyum 칼슘 calcium
k'altchip 칼집 sheath (for knife)
K'ambodia 캄보디아 Cambodia ◊ Cambodian
k'amera 카메라 camera
k'an 칸 compartment; panel; section
k'aneishyŏn 카네이션 carnation
k'anmagi 칸막이 partition
k'anmagirŭl hada 칸막이를 하다 partition off
k'ap'e 카페 café
k'ap'ein 카페인 caffeine
k'ap'eini chegŏdoen 카페인이 제거된 decaffeinated
k'ap'irait'ŏ 카피라이터 copy-writer
k'arat'e 카라테 karate
k'aset'ŭ p'ŭlleiŏ 카셋트 플레이어 tape deck
k'auboi 카우보이 cowboy
k'aunt'ŏ 카운터 counter (in café etc)
k'aunt'ŭ 카운트 count (in baseball, boxing)
k'ech'ŏp 케첩 catsup, ketchup
k'eibŭlk'a 케이블카 cable car
k'eik'ŭ 케이크 cake
k'eisŭ 케이스 case, container
k'i 키 height; key (on keyboard); helm
k'ibodŭ 키보드 keyboard
k'iga chagŭn 키가 작은 short
k'iga k'ŭn 키가 큰 tall
k'ikk'ik-kkŏrida 킥킥거리다 titter
k'ik'op'ŭ 킥오프 kickoff
k'ilk'il ut-tta 킬킬 웃다 chuckle
k'illo 킬로 kilo
k'illobait'ŭ 킬로바이트 kilobyte
k'illogŭraem 킬로그램 kilogram
k'illomit'ŏ 킬로미터 kilometer
k'ing saijŭ 킹 사이즈 king-size(d)
k'irŭl ch'ida 키를 치다 key, key in COMPUT
k'isŭ 키스 kiss
k'isŭhada 키스하다 kiss
k'iuda 키우다 raise, bring up children
k'ŏbŏ 커버 cover, jacket (of book)
k'ŏjida 커지다 grow (of number, amount)
k'ŏmp'ŏsŭ 컴퍼스 (pair of) compasses
k'ŏmp'yut'ŏ 컴퓨터 computer
k'ŏmp'yut'ŏ ch'ulp'an 컴퓨터 출판 DTP, desk-top publishing
k'ŏmp'yut'ŏ keim 컴퓨터 게임 computer game
k'ŏmp'yut'ŏ kwahak 컴퓨터 과학 computer science
k'ŏmp'yut'ŏ kwahaktcha 컴퓨터 과학자 computer scientist
k'ŏmp'yut'ŏ sayong 컴퓨터 사용 computing
k'ŏmp'yut'ŏro t'ongjedoenŭn 컴퓨터로 통제되는 computer-controlled
k'ŏnbeiŏ pelt'ŭ 컨베이어 벨트 conveyor belt

k'ŏnbenshyŏn sent'ŏ 컨벤션 센터 convention center

k'ŏndishyŏn 컨디션 condition, shape

k'ŏnssŏlt'ŏnt'ŭ 컨설턴트 consultant, adviser

k'ŏnssŏlt'ŏnt'ŭŏp 컨설턴트업 consultancy (*company*)

k'ŏnt'einŏ 컨테이너 container

k'ŏnt'ŭri myujik 컨트리 뮤직 country and western (music)

k'ŏnyŏng 커녕 to say nothing of; ...*kinŭn k'ŏnyŏng* ...기는 커녕 let alone

k'ŏp 컵 cup; glass

k'ŏp'i 커피 coffee

k'ŏp'i meik'ŏ 커피 메이커 coffee maker

k'ŏp'i p'ot'ŭ 커피 포트 coffee pot

k'ŏp'i shyop 커피 숍 coffee shop

k'ŏsŏ 커서 cursor

k'ŏt'ŭn 커튼 drapes, curtains

k'o 코 nose; trunk; stitch

k'och'i 코치 coach SP

k'odŭ 코드 code

k'okkiri 코끼리 elephant

k'o kolda 코 골다 snore

k'ok'ain 코카인 cocaine

k'ok'oa 코코아 cocoa

k'ollesŭt'erol 콜레스테롤 cholesterol

k'ol t'aeksshi 콜 택시 radio taxi

k'omidiŏn 코미디언 comedian

k'omp'aekt'ŭ tisŭk'ŭ 콤팩트 디스크 CD, compact disc

k'omp'ŭllekssŭ 콤플렉스 complex PSYCH

k'ondishyŏnŏ 콘디셔너 conditioner

k'ondo 콘도 condo

k'ondom 콘돔 condom, sheath

k'ondominium 콘도미니움 condominium

k'ong 콩 bean; soy bean

k'ongp'at 콩팥 soy and red beans; kidney ANAT

k'onk'ŭrit'ŭ 콘크리트 concrete

k'onmul 콧물 mucus

k'onnoraerro purŭda 콧노래로 부르다 hum

k'onŏk'ik 코너킥 corner kick

k'ont'aekt'ŭrenjŭ 콘택트렌즈 contact lens

k'onyak 코냑 cognac

k'op'i 코피 nosebleed; copy; *nanŭn k'op'iga nanda* 나는 코피가 난다 my nose is bleeding

k'orŭk'ŭ 코르크 cork (*material*)

k'orŭk'ŭ magae 코르크 마개 cork (*in bottle*)

k'osŭ 코스 course, track

k'otkkumŏng 콧구멍 nostril

k'otppanggwi kkwida 콧방귀 뀌다 snort (*disdainfully*)

k'otppulsso 코뿔소 rhinoceros

k'otssori 콧소리 twang

k'otssuyŏm 콧수염 mustache

k'ot'inghan 코팅한 laminated

k'ot'ŭ 코트 court SP

k'ŭda 크다 be big

k'ŭge 크게 large ◊ very, highly; greatly; loudly; *k'ŭge ttŭn* 크게 뜬 wide-open; *k'ŭge ut-tta* 크게 웃다 roar with laughter

k'ŭge hada 크게 하다 enlarge

k'ŭgi 크기 size

k'ŭllaeshik 클래식 classical

k'ŭllarinet 클라리넷 clarinet

k'ŭllenjŏ 클렌저 cleanser

k'ŭllik 클릭 click

k'ŭllik'ada 클릭하다 click on

k'ŭllip 클립 clip; fastener

k'ŭllip-ppodŭ 클립보드 clipboard

k'ŭllŏch'i 클러치 clutch MOT

k'ŭllŏch'irŭl p'ulda 클러치를 풀다 declutch

k'ŭllojuŏp 클로즈업 close-up

k'ŭn 큰 big, large

k'ŭngk'ŭnggŏrida 킁킁거리다 sniff

k'ŭn haengbok-kkam 큰 행복감 euphoria

k'ŭn saejang 큰 새장 aviary

k'ŭn ton 큰 돈 fortune; big money

k'ŭraek'ŏ 크래커 cracker

k'ŭreyong 크레용 crayon

k'ŭrim 크림 cream

k'ŭrim ch'ijŭ 크림 치즈 cream cheese

K'ŭrisŭmasŭ 크리스마스 Christmas

k'udet'a 쿠데타 coup

k'uk tchirŭda 쿡 찌르다 jab, poke

k'uk'i 쿠키 cookie

k'ŭllŏp 클럽 club

k'unghanŭn sori 쿵하는 소리 thud, thump

k'ungk'ung kŏt-tta 쿵쿵 걷다 tramp;

trudge
k'up'on 쿠폰 coupon
k'urisŭt'ŏl 크리스털 crystal (*glass*)
k'ushyŏn 쿠션 cushion
k'waehwalhada 쾌활하다 be lively, be vivacious
k'waejŏk'an 쾌적한 delightful
k'waesoktchŏng 쾌속정 speedboat
k'walk'wal hŭllŏnaoda 콸콸 흘러나오다 gush out
k'wang! 쾅! bang!; *munŭl k'wangk'wang tudŭrida* 문을 쾅쾅 두드리다 hammer at the door
k'wang pudich'ida 쾅 부딪히다 bang, hit
k'wang tach'ida 쾅 닫히다 bang, be slammed shut

k'wang tat-tta 쾅 닫다 bang, slam shut
k'wijŭ 퀴즈 quiz
k'wijŭ p'ŭro 퀴즈 프로 quiz program
k'wik'wihan 퀴퀴한 moldy, musty
k'yabare 캬바레 cabaret
k'yŏda 켜다 switch on *machine*
k'yŏit-tta 켜있다 be on (*of device*)
k'yŏjida 켜지다 be turned on (*of device*)
k'yŏlle 켤레 pair ◊ *countword for shoes and socks*
k'yŏn ch'aero tuda 켠 채로 두다 leave on *machine*
k'yu 큐 cue
k'yureit'ŏ 큐레이터 curator

L

...l ...ㄹ *future particle*
labendŏ 라벤더 lavender
ladiet'ŏ 라디에이터 radiator
ladio 라디오 radio
ladio pangsongguk 라디오 방송국
  radio station
laelli 랠리 rally
laem 램 RAM, random access
  memory
laep 랩 rap MUS
laept'ap 랩탑 laptop
lagŏ piŏ 라거 비어 lager
lago hanŭn kŏsŭn 라고 하는 것은
  so-called
laillak 라일락 lilac
laim 라임 lime (*fruit, tree*)
laim nokssaek 라임 녹색 limegreen
laining 라이닝 lining
lait'ŏ 라이터 lighter
lait'ŭkkŭp sŏnsu 라이트급 선수
  lightweight
lait'ŭ p'en 라이트 펜 light pen
lak 락 rock (music)
lakk'ŭllol 락큰롤 rock'n'roll
laksŭt'a 락스타 rock star
lak'et 라켓 racket
langdebu 랑데부 rendez-vous
lanjeri 란제리 lingerie
laundŭ 라운드 round
launji 라운지 lounge
Laosŭ 라오스 Laos ◊ Laotian
leiausŭl hada 레이아웃을 하다 lay
  out
leida 레이다 radar
leida yŏngsang 레이더 영상 blip
leijyŏ 레이저 laser
leijyŏ kwangsŏn 레이저 광선 laser
  beam
leijyŏ p'urint'ŏ 레이저 프린터 laser
  printer
leisŭ 레이스 lace
lejŏ sent'ŏ 레저 센터 leisure center
lejŭbiŏn 레즈비언 lesbian
lek'odŭ 레코드 record

lemon 레몬 lemon
lemon chussŭ 레몬 주스 lemon juice
lemonch'a 레몬차 lemon tea
lemoneidŭ 레모네이드 lemonade
lench'i 렌치 wrench
lenjŭ 렌즈 lens
lenjŭ k'ong 렌즈 콩 lentil
lenjŭ k'ong süp'ŭ 렌즈 콩 스프
  lentil soup
lenjŭ ttukkŏng 렌즈뚜껑 lens cover
lep'ot'ŭ 레포트 essay
lesŭlling 레슬링 wrestling
lesŭlling kyŏnggi 레슬링 경기
  wrestling bout
lesŭlling sŏnsu 레슬링 선수 wrestler
Libia 리비아 Libya ◊ Libyan
libon 리본 ribbon
libon maedŭp 리본 매듭 bow, knot
lidŭm 리듬 rhythm
lihŏsŏl 리허설 practice; rehearsal
lihŏsŏrhada 리허설하다 rehearse
lik'odŏ 리코더 recorder
lik'yurŭ 리큐르 liqueur
lil 릴 reel
limp'ŭsaem 림프샘 lymph gland
limujin 리무진 limo, limousine
linen 리넨 linen
ling 링 ring
linssŭhada 린스하다 rinse
lipssŭt'ik 립스틱 lipstick
lisait'ŭl 리사이틀 recital
lisepsshyŏn p'at'i 리셉션 파티
  reception
lishibŏ 리시버 receiver (*in tennis*)
lit'ŏ 리터 liter
lit'ŭribŏ 리트리버 retriever (*dog*)
lŏm 럼 rum
lŏmp'ŭ sŭt'eik'ŭ 럼프 스테이크
  rumpsteak
Lŏndŏn 런던 London
lŏning shyŏch'ŭ 러닝 셔츠
  undershirt
lŏp'ŭ 러프 rough (*in golf*)
Lŏshia 러시아 Russia ◊ Russian

Lŏshiain 러시아인 Russian (*person*)

Lŏshiaŏ 러시아어 Russian (*language*)

lobi 로비 lobby

lobot 로봇 robot

lodŭhada 로드하다 load

logo 로고 logo

lok'et 로켓 (space) rocket

lok'ŏ 로커 locker

lol 롤 roll (*of film*)

lollŏ k'osŭt'ŏ 롤러 코스터 roller coaster

lollŏ pŭlleidŭ 롤러 블레이드 roller blade

lollŏ sŭk'eit'ŭ 롤러 스케이트 roller skate

lolppang 롤빵 (bread) roll

lom 롬 ROM, read only memory

lomaensŭ 로맨스 romance; affair

lomaent'ik'ada 로맨틱하다 be romantic

lomaent'ik'an 로맨틱한 romantic

Loma K'at'ollik 로마 카톨릭 Roman Catholic

Loma K'at'ollik-kkyoŭi 로마 카톨릭교의 Roman Catholic

loshyŏn 로션 lotion

lot'ŏri 로터리 traffic circle

loyŏlt'i 로열티 royalty (*on book, recording*)

lubi 루비 ruby

lullet 룰렛 roulette

lum meit'ŭ 룸 메이트 room mate

lum ssŏbissŭ 룸 서비스 room service

lyumat'ijŭm 류마티즘 rheumatism

M

ma 마 jinx, bad luck
mabi 마비 paralysis
mabishik'ida 마비시키다 paralyze
mabŏbe kŏllin 마법에 걸린
  spellbound, enraptured
mabŏbŭi 마법의 occult
mabŏp 마법 the occult; witchcraft
mabŏpsa 마법사 wizard
mabu 마부 groom (*for horse*)
mach'al 마찰 friction
mach'i ...ch'ŏrŏm 마치 ...처럼 as
  though
mach'ida 마치다 end, finish
mach'im 마침 just, exactly
mach'imnae 마침내 finally, at last
mach'imp'yo 마침표 period
  (*punctuation mark*)
mach'ŏllu 마천루 skyscraper
mach'wihada 마취하다 drug
mach'wije 마취제 anesthetic
mach'wisa 마취사 anesthetist
madi 마디 joint; word; phrase;
  ...wa/kwa handu madi marhada
  ...와/과 한두 마디 말하다 have a
  word with
madit'usŏng-iin 마디투성이인
  gnarled
madŏbodŭ 마더보드 motherboard
mae 매 hawk
mae- 매 each, every
maeaehago ulda 매애하고 울다
  bleat
maebok 매복 ambush
maech'e 매체 medium, vehicle
maech'un 매춘 prostitution
maech'unbu 매춘부 prostitute
maech'un-gul 매춘굴 brothel
maeda 매다 knot; tether; tie up
maedalda 매달다 suspend, hang;
  mok maedalda 목 매달다 hang
  person
maedallida 매달리다 cling to
maedalmada 매달마다 monthly
maedarŭi 매달의 monthly

maedogyŏn 맹도견 seeing-eye dog
maedok 매독 syphilis
maedŭp 매듭 knot; decorative tassle
maegagin 매각인 vendor
maehok 매혹 charm; magnetism
maehoksshik'ida 매혹시키다
  fascinate
maehoktchŏgin 매혹적인 charming;
  ravishing; fascinating
maehokttoeda 매혹되다 be
  fascinated by
maehok'ada 매혹하다 charm
maehyŏng 매형 brother-in-law
  (*man's elder sister's husband*)
maeil 매일 every day
maeil maeil kyesok'aesŏ 매일 매일
  계속해서 day in, day out
maeil pame 매일 밤에 nightly
maeiptcha 매입자 purchaser
maeirŭi 매일의 daily
maejang 매장 department (*of store*);
  outlet; burial
maejangmul 매장물 deposit
maejil 매질 beating, hiding
maejindoen 매진된 out of stock
maejŏk'ijŭm 매저키즘 masochism
maejŏk'isŭt'ŭ 매저키스트 masochist
maejŏm 매점 bookstall
maejŏmhada 매점하다 buy up
maejŏnghan 매정한 heartless,
  pitiless
maeju 매주 every week
maejumada 매주마다 weekly
maeju-ŭi 매주의 weekly
makttaehada 막대하다 be huge
maekkŭrŏptta 매끄럽다 be smooth
maekppak 맥박 throb, pulse
maekppak chojŏnggi 맥박 조정기
  pacemaker
maektchu 맥주 beer
maek'ŭro 매크로 macro
maemae 매매 marketing ◊ for sale
maemae changso 매매 장소
  market-place

maemaeshijang 매매시장 market

maemdom 맴돔 curl

maen araetchok 맨 아래쪽 bottom

maenbarida 맨발이다 be barefoot

maeng-in 맹인 the blind

Maengja 맹자 Mencius

maengjang 맹장 appendix

maengjangnyŏm 맹장염 appendicitis

maengnyŏrhan sokttoro 맹렬한 속도로 at a furious pace

maengnyŏrhi pinanhada 맹렬히 비난하다 hit out at, criticize

maengsehada 맹세하다 swear, promise

maengtchŏm 맹점 blind spot

maenik'yuŏ 매니큐어 manicure; nail polish

maenik'yuŏ chiunŭn yak 매니큐어 지우는 약 nail polish remover

maen katchok 맨 가쪽 bottom

maenmaru 맨마루 bare floor

maen mitppadagŭi 맨 밑바닥의 bottom; lowest

maen twittchogŭi 맨 뒷쪽의 rearmost

maenwiŭi 맨위의 top

maenyŏn 매년 yearly

maenyŏnŭi 매년의 yearly

maenyuŏl 매뉴얼 manual

maepok'ayŏ sŭpkkyŏk'ada 매복하여 습격하다 ambush

maepsshi innŭn 맵시있는 spruce, neat

maeptta 맵다 be hot, be spicy

maep'yogyewŏn 매표계원 booking clerk

maep'yoso 매표소 box office, ticket office

maeryŏginnŭn 매력있는 attractive

maeryŏgi nŏmch'inŭn 매력이 넘치는 glamorous

maeryŏk 매력 appeal, attraction

maeryŏktchŏgin 매력적인 engaging; seductive; cute

maeryodoen 매료된 entranced

maeryohada 매료하다 enchant

maesanggo 매상고 turnover, takings

maesang-ŭl ollida 매상을 올리다 turn over FIN

maeshit'ŭ p'ot'eit'o 매시트 포테이토 mashed potatoes

maesŏun 매서운 severe, strict; piercing

maesŭk'ŏm 매스컴 the media

maesŭk'ŏmŭi kwajang 매스컴의 과장 media hype

maesuhada 매수하다 bribe; corrupt

maet-tta 맺다 form, establish

maet'ŭ 매트 mat

maet'ŭrisŭ 매트리스 mattress

maeu 매우 most, tremendously

maeun 매운 hot, spicy

maeunt'ang 매운탕 spicy fish soup

maewŏl 매월 every month

maeyŏn 매연 fumes

magae 마개 plug

magaerŭl ppoptta 마개를 뽑다 uncork

magaerŭl yŏlda 마개를 열다 unscrew

magamil 마감일 deadline (*day*)

magamshigan 마감시간 deadline (*hour*)

maganaeda 막아내다 keep away, ward off

magarin 마가린 margarine

magi 막이 screen, shield

magu charada 마구 자라다 run wild

magu chitppalp'ida 마구 짓밟히다 be trampled underfoot

magujabiŭi 마구잡이의 haphazard

magutkkan 마구간 stable

magu toradanida 마구 돌아다니다 travel; wander

magu ttaerida 마구 때리다 thrash

magu tudŭlgyŏ p'aeda 마구 두들겨 패다 beat, knock around

magu tudŭrida 마구 두드리다 pound on, hammer on

magwŏnŏptcha 마권업자 bookmaker

magyŏnhan 막연한 indefinable

mahŭn 마흔 forty

mahŭn pŏntchaeŭi 마흔 번째의 fortieth

maik'ŭroch'ip 마이크로칩 microchip

maik'ŭrop'illŭm 마이크로필름 microfilm

maik'ŭrop'ŭrosesŏ 마이크로프로세서 microprocessor

maik'ŭ 마이크 mike, microphone
mail 마일 mile
mail su 마일 수 mileage
majak 마작 mah-jong
majayo! 맞아요! that's it!, that's right!
maji 맏이 the eldest
majihada 맞이하다 meet with
majijak-kkŏrida 만지작거리다 fiddle (around) with
majimagesŏ tu pŏntchae 마지막에서 두 번째 second to last, penultimate
majimagŭi 마지막의 final, last
majimagŭro 마지막으로 finally, lastly
majimak 마지막 last
majimak sudanŭro 마지막 수단으로 as a last resort
majimak sun-gane 마지막 순간에 at the last moment, at the eleventh hour
maji mot'ae 마지 못해 reluctantly
majiro t'aeŏnan 맏이로 태어난 first-born, eldest
majok'ago innŭn 만족하고 있는 contented
majŭl li ŏpssŏ 맞을 리 없어 that can't be right
majuboda 마주보다 face
majuch'ida 마주치다 meet
majuhada 마주하다 confront, face
majungnagada 마중나가다 collect, meet
majung naoda 마중 나오다 pick up, collect
mak 막 membrane; slick; curtain; act
mak haryŏgo hada 막 하려고 하다 be on the point of; *nanŭn mak ttŏnaryŏdŏn ch'amiŏssŏyo* 나는 막 떠나려던 참이었어요 I was just about to leave
mak-kkan 막간 interlude
mak-kkŏlli 막걸리 rice wine
makkwŏnŏptcha 마권업자 bookie
makssa 막사 barracks
makssangmak'ae irŭda 막상막하에 이르다 draw level
maksshimhan 막심한 heavy
maktta 막다 block; contain; hold back; prevent
makttae 막대 rod, stick

makttaegi 막대기 bar, stick
makttaegi sat'ang 막대기 사탕 lollipop
makttaehan 막대한 huge, incalculable
makttarŭda 막다르다 be closed off
makttarŭn kil 막다른 길 cul-de-sac
makttarŭn kolmok 막다른 골목 blind alley
mak'ida 막히다 clog up
mak'ige hada 막히게 하다 clog up
mak'im 막힘 congestion
mak'yŏ innŭn kŏt 막혀있는 것 blockage
mal 말 horse; piece (*in board game*); end; word; *idal mare* 이달 말에 at the end of this month; *ch'irwŏl mal* 칠월 말 at the end of July
malbŏl 말벌 wasp; hornet
malch'amgyŏnhada 말참견하다 chip in, interrupt
malda 말다 stop; *kŭnŭn kŭgose salge toego marat-tta* 그는 그곳에 살게 되고 말았다 he finished up living there; *hwanaeji mallagu* 화내지 말라구 don't get angry
maldaekkuhada 말대꾸하다 answer back
maldat'um 말다툼 disagreement, squabble
maldat'umhada 말다툼하다 argue, squabble, bicker
maldŏdŭm 말더듬 stammer
maldo andoenda! 말도 안된다! that's out of the question!
maldo an toenŭn sori 말도 안 되는 소리 nonsense
malgajida 맑아지다 settle; brighten up
malgŭm 맑음 brightness; clearness
malgŭn 맑은 clear; pure; fine
malgup 말굽 horseshoe
malgwallyang-i 말괄량이 tomboy
malkkŭmhan 말끔한 trim, neat
malktta 맑다 be clear; be clean; be honest
Malleiŏ 말레이어 Malay (*language*)
Malleishia 말레이시아 Malaysia ◊ Malaysian
Malleishia saram 말레이시아 사람 Malay (*person*)

mallida 말리다 dry; dissuade; break up *fight*

mallin 말린 dried *fruit etc*

mallin chadu 말린 자두 prune

mallo wihyŏp'ada 말로 위협하다 browbeat

malssŏng 말썽 disturbance, trouble; *malssŏng-ŭl purida* 말썽을 부리다 cause trouble, make a fuss

malssŏng-i nada 말썽이 나다 get into trouble

malssŏngkkun 말썽꾼 troublemaker

malsso 말소 deletion

malssuga chŏgŭn 말수가 적은 reserved

malssuk'aejida 말쑥해지다 clean up, wash

malssuk'age hada 말쑥하게 하다 smarten up

malttuguro chijihada 말뚝으로 지지하다 stake, support

malttuk 말뚝 stake, peg

malttuk ult'ari 말뚝 울타리 picket fence

malt'u 말투 speech, way of speaking

Malŭk'ŭsŭjuŭi 마르크스주의 Marxism

mamalleidŭ 마말레이드 marmalade

mamurihada 마무리하다 finalize, round off

man 만 bay, inlet; gulf; ten thousand ◊ *after* ◊ only, just

manaya 많아야 at (the) most

manbarhada 만발하다 come into full bloom

manch'an 만찬 dinner; feast

manch'an sonnim 만찬 손님 dinner guest

manch'wihan 만취한 drunken

mandŭlda 만들다 ◊ establish, create, form, make ◊ (*causative*): *...ge mandŭlda* ...게 만들다 make

mandu 만두 stuffed dumpling

manek'ing 마네킹 mannequin (*for clothes*)

mang-aji 망아지 colt

mangboda 망보다 keep watch

mangbogi 망보기 lookout

mangch'i 망치 hammer

mangch'ida 망치다 destroy; ruin; spoil

mangch'ijirhada 망치질하다 hammer

mangch'yŏnot'a 망쳐놓다 mess up, spoil; *sŏt'urŭge haesŏ mangch'yŏbŏrida* 서투르게 해서 망쳐버리다 botch, bungle

manggattŭrida 망가뜨리다 ruin

manghada 망하다 fail, fold

man-gi 만기 termination

man-gidoeda 만기되다 expire

man-giga toeda 만기가 되다 mature; run out

mangmyŏng 망명 exile, asylum

mangmyŏngja 망명자 exile (*person*)

mangnani 망나니 bum (*person*)

man-gok 만곡 bend, sweep

mangsa k'ŏt'ŭn 망사 커튼 net curtain

mangsang 망상 myth

mangshinshik'ida 망신시키다 shame, bring dishonor on

mangsŏrida 망설이다 hesitate; *tu taean saiesŏ mangsŏrida* 두 대안 사이에서 망설이다 be torn between two alternatives

mangsŏrim 망설임 hesitation

mang-wŏn-gyŏng 망원경 telescope

mang-wŏn lenjŭ 망원 렌즈 telephoto lens

manhada 만하다 be worth; deserve to; *ilgŭl/pol manhada* 읽을 / 볼 만하다 be worth reading/seeing; *chumŏngmanhan tol* 주먹만한 돌 a rock the size of your fist

manhwa 만화 cartoon

manhwa chaptchi 만화 잡지 comic (book)

manhwa ch'aek 만화 책 comic book

manhwaran 만화란 comics; comic strip

manhwa yŏnghwa 만화 영화 cartoon

mani 많이 a lot, lots, a good deal; much; *aju mani* 아주 많이 very much; *mani tŭseyo* 많이 드세요 please help yourself; enjoy

manjang-ilch'ihada 만장일치하다 be unanimous on

manjang-ilch'iro 만장일치로 unanimously

manjang-ilch'iŭi 만장일치의

unanimous
manjida 만지다 touch, feel
manjijak-kkŏrida 만지작거리다 meddle with, tinker with
manjo 만조 high tide
manjok 만족 satisfaction, contentment; pleasure; *muŏsesŏ manjogŭl nŭkkida* 무엇에서 만족을 느끼다 get satisfaction out of sth
manjok-kkam 만족감 feeling of satisfaction, fulfillment
manjoksshik'ida 만족시키다 satisfy, gratify
manjoksshik'igi 만족시키기 gratification
manjokssŭrŏun 만족스러운 adequate; fulfilling
manjok'ada 만족하다 be satisfied; content oneself with; feel fulfilled; *...ŭro manjok'ada* ...으로 만족하다 make do with
manjok'an 만족한 satisfactory; pleased
manjok'anŭn 만족하는 content
mank'ŭm 만큼 as; *...mank'ŭm chal hada* ...만큼 잘 하다 be as good as; measure up to; *...mank'ŭm mani* ...만큼 많이 as much as ...
mannada 만나다 meet, meet with; join
mannaeda 맛내다 flavor
mannal kwŏllirŭl kat-tta 만날 권리를 갖다 have access to *one's children*
mannam 만남 meeting
mannasŏ pan-gapssŭmnida 만나서 반갑습니다 pleased to meet you; glad to see you
mannŭn 맞는 correct, right; *kŭgŏsŭn uriŭi kyehoege tŭrŏ mannŭnda* 그것은 우리의 계획에 들어 맞는다 it fits in well with our plans
mannŭng 만능 versatility
mannŭng-ŭi 만능의 versatile, all-round
mannŭn saenghwarŭl hada 맞는 생활을 하다 live up to
mannyŏnp'il 만년필 (fountain) pen
mansa 만사 everything
mansa p'yŏnanhan 만사 편안한

hunky-dory
manse! 만세! hurray!
mansŏng-ŭi 만성의 chronic
mant'a 많다 be many
manŭl 마늘 garlic
manŭn 많은 many, a lot of, lots of; much; plenty of; heavy
manŭn chŏngdo 많은 정도 number, quantity
manŭn shigani kŏllinŭn 많은 시간이 걸리는 time-consuming
manura 마누라 wife
manyak ...myŏn 만약 ...면 if; on condition that; *manyak tarŭn hal iri ŏpttamyŏn* 만약 다른 할 일이 없다면 if you've got nothing else to do
manyŏ 마녀 witch
manyŏn 만연 spread; diffusion
manyŏn chashil 망연 자실 stupor
manyŏndoen 만연된 widespread
manyŏnhada 만연하다 spread
Map'ia chojik 마피아 조직 the Mafia
marat'on 마라톤 marathon
marhada 말하다 talk; speak; say; tell; *hago ship'ŭn marŭl hada* 하고 싶은 말을 하다 have one's say
marhagi choahanŭn 말하기 좋아하는 talkative; communicative
marhanŭn nŭngnyŏk 말하는 능력 speech (*ability to speak*)
marharyŏhada 말하려하다 get at; imply; mean
mari 마리 countword for animals
mari andwaeyo 말이 안돼요 not make sense
marihwana 마리화나 marijuana
mari manŭn 말이 많은 talkative
mari nan-gime 말이 난김에 incidentally
maronie yŏlmae 마로니에 열매 horse chestnut
marŭda 마르다 dry; waste away; run out (*of money*)
Marŭk'ŭsŭjuŭija 마르크스주의자 Marxist (*person*)
Marŭk'ŭsŭjuŭiŭi 마르크스주의의 Marxist
marŭl kkŏnaeda 말을 꺼내다 bring up, broach

marŭl kollasŏ ssŭda 말을 골라서 쓰다 put into words, formulate

marŭl ttokttok'i mot'anŭn 말을 똑똑히 못하는 inarticulate

marŭl tŭt-tchi annŭn 말을 듣지 않는 disobedient

marŭl t'ago 말을 타고 on horseback

marŭmjil 마름질 cut

marŭmmokkol 마름모꼴 lozenge

marŭn 마른 dry; thin

marŭn haengju 마른 행주 tea cloth, dishcloth

maru 마루 brow

maru kŏlle 마루 걸레 floor cloth

marutppadak 마룻바닥 floor

maryŏk 마력 horsepower

maryŏnhada 마련하다 lay on, provide

masaji 마사지 massage

mashi chinhan 맛이 진한 rich

mashida 마시다 drink

mashil su innŭn 마실 수 있는 drinkable

mashimaello 마시맬로 marshmallow

mashinnŭn 맛있는 tasty, delicious

mashinŭn mul 마시는 물 drinking water

mashitkke tŭseyo! 맛있게 드세요! enjoy!

mashyŏbŏrida 마셔버리다 consume, drink

masŭk'ara 마스카라 mascara

masŭk'ot'ŭ 마스코트 mascot

masul 마술 magic; conjuring tricks

masuljŏgin 마술적인 magical

masulssa 마술사 magician, conjurer

masurŭi 마술의 magic

mat 맛 flavor, taste; *ammu mat ŏmnŭn* 아무 맛 없는 tasteless *food*

match'uda 맞추다 adjust; fit together; be fitting; be appropriate; *ch'aenŏrŭl match'uda* 채널을 맞추다 tune in; *kŭe match'uŏ* 그에 맞추어 accordingly, appropriately

match'ugi 맞추기 justify *text*

match'umbŏp kŏmsagi 맞춤법 검사기 spell checker

match'um k'ap'et 맞춤 카펫 wall-to-wall carpet

match'um puŏk 맞춤 부엌 fitted kitchen

match'umŭi 맞춤의 custom-made, tailor-made

match'uŏ not'a 맞추어 놓다 set; adjust

matkkida 맡기다 entrust

matpakkuda 맞바꾸다 exchange

matppadach'igi 맞받아치기 tit for tat

matpparam 맞바람 headwind

matppoda 맛보다 taste, sample

matpput'ŏ ssauda 맞붙어 싸우다 grapple with

matssŏda 맞서다 meet, confront, stand up to; oppose

mattakttŭrida 맞닥뜨리다 meet with

mattanghage 마땅하게 justly, deservedly

mattanghan 마땅한 due, proper

mattanghan shillangkkam 마땅한 신랑감 eligible bachelor

mat-tchi ant'a 맞지 않다 be alien to

mat-tta 맞다 be right; fit, go in; take on *job*; suit; match; strike, hit; meet; be exposed to; encounter; be struck by; get, have; *mat-tchiyo?* 맞지요? that's right, isn't it?; *chal mat-tta* 잘 맞다 it's a good fit

mat-ttakttŭrida 맞닥뜨리다 encounter

maŭl 마을 village

maŭl saram 마을 사람 villager

maŭm 마음 heart; mind; spirit; *kŭgŏshi maŭme kŏllyŏssŏyo* 그것이 마음에 걸렸어요 it has been on my conscience; *maŭmi t'onghaetkkunyo!* 마음이 통했군요! you must be telepathic!; *hyŏmnyŏktchŏgin maŭmŭro* 협력적인 마음으로 in a spirit of cooperation; *maŭm p'yŏnhage saenggak'ae!* 마음 편하게 생각해! relax!

maŭmdaero 마음대로: *nuguŭi maŭmdaero toeda* 누구의 마음대로 되다 be at s.o.'s mercy; *muŏsŭl maŭmdaero hada* 무엇을 마음대로 하다 be at liberty to do sth; *maŭmdaero haseyo!* 마음대로 하세요! do what you like!, suit yourself!; *Xŭl/rŭl Yŭi maŭmdaero ssŭge hada* X을/를 Y의 마음대로

쓰게 하다 put X at Y's disposal

maŭme mannŭn 마음에 맞는 congenial, pleasant

maŭme p'umtta 마음에 품다 harbor *grudge*

maŭme tŭlda 마음에 들다 be to s.o.'s liking

maŭme tuda 마음에 두다 mind, heed

maŭmi chobŭn 마음이 좁은 narrow-minded

maŭmi mŏrŏjida 마음이 멀어지다 drift apart (*emotionally*)

maŭmi naek'iji annŭn 마음이 내키지 않는 half-hearted; disinclined; listless

maŭmi nŏlbŭn 마음이 넓은 liberal, broad-minded

maŭmi nugŭrŏjida 마음이 누그러지다 relent

maŭmi ŏjirŏun 마음이 어지러운 disturbed, concerned, worried

maŭm kabyŏun 마음 가벼운 light-hearted

maŭmkkŏt tŭlda 마음껏 들다 help oneself

maŭm soge ttŏollida 마음 속에 떠올리다 visualize

maŭmsoguro 마음속으로 inwardly; privately; mentally

maŭmsshi koun 마음씨 고운 kind-hearted

maŭmŭi 마음의 mental

maŭmŭi sangch'ŏrŭl ibŭn 마음의 상처를 입은 broken-hearted

maŭmŭl chŏnghada 마음을 정하다 make up one's mind

maŭmŭl karaanch'ida 마음을 가라앉히다 pull oneself together, compose oneself

maŭmŭl ŏjirŏp'ida 마음을 어지럽히다 disturb, upset

maŭmŭl ŏjirŏp'inŭn 마음을 어지럽히는 disturbing, upsetting

maŭmŭl pakkuda 마음을 바꾸다 change one's mind

maŭmŭl pakkuge hada 마음을 바꾸게 하다 cause to change his/her mind

maŭmŭl p'yŏnhi noch'i mot'ada 마음을 편히 놓지 못하다 feel ill at ease

maŭmŭl sanghage hada 마음을 상하게 하다 hurt *feelings*

maŭmŭl sarojaptta 마음을 사로잡다 captivate, enthrall

maŭmŭl t'ŏnot'a 마음을 터놓다 come out of one's shell

maundŭ 마운드 mound (*in baseball*)

mausŭ 마우스 mouse COMPUT

mausŭ maet'ŭ 마우스 매트 mouse mat

mayagŭl hada 마약을 하다 be on drugs

mayak 마약 narcotic, drug; dope

mayak kŏrae 마약 거래 drug trafficking

mayak milmaehada 마약 밀매하다 push *drugs*

mayak milmaeja 마약 밀매자 pusher (*of drugs*)

mayak p'anmaeja 마약 판매자 drug dealer

mayak sang-yongja 마약 상용자 drug addict

mayak tansokppan 마약 단속반 narcotics agent

mayak tillŏ 마약 딜러 (drug) dealer

mayonejŭ 마요네즈 mayo, mayonnaise

meari 메아리 echo

medal 메달 medal

medŭlli 메들리 medley

megabait'ŭ 메가바이트 megabyte

meilbakssŭ 메일박스 mailbox

meilmŏji 메일머지 mail merge

meinbodŭ 메인보드 mainboard

Meksshik'o 멕시코 Mexico ◊ Mexican

melodi 멜로디 melody

melodŭramagat'ŭn 멜로드라마같은 melodramatic

melon 멜론 melon

melppang 멜빵 suspenders (*for pants*)

melppang paji 멜빵 바지 dungarees

memo 메모 note; memo

memojich'ŏp 메모지첩 notepad

memori 메모리 memory COMPUT

menyu 메뉴 menu *also* COMPUT

Meri K'ŭrisŭmasŭ 메리 크리스마스! Merry Christmas!

mesiji 메시지 message
mesŭkkŏun 메스꺼운 repulsive
mettugi 메뚜기 grasshopper; locust
meuda 메우다 fill in
mianhae 미안해 (I'm) sorry
mianhamnida 미안합니다 *fml* (I'm) sorry
mibongjŏgŭro koch'ida 미봉적으로 고치다 patch up
mibul 미불 nonpayment
miburŭi 미불의 outstanding *payment*
mich'ida 미치다 become insane; be crazy; reach; happen; match
mich'idŭshi choahada 미치듯이 좋아하다 be mad about, be enthusiastic about
mich'igwang-i 미치광이 lunatic, madman
mich'il tŭshi hwanage hada 미칠 듯이 화나게 하다 madden, infuriate, drive crazy
mich'il tŭshi hwanan 미칠 듯이 화난 mad, angry
mich'il tŭt'an 미칠 듯한 distraught
mich'in 미친 insane, mad, crazy
mich'in tŭshi 미친 듯이 madly, like mad
mich'in tŭt'an 미친 듯한 wild, crazy, frantic
mich'ŏribun 미처리분 backlog
mich'yŏgada 미쳐가다 become insane, go mad
midaji mun 미닫이 문 sliding door
midiŏ 미디어 media
midŏjiji annŭn 믿어지지 않는 incredible, amazing, very good
midŭl manhan 믿을 만한 credible, believable
midŭl su ŏmnŭn 믿을 수 없는 unbelievable; unreliable
midŭm 믿음 belief
midŭng 미등 tail light
migaein 미개인 savage
migaeji 미개지 the wilds
migak 미각 taste (*sense*); palate
Migugin 미국인 American (*person*)
Miguk 미국 USA, America ◊ American
Miguk chung-ang chŏngbobu 미국 중앙 정보부 CIA, Central Intelligence Agency

Miguk kukppangssŏng 미국 국방성 the Pentagon
Miguk nŏguri 미국 너구리 raccoon
Miguk saram 미국 사람 American (*person*)
migyŏltcheŭi 미결제의 unsettled, unpaid
mihaenghada 미행하다 follow, dog
Mihaptchungguk 미합중국 United States of America
mihonŭi 미혼의 unmarried
mijigŭnhan 미지근한 lukewarm, tepid
mijiroŭi yŏhaeng 미지로의 여행 journey into the unknown
mikki 미끼 bait
mikkirŭl mulda 미끼를 물다 bite (*of fish*); get a bite
mikkŭrŏjida 미끄러지다 slip, slither, skid
mikkŭrŏjiji annŭn 미끄러지지 않는 nonslip, nonskid
mikkŭrŏjim 미끄러짐 slip
mikkŭrŏm 미끄럼 skid
mikkŭrŏmt'ŭl 미끄럼틀 slide
mikkŭrŏpkke hada 미끄럽게 하다 lubricate
mikkŭrŏptta 미끄럽다 be smooth; be slippery, be slick
mikkŭrŏun 미끄러운 slippery
mikkŭrojida 미끄러지다 slide, glide
mikssŏ 믹서 food mixer
mikssŏgi 믹서기 blender
mil 밀 wheat
milbong 밀봉 seal
milbonghada 밀봉하다 seal
milda 밀다 push, shove
milgam 밀감 tangerine
milgi 밀기 pushing
milgoja 밀고자 informer
milgo kada 밀고 가다 push along
milkkaru 밀가루 flour
milkkaru panjuk 밀가루 반죽 dough, pastry; batter
milk'ŭ chyok'ollit 밀크 쵸콜릿 milk chocolate
milk'ŭ shweik'ŭ 밀크 쉐이크 milk shake
milligŭraem 밀리그램 milligram
millim 밀림 jungle
millimit'ŏ 밀리미터 millimeter

millyŏdŭnŭn p'ado 밀려드는 파도 surf

millyŏ it-tta 밀려있다 be behind with; be backed up

millyŏnagada 밀려나가다 surge forward

millyŏp'ada 밀렵하다 poach *rabbits etc*

milmul 밀물 incoming tide

milmurida 밀물이다 the tide is out

milsshil kongp'otchŭng 밀실 공포증 claustrophobia

milssu 밀수 smuggling

milssuhada 밀수하다 smuggle; traffic in

milssuŏptcha 밀수업자 smuggler

miltchip 밀짚 straw (*of wheat etc*)

miltchip chiyŏk 밀집 지역 crowded area

miltchip'an 밀집한 dense

miman 미만 under, below; less than

mimang-ini toen 미망인이 된 widowed

mimyohan 미묘한 subtle, delicate

mimyoham 미묘함 delicacy

minapkkŭm 미납금 arrears

minap'ada 미납하다 be in arrears

minbak 민박 vacation home

minbang-wi 민방위 civil defense

minch'ŏp'an 민첩한 snappy

mindalp'aeng-i 민달팽이 slug

min-gamhada 민감하다 be sensitive

min-gamham 민감함 sensitivity

min-gane ŭihae 민간에 의해 privately

min-ganin 민간인 civilian

min-gan pangsong 민간 방송 commercial television

min-gan pumun 민간 부문 private sector

min-ganŭi 민간의 civil

min-gan yoppŏp 민간 요법 folk medicine

mingk'ŭ 밍크 mink (*fur*)

mingk'ŭ k'ot'ŭ 밍크 코트 mink (coat)

minhwa 민화 folk painting

mini sŭk'ot'ŭ 미니 스커트 miniskirt

minjogŭi 민족의 ethnic

minjok 민족 people; race; tribe

minjokchipttan 민족집단 ethnic group

minjoktchuŭi 민족주의 nationalism

Minju Chayudang 민주 자유당 Democratic Liberal Party

Minjudang 민주당 Democratic Party

minjudang chijija 민주당 지지자 democrat

Minjudang-wŏn 민주당원 Democrat

minjujuŭi 민주주의 democracy

minjujuŭija 민주주의자 democrat

minjujuŭiŭi 민주주의의 democratic

minjung shinhak 민중 신학 people's theology

minmurŭi 민물의 freshwater

minsok ch'um 민속 춤 folk dance

minsok ŭmak 민속 음악 folk music

mint'ŭ 민트 mint

mint'ŭ chyok'ollit 민트 쵸콜릿 mint

minyo 민요 folk song

minyo kasu 민요 가수 folk singer

mirae 미래 future; *miraeeŭi kyehoek/saenggak* 미래에의 계획/생각 plan/think ahead

miraehyŏngŭi 미래형의 futuristic

mirhanghada 밀항하다 stow away

mirhangja 밀항자 stowaway

miri 미리 beforehand, in advance

miribogi 미리보기 print preview COMPUT

miri haenghaejida 미리 행해지다 precede

miri mandŭrŏjyŏ innŭn 미리 만들어져 있는 ready-made

miri naeda 미리 내다 advance

miri sŏltchŏngdoen 미리 설정된 default (setting)

mirŏ chech'ida 밀어 제치다 push away

mirŏdakch'yŏ it-tta 밀어닥쳐 있다 be swamped with

mirŏnaeda 밀어내다 shove off, push off; pump

mirŏnŏt'a 밀어넣다 slide; cram

mirŏ puch'ida 밀어 붙이다 squeeze up

mirŏ umjigida 밀어 움직이다 wheel

miro 미로 maze

Mirŭkppul 미륵불 Maitreya Buddha

miruda 미루다 wait

misa 미사 mass

misaegŭi 미색의 off-white

misaengmure ŭihae punhaega toenŭn 미생물에 의해 분해가 되는 biodegradable

misail 미사일 missile

misayŏguŭi 미사여구의 flowery

misehan 미세한 fine

Mishik ch'uk-kku 미식 축구 (American) football

Mishik ch'uk-kku kyŏnggijang 미식 축구 경기장 gridiron

Mishik ch'uk-kku sŏnsu 미식 축구 선수 (American) football player

mishin 미신 superstition

mishinŭl minnŭn 미신을 믿는 superstitious

misŏngnyŏnja 미성년자 minor (*child*)

misŏngnyŏnjaida 미성년자이다 be underage

misŏngnyŏnŭi 미성년의 underage

misŏngsugŭi 미성숙의 immature

miso 미소 smile

misojit-tta 미소짓다 smile; smile at

misshik-kka 미식가 gourmet

misuga 미숙아 premature baby

misuk'an 미숙한 immature, juvenile; unskilled

misulga 미술가 artist, painter

misulgwan 미술관 art gallery

misungnyŏn nodongja 미숙련 노동자 unskilled labor

mit 밑 base, bottom

mitchul kŭt-tta 밑줄 긋다 underline

mitkkŭrim 밑그림 design

mitppadagŭro ttŏrŏjida 밑바닥으로 떨어지다 reach rock bottom

mitppadak 밑바닥 bottom, underside

mit-tta 믿다 believe

mit'e 밑에 underneath; *chang-ŭi / ŏndŏgŭi mit'e* 장의/언덕의 밑에 at the foot of the page / hill

mit'ing 미팅 meeting, session; blind date

mit'ŏ 미터 meter

mit'ŏppŏbŭi 미터법의 metric

mit'ŭ 미트 mitt

mit'ŭro tŏnjyŏ 밑으로 던져 underarm throwing

mium 미움 hate

miwallyo 미완료 imperfect

miwŏhada 미워하다 hate

miyak'an 미약한 feeble

miyak'an chinghu 미약한 징후 hint

miyongsa 미용사 beautician; hairdresser

miyongshil 미용실 beauty parlor

mŏdŏmnŭn 멋없는 tasteless

mŏgi 먹이 prey

mŏgida 먹이다 feed

mŏgirŭl chuda 먹이를 주다 feed

mŏgŏbŏrida 먹어버리다 consume, eat up

mŏgŏboda 먹어보다 try *food*

mŏgŏ ch'iuda 먹어 치우다 eat up

mŏgŭjan 머그잔 mug

mŏgŭl su innŭn 먹을 수 있는 edible

mŏgŭl su ŏmnŭn 먹을 수 없는 uneatable

mŏk-kkie chot'a 먹기에 좋다 nice to eat

mŏk-kko salda 먹고 살다 live on *food*

mŏktta 먹다 eat, have

mŏlda 멀다 be distant, be remote; be unskilled

mŏlli 멀리 far, far away ◊ remotely

mŏlli ttŏrŏjim 멀리 떨어짐 seclusion

mŏlli ttŏrŏjin 멀리 떨어진 far away, remote

mŏlli ttŏrŏjyŏ hanjŏk'an 멀리 떨어져 한적한 secluded

mŏlli ttŏrojyŏ it-tta 멀리 떨어져 있다 it's a long way off

mŏlli ttwigi 멀리 뛰기 broad jump, long jump

mŏlmiga chal nanŭn 멀미가 잘 나는 squeamish

mŏlt'imidiŏ 멀티미디어 multimedia

mŏmch'uda 멈추다 stop; stall; seize up; put a stop to

mŏmch'uge hada 멈추게 하다 stop, halt, bring to a standstill

mŏmch'ul su ŏmnŭn 멈출 수 없는 remorseless, relentless

mŏmch'um chŏngji 멈춤 정지 no stopping

mŏmch'um shinho 멈춤 신호 stop sign

mŏmch'un 멈춘 be at a standstill

mŏmullŏ it-tta 머물러 있다 stick around

mŏmurŭda 머무르다 stay
mŏn 먼 distant, remote
mŏng 멍 bruise
mŏngch'ŏng-i 멍청이 idiot, dope, jerk
mŏngdŭlda 멍들다 bruise
mŏngdŭlge hada 멍들게 하다 bruise
mŏngdŭn nun 멍든 눈 black eye
mŏng-e 멍에 yoke (*for oxen*)
mŏnghage hada 멍하게 하다 stupefy
mŏnghan 멍한 vacant, blank, absent-minded
mŏngk'i sŭp'aenŏ 멍키 스패너 monkey wrench
mŏngmŏng-i 멍멍이 doggie
mŏngnŭn p'iimyak 먹는 피임약 the (contraceptive) pill
mŏnji 먼지 dirt; grit; dust
mŏnji magi tŏpkkae 먼지 막이 덮개 dust cover
mŏnjirŭl t'ŏlda 먼지를 털다 dust
mŏnji tangnŭn hŏnggŏp 먼지 닦는 헝겊 duster
mŏnjit'usŏng-iŭi 먼지투성이의 dusty
mŏnjŏ 먼저 first
mŏnjŏtppŏnŭi 먼젓번의 past, former
mŏn kose(sŏ) 먼 곳에(서) in the distance
mŏp'in 머핀 muffin
mŏri 머리 head; hair; *mŏrirŭl tchada* 머리를 짜다 rack one's brains
mŏriga nappŭn 머리가 나쁜 not clever
mŏriga pŏtkkyŏjinŭn 머리가 벗겨지는 balding
mŏriga saltchak ton 머리가 살짝 돈 be slightly crazy
mŏrihyŏng 머리형 hairstyle, hairdo
mŏri indu 머리 인두 tongs
mŏri kamtta 머리 감다 shampoo
mŏrikkŭch'i tchuppyŏt'aejinŭn 머리끝이 쭈뼛해지는 hair-raising
mŏrik'arak 머리카락 hair
mŏri manŭn lol 머리 마는 롤 roller (*for hair*)
mŏrinmal 머릿말 header (*in text*)
mŏri patch'im 머리 받침 headrest
mŏrip'in 머리핀 hairpin
mŏriro pat-tta 머리로 받다 head *ball*; head-butt; bump one's head

mŏrirŭl charŭda 머리를 자르다 have a haircut, get one's hair cut
mŏrirŭl handae mat-tta 머리를 한대 맞다 get a bump on the head
mŏrirŭl sonjirhada 머리를 손질하다 have one's hair done
mŏri sŭk'ap'ŭ 머리 스카프 headscarf
mŏritkkajuk 머리가죽 scalp
mŏritkkisa 머릿기사 headline
mŏritkkisaro k'ŭge ch'wigŭpttoeda 머릿기사로 크게 취급되다 make the headlines
mŏshinnŭn 멋있는 stylish
mŏsŭl chal naenŭn 멋을 잘 내는 fashionable
mŏtchida 멋지다 be stylish
mŏtchige 멋지게 impeccably
mŏtchin 멋진 smart, elegant; stylish; nice, lovely
mŏt-tta 멎다 let up; stop
mo 모 countword for tofu
moanot'a 모아놓다 collect
mobang 모방 imitation, copying; copy
mobanghada 모방하다 imitate, copy
mobang pŏmjoe 모방 범죄 copycat crime
mobil 모빌 cell phone, *Br* mobile
mobŏmjŏgin 모범적인 exemplary
mobŏmŭi 모범의 model, perfect
modakppul 모닥불 camp fire
model 모델 model
modem 모뎀 modem
moderida 모델이다 be a model, model
moderŭl hada 모델을 하다 model *clothes*
modok 모독 violation
modok'ada 모독하다 violate; blaspheme
modŭ 모드 mode COMPUT
modŭn 모든 all; whole; every
modŭn kwanshimŭl ssot-tta 모든 관심을 쏟다 make a fuss of
modu 모두 everyone; all
mogi 모기 mosquito
mogihyang 모기향 mosquito coil
mogijang 모기장 mosquito net
mogi maeida 목이 매이다 choke
mogi marŭda 목이 마르다 be thirsty
mogi t'ada 목이 타다 be parched

mogong 모공 pore

mogŭl charŭda 목을 자르다 decapitate

mogŭl chorŭda 목을 조르다 choke

mogŭl kilge ppaeda 목을 길게 빼다 crane one's neck

mogŭl kkolttak-kkŏrida 목을 꼴딱거리다 gurgle

mogŭl ppida 목을 삐다 have a crick in the neck

mogugŏ 모국어 native language, mother tongue

moguk 모국 native country

mogyeŭi 모계의 maternal

mogyoil 목요일 Thursday

mogyok 목욕 bath

mogyok kaun 목욕 가운 bathrobe

mogyok sugŏn 목욕 수건 bath towel

mogyokt'ang 목욕탕 public bathhouse

mogyokt'ang kkalgae 목욕탕 깔개 bath mat

mogyok'ada 목욕하다 have a bath, bathe

mohŏm 모험 venture; adventure

mohŏmjŏk 모험적 adventurous

mohŏmŭl chŭlginŭn 모험을 즐기는 adventurous person

mohŏmŭl hada 모험을 하다 venture; take the plunge

mohoesa 모회사 parent company, holding company

mohohage 모호하게 vaguely

mohohan 모호한 vague

mohyŏng 모형 model, miniature; mock-up

mohyŏng-ŭi 모형의 model

moida 모이다 meet; congregate; accumulate

moim 모임 gathering

moirŭl tchoda 모이를 쪼다 pick at one's food

moisch'yŏraijŏ 모이스쳐라이저 moisturizer

moja 모자 hat

mojaik'ŭ 모자이크 mosaic

mojarada 모자라다 be short of, be wanting in; be stupid

mojaran 모자란 useless

mojaranŭn 모자라는 scarce; chigwŏni mojaranŭn 직원이

모자라는 short-staffed

mojik 모직 woolen

mojim 모짐 severity

mojin 모진 severe

mojingmul 모직물 woolen fabric

mojohada 모조하다 forge

mojo posŏngnyu 모조 보석류 costume jewelry

mojop'um 모조품 imitation

mojori 모조리 without exception; completely

mok 목 neck; throat

mok 몫 share, quota

mokch'oji 목초지 field

mokch'ugŏptcha 목축업자 stockbreeder

mok-kkŏri 목걸이 necklace, pendant

mok-kkŏrijul 목걸이줄 chain (jewelry)

mok-kkong 목공 woodwork

mok-kkwanak-kki 목관악기 woodwind

mok-kkyŏktcha 목격자 (eye)witness

mok-kkyŏk'ada 목격하다 witness

mokkumŏng 목구멍 throat

mokp'yo 목표 objective, goal, target

mokp'yo kŭrup 목표 그룹 target group

mokp'yo magamil 목표 마감일 target date

mokp'yoro hada 목표로 하다 target

mokp'yoro samtta 목표로 삼다 aim at; aim to

mok sat'ang 목 사탕 throat lozenges

mokssa 목사 priest

moksshwin 목쉰 hoarse

mokssŏn 목선 neckline

mokssori 목소리 voice, tone of voice; k'ŭn mokssoriro 큰 목소리로 in a loud voice

mokssu 목수 joiner, carpenter

moktchae 목재 timber

moktchang 목장 ranch

moktchangju 목장주 rancher

moktchŏgŏ 목적어 object GRAM

moktchŏk 목적 objective, aim; ...l moktchŏgŭro ...ㄹ목적으로 with a view to

moktchŏktchi 목적지 destination

moktcho pubun 목조 부분 woodwork, wooden part

153 **morŭp'in**

moktchorŭda 목조르다 throttle
mokttari 목다리 crutch
mokttŏlmi 목덜미 nape of the neck
mokttori 목도리 scarf, muffler
mokt'an 목탄 charcoal
molda 몰다 drive
molgo tanida 몰고 다니다 kick
around
mollae 몰래 secretly, privately;
furtively
mollae hanŭn 몰래 하는 stealthy
mollae pekkida 몰래 베끼다
(secretly) copy
mollak 몰락 comedown; downfall
Molmon-gyo 몰몬교 Mormonism
molttudoen 몰두된 engrossed in
molttuhada 몰두하다 immerse
oneself in; *ire molttuhada* 일에
몰두하다 bury oneself in work
molttuhan 몰두한 preoccupied,
absorbed
mom 몸 body; *onmomi ssushida*
온몸이 쑤시다 it hurts all over
momburimch'ida 몸부림치다 writhe,
thrash about; struggle
mome kkok mannŭn 몸에 꼭 맞는
skin-tight
momi choch'i anŭn 몸이 좋지 않은
unwell, poorly
momi chot'a 몸이 좋다 feel well
momi pulp'yŏnhan 몸이 불편한
indisposed, unwell
momi tchibudŭdŭhada 몸이
찌부드드하다 be feeling under the
weather
momjorishik'ida 몸조리시키다 take
good care of
momkkap 몸값 ransom
mommae 몸매 figure, physique
mommae ch'itssu 몸매 치수 vital
statistics
momsŏrich'ida 몸서리치다 shudder
momsusaek'ada 몸수색하다 frisk
momtchibi chagŭn 몸집이 작은
petite
momtchit ŏnŏ 몸짓 언어 body
language
momttung-i 몸뚱이 trunk
momŭi 몸의 bodily
momŭl kuburida 몸을 구부리다
slouch; crouch

momŭl umsshirhada 몸을 움씰하다
cringe
momŭro 몸으로 bodily
momyŏnhada 모면하다 escape;
avoid, evade
monaegi 모내기 rice planting
Monggo 몽고 Mongolia ◊
Mongolian
mongmarŭda 목마르다 be thirsty
mongmarŭn 목마른 thirsty
mongnoge ollida 목록에 올리다 list,
put on a list
mongnok 목록 list, roll, inventory
mongnyuppyŏngja 몽유병자 sleep
walker
mongsangga 몽상가 (day)dreamer
mongsanghada 몽상하다
(day)dream
mongttang chŏjŏt-tta 몽땅 젖었다
wet through
moning k'ol 모닝 콜 wake-up call
monit'ŏ 모니터 monitor COMPUT
monmŏri 못머리 head
monsun 몬순 monsoon
monsun kyejŏl 몬순 계절 monsoon
season
mopsshi 몹시 very, terribly
morae 모래 sand
morae chumŏni 모래 주머니
sandbag
morae ŏndŏk 모래 언덕 sand dune
moraep'an 모래판 sandpit
moraesaegŭi 모래색의 sandy *color*
moranaeda 몰아내다 repel
more 모레 the day after tomorrow
mori 몰이 round-up
morinjŏnghan 몰인정한 inhuman
morŭda 모르다 not know; be ignorant
of; not appreciate; ignore;
morŭgessŭmnida 모르겠습니다 I
don't know; *naega kŏŭi morŭnŭn
kŏt* 내가 거의 모르는 것 the little I
know ◊: *...ltchido morŭnda*
...ㄹ지도 모른다 may, might; *kŭ
yŏjaga kaltchido morŭnda* 그
여자가 갈지도 모른다 I don't know
whether she'll go, she may go
morŭmot'ŭ 모르모트 guinea pig
morŭnŭn 모르는 strange, unknown;
ignorant
morŭp'in 모르핀 morphine

moshida 모시다 attend to, serve; accompany, escort

moshinnŭn 멋있는 good-looking *man*

mosŏng 모성 motherhood

mosŏri 모서리 edge

mossaenggida 못생기다 be ugly

mosshi 모씨: *Pak mosshi* 박 모씨 a certain Mr Park

mosun 모순 contradiction; discrepancy

mosundoen 모순된 contradictory

mosundoenŭn 모순되는 inconsistent

mot 못 nail; peg

mot... 못... cannot; *...ji mot'ada ...*지 못하다 be unable to, cannot

motppoda 못보다 overlook

mot salge kulda 못 살게 굴다 bully

motssaenggin 못생긴 plain, homely

mot-ttoen 못된 nasty; *mot-ttoen chisŭl hada* 못된 짓을 하다 be up to something (bad)

mot'age hada 못하게 하다 discourage; stop, prevent

mot'el 모텔 motel

mot'ŏ 모터 motor

mot'ŏbot'ŭ 모터보트 motorboat

mot'o 모토 motto

mot'ung-i 모퉁이 turning, turn, corner

mot'ung-irŭl tolda 모퉁이를 돌다 turn a corner; corner (*of vehicle*)

moŭda 모으다 collect; gather; accumulate; save; *chogagŭl moŭda* 조각을 모으다 piece together

moŭi 모의 scheme

moŭihada 모의하다 scheme

moŭiŭi 모의의 mock

moŭm 모음 vowel

moŭn 모은 collected

moyang 모양 appearance, look; shape

moyŏ it-tta 모여 있다 be gathered together; be crowded

moyok 모욕 insult

moyok'ada 모욕하다 insult

moyurŭl mŏgida 모유를 먹이다 breastfeed

mu 무 nil

mu... 무... non...

mu 무 radish

muak 무악 shamanistic music

mubangbiŭi 무방비의 defenseless, unprotected

mubŏbŭi 무법의 disorderly; lawless

mubunbyŏl 무분별 indiscretion

mubunbyŏrhan 무분별한 indiscreet

much'abyŏrŭi 무차별의 indiscriminate

much'aegimhan 무책임한 irresponsible

much'ŏk 무척 extremely; *much'ŏk ttokttok'an* 무척 똑똑한 brilliant, very intelligent

much'ŏkch'u tongmul 무척추 동물 invertebrate

mudae 무대 stage

mudae paegyŏng 무대 배경 scenery, scenes

mudang 무당 shaman (*female*)

mudangbŏlle 무당벌레 ladybug

mudan hwoengdan 무단 횡단 jaywalking

mudan kŏjuhada 무단 거주하다 squat (*in building*)

mudan kŏjuja 무단 거주자 squatter

mudan kyŏlssŏk'ada 무단 결석하다 play truant

mudin 무딘 blunt

mudŏm 무덤 grave, tomb

mudŏmdŏmhan 무덤덤한 impervious to

mudŭktchŏm 무득점 love (*in tennis*)

mudujirhada 무두질하다 tan *leather*

muga 무가 shaman song

mugamgak 무감각 insensitivity

mugamgak'an 무감각한 callous, insensitive; numb

muge 무게 weight

mugega nagada 무게가 나가다 weigh

mugero nullyŏjida 무게로 눌려지다 be weighed down with

mugerŭl talda 무게를 달다 weigh

mugi 무기 weapon

mugihanŭro 무기한으로 indefinitely

muginhada 묵인하다 tolerate

mugirŭl ppaeat-tta 무기를 빼앗다 disarm

mugiŭi 무기의 inorganic

mugŏptta 무겁다 be heavy; be important

mugŏun 무거운 heavy
mugŏun 무거운 weighty, hefty
mugonghaeŭi 무공해의 nonpolluting
mugŭbŭi 무급의 unpaid
Mugunghwa 무궁화 Rose of Sharon
mugunghwa nesŭi 무궁화 넷의
four-star
mugwanhada 무관하다 be
unrelated; be irrelevant
mugwanshim 무관심 indifference
mugwanshimhan 무관심한 offhand,
indifferent
muhaehan 무해한 harmless;
inoffensive
muhan 무한 infinity
muhanhan 무한한 infinite
muhanjŏnghan 무한정한 indefinite
muhanŭi 무한의 boundless
muhŏgaŭi 무허가의 unauthorized
muhwagwa 무화과 fig
muhyŏrŭi 무혈의 bloodless
muhyohwahada 무효화하다
invalidate; overrule
muhyorohada 무효로 하다 annul,
revoke
muhyoŭi 무효의 invalid, null and
void
muilp'unŭi 무일푼의 penniless
muinŭi 무인의 unmanned
mujabihan 무자비한 merciless,
remorseless
mujagwi ch'uch'ul kŏmsa 무작위
추출 검사 spot check
mujagwihan 무작위한 arbitrary
mujagwiro 무작위로 at random,
willy-nilly; *mujagwiro kŏmsahada*
무작위로 검사하다 carry out a spot
check
mujagwi saemp'ŭl 무작위 샘플
random sample
mujagwiŭi 무작위의 random
mujang haeje 무장 해제
disarmament
mujang haejeshik'ida 무장
해제시키다 disarm
mujanghan 무장한 armed
mujang kangdo 무장 강도 armed
robbery; gunman
mujangshik'ida 무장시키다 arm
mujang-ŭl haejehada 무장을
해제하다 disarm

muji 무지 ignorance
mujigae 무지개 rainbow
mujilssŏ 무질서 lawlessness;
confusion; disorder
mujilssŏhan 무질서한 disorganized
mujinjanghan 무진장한
inexhaustible
mujiŭi 무지의 plain
mujŏgŭi 무적의 invincible
mujŏltchehan 무절제한 immoderate
mujŏngbu sangt'ae 무정부 상태
anarchy
mujŏnghan 무정한 unfeeling
mujŏn-gi 무전기 walkie-talkie
mujŏnŭro 무전으로 by radio
mujoeimŭl sŏnŏnhada 무죄임을
선언하다 acquit
mujoero hada 무죄로 하다 acquit,
clear
mujoerŭl chŭngmyŏnghada 무죄를
증명하다 exonerate, clear
mujokkŏnŭi 무조건의 unconditional
mujungnyŏgŭi 무중력의 weightless
mujungnyŏk 무중력 weightlessness
mujut'aektcha 무주택자 the
homeless
mukke hada 묵게 하다 take in, put
up, give accommodation
muk-kke hada 묽게 하다 dilute
mukkŏ not'a 묶어 놓다 tie down
mukkŭm 묶음 packet; *han mukkŭm*
한 묶음 batch
mukssang 묵상 meditation
mukssanghada 묵상하다 meditate
muktta 묶다 tie, tie up
mukwanshimhan 무관심한 apathetic
mul 물 water
mulbang-ul p'ojang 물방울 포장
blister pack
mulbinu 물비누 gel, liquid soap
mulbora 물보라 spray
mulch'e 물체 object
mulda 물다 bite
muldŭrida 물들이다 infect
mulgalk'wi 물갈퀴 flipper
mulgalk'wiga tallin 물갈퀴가 달린
webbed
mulgi 물기 nip, bite
mulgŏn 물건 stuff, things
mulgŭn 묽은 thin, watery
mulgŭn sup'ŭ 묽은 수프 broth, soup

mulkka 물가 shore, waterside

mulkkae 물개 seal

mulkkam 물감 paint

mulkkawa yŏndongshik'in 물가와 연동시킨 index-linked

mulkkiga marŭda 물기가 마르다 drain

mulkkirŭl ppaeda 물기를 빼다 drain

mulkkirŭl tudŭryŏ chiuda 물기를 두드려 지우다 blot (dry)

mulkkogi 물고기 fish

mulkkoktchi 물꼭지 faucet

mulkkyŏl 물결 ripple; stream

mulli ch'iryo 물리 치료 physiotherapy

mulli ch'iryosa 물리 치료사 physiotherapist

mullihak 물리학 physics

mullihaktcha 물리학자 physicist

mullŏnada 물러나다 stand down; back away; ...(ŭ)robut'ŏ mullŏna it-tta ...(으)로부터 물러나 있다 keep away from

mullon 물론 certainly, of course, sure; mullon andwaeji! 물론 안돼지! no way!; mullon anijyo! 물론 아니죠! of course not!

mulloniji 물론이지 no problem

mullonimnida 물론입니다 please do, by all means

mullyŏjuda 물려주다 hand down; make over

mulmangch'o 물망초 forget-me-not

mulmul kyohwan 물물 교환 barter

mulmul kyohwanhada 물물 교환하다 barter

mulnaeng-i 물냉이 watercress

mulppang-ul munŭi 물방울 무늬 spot (in pattern)

mulppurigae 물뿌리개 watering can

multchangnanŭl ch'ida 물장난을 치다 paddle

multchibi saenggida 물집이 생기다 blister

multchil 물질 matter

multchip 물집 blister

multchirŭi 물질의 material

mul t'aengk'ŭ 물 탱크 cistern

mul t'winŭn sori 물 튀는 소리 splash

mulyak 물약 mixture; medicine

mumohan 무모한 reckless

mumyŏng-ŭi 무명의 obscure; anonymous

mun 문 door; mune 문에 at the door; kagega munŭl tadat-tta 가게가 문을 닫았다 the store was shut

munbanggu 문방구 stationery

munbanggujŏm 문방구점 stationer's

munch'e 문체 style (literary)

mundan 문단 paragraph

mungch'i 뭉치 bundle, wad

mungch'ida 뭉치다 unite together

mungttuk'an 뭉뚝한 stubby

munhagŭi 문학의 literary

munhak 문학 literature

munhak sŏkssa 문학 석사 Master of Arts

munhakssa 문학사 arts degree

munhŏn mongnok 문헌 목록 bibliography

munhwa 문화 culture

Munhwach'eyukppu 문화체육부 Ministry of Culture and Sports

munhwajŏgin 문화적인 cultural

munhwajŏk ch'unggyŏk 문화적 충격 culture shock

Munhwa Pangsong 문화 방송 Munhwa Broadcasting Corporation, MBC

munhwayesul 문화예술 the arts

munjabi 문잡이 doorknob

munjang 문장 sentence

munjangnon 문장론 syntax

munjap'yo 문자표 character set

munje 문제 problem; trouble; question; tonŭi munjeida 돈의 문제이다 it's a question of money

munje haegyŏl 문제 해결 troubleshooting, problem solving

munje haegyŏlssa 문제 해결사 troubleshooter

munjeŏpsshi 문제없이 without any problems; safely

munjeŭi 문제의 in question

munjillŏ ŏpssaeda 문질러 없애다 rub off

munjillŏ taktta 문질러 닦다 scour

munjirŭda 문지르다 rub, scrub

munkku 문구 phrase

munmaek 문맥 context; Xŭl / rŭl munmaege match'wŏ /

munmaegŭl pŏsŏna poda X을 / 를
문맥에 맞춰/문맥을 벗어나 보다
look at X in context / out of context
munmaeng-ŭi 문맹의 illiterate
munmyŏng 문명 civilization
munŏ 문어 octopus
munŏjida 무너지다 fall down,
collapse, give way
munŏjiltttŭt'an 무너질 듯한
tumbledown
munŏjim 무너짐 crash
munŏttŭrida 무너뜨리다 flatten,
knock out
munppŏp 문법 grammar
munppŏpssang-ŭi 문법상의
grammatical
munshin 문신 tattoo
munsŏ 문서 document
munsŏe ŭihan myŏng-ye hweson
문서에 의한 명예 훼손 libel
munsŏ ŏmmu 문서 업무 paperwork
muntcha 문자 character, letter
muntchibang 문지방 doorstep,
threshold
mun tudŭrinŭn sori 문 두드리는
소리 knock
munŭi 문의 inquiry
munŭi 무늬 pattern, design
munŭihada 문의하다 inquire
munŭi innŭn 무늬 있는 patterned
munŭng 무능 inability
munŭnghada 무능하다 be
incompetent; *muŏsŭl hanŭn kŏse
munŭnghada* 무엇을 하는 것에
무능하다 be incapable of doing sth
munŭnghage hada 무능하게 하다
incapacitate; cripple
munŭngnyŏk 무능력 incompetence
munŭngnyŏktcha 무능력자
incompetent, no-hoper
munŭngnyŏk'an 무능력한
incompetent
muŏnŭi 무언의 mute, silent; tacit
muŏshidŭn 무엇이든 whatever;
...nŭn kosŭn muŏshidŭnji ...는
것은 무엇이든지 whatever
muŏshin-ga 무엇인가 something
muŏt 무엇 something; anything; what
muŏtppodado 무엇보다도 above all
muran-gyŏng 물안경 goggles
mure chamgin 물에 잠긴

waterlogged
muri 무리 group; strain
muri chit-tta 무리 짓다 congregate,
form a group
muri choŭn 물이 좋은 freshwater
murie ŏullida 무리에 어울리다 fit in
(*with a group*)
murihada 무리하다 be unreasonable
murihage ssŭda 무리하게 쓰다
overuse *machine etc*
murihanŭn 무리하는 compulsive
murihan yogu 무리한 요구 excessive
demand, tall order
murijit-tta 무리짓다 group
murirŭl hada 무리를 하다 strain;
injure
muri tŭlda 물이 들다 dye; be stained;
become infected
murŏboda 물어보다 question, quiz
murŏttŭtda 물어뜯다 bite off
murŭda 무르다 take back; be soft
murŭiktta 무르익다 ripen
murŭl chuda 물을 주다 water *plants,
animals*
murŭl naerida 물을 내리다 flush
water
murŭl t'ada 물을 타다 water down
liquor etc
murŭl t'wigida 물을 튀기다 splash
murŭmp'yo 물음표 question mark
murŭp 무릎 knee; lap; *murŭp'ŭl
kkulk'o* 무릎을 꿇고 down on one's
knees
murŭp kkult'a 무릎 꿇다 kneel
murye 무례 rudeness, disrespect
muryehada 무례하다 be rude
muryehan 무례한 rude, disrespectful
muryŏkk'ehada 무력게하다 paralyze
muryŏk'age hada 무력하게 하다
neutralize; overpower
muryŏk'an 무력한 impotent,
powerless, helpless
muryoŭi 무료의 free (*no cost*)
muryo iptchang 무료 입장
admission free
muryo kyŏnbon 무료 견본 free
sample
muryoro 무료로 free of charge, for
free
muryo t'onghwa 무료 통화 toll-free
muryoŭi 무료의 complimentary, free

musaengmurŭi 무생물의 inanimate
musahada 무사하다 be in safety
musahan 무사한 unharmed
musahi 무사히 safely
musahi chinagada 무사히 지나가다
  blow over (*of crisis*)
mushi 무시 disregard
mushihada 무시하다 ignore; dismiss
mushihago 무시하고 in defiance of
mushillonja 무신론자 atheist
mushimushihan 무시무시한
  dreadful; lurid; scary
mushin-gyŏnghan 무신경한
  insensitive, callous
musŏn chŏnhwagi 무선 전화기
  cordless phone; radio telephone
musŏnghan 무성한 overgrown
musŏng-ŭi 무성의 insincerity ◊ silent
  movie
musŏng-ŭihan 무성의한 insincere
musŏnŭi 무선의 wireless
musŏptta 무섭다 be appalling; be
  frightening
musŏwŏhada 무서워하다 be afraid
  of, be scared of
musoe 무쇠 cast iron
musoero mandŭn 무쇠로 만든 cast-
  iron
Musok Shinang 무속 신앙
  Shamanism
musŭn 무슨 any; some; what kind of
  ◊ what; *musŭn il issŏyo?* 무슨 일
  있어요? what's up?; *musŭn soriya?*
  무슨 소리야? what are you saying?
musŭngbu 무승부 dead heat
musuhan 무수한 innumerable
musul 무술 martial arts
mut-tta 묻다 ask; *..ŭi kŭnhwang-ŭl*
  mut-tta ...의 근황을 묻다 ask after
muttukttuk'an 무뚝뚝한 surly;
  brusque
mut'e 물에 ashore
mut'e orŭda 물에 오르다 go ashore
mut'ong-ŭi 무통의 painless
muŭimi 무의미 nonsense
muŭimihan 무의미한 meaningless,
  pointless
mu-ŭishik 무의식 the subconscious
muŭishik sangt'aeŭi 무의식 상태의
  unconscious
muŭishiktchŏgin 무의식적인

involuntary, unconscious
muyŏk 무역 business, trade
muyŏk chŏnshihoe 무역 전시회
  trade fair
muyŏk-kkwan 무역관 trade mission
muyŏk pangnamhoe 무역 박람회
  fair, trade show
muyŏk suji 무역 수지 balance of
  trade
muyŏn hwibaryu 무연 휘발유
  unleaded gasoline
muyŏnŭi 무연의 lead-free
muyong 무용 dancing
muyongga 무용가 dancer
mwŏrago? 뭐라고? what?
mwŏragoyo? 뭐라고요? excuse me?
mwŏraguyo? 뭐라구요? pardon me?
myŏlch'i 멸치 anchovies
myŏltchong 멸종 extinction
myŏltchongdoen 멸종된 extinct
myŏltchongshik'ida 멸종시키다
  exterminate
myŏltchong wigiŭi p'umjong 멸종
  위기의 품종 endangered species
myŏn 면 cotton; aspect; township
myŏndo 면도 shave
myŏndogi 면도기 shaver
myŏndohada 면도하다 shave, have a
  shave
myŏndohaji anŭn 면도하지 않은
  unshaven
myŏndok'al 면도칼 razor
myŏndonal 면도날 razor blade
myŏndoyong pinu 면도용 비누
  shaving soap
myŏndoyong sol 면도용 솔 shaving
  brush
myŏng 명 *countword for people*
myŏngbaek'ada 명백하다 be clear
myŏngbaek'age 명백하게 obviously
myŏngbaek'age hada 명백하게 하다
  make plain, make clear
myŏngbaek'i 명백히 evidently,
  apparently; explicitly
myŏngdanŭi ch'ŏnmŏrie 명단의
  첫머리에 at the head of the list
myŏnggihada 명기하다 specify
myŏngham 명함 business card,
  visiting card
myŏnghwak'age hada 명확하게
  하다 clarify

myŏnghwak'am 명확함 clarity

myŏnghwak'an 명확한 definite; articulate

myŏnghwak'i 명확히 expressly, explicitly; *myŏnghwak'i p'yohyŏnhada* 명확히 표현하다 express clearly

myŏngjak 명작 masterpiece

myŏngminhan 명민한 intelligent, sharp

myŏngnanghada 명랑하다 be bright; be cheerful

myŏngnyŏng 명령 command, order

myŏngnyŏnghada 명령하다 order, command, instruct

myŏngnyŏngjŏgin 명령적인 dictatorial

myŏngnyŏngppŏp 명령법 imperative GRAM

myŏngsa 명사 noun

myŏngsang 명상 meditation

myŏngsanghada 명상하다 meditate

myŏngserŭl palk'ida 명세를 밝히다 itemize

myŏngsesŏ 명세서 specifications

-myŏnsŏ 면서 (*indicates two parallel actions*): *mashimyŏnsŏ iyagihapsshida* 마시면서 이야기합시다 let's talk over a drink

myŏngsŏk'an 명석한 clear

myŏngsŏng 명성 fame; standing; prestige

myŏngsŏng-i nainnŭn 명성이 나있는 prestigious

myŏng-ye 명예 honor

myŏng-ye hwesonhada 명예 훼손하다 libel

myŏng-ye t'oejiksshik'ida 명예 퇴직시키다 pension off

myŏnhada 면하다 look onto

myŏnhŏ pat-tta 면허 받다 be licensed

myŏnhŏtchŭng 면허증 license

myŏnhoe shigan 면회 시간 visiting hours

myŏnje 면제 immunity

myŏnjedoeda 면제되다 be exempt from

myŏnjedoen 면제된 immune; exempt

myŏnjehae chuda 면제해 주다 exempt from, excuse from

myŏnjŏk 면적 area

myŏnjŏnesŏ 면전에서 in the presence of

myŏnjŏp 면접 interview

myŏnjŏpkkwan 면접관 interviewer

myŏnjŏp'ada 면접하다 interview

myŏnmirhada 면밀하다 be detailed, be meticulous

myŏnmirhan 면밀한 rigorous

myŏnmirhi 면밀히 meticulously

myŏnmyŏch'ŭi 몇몇의 several

myŏn samuso 면사무소 township office

myŏnsejŏm 면세점 duty-free shop

myŏnsep'um 면세품 duty-free (*goods*)

myŏnseŭi 면세의 duty-free, tax-free

myŏnŭnim 며느님 (*polite*) daughter-in-law

myŏnŭri 며느리 daughter-in-law

myŏnŭro mandŭn 면으로 만든 cotton

myŏnyŏgŭi 면역의 immune

myŏnyŏk 면역 immunity

myŏnyŏk ch'egye 면역 체계 immune system

myŏt 몇 how many; how much; *onŭl myŏch'irijyo?* 오늘 몇일이죠? what's the date today?

myŏt kae 몇 개 several

myŏt pŏnina kyesok 몇 번이나 계속 time and again

myŏt pun ch'airo 몇 분 차이로 by a couple of minutes

myŏt shiimnikka? 몇 시입니까? what's the time?, what time is it?

myoan 묘안 brainwave

myohage tamtta 묘하게 닮다 have an uncanny resemblance to

myohan 묘한 uncanny

myoji 묘지 cemetery, graveyard

myojong 묘종 seedling (*of plant*)

myomok 묘목 seedling (*of tree*)

myosa 묘사 description

myosahada 묘사하다 describe

myujik'ŏl 뮤지컬 musical (*drama*)

myul 뮬 mule, slipper

N

na 나 I ◊ me ◊ mine
nabang 나방 moth
nabi 나비 butterfly
nabi nekt'ai 나비 넥타이 bow tie
nabip 납입 payment
nabip chabon 납입자본 equity capital
na chashin 나 자신 myself
nach'ehwa 나체화 nude
nach'ejuŭija 나체주의자 nudist
nach'ero 나체로 in the nude
nach'imban 나침반 compass
nach'uda 낮추다 turn down; belittle
nada 나다 it's me ◊ flare up
nadal 낟알 grain
nae 내 my
naebaet-tta 내뱉다 spit out
naebŏrida 내버리다 throw out, dump
naebŏryŏduda 내버려두다 leave alone; leave unattended
naebŏryŏdun 내버려둔 unattended
naebu 내부 inside
naebu chŏngbo 내부 정보 inside information
naebue(sŏ) 내부에(서) inside
naebue innŭn 내부에 있는 inside
naebu haeksshim chipttan 내부 핵심 집단 in-crowd
naebuin 내부인 insider
naebujŏgŭro 내부적으로 internally
naebuŭi 내부의 inner, internal
naeda 내다 provide; serve; spare; give off
naedaboda 내다보다 look out (of)
naedŏnjida 내던지다 fling, throw
naegak 내각 cabinet
naegi 내기 bet, wager; *...e naegirŭl kŏlda* ...에 내기를 걸다 bet
naegusŏng-i innŭn 내구성이 있는 durable
naegusŏng-i kanghan 내구성이 강한 resilient
naehyangjŏgin 내향적인 retiring
naeil 내일 tomorrow; *naeil ach'im*

내일 아침 in the morning, tomorrow morning; *naeil i shigankkaji* 내일 이 시간까지 by this time tomorrow
naejangdoeŏ innŭn 내장되어 있는 built-in
naejangdoeŏ it-tta 내장되어 있다 be supplied with
naejŏn 내전 civil war
naekkwa ŭisa 내과 의사 physician
nae kŏt 내 것 mine
naek'iji annŭn 내키지 않는 reluctant
naeda 내다 pay; *naega naenda* 내가 낸다 I'm paying, this is on me
naekkwa chŏnmun ŭisa 내과 전문 의사 internist
naembi 냄비 pot, saucepan
naemilda 내밀다 extend, stretch
naemirhage 내밀하게 in private, privately
naemsae 냄새 smell; odor; scent
naemsaega nada 냄새가 나다 smell, reek
naemsae nanŭn 냄새 나는 smelly
naemsaerŭl mat-tta 냄새를 맡다 smell, sniff
Naemubu 내무부 Department of the Interior
naenae 내내 all the time, all along; *wŏryoilbut'ŏ kŭmnyoil tong-an naenae* 월요일부터 금요일 동안 내내 Monday through Friday
naengbang 냉방 air-conditioning
naengbangjung 냉방중 air-conditioned
naengdae 냉대 snub
naengdaehada 냉대하다 snub
naengdam 냉담 reserve, aloofness
naengdamhan 냉담한 unfriendly
naengdong 냉동 freezing
naengdong shikp'um 냉동 식품 frozen food
naengdongshil 냉동실 freezer; freezing compartment
naenghok'age 냉혹하게 in cold

blood

naenghok'an 냉혹한 grim

naenghyŏrhage 냉혈하게 in cold blood

naenghyŏrhan 냉혈한 cold-blooded *fig*

naenghyŏrŭi 냉혈의 cold-blooded

naengjanggo 냉장고 fridge, freezer

naengjŏnghada 냉정하다 be cool, be calm

naengjŏnghan 냉정한 dispassionate, objective; calm, impassive; hardheaded

naengmyŏn 냉면 chilled noodles

naeng-ŏmhan 냉엄한 brutal

naengso 냉소 cynicism

naengsojŏgin 냉소적인 cynical

naeng-yuk 냉육 cold cuts

naenot'a 내놓다 set out; *p'allyŏgo naenot'a* 팔려고 내놓다 put up for sale

naepk'in 냅킨 napkin

naeppumtta 내뿜다 blow *smoke*; snort

naep'aenggaech'ida 내팽개치다 throw; toss away

naep'ip 내핍 austerity

naeribeda 내리베다 slash

naerida 내리다 get out (*of car etc*); get off, disembark; come down (*of rain*); lower; wind down; unload; bring in *verdict*; percolate, filter; *araero naerida* 아래로 내리다 scroll down

naerige hada 내리게 하다 bring down

naerimak-kkiri toeda 내리막길이 되다 go downhill, decline

naeri tŏpch'ida 내리 덮치다 swoop; swoop down on

naeryŏant'a 내려앉다 subside; descend

naeryŏ chuda 내려 주다 let off (*from car*)

naeryŏdaboda 내려다보다 overlook; look down

naeryŏgada 내려가다 go down, descend, get down

naeryŏga it-tta 내려가 있다 be down

naeryŏjuda 내려주다 drop; *ch'a-esŏ naeryŏjuda* 차에서 내려주다 drop

off (*from car*)

naeryŏk 내력 personal history, career

naeryŏoda 내려오다 come down

naeryugŭi 내륙의 inland

naeryuk 내륙 interior

naesaek'aji ant'a 내색하지 않다 disguise one's emotions

naeshwida 내쉬다 exhale

naesŏn 내선 extension

naesŏngjŏgin 내성적인 withdrawn; introspective

naetchŏgin 내적인 inner

naetchot-tta 내쫓다 throw out, oust

naeŭi 내의 underwear

naeyŏlssŏng-ŭi 내열성의 heatproof, heat-resistant

naeyŏn-gigwan 내연기관 internal combustion engine

naeyŏnŭi ch'ŏ 내연의 처 common law wife

naeyong 내용 content; contents

nagada 나가다 go out; *kŭnŭn chigŭm chŏng-wŏne nagait-tta* 그는 지금 정원에 나가있다 he's out in the garden; *nagaseyo!* 나가세요! (get) out!; *nagayo!* 나가요! get out!

nagage hada 나가게 하다 let out

naga ttŏrŏjige hada 나가 떨어지게 하다 knock out

nagoja 낙오자 dropout

nagwŏn 낙원 paradise

nagwŏn-gat'ŭn 낙원같은 idyllic

nai 나이 age

nai chigŭt'an 나이 지긋한 elderly

naidŭrŏ kada 나이들어 가다 get on, become old

nai kapssŭl hae! 나이 값을 해! grow up!

naillon 나일론 nylon

naillonŭi 나일론의 nylon

nai tŭlda 나이 들다 low

nait'inggeil 나이팅게일 nightingale

nait'ŭ k'ŭllŏp 나이트클럽 nightclub, nightspot

naje 낮에 by day, in the daytime

najŭn 낮은 low

najŭn kubŭi 낮은 굽의 flat

najŭn tchoguro 낮은 쪽으로 down

najŭn ŭmjarip'yo 낮은 음자리표 bass clef

najung-e 나중에 later, later on, afterward; *najung-e poja!* 나중에 보자! see you later!

najung-e tashi chŏnhwahada 나중에 다시 전화하다 call back TELEC

nakch'ŏnjŏgin 낙천적인 optimistic, happy-go-lucky

nakch'ŏnjuŭi 낙천주의 optimism

nakch'ŏnjuŭija 낙천주의자 optimist

nakka ch'aeda 낚아 채다 nab

nakkda 낚다 fish, angle; lure, entice; *nakkŭn kŏt* 낚은 것 catch *fish*

nakkwanjŏgin 낙관적인 optimistic

naksshi 낚시 fishing

naksshihada 낚시하다 fish

naksshippanŭl 낚시바늘 fish-hook

naksshitchul 낚싯줄 fishing line

naksshit-ttae 낚싯대 fishing rod

nakssŏ 낙서 graffiti

nakssŏndoen 낙선된 unsuccessful

nakssŭng 낙승 walkover

naktcherŭl pat-tta 낙제를 받다 flunk

naktchi 낙지 octopus

nakttam 낙담 dismay, disappointment

nakttamhan 낙담한 despondent, dejected; disheartened

nakttamshik'ida 낙담시키다 discourage; dishearten

nakt'ae 낙태 abortion

nakt'aehada 낙태하다 have an abortion

nakt'aeshik'ida 낙태시키다 terminate a pregnancy

nak'asan 낙하산 parachute

nak'asanbyŏng 낙하산병 paratrooper

nak'asanŭro naeryŏoda 낙하산으로 내려오다 parachute down

nak'asanŭro t'alch'urhada 낙하산으로 탈출하다 bail out (*of airplane*)

nak'asanŭro t'uhahada 낙하산으로 투하하다 parachute

nal 날 day; edge (*of knife*); blade

nalda 날다 fly

nalgae 날개 wing

nalgi 날기 flight; flying

nalgŭn 낡은 old; shabby; outmoded

nalkkŏsŭi 날것의 raw

nalktta 낡다 be old; be old-fashioned

nalk'aroptta 날카롭다 be sharp; be incisive; be cutting

nalk'aroun 날카로운 sharp; incisive; penetrating; pointed; searching

nallibŏpssŏk 난리법석 fuss

nallibŏpssŏk ttŏlda 난리법석 떨다 make a fuss

nallich'ida 난리치다 make a fuss; complain

nallida 날리다 spend, blow

nalsshi 날씨 weather

nalsshinhada 날씬하다 be slim

nalsshinhan 날씬한 slim

naltcha 날짜 date

naltchaga chinan 날짜가 지난 out of date

naltcharŭl chŏktta 날짜를 적다 date *document*, put a date on

nalttwimyŏ toradanida 날뛰며 돌아다니다 rampage, go on the rampage

nama it-tta 남아 있다 linger

Namap'ŭrik'a 남아프리카 South Africa ◊ South African

Namap'ŭrik'ain 남아프리카인 South African

Namap'ŭrik'aŭi 남아프리카의 South African

nambi 남비 pan

nambuŭi 남부의 southern

namch'ang 남창 male prostitute

namdongsaeng 남동생 (younger) brother

namdongtchogŭi 남동쪽의 southeast, southeastern

namdongtchogŭro 남동쪽으로 southeast

namdongtchok 남동쪽 southeast

namgida 남기다 leave; *kŭga namgin tu ttal* 그가 남긴 두 딸 his two surviving daughters

Namgŭk-kkwŏn 남극권 Antarctic

namgyŏjida 남겨지다 remain

namgyŏ tuda 남겨 두다 leave

Namhae 남해 South Sea, Korean Strait

Namhaedo 남해도 Namhae Island

namhakssaeng 남학생 schoolboy

Namhan 남한 South Korea ◊ South

Korean

Namhanin 남한인 South Korean
namhyang-ŭi 남향의 southerly
namja 남자 man, male
namja ch'in-gu 남자 친구 boyfriend
namjadaum 남자다움 manhood
namjadaun 남자다운 manly; macho; virile
namja hwajangshil 남자 화장실 men's room
namja kanhosa 남자 간호사 male nurse
namja paeu 남자 배우 actor
namja suyŏngbok 남자 수영복 swimsuit
namja undongga 남자 운동가 sportsman
namjit 남짓 more than
Nammi 남미 South America ◊ South American
Nammiin 남미인 South American
Nammiŭi 남미의 South American
nam mollae saltchak 남 몰래 살짝 on the sly
nam morŭge 남 모르게 behind the scenes
namnŭn shigan 남는 시간 spare time
namnuhan 남루한 ragged
namnyŏ konghagŭi 남녀 공학의 coeducational
namŏji 나머지 the rest, remainder
namŏji kŏt 나머지 것 the others
namŏjiŭi 나머지의 surplus
namp'yŏn 남편 husband
namsaek 남색 navy blue
namsŏngdaum 남성다움 virility
namsŏngjŏgin 남성적인 masculine
namsŏngmi 남성미 masculinity
namsŏng-ŭi 남성의 male, masculine
namsŏng uwŏltchuŭija 남성 우월주의자 male chauvinist (pig)
namsŏtchogŭi 남서쪽의 southwest, southwestern
namsŏtchoguro 남서쪽으로 southwest
namsŏtchok 남서쪽 southwest
namtchoge 남쪽에 to the south of
namtchogŭi 남쪽의 south
namtchoguro 남쪽으로 south, southward

namtchok 남쪽 south
namtchok chibang 남쪽 지방 south
namtta 남다 be left, remain; *namŭn kŏshi ŏptta* 남은 것이 없다 there isn't/aren't any left
namŭn kŏt 남은 것 left-overs
namu 나무 tree; wood
Namu Amit'abul 나무 아미타불 Namu Amit'abul (*Buddhist chant*)
namuga manŭn 나무가 많은 woody
namuga ugŏjin 나무가 우거진 wooded
namu kkŏptchil 나무 껍질 bark
namukkun 나무꾼 woodcutter
namurada 나무라다 reprimand, give a piece of one's mind
namural te ŏmnŭn 나무랄 데 없는 impeccable, irreproachable
namural te ŏpsshi 나무랄 데 없이 impeccably
namuro toen 나무로 된 wooden
namu sangja 나무 상자 crate
namutkkyŏl 나뭇결 grain
namuttalgi 나무딸기 raspberry
namyong 남용 abuse
nan 난 column
nanari 나날이 day by day
nanbang 난방 heating
nanbang changch'i 난방 장치 heating; heater
nanbanggi 난방기 radiator
nanch'ŏhage hada 난처하게 하다 stump, baffle
nanch'ŏhan 난처한 messy, unpleasant
nanch'ŏng chiyŏgesŏ 난청 지역에서 out of earshot
nanch'o 난초 orchid
nan-gan 난간 handrail
nangbi 낭비 waste
nangbibyŏgi shimhan 낭비벽이 심한 spendthrift
nangbiga shimhan 낭비가 심한 wasteful
nangbihada 낭비하다 waste, squander; *shigan nangbiyeyo* 시간 낭비예요 it's a waste of time
nan-giryu 난기류 turbulence
nangnongjang 낙농장 dairy
nangsonghada 낭송하다 recite
nanhaehan 난해한 obscure

nanjaeng-i 난쟁이 dwarf
nanjangp'an 난장판 madhouse
nanjap'an 난잡한 promiscuous
nanmin 난민 refugee
nanp'a 난파 shipwreck
nanp'adoeda 난파되다 be shipwecked
nanp'ashik'ida 난파시키다 shipwreck
nanp'ok'age 난폭하게 violently
nanp'ok'age milda 난폭하게 밀다 jostle
nanp'ok unjŏnja 난폭 운전자 road hog
nanp'ok'an 난폭한 rough, rowdy
nanso 난소 ovary
nant'u 난투 scuffle
nanŭn 나는 I
nanuda 나누다 divide, distribute
nanul su innŭn 나눌 수 있는 divisible
nanuŏ chuda 나누어 주다 hand out, deal out
nanutssem 나눗셈 division
naoda 나오다 come out, get out; add up to
naogehada 나오게 하다 flush out
nap 납 lead (metal)
napch'i 납치 kidnapping
napch'ibŏm 납치범 kidnapper
napch'ihada 납치하다 abduct, kidnap
nappajida 나빠지다 deteriorate, suffer
nap-ppuhada 납부하다 pay
nappŭda 나쁘다 be wrong, be bad (morally)
nappŭge 나쁘게 badly
nappŭge haengdonghada 나쁘게 행동하다 misbehave
nappŭn 나쁜 bad
nappŭn haengdong 나쁜 행동 misbehavior
nappŭn nyŏn ∨ 나쁜 년 bitch pej
napsseja 납세자 tax payer
napsse shin-gosŏ 납세 신고서 tax return
napttŭk 납득 understanding
nap'al 나팔 brass trumpet
nara 나라 nation, country
naragada 날아가다 fly away, fly off; fly out

naranhi 나란히 side by side
naraŭi 나라의 national
narŭda 나르다 carry
narŭnhan 나른한 drowsy; weak
naruttppae 나룻배 ferry
nasamot 나사못 screw; *muŏsŭl muŏse nasamosŭro kojŏngshik'ida* 무엇을 무엇에 나사못으로 고정시키다 screw sth to sth
nasarŭl p'ulda 나사를 풀다 unscrew
nasasan 나사산 thread (of screw)
nasŏda 나서다 come out, appear
nasŏnhyŏng kyedan 나선형 계단 winding staircase
nasŏnhyŏng-ŭi 나선형의 spiral
nasŏnhyŏng-ŭi ch'ŭnggye 나선형의 층계 spiral staircase
nat 낮 daylight
nat 낫 scythe
natch'uda 낮추다 lower; keep down
natch'un 낮춘 subdued
natch'uŏ poda 낮추어 보다 look down on
natkke hada 낫게 하다 heal
natssŏn saram 낯선 사람 stranger
nattcham 낮잠 nap
nattchamŭl chada 낮잠을 자다 have a nap
nat-tta 낳다 generate, create; *airŭl nat-tta* 아이를 낳다 give birth
nat-tta 낫다 heal, clear up
nat-tta 낮다 be low
nat'a 낳다 bear, give birth to; lay; spawn
nat'aehan 나태한 indolent, idle
nat'anada 나타나다 appear, turn up; manifest itself; haunt
nat'anaeda 나타내다 show, constitute
naŭi 나의 my
ne chashin 네 자신 yourself
Nedŏllandŭin 네덜란드인 the Dutch
Nedŏllandŭŏ 네덜란드어 Dutch (language)
Nedŏllandŭŭi 네덜란드의 Dutch
nekt'ai 넥타이 tie, necktie
neon ssain 네온 싸인 neon light
ne paero hada 네 배로 하다 quadruple

ne pal chimsŭng 네 발 짐승 quadruped

ne pŏn 네 번 four times

ne pŏntchaeŭi 네 번째의 fourth

Nep'al 네팔 Nepal ◊ Nepalese

ne ssangdung-i 네 쌍둥이 quadruplets

net 넷 four

net'ŭ 네트 net (for tennis)

net'ŭwŏk'ŭ 네트워크 network

nik'el 니켈 nickel

nisŭ 니스 varnish

nisŭrŭl ch'irhada 니스를 칠하다 varnish

nit'ŭ weŏ 니트 웨어 knitwear

...nji ...ㄴ지 → **...inji** ...인지

nŏ 너 (informal) you

nŏdobamnamu 너도밤나무 beech

nŏgŭrŏun 너그러운 decent

nŏhŭidŭl chashin 너희들 자신 yourselves

nŏhŭidŭl sŭsŭro 너희들 스스로 by yourselves

nŏkssŭl ilk'e hada 넋을 잃게 하다 devastate

nŏkssŭl ilt'a 넋을 잃다 get carried away

nŏlbi ttwigi 넓이 뛰기 long jump, broad jump

nŏlbŏjida 넓어지다 broaden, widen

nŏlbŭn 넓은 roomy, wide

nŏlbŭn kang-ŏgwi 넓은 강어귀 estuary

nŏlke 넓게 widely; **nŏlkke pyŏlch'yŏjin** 넓게 펼쳐진 a vast expanse of; **nŏlkke yŏllin** 넓게 열린 wide-open

nŏlli p'ŏjyŏ innŭn 널리 퍼져 있는 pervasive

nŏlppanji 널빤지 plank

nŏlptta 넓다 be wide, be broad

nŏlp'ida 넓히다 broaden, widen; expand; dilate

nŏmch'ida 넘치다 exceed; overflow; **kaemidŭllo nŏmch'ida** 개미들로 넘치다 be teeming with ants; **...esŏ nŏmch'yŏ hŭrŭda** ...에서 넘쳐 흐르다 stream out of; **kangttugi nŏmch'ida** 강둑이 넘치다 flood its banks; **kamjŏng-i nŏmch'inŭn** 감정이 넘치는 effusive

nŏmgida 넘기다 turn; **...ege kyŏltchŏng-ŭl / mun-jerŭl nŏmgida** ...에게 결정을 / 문제를 넘기다 refer a decision / problem to

nŏmgyŏjuda 넘겨주다 hand over, surrender

nŏmŏ 넘어 past (in time)

nŏmŏjida 넘어지다 fall, trip up; stumble

nŏmŏjim 넘어짐 fall; stumble

nŏmŏsŏ 넘어서 beyond

nŏmŏttŭrida 넘어뜨리다 knock over; **hŏrŏ nŏmŏttŭrida** 헐어 넘어뜨리다 knock down

nŏmtta 넘어서다 exceed; be past; go over mountain; **ilgop shiga nŏmŏssŏyo** 일곱 시가 넘었어요 it's past 7 o'clock

nŏmu 너무 too; far; **unbanhagie nŏmu mugŏp-tta** 운반하기에 너무 무겁다 too heavy to carry; **nŏmu andwaessŏyo** 너무 안됐어요 that's really too bad; **nega nŏmu chinach'yŏt-tta** 네가 너무 지나쳤다 you've gone too far; **kŭdŭlŭn iri nŏmu millyŏ issŏyo** 그들은 일이 너무 밀려 있어요 they are way behind with their work

nŏmu honjap'an 너무 혼잡한 overcrowded

nŏmu ik'ida 너무 익히다 overdo

nŏmu mani 너무 많이 too much

nŏmu pissan 너무 비싼 too expensive, overpriced

nŏmu ttabunhan irida 너무 따분한 일이다 it's such a bore

nŏngnŏk'an 넉넉한 plentiful

nŏnjishi pich'ida 넌지시 비치다 insinuate, imply

nŏnjishi pich'uda 넌지시 비추다 make out, imply

nŏnŭn 너는 you (informal); as for you

nŏptchŏkttari 넓적다리 thigh

nŏrŏsŏ mallida 널어서 말리다 dripdry

nŏt'a 넣다 put in, inject

nŏt'ŭ 너트 nut

nŏŭi 너의 (informal) your

no 노 oar; paddle

noajuda 놓아주다 disengage

noa pŏrida

noa pŏrida 놓아 버리다 let go of

noa tuda 놓아 두다 put

nobaldaebarhada 노발대발하다 be furious with

nobaldaebarhan 노발대발한 livid

noch'ida 놓치다 miss (*not hit*); lose one's hold on; pass up *opportunity*

noch'ŏn k'ap'e 노천 카페 sidewalk café

no chŏt-tta 노 젓다 row *boat*

noch'ul 노출 exposure

noch'uldoen 노출된 revealing

noch'ulshik'ida 노출시키다 expose

noch'urhada 노출하다 expose; *chinach'ige noch'urhada* 지나치게 노출하다 overexpose

noch'uri pujok'an 노출이 부족한 underexposed

nodong 노동 labor

nodong chaeng-ŭi haeng-wi 노동 쟁의 행위 industrial action

nodong chohap 노동 조합 labor union

nodong hŏga 노동 허가 work permit

nodong in-gu 노동 인구 workforce

nodongja 노동자 laborer, worker

nodongja kyegŭbŭi 노동자 계급의 working-class

nodongja kyegŭp 노동자 계급 working class

Nodongjŏl 노동절 May Day, Labor Day

nodongjohabŭi chiktchangwiwŏn 노동조합의 직장위원 shop steward

noe chŏnmun oekkwa ŭisa 뇌 전문 외과 의사 brain surgeon

noejint'ang 뇌진탕 concussion

noejol 뇌졸 stroke

noemangnyŏm 뇌막염 meningitis

noemul 뇌물 bribe

noemul susu 뇌물 수수 bribery

noemurŭl chuda 뇌물을 주다 pay off, bribe

noerirŭl ttŏnaji annŭn 뇌리를 떠나지 않는 haunting

noeu 뇌우 thunderstorm

nogaut'ŭ 노아웃 knockout

nogida 녹이다 melt; dissolve; defrost

nogi sŭlji annŭn 녹이 슬지 않는 rust-proof

nogi sŭn 녹이 슨 rusty

nogo 노고 toil

nogoltchŏgin 노골적인 direct; point-blank; obvious

nogoltchŏgin p'orŭno 노골적인 포르노 hardcore porn

nogoltchŏgŭro 노골적으로 pointblank

nogonhan 노곤한 lethargic

nogŭm 녹음 recording

nogŭmdoen 녹음된 canned

nogŭmgi 녹음기 cassette player; record player

nogŭmhada 녹음하다 tape

nogŭmshil 녹음실 recording studio

nogŭm t'eip'ŭ 녹음 테이프 cassette

nogŭn 녹은 molten

nohau 노하우 knowhow, expertise

noin 노인 geriatric

noinppyŏng-ŭi 노인병의 geriatric

nojang chŏngmaek 노장 정맥 varicose vein

nojo 노조 (labor) union

nok 녹 rust

nok chejŏje 녹 제거제 rust remover

nokch'a 녹차 green tea

nokch'oga toen 녹초가 된 exhausted

nokch'oga toeŏ 녹초가 되어 dead beat, dead tired

nokch'oro mandŭlda 녹초로 만들다 exhaust

nokch'oro mandŭnŭn 녹초로 만드는 grueling

nokkŭn 노끈 cord, string

nokssaegŭi 녹색의 green

nokssŭlda 녹슬다 rust

noktta 녹다 thaw; dissolve; melt

nok'ŭhada 노크하다 knock; *munŭl nok'ŭhada* 문을 노크하다 knock at the door

nok'wahada 녹화하다 tape, record

nok'washil 녹화실 recording studio

nolda 놀다 play

nolgo chinaeda 놀고 지내다 loaf around

nolgo innŭn 놀고 있는 idle

nollada 놀라다 marvel at; be surprised

nollage hada 놀라게 하다 surprise; shock; rock

nollapk'e 놀랍게 suprisingly

nolla poida 놀라 보이다 look surprised

nollaptta 놀랍다 be surprising

nollaŭn kŏt 놀라운 것 marvel

nollaun 놀라운 surprising; wonderful; *...ranŭn kŏsŭn nollaun irida* ...라는 것은 놀라운 일이다 it's a wonder that ...

nolli 논리 reasoning, argument, logic

nollida 놀리다 make fun of, tease; play a joke on; send up; scoff; quip

nollijŏgin 논리적인 logical

non 논 rice field, rice paddy

nonbat 논밭 rice fields and dry fields

nong-ak 농악 farmer's music

nong-akttae 농악대 traditional farmers' band

nong-aŭi 농아의 deaf-and-dumb

nongbu 농부 farmer

nongch'ukttoen 농축된 concentrated

nongdam 농담 joke

nongdamhada 농담하다 joke, jest

nongdam kŭmanhago 농담 그만하고 joking apart

nongdamŭi p'yojŏk 농담의 표적 butt (*of joke*)

nongdamŭro 농담으로 in jest, jokingly

nongdo 농도 consistency, texture

nongga 농가 farmhouse

nonggu 농구 basketball

nonggyŏng-e almajŭn 농경에 알맞은 arable

nongjang 농장 farm

nongjangmul 농작물 crop

nongjang-ŭi ilkkun 농장의 일꾼 farmworker

nongmal 녹말 cornstarch

nongmin 농민 peasant

nong-ŏbŭi 농업의 agricultural

nong-ŏp 농업 agriculture

nongsa 농사 agriculture, farming; *nongsa chitkko salda* 농사 짓고 살다 make a living from farming

nongsanmul 농산물 produce

nong-yang 농양 abscess

nonhada 논하다 argue, reason

nonjaeng 논쟁 argument; debate; controversy

nonjaenghada 논쟁하다 debate

nonjaengjŏgin 논쟁적인 provocative

nonjaeng-ŭi yŏjiga innŭn 논쟁의 여지가 있는 debatable

nonjaeng-ŭl irŭk'inŭn 논쟁을 일으키는 controversial

nonmun 논문 thesis, academic paper

nonp'iksshyŏn 논픽션 nonfiction

nonp'yŏnghada 논평하다 review

nontchŏm 논점 issue, topic

nonŭi 논의 discussion; *nonŭi sahang* 논의 사항 the point at issue

nonŭihada 논의하다 discuss

nonŭiŭi yŏjiga ŏmnŭn 논의의 여지가 없는 indisputable

nonyŏn 노년 old age

nopkke 높게 high

noptta 높다 be high

nop'i 높이 height; elevation; altitude; *nugurŭl nop'i p'yŏngkkahada* 누구를 높이 평가하다 have a high opinion of s.o.

nop'ida 높이다 increase, turn up; elevate

nop'i ttwigi 높이 뛰기 high jump

nop'ŭn 높은 high

nop'ŭn ponggŭbŭl pat-tta 높은 봉급을 받다 be highly paid

nop'ŭn kubŭi 높은 굽의 high-heeled

nop'ŭn sujun 높은 수준 high (*in statistics*)

norae 노래 song; chant

noraebang 노래방 karaoke room

noraehada 노래하다 sing; chant

noran 노란 yellow

norang 노랑 yellow

noransaegŭro 노란색으로 in yellow

norat'a 노랗다 be yellow

nori 놀이 play ◊ game

norich'in-gu 놀이친구 playmate

norit'ŏ 놀이터 playground

norŭnja 노른자 yolk

norŭnnorŭt'age kuptta 노릇노릇하게굽다 brown (*in cooking*)

norŭnnorŭt'age toeda 노릇노릇하게되다 brown (*in cooking*)

Norŭwei 노르웨이 Norway ◊ Norwegian

Norŭweiin 노르웨이인 Norwegian

Norŭweiŏ 노르웨이어 Norwegian (*language*)

Norŭweiŭi 노르웨이의 Norwegian

noryŏboda 노려보다 glare at
noryŏk 노력 effort, attempt
noryŏk'ada 노력하다 try, exert
oneself; *tangshinŭn tŏ yŏlshimhi
noryŏk'aeya hamnida* 당신은 더
열심히 노력해야 합니다 you must
try harder
nosae 노새 mule
nosaganŭi purhwa 노사간의 불화
industrial dispute
nosahyŏbŭihwoe 노사협의회 works
council
nosang kangdo 노상 강도 mugger
nosang kangdo haeng-wi 노상 강도
행위 mugging
nosang kangdojirŭl hada 노상
강도질을 하다 mug, rob on the
street
nosoe 노쇠 senility
nosoehan 노쇠한 senile
nosuk'ada 노숙하다 sleep rough
notssoe 놋쇠 brass
not'a 놓다 put; put down
not'ŭbuk 노트북 notebook COMPUT
noŭl 노을 twilight
noye 노예 slave
noyŏum 노여움 anger
nŭgŭt'age 느긋하게 in a leisurely
way
nŭgŭt'an 느긋한 easy-going,
laidback; leisurely
nŭjŏjida 늦어지다 lose
nŭjŏjinda 늦어진다 it's getting late
nŭjŭn 늦은 late, overdue
nŭkkida 느끼다 feel, experience
nŭkkim 느낌 feeling; impression
nŭkkimp'yo 느낌표 exclamation
point
nŭkttae 늑대 wolf
nŭl 늘 always, all the time; *nŭl
hanŭn kŏsŭro chushipsshio* 늘
하는 것으로 주십시오 the usual,
please
nŭlda 늘다 expand; mount up;
op'aundŭga nŭlda 5파운드가 늘다
gain 5 pounds
nŭlgŏjida 늙어지다 grow old
nŭlgŭn 늙은 old
nŭlgŭnina chŏlmŭnina ttokkach'i
늙은이나 젊은이나 똑같이 old and
young alike

nŭlktta 늙다 grow old
nŭllida 늘리다 extend, roll over;
raise; lengthen; let out
nŭlsshinhan 늘씬한 trim
...nŭn ... 는 (*contrast particle, also
used to introduce a topic*); *nŏnŭn*
너는 you; as for you; *...nŭn
cheoehago* ... 는 제외하고
excluding ◊ (*relative*) which; who;
whose; *naega kongbuhanŭn
kwamok* 내가 공부하는 과목 the
subject which I'm studying ◊ (*forms
adjectives*): *nurŏputtchi annŭn*
눌어붙지 않는 nonstick
nŭngdongt'aeŭi 능동태의 active
nŭnggahada 능가하다 surpass,
exceed
nŭnggŭlmajŭn usŭm 능글맞은 웃음
smirk
nŭnggŭlmatkke ut-tta 능글맞게
웃다 smirk
nŭngnyŏginnŭn 능력있는 able,
skillful
nŭngnyŏgi ŏmnŭn 능력이 없는
incapable; inept
nŭngnyŏgŭl shihŏmhaebonŭn
능력을 시험해보는 challenging
nŭngnyŏk 능력 capability, ability;
competence; faculty; *...l nŭngnyŏgi
it-tta* ...ㄹ 능력이 있다 be capable
of ...ing
nŭngnyŏk innŭn 능력 있는 capable,
competent
nŭngnyŏng 능력 capacity, ability
nŭngnyul 능률 efficiency
nŭngnyultchŏgin 능률적인 efficient;
streamlined
nŭngnyultchŏguro 능률적으로
efficiently
nŭngsuk 능숙 proficiency
nŭngsuk'ada 능숙하다 be skilled;
muŏse nŭngsuk'ada 무엇에
능숙하다 be good at sth
nŭngsuk'an 능숙한 skillful,
proficient
...nŭn kŏt ...는 것 ◊ (*creates a noun
form*) ...ing; *kongbu hanŭn kŏt*
공부 하는 것 studying ◊ what;
*kŭgŏshi chega choahanŭn
kŏshiyeyo* 그것이 제가 좋아하는
것이에요 that's what I like

nŭp 늪 swamp
nŭp kat'ŭn 늪 같은 swampy
nŭrida 늘이다 extend, stretch; take down
nŭrida 느리다 be slow; be loose
nŭrige hada 느리게 하다 slow down
nŭrin 느린 slow, sluggish
nŭrin malt'u 느린 말투 drawl
nŭrinnŭrit kada 느릿느릿 가다 crawl
nŭrinnŭrit'age 느릿느릿하게 at a crawl
nŭrin tongjagŭro 느린 동작으로 in slow motion
nŭrŏjida 늘어지다 stretch; sag, hang; *ch'uk nŭrŏjida* 축 늘어지다 droop, sag
nŭrŏjin 늘어진 flabby
nŭrŏnada 늘어나다 stretch, give
nŭrŏnot'a 늘어놓다 draw up
nŭrŭmnamu 느릅나무 elm
nŭryŏjida 느려지다 slow down
nŭsŭnhage hada 느슨하게 하다 loosen, slacken
nŭsŭnhan 느슨한 loose, slack; lax
nŭtch'uda 늦추다 slacken
nŭtch'uŏjida 늦추어지다 slacken off
nŭtkkim 느낌 sense, feeling
nŭttcham chada 늦잠 자다 sleep late; oversleep
nŭt-tta 늦다 be late
nubida 누비다 weave; move
nubi ibul 누비 이불 quilt
nubi chaek'it 누비 재킷 quilted jacket
nuch'uham 누추함 squalor
nuch'uhan chip 누추한 집 hovel
nuch'ul 누출 escape, leak
nuch'uldoeda 누출되다 escape
nudŏgiga toeŏ 누더기가 되어 in tatters
nuga 누가 nougat; who; Luke
nugŭrŏjida 누그러지다 ease off
nugu 누구 who; *igŏsŭn nuguegesŏ on kŏshinji palk'yŏittchi ant'a* 이것은 누구에게서 온 것인지 밝혀있지 않다 it doesn't say who it's from
nugudo 누구도 any; *hakssaengdŭl chung kŭ nugudo* 학생들 중 그 누구도 (+ *negative verb*) none of the students; *... nugudŭnji ...* 누구든지 whoever
nuguna 누구나 everybody, everyone
nugun-ga 누군가 somebody; anybody
nugurŭl 누구를 who; somebody
nugurŭl chemŏt-ttaero hage nae-bŏryŏduda 누구를 제멋대로 하게 내버려두다 leave s.o. to his own devices
nuguseyo 누구세요 hello
nuguŭi 누구의 whose; *igŏsŭn nuguŭi kŏshimnikka?* 이것은 누구의 것입니까? whose is this?
nuguŭi kŏt 누구의 것 whose
numyŏng ssŭiuda 누명 씌우다 frame *person*
nun 눈 eye; snow
nunal 눈알 eyeball
nunbora 눈보라 snowstorm
nunbushida 눈부시다 be dazzling; be spectacular
nunbushige hada 눈부시게 하다 dazzle
nunbushige pinnada 눈부시게 빛나다 glare
nunbushin 눈부신 dazzling, spectacular
nunbushinŭn pit 눈부시는 빛 glare
nunch'ich'aeda 눈치채다 observe, notice
nunch'i ŏmnŭn 눈치 없는 clumsy, tactless
nundŏmi 눈더미 drift
nune hwak ttŭinŭn 눈에 확 띄는 glaring
nune kashi 눈에 가시 undesirable element
nune katch'in 눈에 갇힌 snowbound
nune saenggirŭl ilt'a 눈에 생기를 잃다 glaze over (*of eyes*)
nune ttŭida 눈에 띄다 stick out, stand out
nune ttŭige 눈에 띄게 visibly
nune ttŭinŭn 눈에 띄는 visible; *nŏmu nune ttŭinŭn* 너무 눈에 띄는 showy
nun-gama chuda 눈감아 주다 overlook
nun-gŭmp'an 눈금판 dial
nuni ch'imch'imhan 눈이 침침한

bleary-eyed
nuni mŏl chŏngdoŭi 눈이 멀 정도의
blinding
nuni naerida 눈이 내리다 snow
nuni onŭn 눈이 오는 snowy *day*
nuni ssain 눈이 쌓인 snowy *field*
nun karigae 눈 가리개 blindfold
nun kkamtchak'al saie 눈 깜짝할
사이에 in a flash
nunkkŏp'ul 눈꺼풀 eyelid
nunkkŭm 눈금 scale
nun maja taranada 눈 맞아 달아나다
elope
nun mŏlge hada 눈 멀게 하다 blind
nun mŏn 눈 먼 blind
nunmul 눈물 tear
nunmulnage komapkkunyo
눈물나게 고맙군요 thanks a bunch
nunmul ŏrin 눈물 어린 tearful
nunmul pang-ŭl 눈물 방울 teardrop
nunmul tchage hanŭn kŏt 눈물 짜게
하는 것 slush *pej*
nunmuri nada 눈물이 나다 water (*of
eyes*)
nunmurŭl hŭllida 눈물을 흘리다 be
in tears
nunmurŭl taktta 눈물을 닦다 dry
one's eyes
nun pushige hanŭn 눈 부시게 하는
blinding
nunsat'ae 눈사태 avalanche
nunsong-i 눈송이 snowflake
nunssaram 눈사람 snowman

nunssŏp 눈썹 eyebrow
nunttŏng-i 눈덩이 snowball
nunttongja 눈동자 pupil (*in eye*)
nunŭi kashi 눈의 가시 pain in the
neck (*person*)
nunŭi p'iro 눈의 피로 eye strain
nunŭl karida 눈을 가리다 blindfold
nuptta 눕다 lie, lie down
nurŏputtchi annŭn 눌어붙지 않는
nonstick
nurŭda 누르다 push, press; click
COMPUT
nurŭgi 누르기 push COMPUT
nurŭm tanch'ushigŭi 누름 단추식의
push button
nusŏl 누설 disclosure
nusŏldoeda 누설되다 leak out
nusŏrhada 누설하다 divulge
nwiuch'inŭn 뉘우치는 penitent,
remorseful
nyŏn 년 year; woman *pej*
Nyujillaendŭ 뉴질랜드 New Zealand
Nyujillaendŭin 뉴질랜드인 New
Zealander
nyusŭ 뉴스 news; development;
event
nyusŭ pangsonghanŭn saram 뉴스
방송하는 사람 newsreader
nyusŭ pangsong-ŭl hada 뉴스
방송을 하다 newscast
nyusŭ podo 뉴스 보도 news
report
Nyuyok 뉴욕 New York

ŏ

Ŏbŏinal 어버이날 Parents' Day
ŏbu 어부 fisherman
-ŏch'i -어치 worth; **samch'ŏn wŏnŏch'i** 삼천 원어치 three thousand wons' worth
ŏch'ŏguniŏmnŭn 어처구니없는 absurd
ŏdaept'ŏ 어댑터 adapter ELEC
ŏdi 어디 where; **ŏdie noŭlkkayo?** 어디에 놓을까요? where shall I put this?; **ŏdiesŏ wassŭmnikka?** 어디에서 왔습니까? where are you from?; **ŏdiro kamnikka?** 어디로 갑니까? where are you going?; **ŏdi tarŭn kosŭro kapsshida** 어디 다른 곳으로 갑시다 let's go somewhere else; **ŏdirŭl kadŏrado** 어디를 가더라도 wherever you go; **kŭgŏsŭn Hanguk ŏdiena it-tta** 그것은 한국 어디에나 있다 you find them all over Korea
ŏdidŭnji 어디든지 everywhere, wherever
ŏdin-gae 어딘가에 somewhere
ŏditchŭme(sŏ) 어디쯤에(서) whereabouts, where
ŏdŭl su innŭn 얻을 수 있는 obtainable
ŏdŭl su ŏmnŭn 얻을 수 없는 unobtainable
ŏdŭryŏgo noryŏk'ada 얻으려고 노력하다 strive for
ŏduk'ŏmk'ŏmhan 어두컴컴한 gloomy
ŏdum 어둠 darkness
ŏdumch'imch'imhan 어둠침침한 dim
ŏduptta 어둡다 be dark; be in the dark; be weak
ŏduun 어두운 dark; gloomy
ŏduun pitkkarŭi 어두운 빛깔의 dark-colored
ŏduwŏjida 어두워지다 get dark
ŏgan 어간 stem (of word)

ŏgaptchŏgin 억압적인 repressive
ŏgap'ada 억압하다 repress
ŏgŭmni 어금니 molar
ŏgwi 어귀 mouth (of river)
ŏgyang 억양 inflection
ŏhagŭi 어학의 linguistic
ŏhoengnyang 어획량 haul (of fish)
ŏhwi 어휘 vocabulary
ŏje 어제 yesterday
ŏjetppam 어젯밤 last night
...ŏjida ...어 지다 become ..., get ...
ŏjillŏ noŭn 어질러 놓은 disorderly
ŏjirŏptta 어지럽다 feel faint; be dizzy; be chaotic
ŏjirŏun 어지러운 giddy, faint; messy
ŏjirŭda 어지르다 mess up
ŏjo 어조 tone
ŏkkae 어깨 shoulder; **ŏkkaerŭl ŭssŭk-kkŏrida** 어깨를 으쓱거리다 shrug one's shoulders
ŏkssen 억센 strong, tough, robust
ŏkssen sanai 억센 사나이 tough guy
ŏkssugat'ŭn 억수같은 driving, torrential rain; **(piga) ŏkssugach'i p'ŏbunnŭnda** (비가) 억수같이 퍼붓는다 it's pouring (with rain)
ŏktche 억제 constraint, curb, inhibition; restraint
ŏktchedoen 억제된 inhibited
ŏktchedoen p'yohyŏn 억제된 표현 understatement
ŏktchehada 억제하다 check, restrain; control; inhibit; stifle
ŏktchehal su ŏmnŭn 억제할 수 없는 irresistible
ŏktchi 억지 obstinacy
ŏktchiro ppaeda 억지로 빼다 wrench; pull
ŏktchiro ...shik'ida 억지로 ...시키다 compel
ŏlbŏmurida 얼버무리다 manipulate; stall
ŏlda 얼다 freeze
ŏlgul 얼굴 face

ŏlgurŭl pulk'ida 얼굴을 붉히다 blush, go red in the face

ŏlgurŭl tchip'urida 얼굴을 찌푸리다 wince

ŏlk'ida 얽히다 become entangled in

ŏlk'ŭnhage ch'wihan 얼큰하게 취한 tipsy

ŏllida 얼리다 freeze

ŏllon 언론 journalism; the press

ŏllon-gye 언론계 journalism

ŏllonŭi chayu 언론의 자유 free speech

ŏllugi saenggida 얼룩이 생기다 stain

ŏlluk 얼룩 mark; stain; smear; smudge

ŏlluk chegŏje 얼룩 제거제 stain remover

ŏlluktchin 얼룩진 streaky

ŏllungmal 얼룩말 zebra

ŏlma 얼마 how much; how long; how many; how far; **ŏlma andoenŭn** 얼마 안되는 not much; ***...ŭn/nŭn ŏlmaimnikka?** ...은/는 얼마입니까? how much is/are ...?

ŏlmana ...? 얼마나 ...? how much?

ŏlmana chaju? 얼마나 자주? how often?

ŏlmana chŏne? 얼마나 전에? how long ago?

ŏlmana kŏllimnikka? 얼마나 걸립니까? how long does it take?

ŏlmana mani? 얼마나 많이? how many?

ŏlp'it poda 얼핏 보다 catch a fleeting glimpse of

ŏmaŏmahan 어마어마한 huge

ŏmch'ŏng manŭn 엄청 많은 an awful lot

ŏmch'ŏngnada 엄청나다 be preposterous

ŏmch'ŏngnage 엄청나게 very, extraordinarily

ŏmch'ŏngnan 엄청난 extraordinary, amazing; preposterous

ŏmhage 엄하게 severely

ŏmhage hada 엄하게 하다 tighten up

ŏmhage tasŭrida 엄하게 다스리다 crack down on

ŏmhan 엄한 grim; strict, tough

ŏmi 어미 ending GRAM

ŏmji sonkkarak 엄지 손가락 thumb

ŏmjunghan 엄중한 stringent

ŏmkkyŏk 엄격 severity; rigor

ŏmkkyŏk'ada 엄격하다 be strict

ŏmkkyŏk'age 엄격하게 strictly; *kŭgŏsŭn ŏmkkyŏk'age kŭmjidoe-ŏ it-tta* 그것은 엄격하게 금지되어 있다 it is strictly forbidden

ŏmkkyŏk'an 엄격한 strict, stern; straitlaced

ŏmma 엄마 mom

ŏmmang-in sangt'ae 엄망인 상태 muddle, mess

ŏmmirhi 엄밀히 strictly, closely

ŏmmu 업무 affair, business

ŏmmuryang 업무량 workload

ŏmmu shigan 업무 시간 office hours

ŏmmu suhaeng 업무 수행 performance

ŏmni 엄니 fang; tusk

ŏmnŭn 없는 no; ***...i/ga ŏmnŭn** ...이/가 없는 without; *toni hanp'undo ŏmnŭn* 돈이 한푼도 없는 penniless

ŏmŏni 어머니 mother

ŏmŏnigat'ŭn 어머니같은 motherly

ŏmŏninal 어머니날 Mother's Day

ŏmŏniŭi 어머니의 maternal

ŏmp'o 엄포 bluff; deception

ŏmp'orŭl not'a 엄포를 놓다 bluff

ŏmssuk'ada 엄숙하다 be solemn

ŏmssuk'an 엄숙한 solemn

ŏndŏk 언덕 hill

ŏndŏk kkokttaegi 언덕 꼭대기 hilltop

ŏngdŏng-i 엉덩이 bottom, butt; buttocks

ŏnggida 엉기다 clot, coagulate

ŏngk'ida 엉키다 get tangled up

ŏngmang 엉망 mess

ŏngmangjinch'ang 엉망진창 havoc

ŏngmang-ŭro mandŭlda 엉망으로 만들다 wreck, mess up

ŏngmang-ŭro p'agoehada 엉망으로 파괴하다 wreck

ŏngnullin 억눌린 repressed, pent-up

ŏngnurŭda 억누르다 repress

ŏngnurŭl su ŏmnŭn 억누를 수 없는 irrepressible

ŏngnyuja 억류자 detainee

ŏngttunghada 엉뚱하다 be extraordinary
ŏngttunghan shigane 엉뚱한 시간에 at this unearthly hour
ŏngt'ŏri 엉터리 broken *Korean etc*
ŏn-gŭp 언급 comment, remark; mention; reference
ŏn-gŭp'ada 언급하다 comment, remark; mention; refer to
ŏnje 언제 when; *...l ttaenŭn ŏnjedŭnji* ...ㄹ 때는 언제든지 whenever; *ŏnjedŭn malman haseyo* 언제든 말만 하세요 I am at your disposal
ŏnjekkajina 언제까지나 forever
ŏnjena 언제나 always, for ever
ŏnjen-ga 언제가 ever, someday
ŏnŏ 언어 language
ŏnŏ chang-ae 언어 장애 language barrier; speech defect
ŏnŏ ch'iryo chŏnmun-ga 언어 치료 전문가 speech therapist
ŏnŏhaktcha 언어학자 linguist
ŏntchanahada 언짢아하다 mind, object to
ŏnttŭt poda 언뜻 보다 catch sight of
ŏnŭ 어느 what; which; *ŏnŭ chŏngdo* 어느 정도 some, a measure of; *ŏnŭ chŏngdokkaji* 어느 정도까지 to a certain extent
ŏnŭ han tchogŭi 어느 한 쪽의 either; *Xna Y chung ŏnŭ hanarado* X나 Y 중 어느 하나라도 either X or Y
ŏnŭ kŏt 어느 것 which; *... ŏnŭ kŏshidŭn(ji)* ... 어느 것이든(지) whichever
ŏnŭ kot 어느 곳 anywhere
ŏnŭnal 어느날 one day
ŏnŭ tchogina 어느 쪽이나 either
ŏpkkŭreidŭ 업그레이드 upgrade
ŏpkkŭreidŭhada 업그레이드하다 upgrade
ŏppŏp 어법 usage
ŏprait'ŭ p'iano 업라이트 피아노 upright piano
ŏprodŭhada 업로드하다 upload
ŏpssaeda 없애다 remove, get rid of
...ŏpsshi ...없이 without; *...ŏpsshi chinaeda* ...없이 지내다 do without, go without; *...ŏpsshi hada* ...없이

하다 dispense with; *...ŏpsshi saragada* ...없이 살아가다 go without
ŏpssŏjida 없어지다 go; disappear; be missing
ŏpssŏsŏ 없어서 for want of
ŏptchillŏjida 엎질러지다 spill
ŏptchirŭda 엎지르다 spill
ŏptchŏk 업적 achievement
ŏptchongbyŏl chŏnhwa pŏnhobu 업종별 전화 번호부 yellow pages
ŏptta 없다 there is no; not have; lack; be out, not be at home; *k'ŏp'i/ch'aga ŏptta* 커피/차가 없다 there's no coffee/tea; *nanŭn ŏnŏe sojiri ŏptta* 나는 언어에 소질이 없다 I'm no linguist
ŏpttŭrida 엎드리다 get down, duck
ŏp'asŭt'ŭrop'i 어파스트로피 apostrophe
ŏribŏngbŏnghage hada 어리벙벙하게 하다 stun
ŏrida 어리다 be very young
ŏridungjŏrhaejin 어리둥절해진 dazed
ŏrimdo ŏpssŏ! 어림도 없어! no way!
ŏrimjimjak 어림짐작 guesswork
Ŏrininal 어린이날 Children's Day
ŏriniyong chwasŏk 어린이용 좌석 child's seat, car seat
ŏrin nom 어린 놈 monkey, young rascal
ŏrinshijŏl 어린시절 childhood
ŏrisŏgŭn 어리석은 stupid, dumb; foolish
ŏrisŏgŭn chit 어리석은 짓 folly
ŏrisŏktta 어리석다 be foolish
ŏritkkwangdae 어릿광대 clown
ŏrŭm 얼음 ice; *ŏrŭmŭl kyŏt-ttŭryŏ* 얼음을 곁들여 on the rocks, with ice; *ŏrŭmŭl nŏhŭn* 얼음을 넣은 iced
ŏrŭmi ŏrŭn 얼음이 얼은 icy
ŏrŭn 어른 adult, grown-up
ŏrŭn 얼은 frozen
ŏrŭnsŭrŏun 어른스러운 grown-up
ŏryŏmp'ushi nat'anada 어렴풋이 나타나다 loom up
ŏryŏmp'ut'an 어렴풋한 vague
ŏryŏpkke 어렵게 with difficulty
ŏryŏptta 어렵다 be hard, be difficult
ŏryŏum 어려움 difficulty
ŏryŏun 어려운 difficult

ŏsaek'an 어색한 labored

ŏsŏlp'ŭn 어설픈 rough, careless; lame *excuse*

ŏsŏn 어선 fishing boat

ŏsŭllŏnggŏrida 어슬렁거리다 hang about; saunter; prowl

ŏsŭrehage pich'ida 어스레하게 비치다 gleam

ŏsŭrehan pit 어스레한 빛 gleam

ŏsusŏnhada 행동이 어수선다 be in disorder; *haengdong-i ŏsusŏnhan* 행동이 어수선한 clumsy

ŏtchaet-ttŭn 어쨋든 regardless; in any case; anyhow; *ŏtchaet-ttŭn chossŭmnida* 어쨋든 좋습니다 very well, alright then

ŏtchidoen iriya? 어찌된 일이야? how come?

ŏtchihal parŭl morŭda 어찌할 바를 모르다 be at a loss

ŏtchŏl chul morŭda 어쩔 줄 모르다 be overwhelmed by

ŏtchŏl su ŏmnŭn 어쩔 수 없는 unavoidable

ŏtchŏl su ŏpssŏyo 어쩔 수 없어요 it can't be helped

ŏtchŏnji 어쩐지 somehow, for some unknown reason

ŏtkkallida 엇갈리다 miss (*not meet*)

ŏtkkoja hanŭn 얻고자 하는 acquisitive

ŏttaeyo 것은 how; how about; *k'ŏp'i han chan ŏttaeyo?* 커피 한 잔 어때요? how about a cup of coffee?; *yojŭm ŏttaeyo* 요즘 어때요? how are things?

ŏttŏk'e 어떻게 how; *ŏttŏk'e chinae-seyo? – chal issŭmnida* 어떻게 지내세요? - 잘 있습니다 how are you? – fine; *ŏttŏk'e saeng-gak'aseyo?* 어떻게 생각하세요? what do you think?

ŏttŏk'edŭnji 어떻게든지 somehow

ŏttŏn 어떤 any; some; which; what; what kind of; *ŏttŏn myŏnesŏnŭn* 어떤 면에서는 in a way, in certain respects; *ŏttŏn ŭimiesŏnŭn* 어떤 의미에서는 in a sense; *ŏttŏn ...(i)rado* 어떤 ...(이)라도 whatever; any; *ŏttŏn chongnyuŭi ...?* 어떤 종류의 ...? what kind of ...?

ŏttŏn kŏt 어떤 것 something; *ŏttŏn kŏt?* 어떤 것? which one?; what kind of thing?

ŏttŏn tarŭn kosesŏ 어떤 다른 곳에서 elsewhere, somewhere else; *ŏttŏn tarŭn kosŭro* 어떤 다른 곳으로 elsewhere, somewhere else (*motion toward*)

ŏttŏseyo? 어떠세요? how are you?

ŏt-tta 얻다 get, obtain; earn; gain

ŏullida 어울리다 go with, associate with; mix with; get on with; suit; match

ŏullinŭn 어울리는 matching; suitable

...ŏya handa ...어야 한다 have to, must; be bound to

...ŏyaman hada ...어야만 하다 have (got) to; should, must

o

o 오 five; oh!

oashissŭ 오아시스 oasis

obŏdŭraibŭ 오버드라이브 overdrive

obŭn 오븐 oven

och'an 오찬 lunch

oda 오다 come; fall (*of night*); *...esŏ oda* ...에서 오다 come from

odioŭi 오디오의 audio

odishyŏn 오디션 audition

odogado mot'ada 오도가도 못하다 be stranded, be stuck

odohada 오도하다 mislead

odohanŭn 오도하는 misleading

odumak 오두막 hut

odumaktchip 오두막집 shack

oe 외 outside; except; *Sŏul oeg-wage* 서울 외곽에 outside Seoul

oeadŭl 외아들 only son

oebu 외부 outside ◊ external

oebusaram 외부사람 outsider

oech'ida 외치다 cry, exclaim

oech'im 외침 cry, call; scream

oech'yŏ purŭda 외쳐 부르다 cry out

oedongttal 외동딸 only daughter

oegugin 외국인 foreigner

oegugin hyŏmo 외국인 혐오 xenophobia

oegugŏ 외국어 foreign language

oeguk 외국 foreign country ◊ foreign

oeguk'wan 외국환 foreign exchange

oegwan 외관 external appearance

oegwansang-ŭi 외관상의 exterior

oegwanŭl sonsangshik'ida 외관을 손상시키다 disfigure

oegyein 외계인 alien (*from space*)

oegyo 외교 diplomacy ◊ diplomatic

oegyogwan 외교관 diplomat

oegyomyŏnch'aek 외교면책 diplomatic immunity

oegyosul 외교술 diplomacy, tact

oeharabŏji 외할아버지 maternal grandfather

oehwa 외화 foreign currency

oehyangtchŏgin 외향적인 outgoing

oejin 외진 out of the way

oekkwa ŭisa 외과 의사 surgeon

oekkwayong mesŭ 외과용 메스 scalpel

oemu 외무 foreign affairs ◊ foreign

Oemubu 외무부 Department of State

Oemu changgwan 외무 장관 Secretary of State

oemu chŏngch'aek 외무 정책 foreign policy

oemuŏmmu 외무업무 foreign affairs

oemyŏnhada 외면하다 turn away, look away

oensonjabi 왼손잡이 left-handed

oentchoge(sŏ) 왼쪽에(서) on the left

oentchogŭro 왼쪽으로 to the left

oentchok 왼쪽 left

oe pal sŭk'eit'ŭ 외 발 스케이트 scooter (*child's*)

oep'anwŏn 외판원 commercial traveler

oeroptta 외롭다 be solitary, be lonely

oeroum 외로움 loneliness

oeroun 외로운 lonely

oesamch'on 외삼촌 uncle (*mother's brother*)

oesang 외상 credit FIN

oesang kŏrae 외상 거래 charge account

oeshik'ada 외식하다 eat out

oesŏltchŏgin 외설적인 pornographic, obscene

oesungmo 외숙모 aunt (*mother's brother's wife*)

oettan 외딴 isolated, remote

oet'u 외투 overcoat; cloak

oeuda 외우다 memorize

ogap'ada 억압하다 supress

ogoe 옥외 open-air ◊ open air

ohae 오해 misunderstanding, misconception

ohaehada 오해하다 misread, misunderstand

ohiryŏ 오히려 rather, preferably

ohiryŏ naŭn 오히려 나은 preferable

ohu 오후 afternoon; *ohue* 오후에 in the afternoon

oi 오이 cucumber

oil 오일 oil

oji 오지 bush, hinterland

ojik 오직 only, solely

ojing-ŏ 오징어 squid

ojŏn 오전 morning; *ojŏne* 오전에 in the morning

ojon 오존 ozone

ojonch'ŭng 오존층 ozone layer

ojum nuda 오줌 누다 urinate; pee

okp'yŏn 옥편 Chinese character dictionary

oksshin-gaksshinhada 옥신각신하다 argue, squabble

okssusu 옥수수 maize, corn; sweetcorn

ok'esŭt'ŭra 오케스트라 orchestra

ok'ŭ 오크 oak (*wood*)

ok'ŭnamu 오크나무 oak (*tree*)

olbarŭda 올바르다 be straight; be upright; be honest

olbarŭge 올바르게 correctly, right

olbarŭn 올바른 right, proper; just

olch'aeng-i 올챙이 tadpole

olgami 올가미 noose

olk'e 올케 sister-in-law (*woman's brother's wife*)

ollagada 올라가다 go up, climb; *1935nyŏnŭro kŏsŭllŏ ollagasŏ* 1935년으로 거슬러 올라가서 back in 1935

ollain 온라인 on-line

ollain sŏbissŭ 온라인 서비스 on-line service

olla it-tta 올라 있다 be up (*of prices, temperature*)

ollaoda 올라오다 come up

ollibŭ 올리브 olive

ollibŭ kirŭm 올리브 기름 olive oil

ollida 올리다 raise; *p'ŏmp'ŭro p'ŏ ollida* 펌프로 퍼 올리다 pump

ollim 올림 Yours truly, Yours sincerely

Ollimp'ik Keim 올림픽 게임 Olympic Games

olppaemi 올빼미 owl

olt'a 옳다 be right, be correct ◊ OK

omgida 옮기다 move, transfer; carry

omgyŏjigi shwiun 옮겨지기 쉬운 infectious *laughter*

omgyŏt'ada 옮겨타다 transfer

omŭllet 오믈렛 omelet

omŭrida 오므리다 pucker; purse; furl

onch'ŏn 온천 spa

ondo 온도 temperature

ondogye 온도계 thermometer

ondol 온돌 heated floor

ongho 옹호 defense

onghohada 옹호하다 defend

onghoja 옹호자 defender, champion

on-gi 온기 warmth

on-gŏnhan 온건한 moderate

on-gŏnp'a 온건파 moderate party

onhwahan 온화한 mild, gentle; benign

onjŏng 온정 warmth, geniality

onlain 온라인 on-line

onnan chŏnsŏn 온난 전선 warm front

onsang 온상 breeding ground; hotbed

onshil 온실 glasshouse; nursery; conservatory

onshil hyokkwa 온실 효과 greenhouse effect

onsunhan 온순한 gentle, meek

onsu suyŏngjang 온수 수영장 heated swimming pool

ont'ong 온통 entirely

onŭl 오늘 today

onŭl ach'im 오늘 아침 this morning

onŭl chŏnyŏk 오늘 저녁 this evening

onŭllobut'ŏ 오늘로부터 from today on

onŭlnarŭi 오늘날의 present-day

onŭl ohue 오늘 오후에 this afternoon

onŭl pam 오늘 밤 tonight

oppa 오빠 brother (*woman's elder*)

opsshŏn sangp'um 옵션 상품 optional extras

op'era 오페라 opera

op'era haussŭ 오페라 하우스 opera house

op'era kasu 오페라 가수 opera singer

op'era mang-wŏn-gyŏng 오페라 망원경 opera glasses

op'ŏreit'ing shisŭt'em 오퍼레이팅 시스템 operating system
op'ŭnt'ik'et 오픈티켓 open ticket
op'ŭsaidŭ 오프사이드 offside
orae 오래 long, a long while; *orae chŏne* 오래 전에 long ago
oraedoen 오래된 old
orae kanŭn 오래 가는 durable
orae kkŭnŭn 오래 끄는 protracted, lengthy
oraen 오랜 old
orae sayonghan 오래 사용한 old, veteran
oraettong-an 오랫동안 for a long time
orak 오락 entertainment, pleasure
oraksshishŏl 오락시설 amenities
oral sseksssŭ 오랄 섹스 oral sex
orangmul 오락물 amusements, games
orenji 오렌지 orange
orenji chyussŭ 오렌지 쥬스 orange juice
orenjijok 오렌지족 rich kids (*of Seoul's wealthy elite renowned for their extravagant lifestyle*)
ori 오리 duck
orient'eishyŏn 오리엔테이션 orientation; induction ceremony
orit'ŏl ibul 오리털 이불 eiderdown, quilt
orit'ŏl p'ak'a 오리털 파카 padded jacket
orŭda 오르다 climb; mount; increase
orŭgajŭm 오르가즘 orgasm
orŭgan 오르간 organ MUS
orŭn 옳은 correct
orŭnp'yŏne 오른편에 on the right-hand side
orŭnsonjabiŭi 오른손잡이의 right-handed
orŭntchoguro 오른쪽으로 right, to the right

orŭntchok 오른쪽 right; *orŭntchoge(sŏ)* 오른쪽에(서) on the right; *orŭntchok panghyang-ŭro* 오른쪽 방향으로 on your right hand
oryŏdugi 오려두기 cut COMPUT
oryŏnaeda 오려내다 cut out
oryŏnaen kŏt 오려낸 것 cutting
osan 오산 miscalculation
Oseania 오세아니아 Oceania ◊ Oceanian
oship 오십 fifty
osolkkil 오솔길 alley
ossak'an 오싹한 eerie
Osŭk'a shisangshik 오스카 시상식 Oscars ceremony
osŭl iptta 옷을 입다 dress, get dressed
osŭl ip'ida 옷을 입히다 dress *person*
osŭl pŏtkkida 옷을 벗기다 undress, strip *person*
osŭl pŏt-tta 옷을 벗다 undress, strip
Osŭt'ŭria 오스트리아 Austria ◊ Austrian
ot 옷 clothes; clothing; *ot hanbŏl* 옷 한벌 an item of clothing
otchŏm 오점 smear (*on character*)
otkkabang 옷가방 suitcase
otkkaji 옷가지 wardrobe (*clothes*)
otkkam 옷감 material, fabric
otkkŏri 옷걸이 clothes hanger
ot-tchang 옷장 closet
ottŏn 어떤 certain, particular
ot-ttan 옷단 hem
ott'ŏri 옷털이 clothes brush
ot'obai 오토바이 motorbike
ot'ŭmil 오트밀 oatmeal
owŏl 오월 May
oyŏm 오염 pollution; contamination
oyŏmmultchil 오염물질 pollutant
oyŏmshik'ida 오염시키다 pollute, contaminate
oyonghada 오용하다 misuse

P

pa 바 way; thing; crossbar; *naega al pa anida* 내가 알 바 아니다 for all I care

pabek'yu 바베큐 barbecue

pabek'yuyong ch'ŏlp'an 바베큐용 철판 barbecue (*equipment*)

pabo 바보 idiot; *pabojisŭl hada* 바보짓을 하다 behave like an idiot

pabosŭrŏun 바보스러운 idiotic

pach'ida 바치다 dedicate, devote; donate; sacrifice

pach'im chŏpsshi 받침 접시 saucer

pada 바다 sea; ocean

pada chŏkta 받아 적다 take down, write down

padadŭrida 받아들이다 assimilate; accept; come to terms with; keep down; *chok'e / nappŭge padadŭryŏjida* 좋게 / 나쁘게 받아들여지다 go down well / badly

padadŭril su innŭn 받아들일 수 있는 acceptable; admissible

padagŭl pŏsŏnada 바닥을 벗어나다 bottom out

padajŏkta 받아적다 write down

padak 바닥 floor; bottom; sole (*of foot, shoe*)

padassŭgi 받아쓰기 dictation

padatkkajae 바다가재 lobster

padŭl manhada 받을 만하다 deserve

padŭl manhan 받을 만한 be worthy of, deserve

Paduk 바둑 Go

pae 배 stomach, belly; embryo; ship; pear; *han pae saekki* 한 배 새끼 litter (*of animal*); *pae ane* 배 안에 on board

paeban 배반 betrayal, treachery

paebanhada 배반하다 betray, doublecross

paebanhanŭn 배반하는 treacherous

paebanja 배반자 traitor

paebuhada 배부하다 distribute

paeburŭda 배부르다 full up (*with food*)

paech'i 배치 layout; batch (*of data*)

paech'idoeda 배치되다 be stationed at

paech'ihada 배치하다 arrange, position

paech'u 배추 Chinese cabbage

paech'ul 배출 exhaust, fumes

paech'ulgu 배출구 outlet (*of pipe*)

paech'ulshik'ida 배출시키다 drain (off)

paedal 배달 delivery

paedalbu 배달부 messenger, courier

paedalch'a 배달차 delivery van

paedal kuyŏk 배달 구역 round (*of mailman etc*)

paedal naltcha 배달 날짜 delivery date

paedanggŭm 배당금 dividend

paedanghada 배당하다 allot

paedarhada 배달하다 deliver

paedarwŏn 배달원 tradesman

paedŭmint'ŏn 배드민턴 badminton

paedŭmint'ŏn kong 배드민턴 공 shuttlecock

Paegak-kkwan 백악관 White House

paegigwan 배기관 exhaust (pipe); waste pipe

paegi kasŭ 배기 가스 exhaust

paegil 백일 100 day ceremony (*after birth*); one hundred and one

paegilmong 백일몽 daydream

paegin 백인 white (*person*)

paegirhae 백일해 whooping cough

paegŏp 백업 backup

paegŏp tisŭk'ŭ 백업 디스크 backup disk

paegŏp tŭraibŭ 백업 드라이브 backup drive; tape drive

paegŏp'ada 백업하다 back up *file*

paegop'ŭda 배고프다 be hungry

paegop'ŭm 배고픔 hunger

paegop'ŭn 배고픈 hungry; *paega kop'ayo* 배가 고파요 I'm hungry

paegŭbŏptcha 배급업자 distributor COM

paegŭmnyang 배급량 ration

paegŭp'ada 배급하다 ration

paegu 배구 volleyball

paegwan 배관 plumbing, pipes

paegwangong 배관공 plumber

paegyŏl chŏn-gu 배열 전구 light bulb

paegyŏng 배경 background, setting

paegyŏng ŭmak 배경 음악 soundtrack

paehu 배후 background; rear

paehu-esŏ chojonghada 배후에서 조종하다 pull strings

paejehada 배제하다 exclude

paejŏnban 배전반 switchboard

paek 백 hundred; white; back; bag

paek chunyŏn 백 주년 centenary

paek haendŭ 백 핸드 backhand

paek-kkŭm 백금 platinum

paek-kkwa sajŏn 백과 사전 encyclopedia

paekkop 배꼽 navel

paekppal 백발 white hair; gray hair; *paekppari toeda* 백발이 되다 be going gray

paekpparŭi 백발의 gray-haired

paekppunŭi il 백분의 일 hundredth

paekp'odoju 백포도주 white wine

paeksshin 백신 vaccine

paekssüp'eisŭ k'i 백스페이스 키 backspace (key)

paektcha 백자 white porcelain (*Choson*)

paektcho 백조 swan

paek'ap 백합 lily

paek'wajŏm 백화점 department store

paek'yŏlppyŏng 백혈병 leukemia

paelbŭ 밸브 valve

paem 뱀 snake

paemjang-ŏ 뱀장어 eel

paemŏlmi 배멀미 seasickness

paemŏlmiga nan 배멀미가 난 seasick

paemŏlmihada 배멀미하다 get seasick

paenang 배낭 rucksack; *paenang maego yŏhaenghada* 배낭 매고 여행하다 backpack, go backpacking

paenang yŏhaengja 배낭 여행자 backpacker

paendŭ 밴드 (pop) band

paengman 백만 million

paengman changja 백만 장자 millionaire

paengmirŏ 백미러 rear-view mirror

paenmŏri 뱃머리 bow, prow

paennori 뱃놀이 sail

paeran ch'oktchinje 배란 촉진제 fertility drug

paeryŏ 배려 respect; tact; consideration

paesang 배상 compensation, recompense

paesanghada 배상하다 compensate

paeshimwŏn 배심원 juror

paeshimwŏndan 배심원단 jury

paeshimwŏnjang 배심원장 foreman (of the jury)

paesŏhada 배서하다 endorse

paesŏn 배선 wiring

paesok'ada 배속하다 post, transfer, send

paesu 배수 drainage; drains

paesugwan 배수관 drainpipe

paesuro 배수로 drain; storm drain

paetchang 배짱 courage, nerve

paetchi 배지 pin, badge

paet'ajŏgin 배타적인 exclusive

paet'al 배탈 upset stomach

paet'alnada 배탈나다 have an upset stomach

paet'ŏri 배터리 battery

paeŭi k'i 배의 키 rudder

paeŭnmangdŏk 배은망덕 ingratitude

paeuda 배우다 learn

paeuga toeda 배우가 되다 become an actor/actress

paeuja 배우자 partner; spouse

paeunghada 배웅하다 see off

paeyŏng 배영 backstroke

paeyŏrhada 배열하다 arrange, put in order

pagaji kŭltta 바가지 긁다 go on at

pagaji ssŭiuda 바가지 씌우다 overcharge

paguni 바구니 basket

paindŏ 바인더 binder

paiŏ 바이어 buyer

paiollin 바이올린 violin
paiollin yŏnjuja 바이올린 연주자 violinist
paiosŭ 바이오스 BIOS COMPUT
pairŏsŭ 바이러스 virus COMPUT
pairŏsŭ paeksshin p'ŭrogŭraem 바이러스 백신 프로그램 antivirus program
pait'ŭ 바이트 byte
paji 바지 pants
paji ammun 바지 앞문 fly
pak 박 night (*in hotel*)
pakk 밖 outside
pakkach'ŭi 바깥의 outside, external
pakkat'e 바깥에 outside
pakkat myŏn 바깥 면 outside
...pakke ...밖에 outside (of); except
pakkŭro 밖으로 outside
pakkuda 바꾸다 change, exchange; swap; vary; move on
pakkul su innŭn 바꿀 수 있는 interchangeable
pakkuŏ chuda 바꾸어 주다 change *money*
pakkuŏ iptta 바꾸어 입다 change *clothes*
pakkuŏjida 바뀌어지다 change
pakkuŏ not'a 바꾸어 놓다 displace, supplant
pakkuŏ t'ada 바꾸어 타다 change *trains, planes*
pakkwida 바뀌다 switch, change; vary; **...(ŭ)ro pakkwida** ...(으)로 바뀌다 give way to, be replaced by
pakkwŏ chuda 바꿔 주다 put through TELEC
pakkwŏt'ada 바꿔타다 transfer
pakkyŏkp'o 박격포 mortar MIL
pakssa 박사 PhD, Doctor of Philosophy
pakssae 박새 tit (*bird*)
pakssa hagwi 박사 학위 doctorate
pakssallaeda 박살내다 write off, wreck
paksshik'an 박식한 erudite
pakssŭ 박스 carton; booth
pakssurŭl ch'ida 박수를 치다 clap, applaud
pakssurŭl ponaeda 박수를 보내다 applaud
paktcha 박자 tempo, beat

paktchwi 박쥐 bat (*animal*)
paktta 박다 drive in *nail*
pakt'arhada 박탈하다 deprive; **chagyŏgŭl pakt'arhada** 자격을 박탈하다 disqualify
pakt'eria 박테리아 bacteria
pak'a 박하 mint (*herb*)
pak'ae 박해 persecution
pak'aehada 박해하다 persecute, oppress
pak'ahyang 박하향 peppermint (*flavoring*)
pak'a sat'ang 박하 사탕 mint, peppermint
pak'ida 박히다 lodge (*of bullet, ball*)
pak'odŭ 바코드 bar code
pak'wi 바퀴 wheel; lap, circuit
pak'wi pŏlle 바퀴 벌레 cockroach
pak'wiŭi chungshimbu 바퀴의 중심부 hub
pal 발 foot; paw
palbal 발발 eruption
palba munggaeda 밟아 뭉개다 trample on
palbarhada 발발하다 erupt
palbyŏnghada 발병하다 affect
palch'we 발췌 clip, extract (*from movie*)
palgabŏsŭn 발가벗은 naked; bare
palgajida 밝아지다 brighten up, become more cheerful
palgak 발각 detection
palgi 발기 erection (*of penis*)
palgŭm 밝음 lightness
palgŭn 밝은 bright; light; fair
palgŭp'ada 발급하다 issue, give out
palgul 발굴 excavation
palgurhada 발굴하다 discover; excavate, unearth
palgwang taiodŭ 발광 다이오드 LED, light-emitting diode
palgyŏn 발견 discovery
palgyŏnhada 발견하다 discover, find
palkkarak 발가락 toe
palkke hada 밝게 하다 light up, lighten
palkkŏrŭm 발걸음 tread
palktta 밝다 be bright; be keen; be expert; be cheerful; dawn
palkkŭn hwarŭl naeda 발끈 화를 내다 flare up, fly into a rage

palkküt pubun 발끝 부분 toe
palkküt'üro 발끝으로 on tippy-toe
palkkup 발굽 hoof
palk'ida 밝히다 reveal, make known; express
palk'yöjunün 밝혀주는 revealing
palk'yönaeda 밝혀내다 find out, uncover
pallajida 발라지다 straighten out; spread
pallan 반란 mutiny, rebellion
pallanaeda 발라내다 shell; clean; take off; debone
pallan-gun 반란군 rebel troops
pallanül irük'ida 반란을 이르키다 revolt
palle 발레 ballet
palle muyongga 발레 무용가 ballet dancer
pallerina 발레리나 ballerina
pallonhada 반론하다 dispute; disagree with
palmae 발매 launch; release; sale
palmae ch'uk'ayön 발매 축하연 launch; release (event)
palmaehada 발매하다 launch; release; bring out
palmok 발목 ankle; *palmogül ppida* 발목을 삐다 twist one's ankle
palmyöng 발명 invention
palmyöngga 발명가 inventor
palmyönghada 발명하다 invent
palp'an 발판 scaffolding; stepping stone
palp'o 발포 gunshot
palppyöng 발병 bout, attack MED
palppyönghada 발병하다 break out (of disease)
palp'yö chuktta 밟혀 죽다 be trampled to death
palp'yo 발표 release; presentation; statement
palssa 발사 blast-off
palssadae 발사대 launch pad
palssadoeda 발사되다 go off (of gun)
palssaeng 발생 happening
palssaengshik'ida 발생시키다 generate, produce
palssahada 발사하다 launch
palssan 발산 emission

palssashik'ida 발사시키다 blast off
palsshinüm 발신음 dial tone
palssong 발송 shipping
palssonghada 발송하다 dispatch, send
palssong-in 발송인 sender
paltchaguk 발자국 footprint
paltchaguk sori 발자국 소리 footstep
paltchak 발작 fit, seizure
paltchaktchögin 발작적인 hysterical
paltchin 발진 rash MED
paltchint'ip'usü 발진티푸스 typhus
paltchön 발전 development; progression
paltchön-gi 발전기 dynamo; generator
paltchönhada 발전하다 develop; advance, improve
paltchönshik'ida 발전시키다 develop, expand
paltchönso 발전소 power station
paltta 밟다 tread; tread on; *chandirül paltchi mashiyo!* 잔디를 밟지 마시요! keep off the grass!
palttalshik'ida 발달시키다 develop; progress
palttüng 발등 instep
palt'op 발톱 toenail; claw; talon
pam 밤 night; chestnut; *pame* 밤에 at night-time, in the night-time; *pam saie* 밤 사이에 during the night; *naeil pam* 내일 밤 tomorrow night; *pam nüjün* 밤 늦은 late (at night); *pam yöhaeng* 밤 여행 travel by night
pambihaenggi 밤비행기 night flight
pamnanu 밤나무 chestnut (tree)
pamsae 밤새 overnight
pan 반 half; *tushi paniyeyo* 두시 반이예요 it's half past two
panana 바나나 banana
panbaji 반바지 shorts
panbak 반박 retort
panbak'ada 반박하다 contradict; protest; retort
panbal 반발 backlash
panbok 반복 repetition
panbok'ada 반복하다 repeat; *muösül panbok'ada* 무엇을 반복하다 do sth over (again)

panch'an 반찬 side dish
panch'anggo 반창고 adhesive tape; Band-Aid®
panch'igŭi 반칙의 irregular
panch'ik 반칙 foul
pandae 반대 opposite; objection; opposition
pandaedoeda 반대되다 run counter to
pandaehada 반대하다 object; object to; oppose, resist; contest; *wae kŭrŭl pandaehanŭn kŏyeyo?* 왜 그를 반대하는 거예요? what do you have against him?
pandaeja 반대자 opponent; dissident
pandaep'yŏn 반대 편 across
pandaero 반대로 on the other hand; conversely; on the contrary; as opposed to; vice versa
pandae shimmunhada 반대 심문하다 cross-examine
pandae tchogŭi 반대 쪽의 opposite
pandaeŭi 반대의 opposite
pandae ŭigyŏn 반대 의견 dissent
pando 반도 peninsula
pandoch'e 반도체 semiconductor
pandongjuŭija 반동주의자 reactionary (*person*)
pandŭshi 반드시 necessarily; certainly
pang 방 room
pan-gam 반감 antipathy
pang-asoe 방아쇠 trigger
pangbŏp 방법 method; style; formula
pangbu ch'ŏrihada 방부 처리하다 embalm
pangbuje 방부제 preservative
pangch'aek 방책 measure, step
pangch'i 방치 neglect
pangch'ŏp 방첩 counterespionage
pangch'ungje 방충제 insect repellent
pangdaehan 방대한 vast, gigantic
Panggŭlladeshi 방글라데시 Bangladesh ◊ Bangladeshi
panggŭm 방금 just now
panggwang 방광 bladder
panggwanhada 방관하다 stand by (and do nothing)

panggwanja 방관자 bystander
panggwi 방귀 fart
panggwi kkwida 방귀 뀌다 fart
panghae 방해 obstacle; disturbance; *panghaerŭl pat-tta* 방해를 받다 suffer a setback
panghaehada 방해하다 disturb; interrupt, disrupt; hinder, impede; jam
panghaehanŭn 방해하는 obstructive
panghaemul 방해물 obstruction; deterrent
panghan 방한 insulation
panghanhada 방한하다 insulate
panghwa 방화 arson
panghwajangch'i 방화장치 incendiary device
panghyang 방향 direction; directions; *panghyang kamgagŭl irŏbŏrin* 방향 감각을 잃어버린 disoriented, confused
panghyang p'yoshidŭng 방향 표시등 turn signal
pangjŏk'ada 방적하다 spin
pangjŏngshik 방정식 equation
pangjonghan 방종한 dissolute, loose
pangmang-i 방망이 bat (*in baseball*)
pangmang-iro ch'ida 방망이로 치다 bat
pangmulgwan 박물관 museum
pangmun 방문 door; visit
pangmunhada 방문하다 visit, call on; look in on; look up
pangmyŏrhada 박멸하다 eradicate
pangnanghada 방랑하다 rove, wander
pangnangja 방랑자 drifter, hobo
pang-ŏ 방어 defense; *pang-ŏhanŭn chasero* 방어하는 자세로 on the defensive
pang-ŏhada 방어하다 defend
pang-ŏjŏgin 방어적인 defensive
pang-ŏyong-ŭi 방어용의 defensive
pan-gongjuŭi 반공주의 anti-Communism
pangp'ae 방패 shield
pangp'aje 방파제 breakwater
pangsanŭng 방사능 radioactivity
pangsanŭng-i innŭn 방사능이 있는 radioactive
pangsanŭng yoppŏp 방사능 요법

radiotherapy
pangsasŏn 방사선 radiation
pangsasŏng naktchin 방사성 낙진 fallout
pangshik 방식 manner, way; system; method; mode; form; *iltchŏnghan pangshige ttarŭn* 일정한 방식에 따른 methodical
pangsong 방송 broadcast; broadcasting; *pangsong chung-e* 방송 중에 on the air
pangsongguk 방송국 station RAD, TV
pangsonghada 방송하다 broadcast; transmit
pangsong-in 방송인 broadcaster
pangsong p'ŭrogŭraem chaptchi 방송 프로그램 잡지 listings magazine
pangsongshil 방송실 studio
pangsudoenŭn 방수되는 waterproof
pangsu oet'u 방수 외투 mackintosh
pangsup'o 방수포 tarpaulin
pangsuŭi 방수의 watertight; showerproof
pangt'an chokki 방탄 조끼 armor
pangt'ang 방탕 debauchery
pangt'anghan 방탕한 debauched, dissolute
pang-ŭm 방음 soundproofing ◊ soundproof
pang-ŭm changch'i 방음 장치 muffler MOT
pan-gu 반구 hemisphere
pang-ul 방울 drip, drop
pang-wi 방위 defense
pan-gyŏk 반격 return
pang-yŏnghada 방영하다 televise
panhae it-tta 반해 있다 be stuck on; have a crush on
panhal manhan 반할 만한 adorable
panhang 반항 defiance
panhanghada 반항하다 defy
panhangjŏgin 반항적인 defiant; rebellious
panhayŏ 반하여 contrary to
panhwan 반환 return
panil kŭnmu 반일 근무 part-time job
panilla 바닐라 vanilla
panjagyong 반작용 reaction
panjagyonghada 반작용하다 react

panji 반지 ring
panjirŭm 반지름 radius
panjŏm 반점 spot; blotch
panjŭnghada 반증하다 disprove
panju 반주 accompaniment; backing
panjudan 반주단 backing group
panjuk'ada 반죽하다 knead
panjurŭl hada 반주를 하다 accompany MUS
pannŭn chŭksshiro 받는 즉시로 by return (of mail)
panp'arŭi 반팔의 short-sleeved
pansahada 반사하다 reflect
pansa shin-gyŏng 반사 신경 reflex
pansa undong 반사 운동 reflex reaction
pansonghada 반송하다 send back
pantchagida 반짝이다 shine, gleam; twinkle
pantchak 반짝 glint
pantchak-kkŏrida 반짝거리다 shine; glisten
pantchak-kkŏrinŭn 반짝거리는 shiny
pantchakpantchak pinnada 반짝반짝 빛나다 glitter
pantchak pinnada 반짝 빛나다 glint
panŭi 반의 half
panŭjil 바느질 needlework, sewing
panŭjilkkŏri 바느질거리 sewing
panŭjil yongp'um 바느질 용품 notions
panŭjirhada 바느질하다 sew
panŭl 바늘 needle; stitches
panŭlgwi 바늘귀 eye (*of needle*)
panŭlttam 바늘땀 stitch
panŭm naerimŭi 반음 내림의 flat MUS
panŭm nopkke 반음 높게 sharp MUS
panŭng 반응 reaction
panŭnghada 반응하다 react, respond
panŭnghanŭn 반응하는 responsive
panŭro chŏptta 반으로 접다 fold in half
panŭro hada 반으로 하다 halve
panwŏn 반원 semicircle
panwŏnhyŏngŭi 반원형의 semicircular
panyŏk 반역 treason
panyŏktcha 반역자 rebel
pap 밥 rice

pap kŭrŭt 밥 그릇 rice bowl

pappŭda 바쁘다 be busy; busy oneself with, occupy oneself with; *...ŭl/rŭl hanŭra pappŭda* ...을/를 하느라 바쁘다 be busy doing ...

pappŭn 바쁜 busy; full

paraboda 바라보다 view

parada 바라다 hope; wish; hope for; wish for; *...girŭl parada* ...기를 바라다 may ...; *nanŭn ...girŭl paramnida* 나는 ...기를 바랍니다 I wish that ...

paraeda 바래다 fade; take, escort; *munkkaji paraeda chulkkeyo* 문까지 바래다 줄께요 I'll see you to the door

paraedajuda 바래다주다 escort

paraen 바랜 faded

paragŏnde 바라건데 hopefully

param 바람 desire, wish; wind; *parami pulgi shijak'anda* 바람이 불기 시작한다 it's getting windy; *parami shimhan* 바람이 심한 gusty

paramdung-i 바람둥이 womanizer

paramjik'an 바람직한 desirable, advisable

param mach'ida 바람 맞히다 stand up (*on date*)

param multchil 발암 물질 carcinogen

paramnan 바람난 flirtatious

param punŭn 바람 부는 windy

param p'iuda 바람 피우다 have an affair with; fool around; cheat on one's wife

paramsŏng-ŭi 발암성의 carcinogenic

paramŭl p'iuda 바람을 피우다 have an affair; be unfaithful

parhada 발하다 utter

parhaeng 발행 publication

parhaenghada 발행하다 print; issue

parhaeng pusu 발행 부수 circulation

parhwi 발휘 exhibition (*of skill*)

parhwihada 발휘하다 exert; show off; *chagi nŭngnyŏk isang-ŭl parhwihada* 자기 능력 이상을 발휘하다 excel oneself

parhyo 발효 fermentation

parhyohada 발효하다 ferment

parik'ang 바리캉 hair clippers

parik'eidŭ 바리케이드 barricade; roadblock

parŏnhada 발언하다 speak; state

paro 바로 properly; directly; *paro ap'e* 바로 앞에 straight ahead; *paro chŏne* 바로 전에 recently; *paro kakkaie* 바로 가까이에 close at hand; *paro kyŏt'e* 바로 곁에 close by; *ŭnhaeng paro yŏp'ye* 은행 바로 옆에 right next to the bank; *paro kŭgŏya!* 바로 그거야! that's right!; *paro kŭrŏk'e* 바로 그렇게 just like that, exactly like that; *paro kŭ saenggak* 바로 그 생각 the very thought; *paro kŭ sun-gane* 바로 그 순간에 at the very moment; *paro seuda* 바로 세우다 erect; *paro sŏ!* 바로 서! stand up straight!

parŭda 바르다 be straight; be right; stick, paste, plaster; spread; put up *wallpaper*

parŭge hada 바르게 하다 straighten out

parŭl kurŭda 발을 구르다 stamp one's feet

parŭm 발음 pronunciation

parŭmhada 발음하다 pronounce

parŭn 바른 proper, correct; orderly; honest; decent

passak mallida 바싹 말리다 parch

passak marŭda 바싹 마르다 dry up

pasŭk'et 바스켓 basket

pasŭrak-kkŏrida 바스락거리다 rustle

pat 밭 (dry) field

patatkka 바닷가 seaside

patch'imttae 받침대 stand, support, base

pattchul 밧줄 rope

pattchurŭl p'ulda 밧줄을 풀다 cast off

pat-tta 받다 receive, accept; undergo; sustain; butt (*of goat*)

pat'ang 바탕 bout; nature; base; *...e pat'angŭl tuda* ...에 바탕을 두다 base on

pat'endŏ 바텐더 bartender

pawi 바위 rock

peda 베다 cut

pegae 베개 pillow

pegaennit 베갯잇 pillowcase

pegi 베기 cut, slash

peil 베일 veil
peisŭ 베이스 bass
pekkyŏ ssŭda 베껴 쓰다 copy
Pelgie 벨기에 Belgium ◊ Belgian
Pelgiein 벨기에인 Belgian
pench'i 벤치 bench
peniŏ happ'an 베니어 합판 veneer
pen sangch'ŏ 벤 상처 cut (*injury*)
peŏnaeda 베어내다 cut off
peŏring 베어링 bearing TECH
peranda 베란다 balcony; veranda
pesŭt'üsellŏ 베스트셀러 best-seller
pet'erang 베테랑 veteran
Pet'erang 베트남 Vietnam ◊
  Vietnamese
Pet'ŭnamin 베트남인 Vietnamese
Pet'ŭnamŏ 베트남어 Vietnamese
  (*language*)
pi... 비... non..., un...
pi 비 rain
pibang 비방 slur, defamation
pibanghanŭn 비방하는 defamatory
pibarame shidallin 비바람에 시달린
  weather-beaten
pibi kkoda 비비 꼬다 squirm (*in
  embarrassment*)
pibimppap 비빔밥 rice mixed with
  meat and vegetables
pibŏnida 비번이다 be off duty
pich'amhada 비참하다 be miserable
pich'ida 비치다 flash
pich'inŭn 비치는 see-through
pich'ŭl naeda 빛을 내다 glow
pich'ŭl naenŭn 빛을 내는 luminous
pich'uda 비추다 shine; flash; reflect;
  ...e pich'uŏsŏ ...에 비추어서 in the
  light of
pich'uk'ada 비축하다 stockpile,
  hoard; **muŏsŭl pich'uk'ada** 무엇을
  비축하다 keep sth in reserve
pida 비다 be empty
pidan 비단 silk
pidio 비디오 video
pidio k'amera 비디오 카메라 video
  camera
pidio k'aset'ŭ 비디오 카세트 video
  cassette
pidio nok'wa 비디오 녹화 video
  recording
pidio nok'wagi 비디오 녹화기 video
  recorder

pidioro ch'waryŏnghada 비디오로
  촬영하다 video
pidio t'eip'ŭ 비디오 테이프
  videotape
pidodŏktchŏgin 비도덕적인
  unprincipled
pidŭm 비듬 dandruff
pidulgi 비둘기 dove; pigeon
piga oda 비가 오다 rain
piga onŭn 비가 오는 rainy, wet
pigida 비기다 draw SP
pigŏjuja 비거주자 non-resident
pigŏp 비겁 cowardice
pigŏp'an 비겁한 cowardly
pigongshigŭi 비공식의 informal
pigongshik 비공식 informality
pigongshiktchŏgin 비공식적인
  unofficial
pigongshiktchŏgŭro 비공식적으로
  unofficially
pigŭk 비극 tragedy
pigŭktchŏgin 비극적인 tragic
pigwanjŏgin 비관적인 pessimistic
pigwanjuŭi 비관주의 pessimism
pigwanjuŭija 비관주의자 pessimist
pigwansŭptchŏgin 비관습적인
  unconventional
pigyŏl 비결 tip, piece of advice
pigyo 비교 comparison
pigyodoel su innŭn 비교될 수 있는
  comparable
pigyogŭp 비교급 comparative GRAM
pigyohada 비교하다 compare;
  ...wa / gwa pigyohaesŏ ...와 / 과
  비교해서 compared with
pigyojŏgin 비교적인 comparative,
  relative
pigyojŏgŭro 비교적으로
  comparatively
pihaeng 비행 flight; flying; **pihaeng
  chung-ŭi** 비행 중의 in-flight
pihaenggi 비행기 airplane; **pihaenggiro** 비행기로 by air; **pihaenggiro toragada** 비행기로
  돌아가다 fly back
pihaengjang 비행장 airfield
pihaeng kyŏngno 비행 경로 flight
  path
pihal te ŏmnŭn 비할 데 없는
  incomparable
pihamnijŏgin 비합리적인

unreasonable
pihŭbyŏnja 비흡연자 non-smoker
pihyŏnshiltchŏgin 비현실적인
impractical, unrealistic
pihyŏptchojŏgin 비협조적인
uncooperative
piin-ganjŏgin 비인간적인 inhuman
pija 비자 visa
pijagŭm 비자금 slush fund
pijŏngsangtchŏgin moyang-ŭi
비정상적인 모양의 misshapen
pijŏngsang-ŭi 비정상의 abnormal
pijobŭn 비좁은 cramped
pijŭnisŭ k'ŭllaesŭ 비즈니스 클래스
business class
pijŭnisŭ mit'ing 비즈니스 미팅
business meeting
pikkoda 비꼬다 twist; give an ironic
twist to
pikkonŭn 비꼬는 dry; ironic
pik'ida 비키다 get out of the way;
kirŭl pik'yŏjuda 길을 비켜주다
make way
pik'ini 비키니 bikini
pilda 빌다 beg; pray; implore
pillida 빌리다 borrow; lend
pillin 빌린 on loan
pillyŏjuda 빌려주다 lend; rent out
pimanhan 비만한 corpulent
pimil 비밀 confidence; secret;
muŏsŭl pimillie hada 무엇을
비밀리에 하다 do sth in secret; *pimillo* 비밀로 in secret; *nuguege
pimirŭl t'ŏrŏnot'a* 누구에게 비밀을
털어놓다 confide in s.o.
pimil chŏngbo kigwan 비밀 정보
기관 secret service
pimil kyŏngch'al 비밀 경찰 secret
police
pimillie sumgyŏjin 비밀리에 숨겨진
undercover
pimil pŏnho 비밀 번호 PIN
pimirŭi 비밀의 secret; underground,
covert
Pimujang Chidae 비무장 지대
Demilitarized Zone, DMZ
pimun 비문 epitaph
pimyŏng 비명 screech, shriek
pimyŏngŭl chirŭda 비명을 지르다
screech, shriek
pin 빈 empty, free

pinan 비난 blame; accusation;
condemnation, reproach
pinanhada 비난하다 accuse; blame;
condemn
pinanhanŭn 비난하는 reproachful
pinan padŭlmanhan 비난 받을만한
reprehensible
pinanŭi yŏjiga ŏpta 비난의 여지가
없다 be beyond reproach
pinbŏnhada 빈번하다 be frequent
pindungbindung chinaeda 빈둥빈둥
지내다 while away; bum around, be
lazy
pindunggŏrida 빈둥거리다 laze
around
pingbing tolda 빙빙 돌다 circle (*of
plane*)
pingbing tollida 빙빙 돌리다 twirl
pingha 빙하 glacier
pin-gone tchidŭn 빈곤에 찌든
impoverished
pin-gonhan 빈곤한 destitute
pin-got 빈 곳 gap
pingsan 빙산 iceberg
pingtchŏm 빙점 freezing point
pin-gunghan 빈궁한 needy, poor
pinhyŏltchŭng 빈혈증 anemia
pinil pongji 비닐 봉지 plastic bag
pinjŏngdaeda 빈정대다 get at,
criticize
pinjŏngdaenŭn 빈정대는 sarcastic
pin konggan 빈 공간 void
pinmin-ga 빈민가 ghetto, slum
pinnada 빛나다 shine; sparkle,
twinkle
pinnagada 빗나가다 swerve; digress;
misfire; *yŏp killo pinnagada* 옆
길로 빗나가다 stray
pinnagan 빗나간 stray *bullet*
pinollijŏgin 비논리적인 illogical
pint'ŏlt'ŏri 빈털터리 down-and-out
pint'ŭm ŏmnŭn 빈틈 없는 alert,
shrewd, on the ball; scrupulous
pinŭl 비늘 scale (*on fish*)
pinŭngnyultchŏgin 비능률적인
inefficient
pinu 비누 soap; *pinu hanjang* 비누
한 장 a bar of soap
pinyak'an 빈약한 flimsy, skimpy
piŏinnŭn 비어있는 unoccupied
piŏinnŭn shigan 비어있는 시간

(time) slot
piok 비옥 fertility (*of soil*)
piok'an 비옥한 fertile *soil*
pip'anjŏgin 비판적인 critical
pip'anjŏgŭro 비판적으로 critically
pip'anŭl pat-tta 비판을 받다 come in for criticism
pip'ongnyŏgŭi 비폭력의 non-violent
pip'ongnyŏk 비폭력 non-violence
pip'ŭbŏgŏ 비프버거 beefburger
pip'yŏng 비평 criticism, review
pip'yŏngga 비평가 critic
pip'yŏnghada 비평하다 criticize
pirŏmŏgŭl 빌어먹을! blast!
pirok ...-l/-ŭltchirado 비록 ...-ㄹ/-을지라도 although, even if
pirot-ttoeda 비롯되다 originate
pirot'ada 비롯하다 begin, start
piryehada 비례하다 be proportional to
piryehanŭn 비례하는 proportional, in proportion
piryo 비료 fertilizer, manure
pisaengsanjŏgin 비생산적인 unproductive
pisagyojŏgin 비사교적인 unsociable
pisang 비상 emergency
pisang ch'angnyuk 비상 착륙 emergency landing
pisangdŭng 비상등 hazard lights
pisanggu 비상구 emergency exit
pisangnyong hwalgangno 비상용 활강로 escape chute
pisangsat'ae 비상사태 state of emergency
pisangshi 비상시 time of emergency; *pisangshie* 비상시에 in an emergency
pisŏ 비서 secretary
pisŏk 비석 tombstone
pissada 비싸다 be expensive
pissan 비싼 expensive
pisŭdŭmhan 비스듬한 slanting
pisŭk'et 비스켓 biscuit
pisŭt'ada 비슷하다 be alike, be similar
pisŭt'an 비슷한 similar
pisugi 비수기 low season
pit 빗 comb
pit 빛 debt; *piji it-tta* 빚이 있다 be in debt

pit 빛 light; ray
pitchang 빗장 bar, bolt
pitcharu 빗자루 broom
pitchida 빚지다 owe
pitchirhada 빗질하다 brush
pitkkŭm 빗금 slash, oblique
pitppang-ul 빗방울 raindrop
pit-tta 빗다 comb
pitturŏjida 비뚤어지다 be warped
pitturŏjin 비뚤어진 crooked; warped
pit'amin 비타민 vitamin
pit'an 비탄 lament
pit'ong 비통 grief
pit'onghaehada 비통해하다 grieve
pit'onghan 비통한 heartrending; bitter
pit'ŭ 비트 bit COMPUT
pit'ŭlda 비틀다 contort; wrench
pit'ŭlgŏrida 비틀거리다 lurch, stagger; totter
pit'ŭlgŏrinŭn 비틀거리는 unsteady
pit'ŭmaep 비트맵 bitmap
piuda 비우다 empty; vacate; *chip piuranŭn t'ongjirŭl pat-tta* 집 비우라는 통지를 받다 get one's eviction notice
piunnŭn 비웃는 derisive
piusŭm 비웃음 derision; sneer
piut-tta 비웃다 laugh at, mock, deride; sneer
piwisaengjŏgin 비위생적인 unhygienic
piyŏrhan 비열한 petty; nasty; *piyŏrhan ch'aengnyak* 비열한 책략 dirty trick
piyong 비용 expense; *Xege Yŭi piyong-ŭl kyŏnjŏk'ada* X에게 Y의 비용을 견적하다 give X a quotation for Y; *piyong-i ŏlmana tŭmnikka?* 비용이 얼마나 듭니까? how much does it cost?
piyong myŏngse 비용 명세 expense account
piyong-ŭl kaptta 비용을 갚다 reimburse
piyujŏgin 비유적인 figurative
piyul 비율 proportion; percentage; rate
pŏban 법안 bill POL
pŏbin chojigŭi 법인 조직의 incorporated

pŏbin hoesa 법인 회사
incorporated, inc
pŏbwŏn 법원 courthouse
pŏbwŏn myŏngnyŏng 법원 명령
court order
pŏdŭlgaji 버들가지 wicker
pŏdŭnamu 버드나무 willow
pŏdunggŏrida 버둥거리다 squirm,
wriggle
pŏgŭ 버그 bug COMPUT
pŏjŏn 버전 version
pŏk'ŭl 버클 buckle
pŏl 벌 bee; deck, pack; suit; pair; set;
plain; punishment ◊ countword for
suit of clothes; pŏrŭl momyŏnhada
벌을 모면하다 get off scot-free;
pŏrŭl myŏnhada 벌을 면하다 get
off (not be punished); pŏrŭl pat-
tchi ank'o 벌을 받지 않고 with
impunity
pŏlch'unghada 벌충하다 make up
for, compensate for
pŏlda 벌다 earn
pŏlgŏbosŭn 벌거벗은 naked
pŏlgŭm 벌금 fine; penalty
pŏlk'ŏk sŏngnaeda 벌컥 성내다 fly
into a rage
pŏlle 벌레 bug; worm
pŏlle mŏgŭn 벌레 먹은 worm-eaten
pŏllida 벌리다 open
pŏlmok 벌목 woodcut
pŏlssŏ 벌써 already
pŏltchip 벌집 beehive; honeycomb
pŏlttŏk 벌떡 suddenly; pŏlttŏk
irŏnada 벌떡 일어나다 jump to
one's feet
pŏm 범 tiger
Pŏma 버마 Burma ◊ Burmese
pŏmhada 범하다 commit
pŏmin 범인 culprit
pŏmin susaek 범인 수색 manhunt
pŏmjoe 범죄 crime; offense; guilt ◊
criminal
pŏmjoein indo 범죄인 인도
extradition
pŏmjoein indo hyŏptchŏng 범죄인
인도 협정 extradition treaty
pŏmjoeja 범죄자 criminal; offender
pŏmju 범주 category
pŏmnam 범람 flood; flooding
pŏmnamhada 범람하다 flood

pŏmnyŏng 법령 law, statute
pŏmppoptcha 범법자 offender
pŏmp'ŏ 범퍼 bumper
pŏmsŏn 범선 sailing ship
pŏmurida 버무리다 toss
pŏmwi 범위 extent, range; ...ŭi
pŏmwirŭl nŏmŏsŏ ...의 범위를
넘어서 beyond
pŏmyul 법률 legislation
pŏn 번 time, occasion; number; duty;
han pŏn 한 번 once
pŏnch'ang 변창 prosperity
pŏnch'anghada 변창하다 prosper,
flourish
pŏnch'anghanŭn 변창하는
prosperous, flourishing
pŏn-gae 번개 lightning
pŏn-gaech'ŏrŏm tallida 번개처럼
달리다 race; run like the wind;
streak
pŏn-gaetppul 번갯불 bolt of
lightning
pŏn-gara hanŭn 번갈아 하는
alternate
pŏng-ŏri 벙어리 mute; dumb
pŏng-ŏri changgap 벙어리 장갑
mitten
pŏn-gŏrŏun 번거로운 complex
pŏnho 번호 number
pŏnhop'an 번호판 license plate
pŏnhorŭl maegida 번호를 매기다
number, put a number on
pŏnhwahan 번화한 busy, lively,
bustling
pŏnjida 번지다 run (of paint, make-
up etc)
pŏnnamu 벚나무 cherry (tree)
pŏnshik 번식 breeding
pŏnshik'ada 번식하다 breed
pŏnshingnyŏgi ŏmnŭn 번식력이
없는 infertile
pŏntchŏk-kkŏrinŭn 번쩍거리는
flashing
pŏnttŭgida 번득이다 glint
pŏnyŏk 번역 translation
pŏnyŏkka 번역가 translator
pŏnyŏk'ada 번역하다 translate
pŏnyŏnghada 번영하다 bloom,
flourish
pŏp 법 law; method; pŏbe
ŏgŭnnanŭn 법에 어긋나는 against

the law
pŏp-ppok 법복 robe (*of judge*)
pŏptchŏgin 법적인 legal
pŏptchŏk choŏnja 법적 조언자 legal adviser
pŏptchŏng 법정 court; courtroom
pŏp'ak 법학 law (*as subject of study*)
pŏrida 버리다 abandon, leave; discard; dump
pŏrida 벌이다 stage *demo*; start *business*
pŏrigo ttŏnada 버리고 떠나다 abandon
pŏrŭdŏpsshi mandŭlda 버릇없이 만들다 spoil *child*
pŏrŭsŭl karŭch'ida 버릇을 가르치다 discipline
pŏrŭt ŏmnŭn 버릇 없는 impolite; spoilt
pŏryŏduda 버려두다 abandon; *naenoŭn ch'ae pŏryŏduda* 내놓은 채 버려두다 leave out, not put away
pŏryŏjin 버려진 derelict, neglected
pŏsŏnada 벗어나다 break away; elude; outgrow; *...esŏ pŏsŏnada* ...에서 벗어나다 depart from; deviate from
pŏsŏt 버섯 mushroom
pŏsŭ 버스 bus *also* COMPUT; *pŏsŭro* 버스로 by bus
pŏsŭ chŏngnyujang 버스 정류장 bus stop
pŏsŭ t'ŏminŏl 버스 터미널 bus terminal, bus station
pŏtkkida 벗기다 remove; rub away; strip; undress; unveil; shell; *kkŏptchirŭl pŏtkkida* 껍질을 벗기다 skin; peel, pare
pŏtkkyŏjida 벗겨지다 come off; peel off (*of paint*)
pŏt-tta 벗다 remove
pŏt'ida 버티다 hold out, survive; resist
pŏt'ŏ 버터 butter
pŏt'ŏrŭl parŭda 버터를 바르다 butter *bread*
pŏt'ŭn 버튼 button
poan 보안 security
poan-gyŏng 보안경 goggles
poan hwagin 보안 확인 security check

poankkwa 보안과 security (*department*)
poan kyŏnggye 보안 경계 security alert
poanŭl chungshihanŭn 보안을 중시하는 security-conscious
pobae 보배 jewel *fig*
pobok 보복 revenge
poboktchŏgin 보복적인 vindictive
pobok'ada 보복하다 take one's revenge
pobyŏng 보병 infantry soldier
pobyŏngdae 보병대 infantry
poch'ŏnggi 보청기 hearing aid
poch'o 보초 sentry
poch'ung 보충 compensation, reward
poch'unghada 보충하다 supplement
poda 보다 look; look at; eye; make out; see; watch ◊ than; *...poda tŏ mani* ...보다 더 많이; *... ŭl/rŭl poji mot'anŭn* ...을/를 보지 못하는 blind to; *shihŏmŭl poda* 시험을 보다 take an exam
poda chagŭn 보다 작은 minor, slight
poda chungnyohada 보다 중요하다 outweigh
...poda natkke ...보다 낮게 beneath (*in status, value*)
poda nat-tta 보다 낫다 be better than
poda naŭn 보다 나은 better
poda orae salda 보다 오래 살다 survive, outlive
podap'ada 보답하다 repay, return
poda suga mant'a 보다 수가 많다 outnumber
poda tŏ 보다 더 more than, over, above
poda tŏ charhada 보다 더 잘하다 outdo
poda tŏ orae salda 보다 더 오래 살다 outlive
poda ttwiŏnan 보다 뛰어난 superior, better
...poda wi ...보다 위 above, higher than
podisut'ŭ 보디수트 body (suit)
podo 보도 report, coverage
podohada 보도하다 report, cover

podŭ keim 보드 게임 board game

podŭk'a 보드카 vodka

poganghada 보강하다 follow up; reinforce

pogang hoeŭi 보강 회의 follow-up meeting

pogie 보기에 apparently

pogienŭn 보기에는 seemingly; *naega pogienŭn* 내가 보기에는 in my estimation; as far as I'm concerned

pogi hyunghan 보기 흉한 unsightly

pogiwanŭn tarŭn 보기와는 다른 deceptive

pogo 보고 account, report

pogohada 보고하다 report

pogosŏ 보고서 report, account

Pogŭm 복음 the Word REL; Gospels

pogŭm chŏndosa 복음 전도사 evangelist

pogŭmsŏ 복음서 Gospel

pogwan 보관 storage

pogwan changso 보관 장소 storage space

pogwanhada 보관하다 keep, store

pogwansoe matkkida 보관소에 맡기다 check (in checkroom)

pogwŏnhada 복원하다 reinstate

pogyŏl sŏnsu 보결 선수 substitute

pogyongnyang 복용량 dosage

pogyongppŏp 복용법 directions (for medicine)

pogyongshik'ida 복용시키다 administer, give medicine

pogyunja 보균자 carrier (of disease)

pohaenggi 보행기 walker (for baby)

pohaengja 보행자 pedestrian, walker

pohaengja chŏnyong kuyŏk 보행자 전용 구역 pedestrian precinct

pohamhada 포함하다 include, comprise

pohŏm 보험 insurance

pohŏm chŭngsŏ 보험 증서 insurance policy

pohŏme tŭlda 보험에 들다 insure

pohŏm hoesa 보험 회사 insurance company

poho 보호 protection

pohoch'aek 보호책 safeguard

pohohada 보호하다 protect, preserve

pohohanŭn 보호하는 protective

poho kamch'algwan 보호 감찰관 probation officer

poho kuyŏk 보호 구역 (wild animal) sanctuary

poida 보이다 be able to see; be visible; show; seem; *poiji annŭn* 보이지 않는 out of sight

poik'ot 보이콧 boycott

poik'ot'ada 보이콧하다 boycott

poillŏ 보일러 boiler

poinŭn 보이는 visible

poisŭk'aut 보이스카웃 boy scout

pojal kŏt omnŭn 보잘 것 없는 trivial; worthless

pojang 보장 security, guarantee (for investment)

pojanghada 보장하다 guarantee, assure

pojogae 보조개 dimple

pojogŭm 보조금 grant, subsidy; *pojogŭmŭl chigŭp'ada* 보조금을 지급하다 subsidize

pojojŏgin 보조적인 auxiliary, supplementary

pojo kyojae 보조 교재 teaching aid

pojon 보존 preservation, maintenance

pojonhada 보존하다 preserve, maintain; conserve

pojoŭi 보조의 auxiliary

pojŭng 보증 guarantee, warranty; assurance; *pojŭng kigan chung-ida* 보증 기간 중이다 be under warranty

pojŭnghada 보증하다 sponsor; guarantee; underwrite; vouch for

pojŭng-in 보증인 guarantor; sponsor

pojŭng kigan 보증 기간 guarantee period

pojŭngsŏ 보증서 letter of guarantee

pok-kku 복구 restoration

pok-kkuhada 복구하다 restore

pok-kkwihada 복귀하다 make a comeback; return; be restored

pokppu 복부 abdomen ◊ abdominal

pokssa 복사 copy

pokssadoen yŏlssoe 복사된 열쇠 duplicate key

pokssagi 복사기 photocopier

pokssahada 복사하다 copy; take a

photocopy of
pokssappyŏ 복사뼈 ankle bone
poksshik 복식 doubles (*in tennis*)
pokssŭp'ada 복습하다 brush up; review
pokssu 복수 retaliation, reprisal; vengeance
pokssuhada 복수하다 retaliate, take reprisals
pokssuhyŏng 복수형 plural
pokssung-a 복숭아 peach
poktchap'ada 복잡하다 be complicated
poktchap'an 복잡한 complicated; complex
poktche 복제 reproduction
poktchep'um 복제품 replica
poktchi 복지 welfare
poktchiksshik'ida 복직시키다 reinstate
poktchi kuk-kka 복지 국가 welfare state
poktchi saŏp 복지 사업 welfare work
poktchi saŏpkka 복지 사업가 welfare worker
poktchong 복종 obedience; submission
poktta 볶다 stir-fry
poktto 복도 corridor, passage
pokt'ong 복통 stomach-ache
pok'ŏl kŭrup 보컬 그룹 vocal group
pollae 본래 originally; naturally
polling 볼링 bowling
pollinghada 볼링하다 bowl
pollingjang 볼링장 bowling alley
polling kong 볼링 공 bowl
pollingp'in 볼링핀 pin
pol peŏring 볼 베어링 ball bearing
polp'en 볼펜 ballpoint (pen)
polp'umŏmnŭn 볼품없는 unattractive
polt'ŭ 볼트 bolt; volt
polt'ŭro choeda 볼트로 죄다 bolt
pom 봄 look, glance; spring
pomch'ŏl 봄철 springtime
pommaji taech'ŏngso 봄맞이 대청소 spring-cleaning
pomul 보물 treasure

ponaeda 보내다 pass (*of time*); spend *time*; send
ponbogi 본보기 model, pattern
ponbu 본부 base, center; headquarters
ponggoch'a 봉고차 van
ponggŭmnal 봉급날 payday
ponggŭp 봉급 pay check
ponggŭp pongt'u 봉급 봉투 pay envelope
ponggŭp sujun 봉급 수준 salary scale
ponghada 봉하다 seal *letter*
pong-in 봉인 seal
pongji 봉지 packet, sachet; seal
pongni 복리 well-being; compound interest
pongsahada 봉사하다 render a service, serve
pongswae 봉쇄 blockade
pongswaehada 봉쇄하다 blockade; seal off; freeze
pongt'u 봉투 envelope
ponin 본인 oneself; himself; herself; *ponini chiktchŏp* 본인이 직접 in person; *ponin sajin* 본인 사진 a photo of oneself
ponjiltchŏgin 본질적인 fundamental; substantial
ponjiltchŏgŭro 본질적으로 fundamentally, basically, mainly
ponmun 본문 text
ponnŭng 본능 instinct
ponnŭngjŏgin 본능적인 instinctive
ponŏsŭ 보너스 bonus
ponsa 본사 head office
ponttŭda 본뜨다 imitate, emulate
pont'o 본토 mainland
poonbyŏng 보온병 thermos flask
pop'yŏnjŏgin 보편적인 universal, general
pop'yŏnjŏgŭro 보편적으로 universally
porami innŭn 보람이 있는 worthwhile
poram ŏmnŭn 보람 없는 thankless
poratppit 보라빛 violet (*color*)
pori 보리 barley
porich'a 보리차 roasted barley tea
porŭmttal 보름달 full moon
poryŏnji 볼연지 blusher

poryuhada 보류하다 withhold

Posal 보살 Bodhisattva

posalp'ida 보살피다 look after

posalp'im 보살핌 care

posang 보상 reward; compensation; *posangŭl hada* 보상을 하다 make amends, compensate for

posanghada 보상하다 compensate for

poshint'ang 보신탕 dog meat soup

posŏk 보석 bail; jewel, gem; *posŏgŭl patkke hada* 보석을 받게 하다 bail out

posŏk-kkŭm 보석금 bail (*money*)

posŏkssang 보석상 jeweler

posŏngnyu 보석류 jewelry

posŭlbi 보슬비 drizzle

posu 보수 pay; reward, remuneration; conservativeness ◊ conservative

posuga ch'ungbunhan 보수가 충분한 remunerative

posuhada 보수하다 renovate, do up; repair

posujŏgin 보수적인 conservative; conventional

posurŭl chuda 보수를 주다 pay; reward

pot'ong 보통 usual; ordinary ◊ usually

pot'ong chŏngdoŭi 보통 정도의 average, mediocre

pot'ong saram 보통 사람 ordinary person

pot'ongsŏk 보통석 economy class

pot'ong ttaech'ŏrŏm 보통 때처럼 as usual

pot'ong-ŭi 보통의 normal, usual; ordinary; common; standard; mediocre

pot'ong-ŭro 보통으로 normally, usually

pot'ong yegŭm 보통 예금 savings account

pot'ŭ 보트 boat

powanhada 보완하다 complement

powanhanŭn 보완하는 complementary

poyangji 보양지 health resort

poyŏjida 보여지다 appear, seem; show; show up, be visible

poyŏjuda 보여주다 show; expose

poyugŭm 보유금 reserves

poyugwŏn 보육원 kindergarten

poyuja 보유자 holder (*of record*)

ppadŭt'an 빠듯한 full

ppaeat-tta 빼앗다 take by force; *nugurobut'ŏ muŏsŭl ppaeat-tta* 누구로부터 무엇을 빼앗다 take sth away from s.o. (by force), snatch sth from s.o.

ppaeda 빼다 drain off; omit; subtract; *42 ppaegi 18ŭn 24ida* 42 빼기 18은 24이다 42 minus 18 is 24; *...man ppaego* ...만 빼고 all but ..., except ...

ppaedalmŭn mosŭp 빼닮은 모습 image, exact likeness

ppaegi puho 빼기 부호 minus sign

ppaekppaek'age kwak ch'an 빽빽하게 꽉 찬 jam-packed, crowded

ppaenaeda 빼내다 take out; eject; drain

ppaengsoni sago 뺑소니 사고 hit-and-run accident

ppaengsoni unjŏnsu 뺑소니 운전수 hit-and-run driver

ppajida 빠지다 drain away, ebb; sink in; fall in; fall out; pull out; be hooked on; miss; *sarange ppajida* 사랑에 빠지다 fall in love; *muŏse ppajida* 무엇에 빠지다 indulge in sth; give sth a miss

ppajyŏ nagada 빠져 나가다 slip out, go out; ebb away; *sarami ppajyŏt-tta!* 사람이 빠졌다! man overboard!

ppalda 빨다 wash; suck

ppalgaejida 빨개지다 flush, redden

ppalgan 빨간 red

ppalgan pul 빨간 불 red light

ppalgat'a 빨갛다 be red

ppallae 빨래 washing; *ppallaerŭl hada* 빨래를 하다 do the washing

ppallajida 빨라지다 accelerate

ppalli 빨리 quickly

ppalli chinagada 빨리 지나가다 speed by

ppalli hada 빨리 하다 speed up

ppalli hae! 빨리 해! be quick!

ppalli kada 빨리 가다 speed

ppang 빵 bread

ppangjip 빵집 bakery

ppang karu 빵 가루 breadcrumbs (*for cooking*)

ppang pusŭrŏgi 빵 부스러기 breadcrumbs (*for birds*)

ppanhi ch'yŏdaboda 빤히 쳐다보다 stare; stare at

pparadŭrida 빨아들이다 inhale; suck in; absorb

ppara mŏktta 빨아 먹다 suck

pparŭda 빠르다 be fast, be quick

pparŭge 빠르게 fast, quickly

pparŭn 빠른 fast, quick; speedy

ppatppat'an 빳빳한 stiff

ppattŭrida 빠뜨리다 skip, omit

ppida 삐다 sprain

ppigŏk-kkŏrida 삐걱거리다 creak, squeak

ppii hanŭn sori 삐이 하는 소리 bleep

ppŏdŏit-tta 뻗어있다 extend

ppŏdŏnagago innŭn 뻗어나가고 있는 sprawling

ppŏgŭnhan 뻐근한 stiff

ppŏnppŏnhada 뻔뻔하다 be shameless, be impudent

ppŏnppŏnham 뻔뻔함 impudence

ppŏnppŏnhan 뻔뻔한 impudent, fresh

ppŏnppŏnsŭrŏun 뻔뻔스러운 impudent, blatant, shameless

ppŏtch'ida 뻗치다 stretch, spread

ppŏtppŏt'aejida 뻣뻣해지다 stiffen

ppŏtppŏt'age hada 뻣뻣하게 하다 stiffen up

ppŏtppŏt'an 뻣뻣한 stiff, unyielding

ppoppo 뽀뽀 peck, kiss

ppoppohada 뽀뽀하다 give a peck, kiss

ppoptta 뽑다 pull out, extract; pluck; select

ppul 뿔 horn

ppult'e an-gyŏng 뿔테 안경 horn-rimmed spectacles

ppumŏjyŏ naoda 뿜어져 나오다 squirt, spurt

ppumŏnaeda 뿜어내다 squirt

ppun 뿐 nothing but, only; *...l ppun* ...ㄹ 뿐 nothing but; *Xppunman anira Ydo ttohan* X뿐만 아니라 Y도 또한 not only X but Y also

ppuri 뿌리 root

ppuribak'in 뿌리박힌 entrenched, deep-rooted

ppurida 뿌리다 scatter; sprinkle; slop; spray

ppuri kip'ŭn 뿌리 깊은 deep-rooted

ppurut'unghada 뿌루퉁하다 pout

ppyam 빰 cheek

ppyŏ 뼈 bone

ppyŏdae 뼈대 frame

ppyojokt'ap 뾰족탑 spire, steeple

ppyojuk'an kkŭt 뾰죽한 끝 spike

pp'im 삠 wrench (*injury*)

pu 부 copy (*of book*); ministry; wealth

pu- 부- vice-

pŭi ai p'i 브이 아이 피이 VIP

pŭi ssi al 브이 시이 알 VCR

pŭllaek pakssŭ 블랙 박스 black box, flight recorder

pŭllaekrisŭt'ŭe ollida 블랙리스트에 올리다 blacklist

pŭllaindŭ 블라인드 blind, shade

pŭllausŭ 블라우스 blouse

pŭllok 블록 block COMPUT

pŭllogŭl ssŭiuda 블록을 씌우다 highlight COMPUT

pŭraendi 브랜디 brandy

Pŭrajil 브라질 Brazil ◊ Brazilian

Pŭrajil saram 브라질 사람 Brazilian

pŭraujŏ 브라우저 browser COMPUT

pŭreik'ŭ 브레이크 brake

pŭreik'ŭ lait'ŭ 브레이크 라이트 brake light

pŭreik'ŭrŭl kŏlda 브레이크를 걸다 brake, put the brake(s) on

pŭrejiŏ 브레지어 brassière

pŭroch'i 브로치 brooch

pŭrogŭraem 프로그램 program

pŭrogŭraemŏ 프로그래머 programmer

pŭrogŭraem tchada 프로그램 짜다 program

pŭrok'olli 브로콜리 broccoli

pŭroshyŏ 브로셔 brochure

pubu 부부 couple

pubun 부분 part, proportion; portion; segment; slice

pubuntchŏgin 부분적인 segmented

pubuntchŏgŭro 부분적으로 partially, partly, part

puch'ae 부채 fan

puch'aejirhada 부채질하다 fan oneself

puch'ida 붙이다 attach, stick; pin up

puch'igi 붙이기 paste COMPUT

puch'ŏ 부처 Buddha; department

Puch'ŏnim Oshin Nal 부처님 오신 날 Buddha's Birthday

puch'u 부추 leek

puch'ugida 부추기다 encourage

pudae 부대 unit MIL

pudaep'yo 부대표 deputy leader

pudam 부담 burden; *pudamŭl chuda* 부담을 주다 strain *finances, budget*; *nuguege pudamŭl chuda* 누구에게 부담을 주다 impose oneself on s.o.

pudamhada 부담하다 bear *costs etc*

pudanghada 부당하다 be unjust

pudanghage 부당하게 wrongly, mistakenly

pudanghan 부당한 wrongful

pudich'ida 부딪히다 bump into; bump; ram

pudodŏk 부도덕 immorality

pudodŏk'an 부도덕한 immoral; unscrupulous

pudong-aek 부동액 antifreeze

pudongsan 부동산 real estate

pudongsan chunggaein 부동산 중개인 realtor

pudŭrŏpkke 부드럽게 softly

pudŭrŏpkke hada 부드럽게 하다 tone down, soften

pudŭrŏptta 부드럽다 be soft; be gentle

pudŭrŏun 부드러운 soft; gentle; mild; smooth

pudŭrŏwŏjida 부드러워지다 soften

pudu 부두 dock; port; wharf; *pudue taeda* 부두에 대다 dock, put in

pudu nodongja 부두 노동자 stevedore

pudut-kka 부둣가 quayside

pugajŏgin 부가적인 supplementary

pugamul 부가물 trappings; frills

puga yogŭm 부가 요금 surcharge

pugi 부기 swelling; book-keeping

pugŏm 부검 autopsy

pugo 부고 obituary

pugŭp'ada 보급하다 spread; disseminate

pugwahada 부과하다 impose; *nuguege ch'aegimŭl pugwahada* 누구에게 책임을 부과하다 set a task for s.o.

pugyeŭi 부계의 paternal

pugyŏng-yŏng-in 부경영인 assistant manager

pugyŏrhada 부결하다 throw out

pugyosu 부교수 associate professor

puha 부하 load ELEC

puhap'ada 부합하다 correspond with

puhwahada 부화하다 hatch out

puhwal 부활 revival; resurrection

Puhwaltchŏl 부활절 Easter

puhwarhada 부활하다 revive

puinhada 부인하다 contradict; deny

puja 부자 sage; father and son; rich man

pujae 부재 absence

pujagyong 부작용 side effect

pujang 부장 managing director; assistant director

pujayŏnsŭrŏun 부자연스러운 unnatural

pujibaein 부지배인 assistant manager

pujirŏmnŭn marŭl hada 부질없는 말을 하다 waffle

pujirŏnhan 부지런한 diligent

pujirŏnhi irhada 부지런히 일하다 work hard

pujŏgŭngja 부적응자 misfit

pujŏkkyŏgin 부적격인 (morally) unfit

pujŏktchŏrhan 부적절한 improper

pujŏkttanghada 부적당하다 be unsuitable; be unfit; be inadequate; *mŏkkie / mashigie pujŏkttanghada* 먹기에 / 마시기에 부적당하다 be unfit to eat / drink

pujŏkttanghan 부적당한 unsuitable, inappropriate; inadequate

pujŏng 부정 denial; injustice; infidelity

pujŏng haeng-wi 부정 행위 misconduct

pujŏnghal su ŏmnŭn 부정할 수 없는 undeniable

pujŏnghan 부정한 crooked, dishonest; unfaithful

pujŏnghwak'an 부정확한 inaccurate;

indeterminate
pujŏngjik 부정직 dishonesty
pujŏngjik'an 부정직한 dishonest
pujŏngjŏgin 부정적인 destructive; negative
pujŏngsa 부정사 infinitive
pujŏng-ŭi 부정의 negative
pujojongsa 부조종사 copilot
pujok 부족 shortage; shortfall; tribe; *pujok'ami ŏptta* 부족함이 없다 want for nothing
pujok'ada 부족하다 be lacking
pujuŭihan 부주의한 inattentive; slack; sloppy
puk 북 drum; north
pukch'ae 북채 drumstick
puk-kkŭk kom 북극 곰 polar bear
Puk-kkyŏng 북경 Beijing
Pukkŭk 북극 North Pole
Pukkŭkkwŏn 북극권 Arctic
pukkŭrŏptta 부끄럽다 be ashamed; be shy; *...ege pukkŭrŏpkke yŏgida* ...에게 부끄럽게 여기다 be ashamed of; *pukkŭrŏptchido anni!* 부끄럽지도 않니! shame on you!
pukkŭrŏun 부끄러운 shameful
pukppang-e 북방에 north of
Pukppet'ŭnam 북베트남 North Vietnam ◊ North Vietnamese
Pukppet'ŭnamin 북베트남인 North Vietnamese
pukppuŭi 북부의 northern
pukssŏ 북서 northwest
puktchoge 북쪽에 to the north of
puktchoguro 북쪽으로 northward
Pukttaesŏyang Choyak Kigu 북대서양 조약 기구 NATO
pukttoduda 북돋우다 bolster
Puk'an 북한 North Korea ◊ North Korean
Puk'an saram 북한 사람 North Korean (*person*)
puk'yang-ŭi 북향의 northerly
pul 불 fire; dollar; Buddha; France ◊ French; *pul puch'ida* 불 붙이다 light; *pul kat'ŭn* 불 같은 fiery
pul- 불- not; un-; in-; dis-; non-
pulboktchong 불복종 disobedience, insubordination
pulboktchonghanŭn 불복종하는 disobedient, insubordinate

pulch'ansŏng 불찬성 disapproval
pulch'ansŏnghada 불찬성하다 disapprove of
pulch'injŏrhada 불친절하다 be unkind
pulch'injŏrhan 불친절한 unfriendly; unkind; inhospitable
pulch'ippyŏng-ŭi 불치병의 terminally ill
pulch'ungbunhan 불충분한 meager; insufficient
pulch'ungsshil 불충실 disloyalty
pulch'ungsshirhan 불충실한 disloyal
pulda 불다 blow; inflate
puldoujŏ 불도우저 bulldozer
pulgabunŭi 불가분의 indivisible
pulgamtchŭng-ŭi 불감증의 frigid MED
pulgansŏp 불간섭 noninterference, nonintervention
pulganŭng 불가능 impossibility
pulganŭnghada 불가능하다 be impossible
pulganŭnghan 불가능한 impossible
pulgap'ihada 불가피하다 be unavoidable
pulgasari 불가사리 starfish
pulgasaŭi 불가사의 mystery
pulgasaŭihan 불가사의한 mysterious, inscrutable
pulgirhae poinŭn 불길해 보이는 sinister
pulgirhan 불길한 ominous
pulgirhan yegam 불길한 예감 foreboding
pulgŏjida 붉어지다 redden, blush
pulgogi 불고기 barbecued beef
pulgongjŏnghan 불공정한 unfair, unjust; unequal
pulgongp'yŏnghada 불공평하다 be unfair, be biased
pulgŭn 붉은 ruddy; red
pulguhago 불구하고 in spite of
pulgurŭi 불굴의 indomitable
pulguŭi 불구의 disabled
pulgyŏnggi 불경기 recession, slump
Pulgyo 불교 Buddhism ◊ Buddhist
Pulgyo Shinja 불교 신자 Buddhist
pulgyuch'iktchŏgin 불규칙적인 irregular
pulgyunhyŏng 불균형 disparity

pulgyunhyŏnghan 불균형한 disproportionate

pulkkil 불길 flames

pulkkonnori 불꽃놀이 fireworks

pulkkot 불꽃 flame; spark

pulk'wae 불쾌 displeasure

pulk'waehada 불쾌하다 put off, repel

pulk'waehage hada 불쾌하게 하다 displease

pulk'waehan 불쾌한 nasty, unpleasant; undesirable; offensive, repellent; rotten; sick

pulli 분리 division, separation; segregation

pullihada 분리하다 separate; isolate; segregate; partition; unfix

pullihada 불리하다 be prejudicial to

pullihal su innŭn 분리할 수 있는 detachable

pullihal su ŏmnŭn 분리할 수 없는 inseparable

pullihan 불리한 disadvantageous; *pullihan chokkŏn* 불리한 조건 handicap; *pullihan iptchang-e itta* 불리한 입장에 있다 be at a disadvantage

pullishik'ida 분리시키다 disconnect

pullŏ irŭk'ida 불러 일으키다 arouse; summon up; work up

pullŏogi 불러오기 open COMPUT

pullŏ tŭrida 불러 들이다 call in, summon

pulluk'ada 불룩하다 bulge

pullyangbae 불량배 hooligan

pullyang puch'ae 불량 부채 bad debt

pullyangp'um 불량품 inferior goods; reject

pullyŏnsŏng 불연성 non-combustibility ◊ incombustible; fireproof

pullyu 분류 classification

pullyuhada 분류하다 class; classify; sort; break down; itemize

pullyun 불륜 immorality

pullyunŭi kwangye 불륜의 관계 (love) affair

pulman 불만 discontent, dissatisfaction

pulmanida 불만이다 be unhappy with

pulmansŭrŏun 불만스러운 discontented

pulmo 불모 infertility ◊ barren

pulmoji 불모지 unproductive soil

pulmyŏl 불멸 immortality

pulmyŏnghwak'an 불명확한 uncertain

pulmyŏng-ye 불명예 dishonor; disgrace

pulmyŏng-yesŭrŏun 불명예스러운 dishonorable

pulmyŏntchŭng 불면증 insomnia

pulmyŏrŭi 불멸의 immortal

pulppŏp 불법 illegality ◊ illegal

pulppŏp haengwi 불법 행위 unlawful act

pulppŏp koyong 불법 고용 black economy

pulp'iryohan 불필요한 unnecessary

pulp'yŏnhage nŭkkida 불편하게 느끼다 feel ill at ease

pulp'yŏn 불편 inconvenience

pulp'yŏng 불평 complaint

pulp'yŏngdŭng 불평등 inequality

pulp'yŏnghada 불평하다 complain; complain about

pulp'yŏngkkŏri 불평거리 complaint, grievance

pulp'yŏng-ŭl nŭrŏnot-tta 불평을 늘어놓다 complain

pulp'yŏnhada 불편하다 be uncomfortable; be inconvenient

pulp'yŏnhan 불편한 uncomfortable; inconvenient

pulshich'ak 불시착 crash landing

pulssanghada 불쌍하다 be piteous, be wretched

pulssanghaejin 불쌍해진 wretched

pulssanghan 불쌍한 piteous, wretched

pulssanghi yŏgida 불쌍히 여기다 take pity on

pulsshie 불시에 unexpectedly, by surprise; *Xŭl / rŭl pulsshie sŭpkkyŏk'ada* X을 / 를 불시에 습격하다 catch X unawares

pulsshin 불신 mistrust, doubt

pulsshinhada 불신하다 mistrust

pulssonhan 불손한 insolent, arrogant

pulssuk marhada 불쑥 말하다 blurt out

pulssuk naoda 불쑥 나오다 stick out, protrude

pulssuk nat'anada 불쑥 나타나다 pop up, bob up

pulssuk saenggida 불쑥 생기다 shoot up (*of new suburb etc*)

pulssuk t'wiŏ naoda 불쑥 튀어 나오다 protrude

pulssunhan 불순한 impure

pult'anŭn 불타는 alight, burning

pult'aorŭnŭn 불타오르는 ablaze, blazing

pult'umyŏnghan 불투명한 opaque

pult'umyŏnghan yuri 불투명한 유리 frosted glass

pum 붐 boom

pumbida 붐비다 be busy, be crowded

pumbinŭn 붐비는 busy, crowded

pumo 부모 parent

pumok 부목 splint

pumo-ŭi 부모의 parental

pun 분 face powder; minute; flowerpot; anger; person (*respectful*) ◊ countword for people (*respectful*); *pun tang hoejŏn* 분 당 회전 revs per minute

punbae 분배 distribution

punbaehada 분배하다 share, allocate

punbal 분발 spurt

punbiaek 분비액 secretion

punbihada 분비하다 secrete

punbimul 분비물 secretion (*liquid secreted*)

punbyŏl innŭn 분별 있는 sound, prudent; level-headed; reasonable, sensible

punch'im 분침 minute hand

punch'ul 분출 torrent

punch'uldoeda 분출되다 spout

punch'ulgu 분출구 jet

punch'urhada 분출하다 erupt (*of volcano*)

pun-gae 분개 resentment; outrage

pun-gaehada 분개하다 resent

pun-gaehan 분개한 resentful; indignant

pun-ganhada 분간하다 distinguish

pungdae 붕대 bandage, dressing

pungdaerŭl kamtta 붕대를 감다 bandage, dress

punggoe 붕괴 fall, collapse

punggoedoeda 붕괴되다 disintegrate; crash

pun-gitchŏm 분기점 fork (*in road*)

Pungmi 북미 North America ◊ North American

Pungmiin 북미인 North American

Pungmiŭi 북미의 North American

punhaedoeda 분해되다 come apart

punhaehada 분해하다 take to pieces, dismantle

punhal maeip 분할매입 buying on an installment plan

punhongsaek 분홍색 pink

punhwa 분화 eruption

punhwagu 분화구 crater (*of volcano*)

punja 분자 molecule ◊ molecular

punjae 분재 bonsai

punjaeng 분쟁 dispute

punjaeng chiyŏk 분쟁 지역 hot spot

punjaeng chojŏngja 분쟁 조정자 troubleshooter, mediator

punjangshil 분장실 dressing room

punjuhi irhada 분주히 일하다 bustle about, be busy

punkkwa wiwŏnhoe 분과 위원회 subcommittee

punman 분만 delivery (*of baby*); labor; *punman chung-ida* 분만 중이다 be in labor

punmanhada 분만하다 give birth to

punmang 분망 scramble, rush

punmanshik'ida 분만시키다 deliver *baby*

punmanshil 분만실 labor ward

punmugi 분무기 atomizer; spraygun

punmyŏnghada 분명하다 be obvious; be clear

punmyŏnghage 분명하게 plainly, clearly

punmyŏnghan 분명한 clear, obvious

punmyŏnghi 분명히 clearly, evidently; explicitly

punno 분노 wrath

punnŭn 붙는 sticky *label*

pun parŭda 분 바르다 powder

punp'a 분파 sect; splinter group

punp'il 분필 chalk

punsagirŭl sayonghada 분사기를

사용하다 sandblast
punshilmul sent'ŏ 분실물 센터 lost-and-found
punsŏk 분석 analysis
punsŏk'ada 분석하다 analyze
punsu 분수 fraction; fountain
punsuryŏng 분수령 watershed
punswaegi 분쇄기 mill
punwigi 분위기 atmosphere; mood; tone
punya 분야 area, field
punyŏl 분열 division, split
punyŏlsshik'ida 분열시키다 split
punyŏlsshik'inŭn 분열시키는 disruptive
punyŏrhada 분열하다 be divided; be split
puŏk 부엌 kitchen
puŏngbuŏng ulda 부엉부엉 울다 hoot (of owl)
puŏ nŏt'a 부어 넣다 add water, salt etc
puŏorŭn 부어 오른 puffy, swollen
puŏp 부업 sideline, side job
pup'ae 부패 decay
pup'aehada 부패하다 decay
pup'aehan 부패한 rotten; corrupt
pup'aessŏng-ŭi 부패성의 septic
pup'e 부페 buffet
pup'iga k'ŭn 부피가 큰 bulky
pup'ullida 부풀리다 inflate; expand
pup'um 부품 part, piece; unit; spare part
pup'yo 부표 buoy
pural 불알 balls; testicles
puran 불안 alarm, unrest; *puranhae hada* 불안해 하다 feel uneasy about
purangja 부랑자 bum; street people
puranhada 불안하다 be uneasy
puranhaejida 불안해지다 get worked up, get nervous
puranhage hada 불안하게 하다 alarm, worry
puranhan 불안한 insecure, uneasy; unstable
puranjŏng 불안정 insecurity, instability
puranjŏnghage 불안정하게 precariously
puranjŏnghan 불안정한 precarious, unstable

purhaeng 불행 unhappiness; misfortune
purhaenghada 불행하다 be unhappy; be unlucky
puraenghan 불행한 poor, unfortunate; unhappy
purhaenghi 불행히 unfortunately
purhamnihan 불합리한 irrational
purhandang 불한당 ruffian
purhwa 불화 split; feud; discord
purhwaksshilssŏng 불확실성 uncertainty
purhwaksshirhada 불확실하다 be in doubt; be doubtful
purhwaksshirhan 불확실한 uncertain
purhwang-ida 불황이다 be in the doldrums
purhyŏp'waŭm 불협화음 discord, dissonance
puri 부리 beak
purilch'i 불일치 discrepancy; clash (of personalities)
purilch'ihada 불일치하다 clash; be inconsistent
purim 불임 infertility
purimk'ehada 불임케 하다 sterilize
purimŭi 불임의 infertile, sterile
purŏjida 부러지다 break; get broken
purŏjin 부러진 broken
purŏ nallida 불어 날리다 blow off
purŏttŭrida 부러뜨리다 break, snap
purŏumŭl sada 부러움을 사다 be envious of
purŏun 부러운 enviable
purŏwŏhada 부러워하다 be envious of
purŏwŏhanŭn 부러워하는 envious
purok 부록 appendix (in book)
purŭda 부르다 call; summon; *...rago purŭda* ...라고 부르다 address, call; describe as
purŭl puch'ida 불을 붙이다 ignite, light; set on fire
purŭrŏ ponaeda 부르러 보내다 send for
puruhan 불우한 deprived, underprivileged
purun 불운 bad luck; disaster
purunhan 불운한 ill-fated
purut'unghaejida 부루퉁해지다 sulk

purut'unghan 부루퉁한 sulky
purwanjŏnhan 불완전한 imperfect; incomplete
puryŏmŏktta 부려먹다 boss around
puryŏnsŏng-ŭi 불연성의 non(in)flammable
puryu 부류 class, category
pusa 부사 adverb
pusajang 부사장 vice president
Pusan 부산 Pusan
pusang 부상 injury; wound
pusangja 부상자 injured; wounded
pusanmul 부산물 by-product, spin-off
pushik 부식 corrosion
pushik'ada 부식하다 corrode
pusŏ 부서 department, division, unit; post
pusŏhada 부서하다 countersign
pusŏjida 부서지다 break, come apart; shatter, smash
pusŏjigi shwiun 부서지기 쉬운 brittle; fragile
pusŏjin 부서진 broken
pusŏng 부성 paternity ◊ paternal
pusŭrŏgi 부스러기 crumb; *chandon pusŭrŏgi* 잔돈 부스러기 loose change
pusŭrŏttŭrida 부스러뜨리다 crumble
pusŭrojida 부스러지다 crumble
pusuda 부수다 break, shatter; force
pusugo yŏlda 부수고 열다 break down *door*
puttchaptta 붙잡다 hold *prisoner etc*
put-tta 붙다 adhere, stick; *shihŏme put-tta* 시험에 붙다 pass (*in exam*)
put-tta 붓다 swell
put-ttŭlgo iyagihada 붙들고 이야기하다 buttonhole
put-ttŭrŏ tuda 붙들어 두다 keep; detain; keep in
put'ak'ada 부탁하다 ask; ask for; arrange for; *mwŏ chom put'ak'aedo toemnikka?* 뭐 좀 부탁해도 됩니까? can I ask you something?
Put'an 부탄 Bhutan ◊ Bhutanese
put'bagiŭi 붙박이의 built-in
put'ik'ŭ 부티크 boutique
put'ingdoeda 부팅되다 boot (up)
put'inghada 부팅하다 boot (up)

...put'ŏ ... kkaji ...부터 ... 까지 from ... to ...; *...(esŏ)but'ŏ* ... (에서)부터 from (*in time*); *wŏryoilbut'ŏ suyoilkkaji* 월요일부터 수요일까지 from Monday to Wednesday
pu-ŭn 부은 swollen
puyang 부양 support; boost
puyangbi 부양비 maintenance (*money*)
puyanghada 부양하다 support, maintain
puyang kajok 부양 가족 dependents
puyŏhada 부여하다 attach
puyŏjaptta 부여잡다 grab
puyŏnhada 부연하다 elaborate
puyuhada 부유하다 be rich
puyuhan 부유한 rich, wealthy
pyŏk 벽 wall
pyŏkppo 벽보 placard
pyŏktchi 벽지 wallpaper
pyŏkttol 벽돌 brick
pyŏkttolgong 벽돌공 bricklayer
pyŏk'wa 벽화 mural
pyŏl 별 star ◊ different; unusual; *pyŏl il animnida* 별 일 아닙니다 it's no problem
pyŏlgaero 별개로 independently of
pyŏlgaeŭi 별개의 different; separate
pyŏlgŏ 별거 separation
pyŏlgŏhada 별거하다 separate; live apart; be (legally) separated
pyŏlgŏhan 별거한 separated
pyŏlgŏ sudang 별거 수당 alimony
pyŏlgwan 별관 annex
pyŏllada 별나다 be eccentric; be strange
pyŏllan 별난 eccentric, quirky
pyŏllo 별로 nothing much
pyŏllon 변론 defense; justification
pyŏlloyeyo 별로예요 not really, not much
pyŏlmashi ŏmnŭn 별맛이 없는 bland
pyŏlmyŏng 별명 nickname
pyŏlp'yo 별표 asterisk
pyŏlsŭrŏn 별스런 whimsical
pyŏltchong 별종 freak
pyŏnanhada 편안하다 feel at ease
pyŏnapkki 변압기 transformer
pyŏnbi 변비 constipation
pyŏnbie kŏllin 변비에 걸린

constipated
pyŏnbiyak 변비약 laxative
pyŏndŏk 변덕 freak (*event*); whim
pyŏndŏkssŭrŏptta 변덕스럽다 be
  fickle
pyŏndŏkssŭrŏun 변덕스러운
  temperamental; fickle; variable
pyŏndong 변동 variation, fluctuation
pyŏndonghada 변동하다 fluctuate
pyŏndong shisega toeda 변동
  시세가 되다 float FIN
pyŏnduri 변두리 outskirts
pyŏng 병 bottle; flask; illness
pyŏng-ari 병아리 chick
pyŏngch'am ŏmmu 병참 업무
  logistics
pyŏngch'unghae kwalli 병충해 관리
  pest control
pyŏngdong 병동 ward, room (*in
  hospital*)
pyŏngdŭlda 병들다 fall ill, be taken
  ill
pyŏng-e kŏllida 병에 걸리다 catch
  an illness
pyŏngga 병가 sick leave
pyŏng-i chaebarhada 병이 재발하다
  have a relapse
pyŏn-gie naeryŏbonaeda 변기에
  내려보내다 flush down the toilet
pyŏng-i nat-tta 병이 낫다 get better
  (*in health*)
pyŏngja 병자 invalid (*person*)
pyŏngkkahada 평가하다 estimate
pyŏng magae 병 마개 stopper
pyŏngmok 병목 bottleneck
pyŏngnallo 벽난로 fireplace
pyŏngnihak 병리학 pathology
pyŏngnihaktcha 병리학자
  pathologist
pyŏngnyŏk 병력 case history
pyŏngnyŏng 병영 quarters
pyŏngsang-e innŭn 병상에 있는
  bedridden
pyŏngse 병세 case MED
pyŏngtchŏgin 병적인 morbid,
  pathological
pyŏngtchŏk hŭngbun 병적 홍분
  hysterics; hysteria; *pyŏngtchŏk
  hŭngbunsangt'aega toeda* 병적
  홍분상태가 되다 become hysterical

pyŏngtchŏk hŭngbun sangt'aeŭi
  병적 홍분 상태의 hysterical
pyŏngttagae 병따개 bottle-opener
pyŏng-wŏn 병원 hospital
pyŏngyak'an 병약한 sickly
pyŏn-gyŏng 변경 alteration; shift
pyŏn-gyŏnghada 변경하다 be
  deflected from
pyŏnhada 변하다 change, shift
pyŏnhagi shwiun 변하기 쉬운
  unsettled, changeable
pyŏnhohada 변호하다 defend
pyŏnhosa 변호사 attorney, counsel;
  counselor
pyŏnhosabi 변호사비 fee (*of
  lawyer*)
pyŏnhwa 변화 change, shift; variety
pyŏnhwahada 변화하다 change;
  convert
pyŏnhwan 변환 conversion
pyŏnhwashik'ida 변화시키다
  change
pyŏnhyŏng 변형 transformation
pyŏnhyŏngshik'ida 변형시키다
  transform; deform
pyŏnjang 변장 disguise
pyŏnjanghada 변장하다 dress up,
  wear a disguise; dress up as; disguise
  oneself as
pyŏnje 변제 repayment
pyŏnjehada 변제하다 pay back
pyŏnjildoeda 변질되다 degenerate
  into
pyŏnmyŏng 변명 excuse
pyŏnmyŏnghal su ŏmnŭn 변명할 수
  없는 inexcusable
pyŏnsaeksshik'ida 변색시키다
  discolor; tarnish
pyŏnsŏnghada 변성하다 break (*of
  boy's voice*)
pyŏnsokki 변속기 transmission
pyŏnssu 변수 variable
pyŏnt'ae 변태 perversion
pyŏnt'aejŏgin 변태적인 kinky,
  bizarre; perverted
pyŏrak ch'ulssehan nom 벼락
  출세한 놈 upstart
pyŏril ŏmnŭn 별일 없는 uneventful
pyŏruk 벼룩 flea
pyŏt 볏 crest

P'

p'a 파 scallion; faction; par (*in golf*)
p'aak'agi himdŭn 파악하기 힘든
  elusive *meaning*
p'ach'ungnyu 파충류 reptile
p'ada 파다 dig; mine
p'ado 파도 wave
p'aebae 패배 defeat
p'aebaejuŭijŏgin 패배주의적인
  defeatist
p'aebaeshik'ida 패배시키다 defeat
p'aeda 패다 chop; beat
p'aegŏri 패거리 crowd, crew
p'aein kumŏng 패인 구멍 pothole
p'aeja 패자 loser SP
p'aejiŏ konggyŏk'ada 패지어
  공격하다 gang up on
p'aek 팩 carton
p'aek'iji kwangwang 패키지 관광
  package tour
p'aek'iji sangp'um 패키지 상품
  package deal
p'aekssŭ 팩스 fax
p'aekssŭ munsŏ 팩스 문서 fax
p'aekssŭroponaeda 팩스로 보내다
  fax; *Xŭl/rŭl p'aekssŭro Yege
  ponaeda* X을/를 팩스로 Y에게
  보내다 fax X to Y
p'aen 팬 fan, supporter
p'aendŏ kom 팬더 곰 panda
p'aengch'ang 팽창 expansion
p'aengch'anghada 팽창하다
  expand
p'aengi 팽이 spinning top
p'aengp'aenghan 팽팽한 taut
p'aengp'aenghan chul 팽팽한 줄
  tightrope
p'aenji 팬지 pansy
p'aenk'eik'ŭ 팬케이크 pancake
p'aenŏl 패널 panel
p'aenŏlt'i 패널티 penalty
p'aenŏlt'i kuyŏk 패널티 구역 penalty
  area
p'aen pelt'ŭ 팬 벨트 fan belt
p'aent'i 팬티 panties, underpants

p'aent'i sŭt'ak'ing 팬티 스타킹
  pantyhose
p'aesshyŏn 패션 fashion
p'aesshyŏn tijainŏ 패션 디자이너
  fashion designer
p'aesŭ 패스 pass
p'aesŭhada 패스하다 pass
p'aesŭt'ŭp'udŭjŏm 패스트푸드점
  fastfood restaurant
p'aet'ŏn 패턴 pattern
p'agidoenŭn 파기되는 doomed
p'agoe 파괴 destruction, demolition;
  ruin
p'agoehada 파괴하다 destroy,
  demolish; ruin
p'agoejŏgin 파괴적인 destructive
p'agŭp hyokkwa 파급 효과
  repercussion
p'agyŏktchŏgin harin kagyŏk
  파격적인 할인 가격 knockdown
  price
p'ahech'ida 파헤치다 dig up
p'ai 파이 pie
p'ail 파일 file COMPUT
p'aip'ŭ 파이프 pipe
p'ainaep'ŭl 파인애플 pineapple
p'aip'ŭrain 파이프라인 pipeline
p'ajang 파장 wavelength
p'ak'a 파카 parka
P'ak'isŭt'an 파키스탄 Pakistan ◊
  Pakistani
p'al 팔 arm; eight
p'alda 팔다 sell
p'alkkumch'i 팔꿈치 elbow
p'al kup'yŏ p'yŏgi 팔 굽혀 펴기
  push-up
p'allida 팔리다 fetch *price*, be sold for
P'almandaejanggyŏng 팔만대장경
  Tripitaka Koreana
p'alsship 팔십 eighty
p'altchang-ŭl kkida 팔짱을 끼다
  fold one's arms
p'altchi 팔찌 bracelet
p'ama 파마 perm

p'ama hada 파마 하다 perm
p'amp'üllet 팜플렛 pamphlet
p'amut-tta 파묻다 bury
p'amyöl 파멸 destruction, doom
p'amyölshik'ida 파멸시키다 destroy; ruin
p'amyörhan 파멸한 ruined, in ruins
p'an 판 sheet (*of glass, metal*); tray; board; edition
p'anaeda 파내다 extract
p'andan 판단 opinion, judgment
p'andanhada 판단하다 judge; *könmosüburo p'andanhada* 겉모습으로 판단하다 judge by appearances, take at face value
p'andannyök 판단력 judgment, discernment
p'andok chönyong kiök changch'i 판독 전용 기억 장치 ROM, read-only memory
p'andok chönyong p'ail 판독 전용 파일 read-only file
p'andok'ada 판독하다 decipher
p'an-gyöl 판결 ruling, sentence
p'an-györhada 판결하다 judge; *nugurül mujoero / yujoero p'an-györhada* 누구를 무죄로 / 유죄로 판결하다 find a person innocent / guilty; *p'ansanün ...rago p'an-györhaet-tta* 판사는 ...라고 판결했다 the judge ruled that ...
p'an-györül naerida 판결을 내리다 pass sentence; sentence
p'anhwa 판화 engraving
p'anja 판자 board
p'anjaro maktta 판자로 막다 board up
p'anji 판지 cardboard
p'anmae 판매 sale; selling; *p'anmae chung-ida* 판매 중이다 be on sale
p'anmaebusö 판매부서 sales (department)
p'anmae chömwön 판매 점원 sales clerk
p'anmae ch'oktchin 판매 촉진 promotion
p'anmaehada 판매하다 sell, market
p'anmaeja 판매자 seller
p'anmae kagyök 판매 가격 asking price
p'anmae kümaek 판매 금액 sales figures

p'anmae pujang 판매 부장 sales manager
p'anorama 파노라마 panorama
p'ansa 판사 judge
p'ansori 판소리 epic songs
p'antton 판돈 stake
p'aöp 파업 strike
p'aöptcha 파업자 striker
p'apk'on 팝콘 popcorn
p'apssong 팝송 pop song
p'ap'yön 파편 debris
p'aran 파란 blue
p'arangsaek 파랑색 blue
p'aranmanjanghan 파란만장한 checkered
p'arasol 파라솔 parasol, sunshade
p'arat'a 파랗다 be blue
p'ari 파리 fly (*insect*)
p'arwöl 팔월 August
p'aryömch'ihan 파렴치한 shameless
p'asakp'asak'an 파삭파삭한 crisp
p'asan 파산 bankruptcy
p'asangp'ung 파상풍 tetanus
p'asanhada 파산하다 go bankrupt, go bust; be ruined
p'asanshik'ida 파산시키다 bankrupt; ruin
p'ason 파손 breakage
p'asshijüm 파시즘 fascism
p'asshisüt'ü 파시스트 fascist
p'asülli 파슬리 parsley
p'asüt'el 파스텔 pastel
p'at'anhada 파탄하다 fail; go bankrupt
p'at'i 파티 party
p'at'ibok 파티 복 evening wear; evening dress; party dress
p'at'ü 파트 part MUS
p'awö süt'iöring 파워 스티어링 power steering
p'awö yunit 파워 유닛 power unit
p'ayöl 파열 rupture
p'ayöldoeda 파열되다 rupture
p'edal 페달 pedal
p'edarül paltta 페달을 밟다 pedal
p'eiji 페이지 page
p'eint'ü 페인트 paint
p'eint'ü sol 페인트 솔 paintbrush
p'elt'üp'en 펠트펜 felt-tip (pen)
p'eminijüm 페미니즘 feminism

p'eminisŭt'ŭ 페미니스트 feminist
p'endŏ 펜더 fender
p'enishillin 페니실린 penicillin
p'enp'al ch'in-gu 펜팔 친구 pen pal
p'enshing 펜싱 fencing SP
p'i 피 blood
p'ianisŭt'ŭ 피아니스트 pianist
p'iano 피아노 piano
p'ibu 피부 skin
p'ida 피다 open; unroll; blossom
p'igo 피고 the accused
p'igoch'ŭk 피고측 defense
p'igoch'ŭk chŭngin 피고측 증인
  defense witness
p'igoch'ŭk pyŏnhosa 피고측 변호사
  defense lawyer
p'igoin 피고인 defendant
p'igonhada 피곤하다 be tired
p'igonhaejida 피곤해지다 get tired
p'igonhan 피곤한 tired
p'igosŏk 피고석 dock LAW
p'igyŏ sŭk'eit'ing 피겨 스케이팅
  figure skating
p'ihada 피하다 avoid; ward off;
  shelter
p'ihae 피해 damage
p'ihaega makssimhan 피해가
  막심한 disastrous
p'ihae mangsang 피해 망상
  paranoia
p'ihaerŭl ip'ida 피해를 입히다
  damage
p'ihal su innŭn 피할 수 있는
  sheltered
p'ihal su ŏmnŭn 피할 수 없는
  inevitable
p'ihal su ŏpsshi 피할 수 없이
  inevitably
p'ihugyŏnin 피후견인 ward (child)
p'iim 피임 contraception
p'iimhada 피임하다 use
  contraception
p'iim kigu 피임 기구 contraceptive
  device
p'iimyak 피임약 (contraceptive) pill
p'iimyong p'esari 피임용 페사리
  diaphragm
p'ija 피자 pizza
p'ijangp'ajang-i toeda 피장파장이
  되다 be quits with
p'iksel 픽셀 pixel

p'ik'et 피켓 picket
p'ik'et lain 피켓 라인 picket line
p'ik'ŭl 피클 pickles
p'ildŭ kyŏnggi 필드 경기 field events
P'illandŭ 핀란드 Finland ◊ Finnish
P'illandŭŏ 핀란드어 Finnish
  (language)
P'illandŭ saram 핀란드 사람 Finn
p'ille sŭt'eik'ŭ 필레 스테이크 fillet
  steak
P'illip'in 필리핀 Philippines ◊ Filipino
p'illŭm 필름 film
p'ilmyŏng 필명 pen name
p'ilssabon 필사본 manuscript
p'ilssajŏgin 필사적인 desperate
p'ilssu chokkŏn 필수 조건
  precondition
p'ilssujŏgin 필수적인 vital, essential
p'ilssup'um 필수품 necessity
p'ilssuŭi 필수의 indispensable
p'iltchŏk'ada 필적하다 match;
  parallel; equal
p'ilt'ŏ 필터 filter; filter tip
p'ilt'ŏ innŭn tambae 필터 있는 담배
  filter-tipped (cigarettes)
p'imang 피망 pepper, pimiento
p'in 핀 pin ◊ open flower
p'inanch'ŏ 피난처 refuge, shelter;
  retreat
p'inanhada 피난하다 take refuge
p'inggye 핑계 excuse, pretext
p'ing tolda 핑 돌다 whirl
p'i pŭi sshi 피 브이 씨 PVC
p'iri 피리 Korean oboe
p'iro 피로 fatigue
p'iroch'im 피뢰침 lightning rod
p'iryo 필요 need; ...*l p'iryoga it-tta*
  ... ㄹ 필요가 있다 it is necessary to ...
p'iryohada 필요하다 want; need,
  require, call for
p'iryohadamyŏn 필요하다면 if need
  be, as necessary
p'iryohan 필요한 necessary
p'iryoro hada 필요로 하다 need,
  require, take; entail, mean
p'iryossŏng 필요성 necessity
p'isaldanghada 피살당하다 be killed
p'isangjŏgin 피상적인 cursory
p'ishint'agin 피신탁인 trustee
p'isshi 피씨 PC, personal computer
p'isŭt'on 피스톤 piston

p'itchaguk 핏자국 bloodstain

p'it-ttŏng-ŏri 핏덩어리 (blood) clot

p'it'usŏng-iŭi 피투성이의 bloody

p'iuda 피우다 burn; smoke; give off *smell*; play *trick*

p'ŏbut-tta 퍼붓다 pour; pour on; *chilmun kongserŭl p'ŏbut-tta* 질문 공세를 퍼붓다 bombard with questions

p'ŏdakkŏrida 퍼덕거리다 flutter

p'ŏjida 퍼지다 spread

p'ŏjŭl 퍼즐 puzzle (*game*)

p'ŏllŏgida 펄럭이다 flap; flutter; wave

p'ŏlp'ŭ 펄프 pulp

p'ŏltchŏk ttwida 펄쩍 뛰다 jump

p'ŏmp'ŭ 펌프 pump

p'ŏng 펑 pop

p'ŏngk'ŭ 펑크 blow-out

p'ŏngp'ŏng sosanaoda 펑펑 솟아나오다 gush

p'ŏ ollida 퍼 올리다 scoop up

p'ŏreidŭ 퍼레이드 parade, procession

p'ŏsent'ŭ 퍼센트 percent

p'ŏtchi 버찌 cherry

p'ŏttŭrida 퍼뜨리다 spread; circulate *memo*

p'oak'ada 포악하다 be ruthless; be oppressive

p'oak'an 포악한 oppressive; ruthless

p'och'ak'ada 포착하다 capture, portray; seize

p'odae 포대 bag; sack

p'odaegi 포대기 baby quilt (*for carrying baby on mother's back*)

p'odo 포도 grape; *p'odo han song-i* 포도 한 송이 a bunch of grapes

p'odoju 포도주 wine

p'odoju menyu 포도주 메뉴 wine list

p'odoju pyŏng ttagae 포도주 병 따개 corkscrew

p'odonamu 포도나무 grapevine

p'odongp'odonghan 포동포동한 plump

p'odowŏn 포도원 vineyard

p'ogihada 포기하다 give up, renounce

p'ogŭmhada 폭음하다 drink too much

p'ogu 폭우 downpour

p'ogwaltchŏgin 포괄적인 comprehensive

p'ogyŏk 포격 gunfire

p'ogyŏk'ada 포격하다 shell

p'ohamhada 포함하다 include; add on

p'ohamhan 포함한 inclusive

p'ohamhayŏ 포함하여 including

p'ohwa 포화 shellfire

p'ojang 포장 packaging

p'ojang chaeryo 포장 재료 wrapping

p'ojanghada 포장하다 pack, package; giftwrap; *haembŏgo p'ojanghaejuseyo* 햄버거 포장해주세요 hamburger to go

p'ojangji 포장지 wrapper; wrapping paper; tissue paper

p'ojangnyong laep 포장용 랩 clingfilm

p'ojin 포진 herpes

p'ojŭ ch'wihada 포즈 취하다 pose

p'oju 포주 pimp

p'ok 폭 width, breadth; *p'ok shim-mit'ŏ* 폭 10미터 10m across

p'ok-kkun 폭군 tyrant

p'ok-kkyŏk 폭격 bomb attack

p'ok-kkyŏk-kki 폭격기 bomber

p'okkunjŏgin 폭군적인 tyrannical, domineering

p'okŏ 포커 poker

p'okppal 폭발 explosion

p'okppalmul 폭발물 explosive

p'okppal sshik'ida 폭발시키다 detonate

p'okpparhada 폭발하다 explode, go off; blow up; erupt

p'okp'ahada 폭파하다 blow up, bomb

p'okp'ashik'ida 폭파시키다 blast

p'okp'o 폭포 waterfall

p'okp'ung 폭풍 storm

p'okp'ungju-ŭibo 폭풍주의보 storm warning

p'okp'ung-u 폭풍우 rainstorm

p'okp'ung-u-ga ch'inŭn 폭풍우가 치는 stormy

p'oksshik 폭식 gluttony

p'oksshik'ada 폭식하다 eat too much

p'okssorŭl t'ŏttŭrida 폭소를 터뜨리다 burst out laughing

p'okttong 폭동 riot, uprising
p'okttongja 폭동자 rioter
p'okttongŭl irŭk'ida 폭동을 일으키다 riot
p'okt'an 폭탄 bomb
p'ok'aeng 폭행 assault
p'ok'aenghada 폭행하다 assault
p'ok'etyong kyesan-gi 포켓용 계산기 pocket calculator
p'ok'ŭ 포크 fork
p'ok'ŭttaensŭ 포크댄스 folkdance
p'oldŏ 폴더 folder
P'ollandŭ 폴란드 Poland ◊ Polish
P'ollandŭŏ 폴란드어 Polish
p'olliesŭt'erŭ 폴리에스테르 polyester
p'olliet'illen 폴리에틸렌 polyethylene
p'ollisŭt'iren 폴리스티렌 polystyrene
p'omaet'ada 포맷하다 format
p'ongnak'ada 폭락하다 drop sharply (*of stock market*)
p'ongnirŭl ch'wihada 폭리를 취하다 rip off; profiteer
p'ong-nŏlbŭn 폭넓은 wide *experience*
p'ongno 폭로 revelation, disclosure
p'ongnohada 폭로하다 expose; *uyŏnhi p'ongnohada* 우연히 폭로하다 give oneself away
p'ongnyŏk 폭력 force, violence; outrage
p'ongnyŏktchŏgin 폭력적인 violent; outrageous
p'ongnyŏkttanwŏn 폭력단원 mobster
p'o-ong 포옹 cuddle; hug
p'o-onghada 포옹하다 cuddle; hug
p'oro 포로 captive; *nugurŭl p'ororo chaptta* 누구를 포로로 잡다 take s.o. prisoner
p'orŭno 포르노 pornography ◊ pornographic
p'orŭt 버릇 habit
P'orŭt'ugal 포르투갈 Portugal ◊ Portuguese
P'orŭt'ugarin 포르투갈인 Portuguese
P'orŭt'ugarŏ 포르투갈어 Portuguese (*language*)
p'oshik'ada 포식하다 overeat *muŏsŭl p'oshik'ada* 무엇을 포식하다 gorge oneself on sth
p'osŭt'ŏ 포스터 poster

p'ot'eit'o ch'ipssŭ 포테이토 칩스 potato chips
p'ot'ŏbŭl 포터블 portable COMPUT
p'ot'ŭ 포트 port COMPUT
p'owihada 포위하다 surround; close in
p'owi konggyŏk 포위 공격 siege
p'owi konggyŏk'ada 포위 공격하다 lay siege to
p'owŏdŭ 포워드 forward SP
p'oyu tongmul 포유 동물 mammal
p'ŭllaent'eishyŏn 플랜테이션 plantation
p'ŭllaeshwi 플래쉬 flash PHOT
p'ŭllaetp'om 플랫폼 platform
p'ŭllaja 플라자 plaza, shopping mall
p'ŭllasŭt'ik 플라스틱 plastic
p'ŭllŏgŭ 플러그 plug
p'ŭllŏgŭrŭl kkot-tta 플러그를 꽂다 plug in
p'ŭllŏgŭrŭl ppoptta 플러그를 뽑다 unplug
p'ŭllop'i tisŭk'ŭ 플로피 디스크 floppy (disk)
p'ŭllot'ŏ 플로터 plotter COMPUT
p'ŭllut'ŭ 플루트 flute
P'ŭrangssŭ 프랑스 France ◊ French
P'ŭrangssŭin 프랑스인 Frenchman; Frenchwoman
P'ŭrangssŭŏ 프랑스어 French (*language*)
p'ŭrik'ik 프리킥 free kick
p'ŭrima 프리마 creamer (*for coffee*)
p'ŭrimiŏm 프리미엄 premium
p'ŭrint'ŏ 프린터 printer (*machine*)
p'ŭro 프로 professional
p'ŭromp'ŭt'ŭ 프롬프트 prompt COMPUT
p'ŭront'ŭ 프론트 reception, check-in
p'ŭrop'ellŏ 프로펠러 propeller
p'ŭro sŏnsuro 프로 선수로 professionally SP
p'uda 푸다 scoop
p'uk chamdŭlda 푹 잠들다 be (fast) asleep
p'ukssinhan 푹신한 soft
p'ul 풀 glue; grass; *p'urŭl ttŭdŏmŏktta* 풀을 뜯어먹다 graze
p'ulda 풀다 undo; unpack; disentangle; solve; release *brake*; *k'orŭl p'ulda* 코를 풀다 blow one's nose

p'ullida

p'ullida 풀리다 unwind
p'ullin 풀린 frayed
p'ullo puch'ida 풀로 붙이다 glue
p'umhaeng-i tanjŏnghan 품행이
단정한 well-behaved
p'umjil 품질 quality
p'umjil kwalli 품질 관리 quality
control
p'umjiri nappŭn 품질이 나쁜 poor
quality, shoddy
p'umjong 품종 brand; breed
p'umkkyŏk 유행 style, fashion
p'umsa 품사 part of speech
p'umwi innŭn 품위 있는 gracious;
dignified; classy
p'ungbu 풍부 abundance
p'ungbuhada 풍부하다 be abundant
p'ungbuhage hada 풍부하게 하다
enrich
p'ungbuhan 풍부한 abundant; lavish
◊ a wealth of
p'ungch'a 풍차 windmill
p'unggi sabŏm tansokppan 풍기
사범 단속반 vice squad
p'unggyŏng 풍경 scenery
p'unggyŏnghwa 풍경화 landscape
(painting)
p'ungja 풍자 irony; sarcasm; satire
p'ungjagŭi 풍작의 bumper crop, year
p'ungjajŏgin 풍자적인 satirical
p'ungja manhwa 풍자 만화
caricature
p'ungmanhan 풍만한 buxom
p'ungmunŭro 풍문으로 by hearsay
p'ungnyoropkke hada 풍요롭게
하다 enrich
p'ungsŏn 풍선 balloon
p'ungsŏnghan 풍성한 hearty
p'ungsŏnkkŏm 풍선껌 bubble gum
p'ung-yo 풍요 plenty
p'ung-yoroun sahoe 풍요로운 사회
affluent society
p'unnaegi 풋내기 squirt; greenhorn
p'uri chugŭn 풀이 죽은
downhearted; downcast
p'uri ugŏjin 풀이 우거진 grassy
p'urŏjuda 풀어주다 untie
p'urompŭt'ŭ 프롬프트 prompt
COMPUT
p'urŏ naerida 풀어 내리다 let down
p'urŏ poda 풀어 보다 unwrap

p'ushwi maen 푸쉬맨 person who
pushes Seoul commuters into subway
trains at rush hour
p'ye 폐 lung
p'yeam 폐암 lung cancer
p'yegihada 폐기하다 discard, dump
p'yegimul 폐기물 waste, waste
product
p'yegishik'ida 폐기시키다 scrap,
drop, abandon
p'yegyŏnggi 폐경기 menopause
p'yehoeshik 폐회식 closing
ceremony
p'yejihada 폐지하다 abolish
p'yejŏm 폐점 closure
p'yejŏmhada 폐점하다 close down
p'yejŏm shigan 폐점 시간 closing
time
p'yemuri toen 폐물이 된 obsolete
p'yeŏp'ada 폐업하다 close down
p'yeryŏm 폐렴 pneumonia
p'yeswae 폐쇄 closure
p'yeswaehada 폐쇄하다 close; close
up
p'yeswae hoero t'ellebijyŏn 폐쇄
회로 텔레비전 closed-circuit
television
p'yŏda 펴다 unfold; smooth out
p'yŏlch'ida 펼치다 spread, lay
p'yŏlch'ŏjida 펼쳐지다 unfold
p'yŏlli 편리 convenience
p'yŏllihada 편리하다 be convenient
p'yŏllihan 편리한 convenient, handy
p'yŏn 편 side; faction; means;
tendency; editing; volume; part,
section; k'ŭn / chagŭn p'yŏn
큰 / 작은 편 on the big / small side;
nuguŭi p'yŏni toeŏ chuda 누구의
편이 되어 주다 come to s.o.'s
defense
p'yŏnanhada 편안하다 be
comfortable
p'yŏnanhan 편안한 comfortable,
easy, relaxed
p'yŏnanhi hada 편안히 하다 make
oneself at home
p'yŏnch'in kajŏng 편친 가정 one-
parent family
p'yŏndosŏn 편도선 tonsil
p'yŏndosŏnnyŏm 편도선염
tonsillitis

p'yŏndo sŭngch'akkwŏn 편도 승차권 one-way ticket

p'yŏndŭt'ong 편두통 migraine

p'yŏngbang mit'ŏ 평방 미터 square meter

p'yŏngbŏmhan 평범한 plain, regular; commonplace

p'yŏngdŭng 평등 equality

p'yŏngdŭngjuŭiŭi 평등주의의 egalitarian

p'yŏnggyŏl 평결 verdict

p'yŏnggyun 평균 average; *p'yŏnggyun ...(ŭ)ro kyesandoeda* 평균 ...(으)로 계산되다 average out at

p'yŏnggyunnaeda 평균내다 average out

p'yŏnggyunŭi 평균의 average

p'yŏnggyunŭro ... hada 평균으로 ... 하다 average

p'yŏnghaeng 평행 parallel (line)

p'yŏnghaenghanŭn 평행하는 parallel

p'yŏnghwa 평화 peace

p'yŏnghwajuŭi 평화주의 pacifism

p'yŏnghwajuŭija 평화주의자 pacifist; dove

P'yŏnghwa Pongsadan 평화 봉사단 Peace Corps

p'yŏnghwaropkke 평화롭게 peacefully

p'yŏnghwaroptta 평화롭다 be peaceful

p'yŏnghwaroun 평화로운 peaceful

p'yŏnghyŏng 평형 breaststroke

p'yŏng-il 평일 weekday; workday

p'yŏngkka 평가 evaluation; appreciation

p'yŏngkka chŏrha 평가 절하 devaluation

p'yŏngkka chŏrhashik'ida 평가 절하시키다 devalue

p'yŏngkkahada 평가하다 assess; appreciate; rate, rank, consider; rank among

p'yŏngkkajŏlssang 평가절상 revaluation

p'yŏngmyŏndo 평면도 ground plan

p'yŏngnon 평론 write-up, review

p'yŏngnon-ga 평론가 reviewer

P'yŏngnyang 평양 P'yongyang

p'yŏn-gok 편곡 arrangement MUS

p'yŏn-gok'ada 편곡하다 arrange MUS

p'yŏng-on 평온 calm

p'yŏng-onhada 평온하다 be tranquil

p'yŏng-onhan 평온한 serene, tranquil

p'yŏngp'an 평판 reputation

p'yŏngp'ani chōun 평판이 좋은 reputable

p'yŏngp'ani nappŭn 평판이 나쁜 disreputable

p'yŏngp'yŏnghada 평평하다 be even, be flat

p'yŏngp'yŏnghage hada 평평하게 하다 flatten

p'yŏngp'yŏnghan 평평한 flat, level

p'yŏngsaeng 평생 lifetime; *kŭnyŏ p'yŏngsaeng-e* 그녀 평생에 all her life; *nae p'yŏngsaeng-e* 내 평생에 in my lifetime

p'yŏngsaeng-ŭi 평생의 lifelong

p'yŏngsangbok 평상복 casual wear

p'yŏngsangbok ch'arimŭi 평상복 차림의 informal

p'yŏngsangshich'ŏrŏm 평상시처럼 as usual

p'yŏngsang-ŭi 평상의 casual *shirt etc*

p'yŏng-ya 평야 plain; prairie

p'yŏn-gyŏn 편견 bias, prejudice; *...e taehan p'yŏn-gyŏn* ...에 대한 편견 bias against

p'yŏn-gyŏnŏmnŭn 편견없는 unbiased

p'yŏn-gyŏnŭl kajin 편견을 가진 biased, prejudiced

p'yŏnhan 편한 be comfortable; *tangshini p'yŏnhan shigane* 당신이 편한 시간에 at your convenience

p'yŏnhi shwida 편히 쉬다 relax

p'yŏnhyangshik'ida 편향시키다 deflect

p'yŏnida 편이다: *...nŭn p'yŏnida* ...는 편이다 tend to

p'yŏnji 편지 letter; letters, correspondence

p'yŏnjibin 편집인 editor

p'yŏnjihada 편지하다 mail

p'yŏnjiji 편지지 notepaper

p'yŏnjip 편집 editing ◊ editorial

p'yŏnjipkkwang

208

p'yŏnjipkkwang 편집광 paranoia
p'yŏnjiptcha 편집자 editor
p'yŏnjiptchang 편집장 editor
p'yŏnjiptchŏgin 편집적인 paranoid
p'yŏnjip'ada 편집하다 edit, make
corrections to; compile
p'yŏnjirŭl ponaeda 편지를 보내다
mail
p'yŏnjirŭl ssŭda 편지를 쓰다 write a
letter
p'yŏnmo 편모 single mother
p'yŏnmul 편물 knitting
p'yŏnppŏp 편법 expedient
p'yŏnsŭnghada 편승하다 hitchhike
p'yŏnŭl tŭlda 편을 들다 take sides
p'yŏ parŭda 펴 바르다 apply
ointment etc
p'yo 표 table (*of figures*); ticket
p'yobaek 표백 bleach
p'yobaek'ada 표백하다 bleach;
whiten
p'yobŏm 표범 leopard
p'yobon 표본 sample, specimen
p'yo chadong p'anmaegi 표 자동
판매기 ticket machine
p'yogyŏrhada 표결하다 vote on
p'yohyŏn 표현 expression; display;
wording
p'yohyŏnhada 표현하다 express
p'yohyŏnŭi p'ungbuhan 표현이
풍부한 expressive
p'yoje 표제 heading
p'yoji 표지 cover (*of book,
magazine*)
p'yojip'an 표지판 (road) sign
p'yojŏk 표적 target
p'yojŏng 표정 appearance,
expression, look
p'yojŏng-i p'ungbuhan 표정이
풍부한 expressive
p'yojŏrhada 표절하다 pirate *software
etc*
p'yojun 표준 standard; *p'yojune*

midarhada 표준에 미달하다 not
be up to standard; *p'yojune
tarhada* 표준에 달하다 be up to
standard
p'yojune mat-tchi annŭn 표준에
맞지 않는 nonstandard
p'yojun midarŭi 표준 미달의
substandard
p'yojun shiganttae 표준 시간대 time
zone
p'yo kŏmsawŏn 표 검사원 ticket
inspector
p'yok'an 표칸 cell COMPUT
p'yomyŏn 표면 surface
p'yomyŏnghada 표명하다 voice
opinion
p'yomyŏnjŏgin 표면적인 superficial;
cosmetic
p'yop'i 표피 cuticle
p'yoryuhada 표류하다 drift
p'yoshi 표시 indication, sign; *kamsaŭi p'yoshiro* 감사의 표시로 as a
token of my / our appreciation
p'yoshidŭng 표시등 indicator
p'yoshihada 표시하다 display,
indicate; stand for; mark up
p'yujŭ 퓨즈 fuse
p'yujŭrŭl kkŭnt'a 퓨즈를 끊다 (blow
a) fuse

...rago ...라고 that; *chŏnŭn ...rago
saenggak'amnida* 저는 ...라고
생각합니다 I think that ...
...ranŭn ...라는 that; *...ranŭn saenggagŭl kosuhada* ...라는 생각을
고수하다 hold that, believe
...ro ...로 by; from, because of; of;
into; in; with; to; toward
...robut'ŏ ...로부터 from
...rosŏ ...로서 as
...rŭl ...를 *object particle*
...ryŏgo hada ...려고 하다 try to do;
intend to; be going to

S

sa 사 four
saak'an 사악한 wicked; sinister
saam 사암 sandstone
sabang 사방 all directions
sabip kwanggo 삽입 광고 insert (*in magazine etc*)
sabip'ada 삽입하다 insert
sabŏm 사범 (martial arts) instructor
sabŏp 사법 judicature ◊ judicial
sabŏpkkwŏn 사법권 jurisdiction
sabok 사복 plain clothes ◊ plain-clothes
sabon 사본 duplicate, copy; transcript
sabunŭi il 사분의 일 quarter
sabunŭi sam 사분의 삼 three quarters
sabun ŭmp'yo 사분 음표 quarter note
sabyŏng 사병 private MIL
sabyŏrhan 사별한 bereaved
sach'i 사치 luxury, extravagance
sach'inhoe 사친회 parent-teacher association
sach'isŭrŏptta 사치스럽다 be extravagant; be luxurious
sach'isŭrŏun 사치스러운 extravagant; luxurious
sach'on 사촌 cousin
sach'un-gi 사춘기 adolescence; puberty
sach'un-giŭi 사춘기의 adolescent
sada 사다 buy; pay for
sadari 사다리 ladder
sae 새 bird ◊ new
saebarŭi p'i 새발의 피 chickenfeed, peanuts
saebyŏk 새벽 dawn, daybreak
saech'igihada 새치기하다 shove in, cut in *line*
saeda 새다 leak, seep
saedanjanghada 새단장하다 freshen up
saegan-gyŏng 색안경 sunglasses

saegida 새기다 carve; engrave
saegin 색인 index
saegin k'adŭ 색인 카드 index card
Saehae 새해 New Year; *Saehae Pok Mani Padŭseyo!* 새해 복 많이 받으세요! Happy New Year!
Saehae Ch'ŏnnal 새해 첫날 New Year's Day
sae irŭmŭro (chŏjang hagi) 새이름으로 (저장하기) save as
saejang 새장 bird cage
saekch'aega p'ungbuhan 색채가 풍부한 colorful
saekch'aeŭi paehap 색채의 배합 color scheme
saekkaman 새까만 jet-black
saekki 새끼 cub, young animal; kid; brat
saekki koyang-i 새끼 고양이 kitten
saekkiyang 새끼양 lamb
saek-kkal 색깔 color
saek-kkal innŭn 색깔 있는 tinted
saekssŏp'on 색소폰 saxophone
saektchi 색지 tinted paper
saektchŏntchŭng 색전증 embolism
saektcho 색조 shade, tone
saek'omdalk'omhan 새콤달콤한 sweet and sour
saellŏdŭ 샐러드 salad
saem 샘 spring (*water*); envy; jealousy
saendŭl 샌들 sandal
saendŭwich'i 샌드위치 sandwich
saeng-ae 생애 career
saengbangsong 생방송 live broadcast
saengch'e konghak 생체 공학 biotechnology
saengdo 생도 cadet
saenggage chamgida 생각에 잠기다 muse, reflect
saenggage chamgin 생각에 잠긴 pensive

saenggagi kip'ŭn 생각이 깊은 thoughtful

saenggagŏmnŭn 생각없는 mindless, senseless

saenggak 생각 thought, idea; *choŭn saenggagiya!* 좋은 생각이야! good idea!

saenggak'ada 생각하다 think, consider; *...rago saenggakttoenda* ...라고 생각된다 it is considered to be ...

saenggak'aenaeda 생각해내다 come up with, hit on, think up

saenggak'al su choch'a ŏmnŭn 생각할 수 조차 없는 unthinkable; inconceivable

saenggak'al su innŭn 생각할 수 있는 conceivable

saenggang 생강 ginger

saenggangch'a 생강차 ginger tea

saenggi 생기 animation, liveliness

saenggida 생기다 occur; come into existence; *musŭn iri saeng-gyŏssŏyo* 무슨 일이 생겼어요 something has come up

saenggiga nada 생기가 나다 perk up, cheer up

saenggiinnŭn 생기있는 lively, fresh

saenggi tolge hada 생기 돌게 하다 cheer up

saenggye 생계 living, livelihood; *kyŏu saenggyerŭl iŏnagada* 겨우 생계를 이어나가다 eke out a living

saenghwal 생활 life, existence; living

saenghwalbi 생활비 cost of living; maintenance; budget; *saenghwal-birŭl pŏlda* 생활비를 벌다 earn one's living

saenghwal pangsshik 생활 방식 way of life, lifestyle

saenghwal pojo 생활 보조 welfare

saenghwal pojogŭm 생활 보조금 welfare check

saenghwalsa 생활사 life history

saenghwal sujun 생활 수준 standard of living

saeng-il 생일 birthday; *saeng-il ch'uk'ahamnida!* 생일 축하합니다! happy birthday!

saengjonhada 생존하다 exist; survive

saengjonhal ssu innŭn 생존할 수 있는 viable

saengjonja 생존자 survivor

saengjon kyŏngjaeng 생존 경쟁 struggle for survival

saeng k'ŭrim 생 크림 whipped cream

saengmaektchu 생맥주 draft (beer)

saengmaeng 색맹 color-blindness ◊ color-blind

saengmul 생물 organism, being ◊ bio-

saengmurhak 생물학 biology

saengmurhaktchŏgin 생물학적인 biological

saengmyŏng 생명 life

saengmyŏng ŏmnŭn 생명 없는 lifeless

saengmyŏng pohŏm 생명 보험 life assurance

saengmyŏng-ŭl wihyŏp'anŭn 생명을 위협하는 life-threatening

saengni 생리 menstruation; period

saengnidae 생리대 sanitary napkin

saengnihada 생리하다 menstruate

saengnyak'ada 생략하다 leave out, omit

saengnyŏnwŏril 생년월일 date of birth

saengp'ohada 생포하다 capture (alive)

saengsaenghada 생생하다 be vivid

saengsaenghan 생생한 vivid, graphic

saengsan 생산 production, output

saengsanbi 생산비 production costs

saengsanbirŭl kyŏnjŏk'ada 생산비를 견적하다 cost, calculate the cost of

saengsanhada 생산하다 produce, output

saengsanja 생산자 maker, producer

saengsanmul 생산물 product

saengsannyŏk 생산력 production capacity

saengsanssŏng 생산성 productivity

saengsanŭl kadonghada 생산을 가동하다 come into production; come on stream

saengshikki 생식기 genitals

saengshik nŭngnyŏk 생식 능력

virility
saengsŏn 생선 fish
saengsŏnppyŏ 생선뼈 fishbone
saengsu 생수 mineral water
saengt'aegye 생태계 ecosystem
saengt'aehak 생태학 ecology
saengt'aehaktcha 생태학자
  naturalist, ecologist
saengt'aehaktchŏgin 생태학적인
  ecological
saengt'aehaktchŏk kyunhyŏng
  생태학적 균형 ecological balance
saenŭn 새는 leaky
saeŏ naoda 새어 나오다 leak out,
  seep out; filter through
saeppalgak'e tan 새빨갛게 단 red-
  hot
saeppalgan kŏjinmal 새빨간 거짓말
  downright lie
saero koch'im 새로 고침 reload
  COMPUT
saeropkke nŭkkida 새롭게 느끼다
  feel renewed
saeroptta 새롭다 be new
saeroun 새로운 fresh, new
sae tanjanghada 새 단장하다
  redecorate
saeu 새우 shrimp
sagak'yŏng 사각형 square;
  quadrangle
sagi 사기 swindle, fraud, rip-off; con;
  morale, spirits ◊ fraudulent
sagi ch'ida 사기 치다 con, cheat
sagikkun 사기꾼 crook, con man
sagjik'ada 사직하다 resign
sago 사고 accident, mishap; thought;
  sagoro chuktta 사고로 죽다 be
  killed in an accident; **sagorŭl tanghada** 사고를 당하다 have an
  accident
sagwa 사과 apology; apple
sagwa chusŭ 사과 주스 apple juice
sagwahada 사과하다 apologize
sagwan saengdo 사관 생도 cadet
sagwasosŭ 사과소스 apple sauce
sagwida 사귀다 get acquainted,
  make friends; **ch'in-gurŭl sagwida**
  친구를 사귀다 make friends;
  saramgwa sagwida 사람과 사귀다
  socialize
sagyogye saramdŭl 사교계 사람들

glitterati
sagyojŏgin 사교적인 sociable;
  kŭnyŏnŭn sagyossŏng-i chot'a
  그녀는 사교성이 좋다 she's a good
  mixer
sahaktcha 사학자 historian
sahoe 사회 society, community ◊
  social
sahoehak 사회학 sociology
sahoeja 사회자 chairperson;
  chairwoman; host; master of
  ceremonies
sahoejuŭi 사회주의 socialism
sahoejuŭija 사회주의자 socialist
sahoejuŭijŏgin 사회주의적인
  socialist
sahoe kyegŭp 사회 계급 (social)
  class
sahoe poda 사회 보다 preside
sahoe saŏp 사회 사업 social work
sahoe saŏpkka 사회 사업가 social
  worker
sahoe ssŭregi 사회 쓰레기 lowlife
sahyŏng chip'aeng 사형 집행
  execution
sahyŏng chip'aenghada 사형
  집행하다 execute
sahyŏng chip'aeng-in 사형 집행인
  executioner
sahyŏng sŏn-gorŭl pat-tta 사형
  선고를 받다 be sentenced to death
sai 사이 interval, space; relationship;
  kip'ŭn sai 깊은 사이 intimacy
  (sexual); **kip'ŭn saiin** 깊은 사이인
  intimate (sexually)
saie 사이에 between
saiga chot'a 사이가 좋다 get on; be
  friendly with
saiga t'ŭrŏjida 사이가 틀어지다 fall
  out, argue
saijok'e chinaeda 사이좋게 지내다
  get along
saim 사임 resignation
saimhada 사임하다 resign
sain 사인 killer; autograph
sairen 사이렌 siren
saja 사자 lion
sajang 사장 boss; president
sajik 사직 resignation; **sajik'al kŏsŭl
  allida** 사직할 것을 알리다 hand in
  one's notice

sajik'ada 사직하다 resign
sajin 사진 photo(graph); *sajini chal pannŭn* 사진이 잘 받는 photogenic
sajinaelbŏm 사진앨범 photo album
sajin ch'waryŏng 사진 촬영 photography
sajinsa 사진사 photographer
sajin tchiktta 사진 찍다 photograph
sajŏl 사절 delegation; envoy
sajŏn 사전 dictionary
sajŏng kŏri 사정 거리 range
sajŏng-ŏmnŭn 사정없는 relentless; ruthless
sajŏn kyŏnghŏm 사전 경험 foretaste
sajungju 사중주 quartet
sak-kkam 삭감 cut, cutback, reduction
sak-kkamhada 삭감하다 reduce, cut; slash
sakkŏn 사건 affair, matter, case; incident; *sakkŏnŭi sunsŏ* 사건의 순서 the sequence of events
sakpparhan 삭발한 shaven
saktche 삭제 deletion
saktchehada 삭제하다 delete
sak'arin 사카린 saccharin
sal 살 flesh, meat; years of age; arrow; spoke (*of wheel*)
salch'ungje 살충제 pesticide; insecticide
salda 살다 live
salgach'i kŏch'in 살갗이 거친 chapped
salgŭmŏni 살그머니 stealthily, furtively
salgŭmsalgŭm kŏt-tta 살금살금 걷다 creep
salgu 살구 apricot
salgyundoen 살균된 sterile MED
salgyunŭi 살균의 antiseptic
salk'ogi 살코기 lean meat
sallim kyŏngbiwŏn 산림 경비원 forest ranger
sallŏdŭ tŭreshing 샐러드 드레싱 salad dressing
sal ppaeda 살 빼다 slim
salp'yŏboda 살펴보다 see about, look into; check on; examine, look at; observe
salsal 살살 softly, lightly, gently

salssugi 살수기 sprinkler
sal su innŭn 살 수 있는 inhabitable
sal su ŏmnŭn 살 수 없는 uninhabitable
saltchak 살짝 furtively; easily; lightly
saltchak kkaemulda 살짝 깨물다 nibble
saltchak milch'ida 살짝 밀치다 jog *elbow etc*
saltchak sŭch'ida 살짝 스치다 brush, touch lightly
saltchida 살찌다 fill out, get fatter
sam 삼 three
samagwi 사마귀 wart
samak 사막 desert
samang 사망 death
samangjasu 사망자수 death toll
samangnyul 사망률 mortality, death rate
sambunŭi il 삼분의 일 one third
samch'on 삼촌 uncle (*father's brother, single*)
samgahada 삼가하다 refrain, desist
samgak 삼각 triangle ◊ triangular
samgak-kki 삼각기 pennant
samgak-kkŏn 삼각건 sling (*bandage*)
samgakttae 삼각대 tripod
samgak'yŏng 삼각형 triangle
Samguk 삼국 The Three Kingdoms
samgyet'ang 삼계탕 chicken boiled with ginseng
samgyŏpssal kui 삼겹살 구이 barbecued belly of pork
Samiltchŏl 삼일절 1 March Memorial Day
samja 삼자 third party
samjungju 삼중주 trio
samk'ida 삼키다 engulf, swallow
samnyu 삼류 third class ◊ third-rate
samohada 사모하다 adore
samonim 사모님 Madam, Mrs (*respectful*)
Samp'alssŏn 삼팔선 38th Parallel
samship 삼십 thirty
samtta 삶다 boil
samuguk 사무국 bureau, office
samugwan 사무관 clerk
samujang 사무장 steward
samujik sawŏn 사무직 사원 office worker, white-collar worker

samul 사물 thing

samushil 사무실 office (*room*)

samushillyong kŏnmul 사무실용 건물 office (*building*)

samushillyong koch'ŭng piltting 사무실용 고층 빌딩 office block

samwŏl 삼월 March

samyŏn 사면 amnesty, pardon; hill

samyŏng 사명 mission, vocation

samyŏnhada 사면하다 absolve, pardon

san 산 mountain; acid

sana chehan 산아 제한 birth control

sanaee(sŏ) 사내에(서) in-house

sanaeŭi 사내의 in-house

sanagin 산악인 mountaineer

sanapkke morach'ida 사납게 물아치다 rage

sanaptta 사납다 be wild; be fierce; be unlucky

sanaun 사나운 rough, fierce

sanawajida 사나와지다 become abusive

sanbaltchŏgin 산발적인 sporadic; scattered; intermittent

sanbuinkkwa 산부인과 maternity hospital

sanbuinkkwa pyŏngdong 산부인과 병동 maternity ward

sanbuinkkwa ŭisa 산부인과 의사 gynecologist; obstetrician

sanch'aek 산책 ramble; rambling; stroll

sanch'aekshik'ida 산책시키다 walk *the dog*

sanch'aek'ada 산책하다 go for a walk; take a stroll; ramble

sanch'ul 산출 yield

sanch'urhada 산출하다 yield

sanch'urhae naeda 산출해 내다 calculate

sandaejŏguro 상대적으로 relatively

sandŏmi 산더미 mound, pile

sandŭlpparam 산들바람 breeze

sang 상 prize; icon (*cultural*); statue; table; mourning; *sang chung-ida* 상 중이다 be in mourning

sang-a 상아 ivory

sang-ajil 상아질 enamel (*on tooth*)

sangbandoen 상반된 opposite

sangbogŭl iptta 상복을 입다 wear mourning

sangbuŭi 상부의 top

sangbyŏng 상병 corporal

sangch'ŏ 상처 wound; sore; bruise

sangch'ŏ ibŭn 상처 입은 wounded, injured

sangch'ŏ ip'ida 상처 입히다 injure, wound

sangch'ŏnan 상처난 bruising, emotionally painful

sangch'ŏ ŏmnŭn 상처없는 uninjured

sangch'ŏ patkki shwiun 상처 받기 쉬운 vulnerable

sangch'ŏrŭl chuda 상처를 주다 bruise; hurt

sangch'ŏrŭl pat-tta 상처를 받다 get hurt

sangch'u 상추 lettuce

sangdae 상대 opponent; companion

sangdaejŏgin 상대적인 relative

sangdam 상담 consultancy; counseling; advice

sangdambi 상담비 (consultancy) fee

sangdamhada 상담하다 counsel

sangdamnyŏk 상담역 counselor, adviser

sangdanghada 상당하다 be appropriate; be considerable; be reasonable; be equivalent

sangdanghage 상당하게 substantially, considerably

sangdanghan 상당한 substantial, considerable, significant; equivalent

sangdanghi 상당히 reasonably, considerably, quite

sangdanghi choŭn 상당히 좋은 decent, reasonable

... sang-e ... 상에 on

sangga 상가 (shopping) mall

sanggam 상감 inlay

sanggapp'an 상갑판 upper deck

sanggihada 상기하다 recall, remember; relive

sanggishikida 상기시키다 remind

sanggo mŏri 상고 머리 crew cut

Sanggong Hoeŭiso 상공 회의소 Chamber of Commerce

sanggŭm 상금 winnings

sanggŭp 상급 senior rank; advanced level ◊ senior, superior

sanggwanŏmnŭn 상관없는 immaterial, irrelevant; *chŏn, sanggwanŏpssŏyo* 전, 상관없어요 it's all the same to me

sanggwanŏptta 상관없다 be irrelevant; not mind; *chŏnŭn sanggwanŏpssŭmnida* 저는 상관없습니다 I don't mind; *kŭgŏsŭn sanggwanŏptta* 그것은 상관없다 it doesn't matter

sanghada 상하다 go bad; be injured; be emaciated; *muŏse kibun sanghada* 무엇에 기분 상하다 get upset about sth

sanghage hada 상하게 하다 wound

sanghan 상한 sour

sangho chagyong 상호 작용 interaction

sangho chagyonghanŭn 상호 작용하는 interactive

sanghoganŭi 상호간의 mutual; reciprocal

sangho ŭijonhanŭn 상호 의존하는 interdependent

sanghwang 상황 situation, circumstances; *ŏttŏn sanghwang-esŏdo* 어떤 상황에서도 under no circumstances

sanghwanhada 상환하다 redeem, pay off

sang-in 상인 merchant, dealer, trader

san-gisŭlk 산기슭 foot of a mountain

sangja 상자 case, box

sangjing 상징 symbol, emblem

sangjinghada 상징하다 symbolize

sangjingjŏgin 상징적인 symbolic

sangjingjuŭi 상징주의 symbolism

sangjŏm 상점 store, shop

sangk'waehada 상쾌하다 feel fresh

sangk'waehan 상쾌한 refreshing, invigorating; crisp

sangmak'ada 삭막하다 be bleak

sangmak'an 삭막한 stark, severe

sangnil 삯일 piecework

sangnokssu 상록수 evergreen

sangnyŏnghada 상영하다 show *movie*

sangnyu 상류 upper reaches; upper classes ◊ upper-class

sangnyuch'ŭng 상류층 upper classes

sangnyuch'ŭng-ŭi 상류층의 upper-class

sangnyuro 상류로 upstream

sangnyu sahoe 상류 사회 high society

sangnyu sahoeŭi saenghwal 상류 사회의 생활 high life

sangŏ 상어 shark

sang-ŏp 상업 commerce, trade ◊ commercial

sang-ŏpssang-ŭi 상업상의 commercial

sangp'um 상품 goods, merchandise, stock

sangp'umhwahada 상품화하다 commercialize

sangp'umkkwŏn 상품권 token

sangp'umŭi imiji 상품의 이미지 brand image

sangp'yo 상표 brand, make

sangp'yomyŏng 상표명 brand name

sangsa 상사 boss

sangsang 상상 imagination

sangsanghada 상상하다 imagine, conceive of, envisage

sangsanghal su innŭn 상상할 수 있는 imaginable

sangsanghal su ŏmnŭn 상상할 수 없는 unimaginable

sangsangnyŏgi ŏmnŭn 상상력이 없는 unimaginative

sangsangnyŏgi p'ungbuhan 상상력이 풍부한 imaginative

sangsang-ŭl ch'owŏrhanŭn 상상을 초월하는 exorbitant

sangsehada 상세하다 be detailed

sangsehage 상세하게 minutely, in detail

sangsehan 상세한 detailed, full

sangsehi 상세히 fully, in minute detail

sangshik 상식 sense, common sense

sangshil 상실 loss

sangshirhada 상실하다 forfeit, give up, lose

sangsogin 상속인 heir

sangsok 상속 inheritance

sangsok-kkwŏnŭl pakt'arhada 상속권을 박탈하다 disinherit

sangsok'ada 상속하다 inherit

sangsŭng 상승 rise ◊ rising

sangsŭnghada 상승하다 rise, ascend

sangsŭngse-ŭi 상승세의 buoyant

sangsŭptchŏgin 상습적인 habitual

sangsŭrŏptta 상스럽다 be crude, be vulgar

sangsŭrŏun 상스러운 crude, coarse, vulgar

sangsudo 상수도 waterworks

sangt'ae 상태 state, condition; circumstances

sang-ŭi 상의 top (*piece of clothing*); coat; consultation

sang-wŏn 상원 senate

sang-wŏnŭiwŏn 상원의원 senator

sanho 산호 coral

sanhwamul 산화물 oxide

sanjaehanŭn 산재하는 sparse

sanjŏk 산적 bandit; shish kebab

sankkil 산길 pass

sanmaek 산맥 (mountain) range

sanmanhada 산만하다 be loose; be vague

sanmanhage 산만하게 loosely

sanmanhan 산만한 loose, imprecise; vague; *mŏriga sanmanhan* 머리가 산만한 scatterbrained

sanmun 산문 prose

sannamul 산나물 wild greens

sanŏp 산업 industry ◊ industrial

sanŏpp'yegimul 산업폐기물 industrial waste

sanŏp'wahada 산업화하다 industrialize

sansanjogak naeda 산산조각 내다 smash to pieces

sansaram 산사람 hillbilly

sansat'ae 산사태 landslide

sanshin 산신 mountain spirit

sansŏngbi 산성비 acid rain

sanso 산소 oxygen; ancestral grave

sansul 산술 arithmetic

santtŏmi 산더미 heap, pile; *santtŏmigach'i manŭn il* 산더미같이 많은 일 a pile of work

santtŭngsŏng-i 산등성이 ridge

Sant'ak'ŭllosŭ 산타클로스 Santa Claus

sant'okki 산토끼 hare

sanyang 사냥 hunt; hunting

sanyanghada 사냥하다 hunt

sanyangkkun 사냥꾼 hunter

saŏp 사업 business; enterprise, undertaking; project; *saŏpch'a* 사업차 on business

saŏpkka 사업가 businessman

saŏp kwan-gye 사업 관계 business relations

sap 삽 shovel; scoop; spade

sapsshigane 삽시간에 in an instant; *sapsshigane p'ŏjida* 삽시간에 퍼지다 spread like wildfire

sap'aiŏ 사파이어 sapphire

sap'alnun 사팔눈 squint

sap'o 사포 sandpaper

sap'oro taktta 사포로 닦다 sandpaper

sap'oro tangnŭn changch'i 사포로 닦는 장치 sander

sap'wa 삽화 illustration

sap'waga 삽화가 illustrator

sap'warŭl kŭrida 삽화를 그리다 illustrate

saragada 살아가다 live; keep on living

sara innŭn 살아 있는 live, living

sara innŭn tŭt'an 살아 있는 듯한 lifelike

sarait-tta 살아있다 be alive

sarajida 사라지다 disappear; decline; die out

saram 사람 person; man; people; human ◊ *countword for people*

saramdaun 사람다운 humane

sarami salji annŭn 사람이 살지 않는 uninhabited

saramŭi shilssu 사람의 실수 human error

saranada 살아나다 revive; survive

sara nagada 살아 나가다 survive; carry on living

saranamtta 살아남다 survive

sarang 사랑 love

sarang-e ppajida 사랑에 빠지다 fall in love; fall in love with

saranghada 사랑하다 love

saranghanŭn 사랑하는 beloved

sarang-ni 사랑니 wisdom tooth

sarangsŭrŏun 사랑스러운 lovely; lovable, endearing

sarhae 살해 killing, slaying, murder

sarhaehada 살해하다 kill, slay, murder

sari 사리 coil; self-interest; Buddhist saint's relic; reason

sarin 살인 murder, homicide

sarinbŏm 살인범 homicide; murderer

sarinhada 살인하다 murder

sarinja 살인자 killer, murderer

sarisayok 사리사욕 self-interest

sarojaptta 사로잡다 capture

sarojap'ida 사로잡히다 be obsessed by

sarŭl enŭndŭshi 살을 에는듯이 bitterly *cold*

sarŭl enŭn tŭt'an 살을 에는 듯한 sharp, bitter *cold*

saryŏ kip'ŭn 사려 깊은 thoughtful, considerate

saryŏnggwan 사령관 commander

saryŏŏmnŭn 사려없는 inconsiderate

saryo 사료 fodder

saryun-gudong 사륜구동 four-wheel drive

sasaeng-a 사생아 illegitimate child, bastard

sasaenghwal 사생활 privacy

sasandoeda 사산되다 be stillborn

sasang 사상 thought, ideology; in history; death and injury

sasangja 사상자 casualty

sashil 사실 fact; truth

sashilssang 사실상 in fact, actually; virtually, more or less

sashilssang-ŭi 사실상의 actual; virtual

sashiltchuŭi 사실주의 realism

sashiltchuŭija 사실주의자 realist

saship 사십 forty

sashirŭl tŭrŏnaenŭn 사실을 드러내는 telltale *signs*

sashirŭn 사실은 in fact, as a matter of fact, actually

sashiŭi 사시의 cross-eyed

sasŏ 사서 librarian

sasŏham 사서함 PO Box

sasŏl 사설 editorial

sasŏng changgun 사성 장군 four-star general

sasohada 사소하다 be trivial

sasohan 사소한 trivial, minor

sasohan il 사소한 일 detail, trifle

sasohan kŏt 사소한 것 triviality

sasohan sahang 사소한 사항 technicality

sasŭl 사슬 chain

sasŭm 사슴 deer

sasŭm kogi 사슴 고기 venison

Sasunjŏl 사순절 Lent

satchŏgin 사적인 private

satssach'i twijida 샅샅이 뒤지다 comb; ransack

sat'aguni 사타구니 groin

Sat'an 사탄 Satan

sat'ang 사탕 candy

sat'angsusu 사탕 수수 sugar cane

sat'uri 사투리 dialect

Saudi Arabia 사우디 아라비아 Saudi Arabia ◊ Saudi

sauna 사우나 sauna

saundŭ k'adŭ 사운드 카드 sound card

sawi 사위 son-in-law

sawŏl 사월 April

sawŏn 사원 temple REL

sayanghada 사양하다 decline with thanks; ***sayangch'i mashigo ka-jiseyo*** 사양치 마시고 가지세요 please keep it, I insist

sayanghal su ŏmnŭn 사양할 수 없는 irresistible

sayŏrhada 사열하다 review *troops*

sayong 사용 use

sayonghada 사용하다 use, employ; exercise *control, restraint*; work

sayonghagi shwiun 사용하기 쉬운 user-friendly

sayongja 사용자 user

sayongppŏp 사용법 directions, instructions for use

sayong sŏlmyŏngsŏ 사용 설명서 instruction manual

sayuktcha 사육자 breeder

sebaero chŭnggahada 세배로 증가하다 treble

sebal chajŏn-gŏ 세발 자전거 tricycle

sebu chohang 세부 조항 small print

sebunhada 세분하다 subdivide

sebu sahang 세부 사항 detail

sech'ashik'ida 세차시키다 get the car washed

sech'a sŏbissŭ 세차 서비스 valet service

sech'igi 세치기 cutting in line
sech'öktche 세척제 detergent
seda 세다 count (up)
sedae 세대 generation
sedae ch'ai 세대 차이 generation
  gap
sedan 세단 sedan
sege ch'ida 세게 치다 punch; push,
  jolt
segehada 세게 하다 intensify
sege tchirüda 세게 찌르다 thrust
segi 세기 century
següm 세금 tax
següm kiho 세금 기호 tax code
següm kongjega kanünghan 세금
  공제가 가능한 tax deductible
segümül pugwahada 세금을
  부과하다 tax
segümül p'ohamhan 세금을 포함한
  pre-tax
segwan kömsa 세관 검사 customs
  inspection
segwan t'onggwa 세관 통과
  customs clearance
segwanwön 세관원 customs officer
segye 세계 world
segyehwa 세계화 globalization
segyejögin 세계적인 worldwide
segyejöguro 세계적으로 worldwide
segyejök kangdaeguk 세계적
  강대국 world power
segye kyöngje 세계 경제 global
  economy
segye onnanhwa 세계 온난화 global
  warming
Segye P'yojunshi 세계 표준시
  GMT, Greenwich Mean Time
segye shijang 세계 시장 global
  market
segye taejön 세계 대전 world war
segyun 세균 germ
segyunjön 세균전 germ warfare
seil chung-ida 세일 중이다 be on
  sale (at reduced prices)
seiljümaen 세일즈맨 salesman;
  representative
seip 세입 revenue
sellöri 셀러리 celery
sellop'an 셀로판 cellophane
selp'ü set'aksso 셀프세탁소
  laundromat

selp'üssöbisü shikttang 셀프서비스
  식당 self-service restaurant
selp'üssöbisüüi 셀프서비스의 self-
  service
sel su omnün 셀 수 없는 countless
sem 셈 count; intention, design; ...üi
  semül ijöbörida ...의 셈을
  잊어버리다 lose count of; ...ül/rül
  hal semüro ...을/를 할 셈으로 with
  the intention of
semina 세미나 seminar
semirhi chosadoeda 세밀히
  조사되다 come under scrutiny
semüro ch'ida 셈으로 치다 count,
  qualify
semu chosagwan 세무 조사관 tax-
  inspector
semyöndae 세면대 basin
semyöndogu kabang 세면도구 가방
  sponge bag
semyön-gi 세면기 washbasin,
  washbowl
semyönjang 세면장 bathroom
semyön t'awöl 세면 타월 washcloth
semyön yongp'um 세면 용품
  toiletries
senoe 세뇌 brainwashing
senoehada 세뇌하다 brainwash
sensseisyön 센세이션 sensation
sent'i(mit'ö) 센티(미터) centimeter
sent'ö 센터 center
sent'ü 센트 cent
se pöntchae 세 번째 third
se pöntchaeüi 세 번째의 third
sep'o 세포 cell
seriju 세리주 sherry
seroro 세로로 portrait print
serye 세례 baptism
seryehada 세례하다 baptize, christen
seryemyöng 세례명 Christian name
seryök 세력 power, leverage;
  influence
seryöndoen 세련된 cultured,
  sophisticated
seryok-kkwön 세력권 sphere of
  influence
sesang 세상 world; sesang-e!
  세상에! oh God!; sesang-e naenot'a 세상에 내놓다 bring out;
  sesang multchöng-e palgün 세상
  물정에 밝은 worldly; streetwise;

sesang-ŭl ttŏdŭlssŏk'age hanŭn
세상을 떠들썩하게 하는 sensational;
sesang-ŭl ttŭda 세상을 뜨다
depart this world, pass away
seshim 세심; *...ŭl / rŭl*
seshimhage poda ...을 / 를
세심하게 보다 keep a wary eye on ...
seshimhan 세심한 meticulous
sesogŭi 세속의 secular
sesoktchŏgin 세속적인 material,
worldly
se ssangdung-i 세 쌍둥이 triplets
set 셋 three
set'agŭl matkkida 세탁을 맡기다
have laundered
set'ak-kki 세탁기 washing machine
set'ak sŏbissŭ 세탁 서비스 valet
service
set'aksso 세탁소 laundry; dry
cleaner
set'ak'ada 세탁하다 launder
set'ak'age hada 세탁하게 하다 get
one's laundry done
set'angmul 세탁물 laundry (*clothes*)
set'inghada 세팅하다 set up
setŏp 셋업 set-up COMPUT
set'ŭ 세트 set
seuda 세우다 build; erect; establish,
set up; turn up *collar*; stop *person in
street*; *ttokpparo seuda* 똑바로
세우다 stand on end
shi 시 poetry, verse; poem; city;
o'clock; *tasŏt shie* 다섯 시에 at five
o'clock
shiabŏji 시아버지 father-in-law
(*husband's father*)
shibi 십이 twelve
shibil 십일 eleven
shibiwŏl 십이월 December
shibirwŏl 십일월 November
shibo 십오 fifteen
shibobun 십오분 fifteen minutes, a
quarter of an hour
shich'a 시차 time-lag
shich'al 시찰 inspection
shich'arhada 시찰하다 inspect
shich'e 시체 body, corpse, cadaver
shich'ŏng 시청 city hall; town hall
shich'ŏnggagŭi 시청각의
audiovisual
shich'ŏnghada 시청하다 view, tune

in to
shich'ŏngja 시청자 audience; viewer;
follower
shich'o 시초 beginning, dawn
shida 시다 be sour
shidae 시대 era, epoch; *yojŭm
shidaega kŭrŏssŭmnida* 요즘
시대가 그렇습니다 it's a sign of the
times
shidaee twittŏrŏjin 시대에 뒤떨어진
dated, old-fashioned
shidallida 시달리다 be harassed
shidallin 시달린 harassed;
kŏktchŏng-e shidallin 걱정에
시달린 careworn
shido 시도 attempt, endeavor; *saeroun shido* 새로운 시도 new
departure
shidohada 시도하다 try, attempt,
endeavor
shidongdoeda 시동되다 start
shidonggi 시동기 starter MOT
shidongshik'ida 시동시키다 start
shidŭlda 시들다 droop, wilt, wither
shigaji 시가지 built-up area
shigak kyojae 시각 교재 visual aid
shigaktchŏgin 시각적인 visual
shigaktchŏgŭro 시각적으로 visually
shigaktchŏgŭro sonsangdoen
시각적으로 손상된 visually
impaired
shigan 시간 time; hour
shigan chŏryak 시간 절약
timesaving
shiganjero 시간제로 part-time
shigan kan-gyŏk 시간 간격 interval
shiganmada 시간 마다 every hour
shigan ŏmsu 시간 엄수 punctuality
shiganp'yo 시간표 schedule,
timetable
shiganŭl chik'inŭn 시간을 지키는
prompt, on time
shiganŭl hŏbihada 시간을 허비하다
dawdle
shiganŭl match'uda 시간을 맞추다
synchronize
shiganŭl match'uŏ 시간을 맞추어 in
time
shiganŭl ŏmsuhanŭn 시간을
엄수하는 punctual
shigi 시기 phase, period, stage;

timescale
shigirŭl match'ugi 시기를 맞추기 timing
shigisangjoŭi 시기상조의 premature
shigi yoppŏp 식이 요법 diet (*as cure*)
shigol 시골 countryside; hick town; *shigore(sŏ)* 시골에(서) in the country
shigolkkil 시골길 country lane
shigoltchip 시골집 cottage
shigolttŭgi 시골뜨기 lout; hick
shigorŭi 시골의 rural
shigŭmch'i 시금치 spinach
shigurhada 시굴하다 prospect for
shigye 시계 clock; watch
shigye chejoin 시계 제조인 watchmaker
shigye panghyang-ŭro tora 시계 방향으로 돌아 clockwise
shigye panŭl 시계 바늘 hand (*of clock*)
shigyeradio 시계라디오 clock radio
shigye t'aeyŏp changch'i 시계 태엽 장치 clockwork (mechanism)
shigyogŭl todunŭn 식욕을 돋우는 appetizing
shigyok 식욕 appetite
shihan p'okt'an 시한 폭탄 time bomb
shihap 시합 tournament; event; match; bout (*in boxing*)
shihŏm 시험 exam; test, trial
shihŏmgwan 시험관 examiner; test tube
shihŏmgwan agi 시험관 아기 test-tube baby
shihŏmhada 시험하다 examine, test
shihŏmhae poda 시험해 보다 try out; have on trial
shihŏmji 시험지 examination paper
shihŏm kigan 시험 기간 trial period
shihŏm kongjang 시험 공장 pilot plant
shiin 시인 confession; poet
shiinhada 시인하다 admit, confess
shijak 시작 beginning, start; onset; *choŭn / nappŭn shijagŭl hada* 좋은 / 나쁜 시작을 하다 get off to a good / bad start
shijakdoeda 시작되다 begin, start;

break out, start up; break (*of storm*)
shijak pŏt'ŭn 시작 버튼 start button; trigger; on switch
shijakttoeda 시작되다 begin, commence
shijak'ada 시작하다 begin, originate; institute; take up; get down to; log on; *...ki shijak'ada* ...기 시작하다 start ...ing; *irŭl shijak'ada* 일을 시작하다 set to work
shijang 시장 market; marketplace; mayor; *shijang-e* 시장에 on the market; *shijang-ŭl toktchŏmhada* 시장을 독점하다 corner the market
shijangboda 시장보다 store, shop
shijang chŏmnyuyul 시장 점유율 market share
shijang chosa 시장 조사 market research
shijang kyŏngje 시장 경제 market economy
shijangnyŏk 시장력 market forces
shije 시제 tense GRAM
shijŏl 시절 season; time; *kŭ shijŏrenŭn* 그 시절에는 in those days
shijungdŭlda 시중들다 serve
shijung tŭnŭn saram 시중 드는 사람 valet
shijung-ŭl tŭlda 시중을 들다 wait on
shik 식 event; ceremony; eclipse
shikch'o 식초 vinegar
shikkŭrŏptta 시끄럽다 be loud; be noisy
shikkŭrŏun 시끄러운 loud, noisy
shikkŭrŏun sori 시끄러운 소리 din, noise
shikppyŏllyŏgi innŭn 식별력이 있는 discriminating, discerning
shikppyŏrhada 식별하다 spot, identify; discern; distinguish
shikp'umjŏm 식품점 grocery (store)
shikssa 식사 meal
shikssahada 식사하다 dine
shikssa shigan 식사 시간 mealtime; sitting
shikssŏng 식성 taste, preference (*in food*); *shikssŏng-i kkadaroptta* 식성이 까다롭다 be a fussy eater
shiktchahada 식자하다 typeset, set
shiktchungdok 식중독 food

poisoning

shiktta 식다 cool, cool down

shikttan 식단 menu

shikttang 식당 restaurant; dining room

shikttangch'a 식당차 restaurant car

shikttanp'yo 식단표 menu

shiktto 식도 gullet

shikt'ak 식탁 dining table

shikt'akppo 식탁보 tablecloth

shik'ida 식히다 cool down

shik'ida 시키다 (*causative*): *shilmangshik'ida* 실망시키다 disappoint; *t'ürimül shik'ida* 트림을 시키다 burp *baby*

shil 실 yarn, thread

shilch'ehwahada 실체화하다 materialize

shilk'öt mök-kki 실컷 먹기 blowout

shillae 실내 interior

shillae changshik-kka 실내 장식가 interior decorator

shillaee(sö) 실내에(서) indoors

shillae kyöng-ümak 실내 경음악 piped music

shillalgat'ün hüimang 실날같은 희망 glimmer of hope

shillang 신랑 groom, bridegroom

shillang tüllöri 신랑 들러리 best man

shillarhan 신랄한 cutting, stinging; bitter

shillijögin 실리적인 practical, pragmatic

shillijögüro 실리적으로 practically, pragmatically

shillik'on 실리콘 silicon

shillik'on ch'ip 실리콘 칩 silicon chip

shilloe 신뢰 trust, confidence; faith

shilloegam kanün 신뢰감 가는 credible

shilloehada 신뢰하다 trust, believe in

shilloehal su innün 신뢰할 수 있는 trustworthy; trusted; reliable

shilloehanün 신뢰하는 trustful, trusting

shilloessöng 신뢰성 reliability; credibility

shilluet 실루엣 silhouette

shillye 실례 illustration

shillyehamnida 실례합니다 excuse me

shilmang 실망 disappointment

shilmanghada 실망하다 disappoint

shilmanghan 실망한 disappointed

shilmangshik'ida 실망시키다 disappoint

shilmangsüröun 실망스러운 disappointing

shilmari 실마리 clue

shilmul k'ügiüi 실물 크기의 life-sized

shilp'ae 실패 failure; breakdown; reel, spool

shilp'aehada 실패하다 fail; break down; lose out; be out

shilp'aehan 실패한 unsuccessful

shilp'aeja 실패자 loser, failure

shilp'aejagida 실패작이다 flop, fail

shilp'aejak 실패작 flop, failure

shilp'aero kkünnada 실패로 끝나다 end in failure; fall through

shilsshidoeda 실시되다 come into effect

shilsshigan 실시간 real time

shilsshiganüi 실시간의 real-time

shilsshihada 실시하다 carry out

shilssu 실수 mistake

shilssuhada 실수하다 make a mistake, go wrong

shilssuip 실수입 take-home pay

shilssuro 실수로 by mistake

shiltchaehaji annün 실재하지 않는 unreal

shiltche 실제 truth; fact; practice ◊ practical

shiltchejögin 실제적인 practical; down-to-earth

shiltcheüi 실제의 actual, real

shiltchik'ada 실직하다 lose one's job; be unemployed

shiltchik'an 실직한 unemployed, out of work

shiltchiltchögin 실질적인 substantive

shiltchiltchögüro 실질적으로 substantially

shiltchöm 실점 lost points SP

shiltchong 실종 disappearance

shiltchüng nada 싫증 나다 be tired of

shiltta 싣다 load; *chimül shiltta* 짐을 싣다 load

shilt'an 실탄 live ammunition

shilt'ohada 실토하다 confess
shim 심 pith
shimburŭm 심부름 errand
shimburŭmgada 심부름가다 run
errands
shiment'ŭ 시멘트 cement;
shiment'ŭro parŭda 시멘트로
바르다 cement
shimgak'ada 심각하다 be serious
shimgak'an 심각한 serious *illness*;
deep *trouble*; heavy *loss*
shimgiga twit'ŭllin 심기가 뒤틀린
cranky, bad-tempered
shimgyehangjin 심계항진
palpitations
shimhada 심하다 be awful
shimhage 심하게 seriously; badly;
severely
shimhage nappŭn 심하게 나쁜
atrocious
shimham 심함 severity
shimhan 심한 bad, awful; heavy;
severe
shimin 시민 citizen
shimin-gun 시민군 militia
shiminkkwŏn 시민권 citizenship
shiminŭi 시민의 civil; civic
shimjang 심장 heart ◊ cardiac,
coronary
shimjang chŏngji 심장 정지 cardiac
arrest
shimjang ishik 심장 이식 heart
transplant
shimjang mabi 심장 마비 heart
attack, coronary
shimjang pakttong 심장 박동
heartbeat
shimji 심지 wick
shimjiga kujŭn 심지가 굳은 strong-minded, independent
shimmijŏgin 심미적인 esthetic
shimmun 심문 interrogation
shimmunhada 심문하다 interrogate
shimmunja 심문자 interrogator
shimnanhage hada 심란하게 하다
distract
shimnanhan 심란한 distracted,
worried
shimni 심리 hearing LAW
shimnihak 심리학 psychology
shimnihaktcha 심리학자
psychologist
shimnijŏgin 심리적인 psychological
shimnijŏguro 심리적으로
psychologically
shimnya 심야 small hours
shimnyŏngjuŭi 심령주의 spiritualism
shimnyŏngjuŭija 심령주의자
spiritualist
shimnyŏng-ŭi 심령의 psychic
shimoham 심오함 depth (*of thought*)
shimohan 심오한 deep, profound
shimp'an 심판 referee; umpire
shimp'an wiwŏnhoe 심판 위원회
tribunal
shimsahada 심사하다 judge
shimsasuk-kko 심사숙고 reflection
shimsasuk-kkohan 심사숙고한
thoughtful
shimsa wiwŏn 심사 위원 judge
shimsa wiwŏndan 심사 위원단 jury;
panel
shimsulgujŭn 심술궂은 sour; bitchy;
bad-tempered
shimsulgut-tta 심술궂다 be bad-tempered
shimtta 심다 plant
shimŭi 심의 debate
shimuruk'an 시무룩한 glum
shimwŏnhan 심원한 deep
shimyuk 십육 sixteen
shin 신 deity; god ◊ sour
shinae t'onghwa 시내 통화 local call
shinang 신앙 belief, faith
shinangshim-i kip'ŭn 신앙심이 깊은
deeply religious
shinario 시나리오 scenario
shinbal 신발 footwear; shoe
shinbalkkage 신발가게 shoestore
shinbalkkŭn 신발끈 shoelace
shinbi 신비 mystery
shinbihada 신비하다 be mysterious
shinbihage 신비하게 mysteriously
shinbihan 신비한 mysterious
shinbingssŏng 신빙성 credibility;
authenticity
shinbingssŏng-ŭl ttŏrŏttŭrida
신빙성을 떨어뜨리다 discredit
shinbiroun 신비로운 magical;
delightful
shinbongja 신봉자 believer
shinbu 신부 bride; (Catholic) priest

shinbun 신분 rank
shinbun chŭngmyŏngsŏ 신분 증명서 identity card
shinbuntchŭng 신분증 (identity) papers
shinbunŭi sangjing 신분의 상징 status symbol
shinbu tŭllŏri 신부 들러리 bridesmaid
shinbyŏng 신병 recruit
shinchunghan 신중한 discreet
shinch'am 신참 newcomer
shinch'e chang-ae 신체 장애 physical handicap, physical disability
shinch'e chang-aeja 신체 장애자 the disabled; cripple
shinch'e chang-aeja innŭn 신체 장애가 있는 physically handicapped
shinch'e kŏmsa 신체 검사 medical
shinch'ŏng 신청 application
shinch'ŏnghada 신청하다 apply for; teit'ŭ shinch'ŏnghada 데이트 신청하다 ask out, ask for a date
shinch'ŏngsŏ 신청서 application form
shinch'ukssŏng 신축성 elasticity
shinch'ukssŏng innŭn 신축성 있는 stretchy, elastic
shinch'ukssŏng-ŭl kajin 신축성을 가진 elasticized
shindong 신동 child prodigy
shingandang 시간당 hourly rate
Shinggap'orŭ 싱가포르 Singapore ◊ Singaporean
shinggŭt usŭm 싱긋 웃음 grin
shinggŭt ut-tta 싱긋 웃다 grin
shin-giru 신기루 mirage
shingk'ŭ 싱크 sink
shingminji 식민지 colony
shingminjiŭi 식민지의 colonial
Shingmogil 식목일 Arbor Day
shingmul 식물 plant ◊ botanical
shingmurhak 식물학 botany
shingnyo chap'wajŏm 식료 잡화점 grocery store
shin-gohada 신고하다 register; declare; inform; turn in (to police)
shin-gwan 신관 fuse (of bomb)
shin-gwanŭl chegŏhada 신관을 제거하다 defuse
shin-gyŏng 신경 creed; beliefs;

nerve; nuguŭi shin-gyŏng-ŭl kŏndŭrida 누구의 신경을 건드리다 get on s.o.'s nerves
shin-gyŏng enŏji 신경 에너지 nervous energy
shin-gyŏng-i kŏsŭllinŭn 신경이 거슬리는 annoyed
shin-gyŏng-i kwaminhan 신경이 과민한 nervous
shin-gyŏng-i ssŭida 신경이 쓰이다 bother; shin-gyŏng ssŭji maseyo! 신경 쓰지 마세요! don't bother!; shin-gyŏng ssŭl kŏt ŏpssŭmnida! 신경 쓸 것 없습니다! never mind!
shin-gyŏngjiltchŏgin 신경질적인 fussy
shin-gyŏngkkwa ŭisa 신경과 의사 neurologist
shin-gyŏng kwaminŭi 신경 과민의 jumpy, nervous; neurotic
shin-gyŏng soeyage kŏllida 신경 쇠약에 걸리다 crack up, have a nervous breakdown
shin-gyŏng soeyagida 신경 쇠약이다 be a nervous wreck
shin-gyŏng soeyak 신경 쇠약 nervous breakdown
shin-gyŏng soeyaktcha 신경 쇠약자 nervous wreck
shin-gyŏngssŭji annŭn 신경쓰지 않는 unconcerned
shin-gyŏngtchil 신경질 nervousness
shin-gyŏngtchilnage hada 신경질나게 하다 nettle, irritate
shin-gyŏngtchŭng 신경증 neurosis
Shin-gyodo 신교도 Protestant
Shin-gyodoŭi 신교도의 Protestant
shin-gyu mojip 신규 모집 recruitment
shin-gyu mojip k'aemp'ein 신규 모집 캠페인 recruitment drive
shinhak 신학 theology
shinho 신호 signal
shinhodŭng 신호등 traffic light
shinhohada 신호하다 signal
shinhon pubu 신혼 부부 newlyweds
shinhon yŏhaeng 신혼 여행 honeymoon
shinhwa 신화 myth
shinhwahak 신화학 mythology
shinhwaŭi 신화의 mythical

shinip 신입 newcomer

shinip sawŏn 신입 사원 recruit

shinip sawŏnŭl ppoptta 신입 사원을
뽑다 recruit

shinipssaeng 신입생 freshman

shinja 신자 believer

shinjakp'um 신작품 collection

shinjang 신장 kidney ANAT

shinjindaesa 신진대사 metabolism

Shinjŏng 신정 New Year

shinjo 신조 doctrine

shinju 신주 spirit tablet

shinjung 신중 prudence, caution;
good sense

shinjunghada 신중하다 be careful; be
wary

shinjunghage 신중하게 carefully

shinmang innŭn 신망 있는 serious

shinmun 신문 newspaper

shinmun kap'andae 신문 가판대
newsstand

shinmun p'anmaeso 신문 판매소
newsdealer

shinmun p'anmaewŏn 신문 판매원
newsvendor

shinnyŏm 신념 conviction, belief

shinsa 신사 gentleman

shinsabok 신사복 lounge suit

shinse 신세 debt of gratitude;
nuguege shinserŭl chida 누구에게
신세를 지다 be indebted to s.o.

shinsŏndo 신선도 freshness

shinsŏng 신성 sanctity

shinsŏnghan 신성한 divine, sacred

shinsŏnhada 신선하다 be fresh

shinsŏnhan 신선한 fresh

shinssok 신속 rapidity

shinssok'ada 신속하다 be rapid

shinssok'an 신속한 rapid

shintta 신다 put on *shoes*

shinŭmhada 신음하다 groan, moan

shinŭm sori 신음 소리 groan, moan

shinui 시누이 sister-in-law
(*husband's sister*)

shinwŏn 신원 identity

shinwŏn pojŭng-in 신원 보증인
referee (*for job*)

Shinyak Sŏngsŏ 구약 성서 New
Testament

shinyong 신용 credit

shinyong-i ttŏrŏjigehada 신용이
떨어지게 하다 discredit

shinyonginnŭn 신용있는
creditworthy

shinyong k'adŭ 신용 카드 credit
card

shinyong taebu 신용 대부 credit,
loan

shinyong taebuŭi hando 신용
대부의 한도 credit limit

shinyongtchang 신용장 letter of
credit

shinyung 시늉 act, pretense

shiŏmŏni 시어머니 mother-in-law
(*wife's*)

shiŏmŏnim 시어머님 mother-in-law
(*wife's*) (*polite*)

shioe pŏsŭ 시외 버스 bus (*long-
distance*)

ship 십 ten

shipch'il 십칠 seventeen

shipkku 십구 nineteen

ship nyŏn 십 년 decade

ship ŏk 십억 billion

shipp'al 십팔 eighteen

shipssa 십사 fourteen

shipssam 십삼 thirteen

ship ssent'ŭ 십 센트 dime

ship tae 십 대 teens ◊ teenage; *ship
taega toeda* 십 대가 되다 reach
one's teens; *ship tae sonyŏn /
sonyŏ* 십 대 소년 / 소녀 teenage
boy / girl, teenager

ship taeida 십 대이다 be in one's
teens

shiptchaga 십자가 cross; *kasŭme
shiptcharŭl kŭt-tta* 가슴에 십자를
긋다 cross (oneself)

shiptchungp'algu 십중팔구 in all
likelihood; nine times out of ten

shiptta 싶다 want; seem; *...go
ship'ŭn kibunida* ...고 싶은
기분이다 be in the mood for;
...ŭl / rŭl hago shipssŭmnikka?
...을 / 를 하고 싶습니까? would you
like to ...?

ship'ŭt'ŭ k'i 시프트 키 shift key

shirhaeng 실행 fulfillment;
execution (*of plan*); return COMPUT

shirhaenghada 실행하다 carry out;
execute, put into effect; fulfill; run
software

shirhaeng kanŭnghan 실행 가능한 feasible, workable

shirhŏm 실험 experiment

shirhŏm chaeryo 실험 재료 guinea pig *fig*

shirhŏmhada 실험하다 experiment, test

shirhŏmhaeboda 실험해보다 experiment with, try out

shirhŏmshil 실험실 lab, laboratory

shirhŏmshil kisultcha 실험실 기술자 laboratory technician

shirhŏmŭi 실험의 experimental

shirhwang-ŭi 실황의 actual

shirhyŏn 실현 realization (*of goal*)

shirhyŏndoeda 실현되다 come true

shiriŏl 시리얼 cereal

shirŏhada 싫어하다 dislike

shirŏjida 싫어지다 go off, stop liking

shirŏmnŭn 실없는 frivolous

shirŏn 실언 slip of the tongue

shirŏp 시럽 syrup

shirŏp 실업 unemployment

shirŏpkka 실업가 industrialist

shirŏptcha 실업자 the unemployed

shirŭl kkweda 실을 꿰다 thread

shirŭl ppoptta 실을 뽑다 take the stitches out

shirŭm 싫음 distaste

shirŭn 싫은 distasteful

shiryŏk 시력 eyesight, vision

shiryŏn 실연 demonstration

shiryŏn 시련 ordeal

shiryŏnhada 실연하다 demonstrate

shiryongjŏgin 실용적인 practical, functional

shiryongjuŭi 실용주의 pragmatism

shisa 시사 current affairs; preview

shisa p'ŭrograem 시사 프로그램 current affairs program

shisap'ungjaguk 시사풍자극 revue

shishihada 시시하다 be trivial; be wishy-washy; be tame (*of joke etc*); be stupid

shisŏl 시설 establishment; facilities

shisŏn 시선 line of vision; *nuguŭi shisŏnŭl kkŭlda* 누구의 시선을 끌다 catch s.o.'s eye

shiso 시소 seesaw

shisok 시속: *shisok 150mairŭi sokttoro* 시속 150마일의 속도로 at a speed of 150 mph

shisŭt'em 시스템 system

shisŭt'em punsŏk-kka 시스템 분석가 systems analyst

shitta 싣다 embark, go on board ship

shittchŏgin 시적인 poetic

shit'ŭk'om 시트콤 sitcom

shiŭi 시의 municipal, civic

shi ŭihoe 시 의회 town council

shiŭihoe ŭiwŏn 시의회 의원 councilman

shi ŭiwŏn 시 의원 councilman

shiwi 시위 demonstration, protest

shiwi ch'amgaja 시위 참가자 demonstrator, protester

shiwihada 시위하다 demonstrate

shiwŏl 시월 October

shiwŏnhada 시원하다 be cool

shiya 시야 visibility

shiyŏn 시연 preview

shiyŏnhada 시연하다 rehearse, run through

shŏlttŭk'ae poda 설득해 보다 reason with

shwida 쉬다 rest; be off; not be at work; *harurŭl/iltchuirŭl shwida* 하루를/일주일을 쉬다 take a day/week off

shwim ŏpsshi 쉼 없이 without respite

shwimp'yo 쉼표 comma

shwin 쉰 fifty

shwin mokssori 쉰 목소리 croak

shwin mokssoriŭi 쉰 목소리의 husky

shwin pŏntchaeŭi 쉰 번째의 fiftieth

shwinŭn nal 쉬는 날 day off

shwinŭn shigan 쉬는 시간 recess EDU

shwipkke 쉽게 easily

shwipkke hŭngbunhanŭn 쉽게 흥분하는 excitable

shwiptta 쉽다 be easy; *...gi shwiptta* ...기 쉽다 be prone to ...

shwishwihaebŏrida 쉬쉬해버리다 hush up, conceal

shwit sorirŭl naeda 쉿 소리를 내다 hiss

shwiun 쉬운 easy, simple; *...gi shwiun* ...기 쉬운 be easy to ...

shyaemi kajuk 섀미 가죽 chamois

(leather)
shyaeshi 섀시 chassis
shyamp'ein 샴페인 champagne
shyamp'u 샴푸 shampoo
shyam ssangdung-i 샴 쌍둥이
Siamese twins
shyangdŭllie 샹들리에 chandelier
shyawŏ 샤워 shower
shyawŏhada 샤워하다 shower, take
a shower
shyawŏ k'aep 샤워 캡 shower cap
shyawŏ k'ŏt'ŭn 샤워 커튼 shower
curtain
shyeŏweŏ 셰어웨어 shareware
shyŏch'ŭ 셔츠 shirt
shyŏt'ŏ 셔터 shutter PHOT
shyŏt'ŭlppŏsŭ 셔틀버스 shuttlebus
shyŏt'ŭl sŏbissŭ 셔틀 서비스 shuttle
service
shyo 쇼 show; vaudeville
shyok'ŭ 쇼크 shock ELEC
shyol 숄 shawl
shyo pijŭnisŭ 쇼 비즈니스 show
business
shyop'ing 쇼핑 shopping
shyop'inghanŭn saram 쇼핑하는
사람 shopper
shyop'ingssent'ŏ 쇼핑센터 shopping
center, shopping mall
shyo rum 쇼 룸 showroom
shyowindo 쇼윈도 store window
sidŭ 시드 seed (in tennis)
sik'ye 식혜 malted rice drink
Silla 신라 Silla (Ancient Kingdom)
siltchŭngnage hada 싫증나게 하다
bore
singgŭlp'an 싱글판 single MUS
singnyop'um chŏjangso 식료품
저장소 larder
sŏ 서 west
sŏbissŭ 서비스 service
sŏbissŭ chegonghoesa 서비스
제공회사 service provider
sŏbissŭhada 서비스하다 service
machine, car
sŏbissŭryo 서비스료 service charge
sŏbissŭ sanŏp 서비스 산업 service
industry
sŏbissŭ sanŏp pubun 서비스 산업
부분 service sector
sŏbŏ 서버 server COMPUT

sŏbŭ 서브 serve (in tennis)
sŏbŭhada 서브하다 serve
sŏbu 서부 west
sŏbugŭk 서부극 western (movie)
sŏch'i 서치 search COMPUT
sŏch'ihada 서치하다 search, search
for COMPUT
sŏda 서다 stand; stop
sŏdullŏ! 서둘러! come on! hurry up!
sŏdullŏ ttŏnada 서둘러 떠나다 dash
off
sŏdurŭda 서두르다 hurry up, rush
sŏdurŭn 서두른 hurried
sŏgok 서곡 overture
sŏgŭlp'ŭn 서글픈 sad; lamentable
sŏgyŏnch'i anŭn 석연치 않은
dubious, suspect
sŏgyŏng 석영 quartz
sŏgyu 석유 oil; petroleum
sŏgyu hoesa 석유 회사 oil company
sŏgyu hwahak chep'um 석유 화학
제품 petrochemical
sŏgyu kulch'ak changch'i 석유 굴착
장치 oil rig
Sŏgyu Such'ulguk Kigu 석유 수출국
기구 OPEC, Organization of
Petroleum Exporting Countries
Sŏhae 서해 West Sea, Yellow Sea
sŏjae 서재 study (room)
sŏjŏm 서점 bookstore
sŏkkarae 서까래 rafter
sŏkkida 섞이다 blend in
Sŏk-kkamoni 석가모니 Sakyamuni
(Buddha)
sŏk-kkin 섞인 mixed
sŏk-kkosang 석고상 plaster cast
sŏkkŏ not'a 섞어 놓다 mix up,
muddle up
sŏkkŭn kŏt 섞은 것 mix, mixture
sŏkppang 석방 release
sŏkppanghada 석방하다 free,
release
sŏkp'an 석판 slab
sŏkssa(hagwi) 석사(학위) master's
(degree)
sŏkssoe 석쇠 grill
sŏkssoero kuptta 석쇠로 굽다 grill
sŏkssu 석수 mason
sŏktcho 석조 stone (material)
sŏktta 섞다 mix, blend in; mingle
sŏkt'an 석탄 coal

sŏk'ŏsŭ 서커스 circus

sŏk'o 석호 lagoon

sŏk'oe 석회 lime (*substance*)

sŏk'oeam 석회암 chalk (*in soil*)

sŏlbi 설비 fixture

sŏlch'i 설치 installation

sŏlch'ihada 설치하다 install; *chiro-erŭl sŏlch'ihada* 지뢰를 설치하다 mine, lay mines in

sŏlch'in 설친 fitful

sŏlch'iryu 설치류 rodent

sŏldŭngnyŏk innŭn 설득력 있는 forceful

sŏlgŏji hada 설거지하다 wash the dishes

sŏlgŏji kigye 설거지 기계 dishwasher

sŏlgŏji mul 설겆이 물 dishwater

sŏlguwŏjin 설구워진 soggy

sŏlgyedo 설계도 design; plan

sŏlgyehada 설계하다 design; shape

sŏlgyeja 설계자 designer

sŏlgyesa 설계사 architect

sŏlgyesang-ŭi munjetchŏm 설계상의 문제점 design fault

sŏlgyo 설교 sermon

sŏlgyodan 설교단 pulpit

sŏlgyohada 설교하다 preach

sŏlgyoja 설교자 preacher

Sŏllal 설날 Lunar New Year

sŏlliptcha 설립자 founder

sŏllip'ada 설립하다 establish

sŏllo 선로 track; platform

sŏllye 선례 precedent; *nuguŭi sŏllyerŭl ttarŭda* 누구의 선례를 따르다 follow in s.o.'s footsteps

sŏlma! 설마! surely; come on! (*in disbelief*)

sŏlmyŏng 설명 explanation

sŏlmyŏnghada 설명하다 explain; account for; set out; *Xege Ye tae-han kaeyorŭl sŏlmyŏnghada* X에게 Y에 대한 개요를 설명하다 brief X on Y

sŏlmyŏnghal su ŏmnŭn 설명할 수 없는 inexplicable; unaccountable

sŏlmyŏng p'ail 설명파일 readme file

sŏlmyŏngsŏ 설명서 manual

sŏlssa 설사 diarrhea

sŏltchŏng 설정 institution, setting up

sŏlttŭk 설득 persuasion

sŏlttŭk'ada 설득하다 persuade

sŏlttŭngnyŏk innŭn 설득력 있는 convincing, persuasive

sŏlt'ang 설탕 sugar

sŏlt'ang-t'ong 설탕통 sugar bowl

sŏlt'ang-ŭl nŏt'a 설탕을 넣다 sugar; add sugar

sŏm 섬 island

sŏmgwang 섬광 flash

sŏmgwang chŏn-gu 섬광 전구 flashbulb

sŏmnyu 섬유 fiber

sŏmnyujil 섬유질 roughage

sŏmseham 섬세함 delicacy (*of fabric*)

sŏmsehan 섬세한 delicate, dainty; *chinach'ige sŏmsehan* 지나치게 섬세한 finicky

sŏmssaram 섬사람 islander

sŏmttŭk nollam 섬뜩 놀람 consternation

sŏmttŭk'an 섬뜩한 scary

sŏmun 서문 foreword, preface

sŏmyŏng 서명 signature

sŏmyŏnghada 서명하다 sign

sŏmyŏng-in 서명인 signatory

sŏmyŏnŭro 서면으로 in writing

sŏn 선 line; gland; (space) module; Zen; goodness

-sŏn -선 ship, vessel

sŏnbak 선박 boat, craft

sŏnbak soyuja 선박 소유자 shipowner

sŏnbal kwajŏng 선발 과정 selection process

sŏnban 선반 shelf; rack; lathe

sŏnbarhada 선발하다 choose, single out

sŏnbul 선불 advance (*money*) ◊ prepaid; *sŏnbullo* 선불로 cash in advance, cash up front

Sŏnbulgyo 선불교 Zen Buddhism

sŏnbul yogŭm 선불 요금 advance payment

sŏnburhada 선불하다 put down *deposit*

sŏnburŭi 선불의 prepaid

sŏnbyŏrhada 선별하다 screen (*for security reasons*)

sŏnch'e 선체 hull

sŏnch'ŏnjŏgin 선천적인 congenital,

hereditary

sŏnch'urhada 선출하다 vote in

sŏnch'wihada 선취하다 skim off

sŏndonghada 선동하다 stir up, arouse

sŏndongja 선동자 agitator

sŏndu 선두 lead (*in race*); *sŏndue(sŏ)* 선두에(서) in the lead, in front

sŏndu chuja 선두 주자 forerunner; pacemaker

sŏndue sŏda 선두에 서다 lead

sŏnduŭi 선두의 leading

sŏng 성 gender; surname; castle; ministry

sŏngbyŏk 성벽 rampart

sŏngbyŏrhoe 송별회 farewell party

Sŏng Chugan 성 주간 Holy Week

sŏngch'wi 성취 achievement

sŏngch'wihada 성취하다 accomplish, achieve

sŏngdae 성대 vocal cords

sŏngdang 성당 cathedral

sŏngdoch'ak 성도착 perversion

sŏngga 성가 hymn

sŏnggashige hada 성가시게 하다 annoy, provoke; bother

sŏnggashin 성가신 annoying; nagging; cumbersome

sŏngge 성게 sea urchin

sŏnggong 성공 success, hit

sŏnggonghada 성공하다 succeed, make it; prosper; *...ŭl/rŭl hanŭn te sŏnggonghada* ...을/를 하는 데 성공하다 succeed in doing

sŏnggonghaji mot'an 성공하지 못한 unsuccessful

sŏnggonghan 성공한 prosperous

sŏnggongtch'ŏgin 성공적인 successful

sŏnggongtch'ŏgŭro 성공적으로 successfully

sŏnggorham 성골함 shrine

sŏnggŭm 성금 donation, contribution

Sŏnggŭmnyoil 성금요일 Good Friday

sŏnggŭp'ada 성급하다 be impatient

sŏnggŭp'age 성급하게 impatiently

sŏnggŭp'am 성급함 impatience

sŏnggŭp'an 성급한 short-tempered, impatient; rash

sŏnggwan-gye 성관계 relationship (*sexual*)

sŏnggyŏgi choŭn 성격이 좋은 good-natured

Sŏnggyŏng 성경 Bible

sŏnggyo 성교 sexual intercourse, sex

sŏnggyohada 성교하다 have sex; *sŏnggyorŭl hada* 성교를 하다 have sex

sŏnghaeng 성행 epidemic

sŏngham 성함 name

sŏnghongnyŏl 성홍열 scarlet fever

sŏnghŭirong 성희롱 sexual harassment

sŏnghyang 성향 spirit; attitude; inclination, tendency; liking

sŏnghyŏng-oekkwa 성형외과 cosmetic surgery

sŏnghyŏng-oekkwa ŭisa 성형외과 의사 cosmetic surgeon, plastic surgeon

sŏnghyŏng susul 성형 수술 plastic surgery

sŏng-in 성인 adult (*over 20*) ◊ adult; saint

sŏng-i nada 성이 나다 get ruffled

sŏng-in kyoyuk 성인 교육 further education

sŏng-inŭi 성인의 adult (*over 20*)

sŏng-inyŏnghwa 성인영화 adult film

sŏngjang 성장 growth, development

sŏngjanghada 성장하다 grow (*of business*); dress up

sŏngjanghan tongmul 성장한 동물 adult animal

sŏngjiktcha 성직자 clergyman; priest; Reverend

sŏngjiktchadŭl 성직자들 clergy

sŏngjil 성질 characteristic, quality; (bad) temper

sŏngjiri koyak'an 성질이 고약한 vicious

sŏngjŏgŭl naeda 성적을 내다 grade, mark

sŏngjŏk 성적 grade, mark

sŏngjŏkp'yo 성적표 report card

sŏngjŏn 성전 sanctuary

Sŏngjogi 성조기 Stars and Stripes

sŏngkkal innŭn 성깔 있는 bad-tempered

sŏngkkwaga manŭn 성과가 많은 fruitful

sŏngkkyŏgŭl myosahada 성격을 묘사하다 characterize, describe

sŏngkkyŏk 성격 nature, character; personality; *urinŭn sŏngkkyŏgi an mat-tta* 우리는 성격이 안 맞다 we're not compatible; *sŏngkkyŏgi nanp'ok'ada* 성격이 난폭하다 have a violent temper

sŏng kwan-gyerŭl kajida 성 관계를 가지다 make love

sŏngk'ŭmsŏngk'ŭm kŏt-tta 성큼성큼 걷다 stride

sŏngmarŭn 성마른 petulant; prickly, irritable

sŏngmiga koyak'an 성미가 고약한 ill-natured

sŏngmi kŭp'an 성미 급한 bad-tempered, irritable

sŏngmyŏng 성명 declaration, statement; name (*on document*)

sŏngnada 성나다 be angry, be cross

sŏngnan 성난 angry, cross

sŏngnip'ada 성립하다 materialize; be formed; be concluded

sŏngnŭng 성능 capacity, performance

sŏngnŭng-i usuhan ch'a 성능이 우수한 차 performance car

sŏngnyang 성냥 match

sŏngnyangkkap 성냥갑 box of matches

sŏngnyŏn 성년 manhood, maturity

Sŏngnyŏng 성령 Holy Spirit

sŏn-gŏ 선거 election; the polls

sŏn-gŏil 선거일 election day

sŏn-gŏin 선거인 elector

sŏn-gŏ pangshik 선거 방식 electoral system

sŏn-gŏ undong 선거 운동 election campaign

sŏngppyŏng 성병 sexually transmitted disease

sŏng pullŭng 성 불능 impotence (*sexual*)

sŏngsaenghwal 성생활 sex life

sŏngshil 성실 sincerity

sŏngshirhada 성실하다 be sincere

sŏngshirhan 성실한 sincere

sŏngsŏ-ŭi 성서의 biblical

sŏngsŭrŏptta 성스럽다 be holy

sŏngsŭrŏun 성스러운 holy

sŏngsuk-kki 성숙기 maturity, adulthood

sŏngsuk'ada 성숙하다 be mature; ripen; reach maturity

sŏngsuk'am 성숙함 maturity

sŏngsuk'an 성숙한 mature, adult

sŏngtchŏgin 성적인 sexual

sŏngtchŏgŭro hŭironghada 성적으로 희롱하다 molest

sŏngtchŏgŭro hŭngbunhan 성적으로 흥분한 horny

sŏngtchŏgŭro hŭngbunshik'ida 성적으로 흥분시키다 turn on (*sexually*)

sŏngtchŏgŭro hŭngmirŭl ilk'e hada 성적 흥미를 잃게 하다 turn off (*sexually*)

sŏngtchŏk maeryŏgi innŭn 성적 매력이 있는 sexually attractive

sŏngtchŏk yok-kku pulman 성적 욕구 불만 sexual frustration

Sŏngt'anjŏl 성탄절 Christmas; Christmas Day

sŏn-gŭm 선금 cash in advance

sŏn-guja 선구자 pioneer

sŏn-gujŏgin 선구적인 pioneering

sŏng-wŏn 성원 applause

sŏng-wŏnŭl ponaeda 성원을 보내다 applaud

sŏn-gyŏnjimyŏng 선견지명 foresight

sŏn-gyo 선교 bridge (*of ship*)

sŏn-gyosa 선교사 missionary

sŏnho 선호 preference

sŏnhohada 선호하다 prefer

sŏninjang 선인장 cactus

sŏnipkkyŏn 선입견 prejudice; preconception

sŏnjam 선잠 doze

sŏnjang 선장 captain, master, skipper

sŏnjin-guk 선진국 advanced country

sŏnjŏk 선적 shipping

sŏnjŏk hwamul 선적 화물 cargo

sŏnjŏk'ada 선적하다 ship

sŏnjŏn 선전 publicity; promotion; advertisement

sŏnjŏnhada 선전하다 publicize;

promote; advertise

sŏnjŏn hwalttong 선전 활동
propaganda

sŏnjŏn munkku 선전 문구 blurb

sŏnjŏnnyong 선전용 demo

sŏnjŏnnyong tisŭk'ŭ 선전용 디스크
demo disk

sŏnjŏn p'ogo 선전 포고 declaration
of war

sŏnjŏn p'ogohada 선포 하다
declare war

sŏnmul 선물 gift, present

sŏnmul kyeyak 선물 계약 futures

sŏnmul shijang 선물 시장 futures
market

sŏnmyŏngdo 선명도 resolution,
sharpness

sŏnmyŏnghada 선명하다 be vivid

sŏnmyŏngham 선명함 brilliance;
vividness

sŏnmyŏnghan 선명한 vivid

sŏnnyul 선율 melody

sŏnŏn 선언 declaration

sŏnŏnhada 선언하다 declare,
proclaim

sŏnoe mot'ŏ 선외 모터 outboard
motor

sŏnp'ung 선풍 whirlwind

sŏnp'unggi 선풍기 fan

sŏnp'ungŭl irŭk'ida 선풍을 이르키다
create a sensation

sŏnsaeng 선생 teacher

sŏnsaengnim 선생님 teacher; sir; Mr

sŏnsashidaeŭi 선사시대의
prehistoric

sŏnshil 선실 cabin

sŏnshim 선심 linesman

sŏnshimŭl ssŭnŭn tŭt'ada 선심을
쓰는 듯하다 patronize, be
condescending toward

sŏnsŏ 선서 oath

sŏnsŏ chŭng-ŏn 선서 증언
deposition

sŏnsŏhada 선서하다 swear

sŏnsu 선수 athlete; player

sŏnsuch'ida 선수치다 outwit

sŏnsugwŏn 선수권 championship
(*title*)

sŏnsugwŏn taehoe 선수권 대회
championship (*event*)

sŏnttŭt 선뜻 readily

sŏnt'aegŭi 선택의 optional, elective

sŏnt'aegŭi pŏmwi 선택의 범위
choice, selection

sŏnt'aek 선택 choice, selection

sŏnt'aek-kkwŏn 선택권 option

sŏnt'aekttoen 선택된 elected

sŏnt'aek'ada 선택하다 choose, select

sŏnŭiŭi 선의의 well-meaning; well-
meant

sŏnŭl kŭt-tta 선을 긋다 mark out

sŏnŭrhaejida 서늘해지다 cool down

sŏnwŏn 선원 seaman

sŏnyŏl 선열 glandular fever

sŏpsshi 섭씨 Celsius; centigrade

sŏp'ing 서핑 surfing

sŏp'ing podŭ 서핑 보드 surfboard

sŏp'ung 서풍 west wind

sŏrap 서랍 drawer

sŏraptchang 서랍장 bureau, chest of
drawers

sŏri 서리 frost

sŏriga naerinŭn 서리가 내리는
frosty

sŏrirŭl ŏpssaeda 서리를 없애다
defrost *freezer, windshield*

sŏro 서로 one another, each other

sŏro kwan-gyega innŭn 서로 관계가
있는 interrelated

sŏro mannŭn 서로 맞는 compatible

sŏro mannŭn chŏngdo 서로 맞는
정도 compatibility

sŏron 서론 introduction

sŏrŭn 서른 thirty

sŏrŭn pŏntchaeŭi 서른 번째의
thirtieth

sŏryu 서류 documentation, papers;
document

sŏryu chŏlttan-gi 서류 절단기
shredder

sŏryuch'ŏl 서류철 file

sŏryuham 서류함 file cabinet

sŏryu kabang 서류 가방 briefcase

sŏshiktchi 서식지 habitat

sŏshin wangnae 서신 왕래
correspondence

sŏshin wangnaehada 서신 왕래하다
correspond

sŏsŏhi kkŭltta 서서히 끓다 simmer

sŏsŏhi kkŭnnada 서서히 끝나다
wind down, quieten down

sŏsŏhi sarajida 서서히 사라지다

melt away, vanish

sŏsŏngdaeda 서성대다 prowl

sŏsŭp'enshyŏn 서스펜션 suspension

sŏsŭp'ensŭ 서스펜스 suspense

sŏtchogesŏ punŭn 쪽에서 부는 westerly *wind*

sŏtchogŭi 서쪽의 western; westerly

sŏtchoguro 서쪽으로 west, westward

sŏtchok 서쪽 west; *...e sŏtchoge* ...의 서쪽에 west of

Sŏttal Kŭmŭmnal 섣달 그믐날 New Year's Eve

sŏt'un 서툰 rusty

sŏt'urŭda 서투르다 be bad at; be out of practice

sŏt'urŭge hada 서투르게 하다 fumble; make a mess of

sŏt'urŭge mandŭlda 서투르게 만들다 bungle

sŏt'urŭn 서투른 bad, poor; clumsy

Sŏul 서울 Seoul

sŏyak 서약 vow

Sŏyang 서양 the West ◊ Western

sŏyang changgi 서양 장기 checkers

sŏyang changgip'an 서양 장기판 checkerboard

sŏyanghwadoen 서양화된 westernized

Sŏyang saram 서양 사람 Westerner

sŏye 서예 calligraphy

so 소 cattle

soakkwa 소아과 pediatrics

soakkwa ŭisa 소아과 의사 pediatrician

soamabi 소아마비 polio

sobangch'a 소방차 fire truck

sobangsŏ 소방서 fire department

sobangsu 소방수 firefighter, fireman

sobi 소비 consumption

sobihada 소비하다 consume, expend, use

sobija 소비자 consumer, purchaser

sobija sahoe 소비자 사회 consumer society

sobip'um 소비품 consumer goods

sobyŏn 소변 urine

sobyŏnŭl poda 소변을 보다 urinate

soch'aektcha 소책자 booklet

soch'ong 소총 rifle

sodae 소대 platoon

sodok'ada 소독하다 sterilize,

disinfect

sodong 소동 disturbance, uproar

sodongnyak 소독약 disinfectant, antiseptic

sodŭk 소득 income, earnings

sodŭksse 소득세 income tax

soe 쇠 iron

soech'angssal 쇠창살 grill, grille

soegogi 쇠고기 beef

soesalttae 쇠살대 grate

soesasŭl 쇠사슬 chain

soet'oe 쇠퇴 decay

soet'oehada 쇠퇴하다 decay; go downhill; slump

soet'oehanŭn 쇠퇴하는 decaying, dying

sogae 소개 introduction

sogaehada 소개하다 introduce, present

sogak'ae pŏrida 태워버리다 burn down

sogam 소감 opinion; sentiment

sogangno 소각로 incinerator

...soge ...속에

sogida 속이다 deceive, cheat; fiddle; rip off; *namŭl soginŭn* 남을 속이는 deceitful

sogim 속임 deception

sogimsu 속임수 deceit, cheat; hoax; trick; *...ŭi sogimsue kŏllida* ...의 속임수에 걸리다 fall for, be deceived by

sogimsuro yuhok'ada 속임수로 유혹하다 lure

sogimsurŭl ssŭda 속임수를 쓰다 cheat

sogi pich'inŭn 속이 비치는 transparent

sogi pin 속이 빈 hollow

sogi shiwŏnhajiyo! 속이 시원하지요! I hope you're satisfied!

sogŏ 속어 slang

sogogi kukppap 소고기 국밥 beef soup with rice

sogot 속옷 underwear; briefs

sogŭl ch'ae-uda 속을 채우다 stuff

sogŭl ch'aeunŭn chaeryo 속을 채우는 재료 stuffing

sogŭl ppaenaeda 속을 빼내다 core

sogŭm 소금 salt

sogŭm kŭrŭt 소금 그릇 saltcellar

sogŭp'anŭn 소급하는 retroactive
sogŭp'ayŏ chŏgyongshik'ida
소급하여 적용시키다 backdate
sogŭro ssaida 속으로 쌓이다
smolder *fig*
sohorhan 소홀한 negligent
sohwa 소화 digestion
sohwagi 소화기 fire extinguisher
sohwahada 소화하다 digest,
assimilate; extinguish, put out
sohwahagi öryŏun 소화하기 어려운
indigestible
sohwajŏn 소화전 fire hydrant
sohwa kyet'ong 소화 계통 digestive
system
sohwanhada 소환하다 call;
summons, subpoena; recall
sohwantchang 소환장 subpoena,
summons
sohwa pullyang 소화 불량
indigestion
sohyŏng 소형 small size
sohyŏng chadongch'a 소형 자동차
subcompact (car)
sohyŏngch'a 소형차 compact (car)
sohyŏnghwahada 소형화하다
downsize
sohyŏng pŏsŭ 소형 버스 minibus
soin 소인 postmark
sojangp'um 소장품 collection
sojil 소질 talent; temperament;
sojip'ada 소집하다 call, convene;
summon
sojip'um 소지품 belongings
sojŏngŭi 소정의 prescribed; *sojŏngŭi ch'aek* 소정의 책 set book
soju 소주 distilled liquor
sojunghan saram 소중한 사람
treasure (*person*)
sojunghi hada 소중히 하다 take care
of; cherish
sojunghi kanjik'ada 소중히 간직하다
cherish
sojunghi yŏgida 소중히 여기다
value
sok 속 core; filling; stuffing
sokch'ima 속치마 underskirt
sok-kkan shinmun 석간 신문
evening paper
sok-kki 속기 shorthand
sok-kki shwiun 속기 쉬운 gullible

sokkŏsŏ mandŭlda 섞어서 만들다
concoct
sokppo 속보 news flash
sokp'yŏn 속편 sequel
sokssagida 속삭이다 murmur;
whisper
sokssagim 속삭임 murmur; whisper
sokssanghada 속상하다 be upsetting
sokssanghan 속상한 upsetting
sokssŏng 속성 attribute
sokssŏng taiŏt'ŭ 속성 다이어트
crash diet
sokttam 속담 proverb, saying
sokttanhada 속단하다 come to a
hasty conclusion
soktto 속도 speed; pace, tempo;
velocity
soktto chehan 속도 제한 speed limit
soktto chojŏl changch'i 속도 조절
장치 throttle
sokttogye 속도계 speedometer
soktto naeda 속도 내다 speed up
sok'et 소켓 socket
sol 솔 brush, scrubbing brush
solgi 솔기 seam
soljirhada 솔질하다 brush
solmyŏnghal su ŏmnŭn 설명할 수
없는 mystifying
solppang-ul 솔방울 cone
solssŏnhada 솔선하다 lead the way;
muŏsŭl solssŏnhaesŏ hada
무엇을 솔선해서 하다 do sth on
one's own initiative
soltchik'ada 솔직하다 be frank, be
candid; be blunt; be straight; be
outspoken; *soltchik'i malhamyŏn*
솔직히 말하면 to be frank
soltchik'age 솔직하게 bluntly,
plainly; honestly
soltchik'i 솔직히 frankly
som 솜 absorbent cotton
somae 소매 sleeve
somaech'igi 소매치기 shoplifter;
pickpocket
somaega ŏmnŭn 소매가 없는
sleeveless
somae kagyŏk 소매 가격 retail price
somaero 소매로 retail; *...e somaero
p'alda* ...에 소매로 팔다 retail at
somaesang-in 소매상인 shopkeeper;
retailer

somaetppuri 소맷부리 cuff

somo chingmul 소모 직물 worsted

somsat'ang 솜사탕 cotton candy

somsshi 솜씨 workmanship

somsshi choŭn 솜씨 좋은 deft

somsshi innŭn 솜씨 있는 workmanlike

somt'ŏlgat'ŭn 솜털같은 fluffy

somun 소문 rumor

somyŏl 소멸 disappearance; demise

somyŏrhada 소멸하다 die out

son 손 hand; *soni tach'i annŭn kose* 손이 닿지 않는 곳에 out of reach; *soni tannŭn kose* 손이 닿는 곳에 within reach; *son tteseyo!* 손 떼세요! hands off!; *son tŭrŏ!* 손 들어! hands up!

sonagi 소나기 shower (*of rain*)

sonamu 소나무 pine (tree)

sonaraet saram 손아랫 사람 junior, subordinate

sonaraeŭi 손아래의 junior, subordinate

sonbal 손발 limb

sondokki 손도끼 hatchet

sone chwida 손에 쥐다 purchase, grip

son-gabang 손가방 purse, pocketbook

song-aji 송아지 calf

songaji kogi 송아지 고기 veal

songbyŏrhoe 송별회 leaving party

songgŭmhada 송금하다 transfer

songgŭmhwan 송금환 transfer

song-i 송이 cluster ◊ *countword for flowers, bunches of grapes etc*

songmaŭmŭl t'ŏnot'a 속마음을 터놓다 open up (*of person*)

songmul 속물 snob

songmurŭi 속물의 snobbish

songnunssŏp 속눈썹 eyelash

songnyŏgŭl naeda 속력을 내다 lengthen one's stride

songnyŏgŭl nŭllyŏgada 속력을 늘려가다 gather speed

song-ŏ 송어 trout

son-gŏhada 선거하다 elect

songp'yŏn 송편 rice cake steamed with pine needles

songshin-gi 송신기 transmitter

songshinhada 송신하다 transmit, beam

songwanhada 송환하다 repatriate

sonhae 손해 harm; loss

sonhae paesanggŭm 손해 배상금 damages LAW

sonik pun-gijŏm 손익 분기점 break-even point

sonil 손일 manual labor

sonja 손자 grandson

sonjabi 손잡이 handle; knob; stem (*of glass*)

sonjirhada 손질하다 trim; groom; touch up

sonkkabang 손가방 pocketbook, purse

sonkkaragŭro karik'ida 손가락으로 가리키다 point; point to

sonkkarak 손가락 finger; *kŭnyŏnŭn sonkkaraktto kkadak'aji annŭnda* 그녀는 손가락도 까딱하지 않는다 she never lifts a finger

sonkkarak kkŭt 손가락 끝 fingertip

sonkkarak madi 손가락 마디 knuckle

sonmok 손목 wrist

sonmok shigye 손목 시계 wrist watch

sonnim 손님 guest; visitor; company

sonnimnyong ch'imshil 손님용 침실 guestroom

sonnyŏ 손녀 granddaughter

sonppadagŭro ch'alssak ttaerida 손바닥으로 찰싹 때리다 smack, spank

sonppadak 손바닥 palm (*of hand*)

sonppadangmanhan 손바닥만한 scanty

sonsang 손상 damage

sonsangdoeji anŭn 손상되지 않은 undamaged, intact

sonsangshik'ida 손상시키다 damage, prejudice

sonsangshik'inŭn 손상시키는 damaging

sonshil 손실 loss

sonshiri k'ŭn 손실이 큰 costly

sonsugŏn 손수건 handkerchief

sonsu mandŭlgi 손수 만들기 DIY, do-it-yourself

sontchisŭro marhada 손짓으로 말하다 gesticulate

sontchit 손짓 gesture

sontchit'ayŏ purŭda 손짓하여 부르다 beckon

sont'op 손톱 fingernail

sont'opkkak-kki 손톱깎이 nail clippers

sont'op kkangnŭn kawi 손톱 깎는 가위 nail scissors

sont'optchul 손톱줄 nail file

sonŭl hŭndŭlda 손을 흔들다 wave; wave to

sonŭl ppŏtch'ida 손을 뻗치다 reach out

sonŭl taeda 손을 대다 touch; feel up (sexually); **chamkkan sonŭl taeda** 잠깐 손을 대다 dabble in

sonŭl tteda 손을 떼다 back out

sonŭro 손으로 by hand

sonŭro hanŭn 손으로 하는 manual

sonŭro manjida 손으로 만지다 paw

sonŭro ssŭn 손으로 쓴 handwritten

sonŭro tŏdŭmtta 손으로 더듬다 grope

sonwiŭi 손위의 senior, older

sonyŏ 소녀 girl

sonyŏn 소년 juvenile; boy

sonyŏn-kat'ŭn 소년같은 boyish

sonyŏn pŏmjoe 소년 범죄 juvenile delinquency

sonyŏn pŏmjoeja 소년 범죄자 juvenile delinquent

sonyŏnŭi 소년의 juvenile

sonyŏ tanwŏn 소녀단원 girl guide

so-oegam 소외감 sense of alienation

so-oeja 소외자 outcast

sop'a 소파 couch, sofa

sop'a sett'ŭ 소파 셋트 (three-piece) suite

sop'ashik ch'imdae 소파식 침대 sofa bed

sop'o 소포 parcel, package

sop'ŭrano 소프라노 soprano

sop'ŭt'ŭweŏ 소프트웨어 software

sop'um 소품 (stage) prop

sop'ung 소풍 outing, trip; picnic

soran 소란 uproar, tumult, commotion; scene; **soranŭl p'iuda** 소란을 피우다 make a scene

soranhada 소란하다 be noisy

soranhan 소란한 loud, noisy

soransŭrŏun 소란스러운 tumultuous

sori 소리 sound, noise; **k'ŭn soriro iltta** 큰 소리로 읽다 read out loud; **k'ŭn soriro marhada** 큰 소리로 말하다 speak up, speak louder

sorich'ida 소리치다 shout; scream

sorich'yŏ purŭda 소리쳐 부르다 call, call out, shout

sorijirŭm 소리지름 shouting

sorinop'yŏ ut-tta 소리높여 웃다 howl (with laughter)

sori ŏmnŭn 소리 없는 silent

soriŏpsshi kŏt-tta 소리없이 걷다 pad, move quietly

soriptcha 소립자 (elementary) particle

sorirŭl naeŏ 소리를 내어 aloud

sorŭm 소름 gooseflesh; **narŭl sorŭmkkich'ige handa** 나를 소름끼치게 한다 it gives me gooseflesh

soryang 소량 dab, splash; **soryang-ŭi...** 소량의 ... a little ...

Soryŏn 소련 Soviet Union

soryŏng 소령 major MIL

sosaeng 소생 revival

sosaengshik'ida 소생시키다 revive, resuscitate

sosa orŭda 솟아 오르다 soar; lift off; rise

soshiji 소시지 sausage

soshik 소식 news; **...(ŭ)ro put'ŏ soshigŭl tŭt-tta** ...(으)로 부터 소식을 듣다 have news from, hear from

sosŏl 소설 novel; fiction

sosŏlga 소설가 novelist

sosong 소송 lawsuit

sosong sakkŏn 소송 사건 court case

sossŭ 소스 sauce; dressing (for salad)

sosŭrach'ige hada 소스라치게 하다 petrify, terrify

sosŭrach'in 소스라친 petrified

sosu 소수 decimal

sosu minjok 소수 민족 ethnic minority

sosup'a 소수파 minority

sosup'aida 소수파이다 be in the minority

sosutchŏm 소수점 decimal point

sot'anghada 소탕하다 mop up

sot'ongdoeda 소통되다 flow

sot'ŭ 소트 sort COMPUT

soŭm 소음 sound, noise

souju 소우주 microcosm

sowi 소위 so-called *pej* ◊ second lieutenant

sowŏn 소원 wish

sowŏnhada 소원하다 be estranged; petition

sowŏnhaejin 소원해진 estranged

sowŏnhan 소원한 distant, aloof

soyo 소요 disturbances, civil unrest

soyongdori 소용돌이 whirlpool

soyongŏmnŭn 소용없는 pointless, futile, useless; *noryŏk'aedo soyong-ŏpssŏyo* 노력해도 소용없어요 it's pointless trying

soyu 소유 possession, ownership

soyuhada 소유하다 have, own; possess

soyuja 소유자 owner; holder

soyukkwŏn 소유권 ownership

soyukkyŏk 소유격 possessive GRAM

soyumul 소유물 belongings, things; property; possession

soyuŭi 소유의 own

soyuyogi kanghan 소유욕이 강한 possessive

ssaaollida 쌓아올리다 stack, heap up; build up

ssaa ollin tŏmi 쌓아 올린 더미 heap

ssada 싸다 wrap; pack; envelop; be cheap; be fast; excrete

ssaguryŏmulgŏn 싸구려물건 cheap goods

ssain nundŏmi 쌓인 눈더미 snowdrift

ssak 싹 germ; bud

ssal 쌀 rice (*uncooked*)

ssalongch'a 쌀롱차 sedan MOT

ssalssarhada 쌀쌀하다 be chilly

ssalssarhan 쌀쌀한 chilly; fresh; icy; standoffish

ssamjit-tton 쌈짓돈 loose change

ssan 싼 inexpensive, cheap; low

ssang 쌍 pair; couple; *namnyŏ han ssang* 남녀 한 쌍 couple

ssang-an-gyŏng 쌍안경 binoculars

ssangdung-i 쌍둥이 twins

ssang-ŭro toen 쌍으로 된 double

ssan mulgŏn 싼 물건 cheap goods

ssaragi nun 싸라기 눈 sleet

ssat'a 쌓다 stack; run up *debts*

ssauda 싸우다 fight, battle; combat; *...ŭl/rŭl wihae ssauda* ...을/를 위해 싸우다 fight for

ssaum 싸움 fight, scrap, brawl; struggle; row

ssaumjirhada 싸움질하다 brawl

ssayŏjida 쌓여지다 accumulate, build up

sseda 세다 be strong; turn gray; count

ssekssihan 섹시한 sexy

ssekssŭ 섹스 sex

ssen 센 strong

sshi 씨 Mr; Ms; seed, pip, stone; *Hong Kildongsshi* 홍길동씨 Mr Kildong Hong; *I Sunmisshi* 이순미씨 Ms Sunmi Lee

sshibal! ∨ 씨발! fuck!

sshidaek 씨댁 care of

sshidirom 씨디롬 CD-ROM

sshidirom tŭraibŭ 씨디롬 드라이브 CD-ROM drive

sshiep'ŭsshi 씨에프씨 CFC, chlorofluorocarbon

sshigŭn-gŏrida 씨근거리다 wheeze

sshijok 씨족 clan

sshing chinagada 씽 지나가다 whizz by

sshing pulda 씽 불다 whistle (*of wind*)

sshiptta 씹다 chew

sshiriŏl p'ot'ŭ 씨리얼 포트 serial port

sshirŭm 씨름 (Korean-style) wrestling

sshirŭmhada 씨름하다 tackle *problem*; grapple with; wrestle

sshirŭm kyŏnggi 씨름 경기 (Korean-style) wrestling match

sshirŭm sŏnsu 씨름 선수 (Korean-style) wrestler

sshit-tta 씻다 clean; wash

sshit'ŭ 시트 sheet

ssŏbŏrida 써버리다 use, consume

ssŏgŭn 썩은 rotten, bad, rancid

ssŏk-kki shwiun 썩기 쉬운 perishable

ssŏktta 썩다 rot; go bad

ssŏlda 썰다 chop

ssŏlmae 썰매 sled(ge), toboggan; sleigh

ssŏlmul 썰물 ebb tide; low tide

ssŏlmurida 썰물이다 the tide is out

ssŏn k'urim 썬 크림 sun cream

ssŏnt'en 썬텐 suntan

ssoa ttŏrŏttŭrida 쏘아 떨어뜨리다 shoot down, bring down

ssoda 쏘다 fire; shoot; sting; *ch'ongŭl ssoda* 총을 쏘다 fire a gun

ssoda put-tta 쏟아 붓다 pour

ssonsalgach'i chinagada 쏜살같이 지나가다 fly past, pass quickly (*of time*)

ssonsalgach'i naragada 쏜살같이 날아가다 dart

ssŭda 쓰다 use; spend; write; put on *glasses*; be bitter

ssŭdadŭmtta 쓰다듬다 stroke, caress; smooth *hair*

ssŭgi 쓰기 writing; use

ssŭiuda 씌우다 coat, cover; get on; crown *tooth*

ssŭium 씌움 coating, layer

ssŭlda 쓸다 sweep

ssŭlgae 쓸개 gall bladder

ssŭlmo 쓸모 usefulness

ssŭlmoinnŭn 쓸모있는 useful

ssŭlmoŏmnŭn 쓸모없는 useless, worthless; trashy; waste *land, material*

ssŭl su innŭn 쓸 수 있는 usable

ssŭltteŏmnŭn 쓸데없는 futile; idle *threat*

ssŭn 쓴 bitter

ssŭrarige hada 쓰라리게 하다 embitter

ssŭrebatkki 쓰레받기 dustpan

ssŭregi 쓰레기 garbage, litter; scum (*people*); crap

ssŭregi p'yegijang 쓰레기 폐기장 garbage dump

ssŭregi sujip 쓰레기 수집 garbage collection

ssŭregi tŏmi 쓰레기 더미 scrap heap

ssŭregi t'ong 쓰레기 통 garbage can, trashcan

ssŭregi t'ongno 쓰레기 통로 garbage chute

ssŭrŏjida 쓰러지다 fall, fall over; fall down; slump

ssŭrŏttŭrida 쓰러뜨리다 topple, bring down

ssukssuk charada 쑥쑥 자라다 shoot up (*of children*)

ssukttŭm 쑥뜸 moxibustion

ssurŏ moŭda 쓸어 모으다 sweep up

ssushida 쑤시다 prod, poke; have a stitch; hurt, smart

ssushyŏ nŏt'a 쑤셔 넣다 jam, ram

sswabŏrida 쏴버리다 blaze away (*with gun*)

sswaegi 쐐기 wedge

süch'idŭt chinagada 스치듯 지나가다 skim

sŭk'ach'i 스카치 Scotch

sŭk'aen 스캔 scan

sŭk'aendŭl 스캔들 scandal

sŭk'aenhada 스캔하다 scan; scan in

sŭk'aenŏ 스캐너 scanner

sŭk'airain 스카이라인 skyline

sŭk'ap'ŭ 스카프 scarf

sŭk'aut'ŭ 스카우트 (boy) scout

sŭk'ech'i 스케치 sketch

sŭk'ech'ibuk 스케치북 sketchbook

sŭk'ech'ihada 스케치하다 sketch

sŭk'eit'ŭ 스케이트 skate

sŭk'eit'ŭbodŭ 스케이트보드 skateboard

sŭk'eit'ŭjang 스케이트장 ice rink

sŭk'eit'ŭ t'ada 스케이트 타다 skate

sŭk'eit'ŭ t'agi 스케이트 타기 skating

sŭk'i 스키 ski

sŭk'i chip'ang-i 스키 지팡이 ski pole

sŭk'i hwaltchuro 스키 활주로 ski run

sŭk'i k'ŭrosŭk'ŏnt'ŭri 스키 크로스컨트리 cross-country skiing

sŭk'i lip'ŭt'ŭ 스키 리프트 ski lift

sŭk'in taibing 스킨 다이빙 skin diving

sŭk'i t'ada 스키 타다 ski

sŭk'i t'agi 스키 타기 skiing

sŭk'it'o 스키토 ski tow

Sŭk'ot'ŭllaendŭ 스코틀랜드 Scotland ◊ Scottish

sŭk'ŭraep puk 스크랩 북 scrapbook

sŭk'ŭrin 스크린 screen

sŭk'ŭrin t'esŭt'ŭ 스크린 테스트 screen test

sŭk'ubŏ taibing 스쿠버 다이빙 scuba diving

sŭk'ut'ŏ 스쿠터 motorscooter

sŭk'wŏshi 스쿼시 squash SP

sŭlgaegol 슬개골 kneecap

sŭlgŭmŏni 슬그머니 stealthily

sŭllaeshwi 슬래쉬 slash, oblique

sŭllaidŭ 슬라이드 slide, transparency

sŭlleit'ŭ 슬레이트 slate

sŭllip'ing paek 슬리핑 백 sleeping bag

sŭllip'ŏ 슬리퍼 slipper

sŭllogŏn 슬로건 slogan

sŭllot mŏshin 슬롯 머신 slot machine

sŭlloumoshŏn 슬로우모션 slow motion; action replay

sŭlp'ŏhada 슬퍼하다 lament, mourn; *sŭlp'ŏhajima* 슬퍼하지마 don't be sad

sŭlp'ŭda 슬프다 be sad

sŭlp'ŭge 슬프게 sadly

sŭlp'ŭm 슬픔 sadness

sŭlp'ŭme chamgin 슬픔에 잠긴 mournful

sŭlp'ŭn 슬픈 sad

sŭltchŏk kajida 슬쩍 가지다 pocket, take

sŭltchŏk kajyŏgada 슬쩍 가져가다 sneak, steal

sŭltchŏk nagada 슬쩍 나가다 make oneself scarce

sŭmaeshi 스매시 smash (*in tennis*)

sŭmiŏ shihŏm 스미어 시험 smear MED

sŭmogŭ 스모그 smog

sŭmul 스물 twenty

sŭmu pŏntchaeŭi 스무 번째의 twentieth

sŭmyŏnaoda 스며나오다 ooze

sŭnaep sajin 스냅 사진 snap, snapshot

sŭnggaek 승객 passenger; occupant

sŭnggaeksŏk 승객석 passenger seat

sŭngganggi 승강기 elevator

sŭng-in 승인 approval

sŭng-inhada 승인하다 approve; recognize; grant

sŭng-in patta 승인 받다 pass; gain approval

sŭngjin 승진 promotion

sŭngjinhada 승진하다 promote

sŭngma 승마 riding; horse, mount

sŭngmahada 승마하다 ride *horse*

sŭngmuwŏn 승무원 cabin crew, flight crew

sŭngmuwŏn chŏnwŏn 승무원 전원 crew

sŭngmuwŏnshil 승무원실 cabin

sŭngnak 승낙 approval, blessing

sŭngni 승리 win, victory; triumph; *...e taehae sŭngnihada* ...에 대해 승리하다 win a victory over

sŭngnihan 승리한 victorious

sŭngnija 승리자 victor

sŭnok'ŭl 스노클 snorkel

sŭnou ch'ein 스노우 체인 snow chains

sŭpkki 습기 humidity; moisture

sŭpkkich'an 습기찬 damp

sŭpkki innŭn 습기 있는 moist

sŭpkkwan 습관 practice, custom, habit; *kŭŭi sŭpkkwanŭro* 그의 습관으로 as was his custom; *sŭpkkwani toeda* 습관이 되다 become a habit; *...nŭn sŭpkkwani tŭlda* ...는 습관이 들다 take to ...ing, get into the habit of ...ing

sŭpkkwanjŏgin 습관적인 customary, habitual

sŭpkkyŏk 습격 assault, attack

sŭpp'o 습포 compress MED

sŭptchi 습지 marsh

sŭptchin 습진 eczema

sŭptchiŭi 습지의 marshy

sŭpttŭk'ada 습득하다 acquire

sŭp'ai 스파이 spy

sŭp'ai haeng-wi 스파이 행위 espionage

sŭp'aijisŭl hada 스파이짓을 하다 spy

sŭp'an 습한 humid

sŭp'eidŭ 스페이드 spades

Sŭp'ein 스페인 Spain ◊ Spanish

Sŭp'einŏ 스페인어 Spanish (*language*)

sŭp'eisŭ pa 스페이스 바 space bar

sŭp'iamint'ŭ 스피아민트 spearmint

sŭp'ik'ŏ 스피커 speaker

sŭp'och'ŭ 스포츠 sport

sŭp'och'ŭin 스포츠인 athlete

sŭp'och'ŭ kija 스포츠 기자 sports journalist

sŭp'och'ŭ k'a 스포츠 카 sportscar
sŭp'och'ŭ nyusŭ 스포츠 뉴스 sports news
sŭp'och'ŭran 스포츠란 sports page
sŭp'onji 스폰지 sponge
sŭp'onji komu 스폰지 고무 foam rubber
sŭp'onji k'eik'ŭ 스폰지 케이크 sponge cake
sŭp'otŭrait'ŭ 스포트라이트 spotlight
sŭp'ot'ihan 스포티한 sporty
sŭp'ŭredŭshit'ŭ 스프레드시트 spreadsheet
sŭp'ŭrei 스프레이 aerosol, spray
sŭrasoni 스라소니 lynx
sŭrillŏmul 스릴러물 thriller
sŭroin 스로인 throw-in
Sŭsŭng-ŭi nal 스승의 날 Teachers' Day
sŭsŭro 스스로 by oneself
sŭt'a 스타 star
sŭt'aillisŭt'ŭ 스타일리스트 (hair)stylist
sŭt'ak'ing 스타킹 stocking
sŭt'eik'ŭ 스테이크 steak
sŭt'eindŭ kŭllasŭ 스테인드 글라스 stained glass
sŭt'einlesŭ 스테인레스 stainless steel
sŭt'eip'ŭl kŏn 스테이플 건 staple gun
sŭt'ereo 스테레오 stereo
sŭt'eroidŭ 스테로이드 steroids
sŭt'ik'ŏ 스티커 sticker
sŭt'im tarimi 스팀 다리미 steam iron
sŭt'ŏnt'ŭmaen 스턴트맨 stuntman
sŭt'obŭ 스토브 stove
sŭt'ok'ŏ 스토커 stalker
sŭt'op lait'ŭ 스톱 라이트 stoplight
sŭt'op wŏch'i 스톱 워치 stopwatch
sŭt'ŭraik'ŏ 스트라이커 striker
sŭt'ŭraik'ŭ 스트라이크 strike
sŭt'ŭreit'ŭ 스트레이트 straight (up) *whiskey etc*
sŭt'ŭresŭ 스트레스 stress; *sŭt'ŭresŭrŭl pat-tta* 스트레스를 받다 be under stress; *sŭt'ŭresŭga it-tta* 스트레스가 있다 be under pressure
sŭt'ŭresŭ chojŏlppŏp 스트레스 조절법 stress management
sŭt'ŭresŭga shimhan 스트레스가

심한 stressful
sŭt'ŭresŭrŭl shimhage pannŭn 스트레스를 심하게 받는 stressed out
sŭt'ŭripssho 스트립쇼 strip show, striptease
sŭt'ŭrip'ŏ 스트리퍼 stripper
sŭt'ŭro 스트로 straw
sŭt'yu 스튜 stew
sŭt'yudio pakkŭi pangsong 스튜디오 밖의 방송 outside broadcast
sŭt'yuŏdissŭ 스튜어디스 air hostess, stewardess
Sŭweden 스웨덴 Sweden ◊ Swedish
Sŭweden mal 스웨덴 말 Swedish
Sŭweden saram 스웨덴 사람 Swede
Sŭwedenŭi 스웨덴의 Swedish
sŭweidŭ 스웨이드 suede
sŭwet'ŏ 스웨터 sweater
sŭwet'ŭ shyŏch'ŭ 스웨트 셔츠 sweatshirt
sŭwich'i 스위치 switch
Sŭwisŭ 스위스 Switzerland ◊ Swiss
sŭwit'ŭ 스위트 suite
su 수 number; figure; quantity; move (*in chess*) ◊ hydro...
su 수: *...l su it-tta* ...ㄹ 수 있다 can; *...l su ŏptta* ...ㄹ 수 없다 cannot
suabŭi 수압의 hydraulic
suaek 수액 sap
subak 수박 water melon
subanhada 수반하다 involve, mean
subi 수비 defense SP
subisu 수비수 defense player
subunkonggŭpp'aek 수분공급팩 moisturizing face mask
subyŏng 수병 sailor
such'aehwa 수채화 watercolor
such'aehwa mulkkam 수채화 물감 watercolor
such'iga toeda 수치가 되다 disgrace
such'ishim 수치심 shame; *...e such'ishimŭl an-gyŏjuda* ...에 수치심을 안겨주다 bring shame on
such'isŭrŏptta 수치스럽다 be disgraceful
such'isŭrŏun 수치스러운 disgraceful, scandalous
such'ŏk'an 수척한 emaciated; gaunt; haggard
su ch'ŏnŭi 수 천의 thousands of

such'uk p'ojang 수축 포장 shrink-wrapping

such'uk'ada 수축하다 contract, shrink

such'uk p'ojanghada 수축 포장하다 shrink-wrap

such'ul 수출 export, exporting

such'ulguk 수출국 exporter (*country*)

such'ul k'aemp'ein 수출 캠페인 export campaign

such'ulp'um 수출품 export

such'urhada 수출하다 export

such'uröptcha 수출업자 exporter (*person*)

such'wiin 수취인 recipient, receiver; payee

suda 수다 chatter

sudajaeng-i 수다쟁이 chatterbox

sudal 수달 otter

sudan 수단 means, way

sudasŭröun 수다스러운 chatty

suda ttölda 수다 떨다 chatter, talk

sudo 수도 capital (*of country*); metropolis; waterworks

sudongjögin 수동적인 passive

sudong p̆ureik'ŭ 수동 브레이크 parking brake

sudongt'ae 수동태 passive GRAM

sudosa 수도사 monk

sudosŭng kat'ŭn 수도승 같은 monastic

sudowön 수도원 monastery; convent; abbey

sudu 수두 chicken pox

sugaeng 수갱 shaft

sugamja 수감자 inmate

suganghada 수강하다 take a course

sugap 수갑 handcuffs

sugida 숙이다 bow, lower

sugöjip 숙어집 phrasebook

sugön 수건 towel; washcloth

sugön köri 수건 걸이 towel rail

sugo 수고 effort, struggle; *sugo-haseyo* 수고하세요 keep up the good work (*when taking one's leave of s.o. who is working*)

sugong 수공 handiwork

sugong-öptcha 수공업자 artisan

sugongp'um 수공품 handiwork; handmade goods

sugong-ŭi 수공의 handmade

sugong-ye 수공예 handicraft

sugorŭl akkiji annŭn 수고를 아끼지 않는 painstaking

sugŭrödŭlda 수그러들다 die down

sugu 수구 water polo

suhaenghada 수행하다 conduct, carry out

suhage nŭnghan 수학에 능한 mathematical

suhagŭi 수학의 mathematical

suhak 수학 mathematics, math

suhaktcha 수학자 mathematician

suhamul pogwanso 수하물 보관소 (*baggage*) checkroom

suhoja 수호자 protector

suhwa 수화 sign language

suhwagi 수화기 receiver TELEC

suhwak 수확 crop

suhwak'ada 수확하다 reap

suhwamul 수화물 baggage; luggage; hand baggage

suhwamul k'ülleim 수화물 클레임 baggage reclaim

suhwamul pogwantchŭng 수화물 보관증 baggage check

suhwamul unbanch'a 수화물 운반차 baggage cart

suhwamul yölch'a 수화물 열차 baggage car

suhwa pöt'ŭn 수화 버튼 hook TELEC

suhyöl 수혈 blood transfusion

suigi choŭn 수익이 좋은 profitable

suibi ch'ungbunhan 수입이 충분한 financially comfortable

suik 수익 proceeds

suikssöng 수익성 profitability

suimnyo 수임료 retainer

suip 수입 import; receipts FIN

suiptcha 수입자 importer

suip'ada 수입하다 import

sujang 수장 burial at sea

suji 수지 resin

sujiga mat-tta 수지가 맞다 be profitable, pay

sujigŭi 수직의 vertical; perpendicular

sujigŭro ttöröjida 수직으로 떨어지다 plummet

sujip 수집 collection

sujipkka 수집가 collector

sujip'ada 수집하다 collect

sujŏ 수저 spoon and chopsticks

sujŏng 수정 amendment, modification, revision; crystal

sujŏng-aek 수정액 whiteout, correcting fluid

sujŏnghada 수정하다 amend, revise

sujŏngjuŭi 수정주의 revisionism

sujŏngshik'ida 수정시키다 fertilize

sujubŏhada 수줍어하다 be shy

sujubŏhanŭn 수줍어하는 shy; coy

sujubŭm 수줍음 shyness

sujun 수준 level

sujung hohŭpkki 수중 호흡기 air cylinder

sujung-iksŏn 수중익선 hydrofoil

sujung-ŭi 수중의 aquatic

sukch'ŏng 숙청 purge

sukch'ŏnghada 숙청하다 purge

sukch'wi 숙취 hangover

suk-kko 숙고 consideration, thought

suk-kkohada 숙고하다 contemplate, think about, deliberate; debate

sukppak shisŏl 숙박 시설 accommodations

sukssŏng 숙성 ripeness

sukssŏnghan 숙성한 ripe; mellow

suktche 숙제 assignment; homework

suk'ŏsŭi 수컷의 male

suk'ŏt 수컷 male (of animal, bird, fish); cock

suk'oyang-i 수코양이 tomcat

sul 술 liquor; fringe; tassel; tuft

sul chanch'i 술 잔치 drinking party

sul ch'wihan 술 취한 drunk; intoxicated

sulgorae 술고래 heavy drinker

sulkkun 술꾼 drunk

sullye 순례 pilgrimage

sullyeja 순례자 pilgrim

sulp'ŭm 슬픔 sorrow, sadness

sultchan 술잔 stemware

sultchip 술집 bar

sultchip yŏjong-ŏbwŏn 술집 여종업원 bartender

sum 숨 breath; *sumŭl kip'i tŭrŏ mashida* 숨을 깊이 들어 마시다 take a deep breath; *sumi ch'ada* 숨이 차다 be out of breath, pant; *sumŭl chugida* 숨을 죽이다 hold one's breath; gulp; *sumŭl hŏlttŏgida* 숨을 헐떡이다 gasp for

breath; *sumŭl naeshwida* 숨을 내쉬다 breathe out; *sumŭl tŭryŏ mashida* 숨을 들여 마시다 breathe in

sumanŭn 수많은 a great many, a large number of

sumbakkoktchil 숨바꼭질 hide-and-seek

sumch'an 숨찬 breathless

sumgida 숨기다 hide, conceal; hold back

sumgimŏmnŭn 숨김없는 open, honest, frank

sumgimŏpsshi 숨김없이 openly, honestly, frankly

sumgyŏjin 숨겨진 hidden

summak'il chŏngdoŭi 숨막힐 정도의 breathtaking

sumnŭn kot 숨는 곳 hiding place

sumshwida 숨쉬다 breathe

sumtta 숨다 hide; go into hiding

sumt'ong 숨통 windpipe

sumyŏn 수면 surface; *sumyŏni orŏbut-tta* 수면이 얼어붙다 freeze over

sumyŏng 수명 life (of machine)

sumyŏnje 수면제 sleeping pill

sun 순 pure silver, gold; complete, total ◊ ten days; ten years

-sun -순 order; *yŏllyŏngsunŭro* 연령순으로 in order of age

sunch'al 순찰 patrol

sunch'alch'a 순찰차 patrol car

sunch'algwan 순찰관 patrolman

sunch'arhada 순찰하다 patrol; be on patrol

sun-gan 순간 moment, instant

sun-gan chŏngjishik'ida 순간 정지시키다 freeze video

sun-ganŭi 순간의 momentary

sungbae 숭배 worship

sungbaehada 숭배하다 worship; idolize

sungmo 숙모 aunt (father's younger brother's wife)

sungmyŏn 숙면 sound sleep

sungnyŏ 숙녀 lady

sungnyŏndoen 숙련된 skilled, expert

sungnyŏn-gong 숙련공 skilled worker

sun-gyŏrŭl ilt'a 순결을 잃다 lose one's virginity

sun-gyoja 순교자 martyr

sunhada 순하다 be gentle; be mild

sunhan 순한 mild; docile

sunhang 순항 cruise

sunhanghada 순항하다 cruise

sunhangsŏn 순항선 cruise liner

sunhan soktto 순항 속도 cruising speed

sunhwan 순환 cycle; circulation

suniik 순이익 net profit

sunjinhada 순진하다 be innocent, be pure

sunjinham 순진함 innocence

sunjinhan 순진한 innocent; naïve

sunjŏnhan 순전한 unadulterated, absolute

sunjong 순종 obedience

sunjonghada 순종하다 obey

sunjonghanŭn 순종하는 obedient

sunjongjŏgin 순종적인 submissive

sunjoroun 순조로운 smooth

sunmu 순무 turnip

sunnyang 숫양 ram

sunoe hoedam 수뇌 회담 summit POL

sunot'a 수놓다 embroider

sunp'ung 순풍 tail wind

sunshik-kkane 순식간에 in an instant, quickly

sunshik-kkanŭi 순식간의 instantaneous

sunsŏ 순서 sequence; system; *ajik tangshin sunsŏga animnida* 아직 당신 순서가 아닙니다 it's not your turn yet; *sunsŏga pakkwin* 순서가 바뀐 out of order, not in sequence

sunsŏdaero 순서대로 in sequence; *sunsŏdaero chŏngnihada* 순서대로 정리하다 order, put in sequence

sunsuhan 순수한 pure; natural; neat; net

sunsuibŭl ollida 순수입을 올리다 earn; clear, net

sunsuik 순수익 profit margin

sunŭnghada 순응하다 conform; *...e sunŭnghayŏ* ...에 순응하여 in line with

sunyŏ 수녀 nun

suŏbil 수업일 school days

suŏp 수업 tuition; lesson, class

sup 숲 forest; wood

suppŏp 수법 gimmick (*promotional*)

sup'ŏmak'et 수퍼마켓 supermarket

sup'ŭ 수프 soup

sup'ul 수풀 tuft

sup'yŏng kŏnnŏlmok 수평 건널목 grade crossing

sup'yŏngsŏn 수평선 horizon (*at sea*)

sup'yo 수표 check FIN

sup'yoch'aek 수표책 checkbook

surak 수락 *fml* acceptance

surak'ada 수락하다 *fml* take up, accept *offer*; undertake, take on *task*

suran 수란 poached egg

sure ch'wihada 술에 취하다 get drunk

surigong 수리공 repairman

surihada 수리하다 repair, recondition

suri kkaeda 술이 깨다 sober up

surishik'ida 수리시키다 get fixed

suro 수로 waterway, channel; watercourse

surŭl mashida 술을 마시다 drink *alcohol*

surŭl seda 수를 세다 count

suryŏk chŏn-gi 수력 전기 hydroelectricity ◊ hydroelectric

suryŏn 수련 water lily

suryŏng-in 수령인 recipient

suryŏngchŭng 수령증 delivery note

suryut'an 수류탄 grenade

susa 수사 rhetoric

susaek 수색 search, hunt

susaekttae 수색대 search party

susaek yŏngch'ang 수색 영장 search warrant

susaek'ada 수색하다 search for; trace

susaek'anŭn 수색하는 searching

susang 수상 premier

susang ch'angnyuk'ada 수상 착륙하다 splash down

susanghada 수상하다 win a prize; be suspicious

susanghan 수상한 suspicious, fishy

susangja 수상자 prizewinner; medalist

susangsŭk'i 수상스키 waterskiing

suseshik pyŏn-gi 수세식 변기 water closet, flush toilet

sushin 수신 reception (*for phone etc*); for the attention of

sushin-gi 수신기 receiver RAD

sushinin 수신인 addressee

sushinin pudamŭi chŏnhwa 수신인 부담의 전화 collect call

sushinin pudamŭro chŏnhwahada 수신인 부담으로 전화하다 call collect

sushinyŏburŭl allida 수신여부를 알리다 acknowledge

susŏk paiollinisŭt'ŭ 수석 바이올리니스트 concert master

susŏk weit'ŏ 수석 웨이터 head waiter

susŏn 수선 repair; alteration

susŏnhada 수선하다 mend, repair

suso 수소 hydrogen

susong 수송 transport; transportation; *susong chung-in* 수송 중인 in transit

susonghada 수송하다 transport

suso p'okt'an 수소 폭탄 hydrogen bomb

susuham 수수함 modesty

susuhan 수수한 modest; conservative

susukkekki 수수께끼 puzzle, mystery; riddle; enigma

susukkekkigat'ŭn 수수께끼같은 enigmatic

susul 수술 surgery; operation

susulshil 수술실 operating room

susurŭl hada 수술을 하다 operate

susurŭl pat-tta 수술을 받다 have an operation, undergo surgery

susurhada 수술하다 operate on

susuryo 수수료 commission

sut 숱 thickness; *such'i manŭn mŏri* 숱이 많은 머리 thick hair

sut 숯 charcoal

sutcha 숫자 numeral, digit, figure

sutchap'an 숫자판 numeric keys

sutch'onggak 숫총각 virgin (*male*)

sutkkarak 숟가락 spoon

sutppure kuwŏjin 숯불에 구워진 charbroiled

sut'ak 수탉 cock (*chicken*)

suŭisa 수의사 veterinarian

suŭn 수은 mercury, quicksilver

suwi 수위 janitor; water level

suwŏnji 수원지 source

suwŏrhada 수월하다 be easy

suwŏrhan 수월한 easy, simple

suyang pŏdŭl 수양 버들 weeping willow

suyŏhada 수여하다 award, confer

suyŏk 수역 body of water

suyŏm 수염 whiskers; bristles

suyŏng 수영 swimming; swim

suyŏngbok 수영복 swimsuit

suyŏnghada 수영하다 swim

suyŏngjang 수영장 swimming pool

suyŏngppŏp 수영법 stroke (*swimming*)

suyo 수요 demand COM; *suyoga it-tta* 수요가 있다 be in demand

suyoil 수요일 Wednesday

suyong inwŏn 수용 인원 intake (*of people*)

suyongnyŏk 수용력 capacity

suyongso 수용소 camp

swaebingsŏn 쇄빙선 icebreaker

swaedo 쇄도 deluge; stampede

swaedohada 쇄도하다 deluge

swaegol 쇄골 collarbone

T

ta 다 completely, fully; *ta ssŏbŏrida* 다 써버리다 run out of; use up

tabal 다발 wad (*of paper*); wisp (*of hair*)

tabang 다방 café

tabunhi 다분히 no doubt, probably

ta charan 다 자란 full-grown

tach'aeropkke hada 다채롭게 하다 jazz up

tach'aeroun 다채로운 colorful

tach'ida 닫히다 close

tach'ige hada 다치게 하다 hurt

tach'iji anŭn 다치지 않은 unhurt

tach'in 닫힌 shut, closed

tach'in te ŏmnŭn 다친 데 없는 unhurt, unscathed

tach'ŭl naerida 닻을 내리다 anchor

tach'ŭl ollida 닻을 올리다 weigh anchor

tadarŭda 다다르다 span

tado 다도 tea ceremony

tadŭmtta 다듬다 polish, perfect; trim *hair*; smooth out; *k'allo tadŭmtta* 칼로 다듬다 scrape

tae 대 great; huge ◊ versus ◊ stem ◊ countword for vehicles, airplanes, machines, pipe tobacco, cigarettes

taean 대안 alternative

taebon 대본 script

taebu 대부 loan; godfather

taebubun 대부분 most

taebubunŭi 대부분의 most

taebubunŭn 대부분은 mostly, mainly

taebumo 대부모 godparent

taebyŏnin 대변인 spokesperson; mouthpiece

taebyŏnja 대변자 representative

taech'adaejop'yo 대차대조표 balance sheet

taech'ebup'um 대체부품 replacement part

taech'ehal su ŏmnŭn 대체할 수 없는 irreplaceable

taech'e ŏdie 대체 어디에 wherever

taech'ep'um 대체품 replacement

taech'ero 대체로 on the whole, as a rule

taech'ing 대칭 symmetry

taech'ingjŏgin 대칭적인 symmetrical

taech'owŏn 대초원 prairie

taech'u 대추 date (*fruit*)

taech'ung hult'ŏboda 대충 훑어보다 look over

taeda 대다 pad (*with material*)

taedamhada 대담한 be bold

taedanhage 대단하게 enormously

taedanhan 대단한 enormous, tremendous; serious ◊ a great deal of; *kŭnŭn taedanhan inmuriyeyo* 그는 대단한 인물이예요 he's a real character; *tangshinŭn taedanha-gunyo* 당신은 대단하군요 you're incredible

taedanhi 대단히 very, extremely, remarkably; *taedanhi manŭn* 대단히 많은 a great many

taedap 대답 answer, reply

taedap'ada 대답하다 answer, reply

taedasu 대다수 majority

taedoshi 대도시 metropolis

taedoshiŭi 대도시의 metropolitan

taedŭlbo 대들보 girder

taedŭnghada 대등하다 equalize

taegae 대개 principally, mainly, chiefly

taegakssŏnŭi 대각선의 diagonal

taegang 대강 general features ◊ roughly; cursorily

taegang hult'ŏboda 대강 훑어보다 flip through

taegang miruŏ poda 대강 미루어 보다 judge, estimate

taegang-ŭi 대강의 approximate, rough; sweeping *generalization*

taegi 대기 atmosphere

taegihada 대기하다 stand by, be ready

taegihago innŭn 대기하고 있는 on

standby

taegija myŏngdan 대기자 명단 waiting list

taegi oyŏm 대기 오염 atmospheric pollution

taegishil 대기실 waiting room

taegŏlle 대걸레 mop

taegŭm 대금 (large) flute

taegŭmŏptcha 대금업자 money-lender

taegŭm sanghwan 대금 상환 COD, collect on delivery

taegyŏl 대결 confrontation; clash; dispute

taegyumoŭi 대규모의 large scale

taehae(sŏ) 대해(서): *...e taehae(sŏ)* ...에 대해(서) about; regarding

taehagwŏn 대학원 graduate school

taehagwŏnsaeng 대학원생 graduate

taehak 대학 university, school

taehak-kkyo 대학교 university

taehak kyojŏng 대학 교정 university campus

taehakssaeng 대학생 university student

taehakssal 대학살 carnage, slaughter

taehak k'aemp'ŏsŭ 대학 캠퍼스 university campus

taehamul 대하물 epic

taehan 대한: *...e taehan* ...에 대한 about

Taehanjeguk 대한제국 Great Han Empire

Taehanmin-guk 대한민국 Republic of Korea, ROK

taehap chogae 대합 조개 clam

taehapsshil 대합실 departure lounge

taehayŏ 대하여: *...e taehayŏ* ...에 대하여 with respect to, with regard to

taehit'ŭ 대히트 smash hit

taehit'ŭjak 대히트작 blockbuster

taehoe 대회 convention, rally; contest

taehoe ch'amgaja 대회 참가자 conventioneer

taehollan 대혼란 chaos

taehongsu 대홍수 deluge

taehwa 대화 talk; conversation; dialog; *taehwarŭl chungdanhada* 대화를 중단하다 break off, stop talking

taehwasangja 대화상자 dialog box COMPUT

taehyŏng 대형 large size

taeja 대자 godchild; godson

taejesajang 대제사장 high priest

taejŏnhada 대전하다 meet (*in competition*)

taejŏp 대접 dish; bowl; beaker

taejŏp'ada 대접하다 entertain; treat

taejo 대조 contrast

taejohada 대조하다 contrast

taejojŏgin 대조적인 contrasting

taejop'yo 대조표 checklist

taejo p'yoshirŭl hada 대조 표시를 하다 check off

taejung 대중 the public, the masses ◊ popular, mass

taejunggayo 대중가요 pop MUS

taejung kyot'ong 대중 교통 public transportation

taejung maech'e 대중 매체 mass media

taejungtchŏgin 대중적인 popular, general, widespread; mass, downmarket

taema 대마 hemp

taemach'o 대마초 cannabis, hashish

Taeman 대만 Taiwan ◊ Taiwanese

Taemanin 대만인 Taiwanese (*person*)

Taemanŏ 대만어 Taiwanese (*dialect*)

taemŏriŭi 대머리의 bald

taemo 대모 godmother

taemosŭro paktta 대못으로 박다 rivet

taemot 대못 rivet; spike

taemŭro maktta 댐으로 막다 dam

taemun 대문 gate

taemuntcha 대문자 capital (letter)

taemyŏngsa 대명사 pronoun; *...ŭi taemyŏngsaga toeda* ...의 대명사가 되다 be a byword for, be synonymous with

taemyŏnhago 대면하고 face to face

taenaje 대낮에 in broad daylight

taenamu 대나무 bamboo

taenggŭranghanŭn sori 댕그랑하는 소리 chink (*sound*)

taensŭ p'ati 댄스 파티 dance

taenyŏ 대녀 god-daughter

taep'ae 대패 plane (*tool*)
taep'ihada 대피하다 evacuate, leave
taep'iho 대피호 shelter
taep'ishik'ida 대피시키다 evacuate
taep'iro 대피로 pull-in
taep'iso 대피소 shelter
taep'o 대포 artillery
taep'ok ollida 대폭 올리다 bump up
taep'yodan 대표단 delegation
taep'yohada 대표하다 represent, stand for
taep'yoja 대표자 representative, delegate
taep'yojŏgin myŏn 대표적인 면 cross-section
taep'yoro immyŏnghada 대표로 임명하다 delegate
taeri 대리 deputy
taerihada 대리하다 represent, act as
taeriin 대리인 agent, representative, proxy; substitute
taerikkwŏn 대리권 proxy, authority
taerimo 대리모 surrogate mother
taerip 대립 conflict, disagreement
taerisŏk 대리석 marble
taeryagŭi 대략의 approximate
taeryak 대략 approximately
taeryang 대량 large quantity
taeryang hakssal 대량 학살 massacre, slaughter
taeryang saengsan 대량 생산 mass production
taeryang saengsanhada 대량 생산하다 mass-produce
taeryang-ŭi 대량의 wholesale, indiscriminate
taeryang-ŭro 대량으로 in bulk
taeryŏng 대령 colonel
taeryugŭi 대륙의 continental
taeryuk 대륙 continent
taesa 대사 speech; ambassador
taesagwan 대사관 embassy
taesang 대상 object
taesangja myŏngdan 대상자 명단 hit list
taesangp'ojin 대상포진 shingles
taesarŭl illŏjuda 대사를 일러주다 prompt *actor*
taeshi 대시 dash
taeshikka 대식가 glutton
taeshilp'ae 대실패 fiasco

taeshin 대신 substitute; compensation ◊ instead of; *taeshin kiyonghada* 대신 기용하다 make a substitution SP
taeshine 대신에 instead; instead of
taeshinhada 대신하다 replace, stand in for; take over; substitute
taeshinhaesŏ hada 대신해서 하다 stand in for; *narŭl/kŭrŭl taeshinhaesŏ* 나를/그를 대신해서 on my/his behalf
taeshinhal 대신할 alternative
taesŏnggong 대성공 coup
taesŏnggong-ida 대성공이다 be a success
taesŏnggong-ŭl kŏduda 대성공을 거두다 hit the bull's-eye
Taesŏyang 대서양 Atlantic
Taesŏyang hoengdanŭi 대서양 횡단의 transatlantic
taesuroptchi anŭn 대수롭지 않은 peripheral
taet'ongnyŏng 대통령 president
taet'ongnyŏng imgi 대통령 임기 presidency (*term*)
taet'ongnyŏngjik 대통령직 presidency (*office*)
taeŭnghanŭn 대응하는 corresponding, equivalent
taeu 대우 treatment
taeuhada 대우하다 treat, behave toward
taeyŏk 대역 double (*person*)
taeyŏl 대열 file; ranks MIL
taeyong 대용 substitution
taeyongp'um 대용품 substitute
taeyuhaeng 대유행 all the rage, fashionable ◊ craze, fad; *ch'oegŭnŭi taeyuhaeng* 최근의 대유행 the latest craze
tagagada 다가가다 walk up to
tagak'wa 다각화 diversification
tagak'washik'ida 다각화시키다 diversify
tagaoda 다가오다 close in, move closer
tagaonŭn 다가오는 forthcoming
tagugŏŭi 다국어의 multilingual
taguktchŏk 다국적 multinational
taguktchŏk kiŏp 다국적 기업 multinational company

tagwa 다과 refreshments; tea and cookies

ta hada 다 하다 run out (*of time*); carry out, perform

tahaenghido 다행히도 thankfully, luckily

tahaengsŭrŏpkkedo 다행스럽게도 mercifully, thankfully

taiamondŭ 다이아몬드 diamond

taibing 다이빙 (high) diving

taibing tae 다이빙 대 diving board

taibŏ 다이버 diver

tainŏmait'ŭ 다이너마이트 dynamite

taiŏl 다이알 dial; *taiŏrŭl tollida* 다이얼을 돌리다 dial

taiŏri 다이어리 (appointments) diary

taiŏt'ŭ 다이어트 diet

taiŏt'ŭhada 다이어트하다 diet; be on a diet

tajaedanŭnghan 다재다능한 versatile

tajagŭi 다작의 prolific

tajŏngdagamhan 다정다감한 warm-hearted

tajŏnghada 다정하다 be affectionate; be friendly

tajŏnghan 다정한 affectionate, loving; genial; pleasant, friendly

tajung maech'e 다중 매체 multimedia

tak 닭 chicken

takkanaeda 닦아내다 wipe off

tak-kkogi 닭고기 chicken (*as food*)

taktta 닦다 wipe; clean; wash; mop up

takttari 닭다리 drumstick (*of poultry*)

tak'yument'ŏri 다큐멘터리 documentary (program)

tak'yument'ŏri tŭrama 다큐멘터리 드라마 docudrama

tal 달 month; moon ◊ lunar

talch'angnyuksŏn 달착륙선 lunar module

talda 달다 fit, install; attach; be sweet

talge hada 달게 하다 sweeten

talgyal 달걀 egg

talgyal kkŏptchil 달걀 껍질 eggshell

talgyal wansuk 달걀 완숙 hard-boiled egg

talgyarhyŏng 달걀형 oval

talk'e hada 닳게 하다 wear; wear away; damage

talk'omhada 달콤하다 be sweet

tallabut-tta 달라붙다 stick, jam; stick to, adhere to; cling

tallak 단락 passage; short circuit

tallanggŏrida 달랑거리다 dangle

tallida 달리다 hang; depend; be attached; run short; not be enough; run, rush; drive

talligi 달리기 run; running SP

tallŏ 달러 dollar

tallyŏdŭlda 달려들다 tackle

tallyŏk 달력 calendar

tallyŏnhada 단련하다 build up

tallyŏnshik'ida 단련시키다 exercise

talppich'i ŏrin 달빛이 어린 moonlit

talppit 달빛 moonlight

talp'aeng-i 달팽이 snail

taltta 닳다 run down

tam 담 wall

tambae 담배 tobacco; cigarette; *tambaerŭl samgahae chushigi paramnida* 담배를 삼가해 주시기 바랍니다 please refrain from smoking; *tambae p'iuda* 담배 피우다 smoke a cigarette

tambae kkongch'o 담배 꽁초 cigarette butt

tamdamhan 담담한 matter-of-fact, calm; unemotional

tamdang 담당 charge ◊ in charge

tamdanghada 담당하다 take charge of

tamdang-ida 담당이다 be in charge

tamgŭda 담그다 immerse, soak

tamhwangsaek 담황색 cream (*color*)

tamjaeng-i 담쟁이 ivy

tamkko it-tta 담고 있다 contain

tamnyo 담요 blanket

tamsŏk 담석 gallstone

tamtta 담다 hold, contain; resemble, take after; *nuguwa tamtta* 누구와 닮다 be like s.o.

tamyo 담요 rug

tan 단 column (*in newspaper*); rung; hit squad; tuck (*in dress*) ◊ sweet ◊ countword for firewood, spinach etc

tanbaektchil 단백질 protein

tanbal 단발 bob (*haircut*)

tanch'e 단체 society, organization

tanch'e chŏngshin 단체 정신 team spirit

tanch'e hyŏp'oe 단체 협회 association, organization

tanch'e kyosŏp 단체 교섭 collective bargaining

tanch'ŏl 단철 wrought iron

tan ch'ŏri 단처리 braid, trimming

tanch'ŭng 단층 rift (in earth)

tanch'u 단추 button

tanch'ukk'i 단축키 shortcut key COMPUT

tanch'u kumŏng 단추구멍 buttonhole

tanch'urŭl ch'aeuda 단추를 채우다 button (up)

tandanhada 단단하다 be solid; be firm; be tight

tandanhi 단단히 tight

tandanhi choida 단단히 조이다 tighten

tandanhi ch'unggyŏgŭl padŭn 단단히 충격을 받은 shattered, upset

tandanhi muktta 단단히 묶다 lash down (with rope)

tandanhi pak'in 단단히 박힌 stuck fast

tando 단도 dagger

tandogŭi 단독의 single-handed

tang 당 party; faction

tang- 당- this; that; the present; *tangshi* 당시 that time

-tang -당 per; *irindang* 일인당 per head, per person

tangbŏn 당번 rota

tangbun-gan 당분간 for the moment, for the time being

tangch'an 당찬 brisk

tangch'ŏmdoen 당첨된 winning

tangch'ŏmja 당첨자 winner

tangdanghan 당당한 regal

tanggida 당기다 pull

tanggŭn 당근 carrot

tanggu 당구 pool; snooker; billiards

tanggudae 당구대 pool table

tanggujang 당구장 pool hall

tangguk 당국 the authorities

tanghok 당혹 perplexity

tanghok'age hada 당혹하게 하다 perplex, puzzle

tanghok'an 당혹한 perplexed, puzzled

tanghwang 당황 alarm, panic

tanghwanghada 당황하다 be embarrassed; panic, get flustered

tanghwanghae hada 당황해 하다 be baffled

tanghwanghage hada 당황하게 하다 baffle; embarrass; disconcert

tanghwanghage hanŭn 당황하게 하는 embarrassing

tanghwanghan 당황한 embarrassed; disconcerted

tan-gigan 단기간 short-term

tan-gijŏgŭro 단기적으로 in the short term

tang-ilch'igi yŏhaeng 당일치기 여행 daytrip

tangjang 당장 right now, immediately

tangjigida 당직이다 be on duty

tangjwa yegŭm kujwa 당좌 예금 구좌 checking account

tangmil 당밀 molasses

tangnagwi 당나귀 donkey

tangnyŏnhada 당연하다 be natural, be right

tangnyŏnhan 당연한 natural, obvious; *muŏsŭl tang-yŏnhan illo yŏgida* 무엇을 당연한 일로 여기다 take sth for granted

tangnyŏnhi 당연히 naturally, of course; automatically

tangnyoppyŏng 당뇨병 diabetes ◊ diabetic

tan-gŏri yukssang kyŏnggi 단거리 육상 경기 sprint

tan-gŏri yukssang sŏnsu 단거리 육상 선수 sprinter

tan-gol 단골 custom; regular (person)

tan-gollo tanida 단골로 다니다 patronize, be a customer of

tangshin 당신 (polite) you

tangshin chashin 당신 자신 (polite) yourself

tangshindŭl chashin 당신들 자신 (polite) yourselves

tangshinŭi 당신의 (polite) your

tangsŏndoeda 당선되다 be elected; *sŏn-gŏro tangsŏndoen* 선거로

당선된 elected
tangsŏnja 당선자 winner
tan-gye 단계 stage, period, phase
tan-gyejŏguro chegŏhada
단계적으로 제거하다 phase out
tan-gyejŏguro t'uip'ada 단계적으로
투입하다 phase in
tan-gyŏl solidarity
tang-yŏnhae! 당연해! no wonder!
tang-yŏnhi 당연히 of course,
naturally
tan hanaŭi 단 하나의 sole, only;
single, solitary, lone
tanhohan 단호한 decisive, resolute,
emphatic; purposeful, determined,
relentless; stalwart
tanilssŏng 단일성 unity
tanja 단자 terminal ELEC
tanji 단지 only, just ◊ mere ◊ jar;
container; urn; housing development
tanjŏl 단절 rupture
tanjŏnghada 단정하다 determine,
establish; be neat; be decent
tanjŏnghan 단정한 tidy, neat; decent,
upright
tanjŏnghi hada 단정히 하다 tidy
oneself up
tanjŏngtchŏgin 단정적인 assertive
tanjoroptta 단조롭다 be monotonous;
be boring
tanjoroum 단조로움 monotony
tankkwa taehak 단과 대학 college
tanmal changch'i 단말 장치
terminal COMPUT
tanmyŏnghan 단명한 short-lived
tannyŏm 단념 resignation
tannyŏmhada 단념하다 relinquish,
abandon
tannyŏmshik'ida 단념시키다 deter;
Xi/ga Yŭl/rŭl tannyŏmhage hada
X이/가 Y을/를 단념하게 하다 put X
off Y
tanŏ 단어 word
tanp'a 단파 short wave
tanp'ungnamu 단풍나무 maple
tanp'yŏn 단편 fragment, shred
tanp'yŏnsosŏl 단편소설 short story
tanp'yŏntchŏgin 단편적인 sketchy;
piecemeal; fragmentary
tansang 단상 platform, stage
tanshigan 단시간 a short time

tanshik 단식 singles (*in tennis*)
tansŏ 단서 proviso, stipulation
tanso 단소 bamboo flute
tansok 단속 crackdown
tansok'ada 단속하다 crack down,
clamp down
tansu 단수 singular GRAM
tansume 단숨에 at a stretch, non-
stop; *tansume ssŭda* 단숨에 쓰다
dash off, write quickly; *tansume
tallyŏgada* 단숨에 달려가다 dash;
make a dash for
tansunhada 단순하다 be simple; be
unsophisticated
tansunhwahada 단순화하다 simplify
tansuro 단수로 in the singular
tansuŭi 단수의 singular GRAM
tantchŏm 단점 disadvantage,
drawback
tantcho 단조 minor MUS
tanŭl naerida 단을 내리다 let down
dress etc
tanwi 단위 unit (of measurement)
tanwi wŏnkka 단위 원가 unit cost
tanyŏnhi 단연히 easily, by far
tap 답 answer
tapp'ahada 답파하다 cover, travel
tapssahada 답사하다 travel; explore
taptchang 답장 reply (*letter*)
taptchanghada 답장하다 reply (*to
letter*)
tapttap'ada 답답하다 be gloomy; be
stifling; be hidebound; be anxious
tapttap'an 답답한 stifling
tap'ada 답하다 answer
tarajida 닳아지다 wear; wear away,
wear out
tarakppang 다락방 attic, loft
taramjwi 다람쥐 squirrel
taranada 달아나다 run away, rush off
taraorŭda 달아오르다 glow
tarappajin 닳아빠진 well-worn,
worn-out
tara ttŏrŏjida 닳아 떨어지다 wear
out
tari 다리 bridge; leg
tarimi 다리미 iron
tarimjil 다림질 ironing
tarimjilttae 다림질대 ironing board
tarimjirhada 다림질하다 iron; press;
do the ironing

tarimjiri p'iryoŏmnŭn 다림질이 필요없는 non-iron

tarŭda 다르다 differ, be different

tarŭge 다르게 differently; *...wa / kwanŭn tarŭge* ...와 / 과는 다르게 as distinct from

tarŭn 닳은 threadbare; dead *battery*

tarŭn 다른 different; distinct; another; other

tarŭn kŏt 다른 것 another

tarŭn nugun-ga 다른 누군가 someone else

tarŭn ŏttŏn kŏt 다른 어떤 것 something else

taruda 다루다 handle; manage; treat

tarugi himdŭn 다루기 힘든 unruly; tricky

tarugi ŏryŏun 다루기 어려운 awkward *customer*; not user-friendly

tarugi shwiun 다루기 쉬운 manageable; docile

taryang 다량 mass

tasahan 다사한 eventful

tasan 다산 fertility

tasanŭi 다산의 fertile

tashi 다시 again; *tashi han pŏn* 다시 한 번 once more

tashi chada 다시 자다 go back to sleep

tashi ch'aeuda 다시 채우다 refill

tashi ch'irhada 다시 칠하다 repaint

tashi ch'usŭrida 다시 추스리다 reconstruct

tashi hwaginhada 다시 확인하다 doublecheck

tashi kamtta 다시 감다 rewind

tashi nat'anada 다시 나타나다 reappear

tashi padadŭrida 다시 받아들이다 take back, accept back

tashi pangmunhada 다시 방문하다 call back

tashi ssŭda 다시 쓰다 rewrite

tasŏt 다섯 five

tasŏt pŏntchaeŭi 다섯 번째의 fifth

taso 다소 rather, sort of, somewhat

tasŭrida 다스리다 govern, rule

tasuŭi 다수의 many

tat 닻 anchor

tatch'ida 닫히다 shut

tatki 닫기 close COMPUT

tatkki shwiun 닿기 쉬운 easy to reach, accessible

tat-tta 닫다 close; fasten; be closed

tat'a 닿다 reach

tat'ŭ 다트 dart

tat'uda 다투다 fight; quarrel; *...ŭl / rŭl wihae tat'uda* ...을 / 를 위해 다투다 contend for

tat'um 다툼 quarrel

taŭm 다음 next; *taŭmŭi kŏt* 다음의 것 the following

taŭme 다음에 after, next; *taŭme kyesok* 다음에 계속 to be continued; *taŭmgwa kat'ŭn* 다음과 같은 as follows; *taŭm pun?* 다음 분? who's next?

taŭmnal 다음날 the day after

Tau Chonsŭ P'yŏnggyun Chuga 다우 존스 평균 주가 Dow Jones Average

taunnodŭ 다운로드 download

taunnodinghada 다운로딩하다 download

tayanghada 다양하다 be diverse

tayanghage twisŏkkin 다양하게 뒤섞인 miscellaneous

tayanghan 다양한 diverse, varied; multiple

tayangssŏng 다양성 diversity, variety

tayongdoŭi 다용도의 all-purpose; adaptable

-tcha -자 (*suffix for persons*) → *-ja* -자

tchada 짜다 structure, plan; press, squeeze; weave; spin; wring; be salty

tchaenggŭrŏnghanŭn sori 찡그렁하는 소리 clink

tchajangmyŏn 짜장면 noodles and black bean sauce

tchajŭngnadorok 짜증나도록 frustratingly

tchajŭngnage hada 짜증나게 하다 irritate

tchajŭngnage hanŭn 짜증나게 하는 irritating

tchajŭngnanŭn 짜증나는 irritating; frustrating; trying, annoying

tchajŭng-ŭl chal naenŭn 짜증을 잘 내는 irritable

tchak 짝 partner; mate (*of animal*)

tchakssuŭi 짝수의 even *number*
tchaktchit-tta 짝짓다 mate
tchalbŭn 짧은 short
tchalkke charŭda 짧게 자르다 cut shorter; crop
tchalkke hada 짧게 하다 shorten
tchalkke pomyŏn 짧게 보면 in the short run
tchallida 짤리다 ax *employee*
tchalptta 짧다 be short
tcham 짬 slot (*in schedule*)
tcha match'uda 짜 맞추다 piece together
tchan 짠 salty
tchaptcharhan 짭짤한 savory
tchatchŭng 짜증 tantrum
tchiburŏttŭrida 찌부러뜨리다 mangle, crush
tchida 찌다 steam
tchigŏ mŏktta 찍어 먹다 dip, dunk
tchigŏ naegi 찍어 내기 chop
tchigŭrŏttŭrida 찌그러뜨리다 crush; *nullŏ tchigŭrŏttŭrida* 눌러 찌그러뜨리다 squash, crush
tchijŏjida 찢어지다 split
tchijŏjige kananhan 찢어지게 가난한 poverty-stricken
tchijŏjigi shwiun 찢어지기 쉬운 flimsy
tchijŏjin 찢어진 ragged, tattered
tchijŏjin kot 찢어진 곳 slit; tear
tchijŏ yŏlda 찢어 열다 slit; rip open
tchikkŏgi 찌꺼기 dregs
tchiktchigi 찍찍이 Velcro®
tchiktchk-kkŏrida 찍찍거리다 squeak
tchimt'ong 찜통 steamer (*for cooking*)
tchinggŭrida 찡그리다 scowl; contort; screw up *eyes*
tchinggŭrin ŏlgul 찡그린 얼굴 scowl
tchinŭn tŭshi tŏun 찌는 듯이 더운 scorching hot
tchinŭn tŭt'an 찌는 듯한 sweltering
tchip'urida 찌푸리다 frown
tchip'urin 찌푸린 threatening
tchip'urin ŏlgul 찌푸린 얼굴 frown
tchirŭda 찌르다 plunge; thrust; prick; jab; stab; lunge at; *k'allo tchirŭda* 칼로 찌르다 knife, stab
tchirŭregi 찌르레기 blackbird;
starling
tchit-tta 찢다 rip, tear; split
tchit'ŭn 짙은 thick, dense
tchoch'abŏrida 쫓아버리다 chase away; turn away, send away
tchoch'anaeda 쫓아내다 eject; expel; evict
tchoch'a ponaeda 쫓아 보내다 see off, chase away
tchoda 쪼다 peck
tchogaeda 쪼개다 split
tchogaejida 쪼개지다 split
tchok 쪽 page; slice
tchok pŏnho 쪽 번호 page number
tchotkkyŏnada 쫓겨나다 be expelled, be kicked out
-tchŭm -쯤 around, approximately; *tushitchŭm* 두시쯤 around two o'clock
tchugŭlgŏrige hada 쭈글거리게 하다 shrivel
tchuk ppŏt-tta 쭉 뻗다 stretch
tebyu 데뷰 début
teda 데다 get burnt; get scalded
teit'ŏ 데이터 data
teit'ŏ chŏjang 데이터 저장 data storage
teit'ŏ ch'ŏri 데이터 처리 data processing
teit'ŏ peisŭ 데이터 베이스 database
teit'ŏ poho 데이터 보호 data protection
teit'ŏ sujip 데이터 수집 data capture
teit'ŭ 데이트 date, meeting
teit'ŭ hada 데이트하다 date, go out with
teit'ŭ sangdae 데이트 상대 date (*person*)
tek'ŭnosedae 테크노세대 techno music fans
temo 데모 demo, demonstration, protest
temohada 데모하다 demonstrate, protest
temo haengjin 데모 행진 demo, demonstration, march
temo haengjinhada 데모 행진하다 march
temoja 데모자 demonstrator, protester
tenim 데님 denim

Tenishwi p'aesŭch'yuri 데니쉬 패스츄리 Danish pastry
Tenmak'ŭ 덴마크 Denmark ◊ Danish
Tenmak'ŭŏ 덴마크어 Danish
terigo kada 데리고 가다 take, accompany
terigo nagada 데리고 나가다 take out (*to dinner etc*)
terigo oda 데리고 오다 fetch *person, animal*
terirŏ kada 데리러 가다 call for, collect
terirŏ oda 데리러 오다 come for, collect
teryŏdajuda 데려다주다 take back
teryŏgada 데려가다 draw, lead
teryŏoda 데려오다 bring; pick up
teshibel 데시벨 decibel
tesŭk'ŭ 데스크 (reception) desk
teuda 데우다 heat up
teun 데운 heated
tewŏjida 데워지다 warm up
tidimp'an 디딤판 tread
tidimttol 디딤돌 stepping stone
tijain 디자인 design
tijainhada 디자인하다 design, plan
tijain hak-kkyo 디자인 학교 design school
tijainŏ 디자이너 designer
tijel 디젤 diesel
tijit'ŏl 디지털 digital
tillŏ 딜러 dealer (*in card game*)
tinŏ p'at'i 디너 파티 dinner party
tioksshiribo haekssan 디옥시리보 핵산 DNA, deoxyribonucleic acid
tip'olt'ŭkkap 디폴트값 default COMPUT
tisŭk'et 디스켓 disk
tisŭk'et tŭraibŭ 디스켓 드라이브 disk drive
tisŭk'o 디스코 disco
tisŭk'o t'ek 디스코 텍 discotheque
tisŭk'ŭ 디스코 disc
tisŭk'ŭ chak'i 디스크 자키 disc jockey
tisŭp'ŭllei 디스플레이 display COMPUT
tŏ 더 far, much; further; **tŏ chagŭn** 더 작은 fewer; **tŏ chal** 더 잘 better; **chogŭmman tŏ** 조금만 더 a little

more
tŏbinghada 더빙하다 dub
tŏbŭl 더블 double
tŏbŭlbedŭ 더블베드 double bed
tŏbŭlbeisŭ 더블베이스 double-bass
tŏbŭl k'ŭllik 더블클릭 double click COMPUT
tŏch'e kŏllida 덫에 걸리다 be trapped
toch'ŏng 도청 provincial office
tŏch'ŭro chaptta 덫으로 잡다 trap
tŏdŏl ttŏlda 덜덜 떨다 quake, tremble
tŏdŭmgŏrim 더듬거림 impediment (*in speech*)
tŏdŭmgŏrimyŏ ch'at-tta 더듬거리며 찾다 fumble around
tŏdŭmi 더듬이 feeler, antenna
tŏdŭmtta 더듬다 stumble over *words*; **marŭl tŏdŭmtta** 말을 더듬다 stammer, stutter
tŏhada 더하다 add
tŏhagi 더하기 plus (sign)
tŏhayŏ 더하여 plus, in addition to
tŏ isang 더 이상 any more
tŏk 덕 goodness, virtue; **...tŏkt'aege** ...덕택에 thanks to ...; **kŭ tŏkppune** 그 덕분에 because of that
tŏl 덜 less; incompletely
tŏlda 덜다 ease, alleviate, relieve
tŏldŏl ttŏllida 덜덜 떨리다 chatter (*of teeth*)
tŏlgŏdŏk'anŭn sori 덜거덕하는 소리 clatter
tŏl ik'in 덜 익힌 rare, underdone
tŏl'ŏk-kkŏrida 덜컥거리다 rattle; jolt
tŏm 덤 bonus; freebie
tŏ manŭn 더 많은 more
tŏmbida 덤비다 pounce
tŏmbul 덤불 clump, group; undergrowth
tŏmbyŏdŭlda 덤벼들다 go for, attack
tŏmi 더미 pile, heap
tŏ mŏlli 더 멀리 farther
tŏ mŏn 더 먼 further
tŏmp'ŭlling 덤플링 dumpling
tŏ naajida 더 나아지다 be better; be on the mend
tŏ nappajida 더 나빠지다 worsen
tŏ nappŭge 더 나쁘게 worse

tŏ nappŭn 더 나쁜 worse

tŏ natkke 더 낫게 better

tŏnggul shingmul 덩굴 식물 creeper

tŏnggulwŏlgyul 덩굴월귤 cranberry

tŏng-ŏri 덩어리 lump, block; loaf

tŏng-ŏrijida 덩어리지다 cake, solidify

tŏng-ŏri t'usŏng-iŭi 덩어리 투성이의 lumpy

tŏnjida 던지다 throw; *Xege Yŭl/rŭl tŏnjida* X에게 Y을/를 던지다 pelt X with Y

tŏnjigi 던지기 throw

tŏnmun 덧문 shutter

tŏ ŏmnŭn haengbok 더 없는 행복 bliss, no greater happiness

tŏpch'ida 덮치다 pounce; swoop on

tŏpch'iryŏ tŭlda 덮치려 들다 attack, go for

tŏpkkae 덮개 cover, hood; *tŏpkkaerŭl pŏtkkida* 덮개를 벗기다 uncover

tŏpssuruk'an 덥수룩한 shaggy

tŏptta 덥다 be hot (*of weather*); be warm (*of water*)

tŏptta 덮다 cover

tŏp'ida 덮히다 be buried under, be covered by

tŏp'in 덮힌: *k'ŭrimŭro tŏp'in* 크림으로 덮힌 topped with cream

tŏp'ŏ kkŭda 덮어 끄다 smother

tŏrhada 덜하다 ease

tŏrŏptta 더럽다 be dirty; be sordid

tŏrŏp'ida 더럽히다 soil, stain, dirty; smudge; blemish; smear *character*

tŏrŏwŏjida 더러워지다 stain

tŏt 덫 trap

tŏt-ch'angmun 덧창문 storm window

tŏtch'il 덧칠 coat (*of paint etc*)

tŏtppuch'ida 덧붙이다 add

tŏtppuch'yŏ marhada 덧붙여 말하다 add

tŏtssem 덧셈 addition

tŏŭk 더욱 more; *tŏŭk chung-yohan* 더욱 중요한 more important; *tŏŭk tŏ* 더욱 더 more and more, even more

tŏugi 더욱이 moreover; in addition; plus

tŏun 더운 hot; warm

...to ...도 too, also

to 도 province, *do*; degree

toan 도안 engraving

toan-ga 도안가 draftsman

tobaehada 도배하다 paper *room, walls*

tobak 도박 gambling

tobak-kkun 도박꾼 gambler

tobak'ada 도박하다 gamble

tobaldoeji anŭn 도발되지 않은 unprovoked; spontaneous

tobalshik'ida 도발시키다 whip up, arouse

tobo yŏhaeng 도보 여행 walk; walking; hike; hiking; walking tour

tobo yŏhaenghada 도보 여행하다 walk, hike

toboyŏhaengja 도보여행자 hiker

toch'ak 도착 arrival

toch'ak yejŏng shigan 도착 예정 시간 ETA, estimated time of arrival

toch'ak'ada 도착하다 arrive, reach

toch'ak'anŭn 도착하는 incoming

toch'ŏe 도처에 throughout

toch'ŏnggi 도청기 (*electronic*)

toch'ŏnggirŭl sŏlch'ihada 도청기를 설치하다 bug, wire up

toch'ŏnghada 도청하다 bug, tap

todaech'e 도대체 on earth, the hell; *todaech'e muŏsŭl hanŭn/wŏnhanŭn kŏmnikka?* 도대체 무엇을 하는/원하는 겁니까? what the hell are you doing/do you want?

todarhada 도달하다 arrive at

todŏk kwannyŏm 도덕 관념 morals; scruples

todŏkssŏng 도덕성 morality

todŏktchŏgin 도덕적인 moral; scrupulous

toduda 돋우다 boost

toduktchil 도둑질 theft

toduktchirhada 도둑질하다 steal

toebadach'ida 되받아치다 hit back, retaliate

toech'ajŭm 되찾음 recovery

toech'at-tta 되찾다 recover, regain

toeda 되다 amount to; become, get; *...ke/ge toeda* ...게 되다 turn out so that ...; be arranged so that; *ak'wadoeda* 악화되다 get worse, become worse

toedollyŏjuda 252

toedollyŏjuda 되돌려주다 return, give back; take back
toedollyŏnot'a 되돌려놓다 replace, put back
toedoragada 되돌아가다 go back, return; retrace
toedoraoda 되돌아오다 come back, return
toedorok imyŏn 되도록 이면 preferably, if possible
toejŏra! 뒈져라! go to hell!
toel ssu innŭn han 될 수 있는 한 as possible; if possible
toen 된 stiff
toenjang 된장 fermented soya paste
toeŏ it-tta 되어 있다 be scheduled; *taŭmttarre kkŭnmach'igiro toeŏ issŏyo* 다음달에 끝마치기로 되어 있어요 it's scheduled for completion next month; *...giro toeŏ it-tta* ...기로 되어 있다 be supposed to ...
toep'uridoenŭn 되풀이되는 repetitive
toep'urihada 되풀이하다 repeat; go over
toesallida 되살리다 revive; resuscitate; jog *memory*
toetch'atta 되찾다 retrieve
toetollida 되돌리다 reintroduce, bring back
toet'wida 되튀다 rebound
togani 도가니 melting pot
togi 도기 pottery
Togil 독일 Germany ◊ German
Togirin 독일인 German
Togirŏ 독일어 German (*language*)
togong 도공 potter
togŭl t'ada 독을 타다 poison
togu 도구 tool, device
Togyo 도교 Taoism
tohwasŏn 도화선 fuse wire
toip 도입 introduction; injection; input
toip'ada 도입하다 introduce; inject, contribute; input
tojagi 도자기 ceramics; porcelain
tojagiro toen 도자기로 된 ceramic
tojagiryu 도자기류 crockery
tojang 도장 paintwork; stamp, seal
tojang chaguk 도장 자국 stamp
tojang tchiktta 도장 찍다 stamp

tojŏhi 도저히 at all, by no means; *tojŏhi ...l su ŏptta* 도저히 ...ㄹ 수 없다 be completely unable to ...
tojŏn 도전 challenge
tojŏnhada 도전하다 challenge; dare
tojŏnja 도전자 challenger
toju ch'aryang 도주 차량 getaway car
tojung-e 도중에 on the way; *kirŭl kŏnnŏnŭn tojung-e* 길을 건너는 도중에 in crossing the road, while crossing the road
tojung-e tŭllŭda 도중에 들리다 stop off, break a journey
tok 독 poison; pot; dock
tokch'ang 독창 solo
tokch'angja 독창자 soloist
tokch'angjŏgin 독창적인 clever, ingenious
tokch'angnyŏk 독창력 ingenuity
tokch'angssŏng 독창성 originality
tokch'oktchang 독촉장 reminder COM
tokki 도끼 ax
tok-kkam 독감 flu, influenza
tokppaek 독백 monolog
tokppŏsŏt 독버섯 toadstool, poisonous mushroom
...tokppune ...덕분에 through, thanks to
tokssarhada 독살하다 poison
toksshinin 독신인 unattached, single
toksshinja 독신자 single (person)
toksshirhan 독실한 devout
tokssŏ 독서 reading
tokssŏ chang-ae 독서 장애 dyslexia
tokssŏ chang-aeja 독서 장애자 dyslexic (*person*)
tokssŏga 독서가 reader (*person*)
tokssŏl 독설 sharp tongue
tokssŏnjŏgin 독선적인 dogmatic; self-righteous
tokssuri 독수리 eagle; vulture
toktchae chŏngkkwŏn 독재 정권 dictatorship
toktchaeja 독재자 dictator
toktchaejŏgin 독재적인 dictatorial
toktchajŏgin chosa podo 독자적인 조사 보도 investigative journalism
toktchŏm 독점 monopoly
toktchŏmhada 독점하다 monopolize

toktchŏmjŏgin 독점적인 exclusive, sole

toktchu 독주 solo

toktchuja 독주자 soloist

tokttanjŏgin 독단적인 arbitrary

tokt'ŭk'ada 독특하다 be unique

tokt'ŭk'an 독특한 unique

tok'ada 독하다 be poisonous; be strong (*of coffee etc*); be spiteful; be firm

tok'ingshik'ida 도킹시키다 dock

tol 돌 rock, stone; *tori manŭn* 돌이 많은 stony

tol 돐 first birthday

tolbal 돌발 outbreak

tolbarhada 돌발하다 flare up

tolboda 돌보다 look after

tolbom 돌봄 care

tolbwajuda 돌봐주다 watch, look after; *agirŭl tolbwajuda* 아기를 돌봐주다 baby-sit

tolch'ul 돌출 bulge

tolch'urhada 돌출하다 jut out

tolda 돌다 turn, turn around; circulate

toldol mungch'ida 돌돌 뭉치다 screw up *paper etc*

tolgi 돌기 turn

tolgyŏk'ada 돌격하다 charge, attack

tolkkorae 돌고래 dolphin

tollida 돌리다 turn, turn around; pass around; deal; direct

tollyŏbat-tta 돌려받다 have back, get back

tollyŏjuda 돌려주다 return, give back; pass on *costs, savings*

tollyŏnot'a 돌려놓다 return, put back

tollyŏ ponaeda 돌려 보내다 send back

tollyŏsŏ ŏn-gŭp'ada 돌려서 언급하다 allude to

tolp'ari 돌팔이 itinerant tradesman ◊ unqualified, quack

tolp'ung 돌풍 blast; gust, freak wind

tol segong 돌 세공 masonry

tomabaem 도마뱀 lizard

tomae 도매 wholesale

tomaekkapssŭro 도매값으로 wholesale

tomae-ŏptcha 도매업자 wholesaler

tomal p'yobon kŏmsa 도말 표본

검사 smear (test)

tomang 도망 escape

tomangch'ida 도망치다 escape; break away; flee

tomanggada 도망가다 escape; run away; scram

tomangja 도망자 fugitive

ton 돈 money; cash; currency

tonan kyŏngbogi 도난 경보기 burglar alarm

tong 동 sub-district, *dong*

...tong-an ... 동안 during ◊ while; *...nŭn tong-ane* ...는 동안에 while ...ing; *...tong-an naenae* ...동안 내내 throughout, during

tongbanhada 동반하다 accompany

tongbanja 동반자 escort

tongbong 동봉 inclosure ◊ inclosed

tongbonghada 동봉하다 attach, inclose

tongbongmul 동봉물 inclosure (*in letter etc*)

tongbuk 동북 north-east

tongch'e 동체 fuselage

tongdŭnghada 동등하다 be equal

tongdŭnghage 동등하게 equally

tongdŭnghan 동등한 equal, equivalent; *tongdŭnghan kach'iga it-tta* 동등한 가치가 있다 be equivalent to

tonggamhada 동감하다 empathize with

tonggi 동기 incentive, motive

tonggi puyŏ 동기 부여 motivation

tonggirŭl puyŏhada 동기를 부여하다 motivate

tonggisaeng 동기생 contemporary

tonggŏhada 동거하다 live with; cohabit

tonggŭpssaeng 동급생 classmate

tonggŭrami 동그라미 circle; *tonggŭramirŭl ch'ida* 동그라미를 치다 circle, draw a circle around

tonggul 동굴 cave

tonggyŏldoeda 동결되다 ice up

Tonggyŏng 동경 Tokyo

tonggyŏng-ŭi taesang 동경의 대상 heart-throb

tonggyŏrhada 동결하다 freeze

Tonghae 동해 East Sea, Sea of Japan

tonghwa 동화 fairy tale

tonghyŏng-iŭiŏ 동형이의어 homograph

tong-irhan 동일한 identical

tongjaguro p'yohyŏnhada 동작으로 표현하다 mime

tongjak 동작 motion

tongji 동지 comrade

tongjŏn 동전 coin

tongjŏng 동정 pity; virginity; collar

tongjŏnghada 동정하다 pity; commiserate

tongjŏnghanŭn 동정하는 sympathetic, compassionate

tongjŏngshim 동정심 sympathy, pity, compassion

tongjŏngshimi manŭn 동정심이 많은 considerate

tongjoja 동조자 sympathizer

tongjongnyoppŏp 동종요법 homeopathy

tongjong pŏnshik 동종 번식 inbreeding

tongmaek 동맥 artery

tongmaeng 동맹 alliance

tongmaengguk 동맹국 ally (country)

tongmaeng p'aŏp 동맹 파업 strike; *tongmaeng p'aŏp'ada* 동맹 파업하다 go on strike; *tongmaeng p'aŏp chung-ida* 동맹 파업 중이다 be on strike

tongmedal 동메달 bronze medal

tongmu 동무 friend; comrade; companion

tongmul 동물 animal, creature

tongmurhak 동물학 zoology

tongmurhakssang-ŭi 동물학상의 zoological

tongmuro sagwigi 동무로 사귀기 companionship

tongmurwŏn 동물원 zoo

tongmyŏng-iin 동명이인 namesake

tongmyŏnhada 동면하다 hibernate

Tongnam Ashia 동남 아시아 Southeast Asia ◊ Southeast Asian

Tongnam Ashia Kuk-kka Yŏnhap 동남 아시아 국가 연합 ASEAN, Association of South East Asian Nations

tongnip 독립 independence ◊ independent

Tongnip Kinyŏmil 독립 기념일 Independence Day

tongnipkkuk 독립국 independent country

tongniptchŏgin 독립적인 independent, self-reliant

tongniptchŏguro 독립적으로 independently

tongnip'ada 독립하다 break away

tongnŏk 동력 movement; play

Tongnyang 동양 East Asia ◊ East Asian

Tongnyang saram 동양 사람 East Asian

tongnyŏguro chojonghanŭn 동력으로 조종하는 power-assisted

tongnyŏk 동력 power

tongnyo 동료 companion; colleague

tongnyo 동요 nursery rhyme; turbulence; *chŏllyuŭi tongnyo* 전류의 동요 surge ELEC

tongnyohanŭn 동요하는 turbulent

tongnyo kwan-gye 동료 관계 comradeship, friendship

tong-ŏp 동업 partnership

tong-ŏptcha 동업자 partner

tongp'o 동포 fellow citizen, fellow countryman

tongp'ung 동풍 easterly wind

tongsa 동사 verb

tongsamuso 동사무소 sub-district office

tongsang 동상 frostbite; chilblain

tongsang-e kŏllin 동상에 걸린 frostbitten

tongshi 동시 the same time ◊ simultaneous ◊ nursery rhyme

tongshie 동시에 at the same time, simultaneously

tongshie irŏnanŭn 동시에 일어나는 parallel, simultaneous

tongsŏ 동서 sister-in-law (husband's younger / elder brother's wife)

tongsŏng-ae hyŏmotchŭng 동성애 혐오증 homophobia

tongsŏng-aeja 동성애자 homosexual, gay

tongsŏng-aeŭi 동성애의 homosexual, gay

tongtchŏm 동점 draw, tie; *tongtchŏmŭl mandŭlda* 동점을 만들다 even the score; *i tae iro*

tongtchŏmin 이 대 이로 동점인 two all

tongtchŏmi toeda 동점이 되다 draw, tie

tongtchoguro 동쪽으로 east, eastward

tongtchok 동쪽 east

tongtŭnghan chonjae 동등한 존재 equal

tongt'ae chigae 동태 찌개 pollack chowder

tong-ŭi 동의 agreement, consent; arrangement; understanding

tong-ŭihada 동의하다 agree, consent; agree with, support

tong-ŭiŏ 동의어 synonym

tong-yo 동요 agitation

tong-yohan 동요한 agitated

tonŏt 도넛 donut

tonŭl kŏlda 돈을 걸다 back, put money on

tonŭl moktchŏguro hanŭn 돈을 목적으로 하는 mercenary

tonŭl naeda 돈을 내다 pay

tonŭl pŏlda 돈을 벌다 earn money

toŏ maen 도어 맨 doorman

toptta 돕다 help

top'yo 도표 diagram, graph

toragada 돌아가다 go back, return

torang 도랑 ditch; gutter

toraoda 돌아오다 come back, get back

toratanida 돌아다니다 move around; wander, roam

torie mannŭn 도리에 맞는 honorable

torie mat-tta 도리에 맞다 be in the right

torik'il su ŏmnŭn 돌이킬 수 없는 irretrievable

torip'ada 돌입하다 fall, plunge

torirŭl anŭn 도리를 아는 honorable

toro 도로 roadway

toro chido 도로 지도 road map

toro kongsa 도로 공사 road works

toro p'yojip'an 도로 표지판 roadsign

toroŭi chung-ang pullidae 도로의 중앙 분리대 median strip

toroŭi taep'isŏn 도로의 대피선 hard shoulder

torŭrae 도르래 pulley

toryŏnhan 돌연한 freak

tosal 도살 slaughter

tosarhada 도살하다 slaughter

toshi 도시 city; town ◊ urban

toshihwa 도시화 urbanization

toshim-ŭi 도심의 down-town

toshirak 도시락 lunch box

toshiŭi 도시의 city, urban

toshiŭi chungshim 도시의 중심 city center

toshiŭi chungshimbue(sŏ) 도시의 중심부에(서) down-town

tosŏgwan 도서관 library

tot 돛 sail

totkkuda 돋구다 work up, develop

totppogi 돋보기 magnifying glass

tot-ttae 돛대 mast

totuk 도둑 thief

toŭi 도의 (moral) principle; **toŭisang** 도의상 on principle, as a matter of principle

tourŏ moida 도우러 모이다 rally around

toum 도움 help, aid; **toumŭi p'iryohan** 도움이 필요한 in need

toumdatkki 도움닫기 run-up SP

toumi toenŭn 도움이 되는 helpful; conducive to

toummal hwamyŏn 도움말 화면 help screen

tourŏ tallyŏoda 도우러 달려오다 rally around

toyak 도약 leap; vault

toyak sŏnsu 도약 선수 jumper

toye 도예 pottery; ceramics

toyeji 도예지 pottery (*place*)

ttabunhan 따분한 boring

ttada 따다 win; pick; unstop, pop *cork*

ttadollida 따돌리다 leave out; ostracize

ttadollimŭl pat-tta 따돌림을 받다 be alienated; be excluded

ttae 때 occasion; grime; **-l ttae** -ㄹ 때 when; **naega ŏryŏssŭl ttae** 내가 어렸을 때 when I was a child; **...se ttaee** ...세 때에 at the age of ...; **-l ttaemada** -ㄹ 때마다 whenever; **ttaerŭl chal match'un** 때를 잘 맞춘 well-timed

ttae anin 때 아닌 untimely
ttaega toemyŏn 때가 되면 in due course, eventually
ttaekkaji 때까지 until; **-l ttaekkaji** -ㄹ 때까지 until
ttaelnamu 땔나무 firewood
ttaem 댐 dam
ttaemudŭn 때묻은 grimy
...ttaemune ...때문에 because ◊ because of; out of; **...gi ttaemune** ...기 때문에 since, because of; **...ttaemune irŏnada** ...때문에 일어나다 be due to, be caused by
...ttaemunŭro ...때문으로 because of
ttaerida 때리다 hit, beat (up)
ttaerigi 때리기 thrashing, beating
ttaettaero 때때로 sometimes, occasionally
ttagae 따개 tab
ttak 딱 punctually; exactly; just
ttakttak'ada 딱딱하다 be hard; be stiff
ttakkŭmgŏrida 따끔거리다 sting; tingle
ttakkŭmgŏrinŭn 따끔거리는 prickly
ttak tallabut-tta 딱 달라붙다 adhere
ttaktchi 딱지 scab
ttaktchŏngbŏlle 딱정벌레 beetle
ttakttaguri 딱따구리 woodpecker
ttakttak-kkŏrida 딱딱거리다 snap
ttakttak sorirŭl naeda 딱딱 소리를 내다 crackle
ttakttak'an 딱딱한 hard; stiff, stilted
ttakttak'an kkŏptchil 딱딱한 껍질 crust
ttak'anŭn sori 딱하는 소리 snap
ttal 딸 daughter
ttalgi 딸기 strawberry
ttalkkuktchil 딸꾹질 hiccup
ttalkkuktchirhada 딸꾹질하다 have the hiccups
ttallanggŏrida 딸랑거리다 jingle
ttallangttallang 딸랑딸랑 tinkling, jingling
ttam 땀 sweat, perspiration
ttami paen 땀이 밴 sweaty
ttamnae nanŭn 땀내 나는 sweaty
ttamt'usŏng-iin 땀투성이인 covered in sweat
ttamŭl hŭllida 땀을 흘리다 sweat, perspire

ttang 땅 property, land; estate
ttangbŏlle 땅벌레 grub (of insect)
ttangk'ong 땅콩 groundnut, peanut
ttangk'ong pŏt'ŏ 땅콩 버터 peanut butter
ttangttalmak'an 땅딸막한 squat, stocky
ttanim 따님 daughter
ttan 딴 another; different; separate; irrelevant; **ttan tero tollida** 딴 데로 돌리다 divert; **kŭgŏn ttan yaegi-yeyo** 그건 딴 얘기예요 that's beside the point
ttara 따라 down, along
ttaragada 따라가다 follow, come too
ttarajaptta 따라잡다 catch; catch up; overtake
ttarasŏ 따라서 therefore; thus ◊ in accordance with; along
ttarasŏ irŏnan 따라서 일어난 subsequent, later
ttaro 따로 separately, apart ◊ extra, additional; **kakki ttaro salda** 각기 따로 살다 live apart
ttarŭda 따르다 abide by, follow, conform; go along with; pour out liquid; **sanghwang-e ttara tarŭda** 상황에 따라 다르다 that depends (on the circumstances)
ttarŭmyŏn 따르면 according to
ttattŭt'ada 따뜻하다 be warm
ttattŭt'aejida 따뜻해지다 warm up
ttattŭt'age 따뜻하게 warmly
ttattŭt'age iptta 따뜻하게 입다 wrap up
ttattŭt'age kamssada 따뜻하게 감싸다 muffle up
ttattŭt'an 따뜻한 warm
ttat'a 땋다 braid
ttaŭn mŏri 땋은 머리 braid, pigtail
tte 떼 crowd; mob; herd; flock; swarm; **tte tonŭl pŏlda** 떼 돈을 벌다 make a killing; **tterŭl chiŏ moida** 떼를 지어 모이다 huddle together; **tterŭl chiŏ tallyŏdŭlda** 떼를 지어 달려들다 mob; **tterŭl chit-tta** 떼를 짓다 swarm
ttemilgi 떼밀기 shove
ttemilgo tŭrŏgada 떼밀고 들어가다 squeeze into room
ttenmok 뗏목 raft

tteŏnaeda 떼어내다 detach; pull off; separate; *t'ellebijŏnesŏ tteŏ not'a* 텔레비전에서 떼어 놓다 drag oneself away from the TV

tti 띠 sash

ttŏdoradanida 떠돌아다니다 wander, roam

ttŏdori 떠돌이 hobo

ttŏdŭlssŏk'an 떠들썩한 boisterous

ttŏ innŭn 떠 있는 afloat

ttŏk 떡 rice cake

ttŏkch'iri toeda 떡칠이 되다 be plastered with

ttŏk-kkuk 떡국 rice cake soup

ttŏk pŏrŏjin 떡 벌어진 broad

ttŏkppok-kki 떡볶기 rice cake in hot sauce

ttŏlch'yŏbŏrida 떨쳐버리다 dismiss

ttŏlda 떨다 shake, tremble; shiver

ttŏllida 떨리다 quaver, tremble; shudder; throb

ttŏllim 떨림 shudder

ttŏllimŭm 떨림음 throb

ttŏllinŭn 떨리는 wobbly

ttŏmat-tta 떠맡다 take charge

ttŏnada 떠나다 leave, go away

ttŏnaganŭn 떠나가는 outgoing

ttŏnage hada 떠나게 하다 excuse, allow to leave

ttŏngmanduguk 떡만두국 rice cake and dumpling soup

ttŏorŭda 떠오르다 occur to; haunt (*of memory*); surface, come up, rise

ttŏrŏjida 떨어지다 fall, drop, decline; run out; run out of; come off (*of handle etc*); strike (*of disaster*); set (*of sun*); deteriorate; be apart; separate; be left behind; fail *exam*; miscarry; be evenly divisible; get finished; die; get over *illness*; *imail ttŏrŏjyŏit-tta* 2마일 떨어졌다 it's 2 miles away

ttŏrŏjyŏsŏ 떨어져서 apart; *chu-doroesŏ ttŏrŏjyŏ* 주도로에서 떨어져 off the main road; *...put'ŏ ttŏrŏjyŏ it-tta* ...부터 떨어져 있다 stay away from; *...esŏ ttŏrŏjyŏsŏ sŏda* ...에서 떨어져서 서다 stand clear of

ttŏrŏttŭrida 떨어뜨리다 drop, lower; shed *leaves*; strip leaves; throw off

ttŏrŏttŭryŏ 떨어뜨려 aside

tto 또 again; also; *tto poja!* 또 보자! see you!

ttohan 또한 also, too; either; *...to ttohan* ...도 또한 ... (+ *negative verb*) nor

tto hana 또 하나 another, additional

ttokkatchi anŭn 똑같지 않은 unequal

ttokkatkkehada 똑같게하다 equalize

ttok-kkat-tta 똑같다 be exactly like; *soriga ttok-kkat'ayo* 소리가 똑같아요 sound the same

ttokpparo 똑바로 straight; straight ahead; upright; *ttokpparo kada* 똑바로 가다 carry straight on; *ttokpparo antta* 똑바로 앉다 sit up (straight)

ttokpparŭge hada 똑바르게 하다 straighten

ttokpparŭn 똑바른 straight

ttokttak-kkŏrida 똑딱거리다 tick

ttokttok ttŏrŏjida 똑똑 떨어지다 drip, trickle

ttokttok'ada 똑똑하다 be intelligent

ttokttok'an 똑똑한 intelligent, smart, clever

ttolttol kamtta 똘똘 감다 coil

ttong 똥 dung; shit; poop; excrement

ttongkkumŏng 똥구멍 anus, rectum; bottom; butt

ttongppae 똥배 paunch, belly

ttonŭn 또는 or

tto tarŭn 또 다른 further, additional; *tto tarŭn kŏt* 또 다른 것 another (one)

ttŭda 뜨다 float; scoop

ttŭgaejil 뜨개질 knitting

ttŭgaejirhada 뜨개질하다 knit

ttŭgŏptta 뜨겁다 be hot; be burning

ttŭgŏun 뜨거운 hot

ttŭiŏmttŭiŏm 띄엄띄엄 sparsely; intermittently; slowly; *ttŭiŏmttŭiŏm iltta* 띄엄띄엄 읽다 browse through a book

ttŭiuda 띄우다 sail

ttŭkppakkŭi il 뜻밖의 일 contingency

ttŭl 뜰 garden

ttŭnaegi 뜨내기 hobo

ttŭnaegi ilkkun 뜨내기 일꾼 hobo (*itinerant worker*)

ttŭn-gurum chapkki 뜬구름 잡기
wild-goose chase

ttŭsŭl palk'ida 뜻을 밝히다 define,
specify

ttŭsŭl palk'im 뜻을 밝힘 definition

ttŭt 뜻 sense, meaning; intention;
aim, purpose

ttŭtppakk 뜻밖 surprise

ttŭtppakke 뜻밖에 unexpectedly

ttŭtppakkŭi 뜻밖의 unexpected

ttŭtppakkŭi haeng-un 뜻밖의 행운
stroke of luck

ttŭt'aji anŭn chang-ae 뜻하지 않은
장애 snag, problem; twist (*in story*)

ttukkŏng 뚜껑 lid; top, cap; flap

ttukttuk ttŏrŏjida 뚝뚝 떨어지다
dribble

ttulkko nagada 뚫고 나가다
negotiate *obstacles*; weather *crisis*

ttult'a 뚫다 drill; pierce *ears*; unblock

ttungbo 뚱보 fatty

ttungttungbo 뚱뚱보 fatso

ttungttunghada 뚱뚱하다 be fat

ttungttunghan 뚱뚱한 fat

tturŏjige poda 뚫어지게 보다 peer at

tturyŏt'ada 뚜렷하다 be clear,
distinct

tturyŏt'age 뚜렷하게 clearly,
distinctly

tturyŏt'aji anŭn 뚜렷하지 않은
indistinct

tturyŏt'an 뚜렷한 clear; distinct;
definite

ttwida 뛰다 pound, throb

ttwigi 뛰기 spring, jump

ttwiŏdanida 뛰어다니다 jump,
bounce

ttwiŏdŭlda 뛰어들다 dive; *pang
anŭro ttwiŏdŭlda* 방 안으로
뛰어들다 burst into the room

ttwiŏdŭlgi 뛰어들기 dive

ttwiŏdŭm 뛰어듦 plunge, fall

ttwiŏnada 뛰어나다 excel; excel at;
be excellent; *poda ttwiŏnada* 보다
뛰어나다 outperform

ttwiŏ nagada 뛰어 나가다 fly out,
rush out

ttwiŏnage 뛰어나게 extremely

ttwiŏnam 뛰어남 excellence

ttwiŏnan 뛰어난 excellent

ttwiŏnan somsshi 뛰어난 솜씨
prowess

ttwiŏ nŏmtta 뛰어 넘다 jump, vault

ttwiŏ orŭda 뛰어 오르다 jump

ttwiŏorŭgi 뛰어오르기 jump

ttwiŏ orŭm 뛰어 오름 jump

tŭk 득 profit, benefit; *...nŭn kŏshi
tŭgi toeji anayo* ...는 것이 득이
되지 않아요 it doesn't pay to ...

tŭkp'yohada 득표하다 poll, obtain

tŭksshiri ŏpkke toeda 득실이 없게
되다 break even

tŭktchŏm 득점 score; goal;
tŭktchŏm maganaegi 득점
막아내기 save SP

tŭktchŏmhada 득점하다 score; touch
down

tŭktchŏmja 득점자 scorer

tŭlch'angmun 들창문 trapdoor

tŭlch'uŏnaeda 들추어내다 dredge
up, unearth

tŭlda 들다 enter; join *club*; catch
cold; contain; accommodate; get;
begin; dye; be pleased, be satisfied;
cost; put up *hand*; take out *insurance
policy*; cut; grow older; hold *pen*; lift;
cite *example*; eat; drink

tŭlgo kada 들고 가다 carry

tŭlkkae p'ohoegin 들개 포획인 dog
catcher

tŭlkkŏt 들것 stretcher

tŭlkkŭlt'a 들끓다 be overrun with;
smolder

tŭllida 들리다 hear; be audible; be
rumored; be obsessed by; be lifted
up

tŭllinŭn pŏmwi ane(sŏ) 들리는 범위
안에(서) within hearing

tŭllinŭn pŏmwi pakke(sŏ) 들리는
범위 밖에(서) out of hearing

tŭllŏbunnŭn 들러붙는 clingy

tŭllŭda 들르다 drop in, stop by

tŭlppo 들보 beam

tŭlp'an 들판 field

tŭlsso 들소 buffalo

tŭltchungnaltchuk'an 들쭉날쭉한
ragged, jagged

tŭmppuk 듬뿍 plenty, lots

tŭmulda 드물다 be rare

tŭmulge 드물게 rarely, seldom,
unusually

tŭmun 드문 rare; infrequent; unusual

tŭndŭnhan 든든한 stalwart, steadfast

tŭng 등 back, spine (*of book*); light, lantern; *nuguege tŭng-ŭl tollida* 누구에게 등을 돌리다 turn one's back on s.o.

tŭngban 등반 climb

tŭngbanhada 등반하다 climb

tŭngch'yŏmŏkta 등쳐먹다 prey on

tŭngdae 등대 lighthouse

tŭnggamul 등가물 equivalent

tŭnggŭbŭl maegida 등급을 매기다 grade, rank

tŭnggŭp 등급 grade, quality

tŭng-i kuptta 등이 굽다 stoop

tŭngjang 등장 entrance THEAT

tŭngjanghada 등장하다 enter THEAT

tŭngjang inmul 등장 인물 characters, cast THEAT

tŭngjida 등지다 desert

tŭngkkiro puch'ida 등기로 부치다 register; *pyŏnjirŭl tŭngkkiro ponaeda* 편지를 등기로 보내다 send a letter registered

tŭngkki up'yŏn 등기 우편 registered letter

tŭngnogŭl hada 등록을 하다 register

tŭngnok 등록 entry; enrollment, registration

tŭngnok pŏnho 등록 번호 license number

tŭngnok sangp'yo 등록 상표 trademark

tŭngnok'ada 등록하다 register, enroll

tŭngppul 등불 lamp

tŭngsan 등산 mountaineering

tŭngsan-ga 등산가 mountaineer, climber

tŭngsanhwa 등산화 climbing boots

tŭngssu 등수 place, position

tŭngtcha 등자 stirrup

tŭngttaktchi 등딱지 shell (*of tortoise*)

tŭng-yu 등유 kerosene

tŭnŏlbŭn 드넓은 spacious

tŭraibŏ 드라이버 screwdriver; driver COMPUT

tŭraibŭ 드라이브 drive; outing

tŭraik'ŭllining 드라이클리닝 dry-cleaning

tŭraik'ŭllininghada 드라이클리닝하다 dry-clean

tŭraik'ŭllining set'aksso 드라이클리닝 세탁소 dry-cleaner

tŭraiŏro mŏrirŭl mallida 드라이어로 머리를 말리다 blow-dry

tŭrama 드라마 drama

tŭresŭ 드레스 dress

tŭribat-tta 들이받다 knock down; run into

tŭribŭrhada 드리블하다 dribble SP

tŭrida 드리다 give

tŭrimashida 들이마시다 suck in, gulp down; inhale

tŭrishwida 들이쉬다 breathe in; *k'oro tŭrishwida* 코로 들이쉬다 sniff

tŭrŏgada 들어가다 enter, go into; let in

tŭrŏ it-tta 들어 있다 be inside; *nae k'ameraga tŭrŏ issŏt-tta* 내 카메라가 들어 있었다 my camera was in it

tŭrŏjuda 들어주다 accommodate *requirement*; grant *wish*

tŭrŏm 드럼 drum

tŭrŏ mat-tta 들어 맞다 fit

tŭrŏmŏ 드러머 drummer

tŭrŏmt'ong 드럼통 drum (*container*)

tŭrŏnaeda 드러내다 reveal; take out; throw out; *kamjŏng-ŭl tŭrŏnaeda* 감정을 드러내다 be demonstrative

tŭrŏnuptta 드러눕다 lie down

tŭrŏoda 들어오다 come in, enter

tŭrŏ ollida 들어 올리다 lift; heave; hand

tŭrŏsŏda 들어서다 enter; *tarŭn killo tŭrŏsŏda* 다른 길로 들어서다 turn off

tŭryŏda ponŭn kumŏng 들여다 보는 구멍 peephole

tŭryŏnot'a 들여놓다 stock up on

tŭryŏ ponaeda 들여 보내다 send in

tŭt-tta 듣다 hear; listen; listen to; *tŭrŭl su innŭn* 들을 수 있는 audible

tu 두 two

tubu 두부 tofu

tu chari su 두 자리 수 in double figures

tudŭrida 두드리다 beat; knock; pound

tudŭrŏjin 두드러진 conspicuous

tudŭrŏjinŭn 두드러지는 striking, marked

tudunhada 두둔하다 cover up for

tugaegol 두개골 skull

tugoboda 두고보다 watch, keep watch; *nŏ tugo poja!* 너 두고 보자! just you wait!

tugo kada 두고 가다 leave behind

tugo marhada 두고 말하다 be meant for, be aimed at

tugŭndugŭn ttwida 두근두근 뛰다 thump

tugŭn-gŏrida 두근거리다 flutter

tujŏl 두절 disruption

tujŏlshik'ida 두절시키다 disrupt

tuk 둑 dike; embankment; weir

tuk-kkil 둑길 embankment

tukkŏbi 두꺼비 toad

tukkŏbijip 두꺼비집 fusebox

tukkŏun 두꺼운 thick

tukkŏuptta 두껍다 be thick

tu kyŏbŭi 두 겹의 double *layer*

tul 둘 two; *kŭdŭl tul* 그들 둘 the two of them; *...wa / gwa ..., tul ta* ...와 / 과 ..., 둘 다 both... and ...

tulle 둘레 around

tullŏboda 둘러보다 look around; survey; view

tullŏdaeda 둘러대다 beat about the bush; dodge

tullŏdaenŭn kŏjinmal 둘러대는 거짓말 whitewash

tullŏ ssada 둘러 싸다 enclose; surround; *tullŏssaida* 둘러싸이다 be surrounded by

tullŏ ssŭiuda 둘러 씌우다 drape

tul ta 둘 다 both; *kŭdŭl tul ta* 그들 둘 다 both of them

tultchaero 둘째로 secondly

tumal hal kŏt ŏpsshi 두말 할 것 없이 it goes without saying; *tumal hal kŏt ŏpsshi ch'oegoimnida* 두말 할 것 없이 최고입니다 it is simply the best

tumesankkol 두메산골 the sticks, the boonies

tumok haengsehanŭn 두목 행세하는 bossy

tunbu 둔부 haunch

tun-gamhan 둔감한 stolid

tunggŭlda 둥글다 be round

tunggŭlge hada 둥글게 하다 round off *edges*

tunggŭlge ogŭradŭlda 둥글게 오그라들다 curl

tunggŭn 둥근 round, circular

tunggŭn ch'ŏnjang 둥근 천장 dome; vault

tungji 둥지 nest

tunhan 둔한 dull; thick; stupid

tunoe 두뇌 brain

tunt'ak'an 둔탁한 dull

tu pae 두 배 double *amount*

tu paega toeda 두 배가 되다 double

tu paero 두 배로 double

tu paero hada 두 배로 하다 double

tu paeŭi 두 배의 double, twice as much

tu pŏn 두 번 twice

tu pŏntchae 두 번째 second

tu pŏntchaero 두 번째로 second; *tu pŏntchaero chal hanŭn* 두 번째로 잘 하는 second best

tu pŏntchaeŭi 두 번째의 second

tup'yoham 투표함 ballot box

turŏnada 들어나다 emerge

turŏ ollida 들어 올리다 take up *carpet etc*

turŭda 드르다 enclose

turumagi 두루마기 (traditional) long coat

turumari 두루마리 scroll, manuscript

turyŏptta 두렵다 be fearful

turyŏum 두려움 fear

turyŏum ŏmnŭn 두려움 없는 fearless

turyŏwŏhada 두려워하다 be afraid; be afraid of

tusŏnŏ kae 두서너 개 a couple of

tusŏnŏsŭi 두서넛의 a couple of (*people*)

tusŏŏmnŭn 두서없는 incoherent, rambling

tusŏŏpsshi iyagihada 두서없이 이야기하다 ramble

tut'ong 두통 headache

tu t'ong-ŭro 두 통으로 in duplicate

tuyu 두유 soy(a) milk

twaeji 돼지 hog, pig

twaeji chŏgŭmt'ong 돼지 저금통 piggybank

twaeji chokppal 돼지 족발 pig's trotters

twaejigogi 돼지고기 pork

twaeji kajuk 돼지 가죽 pigskin

twaejiuri 돼지우리 pigpen

twaessŏyo 됐어요 that's plenty; that's it

twaessŭmnida 됐습니다 there you are (*completing sth*)

twengbŏl 뒝벌 bumblebee

twesalligi 되살리기 undelete COMPUT

twi 뒤 back, rear; (*ch'aŭi*) **twit chwasŏge**(*sŏ*) (차의) 뒷 좌석에(서) in back (of the car); **pŏsŭ twit chwasŏge**(*sŏ*) 버스 뒷 좌석에(서) at the back of the bus

twibŏmbŏk 뒤범벅 jumble

twich'ŏgida 뒤척이다 stir, move

twich'ŏk-kkŏrida 뒤척거리다 toss and turn; turn over

twich'uk 뒤축 heel (*of shoe*)

twich'yŏjige hada 뒤처지게 하다 set back

twidoraboda 뒤돌아보다 look back

twie(*sŏ*) 뒤에(서) behind; at the back

twie namgida 뒤에 남기다 leave behind

twie namtta 뒤에 남다 stay behind

twiesŏ chidohada 뒤에서 지도하다 mastermind

twiiŭn 뒤이은 succeeding, following

twijibŏjida 뒤집어지다 turn over (*of vehicle*)

twijibŏsŏ 뒤집어서 inside out

twijibŭm 뒤집음 demolition (*of argument*)

twijida 뒤지다 poke around; search

twijiji ank'o ttaragada 뒤지지 않고 따라가다 keep up (*when walking etc*)

twijiptta 뒤집다 upset, overturn *drink, glass*; capsize; fold; back; demolish *argument*; turn inside out

twijip'ida 뒤집히다 overturn, capsize

twijukppaktchugin 뒤죽박죽인 topsy-turvy

twijyŏ ch'ajanaeda 뒤져 찾아내다 rummage around

twijyŏsŏ 뒤져서 behind (*in progress, order*)

twikkumch'i 뒤꿈치 heel (*of foot*)

twinggulda 뒹굴다 roll over

twinmadang 뒷마당 backyard

twinmun 뒷문 backdoor

twinmyŏn 뒷면 back, reverse; *ammyŏn animyŏn twinmyŏn?* 앞면 아니면 뒷면? heads or tails?

twinŭjŭn kkaedarŭm 뒤늦은 깨달음 hindsight

twiŏlk'in 뒤얽힌 intricate

twiŏptta 뒤엎다 overturn, tip over

twiro chŏp'ae it-tta 뒤로 접해 있다 back onto

twiro mungnŭn mŏri 뒤로 묶는 머리 ponytail

twiro tanggida 뒤로 당기다 draw back, pull back

twirŭl paltta 뒤를 밟다 stalk

twisŏk-kkida 뒤섞이다 be mixed up (*of figures, papers*)

twisŏktta 뒤섞다 shuffle; *ilburŏ twisŏktta* 일부러 뒤섞다 scramble *message*

twitchoch'a ch'ajanaeda 뒤쫓아 찾아내다 track down

twitchot-tta 뒤쫓다 chase

twitch'ŭnggye 뒷층계 backstairs

twitjwasŏk 뒷좌석 pillion

twitkkil 뒷길 back road

twitkŭlswe 뒷글쇠 backspace COMPUT

twitppatch'imhae chuda 뒷받침해 주다 back up *claim, argument*

twittchang 뒷장 back, reverse

twittchoge(*sŏ*) 뒷쪽에(서) behind (*in position*)

twittchoge innŭn 뒷쪽에 있는 back, at the back

twittchogŭi 뒷쪽의 backward; rear

twittchogŭro 뒷쪽으로 backward

twittchok 뒷쪽 back

twittchumŏni 뒷주머니 hip pocket

twittŏrŏjida 뒤떨어지다 lag behind

twit-ttŭl 뒷뜰 backyard

twittunggŏrimyŏ kŏt-tta 뒤뚱거리며 걷다 waddle

twiŭi 뒤의 rear

tyusŭ 듀스 deuce (*in tennis*)

T'

t'aak-kki 타악기 percussion; percussion instrument
t'abŏrida 타버리다 burn down
t'abŭlloidŭp'an shinmun 타블로이드판 신문 tabloid (newspaper)
t'ada 타다 get in (to car); board; catch bus etc; mount horse, bicycle; ride horse, bicycle; fly; burn; glow
t'adanghada 타당하다 be just; be valid
t'adanghan 타당한 just; valid
t'adangsŏng 타당성 validity
t'adangsŏng chosa 타당성 조사 feasibility study
t'aea 태아 embryo; fetus
t'aedo 태도 attitude, manner
T'aegugin 태국인 Thai
T'aegugŏ 태국어 Thai (language)
t'aegŭk-kki 태극기 (South Korean) national flag
T'aeguk 태국 Thailand ◊ Thai
T'aekkwŏndo 태권도 T'aekwondo
t'aeksshi 택시 taxi, cab
t'aeksshi sŭngch'ajang 택시 승차장 taxi rank, cab stand
t'aeksshi unjŏnsa 택시 운전사 taxi driver, cab driver
t'aek'ŭl 태클 tackle SP
t'aek'ŭrhada 태클하다 tackle SP
t'aemanhada 태만하다 neglect, omit
t'aenggo 탱고 tango
t'aengk'ŭ 탱크 tank
t'aeŏnada 태어나다 be born
t'aeŏp 태업 slowdown, go-slow
t'aep 탭 tab
t'aepttaensŭ 탭댄스 tap dance
t'aep'ung 태풍 hurricane, typhoon
T'aep'yŏng-yang 태평양 Pacific (Ocean)
T'aep'yŏng-yang yŏnan 태평양 연안 Pacific Rim
t'aetchul 탯줄 umbilical cord
t'aeuda 태우다 burn; give a ride;

ch'a-e t'aeuda 차에 태우다 pick up (in car)
t'aeugi 태우기 ride (in car)
t'aewŏbŏrida 태워버리다 burn out, gut
t'aewŏ chuda 태워 주다 take, drive
t'aeyang 태양 sun
t'aeyang chŏnjip'an 태양 전지판 solar panel
t'aeyang enŏji 태양 에너지 solar energy
t'aeyŏnhan 태연한 nonchalant
t'agae 타개 breakthrough
t'agi shwiun 타기 쉬운 combustible
t'agonan 타고난 innate; natural
t'agonan chaenŭng 타고난 재능 gift, natural ability
t'agonan kŭmbal 타고난 금발 natural blonde
t'agwŏrhan 탁월한 prominent, significant
t'agyŏk 타격 knock, blow
t'ahyŏp 타협 compromise
t'ahyŏpsshik'ida 타협시키다 compromise
t'ahyŏp'ada 타협하다 compromise
t'ahyŏp'aji annŭn 타협하지 않는 uncompromising
t'ail 타일 tile
t'aim aut 타임 아웃 time out
t'aiming 타이밍 timing
t'aimŏ 타이머 timer
t'aim süwich'i 타임 스위치 time switch
t'aiŏ 타이어 tire
t'aip'isŭt'ŭ 타이피스트 typist
t'airŭda 타이르다 preach, moralize
t'aja 타자 batter SP
t'aja ch'ida 타자 치다 type
t'ajagi 타자기 typewriter
t'ajagiro ch'ida 타자기로 치다 type
t'ak-kku 탁구 ping-pong
t'alch'um 탈춤 mask dance
t'alch'urhada 탈출하다 escape; get

away; bail out

t'alch'urhan 탈출한 at large

t'alch'wi 탈취 hijack

t'alch'wibŏm 탈취범 hijacker

t'alch'wihada 탈취하다 hijack

t'alch'wije 탈취제 deodorant

t'algok'ada 탈곡하다 thresh *corn*

t'algushik'ida 탈구시키다 dislocate

t'allak 탈락 elimination

t'allak'ada 탈락하다 be eliminated

t'allo 탄로 exposure

t'allonada 탄로나다 be out (*of secret*)

t'allyŏginnŭn 탄력있는 elastic

t'alsse 탈세 tax evasion

t'alssŏndoeda 탈선되다 be derailed

t'alssudoen 탈수된 dehydrated

t'alssugi 탈수기 spin-dryer

t'alssuhada 탈수하다 spin-dry

t'altchang 탈장 hernia

t'altchimyŏn 탈지면 absorbent cotton

t'altchi uyu 탈지 우유 skimmed milk

t'alt'oehada 탈퇴하다 break away (*from organization*)

t'am 탐 ride

t'amdok'ada 탐독하다 devour

t'amgujŏgin 탐구적인 inquisitive

t'amhŏm 탐험 expedition, exploration

t'amhŏmdae 탐험대 expedition

t'amhŏmga 탐험가 explorer

t'amji 탐지 detection

t'amjigi 탐지기 detector

t'amjihada 탐지하다 detect

t'amjŏng sosŏl 탐정 소설 detective novel

t'amjodŭng 탐조등 searchlight

t'amnanŭn 탐나는 desirable, coveted

t'amnik 탐닉 indulgence

t'amnik'ada 탐닉하다 indulge

t'amp'on 탐폰 tampon

t'amsa 탐사 probe

t'amsaek 탐색 search

t'amsaek'ada 탐색하다 explore, look into, examine; seek, search for

t'amyokssŭroun 탐욕스러운 insatiable

t'ando misail 탄도 미사일 ballistic missile

t'andu 탄두 warhead

t'an-gwang 탄광 coal mine

t'annyak 탄약 ammunition

t'ansaeng 탄생 birth

t'ansansu 탄산수 soda (water)

t'ansanŭi 탄산의 carbonated

t'ansŏng-i innŭn 탄성이 있는 springy

t'ansuhwamul 탄수화물 carbohydrate

t'anyakt'ong 탄약통 cartridge

t'aorŭda 타오르다 blaze; flare up

t'ap 탑 pagoda; tower

t'apssŭnggu 탑승구 gate (*at airport*)

t'apssŭngkkwŏn 탑승권 boarding card

t'apssŭng susogŭl hada 탑승 수속을 하다 check in

t'apssŭng susok k'aunt'ŏ 탑승 수속 카운터 check-in (counter)

t'apssŭng susok shigan 탑승 수속 시간 check-in time

t'apssŭng taegija 탑승 대기자 standby passenger

t'arae 타래 lock (*of hair*)

t'arak 타락 corruption

t'araksshik'ida 타락시키다 corrupt

t'arak'ada 타락하다 degenerate; be corrupt

t'arak'an 타락한 corrupt, sleazy

t'arhwan 탈환 recapture

t'arok'ada 탈옥하다 break out, escape

t'arŭ 타르 tar

t'arŭishil 탈의실 cubicle; changing room

t'aryŏng 탈영 desertion

t'aryŏngbyŏng 탈영병 deserter

t'aryŏnghada 탈영하다 desert MIL

t'at 탓 fault, blame; result; effect; *Xŭl/rŭl Yŭi t'asŭro tollida* X을/를 Y의 탓으로 돌리다 put X down to Y

t'at'ada 탓하다 blame

t'awŏnhyŏng 타원형 ellipse

t'e 테 frame, rim; hoop

t'eduri 테두리 brim, rim

t'eibŭl 테이블 table

t'eibŭl po 테이블 보 table cloth

t'eip'ŭ 테이프 tape

t'eip'ŭ nogŭm 테이프 녹음 tape recording

t'eip'ŭro puch'ida 테이프로 붙이다 tape (*with sticky tape*)

t'eksŭt'ŭ p'ail 텍스트 파일 text file

t'ellebi 텔레비 TV

t'ellebijŏn 텔레비전 television

t'ellebijŏn p'ŭrogŭraem 텔레비전 프로그램 television program

t'ellebijŏn set'ŭ 텔레비전 세트 television (set)

t'ellebijŏn susanggi 텔레비전 수상기 television (set)

t'ema 테마 theme

t'ema kong-wŏn 테마 공원 theme park

t'ema ŭmak 테마 음악 theme tune; signature tune

t'enissŭ 테니스 tennis

t'enissŭ chang 테니스 장 tennis court

t'enissŭ kong 테니스 공 tennis ball

t'enissŭ lak'et 테니스 라켓 tennis racket

t'enissŭ sŏnsu 테니스 선수 tennis player

t'enŏ 테너 tenor

t'erŏbŏm 테러범 terrorist

t'erŏ chojik 테러 조직 terrorist organization

t'erŏrijŭm 테러리즘 terrorism

t'erŭl talda 테를 달다 edge

t'i 티 tee

T'ibet'ŭ 티베트 Tibet ◊ Tibetan

T'ibet'ŭin 티베트인 Tibetan (person)

T'ibet'ŭŏ 티베트어 Tibetan (language)

t'ibi 티비 TV

t'ik'ŭ namu 티크 나무 teak

t'im 팀 team; crew

t'imjang 팀장 team captain

t'ineijŏ 틴에이저 teenager

t'i ŏmnŭn 티 없는 immaculate

t'ip 팁 tip, gratuity

t'ishyŏch'ŭ 티셔츠 T-shirt

t'ŏbin 터빈 turbine

t'ŏch'i 터치 touch SP

t'ŏch'idaun 터치다운 touchdown

t'ŏch'irain 터치라인 touchline

t'ŏjida 터지다 burst

t'ŏjin 터진 burst

t'ŏk 턱 chin; jaw; ledge

t'ŏkppaji 턱받이 bib

t'ŏksshido 턱시도 tuxedo

t'ŏkssuyŏm 턱수염 beard

T'ŏk'i 터키 Turkey ◊ Turkish

T'ŏk'iin 터키인 Turk

T'ŏk'iŏ 터키어 Turkish (language)

t'ŏl 털 hair; fur; bristles

t'ŏlshillo ttŭda 털실로 뜨다 knit

t'ŏlssŏk naeryŏnot'a 털썩 내려놓다 slam down

t'ŏminŏl 터미널 terminal

t'ŏmuniŏmnŭn 터무니없는 outrageous, ridiculous

t'ŏng pin 텅 빈 bare, empty

t'ŏnŏl 터널 tunnel

t'ŏ noch'i annŭn 터 놓지 않는 secretive

t'ŏnot'a 터놓다 pour out, tell troubles; songmaŭmŭl t'ŏnot'a 속마음을 터놓다 speak one's mind

t'ŏnt'eibŭl 턴테이블 turntable

t'ŏpssuruk'an 텁수룩한 bushy

t'ŏri manŭn 털이 많은 woolly

t'ŏri ŏmnŭn 털이 없는 hairless

t'ŏri p'ungsŏnghan 털이 풍성한 furry

t'ŏrŏnaeda 털어내다 brush off dust etc

t'ŏrŏnot'a 털어놓다 confide

t'ŏttŭrida 터뜨리다 burst; give vent to

t'obŭro charŭda 톱으로 자르다 saw

t'obŭro k'yŏda 톱으로 켜다 saw off

t'odae 토대 support

t'oebohada 퇴보하다 go backward; degenerate

t'oebohanŭn 퇴보하는 backward society

t'oegŏ myŏngnyŏng 퇴거 명령 deportation order

t'oehak 퇴학 expulsion

t'oejanghada 퇴장하다 leave; exit (of actor); walk out

t'oejangshik'ida 퇴장시키다 expel from the game

t'oejikkŭm 퇴직금 golden handshake

t'oejik sudang 퇴직 수당 unemployment compensation

t'oejŏkshik'ida 퇴적시키다 deposit

t'oep'yejŏgin 퇴폐적인 decadent

t'oerak'ada 퇴락하다 go to seed, become shabby

t'oetcha 퇴짜 brush-off

t'oewihada 퇴위하다 abdicate

t'oewŏn 퇴원 discharge
t'oewŏnshik'ida 퇴원시키다 discharge
t'ogi 토기 earthenware
t'ohada 토하다 vomit
t'oji kaebarŏptcha 토지 개발업자 property developer
t'okki 토끼 rabbit
t'okt'ok tudŭrida 톡톡 두드리다 rap
t'ok'ŭn 토큰 token
t'omak 토막 fragment, chip
t'omakch'ida 토막치다 cut up
t'omat'o 토마토 tomato
t'omat'o k'ech'ap 토마토 케찹 tomato ketchup
t'omnibak'wi 톱니바퀴 cog
t'omni moyang-ŭi 톱니 모양의 jagged
t'omok kisa 토목 기사 civil engineer
t'on 톤 ton
t'ong 통 pack; tub; barrel; *t'ong, subdivision of a city* ◊ *countword for letters or documents*
t'ongch'al 통찰 insight
t'ongch'allyŏk innŭn 통찰력 있는 perceptive, shrewd
t'ongch'ihada 통치하다 rule (*of monarch*)
t'ongch'ija 통치자 ruler (*of state*)
t'ongdok'ada 통독하다 go through, read through
t'onggi 통기 ventilation
t'onggi kumŏng 통기 구멍 vent
t'onggŭnhada 통근하다 commute
t'onggŭnja 통근자 commuter
t'onggŭn kyot'ong 통근 교통 commuter traffic
t'onggŭn yŏlch'a 통근 열차 commuter train
t'onggwashik'ida 통과시키다 carry *proposal*, approve
t'onggwa yŏgaek 통과 여객 transit passenger
t'onggwa yŏgaek taehapsshil 통과 여객 대합실 transit lounge
t'onggye 통계 statistics, figures ◊ statistical
t'onggyehak 통계학 statistics
t'onggyejŏguro 통계적으로 statistically
t'onghada 통하다 flow; be

understood; be versed in; go through; open onto
t'onghae chinagada 통해 지나가다 pass through
t'onghaengin 통행인 passer-by
t'onghaengkkwŏn 통행권 right of way
t'onghaengnyo 통행료 toll
t'onghaeng usŏnkkwŏn 통행 우선권 priority, right of way
t'onghap'ada 통합하다 integrate
t'onghwa 통화 currency; telephone call
t'onghwa chaep'aengch'ang 통화 재팽창 reflation
t'onghwa chung shinho 통화중 신호 busy signal TELEC
t'onghwahada 통화하다 get through TELEC
t'onghwajung-in 통화중인 busy TELEC
t'onghwajung shinhoŭm 통화중 신호음 busy tone TELEC
t'onghwa p'aengch'angshik'ida 통화 팽창시키다 inflate
t'onghwaryo 통화료 toll TELEC
t'ong-il 통일 unification; reunification
t'ong-irhada 통일하다 unify
t'ongjang 통장 bank book, pass book; head of a *t'ong, subdivision of a city*
t'ongjehada 통제하다 control, regulate; master; *uriga t'ongjehal su ŏmnŭn sanghwang-ida* 우리가 통제할 수 없는 상황이다 these are circumstances beyond our control
t'ongjeshil 통제실 control center
t'ongji 통지 notice (*to leave job, house*); *nuguege chibŭl nagarago t'ongjihada* 누구에게 집을 나가라고 통지하다 give s.o. his/her notice
t'ongjorim 통조림 can
t'ongjorimdoen 통조림된 canned
t'ongjorimhada 통조림 하다 can
t'ongmilppang 통밀빵 wholemeal bread
t'ongnamu 통나무 log
t'ongnamu odumaktchip 통나무 오두막집 log cabin
t'ongno 통로 aisle; passageway;

gangway

t'ongnye 통례 custom
t'ongnyeŭi 통례의 customary
t'ongnyŏrhan 통렬한 scathing
t'ongp'ung 통풍 draft
t'ongp'ung-i chal toenŭn 통풍이 잘 되는 drafty
t'ongshin 통신 communications; telecommunications
t'ongshin p'anmae ch'aektcha 통신 판매 책자 mail-order catalog
t'ongshin p'anmae hoesa 통신 판매 회사 mail-order firm
t'ongshinsa 통신사 news agency
t'ongshin wisŏng 통신 위성 communications satellite
t'ongsollyŏk 통솔력 leadership
t'ongsorhada 통솔하다 lead
t'ongtchaero kuptta 통째로 굽다 barbecue
t'ongt'onghada 통통하다 be chubby
t'ongt'onghan 통통한 chubby
t'ongyŏk 통역 interpretation
t'ongyŏk-kka 통역가 interpreter
t'ongyŏk'ada 통역하다 interpret
t'onik wŏt'ŏ 토닉 워터 tonic water
t'onŏ 토너 toner
t'op 톱 saw
t'opkkiŏ 톱기어 top (gear)
t'op-ppap 톱밥 sawdust
t'op'i 토피 toffee
t'op'ing 토핑 topping
t'op'ŭllisŭ 토플리스 topless
t'oron 토론 discussion, debate
t'osŭt'ŭ 토스트 toast
t'oyoil 토요일 Saturday
t'uda 트다 open *bank account*; sprout (*of seed*)
t'ŭgi ch'ejil 특이 체질 peculiarity
t'ŭgihan 특이한 peculiar to
t'ŭgiŏptcha 투기업자 speculator
t'ŭgyuŭi 특유의 distinctive
t'ŭkch'urhan 특출한 outstanding; high-powered
t'ŭk-kkwŏnŭl kajin 특권을 가진 privileged
t'ŭkppyŏl chosadan 특별 조사단 task force
t'ŭkppyŏl kwallamsŏk 특별 관람석 grandstand
t'ŭkppyŏl poryuji 특별 보류지 reservation (*special area*)
t'ŭkppyŏrhada 특별하다 be special
t'ŭkppyŏrhage 특별하게 particularly, especially
t'ŭkppyŏrhan 특별한 particular, special
t'ŭkppyŏrhan yeoeŭi 특별한 예외의 exceptional, special
t'ŭkppyŏrhi 특별히 especially, in particular, particularly
t'ŭkp'awŏn 특파원 (special) correspondent
t'ŭkssang-ŭi 특상의 choice, top quality
t'ŭkssŏng 특성 characteristic, trait; special quality
t'ŭkssŏng-ŭl nat'anaeda 특성을 나타내다 characterize, be typical of
t'ŭkssŏng-ŭl nat'anaenŭn 특성을 나타내는 characteristic, typical
t'ŭkssu kidongdae 특수 기동대 taskforce
t'ŭktchil 특질 idiosyncrasy
t'ŭktching 특징 character, feature; *...ŭl/rŭl t'ŭktching-ŭro hada* ...을/를 특징으로 하다 make a feature of; emphasize
t'ŭktching-ŏmnŭn 특징없는 nondescript
t'ŭktchŏn 특전 privilege; prerogative
t'ŭktchŏnghada 특정하다 specify
t'ŭktchŏnghan 특정한 particular, specific
t'ŭktchong 특종 scoop (*in journalism*)
t'ŭkttaehyŏng-ŭi 특대형의 outsize
t'ŭk'i 특히 especially; specifically
t'ŭk'i choahanŭn 특히 좋아하는 favorite
t'ŭk'ŏ 특허 patent
t'ŭk'ŏrŭl ŏt-tta 특허를 얻다 patent
t'ŭl 틀 frame; casing; mold
t'ŭlda 틀다 put on, turn on
t'ŭlli 틀니 false teeth
t'ŭllida 틀리다 be wrong; go wrong, make a mistake
t'ŭllige 틀리게 incorrectly
t'ŭllimŏmnŭn 틀림없는 correct; unmistakable
t'ŭllimŏptta 틀림없다 must be; *6shiime t'ŭllimŏptta* 6시임에

틀림없다 it must be about 6 o'clock; ***t'üllimŏpsshi ...l kŏshida* 틀림없이 ...ㄹ 것이다** be bound to, be sure to

t'üllin 틀린 incorrect, wrong, mistaken

t'üllin koshi manün 틀린 곳이 많은 corrupt COMPUT

t'üllin parüm 틀린 발음 mispronunciation

t'üllin parümül hada 틀린 발음을 하다 mispronounce

t'üm 틈 space; gap; opening; ***kip'ün t'üm* 깊은 틈** gulf

t'ümsae 틈새 niche, slot

t'ünt'ünhada 튼튼하다 be robust, be healthy

t'ünt'ünhan 튼튼한 healthy, robust, solid

t'üraek 트랙 track

t'üraekt'ŏ 트랙터 tractor

t'üraemp'ollin 트램폴린 trampoline

t'üraenjisüt'ŏ 트랜지스터 transistor

t'üraenjisüt'ŏ ladio 트랜지스터 라디오 transistor radio

t'üraiaenggül 트라이앵글 triangle MUS

t'üredü 트레드 tread (*of tire*)

t'üreillŏ 트레일러 trailer

t'üre kkiuda 틀에 끼우다 frame

t'üre nŏŏ mandülda 틀에 넣어 만들다 mold

t'ürim 트림 belch

t'ürimhada 트림하다 belch

t'ürŏk 트럭 truck

t'ürŏk unjŏnsa 트럭 운전사 truck driver, teamster

t'ürŏ maktta 틀어 막다 plug *hole*

t'ürŏmbon 트럼본 trombone

t'ürŏmp'et 트럼펫 trumpet

t'ürŏngk'ü 트렁크 trunk

t'ürŏollin mŏri 틀어올린 머리 bun (*in hair*)

t'ürol ŏsŏn 트롤 어선 trawler

t'üwin pedü 트윈 베드 twin beds

t'udŏlgŏrida 투덜거리다 grumble

t'ugi 투기 speculation FIN; jealousy

t'ugihada 투기하다 speculate FIN

t'ugijŏk saŏp 투기적 사업 venture

t'uguhada 투구하다 pitch SP

t'ugwang chomyŏng 투광 조명 floodlight

t'uhahada 투하하다 jettison, throw overboard; drop *bomb*

t'uip chŏnyŏlgi 투입 전열기 immersion heater

t'uja 투자 stake, investment

t'ujaeng 투쟁 fight, conflict

t'ujaengtchŏgin 투쟁적인 militant

t'ujahada 투자하다 invest

t'ujaja 투자자 investor

t'uk t'wiŏ naon 툭 튀어 나온 prominent

t'umyŏnghan 투명한 transparent

t'ungmyŏngsŭrŏptta 퉁명스럽다 be curt, be blunt

t'ungmyŏngssŭrŏun 퉁명스러운 abrupt, curt

t'uok 투옥 imprisonment

t'uok'ada 투옥하다 imprison

t'up'isü 투피스 two-piece

t'up'yo 투표 vote; voting; ***t'up'yokkwŏnül kajida* 투표권을 가지다** have the vote

t'up'yohada 투표하다 vote

t'up'yoro chŏnghada 투표로 정하다 ballot

t'usa 투사 militant

t'usu 투수 pitcher SP

t'usuk shigan 투숙 시간 check-in time (*at hotel*)

t'wida 튀다 bounce; splash

t'wige hada 튀게 하다 bounce

t'wigida 튀기다 splatter; deep-fry

t'wigim 튀김 (deep) fried food

t'winggida 튕기다 twang

t'wiŏ naoda 튀어나오다 bulge, project

t'yubü 튜브 tube

t'yubüga ŏmnün 튜브가 없는 tubeless *tire*

t'yullip 튤립 tulip

t'yunŏ 튜너 tuner

Ŭ

ŭddŭm direkt'ori 으뜸 디렉토리 root
directory
...ŭi ...의 of; kŭ ch'aŭi saek 그 차의
색 the color of the car
ŭi-ahage yŏgida 의아하게 여기다
wonder, think
ŭibok 의복 garment
ŭibudadŭl 의붓아들 stepson
ŭibut-tchamae 의붓자매 stepsister
ŭibut-ttal 의붓딸 stepdaughter
ŭibut'yŏngje 의붓형제 stepbrother
ŭibyŏng 의병 righteous army
ŭichimhaji annŭn 의심하지 않는
unsuspecting
ŭich'i 의치 dentures
ŭido 의도 intention
ŭidohada 의도하다 mean, intend;
muŏsŭl ŭidohada 무엇을 의도하다
intend to do sth, do sth on purpose
ŭidojŏgin 의도적인 intentional
ŭigiyangyang 의기양양 elation
ŭigiyangyanghan 의기양양한 elated
ŭigushim 의구심 doubt, uncertainty;
reservation
ŭigyŏn 의견 opinion; naŭi
ŭigyŏnŭronŭn 나의 의견으로는 in
my opinion
ŭigyŏn ch'ai 의견 차이
disagreement, misunderstanding
ŭigyŏni mat-tchi ant'a 의견이 맞지
않다 disagree with
ŭigyŏnŭl murŏboda 의견을 물어보다
canvass, seek opinion of
ŭigyŏnŭl mut-tta 의견을 묻다
consult, seek the advice of
ŭigyŏnŭl tallihada 의견을 달리하다
differ, dissent from, disagree
ŭihae 의해 by
ŭihak 의학 medicine (science) ◊
medical
ŭihak pakssa 의학 박사 MD, Doctor
of Medicine
ŭihoe 의회 assembly; council;
parliament

ŭihoeŭi 의회의 parliamentary
ŭija 의자 chair
ŭijang 의장 chairman, the chair
ŭijangjigŭl mat-tta 의장직을 맡다
chair; take the chair
ŭiji 의지 will, willpower
ŭijiga kanghan 의지가 강한 strong-
willed
ŭijiga kudŭn 의지가 굳은 resolute
ŭijihada 의지하다 rely on, look to
ŭijiryŏk 의지력 willpower
ŭijŏrhada 의절하다 disown
ŭijonhada 의존하다 depend; muŏse
ŭijonhada 무엇에 의존하다 depend
on sth; nanŭn nŏhant'e ŭijonhago
it-tta 난는 너한테 의존하고 있다 I
depend on you
ŭijonhanŭn 의존하는 dependant
ŭimi 의미 sense, meaning
ŭimihada 의미하다 signify, mean
ŭimiinnŭn 의미있는 meaningful,
constructive
ŭimu 의무 duty; obligation;
responsibility
ŭimujŏgin 의무적인 compulsory,
mandatory
ŭimu kyoyuk 의무 교육 compulsory
education
ŭimun 의문 query
ŭimunsa 의문사 interrogative
ŭimunŭl chegihada 의문을 제기하다
query
ŭimurŭl chiuda 의무를 지우다 bind,
oblige
ŭimuŭi 의무의 obligatory
ŭinonhada 의논하다 discuss, talk
over, talk
ŭiroe 의뢰 commission (job)
ŭiroehada 의뢰하다 commission (for
a job)
ŭiroein 의뢰인 client
ŭirye 의례 protocol, etiquette
ŭiryo pohŏm 의료 보험 medical
insurance

ŭiryu 의류 clothing
ŭisa 의사 doctor
ŭisa chŏndal 의사 전달 communication
ŭisa kyŏltchŏngja 의사 결정자 decision-maker
ŭisang 의상 outfit, costume
ŭisa p'yoshi 의사 표시 gesture
ŭisarok 의사록 minutes (of meeting)
ŭisarŭl sot'onghada 의사를 소통하다 communicate
ŭishigi innŭn 의식이 있는 conscious
ŭishigŭi 의식의 ritual
ŭishigŭl hoebok'ada 의식을 회복하다 come to, regain consciousness
ŭishigŭl ilt'a 의식을 잃다 lose consciousness, black out
ŭishik 의식 ritual, ceremony; consciousness
ŭishik sangshil 의식 상실 blackout
ŭishiktchŏgin 의식적인 conscious, deliberate
ŭishim 의심 suspicion, doubt
ŭishimhada 의심하다 doubt, question, suspect; *ŭishimhal yŏji ŏpsshi* 의심할 여지 없이 undoubtedly, indisputably
ŭishimŏmnŭn 의심없는 unquestioning
ŭishimsŭrŏpkke 의심스럽게 doubtfully
ŭishimsŭrŏptta 의심스럽다 be doubtful (of person)
ŭishimsŭrŏun 의심스러운 dubious; suspicious; questionable
ŭishimtchŏgŭn 의심쩍은 doubtful; in question; shady
ŭishimtchŏk-kke saenggak'ada 의심쩍게 생각하다 doubt
ŭisŏk 의석 seat POL
ŭiwŏn 의원 councilor
ŭiyok 의욕 will, motivation; *nanŭn pyŏllo ŭiyogi annanda* 나는 별로 의욕이 안난다 I don't feel very motivated
ŭkkaeda 으깨다 mash
ŭkkaen kamja 으깬 감자 mashed potatoes
...ŭl ...을 object particle; future particle
-(ŭ)lsurok -(으)ㄹ수록 the more... the

more ...; *manŭlsurok chohayo* 많을수록 좋아요 the more the better
ŭmak 음악 music
ŭmak hak-kkyo 음악 학교 music school, conservatory
ŭmakkat'ŭn 음악같은 musical, melodious
ŭmak-kka 음악가 musician
ŭmaktchŏgin 음악적인 musical person
ŭmaktchŏk sojiri ŏmnŭn 음악적 소질이 없는 unmusical
ŭmban 음반 album
ŭmch'imhan 음침한 bleak, dingy
ŭmgŭgŭi 음극의 negative ELEC
ŭmgye 음계 scale MUS
ŭmgyŏng 음경 penis
ŭmhŏmhan 음험한 underhand, devious; insidious
ŭmhyanghak 음향학 acoustics
ŭmjŏl 음절 syllable
ŭmjŏng-i mannŭn 음정이 맞는 in tune
ŭmjŏng-i t'ŭllin 음정이 틀린 out of tune
ŭmju 음주 drinking
ŭmju ch'ŭktchŏnggi 음주 측정기 Breathalyzer®, breath analyzer
ŭmjuja 음주자 drinker
ŭmju unjŏn 음주 운전 drink driving
ŭmmi 음미 taste, savor
ŭmmihada 음미하다 taste, savor
ŭmmo 음모 conspiracy, intrigue; pubic hair
ŭmmohada 음모하다 plot
ŭmmoja 음모자 conspirator
ŭmmorŭl kkumida 음모를 꾸미다 conspire
ŭmnanhada 음란하다 be obscene
ŭmnanhan 음란한 dirty; obscene; pornographic
ŭmnyang 음량 volume
ŭmnyang 음양 yin and yang
ŭmnyang chojŏlgi 음량 조절기 volume control
ŭmnyŏk 음역 range
ŭmnyŏk 음력 lunar calendar
ŭmnyŏk'ada 음역하다 transliterate
ŭmnyo 음료 beverage, drink
ŭmp'yo 음표 note MUS
ŭmsaek 음색 tone

ŭmsanhan 음산한 dismal

ŭmshik 음식 food

ŭmsŏng up'yŏn 음성 우편 voice mail

ŭn 은 silver

...ŭn ... 은 → **nŭn** 는

ŭnbang-ul kkot 은방울 꽃 lily of the valley

ŭnch'ong 은총 blessing

ŭndunja 은둔자 recluse, hermit

ŭndunsaenghwal 은둔생활 secluded life

ŭngch'uk 응축 condensation

ŭngch'uk'ada 응축하다 condense

ŭngdal 응달 shade; **ŭngdare(sŏ)** 응달에(서) in the shade

ŭngdap 응답 answer

ŭngdap'ada 응답하다 answer

ŭnggohada 응고하다 set, congeal; curdle

ŭnggoshik'ida 응고시키다 coagulate

ŭnggŭp ch'iryo 응급 치료 first aid

ŭnghada 응하다 comply; comply with; **k'waehi ŭnghada** 쾌히 응하다 jump at, take eagerly

ŭngmoja 응모자 applicant

ŭngmojak 응모작 entry (*for competition*)

ŭngmo sŏryu 응모 서류 entry form

ŭngnak 응낙 compliance

ŭn-goe 은괴 silver ingot

ŭngshi 응시 gaze

ŭngshihada 응시하다 gaze; gaze at; contemplate

ŭngshija 응시자 entrant, candidate

ŭn-gŭnhi 은근히 politely; secretly; **...ranŭn ŭishimŭl ŭn-gŭnhi kajida** ...라는 의심을 은근히 가지다 have a sneaking suspicion that

ŭng-wŏnhada 응원하다 cheer on

ŭngyong p'ŭrogŭraem 응용 프로그램 application (program)

ŭnhaeng 은행 bank

ŭnhaeng chan-go 은행 잔고 bank balance

ŭnhaengga 은행가 banker

ŭnhaeng t'ongjang 은행 통장 bank book

ŭnhaeng yungja 은행 융자 bank loan

ŭnhye 은혜 obligation, moral indebtedness; **nuguege ŭnhyerŭl ipkko it-tta** 누구에게 은혜를 입고 있다 be under an obligation to s.o.

ŭnhyerŭl pep'unŭn saram 은혜를 베푸는 사람 benefactor

...(ŭ)nji ...(으)ㄴ지 → **...inji** ...인지

ŭnjong-i 은종이 tinfoil

ŭnmirhi 은밀히 secretly

ŭnnik 은닉 secretion, concealment

ŭnnik'ada 은닉하다 conceal, hide; **chiharo ŭnnik'ada** 지하로 은닉하다 go underground

ŭnŏ 은어 slang

ŭnppich'ŭi 은빛의 silver

ŭnp'ye 은폐 cover-up

ŭnshinch'ŏ 은신처 hideaway

ŭnshinhada 은신하다 be in hiding

ŭn togŭmhan 은 도금한 silver-plated

ŭnt'oe 은퇴 retirement

ŭnt'oehada 은퇴하다 retire

ŭnt'oehan 은퇴한 retired

ŭp 읍 large township

...ŭro ...으로 by; from, because of; of; into; in; with; to; toward

...ŭrobut'ŏ ...으로부터 from

...ŭrosŏ ...으로서 as

ŭrŭrŏnggŏrida 으르렁거리다 growl, snarl

U

uahada 우아하다 be graceful; be elegant

uahan 우아한 graceful; elegant

ubak 우박 hail

ubi 우비 raincoat

Uchahyŏng k'ŏbŭ U자형 커브 hairpin curve

uch'ebu 우체부 mailman

uch'eguk 우체국 post office

uch'et'ong 우체통 mailbox

uch'ŭgŭi 우측의 starboard; right

uch'ŭk haendul unjŏn 우측 핸들 운전 right-hand drive

uch'ŭk konggyŏkssu 우측 공격수 right wing

udaehanŭn 우대하는 preferential

udumŏri 우두머리 head; boss; leader

udunhan 우둔한 dense, dim, stupid

ugŏjin 우거진 dense *foliage*

ugŭlgŏrida 우글거리다 swarm, crowd

uhoe 우회 detour, diversion

uhoehada 우회하다 bypass, circumvent

uhoero 우회로 bypass

uhoeshik'ida 우회시키다 divert

uhoeŭi 우회의 roundabout

uhojŏgin 우호적인 amicable

uigŭi 우익의 right-wing

uik 우익 right, right wing; *uige(sŏ)* 우익에(서) on the right

uik chijija 우익 지지자 right winger

ujŏkujŏk sshiptta 우적우적 씹다 munch

ujŏng 우정 friendship

uju 우주 space, outer space; universe

ujubok 우주복 spacesuit

uju chŏnggŏjang 우주 정거장 space station

ujuin 우주인 astronaut

uju pihaengsa 우주 비행사 cosmonaut

ujusŏn 우주선 spaceship, spacecraft

uju wangbokssŏn 우주 왕복선 space shuttle

ujuyŏhaeng 우주여행 voyage (*in space*)

ulbujit-tta 울부짖다 howl, wail

ulch'anghage charada 울창하게 자라다 thrive

ulda 울다 weep, cry; bawl, bellow

ullida 올리다 go off (*of alarm*); blow; ring; honk

ullim 울림 ring (*of bell*); roll (*of thunder*); echo

Ullŭngdo 울릉도 Ullung Island

ullyŏ p'ŏjida 울려 퍼지다 echo, reverberate; blare out

ultchŏk'ada 울적하다 be melancholy

ult'ari 울타리 fence; railings; hedge; barrier

ult'ariro tullŏ ssada 울타리로 둘러 싸다 fence in

ult'ungbult'unghada 울퉁불퉁하다 be bumpy

ult'ungbult'unghan 울퉁불퉁한 rough; bumpy; lumpy

umch'ŭrida 움츠리다 cower

umch'urida 움추리다 curl up

umjigida 움직이다 move, budge; dislodge; operate, run

umjigim 움직임 motion; move; movement; maneuver

umjiginŭn 움직이는 moving (*which can move*)

umk'yŏjaptta 움켜잡다 grasp

ummorŭl kkumida 음모를 꾸미다 frame, set up

ump'uk kkŏjida 움푹 꺼지다 cave in

ump'uk tŭrŏgage hada 움푹 들어가게 하다 dent

ump'uk tŭrŏgan 움푹 들어간 hollow

umtchirhada 움찔하다 flinch

umul 우물 well

un 운 luck, fortune; rhyme; *une matkkigo haeboda* 운에 맡기고 해보다 take a chance; *uni chot'a* 운이 좋다 be lucky, luck out; *uni mat-tta* 운이 맞다 rhyme with

unban 운반 haulage
unbanhada 운반하다 convey, carry
unbanin 운반인 porter
unban sudan 운반 수단 vehicle
un chok'e 운 좋게 luckily
un choŭn 운 좋은 lucky
undong 운동 campaign, drive; movement; exercise ◊ sporting, athletic
undongga 운동가 athlete; campaigner
undonggyŏnggi 운동경기 athletics
undonghada 운동하다 exercise, take exercise; work out; play SP
undonghwa 운동화 sneakers
undongjang 운동장 arena
undong pujogin 운동 부족인 unfit
undongshik'ida 운동시키다 exercise
undong-ŭl hada 운동을 하다 campaign
ungbyŏn-ga 웅변가 speaker, orator
ungdaehan 웅대한 epic; tremendous; impressive; majestic
ungdŏng-i 웅덩이 pool; puddle
ungjanghada 웅장하다 be grand
ungjangham 웅장함 grandeur
ungjanghan 웅장한 grand
ungk'ŭrida 웅크리다 stoop, bend down
unha 운하 canal
unhaengdoeda 운행되다 run (of trains etc)
unim mit pohŏm p'oham kagyŏk 운임 및 보험 포함 가격 CIF, cost insurance freight
unjŏn 운전 drive; driving
unjŏnhada 운전하다 drive
unjŏn hagwŏn 운전 학원 driving school
unjŏnja 운전자 driver; motorist
unjŏn kyoyuk 운전 교육 driving lesson
unjŏn kyoyuk kangsa 운전 교육 강사 driving instructor
unjŏn myŏnhŏ shihŏm 운전 면허 시험 driving test
unjŏn myŏnhŏtchŭng 운전 면허증 driver's license
unjŏntae 운전대 steering column
unmyŏng 운명 fate, destiny
unmyŏng chiuda 운명 지우다 condemn

unmyŏng yejŏngsŏl 운명 예정설 predestination
unŏmnŭn 운없는 unlucky, unfortunate
unŏpkke 운없게 unluckily
unsŏk 운석 meteorite
unsong hoesa 운송 회사 carrier, haulage company
unsuŏptcha 운수업자 forwarding agent
unttaega mannŭn 운때가 맞는 lucky
unyŏng 운영 operations
unyŏngdoeda 운영되다 operate
unyŏnghada 운영하다 run, manage
up'yŏn 우편 mail ◊ postal; *muŏsŭl up'yŏnŭro ponaeda* 무엇을 우편으로 보내다 put sth in the mail
up'yŏnham 우편함 mailbox
up'yŏnhwan 우편환 money order
up'yŏn pŏnho 우편 번호 zip code
up'yŏn yogŭm 우편 요금 postage
up'yo 우표 stamp
uranyum 우라늄 uranium
uri 우리 we; us ◊ cage; pen; pound
uri chashin 우리 자신 ourselves; *uri chashinŭro* 우리 자신으로 by ourselves; *urikkiriŭi yaegiijiman* 우리끼리의 얘기이지만 between you and me
urida 우리다 infuse
uriŭi 우리의 our; my
uriŭi kŏt 우리의 것 ours; mine
urŏnada 우러나다 well up; soak out; *chinshimesŏ urŏnan* 진심에서 우러난 heartfelt
urŭmŭl t'ŏttŭrida 울음을 터뜨리다 burst into tears
urŭrunggŏrida 우르릉거리다 roar
ururu taranada 우루루 달아나다 stampede
ururu taranam 우루루 달아남 stampede
uryang chushik 우량 주식 blue chip
uryangju 우량주 gilts
uryŏhada 우려하다 worry
usan 우산 umbrella
usang 우상 idol
use 우세 domination, superiority
usehan 우세한 prevailing
usŏn 우선 firstly

usŏng-ŭi 우성의 dominant
usŏn-gwŏnŭl chuda 우선권을 주다
give preference to
usŏnhada 우선하다 take precedence;
take precedence over
usŏnkkwŏni it-tta 우선권이 있다
have priority
usŏnkkwŏnŭl chuda 우선권을 주다
prioritize, give priority to
usŏn sunwirŭl maegida 우선 순위를
매기다 prioritize, put in order of
priority
usŏnŭn 우선은 first of all
usosŭl pŏtko 웃옷을 벗고 in his
shirt sleeves
usŭgae sori 우스개 소리 joke
usŭkkwangsŭrŏun 우스꽝스러운
comical
usŭl iri anida 웃을 일이 아니다 it's
no joke
usŭm 웃음 laugh; laughter
usŭmkkŏriga toeda 웃음거리가 되다
make a fool of oneself, become a
laughing stock
usŭmŭl chaanaenŭn 웃음을
자아내는 hilarious
usŭngja 우승자 winner
usŭngk'ŏp 우승컵 trophy, cup
usŭngp'ae 우승패 shield, trophy
usŭpkkedo 우습게도 funnily enough
usŭpkke yŏgida 우습게 여기다 jeer
at
usŭptta 우습다 be funny
usŭun 우스운 funny, humorous
utchuldaenŭn 우쭐대는 big-headed
utkkida 웃기다 amuse
utkkige 웃기게 comically
utkkinŭn chit 웃기는 짓 farce
utkkinŭn nom 웃기는 놈 joker,
comedian, clown *pej*
uttchuldaeda 우쭐대다 show off *pej*

ut-tta 웃다 laugh
uul 우울 gloom
uultchŭng 우울증 depression
uultchŭng hwanja 우울증 환자
hypochondriac
uurhada 우울하다 be gloomy
uurhaehada 우울해하다 depress, get
down; mope
uurhagehada 우울하게하다 depress,
get down
uurhagehanŭn 우울하게하는
depressing; oppressive
uurhan 우울한 depressed; gloomy;
morose
uusorirŭl naeda 우우소리를 내다
hoot
uyŏn 우연 chance, luck
uyŏnhada 우연하다 be accidental
uyŏnhan 우연한 casual; accidental;
chance
uyŏnhan mannam 우연한 만남
chance encounter
uyŏnhan sakkŏn 우연한 사건
accident
uyŏnhi 우연히 by accident, by chance
uyŏnhi irŏnanŭn 우연히 일어나는
incidental
uyŏnhi majuch'ida 우연히 마주치다
meet by chance
uyŏnhi mannada 우연히 만나다
bump into, meet by chance, run
across
uyŏnhi palgyŏnhada 우연히
발견하다 happen across, find by
chance
uyŏnhi tŭt-tta 우연히 듣다 overhear
uyŏnŭi ilch'i 우연의 일치
coincidence
uyu 우유 milk
uyubudan 우유부단 indecisiveness
uyubyŏng 우유병 bottle (*for baby*)

W

...wa ...와 and
wa! 와! wow!
wae 왜 why, what for; what is it?;
　wae andwae? 왜 안돼? why not?
waegari 왜가리 heron
waegŏn 왜건 station wagon
waegokttoen shigandae 왜곡된
　시간대 timewarp
waegok'ada 왜곡하다 distort
Waegu 왜구 Japanese marauders
waenyahamyŏn ...ki ttaemunida
　왜냐하면 ...기 때문이다 as, because
waip'ŏ 와이퍼 windshield wiper
waip'ŭ 와이프 wife
wajak-wajak soriga nada 와작와작
　소리가 나다 crunch
wakssŭ 왁스 wax
walch'ŭ 왈츠 waltz
wallyohyŏng 완료형 perfect GRAM
wanbyŏk 완벽 perfection
wanbyŏkjuŭija 완벽주의자
　perfectionist
wanbyŏk'ada 완벽하다 be perfect
wanbyŏk'age 완벽하게 perfectly;
　impeccably; soundly *beaten*; *muŏsŭl*
　wanbyŏk'age alda 무엇을 완벽하게
　알다 know sth inside out
wanbyŏk'an 완벽한 perfect;
　impeccable
wanbyŏk'i 완벽히 perfectly
wanch'ung changch'i 완충 장치
　buffer
wanch'unggi 완충기 shock absorber
wanch'ung kiŏk changch'i 완충
　기억 장치 memory buffer
wanch'ungnyŏk 완충역 buffer
wanduk'ong 완두콩 pea
wang 왕 king
wan-ganghada 완강하다 be
　stubborn, be dogged
wan-ganghan 완강한 determined,
　tenacious; stubborn
wangbok pihaenggi 왕복 비행기
　return flight

wangbok yŏhaeng 왕복 여행 round
　trip
wangbok yŏhaengp'yo 왕복 여행표
　round trip ticket
wangbok'ada 왕복하다 shuttle
wangguk 왕국 kingdom
wanggwan 왕관 crown
wangja 왕자 prince
wangjo 왕조 dynasty
wangjok 왕족 royalty
wangjwa 왕좌 throne
wan-gogŏ 완곡어 euphemism
wan-gohan 완고한 inflexible, rigid;
　headstrong; pigheaded
wangsŏnghada 왕성하다 be hearty
wangsŏnghan 왕성한 hearty;
　voracious
wang-wie ollida 왕위에 올리다
　crown
wanhwahada 완화하다 soften,
　cushion
wanhwashik'ida 완화시키다 relax
wanje 완제 wipe out
wanjep'um 완제품 end product
wanjŏnhada 완전하다 be perfect, be
　complete
wanjŏnhage 완전하게 perfectly,
　totally
wanjŏnhan 완전한 complete,
　thorough; pure; outright
wanjŏnhi 완전히 purely, nothing but;
　absolutely, completely; entirely
　fully; outright *win*
wanjŏnhi chami kkaen 완전히 잠이
　깬 wide awake
wanjŏnhi kkŭnnaeda 완전히 끝내다
　terminate
wanjŏnhi mach'ida 완전히 마치다
　complete
wanjŏnhi mich'in 완전히 미친
　raving mad
wanjŏnhi pusuda 완전히 부수다
　completely destroy, wipe out
wanjŏnhi p'agoehada 완전히

파괴하다 obliterate

wank'waehada 완쾌하다 make a complete recovery

wanmanhan 완만한 sluggish

wanp'aeshik'ida 완패시키다 bomb

wansŏng 완성 completion

wansŏngdoen 완성된 complete, finished

wansŏnghada 완성하다 complete

wap'ŭl 와플 waffle

washyŏ 와셔 washer

watta katta hada 왔다 갔다 하다 pace up and down

wat'ŭ 와트 watt

webbŭraujŏ 웹브라우저 web browser

weding k'eik'ŭ 웨딩 케이크 wedding cake

weding tŭresŭ 웨딩 드레스 wedding dress

Weiljŭ 웨일즈 Wales ◊ Welsh

weip'ŏ 웨이퍼 wafer

weit'ŏ 웨이터 waiter

weit'ŭrisŭ 웨이트리스 waitress

wep 웹 the Web

wep p'eiji 웹 페이지 web page

wep sa-it'ŭ 웹 사이트 web site

wi 위 upper side; top; superiority; rank; position; stomach ◊ gastric ◊ over, above

wian 위안 comfort, consolation

wianhada 위안하다 comfort, console

wiban 위반 violation, breach

wibanhada 위반하다 break, violate, contravene

wibŏp 위법 offense ◊ illicit

wich'i 위치 position, location, setting; situation

wich'ihada 위치하다 lie, be situated, be located; stand

wich'irŭl aranaeda 위치를 알아내다 locate

wich'irŭl chŏnghada 위치를 정하다 locate, site

wich'i sŏnjŏng 위치 선정 location, siting

wich'ŭng-e 위층에 upstairs, on the floor above

wich'ŭng-ŭi 위층의 upstairs

widaehada 위대하다 be great

widaeham 위대함 greatness

widaehan 위대한 grand

wido 위도 latitude; parallel

widok'ada 위독하다 be critically ill

widok'an 위독한 critical; critically ill

wie 위에 up; above; on top of; *hanŭl/chibung wie* 하늘/지붕 위에 up in the sky/up on the roof

wigi 위기 crisis; *...a(ŏ, yŏ)ya hal wigie mollyŏ it-tta* ...아(어, 여)야 할 위기에 몰려있다 be under pressure to ...

wigie ch'ŏhada 위기에 처하다 be at stake, be at risk

wigijŏgin 위기적인 critical, serious

wihae 위해 for; *...gi wihae* ...기 위해 to, in order to; *...gi wihayŏ* ...기 위하여 in order to; *...ŭl/rŭl wihaesŏ* ...을/를 위해서 for the sake of ...

wihan 위한 for; *igŏsŭn nŏrŭl wihan kŏshida* 이것은 너를 위한 것이다 this is for you

wihayŏ 위하여 on behalf of; for the sake of; in favor of

wihŏm 위험 risk, chance; danger, peril; *wihŏmŭl murŭpssŭda* 위험을 무릅쓰다 take a risk; *wihŏme ppajige hada* 위험에 빠지게 하다 endanger

wihŏmhada 위험하다 be dangerous

wihŏmhan 위험한 risky, dangerous; hazardous; treacherous

wihŏm inmul 위험 인물 menace; security risk (*person*)

wihŏmjidae 위험 지대 minefield

wihŏm yoso 위험 요소 hazard

wihyŏp 위협 threat, menace

wihyŏp'ada 위협하다 threaten, menace, terrorize

wihyŏp'anŭn 위협하는 threatening, menacing

wiim 위임 delegation

wiimhada 위임하다 delegate

wiimkkwŏn 위임권 power of attorney

wijak 위작 forgery (*painting*)

wijang 위장 disguise, camouflage; insides

wijanghada 위장하다 disguise, camouflage; impersonate

wijaryo 위자료 alimony

wijo 위조 forgery

wijo chip'ye 위조 지폐 forged bill, dud

wijodoen sŏryu 위조된 서류 forgery

wijohada 위조하다 falsify; forge, counterfeit

wijoja 위조자 forger

wijop'um 위조품 forgery

wijoŭi 위조의 counterfeit

wijŭng 위증 perjury

wijŭnghada 위증하다 perjure oneself

windou 윈도우 window COMPUT

windŭsŏp'ing 윈드서핑 windsurfing, sailboarding

windŭsŏp'ing podŭ 윈드서핑 보드 windsurfer, sailboard

wingk'ŭ 윙크 wink

wingk'ŭhada 윙크하다 wink

wing-winggŏrida 윙윙거리다 hum

wing-winghanŭn sori 윙윙하는 소리 buzz, drone

wingwing sorirŭl naeda 윙윙 소리를 내다 buzz

wingwing tolda 윙윙 돌다 whirr

wiŏmminnŭn 위엄있는 dignified, majestic

wiŏp 위업 exploit, feat

wiro 위로 up, upward ◊ consolation

wirohada 위로하다 console

wirohal kil ŏmnŭn 위로할 길 없는 inconsolable

wiro ollida 위로 올리다 scroll up

wiro tŏnjida 위로 던지다 throw up *ball*

wiro unbanhada 위로 운반하다 take up, carry up

wisaeng 위생 hygiene ◊ sanitary

wisaengch'ŏri 위생처리 sanitation

wisaengjŏgin 위생적인 sanitary

wisaengsang-ŭi 위생상의 hygienic

wisaengsŏlbi 위생설비 sanitation, sanitary installation

wishŏme ppattŭrida 위험에 빠뜨리다 risk

wisŏn 위선 hypocrisy

wisŏng t'ibŭi 위성 티브이 satellite TV

wisŏnja 위선자 hypocrite

wisŏnjŏgin 위선적인 hypocritical

wisŭk'i 위스키 whiskey

wit'aeroptta 위태롭다 be in jeopardy

wit'aeroun 위태로운 dangerous

wit'ak 위탁 consignment; trust FIN

witchoge 위쪽에 at the top of

wi tchogŭi 위 쪽의 upper

witppubun 윗부분 top

witssaram 윗사람 superior

wittchari 윗자리 superior position; *Xboda wittcharie innŭn* X보다 윗자리에 있는 be senior to X

wiŭi 위의 upper

wiwŏndan 위원단 panel, committee

wiwŏnhoe 위원회 committee, commission

wŏdŭ p'ŭrosesŏ 워드 프로세서 word processor

wŏdŭ p'ŭrosesŭrŭl sayong 워드 프로세스를 사용 word processing

wŏk'ŭmaen 워크맨 Walkman®

wŏk'ŭshyop 워크숍 workshop

wŏl 월 month; moon

wŏlbu 월부 monthly installment

Wŏldŭwaidŭwep 월드와이드웹 World Wide Web

wŏlganji 월간지 monthly (magazine)

wŏlgŭp 월급 wage; salary

wŏlgŭp pongt'u 월급 봉투 wage packet

wŏlgyesu 월계수 laurel

wŏlgyŏng 월경 menstruation

wŏlgyŏnghada 월경하다 menstruate

wŏllae 원래 originally

wŏllyo 원료 raw materials

Wŏlnam 월남 Vietnam ◊ Vietnamese

Wŏlnamin 월남인 Vietnamese

Wŏlnamŏ 월남어 Vietnamese *(language)*

wŏlsshik 월식 eclipse of the moon

Wŏl Sŭt'ŭrit'ŭ 월 스트리트 Wall Street

wŏn 원 circle; won FIN

wŏnban 원반 discus *(object)*

wŏnbanhyŏng 원반형 disk *(shape)*

wŏnban tŏnjigi 원반 던지기 discus *(event)*

wŏnbon 원본 original manuscript

Wŏnbulgyo 원불교 Won Buddhism

wŏnch'ik 원칙 principle, rule; *wŏnch'iktchŏguro* 원칙적으로 in principle, in theory

wŏnch'ŏn 원천 source

wŏndongnyŏk 원동력 dynamism

wŏn-giwangsŏnghan 원기왕성한

lively, sprightly; forceful
wŏn-gŏri 원거리 long-range
wŏn-go 원고 claimant, plaintiff; manuscript
wŏn-gwang 원광 halo
wŏnhada 원하다 want, desire; *...ŭl / rŭl wŏnhamnikka?* ...을 / 를 원합니까? would you like ...?
wŏnhan 원한 rancor; *nuguege ssain wŏnhanŭl p'ulda* 누구에게 쌓인 원한을 풀다 have a score to settle with s.o.
wŏnhyŏng 원형 circle, ring; prototype
wŏnin 원인 cause; *...ŭihan wŏnini toeda* ...의한 원인이 되다 contribute to
wŏnin kyumyŏng 원인 규명 inquest
wŏnja 원자 atom ◊ atomic
wŏnjak 원작 original *painting etc*
wŏnja p'okt'an 원자 폭탄 atom bomb
wŏnjaro 원자로 nuclear reactor
wŏnjaryŏk 원자력 nuclear power, atomic energy
wŏnjaryŏk paltchŏnso 원자력 발전소 nuclear power station
wŏnjŏng shihap 원정 시합 away game
wŏnjohada 원조하다 assist; *kyŏng-jejŏgŭro wŏnjohada* 경제적으로 원조하다 stake, help financially
wŏnju 원주 circumference
wŏnjumin 원주민 native
wŏnkka 원가 cost, cost price
wŏnkkŭbŭi 원급의 positive GRAM

wŏnkkyŏk chŏpkkŭn 원격 접근 remote access
wŏnkkyŏk chojong 원격 조종 remote control
wŏnmang 원망 resentment
wŏnmanghada 원망하다 resent; bear a grudge; *Xttaemune Yŭl / rŭl wŏnmanghada* X때문에 Y을 / 를 원망하다 hold X against Y
wŏnmanhage haegyŏrhada 원만하게 해결하다 smooth things over
wŏnŏmin 원어민 native speaker
wŏnppul 원뿔 cone
wŏnshijŏgin 원시적인 primitive
wŏnshiŭi 원시의 primitive; far-sighted
wŏnso 원소 element
wŏnsu 원수 enemy
wŏnsuk'ada 원숙하다 mellow
wŏnsuk'an 원숙한 mellow
wŏnsung-i 원숭이 monkey
wŏntchang 원장 ledger
wŏntchŏm 원점 original point, square one; *urinŭn wŏntchŏmŭro torawat-tta* 우리는 원점으로 돌아왔다 we're back to square one
wŏnyang 원양 deep-sea, ocean ◊ ocean-going
wŏnye 원예 gardening; horticulture
wŏnyu 원유 crude (oil)
wŏnt'ong 원통 cylinder
wŏnt'ong moyang-ŭi 원통 모양의 cylindrical
wŏryoil 월요일 Monday
Wŏshingt'ŏn 워싱턴 Washington

XY

Xsŏn X선 X-ray (*picture*)
Xsŏn ch'waryŏng-ŭl hada X선 촬영을 하다 X-ray *patient*

yabihan nom 야비한 놈 jerk
yach'ae 야채 vegetable
yadanbŏpsŏgŭl p'iuda 야단법석을 피우다 play up (*of child*)
yadang 야당 opposition
yadŭ 야드 yard
yagan hak-kkyo 야간 학교 night school
yagan kŭnmu 야간 근무 night shift
yagan kŭnmuida 야간 근무이다 work nights
yagan oech'ul kŭmji 야간 외출 금지 curfew
yagan suŏp 야간 수업 evening classes
yagihada 야기하다 create, bring about, produce, generate
yagishik'ida 야기시키다 precipitate, cause to happen
yagŭn poi 야근 보이 night porter
yagu 야구 ball game, baseball
yagugong 야구공 baseball (*ball*)
yagujang 야구장 ballpark
yagu kŭllŏbŭ 야구 글러브 baseball glove
yagu moja 야구 모자 baseball cap
yagu pangmang-i 야구 방망이 baseball bat
yagu sŏnsu 야구 선수 baseball player
yagyŏngkkun 야경군 watchman
yagyong-ŭi 약용의 medicated
yahan 야한 gaudy; vulgar
yahoebok 야회복 evening dress; suit
yajanamu 야자나무 palm (tree)
yak 약 medicine; medication; drug ◊ in the region of, around; *yak 5,000 tallŏ* 약 5,000 달러 in the region of $5,000; *yak ...tchŭm* 약 ...쯤 around (*with expressions of time*); *yagŭl*

mŏgida 약을 먹이다 give medicine
yakkan 약간 drop, dash, touch ◊ slightly, vaguely
yakkanŭi 약간의 slight, small
yak-kkuk 약국 pharmacy
yak-kkwan 약관 (insurance) policy
yakssa 약사 druggist, pharmacist
yaksshigŭi 약식의 informal
yaksshik 약식 informality
yaksshik ch'ayong chŭngsŏ 약식 차용 증서 IOU
yaksshik yahoebok 약식 야회복 dinner jacket, tuxedo
yakssok 약속 promise, undertaking; engagement, appointment
yakssok changso 약속 장소 meeting place
yakssok'ada 약속하다 promise, pledge; *naega yakssok'agessumnida* 내가 약속하겠습니다 you have my word
yaktcha 약자 weakling; underdog; monogram; abbreviation
yaktchaga saegyŏjin 약자가 새겨진 monogrammed
yaktchang 약장 medicine cabinet
yaktchin 약진 tremor
yaktchŏm 약점 weakness, weak point
yakt'alp'um 약탈품 loot
yakt'altcha 약탈자 looter
yakt'arhada 약탈하다 loot
yak'ada 약하다 be weak; have a weakness for; abridge; omit
yak'aejida 약해지다 weaken
yak'aejinŭn 약해지는 ailing
yak'agehada 약하게 하다 weaken
yak'an 약한 weak, frail; flimsy; muted
yak'on 약혼 engagement
yak'onhada 약혼하다 get engaged
yak'onhan 약혼한 engaged
yak'onja 약혼자 fiancé
yak'onnyŏ 약혼녀 fiancée

yak'on panji 약혼 반지 engagement ring

yak'wadoeda 약화되다 go downhill (*of health*); slacken off

yak'washik'ida 약화시키다 sap

yalbda 얇다 be thin

yalbŭn 얇은 thin, flimsy

yalbŭn p'anyuri 얇은 판유리 laminated glass

yalkke charŭda 얇게 자르다 slice

yamang 야망 ambition

yamjŏnhada 얌전하다 be meek; be gentle; be nice

yamjŏnhan 얌전한 meek; gentle; nice

yang 양 Ms; quantity, amount, level; sheep; tripe; *Kim yang* 김 양 Miss Kim

yangbaech'u 양배추 cabbage

yangban 양반 aristocrat

yangbanghyang t'onghaengno 양방향 통행로 two-way traffic

yangbo 양보 concession, giving in

yangbohada 양보하다 give way, yield; back down, climb down; concede

yangbok 양복 suit (*man's*)

yangbok chokki 양복 조끼 vest

yangbumo 양부모 foster parents

yangbunhwahada 양분화하다 polarize

yangch'iaek 양치액 mouthwash

yangch'ijirhada 양치질하다 brush *teeth*

yangch'iryu 양치류 fern

yangch'o 양초 candle

yangdohada 양도하다 transfer

yangdong-i 양동이 bucket, pail

yanggagŭro 양각으로 in relief

yanggajuk 양가죽 sheepskin

yanggogi 양고기 lamb

yanggŭgŭi 양극의 positive

yanggwibi 양귀비 poppy

yanghoshil 양호실 infirmary

yangjaesa 양재사 dressmaker

yangjohada 양조하다 brew

yangjojang 양조장 brewery

yangjoŏptcha 양조업자 brewer

yangmal 양말 sock

yangmo 양모 wool

yangnip'ada 양립하다 coexist; be compatible

yangnowŏn 양로원 nursing home

yangnyŏm 양념 spice, seasoning; relish; sauce

yangnyŏmtchang 양념장 dip

yangnyŏp'e kŏnŭrida 양옆에 거느리다 be flanked by

yangnyŏp'e tuda 양옆에 두다 be flanked by

yangnyuk-kkwŏn 양육권 custody

yangnyuk'ada 양육하다 bring up *child*

yangp'a 양파 onion

yangshik 양식 form, document; pattern (*in behavior*); style; Western-style food; food ◊ Western-style

yangshik'wahada 양식화하다 format, lay out

yangshim 양심 conscience; *...e taehae yangshimŭi kach'aegŭl pat-tchi ant'a* ...에 대해 양심의 가책을 받지 않다 have no qualms about ...

yangshimjŏgin 양심적인 conscientious

yangshimjŏgŭro 양심적으로 religiously, conscientiously

yangshimtchŏk pyŏngnyŏk kŏbuja 양심적 병역 거부자 conscientious objector

yangshimŭi kach'aek 양심의 가책 qualm; guilty conscience

yangsŏng-aeja 양성애자 bisexual

yangsŏng-ŭi 양성의 positive; benign; bisexual

yangtchok 양쪽 both; both sides

yang-ŭl chaeda 양을 재다 quantify

yaoe 야외 the open air ◊ outdoor, open-air; *yaoe ch'waryŏngjung* 야외 촬영중 on location

yaoeesŏ 야외에서 outdoors, in the open air

yaong 야옹 miaow

yasaeng 야생 wild

yasaeng tongmul 야생 동물 wildlife

yashiminnŭn 야심있는 ambitious

yat-tta 얕다 be shallow; be superficial; be low

yatchababonŭn 얕잡아보는 contemptuous

yat'ŭn 얕은 shallow, superficial

yawida 야위다 waste away

yayŏngji 야영지 campsite, camp ground

yayu 야유 jeer

yayuhada 야유하다 jeer; heckle; boo

yayurŭl ponaeda 야유를 보내다 hiss

ye 예 example, instance; old times; ceremony; courtesy; salute; bow ◊ yes; *choŭn / nappŭn yega toeda* 좋은 / 나쁜 예가 되다 set a good / bad example

yebaedang 예배당 chapel

yebang 예방 prevention; precaution

yebang chŏptchong 예방 접종 vaccination, inoculation; *... yebang chŏptchong chusarŭl mat-tta* ... 예방 접종 주사를 맞다 be vaccinated against

yebang chŏptchonghada 예방 접종하다 vaccinate, inoculate

yebanghada 예방하다 ward off

yebang-ŭi 예방의 preventive, precautionary

yebihada 예비하다 anticipate

yebi kyehoek 예비 계획 pilot scheme

yebi pak'wi 예비 바퀴 spare wheel

yebip'um 예비품 spare (part)

yebisŏn-gŏ 예비선거 primary POL

yebi t'aiŏ 예비 타이어 spare tire

yebiŭi 예비의 preliminary; spare

yebok 예복 robe (of priest)

yech'ŭk'al su ŏmnŭn 예측할 수 없는 unpredictable

yegam 예감 premonition; hunch; idea

yegihada 예기하다 expect, anticipate

yegop'yŏn 예고편 trailer (of movie)

yegŭm 예금 savings; deposit; *yegŭmi it-tta* 예금이 있다 be in credit

yegŭmaek 예금액 credit (payment received)

yegŭmhada 예금하다 bank, deposit; *kyejwae yegŭmhada* 계좌에 예금하다 credit an amount to an account

yegyŏn 예견 prediction

yegyŏnhada 예견하다 predict, foresee, visualize

yeinsŏn 예인선 tug NAUT

yeji 예지 prognosis

yejŏn 예전 former times

yejŏne 예전에 way back

yejŏng 예정 schedule; *yejŏngboda nŭt-tta* 예정보다 늦다 be behind schedule; *yejŏngdaero* 예정대로 as scheduled, duly, as expected; *...l yejŏng-ida* ...ㄹ 예정이다 be due to

yejŏnghada 예정하다 schedule

yennal 옛날 old days; *yennal saenggagi nage handa* 옛날 생각이 나게 한다 that takes me back; *yennal yettchŏge ...i issŏt-tta* 옛날 옛적에 ...이 있었다 once upon a time there was ...

yeŏn 예언 prophecy

yeŏnhada 예언하다 foretell, prophesy

yeoe 예외 exception

yeppŭda 예쁘다 be pretty

yeppŭjanghada 예쁘장하다 be lovely

yeppŭjanghan 예쁘장한 pretty

yeppŭn 예쁜 pretty

yerihada 예리하다 be sharp

yerihan 예리한 sharp; acute

yerŭl tŭlmyŏn 예를 들면 e.g.

yerŭl tŭrŏ 예를 들어 for instance

yerŭl tŭrŏsŏ 예를 들어서 for example

yesan 예산 budget; projection, forecast

yesane nŏt'a 예산에 넣다 budget for

yesang 예상 anticipation; forecast; prospect

yesanghada 예상하다 expect; forecast; anticipate; bargain for

yesang pakke 예상 밖에 unexpectedly

yesang sumyŏng 예상 수명 life expectancy

yesanhada 예산하다 project, work out in advance

yesanŭl seuda 예산을 세우다 budget

yeshihada 예시하다 illustrate (with examples)

yeshiktchang 예식장 wedding hall

yesŏnŭl t'onggwahada 예선을 통과하다 qualify

Yesu(nim) 예수(님) Jesus

yesul 예술 art

yesulga 예술가 artist

yesulp'um 예술품 art; work of art
yesultchŏgin 예술적인 artistic
yesun 예순 sixty
yesun pŏntchaeŭi 예순 번째의 sixtieth
yeŭi 예의 politeness; manners
yeŭiga ŏptta 예의가 없다 have no manners
yeŭi parŭge haengdonghada 예의 바르게 행동하다 behave (oneself)
yeŭi parŭn 예의 바른 polite, well-mannered
yeuhada 예우하다 honor
yeyagi kkwak ch'ada 예약이 꽉 차다 booked up
yeyak 예약 reservation
yeyak-kkŭm 예약금 deposit
yeyaktoen 예약된 reserved
yeyak'ada 예약하다 book, reserve; arrange
yŏbaek 여백 margin
yŏbo 여보 honey (*form of address to husband*)
yŏboge! 여보게! buddy! (*form of address*)
yŏboseyo 여보세요 hello TELEC
yŏbuni nama innŭn hando naeesŏ 여분이 남아 있는 한도 내에서 subject to availability
yŏdŏl 여덟 eight
yŏdŏl pŏntchaeŭi 여덟 번째의 eighth
yŏdŭn 여든 eighty
yŏdŭn pŏntchaeŭi 여든 번째의 eightieth
yŏdŭrŭm 여드름 spot; pimple
yŏdŭrŭmi nan 여드름이 난 spotty
yŏga 여가 leisure
yŏgajang 여가장 matriarch
yŏga shigan 여가 시간 leisure time
yŏgi 여기 here; *yŏgi issŭmnida* 여기 있습니다 here you are, there you are; *yŏgi itkkuna* 여기 있구나 here we are (*finding sth*)
yŏgida 여기다 consider, regard; *charangsŭrŏpkke yŏgida* 자랑스럽게 여기다 pride oneself on
yŏgie(sŏ) 여기에(서) here; in here
yŏgijŏgi 여기저기 here and there
yŏgijŏgi toradanida 여기저기 돌아다니다 wander around

yŏgijŏgi yŏhaenghada 여기저기 여행하다 get about, travel around
yŏgwagi 여과기 filter
yŏgwan 여관 guesthouse; inn; hostel
yŏgyŏng 여경 policewoman
yŏgyojang 여교장 principal, headmistress
yŏhaeng 여행 trip, journey; ride; travel; travels
yŏhaenggaek 여행객 traveler
yŏhaenghada 여행하다 travel
yŏhaengja sup'yo 여행자 수표 traveler's check
yŏhaeng kabang 여행 가방 travel bag; suitcase
yŏhaeng piyong 여행 비용 travel expenses
yŏhaeng pohŏm 여행 보험 travel insurance
yŏhaengsa 여행사 travel agency
yŏhaeng shigan 여행 시간 journey time; flight time
yŏhakssaeng 여학생 schoolgirl
Yŏhowaŭi Chŭng-in 여호와의 증인 Jehovah's Witness
yŏja 여자 woman
yŏja ch'in-gu 여자 친구 girl friend
yŏjadaun 여자다운 womanly
yŏjagat'ŭn 여자같은 effeminate
yŏja hwajangshil 여자 화장실 ladies' room
yŏja hyŏngje 여자 형제 sister
yŏjangbu 여장부 heroine
yŏjang-ŭl hago 여장을 하고 disguised as a woman; in drag
yŏja paeu 여자 배우 actress
yŏja sone chwiyŏ sanŭn 여자 손에 쥐여 사는 henpecked
yŏja undongga 여자 운동가 sportswoman
yŏje 여제 empress
yŏji 여지 scope, latitude
...yŏjida ...여지다 become ..., get ..., go ...
yŏjŏng 여정 itinerary; stage (*of journey*)
yŏjŏnhi 여전히 yet; still; as ever
yŏjong-ŏbwŏn 여종업원 hostess
yŏjuin 여주인 landlady; mistress
yŏk 역 station; part, role; *Haemlit yŏgŭro* 햄릿 역으로 in the role of

Hamlet, as Hamlet
yŏk-kkyŏpkke hada 역겹게 하다
nauseate, disgust
yŏk-kkyŏpta 역겹다 be nauseating;
be nauseated; feel nauseous
yŏk-kkyŏun 역겨운 nauseating
yŏk-kkyŏwŏ hada 역겨워 하다
sicken, disgust
yŏkkŏnaeda 엮어내다 concoct
yŏkkwŏn 여권 passport
yŏkkwŏnjuŭi 여권주의 feminism
yŏkkwŏnjuŭija 여권주의자 feminist
yŏkkwŏnjuŭijaŭi 여권주의자의
feminist
yŏkkwŏnjuŭiŭi 여권주의의 feminist
yŏkkwŏn kwalli 여권 관리 passport
control
yŏkkyŏun 역겨운 foul
yŏkssa 역사 history
yŏkssajŏgin 역사적인 historical
yŏkssasang-ŭro chungnyohan
역사상으로 중요한 historic
yŏksshi 역시 too, also; still; after all;
but, nevertheless; *yŏksshi
isanghagedo* 역시 이상하게도
strangely enough
yŏkssŏl 역설 paradox
yŏkssŏltchŏgin 역설적인
paradoxical
yŏkssŭp 역습 counter-attack
yŏkssŭp'ada 역습하다 counter-
attack
yŏktto 역도 weightlifting
yŏktto sŏnsu 역도 선수 weightlifter
yŏk'al 역할 role
yŏk'yokkwaga nada 역효과가 나다
backfire, rebound
yŏk'yokkwaŭi 역효과의 counter-
productive
yŏl 열 ten; row; line; tier; heat; fever;
temperature
yŏlbyŏngshik 열병식 review
yŏlda 열다 open; be off (*of lid, top*);
inaugurate; throw *party*
yŏldasŏt 열 다섯 fifteen
yŏldasŏt pŏntchaeŭi 열 다섯 번째의
fifteenth
yŏldu kae 열두 개 dozen
yŏldul 열 둘 twelve
yŏldu pŏntchaeŭi 열두 번째의
twelfth

yŏlgi 열기 open
yŏlgŏhada 열거하다 recite
yŏlgwang 열광 fascination;
yŏlgwanghada 열광하다 be crazy
about; go wild
yŏlgwanghan 열광한 delirious,
ecstatic
yŏlgwangtchŏgin 열광적인 wild,
rapturous; feverish; avid
yŏllagi it-tta 연락기 있다
communicate; *nuguwa yŏllagi
kkŭnkkida* 누구와 연락이 끊기다
lose touch with s.o.
yŏllak 연락 contact, liaison,
communication; *...wa / gwa
yŏllagŭl chugo pat-tta* ...와 / 과
연락을 주고 받다 keep in contact
with; *yŏllagŭl ch'wihada* 연락을
취하다 liaise with
yŏllakch'ŏ 연락처 contact number
yŏllak'ada 연락하다 apply to;
contact, get in touch with; *nuguwa
kyesok yŏllak'ada* 누구와 계속
연락하다 keep in touch with s.o.
yŏllet 열 넷 fourteen
yŏllida 열리다 open; take place
yŏllin 열린 open
yŏllip chut'aek 연립 주택 row house
yŏllu 연루 involvement; *nugurŭl
muŏse yŏllu shik'ida* 누구를
무엇에 연루 시키다 involve s.o. in
sth
yŏlludoeda 연루되다 be a party to,
be involved in; *muŏse yŏlludoeda*
무엇에 연루되다 get involved with
sth
yŏllyŏ innŭn 열려 있는 open
yŏllyŏrhan 열렬한 enthusiastic;
ardent, fervent; glowing
yŏllyo 연료 fuel
yŏllyorŭl konggŭp'ada 연료를
공급하다 refuel
yŏllyorŭl pogŭp pat-tta 연료를 보급
받다 refuel
yŏlne pŏntchaeŭi 열 네 번째의
fourteenth
yŏl pat-tta 열 받다 be steamed up
yŏl pŏntchaeŭi 열 번째의 tenth
yŏlp'a 열파 heatwave
yŏlshi pan 열시 반 half past ten, half
after ten

yŏlsoe 열쇠 key
yŏlsoe kori 열쇠 고리 keyring
yŏlsoe kumŏng 열쇠 구멍 keyhole
yŏlsoe mungch'i 열쇠 뭉치 bunch of keys
yŏlssabyŏng 열사병 heatstroke
yŏlsse pŏntchaeŭi 열 세 번째의 thirteenth
yŏlsset 열 셋 thirteen
yŏlsshim 열심 zeal, enthusiasm
yŏlsshimhi 열심히 enthusiastically, eagerly
yŏlsshimhi irhanŭn 열심히 일하는 hard-working
yŏlsshimin 열심인 enthusiastic
yŏlssŏltchŏgŭro 역설적으로 paradoxically
yŏltchŏng 열정 enthusiasm; zest; passion
yŏltchŏngjŏgin 열정적인 passionate; fervent; impassioned
yŏltchunghada 열중하다 be enthusiastic about; be absorbed in; *muŏsŭl hanŭnde yŏltchunghada* 무엇을 하는데 열중하다 concentrate on doing sth
yŏlttae chibang 열대 지방 tropics
yŏlttaeŭi 열대의 tropical
yŏlttae urim 열대 우림 tropical rain forest
yŏlttŭng ŭishik 열등 의식 inferiority complex
yŏlyŏdŏl 열 여덟 eighteen
yŏlyŏdŏl pŏntchaeŭi 열 여덟 번째의 eighteenth
yŏlyŏsŏt 열 여섯 sixteen
yŏlyŏsŏt pŏntchaeŭi 열 여섯 번째의 sixteenth
yŏm mosŭp 옆 모습 profile (*of face*)
yŏmmyŏn 옆면 side
yŏmnyŏ 염려 concern, anxiety; misgiving
yŏmnyŏhada 염려하다 be anxious
yŏmnyŏhanŭn 염려하는 concerned, anxious
yŏmnyo 염료 dye
yŏmsaek 염색 tint
yŏmsaek'ada 염색하다 color; tint; dye
yŏmso 염소 goat; chlorine
yŏmtchŭng 염증 inflammation

yŏn 연 kite
yŏnae 연애 romance
yŏnae kyŏrhon 연애 결혼 love marriage, love match
yŏnae p'yŏnji 연애 편지 love letter
yŏnae sakkŏn 연애 사건 love affair
yŏnan 연안 coast; *yŏnane(sŏ)* 연안에(서) at the coast
yŏnan kyŏngbidae 연안 경비대 coastguard (*organization*)
yŏnan kyŏngbiwŏn 연안 경비원 coastguard (*person*)
yŏnanŭi 연안의 coastal
yŏnbal 연발 torrent (*of words, abuse*)
yŏnbang chŏngbu 연방 정부 federal government
yŏnbang chŏngbuŭi 연방 정부의 federal
Yŏnbang Susaguk 연방 수사국 FBI, Federal Bureau of Investigation
yŏnbong 연봉 annual salary
yŏnbun 연분 bond
yŏnch'ach'onghoe 연차총회 annual general meeting
yŏnch'ak'ada 연착하다 be delayed
yŏnch'ul 연출 direction
yŏnch'ultcha 연출자 director
yŏnch'urhada 연출하다 direct
yŏndae 연대 regiment; chronology; era
yŏndaesunŭi 연대순의 chronological; *yŏndaesunŭro* 연대순으로 in chronological order
yŏndan 연단 podium, dais; rostrum
yŏng 영 zero
yŏng-anshil 영안실 morgue, mortuary
yŏng-anso 영안소 funeral home
yŏnggam 영감 inspiration; old man; husband (*used by elderly persons*); sir; *nuguege / muŏse yŏnggamŭl pat-tta* 누구에게 / 무엇에 영감을 받다 be inspired by s.o. / sth
yŏnggong 영공 airspace
yŏngguch'a 영구차 hearse
Yŏnggugin 영국인 the British; the English
yŏngguhi 영구히 permanently
yŏnggujŏgin 영구적인 permanent
Yŏngguk 영국 Britain; United Kingdom; England ◊ British;

English

Yŏngguk saram 영국 사람 Briton
yŏnggwang 영광 glory; privilege, honor
yŏnggwangsŭrŏptta 영광스럽다 be glorious
yŏnggwangsŭrŏun 영광스러운 glorious; privileged, honored
yŏngha 10to 영하 10도 10 below zero
yŏnghae 영해 waters; territorial waters
yŏngha-ŭi 영하의 subzero
yŏnghon 영혼 soul, spirit
yŏnghwa 영화 movie, film
yŏnghwa chejaktcha 영화 제작자 film-maker
yŏnghwa ch'waryŏngso 영화 촬영소 film studio
yŏnghwagwan 영화관 movie theater
yŏnghwa sanŏp 영화 산업 cinema, movie industry
yŏnghwa sŭt'a 영화 스타 movie star
yŏnghyang 영향 effect, impact; influence; *yŏnghyang-ŭl mich'ida* 영향을 미치다 affect; have an effect; influence; *yŏnghyang-ŭl namgida* 영향을 남기다 leave one's mark
yŏnghyang chuda 영향 주다 influence
yŏnghyang kkich'ida 영향 끼치다 influence
yŏnghyangnyŏk 영향력 impact; influence
yŏnghyangnyŏk innŭn 영향력 있는 influential
yŏn-gi 연기 action; acting (*profession*); portrayal; smoke; delay, postponement
yŏn-gich'ŏrŏm sarajida 연기처럼 사라지다 evaporate; vanish
yŏn-gidoen 연기된 belated
yŏn-giga chauk'an 연기가 자욱한 smoky
yŏn-giga nada 연기가 나다 smoke
yŏn-gihada 연기하다 act; portray; delay, postpone; put off
yŏn-gija 연기자 act; actor
yŏn-giman p'iuda 연기만 피우다 smolder
yŏngmae 영매 medium, spiritualist

yŏngmun morŭl 영문 모를 puzzling
yŏngmunŭl morŭge hada 영문을 모르게 하다 puzzle
yŏngnihada 영리하다 be smart, be clever
yŏngnihan 영리한 smart, clever
yŏngnyang 영양 nutrition
yŏngnyangbujogŭi 영양부족의 underfed
yŏngnyangbun 영양분 nourishment, goodness; nutrient
yŏngnyang-innŭn 영양있는 nourishing, nutritious
yŏngnyang shiltcho 영양 실조 malnutrition
yŏngnyŏk 영역 sector
yŏngnyŏk'ada 역력하다 be clear; *kŭnŭn kamdong padŭn kŏshi yŏngnyŏk'aet-tta* 그는 감동 받은 것이 역력했다 he was visibly moved
Yŏng-ŏ 영어 English (*language*)
yŏn-go 연고 ointment
yŏn-goja 연고자 relative
yŏn-gol 연골 gristle
yŏngsa 영사 consul
yŏngsagi 영사기 projector
yŏngsagwan 영사관 consulate
yŏngsahada 영사하다 project
yŏngsang p'yoshi changch'i 영상 표시 장치 visual display unit
yŏngsujŭng 영수증 receipt; bill of sale
yŏngtchang 영장 warrant, writ
yŏngt'o 영토 territory ◊ territorial
yŏn-gŭk 연극 theater; play ◊ theatrical
yŏn-gŭm 연금 pension
yŏn-gŭm chedo 연금 제도 pension scheme
yŏn-gu 연구 research, study; *...e taehan yŏn-gu* ...에 대한 연구 research into
yŏn-guhada 연구하다 research
yŏn-gu kaebal 연구 개발 R & D, research and development
yŏn-gu kyehoek 연구 계획 research plan
yŏng-ung 영웅 hero
yŏng-ungjŏgin 영웅적인 heroic
yŏn-gu pojowŏn 연구 보조원 research assistant

yŏn-guso 연구소 research institute

yŏn-guwŏn 연구원 researcher

yŏn-gwan 연관 link, connection

yŏn-gwanjit-tta 관련짓다 link

yŏngwŏn 영원 eternity

yŏngwŏnhada 영원하다 be eternal

yŏng-wŏnhage hada 영원하게 하다
perpetuate

yŏngwŏnhan 영원한 eternal,
everlasting

yŏng-wŏnhi 영원히 forever,
eternally

yŏng-ye 영예 kudos

yŏngyŏk 영역 preserve, domain

yŏn-gyŏl 연결 connection; **yŏn-
gyŏldwaessŭmnida** 연결됐습니다
you're through TELEC

yŏn-gyŏlp'yŏn 연결편 connecting
flight, connection

yŏn-gyŏrhada 연결하다 connect,
join, link

yŏnhabŭi 연합의 federal

yŏnhada 연하다 be tender; be soft

yŏnhan 연한 weak; tender *steak*

yŏnhan hŏrisal 연한 허리살 fillet

yŏnhan saektcho 연한 색조 tint

yŏnhap 연합 union, confederation;
coalition; federation

yŏnhapttoen 연합된 united

yŏnhoe 연회 banquet

yŏniŏsŏ 연이어서 consecutively, in a
row

yŏniyul 연이율 APR, annual
percentage rate

yŏnjaeŭi il hoebun 연재의 일 회분
installment, episode

yŏnjang 연장 extension

yŏnjanghada 연장하다 extend,
prolong

yŏnjang k'eibŭl 연장 케이블
extension cable

yŏnjangshik'ida 연장시키다 extend;
kiganŭl yŏnjangshik'ida 기간을
연장시키다 roll over, renew

yŏnju 연주 rendering

yŏnjuhada 연주하다 play (*of
musician*)

yŏnjuhoe 연주회 concert

yŏnjuja 연주자 player, musician

yŏnjung 연중 throughout the year ◊
annual

yŏnjung haengsa 연중 행사 annual
event

yŏnjung-ŭi 연중의 annual

yŏnmaeng 연맹 league

yŏnmahada 연마하다 sharpen *skills*

yŏnminŭl cha-anaenŭn 연민을
자아내는 pitiful

yŏnmot 연못 pond

yŏnnalligi 연날리기 kite flying

yŏnŏ 연어 salmon

yŏnp'il 연필 pencil

yŏnp'il kkak-kki 연필 깍기 pencil
sharpener

yŏnsang 연상 elder

yŏnsanghada 연상하다 associate

yŏnsangshik'ida 연상시키다 be
reminiscent of

yŏnsang-ŭi 연상의 elder

yŏnse 연세 age

yŏnsŏl 연설 speech, address

yŏnsŏlga 연설가 orator

yŏnsŏlmun chakssŏngja 연설문
작성자 speech writer

yŏnsŏltcha 연설자 speaker

yŏnsŏrhada 연설하다 speak; address;
make a speech

yŏnso 연소 combustion

yŏnsohada 연소하다 burn, consume
fuel

yŏnsok 연속 series; succession;
sequence

yŏnsok kong-yŏn 연속 공연 run (*of
play*)

yŏnsok kong-yŏndoeda 연속
공연되다 run (*of play*)

yŏnsok pangyŏnghada 연속
방영하다 serialize

yŏnsok sarhaebŏm 연속 살해범
serial killer

yŏnsokssŏng 연속성 continuity

yŏnsoktchŏgin 연속적인 consecutive

yŏnsok tŭrama 연속 드라마 soap
(opera)

yŏnsongmul 연속물 serial

yŏnsŭp 연습 exercise; drill; practice;
workout

yŏnsŭptchang 연습장 exercise book

yŏnsŭp'ada 연습하다 practice;
exercise; train

yŏnsuip 연수입 annual income

yŏnswae ch'ungdol 연쇄 충돌 pile-up, crash

yŏnswaejŏm 연쇄점 chain store

yŏnswae panŭng 연쇄 반응 chain reaction

yŏntchul 연줄 connection, personal contact; *choŭn yŏntchuri innŭn* 좋은 연줄이 있는 be well-connected

yŏnyak'an 연약한 feeble

yŏnyein 연예인 entertainer

yŏnyu 연유 condensed milk

yŏpch'ong 엽총 shotgun

yŏpkkuri 옆구리 side, flank

yŏp saram 옆 사람 neighbor

yŏpssŏ 엽서 (post)card

yŏptchip 옆집 next door

yŏp'a 여파 hangover

yŏp'e 옆에 next to, beside

yŏp'ŭi 옆의 adjoining

yŏp'ŭro 옆으로 sideways

yŏrahop 열 아홉 nineteen

yŏrahop pŏntchaeŭi 열 아홉 번째의 nineteenth

yŏrhana 열 하나 eleven

yŏrhan pŏntchaeŭi 열 한 번째의 eleventh

yŏri innŭn 열이 있는 feverish

yŏri it-tta 열이 있다 have a temperature

yŏrilgop 열 일곱 seventeen

yŏrilgop pŏntchaeŭi 열 일곱 번째의 seventeenth

yŏrŏ 여러 various; several; *yŏrŏ hae tong-an* 여러 해 동안 for several years; *yŏrŏmoro kŏmt'ohada* 여러모로 검토하다 examine from various angles

yŏrŏbun 여러분 everyone; ladies and gentlemen

yŏrŏgaeŭi sŏnban 여러개의 선반 shelves

yŏrŏgaji 여러가지 all sorts of, various kinds of, various

yŏrŏ myŏnesŏ 여러 면에서 in many respects

yŏrŏ pŏn 여러 번 many times

yŏrŏ puryuŭi saram 여러 부류의 사람 assortment of people

yŏron chosa 여론 조사 poll, survey

yŏron chosawŏn 여론 조사원 pollster

yŏronŭl mut-tta 여론을 묻다 poll

yŏrŭi 열의 enthusiasm

yŏrŭm 여름 summer; *yŏrŭme* 여름에 in the summer

yŏsa 여사 Mrs (*honoring term generally used for famous or accomplished women*)

yŏse 여세 impetus

yŏshin 여신 goddess

yŏsŏng 여성 female (*person*); women; feminine

yŏsŏng haebang undong 여성 해방 운동 women's lib

yŏsŏng haebang undongga 여성 해방 운동가 women's libber

yŏsŏngjŏgin 여성적인 feminine

yŏsŏng kyŏngnyŏng-in 여성 경영인 proprietress

yŏsŏng saŏpkka 여성 사업가 businesswoman

yŏsŏng-ŭi 여성의 female, feminine GRAM

yŏsŏnsaengnim 여선생님 woman teacher

yŏsŏt 여섯 six

yŏsŏt pŏntchaeŭi 여섯 번째의 sixth

yŏsong-yŏn 여송연 cigar

yŏttŭt-tta 엿듣다 intercept *message*; listen in, eavesdrop

yŏt'ŭn 열은 pale; *yŏt'ŭn punhong-saek* 열은 분홍색 pale pink

yŏt'ŭn saektcho 열은 색조 tinge

yŏŭisa 여의사 woman doctor

yŏu 여우 fox

yŏwang 여왕 queen

yŏwangbŏl 여왕벌 queen bee

...yŏya handa ...여야 한다 have to, must; be bound to

...yŏyaman hada ...여야만 하다 have (got) to; should, must

yŏyuga it-tta 여유가 있다 afford

yŏyuitkke hada 여유있게 하다 take things easy

yŏyuroun 여유로운 free and easy

yo 요 Korean-style mattress (*for sleeping on the floor*)

yoch'ŏng 요청 request; *yoch'ŏnge ttara* 요청에 따라 on request

yoch'ŏnghada 요청하다 request, put in for

yoga 요가 yoga

yogŭl hada 옥을 하다 swear; swear at

yogŭm 요금 fare; fee; charge; rate

yogŭm chingsuso 요금 징수소 toll booth

yogŭm kyesan-gi 요금 계산기 meter

yogŭmp'yo 요금표 tariff, price

yogu 요구 demand, requirement

yoguga shimhan 요구가 심한 demanding

yoguhada 요구하다 demand, call for, require; urge

yoguja 요구자 claimant

yogurŭt'ŭ 요구르트 yoghurt

yogyŏk'ada 요격하다 intercept

yohaengsu 요행수: *yohaengsurŭl paraji anssŭmnida* 요행수를 바라지 않습니다 I'm not taking any chances

yoin 요인 factor

yojŏl 요절 premature death

yojŏng 요정 fairy

yojŭŭm 요즈음 nowadays

yok 욕 abuse; abusive language; swearword

yokku 욕구 appetite

yoksshil 욕실 bathroom

yoksshim 욕심 greed

yoksshimi ŏmnŭn 욕심이 없는 selfless

yoksshim manŭn 욕심 많은 greedy

yokssŏl 욕설 bad language; curse, oath; derogatory remark

yoktchŏng 욕정 passion, sexual desire

yoktcho 욕조 tub, bathtub

yok'ada 욕하다 abuse; curse; call names

yomojomo saenggak'ae poda 요모조모 생각해 보다 think through

yong 용 dragon

yongbyŏnboda 용변보다 relieve oneself

yongbyŏng 용병 mercenary MIL

yonggamhada 용감하다 be brave

yonggamham 용감함 bravery

yonggamhan 용감한 brave, valiant

yonggi 용기 container; courage; spirit

yonggi innŭn 용기 있는 courageous

yonggirŭl chunŭn 용기를 주는 encouraging

yonggirŭl naeda 용기를 내다 pluck up courage

yonggol 용골 keel

yonggu 용구 equipment, gear; utensil

yonggwangno 용광로 furnace; blast furnace

yonghaedoeji annŭn 용해되지 않는 insoluble

yong-i 용이 ease, simplicity

yongjŏk 용적 proportions; dimensions; capacity

yongjŏpkkong 용접공 welder

yongjŏp'ada 용접하다 weld

yongk'e haenaeda 용케 해내다 contrive

yongk'e kuhada 용케 구하다 wangle

yongmang 욕망 desire, lust; ambition

yongmo 용모 looks, beauty

yongnap'ada 용납하다 approve; countenance

yongnyang 용량 capacity; memory

yong-ŏ 용어 term, word

yong-ŏ p'uri 용어 풀이 glossary

yongsŏ 용서 forgiveness

yongsŏhada 용서하다 forgive; excuse; let off; condone

yongsŏhal su ŏmnŭn 용서할 수 없는 unforgivable

yongsuch'ŏl 용수철 spring (*device*)

yongtton 용돈 allowance

yoodŭ 요오드 iodine

yoram 요람 cradle

yoranhada 요란하다 be loud

yoranhage ullida 요란하게 울리다 blare out

yori 요리 cooking; dish; food

yorich'aek 요리책 cookbook

yorihada 요리하다 cook

yorippŏp 요리법 cookery

yorisa 요리사 cook

yoriŭi 요리의 culinary

yoriyong ch'ŏlp'an 요리용 철판 burner

yoriyong konno 요리용 곤로 stove

yoryŏng 요령 knack

yosae 요새 fort, fortress

yoso 요소 ingredient

yosul 요술 magic; magic trick

yosulgach'i 요술같이 like magic

yosuljaeng-i 요술쟁이 magician

yosurŭl purida 요술을 부리다 juggle

yotchŏm 요점 point (*in argument*); gist; *yotchŏmŭl marhada* 요점을 말하다 get to the point; *yotchŏmŭl pŏsŏnan* 요점을 벗어난 beside the point, irrelevant

yot'ong 요통 lumbago

yot'ŭ 요트 sailboat, yacht

yot'ŭ chojongja 요트 조종자 yachtsman

yot'ŭ kyeryujang 요트 계류장 marina

yot'ŭ kyŏnggi 요트 경기 sailing

yot'ŭ kyŏnggija 요트 경기자 sailor

yot'ŭ t'agi 요트 타기 yachting

yoyak 요약 summary; précis; round-up

yoyak'ada 요약하다 summarize; sum up; abridge; compress

yoyak'amyŏn 요약하면 in short

yoyangso 요양소 rest home; hospice; sanatorium

yua 유아 infant

yuabŭi 유압의 hydraulic (*using oil*)

yuagi 유아기 infancy

yuayong pyŏn-gi 유아용 변기 potty

yubalshik'ida 유발시키다 cause; prompt

yubal yoin 유발 요인 trigger

yubang 유방 breast

yubarhada 유발하다 provoke, trigger

yuboktcha 유복자 posthumous child

yubok'an 유복한 fortunate

yubunam 유부남 married man

yubyŏlnan kŏt 유별난 것 the odd one out (*thing*)

yubyŏlnan saram 유별난 사람 the odd one out (*person*)

yuch'anghada 유창하다 be fluent

yuch'anghage 유창하게 eloquently, fluently

yuch'anghan 유창한 eloquent, fluent

yuch'anghan hwasul 유창한 화술 eloquence

yuch'ihada 유치하다 be childish

yuch'ihan 유치한 childish, infantile

yuch'iwŏn 유치원 kindergarten

yuch'ung 유충 larva; caterpillar

Yudaegyoŭi 유대교의 Jewish

Yudaein 유대인 Jew ◊ Jewish

yudae kwan-gye 유대 관계 link

yudo 유도 judo

yudok'an 유독한 virulent *disease*; poisonous

yudong-aek 유동액 fluid

yudong chasan 유동 자산 liquidity FIN

yudot'an 유도탄 guided missile

yudu 유두 nipple

Yuen 유엔 UN, United Nations

Yuen-gigu 유엔기구 United Nations

yugam 유감 regret; grudge; *Sŏurŭl ttŏnani yugamimnida* 서울을 떠나니 유감입니다 I will be sorry to leave Seoul; *yugamŭl kajida* 유감을 가지다 bear a grudge

yugamsŭrŏn 유감스런 criminal, shameful

yugamsŭrŏn il 유감스런 일 crime, shameful thing to do

yugamsŭrŏpkkedo 유감스럽게도 regrettably

yugamsŭrŏptta 유감스럽다 be regrettable

yugamsŭrŏun 유감스러운 regrettably

yuganŭronŭn 육안으로는 to the naked eye

yugashil 육아실 nursery

yugi nongppŏbŭi 유기 농법의 organic

Yugio Tongnan 육이오 동란 Korean War

yugiŭi 유기의 organic

yugoe 유괴 kidnapping

yugoebŏm 유괴범 kidnapper

yugoehada 유괴하다 kidnap

yugŭp koyong 유급 고용 paid employment

Yugyo 유교 Confucianism

yuhae 유해 remains

yuhaehada 유해하다 be harmful

yuhaehan kŏt 유해한 것 hazard

yuhaeng 유행 fashion, vogue; *yuhaeng chung-ida* 유행 중이다 be in fashion; *yuhaeng-e twijida* 유행에 뒤지다 be out of fashion; *yuhaeng-e min-gamhan* 유행에 민감한 fashion-conscious; *yuhaeng-i chinada* 유행이 지나다 go out of fashion; *yuhaeng-i chinan* 유행이 지난 old-fashioned, out of fashion

yuhaenghago innŭn 유행하고 있는 in, fashionable, popular

yuhaenghanŭn 유행하는 in fashion

yuhaeng-ida 유행이다 be around (of illness)

yuhaengppyŏng 유행병 epidemic

yuhaeng-ŭi kyŏnghyang 유행의 경향 fashion, trend

yuhaeng-ŭl ttarŭnŭn 유행을 따르는 fashionable, trendy

yuhok 유혹 temptation; seduction; *yuhoge kulbok'ada* 유혹에 굴복하다 succumb to temptation

yuhoktchŏgin 유혹적인 tempting; seductive; alluring

yuhok'ada 유혹하다 tempt, entice; seduce; make advances to

yuhwa 유화 oil painting

yuhwang 유황 sulfur

yuhyŏl 유혈 bloodshed

yuhyŏng 유형 type, sort

yuhyŏrŭi 유혈의 bloody

yuhyohaejida 유효해지다 come into force

yuhyohage hada 유효하게 하다 validate

yuhyohan 유효한 valid

yuhyo mallyoil 유효 만료일 expiry date

yuik'ada 유익하다 be beneficial

yuik'an 유익한 beneficial, salutary

yuinyong 유인용 decoy

yuirhada 유일하다 be unique

yuirhan 유일한 only, sole; unique

yujep'um 유제품 dairy products

yuji 유지 upkeep, maintenance; grease

yujihada 유지하다 hold; stay; keep; keep up; uphold, maintain; *kŏn-gang-ŭl yujihada* 건강을 유지하다 keep fit

yujŏk 유적 ruins, vestige

yujŏn 유전 inheritance (characteristics); oil field

yujŏndoenŭn 유전되는 hereditary

yujŏng 유정 oil well

yujŏnhak 유전학 genetics

yujŏnhaktcha 유전학자 geneticist

yujŏnja 유전자 gene

yujŏnja chimun 유전자 지문 genetic fingerprint

yujŏnjŏgin 유전적인 genetic

yujŏnjŏguro 유전적으로 genetically

yujŏn konghak 유전 공학 genetic engineering

yujoch'a 유조차 tanker, truck

yujoerŭl sŏn-gohada 유죄를 선고하다 convict

yujoeŭi 유죄의 guilty

yujoeŭi p'an-gyŏl 유죄의 판결 conviction

yujok 유족 bereaved family

yujosŏn 유조선 oil tanker

yuk 육 six

yukch'e 육체 flesh ◊ physical

yukch'ejŏguro 육체적으로 physically

yukch'e nodongja 육체 노동자 manual worker, blue-collar worker

yukch'in 육친 blood relative

yukka chŭngkkwŏn 유가 증권 securities

yukka chŭngkkwŏn shijang 유가 증권 시장 securities market

yuk-kkamjŏgin 육감적인 voluptuous

yuk-kkun 육군 army

yuk-kkun hasagwan 육군 하사관 noncommissioned officer

yuk-kkun sagwan hak-kkyo 육군 사관 학교 military academy

yukkwŏnja 유권자 voter; electorate

yukkyo 육교 footbridge, overpass

yukp'il 육필 handwriting

yukssang-e(sŏ) 육상에(서) on shore

yukssang up'yŏnmul 육상 우편물 surface mail

yuksshik tongmul 육식 동물 predator

yuksship 육십 sixty

yuktchi 육지 land, shore; *yuk-tchie(sŏ)* 육지에(서) on land

yuktchi tchogŭi 육지 쪽의 inland

yuktchŭp 육즙 gravy; juice

yukt'anjŏn 육탄전 unarmed combat

yuk'waehada 유쾌하다 be pleasant

yuk'waehan 유쾌한 pleasant, delightful

yulli 윤리 ethics

yullijŏgin 윤리적인 ethical, moral

yumanghan 유망한 rosy future

yumŏ kamgak 유머 감각 sense of humor

yumo 유모 nanny

yumoch'a 유모차 buggy, stroller; baby carriage

yulmuch'a 율무차 Job's tears tea

yumul 유물 remnant, relic

yumullon 유물론 materialism

yumullonja 유물론자 materialist

yumullonjŏgin 유물론적인 materialistic

yumyŏng 유명 fame

yumyŏnghada 유명하다 be famous; be famous for

yumyŏnghaejida 유명해지다 make a name for oneself

yumyŏnghan 유명한 famous, renowned

yumyŏng-in 유명인 personality, celebrity

yumyŏng insa 유명 인사 celebrity

yun 윤 gloss, shine

yunggi 융기 bump

yunghap 융합 fusion

yungja 융자 financing; loan

yungnoro 육로로 by land, overland

yungt'ongssŏng innŭn 융통성 있는 flexible

yun-gwagŭl chaptta 윤곽을 잡다 outline

yun-gwak 윤곽 outline, contour

yunhwaltche 윤활제 lubricant

yunhwalyu 윤활유 grease

yunip'om 유니폼 uniform, strip

yun naeda 윤 내다 rub, polish

yunnyŏn 윤년 leap year

yunyŏm 유념 regard, attention

yunyŏmhada 유념하다 pay heed to

yuraehada 유래하다 stem from

yuri 유리 glass

yuri chŏp'aptche 유리 접합제 putty

yurihada 유리하다 be profitable; be advantageous; *kŭgŏshi nŏege yurihada* 그것이 너에게 유리하다 it's to your advantage

yurihan 유리한 advantageous

yurihan chŏm 유리한 점 advantage

yuriŏptcha 유리업자 glazier

yuri sujokkwan 유리 수족관 aquarium

Yurŏbin 유럽인 European

Yurŏp 유럽 Europe ◊ European

yuryŏhage 유려하게 fluently

yuryŏhan 유려한 fluent

yuryŏk'an 유력한 strong, dominant

yuryŏng 유령 ghost; *igosŭn yuryŏng-i nat'ananŭn koshida* 이곳은 유령이 나타나는 곳이다 this place is haunted

yuryo kosokttoro 유료 고속도로 turnpike

yuryo toro 유료 도로 toll road

yusa 유사 similarity, resemblance; analogy; quicksand

yusahan 유사한 close, similar; comparable

yusan 유산 heritage; estate, legacy; miscarriage MED

yusanŭro namgida 유산으로 남기다 bequeath

yusashie 유사시에 in an emergency

yusassŏng 유사성 affinity

yusattchŏm 유사점 parallel

yusehada 유세하다 canvass POL

yusŏ 유서 will

yusŏng 유성 meteor, falling star

yusŏnggat'ŭn 유성같은 meteoric

yusŏng-ŭi 유성의 oily

yusŏnhyŏng 유선형 streamlined shape ◊ streamlined

yusŭ hosŭt'el 유스 호스텔 youth hostel

yusu 유수 running water

yut 윷 Four-Stick Game

yut'an 유탄 shell MIL

yut'illit'i 유틸리티 utility COMPUT

yut'ŏn U턴 U-turn

yut'ong 유통 distribution

yut'onghada 유통하다 distribute

yut'ong hyŏptchŏng 유통 협정 distribution arrangement

yuwŏl 유월 June

yuwŏnji 원원지 amusement park; recreation ground

yuyak 유약 enamel; glaze

yuyŏnhan 유연한 supple

yuyonghage hada 유용하게 하다 utilize

yuyongssŏng 유용성 utility, usefulness

A

a, an ◊ (*no equivalent in Korean*): *a book about Korea* Han-guge kwanhan ch'aek 한국에 관한 책; *he bought a car* kŭnŭn ch'arŭl sassŏyo 그는 차를 샀어요 ◊ (*with a countword*) hanaǔi 하나의, han 한; *a cup of coffee* k'ŏp'i han chan 커피 한 잔; *five men and a woman* tasŏt namjawa han yŏja 다섯 남자와 한 여자 ◊ (*per*) han 한; *$50 a ride* han pŏne 50tallŏ 한 번에 50달러; *$15 a head* han saram tang 15tallŏ 한 사람 당 15달러

abandon *object* pŏryŏduda 버려두다; *person* pŏrigo ttŏnada 버리고 떠나다; *plan* p'ogihada 포기하다

abbreviate churyŏssŭda 줄여쓰다

abbreviation yaktcha 약자

abdomen pokppu 복부

abdominal pokppuŭi 복부의

abduct napch'ihada 납치하다

♦ **abide by** ttarŭda 따르다

ability nŭngnyŏk 능력

ablaze: be ~ pult'aorŭ it-tta 불타오르고 있다

able (*skillful*) nŭngnyŏginnŭn 능력있는; *be ~ to ...* ...hal su it-tta ...할 수 있다; *I wasn't ~ to see/hear* nanŭn pol/tŭrŭl su ŏpssŏt-tta 나는 볼/들을 수 없었다

abnormal pijŏngsang-ŭi 비정상의

aboard 1 *prep* ...e t'ago ...에 타고 **2** *adv*: *be ~* t'ago it-tta 타고 있다; *go ~* t'ada 타다

abolish p'yejihada 폐지하다

abort *v/t mission, rocket launch,* COMPUT chungjihada 중지하다

abortion nakt'ae 낙태; *have an ~* nakt'aehada 낙태하다

about 1 *prep* (*concerning*) ...e kwanhan ...에 관한, ...e taehan ...에 대한; *what's it ~?* (*book, movie*) muŏse kwanhan kŏshimnikka? 무엇에 관한 것입니까? **2** *adv* (*roughly*) yak 약; (*in the area*) chuwie 주위에; *~ 20 books* yak 20kwŏn 약 20권; *be ~ to ...* mak ...haryŏgo hada 막 ...하려고 하다; *I was just ~ to leave* nanŭn mak ...ttŏnaryŏgo haessŏyo 나는 막 ...떠나려고 했어요; *how ~ ...?* ...i/ga ŏttaeyo? ...이/가 어때요?; *how ~ going to the movies?* yŏnghwagwane kanŭn kŏshi ŏttaeyo? 영화관에 가는 것이 어때요?

above 1 *prep* (*higher than*) ... poda wi ... 보다 위; (*more than*) ... poda tŏ ... 보다 더; *~ all* muŏtppodado 무엇보다도 **2** *adv* wie 위에; *on the floor ~* wich'ŭng-e 위층에

above-mentioned sanggihan 상기한

abrasion pŏtkkyŏjin kot 벗겨진 곳

abrasive *personality* kŏsŭllinŭn 거슬리는

abridge yoyak'ada 요약하다

abroad *live* haeoeesŏ 해외에서; *go* haeoero 해외로

abrupt *departure* kaptchakssŭrŏn 갑작스런; *manner* t'ungmyŏngssŭrŏun 퉁명스러운

abscess nong-yang 농양

absence (*of person*) pujae 부재; (*from school*) kyŏlsŏk 결석; (*from work*) kyŏlgŭn 결근; (*lack*) kyŏlp'ip 결핍

absent *adj* (*from school*) kyŏlssŏk'an 결석한; (*from work*) kyŏlgŭnhan 결근한

absent-minded mŏnghan 멍한

absolute *power* chŏlttaejŏgin 절대적인; *idiot* wanjŏnhan 완전한

absolutely (*completely*) wanjŏnhi 완전히; *~ not!* chŏlttae andoemnida! 절대 안됩니다!; *do you agree?* – *~* tong-ǔihaseyo? – kŭya mullonimnida 동의하세요? – 그야 물론입니다

absolve samyŏnhada 사면하다
absorb *liquid, shock, group* hŭpssuhada 흡수하다; *changes, information* padadŭrida 받아들이다; **~ed in** …e molttuhan …에 몰두한
absorbent hŭpssussŏng-ŭi 흡수성의
absorbent cotton t'altchimyŏn 탈지면, som 솜
abstain (*from voting*) kikkwŏnhada 기권하다
abstention (*in voting*) kikkwŏn 기권
abstract *adj* ch'usangjŏgin 추상적인
absurd ŏrisŏgŭn 어리석은
absurdity ŏrisŏgŭm 어리석음
abundance p'ungbu 풍부
abundant p'ungbuhan 풍부한
abuse[1] *n* (*insults*) yok 욕; (*of child*) hakttae 학대; (*of machine etc*) namyong 남용
abuse[2] *v/t* (*physically, sexually*) hakttaehada 학대하다; (*verbally*) yok'ada 욕하다
abusive: ~ language yok 욕; **become ~** sanawajida 사나와지다
abysmal (*very bad*) hyŏngp'yŏnŏmnŭn 형편없는
abyss kurŏngt'ŏng-i 구렁텅이
academic 1 *n* kyosa 교사 2 *adj* kodŭnggyoyugŭi 고등교육의; *person* hak-kkujŏgin 학구적인; **~ year** hangnyŏn 학년
academy hagwŏn 학원
accelerate 1 *v/i* ppallajida 빨라지다 2 *v/t production* kasokshik'ida 가속시키다
acceleration (*of car*) kasoktto 가속도
accelerator aeksellŏreit'ŏ 액셀러레이터
accent (*when speaking*) akssent'ŭ 악센트; (*emphasis*) kangjo 강조
accentuate kangjohada 강조하다
accept 1 *v/t offer, present* padadŭrida 받아들이다; *behavior, conditions* kyŏndida 견디다 2 *v/i* padadŭrida 받아들이다
acceptable padadŭril su innŭn 받아들일 수 있는
acceptance padadŭrim 받아들임
access 1 *n* (*to secrets, one's children*) chŏpkkŭn 접근; (*to a building*) ch'urip 출입; **have ~ to** *computer*

…e chŏpkkŭnhal su it-tta …에 접근할 수 있다; *child* …ŭl/rŭl mannal kwŏllirŭl kat-tta …을/를 만날 권리를 갖다 2 *v/t* chŏpkkŭnhada 접근하다; COMPUT ipch'ullyŏk'ada 입출력하다
access code COMPUT ipch'ullyŏk k'odŭ 입출력 코드
accessible (*easy to reach*) tatkki shwiun 닿기 쉬운; *house* kagi shwiun 가기 쉬운; *information* ipssuhagi shwiun 입수하기 쉬운
accessory (*for wearing*) changshin-gu 장신구; LAW chongbŏm 종범
access road chinimno 진입로
access time COMPUT hoch'ul shigan 호출 시간
accident uyŏnhan sakkŏn 우연한 사건; (*crash etc*) sago 사고; **by ~** uyŏnhi 우연히
accidental uyŏnhan 우연한
acclimate, acclimatize *v/t* chŏgŭnghada 적응하다
accommodate chinael kosŭl chegonghada 지낼 곳을 제공하다; *special requirements* tŭrŏjuda 들어주다
accommodations sukppak shisŏl 숙박 시설; *have you found ~?* chinael kosŭn ch'ajŭsyŏssŏyo? 지낼 곳은 찾으셨어요?
accompaniment MUS panju 반주
accompany tongbanhada 동반하다; MUS panjurŭl banju를 하다
accomplice kongbŏm 공범
accomplish *task* sŏngch'wihada 성취하다
accomplished (*person*) ttwiŏnan 뛰어난
accord: of one's own ~ chabaltchŭguro 자발적으로
accordance: in ~ with …e ttarasŏ …에 따라서
according: ~ to …e ttarŭmyŏn …에 따르면
accordingly (*consequently*) kŭrŏmŭro 그러므로; (*appropriately*) kŭe match'uŏ 그에 맞추어
account *n* (*financial*) kujwa 구좌; (*report, description*) pogo 보고; *give an ~ of* …ŭi iyagirŭl hada …의

이야기를 하다; *on no ~ must you tell anybody* chŏlttaero amuegedo iyagihaesŏnŭn andoemnida 절대로 아무에게도 이야기해서는 안됩니다; *on ~ of* …ttaemune …때문에; *take ... into ~*, *take ~ of* …ŭl/rŭl koryŏhada …을/를 고려하다

♦ **account for** (*explain*) sŏlmyŏnghada 설명하다; (*make up, constitute*) pijung-ŭl ch'ajihada 비중을 차지하다

accountability ch'aegim 책임

accountable: *be held ~* ch'aegimŭl chida 책임을 지다

accountant hoegyesa 회계사

account number kujwa pŏnho 구좌 번호

accounts hoegye 회계

accumulate 1 *v/t* moŭda 모으다 2 *v/i* moida 모이다

accuracy chŏnghwak 정확

accurate chŏnghwak'an 정확한

accusation pinan 비난

accuse pinanhada 비난하다; *he ~d me of lying* kŭnŭn naega kŏjinmarŭl haet-ttago pinanhaet-tta 그는 내가 거짓말을 했다고 비난했다; *be ~d of* LAW …(ŭ)ro kobaldoeda …(으)로 고발되다

accused: *the ~* LAW p'igo 피고

accustom: *get ~ed to* …e ikssuk'aejida …에 익숙해지다; *be ~ed to* …nŭn supkkwani it-tta …는 습관이 있다

ace (*in cards, tennis: shot*) eisŭ 에이스

ache 1 *n* ap'ŭm 아픔 2 *v/i* ap'ŭda 아프다

achieve sŏngch'wihada 성취하다

achievement (*of ambition*) sŏngch'wi 성취; (*thing achieved*) ŏptchŏk 업적

acid *n* san 산

acid rain sansŏngbi 산성비

acid test *fig* kyŏltchŏngjŏgin kŏmt'o 결정적인 검토

acknowledge injŏnghada 인정하다; *receipt* sushinyŏburŭl allida 수신여부를 알리다

acknowledg(e)ment injŏng 인정; (*of a letter*) sushinyŏburŭl allinŭn kŏt 수신여부를 알리는 것

acoustics ŭmhyanghak 음향학

acquaint: *be ~ed with* (*with person*) …wa/kwa mannan chŏgi it-tta …와/과 만난 적이 있다; (*with things, poem*) …ŭl/rŭl algo it-tta …을/를 알고 있다

acquaintance (*person*) anŭn saram 아는 사람

acquire *skill, knowledge* sŭpttŭk'ada 습득하다; *property* hoektttŭk'ada 획득하다

acquisitive ŏtkkoja hanŭn 얻고자 하는

acquit LAW mujoeimŭl sŏnŏnhada 무죄임을 선언하다

acre eik'ŏ 에이커

acrobat kogyesa 곡예사

acrobatics kogye 곡예

across 1 *prep* ◊ (*on the other side of*) …ŭi majŭn p'yŏne(sŏ) …의 맞은 편에(서); *the person sitting ~ the table from me* shikt'agŭi majŭn p'yŏne anjŭn saram 식탁의 맞은 편에 앉은 사람; *~ the street* kŏriŭi majŭn p'yŏne(sŏ) 거리의 맞은 편에(서) ◊ (*to the other side of*) …ŭi majŭn p'yŏnŭro …의 맞은 편으로; *walk ~ the street* kirŭl kŏnnŏda 길을 건너다; *sail ~ the Pacific* T'aep'yŏng-yang-ŭi majŭn p'yŏnŭro hanghaehada 태평양의 맞은 편으로 항해하다 2 *adv* (*to the other side*) kŏnnŏsŏ 건너서; *10 meters ~* p'ok 10mit'ŏ 폭 10미터

act 1 *v/i* THEA yŏn-gihada 연기하다; (*pretend*) kajanghada 가장하다; (*take action*) haengdonghada 행동하다; *~ as* …ŭl/rŭl taerihada …을/를 대리하다 2 *n* (*deed*) haengdong 행동; (*of play*) mak 막; (*in vaudeville*) yŏn-gija 연기자; (*pretense*) shinyung 시늉; (*law*) pŏmnyŏng 법령

acting 1 *n* yŏn-gi 연기 2 *adj* (*temporary*) imshiŭi 임시의

action haengwi 행위; *out of ~* (*not functioning*) chakttong-i andoenŭn 작동이 안되는; *take ~* choch'wihada 조취하다; *bring an ~ against* LAW kobarhada 고발하다

action replay TV kyŏnggi chaeyŏn

경기 재연; (*in slow motion*)
sŭlloumoshŏn 슬로우모션
active hwalttongjŏgin 활동적인;
GRAM nŭngdongt'aeŭi 능동태의
activist POL hwalttongga 활동가
activity (*being busy*) hwalbarhan
umjigim 활발한 움직임; (*pastime*)
hwalttong 활동
actor namja paeu 남자 배우
actress yŏja paeu 여자 배우
actual (*real*) shiltcheŭi 실제의
actually (*in fact, to tell the truth*)
sashirŭn 사실은; (*surprised*)
chŏngmallo 정말로; ~ *I do know
him* (*stressing converse*) nanŭn
chŏngmallo kŭrŭl arayo 나는 정말로
그를 알아요
acupressure massage chiap 지압
acupuncture ch'imsul 침술
acute *pain* kŭksshimhan 극심한; *sense
of smell* min-gamhan 민감한;
analysis, mind yerihan 예리한
ad kwanggo 광고; (*on TV*) sŏnjŏn
선전
adapt 1 *v/t* chŏk'ap'age hada 적합하게
하다 **2** *v/i* chŏŭnghada 적응하다
adaptable *person, plant*
chŏgŭngnyŏgi innŭn 적응력이 있는;
vehicle etc tayongdoŭi 다용도의
adaptation (*of play etc*) kakssaek
각색
adapter ELEC ŏdaept'ŏ 어댑터
add 1 *v/t* MATH tŏhada 더하다; (*say*)
tŏtppuch'yŏ marhada 덧붙여 말하다;
comment tŏtppuch'ida 덧붙이다;
sugar, salt etc puŏ nŏt'a 부어 넣다
2 *v/i* (*of person*) tŏhada 더하다
♦ **add on** *15% etc* p'ohamhada
포함하다
♦ **add up 1** *v/t* hapkkyehada 합계하다
2 *v/i fig* ihaedoeda 이해되다
addict chungdoktcha 중독자
addicted: *be* ~ *to* ...e chungdogida
...에 중독이다
addiction (*to drugs, TV etc*)
chungdok 중독
addictive: *be* ~ chungdokssŏng-ida
중독성이다
addition MATH tŏtssem 덧셈; (*to list,
company etc*) ch'uga 추가; *in* ~
ch'ugaro 추가로; *in* ~ *to* ...e tŏhayŏ

...에 더하여
additional ch'ugaŭi 추가의
additive (*in food*) ch'ŏmgaje 첨가제
add-on ch'uga hangmok 추가 항목
address 1 *n* chuso 주소;
ch'ingho 칭호 **2** *v/t letter* chusorŭl
ssŭda 주소를 쓰다; *audience*
yŏnsŏrhada 연설하다; *person* ...rago
purŭda ...라고 부르다
address book chusorok 주소록
addressee sushinin 수신인
adequate chŏkttanghan 적당한;
(*satisfactory*) manjokssŭrŏun
만족스러운
adhere ttak tallabut-tta 딱 달라붙다
♦ **adhere to** *surface* ...e tallabut-tta
...에 달라붙다; *rules* ...ŭl/rŭl
chik'ida ...을/를 지키다; *opinion*
...ŭl/rŭl kosuhada ...을/를 고수하다
adhesive *n* chŏpch'aktche 접착제
adhesive plaster panch'anggo
반창고
adhesive tape panch'anggo 반창고
adjacent injŏp'an 인접한
adjective hyŏng-yongsa 형용사
adjoining yŏp'ŭi 옆의
adjourn *v/i* (*of court*) hyujŏngdoeda
휴정되다; (*of meeting*)
chungdandoeda 중단되다
adjust *v/t* match'uda 맞추다
adjustable chojŏnghal su innŭn
조정할 수 있는
administer *medicine* pogyongshik'ida
복용시키다; *company* kwallihada
관리하다; *country* tasŭrida 다스리다
administration (*of company etc*)
kwalli 관리; (*of country*) haengjŏng
행정; (*government*) chŏngbu 정부
administrative haengjŏng-ŭi 행정의
administrator kwalliin 관리인; (*of
company*) kwallija 관리자; (*in
government*) haengjŏnggwan 행정관
admirable hullyunghan 훌륭한
admiral haegun changsŏng 해군 장성
admiration kamt'an 감탄
admire kamt'anhada 감탄하다
admirer ch'anmija 찬미자
admissible padadŭril su innŭn
받아들일 수 있는
admission (*confession*) shiin 시인; (*to
building*) iptchang hŏga 입장 허가;

(to country) ipkkuk hŏga 입국 허가;
(to organization) ip'oe hŏga 입회
허가; *(fee)* iptchangnyo 입장료; ~
free muryo iptchang 무료 입장
admit injŏnghada 인정하다; *(allow in)*
tŭrŏonŭn kŏsŭl hŏgahada 들어오는
것을 허가하다; *(confess)* shiinhada
시인하다; *(accept)* padadŭrida
받아들이다; *he was ~ted to the
hospital* kŭnŭn pyŏng-wŏne
ibwŏnhaet-tta 그는 병원에 입원했다
admittance: *no ~* iptchang kŭmji
입장 금지
adolescence sach'un-gi 사춘기
adolescent 1 *n* sach'un-giŭi namnyŏ
사춘기의 남녀 **2** *adj* sach'un-giŭi
사춘기의
adopt *child* ibyanghada 입양하다;
plan ch'aet'aek'hada 채택하다
adoption *(of child)* ibyang 입양; *(of
plan)* ch'aet'aek 채택
adorable panhal manhan 반할 만한
adore samohada 사모하다
adult 1 *n* ŏrŭn 어른; *(over 20)* sŏng-in
성인; *(animal)* sŏngjanghan tongmul
성장한 동물 **2** *adj* sŏngsuk'an
성숙한; *person* ŏrŭnŭi 어른의; *(over
20)* sŏng-inŭi 성인의; ~ *movie* sŏng-
inyŏnghwa 성인영화
adultery kant'ŏng kwan-gye 간통
관계
advance 1 *n* *(money)* sŏnbul 선불; *(in
science etc)* chinbo 진보; MIL chŏnjin
전진; *in* ~ miri 미리; *get money*
sŏnbullo 선불로; *48 hours in* ~
sashipp'alshigan chŏne 48시간 전에;
make ~*s (progress)* chinbohada
진보하다; *(sexually)* yuhok'ada
유혹하다 **2** *v/i* MIL chŏnjinhada
전진하다; *(make progress)*
chinbohada 진보하다 **3** *v/t* theory
cheanhada 제안하다; *sum of money*
miri naeda 미리 내다; *human
knowledge, a cause* paltchŏnhada
발전하다
advance booking yeyak 예약
advanced ap sŏn 앞 선; ~ *country*
sŏnjin-guk 선진국; ~ *learner*
sanggŭptcha 상급자; ~ *level* sanggŭp
상급
advance payment sŏnbul yogŭm

sŏnbul yogŭm
선불 요금
advantage yurihan chŏm 유리한 점;
it's to your ~ kŭgŏshi nŏege
yurihada 그것이 너에게 유리하다;
take ~ *of sth of opportunity* muŏsŭl
iyonghada 무엇을 이용하다
advantageous yurihan 유리한
adventure mohŏm 모험
adventurous mohŏmjŏk 모험적;
person mohŏmŭl chŭlginŭn 모험을
즐기는
adverb pusa 부사
adversary chŏk 적
advertise *v/t & v/i* kwanggohada
광고하다
advertisement kwanggo 광고
advertiser kwanggoju 광고주
advertising kwanggo 광고; *(industry)*
kwanggo-ŏp 광고업
advertising agency kwanggo
taehaengsa 광고 대행사
advice choŏn 조언; *take s.o.'s* ~
nuguŭi choŏnŭl padadŭrida 누구의
조언을 받아들이다
advisable hyŏnmyŏnghan 현명한
advise *person* choŏnhada 조언하다;
caution etc ch'unggohada 충고하다;
~ *s.o. to* ... nuguege ...rago choŏnhada 누구에게 ...라고 조언하다
adviser komun 고문
aerial 1 *n* ant'ena 안테나 **2** *adj*
kongjung-ŭi 공중의
aerial photograph hanggongsajin
항공사진
aerobics eŏrobik 에어로빅
aerodynamic konggi yŏk'agŭi 공기
역학의
aeronautical hanggonghagŭi
항공학의
aerosol sŭp'ŭrei 스프레이
aerospace industry hanggong-
ujugonghak 항공우주공학
affair *(matter)* il il 일 일; *(business)* ŏmmu
업무; *(love)* pullyun 불륜; *foreign* ~*s*
oemuŏmmu 외무업무; *have an* ~
with ...wa / kwa param p'iuda
...와 / 과 바람피우다; *that's my* ~
kŭgŏsŭn che ŏmmuimnida 그것은 제
업무입니다
affect MED palbyŏnghada 발병하다;
(influence) yŏnghyang-ŭl mich'ida

affection 영향을 미치다; (*concern*) kŏktchŏng-ŭl kkich'ida 걱정을 끼치다

affection aejŏng 애정

affectionate tajŏnghan 다정한

affinity yusassŏng 유사성

affirmative: *answer in the ~* yerago tap'ada 예라고 답하다

affluent puyuhan 부유한; *~ society* p'ung-yoroun sahoe 풍요로운 사회

afford (*financially*) yŏyuga it-tta 여유가 있다

Afghan 1 *adj* Ap'ŭganisŭt'anŭi 아프가니스탄의 **2** *n* (*person*) Ap'ŭganisŭt'anin 아프가니스탄인

Afghanistan Ap'ŭganisŭt'an 아프가니스탄

afloat *boat* ttŏ innŭn 떠 있는

afraid: *be ~* turyŏwŏhada 두려워하다; *be ~ of* ...ŭl/rŭl musŏwŏhada ...을/를 무서워하다; *of upsetting s.o.* ...ŭl/rŭl turyŏwŏhada ...을/를 두려워하다; *I'm ~ ...* (*expressing regret*) choesonghajiman ... 죄송하지만 ...; *I'm ~ he will lose his job* kŭga iltcharirŭl irŭlkkabwa kŏktchŏng imnida 그가 일자리를 잃을까봐 걱정입니다; *I'm ~ so* choesonghajiman, kŭrŏn kŏt kat'ayo 죄송하지만, 그런 것 같아요; *I'm ~ not* choesonghajiman, andoelgŏt kat'ayo 죄송하지만, 안될 것 같아요

Africa Ap'ŭrik'a 아프리카

African 1 *adj* Ap'ŭrik'aŭi 아프리카의 **2** *n* Ap'ŭrik'a saram 아프리카 사람

after 1 *prep* (*in order, time*) hue 후에; (*in position*) taŭme 다음에; *~ all* kyŏlguk 결국; *~ that* kŭ ihue 그 이후에; *it's ten ~ two* tushi shippunimnida 두시 십분입니다 **2** *adv* (*afterward*) taŭme 다음에, hue 후에; *the day ~* taŭmnal 다음날

afternoon ohu 오후; *in the ~* ohue 오후에; *this ~* onŭl ohue 오늘 오후에; *good ~* annyŏnghaseyo 안녕하세요

after sales service aep'ŭt'ŏ sŏbisŭ 애프터 서비스; **aftershave** aep'ŭt'ŏ shyeibŭ loshyŏn 애프터 셰이브 로션; **aftertaste** kkŭnmat 끝맛

afterward najung-e 나중에

again tashi 다시

against (*opposed to*) ...e pandaehayŏ ...에 반대하여; (*leaning on*) ...e kidaeŏ ...에 기대어; *America ~ Brazil* SP Miguk tae Pŭrajil 미국 대 브라질; *I'm ~ the idea* nanŭn kŭ ŭigyŏne pandaehamnida 나는 그 의견에 반대합니다; *what do you have ~ him?* wae kŭrŭl pandaehanŭn kŏyeyo? 왜 그를 반대하는 거예요?; *be ~ the law* pŏbe ŏgŭnnada 법에 어긋나다

age 1 *n* (*of person, object*) nai 나이; (*respectful: of older person*) yŏnse 연세; (*era*) ki 기; *at the ~ of* ...se ttaee ...세 때에; *under ~* misŏngnyŏnŭi 미성년의; *she's five years of ~* kŭnyŏnŭn tasŏt sarimnida 그녀는 다섯 살입니다 **2** *v/i* nai tŭlda 나이 들다

agency chunggaeŏp 중개업

agenda iltchŏng 일정; *on the ~* iltchŏngsang 일정상

agent taeriin 대리인

aggravate ak'washik'ida 악화시키다

aggression konggyŏk 공격

aggressive konggyŏktchŏgin 공격적인; (*dynamic*) chinch'wijŏgin 진취적인

agile chaepparŭn 재빠른

agitated tong-yohan 동요한

agitation tong-yo 동요

agitator sŏndongja 선동자

ago: *3 days ~* samil chŏne 3일 전에; *long ~* orae chŏne 오래 전에; *how long ~?* ŏlmana chŏne? 얼마나 전에?

agonizing kot'ongsŭrŏun 고통스러운

agony kot'ong 고통

agree 1 *v/i* tong-ŭihada 동의하다; (*of figures, accounts*) ilch'ihada 일치하다; (*reach agreement*) habŭihada 합의하다; *I ~* nanŭn tong-ŭihanda 나는 동의한다; *I don't ~* nanŭn tong-ŭihaji annŭnda 나는 동의하지 않는다; *it doesn't ~ with me* (*of food*) nanŭn i ŭmshigi patchi annŭnda 나는 이 음식이 받지 않는다 **2** *v/t price* ilch'ishik'ida 일치시키다; *~ that something should be done* muŏsŭl haeyahamŭl tong-ŭihada 무엇을

해야함을 동의하다
agreeable (*pleasant*) kibunjoŭn
기분좋은; (*in agreement*) tong-ŭihal
manhan 동의할 만한
agreement (*consent*) tong-ŭi 동의;
(*contract*) kyeyak 계약; *reach ~ on*
…e habŭihada …에 합의하다
agricultural nong-ŏbŭi 농업의
agriculture nong-ŏp 농업
ahead: *be ~ of* …ŭi ap'e …의 앞에;
plan/think ~ miraeeŭi
kyehoek/saenggak 미래에의
계획/생각
aid 1 *n* toum 도움 2 *v/t* toptta 돕다
Aids eijŭ 에이즈, huch'ŏnssŏng
myŏnnyŏk kyŏlp'iptchŭng 후천성
면역 결핍증
ailing *economy* yak'aejinŭn 약해지는
aim 1 *n* (*in shooting*) kyŏnyang 겨냥;
(*objective*) moktchŏk 목적 2 *v/i* (*in
shooting*) kyŏnyanghada 겨냥하다; *~
at doing sth, ~ to do sth* muŏsŭl
hanŭn kŏsŭl mokp'yoro samtta
무엇을 하는 것을 목표로 삼다 3 *v/t*:
be ~ed at (*of remark etc*) …ŭl/rŭl
kyŏnun kŏshida …을/를 겨눈
것이다; (*of guns*) …ŭl/rŭl
kyŏnyanghada …을/를 겨냥하다
air 1 *n* kongjung 공중; (*what we
breathe*) konggi 공기; *by ~ travel*
pihaenggiro 비행기로; *send mail*
hanggongp'yŏnŭro 항공편으로; *in
the open ~* yaoeesŏ 야외에서; *on
the ~* RAD, TV pangsong chung-e
방송 중에 2 *v/t room* hwan-
gishik'ida 환기시키다; *fig*: *views*
palk'ida 밝히다
airbase konggun kiji 공군 기지; **air-
conditioned** naengbangjung 냉방중;
air-conditioning naengbang 냉방,
eŏk'on 에어콘; **aircraft** hanggonggi
항공기; **aircraft carrier**
hanggongmoham 항공모함; **air cylinder** sujung hohŭpkki 수중 호흡기;
airfield pihaengjang 비행장; **air
force** konggun 공군; **air hostess**
sŭt'yuŏdissŭ 스튜어디스; **air letter**
hanggongbonghamnyŏpssŏ
항공봉함엽서; **airline** hanggongsa
항공사; **airmail**: *by ~* hanggong-
up'yŏnŭro 항공우편으로; **airplane**

pihaenggi 비행기; **air pollution**
taegioyŏm 대기오염; **airport**
konghang 공항; **airsick**: *get ~*
pihaenggi mŏlmirŭl hada 비행기
멀미를 하다; **airspace** yŏnggong
영공; **air terminal** konghang
t'ŏminŏl 공항 터미널; **airtight**
container konggiga ant'onghanŭn
공기가 안통하는; **air traffic**
hanggong kyot'ong 항공 교통; **air-
traffic control** hanggong kyot'ong
kwanje 항공 교통 관제; **air-traffic
controller** hanggong kyot'ong
kwanjewŏn 항공 교통 관제원
airy *room* konggiga shinsŏnhan
공기가 신선한; *attitude* kabyŏun
가벼운
aisle t'ongno 통로
aisle seat t'ongno tchok chari 통로
쪽 자리
alarm 1 *n* (*feeling*) puran 불안;
(*warning*) kyŏnggo 경고; (*device*)
kyŏngbogi 경보기; *raise the ~*
kyŏnggohada 경고하다 2 *v/t*
puranhage hada 불안하게 하다
alarm clock chamyŏngjong shigye
자명종 시계
album (*for photographs*) aelbŏm
앨범; (*record*) ŭmban 음반
alcohol alk'o-ol 알코올
alcoholic 1 *n* alk'o-ol chungdoktcha
알코올 중독자 2 *adj* alk'o-olssŏng-ŭi
알코올성의
alert 1 *n* (*signal*) kyŏngboŭm 경보음;
be on the ~ kyŏnggyehada 경계하다
2 *v/t* kyŏnggohada 경고하다 3 *adj*
kyŏnggyehanŭn 경계하는
alibi allibai 알리바이
alien 1 *n* (*foreigner*) oegugin 외국인;
(*from space*) oegyein 외계인 2 *adj*
ijiltchŏgin 이질적인; *be ~ to*
…wa/kwa mat-tchi ant'a …와/과
맞지 않다
alienate sowŏnhage hada 소원하게
하다; *be ~d* ttadollimŭl pat-tta
따돌림을 받다
alight *adj*: *be ~* pult'aorŭda
불타오르다
alike 1 *adj*: *be ~* pisŭt'ada 비슷하다
2 *adv*: *old and young ~* nŭlgŭnina
chŏlmŭnina ttokkach'i 늙은이나

젊은이나 똑같이
alimony wijaryo 위자료
alive: *be ~* sarait-tta 살아있다
all 1 *adj* modŭn 모든; *~ the cars* modŭn ch'a 모든 차; *~ the time* hangsang 항상 **2** *pron* modu 모두; *~ of us / them* uridŭl / kŭdŭl modu 우리들 / 그들 모두; *he ate ~ of it* kŭga modu ta mŏgŏssŏyo 그가 모두 다 먹었어요; *that's ~, thanks* twaessŭmnida, kamsahamnida 됐습니다, 감사합니다; *for ~ I care* naega al pa aniyeyo 내가 알 바 아니예요; *for ~ I know* naega anŭn paronŭn 내가 아는 바로는; *~ but ...* (*except*) ...man ppaego ...만 빼고; *~ but John agreed* Chonman ppaego modu tong-ŭihaessŏyo 존만 빼고 모두 동의했어요 **3** *adv*: *~ at once* (*suddenly*) kaptchagi 갑자기; *~ but* (*nearly*) kŏŭi ta 거의 다; *~ right* choayo 좋아요; *be ~ the better* ohiryŏ tŏ nat-tta 오히려 더 낫다; *it is ~ the better for having been cleaned* ch'ongsoga ta toeŏsŏ ohiryŏ tŏ natkkunnyo 청소가 다 되어서 오히려 더 낫군요; *they're not at ~ alike* kŭdŭrŭn chŏnhyŏ tamtchi anassŏyo 그들은 전혀 닮지 않았어요; *not at ~!* (*please do*) chŏnmaneyo! 천만에요!; *two ~* (*in score*) i tae iro tongtchŏm 이 대 이로 동점
allegation chujang 주장
alleged chujangdoen 주장된
allergic: *be ~ to* ...e allerŭgi panŭng-i it-tta ...에 알레르기 반응이 있다
allergy allerŭgi 알레르기
alleviate *pain, suffering* tŏlda 덜다
alley (*between buildings*) kolmok 골목; (*in a garden*) osolkkil 오솔길
alliance tongmaeng 동맹
alligator agŏ 악어
allocate punbaehada 분배하다
allot paebunhada 배분하다
allow (*permit*) hŏrak'ada 허락하다; *money, time* chuda 주다; *it's not ~ed* kŭgŏsŭn kŭmjisahang-imnida 그것은 금지사항입니다; *~ s.o. to ...* nuguege ...ŭl / rŭl hŏrak'ada 누구에게 ...을 / 를 허락하다

♦ **allow for** ...ŭl / rŭl koryŏhada ...을 / 를 고려하다
allowance (*money*) kŭbyŏ 급여; (*pocket money*) yongtton 용돈; *make ~s* (*for differences etc*) koryŏhada 고려하다; (*for person*) kamanhaejuda 감안해주다
alloy hapkkŭm 합금
all-purpose tayongdoŭi 다용도의; **all-round** mannŭng-ŭi 만능의; **all-time**: *be at an ~ low* chŏllyeŏpsshi chŏgŭn 전례없이 적은
♦ **allude to** tollyŏsŏ ŏn-gŭp'ada 돌려서 언급하다
alluring yuhoktchŏgin 유혹적인
all-wheel drive saryun-gudong 사륜구동
ally *n* (*country*) tongmaengguk 동맹국; (*person*) hyŏmnyŏktcha 협력자
almond amondŭ 아몬드
almost kŏŭi 거의
alone honja 혼자
along 1 *prep* ...ŭl / rŭl ttarasŏ ...을 / 를 따라서 **2** *adv* hamkke 함께; *~ with* ...wa / kwa hamkke ...와 / 과 함께; *all ~* (*all the time*) naenae 내내
aloud sorirŭl naeŏ 소리를 내어; *think ~* chung-ŏl kŏrimyŏ 중얼 거리며
alphabet alp'abet 알파벳
alphabetical alp'abesŭi 알파벳의
already pŏlssŏ 벌써, imi 이미
alright: *that's ~* (*doesn't matter*) kwaench'anayo 괜찮아요; (*when s.o. says thank you*) ch'ŏnmaneyo 천만에요; (*is quite good*) choŭndeyo 좋은데요; *I'm ~* (*not hurt*) chŏn, kwaench'anayo 전, 괜찮아요; (*have got enough*) chŏn, kŭman twaessŭmnida 전, 그만 됐습니다; *~, that's enough!* kŭgŏllo twaessŏyo 그걸로 됐어요
also ttohan 또한
altar chedan 제단
alter *v/t* pakkuda 바꾸다
alteration pyŏn-gyŏng 변경; (*to clothes*) susŏn 수선
alternate 1 *v/i* kyoch'ehada 교체하다 **2** *adj* pŏn-gara hanŭn 번갈아 하는; *on ~ days* kyŏgillo 격일로
alternating current kyoryu 교류

alternative 1 *n* taean 대안 **2** *adj* taeshinhal 대신할

alternatively taeshin 대신

although pirok ... haljirado 비록 ...할지라도; **~ I don't like it** pirok naega choahaji anŭltchirado 비록 내가 좋아하지 않을지라도

altitude haebalgodo 해발고도; (*of plane*) kodo 고도

altogether (*completely*) wanjŏnhi 완전히; (*in all*) chŏnbu 전부

altruistic aet'ajŏgin 애타적인

aluminum alluminyum 알루미늄

always hangsang 항상, ŏnjena 언제나, nŭl 늘

a.m. ojŏn 오전

amalgamate *v/i* (*of companies*) happyŏnghada 합병하다

amateur *n* amach'uŏ 아마츄어

amaze kkamtchak nollage hada 깜짝 놀라게 하다

amazement kkamtchak nollam 깜짝 놀람

amazing (*surprising*) aju nollaun 아주 놀라운; (*very good*) aju choŭn 아주 좋은

ambassador taesa 대사

amber: **at ~** hwangsaek shinho-e 황색 신호에

ambiguous aemaemohohan 애매모호한

ambition yamang 야망; (*something desired*) kkum 꿈; *pej* yongmang 욕망

ambitious *person, plan* yashiminnŭn 야심있는

ambulance kugŭpch'a 구급차

ambush 1 *n* maebok 매복 **2** *v/t* maepok'ayŏ sŭpkkyŏk'ada 매복하여 습격하다

amend sujŏnghada 수정하다

amendment sujŏng 수정

amends: **make ~** posangŭl hada 보상을 하다

amenities (*leisure facilities*) oraksshishŏl 오락시설

America Miguk 미국

American 1 *adj* Migugŭi 미국의 **2** *n* Miguk saram 미국 사람

amiable hogamŭl chunŭn 호감을 주는

amicable uhojŏgin 우호적인

Amitabha Buddha Amit'abul 아미타불

ammunition t'annyak 탄약; *fig* mugi 무기

amnesty *n* samyŏn 사면

among(st) kaunde 가운데

amount yang 양; (*sum of money*) kŭmaek 금액

♦ **amount to** ...i/ka toeda ...이/가 되다

ample ch'ungbunhan 충분한

amplifier aemp'ŭ 앰프

amplify *sound* chŭngp'ok'ada 증폭하다

amputate chŏlttanhada 절단하다

amuse (*make laugh etc*) utkkida 웃기다; (*entertain*) chŭlgŏpkkehada 즐겁게하다

amusement (*merriment*) chaemi 재미; (*entertainment*) chŭlgŏum 즐거움; **~s** (*games*) orangmul 오락물; *to our great ~* usŭpkkedo 우습게도

amusement park yuwŏnji 유원지

amusing chaemiinnŭn 재미있는

anabolic steroid kŭnyuk chŭnggangje 근육 증강제

analog COMPUT anallogŭ 아날로그

analogy yusa 유사

analysis punsŏk 분석; PSYCH chŏngshinbunsŏk 정신분석

analyze punsŏk'ada 분석하다

anarchy mujŏngbu sangt'ae 무정부 상태

anatomy haebuhak 해부학

ancestor chosang 조상; **~ worship** chosang sungbae 조상 숭배

ancestral grave sanso 산소

ancestral rite chesa 제사

anchor NAUT **1** *n* tat 닻 **2** *v/i* tach'ŭl naerida 닻을 내리다

anchor man TV aengk'ŏ 앵커

anchovies myŏlch'i 멸치

ancient *adj* kodaeŭi 고대의

and ◊ (*joining nouns*) wa/kwa 와/과; *you ~ me* tangshin-gwa na 당신과 나 ◊ (*joining adjectives*) ...go ...고; *tall ~ thin* k'iga k'ŭgo marŭn 키가 크고 마른 ◊ (*joining verbs*) ...hago ...하고; *I did some exercises ~ had a shower* nanŭn undong-ŭl hago

shyawŏrŭl haet-tta 나는 운동을 하고
샤워를 했다; *they were eating ~
drinking* kŭdŭrŭn mŏk-kko
mashigo issŏssŏyo 그들은 먹고
마시고 있었어요 ◊ (*starting a new
sentence*) kŭrigo 그리고; *And it was
expensive* kŭrigo pissassŏyo 그리고
비쌌어요 ◊ (*expressing a result*)
...haesŏ ...해서; *he fell ~ broke his
leg* kŭnŭn nŏmŏjyŏsŏ tariga
purŏjyŏt-tta 그는 넘어져서 다리가
부러졌다 ◊: *it's getting hotter ~
hotter* chŏmjŏm tŏ tŏwŏjinda 점점
더 더워진다

anemia pinhyŏltchŭng 빈혈증
anemic: *be ~* MED pinhyŏltchŭng-ida
빈혈증이다
anesthetic mach'wije 마취제
anesthetist mach'wisa 마취사
anger 1 *n* noyŏum 노여움 **2** *v/t*
hwanaege hada 화내게 하다
angina hyopsshimtchŭng 협심증
angle *n* kak 각
angry hwaga nan 화가 난; *be ~ with
s.o.* nuguege hwaga nada 누구에게
화가 나다
anguish k'ŭn kot'ong 큰 고통
animal tongmul 동물
animated hwalbarhan 활발한
animated cartoon manhwa yŏnghwa
만화 영화
animation (*liveliness*) saenggi 생기;
(*cinematic*) aenimeishyŏn
애니메이션
animosity chŭng-o 증오
ankle palmok 발목
annex 1 *n* (*building*) pyŏlgwan 별관
2 *v/t state* hap-ppyŏnghada 합병하다
anniversary (*wedding ~*) kinyŏmil
기념일
announce kongshiktchŏgŭro allida
공식적으로 알리다
announcement allim 알림; (*official*)
konggo 공고
announcer TV, RAD anaunsŏ
아나운서
annoy sŏnggashigehada 성가시게
하다; *be ~ed* hwanada 화나다
annoyance (*anger*) hwa 화;
(*nuisance*) sŏnggashim 성가심
annoying sŏnggashin 성가신

annual *adj* (*once a year*) illyŏne han
ponŭi 일년에 한 번의; (*of a year*)
yŏnjung-ŭi 연중의; *~ salary*
yŏnbong 연봉; *an ~ income* yŏnsuip
연수입; *an ~ event* yŏnjung haengsa
연중 행사
annul *marriage* muhyorohada 무효로
하다
anonymous ingmyŏng-ŭi 익명의
anorexia kŏshiktchŭng 거식증
anorexic: *be ~* kŏshiktchŭng-ŭl alt'a
거식증을 앓다
another 1 *adj* (*different*) tarŭn 다른;
(*additional*) tto hana 또 하나 **2** *pron*
(*different one*) tarŭn kŏt 다른 것;
(*additional one*) tto tarŭn kŏt 또
다른 것; *one ~* sŏro 서로
answer 1 *n* tap 답; (*to problem*)
haedap 해답 **2** *v/t* tap'ada 답하다; *~
the door* munŭl yŏllŏ hada 문을
열러 가다; *~ the telephone*
chŏnhwarŭl pat-tta 전화를 받다
♦**answer back 1** *v/t person* ...ege
maldaekkuhada ...에게 말대꾸하다
2 *v/i* maldaekkuhada 말대꾸하다
♦**answer for** ch'aegimŭl chida 책임을
지다
answerphone chadong-ŭngdapkki
자동응답기
ant kaemi 개미
antagonism chŏktaeshim 적대심
Antarctic *n* Namgŭk-kkwŏn 남극권
antenatal ch'ulssan chŏnŭi 출산 전의
antenna (*of insect*) tŏdŭmi 더듬이;
(*for TV*) ant'ena 안테나
antibiotic *n* hangsaeng multchil 항생
물질
antibody hangch'e 항체
anticipate (*expect*) yesanghada
예상하다
anticipation yesang 예상
anti-Communism pan-gongjuŭi
반공주의
antidote haedoktche 해독제
antifreeze pudong-aek 부동액
antipathy pan-gam 반감
antiquated kushigŭi 구식의
antique *n* kolttongp'um 골동품
antique dealer kolttongp'um sang-in
골동품 상인
antiseptic 1 *adj* salgyunŭi 살균의 **2** *n*

sodongnyak 소독약
antisocial pisagyojŏgin 비사교적인;
I'm feeling very ~ nanŭn pyŏllo
nugurŭl mannal kibuni anida 나는
별로 누구를 만날 기분이 아니다
antivirus program COMPUT pairŏsŭ
paeksshin p'ŭrogŭraem 바이러스
백신 프로그램
anxiety kŏktchŏng
anxious kŏktchŏnghanŭn 걱정하는;
(*eager*) maeu paranŭn 매우 바라는;
be ~ for (*for news etc*) ...ŭl/rŭl
kodaehada ...을/를 고대하다
any 1 *adj* ◊ (*no translation*): *are
there ~ diskettes / glasses?*
tisŭk'eshi/ chani issŏyo?
디스켓이/잔이 있어?; *is there ~
bread / improvement?* ppang-
i / hyangsang-i issŭmnikka?
빵이/향상이 있습니까? ◊ (*in
negatives*) amu 아무; *there aren't ~
diskettes / glasses* amu tisŭk'et-
tto / chando ŏpssŏyo 아무
디스켓도/잔도 없어요; *there isn't ~
bread / improvement* amu
ppangdo / hyangsangdo ŏpssŭmnida
아무 빵도/향상도 없습니다; *take ~
one you like* choahanŭn kŏsŭn
muŏidŭn kajiseyo 좋아하는 것은
무엇이든 가지세요 ◊ (*emphatic*)
ŏttŏn 어떤; *have you ~ idea at all?*
ŏttŏn saenggagi issŭmnikka? 어떤
생각이 있습니까? **2** *pron* (*thing*)
amu kŏt 아무 것; (*person*) nugudo
누구도; *don't you have ~?* amu
kŏtto ŏpssŭseyo? 아무 것도
없으세요?; *there isn't / aren't ~ left*
namŭn kŏshi ŏptta 남은 것이 없다;
~ of them could be guilty kŭtŭl
chung nuguegedo choega issŭl su
issŏyo 그들 중 누구에게도 죄가 있을
수 있어요 **3** *adv* chogŭm 조금; *is
that ~ better / easier?*
chogŭmirado tŏ nassŭmnikka /
shwissŭmnikka? 조금이라도 더
낫습니까?/쉽습니까?; *I don't like it ~
more* nanŭn tŏ isang kŭgŏsŭl
choahaji annŭnda 나는 더이상
그것을 좋아하지 않는다
anybody nugun-ga 누군가; *was ~ at
home?* nugun-ga chibe issŏssŏyo?

누군가 집에 있었어요? ◊ (*with
negatives*) amudo ... (+ *negative
verb*) 아무도 ...; *there wasn't ~
there* amudo kŏgi ŏpssŏssŏyo
아무도 거기 없었어요; *wasn't ~ at
home?* amudo chibe ŏpssŏssŏyo?
아무도 집에 없었어요? ◊ (*emphatic*)
nugurado 누구라도; *~ can do that*
kŭgŏsŭn nugurado hal su issŏyo
그것은 누구라도 할 수 있어요
anyhow ŏtchaet-ttŭn 어쨌든
anyone → *anybody*
anything muŏt 무엇; (*with negatives*)
amu kŏt-tto 아무 것도; *I didn't hear
~* nanŭn amu kŏt-tto tŭt-tchi anat-
tta 나는 아무 것도 듣지 않았다; *~
but ...* chŏnhyŏ ...haji ant'a 전혀
...하지 않다; *she was ~ but helpful*
kŭnyŏnŭn chŏnhyŏ toumi toeji
anassŏyo 그녀는 전혀 도움이 되지
않았어요; *~ else?* tarŭn kŏsŭnyo?
다른 것은요?
anyway → *anyhow*
anywhere ŏdidŭnji 어디든지; *if you
see one ~, buy it* ŏdidŭnji kŭgŏsŭl
pomyŏn saseyo 어디든지 그것을
보면 사세요 ◊ (*with negatives*)
amudedo 아무데도; *he won't go ~
without me* kŭnŭn naŏpsshinŭn
amudedo kaji anŭl kŏyeyo 그는 나
없이는 아무데도 가지 않을 거예요
apart (*in distance*) ttŏrŏjyŏsŏ
떨어져서; *live ~* (*of people*) kakki
ttaro salda 각기 따로 살다; *~ from*
(*excepting*) cheoehago 제외하고; (*in
addition to*) ...edaga tŏ ...에다가 더
apartment ap'at'ŭ 아파트
apartment block ap'at'ŭ tanji 아파트
단지
apathetic mukwanshimhan 무관심한
ape *n* k'ŭn wŏnsung-iryu 큰 원숭이류
aperture PHOT kugyŏng 구경
apologize sagwahada 사과하다
apology sagwa 사과
apostrophe GRAM ŏp'asŭt'ŭrop'i
어퍼스트로피
appall chilgŏp'age hada 질겁하게
하다
appalling musŏun 무서운; *language*
chijŏbunhan 지저분한
apparatus changch'i 장치

apparent myŏngbaek'an 명백한;
become ~ that ... ranŭn kŏshi
punmyŏnghaejida ...라는 것이
분명해지다

apparently pogie 보기에; *~ they are
married* pogie kŭdŭrŭn kyŏrhonhan
kŏt kat'ayo 보기에 그들은 결혼한 것
같아요

appeal 1 *n* (*charm*) maeryŏk 매력;
(*for funds etc*) kanch'ŏng 간청; LAW
hangso 항소 **2** *v/i* LAW hangsohada
항소하다

♦ **appeal to** (*be attractive to*) ...ŭl/rŭl
kkŭlda ...을/를 끌다

♦ **appeal for** ...ŭl/rŭl hosohada
...을/를 호소하다

appear nat'anada 나타나다; (*in
movie*) ch'uryŏnhada 출연하다; (*of
new product*) ch'ulsshihada
출시하다; (*in court*) ch'ulttuhada
출두하다; *he ~s calm* kŭnŭn
choyonghae poinda 그는 조용해
보인다; *it ~s that* ...in kŏt kat-tta ...
인 것 같다

appearance (*arrival*) ch'urhyŏn 출현;
(*in movie etc*) ch'uryŏn 출연; (*in
court*) ch'ulttu 출두; (*look*) p'yojŏng
표정; *put in an ~* chamkkan
ch'amsŏk'ada 잠깐 참석하다

appendicitis maengjangnyŏm 맹장염,
ch'ungsuyŏm 충수염

appendix MED maengjang 맹장,
ch'ungsu 충수; (*of book etc*) purok
부록

appetite shigyok 식욕; *fig* yokku 욕구

appetizer (*food*) chŏnch'ae 전채;
(*drink*) shiktchŏnŭi ŭmnyo 식전의
음료

appetizing shigyogŭl todunŭn 식욕을
돋우는

applaud 1 *v/i* sŏng-wŏnŭl ponaeda
성원을 보내다 **2** *v/t* ...ege pakssurŭl
ponaeda ...에게 박수를 보내다; *fig*
ch'ingsonghada 칭송하다

applause sŏng-wŏn 성원; (*praise*)
ch'ingsong 칭송

apple sagwa 사과

apple pie sagwa p'ai 사과 파이

apple sauce sagwasosŭ 사과소스

appliance kigye 기계; (*household*)
kajŏnjep'um 가전제품; *electrical ~*

chŏnja chep'um 전자 제품

applicable chŏgyonghal su innŭn
적용할 수 있는

applicant ŭngmoja 응모자

application (*for job, university etc*)
chiwŏn 지원; (*for passport, visa*)
shinch'ŏng 신청

application form chiwŏnsŏ 지원서;
(*for passport, visa*) shinch'ŏngsŏ
신청서; (*for university*) ip'ak wŏnsŏ
입학 원서

apply 1 *v/t* chŏgyonghada 적용하다;
ointment p'yŏ parŭda 펴 바르다 **2** *v/i*
(*of rule, law*) chŏgyongdoeda
적용되다

♦ **apply for** *job, university*
chiwŏnhada 지원하다; *passport*
shinch'ŏnghada 신청하다

♦ **apply to** *address, department etc*
...(ŭ)ro yŏllak'ada ...(으)로
yŏllak'ada ...에게 연락하다; (*affect*) ...e
chŏgyongdoeda ...에 적용되다

appoint (*to position*) immyŏnghada
임명하다

appointment (*to position*) immyŏng
임명; (*meeting*) yakssok 약속

appointments diary taiŏri 다이어리

appreciate 1 *v/t* (*value*)
p'yŏngkkahada 평가하다; (*be
grateful for*) kamsahada 감사하다;
(*acknowledge*) alda 알다; *thanks, I
~ it* ch'injŏre kamsadŭrimnida
친절에 감사드립니다 **2** *v/i* FIN
kagyŏgi orŭda 가격이 오르다

appreciation (*of kindness etc*) kamsa
감사; (*of music etc*) p'yŏngkka 평가;
as a token of our ~ kamsaŭi
p'yoshiro 감사의 표시로

apprehensive puranhan 불안한

apprentice kyŏnsŭpsaeng 견습생

approach 1 *n* chean 제안; (*offer etc*)
kyosŏp 교섭; (*to problem*) chŏpkkŭn
pangbŏp 접근 방법 **2** *v/t* (*get near
to*) kakkai tagagada 가까이
다가가다; (*contact*) chŏpch'ok'ada
접촉하다; *problem* taruda 다루다

approachable *person* kakkai hagi
shwiun 가까이 하기 쉬운

appropriate *adj* chŏktchŏrhan 적절한

approval sŭng-in 승인

approve 1 v/i ch'ansŏnghada
찬성하다 **2** v/t sŭng-inhada 승인하다
♦**approve of** injŏnghada 인정하다
approximate adj taeryagŭi 대략의
approximately taeryak 대략
APR (= annual percentage rate)
yŏniyul 연이율
apricot salgu 살구
April sawŏl 사월
apt pupil chaenŭng-innŭn 재능있는;
remark chŏkttanghan 적당한; be ~
to (likely) ...hanŭn kyŏnghyang-i it-
tta ...하는 경향이 있다
aptitude chŏkssŏng 적성
aquarium yuri sujokkwan 유리
수족관
aquatic sujung-ŭi 수중의
Arab 1 adj Arabŭi 아랍의 **2** n Arabin
아랍인
Arabic 1 adj Arabŭi 아랍의; ~ numerals Arabia suttcha 아라비아
숫자 **2** n Arabŏ 아랍어
arable nonggyŏng-e almajŭn 농경에
알맞은
arbitrary decision, remark
tokttanjŏgin 독단적인; attack
mujagwihan 무작위한
arbitrate v/i chungjaehada 중재하다
arbitration chungjae 중재
arch n ach'i 아치
archeologist kogohaktcha 고고학자
archeology kogohak 고고학
archer kungsu 궁수
architect sŏlgyesa 설계사
architecture (subject) kŏnch'uk'ak
건축학; (style) kŏnch'ungnyangshik
건축양식
archives kirok 기록
archway ach'i mich'ŭi t'ongno 아치
밑의 통로
Arctic n Pukkŭkkwŏn 북극권
ardent yŏllyŏrhan 열렬한
area (region) chiyŏk 지역; (of activity,
study etc) punya 분야; (square meters
etc) myŏnjŏk 면적
area code TELEC chiyŏk pŏnho 지역
번호
arena SP undongjang 운동장
Argentina Arŭhent'ina 아르헨티나
Argentinian 1 adj Arŭhent'inaŭi
아르헨티나의 **2** n Arŭhent'inain

아르헨티나인
arguably ama t'ŭllimŏpsshi 아마
틀림없이
argue 1 v/i (quarrel) maldat'umhada
말다툼하다; (reason) nonhada 논하다
2 v/t: ~ that ...rago chujanghada
...라고 주장하다
argument (quarrel) nonjaeng 논쟁;
(reasoning) nolli 논리
argumentative nonjaeng-ŭl
choahanŭn 논쟁을 좋아하는
arid land kŏnjohan 건조한
arise (of situation, problem) irŏnada
일어나다
aristocrat kwijok 귀족
arithmetic sansul 산술
arm¹ n (of person) p'al 팔; (of chair)
p'algŏri 팔걸이
arm² v/t mujangshik'ida 무장시키다
armaments kunbi 군비
armchair allak ŭija 안락 의자
armed mujanghan 무장한
armed forces kukkun 국군
armed robbery mujang kangdo 무장
강도
armor pangt'an chokki 방탄 조끼
armored vehicle changgapch'a
장갑차
armpit kyŏdŭrang-i 겨드랑이
arms (weapons) kunbi 군비
army yuk-kun 육군
aroma hyanggi 향기
around 1 prep (in circle) ...ŭi chuwi
...의 주위, ...ŭi tulle ...의 둘레;
(roughly) taeryak ... 대략 ...; (with
expressions of time) yak ... tchŭm 약
... 쯤; it's ~ the corner igŏsŭn chŏ
kusŏktchŭme it-tta 이것은 저 구석
쯤에 있다 **2** adv (in the area)
kŭnch'ŏe kŭnch'ŏe 근처에; (encircling) tullee
둘레에; be ~ (somewhere near)
kŭnch'ŏe it-tta 근처에 있다; he's ~
somewhere kŭnŭn ŏdi kŭnch'ŏe
issŏyo 그는 어디 근처에 있어요;
there are a lot of people ~ sabang-
e manŭn saramdŭri issŏyo 사방에
많은 사람들이 있어요; there's a
nasty flu ~ tok-kkami yuhaeng-ida
독감이 유행이다; he lives ~ here
kŭnŭn i kŭnch'ŏe sanda 그는 이
근처에 산다; walk ~ kŏrŏdanida

걸어다니다; *she has been ~ (has traveled, is experienced)* künyönün insaenggyönghŏmi mant'a 그녀는 인생경험이 많다

arouse *interest, feelings* pullŏ irŭk'ida 불러 일으키다; *(sexually)* chagŭk'ada 자극하다

arrange *(put in order)* paeyŏrhada 배열하다; *furniture* paech'ihada 배치하다; *flowers, books* kajirŏnhi kkot-tta 가지런히 꽂다; *music* p'yŏn-gok'ada 편곡하다; *meeting, party etc* chunbihada 준비하다; *time and place* yeyak'ada 예약하다; *I've ~d to meet him* nanŭn kŭwa mannagiro haet-tta 나는 그와 만나기로 했다

♦ **arrange for** …ege put'ak'ada …에게 부탁하다

arranged marriage chungmae kyŏrhon 중매 결혼

arrangement *(plan)* kyehoek 계획; *(agreement)* tong-ŭi 동의; *(of furniture etc)* paech'i 배치; *(of flowers etc)* kkotkkoji 꽃꽂이; *(of music)* p'yŏn-gok 편곡

arrears minapkkŭm 미납금; *be in ~ (of person)* minap'ada 미납하다; *I'm paid in ~* nanŭn hubullo chigŭppannŭnda 나는 후불로 지급받는다

arrest 1 *n* ch'ep'o 체포; *be under ~* kugŭm sangt'aee it-tta 구금 상태에 있다 **2** *v/t criminal* ch'ep'ohada 체포하다

arrival toch'ak 도착; *~s (at airport)* ipkkuk 입국

arrive toch'ak'ada 도착하다

♦ **arrive at** *place* …e toch'ak'ada …에 도착하다; *decision etc* …e todarhada …에 도달하다

arrogance kŏman 거만

arrogant kŏmanhan 거만한

arrow hwasal 화살

arrow key COMPUT hwasalp'yo kŭlsoe 화살표 글쇠

arson panghwa 방화

art yesul 예술; *(things produced)* yesulp'um 예술품; *(skill)* kisul 기술; *the ~s* munhwayesul 문화예술; *~s degree* munhakssa 문학사

arterial road kansŏndoro 간선도로

artery MED tongmaek 동맥

art gallery misulgwan 미술관

arthritis kwanjŏllyŏm 관절염

article *(item)* han p'ummok 한 품목; *(in newspaper)* kisa 기사; *(section)* chohang 조항; GRAM kwansa 관사

articulate *adj* myŏnghwak'an 명확한

artificial in-gongjŏgin 인공적인; *pearls, leather, flowers* injoŭi 인조의; *(not sincere)* inwijŏgin 인위적인

artificial intelligence in-gongjinŭng 인공지능

artillery taep'o 대포

artisan sugong-ŏptcha 수공업자

artist *(painter)* misulga 미술가; *(artistic person)* yesulga 예술가

artistic yesultchŏgin 예술적인

as 1 *conj* ◊ *(while, when)* …hal ttae …할 때; *he came in ~ I was going out* naega nagaryŏgo hal ttae kŭga tŭrŏwassŏyo 내가 나가려고 할 때 그가 들어왔어요 ◊ *(because)* waenyahamyŏn …(i)ki ttaemunida 왜냐하면 …(이)기 때문이다; *~ it's so rainy today* piga nŏmu ogi ttaemuniyeyo 왜냐하면 오늘 비가 너무 오기 때문이에요 ◊ *(like)* …ch'ŏrŏm …처럼; *she married a miner, ~ her sister had done* kŭnyŏnŭn ŏnnich'ŏrŏm kwangbuwa kyŏrhonhaet-tta 그녀는 언니처럼 광부와 결혼했다; *~ if …* …in-gŏt ch'ŏrŏm …인것 처럼; *don't treat me ~ if I was a child* narŭl aiin-gotch'ŏrŏm ch'igŭp'aji maseyo 나를 아이인것 처럼 취급하지 마세요; *~ usual* p'yŏngsoch'ŏrŏm 평소처럼; *~ necessary* p'iryohadamyŏn 필요하다면 **2** *adv* mank'ŭm 만큼; *~ high/pretty ~ …* …mank'ŭm nop'ŭn/yeppŭn …만큼 높은/예쁜; *~ much ~ that?* kŭrŏke mani? 그렇게 많습니까? **3** *prep* …(ŭ)rosŏ …(으)로서; *~ a child* ŏryŏssŭl ttae 어렸을 때; *work ~ a teacher/translator* sŏnsaengnimŭro/pŏnyŏkkaro irhada 선생님으로/번역가로 일하다; *~ for you* nŏnŭn nŏnŭn 너는; *~ Hamlet* haemlit yŏgŭro 햄릿 역으로

asap (= *as soon as possible*)

kanŭnghanhan ppalli 가능한한 빨리

ASEAN (= *Association of South East Asian Nations*) Tongnam Ashia Kuk-kka Yŏnhap 동남 아시아 국가 연합

ash chae 재; ~**es** chae 재

ashamed: be ~ pukkŭrŏwŏhada 부끄러워하다; be ~ of ...ege pukkŭrŏpkke yŏgida ...에게 부끄럽게 여기다; you should be ~ of yourself tangshinŭn chashinege pukkŭrŏun churŭl arayadoeyo 당신은 자신에게 부끄러운 줄을 알아야되요

ash can ssŭregi t'ong 쓰레기 통

ashore mut'e 뭍에; go ~ mut'e orŭda 뭍에 오르다

ashtray chaettŏri 재떨이

Asia Ashia 아시아

Asian 1 *adj* Ashiaŭi 아시아의 **2** *n* Ashiain 아시아인

aside ttŏrŏttŭryŏ 떨어뜨려; ~ from ...ŭl/rŭl cheoehago ...을/를 제외하고; (*in addition to*) ...edaga tŏ ...에다가 더

ask 1 *v/t* (*put a question to*) ...ege mut-tta ...에게 묻다; (*invite*) ch'odaehada 초대하다; *question* chilmunhada 질문하다; *favor* put'ak'ada 부탁하다; can I ~ you something? mwŏ chom put'ak'aedo toemnikka? 뭐 좀 부탁해도 됩니까?; ~ s.o. about sth nuguege muŏse kwanhayŏ mut-tta 누구에게 무엇에 관하여 묻다; ~ s.o. for nuguege ...ŭl/rŭl put'ak'ada 누구에게 ...을/를 부탁하다; ~ s.o. to nuguege ... haedallago hada 누구에게 ... 해달라고 하다 **2** *v/i* mut-tta 묻다

♦ **ask after** *person* ..ŭi kŭnhwang-ŭl mut-tta ...의 근황을 묻다

♦ **ask for** ...ŭl/rŭl put'ak'ada ...을/를 부탁하다; *person* ...ŭl/rŭl ch'at-tta ...을/를 찾다

♦ **ask out** teit'ŭ shinch'ŏnghada 데이트 신청하다

asking price p'anmae kagyŏk 판매 가격

asleep: be (*fast*) ~ p'uk chamdŭlda 푹 잠들다; fall ~ chamdŭlda 잠들다

asparagus asŭp'aragŏsŭ 아스파라거스

aspect myŏn 면

aspirin asŭp'irin 아스피린

ass[1] (*idiot*) pabo 바보

ass[2] ∨ (*backside*) ŏngdŏng-i 엉덩이; (*sex*) sekssŭ 섹스

assassin amsalbŏm 암살범

assassinate amsarhada 암살하다

assassination amsal 암살

assault 1 *n* p'ok'aeng 폭행 **2** *v/t* p'ok'aenghada 폭행하다

assemble 1 *v/t parts* chorip'ada 조립하다 **2** *v/i* (*of people*) moida 모이다

assembly (*of parts*) chorip 조립; POL ŭihoe 의회

assembly line ilgwanjagŏp yŏl 일관작업 열

assembly plant chorip kongjang 조립 공장

assent *v/i* tong-ŭihada 동의하다

assert: ~ oneself chagirŭl chujanghada 자기를 주장하다

assertive *person* tanjŏngtchŏgin 단정적인

assess *situation, value* p'yŏngkkahada 평가하다

asset FIN, *fig* chasan 자산

asshole ∨ ttongkkumŏng 똥구멍; (*idiot*) kaesaekki 개새끼

assign *task* chuda 주다; *room* halttanghada 할당하다

assignment (*task*) immu 임무; EDU suktche 숙제

assimilate *v/t facts* sohwahada 소화하다; *person into group* padadŭrida 받아들이다

assist toptta 돕다

assistance toum 도움

assistant chosu 조수

assistant director pujang 부장; (*for movie*) chogamdok 조감독

assistant manager pugyŏng-yŏng-in 부경영인; (*of hotel, restaurant, store*) pujibaein 부지배인

associate 1 *v/t* kwallyŏnshik'ida 관련시키다; (*in one's mind*) yŏnsanghada 연상하다 **2** *v/i*: ~ with kyojehada 교제하다 **3** *n* tongnyo 동료

associate professor pugyosu 부교수

association tanch'e hyŏp'oe 단체 협회; *in ~ with* ...wa/kwa hyŏmnyŏk'ayŏ ...와/과 협력하여

assortment kajigaksssaek 가지각색

assume (*suppose*) kajŏnghada 가정하다

assumption kajŏng 가정

assurance pojŭng 보증; (*confidence*) chashin 자신

assure (*reassure*) pojanghada 보장하다

assured (*confident*) hwaksshine ch'an 확신에 찬

asterisk pyŏlp'yo 별표

asthma ch'ŏnshik 천식

astonish kkamtchak nollagehada 깜짝 놀라게하다; *be ~ed* kkamtchak nollada 깜짝 놀라다

astonishing maeu nollaun 매우 놀라운

astonishment kkamtchak nollam 깜짝 놀람

astrologer chŏmsŏngga 점성가

astrology chŏmsŏngsul 점성술

astronaut ujuin 우주인

astronomer ch'ŏnmunhaktcha 천문학자

astronomical ch'ŏnmunhaktchŏgin 천문학적인; *price* ŏmch'ŏngnage nop'ŭn 엄청나게 높은

astronomy ch'ŏnmunhak 천문학

asylum (*mental*) chŏngshinppyŏng-wŏn 정신병원; (*political*) mangmyŏng 망명; *seek political ~* chŏngch'ijŏk mangmyŏng-ŭl shinch'ŏnghada 정치적 망명을 신청하다

at (*with places*) ...e(sŏ) ...에(서); *~ the cleaner's* set'aksssoe(sŏ) 세탁소에(서); *~ Joe's* cho nechibesŏ(sŏ) 조 네집에(서); *~ the door* mune 문에; *~ 10 dollars* 10tallŏro 10달러로; *~ the age of 18* yoryŏdŏl sal ttaee 열여덟 살 때에; *~ 5 o'clock* 5shie 5시에; *~ 150 km/h* shisok 150k'illomit'ŏro 시속 150 킬로미터로; *be good/bad ~ sth* muŏse nŭngsuk'ada/nŭngsuk'aji mot'ada 무엇에 능숙하다/능숙하지 못하다

atheist mushillonja 무신론자

athlete undongga 운동가, sŭp'och'üin 스포츠인

athletic undong-ŭi 운동의; *person* ch'eryŏginnŭn 체력있는

athletics undonggyŏnggi 운동경기

Atlantic n Taesŏyang 대서양

atlas chidoch'aek 지도책

ATM (= *automated teller machine*) hyŏn-gŭm inch'ulgi 현금 인출기

atmosphere (*of earth*) taegi 대기; (*ambiance*) punwigi 분위기

atmospheric pollution taegi oyŏm 대기 오염

atom wŏnja 원자

atom bomb wŏnja p'okt'an 원자 폭탄

atomic wŏnjaŭi 원자의

atomic energy wŏnjaryŏk 원자력

atomic waste haekssŭregi 핵쓰레기

atomizer punmugi 분무기

atrocious shimhage nappŭn 심하게 나쁜

atrocity hyung-ak 흉악

attach puch'ida 붙이다; *importance* puyŏhada 부여하다; (*to letter*) tongbonghada 동봉하다; *be ~ed to* (*fond of*) ...e(ge) maŭmi kkŭllida ...에(게) 마음이 끌리다

attachment (*with e-mail*) ch'ŏmga 첨가

attack 1 n konggyŏk 공격 **2** v/t konggyŏk'ada 공격하다

attempt 1 n shido 시도 **2** v/t shidohada 시도하다

attend ch'amsŏk'ada 참석하다

♦ **attend to** ch'ŏrihada 처리하다; *customer* moshida 모시다; (*pay attention to*) chuŭihada 주의하다

attendance ch'amsŏk 참석; (*at school*) ch'ulssŏk 출석

attendant (*in museum*) chigwŏn 직원

attention chuŭi 주의; *bring X to the ~ of Y* Xe taehan chuŭirŭl Yege hwan-gishik'ida X에 대한 주의를 Y에게 환기시키다; *your ~ please* chumok'ae chushipsshio 주목해 주십시오; *pay ~* chuŭihada 주의하다

attentive *listener* chuŭigip'ŭn 주의깊은

attic tarakppang 다락방

attitude t'aedo 태도
attn (= *for the attention of*) sushin 수신
attorney pyŏnhosa 변호사; *power of ~* wiimkkwŏn 위임권
attract *person, attention* kkŭlda 끌다; *be ~ed to s.o.* nuguege maŭmi kkŭllida 누구에게 마음이 끌리다
attraction (*also romantic*) maeryŏk 매력
attractive maeryŏginnŭn 매력있는
attribute[1] *v/t:* ~ *sth to* muŏshi ... ttaemunŭro ch'ujŏngdoeda 무엇이 ... 때문으로 추정되다; *painting, poem* muŏsŭl ...ŭi chakp'umŭro ch'ujŏnghada 무엇을 ...의 작품으로 추정하다
attribute[2] *n* sokssŏng 속성
auction 1 *n* kyŏngmae 경매 **2** *v/t* kyŏngmaehada 경매하다
♦ **auction off** kyŏngmaehada 경매하다
audacious *plan* taedamhan 대담한
audacity taedamhan haengdong 대담한 행동
audible tŭrŭl su innŭn 들을 수 있는
audience ch'ŏngjung 청중; (*in theater, at show*) kwanjung 관중; TV shich'ŏngja 시청자; (*of radio program*) ch'ŏngch'wija 청취자
audio *adj* odioŭi 오디오의
audiovisual shich'ŏnggagŭi 시청각의
audit 1 *n* kamsa 감사 **2** *v/t* kamsahada 감사하다; *course* ch'ŏngganghada 청강하다
audition 1 *n* odishyŏn 오디션 **2** *v/i* odishyŏnŭl pat-tta 오디션을 받다
auditor FIN kamsagwan 감사관; (*of course*) ch'ŏnggangsaeng 청강생
auditorium (*of theater etc*) kwanjungsŏk 관중석
August p'arwŏl 팔월
aunt (*own, sister of father*) komo 고모; (*own, sister of mother*) imo 이모; (*own, wife of uncle on father's side*) sungmo 숙모; (*own, wife of uncle on mother's side*) oesungmo 외숙모; (*somebody else's*) ajumma 아줌마
austere *interior, style* kkumijianŭn 꾸미지 않은; *person, face*

chunŏmhan 준엄한; *life* kŭmyoktchŏgin 금욕적인
austerity (*economic*) naep'ip 내핍
Australasia Oseania 오세아니아
Australia Hoju 호주
Australian 1 *adj* Hojuŭi 호주의 **2** *n* Hojuin 호주인
Austria Osŭt'ŭria 오스트리아
Austrian 1 *adj* Osŭt'ŭriaŭi 오스트리아의 **2** *n* Osŭt'ŭriain 오스트리아인
authentic chintchaŭi 진짜의
authenticity shinbingssŏng 신빙성
author chakka 작가; (*of report etc*) chipp'iltcha 집필자
authoritative kwŏnwiinnŭn 권위있는
authority kwŏnwi 권위; (*permission*) hŏga 허가; *be an ~ on* ...ŭi kwŏnwijaida ...의 권위자이다; *the authorities* tangguk 당국
authorize kwŏnhanŭl chuda 권한을 주다; *be ~d to* ......l/ŭl hŏga pat-tta ...ㄹ/을 허가 받다
autistic chap'yetchŭng-ŭi 자폐증의
auto *n* chadongch'a 자동차
autobiography chasŏjŏn 자서전
autograph *n* sain 사인
automate chadonghwahada 자동화하다
automatic 1 *adj* chadong-ŭi 자동의 **2** *n* (*car, gun etc*) chadongkigye 자동기계
automatically chadong-ŭro 자동으로
automation chadonghwa 자동화
automobile chadongch'a 자동차
automobile industry chadongch'a sanŏp 자동차 산업
autonomy chach'i 자치
autopilot chadong chojong changch'i 자동 조종 장치
autopsy pugŏm 부검
auxiliary *adj* pojoŭi 보조의
available *facility, service* ŏdŭl su innŭn 얻을 수 있는; *book, information* ch'ajŭl su innŭn 찾을 수 있는; *person* shiganinnŭn 시간있는
avalanche nunsat'ae 눈사태
avenue *also fig* kil 길
average 1 *adj* p'yŏnggyunŭi 평균의; (*ordinary*) pot'ong-ŭi 보통의; (*mediocre*) pot'ong chŏngdoŭi 보통

정도의 2 *n* p'yŏnggyun 평균; *above /
below* ~ p'yŏnggyun wiŭi / araeŭi
평균 위의 / 아래의; *on* ~ pot'ong 보통
3 *v/t* p'yŏnggyunŭro … hada
평균으로 … 하다; *I* ~ *six hours
sleep a night* nanŭn harue
p'yŏnggyun yŏsŏt shiganŭl chanda
나는 하루에 평균 여섯 시간을
잔다
♦ **average out** *v/t* p'yŏnggyunnaeda
평균내다
♦ **average out at** p'yŏnggyun …(ŭ)ro
kyesandoeda 평균 …(으)로
계산되다
aversion: *have an* ~ *to* …ŭl / rŭl aju
shirŏhada …을 / 를 아주 싫어하다
avert *one's eyes* p'ihada 피하다; *crisis*
maktta 막다
aviary k'ŭn saejang 큰 새장
aviation hanggong 항공
avid yŏlgwangtchŏgin 열광적인
avoid p'ihada 피하다
awake *adj* kkaeŏinnŭn 깨어있는; *it's
keeping me* ~ kŭgŏshi chamŭl
sŏlch'ige haet-tta 그것이 잠을
설치게 했다
award 1 *n* (*prize*) sang 상 2 *v/t*
suyŏhada 수여하다; *he was* ~*ed
$10,000 in damages* kŭnŭn
mandallŏŭi sonhae paesang-ŭl
padat-tta 그는 10,000달러의 손해
배상을 받았다
aware: *be* ~ *of sth* muŏsŭl alda
무엇을 알다; *become* ~ *of sth*

muŏsŭl arach'arida 무엇을
알아차리다
awareness inshik 인식
away: *be* ~ (*traveling, sick etc*) ŏptta
없다; *I'll be* ~ *until next Friday*
nanŭn taŭm chu kŭmnyoilkkaji
ŏpssŭl kŏyeyo 나는 다음 주
금요일까지 없을 거에요; *walk / run*
~ kŏrŏgada / tomanggada 걸어가다 /
도망가다; *look* ~ nunkkirŭl tollida
눈길을 돌리다; *it's 2 miles* ~ 2mail
ttŏrŏjyŏit-tta 2마일 떨어져있다;
Christmas is still six weeks ~
Sŏngt'anjŏlkkajinŭn yŏjŏnhi yuk
chuna nama issŏyo 성탄절까지는
여전히 육 주나 남아 있어요; *take
sth* ~ *from s.o.* nugurobut'ŏ
muŏsŭl ppaet-tta 누구로부터
무엇을 빼앗다; *put sth* ~ muŏsŭl
ch'iuda 무엇을 치우다
away game SP wŏnjŏng shihap 원정
시합
awesome F (*terrific*) koengjanghan
굉장한
awful shimhan 심한
awkward (*clumsy*) sŏt'urŭn 서투른;
(*difficult*) himdŭn 힘든;
(*embarrassing*) kŏbuk'an 거북한;
feel ~ kŏbuk'aehada 거북해하다
awning ch'ayang 차양
ax 1 *n* tokki 도끼 **2** *v/t job etc*
tchallida 짤리다; *budget* sak-
kkamhada 삭감하다
axle ch'ach'uk 차축

B

BA (= *Bachelor of Arts*) haksa
hagwi 학사 학위
baboon kaek'owŏnsung-i 개코원숭이
baby *n* agi 아기
baby carriage yumoch'a 유모차;
baby quilt (*for carrying baby*)
p'odaegi 포대기; **baby-sit** agirŭl
tolbwajuda 아기를 돌봐주다; **baby-
sitter** agirŭl tolbwajunŭn saram
아기를 돌봐주는 사람
bachelor ch'onggak 총각
back 1 *n* (*of person, book, knife,
chair*) tŭng 등; (*of car, bus, paper*)
twinmyŏn 뒷면; (*of house*) twittchok
뒷쪽; SP huwi 후위; **in ~** antchoge(sŏ)
안쪽에(서); **in ~** (*of the car*)
(ch'aŭi) twit chwasŏge(sŏ) (차의) 뒷
좌석에(서); **at the ~ of the bus**
pŏsŭ twit chwasŏge(sŏ) 버스 뒷
좌석에(서); **~ to front** kŏkkuro
거꾸로; **at the ~ of beyond** mopsshi
oejin kose(sŏ) 몹시 외진 곳에(서)
2 *adj* twittchoge innŭn 뒷쪽에 있는;
~ road twikkil 뒷길 **3** *adv*: **please
move / stand ~** twiro mullŏna
chushipsshiyo / twie sŏ chushipsshiyo
뒤로 물러나 주십시요 / 뒤에 서
주십시요; **2 meters ~ from the
edge** kajangjariesŏ 2mit'ŏ tŭrŏgasŏ
가장자리에서 2미터 들어가서; **~ in
1935** 1935nyŏnŭro kŏsŭllŏ ollagasŏ
1935년으로 거슬러 올라가서; **give X
~ to Y** Xŭl / rŭl Yege toedollyŏjuda
X을 / 를 Y에게 되돌려주다; **she'll be
~ tomorrow** kŭnyŏnŭn naeil toraol
kŏshimnida 그녀는 내일 돌아올
것입니다; **when are you coming ~?**
ŏnje tora-ol kŏmnikka? 언제 돌아올
겁니까?; **take X ~ to the store**
(*because unsatisfactory*) Xŭl / rŭl
kagee murŭda X을 / 를 가게에
무르다; **they wrote / phoned ~**
kŭdŭrŭn hoeshin haet-tta / hoedap
haet-tta 그들은 회신 했다 / 회답

했다; **he hit me ~** kŭnŭn narŭl
toettaeryŏt-tta 그는 나를 되때렸다
4 *v/t* (*support*) huwŏnhada 후원하다;
car hujinshik'ida 후진시키다; *horse*
tonŭl kŏlda 돈을 걸다 **5** *v/i* (*of car*)
hujinhada 후진하다, ida 이다
♦**back away** mullŏsŏda 물러서다
♦**back down** yangbohada 양보하다
♦**back off** twiro mullŏnada 뒤로
  물러나다; (*from danger*) …esŏ
  mullŏnada …에서 물러나다
♦**back onto** …wa / kwa twiro
  chŏp'ae it-tta …와 / 과 뒤로 접해
  있다
♦**back out** (*of commitment*) sonŭl
  tteda 손을 떼다
♦**back up 1** *v/t* (*support*) huwŏnhada
  후원하다; *claim, argument*
  twitppatch'imhae chuda 뒷받침해
  주다; *file* paegŏp'ada 백업하다; *be
  backed up* (*of traffic*) millyŏ it-tta
  밀려 있다 **2** *v/i* (*in car*) hujinhada
  후진하다
back burner: *put sth on the ~*
muŏsŭl yŏn-gihada 무엇을 연기하다;
backdate sogŭp'ayŏ
chŏgyongshik'ida 소급하여
적용시키다; **backdoor** twinmun
뒷문
backer huwŏnja 후원자
backfire *v/i* fig yŏk'yokkwaga nada
역효과가 나다; **background**
paegyŏng 배경; (*of person*)
ch'ulsshin sŏngbun 출신 성분; (*of
situation*) paehu 배후; *she prefers
to stay in the ~* kŭnyŏnŭn ohiryŏ
nasŏji ank'irŭl choahanda 그녀는
오히려 나서지 않기를 좋아한다;
backhand *n* (*in tennis*) paek
haendŭ 백 핸드
backing (*support*) chiji 지지; MUS
panju 반주
backing group MUS panjudan 반주단
backlash panbal 반발; **backlog**

mich'ŏribun 미처리분; **backpack 1** *n* paenang 배낭 **2** *v/i* paenang maego yŏhaenghada 배낭 매고 여행하다; **backpacker** paenang yŏhaengja 배낭 여행자; **backpedal** *fig* ch'ŏrhoehada 철회하다; **backslash** COMPUT yŏksŭllaeshi 역슬래시; **backspace (key)** COMPUT paekssŭp'eisŭ k'i 백스페이스 키; **backstairs** twitch'ŭnggye 뒷층계; **backstroke** SP paeyŏng 배영; **backup** (*support*) chiwŏn 지원; COMPUT paegŏp 백업; **take a ~** COMPUT paegŏbŭl hada 백업을 하다; **backup disk** COMPUT paegŏp tisŭk'ŭ 백업 디스크

backward 1 *adj child* twittŏrŏjin 뒤떨어진; *society* t'oebohanŭn 퇴보하는; *glance* twittchogŭi 뒷쪽의 **2** *adv* twittchogŭro 뒷쪽으로 **backyard** twit-ttŭl 뒷뜰; *fig* kŭnch'ŏ 근처

bacon peik'ŏn 베이컨

bacteria pakt'eria 박테리아

bad nappŭn 나쁜; *spelling* sŏt'urŭn 서투른; *cold, headache etc* shimhan 심한; (*rotten*) ssŏgŭn 썩은; *it's not ~* kwaench'anayo 괜찮아요; *that's really too ~* (*shame*) nŏmu andwaessŏyo 너무 안됐어요; *feel ~ about* ...e taehae choech'aek-kkamŭl nŭkkida ...에 대해 죄책감을 느끼다; *be ~ at* ...e sŏt'urŭda ...에 서투르다; *Friday's ~, how about Thursday?* kŭmnyoirŭn andoenŭnde, mogyoirŭn ŏttaeyo? 금요일은 안되는데, 목요일은 어때요?

bad debt pullyang puch'ae 불량 부채

badge paeji 배지

badger *v/t* chorŭda 조르다

bad language yokssŏl 욕설

badly nappŭge 나쁘게; (*making mistakes, errors*) chalmot 잘못; *injured, damaged* shimhage 심하게; *he ~ needs a haircut / rest* kŭnŭn chŏngmal mŏrirŭl challayagessŏyo / shwiŏyagessŏyo 그는 정말 머리를 잘라야겠어 요 / 쉬어야겠어요; *he is ~ off* (*poor*) kŭnŭn kananhada 그는 가난하다

badminton paedŭmint'ŏn 배드민턴

baffle tanghwanghage hada 당황하게 하다; *be ~d* tanghwanghae hada 당황해 하다

baffling ihaehal su ŏmnŭn 이해할 수 없는

bag (*travel ~*) yŏhaeng kabang 여행 가방; (*plastic, paper*) kabang 가방; (*for school*) ch'aek-kkabang 책가방; (*pocketbook*) haendŭbaek 핸드백

baggage suhwamul 수화물

baggage car RAIL suhwamul yŏlch'a 수화물 열차; **baggage cart** suhwamul unbanch'a 수화물 운반차; **baggage check** suhwamul pogwantchŭng 수화물 보관증; **baggage reclaim** suhwamul k'ŭlleim 수화물 클레임

baggy hŏllŏnghan 헐렁한

bail *n* LAW posŏk 보석; (*money*) posŏk-kkŭm 보석금; *on ~* posŏk-kkŭmŭl naego 보석금을 내고

♦**bail out 1** *v/t* LAW posŏgŭl patkke hada 보석을 받게 하다; *fig* kon-gyŏng-esŏ ...ŭl / rŭl kuhaenaeda 곤경에서 ...을 / 를 구해내다 **2** *v/i* (*from airplane*) nak'asanŭro t'alch'urhada 낙하산으로 탈출하다

bait *n* mikki 미끼

bake *v/t* kuptta 굽다

baked potato kuŭn kamja yori 구운 감자 요리

baker cheppang-ŏptcha 제빵업자

bakery ppangjip 빵집

balance 1 *n* kyunhyŏng 균형; (*remainder*) chanyŏgŭm 잔여금; (*of bank account*) chan-go 잔고 **2** *v/t* ...ŭi kyunhyŏng-ŭl chaptta ..의 균형을 잡다; *~ the books* hoegye kyŏlssanhada 회계 결산하다 **3** *v/i* kyunhyŏng chaptta 균형 잡다; (*of accounts*) kyŏlssandoeda 결산되다

balanced (*fair*) kongjŏnghan 공정한; *diet* kyunhyŏng chap'in 균형 잡힌; *personality* anjŏngdoen 안정된

balance of payments kuktche suji 국제 수지; **balance of trade** muyŏk suji 무역 수지; **balance sheet** taech'adaejop'yo 대차대조표

balcony (*of house*) peranda 베란다; (*in theater*) ich'ŭng chwasŏk 이층

좌석
bald *man* taemŏriŭi 대머리의; *he's
going ~* kŭnŭn taemŏriga toeŏ
kanda 그는 대머리가 되어 간다
ball kong 공; *on the ~* *fig* pint'ŭm
ŏmnŭn 빈틈 없는; *play ~* *fig*
hyŏmnyŏk'ada 협력하다; *the ~'s in
his court* *fig* taŭmŭn kŭŭi
ch'aryeida 다음은 그의 차례이다
ball bearing pol pŏring 볼 베어링
ballerina pallerina 발레리나
ballet palle 발레
ballet dancer palle muyongga 발레
무용가
ball game (*baseball game*) yagu 야구;
that's a different ~ kŭgŏn tarŭn
chongnyuŭi munjeimnida 그건 다른
종류의 문제입니다
ballistic missile t'ando misail 탄도
미사일
balloon (*child's*) p'ungsŏn 풍선; (*for
flight*) kigu 기구
ballot 1 *n* t'up'yo 투표 **2** *v/t members*
t'up'yoro chŏnghada 투표로 정하다
ballot box tup'yoham 투표함
ballpark (*baseball*) yagujang 야구장;
be in the right ~ *fig* kŏŭi mat-tta
거의 맞다; *~ figure* taegang-ŭi ŏrim
대강의 어림
ballpoint (*pen*) polp'en 볼펜
balls V pural 불알; (*courage*)
paetchang 배짱
bamboo taenamu 대나무
ban 1 *n* kŭmji 금지 **2** *v/t* kŭmjihada
금지하다
banana panana 바나나
band akdan 악단; (*pop*) paendŭ 밴드;
(*of material*) kkŭn 끈
bandage 1 *n* pungdae 붕대 **2** *v/t*
pungdaerŭl kamtta 붕대를 감다
Band-Aid® panch'anggo 반창고
bandit sanjŏk 산적
bandwagon: *jump on the ~*
shiryurŭl t'ada 시류를 타다
bandy *legs* hwin 휜
bang 1 *n* (*noise*) k'wang hanŭn sori
쾅 하는 소리; (*blow*) k'wang
pudich'im 쾅 부딪힘 **2** *v/t door*
k'wang tat-tta 쾅 닫다; (*hit*) k'wang
pudich'ida 쾅 부딪히다 **3** *v/i* (*of
door*) k'wang tach'ida 쾅 닫히다

Bangladesh Panggŭlladeshi
방글라데시
Bangladeshi 1 *adj* Panggŭlladeshiŭi
방글라데시의 **2** *n* Panggŭlladeshiin
방글라데시인
banjo paenjo 밴조
bank[1] (*of river*) chebang 제방
bank[2] **1** *n* FIN ŭnhaeng 은행 **2** *v/i*: *~
with* ...wa/kwa kŏraehada ...와/과
거래하다 **3** *v/t money* yegŭmhada
예금하다
♦**bank on** ...ŭl/rŭl kidaehada
...을/를 기대하다; *don't ~ it* nŏmu
hwaksshinhaji mara 너무 확신하지
마라
bank account ŭnhaeng kujwa 은행
구좌; **bank balance** ŭnhaeng chan-
go 은행 잔고; **bank bill** chip'ye 지폐
banker ŭnhaengga 은행가
banker's card ŭnhaeng shinyong
k'adŭ 은행 신용 카드
banker's order chadong taech'e 자동
대체
bank loan ŭnhaeng yungja 은행 융자;
bank manager ŭnhaeng chijŏmjang
은행 지점장; **bank rate** (chung-ang
ŭnhaengŭi) ijayul (중앙 은행의)
이자율; **bankroll** *v/t* chagŭmŭl taeda
자금을 대다
bankrupt 1 *adj* (*person, company*)
p'asanhan 파산한; *go ~* p'asanhada
파산하다 **2** *v/t* p'asanshik'ida
파산시키다
bankruptcy p'asan 파산
bank statement chan-go chohoe
잔고 조회
banner ki 기
banns kyŏrhon yego 결혼 예고
banquet yŏnhoe 연회
banter *n* kabyŏun nongdam 가벼운
농담
baptism serye 세례
baptize seryehada 세례하다
bar[1] (*iron*) pitchang 빗장; (*of
chocolate*) makttaegi 막대기; (*for
drinks*) sultchip 술집; (*counter*)
kyesandae 계산대; *a ~ of soap* pinu
hanjang 비누 한 장; *be behind ~s*
kamoge it-tta 감옥에 있다
bar[2] *v/t* kŭmhada 금하다
bar[3] *prep* (*except*) ...ŭl/rŭl cheoehago

...을/를 제외하고

barbecue 1 *n* pabek'yu 바베큐;
(*equipment*) pabek'yuyong ch'ŏlp'an
바베큐용 철판 **2** *v/t* t'ongtchaero
kuptta 통째로 굽다

barbecued beef pulgogi 불고기

barbed wire kashi ch'ŏlssa 가시 철사

barber ibalssa 이발사

bar code pak'odŭ 바코드

bare *adj* (*naked*) palgabŏsŭn
발가벗은; *room* t'ŏng pin 텅 빈; ~
floor maenmaru 맨마루

barefoot: *be* ~ maenbarida 맨발이다

bare-headed mojaril ssŭji anŭn
모자를 쓰지 않은

barely kanshinhi 간신히

bargain 1 *n* (*deal*) yakssok 약속;
(*good buy*) ssan mulgŏn 싼 물건; *it's*
a ~! (*deal*) kyŏltchŏngnassŏyo!
결정났어요! **2** *v/i* hŭngjŏnghada
흥정하다

♦ **bargain for** (*expect*) yesanghada
예상하다

barge *n* NAUT kŏrutppae 거룻배

bark¹ **1** *n* (*of dog*) kae chinnŭn sori 개
짖는 소리 **2** *v/i* chit-tta 짖다

bark² (*of tree*) kkŏptchil 껍질

barley pori 보리

barn hŏtkkan 헛간

barometer kiapkkye 기압계; *fig*
chip'yo 지표

barracks MIL maksa 막사

barrel (*container*) t'ong 통

barren *land* pulmoŭi 불모의

barrette mŏrip'in 머리핀

barricade *n* parik'eidŭ 바리케이드

barrier ult'ari 울타리; (*cultural*)
chang-ae 장애; *language* ~ ŏnŏ
chang-ae 언어 장애

bar tender pat'endŏ 바텐더

barter 1 *n* mulmul kyohwan 물물
교환 **2** *v/t* mulmul kyohwanhada
물물 교환하다

base 1 *n* (*bottom*) mit 밑; (*center*)
ponbu 본부; MIL chaktchŏn kiji 작전
기지 **2** *v/t*: ~ *on* ...e pat'angŭl tuda
...에 바탕을 두다; ~ *X on Y* Xŭi
pat'angŭl Y(ŭ)ro hada X의 바탕을
Y(으)로 하다; *be* ~*d in* (*in city,
country*) ...e kŭn-gŏjirŭl tugo it-tta
...에 근거지를 두고 있다

baseball (*ball*) yagugong 야구공;
(*game*) yagu 야구

baseball bat yagu pangmang-i 야구
방망이; **baseball cap** yagu moja
야구 모자; **baseball player** yagu
sŏnsu 야구 선수

base camp peisŭ k'emp'ŭ 베이스
켐프

basement (*of house*) chihashil
지하실; (*of store*) chihach'ŭng 지하층

base rate FIN chung-ang ŭnhaeng-ŭi
kibon kŭmni 중앙 은행의 기본 금리

basic (*rudimentary*) kibonjŏgin
기본적인; (*fundamental*)
kŭnbonjŏgin 근본적인; *level*
kich'ojŏgin 기초적인; *a* ~ *hotel*
susuhan hot'el 수수한 호텔

basically kibonjŏguro 기본적으로

basics: *the* ~ kich'o 기초; *get down*
to ~ kich'obut'ŏ hada 기초부터 하다

basin (*for washing*) semyŏndae
세면대

basis kich'o 기초; (*of argument*) kŭn-
gŏ 근거

bask haetppyŏch'ŭl tchoeda 햇볕을
쬐다

basket paguni 바구니; (*in basketball*)
pasŭk'et 바스켓

basketball nonggu 농구

bass 1 *n* (*part, singer*) peisŭ 베이스;
(*instrument*) pasŭ 바스 **2** *adj*
chŏŭmŭi 저음의; ~ *clef* najŭn
ŭmjarip'yo 낮은 음자리표

bastard sasaeng-a 사생아; F
kaesaekki 개새끼; *poor* / *stupid* ~
pulssanghan / pabokat'ŭn nyŏsŏk
불쌍한 /바보같은 녀석

bat¹ **1** *n* (*for baseball*) pangmang-i
방망이; (*for table tennis*) ch'ae 채
2 *v/i* (*in baseball*) pangmang-iro
ch'ida 방망이로 치다

bat²: *he didn't* ~ *an eyelid* kŭnŭn
nun hana kkamtchak'aji anat-tta
그는 눈 하나 깜짝하지 않았다

bat³ (*animal*) paktchwi 박쥐

batch *n* (*of students*) ilttan 일단; (*of
data*) paech'i 배치; (*of goods
produced*) han mukkŭm 한 묶음; (*of
bread*) han kama 한 가마

bath mogyok 목욕; *have a* ~, *take a*
~ mogyok'ada 목욕하다

bathe *v/i* (*have a bath*) mogyok'ada 목욕하다
bath mat mogyokt'ang kkalgae 목욕탕 깔개; **bathrobe** mogyok kaun 목욕 가운; **bathroom** (*for bath*) yoksshil 욕실; (*for washing hands*) semyŏnjang 세면장; (*toilet*) hwajangshil 화장실; **bath towel** mogyok sugŏn 목욕 수건; **bathtub** yoktcho 욕조
batter[1] *n* (*in cooking*) milkkaru panjuk 밀가루 반죽
batter[2] (*in baseball*) t'aja 타자
battery chŏnji 전지; MOT paet'ŏri 배터리
battle *n* chŏnt'u 전투; *fig* t'ujaeng 투쟁
♦ **battle against** *illness etc* …wa/kwa ssauda …와/과 싸우다
battlefield, battleground chŏnjaengt'ŏ 전쟁터
bawdy oesŏlssŭrŏun 외설스러운
bawl (*shout*) kohamch'ida 고함치다; (*weep*) ulda 울다
♦ **bawl out** *v/t* F hot'ong-ŭl ch'ida 호통을 치다
bay (*inlet*) man 만
bay window naeminch'ang 내민창
BBS (= *Buddhist Broadcasting System*) Pulgyo Pangsong 불교 방송
be ◊ ida 이다; (*exist*) it-tta 있다; *I am a student* nanŭn hakssaeng-iyeyo 나는 학생이에요; *was she there?* kŏgi kŭ yŏjaga itssŏssŏyo? 거기 그 여자가 있었어요?; *it's me* chŏyeyo 저예요; *how much is / are ...?* …ŭn/nŭn ŏlmaimnikka? …은/는 얼마입니까?; *there is*, *there are* …i/ga it-tta …이/가 있다; *there are some books in my bag* nae kabang soge ch'aegi it-tta 내 가방 속에 책이 있다 ◊ (*with adjectives*) …ta …다; *she is pretty* kŭnyŏnŭn yeppŭda 그녀는 예쁘다; *I am tired* nanŭn p'igonhada 나는 피곤하다; *~ careful* choshimhaseyo 조심하세요; *don't ~ sad* sŭlp'ŏhajima 슬퍼하지마 ◊: *has the mailman been?* uch'ebuga tŭllŏt-tta kassŏyo? 우체부가 들렀다 갔어요?; *I've never been to Korea*

nanŭn Han-guge kabon chŏgi ŏptta 나는 한국에 가본 적이 없다; *I've been here for hours* nanŭn yŏgi myŏt shiganina kyesok issŏt-tta 나는 여기 몇 시간이나 계속 있었다 ◊ (*tag questions*) …jiyo? …지요?; *that's right, isn't it?* mat-tchiyo? 맞지요?; *she's Korean, isn't she?* kŭ yŏjanŭn Han-guk saram ijiyo? 그 여자는 한국 사람 이지요? ◊ (*auxiliary*) … hago it-tta … 하고 있다; *I am thinking* nanŭn saenggak'ago issŏyo 나는 생각하고 있어요; *he was running* kŭnŭn ttwigo issŏt-tta 그는 뛰고 있었다; *you're ~ing silly* nŏnŭn pabosŭrŏun chisŭl hago issŏ 너는 바보스러운 짓을 하고 있어 ◊ (*obligation*) … haeya handa … 해야 한다; *you are to do what I tell you* nŏnŭn naega marhanŭn taero haeya handa 너는 내가 말하는 대로 해야 한다; *I was to tell you this* nanŭn nŏege igŏsŭl marhaessŏya haessŏ 나는 너에게 이것을 말했어야 했어; *you are not to tell anyone* amuegedo marhaesŏn andwae 아무에게도 말해선 안돼 ◊ (*passive*): *he was killed* kŭnŭn p'isaldanghaet-tta 그는 피살당했다; *they have been sold* kŭgŏt-ttŭrŭn p'allyŏt-tta 그것들은 팔렸다; *it was discovered* kugŏsŭn palgyŏndoeŏt-tta 그것은 발견되었다
♦ **be in for** …ŭl/rŭl yesanghago it-tta …을/를 예상하고 있다
beach haebyŏn 해변
beachwear pich'iweŏ 비치웨어
beads kusŭl 구슬
beak puri 부리
beaker taejŏp 대접
be-all: *the ~ and end-all* kajang chungnyohan kŏt 가장 중요한 것
beam 1 *n* (*in ceiling etc*) tŭlppo 들보 **2** *v/i* (*smile*) hwaltchak ut-tta 활짝 웃다 **3** *v/t* (*transmit*) songshinhada 송신하다
beans k'ong 콩; *be full of* ~ kiuni nŏmch'yŏ nanŭn 기운이 넘쳐 나는
bear[1] (*animal*) kom 곰
bear[2] **1** *v/t weight* chit'aenghada 지탱하다; *costs* pudamhada 부담하다;

bear
314

(tolerate) kyŏndida 견디다; *child*
ch'ulssanhada 출산하다 **2** *v/i*: ***bring***
pressure to ~ on …e amnyŏgŭl
kahada …에 압력을 가하다
♦**bear out** *(confirm)* chijihada
지지하다
bearable kyŏndil su innŭn 견딜 수
있는
beard t'ŏkssuyŏm 턱수염
bearing *(in machine)* pŏring 베어링;
that has no ~ on the case kŭ
ilgwanŭn amurŏn kwallyŏni ŏpta 그
일과는 아무런 관련이 없다
bear market FIN hahyang shiseŭi
shijang 하향 시세의 시장
beast *(animal)* chimsŭng 짐승
beat 1 *n (of heart)* kodong 고동; *(of
music)* paktcha 박자 **2** *v/i (of heart)*
kodongch'ida 고동치다; *(of rain)*
t'ungt'ung tudŭrida 퉁퉁 두드리다; ~
around the bush tullŏdaeda
둘러대다 **3** *v/t (in competition)* igida
이기다; *(hit)* ttaerida 때리다;
(pound) tudŭrida 두드리다; ~ *it!* F
kkŏjyŏ pŏryŏ! 꺼져 버려!; *it ~s me* F
nanŭn todaech'e ihae hal su ŏpta
나는 도대체 이해할 수 없다
♦**beat up** kut'ahada 구타하다
beaten: *off the ~ track* sandorŭl
pŏsŏnan 상도를 벗어난
beating *(physical)* kut'a 구타
beat-up F nalgŭn 낡은
beautician miyongsa 미용사
beautiful arŭmdaun 아름다운; *day*
mŏtchin 멋진; *weather*
hwach'anghan 화창한; *thanks,
that's just ~!* komawŏyo, nŏmu
mashissŭmnida 고마워요. 너무
맛있습니다
beautifully *cooked, done* hullunghage
훌륭하게; *simple* koengjanghi 굉장히
beauty arŭmdaum 아름다움
beauty parlor miyongshil 미용실
♦**beaver away** pujirŏnhi irhada
부지런히 일하다
because … ttaemune … 때문에; ~ *it
was too expensive* kŭgŏshi nŏmu
pissatkki ttaemunida 그것이 너무
비쌌기 때문이다; ~ *of* … ttaemune
… 때문에; ~ *of the weather* nalsshi
ttaemune 날씨 때문에

beckon *v/i* sontchit'ayŏ purŭda
손짓하여 부르다
become ◊ *(+ adj)* … haejida …
해지다; *the weather became
colder* nalsshiga ch'uwŏjyŏt-tta
날씨가 추워졌다 ◊ *(+ noun)* …i/ga
toeda …이/가 되다; *he became a
priest* kŭnŭn shibuga toeŏt-tta 그는
신부가 되었다; *what's ~ of her?* kŭ
yŏjanŭn ŏttŏk'e toeŏtchiyo? 그
여자는 어떻게 되었지요?
bed ch'imdae 침대; *(of flowers)*
hwadan 화단; *(of sea, river)*
mitppadak 밑바닥; *go to ~*
chamjarie tŭlda 잠자리에 들다; *he's
still in ~* kŭnŭn ajiktto chago it-tta
그는 아직도 자고 있다; *go to ~ with*
…wa/kwa kach'i chada …와/과
같이 자다
bedclothes ch'imgu 침구
bedding ch'imgu 침구
bedridden pyŏngsang-e innŭn 병상에
있는; **bedroom** ch'imshil 침실;
bedspread ch'imdaebo 침대보;
bedtime ch'wich'im shigan 취침
시간
bee pŏl 벌
beech nŏdobamnamu 너도밤나무
beef 1 *n* soegogi 쇠고기; F *(complaint)*
pulp'yŏng 불평 **2** *v/i* F *(complain)*
pulp'yŏnghada 불평하다
♦**beef up** poganghada 보강하다
beefburger pip'ŭbŏgŏ 비프버거
beehive pŏltchip 벌집
beeline: *make a ~ for* …(ŭ)ro kot-
tchang tallyŏgada …(으)로 곧장
달려가다
beep 1 *n* shinhoŭm 신호음 **2** *v/i*
shimhoŭmi ullida 신호음이 울리다
3 *v/t (call on pager)* hoch'urhada
호출하다
beeper hoch'ulgi 호출기
beer maektchu 맥주
beetle ttaktchŏngbŏlle 딱정벌레
before 1 *prep (in time, order)* …
chŏne … 전에; ~ *8 o'clock* 8shi
chŏne 8시 전에 **2** *adv* ijŏne 이전에;
you should have let me know ~
ijŏne na-ege allyŏjuŏssŏya haessŏ
이전에 내게 알려주었어 야 했어; *the
week / day ~* kŭ chŏnjue / chŏnnare

그 전주에/ 전날에 3 *conj* ...hagi chŏne ...하기 전에; **~ he leaves** kŭga ttŏnagi chŏne 그가 떠나기 전에
beforehand miri 미리
beg 1 *v/i* kugŏrhada 구걸하다 **2** *v/t:* **~ s.o. to ...** nuguege ...hae tallago kanch'ŏnghada 누구에게 ... 해 달라고 간청하다
beggar kŏji 거지
begin 1 *v/i* shijakttoeda 시작되다; **to ~ with** (*at first*) ch'ŏumenŭn 처음에는; (*in the first place*) ch'ŏt-tchaero 첫째로 **2** *v/t* shijak'ada 시작하다
beginner ch'oboja 초보자
beginner driver unjŏnŭl paeunŭn saram 운전을 배우는 사람
beginning shijak 시작; (*origin*) shich'o 시초
behalf: on *or* **in ~ of** ...ŭl/rŭl wihayŏ ...을/를 위하여; **on my/his ~** narŭl/kŭrŭl taeshinhaesŏ 나를/그를 대신해서
behave *v/i* haengdonghada 행동하다; **~ (oneself)** yeŭi parŭge haengdonghada 예의 바르게 행동하다; **~ (yourself)!** yeŭi parŭge haengdonghaera 예의바르게 행동해라
behavior haengdong 행동
behind 1 *prep* (*in position*) ...twittchoge(sŏ) ...뒷쪽에(서); (*in progress, order*) ...e twijyŏsŏ ...에 뒤져서; **be ~ ...** (*responsible for*) ...e ch'aegimi it-tta ...에 책임이 있다; (*support*) chijihada 지지하다 **2** *adv* (*at the back*) twie(sŏ) 뒤에(서); **be ~ with ...** ...i/ga millyŏ it-tta ...이/가 밀려있다
Beijing Puk-kkyŏng 북경
being (*existence*) chonjae 존재; (*creature*) saengmul 생물
belated yŏn-gideon 연기된
belch 1 *n* t'ŭrim 트림 **2** *v/i* t'ŭrimhada 트림하다
Belgian 1 *adj* Pelgieŭi 벨기에의 **2** *n* Pelgiein 벨기에인
Belgium Pelgie 벨기에
belief midŭm 믿음; (*religious*) shinang 신앙
believe mit-tta 믿다

♦**believe in** ...ŭl/rŭl mit-tta ...을/를 믿다; *ghosts* ...ŭi chonjaerŭl mit-tta ...의 존재를 믿다; *a person* shilloehada 신뢰하다
believer shinja 신자; *fig* shinbongja 신봉자
bell chong 종
bellhop pelboi 벨보이
belligerent *adj* hojŏnjŏgin 호전적인
bellow 1 *n* koham 고함; (*of bull*) soga unŭn sori 소가 우는 소리 **2** *v/i* kohamch'ida 고함치다; (*of bull*) ulda 울다
belly (*of person*) pae 배; (*fat stomach*) ttongppae 똥배; (*of animal*) wi 위
bellyache *v/i* F pulp'yŏng-ŭl nŭrŏnot-tta 불평을 늘어놓다
belong *v/i*: **where does this ~?** ŏdie noŭlkkayo? 어디에 놓을까요?; **I don't ~ here** nanŭn yŏgie mat-tchi anayo 나는 여기에 맞지 않아요
♦**belong to** ...ŭi kŏshida ...의 것이다; *club, organization* ...ŭi irwŏnida ..의 일원이다
belongings sojip'um 소지품
beloved *adj* saranghanŭn 사랑하는
below 1 *prep* ... araee(sŏ) ... 아래에(서); (*in amount, rate, level*) ... iharo ... 이하로 **2** *adv* araet-tchoge(sŏ) 아랫쪽에(서); (*in text*) araee(sŏ) 아래에(서); **see ~** araet-tchogŭl poseyo 아랫쪽을 보세요; **10 degrees ~** yŏngha shiptto 영하 십도
belt hŏritti 허리띠; **tighten one's ~** *fig* hŏrittirŭl chollamaeda 허리띠를 졸라매다
bench (*seat*) pench'i 벤치; (*work~*) chagŏpttae 작업대
benchmark kijun 기준
bend 1 *n* man-gok 만곡 **2** *v/t* kuburida 구부리다 **3** *v/i* hwida 휘다; (*of person*) kuburida 구부리다
♦**bend down** kuburida 구부리다
bender F sul mashigo hŭngch'ŏnggŏrim 흥청거림; **go on a ~** chint'ang surŭl mashida 진탕 술을 마시다
beneath 1 *prep* ...ŭi araee(sŏ) ...의 아래에(서); (*in status, value*) ... poda natkke ... 보다 낮게 **2** *adv* araee(sŏ) 아래에(서)

benefactor ŭnhyerŭl pep'unŭn saram 은혜를 베푸는 사람
beneficial yuik'an 유익한
benefit 1 *n* iik 이익 **2** *v/t* …ŭi iigi toeda …의 이익이 되다 **3** *v/i* iigŭl ŏt-tta 이익을 얻다
benevolent injŏng manŭn 인정 많은
benign onhwahan 온화한; MED yangsŏng-ŭi 양성의
bequeath yusanŭro namgida 유산으로 남기다; *fig* chŏnhada 전하다
bereaved 1 *adj* sabyŏrhan 사별한; *the ~ family* yujok 유족 **2** *n: the ~* sabyŏrhan saramdŭl 사별한 사람들
berry ttalgiryuŭi yŏlmae 딸기류의 열매
berserk: *go ~* kwangp'ok'aejida 광폭해지다
berth (*for sleeping*) ch'imdaek'an 침대칸; (*for ship*) chŏngbaktchang 정박장; *give a wide ~ to* …ŭl/rŭl p'ihada …을/를 피하다
beside …ŭi kyŏt'e(sŏ) …의 곁에(서); *be ~ oneself* chejŏngshinŭl ilt'a 제정신을 잃다; *that's ~ the point* kŭgŏn ttan yaegiyeyo 그건 딴 얘기예요
besides 1 *adv* kedaga 게다가 **2** *prep* (*apart from*) … ioe-e … 이외에
best 1 *adj* kajang chŏun 가장 좋은, ch'oegoŭi 최고의 **2** *adv* kajang chal 가장 잘, cheil 제일; *it would be ~ if* … hanŭn kŏshi kajang choŭl tŭt'ada … 하는 것이 가장 좋을 듯하다; *I like her ~* nanŭn kŭnyŏrŭl cheil choahanda 나는 그녀를 제일 좋아한다 **3** *n: do one's ~* ch'oesŏnŭl tahada 최선을 다하다; *the ~* (*thing*) ch'oego 최고; (*person*) ch'oegoro chal hanŭn saram 최고로 잘 하는 사람; *make the ~ of* …ŭl/rŭl ch'oedaehanŭro iyonghada …을/를 최대한으로 이용하다; *all the ~!* haeng-uni itkkirŭl! 행운이 있기를!
best before date ch'oego p'umjil pojŭng kigan 최고 품질 보증 기간; **best man** (*at wedding*) shillang tŭllŏri 신랑 들러리; **best-seller** pesŭt'ŭsellŏ 베스트셀러
bet 1 *n* naegi 내기 **2** *v/i* naegirŭl kŏlda

내기를 걸다; *you ~!* mullonijyo! 물론이죠! **3** *v/t* (*reckon*) t'ŭllimŏpsshi …hal kŏshirago saenggak'ada 틀림없이 …할 것이라고 생각하다
betray paebanhada 배반하다
betrayal paeban 배반
better 1 *adj* poda naŭn 보다 나은; *get ~* (*skills*) hyangsangdoeda 향상되다; (*in health*) pyŏng-i nat-tta 병이 낫다; *he's ~* (*in health*) kŭŭi kŏn-gang-i choajyŏt-tta 그의 건강이 좋아졌다 **2** *adv* tŏ chal 더 잘, tŏ natkke 더 낫게; *she sings ~ than I do* kŭnyŏnŭn naboda noraerŭl tŏ chal handa 그녀는 나보다 노래를 더 잘 한다; *you look ~ today* onŭl tŏ naa poinda 오늘 더 나아 보인다; *you'd ~ ask permission* tangshin-ŭn hŏragŭl pannŭn kŏshi natkkessŏyo 당신은 허락을 받는 것이 낫겠어요; *I'd really ~ not* nanŭn haji annŭn p'yŏni natkkessŏyo 나는 하지 않는 편이 낫겠어요; *all the ~ for us* urihant'enŭn tŏ chaldoen irimnida 우리한테는 더 잘된 일입니다; *I like her ~* nanŭn kŭnyŏrŭl tŏ choahamnida 나는 그녀를 더 좋아합니다
better-off yubok'an 유복한
between *prep* saie 사이에: *~ you and me* urikkiriŭi yaegiijiman 우리끼리의 얘기이지만
beverage *fml* ŭmnyo 음료
beware: *~ of* …ŭl/rŭl choshimhada …을/를 조심하다
bewilder tanghwanghage hada 당황하게 하다
beyond 1 *prep* (*in time*) …ŭl/rŭl chinasŏ …을/를 지나서; (*in space*) …ŭl/rŭl nŏmŏsŏ …을/를 넘어서; (*in degree*) …ŭi pŏmwirŭl nŏmŏsŏ …의 범위를 넘어서; *it's ~ me* (*don't understand*) narosŏn al su ŏmnŭn irida 나로선 알 수 없는 일이다; (*can't do it*) nae nŭngnyŏk pakkŭi irida 내 능력 밖의 일이다 **2** *adv* chŏp'yŏnŭro 저편으로
Bhutan Put'an 부탄
Bhutanese 1 *adj* Put'anŭi 부탄의 **2** *n* (*person*) Put'anin 부탄인
bias *n* p'yŏn-gyŏn 편견

bias(s)ed p'yŏn-gyŏnŭl kajin 편견을 가진

bib (*for baby*) t'ŏkppaji 턱받이

Bible Sŏnggyŏng 성경

bibliography munhŏn mongnok 문헌 목록

biceps p'arŭi alt'ong 팔의 알통

bicker v/i maldat'umhada 말다툼하다

bicycle n chajŏn-gŏ 자전거

bid 1 (*at auction*) ipch'al 입찰; (*attempt*) shido 시도 **2** v/i (*at auction*) ipch'arhada 입찰하다

biennial adj kyŏng-nyŏnŭi 격년의

big 1 adj k'ŭn 큰; *my ~ brother/sister* (*man's*) naŭi k'ŭn hyŏng/nuna 나의 큰 형/누나; (*woman's*) naŭi k'ŭn oppa/ŏnni 나의 큰 오빠/언니; *~ name* yumyŏnghan irŭm 유명한 이름 **2** adv: *talk ~* hŏp'ung ttŏlda 허풍 떨다

bigamy chunghon 중혼

big-headed utchuldaenŭn 우쭐대는

bike 1 n chajŏn-gŏ 자전거 **2** v/i chajŏn-gŏrŭl t'ada 자전거를 타다

bikini pik'ini 비키니

bilingual tu nara marŭl hanŭn 두 나라 말을 하는

bill 1 (*money*) chip'ye 지폐; (*for gas, electricity*) ch'ŏnggusŏ 청구서; (*in hotel, restaurant etc*) kyesansŏ 계산서; POL pŏban 법안; (*poster*) kwanggo p'osŭt'ŏ 광고 포스터 **2** v/t (*invoice*) kyesansŏro ch'ŏngguhada 계산서로 청구하다

billboard kwanggop'an 광고판

billfold chigap 지갑

billiards tanggu 당구

billion ship ŏk 십억

bill of exchange hwanŏŭm 환어음

bill of sale yŏngsujŭng 영수증

bin (*for storage*) chŏjangt'ong 저장통

binary ijinppŏbŭi 이진법의

bind v/t (*connect*) kyŏn-gyŏrhada 연결하다; (*tie*) muktta 묶다; (LAW: *oblige*) ...ŭi ŭimurŭl chiuda ...의 의무를 지우다

binder (*for papers*) paindŏ 바인더

binding 1 adj agreement, promise kusongnyŏgi innŭn 구속력이 있는 **2** n (*of book*) changjŏng 장정

binoculars ssang-an-gyŏng 쌍안경

biodegradable misaengmure ŭihae punhaega toenŭn 미생물에 의해 분해가 되는

biography chŏn-gi 전기

biological saengmurhagŭi 생물학의; *~ parents* ch'inbumo 친부모; *~ detergent* ch'inhwan-gyŏng sech'ŏktche 친환경 세척제

biology saengmurhak 생물학

biotechnology saengch'e konghak 생체 공학

bird sae 새

bird of prey sanaun naljimsŭng 사나운 날짐승

bird sanctuary choryu poho kuyŏk 조류 보호 구역

birth (*of child*) t'ansaeng 탄생; (*labor*) ch'ulssan 출산; (*of country*) kiwŏn 기원; *give ~ to child* airŭl nat'a 아이를 낳다; *date of ~* saengnyŏnwŏril 생년월일; *place of ~* ch'ulssaengji 출생지

birth certificate ch'ulssaeng chŭngmyŏngsŏ 출생 증명서; **birth control** sana chehan 산아 제한; **birthday** saeng-il 생일; *happy ~!* saeng-il ch'uk'ahamnida! 생일 축하합니다!; **birthplace** ch'ulssaengji 출생지; **birthrate** ch'ulssaengnyul 출생률

biscuit pisŭk'et 비스켓

bisexual 1 adj yangsŏng-ŭi 양성의 **2** n yangsŏng-aeja 양성애자

bishop chugyo 주교

bit n (*piece*) chogak 조각; (*part of a whole*) pubun 부분; COMPUT pit'ŭ 비트; *a ~* (*a little*) chogŭm 조금; (*a while*) chamkkan 잠깐; *a ~ of* (*a little*) chogŭm 조금; *a ~ of news/advice* yakkanŭi soshik/ch'unggo 약간의 소식/충고; *~ by ~* chogŭmsshik 조금씩; *I'll be there in a ~* nanŭn chamshi hue kŏgi toch'ak'al kŏmnida 나는 잠시 후에 거기 도착할 겁니다

bitch 1 n (*dog*) amk'ae 암캐; F (*woman*) nappŭn nyŏn 나쁜 년 **2** v/i F (*complain*) pulp'yŏnghada 불평하다

bitchy F person, remark shimsulgujŭn

심술궂은

bite 1 *n* mum 묾; (*of food*) han ip 한 입; *get a ~* (*of angler*) mikkirŭl mulda 미끼를 물다; *let's have a ~* (*to eat*) shikssahapsshida 식사합시다 **2** *v/t* mulda 물다 **3** *v/i* mulda 물다; (*of fish*) mikkirŭl mulda 미끼를 물다

bitmap COMPUT pit'ŭmaep 비트맵

bitmap font COMPUT chŏm kŭlkkol 점 글꼴

bitter *taste* ssŭn 쓴; *person* pit'onghan 비통한; *weather* hokttok'an 혹독한; *argument* shillarhan 신랄한

bitterly *cold* sarŭl enŭndŭshi 살을 에는듯이

black 1 *adj* kŏmŭn 검은; *music, history* hŭginŭi 흑인의; *coffee* pŭllaek 블랙; *fig* amdamhan 암담한 **2** *n* (*color*) kŏmjŏngsaek 검정색; (*person*) hŭgin 흑인; *in the ~* FIN hŭktcharo 흑자로

♦**black out** *v/i* ŭishigŭl ilt'a 의식을 잃다

blackberry pŭllaekpperi 블랙베리; **blackbird** tchirŭregi 찌르레기; **blackboard** ch'ilp'an 칠판; **black box** pŭllaek pakssŭ 블랙 박스; **black economy** pulppŏp koyong 불법 고용

blacken *person's name* omyŏng-ŭl ssŭiuda 오명을 씌우다

black eye mŏngdŭn nun 멍든 눈; **black ice** pŭllaek aisŭ 블랙 아이스, *toro wiŭi kŏmke poinŭn pingp'an* 도로 위의 검게 보이는 빙판; **blacklist 1** *n* pŭllaekrisŭt'ŭ 블랙리스트 **2** *v/t* pŭllaekrisŭt'ŭe ollida 블랙리스트 에 올리다; **blackmail 1** *n* konggal 공갈; *emotional ~* shimtchŏk konggal 심적 공갈 **2** *v/t* konggal ch'ida 공갈 치다; **blackmailer** konggal ch'inŭn saram 공갈 치는 사람; **black market** amshijang 암시장

blackness amhŭk 암흑

blackout ELEC chŏngjŏn 정전; MED ŭishik sangshil 의식 상실; **blacksmith** taejangjang-i 대장장이; **black tea** hongch'a 홍차

bladder panggwang 방광

blade (*of knife*) k'allal 칼날; (*of helicopter*) nalgae 날개; (*of grass*) ip 잎

blame 1 *n* pinan 비난; (*responsibility*) ch'aegim 책임 **2** *v/t* pinanhada 비난하다; *~ X for Y* Xŭi ch'aegimi Yege it-ttago pinanhada Y의 책임이 X에게 있다고 비난하다

bland *smile, answer* kimppajin 김빠진; *food* pyŏlmashi ŏmnŭn 별맛이 없는

blank 1 *adj* (*not written on*) kongbaegŭi 공백의; *look* mŏnghan 멍한; *~ tape* kongt'eip'ŭ 공테이프 **2** *n* (*empty space*) kongbaek 공백; *my mind's a ~* chŏngshini mŏnghada 정신이 멍하다

blank check paektchi sup'yo 백지 수표

blanket *n* tamnyo 담요; *a ~ of fig* …(ŭ)ro ont'ong tŏp'in …(으)로 온통 덮인; *a ~ of snow* onnuriŭl tŏp'ŭn nun 온누리를 덮은 눈

blare *v/i* yoranhage ullida 요란하게 울리다

♦**blare out 1** *v/i* ullyŏp'ŏjida 울려퍼지다 **2** *v/t* yoranhage ullida 요란하게 울리다

blaspheme *v/i* modok'ada 모독하다

blast 1 *n* (*explosion*) p'okppal 폭발; (*gust*) tolp'ung 돌풍 **2** *v/t* p'okp'ashik'ida 폭파시키다; *~!* pirŏmŏgŭl 빌어먹을!

♦**blast off** (*of rocket*) palssashik'ida 발사시키다

blast furnace yonggwangno 용광로

blast-off palssa 발사

blatant ppŏnppŏnsŭrŏun 뻔뻔스러운

blaze 1 *n* (*fire*) hwajae 화재; *a ~ of color* manbarhan saek ch'ae man'gbŏn 색채 **2** *v/i* (*of fire*) t'aorŭda 타오르다

♦**blaze away** (*with gun*) sswabŏrida 쏴버리다

blazer pŭlleijyŏ chak'et 블레이져 자켓

bleach 1 *n* p'yobaek 표백; (*for hair*) kŭmballo yŏmsaek 금발로 염색 **2** *v/t* p'yobaek'ada 표백하다; *hair* kŭmballo yŏmsaek'ada 금발로 염색하다

bleak *countryside* hwangnyanghan 황량한; *weather* ŭmch'imhan 음침한;

future ŏduun 어두운
bleary-eyed nuni ch'imch'imhan 눈이 침침한
bleat *v/i* (*of sheep*) maeaehago ulda 매애하고 울다
bleed 1 *v/i* ch'urhyŏrhada 출혈하다; *my nose is ~ing* nanŭn k'op'iga nanda 나는 코피가 난다 **2** *v/t fig* tonŭl ch'akch'wihada ton을 착취하다
bleeding *n* ch'urhyŏl 출혈
bleep 1 *n* ppii hanŭn sori 삐이 하는 소리 **2** *v/i* ppii hanŭn soriga nada 삐이 하는 소리가 나다
bleeper hoch'ulgi 호출기
blemish 1 *n* hŭm 흠 **2** *v/t* hŭmnaeda 흠내다; *reputation* tŏrŏp'ida 더럽히다
blend 1 *n* honhap 혼합 **2** *v/t* honhap'ada 혼합하다
♦ **blend in 1** *v/i* sŏkkida 섞이다 **2** *v/t* (*in cooking*) sŏkta 섞다
blender mikssŏgi 믹서기
bless ch'ukppok'ada 축복하다; ~ *you!* (*when s.o. sneezes*) chŏrŏn! 저런!; *be ~ed with* ...(ŭ)ro ch'ukppok pat-tta ...(으)로 축복 받다
blessing REL ŭnch'ong 은총; *fig* (*approval*) sŭngnak 승낙
blind 1 *adj* nun mŏn 눈 먼; *corner* ap'i poiji annŭn 앞이 보이지 않는; ~ *to* ...ŭl/rŭl poji mot'anŭn ...을/를 보지 못하는 **2** *n: the ~* maeng-in 맹인; **3** *v/t* nun mŏlge hada 눈 멀게 하다; *fig* poji mot'age hada 보지 못하게 하다
blind alley makttarŭn kolmok 막다른 골목; **blind date** p'ŭllaindŭ teit'ŭ 블라인드 데이트, mit'ing 미팅; **blindfold 1** *n* nun karigae 눈 가리개 **2** *v/t* nunŭl karida 눈을 가리다 **3** *adv* nunŭl karigo 눈을 가리고
blinding *light* nun pushige hanŭn 눈 부시게 하는; *headache* nuni mŏl chŏngdoŭi 눈이 멀 정도의
blind spot (*in road*) chadongch'a unjŏnjaŭi sagak 자동차 운전자의 사각; *fig* maengchŏm 맹점
blink *v/i* (*of person, light*) kkamppakkŏrida 깜박거리다
blip (*on radar screen*) leida yŏngsang 레이더 영상; *fig* ilsshijŏk pyŏndong 일시적 변동

bliss tŏ ŏmnŭn haengbok 더 없는 행복
blister 1 *n* multchip 물집 **2** *v/i* multchibi saenggida 물집이 생기다; (*of paint*) kip'oga saenggida 기포가 생기다
blizzard shimhan nunbora 심한 눈보라
bloated puŭn 부은
blob (*of liquid*) han pang-ul 한 방울
bloc POL kwŏn 권
block 1 *n* tŏng-ŏri 덩어리; (*in town*) kuhoek 구획; (*of shares*) han cho 한 조; (*blockage*) chang-aemul 장애물 **2** *v/t* makta 막다
♦ **block in** (*with vehicle*) pongswaehada 봉쇄하다
♦ **block out** *light* ch'adanhada 차단하다
♦ **block up** *sink etc* makta 막다
blockade 1 *n* pongswae 봉쇄 **2** *v/t* pongswaehada 봉쇄하다
blockage mak'yŏ innŭn kŏt 막혀있는 것
blockbuster taehit'ŭjak 대히트작
block letters taemuntcha 대문자
blond *adj* kŭmbarŭi 금발의
blonde *n* (*woman*) kŭmbal mŏri yŏja 금발 머리 여자
blood p'i 피; *in cold ~* naenghok'age 냉혹하게
blood bank hyŏraek ŭnhaeng 혈액 은행; **blood donor** hŏnhyŏltcha 헌혈자; **blood group** hyŏraek'yŏng 혈액형
bloodless *coup* muhyŏrŭi 무혈의
blood poisoning p'yehyŏltchŭng 폐혈증; **blood pressure** hyŏrap 혈압; **blood relation, blood relative** yukch'in 육친; **blood sample** hyŏraek saemp'ŭl 혈액 샘플; **bloodshed** yuhyŏl 유혈; **bloodshot** ch'unghyŏldoen 충혈된; **bloodstain** p'itchaguk 핏자국; **bloodstream** hyŏllyu 혈류; **blood test** hyŏraek kŏmsa 혈액 검사; **blood transfusion** suhyŏl 수혈; **blood vessel** hyŏlgwan 혈관
bloody *hands etc* p'it'usŏng-iŭi 피투성이의; *battle* yuhyŏrŭi 유혈의
bloody mary p'ŭllŏdi maeri 블러디

bloom 320

매리
bloom 1 *n* kkot 꽃; *in full ~*
hwaltchak p'in 활짝 핀 **2** *v/i* kkoch'i
p'ida 꽃이 피다; *fig* pŏnyŏnghada
번영하다
blossom 1 *n* kkot 꽃 **2** *v/i* p'ida 피다;
fig k'waehwarhaejida 쾌활해지다
blot 1 *n* ŏlluk 얼룩; *fig* hŭm 흠 **2** *v/t*
(*dry*) mulkkirŭl tudŭryŏ chiuda
물기를 두드려 지우다
♦**blot out** *memory* chiuda 지우다;
view kamch'uda 감추다; *sun* karida
가리다
blotch panjŏm 반점
blotchy ŏllukt'usŏng-iŭi 얼룩투성이의
blouse pŭllausŭ 블라우스
blow¹ kangt'a 강타; (*shock*)
ch'unggyŏk 충격
blow² 1 *v/t* (*of wind, whistle*) pulda
불다; *smoke* naeppumtta 내뿜다; F
(*spend*) nallida 날리다; F *opportunity*
nallyŏ pŏrida 날려 버리다; *~ one's
nose* k'orŭl p'ulda 코를 풀다 **2** *v/i*
(*of wind*) pulda 불다; (*of whistle*)
ullida 울리다; (*breathe out*) ipkkimŭl
pulda 입김을 불다; (*of fuse*)
kkŭnŏjida 끊어지다; (*of tire*) t'ŏjida
터지다
♦**blow off 1** *v/t* purŏ nallida 불어
날리다 **2** *v/i* parame nallida 바람에
날리다
♦**blow out 1** *v/t candle* kkŭda 끄다
2 *v/i* (*of candle*) kkŏjida 꺼지다
♦**blow over 1** *v/t* purŏ nŏmŏttŭrida
불어 넘어뜨리다 **2** *v/i* karaantta
가라앉다; (*of argument*) musahi
chinagada 무사히 지나가다
♦**blow up 1** *v/t* (*with explosives*)
p'okp'ahada 폭파하다; *balloon* pulda
불다; *photograph* hwakttaehada
확대하다 **2** *v/i* p'okpparhada
폭발하다; F (*get angry*) hwanaeda
화내다
blow-dry *v/t* tŭraiŏro mŏrirŭl mallida
드라이어로 머리를 말리다; **blow job**
V p'ellach'io 펠라치오; **blow-out** (*of
tire*) p'ŏngk'ŭ 펑크; F (*big meal*)
shilk'ŏt mŏk-kki 실컷 먹기; **blow-
up** (*of photo*) hwakttae 확대
blue 1 *adj* p'aran 파란; *movie* p'orŭno
포르노 **2** *n* p'arangsaek 파랑색

blueberry pŭlluberi 블루베리; **blue
chip** uryang chushik 우량 주식;
blue-collar worker yukch'e
nodongja 육체 노동자; **Blue House**
Ch'ŏng-wadae 청와대; **blueprint**
ch'ŏngsajin 청사진; *fig* (*plan*)
sangsehan kyehoek 상세한 계획
blues MUS pŭllusŭ 블루스; *have the ~*
ultchŏk'ada 울적하다
blues singer pŭllusŭ kasu 블루스
가수
bluff 1 *n* (*deception*) ŏmp'o 엄포 **2** *v/i*
ŏmp'orŭl not'a 엄포를 놓다
blunder 1 *n* k'ŭn shilssu 큰 실수 **2** *v/i*
k'ŭn shilssurŭl hada 큰 실수를 하다
blunt *adj* mudin 무딘; *person*
soltchik'an 솔직한
bluntly *speak* soltchik'age 솔직하게
blur 1 *n* hŭrim 흐림 **2** *v/t* hŭrige hada
흐리게 하다
blurb (*on book*) sŏnjŏn munkku 선전
문구
♦**blurt out** pulssuk marhada 불쑥
말하다
blush 1 *n* hongjo 홍조 **2** *v/i* ŏlgurŭl
pulk'ida 얼굴을 붉히다
blusher (*cosmetic*) poryŏnji 볼연지
BO (= *body odor*) amnae 암내
board 1 *n* p'anja 판자; (*for game*)
p'an 판; (*for notices*) keship'an
게시판; *~* (*of directors*) isahoe
이사회; *on ~* (*on plane*) pihaenggi
ane 비행기 안에; (*on train*) kich'a
ane 기차 안에; (*on boat*) pae ane 배
안에; *take on ~ comments etc*
koryŏhada 고려하다; (*fully realize
truth of*) hwaksshirhi ihaehada
확실히 이해하다; *across the ~*
chŏnmyŏnjŏguro 전면적으로 **2** *v/i*
airplane etc t'ada 타다 **3** *v/i* t'ada
타다
♦**board up** p'anjaro maktta 판자로
막다
♦**board with** ...e hasuk'ada ...에
하숙하다
board and lodging hasuk 하숙
boarder hasugin 하숙인; EDU
hasukssaeng 하숙생
board game podŭ keim 보드 게임
boarding card t'apssŭngkkwŏn
탑승권; **boarding house** hasuktchip

하숙집; **boarding pass**
t'apssŭngkkwŏn 탑승권; **boarding
school** kisuk hak-kkyo 기숙 학교
board meeting isa hoeŭi 이사 회의;
board room isa hoeŭishil 이사
회의실; **boardwalk** p'anjarŭl kkan
podo 판자를 깐 보도
boast 1 n charang kŏri 자랑 거리 2 v/i
charanghada 자랑하다
boat pae 배; (small, for leisure) pot'ŭ
보트; **go by ~** paero kada 배로 가다
bob[1] (haircut) tanbal 단발
bob[2] v/i (of boat etc) wi araero
kabyŏpkke umjigida 위 아래로
가볍게 움직이다
♦**bob up** pulssuk nat'anada 불쑥
나타나다
bobsleigh, bobsled popsŭllei
봅슬레이
bodhisattva posal 보살
bodily 1 adj momŭi 몸의 2 adv eject
momŭro 몸으로
body mom 몸; (dead) shich'e 시체; ~
of water suyŏk 수역; ~ (suit)
(undergarment) podisut'ŭ 보디수트
bodyguard kyŏnghowŏn 경호원;
body language momtchit ŏnŏ 몸짓
언어; **body odor** amnae 암내; **body
shop** MOT ch'ach'e kongjang 차체
공장; **bodywork** MOT ch'ach'e 차체
boggle: it ~s the mind! sangsangdo
hal su ŏmnŭn irida! 상상도 할 수
없는 일이다!
bogus katchaŭi 가짜의
boil[1] n (swelling) chonggi 종기
boil[2] 1 v/t liquid kkŭrida 끓이다; egg,
vegetables samtta 삶다 2 v/i kkŭlt'a
끓다
♦**boil down to** kyŏlguk …(ŭ)ro
toeda 결국 …(으) 로 되다
♦**boil over** (of milk etc) kkŭrŏ
nŏmch'ida 끓어 넘치다
boiler poillŏ 보일러
boisterous ttŏdŭlssŏk'an 떠들썩한
bold 1 adj taedamhan 대담한 2 n
(print) kulgŭn kŭlsshich'e 굵은
글씨체; **in ~** kulgŭn kŭlsshich'ero
굵은 글씨체로
bolster v/t confidence pukttoduda
북돋우다
bolt 1 n polt'ŭ 볼트; (on door)

chamulssoe 자물쇠; (of lightning)
pŏn-gae 번개; **like a ~ from the
blue** ch'ŏngch'ŏnbyŏngnyŏk-kkwa
kach'i 청천벽력과 같이 2 adv: ~
upright ttokpparo 똑바로 3 v/t (fix
with bolts) polt'ŭro choeda 볼트로
죄다; (close) chamulssoero
chamgŭda 자물쇠로 잠그다 4 v/i
(run off) tomangch'ida 도망치다
bomb 1 n p'okt'an 폭탄 2 v/t
p'okp'ahada 폭파하다
bombard: ~ **with questions** chilmun
kongserŭl p'ŏbut-tta 질문 공세를
퍼붓다
bomb attack p'ok-kkyŏk 폭격
bomber (airplane) p'ok-kkyŏk-kki
폭격기; (terrorist) p'okp'abŏm
폭파범
bomber jacket kunnyong chamba
군용 잠바
bomb scare p'okt'anŭi uryŏ 폭탄의
우려
bond 1 n (tie) kkŭn 끈; (of
matrimony) yŏnbun 연분; FIN
ch'aekkwŏn 채권 2 v/i (of glue)
chŏpch'ak'ada 접착하다
bone 1 n ppyŏ 뼈 2 v/t meat, fish
ppyŏrŭl pallanaeda 뼈를 발라내다
bonfire modakppul 모닥불
bonsai punjae 분재
bonus (money) ponŏsŭ 보너스;
(something extra) tŏm 덤
boo 1 n yayuhanŭn sori 야유하는 소리
2 v/t & v/i yayuhada 야유하다
book 1 n ch'aek 책; ~ **of matches**
sŏngnyangkkap 성냥갑 2 v/t
(reserve) yeyak'ada 예약하다; (for
crime) pŏlgŭm changbue ollida 벌금
장부에 올리다 3 v/i (reserve)
yeyak'ada 예약하다
bookcase ch'aektchang 책장
booked up hotel, flight yeyagi kkwak
ch'ada 예약이 꽉 차다; person
iltchŏng-i kkwak ch'ada 일정이 꽉
차다
bookie F makkwŏnŏptcha 마권업자
booking (reservation) yeyak 예약
booking clerk maep'yogyewŏn
매표계원
bookkeeper hoegyejangburŭl
chŏngnihanŭn saram 회계장부를

bookkeeping 322

정리하는 사람
bookkeeping pugi 부기
booklet soch'aektcha 소책자
bookmaker magwŏnŏptcha 마권업자
books (*accounts*) hoegyejangbu
회계장부; *do the ~* hoegyejangburŭl
chŏngnihada 회계장부를 정리하다
bookseller ch'aek changsa 책 장사;
bookstall maejŏm 매점; **bookstore**
sŏjŏm 서점
boom[1] **1** *n* (*economic*) kyŏnggi
p'oktttŭng 경기 폭등, pum 붐 **2** *v/i* (*of
business*) kyŏnggiga p'oktttŭnghada
경기가 폭등하다
boom[2] *n* (*noise*) koeng-ŭm 굉음
boonies: *out in the ~* F ojie(sŏ)
오지에(서)
boost 1 *n* (*to sales*) ch'oktchin 촉진;
(*to confidence*) kyŏngnyŏ 격려; (*to
economy*) puyang 부양 **2** *v/t
production, sales* ch'oktchinshik'ida
촉진시키다; *prices* kkŭrŏ ollida 끌어
올리다; *confidence, morale* toduda
돋우다
boot *n* changhwa 장화; *climbing ~s*
tŭngsanhwa 등산화
◆**boot out** F naetchot-tta 내쫓다
◆**boot up 1** *v/t* COMPUT put'inghada
부팅하다 **2** *v/i* COMPUT put'ingdoeda
부팅되다
booth (*at market, fair*) chŏmp'o 점포;
(*in restaurant*) k'anmagihan
chwasŏk 칸막이한 좌석; (*at
exhibition*) kwallamsŏk 관람석
booze *n* F sul 술
booze-up *Br* F sul chanch'i 술 잔치
border 1 *n* (*between countries*) kuk-
kkyŏng 국경; (*edge*) kajangjari
가장자리 **2** *v/t country, river* ...e
chŏp'ae it-tta ...에 접해 있다
◆**border on** *country* ...e iut'ada ...에
이웃하다; (*be almost*) kŏŭi ...ida
거의 ...이다
borderline: *a ~ case* idojŏdo anin
kyŏng-u 이도저도 아닌 경우
bore[1] *v/t hole* ttult'a 뚫다
bore[2] **1** *n* (*person*) ttabunhan saram
따분한 사람 **2** *v/t* siltchŭngnage hada
싫증나게 하다; *be ~d* chiruhaejida
지루해지다
boredom kwŏnt'ae 권태

boring ttabunhan 따분한
born: *be ~* t'aeŏnada 태어나다;
where were you ~? kohyang-i
ŏdiimnikka? 고향이 어디입니까?; *be
a ~ ...* t'agonan ... ida 타고난 ...
이다
borrow pilda 빌다
bosom (*of woman*) chŏtkkasŭm
젖가슴
boss (*one's own*) sangsa 상사; (*of
company*) sajang 사장
◆**boss around** puryŏmŏktta
부려먹다
bossy tumok haengsehanŭn 두목
행세하는
botanical shingmulŭi 식물의
botany shingmurhak 식물학
botch *v/t* sŏt'urŭge haesŏ
mangch'yŏbŏrida 서투르게 해서
망쳐버리다
both 1 *adj* yangtchogŭi 양쪽의 **2** *pron*
tul ta 둘 다; *I know ~ of the brothers* nanŭn kŭ hyŏngjerŭl tul ta algo
issŏyo 나는 그 형제를 둘 다 알고
있어요; *~ of the brothers were
there* tu hyŏngjega ta kŏgie
issŏssŏyo 두 형제가 다 거기에
있었어요; *~ of them* (*things*) kŭgŏt
tul ta 그것 둘 다; (*people*) kŭdŭl tul
ta 그들 둘 다 **3** *adv*: *~ ... and ...*
(*with nouns*) ...wa/kwa ..., tul ta ...
와/과 ..., 둘 다; (*with adjs*) ... go
...ta ... 고 ... 다; *~ my sister and I*
ŏnni wa na, tul ta 언니와 나, 둘 다;
it's ~ easy and interesting
kŭgŏsŭn shwipkko chaemiit-tta
그것은 쉽고 재미있다; *is it business
or pleasure? - ~* illo hanŭn
kŏmnikka, animyŏn chaemiro
hanŭn kŏmnikka? - tul tayeyo 일로
하는 겁니까, 아니면 재미로 하는
겁니까? - 둘 다예요
bother 1 *n* kolch'itkkŏri 골칫거리; *it's
no ~* pyŏl il animnida 별 일
아닙니다 **2** *v/t* (*disturb*) kwich'ank'e
hada 귀찮게 하다; *person working*
sŏnggashige hada 성가시게 하다;
(*worry*) kŏktchŏngdoege hada
걱정되게 하다 **3** *v/i* shin-gyŏng-i
ssŭida 신경이 쓰이다; *don't ~!* shin-
gyŏng ssŭji maseyo! 신경 쓰지

마세요!; *you needn't have ~ed*
shin-gyŏng ssŭl p'iryo ŏpssŏssŏyo
신경 쓸 필요 없었어요
bottle 1 *n* pyŏng 병; (*for baby*)
uyubyŏng 우유병 **2** *v/t* pyŏng-e
tamtta 병에 담다
◆ **bottle up** *feelings* ŏngnurŭda
억누르다
bottle bank chaehwaryongppyŏng
sujipsso 재활용병 수집소
bottled water p'anŭn mul 파는 물
bottleneck *n* (*in road*) pyŏngmok
병목; (*in production*) aero sahang
애로 사항
bottle-opener pyŏngttagae 병따개
bottom 1 *adj* maen mitppadagŭi 맨
밑바닥의 **2** *n* (*on the inside*) antchok
ppadak 안쪽 바닥; (*underside*)
mitppadak 밑바닥; (*of hill*) ŭi kajang
araetppubun 가장 아랫부분; (*of pile*)
maen araetchok 맨 아래쪽; (*of
street*) kkŭt 끝; (*of garden*) maen
katchok 맨 가쪽; (*buttocks*)
ŏngdŏng-i 엉덩이; *at the ~ of the
screen* hwamyŏnŭi hadane 화면의
하단에
◆ **bottom out** padagŭl pŏsŏnada
바닥을 벗어나다
bottom line *fig* (*financial outcome*)
ch'ongkyŏlssan 총결산; (*the real
issue*) kajang chungnyohan sahang
가장 중요한 사항
boulder k'ŭn chagal 큰 자갈
bounce 1 *v/t ball* t'wige hada 튀게
하다 **2** *v/i* (*of ball, rain etc*) t'wida
튀다; (*on sofa etc*) ttwiŏdanida
뛰어다니다; (*of check*) pudoga toeŏ
toedoraoda 부도가 되어 되돌아오다
bouncer kyŏngbiwŏn 경비원
bound¹: *be ~ to ...* (*sure to*)
t'ŭllimŏpsshi ...hal kŏshida 틀림없이
...할 것이다; (*obliged to*) ... haeya
handa ... 해야 한다
bound²: *be ~ for* (*of ship*) ... haeng
... 행; *a plane ~ for Seoul*
Sŏurhaeng pihaenggi 서울행 비행기
bound³ 1 *n* (*jump*) ttwiŏrŭgi
뛰어오르기 **2** *v/i* ttwiŏdanida
뛰어다니다
boundary kyŏnggye 경계
boundless muhanŭi 무한의

bouquet (*flowers*) kkot-ttabal 꽃다발;
(*of wine*) hyanggi 향기
bourbon pŏbon wisŭk'i 버본 위스키
bout MED palppyŏng 발병; (*in boxing*)
shihap 시합
boutique put'ik'ŭ 부티크
bow¹ 1 *n* (*as greeting*) chŏl 절 **2** *v/i*
insahada 인사하다 **3** *v/t head* sugida
숙이다
bow² (*knot*) maedŭp 매듭; MUS,
(*weapon*) hwal 활
bow³ (*of ship*) paenmŏri 뱃머리
bowels ch'angja 창자
bowl¹ (*container*) kŭrŭt 그릇; (*for
rice*) konggi 공기; (*for soup*) taejŏp
대접; (*for cooking, salad*) k'ŭn kŭrŭt
큰 그릇
bowl² *v/i* (*in bowling*) pollinghada
볼링하다
◆ **bowl over** *fig* ...ŭl/rŭl kkamtchak
nollage hada ...을/를 깜짝 놀라게
하다
bowling polling 볼링
bowling alley pollingjang 볼링장
bow tie nabi nekt'ai 나비 넥타이
box¹ *n* (*container*) sangja 상자; (*on
form*) pin k'an 빈 칸
box² *v/i* kwŏnt'uhada 권투하다
boxer kwŏnt'u sŏnsu 권투 선수
boxing kwŏnt'u 권투
boxing match kwŏnt'u shihap 권투
시합
box office maep'yoso 매표소
boy sonyŏn 소년; (*son*) adŭl 아들
boycott 1 *n* poik'ot 보이콧 **2** *v/t*
poik'ot'ada 보이콧하다
boyfriend namja ch'in-gu 남자 친구;
(*lover*) aein 애인
boyish sonyŏn-kat'ŭn 소년같은
boyscout poisŭk'aut 보이스카웃
bra pŭrejiŏ 브레지어
brace (*on teeth*) ch'iyŏl kyojŏnggi
치열 교정기
bracelet p'altchi 팔찌
bracket (*for shelf*) kkach'ibal 까치발;
(*in text*) kwaho 괄호
brag *v/i* charanghada 자랑하다
braid *n* (*in hair*) ttaŭn mŏri 땋은 머리;
(*trimming*) tan ch'ŏri 단처리
braille chŏmtcha 점자
brain tunoe 두뇌

brainless F mŏriga nappŭn 머리가 나쁜

brains (*intelligence*) chinŭng 지능

brainstorm → *brainwave*; **brainstorming** pŭreinsŭt'oming 브레인스토밍; **brain surgeon** noe chŏnmun oekkwa ŭisa 뇌 전문 외과 의사; **brainwash** senoehada 세뇌하다; **brainwashing** senoe 세뇌; **brainwave** (*brilliant idea*) myoan 묘안

brainy F ch'ongmyŏnghan 총명한

brake 1 *n* pŭreik'ŭ 브레이크; *fig* kyŏnje 견제 **2** *v/i* pŭreik'ŭrŭl kŏlda 브레이크를 걸다

brake light pŭreik'ŭ lait'ŭ 브레이크 라이트

brake pedal pŭreik'ŭ p'edal 브레이크 페달

branch *n* (*of tree*) kaji 가지; (*of bank, company*) chijŏm 지점

♦**branch off** (*of road*) kallajida 갈라지다

♦**branch out** saŏbŭl hwaktchanghada 사업을 확장하다

brand 1 *n* (*of product*) sangp'yo 상표 **2** *v/t*: ~ *s.o. a liar* nuguege kŏjitmaltchang-iŭi numyŏng-ŭl ssŭiuda 누구에게 거짓말장이의 누명을 씌우다

brand image sangp'umŭi imiji 상품의 이미지

brandish hwidurŭda 휘두르다

brand leader kajang chal naganŭn sangp'yo 가장 잘 나가는 상표; **brand loyalty** pŭraendŭ loyŏlt'i 브랜드 로열티; **brand name** sangp'yomyŏng 상표명

brand-new shinp'umŭi 신품의

brandy pŭraendi 브랜디

brass (*alloy*) notssoe 놋쇠

brass band ch'wiji akttan 취주 악단

brassière pŭrejiŏ 브레지어

brat *pej* saekki 새끼

bravado hŏse 허세

brave *adj* yonggamhan 용감한

bravery yonggamham 용감함

brawl 1 *n* ssaum 싸움 **2** *v/i* ssaumjirhada 싸움질하다

brawny kŏnjanghan 건장한

Brazil Pŭrajil 브라질

Brazilian 1 *adj* Pŭrajirŭi 브라질의 **2** *n* Pŭrajil saram 브라질 사람

breach (*violation*) wiban 위반; (*in party*) purhwa 불화

breach of contract LAW kyeyak wiban 계약 위반

bread *n* ppang 빵

breadcrumbs (*for cooking*) ppang karu 빵 가루; (*for birds*) ppang pusŭrŏgi 빵 부스러기

breadth p'ok 폭

breadwinner chibanŭi pŏrihanŭn saram 집안의 벌이하는 사람

break 1 *n* (*in bone etc*) kŭm 금; (*rest*) hyushik 휴식; (*in relationship*) hyushik-kki 휴식기; *give ... a ~* (*opportunity*) ...ege kihoerŭl chuda ...에게 기회를 주다; *take a ~* chamshi chungdanhada 잠시 중단하다; *without a ~* work, travel shwiji ank'o 쉬지 않고 **2** *v/t* machine, device, toy pusuda 부수다; stick, arm, leg purŏttŭrida 부러뜨리다; china, glass, egg kkaettŭrida 깨뜨리다; rules, law, promise wibanhada 위반하다; news chŏnhada 전하다; record kkaeda 깨다 **3** *v/i* (*of machine, device, toy*) pusŏjida 부서지다; (*of china, glass, egg*) kkaejida 깨지다; (*of stick*) purŏjida 부러지다; (*of news*) allyŏjida 알려지다; (*of storm*) shijakdoeda 시작되다; (*of boy's voice*) pyŏnsŏnghada 변성되다

♦**break away** *v/i* (*escape*) tomangch'ida 도망치다; (*from family*) tongnip'ada 독립하다; (*from organization*) t'alt'oehada 탈퇴하다; (*from tradition*) pŏsŏnada 벗어나다

♦**break down 1** *v/i* (*of vehicle, machine*) kojangnada 고장나다; (*of talks*) shilp'aehada 실패하다; (*in tears*) urŭmŭl t'ŏttŭrida 울음을 터뜨리다; (*mentally*) shin-gyŏng-i soeyak'aejida 신경이 쇠약해지다 **2** *v/t door* pusugo yŏlda 부수고 열다; figures pullyuhada 분류하다

♦**break even** COM tŭksshiri ŏpkke toeda 득실이 없게 되다

♦**break in** (*interrupt*) pyŏran-gan malch'amgyŏnhada 별안간

말참견하다; (*of burglar*) ch'imip'ada
침입하다

♦**break off 1** *v/t* kkŏkkŏnaeda
꺾어내다; *branch* kkŏkktta 꺾다;
relationship kkaettŭrida 깨뜨리다;
they've broken it off kŭdŭl saiga
kkaejyŏt-tta 그들 사이가 깨어졌다
2 *v/i* (*stop talking*) taehwarŭl
chungdanhada 대화를 중단하다

♦**break out** (*start up*) shijakdoeda
시작되다; (*of disease*)
palppyŏnghada 발병하다; (*of
prisoners*) t'arok'ada 탈옥하다; ***he
broke out in a rash*** kŭnŭn
kaptchagi paltchini nat-tta 그는
갑자기 발진이 났다

♦**break up 1** *v/t* (*into component
parts*) haech'ehada 해체하다; *fight*
mallida 말리다 **2** *v/i* (*of ice*)
kkaeŏjida 깨어지다; (*of couple*)
heŏjida 헤어지다; (*of band, meeting*)
haech'ehada 해체하다

breakable kkaeŏjigi shiun 깨어지기
쉬운

breakage p'ason 파손

breakdown (*of vehicle, machine*)
kojang 고장; (*of talks*) shilp'ae 실패;
(*nervous* ~) shin-gyŏng soeyak 신경
쇠약; (*of figures*) punsŏk 분석

break-even point sonik pun-gitchŏm
손익 분기점

breakfast *n* ach'im 아침; ***have ~***
ach'imŭl mŏktta 아침을 먹다

break-in ch'imip 침입

breakthrough (*in talks*) t'agae 타개;
(*in science, technology*) k'ŭn
paltchŏn 큰 발전

breakup (*of partnership etc*) purhwa
불화

breast (*of woman*) yubang 유방

breastfeed *v/t* moyurŭl mŏgida
모유를 먹이다

breaststroke p'yŏnghyŏng 평형

breath sum 숨; ***be out of ~*** sumi
ch'ada 숨이 차다; ***take a deep ~***
sumŭl kip'i tŭrŏ mashida 숨을 깊이
들어 마시다

Breathalyzer®, breath analyzer
ŭmju ch'ŭktchŏnggi 음주 측정기

breathe 1 *v/i* sumshwida 숨쉬다 **2** *v/t*
(*inhale*) tŭri mashida 들이 마시다;

(*exhale*) naeshwida 내쉬다

♦**breathe in 1** *v/i* sumŭl tŭryŏ
mashida 숨을 들여 마시다 **2** *v/t*
tŭrishwida 들이쉬다

♦**breathe out** *v/i* sumŭl naeshwida
숨을 내쉬다

breathing hohŭp 호흡

breathless sumch'an 숨찬

breathlessness hohŭp kollan 호흡
곤란

breathtaking summak'il chŏngdoŭi
숨막힐 정도의

breed 1 *n* p'umjong 품종 **2** *v/t* kirŭda
기르다; *fig* irŭk'ida 일으키다 **3** *v/i* (*of
animals*) pŏnshik'ada 번식하다

breeding (*of animals*) pŏnshik 번식

breeding ground *fig* onsang 온상

breeze sandŭlpparam 산들바람

brew 1 *v/t* *beer* yangjohada 양조하다;
tea kkŭrida 끓이다 **2** *v/i* (*of storm*)
ilda 일다; (*of trouble*) irŏnaryŏgo
hada 일어나려고 하다

brewer yangjoŏptcha 양조업자

brewery yangjojang 양조장

bribe 1 *n* noemul 뇌물 **2** *v/t*
maesuhada 매수하다

bribery noemul susu 뇌물 수수

brick pyŏkttol 벽돌

bricklayer pyŏktttolgong 벽돌공

bride shinbu 신부

bridegroom shillang 신랑

bridesmaid shinbu tŭllŏri 신부
들러리

bridge[1] **1** *n* tari 다리; (*of nose*)
k'onmaru 콧마루; (*of ship*) sŏn-gyo
선교 **2** *v/t* *gap* chunggae yŏk'arŭl
hada 중개 역할을 하다

bridge[2] (*card game*) pŭritchi 브릿지

brief[1] *adj* kan-gyŏryŏn 간결한; *time*
tanshiganŭi 단시간의

brief[2] **1** *n* (*mission*) immu 임무 **2** *v/t*: ***~
X on Y*** Xege Ye taehan kaeyorŭl
sŏlmyŏnghada X에게 Y에 대한
개요를 설명하다

briefcase sŏryu kabang 서류 가방

briefing pŭrip'ing 브리핑

briefly (*for a short period of time*)
chamshidong-an 잠시동안; (*in a few
words*) kan-gyŏrhage 간결하게; (*to
sum up*) yoyak'ajamyŏn 요약하자면

briefs p'aench'ŭ 팬츠

bright *color, future, room* palgŭn
밝은; *smile* hwanhan 환한; (*sunny*)
hwach'anghan 화창한; (*intelligent*)
ttokttok'an 똑똑한
♦ **brighten up 1** *v/t* hwanhage hada
환하게 하다 **2** *v/i* (*of weather*)
malgajida 맑아지다
brighten (*of face, person*) palgajida
밝아지다
brightly hwanhage 환하게
brightness (*of weather*) malgŭm
맑음; (*of smile*) hwanham 환함;
(*intelligence*) ch'ongmyŏngham
총명함
brilliance (*of person*) chitch'ŏgin
t'agwŏrham 지적인 탁월함; (*of
color*) sŏnmyŏngham 선명함
brilliant *sunshine etc* palgŭn 밝은;
(*very good*) hullyunghan 훌륭한;
(*very intelligent*) much'ŏk
ttokttok'an 무척 똑똑한; *idea* aju
hullyunghan 아주 훌륭한
brim (*of container*) kajangjari
가장자리; (*of hat*) t'eduri 테두리
brimful nŏmch'ildŭt'an 넘칠듯한
bring *object* kajyŏoda 가져오다;
person teryŏoda 데려오다; *peace,
happiness* ch'oraehada 초래하다; **~ it
here, will you?** iriro kŭgŏsŭl
kajyŏda chullaeyo? 이리로 그것을
가져다 줄래요?; **can I ~ a friend?**
ch'in-gurŭl terigo kado twaeyo?
친구를 데리고 가도 돼요?
♦ **bring about** yagihada 야기하다
♦ **bring around** *from a faint* chŏnsin
ch'arigehada 정신 차리게 하다;
(*persuade*) sŏlttŭk'ada 설득하다
♦ **bring back** (*return*) tollyŏjuda
돌려주다; (*re-introduce*) toetollida
되돌리다; *memories* saenggangnage
hada 생각나게 하다
♦ **bring down** *fence, tree* ssŭrŏjige
hada 쓰러지게 하다; *government*
chŏnbokshik'ida 전복시키다; *bird,
airplane* ssoa ttŏrŏttŭrida 쏘아
떨어뜨리다; *rates, inflation, price*
naerige hada 내리게 하다
♦ **bring in** *interest, income* kajyŏoda
가져오다; *legislation* chech'urhada
제출하다; *verdict* naerida 내리다;
(*involve*) kwallyŏnshik'ida

관련시키다
♦ **bring out** *sesang-e naenot'a* 세상에
내놓다; *book* ch'ulp'anhada
출판하다; *video, CD* ch'ulsshihada
출시하다; *new product* palmaehada
발매하다
♦ **bring to** (*from a faint*) chŏnsin
ch'arigehada 정신 차리게 하다
♦ **bring up** *child* yangnyuk'ada
양육하다; *subject* marŭl kkŏnaeda
말을 꺼내다; (*vomit*) t'ohada 토하다
brink kajangjari 가장자리; *fig*
kyŏltchŏngjŏk shigi 결정적 시기
brisk *person, voice, walk* tangch'an
당찬; *trade* hwalbarhan 활발한
bristles (*on chin*) suyŏm 수염; (*of
brush*) t'ŏl 털
bristling: **be ~ with** ...(ŭ)ro kadŭk
ch'ait-tta ...(으)로 가득 차있다
Britain Yŏngguk 영국
British 1 *adj* Yonggugŭi 영국의 **2** *n*:
the ~ Yŏnggugin 영국인,
Yŏngguginŭi 영국인의
Briton Yŏngguk saram 영국 사람
brittle *adj* pusŏjigi shwiun 부서지기
쉬운
broach *subject* marŭl kkŏnaeda 말을
꺼내다
broad 1 *adj* *street, hips* p'ok nŏlbŭn
폭 넓은; *shoulders* ttŏk pŏrŏjin 떡
벌어진; *smile* hwanhan 환한;
(*general*) ilbanjŏgin 일반적인; **in ~
daylight** taenaje 대낮에 **2** *n* F
(*woman*) yŏja 여자
broadcast 1 *n* pangsong 방송 **2** *v/t*
pangsonghada 방송하다
broadcaster pangsong-in 방송인
broadcasting pangsong 방송
broaden 1 *v/i* nŏlbŏjida 넓어지다 **2** *v/t*
nŏlp'ida 넓히다
broadly: **~ speaking** ilbanjŏguro
marhajamyŏn 일반적으로 말하자면
broadminded kwandaehan 관대한
broccoli pŭrok'olli 브로콜리
brochure pŭroshyŏ 브로셔
broil *v/t* kuptta 굽다
broiler *n* (*on stove*) kumnŭn kigu 굽는
기구; (*chicken*) kuiyong yŏnggye
구이용 영계
broke F muilp'unŭi 무일푼의;

(*bankrupt*) p'asanhan 파산한; *go ~* p'asanhada 파산하다

broken *adj* pusŏjin 부서진; *window, promise* kkaejin 깨진; *neck, arm* purŏjin 부러진; *home* kyŏlssonŭi 결손의; *English etc* ŏngt'ŏriŭi 엉터리의

broken-hearted maŭmŭi sangch'ŏrŭl ibŭn 마음의 상처를 입은

broker chunggaeŏptcha 중개업자

bronchitis kigwanjiyŏm 기관지염

bronze *n* (*metal*) ch'ŏngdong 청동; (*color*) ch'ŏngdongsaek 청동색; *~ medal* tongmedal 동메달

brooch pŭroch'i 브로치

brood *v/i* (*of person*) komgomhi saenggak'ada 곰곰히 생각하다

broom pitcharu 빗자루

broth (*soup*) mulgŭn sup'ŭ 묽은 수프; (*stock*) kungmul 국물

brothel maech'un-gul 매춘굴

brother (*man's elder*) hyŏng 형; (*woman's elder*) oppa 오빠; (*younger*) namdongsaeng 남동생; *they're ~s* kŭdŭrŭn hyŏngjeyeyo 그들은 형제예요; *~s and sisters* hyŏngje chamae 형제 자매

brother-in-law (*woman's elder sister's husband*) hyŏngbu 형부; (*wife's younger brother*) ch'ŏ-nam 처남; (*man's elder sister's husband*) maehyŏng 매형

brotherly hyŏngjeŭi 형제의

browbeat mallo wihyŏp'ada 말로 위협하다

brow (*forehead*) ima 이마; (*of hill*) maru 마루

brown 1 *n* kalsaek 갈색 2 *adj* kalsaegŭi 갈색의; (*tanned*) haetpyŏch'e t'an 햇볕에 탄 3 *v/t* (*in cooking*) norŭnnorŭt'age kuptta 노릇노릇하 게굽다 4 *v/i* (*in cooking*) norŭnnorŭt'age toeda 노릇노릇하 게되다

brownbag: *~ it* toshiragŭl ssaoda 도시락을 싸오다

brownie kŏlsŭk'aut'ŭŭi yunyŏn tanwŏn 걸스카우트의 유년 단원; (*cake*) ch'ok'ollit k'eik 초콜릿 케익

brownie points: *earn ~* ach'ŏmŭro ŏdŭn shinyong 아첨으로 얻은 신용

brown-nose *v/t* F ...ege ach'ŏmhada ...에게 아첨하다

browse (*in store*) kugyŏngman hago tanida 구경만 하고 다니다; *~ through a book* ttŭiŏmttŭiŏm iltta 띄엄띄엄 읽다

browser COMPUT pŭraujŏ 브라우저

bruise 1 *n* mŏng 멍; (*emotional*) sangch'ŏ 상처 2 *v/t person, fruit* mŏngdŭlge hada 멍들게 하다 3 *v/i* (*of person*) mŏngdŭlda 멍들다; (*of fruit*) hŭmi saenggida 흠이 생기다

bruising *adj fig* sangch'ŏnan 상처난

brunch ach'im kyŏm chŏmshim 아침 겸 점심

brunette kalsaek mŏriŭi yŏja 갈색 머리의 여자

brunt: *bear the ~ of* ...(ŭ)ro cheil shimhage kot'ongbat-tta ...(으)로 제일 심하게 고통받다

brush 1 *n* sol 솔; (*conflict*) yakkanŭi ch'ungdol 약간의 충돌 2 *v/t hair, floor* pitcharjirhada 빗잘하다; *teeth* yangch'ijirhada 양치질하다; *jacket* soljirhada 솔질하다; (*touch lightly*) saltchak sŭch'ida 살짝 스치다; (*remove*) ch'iuda 치우다

♦**brush against** saltchak sŭch'imyŏnsŏ chinagada 살짝 스치면서 지나가다

♦**brush aside** mushihada 무시하다

♦**brush off** t'ŏrŏnaeda 털어내다; *criticism* mushihada 무시하다

♦**brush up** pokssŭp'ada 복습하다

brushoff F t'oetcha 퇴짜; *get the ~* t'oetacharŭl mat-tta 퇴짜를 맞다

brusque muttukttuk'an 무뚝뚝한

Brussels sprouts yangbaech'uŭi iltchong 양배추의 일종

brutal *person* chaninhan 잔인한; *treatment* hokttok'an 혹독한; *honesty* naeng-ŏmhan 냉엄한

brutality chaninham 잔인함

brutally chaninhage 잔인하게; *be ~ frank* chinach'ige soltchik'ada 지나치게 솔직하다

brute chimsŭng kat'ŭn saram 짐승 같은 사람

brute force p'ongnyŏk 폭력

bubble *n* kŏp'um 거품

bubble gum p'ungsŏnkkŏm 풍선껌

buck 328

buck¹ *n* F (*dollar*) tallŏ 달러

buck² *v/i* (*of horse*) p'ŏltchŏk ttwida 펄쩍 뛰다

buck³: pass the ~ ch'aegimŭl chŏn-gahada 책임을 전가하다

bucket *n* yangdong-i 양동이

buckle¹ 1 *n* pŏk'ŭl 버클 2 *v/t belt* pelt'ŭrŭl maeda 벨트를 매다

buckle² *v/i* (*of wood, metal*) kuburŏjida 구부러지다

bud *n* BOT ssak 싹

Buddha Puch'ŏ 부처

Buddha's Birthday Puch'ŏnim Oshin Nal 부처님 오신 날

Buddhism Pulgyo 불교

Buddhist 1 *n* pulgyo shinja 불교 신자 2 *adj* pulgyoŭi 불교의

Buddhist Broadcasting System Pulgyo Pangsong 불교 방송

buddy F ch'in-gu 친구; (*form of address*) yŏboge 여보게

budge 1 *v/t* umjigida 움직이다; (*make reconsider*) maŭmŭl pakkuge hada 마음을 바꾸게 하다 2 *v/i* umjigida 움직이다; (*change one's mind*) maŭmŭl pakkuda 마음을 바꾸다

budgerigar ingkko 잉꼬

budget 1 *n* yesan 예산; (*of a family*) saenghwalbi 생활비; *be on a ~* kyŏlp'ip saenghwarŭl hada 결핍 생활을 하다 2 *v/i* yesanŭl seuda 예산을 세우다

♦**budget for** yesane nŏt'a 예산에 넣다

buff¹ *adj color* hwanggalssaek 황갈색

buff²: a movie / jazz ~ yŏnghwagwang / chaejŭgwang 영화광 / 재즈광

buffalo tŭlsso 들소

buffer RAIL wanch'ung changch'i 완충 장치; *fig* wanch'ungnyŏk 완충역; *memory ~* COMPUT wanch'ung kiŏk changch'i 완충 기억 장치

buffet¹ *n* (*meal*) pup'e 부페

buffet² *v/t* (*of wind*) ch'ida 치다

bug 1 *n* (*insect*) pŏlle 벌레; (*virus*) pairŏsŭ 바이러스; (*spying device*) toch'ŏnggi 도청기; COMPUT pŏgŭ 버그 2 *v/t room* toch'ŏnggirŭl sŏlch'ihada 도청기를 설치하다; *telephones* toch'ŏnghada 도청하다; F

(*annoy*) koerop'ida 괴롭히다

buggy (*for baby*) yumoch'a 유모차

build 1 *n* (*of person*) ch'egyŏk 체격 2 *v/t* seuda 세우다

♦**build up** 1 *v/t strength* tallyŏnhada 단련하다; *relationship* ssaa ollida 쌓아 올리다; *collection* moŭda 모으다 2 *v/i* ssayŏjida 쌓여지다

builder (*company*) kŏnch'ugŏp 건축업; (*person*) kŏnch'ugŏptcha 건축업자

building kŏnmul 건물; (*activity*) kŏnch'uk 건축

building site kongsajang 공사장

building trade kŏnch'ugŏp 건축업

build-up (*accumulation*) ssayŏjim 쌓여짐; (*publicity*) sŏnjŏn 선전

built-in put'bagiŭi 붙박이의; *flash* naejangdoeŏ innŭn 내장되어 있는

built-up area shigaji 시가지

bulb BOT kugŭn 구근; (*light ~*) chŏn-gu 전구

bulge 1 *n* tolch'ul 돌출; (*in number, quantity*) ilsshijŏk chŭngga 일시적 증가 2 *v/i* (*of pocket*) pulluk'ada 불룩하다; (*of wall, eyes*) t'wiŏ naoda 튀어 나오다

bulk taebubun 대부분; *in ~* taeryang-ŭro 대량으로

bulky pup'iga k'ŭn 부피가 큰

bull hwangso 황소

bulldoze (*demolish*) puldoujŏro chegŏhada 불도우저로 제거하다; *~ X into Y fig* Xŭl / rŭl kangjero Yhadorok mandŭlda X을 / 를 강제로 Y하도록 만들다

bulldozer puldoujŏ 불도우저

bullet ch'ong-al 총알

bulletin keshi 게시

bulletin board (*on wall*) keship'an 게시판; COMPUT chŏnja keship'an 전자 게시판

bullet-proof pangt'anŭi 방탄의

bull market FIN kangse chusik shijang 강세 주식 시장

bull's-eye kwanyŏgŭi hanbokp'an 과녁의 한복판; *hit the ~* kwanyŏgŭl match'uda 과녁을 맞추다; *fig* taesŏnggong-ŭl kŏduda 대성공을 거두다

bullshit V 1 *n* hŏp'ung 허풍 2 *v/i*

hŏp'ung-ŭl ttŏlda 허풍을 떨다
bully 1 *n* kkangp'ae 깡패 **2** *v/t* mot
salge kulda 못 살게 굴다
bum 1 *n* F (*tramp*) puranja 부랑자;
(*worthless person*) mangnani 망나니
2 *adj* (*useless*) ssŭlmoŏmnŭn
쓸모없는 **3** *v/t* cigarette etc kŏjŏ ŏt-tta
거저 얻다
♦**bum around** F (*travel*)
pangnanghada 방랑하다; (*be lazy*)
pindungbindung chinaeda 빈둥빈둥
지내다
bumblebee twengbŏl 뒝벌
bump 1 *n* (*swelling*) hok 혹; (*in road*)
yunggi 융기; *get a ~ on the head*
mŏrirŭl handae mat-tta 머리를 한대
맞다 **2** *v/t* puditch'ida 부딪히다
♦**bump into** …e puditch'ida …에
부딪히다; (*meet*) …wa / kwa uyŏnhi
mannada …와 / 과 우연히 만나다
♦**bump off** F (*murder*) chugida
죽이다
♦**bump up** F prices taep'ok ollida
대폭 올리다
bumper *n* MOT pŏmp'ŏ 범퍼
bumpy *flight* tŏlk'ŏk-kkŏrinŭn
덜컥거리는; *road* ult'ungbult'unghan
울퉁불퉁한
bun (*hairstyle*) t'ŭrŏollin mŏri
틀어올린 머리; (*for eating*) chagŭn
lolppang 작은 롤빵
bunch (*of people*) muri 무리; *a ~ of
keys* yŏlsoe mungch'i 열쇠 뭉치; *a ~
of flowers* kkot hantabal 꽃 한
다발; *a ~ of grapes* p'odo han song-
i 포도 한 송이; *thanks a ~* (*ironic*)
nunmulnage komapkkunyo 눈물나게
고맙군요
bundle (*of clothes*) kkurŏmi 꾸러미;
(*of wood*) mungch'i 뭉치
♦**bundle up** kkurida 꾸리다; (*dress
warmly*) ttattŭt'a-ge ip'ida 따뜻하게
입히다
bungle *v/t* sŏt'urŭge mandŭlda
서투르게 만들다
bunk sŏnban moyang-ŭi ch'imdae
선반 모양의 침대
bunk beds ich'ŭng ch'imdae 이층
침대
buoy *n* pup'yo 부표
buoyant hwallyŏgi innŭn 활력이

innŭn; *fig* sangsŭngse-ŭi 상승세의
burden 1 *n* chim 짐; *fig* pudam 부담
2 *v/t*: *~ X with Y* Xŭl / rŭl Y(ŭ)ro
pudam chiuda X을 / 를 Y(으)로 부담
지우다
bureau (*chest of drawers*)
sŏraptchang 서랍장; (*office*)
samuguk 사무국
bureaucracy (*red tape*) pŏn-gŏroun
haengjŏng chŏlch'a 번거로운 행정
절차; (*system*) kwallyoje 관료제
bureaucrat kwallyo 관료
bureaucratic kwallyojŏgin 관료적인
burger haembŏgŏ 햄버거
burglar kangdo 강도
burglar alarm tonan kyŏngbogi 도난
경보기
burglarize kangdojirhada 강도질하다
burglary kangdo 강도
burial maejang 매장; *~ at sea* sujang
수장
burly kŏnjanghan 건장한
Burma Pŏma 버마
Burmese 1 *adj* Pŏmaŭi 버마의 **2** *n*
(*person*) Pŏmain 버마인; (*language*)
Pŏmaŏ 버마어
burn 1 *n* hwasang 화상 **2** *v/t* t'aeuda
태우다; *fuel* yŏnsohada 연소하다 **3** *v/i*
t'ada 타다
♦**burn down 1** *v/t* t'aewŏbŏrida
태워버리다 **2** *v/i* t'abŏrida 타버리다
♦**burn out** *v/t*: *burn oneself out*
chŏngnyŏgŭl tahada 정력을 다하다;
a burned-out car pult'abŏrin ch'a
불타버린 차
burner (*on cooker*) naembirŭl
ollyŏdunŭn tae 냄비를 올려두는 대
burp 1 *n* t'ŭrim 트림 **2** *v/i* t'ŭrimhada
트림하다 **3** *v/t* baby t'ŭrimŭl shik'ida
트림을 시키다
burst 1 *n* (*in water pipe*) p'ayŏl 파열;
(*of gunfire*) chiptchung sagyŏk 집중
사격; *in a ~ of energy* kiuni p'ŏlp'ŏl
nŏmch'yŏnasŏ 기운이 펄펄 넘쳐나서
2 *adj tire* t'ŏjin 터진 **3** *v/t balloon*
t'ŏttŭrida 터뜨리다 **4** *v/i* (*of balloon,
tire*) t'ŏjida 터지다; *~ into a room*
pang anŭro ttwiŏdŭlda 방 안으로
뛰어들다; *~ into tears* urŭmŭl
t'ŏttŭrida 울음을 터뜨리다; *~ out
laughing* p'oksosŭrŭl t'ŏttŭrida

폭소를 터뜨리다

bury *person, animal* p'amut-tta
파묻다; (*conceal*) sumgida 숨기다; *be*
buried under (*covered by*) …(ŭ)ro
tŏp'ida …(으)로 덮히다; ~ *oneself*
in one's work ire molttuhada 일에
몰두하다

bus[1] **1** *n* (*local*) pŏsŭ 버스; (*long
distance*) shioe pŏsŭ 시외 버스 **2** *v/t*
pŏsŭro idonghada 버스로
이동하다

bus[2] COMPUT pŏsŭ 버스

busboy weit'ŏŭi chosu 웨이터의 조수

bush (*plant*) kwanmok 관목; (*terrain*)
oji 오지

bushed F (*tired*) p'igonhan 피곤한

bushy *beard* t'ŏpssuruk'an 텁수룩한

business (*trade*) muyŏk 무역;
(*company*) hoesa 회사; (*work*) il 일;
(*sector*) saŏbŭi chongnyu 사업의
종류; (*affair, matter*) sakkŏn 사건; (*as
subject of study*) kyŏngnyŏnghak
경영학; *on* ~ saŏpch'a 사업차; *that's
none of your* ~! nega sanggwan hal
paga anida! 네가 상관 할 바가
아니다!; *mind your own* ~! ne irina
haera! 네 일이나 해라!

business card myŏngham 명함;
business class pijŭnisŭ k'ŭllaesŭ
비즈니스 클래스; **business hours**
ŏmmu shigan 업무 시간;
businesslike nŭngnyultchŏgin
능률적인; **business lunch** saŏpch'a
hanŭn shikssa 사업차 하는 식사;
businessman saŏpkka 사업가;
business meeting pijŭnisŭ mit'ing
비즈니스 미팅; **business school**
kyŏngnyŏng taehagwŏn 경영 대학원;
business studies kyŏngnyŏnghak
경영학; **business trip** ch'ultchang
출장; **businesswoman** yŏsŏng
saŏpkka 여성 사업가

bus station pŏsŭ t'ŏminŏl 버스
터미널

bus stop pŏsŭ chŏngnyujang 버스
정류장

bust[1] *n* (*of woman*) kasŭm 가슴

bust[2] **1** *adj* F (*broken*) pusŏjin 부서진;
go ~ (*bankrupt*) p'asanhada
파산하다 **2** *v/t* pusuda 부수다

♦**bustle around** punjuhi irhada

분주히 일하다

bust-up F kyŏlbyŏl 결별

busty kasŭmi p'ungmanhan 가슴이
풍만한

busy 1 *adj* pappŭn 바쁜; *street*
pŏnhwahan 변화한; (*making money*)
pumbinŭn 붐비는; (*full of people*)
saramdŭri puktchŏkttaenŭn
사람들이 북적대는; TELEC
t'onghwajung-in 통화중인; *be* ~
doing … …ŭl/rŭl hanŭra pappŭda
…을/를 하느라 바쁘다 **2** *v/t*: ~ *oneself with* …(ŭ)ro pappŭda …(으)로
바쁘다

busybody ch'am-gyŏn chal hanŭn
saram 참견 잘 하는 사람

busy signal TELEC t'onghwa chung
shinho 통화중 신호

but 1 *conj* …hajiman …하지만; *I tried
to tell him* ~ *he wouldn't listen*
kŭege marharyŏgo haet-tchiman tŭt-
tchi anassŏyo 그에게 말하려고
했지만 듣지 않았어요; *it's not me* ~
my father you want tangshini
wŏnhan saramŭn naega anira nae
abŏjigunyo 당신이 원한 사람은 내가
아니라 내 아버지군요; ~ *then*
(*again*) kŭrŏt'a hadŏrado 그렇다
하더라도; ~ *that's not fair* hajiman
kŭgŏn kongp'yŏnghaji anayo 하지만
그건 공평하지 않아요 **2** *prep*: *all* ~
him kŭ saramŭl cheoehago modŭ ta
그 사람을 제외하고 모두 다; *the
last* ~ *one* hana ppaego maen
majimak 하나 빼고 맨 마지막; *the
next* ~ *one* hana kŏnnŏ ap'e 하나
건너 앞에; ~ *for you* nega
ŏpssŭmyŏn 네가 없으면; *nothing* ~
the best ojik ch'oegoman 오직
최고만

butcher chŏngnyuktchŏm chuin
정육점 주인; (*murderer*) hakssaltcha
학살자

butt 1 *n* (*of cigarette*) tambae
kkongch'o 담배 꽁초; (*of joke*)
nongdamŭi p'yojŏk 농담의 표적; F
(*buttocks*) ŏngdŏng-i 엉덩이 **2** *v/t*
mŏriro pat-tta 머리로 받다; (*of goat,
bull*) pat-tta 받다

♦**butt in** panghaehada 방해하다

butter 1 *n* pŏt'ŏ 버터 **2** *v/t* pŏt'ŏrŭl

parŭda 버터를 바르다
♦**butter up** F ach'ŏmhada 아첨하다
butterfly (*insect*) nabi 나비
buttocks ŏngdŏng-i 엉덩이
button 1 *n* tanch'u 단추; (*on machine*)
pŏt'ŭn 버튼; (*badge*) paeji 배지 **2** *v/t*
tanch'urŭl ch'aeuda 단추를 채우다
♦**button up** → *button*
buttonhole 1 *n* (*in suit*) tanch'u
kumŏng 단추구멍 **2** *v/t* put-ttŭlgo
iyagihada 붙들고 이야기하다
buxom p'ungmanhan 풍만한
buy 1 *n* san mulgŏn 산 물건 **2** *v/t* sada
사다; *can I ~ you a drink?* chega
han chan sado toelkkayo? 제가 한
잔 사도 될까요?; *$50 doesn't ~
much* 50tallŏronŭn pyŏllo sal kŏshi
ŏptta 50달러로는 별로 살 것이 없다
♦**buy off** (*bribe*) maesuhada
매수하다
♦**buy out** COM hoesa chibunŭl
sadŭrida 회사 지분을 사들이다
♦**buy up** maejŏmhada 매점하다
buyer kumaeja 구매자; (*for a
company*) paiŏ 바이어
buzz 1 *n* wing-winghanŭn sori
윙윙하는 소리; F (*thrill*) sŭril 스릴
2 *v/i* (*of insect*) wingwing sorirŭl
naeda 윙윙 소리를 내다; (*with
buzzer*) pujŏrŭl ullida 부저를 울리다
3 *v/t* (*with buzzer*) pujŏro purŭda
부저로 부르다
♦**buzz off** F kkŏjyŏ pŏrida 꺼져
버리다; *~!* kkŏjyŏ pŏryŏ! 꺼져 버려!
buzzer pujŏ 부저
by 1 *prep* ◊ (*agency*) …e ŭihae …에
의해; *she was murdered ~ her
husband* kŭnyŏnŭn namp'yŏne
ŭihae sarhaedanghaet-tta 그녀는

남편에 의해 살해당했다 ; *a play ~ …*
…i / ga ssŭn yŏn-gŭk …이 / 가 쓴 연극
◊ (*near, next to*) …yŏp'e …옆에; *a
seat ~ the window* ch'angmun
yŏp'e innŭn chari 창문 옆에 있는
자리; *side ~ side* naranhi 나란히 ◊
(*no later than*) …kkaji …까지; *~
midnight* chajŏngkkaji 자정까지; *~
this time tomorrow* naeil i
shigankkaji 내일 이 시간까지 ◊
(*past*) …ŭl / rŭl chinasŏ …을 / 를
지나서; *as we walked ~ the
church* uriga kyohoerŭl china
kŏrŏgassŭl ttae 우리가 교회를 지나
걸어갔을 때 ◊ (*mode of transport*)
…(ŭ)ro …(으)로; *~ bus / train*
pŏsŭro / kich'aro 버스로 / 기차로; *~
day / night* naje / pame 낮에 / 밤에 ◊
(*measuring*): *~ the hour / ton*
shigandang / t'ondang 시간당 / 톤당; *~
a couple of minutes* myŏt pun
ch'airo 몇 분 차이로; *2 ~ 4* p'ogi 2,
kiriga 4in nŏlbi 폭이 2, 길이가 4인
넓이; *~ my watch* nae shigyero 내
시계로 ◊: *~ oneself* honjasŏ 혼자서
2 *adv*: *~ and ~* (*soon*) kot 곧
bye(-bye) annyŏng 안녕
bygone: *let ~s be ~s* chinan irŭn
kŭnyang chŏbŏduja 지난 일은 그냥
접어두자
bypass 1 *n* (*road*) uhoero 우회로;
MED hyŏlgwan ishik 혈관 이식 **2** *v/t*
uhoehada 우회하다
by-product pusanmul 부산물
bystander panggwanja 방관자
byte COMPUT pait'ŭ 바이트
byword: *be a ~ for* …ŭi
taemyŏngsaga toeda …의 대명사가
되다

C

cab (*taxi*) t'aeksshi 택시; (*of truck*) unjŏnsŏk 운전석
cabaret k'yabare 카바레
cabbage yangbaech'u 양배추
cab driver t'aeksshi unjŏnsa 택시 운전사
cabin (*of plane, for crew*) sŭngmuwŏnshil 승무원실; (*of plane, for passengers*) kaeksshil 객실; (*on ship*) sŏnshil 선실
cabin crew sŭngmuwŏn 승무원
cabinet changshiktchang 장식장; POL naegak 내각; *medicine* ~ yaktchang 약장
cable (*of electrical appliance, telephone etc*) k'eibŭl 케이블; ~ (*TV*) yusŏn pangsong 유선 (방송)
cable car k'eibŭlk'a 케이블카
cable television yusŏn pangsong 유선 방송
cab stand t'aeksshi t'anŭn kot 택시 타는 곳
cactus sŏninjang 선인장
cadaver shich'e 시체
CAD-CAM k'aedŭ/k'aem 캐드/캠
caddie 1 *n* (*in golf*) k'aedi 캐디 2 *v/i*: ~ *for* ...ŭl/rŭl wihan k'aediro irhada ...을/를 위한 캐디로 일하다
cadet (*in police etc*) saengdo 생도; MIL sagwan saengdo 사관 생도
cadet corps hakssaeng kunsa kyoryŏndan 학생 군사 교련단
cadge: ~ *X from Y* Y(ŭ)robut'ŏ Xŭl/rŭl kugŏrhada Y(으)로부터 X을/를 구걸하다
café tabang 다방
cafeteria k'ap'et'eria 카페테리아
caffeine k'ap'ein 카페인
cage (*for bird*) saejang 새장; (*for lion*) uri 우리
cagey t'ŏnoŭryŏ haji annŭn 터놓으려 하지 않는
cahoots: *be in ~ with* ...wa/kwa kongmohada ...와/과 공모하다

cake 1 *n* k'eik'ŭ 케이크; *be a piece of* ~ *fig* maeu shwiun irida 매우 쉬운 일이다 2 *v/i* tŏng-ŏrijida 덩어리지다
calcium k'alshyum 칼슘
calculate (*work out*) sanch'urhae naeda 산출해 내다; (*in arithmetic*) kyesanhada 계산하다
calculating *adj* kyesanjŏgin 계산적인
calculation kyesan 계산
calculator kyesan-gi 계산기
calendar tallyŏk 달력
calf[1] (*young cow*) song-aji 송아지
calf[2] ANAT chong-ari 종아리
caliber (*of gun*) kugyŏng 구경; *a man of his* ~ suwan choŭn saram 수완 좋은 사람
call 1 *n* TELEC chŏnhwa 전화; (*shout*) oech'im 외침; (*demand*) yogu 요구; *there's a ~ for you* tangshinhant'e chŏnhwaga wassŏyo 당신한테 전화가 왔어요 2 *v/t* TELEC chŏnhwarŭl kŏlda 전화를 걸다; (*summon*) purŭda 부르다; *meeting* sojip'ada 소집하다; (*summons*) sohwanhada 소환하다; (*describe as*) ...rago purŭda ...라고 부르다; (*shout*) sorich'yŏ purŭda 소리쳐 부르다; *what have they ~ed the baby?* kŭdŭrŭn agi irŭmŭl mwŏrago chiŏt-tchiyo? 그들은 아기 이름을 뭐라고 지었지요?; *but we ~ him Tom* kŭrŏch'iman urinŭn kŭrŭl T'omirago pullŏyo 그렇지만 우리는 그를 토미라고 불러요; ~ *s.o. names* nugurŭl yok'ada 누구를 욕하다 3 *v/i* TELEC chŏnhwahada 전화하다; (*shout*) sorich'yŏ purŭda 소리쳐 부르다; (*visit*) pangmunhada 방문하다
♦ **call at** (*stop at*) ...e tŭllida ...에 들리다; (*of train*) ...e chŏngch'ahada ...에 정차하다
♦ **call back** 1 *v/t* TELEC najung-e tashi chŏnhwahada 나중에 다시 전화하다;

(*summon*) pullŏsŏ toedoraoge hada 불러서 되돌아오게 하다 2 *v/i* TELEC najung-e tashi chŏnhwahada 나중에 다시 전화하다; (*visit*) tashi pangmunhada 다시 방문하다

♦ **call for** (*collect*) ...ŭl/rŭl kajirŏ kada ...을/를 가지러 가다; *person* ...ŭl/rŭl terirŏ kada ...을/를 데리러 가다; (*demand*) yoguhada 요구하다; (*require*) ...i/ga p'iryohada ...이/가 필요하다

♦ **call in 1** *v/t* (*summon*) pullŏ tŭrida 불러 들이다 2 *v/i* TELEC chŏnhwaro allida 전화로 알리다

♦ **call off** (*cancel*) ch'wisohada 취소하다

♦ **call on** (*urge*) yoguhada 요구하다; (*visit*) pangmunhada 방문하다

♦ **call out** sorich'yŏ purŭda 소리쳐 부르다; (*summon*) ch'ulttongshik'ida 출동시키다

♦ **call up** *v/t* TELEC chŏnhwahada 전화하다; COMPUT yŏlda 열다

caller TELEC chŏnhwa kŏn saram 전화 건 사람; (*visitor*) sonnim 손님

call girl maech'unbu 매춘부

calligraphy sŏye 서예

callous mugamgak'an 무감각한

calm 1 *adj sea, weather* koyohan 고요한; *person* ch'imch'ak'an 침착한 2 *n* (*of the countryside etc*) p'yŏng-on 평온; (*of person*) ch'imch'ak 침착

♦ **calm down 1** *v/t* karaanch'ida 가라앉히다 2 *v/i* (*of sea, weather*) koyohaejida 고요해지다; (*of person*) ch'imch'ak'aejida 침착해지다

calorie k'allori 칼로리

Cambodia K'ambodia 캄보디아

Cambodian 1 *adj* K'ambodiaŭi 캄보디아의 2 *n* (*person*) K'ambodia saram 캄보디아 사람

camcorder k'aemk'odŏ 캠코더

camera k'amera 카메라

cameraman ch'waryŏng kisa 촬영 기사

camouflage 1 *n* wijang 위장 2 *v/t* wijanghada 위장하다

camp 1 *n* k'aemp'ŭ 캠프; (*for prisoners, refugees*) suyongso 수용소 2 *v/i* ch'ŏnmagŭl ch'ida 천막을 치다

campaign 1 *n* undong 운동 2 *v/i* undong-ŭl hada 운동을 하다

campaigner undongga 운동가

camper (*person*) k'aemp'inghanŭn saram 캠핑하는 사람; (*vehicle*) k'aemp'ŭyong t'ŭreillŏ 캠프용 트레일러

camp ground yayŏngji 야영지

camping k'aemp'ing 캠핑

campsite yayŏngji 야영지

campus: *university* ~ taehak kyojŏng 대학 교정, taehak k'aemp'ŏsŭ 대학 캠퍼스

can¹ ◊ (*ability*) ...hal su it-tta ...할 수 있다; ~ *you hear me?* nae marŭl tŭrŭl su issŏyo? 내 말을 들을 수 있어요?; ~ *you speak French?* Puŏrŭl marhal su issŏyo? 불어를 말할 수 있어요?; ~ *you help me?* towajul su issŏyo? 도와줄 수 있어요?; ~ *he call me back?* kŭnŭn na-ege najung-e chŏnhwahae chul su issŏyo? 그는 내게 나중에 전화해 줄 수 있어요?; *I* ~ *do it by tomorrow* naeil kkaji hal su issŏyo 내일까지 할 수 있어요 ◊ (*in negative*) ...hal su ŏptta ...할 수 없다; *I* ~'*t see* pol su ŏpssŏyo 볼 수 없어요; *you* ~'*t give up now* tangshinŭn chigŭm p'ogihal su ŏpssŏyo 당신은 지금 포기할 수 없어요; *that* ~*t be right* majŭl li ŏpssŏ 맞을 리 없어 ◊ (*permission*) ...hayŏdo chot'a ...하여도 좋다; ~ *I use the phone?* chŏnhwarŭl ssŏdo toemnikka? 전화를 써도 됩니까?; ~ *I help you?* towadŭrilkkayo? 도와드릴까요?; ~ *I have a beer / coffee?* maektchuga / k'ŏp'iga issŏyo? 맥주가 / 커피가 있어요?

can² **1** *n* (*for drinks etc*) kkangt'ong 깡통; (*of preserved food*) t'ongjorim 통조림 2 *v/t* t'ongjorimhada 통조림

Canada K'aenada 캐나다

Canadian 1 *adj* K'aenadaŭi 캐나다의 2 *n* K'aenada saram 캐나다 사람

canal (*waterway*) unha 운하

canary k'anaria 카나리아

cancel ch'wisohada 취소하다

cancellation ch'wiso 취소

cancer am 암

c & f

c & f (= *cost and freight*) unim p'oham kagyŏk 운임 포함 가격
candid soltchik'an 솔직한
candidacy ip'ubo 입후보
candidate (*for position*) huboja 후보자; (*in exam*) ŭngshija 응시자
candle yangch'o 양초
candlestick ch'ot-ttae 촛대
candor hŏshim t'anhoe 허심 탄회
candy sat'ang 사탕
cannabis taemach'o 대마초
canned *fruit etc* t'ongjorimdoen 통조림된; (*recorded*) nogŭmdoen 녹음된
cannot → *can*[1]
canoe k'anu 카누
can opener kkangt'ong ttagae 깡통 따개
can't → *can*[1]
canteen (*in factory*) kunae shikttang 구내 식당
canvas (*for painting*) kaenbŏsŭ 캔버스; (*material*) chŭk'ŭ 즈크
canvass 1 *v/t* (*seek opinion of*) ...ŭi ŭigyŏnŭl murŏboda ...의 의견을 물어보다 **2** *v/i* POL yusehada 유세하다
canyon kip'ŭn hyŏpkkok 깊은 협곡
cap (*hat*) k'aep 캡; (*of bottle, pen, lens etc*) ttukkŏng 뚜껑
capability (*of person*) nŭngnyŏk 능력; (*of military*) kunsaryŏk 군사력
capable (*efficient*) nŭngnyŏk innŭn 능력 있는; *be ~ of* ...hal nŭngnyŏgi it-tta ...할 능력이 있다
capacity (*of container, engine*) yongnyang 용량; (*of building*) yongjŏk 용적; (*of elevator*) suyongnyŏk 수용력; (*of factory*) ch'oedae saengsannyŏk 최대 생산력; (*ability*) nŭngnyŏng 능력; *in my ~ as* nanŭn ...(ŭ)rosŏ 나는 ...(으)로서
capital *n* (*of country*) sudo 수도; (*letter*) taemuntcha 대문자; (*money*) chabon 자본
capital expenditure ch'ongbiyong 총비용; **capital gains tax** chasan sodŭksse 자산 소득세; **capital growth** chabon chŭngga 자본 증가
capitalism chabonjuŭi 자본주의
capitalist 1 *adj* chabonjuŭijŏk

자본주의적 **2** *n* chabonjuŭija 자본주의자; (*businessman*) chabon-ga 자본가
capital letter taemuntcha 대문자
capital punishment kŭk'yŏng 극형
capitulate hangbok'ada 항복하다
capsize 1 *v/i* twijip'ida 뒤집히다 **2** *v/t* twijiptta 뒤집다
capsule MED, (*in space*) k'aepsshyul 캡슐
captain *n* (*of ship*) sŏnjang 선장; (*of aircraft*) kijang 기장; (*of team*) t'imjang 팀장
caption *n* k'aepsshyŏn 캡션
captivate maŭmŭl sarojaptta 마음을 사로잡다
captive (*of war*) p'oro 포로
captivity kamgŭm 감금
capture 1 *n* (*of city*) chŏmnyŏng 점령; (*of criminal*) saengp'o 생포; (*of animal*) p'ohoek 포획 **2** *v/t person, animal* sarojaptta 사로잡다; *city, building* chŏmnyŏnghada 점령하다; *market share etc* hoektŭk'ada 획득하다; (*portray*) p'och'ak'ada 포착하다
car chadongch'a 자동차; (*of train*) ch'aryang 차량; *by ~* chadongch'aro 자동차로
carafe pyŏng 병
carat k'aerŏt 캐럿
carbohydrate t'ansuhwamul 탄수화물
carbonated *drink* t'ansanŭi 탄산의
carbon monoxide ilssanhwat'anso 일산화탄소
carbureter, carburetor k'aburet'ŏ 카부레터
carcinogen param multchil 발암 물질
carcinogenic paramsŏng-ŭi 발암성의
card k'adŭ 카드; (*post~*) yŏpssŏ 엽서; (*business ~*) myŏngham 명함
cardboard p'anji 판지
cardiac shimjang-ŭi 심장의
cardiac arrest shimjang chŏngji 심장 정지
cardigan k'adigŏn 카디건
card index k'adŭshik saegin 카드식 색인

card key k'adŭro toen yŏlssoe 카드로 된 열쇠

care 1 n (of baby, pet) tolbom 돌봄; (of the elderly) posalp'im 보살핌; (of sick person) kanho 간호; (medical ~) ch'iryo 치료; (worry) kŏkchŏng 걱정; ~ **of** → c/o; **take ~** (be cautious) choshimhada 조심하다; **take ~** (**of yourself**)! (goodbye) choshimhaesŏ kaseyo! 조심해서 가세요!; **take ~ of** baby, dog tolboda 돌보다; tool, house, garden sojunghi hada 소중히 하다; (deal with) ch'ŏrihada 처리하다; (**handle**) **with ~!** (on label) ch'wigŭp chuŭi 취급 주의 **2** v/i kwanshimŭl kajida 관심을 가지다; **I don't ~!** sanggwan ŏpssŏ! 상관 없어!; **I couldn't ~ less** chŏnhyŏ kwanshimi ŏpssŏ 전혀 관심이 없어
♦ **care about** ...e kwanshimŭl kajida ...에 관심을 가지다
♦ **care for** (look after) tolboda 돌보다; (like, be fond of) choahada 좋아하다; **would you ~ ...?** ...ŭl/rŭl chom tŭshigessŏyo? ...을/를 좀 드시겠어요?

career (profession) kyŏngnyŏk 경력; (path through life) saeng-ae 생애

carefree amu kŏktchŏng ŏmnŭn 아무 걱정 없는

careful (cautious) choshimsŏng innŭn 조심성 있는; (thorough) shinjunghan 신중한; (**be**) ~! choshimhae! 조심해!

carefully (with caution) choshimsŭrŏpkke 조심스럽게; worded etc shinjunghage 신중하게

careless choshimsŏng ŏmnŭn 조심성 없는; **you are so ~!** nŏnŭn nŏmu choshimsŏng-i ŏpkkuna! 너는 너무 조심성이 없구나!

caress 1 n aemu 애무 **2** v/t aemuhada 애무하다

caretaker kwalliin 관리인

careworn kŏktchŏng-e shidallin 걱정에 시달린

cargo sŏnjŏk hwamul 선적 화물

caricature n p'ungja manhwa 풍자 만화

caring adj chal tolbonŭn 잘 돌보는

carnage taehakssal 대학살

carnation k'aneishyŏn 카네이션

carnival ch'uktche 축제; (amusement park) yuwŏnji 유원지

carol n ch'uk-kka 축가

carousel (at airport) hoejŏnshik k'onbeiŏ 회전식 콘베이어; (for slide projector) hwandŭnggi p'illŭm k'arusel 환등기 필름 카루셀; (merry-go-round) hoejŏn mongma 회전 목마

carpenter mokssu 목수

carpet k'ap'et 카펫

carpool 1 n chagayong-ŭi hapssŭng iyong 자가용의 합승 이용 **2** v/i chagayong-ŭl hapssŭng-ŭro iyonghada 자가용을 합승으로 이용하다

car port kani ch'ago 간이 차고

carrier (company) unsong hoesa 운송 회사; (of disease) pogyunja 보균자

carrot tanggŭn 당근

carry 1 v/t (in hand) tŭlgo kada 들고 가다; (from one place to another) narŭda 나르다; (have on one's person) chinigo tanida 지니고 다니다; (of pregnant woman) paego it-tta 배고 있다; disease omgida 옮기다; (of ship, plane, bus etc) narŭda 나르다; proposal t'onggwashik'ida 통과시키다; **get carried away** nŏkssŭl ilt'a 넋을 잃다 **2** v/i (of sound) irŭda 이르다
♦ **carry on 1** v/i (continue) kyesok'ada 계속하다; (make a fuss) soranŭl p'iuda 소란을 피우다; (have an affair) paramŭl p'iuda 바람을 피우다 **2** v/t (conduct) haenagada 해나가다
♦ **carry out** survey etc shilsshihada 실시하다; orders etc shirhaenghada 실행하다

car seat (for child) ŏriniyong chwasŏk 어린이용 좌석

cart chimmach'a 짐마차

cartel k'arŭt'el 카르텔

carton (for storage, transport) pakssŭ 박스; (for eggs) kwak 곽; (for milk etc) p'aek 팩; (of cigarettes) kap 갑

cartoon (in newspaper, magazine) manhwa 만화; (on TV, movie) manhwa yŏnghwa 만화 영화

cartridge (*for gun*) t'anyakt'ong 탄약통

carve *meat* charŭda 자르다; *wood* saegida 새기다

carving (*figure*) chogak 조각

car wash ch'a sech'ŏk 차 세척

case¹ (*container*) k'eisŭ 케이스; (*of Scotch, wine*) sangja 상자; *Br* (*suitcase*) otkkabang 옷가방

case² *n* (*instance*) kyŏng-u 경우; (*argument*) chujang 주장; (*for investigation*) sakkŏn 사건; MED pyŏngse 병세; LAW sosong sakkŏn 소송 사건; *in ~ ...* manil ... hal kyŏng-urŭl saenggak'ayŏ 만일 ... 할 경우를 생각하여; *in ~ it rains* manil piga ol kyŏng-urŭl saenggak'ayŏ 만일 비가 올 경우를 생각하여; *in any ~* ŏtchaettŭn 어쨌든; *in that ~* kŭrŏn kyŏng-ue 그런 경우에

case history MED pyŏngnyŏk 병력

cash 1 *n* hyŏn-gŭm 현금; *~ down* kŭ chariesŏ hyŏn-gŭmŭro 그 자리에서 현금으로; *pay (in) ~* hyŏn-gŭmŭro naeda 현금으로 내다; *~ in advance* sŏn-gŭm 선금 **2** *v/t* check hyŏn-gŭmŭro pakkuda 현금으로 바꾸다
♦ **cash in on** ...(ŭ)ro tonŭl pŏlda ...(으)로 돈을 벌다

cash cow kiŏbŭi hŭktcha hoesa 기업의 흑자 회사; **cash desk** kyesandae 계산대; **cash discount** hyŏn-gŭm harin 현금 할인; **cash flow** hyŏn-gŭm yuch'urip 현금 유출입

cashier *n* (*in store etc*) ch'ullabwŏn 출납원

cash machine hyŏn-gŭm inch'ulgi 현금 인출기

cashmere *adj* k'aeshimiŏ 캐시미어

cash register kŭmjŏn tŭngnok-kki 금전 등록기

casino k'ajino 카지노

casket (*coffin*) kwan 관

cassette nogŭm t'eip'ŭ 녹음 테이프

cassette player nogŭmgi 녹음기

cassette recorder nogŭmgi 녹음기

cast 1 *n* (*of play*) ch'uryŏnjin 출연진; (*mold*) chuhyŏng 주형 **2** *v/t* play paeurŭl chohada 배역을 정하다; *actor* paeyŏgŭl chŏnghada 배역을 정하다
♦ **cast off** *v/i* (*of ship*) pattchurŭl p'ulda 밧줄을 풀다

caste k'asŭt'ŭ chedo 카스트 제도

caster (*on chair etc*) tari pak'wi 다리 바퀴

cast iron *n* musoe 무쇠

cast-iron *adj* musoero mandŭn 무쇠로 만든

castle sŏng 성

castrate kŏsehada 거세하다

casual (*chance*) uyŏnhan 우연한; (*offhand*) mugwanshimhan 무관심한; (*not formal*) p'yŏngsang-ŭi 평상의; (*not permanent*) ilsshijŏgin 일시적인

casualty sasangja 사상자

casual wear p'yŏngsangbok 평상복

cat koyang-i 고양이

catalog *n* mongnok 목록

catalyst *fig* ch'oktchinje 촉진제

catalytic converter ch'ongmae k'ŏnbŏt'ŏ 촉매 컨버터

catastrophe ch'ŏnjaejibyŏn 천재지변

catch 1 *n* chapkki 잡기; (*of fish*) nakkŭn kŏt 낚은 것; (*locking device*) kori 고리; (*problem*) munje 문제 **2** *v/t* ball, escaped prisoner, fish chaptta 잡다; (*bus, train*) chaba t'ada 잡아 타다; (*in order to speak to*) ttarajaptta 따라잡다; (*hear*) ara tŭt-tta 알아 듣다; *illness* ...e kŏllida ...에 걸리다; *~ (a) cold* kamgie kŏllida 감기에 걸리다; *~ s.o.'s eye* (*of person, object*) nuguŭi shisŏnŭl kkŭlda 누구의 시선을 끌다; *~ sight of* ...ŭl/rŭl hŭlkkŭt poda ...을/를 흘깃 보다; *~ X doing Y* Xi/ga Yhago innŭn changmyŏnŭl puttchaptta X이/가 Y하고 있는 장면을 붙잡다
♦ **catch on** (*become popular*) in-girŭl ŏt-tta 인기를 얻다; (*understand*) ihaehada 이해하다
♦ **catch up** *v/i* ttarajaptta 따라잡다
♦ **catch up on** ...ŭl/rŭl poch'unghada ...을/를 보충하다

catch-22: *it's a ~ situation* pujorihan sanghwang-ida 부조리한 상황이다

catcher (*in baseball*) k'aech'ŏ 캐처

catching *disease* chŏnyŏmsŏng-ŭi 전염성의; *fear, panic* ŏmssŭp'anŭn 엄습하는

catchy *tune* kŭmbang shwipkke oewŏjinŭn 금방 쉽게 외워지는

category pŏmju 범주

♦cater for (*meet the needs of*) ...ŭi kumie mat-tta ...의 구미에 맞다; (*provide food for*) ...ŭl/rŭl wihan yorirŭl chegonghada ...을/를 위한 요리를 제공하다

caterer yori chodaltcha 요리 조달자

caterpillar yuch'ung 유충

cathedral sŏngdang 성당

Catholic 1 *adj* Ch'ŏnjugyoŭi 천주교의, 2 *n* Ch'ŏnjugyo shinja 천주교 신자

catsup k'ech'ŏp 케첩

cattle so 소

catty pianyanggŏrinŭn 비아냥거리는

cauliflower k'ollip'ŭllawŏ 콜리플라워

cause 1 *n* wŏnin 원인; (*grounds*) iyu 이유; (*aim of movement*) moktchŏk 목적 2 *v/t* irŭk'ida 일으키다

caution 1 *n* (*care*) choshim 조심; ~ *is advised* choshimhaeya hamnida 조심해야 합니다 2 *v/t* (*warn*) chuŭishik'ida 주의시키다

cautious choshimsŭrŏun 조심스러운

cave tonggul 동굴

♦cave in (*of roof*) ump'uk kkŏjida 움푹 꺼지다

caviar ch'ŏlgap sang-ŏ aljŏt 철갑 상어 알젓

cavity ch'ungch'i 충치

CBS (= *Christian Broadcasting System*) Kidok-kkyo Pangsong 기독교 방송

cc 1 *n* saboni ponaejim 사본이 보내짐 2 *v/t* sabonŭl ponaeda 사본을 보내다

CD (= *compact disc*) k'omp'aekt'ŭ tisŭk'ŭ 콤팩트 디스크

CD player CD p'ŭlleiŏ CD 플레이어

CD-ROM sshidirom 씨디롬

CD-ROM drive sshidirom tŭraibŭ 씨디롬 드라이브

cease 1 *v/i* chungdanhada 중단하다 2 *v/t* chungdanshik'ida 중단시키다

ceasefire hyujŏn 휴전

ceiling (*of room*) ch'ŏnjang 천장; (*limit*) ch'oego hando 최고 한도

celadon ware ch'ŏngja 청자

celebrate 1 *v/i* ch'uk'ahada 축하하다 2 *v/t* ch'uk'ahada 축하하다; (*observe*) chinaeda 지내다

celebrated yumyŏnghan 유명한; *be ~ for* ...(ŭ)ro yumyŏnghada ...(으)로 유명하다

celebration ch'uk'ayŏn 축하연

celebrity yumyŏng insa 유명 인사

celery sellŏri 셀러리

cell (*for prisoner*) kambang 감방; BIO sep'o 세포; COMPUT p'yok'an 표칸

cellar chihashil 지하실

cello ch'ello 첼로

cellophane sellop'an 셀로판

cell(ular) phone haendŭp'on 핸드폰, idong chŏnhwa 이동 전화

Celsius sŏpsshi 섭씨

cement 1 *n* shiment'ŭ 시멘트 2 *v/t* shiment'ŭro parŭda 시멘트로 바르다; *friendship* kuch'ida 굳히다

cemetery myoji 묘지

censor *v/t* kŏmyŏrhada 검열하다

censorship kŏmyŏl chedo 검열 제도

cent sent'ŭ 센트

centennial paek chunyŏn 백 주년

center 1 *n* (*middle*) han-gaunde 한가운데; (*building*) sent'ŏ 센터; (*region*) chungshimji 중심지; POL chungdop'a 중도파; *in the ~ of* ...ŭi han-gaundee(sŏ) ...의 한가운데에(서) 2 *v/t* han-gaundero tuda 한가운데로 두다

♦center on ...e chungshimŭl tuda ...에 중심을 두다

centigrade sŏpsshi 섭씨; *10 degrees ~* sŏpsshi 10to 섭씨 10도

centimeter sent'i(mit'ŏ) 센티(미터)

central chungshimŭi 중심의; *location, apartment* chungshimbue innŭn 중심부에 있는; (*main*) chuyohan 주요한; *~ France* P'ŭrangsŭ chungbu 프랑스 중부; *be ~ to sth* muŏse chungshimjŏgida 무엇에 중심적이다

central heating chung-ang chamgŭm changch'i 중앙 잠금 장치

centralize chiptchung kyŏrŭihada 집중 결의하다

central locking MOT chung-ang anjŏn changch'i 중앙 안전 장치

central processing unit → *CPU*

century segi 세기

CEO (= *Chief Executive Officer*)
ch'oego kyŏngnyŏngja 최고 경영자

ceramic tojagiro toen 도자기로 된

ceramics (*objects*) tojagi 도자기; (*art*)
toye 도예

cereal (*grain*) kongmul 곡물; *breakfast* ~ shiriŏl 시리얼

ceremonial 1 *adj* ŭishigŭl wihan
의식을 위한 2 *n* ŭishik 의식

ceremony (*event*) shik 식; (*ritual*)
ŭishik 의식; *the Oscars* ~ Osŭk'a
shisangshik 오스카 시상식; *opening
~/closing* ~ kaehoeshik /
p'yehoeshik 개회식 / 폐회식

certain (*sure*) hwaksshinhanŭn
확신하는; (*particular*) ottŏn 어떤;
(*specific*) iltchŏnghan 일정한; *it's ~
that* ...ranŭn kŏsŭn hwaksshirada
...라는 것은 확실하다; *a ~ Mr Park*
Pak mosshi 박 모씨; *make ~*
hwaginhada 확인하다; *know/say
for* ~ hwaksshirhi alda/marhada
확실히 알다 /말하다

certainly (*definitely*) hwaksshirhi
확실히; (*of course*) mullon 물론; ~
not! mullon andwaeji! 물론 안돼지!

certainty (*confidence*) hwaksshin
확신; (*inevitability*) hwaksshilssŏng
확실성; *it's/he's a ~*
kŭgŏsŭn/kŭnŭn hwaksshirhada
그것은/그는 확실하다

certificate (*qualification*)
chagyŏktchŭng 자격증; (*official
paper*) chŭngmyŏngsŏ 증명서

certified public accountant kong-in
hoegyesa 공인 회계사

certify pojŭnghada 보증하다

Cesarean *n* chewang chŏlgae 제왕
절개

cessation chungji 중지; ~ *of hostilities* hyujŏn 휴전

CFC (= *chlorofluorocarbon*)
sshiep'ŭsshi 씨에프씨

chain 1 *n* (*for animal, anchor*)
soesasŭl 쇠사슬; (*jewelry*) mok-
kkŏrijul 목걸이줄; (*for bicycle, tire*)
ch'ein 체인; (*of stores, hotels*)
ch'einjom 체인점 2 *v/t*: ~ *X to Y*
Xŭl/rŭl Ye sasŭllo muktta X을/를

Y에 사슬로 묶다

chain reaction yŏnswae panŭng 연쇄
반응; **chain smoke** chuldambaerŭl
p'iuda 줄담배를 피우다; **chain
smoker** chuldambaerŭl p'iunŭn
saram 줄담배를 피우는 사람; **chain
store** yŏnswaejŏm 연쇄점

chair 1 *n* ŭija 의자; (*arm~*) allak ŭija
안락 의자; (*at university*)
chŏnggyosujik 정교수직; *the ~*
(*electric*) chŏn-gi ŭija 전기 의자; (*at
meeting*) ŭijang 의장; *take the ~*
ŭijangjigŭl mat-tta 의장직을 맡다
2 *v/t meeting* ŭijangjigŭl mat-tta
의장직을 맡다

chair lift ch'eŏ lip'ŭt'ŭ 체어 리프트;
chairman ŭijang 의장; **chairperson**
sahoeja 사회자; **chairwoman**
sahoeja 사회자

chalk (*for writing*) punp'il 분필; (*in
soil*) sŏk'oeam 석회암

challenge 1 *n* (*difficult task*) haebol
manhan il 해볼 만한 일; (*in race,
competition*) tojŏn 도전 2 *v/t* (*to
race, debate*) tojŏnhada 도전하다;
(*call into question*) hwan-gishik'ida
환기시키다

challenger tojŏnja 도전자

challenging nŭngnyŏgŭl
shihŏmhaebonŭn 능력을 시험해보는

chambermaid kaekshil tamdang
yŏjong-ŏbwŏn 객실 담당 여종업원

Chamber of Commerce Sanggong
hoeŭiso 상공 회의소

chamois (*leather*) shyaemi kajuk
섀미 가죽

champagne shyamp'ein 샴페인

champion 1 *n* SP ch'aemp'iŏn 챔피언;
(*of cause*) onghoja 옹호자 2 *v/t*
(*cause*) onghohada 옹호하다

championship (*event*) sŏnsugwŏn
taehoe 선수권 대회; (*title*)
sŏnsugwŏn 선수권

chance (*possibility*) kamang 가망;
(*opportunity*) kihoe 기회; (*risk*)
wihŏm 위험; (*luck*) uyŏn 우연; *by ~*
uyŏnhi 우연히; *take a ~* une
matkkigo haeboda 운에 맡기고
해보다; *I'm not taking any ~s*
yohaengsurŭl paraji anssŭmnida
요행수를 바라지 않습니다

chandelier shyangdŭllie 샹들리에

change 1 n (to plan, idea etc)
pyŏnhwa 변화; (small coins, from
purchase) chandon 잔돈; (different
situation etc) kibun chŏnhwan 기분
전환; for a ~ kibun chŏnhwanŭro
기분 전환으로; a ~ of clothes
karaibŭl ot 가라입는 옷 2 v/t (alter)
pakkuda 바꾸다; world, society
pyŏnhwashik'ida 변화시키다;
bankbill pakkuŏ chuda 바꾸어 주다;
(replace) kalda 갈다; trains, planes
karat'ada 갈아타다; one's clothes
pakkuŏ iptta 바꾸어 입다 3 v/i
pakkuŏjida 바뀌어지다; (of world,
society) pyŏnhwahada 변화하다; (put
on different clothes) pakkuŏ iptta
바꾸어 입다; (take different train etc)
karat'ada 갈아타다

channel (on TV, radio) ch'aenŏl
채널; (waterway) suro 수로

chant 1 n norae 노래 2 v/i noraehada
노래하다

chaos taehollan 대혼란

chaotic hollansŭrŏun 혼란스러운

chapel yebaedang 예배당

chapped salgach'i t'ŭn 살갗이 튼

chapter (of book) chang 장; (of
organization) chibu 지부

character (nature) sŏngkkyŏk 성격;
(person) inmul 인물; (in book, play)
tŭngjang inmul 등장 인물; (special
aura) t'ŭktching 특징; (letter)
muntcha 문자; he's a real ~ kŭnŭn
taedanhan inmuriyeyo 그는 대단한
인물이에요

characteristic 1 n t'ŭkssŏng 특성
2 adj t'ŭkssŏng-ŭl nat'anaenŭn
특성을 나타내는

characterize (be typical of) …ŭi
t'ŭkssŏng-ŭl nat'anaeda …의 특성을
나타내다; (describe) sŏngkkyŏgŭl
myosahada 성격을 묘사하다

character set COMPUT munjap'yo
문자표

charbroiled sutppure kuwŏjin 숯불에
구워진

charcoal (for barbecue) sut 숯; (for
drawing) mokt'an 목탄

charge 1 n (fee) yogŭm 요금; LAW
hyŏmŭi 혐의; free of ~ muryoro

무료로; will that be cash or ~?
hyŏn-gŭmimnikka, oesang-imnikka?
현금입니까, 외상입니까?; be in ~
tamdang-ida 담당이다; take ~
ttŏmat-tta 떠맡다 2 v/t sum of money
ch'ŏngguhada 청구하다; (put on
account) ap'ŭro taranot'a 앞으로
달아놓다; LAW kobarhada 고발하다;
battery ch'ungjŏnshik'ida 충전시키다
3 v/i (attack) tolgyŏk'ada 돌격하다

charge account oesang kŏrae 외상
거래

charge card shinyong k'adŭ 신용
카드

charisma k'arisŭma 카리스마

charitable institution, donation
chasŏnŭi 자선의; person chasŏnshimi
manŭn 자선심이 많은

charity (assistance) chasŏn 자선;
(organization) chasŏn tanch'e 자선
단체

charm 1 n (appealing quality)
maeryŏk 매력 2 v/t (delight)
maehok'ada 매혹하다

charming maehoktchŏgin 매혹적인

charred kŭsŭllin 그슬린

chart (diagram) top'yo 도표; NAUT
haedo 해도; (for airplane) ch'yat'ŭ
차트; the ~s MUS hit'ŭgok sunwi
히트곡 순위

charter v/t chŏnse naeda 전세 내다

charter flight chŏnsegi 전세기

chase 1 n ch'ugyŏk 추격 2 v/t
twitchot-tta 뒤쫓다

♦**chase away** tchoch'abŏrida
쫓아버리다

chaser (drink) ch'eisŏ 체이서

chassis (of car) shyaeshi 섀시

chat 1 n chapttam 잡담 2 v/i
chapttamhada 잡담하다

chatter 1 n suda 수다 2 v/i (talk) suda
ttŏlda 수다 떨다; (of teeth) tŏldŏl
ttŏllida 덜덜 떨리다

chatterbox sudajaeng-i 수다쟁이

chatty person sudasŭrŏun 수다스러운;
letter hŏmurŏmnŭn 허물없는

chauffeur n chagayong unjŏnsa
자가용 운전사

chauvinist (male ~) namsŏng
uwŏltchuŭija 남성 우월주의자

cheap adj (inexpensive) ssan 싼;

(*nasty*) piyŏrhan 비열한; (*mean*) insaek'an 인색한

cheat 1 *n* (*person*) sogimsu 속임수 **2** *v/t* sogida 속이다; **~ X out of Y** Yŭl/rŭl sogyŏsŏ Xŭl/rŭl ppaeat-tta Y을/를 속여서 X을/를 빼앗다 **3** *v/i* (*in exam, cards etc*) sogimsurŭl ssŭda 속임수를 쓰다; **~ on one's wife** anae mollae param p'iuda 아내 몰래 바람 피우다

check¹ 1 *adj* shirt ch'ek'ŭ munŭiŭi 체크 무늬의 **2** *n* ch'ek'ŭ munŭi 체크 무늬

check² FIN sup'yo 수표; (*in restaurant etc*) kyesansŏ 계산서; **~ please** kyesanhae chuseyo 계산해 주세요

check³ 1 *n* (*to verify sth*) hwagin 확인; **keep in ~, hold in ~** ŏktchehada 억제하다; **keep a ~ on** hwaginhae tuda 확인해 두다 **2** *v/t* (*verify*) hwaginhada 확인하다; (*inspect*) chŏmgŏmhada 점검하다; (*restrain*) ŏktchehada 억제하다; (*stop*) maktta 막다; (*with a ~mark*) ch'ek'ŭ p'yoshirŭl hada 첵크 표시를 하다; *coat, package etc* pogwansoe matkkida 보관소에 맡기다 **3** *v/i* hwaginhae chuda 확인해 주다; **~ for** hwaginhada 확인하다

♦ **check in** (*at airport*) t'apssŭng susogŭl hada 탑승 수속을 하다; (*at hotel*) ch'ek'ŭinhada 체크인하다

♦ **check off** taejo p'yoshirŭl hada 대조 표시를 하다

♦ **check on** salp'yŏboda 살펴보다

♦ **check out 1** *v/i* (*of hotel*) ch'ek'ŭaut'ada 체크아웃하다 **2** *v/t* (*look into*) chosahada 조사하다; *club, restaurant etc* tŭllyŏboda 들려보다

♦ **check up on** ... ŭl/rŭl naeryŏgŭl chosahada ...을/를 내력을 조사하다

♦ **check with** (*of person*) ...wa/kwa mŏnjŏ araboda ... 와 / 과 먼저 알아보다; (*of information*) ...wa/kwa ilch'ihada ...와/과 일치하다

checkbook sup'yoch'aek 수표책
checked *material* ch'ek'ŭ munŭiŭi 체크 무늬의
checkerboard sŏyang changgip'an 서양 장기판

checkered *pattern* ch'ek'ŭ munŭiŭi 체크 무늬의; *career* p'aranmanjanghan 파란만장한

checkers sŏyang changgi 서양 장기

check-in (**counter**) t'apssŭng susok k'aunt'ŏ 탑승 수속 카운터

checking account tangjwa yegŭm kujwa 당좌 예금 구좌

check-in time (*in hotel*) t'usuk shigan 투숙 시간; (*at airport*) t'apssŭng susok shigan 탑승 수속 시간; **checklist** taejop'yo 대조표; **checkmark** ch'ek'ŭ p'yoshi 체크 표시; **checkmate** *n* changgun 장군; **checkout** kyesandae 계산대; **checkout time** pang-ŭl naeŏjul shigan 방을 내어줄 시간; **check-point** MIL kŏmmunso 검문소; (*in race etc*) ch'ek'ŭp'oint'ŭ 체크포인트; **checkroom** (*for coats*) hyudaep'um pogwanso 휴대품 보관소; (*for baggage*) suhamul pogwanso 수하물 보관소; **checkup** MED kŏn-gang chindan 건강 진단; (*dental*) ch'ia kŏmsa 치아 검사

cheek (*of face*) ppyam 뺨
cheekbone kwangdaeppyŏ 광대뼈
cheer 1 *n* hwanho 환호; **~s!** (*toast*) kŏnbae! 건배! **2** *v/t & v/i* hwanhohada 환호하다

♦ **cheer on** ŭng-wŏnhada 응원하다

♦ **cheer up 1** *v/i* kiuni nada 기운이 나다; **~!** kiun nae! 기운 내! **2** *v/t* kiunŭl na-ege hada 기운을 내게 하다

cheerful myŏngnanghan 명랑한
cheering hwanho 환호
cheerleader ch'iŏridŏ 치어리더
cheese ch'ijŭ 치즈
cheeseburger ch'ijŭbŏgŏ 치즈버거
cheesecake ch'ijŭk'eik 치즈케익
chef chubangjang 주방장
Cheju Island Chejudo 제주도
chemical 1 *adj* hwahagŭi 화학의 **2** *n* hwahak chep'um 화학 제품
chemical warfare hwahaktchŏn 화학전
chemist hwahaktcha 화학자
chemistry hwahak 화학; *fig* sŏnggyŏgi mannŭn yŏbu 성격이 맞는 여부

chemotherapy hwahak yoppŏp 화학요법

cherish sojunghi hada 소중히 하다; *memory, hope* sojunghi kanjik'ada 소중히하다

cherry (*fruit*) p'ŏtchi 버찌; (*tree*) pŏnnamu 벚나무

chess ch'esŭ 체스

chessboard ch'esŭp'an 체스판

chest (*of person*) kasŭm 가슴; (*box*) changnong 장롱

chestnut pam 밤; (*tree*) pamnamu 밤나무

chest of drawers sŏraptchang 서랍장

chew *v/t* sshiptta 씹다

♦**chew out** F hodoege kkujit-tta 호되게 꾸짖다

chewing gum kkŏm 껌

chick pyŏng-ari 병아리; F (*girl*) kyejibae 계집애

chicken 1 *n* tak 닭; (*food*) tak-kkogi 닭고기; F kŏptchaeng-i 겁쟁이 **2** *adj* F (*cowardly*) kŏbŭl mŏgŭn 겁을 먹은

♦**chicken out** kŏbŭl mŏk-kko mullŏsŏda 겁을 먹고 물러서다

chickenfeed F saebarŭi p'i 새발의 피

chicken pox sudu 수두

chief 1 *n* (*head*) chang 장; (*of tribe*) choktchang 족장 **2** *adj* chuyohan 주요한

chiefly churo 주로

chilblain tongsang 동상

child ai 아이; *pej* yuch'ihan saram 유치한 사람

childbirth haesan 해산

childhood ŏrinshijŏl 어린시절

childish *pej* yuch'ihan 유치한

childless ai ŏmnŭn 아이 없는

childlike ch'ŏnjinhan 천진한

Children's Day Ŏrininal 어린이날

chill 1 *n* (*in air*) han-gi 한기; (*illness*) kamgi 감기 **2** *v/t* (*wine*) ch'age hada 차게 하다

chilli (**pepper**) koch'u 고추

chilli (**pepper**) **powder** koch'ugaru 고추가루

chilly *weather* ssalssarhan 쌀쌀한; *welcome* naengdamhan 냉담한; *I'm ~* ssalssarhaneyo 쌀쌀하네요

chime *v/i* chong-i ullida 종이 울리다

chimney kulttuk 굴뚝

chimpanzee ch'imp'anji 침판지

chin t'ŏk 턱

China Chungguk 중국

china chagi 자기; (*material*) chagi kŭrŭt 자기 그릇

Chinese 1 *adj* Chunggugŭi 중국의 **2** *n* (*language*) Chunggugŏ 중국어; (*person*) Chungguk saram 중국 사람

Chinese cabbage paech'u 배추; **Chinese character** hantcha 한자; **Chinese character dictionary** okp'yŏn 옥편; **Chinese herbal medicine** hanyak 한약; **Chinese medicine clinic** hanŭiwŏn 한의원

Chin Island Chindo 진도

chink (*gap*) t'ŭm 틈; (*sound*) taenggŭranghanŭn sori 댕그랑하는 소리

chip 1 *n* (*fragment*) t'omak 토막; (*damage*) i ppajin chaguk 이 빠진 자국; (*in gambling*), COMPUT ch'ip 칩; **~s** p'ot'eit'o ch'ipssŭ 포테이토 칩스 **2** *v/t* (*damage*) iga ppajida 이가 빠지다

♦**chip in** (*interrupt*) malch'amgyŏnhada 말참견하다; (*with money*) chogŭmsshik tonŭl naeda 조금씩 돈을 내다

chipset COMPUT ch'ipset 칩셋

chiropractor ch'ŏkch'u chiapssa 척추지압사

chirp *v/i* chijŏgwida 지저귀다

chisel *n* kkŭl 끌

chivalrous kisadojŏgin 기사도적인

chives kolp'aŭi ip 골파의 잎

chlorine yŏmso 염소

chockfull kkwak tŭrŏch'an 꽉 들어찬

chocolate ch'ok'ollit 초콜릿; *hot ~* hat ch'ok'ollit 핫 초콜릿

chocolate cake ch'ok'ollit k'eik 초콜릿 케익

choice 1 *n* sŏnt'aek 선택; (*selection*) sŏnt'aegŭi pŏmwi 선택의 범위; *I had no ~* sŏnt'aegŭi yŏjiga ŏpssŏt-tta 선택의 여지가 없었다 **2** *adj* (*top quality*) t'ŭkssang-ŭi 특상의

choir hapch'angdan 합창단

choke 1 *n* MOT ch'ok'ŭ 초크 **2** *v/i* mogi maeida 목이 매이다; *he ~d on a bone* kŭnŭn kashiga kŏllyŏ mogi

maeyŏt-tta 그는 가시가 걸려 목이
매었다 **3** *v/t* mogŭl chorŭda 목을
조르다

cholesterol k'ollesŭt'erol 콜레스테롤

choose *v/t* & *v/i* sŏnt'aek'ada
선택하다

choosey F kkadaroun 까다로운

chop 1 *n* chigŏ naegi 찍어 내기;
(*meat*) tukkŏpke charŭn
kogittchŏm 두껍게 자른 고깃점 **2** *v/t*
wood p'aeda 패다; *meat, vegetables*
ssŏlda 썰다

♦**chop down** *tree* p'aenŏmgida
패넘기다

chopper (*tool*) tokki 도끼; F
(*helicopter*) hellik'opt'ŏ 헬리콥터

chopsticks chŏtkkarak 젓가락

chord MUS hyŏn 현

chore chiban il 집안 일

choreographer anmuga 안무가

choreography anmu 안무

chorus (*singers*) hapch'angdan
합창단; (*of song*) hapch'ang 합창

Choson Chosŏn 조선

Christ Kŭrisŭdo 그리스도; ~!
chegirŏl! 제기랄!

christen seryehada 세례하다

Christian 1 *n* Kidok-kkyo shinja
기독교 신자 **2** *adj* Kidok-kkyoŭi
기독교의; *attitude* in-ganjŏgin
인간적인

Christian Broadcasting System
Kidok-kkyo Pangsong 기독교 방송

Christianity Kidok-kkyo 기독교

Christian name seryemyŏng 세례명

Christmas Sŏngt'anjŏl 성탄절; *at ~*
Sŏngt'anjŏre 성탄절에; *Merry ~!*
meri K'ŭrisŭmasŭ! 메리 크리스마스!

Christmas card K'ŭrisŭmasŭ k'adŭ
크리스마스 카드; **Christmas Day**
Sŏngt'anjŏl 성탄절; **Christmas Eve**
K'ŭrisŭmasŭ ibŭ 크리스마스 이브;
Christmas present K'ŭrisŭmasŭ
sŏnmul 크리스마스 선물; **Christmas
tree** K'ŭrisŭmasŭ t'ŭri 크리스마스
트리

chrome, chromium k'ŭrom 크롬

chronic mansŏng-ŭi 만성의

chronological yŏndaesunŭi 연대순의;
in ~ order yŏndaesunŭro 연대순으로

chrysanthemum kuk'wa 국화

chubby t'ongt'onghan 통통한

chuck *v/t* F naedŏnjida 내던지다

♦**chuck out** *object* naebŏrida
내버리다; *person* naetchot-tta 내쫓다

chuckle 1 *n* k'ilk'il usŭm 킬킬 웃음
2 *v/i* k'ilk'il ut-tta 킬킬 웃다

chunk k'ŭn tŏng-ŏri 큰 덩어리

church kyohoe 교회

chute hwalgangno 활강로; (*for
garbage*) ssŭregi t'ongno 쓰레기
통로

CIA (= *Central Intelligence
Agency*) Miguk chung-ang
chŏngbobu 미국 중앙 정보부

cider sagwa chusŭ 사과 주스

CIF (= *cost insurance freight*) unim
mit pohŏm p'oham kagyŏk 운임 및
보험 포함 가격

cigar yŏsong-yŏn 여송연

cigarette tambae 담배

cinema (*industry*) yŏnghwa sanŏp
영화 산업; *Br* (*building*)
yŏnghwagwan 영화관

cinnamon kyep'i 계피

circle 1 *n* wŏn 원; (*group*) chipttan
집단 **2** *v/t* (*draw circle around*)
tonggŭramirŭl ch'ida 동그라미를
치다 **3** *v/i* (*of plane, bird*) pingbing
tolda 빙빙 돌다

circuit hoero 회로

circuit board hoero kyegip'an 회로
계기판

circuit breaker hoero ch'adan-gi
회로 차단기

circular 1 *n* (*giving information*)
hoeram 회람 **2** *adj* tunggŭn 둥근

circulate 1 *v/i* tolda 돌다 **2** *v/t*
(*memo*) p'ŏttŭrida 퍼뜨리다

circulation BIO sunhwan 순환; (*of
newspaper, magazine*) parhaeng
pusu 발행 부수

circumference wŏnju 원주

circumstances sanghwang 상황;
(*financial*) sangt'ae 상태; *under no
~* ŏttŏn sanghwang-esŏdo
(+ *negative verb*) 어떤 상황에서도;
under the ~ kŭrŏn sanghwang-
esŏnŭn 그런 상황에서는

circus sŏk'ŏsŭ 서커스

cistern mul t'aengk'ŭ 물 탱크

citizen shimin 시민

citizenship shiminkkwŏn 시민권
city toshi 도시; **~ center** toshiŭi chungshim 도시의 중심; **~ hall** shich'ŏng 시청
civic *adj* shiŭi 시의; *pride, responsibilities* shiminŭi 시민의
civil (*not military*) min-ganŭi 민간의; *disobedience etc* shiminŭi 시민의; (*polite*) yeŭi parŭn 예의 바른
civil defense minbang-wi 민방위
civil engineer t'omok kisa 토목 기사
civilian 1 *n* min-ganin 민간인 **2** *adj clothes* ilbanŭi 일반의
civilization munmyŏng 문명
civilize *person* kaehwahada 개화하다
civil rights kongmin p'yŏngdŭngkkwŏn 공민 평등권; **civil servant** kongmuwŏn 공무원; **civil service** haengjŏng samu 행정 사무; **civil war** naejŏn 내전
claim 1 *n* (*for damages*) ch'ŏnggu 청구; (*right*) kwŏlli 권리; (*assertion*) chujang 주장 **2** *v/t* (*ask for as a right*) ch'ŏngguhada 청구하다; (*assert*), *property* chujanghada 주장하다; **they have ~ed responsibility for the attack** kŭdŭrŭn konggyŏge taehan ch'aegimŭl yoguhaetta 그들은 공격에 대한 책임을 요구했다
claimant yoguja 요구자; LAW wŏn-go 원고
clam taehap chogae 대합 조개
♦**clam up** F ibŭl tamulda 입을 다물다
clammy ch'ago kkŭnjŏk-kkŭnjŏk'an 차고 끈적끈적한
clamor (*noise*) ttŏdŭlssŏk'am 떠들썩함; (*outcry*) ausŏng 아우성
♦**clamor for** shikkŭrŏpkke yoguhada 시끄럽게 요구하다
clamp 1 *n* (*fastener*) choemsoe 죔쇠 **2** *v/t* (*fasten*) choemsoero choeda 죔쇠로 죄다
♦**clamp down** tansok'ada 단속하다
♦**clamp down on** kangnyŏk'i tansok'ada 강력히 단속하다
clan sshijok 씨족
clandestine pimirŭi 비밀의
clang 1 *n* ch'ŏlk'ŏdŏnghanŭn sori 철커덩하는 소리 **2** *v/i* ch'ŏlk'ŏdŏnghanŭn soriga nada 철커덩하는 소리가 나다

clap 1 *v/i* (*applaud*) paksusŭrŭl ch'ida 박수를 치다 **2** *v/t* paksu ch'ida 박수 치다
clarify myŏnghwak'age hada 명확하게 하다
clarinet k'ŭllarinet 클라리넷
clarity myŏnghwak'am 명확함
clash 1 *n* ch'ungdol 충돌; (*of personalities*) ch'ungdorhada 충돌하다; (*of opinions*) purilch'ihada 불일치하다; (*of colors*) ŏulliji ant'a 어울리지 않다; (*of events*) kyŏpch'ida 겹치다
clasp 1 *n* kŏlssoe 걸쇠 **2** *v/t* (*in hand*) kkwak chwida 꽉 쥐다; (*to self*) kkyŏantta 껴안다
class 1 *n* (*lesson*) suŏp 수업; (*students in a ~*) hak-kkŭp 학급; (*social*) kyegŭp 계급; (*category*) puryu 부류 **2** *v/t* pullyuhada 분류하다
classic 1 *adj* (*typical*) chŏnhyŏngjŏgin 전형적인; (*definitive*) kwŏnwi innŭn 권위 있는 **2** *n* kojŏn 고전
classical *music* k'ŭllaeshik 클래식
classification (*activity*) tŭnggŭbŭl maegim 등급을 매김; (*category*) pullyu 분류
classified *information* kimirŭi 기밀의
classified ad(**vertisement**) hangmokppyŏl kwanggo 항목별 광고
classify (*categorize*) pullyuhada 분류하다
classmate tonggŭpssaeng 동급생; **classroom** kyoshil 교실; **class warfare** kyegŭp t'ujaeng 계급 투쟁
classy F kogŭbin 고급인; *person* p'umwi innŭn 품위 있는
clatter 1 *n* tŏlgŏdŏk'anŭn sori 덜거덕하는 소리 **2** *v/i* soransŭrŏn sorirŭl naemyŏ ppalli umjigida 소란스런 소리를 내며 빨리 움직이다
clause (*in agreement*) chohang 조항; GRAM chŏl 절
claustrophobia milsshil kongp'otchŭng 밀실 공포증
claw 1 *n* palt'op 발톱; *fig* ansanghage marŭn son-garak 앙상하게 마른 손가락 **2** *v/t* (*scratch*) halk'wida 할퀴다

clay 344

clay chinhŭk 진흙
clean 1 *adj* kkaekkŭt'an 깨끗한 **2** *adv*
F (*completely*) kkaekkŭshi 깨끗이
3 *v/t* kkaekkŭt'age hada 깨끗하게
하다; *teeth, shoes* taktta 닦다; *house,
room* ch'ŏngsohada 청소하다; *car,
hands, face* sshit-tta 씻다; *clothes*
ppalda 빨다; *have sth ~ed* muŏsŭl
set'age matkkida 무엇을 세탁에
맡기다
♦ **clean out** *room, cupboard*
kkaekkŭt'age ch'ŏngsohada
깨끗하게 청소하다; *fig* pint'ŏlt'ŏriro
mandŭlda 빈털털이로 만들다
♦ **clean up 1** *v/t* ch'ŏngsohada
청소하다; *fig* ilssohada 일소하다 **2** *v/i*
ch'ŏngsohada 청소하다; (*wash*)
malssuk'aejida 말쑥해지다; (*on stock
market etc*) k'ŭn tonŭl pŏlda 큰 돈을
벌다
cleaner ch'ŏngsobu 청소부; *dry ~*
tŭraik'ŭllining set'aksso
드라이클리닝 세탁소
cleaning woman ch'ŏngsohanŭn
ajumma 청소하는 아줌마
cleanse (*skin*) kkaekkŭt'age sshit-tta
깨끗하게 씻다
cleanser (*for skin*) k'ŭllenjŏ 클렌저
clear 1 *adj voice, weather, water, skin*
malgŭn 맑은; (*bright*) palgŭn 밝은;
photograph, vision tturyŏt'an 뚜렷한;
(*easy to understand*) punmyŏnghan
분명한; (*obvious*) myŏngbaek'an
명백한; *thinker* myŏngsŏk'an 명석한;
I'm not ~ about it musŭn irinji
punmyŏnghaji anayo 무슨 일인지
분명하지 않아요; *I didn't make
myself ~* nae shimjung-ŭl
tturyŏt'age marhaji anassŏ 내 심중을
뚜렷하게 말하지 않았어 **2** *adv:*
stand ~ of ...esŏ ttŏrŏjyŏsŏ sŏda
...에서 떨어져서 서다; *steer ~ of*
...e chŏpkkŭnhaji ant'a ...에
접근하지 않다 **3** *v/t roads etc* ch'iuda
치우다; (*acquit*) mujoero hada
무죄로 하다; (*authorize*) hŏgahada
허가하다; (*earn*) ...ŭi sunsuibŭl
ollida ...의 순수입을 올리다; *~
one's throat* hŏtkkich'imhada
헛기침하다 **4** *v/i* (*of sky, mist*) kaeda
개다; (*of face*) palgajida 밝아지다

♦ **clear away** *v/t* ch'iuda 치우다
♦ **clear off** *v/i* sarajida 사라지다
♦ **clear out 1** *v/t closet* piuda 비우다
2 *v/i* kabŏrida 가버리다
♦ **clear up 1** *v/i* chŏngdonhada
정돈하다; (*of weather*) kaeda 개다;
(*of illness, rash*) nat-tta 낫다 **2** *v/t*
(*tidy*) chŏngdonhada 정돈하다;
mystery, problem p'ulda 풀다
clearance (*space*) t'ŭm 틈;
(*authorization*) hŏga 허가
clearance sale chaego chŏngni seil
재고 정리 세일
clearly (*with clarity*) tturyŏt'age
뚜렷하게; (*evidently*) punmyŏnghi
분명히
clemency kwannyong 관용
clench *teeth* angmulda 악물다; *fist*
kkwak chwida 꽉 쥐다
clergy sŏngjiktchadŭl 성직자들
clergyman sŏngjiktcha 성직자
clerk (*administrative*) samugwan
사무관; (*in store*) chŏmwŏn 점원
clever *person, animal* ttokttok'an
똑똑한; *idea* hyŏnmyŏnghan 현명한;
gadget tokch'angjŏgin 독창적인
click 1 *n* COMPUT k'ŭllik 클릭 **2** *v/i*
(*make noise*) ch'alk'ak'anŭn soriga
nada 찰칵하는 소리가 나다
♦ **click on** COMPUT k'ŭllik'ada
클릭하다
client (*of lawyer etc*) ŭiroein 의뢰인;
(*customer*) kogaek 고객
cliff chŏlbyŏk 절벽
climate kihu 기후
climax *n* chŏltchŏng 절정
climb 1 *n* (*up mountain*) tŭngban
등반 **2** *v/t* orŭda 오르다 **3** *v/i* orŭda
오르다; *mountain* tŭngbanhada
등반하다; *fig* (*of inflation etc*)
chŭnggahada 증가하다
♦ **climb down** naerida 내리다; *fig*
yangbohada 양보하다
climber (*person*) tŭngsan-ga 등산가
clinch *~ a deal* kŏraerŭl maedŭp
chit-tta 거래를 매듭 짓다
cling (*of clothes*) tallabut-tta 달라붙다
♦ **cling to** (*of child*) ...e maedallida
...에 매달리다; *ideas, tradition* ...e
chipch'ak'ada ...에 집착하다
clingfilm p'ojangnyong laep 포장용

랩

clingy *child, boyfriend* tŭllŏbunnŭn 들러붙는

clinic chillyoso 진료소

clinical imsang-ŭi 임상의

clink 1 *n (noise)* tchaenggŭrŏnghanŭn sori 쩽그렁하는 소리 **2** *v/i* tchaenggŭrŏnghanŭn soriga nada 쩽그렁하는 소리가 나다

clip¹ 1 *n (fastener)* k'ŭllip 클립 **2** *v/t* k'ŭllibŭro kojŏngshik'ida 클립으로 고정시키다; ~ *X to Y* Xŭl/rŭl Ye k'ŭllibŭro kojŏngshik'ida X을/를 Y에 클립으로 고정시키다

clip² 1 *n (extract)* palch'we 발췌 **2** *v/t hair, hedge, grass* kawiro charŭda 가위로 자르다

clipboard k'ŭllip-ppodŭ 클립보드

clippers (*for hair*) parik'ang 바리캉; (*for nails*) sont'op kkak-kki 손톱 깎기; (*for gardening*) chŏng-wŏnnyong kawi 정원용 가위

clipping (*from newspaper etc*) oryŏnaen kŏt 오려낸 것

clock shigye 시계

clock radio shigyega innŭn ladio 시계가 있는 라디오

clockwise shigye panghyang-ŭro tora 시계 방향으로 돌아

clockwork shigye t'aeyŏp changch'i 시계 태엽 장치; *it went like ~* mansaga chal chinhaengdoeŏt-tta 만사가 잘 진행되었다

♦**clog up 1** *v/i* mak'ida 막히다 **2** *v/t* mak'ige hada 막히게 하다

close¹ 1 *adj family* kakkaun 가까운; *friend* ch'inhan 친한; *resemblance* yusahan 유사한 **2** *adv* kakkapkke 가깝게; ~ *at hand* paro kakkaie 바로 가까이에; ~ *by* paro kyŏt'e 바로 곁에; *be ~ to* (*emotionally*) ...wa/kwa ch'inhada ...와/과 친하다

close² 1 *v/t* tat-tta 닫다; *eyes* kamtta 감다; *factory* p'yeswaehada 폐쇄하다; (*permanently*) p'yeŏp'ada 폐업하다 **2** *v/i* (*of door, store*) tach'ida 닫히다; (*of eyes*) kamgida 감기다; (*of store: permanently*) p'yeŏp'ada 폐업하다

♦**close down 1** *v/t* p'yeŏpsshik'ida 폐업시키다 **2** *v/i* (*permanently*)

p'yeŏp'ada 폐업하다

♦**close in** *v/i* (*of fog*) tagaoda 다가오다; (*of troops*) p'owihada 포위하다

♦**close up 1** *v/t building* p'yeswaehada 폐쇄하다 **2** *v/i* (*move closer*) tagaoda 다가오다

closed *store* tach'in 닫힌; *eyes* kamgin 감긴

closed-circuit television p'yeswae hoero t'ellebijyŏn 폐쇄 회로 텔레비전

closely *listen, watch* yŏlsshimhi 열심히; *cooperate* ŏmmirhi 엄밀히

closet ot-tchang 옷장

close-up k'ŭllojŭŏp 클로즈업

closing time (*of store*) p'yejŏm shigan 폐점 시간; (*of museum, library*) p'yegwan shigan 폐관 시간

closure *permanent* p'yeswae 폐쇄; (*of shop*) p'yejŏm 폐점

clot 1 *n (of blood)* p'it-ttŏng-ŏri 핏덩어리 **2** *v/i* (*of blood*) ŏnggida 엉기다

cloth (*fabric*) ch'ŏn 천; (*for kitchen*) haengju 행주; (*for cleaning*) kŏlle 걸레

clothes ot 옷

clothes brush ott'ŏri 옷털이

clothes hanger otkkŏri 옷걸이

clothing ŭiryu 의류

cloud *n* kurŭm 구름; *a ~ of smoke/dust* sabang-e kkin yŏn-gi/mŏnji 사방에 낀 연기/먼지

♦**cloud over** ont'ong hŭryŏjida 온통 흐려지다

cloudburst p'ogu 폭우

cloudy hŭrin 흐린

clout *fig (influence)* yŏnghyangnyŏk 영향력

clown (*in circus*) ŏritkkwangdae 어릿광대; (*joker*) chaemiinnŭn saram 재미있는 사람; *pej* utkkinŭn nom 웃기는 놈

club *n (weapon)* konbong 곤봉; (*golf iron, organization*) k'ŭllŏp 클럽; ~*s* (*in cards*) k'ŭllŏp 클럽

clue shilmari 실마리; *I haven't a* ~ orimujung-iya 오리무중이야

clued-up F ...e taehae chal algo it-tta ...에 대해 잘 알고 있다

p'yeŏp'ada 폐업하다

clump *n* (*of earth*) hŭkttŏng-ŏri 흙덩어리; (*group*) tŏmbul 덤불
clumsiness kkolsanaum 꼴사나움; (*lack of tact*) sŏt'urŭm 서투름
clumsy *person* haengdong-i ŏsusŏnhan 행동이 어수선한; (*tactless*) nunch'i ŏmnŭn 눈치 없는
cluster 1 *n* (*of people*) muri 무리; (*of houses*) miltchip chiyŏk 밀집 지역 **2** *v/i* (*of people*) muri chit-tta 무리 짓다; (*of houses*) moyŏ it-tta 모여 있다
clutch 1 *n* MOT k'ŭllŏch'i 클러치 **2** *v/t* kkwak chaptta 꽉 잡다
♦**clutch at** chabŭryŏ tŭlda 잡으려 들다
Co. (= *Company*) hoesa 회사
c / o (= *care of*) ...sshidaek ...씨댁
coach 1 *n* (*trainer*) k'och'i 코치 **2** *v/t* karŭch'ida 가르치다
coagulate (*of blood*) ŭnggoshik'ida 응고시키다
coal sŏkt'an 석탄
coalition yŏnhap 연합
coalmine t'an-gwang 탄광
coarse kŏch'in 거친
coast *n* yŏnan 연안; *at the ~* yŏnane(sŏ) 연안에(서)
coastal yŏnanŭi 연안의
coastguard yŏnan kyŏngbidae 연안 경비대; (*person*) yŏnan kyŏngbiwŏn 연안 경비원
coastline haeansŏn 해안선
coat 1 *n* sang-ŭi 상의; (*over~*) oet'u 외투; (*of animal*) oep'i 외피; (*of paint etc*) tŏtch'il 덧칠 **2** *v/t* (*cover*) ssŭiuda 씌우다; (*of paint*) ch'irhada 칠하다
coathanger otkkŏri 옷걸이
coating ssŭium 씌움
coax kusŭllida 구슬리다
cobweb kŏmijul 거미줄
cocaine k'ok'ain 코카인
cock *n* (*chicken*) sut'ak 수탉; (*any male bird*) suk'ŏt 수컷
cockeyed *idea etc* ŏch'ŏguniŏmnŭn 어처구니없는
cockpit (*of plane*) chojongshil 조종실
cockroach pak'wi pŏlle 바퀴 벌레
cocktail k'akt'eil 칵테일
cocoa (*plant, drink*) k'ok'oa 코코아
coconut k'ok'oyaja yŏlmae 코코야자 열매
coconut palm k'ok'oyaja namu 코코야자 나무
COD (= *collect on delivery*) taegŭm sanghwan 대금 상환
coddle *sick person* momjorishik'ida 몸조리시키다; *child* kwaing pohohada 과잉 보호하다
code *n* k'odŭ 코드
coeducational namnyŏ konghagŭi 남녀 공학의
coerce kangyohada 강요하다
coexist kongjonhada 공존하다
coexistence kongjon 공존
coffee k'ŏp'i 커피; *two ~s please* k'ŏp'i tu jan chuseyo 커피 두 잔 주세요
coffee break kabyŏun hyushik shigan 가벼운 휴식 시간; **coffee maker** k'ŏp'i kkŭrinŭn kigu 커피 끓이는 기구; **coffee pot** k'ŏp'i p'ot'ŭ 커피 포트; **coffee shop** k'ŏp'i shyop 커피 숍; **coffee table** k'ŏp'iyong chagŭn t'aktcha 커피용 작은 탁자
coffin kwan 관
cog t'omnibak'wi 톱니바퀴
cognac k'onyak 코냑
cogwheel manmullinŭn t'omnibak'wi 맞물리는 톱니바퀴
cohabit tonggŏhada 동거하다
coherent chŏnghaptchŏgin 정합적인; (*in speech*) choriga sŏnŭn 조리가 서는
coil 1 *n* (*of rope*) sari 사리 **2** *v/t* kamtta 감다
coin *n* tongjŏn 동전
coincide tongshie irŏnada 동시에 일어나다
coincidence uyŏnŭi ilch'i 우연의 일치
coke F (*cocaine*) k'ok'ain 코카인
Coke® k'ok'a k'olla 코카 콜라
cold 1 *adj weather, day, room* ch'uun 추운; *air, water, character* ch'agaun 차가운; *I'm (feeling) ~* ch'uwŏyo 추워요; *it's ~* ch'uptta 춥다; *in ~ blood* naenghyŏrhage 냉혈하게; *get ~ feet fig* kŏmmŏktta 겁먹다 **2** *n* ch'uwi 추위; *I have a ~* kamgi kŏllyŏt-tta 감기 걸렸다

cold-blooded naenghyŏrŭi 냉혈의;
  fig naenghyŏrhan 냉혈한; **cold cuts**
  naeng-yuk 냉육; **cold sore** ipkkaŭi
  paltchin 입가의 발진
coleslaw k'osŭllo 코슬로
collaborate kongdong-ŭro irhada
  공동으로 일하다; (*with enemy*)
  hyŏmnyŏk'ada 협력하다; (*in
  research*) kongdong yŏn-guhada
  공동 연구하다; (*on book etc*)
  kongdong-ŭro chŏjak'ada 공동으로
  저작하다
collaboration hyŏpttong 협동; (*on
  book etc*) kongjŏ 공저
collaborator hyŏmnyŏktcha 협력자;
  (*with enemy*) ijŏk haeng-wija 이적
  행위자; (*in writing book etc*)
  kongdong chŏja 공동 저자
collapse munŏjida 무너지다; (*of
  person*) chwajŏrhada 좌절하다
collapsible chŏbŭl su innŭn 접을 수
  있는
collar kit 깃; (*for dog*) kae mok-kkŏri
  개 목걸이
collarbone swaegol 쇄골
colleague tongnyo 동료
collect 1 *v/t* person terirŏ kada 데리러
  가다; *tickets, cleaning etc* kajirŏ kada
  가지러 가다; (*as hobby*) sujip'ada
  수집하다; (*gather*) moŭda 모으다
  2 *v/i* (*gather together*) moida 모이다
  3 *adv*: **call ~** sushinin pudamŭro
  chŏnhwahada 수신인 부담으로
  전화하다
collect call sushinin pudamŭi
  chŏnhwa 수신인 부담의 전화
collected moŭn 모은; *person*
  ch'imch'ak'an 침착한; **~ works**
  chŏnjip 전집
collection sujip 수집; (*in church*)
  kibugŭm mojip 기부금 모집; (*in art*)
  sojangp'um 소장품; (*in fashion*)
  shinjakp'um 신작품
collective chipttanjŏgin 집단적인
collective bargaining tanch'e
  kyosŏp 단체 교섭
collector sujipkka 수집가
college tankkwa taehak 단과 대학
collide ch'ungdorhada 충돌하다
collision ch'ungdol 충돌
colloquial ilssang hoehwaŭi 일상

회화의
colon (*punctuation*) k'ollon 콜론;
  ANAT kyŏltchang 결장
colonel taeryŏng 대령
colonial *adj* shingminjiŭi 식민지의
colonize shingminjiro mandŭlda
  식민지로 만들다
colony shingminji 식민지
color 1 *n* saek-kkal 색깔; (*in cheeks*)
  ansaek 안색; *in ~ movie* k'allaro
  toen 칼라로 된; **~s** MIL kun-gi 군기
  2 *v/t* hair yŏmsaek'ada 염색하다
color-blind saengmaeng-ŭi 색맹의
colored *adj* person hŭginŭi 흑인의
color fast paraeji annŭn 바래지 않는
colorful saekch'aega p'ungbuhan
  색채가 풍부한; *fig* tach'aeroun
  다채로운
coloring ansaek 안색
color photograph k'alla sajin 칼라
  사진; **color scheme** saekch'aeŭi
  paehap 색채의 배합; **color TV** k'alla
  t'ellebijŏn 칼라 텔레비전
colt mang-aji 망아지
column (*of figures, people*) chul 줄;
  (*architectural*) kidung 기둥; (*of text*)
  tan 단; (*newspaper feature*) nan 난
columnist kigoga 기고가
coma honsu sangt'ae 혼수 상태
comb 1 *n* pit 빗 2 *v/t* pit-tta 빗다; *area*
  satssach'i twijida 샅샅이 뒤지다
combat 1 *n* chŏnt'u 전투 2 *v/t* ssauda
  싸우다
combination kyŏrhap 결합; (*of safe*)
  chamulssoeŭi pŏnho 자물쇠의 번호
combine 1 *v/t* kyŏrhap'ada 결합하다;
  ingredients hapch'ida 합치다 2 *v/i* (*of
  chemical elements*) kyŏrhap'ada
  결합하다
combine harvester k'ombain 콤바인
combustible t'agi shwiun 타기 쉬운
combustion yŏnso 연소
come (*toward speaker*) oda 오다;
  (*toward listener*) kada 가다; *you'll ~
  to like it* choahage toel kŏyeyo
  좋아하게 될 거예요; *how ~?* F
  ŏtchidoen iriya? 어찌된 일이야?
♦**come about** (*happen*) irŏnada
  일어나다
♦**come across** 1 *v/t* (*find*)
  palgyŏnhada 발견하다 2 *v/i* (*of idea,*

humor) ihaedoeda 이해되다; *she comes across as ...* künyŏnün ... chŏrŏm poinda 그녀는 ... 처럼 보인다

♦ **come along** (*come too*) kach'i oda 같이 오다; (*turn up*) nat'anada 나타나다; (*progress*) chinhaengdoeda 진행되다

♦ **come apart** punhaedoeda 분해되다; (*break*) pusŏjida 부서지다

♦ **come around** (*to s.o.'s home*) tŭllida 들리다; (*regain consciousness*) ŭishigŭl hoebok'ada 의식을 회복하다

♦ **come away** (*leave*) ttŏnada 떠나다; (*of button etc*) ttŏrŏjida 떨어지다

♦ **come back** toraoda 돌아오다; *it came back to me* tashi saenggangnassŏ 다시 생각났어

♦ **come by 1** *v/i* tŭllida 들리다 **2** *v/t* (*acquire*) ŏt-tta 얻다; (*find*) kuhada 구하다

♦ **come down** *v/i* naeryŏoda 내려오다; (*in price, amount etc*) ttŏrŏjida 떨어지다; (*of rain, snow*) naerida 내리다; *he came down the stairs* kŭnŭn kyedanŭl naeryŏwat-tta 그는 계단을 내려왔다

♦ **come for** (*collect*) kaijrŏ oda 가지러 오다; *person* terirŏ oda 데리러 오다; (*attack*) tŏpch'iryŏ tŭlda 덮치려 들다

♦ **come forward** (*present oneself*) ap'ŭro nasŏda 앞으로 나서다

♦ **come from** ...esŏ oda ...에서 오다

♦ **come in** tŭrŏoda 들어오다; *~!* tŭrŏooseyo! 들어오세요!

♦ **come in for**: *~ criticism* pip'anŭl pat-tta 비판을 받다

♦ **come in on**: *~ a deal* kŏrae ch'amgahada 거래에 참가하다

♦ **come off** (*of handle etc*) ttŏrŏjida 떨어지다

♦ **come on** (*progress*) chinhaengdoeda 진행된다; *~!* sŏdullŏ! 서둘러!; (*in disbelief*) sŏlma! 설마!

♦ **come out** (*of person, sun, results, new product*) naoda 나오다; (*of stain*) ppajida 빠지다

♦ **come to 1** *v/t place* ...e irŭda ...에 이르다; (*of hair, dress, water*) ...kkaji irŭda ...까지이르다; *that comes to $70* chŏgŏsŭn 70tallŏe irŭnda 저것은 70달러에 이른다 **2** *v/i* (*regain consciousness*) ŭishigŭl hoebok'ada 의식을 회복하다

♦ **come up** ollaoda 올라오다; (*of sun*) ttŏrŭda 떠오르다; *something has come up* musŭn iri saenggyŏssŏyo 무슨 일이 생겼어요

♦ **come up with** *new idea etc* saenggak'aenaeda 생각해내다

comeback: *make a ~* pok-kkwihada 복귀하다

comedian k'omidiŏn 코미디언; *pej* utkkinŭn nyŏsŏk 웃기는 녀석

comedown mollak 몰락

comedy hŭigŭk 희극

comet hyesŏng 혜성

comeuppance: *he'll get his ~* kŭnŭn ŭngborŭl padŭl kŏshida 그는 응보를 받을 것이다

comfort 1 *n* allak 안락; (*consolation*) wian 위안 **2** *v/t* wianhada 위안하다

comfortable *chair* p'yŏnhan 편안한; *house, room* allak'an 안락한; *be ~* (*of person*) p'yŏnhan 편한; (*financially*) suibi ch'ungbunhan 수입이 충분한

comic 1 *n* (*magazine*) manhwa chaptchi 만화 잡지 **2** *adj* hŭigŭgŭi 희극의

comical usŭkkwangsŭrŏun 우스꽝스러운

comic book manhwa ch'aek 만화 책

comics manhwaran 만화란

comma shwimp'yo 쉼표

command 1 *n* myŏngnyŏng 명령 **2** *v/t* myŏngnyŏnghada 명령하다

commander saryŏnggwan 사령관

commander-in-chief ch'oego saryŏnggwan 최고 사령관

commemorate kinyŏmhada 기념하다

commemoration: *in ~ of* ...ŭi kinyŏmŭro ...의 기념으로

commence 1 *v/i* shijakttoeda 시작되다 **2** *v/t* shijak'ada 시작하다

comment 1 *n* ŏn-gŭp 언급; *no ~* hal mal ŏpssŭmnida 할 말 없습니다 **2** *v/i* ŏn-gŭp'ada 언급하다

commentary haesŏl 해설

commentator haesŏltcha 해설자

commerce sang-ŏp 상업
commercial 1 adj sang-ŏbŭi 상업의; *success, failure* sang-ŏpssang-ŭi 상업상의 2 n (*advert*) kwanggo 광고
commercial break kwanggo pangsong 광고 방송
commercialize v/t sangp'umhwahada 상품화하다
commercial traveler oep'anwŏn 외판원
commiserate tongjŏnghada 동정하다
commission 1 n (*payment*) susuryo 수수료; (*job*) ŭiroe 의뢰; (*committee*) wiwŏnhoe 위원회 2 v/t (*for a job*) ŭiroehada 의뢰하다
commit *crime* pŏmhada 범하다; *money* halttanghada 할당하다; ~ *oneself* ŏnjirŭl chuda 언질을 주다
commitment (*in professional relationship*) chŏllyŏm 전렴; (*in personal relationship*) hŏnshin 헌신; (*responsibility*) ch'aegim 책임
committee wiwŏnhoe 위원회
commodity iryongp'um 일용품
common (*not rare*) pot'ong-ŭi 보통의; (*shared*) kongt'ong-ŭi 공통의; *in* ~ kongt'ong-ŭro 공통으로; *have sth in* ~ *with s.o.* muŏsŭl nuguwa kongt'ong-ŭro kajigo it-tta 무엇을 누구와 공통으로 가지고 있다
common law wife naeyŏnŭi ch'ŏ 내연의 처; commonplace adj p'yŏngbŏmhan 평범한; common sense sangshik 상식
commotion soran 소란
communal kongdong-ŭi 공동의
communicate 1 v/i (*be in contact*) yŏllagi it-tta 연락이 있다; (*make self understood*) ŭisarŭl sot'onghada 의사를 소통하다 2 v/t chŏndarhada 전달하다
communication ŭisa chŏndal 의사 전달
communications t'ongshin 통신
communications satellite t'ongshin wisŏng 통신 위성
communicative *person* marhagi choahanŭn 말하기 좋아하는
Communism Kongsanjuŭi 공산주의
Communist 1 adj Kongsanjuŭiŭi 공산주의의; (*of Communist party*) Kongsandang-ŭi 공산당의 2 n Kongsanjuŭija 공산주의자
Communist Party Kongsandang 공산당
community kongdongch'e 공동체; (*social group*) sahoe 사회
commute 1 v/i t'onggŭnhada 통근하다 2 v/t LAW kamhyŏnghada 감형하다
commuter t'onggŭnja 통근자
commuter traffic t'onggŭn kyot'ong 통근 교통
commuter train t'onggŭn yŏlch'a 통근 열차
compact 1 adj apch'ukttoen 압축된; *house* adamhan 아담한; MOT sohyŏng-ŭi 소형의 2 n MOT sohyŏngch'a 소형차
compact disc k'omp'aekt'ŭ tisŭk'ŭ 콤팩트 디스크
companion tongnyo 동료
companionship tongmuro sagwigi 동무로 사귀기
company COM hoesa 회사; (*companionship*) tongmuro sagwigi 동무로 사귀기; (*guests*) sonnim 손님; *keep ...* ~ ...wa / kwa kyojehada ...와/과 교제하다
company car hoesa ch'a 회사 차
company law hoesapŏp 회사법
comparable (*can be compared*) pigyodoel su innŭn 비교될 수 있는; (*similar*) yusahan 유사한
comparative 1 adj (*relative*) pigyojŏgin 비교적인; *study* pigyoŭi 비교의; GRAM pigyogŭbŭi 비교급의 2 n GRAM pigyogŭp 비교급
comparatively pigyojŏgŭro 비교적으로
compare 1 v/t pigyohada 비교하다; ~ *X with Y* Xŭl / rŭl Ywa / gwa pigyohada X을/를 Y와/과 비교하다; ~*d with* ...wa / kwa pigyohaesŏ ...와/과 비교해서 2 v/i pigyodoeda 비교되다
comparison pigyo 비교; *there's no* ~ pigyohal su ŏpssŏyo 비교할 수 없어요
compartment k'an 칸
compass nach'imban 나침반; (*for geometry*) k'ŏmp'ŏsŭ 컴퍼스

compassion tongjŏngshim 동정심
compassionate tongjŏnghanŭn
동정하는
compatibility sŏro mannŭn chŏngdo
서로 맞는 정도; (*of systems*)
chŏk'apssŏng 적합성; (*of software*)
hohwansŏng 호환성; (*of blood types*)
ilch'i yŏbu 일치 여부
compatible *people* sŏro mannŭn 서로
맞는; *blood types, lifestyles*
ilch'ihanŭn 일치하는; COMPUT
hohwanhal su innŭn 호환할 수 있는;
we're not ~ urinŭn sŏngkkyŏgi an
mat-tta 우리는 성격이 안 맞다
compel ŏktchiro ...shik'ida 억지로
...시키다; *be ~led to* hal su ŏpsshi
... hada 할 수 없이 ... 하다
compelling *argument* sŏlttŭngnyŏk
innŭn 설득력 있는; *movie, book*
hŭngmirŭl todunŭn 흥미를 돋우는
compensate 1 *v/t* (*with money*)
paesanghada 배상하다 **2** *v/i*: *~ for*
...ŭl/rŭl posanghada ...을/를
보상하다
compensation (*money*) paesang
배상; (*reward*) poch'ung 보충;
(*comfort*) posang 보상
compete kyŏngjaenghada 경쟁하다;
(*take part*) ch'ultchŏnhada 출전하다;
~ for ...ŭl/rŭl wihae
kyŏngjaenghada ...을/를 위해
경쟁하다
competence, competency
nŭngnyŏk 능력
competent *person* nŭngnyŏk innŭn
능력 있는; *work* chungbunhan
충분한; *I'm not ~ to judge* nanŭn
p'andanhal chagyŏgi ŏptta 나는
판단할 자격이 없다
competition kyŏngjaeng 경쟁;
(*competitors*) kyŏngjaengja 경쟁자;
*the government wants to en-
courage ~* chŏngbunŭn
kyŏngjaeng-ŭl puch'uk'igo
ship'ŏhanda 정부는 경쟁을 부추기고
싶어한다
competitive kyŏngjaengjŏgin
경쟁적인; *price, offer*
kyŏngjaengnyŏk innŭn 경쟁력 있는
competitor (*in contest*) kyŏngjaengja
경쟁자; COM kyŏngjaeng sangdae

compile p'yŏnjip'ada 편집하다
complacency chagi manjok 자기
만족
complacent chagi manjoktchŏgin
자기 만족적인
complain *v/i* pulp'yŏnghada
불평하다; *~ of* MED ...ŭl/rŭl
hosohada ...을/를 호소하다
complaint pulp'yŏng 불평; MED
pyŏng 병
complement *v/t* powanhada
보완하다; *they ~ each other*
kŭdŭrŭn sŏro powanhanda 그들은
서로 보완한다
complementary powanhanŭn
보완하는
complete 1 *adj* (*utter*) wanjŏnhan
완전한; (*whole, entire*) chŏnbuŭi
전부의; (*finished*) wansŏngdoen
완성된 **2** *v/t task, building etc*
wansŏnghada 완성하다; *course*
wanjŏnhi mach'ida 완전히 마치다;
form ch'aeuda 채우다
completely wanjŏnhi 완전히
completion wansŏng 완성
complex 1 *adj* poktchap'an 복잡한
2 *n* PSYCH k'omp'ŭllekssŭ 콤플렉스;
(*of buildings*) chip'apch'e 집합체
complexion (*facial*) ansaek 안색
compliance ŭngnak 응낙
complicate poktchap'age hada
복잡하게 하다
complicated poktchap'an 복잡한
complication poktchap'age hanŭn
kŏt 복잡하게 하는 것; *~s* MED hap-
ppyŏngtchŭng 합병증
compliment 1 *n* ch'ansa 찬사 **2** *v/t*
ch'ansahada 찬사하다
complimentary ch'ansahanŭn
찬사하는; (*free*) muryoŭi 무료의
compliments slip kŭnjŏng tchoktchi
근정 쪽지
comply ŭnghada 응하다; *~ with* ...e
ŭnghada ...에 응하다
component (*constituent part*) kusŏng
yoso 구성 요소; (*of machine etc*)
pup'um 부품
compose *v/t* kusŏnghada 구성하다;
MUS chak-kkok'ada 작곡하다; *be ~d
of* ...(ŭ)ro kusŏngdoeŏ it-tta

...(으)로 구성되어 있다; ~ *oneself*
maŭmŭl karaanch'ida 마음을
가라앉히다
composed (*calm*) ch'imch'ak'an
침착한
composer MUS chak-kkok-kka
작곡가
composition (*make-up*) kusŏng 구성;
MUS chak-kkok 작곡; (*essay*)
changmun 작문
composure ch'imch'ak 침착
compound *n* CHEM hapssŏngmul
합성물
compound interest pongni 복리
comprehend (*understand*) ihaehada
이해하다
comprehension ihae 이해
comprehensive p'ogwaltchŏgin
포괄적인
comprehensive insurance
chonghap pohŏm 종합 보험
compress 1 *n* MED sŭpp'o 습포 **2** *v/t*
air, gas, file apch'uk'ada 압축하다;
information yoyak'ada 요약하다
comprise kusŏngdoeda 구성되다; *be*
~d of ...(ŭ)ro kusŏngdoeŏ it-tta
...(으)로 구성되어 있다
compromise 1 *n* t'ahyŏp 타협 **2** *v/i*
t'ahyŏp'ada 타협하다 **3** *v/t principles*
t'ahyŏpsshik'ida 타협시키다;
(*damage: reputation etc*)
sonsangshik'ida 손상시키다; *~ one-*
self chagiŭi ch'emyŏnŭl
sonsangshik'ida 자기의 체면을
손상시키다
compulsion PSYCH kangbak
kwannyŏm 강박 관념
compulsive *behavior* kangbak
kwannyŏme sarojap'in 강박 관념에
사로잡힌; *reading* murihanŭn
무리하는
compulsory ŭimujŏgin 의무적인; *~*
education ŭimu kyoyuk 의무 교육
computer k'ŏmp'yut'ŏ 컴퓨터; *put*
sth on ~ muŏsŭl k'ŏmp'yut'ŏe
imnyŏksshik'yŏ not'a 무엇을
컴퓨터에 입력시켜 놓다
computer-controlled k'ŏmp'yut'ŏro
t'ongjedoenŭn 컴퓨터로 통제되는
computer game k'ŏmp'yut'ŏ keim
컴퓨터 게임

computerize chŏnsanhwahada
전산화하다
computer literate k'ŏmp'yut'ŏrŭl
tarul chul anŭn 컴퓨터를 다룰 줄
아는; **computer science**
k'ŏmp'yut'ŏ kwahak 컴퓨터 과학;
computer scientist k'ŏmp'yut'ŏ
kwahaktcha 컴퓨터 과학자
computing k'ŏmp'yut'ŏ sayong
컴퓨터 사용
comrade (*friend*) tongnyo 동료; POL
tongji 동지
comradeship tongnyo kwan-gye 동료
관계
con F **1** *n* (*trick*) sagi 사기 **2** *v/t* sagi
ch'ida 사기 치다
conceal kamch'uda 감추다
concede *v/t* (*admit*) injŏnghada
인정하다
conceit chaman 자만
conceited chamanhanŭn 자만하는
conceivable saenggak'al su innŭn
생각할 수 있는
conceive *v/i* (*of woman*) imshinhada
임신하다; *~ of* (*imagine*) ...ŭl/rŭl
sangsanghada ...을/를 상상하다
concentrate 1 *v/i* chiptchunghada
집중하다; (*on task*) chŏnnyŏmhada
전념하다 **2** *v/t one's attention,*
energies chiptchungshik'ida
집중시키다
concentrated *juice etc*
nongch'ukttoen 농축된
concentration chiptchung 집중
concept kaenyŏm 개념
conception (*of child*) imshin 임신
concern 1 *n* (*anxiety*) kŏktchŏng
걱정; (*care*) yŏmnyŏ 염려; (*business*)
kwanshimsa 관심사; (*company*)
hoesa 회사 **2** *v/t* (*involve*) ...e kwan-
gyehada ...에 관계하다; (*worry*)
kŏktchŏnghada 걱정하다; *~ oneself*
with ...e kwanyŏhada ...에 관여하다
concerned (*anxious*)
kŏktchŏnghanŭn 걱정하는; (*caring*)
yŏmnyŏhanŭn 염려하는; (*involved*)
kwan-gyedoenŭn 관계되는; *as far*
as I'm ~ naega pogienŭn 내가
보기에는
concerning *prep* ...e kwanhayŏ ...에
관하여

concert yŏnjuhoe 연주회
concerted (*joint*) habŭidoen 합의된
concertmaster susŏk paiollinisŭt'ŭ
수석 바이올리니스트
concerto hyŏptchugok 협주곡
concession (*giving in*) yangbo 양보
conciliatory hoeyujŏgin 회유적인
concise kan-gyŏrhan 간결한
conclude 1 *v/t* (*deduce*) kyŏllonŭl
naerida 결론을 내리다; (*end*)
kkŭnnaeda 끝내다; **~ X from Y**
Y(ŭ)robut'ŏ Xranŭn kyŏllonŭl
naerida Y(으)로부터 X라는 결론을
내리다 **2** *v/i* kkŭnnada 끝나다
conclusion (*deduction*) kyŏllon 결론;
(*end*) kyŏlmal 결말; **in ~** kkŭt'ŭro
끝으로
conclusive kyŏltchŏngjŏgin 결정적인
concoct *meal, drink* sokkŏsŏ
mandŭlda 섞어서 만들다; *excuse,
story* yŏkkŏnaeda 엮어내다
concoction (*food, drink*)
honhammul 혼합물
concrete[1] *adj* (*not abstract*)
kuch'ejŏgin 구체적인
concrete[2] *n* k'onk'ŭrit'ŭ 콘크리트
concur *v/i* tong-ŭihada 동의하다
concussion noejint'ang 뇌진탕
condemn *action* pinanhada 비난하다;
building p'yegi ch'ŏbunŭl sŏn-
gohada 폐기 처분을 선고하다; (*fate*)
unmyŏng chiuda 운명 지우다
condemnation (*of action*) pinan 비난
condensation ŭngch'uk 응축
condense 1 *v/t* (*shorten*) apch'uk'ada
압축하다 **2** *v/i* (*of steam*)
ŭngch'uk'ada 응축하다
condensed milk yŏnyu 연유
condescend: *he ~ed to speak to
me* kŭnŭn hwangsonghagedo na-ege
marŭl kŏrŏssŏ 그가 황송하게도 내게
말을 걸었어
condescending kyŏmsonhan
ch'ŏk'anŭn 겸손한 척하는
condition 1 *n* (*state*) sangt'ae 상태;
(*of health*) kŏn-gang sangt'ae 건강
상태; MED chirhwan 질환;
(*requirement, term*) chokkŏn 조건;
~s (*circumstances*) hwan-gyŏng
환경; **on ~ that** …ranŭn
chokkŏnŭro …라는 조건으로 **2** *v/t*

PSYCH chokkŏn pansarŭl irŭk'ige
hada 조건 반사를 일으키게 하다
conditional 1 *adj acceptance*
chokkŏnbuŭi 조건부의 **2** *n* GRAM
chokkŏnppŏp 조건법
conditioner (*for hair, fabric*)
k'ondishyŏnŏ 콘디셔너
conditioning PSYCH chŏgŭngshik'igi
적응시키기
condo k'ondo 콘도
condolences aedo 애도
condom k'ondom 콘돔
condominium k'ondominium
콘도미니움
condone *actions* yongsŏhada
용서하다
conducive: **~ to** …e toumi toenŭn
…에 도움이 되는
conduct 1 *n* (*behavior*) haeng-wi
행위 **2** *v/t* (*carry out*) suhaenghada
수행하다; ELEC chŏndohada
전도하다; MUS chihwihada 지휘하다;
~ oneself ch'ŏshinhada 처신하다
conducted tour kwan-gwang annae
관광 안내
conductor MUS chihwija 지휘자; (*on
train*) ch'ajang 차장
cone (*in geometry*) wŏnppul 원뿔;
(*for ice cream*) k'on 콘; (*of pine tree*)
solppang-ul solbang울; (*on highway*)
wŏnppul 원뿔
confectioner (*shop*) chegwajŏm
제과점
confectioners' sugar chŏngje
sŏlt'ang 정제 설탕
confectionery (*candy*) kwajaryu
과자류
confederation yŏnhap 연합
confer 1 *v/t* (*bestow*) suyŏhada
수여하다 **2** *v/i* (*discuss*) hyŏbŭihada
협의하다
conference hoeŭi 회의
conference room hoeŭishil 회의실
confess 1 *v/t* *sin, guilt* kobaek'ada
고백하다; (*to police*) chabaek'ada
자백하다; REL kohaehada 고해하다; **I
~ I don't know** morŭndanŭn kŏsŭl
kobaek'amnida 모른다는 것을
고백합니다 **2** *v/i* kobaek'ada
고백하다; (*to police*) chabaek'ada
자백하다; REL kohaehada 고해하다;

~ to a weakness for sth muŏse yak'adanŭn kŏsŭl shilt'ohada 무엇에 약하다는 것을 실토하다

confession kobaek 고백; (*to police*) chabaek 자백; REL kohae 고해

confessional REL kohaeshil 고해실

confessor REL kohae shinbu 고해 신부

confide 1 *v/t* t'ŏrŏnot'a 털어놓다 **2** *v/i*: *~ in s.o.* nuguege pimirŭl t'ŏrŏnot'a 누구에게 비밀을 털어놓다

confidence (*assurance*) hwaksshin 확신; (*trust*) shilloe 신뢰; (*secret*) pimil 비밀; *in ~* pimillo 비밀로

confident (*self-assured*) chashinhanŭn 자신하는; (*convinced*) hwaksshinhanŭn 확신하는

confidential kŭkppiŭi 극비의

confine (*imprison*) kamgŭmhada 감금하다; (*restrict*) chehanhada 제한하다; *be ~d to one's bed* ara nuwŏ it-tta 앓아 누워 있다

confined *space* chehandoen 제한된

confinement (*imprisonment*) kamgŭm 감금; MED haesan 해산

confirm *v/t* hwaginhada 확인하다; *theory, statement, fears* hwaktchŭnghada 확증하다

confirmation hwagin 확인; (*of theory, statement, fears*) hwaktchŭng 확증

confirmed (*inveterate*) kudŏbŏrin 굳어버린

confiscate apssuhada 압수하다

conflict 1 *n* (*disagreement*) taerip 대립; (*clash*) ch'ungdol 충돌; (*war*) t'ujaeng 투쟁 **2** *v/i* (*clash*) ch'ungdorhada 충돌하다

conform sunŭnghada 순응하다; (*of product*) ttarŭda 따르다; *~ to government standards* chŏngbu kyugyŏge ttarŭda 정부 규격에 따르다

conformist *n* chunsuja 준수자

confront (*face*) majuhada 마주하다; (*tackle*) matssŏda 맞서다

confrontation taegyŏl 대결

Confucianism Yugyo 유교

Confucius Kongja 공자

confuse (*muddle*) hollanshik'ida 혼란시키다; (*one thing with another*) hondonghada 혼동하다; *~ X with Y* Xŭl/rŭl Ywa/gwa hondonghada X을/를 Y와/과 혼동하다

confused hollansŭrŏun 혼란스러운

confusing hollanshik'inŭn 혼란시키는

confusion hollan 혼란

congeal ŭnggohada 응고하다

congenial maŭme mannŭn 마음에 맞는

congenital MED sŏnch'ŏnjŏgin 선천적인

congested *roads* honjap'an 혼잡한

congestion (*on roads*) honjap 혼잡; (*in chest*) mak'im 막힘; *traffic ~* kyot'ong honjap 교통 혼잡

conglomerate chaebŏl 재벌

congratulate ch'uk'ahada 축하하다

congratulations ch'uk'a 축하; *~ on* …ŭl/rŭl ch'uk'ahamnida …을/를 축하합니다

congregate (*gather*) moida 모이다

congregation REL chip'oe 집회

congress (*conference*) hoeŭi 회의; *Congress* (*of US*) Kuk'oe 국회

congressional kuk'oeŭi 국회의

congressman kuk'oe ŭiwŏn 국회 위원

congresswoman yŏja kuk'oe ŭiwŏn 여자 국회 의원

conifer ch'imnyŏpssu 침엽수

conjecture *n* (*speculation*) ch'uch'ŭk 추측

conjugate *v/t* GRAM hwaryongshik'ida 활용시키다

conjunction GRAM chŏpssoksa 접속사; *in ~ with* …wa/kwa hamkke …와/과 함께

conjunctivitis kyŏlmangnyŏm 결막염

♦ **conjure up** (*produce*) nun kkamtchak'al saie mandŭlda 눈 깜짝할 사이에 만들다; (*evoke*) pullŏ irŭk'ida 불러 일으키다

conjurer, conjuror masulsa 마술사

conjuring tricks masul 마술

con man sagikkun 사기꾼

connect (*join*), TELEC yŏn-gyŏrhada 연결하다; (*link*) kwallyŏnshik'ida 관련시키다; (*to power supply*) chŏpssoksshik'ida 접속시키다

connected: *be well-~* chŏun yŏntchuri innŭn 좋은 연줄이 있는; *be ~ with* …wa/kwa kwallyŏndoeda …와/과 관련되다

connecting flight yŏn-gyŏlp'yŏn
연결편

connection (*in wiring*) yŏn-gyŏl 연결;
(*link*) kwallyŏn 관련; (*when
traveling*) yŏn-gyŏlp'yŏn 연결편;
(*personal contact*) yŏntchul 연출; *in
~ with* …wa/kwa kwallyŏnhayŏ
…와/과 관련하여

connoisseur kamjŏngga 감정가

conquer chŏngbok'ada 정복하다; *fear
etc* kŭkppok'ada 극복하다

conqueror chŏngboktcha 정복자

conquest (*of territory*) chŏngbok
정복

conscience yangshim 양심; *a guilty
~* yangshimŭi kach'aek 양심의 가책;
it has been on my ~ kŭgŏshi
maŭme kŏllyŏssŏyo 그것이 마음에
걸렸어요

conscientious yangshimjŏgin
양심적인

conscientious objector
yangshimtchŏk pyŏngnyŏk kŏbuja
양심적 병역 거부자

conscious *adj* (*aware*) chigagi innŭn
지각이 있는; (*deliberate*)
ŭishiktchŏgin 의식적인; MED ŭishigi
innŭn 의식이 있는; *be ~ of* …ŭl/rŭl
algo it-tta …을/를 알고 있다

consciousness (*awareness*) chigak
지각; MED ŭishik 의식; *lose/regain
~* ŭishigŭl ilt'a/hoebok'ada 의식을
잃다/회복하다

consecutive yŏnsoktchŏgin 연속적인

consensus ilch'i 일치

consent 1 *n* tong-ŭi 동의 **2** *v/i* tong-
ŭihada 동의하다

consequence (*result*) kyŏlkwa 결과

consequently (*therefore*) ttarasŏ
따라서

conservation (*preservation*) pojon
보존

conservationist *n* chawŏn pohoronja
자원 보호론자

conservative *adj* (*conventional*)
posujŏgin 보수적인; *clothes* susuhan
수수한; *estimate* chuljabŭn 줄잡은

conservatory (*for plants*) onshil
온실; MUS ŭmak hak-kkyo 음악 학교

conserve 1 *n* (*jam*) chaem 쨈 **2** *v/t*

energy, strength pojonhada 보존하다

consider (*regard*) yŏgida 여기다;
(*show regard for*) koryŏhada
고려하다; (*think about*)
saenggak'ada 생각하다; *it is ~ed to
be* …rago saenggakttoenda …라고
생각된다

considerable sangdanghan 상당한

considerably sangdanghi 상당히

considerate tongjŏngshimi manŭn
동정심이 많은

consideration (*thought*) suk-kko
숙고; (*thoughtfulness, concern*)
koryŏ 고려; (*factor*) koryŏhal sahang
고려할 사항; *take X into ~* Xŭl/rŭl
koryŏhada X을/를 고려하다

consignment COM wit'ak 위탁

♦**consist of** …(ŭ)ro iruŏjyŏ it-tta
…(으)로 이루어져 있다

consistency (*texture*) nongdo 농도;
(*of attitude, behavior*) ilgwansŏng
일관성

consistent *attitude, behavior*
ilgwansŏng innŭn 일관성 있는

consolation wiro 위로

console *v/t* wirohada 위로하다

consonant *n* GRAM chaŭm 자음

consortium ch'agwandan 차관단

conspicuous tudŭrŏjin 두드러진

conspiracy ŭmmo 음모

conspire ŭmmorŭl kkumida 음모를
꾸미다

constant (*continuous*)
kyesokttoenŭn 계속되는

consternation sŏmttŭk nollam 섬뜩
놀람

constipated pyŏnbie kŏllin 변비에
걸린

constipation pyŏnbi 변비

constituent *n* (*component*) kusŏng
yoso 구성 요소

constitute (*account for*) kusŏnghada
구성하다; (*represent*) nat'anaeda
나타내다

constitution POL hŏnppŏp 헌법; (*of
person*) ch'ejil 체질

constitutional *adj* POL
hŏnppŏpssang-ŭi 헌법상의

Constitution Day Chaehŏnjŏl 재헌절

constraint (*restriction*) ŏktche 억제

construct *v/t building etc* seuda

세우다
construction (*of building etc*) kŏnsŏl
건설; (*building etc*) kŏnch'ungmul
건축물; (*trade*) kŏnsŏrŏp 건설업;
under ~ kongsa chung 공사 중
construction industry kŏnsŏrŏp
건설업; **construction site**
kongsajang 공사장; **construction
worker** kongsajang inbu 공사장
인부
constructive kŏnsŏltchŏgin 건설적인
consul yŏngsa 영사
consulate yŏngsagwan 영사관
consult (*seek the advice of*) …ŭi
ŭigyŏnŭl mut-tta …의 의견을 묻다;
dictionary ch'amgohada 참고하다
consultancy (*company*)
k'ŏnssŏlt'ŏnt'ŭŏp 컨설턴트업;
(*advice*) sangdam 상담
consultant (*adviser*) k'ŏnssŏlt'ŏnt'ŭ
컨설턴트
consultation sang-ŭi 상의
consume (*eat*) mŏgŏbŏrida
먹어버리다; (*drink*) mashyŏbŏrida
마셔버리다; (*use*) ssŏbŏrida 써버리다
consumer (*purchaser*) sobija 소비자
consumer confidence kumae ŭiji
구매 의지; **consumer goods**
sobip'um 소비품; **consumer society** sobija sahoe 소비자 사회
consumption sobi 소비
contact 1 *n* (*person*) chunggyein
중계인; (*communication*) yŏllak
연락; (*social*) kyoje 교제; (*by radio*)
kyoshin 교신; (*physical*) chŏpch'ok
접촉; *keep in ~ with X* Xwa / gwa
yŏllagŭl chugo pat-tta X와 / 과 연락을
주고 받다 **2** *v/t* yŏllak'ada 연락하다;
(*by radio*) kyoshinhada 교신하다
contact lens k'ont'aekt'ŭrenjŭ
콘택트렌즈
contact number yŏllakch'ŏ 연락처
contagious *illness, laughter*
chŏnyŏmdoenŭn 전염되는
contain tamkko it-tta 담고 있다;
tears, laughter ch'amtta 참다; *flood*
maktta 막다; *it ~ed my camera* nae
k'ameraga tŭrŏ issŏt-tta 내 카메라가
들어 있었다; *~ oneself* ch'amtta
참다
container (*recipient*) yonggi 용기;

COM k'ŏnt'einŏ 컨테이너
container ship k'ŏnt'einŏsŏn
컨테이너선
contaminate oyŏmshik'ida
오염시키다
contamination oyŏm 오염
contemplate *v/t* (*look at*) ŭngshihada
응시하다; (*think about*) suk-kkohada
숙고하다
contemporary 1 *adj* hyŏndaeŭi
현대의 **2** *n* tongnyŏnbaeŭi saram
동년배의 사람; (*at school*)
tonggisaeng 동기생
contempt kyŏngmyŏl 경멸; *be beneath ~* kyŏngmyŏrhal kach'ijoch'a
ŏmnŭn 경멸할 가치조차 없는
contemptible kyŏngmyŏrhal manhan
경멸할 만한
contemptuous yatchababonŭn
얕잡아보는
contend: ~ for …ŭl / rŭl wihae
tat'uda …을 / 를 위해 다투다; *~ with*
ch'ŏrihada 처리하다
contender (*in sport, competition*)
kyŏngjaengja 경쟁자; (*against
champion*) tojŏnja 도전자
content¹ *n* naeyong 내용
content² **1** *adj* manjok'anŭn 만족하는
2 *v/t:* **~ oneself with** …(ŭ)ro
manjok'ada …(으)로 만족하다
contented majok'ago innŭn 만족하고
있는
contention (*assertion*) chujang 주장;
be in ~ for …ŭl / rŭl wihae
kyŏngjaenghada …을 / 를 위해
경쟁하다
contentment manjok 만족
contents naeyong 내용
contest¹ (*competition*) taehoe 대회;
(*struggle, for power*) kyŏngjaeng
경쟁
contest² *leadership etc* kyŏruda
겨루다; (*oppose*) pandaehada
반대하다
contestant kyŏngjaengja 경쟁자
context munmaek 문맥; *look at X in
~ / out of ~* Xŭl / rŭl munmaege
match'wŏ / munmaegŭl pŏsŏna poda
X을 / 를 문맥에 맞춰 / 문맥을 벗어나
보다
continent *n* taeryuk 대륙

continental taeryugŭi 대륙의
contingency ttŭkppakkŭi il 뜻밖의 일
continual kyesoktchŏgin 계속적인
continuation kyesok 계속
continue 1 v/t kyesok'ada 계속하다; *to be ~d* taŭme kyesok 다음에 계속 **2** v/i kyesokttoeda 계속되다
continuity yŏnsoksŏng 연속성
continuous kkŭnimŏmnŭn 끊임없는
contort *face* tchinggŭrida 찡그리다; *body* pit'ŭlda 비틀다
contour yun-gwak 윤곽
contraception p'iim 피임
contraceptive n (*device*) p'iim kigu 피임 기구; (*pill*) p'iimyak 피임약
contract[1] n kyeyak 계약
contract[1] **1** v/i (*shrink*) such'uk'ada 수축하다 **2** v/t *illness* ...e kŏllida ...에 걸리다
contractor kyeyaktcha 계약자
contractual kyeyakssang-ŭi 계약상의
contradict *statement* puinhada 부인하다; *person* panbak'ada 반박하다
contradiction mosun 모순
contradictory *account* mosundoen 모순된
contraption F sae koanmul 새 고안물
contrary[1] **1** adj pandaeŭi 반대의; *~ to* ...e panhayŏ ...에 반하여 **2** n: *on the ~* pandaero 반대로
contrary[2] (*perverse*) pandaeroman hanŭn 반대로만 하는
contrast 1 n taejo 대조 **2** v/t taejohada 대조하다 **3** v/i taejodoeda 대조되다
contrasting taejojŏgin 대조적인
contravene wibanhada 위반하다
contribute 1 v/i (*with money, material*) kibuhada 기부하다; (*with time*) konghŏnhada 공헌하다; (*to magazine, paper*) kigohada 기고하다; (*to discussion*) kiyŏhada 기여하다; *~ to* (*help to cause*) ...ŭihan wŏnini toeda ...의한 원인이 되다 **2** v/t *money* kibuhada 기부하다
contribution (*money*) kibu 기부; (*of time, effort*) konghŏn 공헌; (*to discussion*) kiyŏ 기여; (*to magazine*) kigo 기고

contributor (*of money*) kibuja 기부자; (*to magazine*) kigoga 기고가
contrive yongk'e haenaeda 용케 해내다
control 1 n (*of country, organization*) chibae 지배; (*of emotions*) cheŏ 제어; (*of ball*) cheguryŏk 제구력; *be in ~ of* ...ŭl/rŭl chibaehada ...을/를 지배하다; *bring X under ~* Xŭl/rŭl cheŏhada X을/를 제어하다; *get out of ~* cheŏhal su ŏpkke toeda 제어할 수 없게 되다; *lose ~ of* ...ŭl/rŭl cheŏhal su ŏpkke toeda ...을/를 제어할 수 없게 되다; *lose ~ of oneself* chashinŭl ŏktchehal su ŏpkke toeda 자신을 억제할 수 없게 되다; *the situation is under ~* sanghwang-ŭn t'ongjedoeŏt-tta 상황은 통제되었다; *circumstances beyond our ~* uriga t'ongjehal su ŏmnŭn sanghwang-ida 우리가 통제할 수 없는 상황이다; *~s* (*of aircraft, vehicle*) chojong changch'i 조종 장치; (*restrictions*) chehan 제한 **2** v/t (*govern*) chibaehada 지배하다; (*restrict*) chehanhada 제한하다; (*regulate*) t'ongjehada 통제하다; *~ oneself* chajehada 자제하다
control center t'ongjeshil 통제실
control freak F kwŏllyŏk chungdoktcha 권력 중독자
controlled substance kyuje yangmul 규제 약물
controlling interest FIN chibaejŏk ikkwŏn 지배적 이권
control panel cheŏban 제어반
control tower kwanjet'ap 관제탑
controversial nonjaeng-ŭl irŭk'inŭn 논쟁을 일으키는
controversy nonjaeng 논쟁
convalesce kŏn-gang-ŭl hoebok'ada 건강을 회복하다
convalescence hoebok-kki 회복기
convene v/t sojip'ada 소집하다
convenience (*of location, time*) p'yŏlli 편리; *at your/my ~* tangshini/naega p'yŏllihan ttae 당신이/내가 편리한 때에; *all (modern) ~s* modŭn hyŏndaejŏgin p'yŏnŭi shisŏl 모든 현대적인 편의 시설

convenience food insŭt'ŏnt'ŭ shikp'um 인스턴트 식품
convenience store iryong chap'wa shikp'umjŏm 일용 잡화 식품점
convenient p'yŏllihan 편리한
convent sudowŏn 수도원
convention (*tradition*) kwansŭp 관습; (*conference*) taehoe 대회
conventional chŏnt'ongjŏgin 전통적인
convention center k'ŏnbenshyŏn sent'ŏ 컨벤션 센터
conventioneer taehoe ch'amgaja 대회 참가자
conversant: *be ~ with* ...ŭl/rŭl chal anŭn ...을/를 잘 아는
conversation taehwa 대화
conversational hoehwaŭi 회화의
converse *n* (*opposite*) pandae 반대
conversely pandaero 반대로
conversion chŏnhwan 전환; (*of unit of measurement*) hwansan 환산; (*of building*) kaejo 개조
conversion table hwansanp'yo 환산표
convert 1 *n* chŏnhyang 전향 **2** *v/t* pyŏnhage hada 변하게 하다; *unit of measurement* hwansanhada 환산하다; *building* kaejohada 개조하다; *person* chŏnhyangshik'ida 전향시키다
convertible *n* (*car*) kŏnbŏt'ŏbŭl 컨버터블
convey (*transmit*) chŏndarhada 전달하다; (*carry*) unbanhada 운반하다
conveyor belt k'ŏnbeiŏ pelt'ŭ 컨베이어 벨트
convict 1 *n* kigyŏlssu 기결수 **2** *v/t* LAW yujoerŭl sŏn-gohada 유죄를 선고하다; *~ X of Y* Xege Yŭi p'an-gyŏrŭl naerida X에게 Y의 판결을 내리다
conviction LAW yujoeŭi p'an-gyŏl 유죄의 판결; (*belief*) shinnyŏm 신념
convince hwacksshinshik'ida 확신시키다
convincing sŏltŭngnyŏk innŭn 설득력 있는
convivial (*friendly*) k'waehwarhan 쾌활한

convoy (*of ships*) hosonghada 호송하다; (*of vehicles*) howihada 호위하다
convulsion MED kyŏngnyŏn 경련
cook 1 *n* yorisa 요리사 **2** *v/t* yorihada 요리하다; *a ~ed meal* yoridoen shikssa 요리된 식사 **3** *v/i* yorihada 요리하다
cookbook yorich'aek 요리책
cookery yorippŏp 요리법
cookie k'uk'i 쿠키
cooking (*food*) yori 요리
cool 1 *n* F *keep one's ~* ch'imch'ak'ada 침착하다; *lose one's ~* hŭngbunhada 흥분하다 **2** *adj weather, breeze* shiwŏnhan 시원한; *drink* ch'agaun 차가운; (*calm*) naengjŏnghan 냉정한; (*unfriendly*) naengdamhan 냉담한; F (*great*) kimak'ige kŭnsahan 기막히게 근사한 **3** *v/i* (*of food*) shiktta 식다; (*of tempers, interest*) karaantta 가라앉다 **4** *v/t* F: *~ it* ch'imch'ak'aseyo 침착하세요
♦ **cool down 1** *v/i* (*of food, person*) shiktta 식다; (*of weather*) sŏnŭrhaejida 서늘해지다; (*of tempers*) karaantta 가라앉다 **2** *v/t food* shik'ida 식히다; *fig* karaanch'ida 가라앉히다
cooperate hyŏmnyŏk'ada 협력하다
cooperation hyŏmnyŏk 협력
cooperative 1 *n* COM hyŏpttong chohap 협동 조합 **2** *adj* COM hyŏpttong-ŭi 협동의; (*helpful*) hyŏmnyŏktchŏgin 협력적인
coordinate *activities* chojŏng chohwashik'ida 조정 조화시키다
coordination (*of activities*) chojŏng chohwa 조정 조화; (*of body*) undong shingyŏng 운동 신경
cop F kyŏngch'al 경찰
cope ch'ŏrihada 처리하다; *~ with* ...ŭl/rŭl ch'ŏrihada ...을/를 처리하다
copier (*machine*) pokssagi 복사기
copilot pujojongsa 부조종사
copious *amount* p'ungbuhan 풍부한; *notes* chasehan 자세한
copper *n* (*metal*) kuri 구리
copy 1 *n* (*duplicate, photocopy*)

poksssa 복사; (*imitation*) mobang
모방; (*of book*) pu 부; (*of record,
CD*) chang 장; (*written material*) kisa
kŏri 기사 거리; (*in advertisement*)
kwanggo munan 광고 문안; **make a
~ of a file** COMPUT p'airŭl
pokssahada 파일을 복사하다 **2** *v/t*
(*imitate*) mobanghada 모방하다;
(*duplicate, photocopy*) pokssahada
복사하다; (*in writing*) pekkyŏ ssŭda
베껴 쓰다; (*in order to cheat*) mollae
pekkida 몰래 베끼다

copy cat F mobanghanŭn saram
모방하는 사람; **copycat crime**
mobang pŏmjoe 모방 범죄; **copyright** *n* chŏjak-kkwŏn 저작권; **copy-
writer** k'ap'irait'ŏ 카피라이터

coral (*on seabed*) sanho 산호

cord (*string*) nokkŭn 노끈; (*cable*)
chŏnsŏn 전선

cordial *adj* ch'ungshimŭrobut'ŏŭi
충심으로부터의

cordless phone musŏn chŏnhwagi
무선 전화기

cordon pisang kyŏnggyesŏn 비상
경계선

♦**cordon off** pisang kyŏnggyesŏnŭl
ch'ida 비상 경계선을 치다

cords (*pants*) kolden paji 골덴 바지

corduroy kolden 골덴

core 1 *n* (*of fruit*) sok 속; (*of
problem*) koltcha 골자; (*of
organization, party*) haekssim 핵심
2 *adj* issue haekssimjŏgin 핵심적인

cork (*in bottle*) k'orŭk'ŭ magae
코르크 마개; (*material*) k'orŭk'ŭ
코르크

corkscrew p'odoju pyŏng ttagae
포도주 병 따개

corn oksssusu 옥수수

corner 1 *n* (*of page, room*) kusŏk
구석; (*of table, street*) mot'ung-i
모퉁이; (*bend: on road*) kilmot'ung-i
길모퉁이; (*in soccer*) k'onŏk'ik
코너킥; **in the ~** kusŏge(sŏ)
구석에(서); **on the ~** (*of street*)
mot'ung-ie(sŏ) 모퉁이에(서) **2** *v/t*
person kusŏgŭro molda 구석으로
몰다; **the market** shijang-ŭl
toktchŏmhada 시장을 독점하다 **3** *v/i*
(*of driver, car*) mot'ung-irŭl tolda

모퉁이를 돌다

corner kick k'onŏk'ik 코너킥

cornstarch nongmal 녹말

corny F (*trite*) chinbuhan 진부한;
(*sentimental*) kamsangjŏgin 감상적인

coronary 1 *adj* shimjang-ŭi 심장의 **2** *n*
shimjang mabi 심장 마비

coroner kŏmshigwan 검시관

corporal *n* sangbyŏng 상병

corporal punishment ch'ehyŏng
체형

corporate COM pŏbinŭi 법인의; **~
image** kiŏp imiji 기업 이미지;
sense of ~ loyalty kiŏbe taehan
ch'ungsŏngshim 기업에 대한 충성심

corporation (*business*) chushik hoesa
주식 회사

corps kundan 군단

corpse shich'e 시체

corpulent pimanhan 비만한

corpuscle hyŏlgu 혈구

corral *n* kach'uk uri 가축 우리

correct 1 *adj* orŭn 옳은; *time*
chŏnghwak'an 정확한 **2** *v/t* koch'ida
고치다; *proofs* kyojŏnghada 교정하다

correction koch'in kŏt 고친 것

correspond (*match*) ilch'ihada
일치하다; (*write letters*) sŏshin
wangnaehada 서신 왕래하다; **~ to**
...e haedanghada ...에 해당하다; **~
with** ...wa/kwa puhap'ada ...와/과
부합하다

correspondence (*match*) ilch'i 일치;
(*letters*) p'yŏnji 편지; (*exchange of
letters*) sŏshin wangnae 서신 왕래

correspondent (*letter writer*)
p'yŏnjirŭl ssŭnŭn saram 편지를 쓰는
사람; (*reporter*) t'ŭkp'awŏn 특파원

corresponding *adj* taeŭnghanŭn
대응하는

corridor (*in building*) poktto 복도

corroborate hwakssirhage hada
확실하게 하다

corrode *v/t* & *v/i* pushik'ada 부식하다

corrosion pushik 부식

corrugated cardboard kolp'anji
골판지

corrugated iron korhamsŏk 골함석

corrupt 1 *adj* t'arak'an 타락한;
COMPUT t'ŭllin koshi manŭn 틀린
곳이 많은 **2** *v/t* t'araksshik'ida

타락시키다; (*bribe*) maesuhada
매수하다
corruption t'arak 타락
cosmetic *adj* hwajangnyŏng-ŭi
화장용의; *fig* p'yomyŏnjŏgin
표면적인
cosmetics hwajangp'um 화장품
cosmetic surgeon sŏnghyŏng-
oekkwa ŭisa 성형외과 의사
cosmetic surgery sŏnghyŏng-
oekkwa 성형외과
cosmonaut uju pihaengsa 우주
비행사
cosmopolitan *city* taguktchogŭi
다국적의
cost 1 *n* kagyŏk 가격; (*~ price, in
manufacturing*) wŏnka 원가; *fig*
hŭisaeng 희생; **~s** piyong 비용 **2** *v/t
money, time* tŭlda 들다; FIN *project*
saengsanbirŭl kyŏnjŏk'ada 생산비를
견적하다; *how much does it ~?*
piyong-i ŏlmana tŭmnikka? 비용이
얼마나 듭니까?; *it ~ me my health*
kŭgot-ttaemune kŏn-gang-ŭl irŏt-tta
그것때문에 건강을 잃었다
cost and freight COM unim p'oham
kagyŏk 운임 포함 가격; **cost-
conscious** kyŏngbirŭl
chŏlgamhanŭn 경비를 절감하는;
cost-effective piyong
hyokkwajŏgin 비용 효과적인; **cost,
insurance and freight** COM pohŏm
mit unim p'oham kagyŏk 보험 및
운임 포함 가격
costly *error* sonshiri k'ŭn 손실이 큰
cost of living saenghwalbi 생활비
cost price wŏnka 원가
costume (*for actor*) ŭisang 의상
costume jewelry mojo posŏngnyu
모조 보석류
cot (*camp-bed*) kani ch'imdae 간이
침대
cottage shigoltchip 시골집
cotton 1 *n* myŏn 면 **2** *adj* myŏnŭro
mandŭn 면으로 만든
♦**cotton on** F ihaehada 이해하다
♦**cotton on to** F ...ŭl/rŭl
kkaedatkke toeda ...을/를 깨닫게
되다
♦**cotton to** F ...ege hogamŭl kajida
...에게 호감을 가지다

cotton candy somsat'ang 솜사탕
couch *n* sop'a 소파
couch potato F t'edori 테돌이
couchette chimdaech'atkkan
침대찻간
cough 1 *n* kich'im 기침; (*to get
attention*) kich'im sori 기침 소리
2 *v/i* kich'imhada 기침하다; (*to get
attention*) kich'im sorirŭl naeda 기침
소리를 내다
♦**cough up 1** *v/t blood etc*
kich'imhayŏ naebaet-tta 기침하여
내뱉다; F *money* maji mot'ae
naejuda 마지 못해 내주다 **2** *v/i* F
(*pay*) maji mot'ae naeda 마지 못해
내다
cough medicine, cough syrup
kich'im yak / shirŏp 기침 약 / 시럽
could: *I have my key?* che
yŏlsoerŭl chushigessŏyo? 제 열쇠를
주시겠어요?; *~ you help me?* chŏl
towajushil su issŏyo? 절 도와주실 수
있어요?; *this ~ be our bus* uri
pŏsŭinjido morŭnda 우리
버스인지도 모른다; *you ~ be right*
nega majŭl sudo issŏ 네가 맞을 수도
있어; *I ~n't say for sure*
hwaksshirhadago marhal sunŭn
ŏpssŏyo 확실하다고말할 수는
없어요; *he ~ have got lost* kŭnŭn
kirŭl irŏbŏryŏssŭltchido morŭnda
그는 길을 잃어버렸을지도 모른다;
you ~ have warned me! nahant'e
miri yaegirŭl haessŏyaji! 나한테 미리
얘기를 했어야지!
council (*assembly*) hoeŭi 회의; POL
ŭihoe 의회
councilman shiŭihoe ŭiwŏn 시의회
의원
councilor ŭiwŏn 의원
counsel 1 *n* (*advice*) choŏn 조언;
(*lawyer*) pyŏnhosa 변호사 **2** *v/t*
(*advise*) choŏnhada 조언하다;
(*because of problems*) ...wa/kwa
sangdamhada ...와/과 상담하다
counseling sangdam 상담
counselor (*adviser*) sangdamnyŏk
상담역; LAW pyŏnhosa 변호사
count 1 *n* (*number arrived at*)
ch'onggye 총계; (*counting*) sem 셈;
(*in baseball, boxing*) k'aunt'ŭ

카운트; *keep ~ of* ...ŭl/rŭl kyesok seda ...을/를 계속 세다; *lose ~ of* ...ŭi semŭl ijŏbŏrida ...의 셈을 잊어버리다; *at the last ~* ch'oejongsuro 최종수로 2 *v/i (to ten etc)* surŭl seda 수를 세다; *(calculate)* kyesanhada 계산하다; *(be important)* kach'iga it-tta 가치가 있다; *(qualify)* semŭro ch'ida 셈으로 치다 3 *v/t (~ up)* seda 세다; *(calculate)* kyesanhada 계산하다; *(include)* ch'ida 치다

♦**count on** ...ege kidaeda ...에게 기대다

countdown ch'o ilkki 초 읽기
countenance *v/t* yongnap'ada 용납하다
counter[1] *(in shop, café)* k'aunt'ŏ 카운터; *(in game)* san-gaji 산가지
counter[2] 1 *v/t* ...ŭi hyokkwarŭl churida ..의 효과를 줄이다 2 *v/i (retaliate)* matssŏda 맞서다
counter[3]: *run ~ to* ...e pandaedoeda ...에 반대되다
counteract chunghwahada 중화하다; **counter-attack** 1 *n* yŏkssŭp 역습 2 *v/i* yŏkssŭp'ada 역습하다; **counterclockwise** panshigye panghyang 반시계 방향; **counterespionage** pangch'ŏp 방첩
counterfeit 1 *v/t* wijohada 위조하다 2 *adj* wijoŭi 위조의
counterpart *(person)* kat'ŭn chiwiŭi saram 같은 지위의 사람; **counter-productive** yŏk'yokkwaŭi 역효과의; **countersign** *v/t* pusŏhada 부서하다
countless sel su ŏmnŭn 셀 수 없는
country nara 나라; *(not town)* shigol 시골; *in the ~* shigore(sŏ) 시골에(서)
country and western MUS k'ŏnt'ŭri myujik 컨트리 뮤직
countryman *(fellow ~)* kat'ŭn nara saram 같은 나라 사람
countryside shigol 시골
county kun 군
coup POL k'udet'a 쿠데타; *fig* taesŏnggong 대성공
couple *(married)* pubu 부부; *(man & woman)* namnyŏ han ssang 남녀 한 쌍; *(two people)* han ssang 한 쌍; *just a ~* chogŭm 조금; *a ~ of*

(people) tusŏnŏsŭi 두서넛의; *(things)* tusŏnŏ kae 두서너 개; *a ~ of days* isahŭl 이사흘
coupon *(form)* shinch'ŏngkkwŏn 신청권; *(voucher)* k'up'on 쿠폰
courage yonggi 용기
courageous yonggi innŭn 용기 있는
courier *(messenger)* paedal 배달; *(with tourist party)* annaewŏn 안내원
course *n (series of lessons)* kyokkwa kwajŏng 교과 과정; *(part of meal, for race)* k'osŭ 코스; *(of ship, plane)* haengno 행로; *of ~ (certainly)* mullon 물론; *(naturally)* tang-yŏnhi 당연히; *of ~ not* mullon anijyo 물론 아니죠; *~ of action* haengdong pangch'im 행동 방침; *~ of treatment* chillyo kwajŏng 진료 과정; *in the ~ of* tong-ane ... 동안에
court *n* LAW pŏptchŏng 법정; *(courthouse)* pŏbwŏn 법원; SP k'ot'ŭ 코트; *take X to ~* Xŭl/rŭl chaep'ane kŏlda X을/를 재판에 걸다
court case sosong sakkŏn 소송 사건
courteous chŏngjunghan 정중한
courtesy chŏngjungham 정중함
courthouse pŏbwŏn 법원; **court martial** 1 *n* kunppŏp hoeŭi 군법 회의 2 *v/t* kunppŏp hoeŭie hoebuhada 군법 회의에 회부하다; **court music** aak 아악; **court order** pŏbwŏn myŏngnyŏng 법원 명령; **courtroom** pŏptchŏng 법정; **courtyard** anmadang 안마당
cousin sach'on 사촌
cove *(bay)* humijin kot 후미진 곳
cover 1 *n (protective)* tŏpkkae 덮개; *(of book, magazine)* p'yoji 표지; *(for bed)* ch'imdaeppo 침대보; *(shelter)* ŏmhomul 엄호물; *(shelter from rain etc)* p'inanch'ŏ 피난처; *(insurance)* pohŏm 보험 2 *v/t* tŏpta 덮다; *(in blood, mud etc)* ssŭiuda 씌우다; *(hide)* sumgida 숨기다; *(of insurance policy)* pohŏme kŏlda 보험에 걸다; *distance* tapp'ahada 답파하다; *(of journalist)* podohada 보도하다

♦**cover up** 1 *v/t* tŏpta 덮다; *fig* kamch'uda 감추다 2 *v/i* fig kamch'uda 감추다; *~ for X* Xŭl/rŭl tudunhada X을/를 두둔하다

coverage (*by media*) podo 보도
covering letter ch'ŏmbusŏ 첨부서
covert pimirŭi 비밀의
coverup (*of crime*) ŭnp'ye 은폐
cow *n* amso 암소
coward kŏptchaeng-i 겁쟁이
cowardice pigŏp 비겁
cowardly pigŏp'an 비겁한
cowboy k'auboi 카우보이
cower umch'ŭrida 움츠리다
coy (*evasive*) hoep'ihanŭn 회피하는;
  (*flirtatious*) sujubŏhanŭn 수줍어하는
cozy anŭk'an 아늑한
CPU (= *central processing unit*)
  chung-ang ch'ŏri changch'i 중앙
  처리 장치
crab *n* ke 게
crack 1 *n* kallajin kŭm 갈라진 금;
  (*joke*) pikkonŭn nongdam 비꼬는
  농담 **2** *v/t* cup, glass kŭmgage hada
  금가게 하다; *nut* kkaeda 깨다; *code*
  p'ulda 풀다; F (*solve*) haegyŏrhada
  해결하다; **~ a joke** nongdamhada
  농담하다 **3** *v/i* kŭmi kada 금이 가다;
  get ~ing F irŭl shijak'ada 일을
  시작하다
♦ **crack down on** ...ŭl/rŭl ŏmhage
  tasŭrida ...을/를 엄하게 다스리다
♦ **crack up** *v/i* (*have breakdown*)
  shin-gyŏng soeyage kŏllida 신경
  쇠약에 걸리다; F (*laugh*) kaptchagi
  utkki shijak'ada 갑자기 웃기
  시작하다
crackdown tansok 단속
cracked cup, glass kŭmi kan 금이 간
cracker (*to eat*) k'ŭraek'ŏ 크래커
crackle *v/i* (*of fire*) ttaktttak sorirŭl
  naeda 딱딱 소리를 내다
cradle *n* (*for baby*) yoram 요람
craft¹ NAUT sŏnbak 선박
craft² (*art*) kong-ye 공예; (*skill*)
  kinŭng 기능
craftsman chang-in 장인
crafty kyohwarhan 교활한
crag (*rock*) hŏmhan pawi 험한 바위
cram *v/t* mirŏ nŏt'a 밀어 넣다
cramped room pijobŭn 비좁은
cramps pŏlkkyŏk'an pokt'ong
  급격한 복통
cranberry tŏnggulwŏlgyul 덩굴월귤
crane 1 *n* (*machine*) kijunggi 기중기;

  (*bird*) hak 학 **2** *v/t*: ~ **one's neck**
  mogŭl kilge ppaeda 목을 길게 빼다
crank *n* (*strange person*) koetcha 괴짜
crankshaft kŭraengk'ŭch'uk
  크랭크축
cranky (*bad-tempered*) shimgiga
  twit'ŭllin 심기가 뒤틀린
crap F (*garbage*) ssŭregi 쓰레기
crash 1 *n* (*noise*) k'wang hanŭn sori
  쾅 하는 소리; (*accident*) ch'ungdol
  충돌; (*plane ~*) ch'urak 추락; COM
  munŏjim 무너짐; COMPUT kojang
  고장 **2** *v/i* (*make noise*) k'wang
  hanŭn sorirŭl naeda 쾅 하는 소리를
  내다; (*of thunder*) ch'ida 치다; (*of
  car*) ch'ungdorhada 충돌하다; (*of
  airplane*) ch'urak'ada 추락하다;
  (COM: *of market*) punggoehada
  붕괴하다; COMPUT kojangnada
  고장나다; F (*sleep*) chada 자다 **3** *v/t*
  car ch'ungdolshik'ida 충돌시키다
♦ **crash out** F (*fall asleep*) kora
  ttŏrŏjida 곯아 떨어지다
crash course chiptchung kangjwa
  집중 강좌; **crash diet** sokssŏng
  taiŏt'ŭ 속성 다이어트; **crash helmet**
  anjŏn helmet 안전 헬멧; **crash
  landing** pulshich'ak 불시착
crate namu sangja 나무 상자
crater (*of volcano*) punhwagu 분화구
crave kalmanghada 갈망하다
craving kalmang 갈망
crawl 1 *n* (*stroke*) k'ŭrol suyŏng 크롤
  수영; *at a* ~ (*slowly*) nŭrinnŭrit'age
  느릿느릿하게 **2** *v/i* (*on floor*) kida
  기다; (*move slowly*) nŭrinnŭrit kada
  느릿느릿 가다
♦ **crawl with** ...(ŭ)ro ugŭlgŏrida
  ...(으)로 우글거리다
crayon k'ŭreyong 크레용
craze ilsshijŏk taeyuhaeng 일시적
  대유행; **the latest** ~ ch'oegŭnŭi
  taeyuhaeng 최근의 대유행
crazy *adj* mich'in 미친; **be ~ about**
  ...e yŏlgwanghada ...에 열광하다
creak 1 *n* ppigŏk-kkŏrinŭn sori
  삐걱거리는 소리 **2** *v/i* ppigŏk-
  kkŏrida 삐걱거리다
cream 1 *n* (*for skin, coffee, cake*)
  k'ŭrim 크림; (*color*) tamhwangsaek
  담황색 **2** *adj* tamhwangsaegŭi

담황색의

cream cheese k'ŭrim ch'ijŭ 크림 치즈

creamer (*pitcher*) k'ŭrim kŭrŭt 크림 그릇; (*for coffee*) p'ŭrima 프리마

creamy (*with lots of cream*) k'ŭrimi mani tŭrŏgan 크림이 많이 들어간

crease 1 n (*accidental*) kugimsal 구김살; (*deliberate*) churŭm 주름 **2** v/t (*accidentally*) kugida 구기다

create 1 v/t ch'angjohada 창조하다; *uncertainty, problem* yagihada 야기하다 **2** v/i ch'angjohada 창조하다

creation ch'angjo 창조; (*sth created*) ch'angjomul 창조물; *the Creation* REL Ch'ŏnji ch'angjo 천지 창조

creative ch'angjojŏgin 창조적인

creator ch'angjoja 창조자; (*author*) ch'angjaktcha 창작자; (*founder*) ch'angsŏltcha 창설자; *the Creator* REL Chomultchu 조물주

creature (*animal*) tongmul 동물; (*person*) saram 사람

credibility (*of person*) shilloesŏng 신뢰성; (*of story*) shinbingsŏng 신빙성

credible (*believable*) midŭl manhan 믿을 만한; *candidate etc* shilloegam kanŭn 신뢰감 가는

credit 1 n FIN oesang 외상; (*loan*) shinyong taebu 신용 대부; (*honor*) kongno 공로; (*payment received*) yegŭmaek 예금액; *be in ~* yegŭmi it-tta 예금이 있다; *get the ~ for X* Xe taehan kongnorŭl injŏngpat-tta X에 대한 공로를 인정받다 **2** v/t (*believe*) mit-tta 믿다; *~ an amount to an account* kyejwae yegŭmhada 계좌에 예금하다

creditable ch'ingch'anhal manhan 칭찬할 만한

credit card shinyong k'adŭ 신용 카드

credit limit (*of credit card*) shinyong taebuŭi hando 신용 대부의 한도

creditor ch'aegwŏnja 채권자

creditworthy shinyonginnŭn 신용있는

credulous chal minnŭn 잘 믿는

creed (*beliefs*) shin-gyŏng 신경

creek (*stream*) chagŭn nae 작은 내

creep 1 n pej anikkoun saram

아니꼬운 사람 **2** v/i salgŭmsalgŭm kŏt-tta 살금살금 걷다

creeper BOT tŏnggul shingmul 덩굴 식물

creeps: *the house/he gives me the ~* kŭ chibi/kŭga narŭl sŏmttŭk'age handa 그 집이/그가 나를 섬뜩하게 한다

creepy sŏmttŭk'an 섬뜩한

cremate hwajanghada 화장하다

cremation hwajang 화장

crematorium hwajangjang 화장장

crescent ch'osŭngttal moyang 초승달 모양

crest (*of hill*) kkokttaegi 꼭대기; (*of bird*) pyŏt 볏

crestfallen p'uri chugŭn 풀이 죽은

crevice kallajin t'ŭm 갈라진 틈

crew n (*of ship, airplane*) sŭngmuwŏn chŏnwŏn 승무원 전원; (*of repairmen etc*) t'im 팀; (*group*) p'aegŏri 패거리

crew cut sanggo mŏri 상고 머리

crew neck swet'aŭi tunggŭn mok 쉐타의 둥근 목

crib n (*for baby*) yuayong ch'imdae 유아용 침대

crick: *~ in the neck* mogŭl ppida 목을 삐다

cricket (*insect*) kwitturami 귀뚜라미

crime pŏmjoe 범죄; (*shameful act*) yugamsŭrŏn il 유감스런 일

criminal 1 n pŏmjoeja 범죄자 **2** adj pŏmjoeŭi 범죄의; (LAW: *not civil*) hyŏngsasang-ŭi 형사상의; (*shameful*) yugamsŭrŏn 유감스런

crimson adj chinhongsaegŭi 진홍색의

cringe momŭl umsshirhada 몸을 움씰하다

cripple 1 n (*disabled person*) shinch'e chang-aeja 신체 장애자 **2** v/t person pulguga toege hada 불구가 되게 하다; *fig* munŭnghage hada 무능하게 하다

crisis wigi 위기

crisp adj *weather, air* sangk'waehan 상쾌한; *apple, bacon* p'asakp'asak'an 파삭파삭한; *new shirt, bills* ppatppat'an 빳빳한

criterion (*standard*) kijun 기준

critic pip'yŏngga 비평가

critical (*making criticisms*)
pip'anjŏgin 비판적인; (*serious*)
wigijŏgin 위기적인; *moment etc*
kyŏltchŏngjŏgin 결정적인; MED
widok'an 위독한
critically *speak etc* pip'anjŏguro
비판적으로; ~ *ill* widok'an 위독한
criticism pip'yŏng 비평
criticize *v/t* pip'yŏnghada 비평하다
croak *v/i* (*of frog*) kaegulgaegul ulda
개굴개굴 울다; (*of person*) shwin
mokssoriŭl naeda 쉰 목소리를 내다
crockery tojagiryu 도자기류
crocodile agŏ 악어
crony F ch'in-gu 친구
crook *n* (*dishonest*) sagikkun 사기꾼
crooked (*twisting*) kuburŏjin
구부러진; *necktie, picture* pitturŏjin
비뚤어진; (*dishonest*) pujŏnghan
부정한
crop 1 *n* nongjangmul 농작물; *fig*
suhwak 수확 **2** *v/t hair, photo*
tchalkke charŭda 짧게 자르다
♦ **crop up** kaptchagi saenggida 갑자기
생기다
cross 1 *adj* (*angry*) sŏngnan 성난 **2** *n*
(X) kopp'yo 곱표; (*Christian
symbol*) shiptchaga 십자가 **3** *v/t* (*go
across*) kŏnnŏgada 건너가다; ~ *oneself* REL kasŭme shiptcharŭl kŭt-tta
가슴에 십자를 긋다; ~ *one's legs*
tarirŭl kkoda 다리를 꼬다; *keep
one's fingers ~ed* haeng-unŭl pilda
행운을 빌다; *it never ~ed my mind*
kŭ saenggagŭn na-ege ttŏorŭji anat-
tta 그 생각은 내게 떠오르지 않았다
4 *v/i* (*go across*) kŏnnŏgada
건너가다; (*of lines*) kyoch'ahada
교차하다
♦ **cross off, cross out** chiuda 지우다
crossbar (*of goal*) kolttae 골대; (*of
bicycle*) chungshimdae 중심대; (*in
high jump*) pa 바
cross-country (**skiing**) sŭk'i
k'ŭrosŭk'ŏnt'ŭri 스키 크로스컨트리
crossed check hoengsŏn sup'yo
횡선 수표
cross-examine LAW pandae
shimmunhada 반대 심문하다
cross-eyed sashiŭi 사시의
crossing NAUT hoengdan 횡단

crossroads kyoch'aro 교차로; **cross-
section** (*of people*) taep'yojŏgin
myŏn 대표적인 면; **crosswalk**
hoengdan podo 횡단 보도; **crossword** (**puzzle**) kŭltcha match'ugi
nori 글자 맞추기 놀이
crouch *v/i* momŭl kuburida 몸을
구부리다
crow *n* (*bird*) kkamagwi 까마귀; *as
the ~ flies* iljikssŏnŭro 일직선으로
crowd *n* kunjung 군중; (*at sports
event*) kwanjung 관중
crowded pumbinŭn 붐비는
crown 1 *n* wanggwan 왕관; (*on tooth*)
ch'igwan 치관 **2** *v/t* wang-wie ollida
왕위에 올리다; *tooth* ssŭiuda 씌우다
crucial kyŏltchŏngjŏgin 결정적인
crude 1 *adj* (*vulgar*) sangsŭrŏun
상스러운; (*unsophisticated*)
chojap'an 조잡한 **2** *n*: ~ (**oil**) wŏnyu
원유
cruel chaninhan 잔인한
cruelty chaninham 잔인함
cruise 1 *n* sunhang 순항 **2** *v/i* (*in ship*)
sunhanghada 순항하다; (*of car*)
kyŏngje sokttoro kada 경제 속도로
가다; (*of plane*) sunhang sokttoro
nalda 순항 속도로 날다
cruise liner sunhangsŏn 순항선
cruising speed sunhan soktto 순항
속도; (*of project*) sunjoroun soktto
순조로운 속도
crumb pusŭrŏgi 부스러기
crumble 1 *v/t* pusŭrŏttŭrida
부스러뜨리다 **2** *v/i* (*of bread, stone*)
pusŭrojida 부스러지다; *fig* (*of
opposition etc*) munŏjida 무너지다
crumple 1 *v/t* (*crease*) kugida 구기다
2 *v/i* (*collapse*) munŏjida 무너지다
crunch 1 *n*: *when it comes to the ~*
F kyŏltchŏngjŏgin shigiga omyŏn
결정적인 시기가 오면 **2** *v/i* (*of snow,
gravel*) wajak-wajak soriga nada
와작와작 소리가 나다
crusade *n fig* kaehyŏk undong 개혁
운동
crush 1 *n* (*crowd*) kunjung 군중;
have a ~ on ...ege holttak panhada
...에게 홀딱 반하다 **2** *v/t* pakssarŭl
naeda 박살을 내다; (*crease*) kugida
구기다; *they were ~ed to death*

küdŭrŭn pakssalla chugŏt-tta 그들은
박살나 죽었다 3 v/i (crease)
kugyŏjida 구겨지다
crust (on bread) ttakttak'an
kkŏptchil 딱딱한 껍질
crutch (for walking) mokttari 목다리
cry 1 n (call) oech'im 외침; **have a ~**
ulda 울다 **2** v/t (call) oech'ida 외치다
3 v/i (weep) ulda 울다
♦ **cry out 1** v/t oech'yŏ purŭda 외쳐
부르다 **2** v/i koham chirŭda 고함
지르다
♦ **cry out for** (need) …ŭl/rŭl p'iryoro
hada …을/를 필요로 하다
crystal (mineral) sujŏng 수정; (glass)
k'ŭrisŭt'ŏl 크리스털
crystallize v/t & v/i kuch'ehwahada
구체화하다
cub saekki 새끼
cube (shape) ip-ppangch'e 입방체
cubic ip-ppang-ŭi 입방의
cubic capacity TECH ip-ppang
yongnyang 입방 용량
cubicle (changing room) t'arŭishil
탈의실
cucumber oi 오이
cuddle 1 n p'oong 포옹 **2** v/t kkok
kkyŏantta 꼭 껴안다
cuddly kitten etc kkyŏankko ship'ŭn
껴안고 싶은; (liking cuddles)
kkyŏankko ship'ŏhanŭn 껴안고
싶어하는
cue n (for actor, pool etc) k'yu 큐
cuff 1 n (of shirt) somaetppuri
소맷부리; (of pants) pajittan 바지단;
(blow) ch'alssak ttaerim 찰싹 때림;
off the ~ chŭkssŏgŭi 즉석의 **2** v/t
(hit) ch'alssak ttaerida 찰싹 때리다
cuff link k'ŏp'ŭsŭ tanch'u 커프스 단추
culinary yoriŭi 요리의
culminate: ~ in …(ŭ)ro chŏltchŏng-e
tarhada …(으)로 절정에 달하다
culmination chŏltchŏng 절정
culprit pŏmin 범인
cult (sect) sagyo chipttan 사교 집단
cultivate land kyŏngjak'ada 경작하다;
person chal sagwida 잘 사귀다
cultivated person seryŏndoen 세련된
cultivation (of land) kyŏngjak 경작
cultural munhwajŏgin 문화적인
culture n munhwa 문화

cultured (cultivated) seryŏndoen
세련된
culture shock munhwajŏk
ch'unggyŏk 문화적 충격
cumbersome sŏnggashin 성가신
cunning 1 n kyohwaram 교활함
2 adj kyohwarhan 교활한
cup n chan 잔; (trophy) usŭngk'ŏp
우승컵; **a ~ of tea** ch'a han chan 차
한 잔
cupboard ch'antchang 찬장
curable ch'iryohal su innŭn 치료할 수
있는
curator k'yureit'ŏ 큐레이터
curb 1 n (of street) yŏnsŏk 연석; (on
powers etc) ŏktche 억제 **2** v/t
ŏktchehada 억제하다
curdle v/i (of milk) ŭnggohada
응고하다
cure 1 n MED ch'iryo 치료 **2** v/t MED
ch'iryohada 치료하다; meat, fish
pojon ch'ŏrihada 보존 처리하다
curfew yagan oech'ul kŭmji 야간
외출 금지
curiosity (inquisitiveness) hogishim
호기심
curious (inquisitive) hogishim manŭn
호기심 많은; (strange) isanghan
이상한
curiously (inquisitively) hogishimsŏ
호기심에서; (strangely) isanghage
이상하게; **~ enough** isanghagedo
이상하게도
curl 1 n (in hair) kopssŭlgŏrim
곱슬거림; (of smoke) maemdom 맴돔
2 v/t hair kopssŭlgŏrige hada
곱슬거리게 하다; (wind) kamtta 감다
3 v/i (of hair) kopssŭlgŏrida
곱슬거리다; (of paper etc) tunggŭlge
ogŭradŭlda 둥글게 오그라들다
♦ **curl up** umch'urida 움추리다
curly hair kopssŭlgŏrinŭn 곱슬거리는;
tail kkobulgŏrinŭn 꼬불거리는
currant (dried fruit) kŏnp'odo 건포도
currency (money) t'onghwa 통화;
foreign ~ oehwa 외화
current 1 n hŭrŭm 흐름; (tidal)
choryu 조류; ELEC chŏllyu 전류 **2** adj
(present) chigŭmŭi 지금의
current affairs shisa 시사
current affairs program shisa

p'ŭrograem 시사 프로그램
currently chigŭm 지금
curriculum kyokkwa kwajŏng 교과
과정
curse 1 n (spell) chŏju 저주; (swear-word) yoksŏl 욕설 **2** v/t chŏjuhada
저주하다; (swear at) yok'ada 욕하다
3 v/i (swear) yok'ada 욕하다
cursor COMPUT k'ŏsŏ 커서
cursory p'isangjŏgin 피상적인
curt t'ungmyŏngsŭrŏun 퉁명스러운
curtail churida 줄이다
curtain k'ŏt'ŭn 커튼; THEA mak 막
curve 1 n koksssŏn 곡선 **2** v/i (bend)
kuburŏjida 구부러지다
cushion 1 n (for couch etc) k'ushyŏn
쿠션 **2** v/t fall wanhwahada 완화하다
custard k'ŏsŭt'ŏdŭ 커스터드
custody (of children) yangnyuk-
kkwŏn 양육권; in ~ LAW kuryu
chung 구류 중
custom (tradition) kwansŭp 관습;
COM tan-gol 단골; as was his ~ kŭŭi
sŭpkkwanŭro 그의 습관으로
customary sŭpkkwanjŏgin 습관적인;
(socially) t'ongnyeŭi 통례의; it is ~
to ... ... hanŭn kŏshi t'ongnyeida ...
하는 것이 통례이다
customer kogaek 고객
customer relations kogaek kwalli
고객 관리
customs kwanse 관세
customs clearance segwan
t'onggwa 세관 통과; **customs inspection** segwan kŏmsa 세관 검사;
customs officer segwanwŏn 세관원
cut 1 n (with knife) pegi 베기; (with
scissors) charŭgi 자르기; (injury) pen
sangch'ŏ 벤 상처; (of garment, hair)
marŭmjil 마름질; (reduction) sak-
kkam 삭감; my hair needs a ~
nanŭn mŏrirŭl challayagessŏyo 나는
머리를 잘라야겠어요 **2** v/t (with
knife) peda 베다; (with scissors)
charŭda 자르다; (reduce) sak-
kkamhada 삭감하다; get one's hair
~ mŏrirŭl charŭda 머리를 자르다
♦ **cut back 1** v/i (in costs)
ch'uksssohada 축소하다 **2** v/t
employees sak-kkamhada 삭감하다
♦ **cut down 1** v/t peŏ nŏmŏttŭrida

베어 넘어뜨리다 **2** v/i (in smoking
etc) churida 줄이다
♦ **cut down on** smoking etc ...ŭl/rŭl
churida ...을/를 줄이다
♦ **cut off** (with knife etc) peŏnaeda
베어내다; (with scissors) challanaeda
잘라내다; (isolate) koripsshik'ida
고립시키다; TELEC kkŭnt'a 끊다; we
were ~ chŏnhwaga kkŭnk'yŏssŏyo
전화가 끊겼어요
♦ **cut out** (with scissors) oryŏnaeda
오려내다; (eliminate) chungdanhada
중단하다; (exclude) ch'adanhada
차단하다; cut that out! F kŭman
twŏ! 그만 뒤!; be ~ for X Xe ttak
chŏk'ap'ada X에 딱 적합하다
♦ **cut up** v/t meat etc t'omakch'ida
토막치다
cutback sak-kkam 삭감
cute (pretty) kwiyŏun 귀여운;
(sexually) maeryŏktchŏgin 매력적인;
(clever) yŏngnihan 영리한
cuticle p'yop'i 표피
cut-price harinkkaŭi 할인가의
cut-throat competition ch'iyŏrhan
치열한
cutting 1 n (from newspaper)
oryŏnaen kŏt 오려낸 것 **2** adj
remark shillarhan 신랄한
cyberspace kasang konggan 가상
공간
cycle 1 n (bicycle) chajŏn-gŏ 자전거;
(series of events) sunhwan 순환 **2** v/i
chajŏn-gŏro kada 자전거로 가다
cycling chajŏn-gŏ t'agi 자전거
타기
cyclist chajŏn-gŏ t'anŭn saram 자전거
타는 사람
cylinder (container) wŏnt'ong 원통;
(in engine) kit'ong 기통
cylindrical wŏnt'ong moyang-ŭi 원통
모양의
cynic pikkonŭn saram 비꼬는 사람
cynical naengsojŏgin 냉소적인
cynicism naengso 냉소
cyst p'onang 포낭
Czech 1 adj Ch'ek'oŭi 체코의; the ~
Republic Ch'ek'o konghwaguk 체코
공화국 **2** n (person) Ch'ek'o saram
체코 사람; (language) Ch'ek'oŏ
체코어

D

DA (= *district attorney*) chibang kŏmsa 지방 검사

dab 1 *n* (*small amount*) soryang 소량 **2** *v/t* (*remove*) saltchak takkkanaeda 살짝 닦아내다; (*apply*) kabyŏpkke parŭda 가볍게 바르다

♦ **dabble in** chamkkan sonŭl taeda 잠깐 손을 대다

dad appa 아빠

dagger tando 단도

daily 1 *n* (*paper*) shinmun 신문 **2** *adj* maeirŭi 매일의; **~ newspaper** ilgan shinmun 일간 신문

dainty sŏmsehan 섬세한

dairy products yujep'um 유제품

dais yŏndan 연단

dam 1 *n* (*for water*) ttaem 댐 **2** *v/t river* taemŭro maktta 댐으로 막다

damage 1 *n* p'ihae 피해; *fig* (*to reputation etc*) sonsang 손상 **2** *v/t* p'ihaerŭl ip'ida 피해를 입히다; *fig: reputation etc* sonsangshik'ida 손상시키다

damages LAW sonhae paesanggŭm 손해 배상금

damaging sonsangshik'inŭn 손상시키는

dame F (*woman*) yŏja 여자

damn 1 *interj* F chegirŭl 제기랄 **2** *n* F: *I don't give a* **~!** naega alkke mwŏya! 내가 알게 뭐야! **3** *adj* F pirŏmŏgŭl 빌어먹을 **4** *adv* F pirŏmŏk-kke 빌어먹게 **5** *v/t* (*condemn*) hŏltttŭt-tta 헐뜯다; **~ it!** F chenjanghal! 젠장할!; *I'm* **~ed if** F nanŭn chŏlttaero ... haji ank'et-tta 나는 절대로 ... 하지 않겠다

damned → *damn adj & adv*

damp *cloth* ch'ukch'uk'an 축축한; *building, room* sŭpkkich'an 습기찬

dampen ch'ukch'uk'age hada 축축하게 하다

dance 1 *n* ch'um 춤; (*social event*) taensŭ p'ati 댄스 파티 **2** *v/i*

ch'umch'uda 춤추다; *would you like to* **~?** ch'um ch'ushigessŏyo? 춤 추시겠어요?

dancer ch'umch'unŭn saram 춤추는 사람; (*performer*) muyongga 무용가

dancing muyong 무용

dandruff pidŭm 비듬

Dane Tenmak'ŭ saram 덴마크 사람

danger wihŏm 위험; *out of* **~** (*of patient*) chungt'ae-esŏ pŏsŏnan 중태에서 벗어난

dangerous wihŏmhan 위험한; *assumption* wit'aeroun 위태로운

dangle *v/t & v/i* tallanggŏrida 달랑거리다

Danish 1 *adj* Tenmak'ŭŭi 덴마크의 **2** *n* (*language*) Tenmak'ŭŏ 덴마크어

Danish (**pastry**) tenishwi p'aesŭch'yuri 데니쉬 패스츄리

dare 1 *v/i: he didn't* **~** kŭnŭn kamhi hal su ŏpssŏssŏyo 그는 감히 할 수 없었어요; *how* **~** *you!* nega kamhi ŏttŏk'e! 네가 감히 어떻게! **2** *v/t:* **~** *X to do Y* Xege Yŭl/rŭl tojŏnhae porago hada X에게 Y을/를 도전해 보라고 하다

daring *adj* taedamhan 대담한

dark 1 *n* ŏdum 어둠; *after* **~** haejin hue 해진 후에; *keep s.o. in the* **~** *fig* nuguege morŭge hada 누구에게 모르게 하다 **2** *adj room, night* ŏduun 어두운; *hair, eyes* kŏmusŭrŭmhan 거무스름한; *color* chinhan 진한; *clothes* ŏduun pitkkarŭi 어두운 빛깔의; **~ green/blue** chinhan ch'orokssaek/p'aransaek 진한 초록색/파란색

darken (*of sky*) ŏduwŏjida 어두워지다

dark glasses saegan-gyŏng 색안경

darkness amhŭk 암흑

darling 1 *n* kajang sarangsŭrŏn saram 가장 사랑스런 사람; **~!** chagiya!

자기야! **2** *adj* kajang saranghanŭn 가장 사랑하는

darn[1] **1** *n* (*mend*) kkwemaen chari 꿰맨 자리 **2** *v/t* (*mend*) kkwemaeda 꿰매다

darn[2], **darned** → **damn**

dart 1 *n* (*for throwing*) tat'ŭ 다트 **2** *v/i* ssonsalgach'i naragada 쏜살같이 날아가다

dash 1 *n* (*punctuation*) taeshi 대시; (*small amount*) yakkan 약간; (MOT: *dashboard*) kyegip'an 계기판; *a ~ of brandy* yakkanŭi pŭraendi 약간의 브랜디; *make a ~ for* ...(ŭ)ro tansume tallyŏgada ...(으)로 단숨에 달려가다 **2** *v/i* tansume tallyŏgada 단숨에 달려가다 **3** *v/t hopes* kkŏkta 꺾다

♦**dash off 1** *v/i* sŏdullŏ ttŏnada 서둘러 떠나다 **2** *v/t* (*write quickly*) tansume ssŭda 단숨에 쓰다

dashboard kyegip'an 계기판

data charyo 자료, teit'ŏ 데이터; (*information*) chŏngbo 정보

database teit'ŏ peisŭ 데이터 베이스; **data capture** teit'ŏ sujip 데이터 수집; **data processing** teit'ŏ ch'ŏri 데이터 처리; **data protection** teit'ŏ poho 데이터 보호; **data storage** teit'ŏ chŏjang 데이터 저장

date[1] (*fruit*) taech'u 대추

date[2] **1** *n* naltcha 날짜; (*meeting*) teit'ŭ 데이트; (*person*) teit'ŭ sangdae 데이트 상대; *what's the ~ today?* onŭl myŏch'irijyo? 오늘 몇일이죠?; *out of ~ clothes* yuhaeng-i chinan 유행이 지난; *passport* naltchaga chinan 날짜가 지난; *up to ~* ch'oeshinŭi 최신의 **2** *v/t letter, check* naltcharŭl chŏkta 날짜를 적다; (*go out with*) ...wa/kwa teit'ŭ hada ...와/과 데이트하다; *that ~s you* kŭgŏsŭro nŏŭi nairŭl kanŭmhal su it-tta 그것으로 너의 나이를 가늠할 수 있다

dated shidaee twittŏrŏjin 시대에 뒤떨어진

daub *v/t* sŏt'urŭge ch'irhada 서투르게 칠하다; *~ paint on a wall* pyŏge sŏt'urŭge p'eint'ŭ ch'irŭl hada 벽에 서투르게 페인트 칠을 하다

daughter ttal 딸; (*somebody else's*) ttanim 따님

daughter-in-law myŏnŭri 며느리; (*somebody else's*) myŏnŭnim 며느님

daunt *v/t* kirŭl kkŏkta 기를 꺾다

dawdle (*waste time*) shiganŭl hŏbihada 시간을 허비하다; (*move slowly*) kkumulgŏrida 꾸물거리다; *~ over* nŭgŭt'age ... hada 느긋하게 ... 하다

dawn 1 *n* saebyŏk 새벽; *fig* (*of new age*) shich'o 시초 **2** *v/i: it ~ed on me that* ...ranŭn kŏsŭl nanŭn kkaedatkki shijak'aet-tta ...라는 것을 나는 깨닫기 시작했다

day nal 날; *all ~* haru chong-il 하루 종일; *what ~ is it today?* onŭrŭn musŭn yoiriyeyo? 오늘은 무슨 요일이예요?; *~ off* shwinŭn nal 쉬는 날; *by ~* naje 낮에; *~ by ~* nanari 나날이; *the ~ after* kŭ taŭmnal 그 다음날; *the ~ after tomorrow* more 모레; *the ~ before* kŭ chŏnnal 그 전날; *the ~ before yesterday* kŭjŏkke 그저께; *~ in ~ out* maeilmaeil kyesok'aesŏ 매일 매일 계속해서; *in those ~s* kŭ shijŏrenŭn 그 시절에는; *one ~* ŏnjen-ganŭn 엔젠가는; *the other ~* (*recently*) iltchŏne 일전에; *let's call it a ~!* kŭman kkŭnnaepsshida! 그만 끝냅시다!

daybreak saebyŏk 새벽; **daydream 1** *n* paegilmong 백일몽 **2** *v/i* kongsang-e chamgida 공상에 잠기다; **daylight** nat 낮; **daytime**: *in the ~* naje 낮에; **daytrip** tang-ilch'igi yŏhaeng 당일치기 여행

dazed (*by news*) ŏridungjŏrhaejin 어리둥절해진; (*by a blow*) chŏngshini mŏnghan 정신이 멍한

dazzle *v/t* nunbushige hada 눈부시게 하다; *fig* apttodanghada 압도당하다

dead 1 *adj person, plant* chugŭn 죽은; *battery* tarŭn 닳은; *phone* kkŭnjin 끊어진; *flashlight, engine* kkŏjin 꺼진; *bulb* nagan 나간; F (*boring: place*) hwalgi ŏmnŭn 활기 없는 **2** *adv* F (*very*) ŏmch'ŏngnage 엄청나게; *~ beat, ~ tired* nokch'oga toeŏ 녹초가 되어; *that's ~ right* chŏntchŏgŭro

matsŭmnida 전적으로 맞습니다 **3** *n*:
the ~ koin 고인; *in the ~ of night*
han pamtchung-e 한 밤중에
deaden *pain*, *sound* chugida 죽이다
dead end (*street*) makktarŭn 막다른;
  dead-end job changnaesŏng
  ŏmnŭn chigŏp 장래성 없는 직업;
  dead heat musŭngbu 무승부; **deadline** (*day*) magamil 마감일; (*hour*)
  magamshigan 마감시간; **deadlock** *n*
  (*in talks*) kyoch'ak sangt'ae 교착
  상태
deadly *adj* (*fatal*) ch'imyŏngjŏgin
  치명적인; F (*boring*) chiruhaesŏ
  mich'ilkkŏt kat'ŭn 지루해서 미칠것
  같은
deaf kwimŏgŭn 귀먹은
deaf-and-dumb nong-aŭi 농아의
deafen kwimŏk-kke hada 귀먹게
  하다
deafening kwich'ŏng-i ttŏrŏjil ttŭt'an
  귀청이 떨어질 듯한
deafness ch'ŏnggak chang-ae 청각
  장애
deal 1 *n* (*contract*) kyeyak 계약; (*in
  business*) kŏrae 거래; *it's a ~!*
  (*agreed*) habŭidoen kŏmnida! 합의된
  겁니다!; (*it's a promise*) yakssok'an
  kŏmnida! 약속한 겁니다!; *a good ~*
  (*bargain*) charhan hŭngjŏng 잘한
  흥정; (*a lot*) mani 많이; *a great ~ of*
  (*lots*) manŭn 많은 **2** *v/t cards* tollida
  돌리다; *~ a blow to* …ege t'agyŏgŭl
  chuda …에게 타격을 주다
♦**deal in** (*trade in*) kŏraehada
  거래하다
♦**deal out** *cards* nanuŏ chuda 나누어
  주다
♦**deal with** (*handle*) ch'ŏrihada
  처리하다; (*do business with*)
  kŏraehada 거래하다
dealer (*merchant*) sang-in 상인; (*drug
  ~*) mayak tillŏ 마약 딜러; (*in cards*)
  tillŏ 딜러
dealing (*drug ~*) mayak kŏrae 마약
  거래
dealings (*business*) kŏrae 거래
dean (*of college*) haktchang 학장
dear *adj* ch'inaehanŭn 친애하는;
  (*expensive*) kagyŏgi pissan 가격이
  비싼; *Dear Sir* chon-gyŏnghanŭn

sŏnsaengnimkke chon-gyŏnghanŭn 선생님께;
Dear Richard / Margaret
saranghanŭn Rich'adŭ / Magaret
사랑하는 리차드 / 마가 렛; (*oh*) ~!, ~
me! irŏn, sesange! 이런, 세상에!
dearly *love* kkŭmtchigi 끔찍이
death chugŭm 죽음; *~s* (*fatalities*)
  samangja 사망자; *be sentenced to
  ~* sahyŏng sŏn-gorŭl pat-tta 사형
  선고를 받다
death penalty sahyŏng 사형
death toll samangjasu 사망자수
debatable nonjaeng-ŭi yŏjiga innŭn
  논쟁의 여지가 있는
debate 1 *n* nonjaeng 논쟁; POL shimŭi
  심의 **2** *v/i* suk-kkohada 숙고하다 **3** *v/t*
  nonjaenghada 논쟁하다
debauchery pangt'ang 방탕
debit 1 *n* chan-goran 잔고란 **2** *v/t*
  account, amount chan-gorane
  kiip'ada 잔고란에 기입하다
debris p'ap'yŏn 파편
debt pit 빚; *be in ~* piji it-tta 빚이
  있다
debtor ch'aemuja 채무자
debug *room* toch'ŏng changch'irŭl
  chegŏhada 도청 장치를 제거하다;
  COMPUT kyŏrhamŭl koch'ida 결함을
  고치다
début *n* tebyu 데뷔
decade ship nyŏn 십 년
decadent t'oep'yejŏgin 퇴폐적인
decaffeinated k'ap'eini chegŏdoen
  카페인이 제거된
decapitate mogŭl charŭda 목을
  자르다
decay 1 *n* (*process*) pup'ae 부패; (*of
  civilization*) soet'oe 쇠퇴; (*decayed
  matter*) ssŏgŭm 썩음 **2** *v/i*
  pup'aehada 부패하다; (*of
  civilization*) soet'oehada 쇠퇴하다;
  (*of teeth*) ch'ungch'iga saenggida
  충치가 생기다
deceased: *the ~* chugŭn saram 죽은
  사람
deceit sogimsu 속임수
deceitful namŭl soginŭn 남을 속이는
deceive sogida 속이다
December shibiwŏl 십이월
decency yeŭi parŭm 예의 바름; *he
  had the ~ to …* kŭnŭn … hal

chŏngdoŭi yeŭinŭn issŏt-tta 그는 …
활 정도의 예의는 있었다

decent *person* nŏgŭrŏun 너그러운;
(*acceptable*) kwaench'anŭn
chŏngdoŭi 괜찮은 정도의;
(*reasonable*) sangdanghi choŭn
상당히 좋은; (*meal, sleep*)
chŏkttanghan 적당한

decentralize *administration* chibang
punkkwŏnhwa hada 지방 분권화
하다

deception sogim 속임

deceptive (*in appearance*)
pogiwanŭn tarŭn 보기와는 다른

deceptively: *it looks ~ simple*
pogiwanŭn tarŭge kandanhaji ant'a
보기와는 다르게 간단하지 않다

decibel teshibel 데시벨

decide 1 *v/t* (*make up one's mind*)
kyŏlsshimhada 결심하다; (*conclude*)
kyŏltchŏnghada 결정하다; (*settle*)
kyŏltchŏng-ŭl naerida 결정을 내리다
2 *v/i* kyŏltchŏnghada 결정하다; *you
~ nega kyŏltchŏnghae* 네가 결정해

decided (*definite*) tturyŏt'an 뚜렷한

decider (*match etc*) kyŏlssŭngjŏn
결승전

decimal *n* sosu 소수

decimal point sosutchŏm 소수점

decimate manŭn surŭl chugida 많은
수를 죽이다

decipher p'andok'ada 판독하다

decision kyŏltchŏng 결정;
(*conclusion*) kyŏllon 결론; *come to
a ~* kyŏllone irŭda 결론에 이르다

decision-maker ŭisa kyŏltchŏngja
의사 결정자

decisive (*resolute*) tanhohan 단호한;
(*crucial*) kyŏltchŏngjŏgin 결정적인

deck (*of ship*) kapp'an 갑판; (*of bus*)
ch'ŭng 층; (*of cards*) han pŏl 한 벌

deckchair hyudaeyong ŭija 휴대용
의자

declaration (*statement*) sŏngmyŏng
성명; (*of independence*) sŏnŏn 선언;
~ of war sŏnjŏn p'ogo 선전 포고

declare (*state*) kongp'yohada
공표하다; *independence* sŏnŏnhada
선언하다; (*at customs*) shin-gohada
신고하다; *~ war* sŏnjŏn p'ogohada
선전 포고하다

decline 1 *n* (*fall*) kamso 감소; (*in
standards*) harak 하락; (*in health*)
ak'wa 악화 2 *v/t invitation* kŏjŏrhada
거절하다; *~ to comment* ŏn-gŭbŭl
kŏbuhada 언급을 거부하다; *~ to
accept* padadŭriji ant'a 받아들이지
않다 3 *v/i* (*refuse*) kŏjŏrhada
거절하다; (*decrease*) kamsohada
감소하다; (*of health*) ak'wadoeda
악화되다

declutch k'ŭllŏch'irŭl p'ulda 클러치를
풀다

decode haedok'ada 해독하다

decompose pup'aehada 부패하다

décor changsshik 장식

decorate (*with paint, paper*)
changsshik'ada 장식하다; (*adorn*)
kkumida 꾸미다; *soldier* hunjang-ŭl
suyŏhada 훈장을 수여하다

decoration (*paint, paper, ornament*)
changshik 장식

decorative changshingnyong-ŭi
장식용의

decorator (*interior ~*) shillae
changshik-kka 실내 장식가

decoy *n* yuinyong 유인용

decrease 1 *n* kamso 감소 2 *v/t*
churida 줄이다 3 *v/i* chulda 줄다

dedicate *book etc* pach'ida 바치다; *~
oneself to* …e chŏnnyŏmhada …에
전념하다

dedication (*in book*) hŏnjŏngsa
헌정사; (*to cause, work*) chŏnnyŏm
전념

deduce ch'uronhada 추론하다

deduct: *~ X from Y* Yesŏ Xŭl / rŭl
ppaeda Y에서 X을 / 를 빼다

deduction (*from salary*) kongje 공제;
(*conclusion*) ch'uron 추론

deed *n* (*act*) haeng-wi 행위; LAW
kimyŏng narinhan chŭngsŏ 기명
날인한 증서

deep *hole, water, sleep* kip'ŭn 깊은;
trouble shimgak'an 심각한; *voice*
chŏŭmŭi 저음의; *color* chinhan 진한;
thinker shimwŏnhan 심원한

deepen 1 *v/t* kipkke hada 깊게 하다
2 *v/i* kip'ŏjida 깊어지다; (*of crisis,
mystery*) shimgak'aejida 심각해지다

deep freeze *n* kŭpssok naengdong
naengjanggo 급속 냉동 냉장고;

deep-frozen food naengdong shikp'um 냉동 식품; **deep-fry** tŭmppuk t'wigida 듬뿍 튀기다

deer sasŭm 사슴

deface woegwanŭl sonsangshik'ida 외관을 손상시키다

defamation pibang 비방

defamatory pibanghanŭn 비방하는

default adj COMPUT miri sŏltchŏngdoen 미리 설정된; ~ value tip'olt'ŭkkap 디폴트값

defeat 1 n p'aebae 패배 **2** v/t p'aebaeshik'ida 패배시키다; (of task) chwajŏlsshik'ida 좌절시키다

defeatist adj attitude p'aebaejuŭijŏgin 패배주의적인

defect n kyŏltchŏm 결점

defective kyŏltchŏmi innŭn 결점이 있는

defend chik'ida 지키다; (back up) onghohada 옹호하다; (justify) chŏngdanghwahada 정당화하다; LAW pyŏnhohada 변호하다

defendant (in criminal case) p'igoin 피고인

defense n (protection) pang-ŏ 방어; MIL, POL pang-wi 방위; SP subi 수비; LAW p'igoch'ŭk 피고측; (justification) pyŏllon 변론; (of cause, support) ongho 옹호; come to s.o.'s ~ nuguŭi p'yŏni toeŏ chuda 누구의 편이 되어 주다

defense budget POL kukppangbi yesan 국방비 예산

defense lawyer p'igoch'ŭk pyŏnhosa 피고측 변호사

defenseless mubangbiŭi 무방비의

defense player SP subisu 수비수; **Defense Secretary** POL Kukppangbuhanggwan 국방부 장관; **defense witness** LAW p'igoch'ŭk chŭng-in 피고측 증인

defensive 1 n: on the ~ pang-ŏhanŭn chasero 방어하는 자세로; go on the ~ pangŏjŏgin chaserŭl ch'wihada 방어적인 자세를 취하다 **2** adj weaponry pang-ŏyong-ŭi 방어용의; person pang-ŏjŏgin 방어적인

defer v/t yŏn-gihada 연기하다

deference chon-gyŏng 존경

deferential chŏngjunghan 정중한

defiance panhang 반항; in ~ of ...ŭl/rŭl mushihago ...을/를 무시하고

defiant panhangjŏgin 반항적인

deficiency (lack) kyŏlp'ip 결핍

deficient: be ~ in ...i/ga kyŏlp'ipttoeda ...이/가 결핍되다

deficit chŏktcha 적자

define word chŏng-ŭirŭl naerida 정의를 내리다; objective ttŭsŭl palk'ida 뜻을 밝히다

definite date, time chŏnghwak'an 정확한; answer, improvement myŏnghwak'an 명확한; (certain) hwaksshinhanŭn 확신하는; are you ~ about that? hwaksshin-hamnikka? 확신합니까?; nothing ~ has been arranged hwaktchŏng-doen kŏn, amu kŏtto ŏpssŭmnida 확정된 건, 아무 것도 없습니다

definite article chŏnggwansa 정관사

definitely hwaksshirhi 확실히

definition (of word) chŏng-ŭi 정의; (of objective) ttŭsŭl palk'im 뜻을 밝힘

definitive kyŏltchŏngjŏgin 결정적인

deflect ball, blow pinnagage hada 빗나가게 하다; criticism p'yŏnhyang-shik'ida 편향시키다; (from course of action) pŏsŏnage hada 벗어나게 하다; be ~ed from ...ŭl/rŭl pyŏn-gyŏnghada ...을/를 변경하다

deform pyŏnhyŏngshik'ida 변형시키다

deformity kihyŏng 기형

defraud sach'wihada 사취하다

defrost v/t food nogida 녹이다; fridge sŏrirŭl ŏpssaeda 서리를 없애다

deft person somsshi choŭn 솜씨 좋은; fingers nŭngsuk'an 능숙한

defuse bomb shin-gwanŭl chegŏhada 신관을 제거하다; situation chinjŏngshik'ida 진정시키다

defy panhanghada 반항하다

degenerate v/i t'arak'ada 타락하다; ~ into ...(ŭ)ro pyŏnjildoeda ...(으)로 변질되다

degrade ch'emyŏnŭl sonsangshik'ida 체면을 손상시키다

degrading position, work ch'emyŏnŭl sonsangshik'inŭn 체면을 손상시키는

degree (*from university*) hagwi 학위; (*of temperature, angle, latitude*) to 도; (*amount*) chŏngdo 정도; **by ~s** ch'ach'a 차차; **get one's ~** hagwirŭl ttada 학위를 따다

dehydrated t'alssudoen 탈수된

de-ice *windshield* chebinghada 제빙하다; *airplane wings* pangbinghada 방빙하다

de-icer (*spray*) chebingje 제빙제

deign: ~ to komapkkedo … hae chushida 고맙게도 … 해 주시다

deity shin 신

dejected nakttamhan 낙담한

delay 1 *n* yŏn-gi 연기 **2** *v/t* yŏn-gihada 연기하다; **be ~ed** (*of person*) chigak'ada 지각하다; (*of train, plane*) yŏnch'ak'ada 연착하다 **3** *v/i* chich'ehada 지체하다

delegate 1 *n* taep'yoja 대표자 **2** *v/t task* wiimhada 위임하다; *person* taep'yoro immyŏnghada 대표로 임명하다

delegation (*of task*) wiim 위임; (*people*) taep'yodan 대표단

delete saktchehada 삭제하다; (*cross out*) chiuda 지우다

deletion (*act*) malsso 말소; (*that deleted*) saktche 삭제

deli shikp'umjŏm 식품점

deliberate 1 *adj* koŭijŏgin 고의적인 **2** *v/i* suk-kkohada 숙고하다

deliberately ilburŏ 일부러

delicacy (*of fabric*) sŏmseham 섬세함; (*of problem*) mimyoham 미묘함; (*of health*) hŏyak'am 허약함; (*tact*) paeryŏ 배려; (*food*) chinmi 진미

delicate *fabric* sŏmsehan 섬세한; *problem* mimyohan 미묘한; *health* hŏyak'an 허약한

delicatessen shikp'umjŏm 식품점

delicious mashinnŭn 맛있는; *that was ~* mashissŏssŏyo 맛있었어요

delight *n* kippŭm 기쁨

delighted kippŏhanŭn 기뻐하는

delightful *evening* chŭlgŏun 즐거운; *person* yuk'waehan 유쾌한; *house* k'waejŏk'an 쾌적한

delimit han-gyerŭl chŏnghada 한계를 정하다

delirious MED ilsshijŏk chŏngshin ch'angnanŭi 일시적 정신 착란의; (*ecstatic*) yŏlgwanghan 열광한

deliver paedarhada 배달하다; *message* chŏndarhada 전달하다; *baby* punmanshik'ida 분만시키다; **~ a speech** yŏnsŏrŭl hada 연설을 하다

delivery (*of goods, mail*) paedal 배달; (*of baby*) punman 분만

delivery date paedal naltcha 배달 날짜; **delivery note** suryŏngtchŭng 수령증; **delivery van** paedalch'a 배달차

delude sogida 속이다; *you're deluding yourself* tangshin sŭsŭro ch'ak-kkak'ago innŭn kŏyeyo 당신 스스로 착각하고 있는 거예요

deluge 1 *n* taehongsu 대홍수; *fig* swaedo 쇄도 **2** *v/t fig* swaedohada 쇄도하다

delusion ch'ak-kkak 착각

de luxe hohwaroun 호화로운

demand 1 *n* yogu 요구; COM suyo 수요; **be in ~** suyoga it-tta 수요가 있다 **2** *v/t* yoguhada 요구하다; (*require*) yoguhada 요구하다

demanding *job* sangdanghan noryŏgi yogudoenŭn 상당한 노력이 요구되는; *person* yoguga shimhan 요구가 심한

demented chŏngshin ch'angnane kŏllin 정신 착란에 걸린

Demilitarized Zone Pimujang Chidae 비무장 지대

demise samang 사망; *fig* somyŏl 소멸

demitasse chagŭn k'ŏp'itchan 작은 커피잔

demo (*protest*) temo 데모; (*of video etc*) sŏnjŏnnyong 선전용

democracy minjujuŭi 민주주의

democrat minjujuŭija 민주주의자; *Democrat* POL Minjudang-wŏn 민주당원; (*supporter*) Minjudang chijija 민주당 지지자

democratic minjujuŭiŭi 민주주의의

Democratic People's Republic of Korea Chosŏn Minjujuŭi Inmin Konghwaguk 조선 민주주의 인민 공화국

demo disk sŏnjŏnnyong tisŭk'ŭ 선전용 디스크

demolish *building* p'agoehada
파괴하다; *argument* twijiptta 뒤집다
demolition (*of building*) p'agoe 파괴;
(*of argument*) twijibŭm 뒤집음
demon angma 악마
demonstrate 1 *v/t* (*prove*)
iptchŭnghada 입증하다; *machine*
shiryŏnhada 실연하다 **2** *v/i*
(*politically*) shiwihada 시위하다
demonstration (*display*) kwashi
과시; (*protest*) shiwi 시위; (*of
machine*) shiryŏn 실연
demonstrative: be ~ kamjŏng-ŭl
tŭrŏnaeda 감정을 드러내다
demonstrator (*protester*) shiwi
ch'amgaja 시위 참가자
demoralized kiga kkŏkkin 기가 꺾인
demoralizing kirŭl kkŏngnŭn 기를
꺾는
den (*study*) sŏjae 서재
denial (*of rumor, accusation*) pujŏng
부정; (*of request*) kŏjŏl 거절
denim tenim 데님
denims (*jeans*) ch'ŏngbaji 청바지
Denmark Tenmak'ŭ 덴마크
denomination (*of money*) aengmyŏn
kŭmaek 액면 금액; (*religious*)
chongp'a 종파
dense tchit'ŭn 짙은; *foliage* ugŏjin
우거진; *crowd* miltchip'an 밀집한;
(*stupid*) udunhan 우둔한
densely: ~ populated in-guga
chomirhan 인구가 조밀한
density (*of population*) in-gu miltto
인구 밀도
dent 1 *n* ump'uk p'aein kot 움푹 패인
곳 **2** *v/t* ump'uk tŭrŏgage hada 움푹
들어가게 하다
dental *treatment* ch'iaŭi 치아의;
school etc ch'ikkwa 치과; **~ clinic**
ch'ikkwa 치과
dentist ch'ikkwa ŭisa 치과 의사
dentures ŭich'i 의치
deny *charge, rumor* puinhada
부인하다; *right, request* kŏjŏrhada
거절하다
deodorant t'alch'wije 탈취제
depart ch'ulbarhada 출발하다; **~
from** (*deviate*) ...esŏ pŏsŏnada
...에서 벗어나다
department (*of company*) pusŏ 부서;

(*of university*) hak-kwa 학과; (*of
government*) puch'ŏ 부처; (*of store*)
maejang 매장; **Department of Defense** Kukppangbu 국방부; **Department of the Interior** Hwan-
gyŏngch'ŏ 환경처; **Department of
State** (Mi)Kungmusŏng (미)국무성
department store paek'wajŏm
백화점
departure (*of train, bus etc*) ch'ulbal
출발; (*of person from job*)
kŭmandum 그만둠; (*deviation*) it'al
이탈; **a new ~** (*for goverment,
organization*) sae ch'ulbŏm 새 출범;
(*for company*) sae ch'ulbal 새 출발;
(*for actor, artist, writer*) saeroun
shido 새로운 시도
departure lounge taehapsshil
대합실
departure time ch'ulbal shigak 출발
시각
depend ŭijonhada 의존하다; **that ~s**
sanghwang-e ttara tarŭda 상황에
따라 다르다; **it ~s on the weather**
nalsshie tallyŏit-tta 날씨에 달려있다;
~ on sth (*need*) muŏse ŭijonhada
무엇에 의존하다; **I ~ on you** nanŭn
nŏhant'e ŭijonhago it-tta 나는
너한테 의존하고 있다
dependable ŭijonhal su innŭn 의존할
수 있는
dependence, dependency ŭijon
의존
dependent 1 *n* puyang kajok 부양
가족 **2** *adj* ŭijonhanŭn 의존하는
depict myosahada 묘사하다
deplorable hant'anhal 한탄할
deplore hant'anhada 한탄하다
deport kugoero ch'ubanghada 국외로
추방하다
deportation kugoe ch'ubang 국외
추방
deportation order t'oegŏ
myŏngnyŏng 퇴거 명령
deposit 1 *n* (*in bank*) yegŭm 예금; (*of
mineral*) maejangmul 매장물; (*on
purchase*) yeyak-kkŭm 예약금; (*for
the lease on an apartment*)
chŏnsegŭm 전세금 **2** *v/t money*
yegŭmhada 예금하다; (*put down*)
not'a 놓다; *silt, mud* t'oejŏkshik'ida

퇴적시키다
deposition LAW sŏnsŏ chŭng-ŏn 선서
증언
depot (*train station*) chŏnggŏjang
정거장; (*bus station*) chŏngnyujang
정류장; (*for storage*) ch'anggo 창고
depreciate v/i FIN kach'iga ttŏrŏjida
가치가 떨어지다
depreciation FIN kach'i harak 가치
하락
depress *person* uurhagehada
우울하게하다
depressed *person* uurhan 우울한
depressing uurhagehanŭn
우울하게하는
depression MED uultchŭng 우울증;
(*economic*) pulgyŏnggi 불경기;
(*meteorological*) chŏgiap
저기압
deprive: ~ X *of* Y Xegesŏ Yŭl/rŭl
ppaeat-tta X에게서 Y을/를 빼앗다
deprived *child* puruhan 불우한; *area*
kananhan 가난한
depth kip'i 깊이; (*of shelf*) kip'ŭm
깊음; (*of color*) chit'ŭm 짙음; (*of
thought*) shimoham 심오함; **in ~**
ch'ŏltchŏhage 철저하게; **in the ~s of
winter** han kyŏure 한 겨울에; **he
was out of his ~** (*in water*) kŭŭi
k'irŭl nŏmnŭn kip'iyŏt-tta 그의 키를
넘는 깊이였다; (*in discussion*) kŭŭi
ihaega mich'iji anat-tta 그의 이해가
미치지 않았다
deputation taep'yodan 대표단
♦**deputize for** ...ŭl/rŭl taerihada
...을/를 대리하다
deputy taeri 대리
deputy leader pudaep'yo 부대표
derail: **be ~ed** (*of train*)
t'alssŏndoeda 탈선되다
deranged hollandoen 혼란된
derelict *adj building* pŏryŏjin 버려진
deride piut-tta 비웃다
derision piusŭm 비웃음
derisive *remarks, laughter* piunnŭn
비웃는
derisory *amount* chwikkorimanhan
쥐꼬리만한
derivative (*not original*)
tokch'angjŏgi anin 독창적이 아닌
derive v/t ŏt-tta 얻다; **be ~d from** (*of*

word) ...esŏ yuraedoeda ...에서
유래되다
derogatory kyŏngmyŏrhanŭn
경멸하는; ~ **remark** kyŏngsŏl 욕설
descend 1 v/t naeryŏgada 내려가다;
she ~ed the staircase kŭnyŏnŭn
kyedanŭl naeryŏgat-tta 그녀는
계단을 내려갔다; **be ~ed from** ...ŭi
chasonida ...의 자손이다 **2** v/i (*of
airplane*) haganghada 하강하다; (*of
climber*) naeryŏgada 내려가다; (*of
road*) kyŏngsajida 경사지다; (*of
darkness*) naeryŏantta 내려앉다
descendant chason 자손
descent (*from mountain*) hasan 하산;
(*of airplane*) hagang 하강; (*ancestry*)
kagye 가계; **of Korean ~** Han-guk-
kkyeŭi 한국계의
describe myosahada 묘사하다; ~ X
as Y Xŭl/rŭl Y(ŭ)ro myosahada
X을/를 Y(으)로 묘사하다
description myosa 묘사
desegregate injong ch'abyŏl p'yeji
인종 차별 폐지
desert¹ n samak 사막; *fig* hwangmuji
황무지
desert² 1 v/t (*abandon*) pŏrida 버리다;
friends tŭngjida 등지다 **2** v/i (*of
soldier*) t'aryŏnghada 탈영하다
deserted injŏgi kkŭnk'in 인적이 끊긴
deserter MIL t'aryŏngbyŏng 탈영병
desertion (*abandoning*) pŏrim 버림;
MIL t'aryŏng 탈영
deserve padŭl manhada 받을 만하다;
~ **to ...** ... hal manhada ... 할 만하다
design 1 n tijain 디자인; (*drawing*)
mitkkŭrim 밑그림; (*for building, car
etc*) sŏlgyedo 설계도; (*pattern*)
munŭi 무늬 **2** v/t tijainhada
디자인하다; *building, car, machine*
sŏlgyehada 설계하다; **not ~ed for
use in the home** kajŏngnyŏng-i
anin 가정용이 아닌
designate v/t *person* immyŏnghada
임명하다; *area etc* chijŏnghada
지정하다
designer tijainŏ 디자이너; (*of car,
building*) sŏlgyeja 설계자
designer clothes yumyŏng tijainŏŭi
ot 유명 디자이너의 옷
design fault sŏlgyesang-ŭi

munjetchŏm 설계상의 문제점

design school tijain hak-kkyo 디자인 학교

desirable (*advisable*) paramjik'an 바람직한; (*coveted*) t'amnanŭn 탐나는

desire *n* param 바람; (*sexual*) yongmang 욕망

desk ch'aekssang 책상; (*in hotel*) tesŭk'ŭ 데스크

desk clerk chŏpssu kyewŏn 접수 계원

desktop publishing kŏmp'yut'ŏ ch'ulp'an 컴퓨터 출판

desolate *adj place* hwangnyanghan 황량한

despair 1 *n* chŏlmang 절망; **in ~** chŏlmanghayŏ 절망하여 **2** *v/i* chŏlmanghada 절망하다; **~ of** ...e taehae chŏlmanghada ...에 대해 절망하다

desperate *person, action* p'ilssajŏgin 필사적인; *situation* chŏlmangjŏgin 절망적인; **be ~ for a drink / cigarette** surŭl mashigo / tambaerŭl p'iugo ship'ŏ chugŭl chigyŏng-ida 술을 마시고 / 담배를 피우고 싶어 죽을 지경이다

desperation p'ilssajŏgim 필사적임; **an act of ~** chap'ojagishig-ŭi haengdong 자포자기식의 행동

despise kyŏngmyŏrhada 경멸하다

despite ...edo pulguhago ...에도 불구하고

despondent nakttamhan 낙담한

despot p'ok-kkun 폭군

dessert hushik 후식

destination moktchŏkchi 목적지

destiny unmyŏng 운명

destitute pin-gonhan 빈곤한

destroy p'agoehada 파괴하다; *fig* p'amyŏlshik'ida 파멸시키다; *trust, friendship, marriage* mangch'ida 망치다

destroyer NAUT kuch'uk'am 구축함

destruction p'agoe 파괴; *fig* p'amyŏl 파멸

destructive *power* p'agoejŏgin 파괴적인; *criticism* pujŏngjŏgin 부정적인

detach tteŏnaeda 떼어내다

detachable pullihal su innŭn 분리할 수 있는

detached (*objective*) kongp'yŏnghan 공평한

detachment (*objectivity*) kongp'yŏngham 공평함

detail *n* (*small point*) sebu sahang 세부 사항; (*piece of information*) chasehan naeyong 자세한 내용; (*trifle*) sasohan il 사소한 일; **in ~** chasehage 자세하게

detailed sangsehan 상세한

detain chich'eshik'ida 지체시키다; (*as prisoner*) kamgŭmhada 감금하다

detainee ŏngnyuja 억류자

detect arach'aeda 알아채다; (*of device*) t'amjihada 탐지하다

detection (*of criminal*) palgyŏn 발견; (*of crime*) palgak 발각; (*of smoke*) t'amji 탐지

detective (*policeman*) hyŏngsa 형사

detective novel t'amjŏng sosŏl 탐정 소설

detector t'amjigi 탐지기

détente POL kinjang wanhwa 긴장 완화

detention (*imprisonment*) kamgŭm 감금

deter tannyŏmshik'ida 단념시키다; **~ X from doing Y** Xi / ga Yhanŭn kŏsŭl mot'age hada X이/가 Y하는 것을 못하게 하다

detergent sech'ŏktche 세척제

deteriorate ak'wadoeda 악화되다

determination (*resolution*) kyŏlsshim 결심

determine (*decide*) kyŏltchŏnghada 결정하다; (*establish*) tanjŏnghada 단정하다

determined kyŏlsshimhan 결심한; *effort* hwakkohan 확고한

deterrent *n* panghaemul 방해물

detest hyŏmohada 혐오하다

detonate 1 *v/t* p'okppal shik'ida 폭발시키다 **2** *v/i* p'okpparhada 폭발하다

detour *n* uhoe 우회; (*diversion*) tarŭn kil 다른 길

detract: **~ from** ...ŭi kach'irŭl ttŏrŏttŭrida ...의 가치를 떨어뜨리다

detriment: **to the ~ of** ...e haerŭl

ip'igo ...에 해를 입히고
detrimental haeroun 해로운
deuce (*in tennis*) tyusŭ 듀스
devaluation FIN p'yŏngkka chŏrha 평가 절하
devalue *currency* p'yŏngkka chŏrhashik'ida 평가 절하시키다
devastate p'agoehada 파괴하다; *fig: person* nŏkssŭl ilk'e hada 넋을 잃게 하다
devastating apttohanŭn 압도하는
develop 1 *v/t land*, (*invent*) kaebarhada 개발하다; *activity*, *business* paltchŏnshik'ida 발전시키다; *film* hyŏnsanghada 현상하다; (*progress*) palttalshik'ida 발달시키다; *illness*, *cold* ...e kŏllida ...에 걸리다 **2** *v/i* (*grow*) paltchŏnhada 발전하다; (*of country*, *business*) kaebarhada 개발하다
developer (*of property*) kaebaltcha 개발자
developing country kaebaldosangguk 개발도상국
development (*of land*) kaebal 개발; (*of business*, *country*) sŏngjang 성장; (*event*) nyussŭ 뉴스; (*of film*) hyŏnsang 현상; (*progression*) paltchŏn 발전
device changch'i 장치; (*tool*) togu 도구
devil angma 악마
devious (*sly*) kyohwarhan 교활한
devise koanhada 고안하다
devoid: ~ *of* ...i/ga chŏnhyŏ ŏmnŭn ...이/가 전혀 없는
devote *time*, *money*, *life* pach'ida 바치다; *effort* son etc hŏnshinjŏgin 헌신적인; *be ~ to s.o.* nuguege hŏnshinjŏgida 누구에게 헌신적이다
devotion (*to a person*) hŏnshin 헌신; (*to one's job*) chŏnnyŏm 전념
devour *food* kegŏlssŭrŏpkke mŏktta 게걸스럽게 먹다; *book* t'amdok'ada 탐독하다
devout toksshirhan 독실한
dew isŭl 이슬
dexterity somsshi choŭm 솜씨 좋음
diabetes tangnyoppyŏng 당뇨병
diabetic 1 *n* tangnyoppŏng hwaja

당뇨병 환자 **2** *adj* tangnyoppyŏng-ŭi 당뇨병의
diagonal *adj* taegakssŏnŭi 대각선의
diagram top'yo 도표
dial 1 *n* (*of clock*) chap'an 자판; (*of meter*) nun-gŭmp'an 눈금판 **2** *v/i* TELEC chŏnhwarŭl kŏlda 전화를 걸다 **3** *v/t* TELEC: *number* taiŏrŭl tollida 다이얼을 돌리다
dialect sat'uri 사투리
dialog taehwa 대화
dial tone palsshinŭm 발신음
diameter chik-kkyŏng 직경
diametrically: ~ *opposed* chŏngbandaeŭi 정반대의
diamond (*jewel*, *in cards*) taiamondŭ 다이아몬드; (*shape*) taiamondŭ moyang 다이아몬드 모양
Diamond Sutra Kŭmganggyŏng 금강경
diaper kijogwi 기저귀
diaphragm ANAT hoenggyŏngmak 횡격막; (*contraceptive*) p'iimyong p'esari 피임용 페사리
diarrhea sŏlssa 설사
diary (*for thoughts*) ilgi 일기; (*for appointments*) iltchi 일지
dice 1 *n* chusawi 주사위 **2** *v/t* (*cut*) kkakttugi moyang-ŭro ssŏlda 깍두기 모양으로 썰다
dichotomy ibunppŏp 이분법
dictate *v/t letter*, *novel* kusurhada 구술하다
dictation padassŭgi 받아쓰기
dictator POL toktchaeja 독재자
dictatorial *tone of voice* myŏngnyŏngjŏgin 명령적인; *person* toktchaejŏgin 독재적인; *powers* hoengp'orŭl purinŭn 횡포를 부리는
dictatorship toktchae chŏngkkwŏn 독재 정권
dictionary sajŏn 사전
die chuktta 죽다; ~ *of cancer / aids* amŭro / eijŭro chuktta 암으로 / 에이즈로 죽다; *I'm dying to know / leave* algo / ttŏnago ship'ŏ chuk-kket-tta 알고 / 떠나고 싶어 죽겠다
♦ **die away** (*of noise*) chŏmjŏm sarajida 점점 사라지다
♦ **die down** (*of noise*) churŏdŭlda

줄어들다; (*of storm, fire*)
sugŭrŏdŭlda 수그러들다; (*of excitement*) chŏmjŏm sarajida 점점 사라지다
♦ **die out** (*of custom*) sarajida 사라지다; (*of species*) somyŏrhada 소멸하다
diesel (*fuel*) tijel 디젤
diet 1 *n* (*regular food*) shikttan 식단; (*for losing weight*) taiŏt'ŭ 다이어트; (*for health reasons*) shigi yoppŏp 식이 요법 **2** *v/i* (*to lose weight*) taiŏt'ŭhada 다이어트하다
differ (*be different*) tarŭda 다르다; (*disagree*) ŭigyŏnŭl tallihada 의견을 달리하다
difference ch'ai 차이; (*disagreement*) igyŏn 이견; *it doesn't make any ~* (*doesn't change anything*) amurŏn ch'aiga ŏptta 아무런 차이가 없다; (*doesn't matter*) sanggwan ŏpssŏyo 상관 없어요
different tarŭn 다른, pyŏlgaeŭi 별개의
differentiate: *~ between people* ch'abyŏrhada 차별하다; *~ between X and Y* Xwa/kwa Yŭl/rŭl kubyŏrhada X와/과 Y을/를 구별하다
differently tarŭge 다르게
difficult himdŭn 힘든
difficulty ŏryŏum 어려움; *with ~* ŏryŏpkke 어렵게
dig 1 *v/t* p'ada 파다 **2** *v/i*: *it was ~ging into me* narŭl k'ukk'uk tchillŏt-tta 나를 쿡쿡 찔렀다
♦ **dig out** (*find*) ch'ajanaeda 찾아내다
♦ **dig up** p'ahech'ida 파헤치다; *information* ch'ajanaeda 찾아내다
digest *v/t* sohwahada 소화하다
digestible *food* sohwaga chal toenŭn 소화가 잘 되는
digestion sohwa 소화
digit (*number*) arabia suttcha 아라비아 숫자; *a four ~ number* arabia suttcha negae 아라비아 숫자 네개
digital tijit'ŏl 디지털; *~ camera* tijit'ŏl k'amera 디지털 카메라
dignified wiŏm innŭn 위엄 있는
dignitary kowi insa 고위 인사
dignity chonŏm 존엄

digress pinnagada 빗나가다
digression pinnagam 빗나감
dike (*wall*) tuk 둑
dilapidated *house* hŏmurŏjin 허물어진; *car, sofa* hŏrŏppajin 헐어빠진
dilate (*of pupils*) nŏlp'ida 넓히다
dilemma chint'oeyangnan 진퇴양난; *be in a ~* chint'oeyangnane ch'ŏhada 진퇴양난에 처하다
diligent pujirŏnhan 부지런한
dilute *v/t* muk-kke hada 묽게 하다
dim 1 *adj room, light* ŏdumch'imch'imhan 어둠침침한; *outline* hŭrit'an 흐릿한; (*stupid*) udunhan 우둔한; *prospects* irŏnal kŏt kattchi anŭn 일어날 것 같지 않은 **2** *v/t*: *~ the headlights* hedŭrait'ŭrŭl kŭn-gŏriyong-ŭro pakkuda 헤드라이트를 근거리용으로 바꾸다 **3** *v/i* (*of lights*) hŭrige hada 흐리게 하다
dime ship ssent'ŭ 십 센트
dimension (*measurement*) ch'isu 치수
diminish 1 *v/t* churida 줄이다 **2** *v/i* chulda 줄다
diminutive 1 *n* churin irŭm 줄인 이름 **2** *adj* chagŭmahan 자그마한
dimple pojogae 보조개
din *n* shikkŭrŏun sori 시끄러운 소리
dine shikssahada 식사하다
diner (*person*) shikssahanŭn saram 식사하는 사람
dinghy chagŭn pae 작은 배
dingy (*gloomy*) ŭmch'imhan 음침한; (*dirty*) tŏrŏun 더러운; *a rather ~ white* taso ch'ikch'ik'an hayanssaek 다소 칙칙한 하얀색
dining car shikttangch'a 식당차; **dining room** shikttang 식당; **dining table** shikt'ak 식탁
dinner (*in the evening*) manch'an 만찬; (*at midday*) och'an 오찬; (*gathering*) hyang-yŏn 향연
dinner guest manch'an sonnim 만찬 손님; **dinner jacket** yaksshik yahoebok 약식 야회복; **dinner party** tinŏ p'at'i 디너 파티
dinosaur kongnyong 공룡
dip 1 *n* (*swim*) mure ttwiŏdŭm 물에 뛰어듦; (*for food*) yangnyŏmtchang

양념장; (*in road*) kyŏngsajin kot
경사진 곳 **2** *v/t* (*in liquid etc*)
saltchak tamgŭda 살짝 담그다; ~ *the*
headlights hedŭrait'ŭrŭl kŭn-
gŏriyong-ŭro pakkuda 헤드라이트를
근거리용으로 바꾸다 **3** *v/i* (*of road*)
kyŏngsaga chida 경사가 지다
diploma chŭngsŏ 증서
diplomacy oegyo 외교; (*tact*)
oegyosul 외교술
diplomat oegyogwan 외교관
diplomatic oegyoŭi 외교의; (*tactful*)
suwani choŭn 수완이 좋은
dire (*appalling*) hyŏngp'yŏnŏmnŭn
형편없는; (*extreme*) kŭkttanjŏgin
극단적인
direct 1 *adj* chiktchŏptchŏgin
직접적인; *flight, train* chik'aeng-ŭi
직행의; *person* nogoltchŏgin
노골적인; *a ~ descendant of ...*
...ŭi chik-kkye chason ...의 직계
자손 **2** *v/t* (*to a place*) annaehada
안내하다; *play* yŏnch'urhada
연출하다; *movie* kamdok'ada
감독하다; *attention* tollida 돌리다
direct current ELEC chingnyu 직류
direction panghyang 방향; (*of movie*)
kamdok 감독; (*of play*) yŏnch'ul
연출; ~s (*instructions*) annae 안내;
(*to a place*) panghyang 방향; (*for
use*) sayongppŏp 사용법; (*for
medicine*) pogyongppŏp 복용법
direction indicator MOT panghyang
p'yoshidŭng 방향 표시등
directly 1 *adv* (*straight*) paro 바로;
(*soon*) kot 곧; (*immediately*)
kŭmbang 금방 **2** *conj* ...hajamaja
...하자마자; ~ *I've finished* naega
kkŭnnaejamaja 내가 끝내자마자
director (*of company*) isa 이사; (*of
play*) yŏnch'ultcha 연출자; (*of
movie*) kamdok 감독
directory chuso sŏngmyŏngnok 주소
성명록; TELEC chŏnhwa pŏnhobu
전화 번호부; COMPUT tirekt'ori
디렉토리
dirt mŏnji 먼지
dirt cheap aju hŏlkkapssŭi 아주
헐값의
dirty 1 *adj* tŏrŏun 더러운;
(*pornographic*) ŭmnanhan 음란한

2 *v/t* ...ŭl / rŭl tŏrŏp'ida ...을 / 를
더럽히다
dirty trick piyŏrhan ch'aengnyak
비열한 책략
disability shinch'e chang-ae 신체
장애
disabled 1 *n: the* ~ shinch'e chang-
aeja 신체 장애자 **2** *adj* pulguŭi
불구의
disadvantage (*drawback*) tantchŏm
단점; *be at a* ~ pullihan iptchang-e
it-tta 불리한 입장에 있다
disadvantaged hyet'aekppat-tchi
mot'an 혜택받지 못한
disadvantageous pullihan 불리한
disagree ŭigyŏni tarŭda 의견이
다르다
♦**disagree with** ...wa / gwa ŭigyŏni
mat-tchi ant'a ...와 / 과 의견이 맞지
않다; (*of food*) ...ŭi soge mat-tchi
ant'a ...누 구의 속에 맞지 않다
disagreeable pulk'waehan 불쾌한
disagreement ŭigyŏn ch'ai 의견
차이; (*argument*) maldat'um 말다툼
disappear sarajida 사라지다; (*run
away*) chach'wi-rŭl kamch'uda
자취를 감추다
disappearance (*of thing*) somyŏl
소멸; (*of person*) shiltchong 실종
disappoint shilmangshik'ida
실망시키다
disappointed shilmanghan 실망한
disappointing shilmangsŭrŏun
실망스러운
disappointment shilmang 실망
disapproval pulch'ansŏng 불찬성
disapprove pulch'ansŏnghada
불찬성하다; ~ *of* ...e
pulch'ansŏnghada ...에 불찬성하다
disarm 1 *v/t robber* mugirŭl ppaeat-
tta 무기를 빼앗다; *militia* mujang
haejeshik'ida 무장 해제시키다 **2** *v/i*
mujang-ŭl haejehada 무장을
해제하다
disarmament mujang haeje 무장
해제
disarming ch'ŏnjinhan 천진한
disaster (*natural*) ch'ŏnjaejibyŏn
천재지변; (*fiasco*) shilp'ae 실패
disaster area chaehae chiyŏk 재해
지역; *fig* (*person*) kujebullŭng-in

disastrous 378

saram 구제불능인 사람
disastrous p'ihaega maksshimhan
피해가 막심한
disbelief: *in* ~ mitkkiji annŭn
mosŭbŭro 믿기지 않는 모습으로
disc tisŭk'ŭ 디스크
discard *old clothes* pŏrida 버리다;
boyfriend ch'abŏrida 차버리다;
theory, habits p'yegihada 폐기하다
discern (*see*) shikppyŏrhada 식별하다
discernible arabol su innŭn 알아볼
수 있는
discerning anmogi nop'ŭn 안목이
높은
discharge 1 *n* (*from hospital*)
t'oewŏn 퇴원; (*from army*) chedae
제대 **2** *v/t* (*from hospital*)
t'oewŏnshik'ida 퇴원시키다; (*from
army*) chedaeshik'ida 제대시키다;
(*from job*) haegoshik'ida 해고시키다
disciple (*religious*) cheja 제자
disciplinary chinggyeŭi 징계의
discipline 1 *n* kyuyul 규율 **2** *v/t*
pŏrŭsŭl karŭch'ida 버릇을 가르치다;
employee chinggyehada 징계하다
disc jockey tisŭk'ŭ chak'i 디스크
자키
disclaim puinhada 부인하다
disclose tŭrŏnaeda 드러내다
disclosure (*of information*) nusŏl
누설; (*about scandal*) p'ongno 폭로
disco tisŭk'o 디스코
discolor pyŏnsaeksshik'ida
변색시키다
discomfort (*pain*) ap'ŭm 아픔;
(*embarrassment*) ŏsaek'am 어색함
disconcert tanghwanghage hada
당황하게 하다
disconcerted tanghwanghan 당황한
disconnect pullishik'ida 분리시키다;
(*supply*) chungdanshik'ida
중단시키다; *telephone* kkŭnt'a 끊다
disconsolate sŏgŭlp'ŭn 서글픈
discontent pulman 불만
discontented pulmansŭrŏun
불만스러운
discontinue chungjihada 중지하다
discord MUS purhyŏp'waŭm
불협화음; (*in relations*) purhwa 불화
discotheque tisŭk'o t'ek 디스코 텍
discount 1 *n* harin 할인 **2** *v/t goods*

harinhada 할인하다; *theory*
mushihada 무시하다
discourage (*dissuade*) mot'age hada
못하게 하다; (*dishearten*)
nakttamshik'ida 낙담시키다
discover palgyŏnhada 발견하다;
talent palgurhada 발굴하다
discoverer palgyŏnhan saram 발견한
사람
discovery palgyŏn 발견
discredit *v/t person* ...ŭi shinyong-i
ttŏrŏjigehada ...의 신용이 떨어지게
하다; *theory* ...ŭi shinbingssŏng-ŭl
ttŏrŏttŭrida ...의 신빙성을
떨어뜨리다
discreet *person* shinjunghan 신중한
discrepancy (*in story*) mosun 모순;
(*in accounts etc*) purilch'i 불일치
discretion shinjungham 신중함; *at
your* ~ tangshinŭi chaeryang-ŭro
당신의 재량으로
discriminate: ~ *against* ...ŭl/rŭl
ch'abyŏrhada ...을/를 차별하다; ~
between X and Y (*distinguish*)
Xwa/gwa Yŭl/rŭl kubyŏrhada
X와/과 Y을/를 구별하다
discriminating shikppyŏllyŏgi innŭn
식별력이 있는
discrimination (*sexual, racial etc*)
ch'abyŏl 차별
discus (*object*) wŏnban 원반; (*event*)
wŏnban tŏnjigi 원반 던지기
discuss (*talk about*) hwaje sama
yaegihada 화제 삼아 얘기하다; (*of
article*) nonŭihada 논의하다; (*in
negotiations*) ŭinonhada 의논하다
discussion (*debate*) t'oron 토론;
have a ~ *with s.o.* nuguwa
ŭinonhada 누구와 의논하다; *it's still
under* ~ ajik nonŭijung-ida 아직
논의중이다
disease chilbyŏng 질병
disembark *v/i* naerida 내리다
disenchanted: ~ *with* ...e tŏ isang
maeryŏgŭl nŭkkiji mot'anŭn ...에 더
이상 매력을 느끼지 못하는
disengage noajuda 놓아주다
disentangle p'ulda 풀다
disfigure *person* oemorŭl ch'uhage
mandŭlda 외모를 추하게 만들다;
thing oegwanŭl sonsangshik'ida

외관을 손상시키다

disgrace 1 *n* pulmyŏng-ye 불명예; *a ~* (*person*) ch'iyok 치욕; *it's a ~* ch'iyoktchŏgin iriyeyo 치욕적인 일이에요; *in ~* pulmyŏng-yesŭrŏpke myŏnmogŭl irŭn 불명예스럽게 면목을 잃은, ch'emyŏnŭl irŭn 체면을 잃은 **2** *v/t* ...ŭi such'iga toeda ...의 수치가 되다

disgraceful such'isŭrŏun 수치스러운

disgruntled pulmansŭrŏun 불만스러운

disguise 1 *n* wijang 위장; (*costume, make-up*) pyŏn-jang 변장 **2** *v/t* wijanghada 위장하다; *fear, anxiety* naesaek'aji ant'a 내색하지 않다; *~ oneself as* ...(ŭ)ro pyŏnjanghada ...(으)로 변장하다; *he was ~d as* kŭnŭn ...(ŭ)ro wijanghaet-tta 그는 ...(으)로 위장했다

disgust 1 *n* hyŏmo 혐오 **2** *v/t* hyŏmogamŭl irŭk'ida 혐오감을 일으키다

disgusting *habit* hyŏmosŭrŏun 혐오스러운; *smell, food* kuyŏktchil nanŭn 구역질 나는; *it is ~ that ...* ...ranŭn kŏsŭn hyŏmosŭrŏptta ...라는 것은 혐오스럽다

dish (*part of meal*) yori 요리; (*container*) kŭrŭt 그릇; (*for rice*) konggi 공기; (*for soup*) taejŏp 대접

dishcloth haengju 행주

disheartened nakttamhan 낙담한

disheartening nakttam shik'inŭn 낙담시키는

disheveled *hair* hŏngk'ŭrŏjin 헝클어진; *clothes* tanjŏngch'i mot'an 단정치 못한; *person* hŭt'ŭrŏjin 흐트러진

dishonest pujŏngjik'an 부정직한

dishonesty pujŏngjik 부정직

dishonor *n* pulmyŏng-ye 불명예; *bring ~ on* ...ŭl/rŭl mangshinshik'ida ...을/를 망신시키다

dishonorable pulmyŏng-yesŭrŏun 불명예스러운

dishwasher (*person*) sŏlgŏjihanŭn saram 설거지하는 사람; (*machine*) sŏlgŏji kigye 설거지 기계

dishwashing liquid chubangyong

seje 주방용 세제

dishwater sŏlgŏji mul 설겆이 물

disillusion *v/t* hwansang-ŭl pŏrige hada 환상을 버리게 하다

disillusionment hwanmyŏl 환멸

disinclined maŭmi naek'iji annŭn 마음이 내키지 않는

disinfect sodok'ada 소독하다

disinfectant sodongnyak 소독약

disinherit sangsok-kkwŏnŭl pakt'arhada 상속권을 박탈하다

disintegrate hŏmurŏjida 허물어지다; (*of marriage, building*) punggoedoeda 붕괴되다

disinterested (*unbiased*) kongp'yŏnghan 공평한

disjointed chal yŏn-gyŏri toeji anŭn 잘 연결이 되지 않은

disk (*shape*) wŏnbanhyŏng 원반형; COMPUT tisŭk'et 디스켓; *on ~* tisŭk'ese chŏjangdoen 디스켓에 저장된

disk drive COMPUT tisŭk'et tŭraibŭ 디스켓 드라이브

diskette tisŭk'et 디스켓

dislike 1 *n* shirŏham 싫어함 **2** *v/t* shirŏhada 싫어하다

dislocate t'algushik'ida 탈구시키다

dislodge umjigida 움직이다

disloyal pulch'ungsshirhan 불충실한

disloyalty pulch'ungsshil 불충실

dismal *weather* ŭmsanhan 음산한; *news, prospect* ch'imurhan 침울한; (*depressed*) uurhan 우울한; (*pessimistic*) pujŏngjŏgin 부정적인; *failure* hyŏngp'yŏnŏmnŭn 형편없는

dismantle haech'ehada 해체하다

dismay 1 *n* (*alarm*) tanghwang 당황; (*disappointment*) nakttam 낙담 **2** *v/t* tanghwanghage hada 당황하게 하다

dismiss *employee* haegoshik'ida 해고시키다; *suggestion* kŏjŏrhada 거절하다; *idea, thought* ttŏlch'yŏbŏrida 떨쳐버리다; *possibility* mushihada 무시하다

dismissal (*of employee*) haego 해고

disobedience pulboktchong 불복종

disobedient marŭl tŭt-tchi annŭn 말을 듣지 않는

disobey kŏyŏk'ada 거역하다

disorder (*untidiness*) chijŏbunham

지저분함; (unrest) hollan 혼란; MED chang-ae 장애

disorderly room, desk ŏjillŏ noŭn 어질러 놓은; (unruly) mubŏbŭi 무법의

disorganized mujilssŏhan 무질서한

disoriented panghyang kamgagŭl irŏbŏrin 방향 감각을 잃어버린

disown ŭijŏrhada 의절하다

disparaging hŏltttŭnnŭn 헐뜯는

disparity pulgyunhyŏng 불균형

dispassionate naengjŏnghan 냉정한

dispatch v/t (send) palssonghada 발송하다

dispensary (in pharmacy) chojeshil 조제실

dispense: ~ with ... ŏpsshi hada ... 없이 하다

disperse 1 v/t hŭt'ŏjige hada 흩어지게 하다 2 v/i (of crowd) hŭt'ŏjida 흩어지다; (of mist) hŭt'ŏ ŏpssŏjida 흩어 없어지다

displace (supplant) pakkuŏ not'a 바꾸어 놓다

display 1 n chŏnshi 전시; (in store window) chinyŏl 진열; COMPUT tisŭp'ŭllei 디스플레이; **be on ~** (at exhibition) chŏnshi chung-ida 전시 중이다; (in store) chinyŏl chung-ida 진열 중이다 2 v/t emotion p'yoshihada 표시하다; (at exhibition) chŏnshihada 전시하다; (in store) chinyŏrhada 진열하다; COMPUT hwamyŏne p'yoshihada 화면에 표시하다

display cabinet chinyŏltchang 진열장

displease pulk'waehage hada 불쾌하게 하다

displeasure pulk'wae 불쾌

disposable ssŭgo pŏril su innŭn 쓰고 버릴 수 있는; **~ income** kach'ŏbun sodŭk 가처분 소득

disposal ch'ŏbun 처분; (of pollutants, nuclear waste) p'yegi 폐기; **I am at your ~** ŏnjedŭn malman haseyo 언제든 말만 하세요; **put X at Y's ~** Xŭl/rŭl Yŭi maŭmdaero ssŭge hada X을/를 Y의 마음대로 쓰게 하다

dispose: ~ **of** ...ŭl/rŭl ch'ŏbunhada ...을/를 처분하다

disposed: **be ~ to do ...** (willing) ...

hagop'ŭ maŭmi nada ... 하고픈 마음이 나다; **be well ~ toward** ...ege hogamŭl kajida ...에게 호감을 가지다

disposition (nature) kijil 기질

disproportionate pulgyunhyŏnghan 불균형한

disprove panjŭnghada 반증하다

dispute 1 n nonjaeng 논쟁; (between countries) punjaeng 분쟁; (industrial) chaeng-ŭi 쟁의 2 v/t (disagree with) pallonhada 반론하다; (fight over) ...ŭl/rŭl ŏdŭryŏgo ssauda ...을/를 얻으려고 싸우다

disqualify chagyŏgŭl pakt'arhada 자격을 박탈하다

disregard 1 n mushi 무시 2 v/t mushihada 무시하다

disrepair: **in a state of ~** hwangp'yehan sangt'aee 황폐한 상태에

disreputable person hyŏngp'yŏnŏmnŭn 형편없는; area p'yŏngp'ani nappŭn 평판이 나쁜

disrespect murye 무례

disrespectful muryehan 무례한

disrupt train service tujŏlshik'ida 두절시키다; meeting, class chungdanshik'ida 중단시키다

disruption (of train service) tujŏl 두절; (of meeting, class) chungdan 중단

disruptive punyŏlsshik'inŭn 분열시키는

dissatisfaction pulman 불만

dissatisfied pulmansŭrŏun 불만스러운

dissension ŭigyŏnŭi ch'ai 의견의 차이

dissent 1 n pandae ŭigyŏn 반대 의견 2 v/i: ~ **from** ...e pandaehada ...에 반대하다

dissident n pandaeja 반대자

dissimilar tarŭn 다른

dissociate: ~ **oneself from** ...wa/kwa kwan-gyerŭl kkŭnt'a ...와/과 관계를 끊다

dissolute pangt'anghan 방탕한

dissolve 1 v/t substance nogida 녹이다 2 v/i (of substance) noktta 녹다

dissuade mallida 말리다; ~ **X from Y**

Xi/ga Yhanŭn kŏsŭl mallida X이/가 Y하는 것을 말리다

distance 1 *n* kŏri 거리; *in the ~* mŏn kose(sŏ) 먼 곳에(서) **2** *v/t:* ~ *oneself from* …(ŭ)robut'ŏ kŏrirŭl tuda …(으) 로부터 거리를 두다

distant *place, time* mŏn 먼; *fig (aloof)* sowŏnhan 소원한

distaste shirŭm 싫음

distasteful shirŭn 싫은

distilled liquor soju 소주

distilled rice wine chŏngjong 정종

distinct *(clear)* tturyŏt'an 뚜렷한; *(different)* tarŭn 다른; *as ~ from* …wa/kwanŭn tarŭge …와/과는 다르게

distinction *(differentiation)* kubyŏl 구별; *hotel/product of ~* t'agwŏhan hot'el/sangp'um 탁월한 호텔/상품

distinctive t'ŭgyuŭi 특유의

distinctly tturyŏt'age 뚜렷하게; *(decidedly)* hwaksshirhi 확실히

distinguish *(see)* punganhada 분간하다; ~ *between X and Y* Xwa/gwa Yŭl/rŭl shikppyŏrhada X와/과 Y을/를 식별하다

distinguished *(famous)* chŏmyŏnghan 저명한; *(dignified)* kip'um innŭn 기품 있는

distort waegok'ada 왜곡하다

distract *person* shimnanhage hada 심란하게 하다; *attention* ttan tero tollige hada 딴 데로 돌리게 하다

distracted *(worried)* shimnanhan 심란한

distraction *(of attention)* ttan tero tollim 딴 데로 돌림; *(amusement)* kibun chŏnhwan 기분 전환; *drive s.o. to* ~ nugurŭl mich'ige mandŭlda 누구를 미치게 만들다

distraught mich'il tŭt'an 미칠 듯한

distress 1 *n (mental)* komin 고민; *(physical pain)* kot'ong 고통; *in ~ ship, aircraft* chonan sangt'aeŭi 조난 상태의 **2** *v/t (upset)* koerop'ida 괴롭히다

distress signal chonan shinho 조난 신호

distribute nanuda 나누다; *wealth* punbaehada 분배하다; COM

yut'onghada 유통하다

distribution *(handing out)* nanuŏ chum 나누어 줌; *(of wealth)* punbae 분배; COM yut'ong 유통

distribution arrangement COM yut'ong hyŏptchŏng 유통 협정

distributor COM paegŭbŏptcha 배급업자

district chiyŏk 지역; *(of city)* ku 구

district attorney chibang kŏmsa 지방 검사

district office kuch'ŏng 구청

distrust 1 *n* pulsshin 불신 **2** *v/t* pulsshinhada 불신하다

disturb *(interrupt)* panghaehada 방해하다; *(upset)* …ŭi maŭmŭl ŏjirŏp'ida …의 마음을 어지럽히다; *do not ~* panghaehaji mashio 방해하지 마시오

disturbance *(interruption)* panghae 방해; ~*s* soyo 소요

disturbed *(concerned, worried)* maŭmi ŏjirŏun 마음이 어지러운; *(mentally)* chŏngshin isang-ŭi 정신 이상의

disturbing maŭmŭl ŏjirŏp'inŭn 마음을 어지럽히는

disused sayongdoeji annŭn 사용되지 않는

ditch 1 *n* torang 도랑 **2** *v/t* F *(get rid of)* pŏrida 버리다; *(drop)* kŭmanduda 그만두다

dive 1 *n* ttwiŏdŭlgi 뛰어들기; *(underwater)* chamsu 잠수; *(of plane)* kŭpkkangha 급강하; F *(bar)* ssaguryŏ sultchip 싸구려 술집; *take a ~ (of dollar etc)* p'ongnak'ada 폭락하다 **2** *v/i* ttwiŏdŭlda 뛰어들다; *(underwater)* chamsuhada 잠수하다; *(of plane)* kŭpkkanghahada 급강하하다

diver *(off board)* taibŏ 다이버; *(underwater)* chamsubu 잠수부

diverge kallajida 갈라지다

diverse tayanghan 다양한

diversification COM saŏbŭi tagak'wa 사업의 다각화

diversify *v/i* COM saŏbŭl tagak'washik'ida 사업을 다각화시키다

diversion *(for traffic)* uhoe 우회; *(to*

distract attention) chuŭirŭl ttan tero tollim 주의를 딴 데로 돌림

diversity tayangssŏng 다양성

divert *traffic* uhoeshik'ida 우회시키다; *attention* ttan tero tollida 딴 데로 돌리다

divest: ~ *X of Y* Xegesŏ Yŭl/rŭl ppaeat-tta X에게서 Y을/를 빼앗다

divide nanuda 나누다

dividend FIN paedanggŭm 배당금; *pay ~s* fig idŭgi toeda 이득이 되다

divine REL shinsŏnghan 신성한; F aju mŏtchin 아주 멋진

diving (*from board*) taibing 다이빙; (*scuba*) sŭk'ubŏ taibing 스쿠버 다이빙

diving board taibing tae 다이빙 대

divisible nanul su innŭn 나눌 수 있는

division MATH nanutssem 나눗셈; (*in party etc*) punyŏl 분열; (*splitting into parts*) pulli 분리; (*of company*) pusŏ 부서

divorce 1 *n* ihon 이혼; *get a ~* ihonhada 이혼하다 **2** ...wa/kwa ihonhada ...와/과 이혼하다 **3** *v/i* ihonhada 이혼하다

divorced ihonhan 이혼한; *get ~d* ihonhada 이혼하다

divorcee (*man*) ihonnam 이혼남; (*woman*) ihonnyŏ 이혼녀

divulge nusŏrhada 누설하다; *secret* palk'ida 밝히다

DIY (= *do-it-yourself*) sonsu mandŭlgi 손수 만들기

DIY store tiaiwai kage 디아이와이 가게

dizzy: *feel ~* hyŏn-gitchŭng-i nada 현기증이 나다

DMZ (= *Demilitarized Zone*) Pimujang Chidae 비무장 지대

DNA (= *deoxyribonucleic acid*) tioksshiribo haekssan 디옥시리보 핵산

do 1 *v/t* hada 하다; *one's hair* sonjirhada 손질하다; *French, chemistry* kongbuhada 공부하다; *100mph etc* ...ŭi sokttorŭl naeda ...의 속도를 내다; *what are you ~ing tonight?* onŭl chŏnyŏk mwŏ halkkŏyeyo? 오늘 저녁에 뭐 할꺼예요?; *I don't know what to ~*

ŏttŏk-kke haeya haltchi morŭgessŏyo 어떻게 해야 할지 모르겠어요; *no, I'll ~ it* aniyo, chega hagessŭmnida 아니요, 제가 하겠습니다; *~ it right now!* chigŭm tangjang hae! 지금 당장 해!; *have you done this before?* chŏne hae pon chŏgi issŏyo? 전에 해 본 적이 있어요?; *have one's hair done* mŏrirŭl sonjirhada 머리를 손질하다 **2** *v/i* (*be suitable, enough*) kwaench'ant'a 괜찮다; *that will ~!* kŭ chŏngdomyŏn twaessŏ! 그 정도면 됐어!; *~ well* (*of person*) chal haenaeda 잘 해내다; (*of business*) saŏbi chal toeda 사업이 잘 되다; *well done!* (*congratulations!*) chal haessŏyo! 잘 했어요!; *how ~ you ~* chŏŭm poepkkessŭmnida 처음 뵙겠습니다 **3** (*auxiliary*): *~ you know him?* kŭ saramŭl algo issŭmnikka? 그 사람을 알고 있습니까?; *I don't know* morŭgessŏyo 모르겠어요; *~ you like Seoul? - yes I ~* Sŏurŭl choahaeyo? - ne, choahaeyo 서울을 좋아해요? - 네, 좋아해요; *he works hard, doesn't he?* kŭnŭn chŏngmal yŏlsshimhiirhajyo? 그는 정말 열심히 일하죠?; *don't you believe me?* narŭl mittchi annayo? 나를 믿지 않아요?; *you ~ believe me, don't you?* narŭl mittchyo? 나를 믿죠?

♦**do away with** p'yejihada 폐지하다

♦**do in**: *I'm done in* F nanŭn nokch'oga toeŏt-tta 나는 녹초가 되었다

♦**do out of**: *do X out of Y* Xŭl/rŭl sogyŏ Yŭl/rŭl ppaeat-tta X을/를 속여 Y을/를 빼앗다

♦**do over** (*do again*) toep'urihada 되풀이하다

♦**do up** (*renovate*) posuhada 보수하다; (*fasten*) chamgŭda 잠그다; *buttons* ch'aeuda 채우다; *laces* muktta 묶다

♦**do with**: *I could ~ ...* nanŭn ...i/ga p'iryohada 나는 ...이/가 필요하다; *he won't have anything to ~ it* kŭnŭn kŭ ilgwa mugwanhada 그는 그 일과 무관하다

♦ **do without 1** *v/i* kyŏndida 견디다
  2 *v/t* … ŏpsshi chinaeda … 없이
  지내다

docile *person* sunhan 순한; *animal*
  tarugi shwiun 다루기 쉬운

dock¹ 1 *n* NAUT pudu 부두 **2** *v/i* (*of
  ship*) pudue taeda 부두에 대다; (*of
  spaceship*) tok'ingshik'ida
  도킹시키다

dock² LAW p'igosŏk 피고석

dockyard chosŏnso 조선소

doctor *n* MED ŭisa 의사; (*form of
  address*) ŭisa sŏnsaengnim 의사
  선생님

doctorate paksa hagwi 박사 학위

doctrine shinjo 신조

docudrama tak'yument'ŏri tŭrama
  다큐멘터리 드라마

document *n* sŏryu 서류

documentary (*program*)
  tak'yument'ŏri 다큐멘터리

documentation (*documents*) sŏryu
  서류

dodge *v/t blow* p'ihada 피하다;
  person, issue kyomyohi hoep'ihada
  교묘히 회피하다; *question* tullŏdaeda
  둘러대다

doe (*deer*) amssasŭm 암사슴

dog 1 *n* kae 개 **2** *v/t* (*follow*)
  mihaenghada 미행하다; (*of bad
  luck*) kyesok'aesŏ irŏnada 계속해서
  일어나다

dog catcher tŭlkkae p'ohoegin 들개
  포획인

dogged kkŭnjilgin 끈질긴

doggie mŏngmŏng-i 멍멍이

doggy bag namŭn ŭmshigŭl ssajunŭn
  kŏt 남은 음식을 싸주는 것

doghouse: *be in the* ~ ch'emyŏnŭl
  ilt'a 체면을 잃다

dogma kyori 교리

dogmatic toksssŏnjŏgin 독선적인

do-gooder kongsangjŏk sahoe
  kaeryangga 공상적 사회 개량가

dog tag MIL kuninŭi insshikp'yo
  군인의 인식표

dog-tired kijinmaektchinhan
  기진맥진한

do-it-yourself sonsu mandŭlgi 손수
  만들기

doldrums: *be in the* ~ (*of economy*)

purhwang-ida 불황이다; (*of person*)
  ch'imurhae it-tta 침울해 있다

♦ **dole out** paebunhada 배분하다

doll (*toy*) inhyŏng 인형; F (*woman*)
  maeryŏktchŏgin yŏja 매력적인 여자

♦ **doll up**: *get dolled up* mŏttchige
  ch'aryŏ iptta 멋지게 차려 입다

dollar tallŏ 달러

dollop *n* tŏng-ŏri 덩어리

dolmen koindol 고인돌

dolphin tolkkorae 돌고래

dome (*of building*) tunggŭn
  ch'ŏnjang 둥근 천장

domestic *adj chores* kasaŭi 가사의;
  news, policy kungnaeŭi 국내의

domestic animal (*for agriculture*)
  kach'uk 가축

domesticate *animal* kiltŭrida
  길들이다; *be ~d* (*of person*) kasa irŭl
  hada 가사 일을 하다

domestic flight kungnaesŏn
  pihaenggi 국내선 비행기

dominant chuyohan 주요한;
  (*influential*) yuryŏk'an 유력한; BIO
  usŏng-ŭi 우성의

dominate chibaehada 지배하다;
  landscape apttohada 압도하다

domination (*control*) chibae 지배;
  (*superiority*) use 우세

domineering chibaejŏgin
  지배적인; *husband* p'okkunjŏgin
  폭군적인

donate *money* kibuhada 기부하다;
  time pach'ida 바치다; *toys, books*
  hŭisahada 희사하다; MED kijŭnghada
  기증하다

donation (*of money*) kibuhada 기부;
  (*of time*) hŏnsshin 헌신; (*of toys,
  books*) hŭisa 희사; MED kijŭng 기증

donkey tangnagwi 당나귀

donor (*of money*) kibuja 기부자; MED
  kijŭngja 기증자

donut tonŏt 도넛

doom *n* (*fate*) agun 악운; (*ruin*)
  p'amyŏl 파멸

doomed *project* p'agidoenŭn
  파기되는; *we are* ~ (*bound to fail*)
  urinŭn shilp'aehage toeŏit-tta 우리는
  실패하게 되어있다; (*going to die*)
  urinŭn chukke toeŏit-tta 우리는
  죽게 되어있다; *the* ~ *ship* nanp'ahal

unmyŏng-ŭi pae 난파할 운명의 배
door mun 문; (*entrance, exit*)
ch'urimmun 출입문; ***there's someone at the*** ~ nugun-ga mune it-tta
누군가 문에 있다
doorbell ch'oinjong 초인종; **doorknob** munjabi 문잡이; **doorman** tŏ
maen 도어 맨; **doormat** hyŏn-
gwane innŭn kudu tak-kkae 현관에
있는 구두 닦개; **doorstep**
muntchibang 문지방; **doorway**
ch'uripku 출입구
dope 1 n (*drugs*) mayak 마약; F
(*idiot*) mŏngch'ŏng-i 멍청이; F
(*information*) pimil chŏngbo 비밀
정보 **2** v/t yagŭl mŏgida 약을 먹이다
dormant *plant* paryuk chŏngji chung-
in 발육 정지 중인; ~ *volcano*
hyuhwasan 휴화산
dormitory kisukssa 기숙사
dosage pogyongnyang 복용량
dose n irhoe pogyongnyang 일회
복용량
dot n (*also in e-mail address*) chŏm
점; **on the ~** chŏnghwak'i 정확히
♦**dote on** ...e holttak ppajida ...에
홀딱 빠지다
dotted line chŏmsŏn 점선
double 1 n (*amount*) tu pae 두 배;
(*person*) kkok talmŭn saram 꼭 닮은
사람; (*of movie star*) taeyŏk 대역;
(*room*) iinyong pang 이인용 방 **2** *adj*
(*twice as much*) tu paeŭi 두 배의;
whiskey tŏbŭl 더블; *sink, oven* ssang-
ŭro toen 쌍으로 된; *doors*
yangtchoguro yŏnŭn mun 양쪽으로
여는 문; *layer* tu kyŏbŭi 두 겹의; **in
~ figures** tu chari su 두 자리 수
3 *adv* tu paero 두 배로 **4** v/t tu paero
hada 두 배로 하다; (*fold*) panŭro
chŏptta 반으로 접다 **5** v/i tu paega
toeda 두 배가 되다
♦**double back** v/i (*go back*)
toedoragada 되돌아가다
♦**double up** (*in pain*) ap'asŏ momŭl
kuburida 아파서 몸을 구부리다;
(*share a room*) pang-ŭl nanuŏ ssŭda
방을 나누어 쓰다
double-bass tŏbŭlbeisŭ 더블베이스;
double bed tŏbŭlbedŭ 더블베드;
double-breasted tanch'uga

yangtchoguro tallin 단추가 양쪽으로
달린; **doublecheck** v/t & v/i tashi
hwaginhada 다시 확인하다; **double
chin** ijungt'ŏk 이중턱; **double click**
n tŏbŭl k'ŭllik 더블클릭; **doublecross** v/t paebanhada 배반하다;
double glazing ijung yuri 이중
유리; **doublepark** v/i ijung
chuch'ashik'ida 이중 주차시키다;
double-quick: in ~ time
hwanggŭp'i 황급히; **double room**
iinyong pang 이인용 방
doubles (*in tennis*) poksshik 복식
doubt 1 n (*suspicion*) ŭisim 의심;
(*mistrust*) pulsshin 불신;
(*uncertainty*) ŭigushim 의구심; **be in
~** purhwaksshirhada 불확실하다; **no
~** (*probably*) tabunhi 다분히 **2** v/t
ŭisimhada 의심하다
doubtful *remark, look* ŭisimtchŏgŭn
의심쩍은; **be ~** (*of person*)
ŭisimsurŏptta 의심스럽다; **it is ~
whether** ... halji purhwaksshirhada
... 할지 불확실하다
doubtfully ŭisimsurŏpkke
의심스럽게
doubtless hwaksshirhi 확실히
dough milkkaru panjuk 밀가루 반죽;
F (*money*) ton 돈
dove pidulgi 비둘기; *fig*
p'yŏnghwajuŭija 평화주의자
dowdy ch'onsŭrŏun 촌스러운
Dow Jones Average Tau Chonsŭ
p'yŏnggyun chuga 다우 존스 평균
주가
down¹ n (*feathers*) kitt'ŏl 깃털
down² **1** *adv* (*downward*) najŭn
tchoguro 낮은 쪽으로; (*onto the
ground*) araetchoguro 아래쪽으로; ~
there chŏgi araetchoge 저기
아래쪽에; *fall* ~ ttŏrŏjida 떨어지다;
look ~ naeryŏda poda 내려다 보다;
$200 ~ (*as deposit*) kyeyak-kkŭm
200tallŏ 계약금 200달러; *go* ~ *south*
namtchoguro naeryŏgada 남쪽으로
내려가다; *be* ~ (*of price, rate*)
naerida 내리다; (*of numbers,
amount*) churŏdŭrŏ it-tta 줄어들어
있다; (*not working*) kojangna it-tta
고장나 있다; (*depressed*) ultchŏk'ae
hada 울적해 하다 **2** *prep* ...ŭi

araetchogŭro ...의 아래쪽으로;
(*along*) ...ŭl / rŭl ttara ...을 / 를 따라;
run ~ the stairs kyedanŭi
araetchogŭro tallyŏ naeryŏgada
계단의 아래쪽으로 달려 내려가다;
walk ~ the road kirŭl ttara kŏt-tta
길을 따라 걷다 **3** *v/t* (*swallow*)
mashida 마시다; (*destroy*) ssoa
nŏmŏttŭrida 쏘아 넘어뜨리다
down-and-out *n* pint'ŏlt'ŏri
빈털터리; **downcast** (*dejected*) p'uri
chugŭn 풀이 죽은; **downfall** *n*
mollak 몰락; (*cause of ruin*)
shilp'aeŭi wŏnin 실패의 원인;
downgrade *v/t person*
kangdŭngshik'ida 강등시키다;
document, forecast chŏngdorŭl
ttŏrŏttŭrida 정도를 떨어뜨리다;
downhearted p'uri chugŭn 풀이
죽은; **downhill** *adv: go ~* (*of road*)
naerimak-kkiri toeda 내리막길이
되다; (*of quality of work*) ttŏrŏjida
떨어지다; (*of health*) yak'wadoeda
약화되다; (*of country*) soet'oehada
쇠퇴하다; **downhill skiing** hwalgang
sŭk'i 활강 스키; **download** COMPUT
taunrodinghada 다운로딩하다;
downmarket *adj* taejungtchŏgin
대중적인; **down payment** kyeyak-
kkŭm 계약금; **downplay**
kyŏngshihada 경시하다; **downpour**
p'ogu 폭우; **downright 1** *adj idiot*
wanjŏnhan 완전한; *~ lie* saeppalgan
kŏjinmal 새빨간 거짓말 **2** *adv*
dangerous, stupid etc aju 아주;
downside (*disadvantage*) tantchŏm
단점; **downsize 1** *v/t car*
sohyŏnghwahada 소형화하다;
company kyumorŭl churida 규모를
줄이다 **2** *v/i* (*of company*) kyumoga
chulda 규모가 줄다; **downstairs**
1 *adj* araech'ŭng-ŭi 아래층의 **2** *adv*
araech'ung-e(sŏ) 아래층에(서);
down-to-earth *approach*
shiltchejŏgin 실제적인; *person*
hyŏnshiljŏgin 현실적인; **down-town**
1 *adj* toshim-ŭi 도심의 **2** *adv* toshiŭi
chungshimbue(sŏ) 도시의
중심부에(서); **downturn** (*economic*)
kyŏnggi ch'imch'e 경기 침체
downward 1 *adj* araetchogŭroŭi

아래쪽으로의 **2** *adv* araetchogŭro
아래쪽으로
doze 1 *n* sŏnjam 선잠 **2** *v/i* cholda
졸다
♦**doze off** kkubŏk-kkubŏk cholda
꾸벅꾸벅 졸다
dozen yŏldu kae 열두 개; *~s of* aju
manŭn 아주 많은
DPRK (= *Democratic People's
Republic of Korea*) Chosŏn
Minjujuŭi Inmin Konghwaguk 조선
민주주의 인민 공화국
drab tanjoroun 단조로운
draft 1 *n* (*of air*) t'ongp'ung 통풍; (*of
document*) ch'ogo 초고; MIL
chingbyŏng 징병; *~* (*beer*)
saengmaektchu 생맥주 **2** *v/t*
document ch'ogorŭl chakssŏnghada
초고를 작성하다; MIL
chingbyŏnghada 징병하다
draft dodger chingbyŏng kip'ija 징병
기피자
draftee chingjip-ppyŏng 징집병
draftsman (*of technical drawing*)
toan-ga 도안가; (*of plan*) ibanja
입안자
drafty t'ongp'ung-i chal toenŭn
통풍이 잘 되는
drag 1 *n: it's a ~ having to ...* ...
haeya hanŭn kŏshi sŏnggashida ...
해야 하는 것이 성가시다; *he's a ~*
kŭnŭn ttabunhan saramida 그는
따분한 사람이다; *the main ~* han-gil
한길; *in ~* yŏjang-ŭl hago yŏjada
를 하고 **2** *v/t* (*pull*) kkŭrŏ tanggida 끌어
당기다; *person, oneself* kkŭrŏ tŭrida
끌어 들이다; (*search*) hultta 훑다; *~
X into Y* (*involve*) Xŭl / rŭl Y(ŭ)ro
kkŭrŏ tŭrida X을 / 를 Y(으)로 끌어
들이다; *~ X out of Y* (*get
information from*) Y(ŭ)robut'ŏ
Xŭl / rŭl kanshinhi ppaenaeda
Y(으)로부터 X을 / 를 간신히 빼내다
3 *v/i* (*of time*) kkŭlda 끌다; (*of show,
movie*) chiruhada 지루하다
♦**drag away**: *drag oneself away
from the TV* t'ellebijŏnesŏ tteŏ
not'a 텔레비전에서 떼어 놓다
♦**drag in** (*into conversation*) ...e
taehan marŭl kkŏnaeda ...에 대한
말을 꺼내다

♦**drag on** chijil kkŭlda 질질 끌다
♦**drag out** (*prolong*) kkŭlda 끌다
♦**drag up** (*mention*) kkŭjibŏ naeda
끄집어 내다
dragon yong 용; *fig* ŏmkkyŏk'an
saram 엄격한 사람
drain 1 n (*pipe*) paesuro 배수로;
(*under street*) hasugu 하수구; *a ~ on
resources* chawŏn kogal 자원 고갈
2 v/t *water* ppaenaeda 빼내다; *engine
oil* paech'ulshik'ida 배출시키다;
vegetables mulkkirŭl ppaeda 물기를
빼다; *land* paesu shisŏrŭl hada 배수
시설을 하다; *glass, tank* piuda
비우다; (*exhaust: person*) chich'ige
hada 지치게 하다 **3** v/i (*of dishes*)
mulkkiga marŭda 물기가 마르다
♦**drain away** (*of liquid*) ppajida
빠지다
♦**drain off** *water* ppaeda 빼다
drainage (*drains*) paesu 배수; (*of
water from soil*) ppajim 빠짐
drainpipe paesugwan 배수관
drama (*art form*) hŭigok 희곡;
(*excitement*) kŭktchŏgin sanghwang
극적인 상황; (*play: on TV*) tŭrama
드라마
dramatic yŏn-gŭgŭi 연극의; (*exciting*)
kŭktchŏgin 극적인; *gesture*
kwajangdoen 과장된
dramatist kŭktchak-kka 극작가
dramatization (*play*) kŭk'wa 극화
dramatize *story* kŭk'wahada
극화하다; *fig* kwajanghayŏ
p'yohyŏnhada 과장하여 표현하다
drape v/t *cloth, coat* tullŏ ssŭiuda 둘러
씌우다; *~d in* (*covered with*) ...(ŭ)ro
tullŏ ssayŏjin ...(으)로 둘러 싸여진
drapery hwijang 휘장
drapes k'ŏt'ŭn 커튼
drastic (*extreme*) chinach'in 지나친;
measures kwagamhan 과감한;
change kyŏngnyŏrhan 격렬한
draw 1 n (*in match, competition*)
tongtchŏm 동점; (*in lottery*) chebi
ppopkki 제비 뽑기; (*attraction*)
inkkiinnŭn kŏt 인기있는 것 **2** v/t
picture, map kŭrida 그리다; *cart*
kkŭrŏ tanggida 끌어 당기다; *curtain*
ch'ida 치다; *gun, knife* ppaeda 빼다;
(*attract*) ...ŭi chuŭirŭl kkŭlda ...의

주의를 끌다; (*lead*) teryŏgada
데려가다; (*from bank account*)
inch'urhada 인출하다 **3** v/i kŭrimŭl
kŭrida 그림을 그리다; (*in match,
competition*) pigida 비기다; *~ near*
kakkai tagagada 가까이 다가가다; (*of
time*) kakkai tagaoda 가까이
다가오다
♦**draw back 1** v/i (*recoil*) twiro
mullŏnada 뒤로 물러나다 **2** v/t (*pull
back*) twiro tanggida 뒤로 당기다
♦**draw on 1** v/i (*advance*) kip'ŏgada
깊어가다 **2** v/t (*make use of*)
iyonghada 이용하다
♦**draw out** v/t *pocketbook* kkŏnaeda
꺼내다; *money from bank*
inch'urhada 인출하다
♦**draw up 1** v/t *document*
chakssŏnghada 작성하다; *chair*
nŭrŏnot'a 늘어놓다 **2** v/i (*of vehicle*)
mŏmch'uda 멈추다
drawback kyŏltchŏm 결점
drawer[1] (*of desk etc*) sŏrap 서랍
drawer[2] (*person*) hwaga 화가
drawing kŭrim 그림
drawing board chedop'an 제도판; *go
back to the ~* ch'ŏŭmbut'ŏ tashi
shijak'ada 처음부터 다시 시작하다
drawl n nŭrin malt'u 느린 말투
dread v/t turyŏwŏhada 두려워하다
dreadful *movie, book*
mushimushihan 무시무시한; *weather,
pity* chidok'an 지독한
dreadfully (*extremely*) mopsshi 몹시;
behave hyŏngp'yŏnŏpsshi 형편없이
dream 1 n kkum 꿈 **2** adj *house etc*
kkumgat'ŭn 꿈같은 **3** v/t kkumkkuda
꿈꾸다; (*day~*) mongsanghada
몽상하다 **4** v/i kkumŭl kkuda 꿈을
꾸다; (*day~*) mongsanghada
몽상하다
♦**dream up** ŏngttunghan saenggagŭl
haenaeda 엉뚱한 생각을 해내다
dreamer (*day~*) mongsangga 몽상가
dreamy *voice, look* kkumkkyŏlgat'ŭn
꿈꼴같은
dreary chiruhan 지루한
dredge *harbor, canal* chunsŏrhada
준설하다
♦**dredge up** *fig* tŭlch'uŏnaeda
들추어내다

dregs (of coffee) tchikkŏgi 찌꺼기; **the ~ of society** sahoe ssŭregi 사회 쓰레기

drench v/t hŭmppŏk chŏksshida 흠뻑 적시다; **get ~ed** hŭmppŏk chŏt-tta 흠뻑 젖다

dress 1 n (for woman) tŭresŭ 드레스; (clothing) ot 옷 **2** v/t person osŭl ip'ida 옷을 입히다; wound pungdaerŭl kamtta 붕대를 감다; **get ~ed** osŭl iptta 옷을 입다 **3** v/i (get ~ed) ot iptta 옷 입다; **~ in black / conservatively** kkaman saegŭro / posujŏgŭro osŭl iptta 까만 색으로 / 보수적으로 옷을 입다; **~ well** osŭl chal iptta 옷을 잘 입다
♦**dress up** v/i sŏngjanghada 성장하다; (wear a disguise) pyŏnjanghada 변장하다; **~ as** ...(ŭ)ro pyŏnjanghada ...(으)로 변장하다

dress circle kŭktchang-ŭi t'ŭkppyŏlssŏk 극장의 특별석

dresser (dressing table) hwajangdae 화장대; (in kitchen) ch'antchang 찬장

dressing (for salad) sosŭ 소스; (for wound) pungdae 붕대

dressing room THEA punjangshil 분장실

dressing table hwajangdae 화장대

dressmaker yangjaesa 양재사

dress rehearsal ŭisang lihŏsŏl 의상 리허설

dressy uahan 우아한

dribble v/i (of person, baby) ch'imŭl hŭllida 침을 흘리다; (of liquid) ttukttuk ttŏrŏjida 뚝뚝 떨어지다; SP tŭribŭrhada 드리블하다

dried fruit etc mallin 말린

drier kŏnjogi 건조기

drift 1 n (of snow) nundŏmi 눈더미 **2** v/i (of snow) parame nallyŏ ssaida 바람에 날려 쌓이다; (of ship) p'yoryuhada 표류하다; (go off course) hangnoesŏ pŏsŏnada 항로에서 벗어나다; (of person) chŏngch'ŏŏpsshi pangnanghada 정처없이 방랑하다
♦**drift apart** (of couple) maŭmi mŏrŏjida 마음이 멀어지다

drifter pangnangja 방랑자

drill 1 n (tool) ch'ŏn-gonggi 천공기; (exercise) yŏnssŭp 연습; MIL hullyŏn 훈련 **2** v/t hole ttult'a 뚫다 **3** v/i (for oil) kumŏng naeda 구멍 내다; MIL hullyŏnhada 훈련하다

drilling rig (platform) chŏn-gongdae 천공대

drily remark pikkoasŏ 비꼬아서

drink 1 n mashil kŏt 마실 것; **a ~ of ... han chan** ... 한 잔; **a ~ of water** mul han chan 물 한 잔; **go for a ~** han chan harŏ kada 한 잔 하러 가다 **2** v/t mashida 마시다 **3** v/i mashida 마시다; (consume alcohol) surŭl mashida 술을 마시다; **I don't ~** nanŭn surŭl ibe taeji anssŭmnida 나는 술을 입에 대지 않습니다
♦**drink up** v/t & v/i ta mashida 다 마시다

drinkable mashil su innŭn 마실 수 있는

drinker ŭmjuja 음주자

drinking (of alcohol) ŭmju 음주

drinking water mashinŭn mul 마시는 물

drip 1 n pang-ul 방울; MED chŏmjŏk 점적 **2** v/i ttokttok ttŏrŏjida 똑똑 떨어지다

dripdry nŏrŏsŏ mallida 널어서 말리다

dripping: **~ (wet)** hŭmppŏk chŏjŭn 흠뻑 젖은

drive 1 n unjŏn 운전; (outing) tŭraibŭ 드라이브; (energy) hwallyŏk 활력; COMPUT tŭraibŭ 드라이브; (campaign) undong 운동; **it's a long ~ to the station from here** yŏgisŏ yŏk-kkajinŭn ch'aro orae kayo 여기서 역까지는 차로 오래 가요; **left- / right-hand ~** MOT oenson / orŭnson chabi unjŏn 왼손 / 오른손 잡이 운전 **2** v/t vehicle molda 몰다; (take in car) ch'aro teryŏda chuda 차로 데려다 주다; TECH chakttongshik'ida 작동시키다; **that noise / he is driving me mad** chŏ soŭmi / kŭga narŭl mich'ige mandŭrŏyo 저 소음이 / 그가 나를 미치게 만들어요 **3** v/i unjŏnhada 운전하다
♦**drive at**: **what are you driving at?** musŭn marŭl haryŏnŭn kŏyeyo?

무슨 말을 하려는 거예요?

♦ **drive away 1** v/t ch'ae t'aeugo
kabŏrida 차에 태우고 가버리다;
(chase off) tchoch'abŏrida
쫓아버리다 **2** v/i ch'arŭl t'ago
kabŏrida 차를 타고 가버리다
♦ **drive in** v/t nail paktta 박다
♦ **drive off** → **drive away**
drive-in n (movie theater) tŭraibŭin
kŭktchang 드라이브인 극장
driver unjŏnja 운전자; COMPUT
tŭraibŏ 드라이버
driver's license unjŏn
myŏnhŏtchŭng 운전 면허증
driveway ch'ado 차도
driving 1 n unjŏn 운전 **2** adj rain
ŏkssugat'ŭn 억수같은
driving force ch'ujinnyŏk 추진력;
driving instructor unjŏn kyoyuk
kangsa 운전 교육 강사; **driving lesson** unjŏn kyoyuk 운전 교육; **driving school** unjŏn hagwŏn 운전
학원; **driving test** unjŏn myŏnhŏ
shihŏm 운전 면허 시험
drizzle 1 n isŭlbi 이슬비 **2** v/i isŭlbiga
naerida 이슬비가 내리다
drone n (noise) wingwinghanŭn sori
윙윙하는 소리
droop v/i ch'uk nŭrŏjida 축 늘어지다;
(of plant) shidŭlda 시들다
drop 1 n (of rain) pang-ul 방울; (small
amount) yakkan 약간; (in price,
temperature) harak 하락; (in
number) kamso 감소 **2** v/t object
ttŏrŏttŭrida 떨어뜨리다; person from
car naeryŏjuda 내려주다; person
from team chemyŏngshik'ida
제명시키다; (stop seeing) …wa/kwa
chŏlgyohada …와/과 절교하다;
(give up) kŭmanduda 그만두다;
charges, demand etc ch'wisohada
취소하다; **~ a line to** …ege kallyak'i
p'yŏnjirŭl ssŭda …에게 간략히 편지를
쓰다 **3** v/i ttŏrŏjida 떨어지다; (of
prices, inflation) harak'ada 하락하다;
(of wind) chada 자다
♦ **drop in** (visit) tŭllŭda 들리다
♦ **drop off 1** v/t person ch'a-esŏ
naeryŏjuda 차에서 내려주다;
(deliver) chŏndarhada 전달하다 **2** v/i
(fall asleep) chami tŭlda 잠이 들다;

(decline) sarajida 사라지다
♦ **drop out** (withdraw) kŭmanduda
그만두다; (of school) chungt'oehada
중퇴하다
dropout (from school) chungt'oeja
중퇴자; (from society) nagoja 낙오자
drops (for eyes) chŏmanje 점안제
drought kamum 가뭄
drown 1 v/i ikssahada 익사하다 **2** v/t
person ikssashik'ida 익사시키다;
sound tŭlliji ank'e hada 들리지 않게
하다; **be ~ed** ikssahada 익사하다
drowsy narŭnhan 나른한
drudgery tanjoroun il 단조로운 일
drug 1 n MED yak 약; (illegal) mayak
마약; **be on ~s** mayagŭl hada 마약을
하다 **2** v/t mach'wihada 마취하다
drug addict mayak sang-yongja 마약
상용자
drug dealer mayak p'anmaeja 마약
판매자
druggist yaksa 약사
drugstore yak-kkugi ttallin
chap'wajŏm 약국이 딸린 잡화점
drug trafficking mayak kŏrae 마약
거래
drum 1 n MUS puk 북; (in western
music) tŭrŏm 드럼; (container)
tŭrŏmt'ong 드럼통
♦ **drum into: drum X into Y** Xŭl/rŭl
Yege panbok'ayŏ karŭch'ida X을/를
Y에게 반복하여 가르치다
♦ **drum up: ~ support** chijirŭl
kwŏnyuhada 지지를 권유하다
drummer pugŭl ch'inŭn saram 북을
치는 사람; (western or ethnic music)
tŭrŏmŏ 드러머; (Korean music) kosu
고수
drumstick MUS pukch'ae 북채; (of
poultry) takttari 닭다리
drunk 1 n (habitually) sulkkun 술꾼;
(on one occasion) sul ch'wihan
saram 술 취한 사람 **2** adj sul
ch'wihan saram 술 취한; **get ~** sure
ch'wihada 술에 취하다
drunk driving ŭmju unjŏn 음주 운전
drunken voices, laughter ch'wijung-ŭi
취중의; party manch'wihan 만취한
dry 1 adj clothes marŭn 마른; skin,
mouth, ground kŏnjohan 건조한;
wine talji anŭn 달지 않은; (ironic)

pikkonŭn 비꼬는; (*where alcohol is banned*) kŭmjuŭi 금주의 **2** *v/t clothes* mallida 말리다; *dishes* mallida 말리다; **~ one's eyes** nunmurŭl taktta 눈물을 닦다 **3** *v/i* marŭda 마르다

♦ **dry out** (*of alcoholic*) alk'ool chungdok ch'iryorŭl pat-tta 알코올 중독 치료를 받다

♦ **dry up** (*of river*) passak marŭda 바싹 마르다; (*be quiet*) choyonghi hada 조용히 하다

dry-clean *v/t* tŭraik'ŭllininghada 드라이클리닝하다

dry-cleaner set'aksso 세탁소

dry-cleaning (*clothes*) tŭraik'ŭllining 드라이클리닝

dryer (*machine*) kŏnjogi 건조기

dry field pat 밭

DTP (= *desktop publishing*) k'ŏmp'yut'ŏ ch'ulp'an 컴퓨터 출판

dual ijung-ŭi 이중의; **have ~ nationality** ijung kuktchŏgŭl kajida 이중 국적을 가지다

dub *movie* tŏbinghada 더빙하다

dubious (*suspect*) sŏgyŏnch'i anŭn 석연치 않은; (*having doubts*) ŭishimsŭrŏun 의심스러운

duck 1 *n* ori 오리 **2** *v* mŏrirŭl hwaek sugida 머리를 홱 숙이다 **3** *v/t head* hwaek sugŭrida 홱 수그리다; *question* p'ihada 피하다

dud *n* (*false bill*) wijo chip'ye 위조 지폐

due (*owed*) chiburhagiro toeŏ innŭn 지불하기로 되어 있는; (*proper*) mattanghan 마땅한; **be ~** (*of train, baby etc*) ... hal yejŏng-ida ... 할 예정이다; **when is your husband ~?** namp'yŏnŭn ŏnje ol yejŏng-iyeyo? 남편은 언제 올 예정이에요?; **when is the baby ~?** ainŭn ŏnje t'aeŏnal yejŏng-in-gayo? 아이는 언제 태어날 예정인가요?; **~ to** (*because of*) ... ttaemune ... 때문에; **be ~ to** (*be caused by*) ... ttaemune irŏnada ... 때문에 일어나다; **in ~ course** ttaega toemyŏn 때가 되면

dull *weather* hŭrin 흐린; *sound* tunt'ak'an 둔탁한; *pain* tunhan 둔한; (*boring*) chiruhan 지루한

duly (*as expected*) yejŏngdaero 예정대로; (*properly*) ch'ungbunhi 충분히

dumb (*mute*) pŏng-ŏriŭi 벙어리의; (*stupid*) ŏrisŏgŭn 어리석은

dummy (*for clothes*) manek'ing 마네킹

dump 1 *n* (*for garbage*) ssŭregi pŏrinŭn kot 쓰레기 버리는 곳; (*unpleasant place*) chijŏbunhan changso 지저분한 장소 **2** *v/t* (*throw away*) naebŏrida 내버리다; (*dispose of*) pŏrida 버리다; *toxic waste, nuclear waste* p'yegihada 폐기하다

dumpling tŏmp'ŭlling 덤플링

dune morae ŏndŏk 모래 언덕

dung ttong 똥

dungarees melppang paji 멜빵 바지

dunk *biscuit* tchigŏ mŏktta 찍어 먹다

duo (*singers*) ijungch'ang 이중창; (*instrumentalists*) ijungju 이중주

duplex (**apartment**) chungch'ŭnghyŏng-ŭi ap'at'ŭ 중층형의 아파트

duplicate 1 *n* sabon 사본; **in ~** tu t'ong-ŭro 두 통으로 **2** *v/t* (*copy*) pokssahada 복사하다; (*repeat*) toep'urihada 되풀이하다

duplicate key pokssadoen yŏlssoe 복사된 열쇠

durable *material* naegusŏng-i innŭn 내구성이 있는; *relationship* orae kanŭn 오래 가는

duration chisok kigan 지속 기간

duress: under ~ hyŏp-ppagŭl pada 협박을 받아

during ... tong-an ... 동안; **~ the week** chu tong-an 주 동안

dusk haejil muryŏp 해질 무렵

dust 1 *n* mŏnji 먼지 **2** *v/t* mŏnjirŭl t'ŏlda 먼지를 털다; **~ X with Y** (*sprinkle*) Yŭl/rŭl Xe ppurida Y을/를 X에 뿌리다

dust cover (*for furniture*) mŏnji magi tŏpkkae 먼지 막이 덮개

duster (*cloth*) mŏnji tangnŭn hŏnggŏp 먼지 닦는 헝겊

dust jacket (*of book*) ch'aek k'ŏbŏ 책 커버

dustpan ssŭrebatkki 쓰레받기

dusty mŏnjit'usŏng-iŭi 먼지투성이의

Dutch 1 *adj* Nedŏllandŭŭi 네덜란드의;
go ~ kaktcha tonŭl naeda 각자 돈을
내다 **2** *n* (*language*) Nedŏllandŏ
네덜란드어; *the ~* Nedŏllandŭin
네덜란드인

duty ŭimu 의무; (*task*) immu 임무; (*on
goods*) kwanse 관세; *be on ~*
tangjigida 당직이다; *be off ~*
pibŏnida 비번이다

duty-free 1 *adj* myŏnseŭi 면세의 **2** *n*
myŏnsep'um 면세품

duty-free shop myŏnsejŏm 면세점

dwarf 1 *n* nanjaeng-i 난쟁이 **2** *v/t*
chaga poige hada 작아 보이게
하다

♦**dwell on** ...e taehae komgomhi
saenggak'ada ...에 대해 곰곰히
생각하다

dwindle chŏmjŏm chagajida 점점
작아지다

dye 1 *n* yŏmnyo 염료 **2** *v/t*
yŏmsaek'ada 염색하다

dying *person* chugŏganŭn 죽어가는;
industry, tradition soet'oehanŭn
쇠퇴하는

dynamic *person* hwalttongjŏgin
활동적인

dynamism wŏndongnyŏk 원동력

dynamite *n* tainŏmait'ŭ
다이너마이트

dynamo TECH paltchŏn-gi 발전기

dynasty wangjo 왕조

dyslexia tokssŏ chang-ae 독서 장애

dyslexic 1 *adj* tokssŏ chang-aeŭi 독서
장애의 **2** *n* tokssŏ chang-aeja 독서
장애자

E

each 1 *adj* kak-kkagŭi 각각의 **2** *adv* kak-kkak 각각; *they're $1.50 ~* kŭgŏttŭrŭn kak-kkak hana-e 1.50 tallŏida 그것들은 각각 하나에 1.50 달러이다 **3** *pron* kak-kkak 각각; *~ other* sŏro 서로; *we don't like ~ other* urinŭn sŏro joahaji annŭnda 우리는 서로 좋아하지 않는다

eager kanjŏrhan 간절한; *be ~ to do X* Xhanŭn kŏse yŏlsshimida X하는 것에 열심이다

eager beaver ilbŏlle 일벌레

eagerly kanjŏrhi 간절히

eagerness kalmang 갈망

eagle tokssuri 독수리

ear¹ (*of person, animal*) kwi 귀

ear² (*of corn*) isak 이삭

earache kwiari 귀앓이

eardrum komak 고막

early 1 *adj* (*not late*) iltchigin 일찍인; (*ahead of time*) irŭn 이른; (*farther back in time*) ch'ogiŭi 초기의; (*in the near future*) pparŭn 빠른; *in the ~ hours of the morning* ojŏn irŭn shigane 오전 이른 시간에; *in ~ March / June* samwŏl / yuwŏl ch'oe 삼월 / 유월 초에 **2** *adv* (*not late*) iltchik 일찍; (*ahead of time*) irŭge 이르게

early bird (*in the morning*) iltchik irŏnanŭn saram 일찍 일어나는 사람; (*who arrives early*) iltchik onŭn saram 일찍 오는 사람

earmark: *~ X for Y* Xŭl / rŭl Yro paedanghada X을 / 를 Y로 배당하다

earn pŏlda 벌다; *holiday, drink etc* ŏt-tta 얻다; *respect* pat-tta 받다

earnest chinjihan 진지한; *in ~* chinjihage 진지하게

earnings sodŭk 소득

earphones hedŭp'on 헤드폰; (*inside ear*) iŏp'on 이어폰; **ear-piercing** *adj* kwich'ŏng-i ttŏrŏjil tŭt'an 귀청이 떨어질 듯한; **earring** kwigori 귀고리;

earshot: *within ~* kach'ŏng chiyŏgesŏ 가청 지역에서; *out of ~* nanch'ŏng chiyŏgesŏ 난청 지역에서

earth (*soil*) hŭk 흙; (*world, planet*) chigu 지구; *where on ~ have you been?* todaech'e ŏdie issŏssŏyo? 도대체 어디에 있었어요?

earthenware *n* t'ogi 토기

earthly chisang-ŭi 지상의; *it's no ~ use ...* ...ŭn / nŭn chŏnhyŏ ssŭlmoŏmnŭn irida ...은 / 는 전혀 쓸모없는 일이다

earthquake chijin 지진

earth-shattering ch'unggyŏktchŏgin 충격적인

ease 1 *n* (*comfort*) p'yŏnanham 편안함; (*simplicity*) yong-i 용이; *feel at ~* p'yŏnanhada 편안하다; *feel ill at ~* maŭmŭl p'yŏnhi noch'i mot'ada 마음을 편히 놓지 못하다 **2** *v/t* (*relieve*) tŏlda 덜다 **3** *v/i* (*of pain*) tŏrhada 덜하다

♦ **ease off 1** *v/t* (*remove*) salsal pŏtkkida 살살 벗기다 **2** *v/i* (*of pain, rain*) nugŭrŏjida 누그러지다

easel ijel 이젤

easily (*with ease*) shwipkke 쉽게; (*by far*) tanyŏnhi 단연히

east 1 *n* tongtchok 동쪽 **2** *adj* tongtchogŭi 동쪽의 **3** *adv travel* tongtchogŭro 동쪽으로

East Asia Tongnyang 동양

East Asian 1 *adj* Tongnyang 동양 **2** *n* Tongnyang saram 동양 사람

Easter Puhwaltchŏl 부활절

easterly tongtchogŭrobut'ŏŭi 동쪽으로부터의; *an ~ wind* tongp'ung 동풍

eastern tongbuŭi 동부의; (*Oriental*) tongnyang-ŭi 동양의

easterner tongbu saram 동부 사람

East Sea Tonghae 동해

eastward(s) tongtchogŭro 동쪽으로

easy (*not difficult*) shwiun 쉬운;

(relaxed) p'yŏnanhan 편안한; **take things ~** *(slow down)* yŏyuitke hada 여유있게 하다; **take it ~!** *(calm down)* nŏmu hŭngbunhaji maseyo! 너무 흥분하지 마세요!

easy-chair allak ŭija 안락 의자

easy-going nŭgŭt'an 느긋한

eat v/t & v/i mŏktta 먹다

♦ **eat out** oeshik'ada 외식하다

♦ **eat up** *food* ta mŏgŏ pŏrida 다 먹어 버리다; *fig* ta ssŭge hada 다 쓰게 하다

eatable mŏgŭl su innŭn 먹을 수 있는

eaves ch'ŏma 처마

eavesdrop yŏt-ttŭt-tta 엿듣다

ebb v/i *(of tide)* ppajida 빠지다

♦ **ebb away** *fig* ppajyŏ yŏttŭt-tta 빠져 나가다

ebb tide ssŏlmul 썰물

eccentric 1 *adj* pyŏllan 별난 **2** *n* koetcha 괴짜

echo 1 *n* ullim 울림; *(in mountains)* meari 메아리 **2** v/i ullyŏ p'ŏjida 울려 퍼지다 **3** v/t *words* toep'uri hada 되풀이 하다; *views* tong-ŭihada 동의하다

eclipse 1 *n* shik 식; **~ of the sun** ilsshik 일식; **~ of the moon** wŏlsshik 월식 **2** v/t *fig* kŭnŭljige hada 그늘지게 하다

ecological saengt'aehaktchŏgin 생태학적인

ecological balance saengt'aehaktchŏk kyunhyŏng 생태학적 균형

ecologically friendly ch'inhwan-gyŏngjŏgin 친환경적인

ecologist saengt'aehaktcha 생태학자

ecology saengt'aehak 생태학

economic kyŏngjeŭi 경제의

economical *(cheap)* kyŏngjejŏgin 경제적인; *(thrifty)* chŏryak'anŭn 절약하는

economically *(in terms of economics)* kyŏngjejŏguro 경제적으로; *(thriftily)* chŏryak'ayŏ 절약하여

economics *(science)* kyŏngjehak 경제학; *(financial aspects)* kyŏngjejŏk ch'ŭngmyŏn 경제적 측면

economist kyŏngjehaktcha 경제학자

economize chŏryak'ada 절약하다

♦ **economize on** ...ŭl/rŭl chŏryak'ada ...을/를 절약하다

economy *(of a country)* kyŏngje 경제; *(saving)* chŏryak 절약

economy class pot'ongsŏk 보통석; **economy drive** chŏryak undong 절약 운동; **economy size** chŏryak'yŏng 절약형

ecosystem saengt'aegye 생태계

ecstasy hwanghol 황홀

ecstatic hwanghorhan 황홀한

eczema sŭptchin 습진

edge 1 *n* *(of knife)* nal 날; *(of table, seat)* mosŏri 모서리; *(of lawn, road)* kajang chari 가장 자리; *(of cliff)* kkŭt kkŭt 끝; *(in voice)* nalk'aroum 날카로움; **on ~** ch'ojohan 초조한 **2** v/t ...e t'erŭl talda ...에 테를 달다 **3** v/i *(move slowly)* ch'ŏnch'ŏnhi umjigida 천천히 움직이다

edgewise: I couldn't get a word in ~ nanŭn mal han madi hal su ŏpssŏssŏyo 나는 말 한 마디 할 수 없었어요

edgy ch'ojohan 초조한

edible mŏgŭl su innŭn 먹을 수 있는

edit p'yŏnjip'ada 편집하다

edition p'an 판

editor p'yŏnjiptcha 편집자; *(of newspaper)* p'yŏnjiptchang 편집장; **sports / political ~** sŭp'och'ŭran / chŏngch'iran p'yŏnjibwiwŏn 스포츠란 / 정치란 편집위원

editorial 1 *adj* p'yŏnjibŭi 편집의 **2** *n* sasŏl 사설

EDP *(= electronic data processing)* chŏnja chŏngbo ch'ŏri 전자 정보 처리

educate *children, consumers* kyoyuk'ada 교육하다

educated *person* kyoyukppadŭn 교육받은

education kyoyuk 교육

educational kyoyuge kwanhan 교육에 관한; *(informative)* kyoyuktchŏgin 교육적인

eel chang-ŏ 장어

eerie ossak'an 오싹한

effect *n* yŏnghyang 영향; **take ~** *(of medicine, drug)* hyoryŏgŭl nat'anaeda 효력을 나타내다; **come**

into ~ (*of law*) shilsshidoeda 실시되다

effective (*efficient*) hyokkwajŏgin 효과적인; (*striking*) insangjŏgin 인상적인; ~ *May 1* owŏl irilbut'ŏ yuhyohan 오월 일일부터 유효한

effeminate yŏjagat'ŭn 여자같은

effervescent kŏp'umnanŭn 거품나는; *personality* hwalgich'an 활기찬

efficiency (*of person*) nŭngnyul 능률; (*of machine, method*) hyoyul 효율

efficient *person* nŭngnyultchŏgin 능률적인; *machine, method* hyoyultchŏgin 효율적인

efficiently nŭngnyultchŏgŭro 능률적으로

effort (*struggle*) sugo 수고; (*attempt*) noryŏk 노력; *make an ~ to ...* ...ŭl/rŭl hagi wihae noryŏk'ada ...을/를 하기 위해 노력하다

effortless suwŏrhan 수월한

effrontery ppŏnppŏnham 뻔뻔함

effusive kamjŏng-i nŏmch'inŭn 감정이 넘치는

e.g. yerŭl tŭlmyŏn 예를 들면

egalitarian *adj* p'yŏngdŭngjuŭiŭi 평등주의의

egg al 알; (*of chicken*) talgyal 달걀, kyeran 계란

♦ **egg on** puch'ugida 부추기다

eggcup salmŭn talgyarŭl nonnŭn k'ŏp 삶은 달걀을 놓는 컵; **egghead** F int'elli 인텔리; **eggplant** kaji 가지; **eggshell** talgyal kkŏptchil 달걀 껍질

ego PSYCH chaa 자아; (*self-esteem*) chabushim 자부심

egocentric chagi chungshimŭi 자기 중심의

Egypt Ijipt'ŭ 이집트

Egyptian 1 *adj* Ijipt'ŭŭi 이집트의 2 *n* Ijipt'ŭ saram 이집트 사람

eiderdown (*quilt*) orit'ŏl ibul 오리털 이불

eight yŏdŏl 여덟, p'al 팔

eighteen yŏlyŏdŏl 열 여덟, shipp'al 십팔

eighteenth yŏlyŏdŏl pŏntchaeŭi 열 여덟 번째의

eighth yŏdŏl pŏntchaeŭi 여덟 번째의

eightieth yŏdŭn pŏntchaeŭi 여든 번째의

eighty yŏdŭn 여든, p'alsship 팔십

either 1 *adj* ŏnŭ han tchogŭi 어느 한 쪽의; (*both*) yangtchogŭi 양쪽의; *which one do you want? - ~ one* ŏnŭ kŏsŭl hashigessŏyo? - ŏnŭ tchoidŭn kwaench'anayo 어느 것을 하시겠어요? - 어느 쪽이든 괜찮아요 2 *pron* ŏnŭ tchogina 어느 쪽이나; ~ *can do it* ŏnŭ tchogina kŭirŭl hal su it-tta 어느 쪽이나 그 일을 할 수 있다 3 *adv* ttohan 또한; *I won't go ~* na ttohan kaji ank'essŏyo 나 또한 가지 않겠어요 4 *conj*: ~ *X or Y* Xna Y X나 Y; ~ *my mother or my sister will come* uri ŏmŏnina nae tongsaeng-i olgŏyeyo 우리 어머니나 내 동생이 올 거에요

eject 1 *v/t demonstrators* tchoch'anaeda 쫓아내다; *cartridge, diskette* ppaenaeda 빼내다 2 *v/i* (*from plane*) t'alch'urhada 탈출하다

♦ **eke out** ...ŭi pujogŭl meuda ...의 부족을 메우다; ~ *a living* kyŏu saenggyerŭl iŏnagada 겨우 생계를 이어나가다

el → *elevated railroad*

elaborate 1 *adj* kongdŭrin 공들인 2 *v/i* puyŏnhada 부연하다

elapse kyŏnggwahada 경과하다

elastic 1 *adj* t'allyŏginnŭn 탄력있는 2 *n* komujul 고무줄

elastic band komu paendŭ 고무 밴드

elasticity shinch'ukssŏng 신축성

elasticized shinch'ukssŏng-ŭl kajin 신축성을 가진

elated ŭigiyanyanghan 의기양양한

elation ŭigiyangnyang 의기양양

elbow 1 *n* p'alkkumch'i 팔꿈치 2 *v/t*: ~ *s.o. out of the way* nugurŭl p'alkkumch'iro mirŏjech'ida 누구를 팔꿈치로 밀어제치다

elder 1 *adj* yŏnsang-ŭi 연상의 2 *n* yŏnsang 연상

elderly nai chigŭt'an 나이 지긋한

eldest 1 *adj* naiga kajang manŭn 나이가 가장 많은 2 *n*: *the ~* (*in family*) maji 맏이

elect *v/t* son-gŏhada 선거하다; ~ *to ...* ...ŭl/rŭl sŏnt'aek'ada ...을/를 선택하다

elected sŏn-gŏro tangsŏndoen 선거로

당선된

election sŏn-gŏ 선거

election campaign sŏn-gŏ undong 선거 운동

election day sŏn-gŏil 선거일

elective sŏnt'aegŭi 선택의

elector sŏn-gŏin 선거인

electoral system sŏn-gŏ pangshik 선거 방식

electorate yukkwŏnja 유권자

electric chŏn-giŭi 전기의; *fig* chagŭktchŏgin 자극적인

electrical chŏn-giŭi 전기의

electric blanket chŏn-gi tamnyo 전기 담요

electric chair chŏn-gi ŭija 전기 의자

electrician chŏn-gi kisa 전기 기사

electricity chŏn-gi 전기

electrify chŏn-girŭl t'onghage hada 전기를 통하게 하다; *fig* hŭngbunshik'ida 흥분시키다

electrocute kamjŏnsashik'ida 감전사시키다

electrode chŏn-gŭk 전극

electron chŏnja 전자

electronic chŏnjaŭi 전자의

electronic data processing chŏnja chŏngbo ch'ŏri 전자 정보 처리

electronic mail chŏnja up'yŏn 전자 우편

electronics chŏnja konghak 전자 공학

electronics industry chŏnja sanŏp 전자 산업

elegance kosang 고상

elegant kosanghan 고상한

element CHEM wŏnso 원소

elementary (*rudimentary*) kibonŭi 기본의

elementary school ch'odŭnghak-kkyo 초등학교

elementary teacher ch'odŭnghak-kkyo kyosa 초등학교 교사

elephant k'okkiri 코끼리

elevate nop'ida 높이다

elevated railroad koga ch'ŏltto 고가 철도

elevation (*altitude*) nop'i 높이

elevator sŭngganggi 승강기, ellibeit'ŏ 엘리베이터

eleven yŏrhana 열 하나, shibil 십일

eleventh yŏrhan pŏntchaeŭi 열 한 번째의; *at the ~ hour* majimak sun-gane 마지막 순간에

eligible chagyŏgi innŭn 자격이 있는

eligible bachelor mattanghan shillangkkam 마땅한 신랑감

eliminate (*get rid of*) chegŏhada 제거하다; (*rule out*) cheoehada 제외하다; (*kill*) chugyŏ ŏpssaeda 죽여 없애다; *be ~d* (*from competition etc*) t'allak'ada 탈락하다

elimination (*from competition*) t'allak 탈락; (*of poverty*) chegŏ 제거; (*murder*) sarin ch'ŏngbu 살인 청부

elite 1 *n* chŏng-ye 정예 **2** *adj* chŏng-yeŭi 정예의

elk k'ŭn sasŭm 큰 사슴

ellipse t'awŏnhyŏng 타원형

elm nŭrŭmnamu 느릅나무

elope nun maja taranada 눈 맞아 달아나다

eloquence yuch'anghan hwasul 유창한 화술

eloquent yuch'anghan 유창한

eloquently yuch'anghage 유창하게

else: *anything ~?* kŭbakkŭi tarŭn kŏsŭn? 그밖의 다른 것은?; *if you have nothing ~ to do* manyak tarŭn hal iri ŏpttamyŏn 만약 다른 할 일이 없다면; *no one ~ spoke / came* tarŭn nugudo marhaji / oji anat-tta 다른 누구도 말하지 / 오지 않았다; *everyone ~ is going* kŭbakke moduga kanda 그밖에 모두가 간다; *who ~ was there?* kŭgose ttonuga issŏssŏyo? 그곳에 또누가 있었어요?; *someone ~* tarŭn nugun-ga 다른 누군가; *something ~* tarŭn ŏttŏn kŏt 다른 어떤 것; *let's go somewhere ~* ŏdi tarŭn kosŭro kapsshida 어디 다른 곳으로 갑시다; *or ~* kŭrŏch'i anŭmyŏn 그렇지 않으면

elsewhere (*position*) ŏttŏn tarŭn kosesŏ 어떤 다른 곳에서; (*motion toward*) ŏttŏn tarŭn kosŭro 어떤 다른 곳으로

elude (*escape from*) pŏsŏnada 벗어나다; (*avoid*) p'ihada 피하다; *her name ~s me* kŭnyŏŭi irŭmi saenggangnaji anat-tta 그녀의

이름이 생각나지 않았다
elusive (*hard to define*) p'aak'agi himdŭn 파악하기 힘든; *person* ch'atkki himdŭn 찾기 힘든
emaciated such'ŏk'an 수척한
e-mail 1 *n* imeil 이메일 **2** *v/t person* ...ege imeirŭl ponaeda ...에게 이메일을 보내다; *text* imeillo ponaeda 이메일로 보내다
e-mail address imeil chuso 이메일 주소
emancipated haebangdoen 해방된; *woman* chayurowajin 자유로와진
emancipation haebang 해방
embalm pangbu ch'ŏrihada 방부 처리하다
embankment *of river* tuk 둑; RAIL tuk-kkil 둑길
embargo *n* ch'urip'ang kŭmji 출입항 금지
embark shitta 싣다
♦**embark on** shijak'ada 시작하다
embarrass tanghwanghage hada 당황하게 하다
embarrassed tanghwanghan 당황한
embarrassing tanghwanghage hanŭn 당황하게 하는
embarrassment tanghwangham 당황함
embassy taesagwan 대사관
embellish changshik'ada 장식하다; *story* kkumida 꾸미다
embers kkambugibul 깜부기불
embezzle hoengnyŏnghada 횡령하다
embezzlement hoengnyŏng 횡령
embitter ssŭrarige hada 쓰라리게 하다
emblem sangjing 상징
embodiment hwashin 화신
embody kuch'ehwahada 구체화하다
embolism MED saektchŏntchŭng 색전증
emboss *metal, paper, fabric* todŭrajinŭn saegimŭl hada 도드라지는 새김을 하다
embrace 1 *n* po-ong 포옹 **2** *v/t* (*hug*) p'o-onghada 포옹하다; (*take in*) p'ohamhada 포함하다 **3** *v/i* (*of two people*) p'o-onghada 포옹하다
embroider sunot'a 수놓다; *fig* kkumida 꾸미다
embroidery chasu 자수

embryo pae 배; (*of human*) t'aea 태아
emerald (*precious stone*) emeraldŭ 에메랄드; (*color*) palgŭn ch'orokssaek 밝은 초록색
emerge (*appear*) nat'anada 나타나다; *it has ~d that* ...ranŭn kŏshi turŏnat-tta ...라는 것이 들어났다
emergency pisang 비상; *in an* ~ pisangshie 비상시에
emergency exit pisanggu 비상구
emergency landing pisang ch'angnyuk 비상 착륙
emigrant *n* imin 이민
emigrate iminhada 이민하다
emigration iju 이주
eminent chŏmyŏnghan 저명한
eminently (*extremely*) ttwiŏnage 뛰어나게
emission (*of gases*) palssan 발산
emotion kamjŏng 감정
emotional *problems, development* kamjŏngjŏgin 감정적인; (*full of emotion*) kamdongjŏgin 감동적인
empathize: ~ *with* ...ŭl/rŭl tonggamhada ...을/를 동감하다
emperor hwangje 황제
emphasis kangjo 강조
emphasize kangjohada 강조하다
emphatic tanhohan 단호한
empire *also fig* cheguk 제국
employ koyonghada 고용하다; (*use*) sayonghada 사용하다; *he's ~ed as a* ... kŭnŭn ...(ŭ)ro koyongdoeŏ it-tta 그는 ...(으)로 고용되어 있다
employee koyong-in 고용인
employer koyongju 고용주
employment chigŏp 직업; (*work*) il 일; *be seeking* ~ kujik'ada 구직하다
employment agency chigŏp annaeso 직업 안내소
empress yŏje 여제
emptiness konghŏham 공허함
empty 1 *adj* pin 빈; *promises* muŭimihan 무의미한 **2** *v/t drawer, pockets, glass* piuda 비우다; **3** *v/i* (*of room, street*) pida 비다
emulate ponttŭda 본뜨다
enable kanŭnghage hada 가능하게 하다
enact *law* chejŏnghada 제정하다; THEA kongnyŏnhada 공연하다

enamel *n* enamel 에나멜; (*on tooth*) sang-ajil 상아질; (*paint*) yuyak 유약
enchanting maehoktchŏgin 매혹적인
encircle ewŏssada 에워싸다
encl (= *enclosure(s)*) tongbong 동봉
enclose (*in letter*) tongbonghada 동봉하다; *area* turǔda 두르다; *please find ~d ...* tongbonghan ...ǔl/rǔl poseyo 동봉한 ...을/를 보세요
enclosure (*with letter*) tongbongmul 동봉물
encore *n* angk'orǔ 앙코르, chaech'ŏng 재청
encounter 1 *n* uyŏnhan mannam 우연한 만남 **2** *v/t person* uyŏnhi mannada 우연히 만나다; *problem* mat-ttakttǔrida 맞닥뜨리다
encourage kyŏngnyŏhada 격려하다
encouragement kyŏngnyŏ 격려
encouraging yonggirǔl chunǔn 용기를 주는
♦ **encroach on** *land* ch'imip'ada 침입하다; *rights* ch'imhaehada 침해하다; *time* ppaeat-tta 빼앗다
encyclopedia paek-kkwa sajŏn 백과사전
end 1 *n* (*extremity, conclusion*) kkǔt 끝; (*of month, year*) mal 말; (*purpose*) moktchŏk 목적; *at the ~ of this month* idal mare 이달 말에; *in the ~* mach'imnae 마침내; *for hours on ~* kyesok myŏt shigan tong-an 계속 몇 시간 동안; *stand X on ~* Xǔl/rǔl ttokpparo seuda X을/를 똑바로 세우다; *at the ~ of July* ch'irwŏl mal 칠월 말; *put an ~ to* ...ǔl/rǔl kkǔttchangnaeda ...을/를 끝장내다 **2** *v/t* kkǔnnaeda 끝내다 **3** *v/i* kkǔnnada 끝나다
♦ **end up:** *you'll ~ in the hospital* tangshinǔn pyŏng-wŏnesŏ insaeng-ǔl mach'ige toelkkŏyeyo 당신은 병원에서 인생을 마치게 될거예요; *we ended up going to his place* urinǔn kyŏlguk kǔǔi chibe kage toego marat-tta 우리는 결국 그의 집에 가게 되고 말았다
endanger wihŏme ppajigehada 위험에 빠지게 하다
endangered species myŏltchong wigiǔi p'umjong 멸종 위기의 품종

endearing sarangsǔrŏun 사랑스러운
endeavor 1 *n* shido 시도 **2** *v/t* shidohada 시도하다; *~ to be early* ppalli odorok hada 빨리 오도록 하다
ending kyŏlmal 결말; GRAM ŏmi 어미
endless kkǔdŏmnǔn 끝없는
endorse *check* isŏhada 이서하다; *candidacy* chijihada 지지하다; *product* ch'uch'ŏnhada 추천하다
endorsement (*of check*) isŏ 이서; (*of candidacy*) chiji 지지; (*of product*) ch'uch'ŏn 추천
end product wanjep'um 완제품
end result ch'oejong kyŏlgwa 최종 결과
endurance chiguryŏk 지구력
endure 1 *v/t* kyŏndida 견디다 **2** *v/i* (*last*) chisok'ada 지속하다
enduring chisoktchŏgin 지속적인
end-user ch'oejong sayongja 최종 사용자
enemy chŏk 적
energetic hwalttongjŏgin 활동적인; *fig: measures* kangnyŏk'an 강력한
energy (*gas, electricity etc*) enŏji 에너지; (*of person*) him 힘
energy-saving *device* enŏjirǔl chŏryak'anǔn 에너지를 절약하는
enforce kangnyŏk shilsshihada 강력 실시하다
engage 1 *v/t* (*hire*) koyonghada 고용하다 **2** *v/i* TECH chakttonghada 작동하다
♦ **engage in** ...e kwallyŏndoeda ...에 관련되다
engaged (*to be married*) yak'onhan 약혼한; *get ~* yak'onhada 약혼하다
engagement (*appointment*) yakssok 약속; (*to be married*) yak'on 약혼; MIL kyojŏn 교전
engagement ring yak'on panji 약혼 반지
engaging maeryŏktchŏgin 매력적인
engine enjin 엔진
engineer 1 *n* kisa 기사; NAUT, RAIL kigwansa 기관사 **2** *v/t coup, meeting* kkoehada 꾀하다
engineering konghak 공학
England Yŏngguk 영국
English 1 *adj* Yŏnggugǔi 영국의 **2** *n* (*language*) Yŏng-ŏ 영어; *the ~*

Yŏnggugin 영국인

Englishman Yŏngguk namja 영국 남자

Englishwoman Yŏngguk yŏja 영국 여자

engrave saegida 새기다

engraving (*drawing*) p'anhwa 판화; (*design*) toan 도안

engrossed: ~ *in* ...e molttudoen ...에 몰두된

engulf samk'ida 삼키다

enhance nop'ida 높이다

enigma susukkekki 수수께끼

enigmatic susukkekkigat'ŭn 수수께끼같은

enjoy chŭlgida 즐기다; ~ *oneself* chŭlgŏpkke chinaeda 즐겁게 지내다; ~*!* (*said to s.o. eating*) mashitkke tŭseyo! 맛있게 드세요!

enjoyable chŭlgŏun 즐거운

enjoyment chŭlgŏum 즐거움

enlarge k'ŭge hada 크게 하다

enlargement hwaktttae 확대

enlighten kyemonghada 계몽하다

enlightened (*liberal*) kyemongdoen 계몽된

enlist 1 *v/i* MIL chawŏn ipttaehada 자원 입대하다 **2** *v/t:* ~ *the help of* ...ŭi toumŭl ŏt-tta ...의 도움을 얻다

enliven hwalgirŭl purŏnŏt'a 활기를 불어넣다

enormity (*of crime*) hyung-akssŏng 흉악성; (*of task*) kŏdaeham 거대함

enormous kŏdaehan 거대한; *satis-faction, patience* taedanhan 대단한

enormously taedanhage 대단하게

enough 1 *adj* ch'ungbunhan 충분한 **2** *pron* ch'ungbunhan yang 충분한 양; *will $50 be* ~*?* 50tallŏmyŏn ch'ungbunhamnikka? 50달러면 충분합니까?; *I've had* ~*!* ije kŭmanhae! 이제 그만해!; *that's* ~, *calm down!* ije twaessŭnikka kŭmanhae! 이제 됐으니까 그만해! **3** *adv* ch'ungbunhi 충분히; *big* / *old* ~ ch'ungbunhi k'ŭn / naidŭn 충분히 큰 / 나이든; *strangely* ~ yŏkssi isanghagedo 역시 이상하게도

enquire, enquiry → *inquire, inquiry*

enraged hwaga nan 화가 난

enrich *vocabulary* p'ungbuhage hada

풍부하게 하다; *s.o.'s life* p'ungnyoropkke hada 풍요롭게 하다

enroll *v/i* tŭngnok'ada 등록하다

enrollment tŭngnok 등록

ensure hwaksshirhage hada 확실하게 하다

entail p'iryoro hada 필요로 하다

entangle: *become* ~*d in* (*in rope*) ...wa / kwa ŏlk'ida ...와 / 과 얽히다; (*in love affair*) ...e kkomtchagŏpsshi yŏlludoeda ...에 꼼짝없이 연루되다

enter 1 *v/t* (*go into*) ...e tŭrŏgada ...에 들어가다; (*come into*) ...(ŭ)ro tŭrŏoda ...(으)로 들어오다; *competition* ...e ch'amgahada ...에 참가하다; *person, horse in race* ch'amgashik'ida 참가시키다; (*write down*) kiip'ada 기입하다; COMPUT imnyŏkshik'ida 입력시키다 **2** *v/i* (*go in*) tŭrŏgada 들어가다; (*come in*) tŭrŏoda 들어오다; THEA tŭngjanghada 등장하다; (*in competition*) ch'amgahada 참가하다 **3** *n* COMPUT imnyŏk 입력

enterprise (*initiative*) chinch'wijŏk kisang 진취적 기상; (*venture*) saŏp 사업

enterprising chinch'wijŏgin 진취적인

entertain 1 *v/t* (*amuse*) chŭlgŏpkke hada 즐겁게 하다; *idea* saenggak'ada 생각하다 **2** *v/i* (*have guests*) taejŏp'ada 대접하다

entertainer yŏnyein 연예인

entertaining *adj* chaemiinnŭn 재미있는

entertainment orak 오락

enthrall ...ŭi maŭmŭl sarojaptta ...의 마음을 사로잡다

enthusiasm yŏltchŏng 열정

enthusiast: ... ~ ...kwang ...광; *jazz* ~ chaejŭgwang 재즈광

enthusiastic yŏllyŏrhan 열렬한

entice yuhok'ada 유혹하다; (*persuade*) kkoeda 꾀다

entire chŏnch'eŭi 전체의

entirely wanjŏnhi 완전히

entitle chagyŏgŭl chuda 자격을 주다

entitled *book* ...(i)ranŭn chemogŭi ...(이)라는 제목의

entrance *n* ipku 입구; (*entering, admission*) iptchang 입장; THEA tŭngjang 등장

entranced maeryodoen 매료된
entrance fee iptchangnyo 입장료
entrant (*in competition*) ch'amgaja 참가자; (*for exam*) ŭngshija 응시자
entrenched *attitudes* ppuribak'in 뿌리박힌
entrepreneur kiŏpka 기업가
entrepreneurial kiŏpkaŭi 기업의
entrust: ~ *X with Y*, ~ *Y to X* Xege Yŭl/rŭl matkkida X에게 Y을/를 맡기다
entry (*way in*) ipkku 입구; (*act of entering*) iptchang 입장; (*to country*) ipkkuk 입국; (*for competition: person*) ch'amgaja 참가자; (*for competition: item submitted*) ŭngmojak 응모작; (*in diary, accounts*) tŭngnok 등록
entry form ŭngmo sŏryu 응모 서류
entry visa ipkkukpija 입국비자
envelop ssada 싸다
envelope pongt'u 봉투
enviable purŏun 부러운
envious purŏwŏhanŭn 부러워하는; *be ~ of s.o.* nugurŭl purŏwŏhada 누구를 부러워하다
environment hwan-gyŏng 환경
environmental hwan-gyŏng-ŭi 환경의
environmentalist hwan-gyŏngbohoronja 환경보호론자
environmentally friendly ch'inhwan-gyŏngjŏgin 친환경적인
environmental pollution hwan-gyŏng-oyŏm 환경오염
environmental protection hwan-gyŏngboho 환경보호
environs kŭn-gyo 근교
envisage sangsanghada 상상하다
envoy sajŏl 사절
envy 1 *n* saem 샘; *be the ~ of* ...ŭi purŏumŭl sada ...의 부러움을 사다 2 *v/t*: ~ *s.o. sth* nuguŭi muŏsŭl purŏwŏhada 누구의 무엇을 부러워하다
epic 1 *n* taehamul 대하물 2 *adj voyage, deed* ungdaehan 웅대한; ~ *journey* changjŏng 장정; ~ *songs* p'ansori 판소리; *a task of ~ proportions* ŏmch'ongnan halttangnyang-ŭi il 엄청난

halttangnyang-ŭi il

epicenter chinwŏnji 진원지
epidemic *n* (*of flu, measles*) yuhaengppyŏng 유행병; *fig* sŏnghaeng 성행
epilepsy kanjilppyŏng 간질병
epileptic *n* kanjilppyŏng hwanja 간질병 환자
epileptic fit kanjirŭi paltchak 간질의 발작
epilog hugi 후기
episode (*of story, soap opera*) sap'wa 삽화; (*happening*) ep'isodŭ 에피소드
epitaph pimun 비문
epoch shidae 시대
epoch-making hoek-kkijŏgin 획기적인
equal 1 *adj* kat'ŭn 같은; *standing, rank* tongdŭnghan 동등한; *be ~ to task* ...ŭl/rŭl ch'ungbunhi hal su itta ...을/를 충분히 할 수 있다 2 *n* tongtŭnghan chonjae 동등한 존재 3 *v/t* MATH ...wa/kwa kat-tta ...와/과 같다; (*be as good as*) p'iltchŏk'ada 필적하다; *four plus five ~s nine* sa toehagi onŭn kuda 4 더하기 5는 9이다
equality p'yŏngdŭng 평등
equalize 1 *v/t* ttokgatkkehada 똑같게하다 2 *v/i* SP taedŭnghada 대등하다
equally kyundŭnghage 균등하게; ~, ... tongdŭnghage, ... 동등하게, ...
equate: ~ *X with Y* Xŭl/rŭl Ywa/kwa kat-ttago saenggak'ada X을/를 Y와/과 같다고 생각하다
equation MATH pangjŏngshik 방정식
equator chŏkto 적도
equilibrium kyunhyŏng 균형
equinox chuya p'yŏngbunshi 주야 평분시; *the autumnal ~* ch'ubun 추분; *the spring ~* ch'unbun 춘분
equip *v/t* katch'uŏ chuda 갖추어 주다; *he's not ~ped to handle it* fig kŭnŭn kŭirŭl halmanhan yŏngnyang-i katch'uŏjyŏ it-tchi antta 그는 그일을 할만한 역량이 갖추어져 있지 않다
equipment changbi 장비
equity capital FIN chagi chabon 자기 자본

equivalent 1 adj tongdŭnghan 동등한;
  be ~ to …wa / kwa tongdŭnghan
  kach'iga it-tta …와 / 과 동등한
  가치가 있다 **2** n tŭnggamul 등가물
era shidae 시대
eradicate pangmyŏrhada 박멸하다
erase chiuda 지우다
eraser chiugae 지우개
erect 1 adj kotpparo sŏn 곧바로 선
  2 v/t paro seuda 바로 세우다
erection (of building etc) paro seugi
  바로 세우기; (of penis) palgi 발기
erode ch'imshik'ada 침식하다; rights,
  power chommŏktta 좀먹다
erosion ch'imshik 침식; fig
  chommŏgŭm 좀먹음
erotic kwannŭngjŏgin 관능적인
eroticism kwannŭngjuŭi 관능주의
errand shimburŭm 심부름; **run ~s**
  shimburŭmgada 심부름가다
erratic driving chigŭjaegŭshigŭi
  지그재그식의; performance, behavior
  iltchŏnghaji anŭn 일정하지 않은
error chalmot 잘못
error message COMPUT erŏ meseji
  에러 메세지
erupt (of volcano) punch'urhada
  분출하다; (of violence) palbarhada
  발발하다; (of person) pokpparhada
  폭발하다
eruption (of volcano) punhwa 분화;
  (of violence) palbal 발발
escalate hwakttaehada 확대하다
escalation hwakttae 확대
escalator esŭk'ŏlleitŏ 에스컬레이터
escape 1 n (of prisoner, animal)
  tomang 도망; (of gas) nuch'ul 누출;
  COMPUT isŭk'eip'ŭ 이스케이프; **have
  a narrow ~** (from death) kkakkasŭro
  saranamtta 가까스로 살아남다;
  (from arrest) kkakkasŭro
  ppajyŏnagada 가까스로 빠져나가다
  2 v/i (of prisoner, animal)
  tomanggada 도망가다; (of gas)
  nuch'uldoeda 누출되다 **3** v/t: **the
  word ~s me** kŭ mari saenggangnaji
  anssŭmnida 그 말이 생각나지
  않습니다
escape chute pisangnyong
  hwalgangno 비상용 활강로
escort 1 n tongbanja 동반자; (guard)

kyŏnghowŏn 경호원 **2** v/t (socially)
  paraedajuda 바래다주다; (act as
  guard to) kyŏnghohada 경호하다
especial → **special**
especially t'ŭkpyŏrhi 특별히
espionage sŭp'ai haeng-wi 스파이
  행위
essay n changmun 작문; (at
  university) lep'ot'ŭ 레포트
essential adj (necessary)
  p'ilssuujŏgin 필수적인; (very
  important) haekssimjŏgin 핵심적인
essentially ponjiltchŏgŭro 본질적으로
establish company sŏllip'ada
  설립하다; (create) mandŭlda 만들다;
  (determine) iptchŭnghada 입증하다;
  ~ oneself as …(ŭ)ro
  yumyŏnghaejida …(으)로
  유명해지다
establishment (firm, store etc) shisŏl
  시설; **the Establishment** kwŏllyŏk
  chipttan 권력 집단
estate (land) ttang 땅; (of dead
  person) yusan 유산
esthetic shimmijŏgin 심미적인
estimate 1 n kyŏnjŏk 견적 **2** v/t
  pyŏngkkahada 평가하다
**estimation: he has gone up / down
  in my ~** kŭedaehan naŭi
  p'yŏngganŭn tŏ nop'ajyŏt-tta /
  najajyŏt-tta 그에대한 나의 평가는 더
  높아졌다 / 낮아졌다; **in my ~** naega
  pogienŭn 내가 보기에는
estranged wife, husband
  sowŏnhaejin 소원해진
estuary nŏlbŭn kang-ŏgwi 넓은
  강어귀
ETA (= estimated time of arrival)
  toch'ak yejŏng shigan 도착 예정 시간
etching ech'ing 에칭
eternal yŏngwŏnhan 영원한
eternity yŏngwŏn 영원
ethical yullijŏgin 윤리적인
ethics yulli 윤리
ethnic minjogŭi 민족의
ethnic group minjokchipttan
  민족집단
ethnic minority sosu minjok 소수
  민족
euphemism wan-gogŏ 완곡어
euphoria k'ŭn haengbok-kkam 큰

행복감

Europe Yurŏp 유럽

European 1 *adj* Yurŏbŭi 유럽의 **2** *n*
Yurŏbin 유럽인

euthanasia allakssa 안락사

evacuate (*clear people from*)
taep'ishik'ida 대피시키다; (*leave*)
taep'ihada 대피하다

evade kyomyohi hoep'ihada 교묘히
회피하다

evaluate p'yŏngkkahada 평가하다

evaluation p'yŏngkka 평가

evangelist pogŭm chŏndosa 복음
전도사

evaporate (*of water*) chŭngbarhada
증발하다; (*of confidence*) yŏn-
gich'ŏrŏm sarajida 연기처럼
사라지다

evasion (*of responsibilities etc*) hoep'i
회피

evasive aemaehan 애매한

eve chŏnya 전야

even 1 *adj* (*regular*) korŭn 고른;
(*level*) p'yŏngp'yŏnghan 평평한;
number tchakssuŭi 짝수의; *get ~
with* ...ege anggap'ŭmŭl hada
...에게 앙갚음을 하다 **2** *adv*
choch'ado 조차도; *~ my father* naŭi
abŏji choch'ado 나의 아버지 조차도;
~ bigger / better tŏuk tŏ k'ŭn / naŭn
더욱 더 큰 / 나은; *not ~* choch'a
ant'a 조차 않다; *~ so* kŭrŏt'a
hadŏrado 그렇다 하더라도; *~ if ...*
pirok ...l / ŭltchirado 비록
...ㄹ / 을지라도 **3** *v/t*: *~ the score*
tongtchŏmŭl mandŭlda 동점을
만들다

evening chŏnyŏk 저녁; *in the ~*
chŏnyŏge 저녁에; *this ~* onŭl
chŏnyŏk 오늘 저녁; *good ~*
annyŏnghaseyo 안녕하세요

evening classes yagan suŏp 야간
수업; **evening dress** (*for woman,
man*) yahoebok 야회복; **evening
paper** sok-kkan shinmun 석간 신문

evenly (*regularly*) korŭge 고르게

event haengsa 행사; SP shihap 시합; *at
all ~s* amut'ŭn 아무튼

eventful tasahan 다사한

eventual kunggŭktchŏgin 궁극적인

eventually kunggŭktchŏgŭro 궁극적으로

궁극적으로

ever *adv* ◊ (*with if, in future*) ŏnjen-ga
언젠가; *if you ~ visit here, please
call me* ŏnjen-ga yŏgi oshimyŏn
chege chŏnhwarŭl chuseyo 언젠가
여기 오시면 제게 전화를 주세요 ◊
(*with past tense*) chigŭmkkaji
지금까지; *have you ~ been to Korea?* chigŭmkkaji Han-guge kabon
chŏgi issŏyo? 지금까지 한국에 가본
적이 있어요? ◊ *for ~* ŏnjena
언제나; *~ since* kŭ hu chulgot 그 후
줄곧

evergreen *n* sangnokssu 상록수

everlasting yŏng-wŏnhan 영원한

every modŭn 모든; onŭ ...(i)na
어느 ...(이)나 다; *~ day / week /
month / year* maeil / maeju /
maewŏl / maenyŏn 매일 / 매주 / 매월 /
매년; *~ other day* it'ŭlmada
이틀마다; *~ now and then*
ttaettaero 때때로

everybody → *everyone*

everyday ilsangjŏgin 일상적인

everyone nuguna 누구나, modu 모두

everything modŭn kŏt 모든 것

everywhere modŭn kot 모든 곳;
(*wherever*) ŏdidŭnji 어디든지

evict tchoch'anaeda 쫓아내다

evidence chŭnggŏ 증거; LAW chŭng-
ŏn 증언; *give ~* chŭng-ŏnhada
증언하다

evident myŏngbaek'an 명백한

evidently punmyŏnghi 분명히

evil 1 *adj* ak'an 악한 **2** *n* ak 악

evoke *image* hwan-gishik'ida
환기시키다

evolution chinhwa 진화

evolve *v/i* (*of animals*) chinhwahada
진화하다; (*develop*) paltchŏnhada
발전하다

ewe amnyang 암양

ex- ijŏnŭi 이전의

ex *n* F (*former wife*) chŏnbuin 전부인;
(*former husband*) chŏnnamp'yŏn
전남편

exact *adj* chŏnghwak'an 정확한

exactly chŏnghwak'i 정확히; *~!* paro
kŭrŏssŭmnida! 바로 그렇습니다!;
not ~ pandŭshi kŭroch'inŭn
anssŭmnida 반드시 그렇지는

않습니다

exaggerate v/t & v/i kwajanghada
과장하다

exaggeration kwajang 과장

exam shihŏm 시험; **take an ~**
shihŏmŭl poda 시험을 보다;
pass/fail an ~ shihŏme put-tta /
ttŏrŏjida 시험에 붙다/떨어지다

examination (of facts, patient) kŏmsa
검사; EDU shihŏm 시험

examine (study) chosahada 조사하다;
patient chinch'arhada 진찰하다; EDU
shihŏmhada 시험하다

examiner EDU shihŏmgwan 시험관

example ye 예; **for ~** yerŭl tŭrŏsŏ
예를 들어서; **set a good/bad ~**
choŭn / nappŭn yega toeda
좋은/나쁜 예가 되다

exasperated hwanan 화난

excavate v/t (dig) p'ada 파다; (of
archeologist) palgurhada 발굴하다

excavation palgul 발굴

excavator kulch'ak-kki 굴착기

exceed (be more than) ch'ogwahada
초과하다; (go beyond) nŏmŏsŏda
넘어서다

exceedingly taedanhi 대단히

excel 1 v/i ttwiŏnada 뛰어나다; **~ at**
...e ttwiŏnada ...에 뛰어나다 2 v/t: **~**
oneself chagi nŭngnyŏk isang-ŭl
parhwihada 자기 능력 이상을
발휘하다

excellence ttwiŏnam 뛰어남

excellent ttwiŏnan 뛰어난

except ...ŭl/rŭl cheoehago ...을/를
제외하고; **~ for** ...i/ga ŏpssŭmyŏn
...이/가 없으면; **~ that ...** ...ranŭn
kosŭl cheoehamyŏn ...라는 것을
제외하면

exception yeoe 예외; **with the ~ of**
...ŭl/rŭl cheoehagonŭn ...을/를
제외하고는; **take ~ to** ...e taehan
iŭirŭl shinch'ŏnghada ... 에 대한
이의를 신청하다

exceptional (very good) iryejŏgŭro
ttwiŏnan 이례적으로 뛰어난;
(special) t'ŭkppyŏrhan yeoeŭi
특별한 예외의

exceptionally (extremely) maeu
yeoejŏgŭro 매우 예외적으로

excerpt palch'we 발췌

excess 1 n: **eat to ~** p'oksshik'ada
폭식하다; **drink to ~** p'ogŭmhada
폭음하다; **in ~ of** ...ŭl/rŭl
ch'ogwahanŭn ...을/를 초과하는
2 adj kwadahan 과다한

excess baggage ch'ogwa suhamul
초과 수하물

excess fare ch'ogwa yogŭm 초과
요금

excessive chinach'in 지나친

exchange 1 n (of views, between
schools) kyohwan 교환; **in ~**
kyohwanŭro 교환으로; **in ~ for**
...wa/kwa kyohwanŭro ...와/과
교환으로 2 v/t (in store) pakkuda
바꾸다, kyohwanhada 교환하다;
addresses matpakkuda 맞바꾸다,
kyohwanhada 교환하다; currency
hwanjŏnhada 환전하다; **~ X for Y**
Xŭl/rŭl Y(ŭ)ro kyohwanhada
X을/를 Y(으)로 교환하다

exchange rate FIN hwannyul 환율

excitable shwipkke hŭngbunhanŭn
쉽게 흥분하는

excite (make enthusiastic)
hŭngbunshik'ida 흥분시키다

excited hŭngbundoen 흥분된; **get ~**
hŭngbunhada 흥분하다; **get ~ about**
...e hŭngbunhada ...에 흥분하다

excitement hŭngbun 흥분

exciting hŭngbunshik'inŭn
흥분시키는

exclaim oech'ida 외치다

exclamation kamt'an 감탄

exclamation point nŭkkimp'yo
느낌표

exclude (not include) cheoehada
제외하다; possibility paejehada
배제하다; (from club etc) tŭrŏoji
mot'age hada 들어오지 못하게 하다

excluding ...ŭn/nŭn cheoehago
...은/는 제외하고

exclusive restaurant etc paet'ajŏgin
배타적인; rights, interview
toktchŏmjŏgin 독점적인

excruciating pain komun pannŭn
tŭt'an 고문 받는 듯한

excursion tchalbŭn yŏhaeng 짧은
여행

excuse 1 n pyŏnmyŏng 변명 2 v/t
(forgive) yongsŏhada 용서하다;

execute (*allow to leave*) ttönage hada 떠나게 하다; *~ X from Y* Xŭl/rŭl Yesŏ myŏnjehae chuda X을/를 Y에서 면제해 주다; *~ me* (*to get attention, to get past, interrupting s.o.*) shillyehamnida 실례합니다; (*apologizing*) choesonghamnida 죄송합니다; *~ me?* (*what did you say?*) mwŏragoyo? 뭐라고요?

execute *criminal* sahyŏng chip'aenghada 사형 집행하다; *plan* shirhaenghada 실행하다

execution (*of criminal*) sahyŏng chip'aeng 사형 집행; (*of plan*) shirhaeng 실행

executioner sahyŏng chip'aeng-in 사형 집행인

executive *n* kanbu 간부

executive briefcase kanbuyong sŏryu kabang 간부용 서류 가방

executive washroom kanbuyong hwajangshil 간부용 화장실

exemplary mobŏmjŏgin 모범적인

exempt: *be ~ from* …(ŭ)ro put'ŏ myŏnjedoeda …(으)로 부터 면제되다

exercise 1 *n* (*physical*) undong 운동; EDU yŏnsŭp 연습; MIL hullyŏn 훈련; *take some ~* undonghada 운동하다 **2** *v/t dog* undongshik'ida 운동시키다; *muscle* tallyŏnshik'ida 단련시키다; *caution, restraint* sayonghada 사용하다 **3** *v/i* undonghada 운동하다

exercise book EDU yŏnsŭptchang 연습장

exert *authority* parwihada 발휘하다; *~ oneself* noryŏk'ada 노력하다

exertion noryŏk 노력

exhale naeswida 내쉬다

exhaust 1 *n* (*fumes*) paech'ul 배출; (*pipe*) paegigwan 배기관 **2** *v/t* (*tire*) nokch'oro mandŭlda 녹초로 만들다; (*use up*) ta ssŏ pŏrida 다 써 버리다

exhausted (*tired*) nokch'oga toen 녹초가 된

exhaust fumes paegi kasŭ 배기 가스

exhausting nokch'oga toege hanŭn 녹초가 되게 하는

exhaustion kŭkttoŭi p'iro 극도의 피로

exhaustive ch'ŏltchŏhan 철저한

exhaust pipe paegigwan 배기관

exhibit 1 *n* (*in exhibition*) chŏnshi'um 전시품 **2** *v/t* (*of gallery, artist*) chŏnshihada 전시하다; (*give evidence of*) poida 보이다

exhibition chŏnshi 전시; (*of bad behavior*) ch'ut'ae 추태; (*of skill*) parhwi 발휘

exhibitionist chagi sŏnjŏn-ga 자기 선전가

exhilarating kibunŭl todunŭn 기분을 돋우는

exile 1 *n* (*forced*) ch'ubang 추방; (*political, voluntary*) mangmyŏng 망명; (*person*) ch'ubangja 추방자; (*person: voluntary*) mangmyŏngja 망명자 **2** *v/t* ch'ubanghada 추방하다

exist chonjaehada 존재하다; *~ on* …(ŭ)ro saragada …(으)로 살아가다

existence chonjae 존재; (*life*) saenghwal 생활; *in ~* hyŏnjonhanŭn 현존하는; *come into ~* saenggida 생기다

existing hyŏnjonhanŭn 현존하는

exit *n* ch'ulgu 출구

exonerate mujoerŭl chŭngmyŏnghada 무죄를 증명하다

exorbitant sangsang-ŭl ch'owŏrhanŭn 상상을 초월하는

exotic iguktchŏgin 이국적인

expand 1 *v/t* nŏlp'ida 넓히다 **2** *v/i* nŭlda 늘다; (*of metal*) p'aengch'anghada 팽창하다

♦ **expand on** tŏ chasehi sŏlmyŏnghada 더 자세히 설명하다

expanse: *a vast ~ of* nŏlkke p'yŏlch'yŏjin 넓게 펼쳐진

expansion hwaktchang 확장; (*of metal*) p'aengch'ang 팽창

expansion card COMPUT hwakchang k'adŭ 확장카드

expect 1 *v/t* kidaehada 기대하다; *baby* imshinhada 임신하다; (*suppose*) ch'uch'ŭk'ada 추측하다; (*demand*) yoguhada 요구하다 **2** *v/i:* *be ~ing* imshinjung-ida 임신 중이다; *I ~ so* kŭrŏl kŏyeyo 그럴 거예요

expectant yegihago innŭn 예기하고 있는

expectant mother imshinbu 임신부

expectation kidae 기대; ~*s*
(*demands*) changnaeŭi hŭimang
장래의 희망
expedient *n* p'yŏnppŏp 편법
expedition t'amhŏm 탐험; (*group*)
t'amhŏmdae 탐험대; (*to do
shopping, sightseeing*) tchalbŭn
yŏhaeng 짧은 여행
expel *person* tchoch'anaeda 쫓아내다
expend *energy* sobihada 소비하다
expendable *person* hŭisaengdoel su
innŭn 희생될 수 있는
expenditure chich'ul 지출
expense piyong 비용; *at the company's ~* hoesa piyong-ŭro 회사
비용으로; *a joke at my ~* narŭl tugo
han nongdam 나를 두고 한 농담; *at
the ~ of his health* kŭŭi kŏn-gang-
ŭl haech'imyŏnsŏ 그의 건강을
해치면서
expense account piyong myŏngse
비용 명세
expenses kyŏngbi 경비
expensive pissan 비싼
experience 1 *n* (*event*) ch'ehŏm 체험;
(*in life*) kyŏnghŏm 경험; (*in
particular field*) kyŏngnyŏk 경력
2 *v/t pain, pleasure* nŭkkida 느끼다;
difficulty kyŏktta 겪다
experienced kyŏnghŏminnŭn
경험있는
experiment 1 *n* shirhŏm 실험 **2** *v/i*
shirhŏmhada 실험하다; *~ on ani-
mals* tongmul shirhŏmŭl hada 동물
실험을 하다; *~ with* (*try out*)
...ŭl/rŭl shirhŏmhaeboda ...을/를
실험해보다
experimental shirhŏmŭi 실험의
expert 1 *adj* sungnyŏndoen; *~ advice*
chŏnmun-gaŭi ch'unggo 전문가의
충고 **2** *n* chŏnmun-ga 전문가
expertise chŏnmun chishik/kisul
전문 지식/기술
expire man-gidoeda 만기되다
expiry kihan mallyo 기한 만료
expiry date yuhyo mallyoil 유효
만료일
explain *v/t & v/i* sŏlmyŏnghada
설명하다
explanation sŏlmyŏng 설명
explicit *instructions* myŏngbaek'an

명백한
explicitly *state* myŏngbaek'i 명백히;
forbid punmyŏnghi 분명히
explode 1 *v/i* (*of bomb*)
p'okpparhada 폭발하다 **2** *v/t bomb*
p'okp'ashik'ida 폭파시키다
exploit[1] *n* wiŏp 위업
exploit[2] *v/t person* ch'akch'wihada
착취하다; *resources* kaebarhayŏ
iyonghada 개발하여 이용하다
exploitation (*of person*) ch'akch'wi
착취
exploration t'amhŏm 탐험
exploratory *surgery* kŏmsa 검사
explore *country etc* tapssahada
답사하다; *possibility* t'amsaek'ada
탐색하다
explorer t'amhŏmga 탐험가
explosion p'okppal 폭발; (*in
population*) kŭptchŭng 급증
explosive *n* p'okppalmul 폭발물
export 1 *n* (*action*) such'ul 수출;
(*item*) such'ulp'um 수출품 **2** *v/t
goods* such'urhada 수출하다;
COMPUT chŏnsonghada 전송하다
export campaign such'ul k'aemp'ein
수출 캠페인
exporter (*person*) such'urŏptcha
수출업자; (*country*) such'ulguk
수출국
expose (*uncover*) tŭrŏnaeda
드러내다; *scandal* p'ongnohada
폭로하다; *person* poyojuda 보여주다;
he's been ~d as ... kŭga ... imi
tŭrŏnat-tta 그가 ... 임이 드러났다; *~
X to Y* Xŭl/rŭl Ye noch'ulshik'ida
X을/를 Y에 노출시키다
exposure noch'ul 노출; (*of dishonest
behavior*) t'allo 탄로; (*part of film*)
chang 장
express 1 *adj* (*fast*) kŭp'aeng-ŭi
급행의; (*explicit*) myŏngbaek'an
명백한; *~ train/bus* kŭp'aeng
yŏlch'a/pŏssŭ 급행 열차/버스 **2** *n*
kŭp'aeng 급행 **3** *v/t* (*speak of, voice*)
mallo p'yohyŏnhada 말로 표현하다;
feelings p'yohyŏnhada 표현하다; *~
oneself well/clearly* chagi
chashinŭl chal/punmyŏnghi
p'yohyŏnhada 자기 자신을
잘/분명히 표현하다

express elevator kosok ellibeit'ŏ 고속 엘리베이터

expression (*voicing, phrase*) p'yohyŏn 표현; (*on face*) p'yojŏng 표정; *with* ~ p'yohyŏni p'ungbuhage 표현이 풍부하게

expressive p'yohyŏni p'ungbuhan 표현이 풍부한; *face* p'yojŏng-i p'ungbuhan 표정이 풍부한

expressly (*explicitly*) myŏnghwak'i 명확히; (*deliberately*) ilburŏ 일부러

expressway kosokttoro 고속도로

expulsion (*from school*) t'oehak 퇴학; (*of diplomat*) ch'ubang 추방

exquisite (*beautiful*) chŏlmyohan 절묘한

extend 1 *v/t* nŏlp'ida 넓히다; *runway, path* nŭrida 늘이다; *contract, visa* yŏnjanghada 연장하다; *thanks, congratulations* p'yohyŏnhada 표현하다 **2** *v/i* (*of garden etc*) ppŏdŏit-tta 뻗어있다

extension (*to house*) hwaktchang 확장; (*of contract, visa*) yŏnjang 연장; TELEC naesŏn 내선

extension cable yŏnjang k'eibŭl 연장 케이블

extensive kwangbŏmwihan 광범위한

extent pŏmwi 범위; *to such an ~ that* ...ranŭn hankkajinŭn ...라는 한까지는; *to a certain ~* ŏnŭ chŏngdokkaji 어느 정도까지

exterior 1 *adj* oegwansang-ŭi 외관상의 **2** *n* (*of building*) oegwan 외관; (*of person*) kŏnmosŭp 겉모습

exterminate *vermin* chŏnmyŏlshik'ida 전멸시키다; *race* myŏltchongshik'ida 멸종시키다

external (*outside*) oebuŭi 외부의

extinct *species* myŏltchongdoen 멸종된

extinction (*of species*) myŏltchong 멸종

extinguish *fire, light* kkŭda 끄다

extinguisher sohwagi 소화기

extort: ~ *money from* ...(ŭ)robut'ŏ tonŭl kangyohada ...(으)로부터 돈을 강요하다

extortion kangt'al 강탈

extortionate t'ŏmuniŏpsshi manŭn 터무니없이 많은

extra 1 *n* ch'ugaŭi kŏt 추가의 것 **2** *adj* ch'ugaŭi 추가의; *be* ~ (*cost more*) ch'ugaida 추가이다 **3** *adv* t'ŭkppyŏrhi 특별히

extra charge ch'uga yogŭm 추가 요금

extract 1 *n* inyong 인용 **2** *v/t* kkŏnaeda 꺼내다; *coal, oil* p'anaeda 파내다; *tooth* ppoptta 뽑다; *information* ŏryŏpkke ŏdŏnaeda 어렵게 얻어내다

extraction (*of oil, coal*) ch'uch'ul 추출; (*of tooth*) ppopkki 뽑기

extradite indohada 인도하다

extradition pŏmjoein indo 범죄인 인도

extradition treaty pŏmjoein indo hyŏptchong 범죄인 인도 협정

extramarital kant'ong-ŭi 간통의

extraordinarily ŏmch'ŏngnage 엄청나게

extraordinary ŏmch'ŏngnan 엄청난

extravagance sach'i 사치

extravagant (*with money*) sach'isŭrŏun 사치스러운

extreme 1 *n* kŭkttan 극단 **2** *adj* kŭksshiman 극심한; *views* kŭkttanjŏgin 극단적인

extremely taedanhi 대단히

extremist *n* kwagyŏngnonja 과격론자

extricate kuch'urhada 구출하다

extrovert *n* oehyangtchŏgin saram 외향적인 사람

exuberant hwalgiga ch'ungmanhan 활기가 충만한

exult kippŏnalttwida 기뻐날뛰다

eye 1 *n* nun 눈; (*of needle*) panŭlgwi 바늘귀; *keep an ~ on* (*look after*) ...ŭl/rŭl chik'yŏboda ...을/를 지켜보다; (*monitor*) ...ŭl/rŭl kamshihada ...을/를 감시하다 **2** *v/t* poda 보다

eyeball nunal 눈알; **eyebrow** nunssŏp 눈썹; **eyeglasses** an-gyŏng 안경; **eyelash** songnunssŏp 속눈썹; **eyelid** nunkkŏp'ul 눈꺼풀; **eyeliner** airainŏ 아이라이너; **eyeshadow** aishyaedou 아이섀도우; **eyesight** shiryŏk 시력; **eyesore** pogi hyunghan kŏt 보기 흉한 것; **eye strain** nunŭi p'iro 눈의 피로; **eyewitness** mok-kkyŏktcha 목격자

F

F (= *Fahrenheit*) Hwasshi 화씨; *45° ~* Hwasshi 45to 화씨 45도
fabric chingmul 직물
fabulous koengjanghan 굉장한
façade (*of building*) chŏngmyŏn 정면; (*of person*) kŏnmosŭp 겉모습
face 1 *n* ŏlgul 얼굴; (*look, expression*) p'yojŏng 표정; *~ to ~* taemyŏnhago 대면하고; *lose ~* ch'emyŏnŭl ilt'a 체면을 잃다 **2** *v/t person, the sea* majuboda 마주보다; *fact* chingmyŏnhada 직면하다
facelift churŭm chegŏsul 주름 제거술
face value aengmyŏnkka 액면가; *take at ~* kŏnmosŭburo p'andanhada 겉모습으로 판단하다
facilitate shwipkke hada 쉽게 하다
facilities shisŏl 시설
fact sashil 사실; *in ~, as a matter of ~* sashirŭn 사실은
factor yoin 요인; MATH insu 인수
factory kongjang 공장
faculty (*hearing etc*) nŭngnyŏk 능력; (*at university*) hakppu 학부; (*teaching staff*) kyojigwŏn 교직원
fade *v/i* (*of colors*) paraeda 바래다; (*of sounds, memories*) hŭimihaejida 희미해지다
faded *color, jeans* paraen 바랜
fag F (*homosexual*) homo 호모
Fahrenheit Hwasshi 화씨
fail *v/i* shilp'aehada 실패하다; (*in exam*) ttŏrŏjida 떨어지다
failure shilp'ae 실패
faint 1 *adj* hŭimihan 희미한; *feel ~* ŏjirŏptta 어지럽다 **2** *v/i* kijŏrhada 기절하다
fair¹ *n* (*trade show*) muyŏk pangnamhoe 무역 박람회; (*agricultural*) p'ump'yŏnghoe 품평회
fair² *adj* *hair* kŭmbarŭi 금발의; *complexion* palgŭn 밝은; (*just*) kongjŏnghan 공정한; *it's not ~* kŭgŏsŭn kongjŏnghaji anssŭmnida

그것은 공정하지 않습니다
fairly *treat* kongjŏnghage 공정하게; (*quite*) kkwae 꽤
fairness (*of treatment*) kongjŏngham 공정함
fairy yojŏng 요정
fairy tale tonghwa 동화
faith shilloe 신뢰; REL shinang 신앙
faithful ch'ungshirhan 충실한; *be ~ to one's partner* sangdaeege ch'ungshirhada 상대에게 충실하다
fake 1 *n* katcha 가짜 **2** *adj* katchaŭi 가짜의
fall¹ 1 *v/i* (*of person, price, temperature etc*) ttŏrŏjida 떨어지다; (*stumble*) nŏmŏjida 넘어지다; (*of building, government*) munŏjida 무너지다; (*of tree*) ssŭrŏjida 쓰러지다; (*of night*) oda 오다; *my birthday ~s on a Tuesday this year* nae saeng-irŭn orhae hwayoirida 내 생일은 올해 화요일이다; *~ ill* pyŏng-e kŏllida 병에 걸리다 **2** *n* (*from high place*) ch'urak 추락; (*stumble*) nŏmŏjim 넘어짐; (*of government*) punggoe 붕괴; (*in temperature*) hagang 하강; (*of minister*) saim 사임; (*in price*) harak 하락
♦ **fall back on** pisangshie sayonghada 비상시에 사용하다
♦ **fall down** (*trip*) nŏmŏjida 넘어지다; (*because ill*) ssŭrŏjida 쓰러지다; (*of wall, building*) munŏjida 무너지다
♦ **fall for** *person* …wa/kwa sarang-e ppajida …와/과 사랑에 빠지다; (*be deceived by*) …ŭi sogimsue kŏllida …의 속임수에 걸리다
♦ **fall out** (*of hair*) ppajida 빠지다; (*argue*) saiga t'ŭrŏjida 사이가 틀어지다
♦ **fall over** (*of person*) nŏmŏjida 넘어지다; (*of tree*) ssŭrŏjida 쓰러지다
♦ **fall through** (*of plans*) shilp'aero

kkŭnnada 실패로 끝나다
fall[2] n (*autumn*) kaŭl 가을
fallout pangsasŏng naktchin 방사성 낙진
false kŭrŭttoen 그릇된
false teeth t'ŭlli 틀니
falsify wijohada 위조하다
fame myŏngsŏng 명성
familiar adj (*intimate*) ch'in-gŭnhan 친근한; (*well-known*) chal anŭn 잘 아는; *form of address* hŏmul ŏmnŭn 허물 없는; *be ~ with X* Xŭl/rŭl chal alda X을/를 잘 알다
familiarity (*with subject etc*) chŏngt'ong 정통; (*of behavior*) hŏmul ŏpssŭm 허물 없음
familiarize ik'ida 익히다; *~ oneself with* …wa/kwa ikssuk'aejida …와/과 익숙해지다
family kajok 가족
family doctor chuch'iŭi 주치의; **family name** sŏng 성; **family planning** kajok kyehoek 가족 계획
famine kigŭn 기근
famous yumyŏnghan 유명한; *be ~ for* …(ŭ)ro yumyŏnghada …(으)로 유명하다
fan[1] n (*supporter*) p'aen 팬
fan[2] 1 n (*for cooling: electric*) sŏnp'unggi 선풍기; (*handheld*) puch'ae 부채; (*on cooker*) hwanp'unggi 환풍기 2 v/t: *~ oneself* puch'aejilhada 부채질하다
fanatic n kwangshinja 광신자
fanatical kwangshinjŏgin 광신적인
fan belt MOT p'aen pelt'ŭ 팬 벨트
fancy adj design mŏtchin 멋진
fancy dress kajang mudobok 가장 무도복
fancy-dress party kajang mudohoe 가장 무도회
fan dance puch'aech'um 부채춤
fang ŏmni 엄니
fanny pack hŏri chigap 허리 지갑
fantastic (*very good*) hwansangjŏgin 환상적인; (*very big*) ŏmch'ŏngnan 엄청난
fantasy hwansang 환상
far adv mŏlli 멀리; (*much*) tŏ tŏ; *~ away* mŏlli ttŏrŏjin 멀리 떨어진; *how ~ is it to …?* … kkaji ŏlmana

mŏn-gayo? … 까지 얼마나 먼가요?; *as ~ as the corner/hotel* kusŏkkaji/hot'elkkaji 구석까지/호텔까지; *as ~ as I can see* naega pol su innŭn han 내가 볼 수 있는 한; *as ~ as I know* naega anŭn han 내가 아는 한; *you've gone too ~* (*in behavior*) nega nŏmu chinach'yŏtta 네가 너무 지나쳤다; *so ~ so good* chigŭmkkajinŭn choayo 지금까지는 좋아요
farce (*ridiculous goings-on*) utkkinŭn chit 웃기는 짓
fare n (*for travel*) yogŭm 요금
Far East Kŭkttong 극동
farewell n ibyŏl 이별
farewell party sŏngbyŏrhoe 송별회
farfetched murihan 무리한; *a ~ story* hŏhwangdoen iyagi 허황된 이야기
farm n nongjang 농장
farmer nongbu 농부
farmhouse nongga 농가
farmworker nongjang-ŭi ilkkun 농장의 일꾼
farsighted sŏn-gyŏnjimyŏng-i innŭn 선견지명이 있는; (*optically*) wŏnshiŭi 원시의
fart F 1 n panggwi 방귀 2 v/i panggwi kkwida 방귀 뀌다
farther adv tŏ mŏlli 더 멀리
farthest travel etc kajang mŏlli 가장 멀리
fascinate v/t maehokssik'ida 매혹시키다; *be ~d by* …e maehokttoeda …에 매혹되다
fascinating maehoktchŏgin 매혹적인
fascination (*with subject*) yŏlgwang 열광
fascism p'asshijŭm 파시즘
fascist 1 n p'asshisŭt'ŭ 파시스트 2 adj p'asshijŭmŭi 파시즘의
fashion n yuhaeng 유행; (*in clothes*) p'aesshyŏn 패션; (*manner*) pangshik 방식; *in ~* yuhaenghanŭn 유행하는; *out of ~* yuhaeng-i chinan 유행이 지난
fashionable clothes yuhaeng-ŭl ttarŭnŭn 유행을 따르는; idea, restaurant inkkiinnŭn 인기있는; person mŏsŭl chal naenŭn 멋을 잘 내는

fashion-conscious yuhaeng-e min-gamhan 유행에 민감한
fashion designer p'aesshyŏn tijainŏ 패션 디자이너
fast¹ 1 *adj* pparŭn 빠른; *be ~ (of clock)* pparŭda 빠르다 2 *adv* pparŭge 빠르게; *stuck ~* tandanhi pak'in 단단히 박힌; *~ asleep* kip'i chamdŭn 깊이 잠든
fast² *n (not eating)* kŭmshik 금식
fasten 1 *v/t (fix)* kojŏnghada 고정하다; *belt, zipper* chaeuda 채우다; *dress, bag* chamgŭda 잠그다; *lid, window* tat-tta 닫다; *~ your seatbelt* anjŏnbelt'ŭrŭl ch'agyonghashio 안전벨트를 착용하시오; *~ X onto Y* Xŭl/rŭl Ye kojŏnghada X을/를 Y에 고정하다 2 *v/i (of dress etc)* chamgida 잠기다
fastener *(for dress, lid)* chamgŭnŭn kŏt 잠그는 것
fast food chŭkssŏk shikp'um 즉석 식품; *(hamburger, fried chicken)* p'aesŭt'ŭp'udŭ 패스트푸드; **fast-food restaurant** p'aesŭt'ŭp'udŭjŏm 패스트푸드점; **fast forward** 1 *n (on video etc)* kosok kamkki 고속 감기 2 *v/i* kosogŭro kamtta 고속으로 감다; **fast lane** *(on road)* kosok ch'asŏn 고속 차선; **fast train** kosok yŏlch'a 고속 열차
fat 1 *adj* ttungttunghan 뚱뚱한 2 *n (on meat)* chibang 지방
fatal *illness, error* ch'imyŏngjŏgin 치명적인
fatality samangja 사망자
fatally: *~ injured* ch'imyŏngsang-ŭi 치명상의
fate unmyŏng 운명
father *n* abŏji 아버지
fatherhood abŏji toegi 아버지 되기
father-in-law *(husband's father)* shiabŏji 시아버지; *(wife's father)* chang-in 장인
fatherly abŏji kat'ŭn 아버지 같은
fathom *n* NAUT kil 길
fatigue *n* p'iro 피로
fatso *n* F ttungttungbo 뚱뚱보
fatty 1 *adj* chibang-i manŭn 지방이 많은 2 *n* F *(person)* ttungbo 뚱보
faucet mulkkoktchi 물꼭지

fault *n (defect)* kyŏltchŏm 결점; *it's your/my ~* nŏŭi/naŭi chalmoshida 너의/나의 잘못이다; *find ~ with* ...ŭl/rŭl hŭmjaptta ...을/를 흠잡다
faultless *person, performance* hŭmjabŭlde ŏmnŭn 흠잡을데 없는
faulty *goods* kyŏltchŏm innŭn 결점 있는
favor hoŭi 호의; *in ~ of (resign, withdraw)* ...ŭl/rŭl wihayŏ ...을/를 위하여; *be in ~ of* ...e ch'ansŏnghada ...에 찬성하다; *do s.o. a ~* nuguege hoŭirŭl pep'ulda 누구에게 호의를 베풀다; *do me a ~!* (don't be stupid) utkkinŭn sori hajima! 웃기는 소리 하지마!
favorable *reply etc* hoŭijŏgin 호의적인
favorite 1 *n (thing)* cheil choahanŭn kŏt 제일 좋아하는 것; *(person)* cheil choahanŭn saram 제일 좋아하는 사람; *(food)* cheil choahanŭn ŭmshik 제일 좋아하는 음식 2 *adj* cheil choahanŭn 제일 좋아하는
fax 1 *n (machine)* p'aekssŭ 팩스; *(document)* p'aekssŭ munsŏ 팩스 문서; *send X by ~* p'aekssŭro Xŭl/rŭl ponaeda 팩스로 X을/를 보내다 2 *v/t* p'aekssŭroponaeda 팩스로 보내다; *~ X to Y* Xŭl/rŭl p'aekssŭroYege ponaeda X을/를 팩스로 Y에게 보내다
FBI (= *Federal Bureau of Investigation*) Yŏnbang Susaguk 연방 수사국
fear 1 *n* turyŏum 두려움 2 *v/t* turyŏwŏhada 두려워하다
fearless turyŏum ŏmnŭn 두려움 없는
feasibility study t'adangsŏng chosa 타당성 조사
feasible shirhaeng kanŭnghan 실행 가능한
feast *n (meal)* manch'an 만찬; *(event)* ch'uktche 축제
feat wiŏp 위업
feather kit'ŏl 깃털
feature 1 *n (on face, of city, style etc)* t'ŭktching 특징; *(article in paper)* kisa 기사; *(movie)* changp'yŏn yŏnghwa 장편 영화; *make a ~ of* ...ŭl/rŭl t'ŭktching-ŭro hada

...을/를 특징으로 하다 2 *v/t* (*of movie*) chuyŏnŭro hada 주연으로 하다

February iwŏl 이월

federal (*allied*) yŏnhabŭi 연합의; *court, police* yŏnbang chŏngbuŭi 연방 정부의; **~ government** yŏnbang chŏngbu 연방 정부

federation (*alliance*) yŏnhap 연합

fed up *adj* F chillin 질린; **be ~ with** ...e(ge) chillida ...에(게) 질리다

fee (*of doctor*) chillyobi 진료비; (*of consultant*) sangdambi 상담비; (*for entrance*) iptchangnyo 입장료; (*for school*) ip'akkŭm 입학금; (*for membership*) hoewŏnnyo 회원료

feeble *person* yŏnyak'an 연약한; *attempt* miyak'an 미약한; *laugh* himŏmnŭn 힘없는

feed *v/t* mŏgida 먹이다; *animal* mŏgirŭl chuda 먹이를 주다

feedback p'idŭbaek 피드백

feel 1 *v/t* (*touch*) manjida 만지다; *pain, pleasure, sensation* nŭkkida 느끼다; (*think*) saenggak'ada 생각하다 2 *v/i* (*of cloth etc*) nŭkkimi it-tta 느낌이 있다; **it ~s like silk/cotton** shilk'ŭwa/myŏn-gwa kat'ŭn kamch'ogida 실크와/면과 같은 감촉이다; **your hand ~s hot/cold** tangshin soni ttŭgŏpkkunyo/ch'agapkkunyo 당신 손이 뜨겁군요/차갑군요; **I ~ hungry/tired** nanŭn paegop'ŭda/p'igonhada 나는 배고프다/피곤하다; **how are you ~ing today?** onŭl kibuni ŏttŏseyo? 오늘 기분이 어떠세요?; **how does it ~ to be rich?** pujaga toenikka ŏttŏn kibuni tŭseyo? 부자가 되니까 어떤 기분이 드세요?; **do you ~ like a drink/meal?** mwŏ mashirŏ/mŏgŭrŏ kallaeyo? 뭐 마시러/먹으러 갈래요?; **I ~ like going/staying** nanŭn kago/mŏmulgo ship'ŏyo 나는 가고/머물고 싶어요; **I don't ~ like it** pyŏllo naek'iji anneyo 별로 내키지 않네요

♦**feel up to** ...hal su issŭl kŏt kat-tta ...할 수 있을 것 같다

feeler (*of insect*) tŏdŭmi 더듬이

feelgood factor hoŭng 호응

feeling (*of happiness etc*) nŭkkim 느낌; (*emotion*) kamjŏng 감정; (*sensation*) kamgak 감각; **what are your ~s about it?** igŏse taehayŏ ŏttŏk'e saenggak'ashimnikka? 이것에 대하여 어떻게 생각하십니까?; **I have mixed ~s about him** nanŭn kŭege ch'aktchap'an shimjŏng-ŭl kajigo it-tta 나는 그에게 착잡한 심정을 가지고 있다

fellow *n* (*man*) saram 사람

fellow citizen kat'ŭn shimin 같은 시민; **fellow countryman** tongp'o 동포; **fellow man** kat'ŭn in-gan 같은 인간

felony chungjoe 중죄

felt p'elt'ŭ 펠트

felt tip, felt-tip(ped) pen p'elt'ŭp'en 펠트펜

female 1 *adj animal, plant* amk'ŏsŭi 암컷의; (*relating to people*) yŏsŏng-ŭi 여성의 2 *n* (*of animals, plants*) amk'ŏt 암컷; (*person*) yŏsŏng 여성; (*pej: woman*) kyejip 계집

feminine 1 *adj qualities* yŏsŏngjŏgin 여성적인; GRAM yŏsŏng-ŭi 여성의; **she's very ~** kŭnyŏnŭn aju yŏsŏngjŏgida 그녀는 아주 여성적이다 2 *n* GRAM yŏsŏng 여성

feminism yŏkkwŏnjuŭi 여권주의, p'eminijŭm 페미니즘

feminist 1 *n* yŏkkwŏnjuŭija 여권주의자, p'eminisŭt'ŭ 페미니스트 2 *adj group* yŏkkwŏnjuŭijaŭi 여권주의자의; *ideas* yŏkkwŏnjuŭiŭi 여권주의의

fence *n* ult'ari 울타리

♦**fence in** *land* ult'ariro tullŏ ssada 울타리로 둘러 싸다

fencing SP p'enshing 펜싱

fend: ~ for oneself che himŭro kkuryŏnagada 제 힘으로 꾸려나가다

fender MOT p'endŏ 펜더

ferment[1] *v/i* (*of liquid*) parhyohada 발효하다

ferment[2] *n* (*unrest*) puran 불안

fermentation parhyo 발효

fermented soya paste toenjang 된장

fern yangch'iryu 양치류

ferocious *animal* hyungp'ohan 흉포한; *attack* chaninhan 잔인한

ferry *n* narutppae 나룻배

fertile *soil* piok'an 비옥한; *woman, animal* tasanŭi 다산의

fertility (*of soil*) piok 비옥; (*of woman, animal*) tasan 다산

fertility drug paeran ch'oktchinje 배란 촉진제

fertilize *v/t ovum* sujŏngshik'ida 수정시키다

fertilizer (*for soil*) piryo 비료

fervent *admirer* yŏllyŏrhan 열렬한

fester *v/i* (*of wound*) komtta 곪다

festival ch'uktche 축제

festive ch'uktcheŭi 축제의; *the ~ season* sŏngt'anjŏl kigan 성탄절 기간

festivities ch'uk'a haengsa 축하 행사

fetch *person* terigo oda 데리고 오다; *thing* kajyŏ oda 가져 오다; *price* …e p'allida …에 팔리다

fetus t'aea 태아

feud *n* purhwa 불화

fever yŏl 열

feverish yŏri innŭn 열이 있는; *fig: excitement* yŏlgwangtchŏgin 열광적인

few 1 *adj* (*not many*) manch'i anŭn 많지 않은; *a ~* (*things*) chogŭmŭi 조금의; *quite a ~*, *a good ~* (*a lot*) kkwae manŭn 꽤 많은; *we have ~ friends* urinŭn ch'in-guga manch'i ant'a 우리는 친구가 많지 않다; *we have a ~ friends* urinŭn ch'in-guga chom it-tta 우리는 친구가 좀 있다 **2** *pron* (*not many people*) chŏgŭn suŭi saram 적은 수의 사람; (*not many: things*) chŏgŭn suŭi kŏt 적은 수의 것; *a ~* (*people*) myŏnmyŏt saram 몇몇 사람; (*things*) myŏnmyŏsŭi kŏt 몇몇의 것; *quite a ~*, *a good ~* (*people*) kkwae manŭn saram 꽤 많은 사람; (*things*) kkwae manŭn kŏt 꽤 많은 것

fewer *adj* tŏ chagŭn 더 작은; *~ than* … poda chagŭn … 보다 작은

fiancé yak'onja 약혼자

fiancée yak'onnyŏ 약혼녀

fiasco taeshilp'ae 대실패

fib *n* sasohan kŏjinmal 사소한 거짓말

fiber *n* sŏmnyu 섬유

fiberglass *n* sŏmnyu yuri 섬유 유리; **fiber optic** kwangsŏmnyuŭi 광섬유의; **fiber optics** kwangsŏmnyu 광섬유

fickle pyŏndŏkssŭrŏun 변덕스러운

fiction (*novels*) sosŏl 소설; (*made-up story*) kkumin iyagi 꾸민 이야기

fictitious hŏguŭi 허구의

fiddle 1 *n* F (*violin*) kkaengkkaeng-i 깽깽이 **2** *v/i: ~ around with* …ŭl/rŭl majijak-kkŏrida …을/를 만지작거리다 **3** *v/t accounts* sogida 속이다

fidelity ch'ungshil 충실

fidget *v/i* anjŏlbujŏl mot'ada 안절부절 못하다

field *n* tŭlp'an 들판; (*for crops*) pat 밭; (*for animals*) mokch'oji 목초지; (*of rice*) non 논; (*for sport*) kyŏnggijang 경기장; (*competitors in race*) kyŏnggi ch'amgaja 경기 참가자; (*of research, knowledge etc*) punya 분야; *that's not my ~* che punyaga animnida 제 분야가 아닙니다

field events p'ildŭ kyŏnggi 필드 경기

fierce sanaun 사나운

fiery *personality, temper* pul kat'ŭn 불 같은

fifteen yŏldasŏt 열 다섯, shibo 십오

fifteenth yŏldasŏt pŏntchaeŭi 열 다섯 번째의

fifth tasŏt pŏntchaeŭi 다섯 번째의

fiftieth shwin pŏntchaeŭi 쉰 번째의

fifty shwin 쉰, oship 오십

fifty-fifty *adv* oship tae oshibŭro 오십 대 오십으로

fig muhwagwa 무화과

fight 1 *n* ssaum 싸움; *in war* chŏnt'u 전투; *fig* (*for survival, championship etc*) t'ujaeng 투쟁; (*in boxing*) kyŏnggi 경기 **2** *v/t enemy, person, disease, injustice* …wa/kwa ssauda …와/과 싸우다; (*in boxing*) …wa/kwa kyŏruda …와/과 겨루다 **3** *v/i* ssauda 싸우다

♦ **fight for** *one's rights, a cause* …ŭl/rŭl wihae ssauda …을/를 위해 싸우다

fighter chŏnsa 전사; (*airplane*)

chŏnt'ugi 전투기; (*boxer*) sŏnsu 선수; **she's a ~** kŭnyŏnŭn pulgurŭi ŭijirŭl kajigo it-tta 그녀는 불굴의 의지를 가지고 있다

figurative *use of word* piyujŏgin 비유적인; *art* chohyŏngjŏgin 조형적인

figure 1 *n* (*digit*) sutcha 숫자; (*of person*) mommae 몸매; (*form, shape*) hyŏngsang 형상 **2** *v/t* (*think*) saenggak'ada 생각하다

♦**figure on** F (*plan*) kyehoek'ada 계획하다

♦**figure out** (*understand*) ihaehada 이해하다; *calculation* kyesanhada 계산하다

figure skating p'igyŏ sŭk'eit'ing 피겨 스케이팅

file¹ 1 *n* (*of documents*) sŏryuch'ŏl 서류철; COMPUT hwail 화일 **2** *v/t documents* ch'ŏrhada 철하다

♦**file away** *documents* ch'ŏrhayŏ pogwanhada 철하여 보관하다

file² *n* (*for wood, fingernails*) chul 줄

file cabinet sŏryuham 서류함

file manager COMPUT hwail maenijŏ 화일 매니저

filial piety hyo 효

Filipino 1 *adj* P'illip'inŭi 필리핀의 **2** *n* (*person*) P'illip'in saram 필리핀 사람

fill 1 *v/t* ch'aeuda 채우다 **2** *n*: *eat one's* ~ chanttŭk mŏktta 잔뜩 먹다

♦**fill in** *form* kiip'ada 기입하다; *hole* meuda 메우다

♦**fill in for** ...ŭl / rŭl taeshinhada ...을 / 를 대신하다

♦**fill out 1** *v/t form* kiip'ada 기입하다 **2** *v/i* (*get fatter*) saltchida 살찌다

♦**fill up 1** *v/t* kadŭk ch'aeuda 가득 채우다 **2** *v/i* (*of stadium, theater*) kadŭk ch'ada 가득 차다

fillet *n* ppyŏ parŭn saltchŏm 뼈 바른 살점

fillet steak p'ille sŭt'eik'ŭ 필레 스테이크

filling 1 *n* (*in sandwich*) sok 속; (*in tooth*) p'illing 필링 **2** *adj food* paeburŭge hanŭn 배부르게 하는

filling station chuyuso 주유소

film 1 *n* (*for camera*) p'illŭm 필름;

(*movie*) yŏnghwa 영화 **2** *v/t person, event* ch'waryŏnghada 촬영하다

film-maker yŏnghwa chejaktcha 영화 제작자

film star yŏnghwa sŭt'a 영화 스타

filter 1 *n* p'ilt'ŏ 필터, yŏgwagi 여과기 **2** *v/t coffee, liquid* kŏrŭda 거르다

♦**filter through** (*of news reports*) saeŏ naoda 새어 나오다

filter tip (*cigarette*) p'ilt'ŏ 필터

filth pulgyŏrhan kŏt 불결한 것

filthy pulgyŏrhan 불결한; *language etc* sangsŭrŏun 상스러운

fin (*of fish*) chinŭrŏmi 지느러미

final 1 *adj* (*last*) majimagŭi 마지막의; *decision* ch'oejŏng-ŭi 최종의 **2** *n* SP kyŏlssŭng 결승

finalist kyŏlssŭngjŏn ch'ultchŏn sŏnsu 결승전 출전 선수

finalize mamurihada 마무리하다

finally majimagŭro 마지막으로; (*at last*) mach'imnae 마침내

finance 1 *n* chaejŏng 재정; (*provision of funds*) kŭmnyung 금융 **2** *v/t* ...e chagŭm chiwŏnŭl hada ...에 자금 지원을 하다

financial chaejŏng-ŭi 재정의; *a ~ magazine* kyŏngje chaptchi 경제 잡지

financial year hoegye yŏndo 회계 연도

financier chaejŏngga 재정가

find *v/t* ch'at-tta 찾다; *if you ~ it too hot weather* nŏmu tŏpttago saenggakttoemyŏn 너무 덥다고 생각되면; *food* nŏmu ttŭgŏpttago saenggaktoemyŏn 너무 뜨겁다고 생각되면; *~ s.o. innocent / guilty* LAW nugurŭl mujoero / yujoero p'an-gyŏrhada 누구를 무죄로 / 유죄로 판결하다

♦**find out 1** *v/t* aranaeda 알아내다 **2** *v/i* (*inquire*) palk'yŏnaeda 밝혀내다; (*discover*) aranaeda 알아내다

fine¹ *adj day, weather* malgŭn 맑은; *wine, performance, city* hullyunghan 훌륭한; *distinction* misehan 미세한; *line* kanŭn 가는; *powder* koun 고운; *print* chŏnggyohan 정교한; *how's that? – that's ~* ŏttŏssŭmnikka? –

chossŭmnida 어떻습니까? -
좋습니다; *that's ~ by me* nanŭn
choŭndeyo 나는 좋은데요; *how are
you?* - ~ ŏttŏk'e chinaeseyo? – chal
issŭmnida 어떻게 지내세요? - 잘
있습니다

fine² *n* pŏlgŭm 벌금

finger *n* sonkkarak 손가락

fingernail sont'op 손톱; **fingerprint** *n*
chimun 지문; **fingertip** sonkkarak
kkŭt 손가락 끝; *have X at one's ~s*
Xŭl/rŭl hwŏnhi alda X을/를 훤히
알다

finicky *person* kkadaroun 까다로운;
design chinach'ige sŏmsehan
지나치게 섬세한

finish 1 *v/t* kkŭnnaeda 끝내다; ~
doing sth muŏt'agirŭl kkŭnnaeda
무엇하기를 끝내다 2 *v/i* kkŭnnada
끝나다 3 *n* (*of product*) kkŭnmaejŭm
끝맺음; (*of race*) kyŏlssŭngjŏm
결승점

♦**finish off** *v/t* kkŭnmach'ida
끝마치다

♦**finish up** *v/t* ta kkŭnnaebŏrida 다
끝내버리다; *he finished up liking
it/living there* kŭnŭn kŭgŏsŭl
choahage toego/kŭgose salge toego
marat-tta 그는 그것을 좋아하게
되고/그곳에 살게 되고 말았다

♦**finish with** *boyfriend etc*
...wa/kwaŭi kwan-gyerŭl
kkŭnnaeda ...와/과의 관계를 끝내다

finishing line kyŏlssŭngsŏn 결승선

Finland P'illandŭ 핀란드

Finn P'illandŭ saram 핀란드 사람

Finnish 1 *adj* P'illandŭŭi 핀란드의 2 *n*
(*language*) P'illandŏ P'illandŭŏ 핀란드어

fir chŏnnamu 전나무

fire 1 *n* pul 불; (*electric, gas*) nanbang
난방; (*blaze*) hwajae 화재; *be on ~*
pul t'ago it-tta 불 타고 있다; *catch
~* pur put-tta 불 붙다; *set X on ~,
set ~ to X* Xe purŭl puch'ida X에
불을 붙이다 2 *v/i* (*shoot*) ssoda 쏘다
3 *v/t* F (*dismiss*) haegohada 해고하다;
be ~d haegodoeda 해고되다

fire alarm hwajae kyŏngbogi 화재
경보기; **firearm** ch'ong 총; **fire department** sobangsŏ 소방서; **fire
escape** hwajae p'inan changch'i

화재 피난 장치; **fire extinguisher**
sohwagi 소화기; **firefighter, fireman**
sobangsu 소방수; **fireplace**
pyŏngnallo 벽난로; **fire truck**
sobangch'a 소방차; **firewood**
ttaelnamu 땔나무; **fireworks**
pulkkonnori 불꽃놀이

firm¹ *adj grip, handshake* himinnŭn
힘있는; *flesh, muscles* tandanhan
단단한; *voice, decision* hwakkohan
확고한; *a ~ deal* hwakssŏhirage toen
kŏrae 확실하게 된 거래

firm² *n* COM hoesa 회사

first 1 *adj* ch'ŏŭmŭi 처음의; *who's
please?* ŏnŭ pun mŏnjŏimnikka?
어느 분 먼저입니까? 2 *n* (*person*)
ch'ŏŭmŭi saram 처음의 사람; (*thing*)
ch'ŏŭmŭi kŏt 처음의 것; ~, *please*
ch'ŏŭm pun oshipsshio 처음 분
오십시오 3 *adv arrive, finish*
ch'ŏŭmŭro 처음으로; (*beforehand*)
mŏnjŏ 먼저; ~ *of all* (*for one reason*)
usŏnŭn 우선은; *at* ~ ch'ŏŭme 처음에

first aid ŭnggŭp ch'iryo 응급 치료;
first-aid box, first-aid kit
kugŭmnyak sangja 구급약 상자; **first
birthday** tol 돐; **first-born** *adj*
majiro t'aeŏnan 맏이로 태어난; **first
class** 1 *adj ticket* ilttŭngshirŭi
일등실의; (*very good*) ch'oegogŭbŭi
최고급의 2 *adv travel* ilttŭngshillo
일등실로; **first floor** ilch'ŭng 일층;
firsthand *adj* chiktchŏptchŏgin
직접적인

firstly usŏn 우선

first name irŭm 이름

first-rate illyuŭi 일류의

fiscal *policy, measures* choseŭi
조세의

fiscal year hoegye yŏndo 회계 연도

fish 1 *n* mulkkogi 물고기; (*to eat*)
saengsŏn 생선 2 *v/i* naksshihada
낚시하다

fishbone saengsŏnppyŏ 생선뼈

fisherman ŏbu 어부

fishing naksshi 낚시

fishing boat ŏsŏn 어선; **fishing line**
nakssitchul 낚싯줄; **fishing rod**
nakssit-ttae 낚싯대

fishmonger saengsŏn changsu 생선
장수

fish stick saengsŏn t'wigim 생선 튀김

fishy F (*suspicious*) susanghan 수상한

fist chumŏk 주먹

fit¹ n MED paltchak 발작; *a ~ of rage / jealousy* sun-ganjŏgin poksssushim / chilt'ushim 순간적인 복수심 / 질투심

fit² adj (*physically*) kŏn-ganghan 건강한; (*morally*) chŏk'ap'an 적합한; *keep ~* kŏn-gang-ŭl yujihada 건강을 유지하다

fit³ 1 v/t (*of clothes*) …ege mat-tta …에게 맞다; (*attach*) talda 달다 2 v/i (*of clothes*) mat-tta 맞다; (*of piece of furniture etc*) tŭrŏ mat-tta 들어 맞다 3 n: *it's a good ~* chal mat-tta 잘 맞다; *it's a tight ~* kkok mat-tta 꼭 맞다

♦ **fit in** (*of person in group*) murie ŏullida 무리에 어울리다; *it fits in with our plans* kŭgŏsŭn uriŭi kyehoege tŭrŏ mannŭnda 그것은 우리의 계획에 들어 맞는다

fitful *sleep* sŏlch'in 설친

fitness (*physical*) kŏn-gangham 건강함

fitness center helssŭ k'ŭllŏp 헬스 클럽

fitted kitchen match'um puŏk 맞춤 부엌

fitter n chŏngbigong 정비공

fitting adj chŏktchŏrhan 적절한

fittings kŏnmul naebu changch'i 건물 내부 장치

five tasŏt 다섯, o 오

fix 1 n (*solution*) haegyŏl 해결; *be in a ~* F kon-gyŏng-e ch'ŏhae it-tta 곤경에 처해 있다 2 v/t (*attach*) kojŏnghada 고정하다; (*repair*) koch'ida 고치다; (*arrange: meeting etc*) ilsshirŭl chŏnghada 일시를 정하다; *lunch* chunbihada 준비하다; (*dishonestly: match etc*) chojak'ada 조작하다; *~ X onto Y* Xŭl / rŭl Ye kojŏngshik'ida X을 / 를 Y에 고정시키다; *I'll ~ you a drink* chega mashil kŏsŭl mandŭrŏ tŭrigesssŭmnida 제가 마실 것을 만들어 드리겠습니다

♦ **fix up** *meeting* ilsshirŭl chŏnghada 일시를 정하다; *it's all fixed up* ta

chŏnghaejyŏt-tta 다 정해졌다

fixed *part, exchange rate* kojŏngdoen 고정된

fixture (*in room*) sŏlbi 설비; SP chŏnggijŏn 정기전

flab (*on body*) kunsal 군살

flabbergast: *be ~ed* F ch'unggyŏgŭl pat-tta 충격을 받다

flabby *muscles, stomach* nŭrŏjin 늘어진

flag¹ n kitppal 깃발; (*national ~*) kukki 국기

flag² v/i (*tire*) chich'ida 지치다

flair (*talent*) chaenŭng 재능; *have a natural ~ for* …e t'agonan chaenŭng-i it-tta …에 타고난 재능이 있다

flake n yalbŭn chogak 얇은 조각

♦ **flake off** v/i pŏtkkyŏjyŏ ttŏrŏjida 벗겨져 떨어지다

flaky adj pŏtkkyŏjigi shwiun 벗겨지기 쉬운; F (*odd*) pyŏllan 별난

flaky pastry p'asak'an p'aiyong panjuk 파삭한 파이용 반죽

flamboyant *personality* chashini nŏmch'yŏboinŭn 자신이 넘쳐보이는

flame n pulkkot 불꽃; *~s* pulkkil 불길

flammable kayŏnssŏng-ŭi 가연성의

flan op'ŭn p'ai 오픈 파이

flank 1 n (*of horse etc*) yŏpkkuri 옆구리; MIL taeyŏrŭi ch'ŭngmyŏn 대열의 측면 2 v/t: *be ~ed by* (*by person*) …ŭl / rŭl yangnyŏp'e kŏnŭrida …을 / 를 양옆에 거느리다; (*by building, person etc*) …ŭl / rŭl yangnyŏp'e tuda …을 / 를 양옆에 두다

flap 1 n (*of envelope, pocket*) ttukkŏng 뚜껑; *be in a ~* F anjŏlbujŏl mot'ada 안절부절 못하다 2 v/t *wings* p'ŏllŏgida 펄럭이다 3 v/i (*of flag etc*) p'ŏllŏgida 펄럭이다; F (*panic*) ch'ojohaehada 초조해하다

flare 1 n (*distress signal*) chomyŏngt'an 조명탄; (*in dress*) p'ŭllleŏ 플레어 2 v/t *nostrils* pŏrida 벌리다

♦ **flare up** (*of violence, illness*) tolbarhada 돌발하다; (*of fire*) t'aorŭda 타오르다; (*get very angry*) hwaga ch'isot-tta 화가 치솟다

flash 1 n (of light) sŏmgwang 섬광; PHOT p'ŭllaeshwi 플래쉬; *in a ~* F nun kkamtchak'al saie 눈 깜짝할 사이에; *have a ~ of inspiration* yŏnggami pŏntchŏk ttorŭda 영감이 번쩍 떠오르다; *~ of lightning* pŏn-gaetppurŭi pŏntchŏgim 번갯불의 번쩍임 **2** v/i (of light) pich'ida 비치다 **3** v/t headlights pich'uda 비추다

flashback n (in movie) kwagŏ hoesang changmyŏn 과거 회상 장면

flashbulb sŏmgwang chŏn-gu 섬광 전구

flasher MOT chadong chŏmmyŏl changch'i 자동 점멸 장치

flashlight hoejung chŏndŭng 회중 전등; PHOT p'ŭllaeshwi 플래쉬

flashy pej yoranhan 요란한

flask pyŏng 병

flat 1 adj surface, land p'yŏngp'yŏnghan 평평한; beer kim ppajin 김 빠진; battery, tire ta tarŭn 다 닳은; shoes najŭn kubŭi 낮은 굽의; MUS panŭm naerimŭi 반음 내림의; *and that's ~* F tŏ isang-ŭn marhaji ank'essŏ 더 이상은 말하지 않겠어 **2** adv MUS panŭm naerimŭro 반음 내림으로; *~ out* chŏnsongnyŏgŭro hada 전속력으로 하다

flat-chested kasŭmi pinyak'an 가슴이 빈약한

flat rate iltchŏng-aek 일정액

flatten v/t land, road p'yŏngp'yŏnghage hada 평평하게 하다; (by bombing, demolition) munŏttŭrida 무너뜨리다

flatter v/t ach'ŏmhada 아첨하다

flattering comments ach'ŏmhanŭn 아첨하는; color, clothes shilmulboda totppoige hanŭn 실물보다 돋보이게 하는

flattery ach'ŏm 아첨

flavor 1 n mat 맛 **2** v/t food mannaeda 맛내다

flavoring chomiryo 조미료

flaw n hŭm 흠

flawless hŭmŏmnŭn 흠없는

flea pyŏruk 벼룩

flee v/i tomangch'ida 도망치다

fleet n NAUT hamdae 함대

fleeting visit etc chamkkan tong-anŭi 잠깐 동안의; *catch a ~ glimpse of* ŏlp'it poda 얼핏 보다

flesh (of people, fruit etc) sal 살; *the ~* yukch'e 육체; *meet / see a person in the ~* nugurŭl shiltchero mannada / poda 누구를 실제로 만나다 / 보다

flex v/t muscles such'ukssik'ida 수축시키다

flexible material kuburigi shwiun 구부리기 쉬운; arrangement, hours yungt'ongssŏng innŭn 융통성 있는; *I'm quite ~ about the timing* chŏnŭn amu ttaerado chossŭmnida 저는 아무 때라도 좋습니다

flick v/t tail hwidurŭda 휘두르다; *he ~ed a fly off his hand* kŭnŭn sonŭl hwidullŏsŏ p'arirŭl naetchoch'at-tta 그는 손을 휘둘러서 파리를 내쫓았다; *she ~ed her hair out of her eyes* kŭnŭn shiyarŭl karinŭn mŏrik'aragŭl ssŭrŏnŏmgyŏt-tta 그는 시야를 가리는 머리카락을 쓸어넘겼다

♦ **flick through** book, magazine taegang hult'ŏboda 대강 훑어보다

flicker v/i (of light, screen) kkamppagida 깜박이다

flies (on pants) paji ammun 바지 앞문

flight (in airplane) pihaeng 비행; (flying) nalgi 날기; (fleeing) tomang 도망; *~ of stairs* han churŭi kyedan 한 줄의 계단; *three ~s a day* iril samhoeŭi hanggongp'yŏn 1일 3회의 항공편; *a direct ~* chik'ang 직항; *it's a long ~* kin yohaeng-iyeyo 이것은 긴 여행이예요; *when is your ~?* tangshinŭi pihaenggi shiganŭn ŏnjeimnikka? 당신의 비행기 시간은 언제입니까?

flight crew sŭngmuwŏn 승무원; **flight deck** (in airplane) chojongshil 조종실; **flight number** hanggongp'yŏn pŏnho 항공편 번호; **flight path** pihaeng kyŏngno 비행 경로; **flight recorder** pŭllaek pakssŭ 블랙 박스; **flight time** (departure) ch'ulbal shigan 출발 시간; (duration) yŏhaeng shigan 여행 시간

flighty pyŏndŏkssŭrŏun 변덕스러운

flimsy *structure, furniture* yak'an 약한; *dress* yalbŭn 얇은; *material* tchijŏjigi shwiun 찢어지기 쉬운; *excuse* pinyak'an 빈약한

flinch umtchirhada 움찔하다

fling *v/t* naedŏnjida 내던지다; ~ *open* kŏch'ilge yŏlda 거칠게 열다; ~ *oneself into a chair* ŭijae t'ŏlssŏk ant'a 의자에 털썩 앉다

♦ flip through *book, magazine* taegang hult'ŏboda 대강 훑어보다

flipper (*for swimming*) mulgalk'wi 물갈퀴

flirt 1 *v/i* saeronggŏrida 새롱거리다 2 *n* saeronggŏrinŭn saram 새롱거리는 사람

flirtatious saeronggŏrinŭn 새롱거리는

float *v/i* ttŭda 뜨다; FIN pyŏndong shisega toeda 변동 시세가 되다

flock *n* (*of sheep*) tte 떼

flog *v/t* (*whip*) ch'aetchiktchirhada 채찍질하다

flood 1 *n* hongsu 홍수; (*of river*) pŏmnam 범람 2 *v/t* (*of river*) pŏmnamhada 범람하다; ~ *its banks* kangttugi nŏmch'ida 강둑이 넘치다

flooding pŏmnam 범람

floodlight *n* t'ugwang chomyŏng 투광 조명

floor *n* (*of room*) marutppadak 마룻바닥; (*story*) ch'ŭng 층

floorboard padangnŏl 바닥널; floor cloth maru kŏlle 마루 걸레; floor lamp sŭt'aendŭ 스탠드

flop 1 *v/i* t'ŏlssŏk momŭl tŏnjida 털썩 몸을 던지다; F (*fail*) shilp'aejagida 실패작이다 2 *n* F (*failure*) shilp'aejak 실패작

floppy *adj* (*not stiff*) hŏllŏnghan 헐렁한; (*weak*) narŭnhan 나른한

floppy (disk) p'ŭllop'i tisŭk'ŭ 플로피 디스크

florist kkotchangsu 꽃장수

flour milkkaru 밀가루

flourish *v/i* (*of plants*) chal charada 잘 자라다; (*of business*) pŏnch'anghada 번창하다; (*of civilization*) pŏnyŏnghada 번영하다

flourishing *business, trade*

pŏnch'anghanŭn 번창하는

flow 1 *v/i* (*of river*) hŭrŭda 흐르다; (*of electric current*) t'onghada 통하다; (*of traffic*) sot'ongdoeda 소통되다; (*of work*) chinhaengdoeda 진행되다; *the traffic ~s better* kyot'ong sot'ong-i wŏnhwarhaejida 교통 소통이 원활해지다 2 *n* (*of river, information*) hŭrŭm 흐름; (*of ideas*) kyohwan 교환

flowchart chagŏp kongjŏngdo 작업 공정도

flower 1 *n* kkot 꽃 2 *v/i* kkoch'i p'ida 꽃이 피다

flowerbed hwadan 화단; Flower Garland Sutra Hwaŏmgyŏng 화엄경; flowerpot hwabyŏng 화병

flowery *pattern* kkŏnmunŭiŭi 꽃무늬의; *style of writing* misayŏguŭi 미사여구의

flu tok-kkam 독감

fluctuate *v/i* pyŏndonghada 변동하다

fluctuation pyŏndong 변동

fluency yuch'angham 유창함

fluent *adj speaker* yuch'anghan 유창한; *he speaks ~ Korean* kŭnŭn Han-gungmarŭl yuch'anghage handa 그는 한국말을 유창하게 한다

fluently *speak* yuch'anghage 유창하게; *write* yuryŏhage 유려하게

fluff: *a bit of ~* (*material*) yakkanŭi pop'ul 약간의 보풀

fluffy *adj material, hair* somt'ŏlgat'ŭn 솜털같은; ~ *clouds* somt'ŏl kurŭm 솜털 구름

fluid *n* (*in body*) aek 액; (*for brakes*) yudong-aek 유동액

flunk *v/t* F (*subject*) ...e naktcherŭl pat-tta ...에 낙제를 받다

fluorescent hyŏnggwang-ŭi 형광의

flush 1 *v/t toilet* ...ŭi murŭl naerida ...의 물을 내리다; ~ *X down the toilet* Xŭl/rŭl pyŏn-gie naeryŏ ponaeda X을/를 변기에 내려 보내다 2 *v/i* (*of toilet*) muri naeryŏgada 물이 내려가다; (*go red in the face*) ppalgaejida 빨개지다 3 *adj* (*level*) kat'ŭn nop'iŭi 같은 높이의; *be ~ with* ...wa/kwa kat'ŭn nop'iida ...와/과 같은 높이이다

♦ flush away (*down toilet*) pyŏn-gie

naeryŏ ponaeda 변기에 내려 보내다
♦**flush out** *rebels etc* naogehada
나오게 하다
fluster *v/t* tanghwanghage hada
당황하게 하다; *get ~ed*
tanghwanghada 당황하다
flute p'ŭllut'ŭ 플루트; (*large*) taegŭm
대금; (*bamboo*) tanso 단소
flutter *v/i* (*of bird, wings*)
p'ŏdŏkkŏrida 퍼덕거리다; (*of flag*)
p'ŏllŏgida 펄럭이다; (*of heart*)
tugŭn-gŏrida 두근거리다
fly¹ *n* (*insect*) p'ari 파리
fly² *n* (*on pants*) paji ammun 바지
앞문
fly³ 1 *v/i* (*of bird, airplane*) nalda 날다;
(*in airplane*) pihaenggiro
yŏhaenghada 비행기로 여행하다; (*of
flag*) keyangdoeda 게양되다; (*rush*)
ttwiŏ nagada 뛰어 나가다; *~ into a
rage* pŏlk'ŏk sŏngnaeda 벌컥
성내다 **2** *v/t airplane* chojonghada
조종하다; *airline* t'ada 타다;
(*transport by air*) hanggong
unsonghada 항공 운송하다
♦**fly away** naragada 날아가다
♦**fly back** *v/i* (*travel back*)
pihaenggiro toragada 비행기로
돌아가다
♦**fly in 1** *v/i* (*of airplane, passengers*)
toch'ak'ada 도착하다 **2** *v/t supplies
etc* pihaenggiro unbanhada 비행기로
운반하다
♦**fly off** (*of hat etc*) naragada
날아가다
♦**fly out** *v/i* naragada 날아가다
♦**fly past** (*in formation*) kongjung
pihaenghada 공중 비행하다; (*of
time*) ssonsalgach'i chinagada
쏜살같이 지나가다
flying *n* pihaeng 비행
foam *n* (*on liquid*) kŏp'um 거품
foam rubber sŭp'onji komu 스폰지
고무
FOB (= *free on board*) ponsŏn indo
본선 인도
focus *n* (*of attention*), PHOT
ch'otchŏm 초점; *be in ~ / out of ~*
PHOT ch'otchŏmi mat-tta / mat-tchi
ant'a 초점이 맞다 / 맞지 않다
♦**focus on** *also fig* ...e ch'otchŏmŭl

match'uda ...에 초점을 맞추다
fodder saryo 사료
fog an-gae 안개
foggy an-gae kkin 안개 낀
foil¹ *n* (*silver ~ etc*) hoil 호일
foil² *v/t* (*thwart*) chwajŏlsshik'ida
좌절시키다
fold 1 *v/t paper* chŏptta 접다; *cloth*
kaeda 개다; *~ one's arms*
p'altchang-ŭl kkida 팔짱을 끼다
2 *v/i* (*of business*) manghada 망하다
3 *n* (*in cloth etc*) chŏbŭn chari 접은
자리
♦**fold up 1** *v/t* chŏptta 접다 **2** *v/i* (*of
chair, table*) chŏp'ida 접히다
folder *also* COMPUT p'oldŏ 폴더
folding *adj* chŏmnŭn 접는
foliage ip 잎
folk (*people*) saram 사람; *my ~s*
(*family*) nae kajok 내 가족; *come
in, ~s* F tŭrŏoseyo, yŏrŏbun
들어오세요, 여러분
folk dance (*traditional*) minsok
ch'um 민속 춤; (*western*) minsok
p'ok'ŭttaensŭ 포크댄스; **folk medicine** min-gan yoppŏp 민간 요법;
folk music minsok ŭmak 민속 음악;
folk painting minhwa 민화; **folk
singer** minyo kasu 민요 가수; **folk
song** minyo 민요
follow 1 *v/t person, road* ttaragada
따라가다; *guidelines, instructions*
ttarŭda 따르다; *TV series, news*
kyesok shich'ŏnghada 계속
시청하다; (*understand*) ihaehada
이해하다; *~ me* (*come*) chŏrŭl
ttaraoseyo 저를 따라오세요 **2** *v/i*
ttaragada 따라가다; (*logically*)
sŏngnip'ada 성립하다; *it ~s from
this that ...* kŭraesŏ ...ranŭn mari
mat-tta 그래서 ...라는 말이 맞다; *as
~s* taŭmgwa kat'ŭn 다음과 같은
♦**follow up** *v/t inquiry* poganghada
보강하다
follower (*of politician etc*) chijija
지지자; (*of football team*) p'aen 팬;
(*of TV program*) shich'ŏngja 시청자
following 1 *adj day, night* kŭ taŭmŭi
그 다음의; *pages* taŭmŭi 다음의 **2** *n*
(*people*) chijija 지지자; *the ~* taŭmŭi
kŏt 다음의 것

follow-up meeting pogang hoeŭi 보강 회의

follow-up visit chaebangmun 재방문; (*to doctor*) chaejin 재진

folly (*madness*) ŏrisŏgŭn chit 어리석은 짓

fond (*loving*) tajŏnghan 다정한; *memory* arŭmdaun 아름다운; *be ~ of* ...ŭl/rŭl choahada ...을/를 좋아하다

fondle v/t ssŭdadŭmtta 쓰다듬다

fondness aejŏng 애정; (*for wine, food*) aeho 애호

font (*in printing*) kŭltchach'e 글자체

food ŭmshik 음식

food freak F misshik-kka 미식가; **food mixer** miksssŏ 믹서; **food poisoning** shiktchungdok 식중독

fool n pabo 바보; *make a ~ of oneself* usŭmkkŏriga toeda 웃음거리가 되다

♦ **fool around** changnanch'ida 장난치다; (*sexually*) param p'iuda 바람피우다

♦ **fool around with** *knife, drill etc* ...ŭl/rŭl kajigo changnanch'ida ...을/를 가지고 장난치다

foolish ŏrisŏgŭn 어리석은

foolproof chalmot toel suga ŏmnŭn 잘못 될 수가 없는

foot pal 발; (*measurement*) p'it'ŭ 피트; *on ~* kŏrŏsŏ 걸어서; *at the ~ of the page*/*hill* chang-ŭi/ŏndŏgŭi mit'e 장의/언덕의 밑에; *put one's ~ in it* F k'ŭn shilssurŭl hada 큰 실수를 하다

football (*soccer*) ch'uk-kku 축구; (*American-style*) mishik ch'uk-kku 미식 축구; (*ball*) ch'uk-kkugong 축구공; **football player** (*soccer*) ch'uk-kku sŏnsu 축구 선수; (*American-style*) mishik ch'uk-kku sŏnsu 미식 축구 선수; **footbridge** yukkyo 육교; **foothills** san-gisŭlgŭi chagŭn ŏndŏk 산기슭의 작은 언덕

footing (*basis*) kiban 기반; *lose one's ~* hŏt-ttidida 헛디디다; *be on the same*/*a different ~* tongdŭnghan/tarŭn chagyŏgida 동등한/다른 자격이다; *be on a friendly ~ with* ...wa/kwa uhojŏk kwan-gyerŭl kajida ...와/과 우호적 관계를 가지다

footlights kak-kkwang 각광; **footnote** kaktchu 각주; **footpath** indo 인도; **footprint** paltchaguk 발자국; **footstep** paltchaguk sori 발자국 소리; **follow in s.o.'s ~s** nuguŭi sŏllyerŭl ttarŭda 누구의 선례를 따르다; **footwear** shinbal 신발

for ◊ (*purpose, destination*) ...ŭl/rŭl wihan ...을/를 위한; *clothes ~ children* aidŭrŭl wihan ot 아이들을 위한 옷; *I did it ~ John* Jonŭl wihaesŏ hassŏyo 존을 위해서 했어요; *a train ~ Seoul* Sŏullo kanŭn kich'a 서울로 가는 기차; *it's too big*/*small ~ you* kŭgŏsŭn nŏege nŏmu k'ŭda/chaktta 그것은 너에게 너무 크다/작다; *here's a letter ~ you* yŏgi nŏege on p'yŏnjiga it-tta 여기 너에게 온 편지가 있다; *this is ~ you* ikŏsŭn nŏrŭl wihan kŏshida 이것은 너를 위한 것이다; *what is there ~ lunch?* chŏmshimŭro muŏshi issŭmnikka? 점심으로 무엇이 있습니까?; *the steak is ~ me* kŭ sŭt'eik'ŭnŭn che kŏshimnida 그 스테이크는 제 것입니다; *what is this ~?* ikŏsŭn muŏse sayongdoennŭn kŏshimnikka? 이것은 무엇에 사용되는 것입니까?; *what ~?* wae kŭron-gayo? 왜 그런가요? ◊ (*time*) ... tong-an 동안; *~ three days*/*two hours* sam il/tu shikan tong-an 삼 일/두 시간 동안; *please get it done ~ Monday* wŏryoire kkŭnnaejuseyo 월요일에 끝내주세요 ◊ (*distance*): *I walked ~ a mile* nanŭn il mairŭ kŏrŏtssŏyo 나는 일 마일을 걸었어요; *it stretches ~ 100 miles* kŭgŏsŭn 100mairina ppŏdŏ issŏyo 그것은 100마일이나 뻗어 있어요 ◊ (*in favor of*): *I am ~ the idea* nanŭn kŭ saenggagi choayo 나는 그 생각이 좋아요 ◊ (*instead of, in behalf of*): *let me do that ~ you* chega taeshin haedŭrigessŭmnida 제가 대신 해드리겠습니다; *we are agents ~ ...* urinŭn ...ŭl/rŭl taehaenghamnida 우리는 ...을/를 대행합니다 ◊ (*in* *exchange for*): **I bought it ~ $25** 25tallŏrŭl chugo sat-tta 25달러를 주고 샀다; **how much did you sell it ~?** kŭgŏsŭl ŏlmae p'aratssŭmnikka? 그것을 얼마에 팔았습니까?

forbid kŭmjihada 금지하다; **~ X to do Y** Xege Yhanŭn kŏsŭl kŭmjihada X에게 Y하는 것을 금지하다

forbidden *adj* kŭmjidoen 금지된; **~ city** chagŭmsŏng 자금성; **it's ~** kŭgŏsŭn kŭmjidoeŏ issŭmnida 그것은 금지되어 있습니다; **smoking / parking ~** kŭmnyŏn / chuch'a kŭmji 금연 / 주차 금지

forbidding hŏmak'an 험악한

force 1 *n* (*violence*) p'ongnyŏk 폭력; (*of explosion, wind, punch*) him 힘; **come into ~** (*of law etc*) yuhyohaejida 유효해지다; **the ~s** MIL chŏn-gun 전군 **2** *v/t door, lock* pusuda 부수다; **~ X to do Y** Xege Yhal kŏsŭl kangyohada X에게 Y할 것을 강요하다; **~ X open** Xŭl / rŭl ŏktchiro yŏlda X을 / 를 억지로 열다

forced *laugh, smile* ŏktchiŭi 억지의; *confession* kangjejŏgin 강제적인

forced landing pisang ch'angnyuk 비상 착륙

forceful *argument* himch'an 힘찬; *speaker* sŏldŭngnyŏk innŭn 설득력 있는; *character* wŏn-giwangsŏnghan 원기왕성한

forceps kyŏmja 겸자

forcible *entry* kangjejŏgin 강제적인; *argument* kangnyŏk'an 강력한

ford *n* yat'ŭn yŏul 얕은 여울

fore: **come to the ~** yumyŏnghaejida 유명해지다

foreboding pulgirhan yegam 불길한 예감; **forecast 1** *n* yesang 예상; (*of weather*) kisang yebo 기상 예보 **2** *v/t* yesanghada 예상하다; **forecourt** (*of service station*) kŭbyuhanŭn kot 급유하는 곳; **forefathers** chosang 조상; **forefinger** chipkke sonkkarak 집게 손가락; **foregone: that's a ~ conclusion** kŭgŏsŭn ch'ŏŭmbut'ŏ ppŏnhan kyŏllonida 그것은 처음부터 뻔한 결론이다; **foreground** chŏn-gyŏng 전경; **forehand** (*in tennis*)

p'ohaendŭ 포핸드; **forehead** ima 이마

foreign oegugŭi 외국의

foreign affairs oemu 외무

foreign currency oehwa 외화

foreigner oegugin 외국인

foreign exchange oeguk'wan 외국환; **foreign language** oegugŏ 외국어; **Foreign Office** *Br* Oemubu 외무부; **foreign policy** oemu chŏngch'aek 외무 정책; **Foreign Minister** *Br* oemu changgwan 외무 장관

foreman kongjangjang 공장장; LAW paeshimwŏnjang 배심원장; **foremost** kajang chungnyohan 가장 중요한; **forerunner** sŏndu chuja 선두 주자; **foresee** yegyŏnhada 예견하다; **foreseeable** yegyŏnhal su innŭn 예견할 수 있는; **in the ~ future** kakkaun changnaee 가까운 장래에; **foresight** sŏn-gyŏnjimyŏng 선견지명

forest sup 숲

forestry imhak 임학

foretaste sajŏn kyŏnghŏm 사전 경험

foretell yeŏnhada 예언하다

forever yŏng-wŏnhi 영원히

foreword sŏmun 서문

forfeit *v/t* sangshirhada 상실하다

forge *v/t* (*counterfeit*) mojohada 모조하다; *signature* wijohada 위조하다

forger wijoja 위조자

forgery (*bank bill, document*) wijo 위조

forget it-tta 잊다

forgetful chal ijŏbŏrinŭn 잘 잊어버리는

forget-me-not (*flower*) mulmangch'o 물망초

forgive *v/t & v/i* yongsŏhada 용서하다

forgiveness yongsŏ 용서

fork *n* p'ok'ŭ 포크; (*in road*) pun-gitchŏm 분기점

♦**fork out** *v/i* F (*pay*) tonŭl naeda 돈을 내다

forklift (**truck**) chigech'a 지게차

form 1 *n* (*shape*) hyŏngt'ae 형태; (*document*) yangshik 양식 **2** *v/t* (*in clay etc*) mandŭlda 만들다; *friendship* maet-tta 맺다; *opinion* seuda 세우다; *past tense etc* hwaryonghada 활용하다 3 *v/i* (*take shape, develop*) kuch'ehwadoeda 구체화되다

formal hyŏngshiktchŏgin 형식적인; *recognition etc* kongtchŏgin 공적인

formality hyŏngshik 형식; *it's just a* ~ künyang hyŏngshigil ppunimnida 그냥 형식일 뿐입니다

formally *adv speak, behave* hyŏngshiktchŏgüro 형식적으로; *recognized* kongtchŏgüro 공적으로

format 1 *v/t diskette* p'omaet'ada 포맷하다; *document* yangshik'wahada 양식화하다 **2** *n* (*size: of magazine, paper etc*) k'ügi 크기; (*make-up: of program*) hyŏngshik 형식

formation (*act of forming*) hyŏngsŏng 형성; ~ *flying* p'yŏndae pihaeng 편대 비행

formative hyŏngsŏnghanün 형성하는; *in his* ~ *years* küüi in-gyŏk hyŏngsŏnggie 그의 인격 형성기에

former chŏnüi 전의; *the* ~ chŏnja 전자

formerly ijŏne 이전에

formidable musŏun 무서운

formula MATH, CHEM kongshik 공식; (*for success etc*) pangbŏp 방법

formulate (*express*) myŏnghwak'i p'yohyŏnhada 명확히 표현하다

fort MIL yosae 요새

forth: *back and* ~ apttwiro 앞뒤로; *and so* ~ kit'a tüngdüng 기타 등등

forthcoming (*future*) tagaonün 다가오는; *personality* saenggagül t'ŏnonnün 생각을 터놓는

fortieth mahün pŏntchaeüi 마흔 번째의

fortnight *Br* tu chu 두 주

fortress MIL yosae 요새

fortunate un chŏun 운 좋은

fortunately un chok'edo 운 좋게도

fortune un 운; (*lot of money*) k'ün ton 큰 돈; *good* ~ haeng-un 행운

fortune-teller chŏmjaeng-i 점쟁이

forty mahün 마흔, saship 사십

forward 1 *adv* ap'üro 앞으로 **2** *adj pej*: *person* kŏnbangjin 건방진 **3** *n* SP p'owŏdü 포워드 **4** *v/t letter* hoesonghada 회송하다

forwarding agent COM unsuŏptcha 운수업자

fossil hwasŏk 화석

foster child ibyang-a 입양아

foster parents yangbumo 양부모

foul 1 *n* SP panch'ik 반칙 **2** *adj smell, taste* yŏkkyŏun 역겨운; *weather* chidok'an 지독한 **3** *v/t* SP panch'igüro panghaehada 반칙으로 방해하다

found *v/t school etc* sŏllip'ada 설립하다

foundation (*of theory etc*) kün-gŏ 근거; (*organization*) chaedan 재단

foundations (*of building*) kich'o 기초

founder *n* sŏlliptcha 설립자

foundry chujo kongjang 주조 공장

fountain punsu 분수

four net 넷, sa 사

four-star *hotel* mugunghwa nesüi 무궁화 넷의

four-stick game yut 윷

fourteen yŏllet 열 넷, shipssa 십사

fourteenth yŏlne pŏntchaeüi 열 네 번째의

fourth ne pŏntchaeüi 네 번째의

fowl kagümnyu 가금류

fox *n* yŏu 여우

fraction ilbubun 일부분; (*decimal*) punsu 분수

fracture 1 *n* küm 금 **2** *v/t* ...e kümgage hada ...에 금가게 하다

fragile kkaejigi shwiun 깨지기 쉬운

fragment *n* (*of vase etc*) chogak 조각; (*of story, conversation*) tanp'yŏn 단편

fragmentary tanp'yŏntchŏgin 단편적인

fragrance hyanggi 향기

fragrant hyangginanün 향기나는

frail yak'an 약한

frame 1 *n* (*of picture, window*) t'ül 틀; (*of eyeglasses*) t'e 테; (*of bicycle*) ppyŏdae 뼈대; ~ *of mind* kibun 기분 **2** *v/t picture* t'üre kkiuda 틀에 끼우다; F *person* numyŏng ssüiuda 누명 씌우다

framework kusang 구상

France P'ŭrangssü 프랑스

frank soltchik'an 솔직한

frankly soltchik'i 솔직히

frantic mich'in tŭt'an 미친 듯한
fraternal hyŏngjeŭi 형제의
fraud sagi 사기; (*person*) sagikkun 사기꾼
fraudulent sagiŭi 사기의
frayed *cuffs* p'ullin 풀린
freak 1 *n* (*unusual event*) pyŏndŏk 변덕; (*two-headed person, animal etc*) kihyŏng 기형; F (*strange person*) pyŏltchong 별종; *movie* / *jazz* ~ F (*fanatic*) yŏnghwagwang / chaejŭgwang 영화광 / 재즈광 **2** *adj* *storm etc* toryŏnhan 돌연한; ~ **wind** tolp'ung 돌풍
freckle chugŭnkkae 주근깨
free 1 *adj* (*at liberty*) chayuŭi 자유의; (*no cost*) muryoŭi 무료의; *room, table* pin 빈; **are you ~ this afternoon?** onŭl ohue shigan issŭseyo? 오늘 오후에 시간 있으세요?; ~ **and easy** yŏyuroun 여유로운; **for ~** muryoro 무료로 **2** *v/t* *prisoners* sŏkppanghada 석방하다
freebie F tŏm 덤
freedom chayu 자유
freedom of the press ŏllonŭi chayu 언론의 자유
free kick (*in soccer*) p'ŭrik'ik 프리킥;
freelance 1 *adj* chayu kyeyagŭi 자유 계약의 **2** *adv* *work* chayu kyeyaguro 자유 계약으로; **freelancer** p'ŭriraensŏ 프리랜서; **free market economy** chayu shijang kyŏngje 자유 시장 경제; **free sample** muryo kyŏnbon 무료 견본; **free speech** ŏllonŭi chayu 언론의 자유; **freeway** kosokttoro 고속도로; **freewheel** *v/i* (*on bicycle*) p'edarŭl tteda 페달을 떼다
freeze 1 *v/t* *food, river* ŏllida 얼리다; *wages, bank account* tonggyŏrhada 동결하다; *video* sun-gan chŏngjishik'ida 순간 정지시키다 **2** *v/i* (*of water*) ŏlda 얼다
♦**freeze over** (*of river*) sumyŏni orŏbut-tta 수면이 얼어붙다
freezer naengdongshil 냉동실
freezing 1 *adj* mopsshi ch'uun 몹시 추운; *water* mopsshi ch'agaun 몹시 차가운; **it's ~** (*cold*) (*of weather*) mopsshi ch'upssŭmnida 몹시

ch'upssŭmnida; (*of water*) mopsshi ch'agapssŭmnida 몹시 차갑습니다; **I'm ~** (*cold*) chŏnŭn mopsshi ch'uwŏyo 저는 몹시 추워요 **2** *n* naengdong 냉동; **10 below ~** yŏngha 10to 영하 10도
freezing compartment naengdongshil 냉동실
freezing point pingtchŏm 빙점
freight *n* hwamul 화물; (*costs*) hwamul unsongnyo 화물 운송료
freight car hwamulch'a 화물차
freighter (*ship*) hwamulsŏn 화물선; (*airplane*) hwamul pihaenggi 화물 비행기
freight train hwamul yŏlch'a 화물 열차
French 1 *adj* P'ŭrangssŭŭi 프랑스의 **2** *n* (*language*) P'ŭrangssŏ 프랑스어; **the ~** P'ŭrangssŭin 프랑스인
French doors ssang-yŏdaji yurimun 쌍여닫이 유리문; **French fries** kamja t'wigim 감자 튀김; (*fast food*) hurench'ihurai 후렌치후라이; **Frenchman** P'ŭrangssŭ namja 프랑스 남자; **Frenchwoman** P'ŭrangssŭ yŏja 프랑스 여자
frequency pinbŏnham 빈번함; RAD chup'asu 주파수; **the increasing ~ of X** Xi / ga palsaenghanŭn hoessuŭi chŭngga X이 / 가 발생하는 횟수의 증가
frequent[1] *adj* chajŭn 잦은; *visitor* chaju onŭn 자주 오는
frequent[2] *v/t* *bar* chaju ch'at-tta 자주 찾다
frequently chaju 자주
fresh *air, water, food* shinsŏnhan 신선한; *complexion* saenggiinnŭn 생기있는; (*cold*) ssalssarhan 쌀쌀한; *start* saeroun 새로운; (*impertinent*) kŏnbangjin 건방진; *feel* ~ sangk'waehada 상쾌하다
♦**freshen up 1** *v/i* sshit-tta 씻다 **2** *v/t* *room, paintwork* saedanjanghada 새단장하다
freshman shinipssaeng 신입생
freshness (*of fruit, meat*) shinsŏndo 신선도; (*of style, approach*) shinsŏnham 신선함; (*of weather*) ssalssarham 쌀쌀함

freshwater *adj* minmurŭi 민물의
fret *v/i* kominhada 고민하다
friction mach'al 마찰
friction tape chŏn-gisŏnyong komut'eip'ŭ 전기선용 고무테이프
Friday kŭmnyoil 금요일
fridge naengjanggo 냉장고
friend ch'in-gu 친구; *make ~s (of one person)* ch'in-gurŭl sagwida 친구를 사귀다; *(of two people)* ch'in-guga toeda 친구가 되다; *make ~s with X* Xwa/kwa ch'in-guga toeda X와/과 친구가 되다
friendly *adj atmosphere* tajŏnghan 다정한; *person* ch'inhan 친한; *(easy to use)* shwiun 쉬운; *be ~ with X (be friends)* Xwa/kwa ch'inhage toeda X와/과 친하게 되다
friendship ujŏng 우정
fries hurench'ihurai 후렌치후라이
fright kkamtchak nollam 깜짝 놀람; *give X a ~* Xŭl/rŭl kkamtchak nollage hada X을/를 깜짝 놀라게 하다
frighten *v/t* kŏptchuda 겁주다; *be ~ed* kŏmnada 겁나다; *don't be ~ed* kŏmnaeji maseyo 겁내지 마세요; *be ~ed of* ... i/ga kŏmnada ...이/가 겁나다
frightening kŏmnanŭn 겁나는
frigid *(sexually)* pulgamtchŭng-ŭi 불감증의
frill *(on dress etc)* p'ŭril 프릴; *(fancy extra)* pugamul 부가물
fringe *(on dress, curtains etc)* sul 술; *(in hair)* ammŏri 앞머리; *(edge)* kajangjari 가장자리
frisk *v/t* momsusaek'ada 몸수색하다
frisky *puppy etc* kiun chok'e ttwiŏdaninŭn 기운 좋게 뛰어다니는
♦**fritter away** *time, fortune* hŏbihada 허비하다
frivolous shirŏmnŭn 실없는
frizzy *hair* kopssŭlgŏrinŭn 곱슬거리는
frog kaeguri 개구리
frogman chamsubu 잠수부
from ◊ *(in time)* ...(esŏ)but'ŏ ...(에서)부터; *~ 9 to 5 (o'clock)* ahopshibut'ŏ tasŏsshikkaji 9시부터 5시까지; *~ the 18th century* 18segibut'ŏ 18세기부터; *~ today on*

onŭlbut'ŏ 오늘부터; *~ next Tuesday* taŭm chu hwayoilbut'ŏ 다음 주 화요일부터 ◊ *(in space)* ...esŏ(but'ŏ) ...에서(부터); *~ here to there* yŏgiesŏ chŏgiro 여기에서 저기로; *we drove here ~ Seoul* urinŭn Sŏuresŏ yŏgikkaji unjŏnhae wassŭmnida 우리는 서울에서 여기까지 운전해 왔습니다 ◊ *(origin: of people)* ...(ŭ)robut'ŏ ...(으)로부터; *a letter ~ Jo* Chorobut'ŏ on p'yŏnji 조로부터 온 편지; *a gift ~ the management* kyŏng-yŏngjinŭrobut'ŏŭi sŏnmul 경영진으로부터의 선물; *it doesn't say who it's ~* igŏsŭn nuguegesŏ on kŏshinji palk'yŏit-tchi ant'a 이것은 누구에게서 온 것인지 밝혀있지 않다; *I am ~ New Jersey* chŏnŭn Nyujŏji ch'ulsshinimnida 저는 뉴저지 출신입니다; *made ~ bananas* pananaro mandŭn 바나나로 만든 ◊ *(because of)* ...(ŭ)ro ...(으)로; *tired ~ the journey* yŏhaeng-ŭro chich'in 여행으로 지친; *it's ~ overeating* nŏmu mani mŏgŭsŏ kŭrŏt'a 너무 많이 먹어서 그렇다
front 1 *n (of building, book)* ap 앞; *(cover organization)* kanp'an 간판; MIL, *(of weather)* chŏnsŏn 전선; *a cold/warm ~* hannaeng/onnan chŏnsŏn 한랭/온난 전선; *in ~* ap'e(sŏ) 앞에(서); *(in a race)* sŏndue(sŏ) 선두에(서); *in ~ of* ...ŭi ap'e(sŏ) ...의 앞에(서); *at the ~* ap'e(sŏ) 앞에(서); *at the ~ of* ...ŭi aptchoge(sŏ) ...의 앞쪽에(서)
2 *adj wheel, seat* aptchogŭi 앞쪽의
3 *v/i TV program* chinhaenghada 진행하다
front cover p'yoji 표지; **front door** ammun 앞문; **front entrance** chŏngmun 정문
frontier kuk-kkyŏng 국경; *fig (of knowledge, science)* ch'oech'ŏmdan 최첨단
front page *(of newspaper)* ilmyŏn 일면; **front page news** ilmyŏn kisa 일면 기사; **front row** aptchul 앞줄; **front seat passenger** *(in car)* aptchwasŏk sŭnggaek 앞좌석 승객; **front-wheel drive** ap-ppak'wi

kullim 앞바퀴 굴림

frost sŏri 서리

frostbite tongsang 동상

frostbitten tongsang-e kŏllin 동상에 걸린

frosted glass pult'umyŏnghan yuri 불투명한 유리

frosting (on cake) sŏlt'ang-ŭl ip'im 설탕을 입힘

frosty weather sŏriga naerinŭn 서리가 내리는; welcome naengdamhan 냉담한

froth n kŏp'um 거품

frothy cream etc kŏp'umi manŭn 거품이 많은

frown 1 n tchip'urin ŏlgul 찌푸린 얼굴 **2** v/i tchip'urida 찌푸리다

frozen ŏrŭn 얼은; wastes of Siberia kŭk'anŭi kŭk'ŏi 극한의; **I'm ~** F ch'uwŏsŏ ŏl chigyŏng-iyeyo 추워서 얼 지경이예요; **a ~ chicken / pizza** naengdong tak / p'ija 냉동 닭 / 피자

frozen food naengdong shikp'um 냉동 식품

fruit kwail 과일

fruitful discussions etc sŏngkkwaga manŭn 성과가 많은

fruit juice kwail chussŭ 과일 쥬스

fruit salad kwail saellŏdŭ 과일 샐러드

frustrate v/t person, plans chwajŏlsshik'ida 좌절시키다

frustrated look, sigh chwajŏldoen 좌절된

frustrating tchajŭngnanŭn 짜증나는

frustratingly slow, hard tchajŭngnadorok 짜증나도록

frustration chwajŏlgam 좌절감; sexual ~ sŏngchŏk yok-kku pulman 성적 욕구 불만; the ~s of modern life hyŏndaejŏk salme taehan chwajŏl 현대적 삶에 대한 좌절

fry v/t chijida 지지다; (stir-~) poktta 볶다; (deep-~) t'wigida 튀기다

fried egg kyeran hurai 계란 후라이

fried potatoes kamja t'wigim 감자 튀김

frying pan huraip'aen 후라이팬

fuck v/t V ...wa / kwa sŏnggyohada ...와 / 과 성교하다; ~! sshibal 씨발!; ~ him / that! sshibal nom / nomŭi kŏt! 씨발 놈 / 놈의 것!

♦**fuck off** V kkŏjida 꺼지다; ~! kkojyŏbŏryŏ! 꺼져버려!

fucking V **1** adj chidok'an 지독한 **2** adv chidok'age 지독하게

fuel n yŏllyo 연료

fugitive n tomangja 도망자

fulfill shirhaenghada 실행하다; feel ~ed (in job, life) manjok'ada 만족하다

fulfilling job manjokssŭroun 만족스러운

fulfillment (of contract etc) shirhaeng 실행; (spiritual) manjok-kkam 만족감

full bottle kadŭk ch'an 가득 찬; hotel, bus, diskette kkwak ch'an 꽉 찬; account, report sangsehan 상세한; life pappŭn 바쁜; schedule, day ppadŭt'an 빠듯한; ~ of ...(ŭ)ro kadŭk'an ...(으)로 가득한; ~ up hotel etc kadŭk ch'ada 가득 차다; (with food) paeburŭda 배부르다; pay in ~ chŏnaegŭl naeda 전액을 내다; sorry, we're ~ (at hotel) choesonghajiman, ta ch'assŭmnida 죄송하지만, 다 찼습니다

full cover (insurance) chonghap pohŏm 종합 보험; **full-grown** ta charan 다 자란; **full-length** dress chŏnshindaeŭi 전신대의; movie changp'yŏnŭi 장편의; **full moon** porŭmttal 보름달; **full stop** mach'imp'yo 마침표; **full-time 1** adj worker, job chŏnshiganjeŭi 전시간제의 **2** adv work chŏnshiganjero 전시간제로

fully ta 다, wanjŏnhi 완전히; describe sangsehi 상세히

fumble v/t catch sŏt'urŭge chaptta 서투르게 잡다

♦**fumble around** tŏdŭmgŏrimyŏ ch'at-tta 더듬거리며 찾다

fume: be fuming F kyŏngnohada 격노하다

fumes maeyŏn 매연

fun chaemi 재미; it was great ~ kŭgŏsŭn chŏngmal chaemiissŏssŏyo 그것은 정말 재미있었어요; bye, have ~! annyŏnghi kyeseyo, chaemiitkke chinaeseyo! 안녕히

계세요, 재미있게 지내세요!; *for ~*
chaemiro 재미로; *make ~ of*
…ŭl/rŭl nollida …을/를 놀리다
function 1 *n* (*of employee*) chingnŭng
직능 기능; (*of machine part*) kinŭng 기능;
(*reception etc*) haengsa 행사 2 *v/i*
chakttonghada 작동하다; *~ as* …ŭi
kinŭng-ŭl hada …의 기능을 하다
function key COMPUT kinŭngk'i
기능키
fund 1 *n* chagŭm 자금 2 *v/t project etc*
…e chagŭmŭl chegonghada …에
자금을 제공하다
fundamental (*basic*) kibonjŏgin
기본적인; (*substantial*) ponjiltchŏgin
본질적인; (*crucial*) chung-yohan
중요한
fundamentally *different, altered*
ponjiltchŏgŭro 본질적으로
funeral changnyeshik 장례식
funeral home yŏng-anso 영안소
funfair yuwŏnji 유원지
funicular (*railway*) k'eibŭl ch'ŏltto
케이블 철도
funnel *n* (*of ship*) kulttuk 굴뚝
funnily (*oddly*) isanghage 이상하게;
(*comically*) utkkige 웃기게; *~
enough* isanghagedo 이상하게도
funny (*comical*) usŭun 우스운; (*odd*)
isanghan 이상한
fur (*of coat, animal*) t'ŏl 털
furious (*angry*) kyŏngnohanŭn
격노하는; *at a ~ pace*
maengnyŏrhan sokttoro 맹렬한
속도로
furnace hwadŏk 화덕; (*for metal*)
yonggwangno 용광로
furnish *room* …e kagurŭl tŭryŏ not'a
…에 가구를 들여 놓다; (*supply*)
konggŭp'ada 공급하다
furniture kagu 가구; *a piece of ~*
kagu han chŏm 가구 한 점
furry *animal, coat* t'ŏri p'ungsŏnghan
털이 풍성한
further 1 *adj* (*additional*) tto tarŭn 또
다른; (*more distant*) tŏ mŏn 더 먼;

until ~ notice ch'uhu t'ongjiga issŭl
ttaekkaji 추후 통지가 있을 때까지;
have you anything ~ to say? tŏ
marhal kŏshi issŭshimnikka? 더
말할 것이 있으십니까? 2 *adv walk,
drive* tŏ 더; *~, I want to say …*
chega tŏtppuch'yŏ marhago ship'ŭn
kŏsŭn … imnida 제가 덧붙여 말하고
싶은 것은 … 입니다; *2 miles ~ (on)*
2mailboda tŏ mŏn 2마일보다 더 먼
3 *v/t cause etc* chojanghada 조장하다
furthest 1 *adj* kajang mŏn 가장 먼
2 *adv* kajang mŏlli 가장 멀리
furtive *glance* ŭnmirhan 은밀한
fury (*anger*) kyŏngno 격노
fuse ELEC 1 *n* p'yujŭ 퓨즈 2 *v/i*
p'yujŭga kkŭnk'ida 퓨즈가 끊기다
3 *v/t* p'yujŭrŭl kkŭnt'a 퓨즈를 끊다
fusebox tukkŏbijip 두꺼비집
fuselage tongch'e 동체
fuse wire tohwasŏn 도화선
fusion yunghap 융합
fuss *n* nalliböpssök 난리법석; *make a
~* (*complain*) nallich'ida 난리치다;
(*behave in exaggerated way*)
nalliböpssök ttölda 난리법석 떨다;
make a ~ of (*be very attentive to*)
…ege modŭn kwanshimŭl ssot-tta
…에게 모든 관심을 쏟다
fussy *person* kkadaroun 까다로운;
design etc chinach'ige kkumin
지나치게 꾸민; *be a ~ eater*
shikssŏng-i kkadaroptta 식성이
까다롭다
futile ssŭltte ŏmnŭn 쓸데 없는
future *n* mirae 미래; GRAM
miraehyŏng 미래형; *in ~* miraeenŭn
미래에는
futures FIN sŏnmul kyeyak 선물 계약
futures market FIN sŏnmul shijang
선물 시장
futuristic *design* ch'ohyŏndaejŏgin
초현대적인
fuzzy *hair* kopssŭlgopssŭrhan
곱슬곱슬한; (*out of focus*) hŭrit'an
흐릿한

G

gadget kanttanhan togu 간단한 도구
gag 1 n chaegal 재갈; (*joke*) kaegŭ
개그 **2** v/t person …ege chaegarŭl
mullida …에게 재갈을 물리다; *the
press* ogap'ada 억압하다
gain v/t (*acquire*) ŏt-tta 얻다; ~ *speed*
sokttorŭl naeda 속도를 내다; ~ *5
pounds* op'aundŭga nŭlda
5파운드가 늘다
gale kangp'ung 강풍
gall bladder ssŭlgae 쓸개
gallery (*for art*) hwarang 화랑; (*in
theater*) maen wich'ŭng kwallamsŏk
맨 위층 관람석
galley (*on ship*) chubang 주방
gallon kaellŏn 갤런
gallop v/i chiltchuhada 질주하다
gallows kyosudae 교수대
gallstone tamsŏk 담석
gamble tobak'ada 도박하다
gambler tobak-kkun 도박꾼
gambling tobak 도박
game n shihap 시합; (*of baseball,
football*) kyŏnggi 경기; (*children's*)
nori 놀이; (*in tennis*) keim 게임
gang p'aegŏri 패거리; (*of criminals*)
kaeng 갱
♦**gang up on** p'aejiŏ konggyŏk'ada
패지어 공격하다
gangster nappŭn muri 나쁜 무리
gangway t'ongno 통로
gap (*in wall, teeth*) t'ŭm 틈; (*for
parking, in figures*) pin-got 빈 곳; (*in
time, conversation*) kongbaek 공백;
(*between opinions, characters*) ch'ai
차이
gape v/i (*of person*) ibŭl ttak pŏlligo
paraboda 입을 딱 벌리고 바라보다
♦**gape at** ibŭl ttak pŏllin ch'ae
nŏksŭl ilk'o ch'yŏdaboda 입을 딱
벌린 채 넋을 잃고 쳐다보다
gaping: ~ *hole* k'ŭge pŏrŏjin kumŏng
크게 벌어진 구멍
garage (*for parking*) ch'ago 차고;

(*for gas*) chuyuso 주유소; (*for
repairs*) chadongch'a suriso 자동차
수리소
garbage ssŭregi 쓰레기; *fig* (*useless
stuff*) ssŭlmoŏmnŭn kŏt 쓸모없는
것; (*poor quality item*)
pullyangp'um 불량품; (*nonsense*)
maldo an toenŭn sori 말도 안 되는
소리; *don't talk ~!* mal katchi anŭn
sori hajido mara! 말 같지 않은 소리
하지도 마라!
garbage can ssŭregi t'ong 쓰레기 통;
garbage collection ssŭregi sujip
쓰레기 수집; **garbage dump**
ssŭregi p'yegijang 쓰레기 폐기장
garden chŏng-wŏn 정원, ttŭl 뜰
gardener (*professional*) chŏng-wŏnsa
정원사; *he's an enthusiastic ~*
kŭnŭn chŏng-wŏnesŏ irhanŭn kŏsŭl
choahaeyo 그는 정원에서 일하는
것을 좋아해요
gardening wŏnye 원예
gargle v/i ibanŭl kashida 입안을
가시다
garish chinach'ige hwaryŏhan
지나치게 화려한
garland n hwahwan 화환
garlic manŭl 마늘
garment ŭibok 의복
garnish v/t komyŏng-ŭro
changshik'ada 고명으로 장식하다
garrison n (*place*) kun chudunji 군
주둔지; (*troops*) chudun-gun 주둔군
garter kat'ŏ 가터
gas n kich'e 기체; (*for cooking*) kasŭ
가스; (*gasoline*) hwibaryu 휘발유
gash n kilgo kipkke pein sangch'ŏ
길고 깊게 베인 상처
gasket kasŭk'et 가스켓
gasoline hwibaryu 휘발유
gasp 1 n hŏltttŏk-kkŏrim 헐떡거림;
with a ~ hŏltttŏk-kkŏrimyŏ
헐떡거리며 **2** v/i hŏltttŏk-kkŏrida
헐떡거리다; ~ *for breath* sumŭl

hŏlttŏgida 숨을 헐떡이다
gas pedal aekssellŏreit'ŏ p'edal
액셀러레이터 페달; **gas pump**
chuyu p'ŏmp'ŭ 주유 펌프; **gas sta-tion** chuyuso 주유소
gate taemun 대문; (*at airport*)
t'apssŭnggu 탑승구
gatecrash ch'odaebat-tchi ank'o
kada 초대받지 않고 가다
gateway (*entrance*) ipkku 입구;
(*passage*) t'ongno 통로; *fig*
kwanmun 관문
gather 1 *v/t facts, information* moŭda
모으다; ~ **speed** songnyŏgŭl
nŭllyŏgada 속력을 늘려다; *am I to*
~ *that ...?* ...rago ihaehamyŏn
matssŭmnikka? ...라고 이해하면
맞습니까? **2** *v/i* (*understand*)
ch'uch'ŭk'ada 추측하다
♦**gather up** *possessions* ...ŭl/rŭl
chuwŏ moŭda ...을/를 주워 모으다
gathering *n* (*group of people*) moim
모임
gaudy ch'onsŭrŏpkke hwaryŏhan
촌스럽게 화려한
gauge 1 *n* kyegi 계기 **2** *v/t pressure*
ch'ŭktchŏnghada 측정하다; *opinion*
p'andanhada 판단하다
gaunt such'ŏk'an 수척한
gauze kŏju 거즈
gay 1 *n* (*homosexual*) tongsŏngaeja
동성애자 **2** *adj* tongsŏngaeŭi
동성애의
gaze 1 *n* ŭngshi 응시 **2** *v/i* ŭngshihada
응시하다
♦**gaze at** ...ŭl/rŭl ŭngshihada
...을/를 응시하다
GB (= *Great Britain*) Yŏngguk 영국
GDP (= *gross domestic product*)
kungnae ch'ongsaengsan 국내
총생산
gear *n* (*equipment*) yonggu 용구; (*in
vehicles*) kiŏ 기어
gear shift kiŏ chŏnhwan changch'i
기어 전환 장치
gel (*for hair*) chel 젤; (*for shower*)
mulbinu 물비누
gem posŏk 보석; *fig* (*book etc*)
myŏngjak 명작; (*person*)
pobaegat'ŭn saram 보배같은 사람
gender sŏng 성

gene yujŏnja 유전자; *it's in his ~s* kŭ
saramŭi ch'ŏnsŏng-ida 그 사람의
천성이다
genealogy book chokppo 족보
general 1 *n* (*in army*) changgun 장군;
in ~ ilbanjŏgŭro 일반적으로 **2** *adj*
ilbanjŏgin 일반적인; (*overall*)
chŏnch'ejŏgin 전체적인
general anesthetic chŏnshin
mach'wi 전신 마취
general election ch'ongsŏn-gŏ
총선거
generalization ilbanhwa 일반화
generalize ilbanhwahada 일반화하다
generally ilbanjŏgŭro 일반적으로
generate (*create*) nat-tta 낳다;
electricity palssaengshik'ida
발생시키다; (*in linguistics*)
saengsŏnghada 생성하다; *feeling*
irŭk'ida 일으키다; *accident, new
situation etc* yagihada 야기하다
generation (*of family*) sedae 세대
generation gap sedae ch'ai 세대
차이
generator paltchŏn-gi 발전기
generosity nŏgŭrŏum 너그러움
generous (*with money*) inshim choŭn
인심 좋은; (*not too critical*)
kwandaehan 관대한; *portion etc*
p'ungbuhan 풍부한
genetic yujŏnjŏgin 유전적인
genetically yujŏnjŏgŭro 유전적으로
genetic engineering yujŏn konghak
유전 공학
genetic fingerprint yujŏnja chimun
유전자 지문
geneticist yujŏnhaktcha 유전학자
genetics yujŏnhak 유전학
genial *person, company* tajŏnghan
다정한
genitals saengshikki 생식기
genius ch'ŏnjae 천재
gentle pudŭrŏun 부드러운; *person*
onhwahan 온화한
gentleman shinsa 신사
gents (*toilet*) namja hwajangshil 남자
화장실
genuine chintchaŭi 진짜의; *person*
chinshirhan 진실한
geographical *features* chirijŏk 지리적
geography (*of area, subject*) chiri

지리
geological *features* chijirŭi 지질의;
survey chijirhaktchŏk 지질학적
geologist chijirhaktcha 지질학자
geology (*of area*) chijil 지질; (*subject*)
chijirhak 지질학
geometric(al) kihahaktchŏk
기하학적
geometry kihahak 기하학
geriatric 1 *adj* noinppyŏng-ŭi
노인병의 **2** *n* noin 노인
germ segyun 세균; (*of idea etc*) ssak
싹
German 1 *adj* Togirŭi 독일의 **2** *n*
(*person*) Togirin 독일인; (*language*)
Togirŏ 독일어
Germany Togil 독일
germ warfare segyunjŏn 세균전
gesticulate sontchisŭro marhada
손짓으로 말하다
gesture *n* (*with hand*) sontchit 손짓;
fig (*of friendship*) ŭisa p'yoshi 의사
표시
get 1 *v/t* ◊ (*obtain*) ŏt-tta 얻다; (*fetch*)
kajyŏoda 가져오다; (*receive*) pat-tta
받다; (*catch: bus, train etc*) t'ada
타다; (*understand*) alda 알다; **I don't
~ it** (*don't understand*) ihaehal su
ŏpssŏyo 이해할 수 없어요 ◊
(*become*) ...haejida ...해지다; **~
tired / careless** p'igonhaejida /
pujuŭihaejida 피곤해지다 /
부주의해지다; **be ~ting older /
warmer** chŏmjŏm nŭlgŏjida /
tŏwŏjida 점점 늙어가다 / 더워지다 ◊
(*causative*): **~ sth done** muŏsŭl
hage hada 무엇을 하게 하다; **~ s.o.
to do sth** nuguege muŏsŭl harago
hada 누구에게 무엇을 하라고 하다;
you must ~ him to agree kŭrŭl
pandŭshi sŏlttŭkshik'yŏya hamnida
그를 반드시 설득시켜야 합니다; **~
one's hair cut** mŏrirŭl charŭda
머리를 자르다; **the car washed**
sech'ashik'ida 세차시키다; **~ the car
fixed** ch'arŭl surishik'ida 차를
수리시키다; **~ sth ready** muŏsŭl hal
chunbirŭl kach'uda 무엇을 할
준비를 갖추다; **~ going** (*leave*)
ttŏnada 떠나다 ◊ (*have
opportunity*): **~ to do sth** muŏsŭl

haepoda 무엇을 해보다; **~ to know**
alge toeda 알게 되다 ◊: **have got**
kajida 가지다; **I've got some
money** tonŭl chom kajigo issŏyo
돈을 좀 가지고 있어요; **I've got
something for you** tangshinhant'e
chul kŏshi issŏyo 당신한테 줄 것이
있어요; **I've got a headache**
mŏriga ap'ayo 머리가 아파요
◊ (*have ~ to*) ...haeya hada ...해야
하다; **I have got to study / see him**
nanŭn kongbuhaeya hamnida / kŭrŭl
mannaboaya hamnida 나는 공부해야
합니다 / 그를 만나보아야 합니다; **I
don't want to, but I've got to**
wŏnhajinŭn anch'iman
haeyahamnida 원하지는 않지만
해야합니다 **2** *v/i* (*arrive*) toch'ak'ada
도착하다
♦ **get about** (*travel*) yŏgijŏgi
yŏhaenghada 여기저기 여행하다; (*be
mobile*) toratanida 돌아다니다
♦ **get along** (*progress*) chinaeda
지내다; (*to party etc*) kada 가다;
(*with s.o.*) saiga chot'a 사이가 좋다
♦ **get at** (*criticize*) pinjŏngdaeda
빈정대다; (*imply, mean*)
marharyŏhada 말하려하다
♦ **get away 1** *v/i* (*leave*) ttŏnada
떠나다 **2** *v/t*: **get sth away from
s.o.** nuguegesŏ muŏsŭl ppaeat-tta
누구에게서 무엇을 빼앗다
♦ **get away with** *crime etc* pŏl pat-
tchi ank'o haenaeda 벌 받지 않고
해내다
♦ **get back 1** *v/i* toraoda 돌아오다; **I'll
~ to you on that** kŭgŏse taehan
ŭngdabŭl tŭrigessŭmnida 그것에
대한 응답을 드리겠습니다 **2** *v/t*
(*obtain again*) toech'at-tta 되찾다
♦ **get by** (*pass*) chinagada 지나가다;
(*financially*) kkuryŏnagada
꾸려나가다
♦ **get down 1** *v/i* (*from ladder etc*)
naeryŏgada 내려가다; (*duck etc*)
ŏpttŭrida 엎드리다 **2** *v/t* (*depress*)
uurhaehada 우울해하다
♦ **get down to** *work* shijak'ada
시작하다; *real facts* tat'a 닿다
♦ **get in 1** *v/i* (*of train, plane*)
toch'ak'ada 도착하다; (*come home*)

chibe tŭrŏoda 집에 들어오다; (*to car*) t'ada 타다; *how did they ~?* (*of thieves, snakes etc*) ŏttŏk'e tŭrŏgassŭlkkayo? 어떻게 들어갔을까요? 2 *v/t* (*to suitcase etc*) chibŏ nŏt'a 집어 넣다

♦ **get off 1** *v/i* (*from bus etc*) naerida 내리다; (*finish work*) iri kkŭnnada 일이 끝나다; (*not be punished*) pŏrŭl myŏnhada 벌을 면하다 2 *v/t clothes, hat, footwear* pŏt-tta 벗다; *lid, top* pŏtkkida 벗기다; *~ the grass!* chandie tŭrŏgaji mashio! 잔디에 들어가지 마시오!

♦ **get off with** *Br* (*sexually*) …wa/kwa chŭlgida …와/과 즐기다; *~ a small fine* kabyŏun pŏlgŭmŭro momyŏnhada 가벼운 벌금으로 모면하다

♦ **get on 1** *v/i* (*to bike, bus, train*) t'ada 타다; (*be friendly*) saiga chot'a 사이가 좋다; (*become old*) naidŭrŏ kada 나이들어 가다; (*make progress*) chinch'ŏkttoeda 진척되다; *it's getting on* (*late*) shigani nŭjŏjinda 시간이 늦어진다; *he's getting on* kŭnŭn kkwae naidŭrŏganda 그는 꽤 나이들어간다; *he's getting on for 50* kŭnŭn nai oshibi ta toeŏt-tta 그는 나이 50이 다 되었다; *he's getting on well at school* kŭnŭn hak-kkyoesŏ chal haenagago it-tta 그는 학교에서 잘 해나가고 있다 2 *v/t lid, top of box* ssŭiuda 씌우다; *boots* shintta 신다; *~ the bus / one's bike* pŏssŭe/chajŏn-gŏe t'ada 버스에/자전거에 타다; *I can't get these pants on* i pajirŭl ibŭl suga ŏpssŭmnida 이 바지를 입을 수가 없습니다

♦ **get out 1** *v/i* (*from car etc*) naerida 내리다; (*of prison*) naoda 나오다; *~!* nagayo! 나가요!; *let's ~ of here* yŏgiesŏ nagapsshida 여기에서 나갑시다; *I don't ~ much these days* yojŭm pyŏllo pakke nagaji ansŭmnida 요즘 별로 밖에 나가지 않습니다 2 *v/t nail, sth jammed, gun, pen* ppaenaeda 빼내다; *stain* ŏpssaeda 없애다

♦ **get over** *fence, disappointment etc* igyŏnaeda 이겨내다, kŭkppok'ada 극복하다; *lover* it-tta 잊다

♦ **get over with:** *let's get it over with* kŭnyang huttak haebŏripsshida 그냥 후딱 해버립시다

♦ **get through** (*on telephone*) t'onghwahada 통화하다; (*make self understood*) ihaeshik'ida 이해시키다

♦ **get up 1** *v/i* (*in morning, from chair etc*) irŏnada 일어나다; (*of wind*) ilda 일다 2 *v/t hill* orŭda 오르다

getaway (*from robbery*) tomang 도망; *~ car* toju ch'aryang 도주 차량

get-together ch'in-gyo moim 친교 모임

ghastly (*horrible*) chidok'an 지독한

gherkin chagŭn oi 작은 오이

ghetto pinmin-ga 빈민가

ghost kwishin 귀신

ghostly kwishin-gat'ŭn 귀신같은

giant 1 *n* kŏin 거인; *fig* kŏjang 거장 2 *adj* kŏdaehan 거대한

gibberish hoengsŏlsusŏl 횡설수설

giblets choryuŭi naejang 조류의 내장

giddiness hyŏn-gitchŭng 현기증

giddy ŏjirŏun 어지러운

gift sŏnmul 선물; (*natural ability*) t'agonan chaenŭng 타고난 재능

gifted t'agonan chaenŭng-i innŭn 타고난 재능이 있는

giftwrap *v/t* p'ojanghada 포장하다

gigabyte COMPUT kigabait'ŭ 기가바이트

gigantic pangdaehan 방대한

giggle 1 *v/i* kkilkkil ut-tta 낄낄 웃다 2 *n* kkilkkil usŭm 낄낄 웃음

gill (*of fish*) agami 아가미

gilt *n* kŭmbak 금박; *~s* FIN uryangju 우량주

gimmick (*promotional*) suppŏp 수법; (*new invention*) koanmul 고안물

gin chin 진; *~ and tonic* chint'onik 진토닉

ginger *n* (*spice*) saenggang 생강

gingerbeer chinjŏ piŏ 진저 비어; **gingerbread** saenggangppang 생강빵; **ginger tea** saenggangch'a 생강차

ginseng insam 인삼

gipsy chipsshi 집시

giraffe kirin 기린

girder *n* taedŭlbo 대들보

girl yŏja 여자; (*young*) sonyŏ 소녀

girl friend yŏja ch'in-gu 여자 친구; (*lover*) aein 애인

girl guide sonyŏ tanwŏn 소녀단원

girlie magazine p'orŭno chaptchi 포르노 잡지

girl scout kŏlsŭk'aut'ŭ 걸스카우트

gist yotchŏm 요점

give chuda 주다; *fml* tŭrida 드리다; (*supply: electricity etc*) konggŭp'ada 공급하다; *~ a talk* iyagirŭl haejuda 이야기를 해주다; *~ a cry* ulda 울다; *~ a groan* shinŭmhada 신음하다; *~ her my regards* kŭnyŏege anburŭl chŏnhaejuseyo 그녀에게 안부를 전해주세요

◆**give away** (*as present*) chuda 주다; (*betray*) paebanhada 배반하다; *give oneself away* uyŏnhi p'ongnohada 우연히 폭로하다

◆**give back** tollyŏjuda 돌려주다

◆**give in 1** *v/i* (*surrender*) kulbok'ada 굴복하다 **2** *v/t* (*hand in*) chech'urhada 제출하다

◆**give off** *smell, fumes* naeda 내다

◆**give onto** (*open onto*) ...(ŭ)ro t'onghada ...(으)로 통하다

◆**give out 1** *v/t leaflets etc* paebuhada 배부하다 **2** *v/i* (*of supplies, strength*) tahada 다하다

◆**give up 1** *v/t smoking etc* kkŭnt'a 끊다; *give oneself up to the police* kyŏngch'are chasuhada 경찰에 자수하다 **2** *v/i* (*cease habit*) kkŭnt'a 끊다; (*stop making effort*) p'ogihada 포기하다

◆**give way** (*of bridge etc*) munŏjida 무너지다

given name sŏng-ŭl cheoehan irŭm 성을 제외한 이름

glacier pingha 빙하

glad kippŭn 기쁜; *~ to see you* mannasŏ pan-gapssŭmnida 만나서 반갑습니다; *yes, I will be ~ to* ye, kikkŏi hagessŏyo 예, 기꺼이 하겠어요

gladly kikkŏi 기꺼이

glamor maeryŏk 매력

glamorous maeryŏgi nŏmch'inŭn 매력이 넘치는

glance 1 *n* hŭlgŭt pom 흘긋 봄 **2** *v/i: ~ at* ...ŭl/rŭl hŭlgŭt poda ...을/를 흘긋 보다

gland sŏn 선

glandular fever sŏnyŏl 선열

glare 1 *n* (*of sun, headlights*) nunbushinŭn pit 눈부시는 빛 **2** *v/i* (*of sun, headlights*) nunbushige pinnada 눈부시게 빛나다

◆**glare at** noryŏboda 노려보다

glaring *adj mistake* nune hwak ttŭinŭn 눈에 확 띄는

glass (*material*) yuri 유리; (*for drink*) k'ŏp 컵

glasses an-gyŏng 안경

glaze *n* yuyak 유약

◆**glaze over** (*of eyes*) nune saenggirŭl ilt'a 눈에 생기를 잃다

glazed *expression* hŭrit'an 흐릿한

glazier yuriŏptcha 유리업자

glazing (*glass*) yuri 유리

gleam 1 *n* ŏsŭrehan pit 어스레한 빛 **2** *v/i* ŏsŭrehage pich'ida 어스레하게 비치다

glee kippŭm 기쁨

gleeful kippŏhanŭn 기뻐하는

glib ipsshim choŭn 입심 좋은

glide (*of bird, plane*) hwalgonghada 활공하다; (*of person, furniture*) mikkŭrojida 미끄러지다

glider SP küllaidŏ 글라이더

gliding *n* SP küllaidŏ kyŏnggi 글라이더 경기

glimmer 1 *n* (*of light*) hŭimihan pit 희미한 빛; *~ of hope* shillalgat'ŭn hŭimang 실낱같은 희망 **2** *v/i* kkamppagida 깜빡이다

glimpse 1 *n* hŭlkkŭt pom 흘끗 봄; *catch a ~ of* ...ŭl/rŭl hŭlkkŭt poda ...을/를 흘끗 보다 **2** *v/t* hŭlkkŭt poda 흘끗 보다

glint 1 *n* pantchak 반짝 **2** *v/i* (*of light*) pantchak pinnada 반짝 빛나다; (*of eyes*) pŏnttŭgida 번득이다

glisten *v/i* pantchak-kkŏrida 반짝거리다

glitter *v/i* pantchakpantchak pinnada 반짝반짝 빛나다

glitterati sagyogye saramdŭl 사교계 사람들

gloat *v/i* kosohaehada 고소해하다; *~*

over kosohaehada 고소해하다

global (*worldwide*) chŏnsegyeŭi 전세계의; (*without exception*) t'onggwaljŏgin 통괄적인

global economy segye kyŏngje 세계 경제

globalization segyehwa 세계화

global market segye shijang 세계 시장

global warming segye onnanhwa 세계 온난화

globe (*the earth*) chigu 지구; (*model of earth*) chigubon 지구본

gloom (*darkness*) ŏduk'ŏmk'ŏmham 어두컴컴함; (*mood*) uul 우울

gloomy *room* ŏduk'ŏmk'ŏmhan 어두컴컴한; *mood, person* uurhan 우울한

glorious *weather* malgŭn 맑은; *victory* yŏnggwangsŭrŏun 영광스러운

glory *n* yŏnggwang 영광

gloss *n* (*shine*) yun 윤; (*general explanation*) chusŏk 주석

glossary yong-ŏ p'uri 용어 풀이

gloss paint kwangt'aek p'eint'ŭ 광택 페인트

glossy 1 *adj paper* kwangt'aek nanŭn 광택 나는 **2** *n* (*magazine*) kogŭp chaptchi 고급 잡지

glove changgap 장갑; (*in baseball*) yagu kŭllŏbŭ 야구 글러브

glow 1 *n* (*of light*) paengnyŏl 백열; (*of fire*) t'aorŭm 타오름; (*in cheeks*) taraorŭm 달아오름 **2** *v/i* (*light*) pich'ŭl naeda 빛을 내다; (*fire*) t'ada 타다 **2** *v/i* (*cheeks*) taraorŭda 달아오르다

glowing *description* yŏllyŏrhan 열렬한

glue 1 *n* p'ul 풀 **2** *v/t* p'ullo puch'ida 풀로 붙이다; **~ X to Y** Xŭl/rŭl Ye p'ullo puch'ida X을/를 Y에 풀로 붙이다

glum shimuruk'an 시무룩한

glutinous rice ch'apssal 찹쌀

glutton taeshikka 대식가

gluttony p'oksshik 폭식

GMT (= *Greenwich Mean Time*) segye p'yojunshi 세계 표준시

gnarled *branch* madit'usŏng-iin 마디투성이인; *hands* kŏch'in 거친

gnat kakttagwi 각다귀

gnaw *v/t bone* kaltta 갉다

GNP (= *gross national product*) kungmin ch'ongsaengsan 국민 총생산

Go (*game*) Paduk 바둑

go 1 *n*: **on the ~** chulgot irhayŏ 줄곧 일하여 **2** *v/i* kada 가다; (*leave: of train, plane*) ch'ulbarhada 출발하다; (*leave: of people*) ttŏnada 떠나다; (*work, function*) chakttonghada 작동하다; (*become*) ...haejida ...해지다; (*come out: of stain etc*) ŏpssŏjida 없어지다; (*cease: of pain etc*) sarajida 사라지다; (*match: of colors etc*) ŏullida 어울리다; **~ quiet** choyonghaejida 조용해지다; **~ shopping** / **jogging** shyop'ingharŏ / chogingharŏ kada 쇼핑하러 / 조깅하러 가다; **I must be ~ing** ije kayaman hamnida 이제 가야만 합니다; **let's ~!** kapsshida! 갑시다!; **~ for a walk** sanch'aek'ada 산책하다; **~ to bed** charŏ kada 자러 가다; **~ to school** hak-kkyoe kada 학교에 가다; **how's the work ~ing?** iri ŏttŏk'e toeŏgamnikka? 일이 어떻게 되어갑니까?; **they're ~ing for $50** kŭgŏsŭn 50tallŏe p'amnida 그것은 50달러에 팝니다; **hamburger to ~** haembŏgo p'ojanghaejuseyo 햄버거 포장해주세요; **it's all gone** ta ŏpssŏjyŏt-tta 다 없어졌다; **be ~ing to do sth** muŏsŭl hal kŏshida 무엇을 할 것이다

♦ **go ahead** kŭrŏk'e haseyo 그렇게 하세요

♦ **go ahead with** *plans etc* ch'ujinhada 추진하다

♦ **go along with** *suggestion* ...e ttarŭda ...에 따르다

♦ **go at** (*attack*) tŏmbyŏdŭlda 덤벼들다

♦ **go away** (*of person*) ttŏnada 떠나다; (*of rain*) kŭch'ida 그치다; (*of pain, clouds*) sarajida 사라지다

♦ **go back** (*return*) toragada 돌아가다; (*date back*) kŏsŭllŏ ollagada 거슬러 올라가다; **~ to sleep** tashi chada 다시 자다; **we ~ a long way** urinŭn orae algo chinaen saiyeyo 우리는

오래 알고 지낸 사이예요
♦ **go by** (*go past*) chinagada 지나가다
♦ **go down 1** *v/t stairs etc* naeryŏgada
내려가다 **2** *v/i* (*of sun*) chida 지다; (*of
ship, swelling*) karaantta 가라앉다; ~
well / badly (*of suggestion etc*)
chok'e / nappŭge padadŭryŏjida
좋게 / 나쁘게 받아들여지다
♦ **go for** (*attack*) tŏmbyŏdŭlda
덤벼들다; (*like*) choahada 좋아하다
♦ **go in** (*to room, of sun*) turŏgada
들어가다; (*fit: of part etc*) mat-tta
맞다
♦ **go in for** *competition, race*
ch'ulchŏnhada 출전하다; (*like*)
chŭlgida 즐기다
♦ **go off 1** *v/i* (*leave*) kabŏrida
가버리다; (*of bomb*) p'okpparhada
폭발하다; (*of gun*) palssadoeda
발사되다; (*of alarm*) ullida 울리다;
(*of milk etc*) sanghada 상하다 **2** *v/t*
(*stop liking*) ...i / ga shirŏjida
...이 / 가 싫어지다
♦ **go on** (*continue*) kyesok'ada
계속하다; (*happen*) irŏnada 일어나다;
~, *do it!* (*encouraging*)
kwaench'anayo, haeboseyo!
괜찮아요, 해보세요!; *what's going
on?* musŭn il issŏyo? 무슨 일
있어요?; ~ *about* ...e taehae kyesok
ttŏdŭrŏdaeda ...에 대해 계속
떠들어대다
♦ **go on at** (*nag*) ...ege chansorihada
...에게 잔소리하다; *husband*
...ŭl / rŭl pagaji kŭltta ...을 / 를
바가지 긁다
♦ **go out** (*of person*) nagada 나가다;
(*of light, fire*) kkŏjida 꺼지다
♦ **go over** *v/t* (*check*) kŏmt'ohada
검토하다
♦ **go through** *v/t illness, hard times*
kyŏktta 겪다; (*check*) myŏnmirhi
chosahada 면밀히 조사하다; (*read
through*) t'ongdok'ada 통독하다
♦ **go under** (*sink*) karaantta
가라앉다; (*of company*) manghada
망하다
♦ **go up** (*climb, in price*) ollagada
올라가다
♦ **go without 1** *v/t food etc* ... ŏpsshi
saragada ... 없이 살아가다 **2** *v/i*

ŏpsshi chinaeda 없이 지내다
goad *v/t* koerop'ida 괴롭히다
go-ahead 1 *n* hŏga 허가; *get the ~*
hŏgabat-tta 허가받다 **2** *adj*
(*enterprising, dynamic*)
chinch'wijŏgin 진취적인
goal SP (*target*) kol 골; (*points*)
tŭktchŏm 득점; (*objective*) mokp'yo
목표
goalkeeper kolk'ip'ŏ 골키퍼
goalpost kolttae 골대
goat yŏmso 염소
♦ **gobble up** kegŏlsŭrŏpkke mŏktta
게걸스럽게 먹다
go-between chunggaeja 중개자
God Hanŭnim 하느님; *thank ~!* a,
sarat-tta 아, 살았다; *oh ~!* sesang-e!
세상에!
god shin 신
goddess yŏshin 여신
godfather taebu 대부
godforsaken *place, town*
hwangnyanghan 황량한
goggles poan-gyŏng 보안경; (*for
skiing*) kogŭl 고글; (*for swimming*)
muran-gyŏng 물안경
going *adj price etc* hyŏnjaeŭi 현재의;
~ *concern* sujiga mannŭn saŏp
수지가 맞는 사업
goings-on pinan padŭl manhan
haeng-wi 비난 받을 만한 행위
gold 1 *n* kŭm 금 **2** *adj* kŭmŭi 금의
golden *hair* kŭmsaegŭi 금색의
golden handshake t'oejikkŭm
퇴직금
golden wedding anniversary
kŭmhonshik 금혼식
goldfish kŭmbung-ŏ 금붕어; **gold
medal** kŭmmedal 금메달; **goldsmith** kŭmsegongsa 금세공사
golf kolp'ŭ 골프
golf club (*organization, stick*) kolp'ŭ
k'ŭllŏp 골프 클럽
golf course kolp'ŭjang 골프장
golfer kolp'ŭ ch'inŭn saram 골프 치는
사람
gong (*iron*) ching 징; (*brass*)
kkwaenggwari 꽹과리
good choŭn 좋은; *a ~ many* aju
manŭn 아주 많은; *be ~ at* ...ŭl / rŭl
charhada ...을 / 를 잘하다; *be ~ for*

s.o. nuguege chot'a 누구에게 좋다
goodbye annyŏng 안녕; (*polite: to the
person who is leaving*) annyŏnghi
kaseyo 안녕히 가세요; (*polite: to the
person who is staying*) annyŏnghi
kyeseyo 안녕히 계세요; **say ~ to
s.o.** nuguege chakppyŏl insarŭl hada
누구에게 작별 인사를 하다
good-for-nothing n amu ssŭlmo
ŏmnŭn saram 아무 쓸모없는 사람;
Good Friday Sŏnggŭmnyoil
성금요일; **good-humored**
myŏngnanghan 명랑한; **good-
looking** chal saenggin 잘 생긴;
good-natured sŏnggyŏgi choŭn
성격이 좋은
goodness (*moral*) tŏk 덕;
(*nutritional*) yŏngnyangbun 영양분;
thank ~! komawŏra! 고마워라!
goods COM sangp'um 상품
goodwill hoŭi 호의
goody-goody n F ch'ak'an
ch'ŏk'anŭn saram 착한 척하는 사람
gooey kkŭnjŏk-kkŭnjŏk'an
끈적끈적한
goof v/i F pabojisŭl hada 바보짓을
하다
goose kŏwi 거위
gooseberry kujŭberi 구즈베리
gooseflesh: it gives me ~ narŭl
sorŭmkkich'ige handa 나를
소름끼치게 한다
gorge 1 n hyŏpkkok 협곡 **2** v/t: ~
oneself on sth muŏsŭl p'oshik'ada
무엇을 포식하다
gorgeous *weather* hwach'anghan
화창한; *dress, woman, hair, smell*
kŭnsahan 근사한
gorilla korilla 고릴라
go-slow t'aeŏp 태업
Gospel (*in Bible*) Pogŭmsŏ 복음서
gossip 1 n chapttam 잡담; (*person*)
hŏmdam 험담 **2** v/i chapttamhada
잡담하다
govern *country* tasŭrida 다스리다
government chŏngbu 정부
governor (*of province*) chisa 지사
gown (*long dress*) kin kŏt'ot 긴 겉옷;
(*wedding dress*) weding tŭresŭ 웨딩
드레스; (*of judge*) pŏp-ppok 법복; (*of
surgeon*) kaun 가운

grab v/t puyŏjaptta 부여잡다; ~
something to eat kanshigŭl mŏktta
간식을 먹다; ~ **a nap** hansum chada
한숨 자다
grace (*quality*) ua 우아
graceful uahan 우아한
gracious *person, style, living* p'umwi
innŭn 품위 있는; **good ~!** chŏrŏn!
저런!
grade 1 n (*quality*) tŭnggŭp 등급;
(*year in school*) hangnyŏn 학년; (*in
exam*) sŏngjŏk 성적 **2** v/t tŭnggŭbŭl
maegida 등급을 매기다; EDU *papers*
sŏngjŏgŭl ŏt-tta 성적을 얻다;
grade crossing RAIL sup'yŏng
kŏnnŏlmok 수평 건널목
gradient kyŏngsado 경사도
gradual chŏmch'ajŏgin 점차적인
gradually chŏmch'ajŏgŭro 점차적으로
graduate 1 n chorŏpssaeng 졸업생;
(*at graduate school*) taehagwŏn
hakssaeng 대학원 학생 **2** v/i
chorŏp'ada 졸업하다
graduate school taehagwŏn 대학원
graduation chorŏp 졸업
graffiti nakssŏ 낙서
graft n BOT chŏppuch'igi 접붙이기;
MED ishik chojik 이식 조직; F
(*corruption*) pujŏng pup'ye 부정
부폐
grain nadal 낟알; (*in wood*)
namutkkyŏl 나뭇결; **go against the
~** sŏngjire mat-tchi ant'a 성질에 맞지
않다
gram kŭraem 그램
grammar munppŏp 문법
grammatical munppŏpssang-ŭi
문법상의
grand 1 adj ungjanghan 웅장한; F
(*very good*) widaehan 위대한 **2** n F
(*$1000*) ch'ŏn tallŏ 천 달러
grandad haraboji 할아버지; **grand-
child** (*male*) sonja 손자; (*female*)
sonnyŏ 손녀; **granddaughter**
sonnyŏ 손녀
grandeur ungjangham 웅장함
grandfather haraboji 할아버지;
grandma halmŏni 할머니; **grandmother** halmŏni 할머니; **grandpa**
haraboji 할아버지; **grandparents**
chobumo 조부모; **grand piano**

kŭraendŭ p'iano 그랜드 피아노;
grandson sonja 손자; **grandstand**
t'ŭkppyŏl kwallamsŏk 특별 관람석
granite hwagang-am 화강암
granny halmŏni 할머니
grant 1 n (money) pojogŭm 보조금;
(for university, school) changhak-
kkŭm 장학금 **2** v/t wish, peace
tŭrŏjuda 들어주다; visa hŏgahada
허가하다; request sŭng-inhada
승인하다; *take sth for ~ed* muŏsŭl
tang-yŏnhan illo yŏgida 무엇을
당연한 일로 여기다; *take s.o. for
~ed* nugurŭl tang-yŏnhage yŏgida
누구를 당연하게 여기다
granule chagŭn algaeng-i 작은 알갱이
grape p'odo 포도
grapefruit kŭreip'ŭp'ŭrut'ŭ
그레이프프루트; **grapefruit juice**
kŭreip'ŭp'ŭrut'ŭ chusŭ
그레이프프루트 주스; **grapevine:**
hear sth through the ~ muŏsŭl
somunŭro tŭt-tta 무엇을 소문으로
듣다
graph top'yo 도표
graphic 1 adj (vivid) saengsaenghan
생생한 **2** n COMPUT kŭraep'ik 그래픽
graphics COMPUT kŭraep'iksŭ
그래픽스
♦ **grapple with** attacker …wa/kwa
matpput'ŏ ssauda …와/과 맞붙어
싸우다; problem etc …wa/kwa
sshirŭmhada …와/과 씨름하다
grasp 1 n (physical) umk'yŏjapkki
움켜잡기; (mental) ihaeryŏk 이해력
2 v/t (physically) umk'yŏjaptta
움켜잡다; (understand) ihaehada
이해하다
grass p'ul 풀
grasshopper mettugi 메뚜기; **grass
widow** kwabugat'ŭn shinse 과부같은
신세; **grass widower** horabigat'ŭn
shinse 홀아비같은 신세
grassy p'uri ugŏjin 풀이 우거진
grate¹ n (metal) soesalttae 쇠살대
grate² **1** v/t carrots etc pibyŏ
pusŭrŏt-tŭrida 비벼 부스러뜨리다
2 v/i (of sound) kŏsŭllida 거슬리다
grateful komapkke yŏginŭn 고맙게
여기는; *be ~ to* …ŭl/rŭl komapkke
yŏgida …을/를 고맙게 여기다

grater kangp'an 강판
gratification manjoksshik'igi
만족시키기
gratify manjoksshik'ida 만족시키다
grating 1 n soe kyŏktcha ttukkŏng 쇠
격자 뚜껑 **2** adj sound, voice kwie
kŏsŭllinŭn 귀에 거슬리는
gratitude kamsa 감사
gratuity t'ip 팁
grave¹ n mudŏm 무덤
grave² adj error chungdaehan 중대한;
face, voice kŭnŏmhan 근엄한
gravel n chagal 자갈
gravestone chagal 자갈
graveyard myoji 묘지
gravity PHYS chungnyŏk 중력
gravy yuktchŭp 육즙
gray adj hoesaegŭi 회색의; *be going
~* paekppari toeda 백발이 되다
gray-haired paekpparŭi 백발의
grayhound kŭreihaundŭ
그레이하운드
graze¹ v/i (of cow, horse) p'urŭl
ttŭdŏmŏktta 풀을 뜯어먹다
graze² **1** v/t arm etc kabyŏpkke
sŭch'ida 가볍게 스치다 **2** n (on arm
etc) ch'algwasang 찰과상
grease (for cooking) yuji 유지; (for
car) yunhwalyu 윤활유
greasy kirŭmkki manŭn 기름기 많은
great (in size) koengjanghi k'ŭn
굉장히 큰; (in amount) koengjanghi
manŭn 굉장히 많은; (outstanding)
hyŏnjŏhan 현저한; (very important)
chungdaehan 중대한; composer,
writer tae… 대…; F (very good)
koengjanghi chʼoŭn 굉장히 좋은; ~
composer taejak-kkok-kka
대작곡가; *how was it? - ~*
ŏttaessŏyo? - koengjanghi
chʼoassŏyo 어땠어요? - 굉장히
좋았어요; *~ to see you!* mannasŏ
nŏmu pan-gapssŭmnida! 만나서
너무 반갑습니다!
Great Britain Yŏngguk 영국
Great Han Empire Taehanjeguk
대한제국
greatly koengjanghi 굉장히
greatness widaeham 위대함
greed yoksshim 욕심
greedy yoksshim manŭn 욕심 많은

green

green nokssaegŭi 녹색의; (*environmentally*) hwan-gyŏng pohoŭi 환경 보호의

greenhorn F p'unnaegi 풋내기; **greenhouse** onshil 온실; **greenhouse effect** onshil hyokkwa 온실 효과; **greenhouse gas** isanhwat'anso 이산화탄소; **green tea** nokch'a 녹차

greet insahada 인사하다

greeting insa 인사

grenade suryut'an 수류탄

grid kyŏktcha 격자

gridiron SP mishik ch'uk-kku kyŏnggijang 미식 축구 경기장

gridlock (*in traffic*) kyot'ongmang chŏngch'e 교통망 정체

grief pit'ong 비통

grievance pulp'yŏngkkŏri 불평거리

grieve pit'onghaehada 비통해하다; ~ **for s.o.** nugurŭl irŏ pit'onghaehada 누구를 잃어 비통해하다

grill 1 *n* (*on window*) soech'angssal 쇠창살 **2** *v/t* (*interrogate*) shimmunhada 심문하다

grille soech'angssal 쇠창살

grim *look, person* ŏmhan 엄한; *prospect, future* naenghok'an 냉혹한

grimace *n* ŏlgurŭl tchip'urim 얼굴을 찌푸림

grime ttae 때

grimy ttaemudŭn 때묻은

grin 1 *n* shinggŭt usŭm 싱긋 웃음 **2** *v/i* shinggŭt ut-tta 싱긋 웃다

grind *v/t* coffee, meat kalda 갈다

grip 1 *n* (*on rope etc*) kkwak chabŭm 꽉 잡음; *be losing one's* ~ (*losing one's skills*) nŭngnyŏgi ŏpssŏjida 능력이 없어지다 **2** *v/t* kkwak chaptta 꽉 잡다

gristle yŏn-gol 연골

grit *n* (*dirt*) mŏnji 먼지; (*for roads*) chan morae 잔 모래

groan 1 *n* shinŭm sori 신음 소리 **2** *v/i* shinŭmhada 신음하다

grocer shingnyo chap'wasang 식료 잡화상

groceries shingnyo chap'waryu 식료 잡화류

grocery store shingnyo chap'wajŏm 식료 잡화점

groin sat'aguni 사타구니

groom 1 *n* (*for bride*) shillang 신랑; (*for horse*) mabu 마부 **2** *v/t* horse sonjirhada 손질하다; (*train, prepare*) hullyŏnshik'ida 훈련시키다; *well* ~*ed* (*in appearance*) chal sonjildoen 잘 손질된

groove *n* hŭm 홈

grope 1 *v/i* (*in the dark*) sonŭro tŏdŭmtta 손으로 더듬다 **2** *v/t* (*sexually*) sonŭro tŏdŭmtta 손으로 더듬다

♦ **grope for** *door, word* ch'at-tta 찾다

gross *adj* (*coarse, vulgar*) sangsŭrŏun 상스러운; *exaggeration* ŏmch'ŏngnan 엄청난; FIN ch'onggye 총계

gross domestic product kungnae ch'ongsaengsan 국내 총생산

gross national product kungmin ch'ongsaengsan 국민 총생산

ground 1 *n* ttang 땅; (*reason*) kŭn-gŏ 근거; ELEC chŏptchi 접지; *on the* ~ hyŏnjang-e(sŏ) 현장에(서) **2** *v/t* ELEC chŏptchihada 접지하다

ground control chisang kwanje 지상 관제

ground crew chisang kŭnmuwŏn 지상 근무원

groundless kŭn-gŏ ŏmnŭn 근거 없는

ground meat kan kogi 간 고기; **groundnut** ttangk'ong 땅콩; **ground plan** p'yŏngmyŏndo 평면도; **ground staff** SP chŏngbiwŏn 정비원; (*at airport*) chisang kŭnmuwŏn 지상 근무원; **groundwork** kich'o chagŏp 기초 작업

group 1 *n* muri 무리; (*of companies*) kŭrup 그룹 **2** *v/t* murijit-tta 무리짓다

grow 1 *v/i* charada 자라다; (*of number, amount*) k'ŏjida 커지다; (*of business*) sŏngjanghada 성장하다; ~ *old / ~ tired* nŭlgŏjida / p'igonhaejida 늙어지다 / 피곤해지다 **2** *v/t* flowers kirŭda 기르다

♦ **grow up** (*of person*) charanada 자라나다; (*of city*) paltchŏnhada 발전하다; ~*!* nai kapssŭl hae! 나이 값을 해!

growl 1 *n* ŭrŭrŏnggŏrinŭn sori 으르렁거리는 소리 **2** *v/i* ŭrŭrŏnggŏrida 으르렁거리다

grown-up 1 *n* ŏrŭn 어른 **2** *adj*
ŏrŭnsŭrŏun 어른스러운
growth (*of person, company*)
sŏngjang 성장; (*increase*) chŭngga
증가; MED chongyang 종양
grub (*of insect*) ttangbŏlle 땅벌레
grubby tŏrŏun 더러운
grudge 1 *n* yugam 유감; *bear a ~*
yugamŭl kajida 유감을 가지다 **2** *v/t*:
I don't ~ him his success kŭga
sŏnggonghaedo pae anap'ayo 그가
성공해도 배 안아파요
grudging insaek'an 인색한
grueling *climb*, *task* nokch'oro
mandŭnŭn 녹초로 만드는
gruff kulkko t'ak'an mokssori 굵고
탁한 목소리
grumble *v/i* t'udŏlgŏrida 투덜거리다
grumbler t'udŏlgŏrinŭn saram
투덜거리는 사람
grunt 1 *n* (*of pig*) kkulkkulgŏrim
꿀꿀거림; (*of person*) kŏch'in shinŭm
거친 신음 **2** *v/i* (*of pig*)
kkulkkulgŏrida 꿀꿀거리다; (*of
person*) kŏch'ilge shinŭmhada
거칠게 신음하다
guarantee 1 *n* pojŭng 보증; *~ period*
pojŭng kigan 보증 기간 **2** *v/t*
pojŭnghada 보증하다
guarantor pojŭng-in 보증인
guard 1 *n* (*security ~*) kyŏngbiwŏn
경비원; MIL poch'o 보초; (*in prison*)
kyodogwan 교도관; *be on one's ~
against* ...ŭl/rŭl kyŏnggyehada
...을/를 경계하다 **2** *v/t* chik'ida
지키다
♦ **guard against** ...ŭl/rŭl
choshimhada ...을/를 조심하다
guarded *reply* choshimsŏng innŭn
조심성 있는
guardian LAW hugyŏnin 후견인
guerrilla kerilla 게릴라
guess 1 *n* ch'uch'ŭk 추측 **2** *v/t* *answer*
ch'uch'ŭk'ada 추측하다; *I ~ so*
kŭrŏn kŏt kat'ayo 그런 것 같아요; *I
~ not* kŭrŏch'i anŭn kŏt kat'ayo
그렇지 않은 것 같아요 **2** *v/i*
ch'uch'ŭk'ada 추측하다
guesswork ŏrimjimjak 어림짐작
guest sonnim 손님
guesthouse yŏgwan 여관

guestroom sonnimnyong ch'imshil
손님용 침실
guffaw 1 *n* kaptchakssŭrŏn k'ŭn
usŭm 갑작스런 큰 웃음 **2** *v/i*
kaptchagi k'ŭge ut-tta 갑자기 크게
웃다
guidance annae 안내
guide 1 *n* (*person*) annaeja 안내자;
(*book*) annaesŏ 안내서 **2** *v/t*
annaehada 안내하다
guidebook annaesŏ 안내서
guided missile yudot'an 유도탄
guided tour kaidŭ t'uŏ 가이드 투어
guidelines chich'im 지침
guilt LAW pŏmjoe 범죄; (*moral*) choe
죄; (*guilty feeling*) choech'aek-kkam
죄책감
guilty LAW yujoeŭi 유죄의;
(*responsible*) choe chiŭn 죄 지은;
look, *smile* choe chiŭndŭt'an 죄
지은듯한; *have a ~ conscience*
choech'aek-kkamŭl nŭkkida
죄책감을 느끼다
guinea pig morŭmot'ŭ 모르모트; *fig*
shirhŏm chaeryo 실험 재료
guitar kit'a 기타
guitarist kit'a yŏnjuga 기타 연주가
gulf man 만; *fig* kip'ŭn t'ŭm 깊은 틈
gull kalmaegi 갈매기
gullet shiktto 식도
gullible sok-kki shwiun 속기 쉬운
gulp 1 *n* (*of water etc*) kkulkkŏk-
kkulkkŏk mashim 꿀꺽꿀꺽 마심
2 *v/i* (*in surprise*) sumŭl chugida
숨을 죽이다
♦ **gulp down** *drink*, kkulkkŏk-
kkulkkŏk mashida 꿀꺽꿀꺽 마시다;
breakfast, *food* kŭp'i mŏktta 급히
먹다
gum[1] (*in mouth*) inmom 잇몸
gum[2] *n* (*glue*) chŏmsŏng komu 점성
고무; (*chewing ~*) kkŏm 껌
gun ch'ong 총
♦ **gun down** ssoa nomŏttŭrida 쏘아
넘어뜨리다
gunfire p'ogyŏk 포격; **gunman**
ch'onggi hyudaeja 총기 휴대자;
(*robber*) mujang kangdo 무장 강도;
gunpowder hwayak 화약; **gunshot**
palp'o 발포; *~ wound* ch'ongsang
총상

gurgle *v/i* (*of baby*) mogŭl kkolttak-kkŏrida 목을 꼴딱거리다; (*of drain*) k'walk'wal hŭllŏnaoda 콸콸 흘러나오다

gush *v/i* (*of liquid*) p'ŏngp'ŏng sosanaoda 펑펑 솟아나오다

gushy F (*very enthusiastic*) chinach'ige kamsangjŏgin 지나치게 감상적인

gust *n* tolp'ung 돌풍

gusty *weather* parami shimhan 바람이 심한; **~ wind** tolp'ung 돌풍

gut 1 *n* ch'angja 창자; F (*stomach*) pae 배; **~s** F (*courage*) yonggi 용기 **2** *v/t* (*of fire*) t'aewŏbŏrida 태워버리다

gutter (*on sidewalk*) torang 도랑; (*on roof*) homt'ong 홈통

guy F namja 남자; **hey, you ~s** ŏi, yŏrŏbun 어이, 여러분

gym ch'eyuk-kkwan 체육관

gymnasium ch'eyuk-kkwan 체육관

gymnast ch'eyuk kyosa 체육 교사

gymnastics ch'ejo 체조

gynecologist sanbuinkkwa ŭisa 산부인과 의사

gypsy chipsshi 집시

H

habit p'orŭt 버릇, sŭpkkwan 습관
habitable kŏjuhal su innŭn 거주할 수 있는
habitat sŏshiktchi 서식지
habitual sŭpkkwanjŏgin 습관적인; *smoker*, *drinker* sangsŭptchŏgin 상습적인
hack n (*poor writer*) samnyu chak-kka 삼류 작가
hacker COMPUT haek'ŏ 해커
hackneyed chinbuhan 진부한
haddock taeguŭi iltchong 대구의 일종
haggard such'ŏk'an 수척한
haggle (*over price*) kkaktta 깎다
hail n ubak 우박
hair t'ŏl 털; (*on person's head*) mŏri 머리; (*single human ~*) mŏrik'arak 머리카락; *short ~* / *long ~* tchalbŭn / kin mŏri 짧은 / 긴 머리
hairbrush mŏri sol 머리 솔; **haircut:** *have a ~* mŏrirŭl charŭda 머리를 자르다; **hairdo** mŏrihyŏng 머리형; **hairdresser** miyongsa 미용사; *at the ~'s* miyongshiresŏ 미용실에서; **hairdrier, hairdryer** heŏdŭraiŏ 헤어드라이어
hairless t'ŏri ŏmnŭn 털이 없는
hairpin mŏrip'in 머리핀; **hairpin curve** Uchahyŏng k'ŏbŭ U자형 커브; **hair-raising** mŏrikkŭch'i tchuppyŏt'aejinŭn 머리끝이 쭈뼛해지는; **hair remover** chemoyongp'um 제모용품; **hair-splitting** n: *that's just ~* sasohan ire shin-gyŏngssŭnŭn kŏshiyeyo 사소한 일에 신경쓰는 것이에요; **hairstyle** mŏrihyŏng 머리형
hairy *arm*, *animal* t'ori manŭn 털이 많은; F *frightening* musŏun 무서운
half 1 n pan 반; ~ (*past*) *ten* yŏlshi pan 열시 반; ~ *an hour* pan shigan 반 시간; ~ *a pound* pan p'aundŭ 반 파운드 **2** adj panŭi 반의 **3** adv: ~

eaten / *finished* panŭn mŏgŭn / kkŭnnan 반은 먹은 / 끝난; *only ~ understood* panman ihaedoen 반만 이해된
half-hearted maŭmi naek'iji annŭn 마음이 내키지 않는; **half time** n SP chunggan hyushik 중간 휴식; **half-way 1** adj *stage*, *point* chunggan chijŏmŭi 중간 지점의 **2** adv chunggane 중간에
hall (*large room*) hol 홀; (*hallway in house*) poktto 복도
halo wŏn-gwang 원광
halt 1 v/i mŏmch'uda 멈추다 **2** v/t mŏmch'ugehada 멈추게하다 **3** n chŏngji 정지; *come to a ~* mŏmch'uda 멈추다
halve v/t panŭro hada 반으로 하다
ham haem 햄
hamburger haembŏgŏ 햄버거
hammer 1 n mangch'i 망치 **2** v/i mangch'ijirihada 망치질하다; *~ at the door* munŭl k'wangk'wang tudŭrida 문을 쾅쾅 두드리다
hammock haemŏk 해먹
hamper[1] n (*for food*) paguni 바구니
hamper[2] v/t (*obstruct*) panghaehada 방해하다
hamster haemsŭt'ŏ 햄스터
hand 1 n son 손; (*of clock*) shigye panŭl 시계 바늘; (*worker*) ilsson 일손; *at ~*, *to ~* kakkaie 가까이에; *at first ~* chiktchŏptchoguro 직접적으로; *by ~* sonŭro 손으로; *deliver* inp'yŏnŭro 인편으로; *on the one ~ ..., on the other* hanp'yŏnŭronŭn ..., tarŭn hanp'yŏnŭronŭn 한편으로는 ..., 다른 한편으로는; *in ~* (*being done*) kkŭnnanŭn chung-in 끝나는 중인; *on your right* orŭntchok panghyang-ŭro 오른쪽 방향으로; *~s off!* son tteseyo! 손 떼세요!; *~s up!* son tŭrŏ! 손 들어!; *change ~s*

imjaga pakkwida 임자가 바뀌다
♦**hand down** *heirloom etc*
mullyŏjuda 물려주다
♦**hand in** chech'urhada 제출하다
♦**hand on** chŏnhada 전하다
♦**hand out** nanuŏ chuda 나누어 주다
♦**hand over** kŏnnejuda 건네주다; (*to
authorities*) nŏmgyŏjuda 넘겨주다
handbag *Br* son-gabang 손가방,
haendŭbag 핸드백; **handbook**
annaech'aektcha 안내책자; **handcuffs** sugap 수갑
handicap *n* (*physical*) shinch'e
chang-ae 신체 장애; *fig* pullihan
chokkŏn 불리한 조건
handicapped (*physically*) shinch'e
chang-aeja innŭn 신체 장애가 있는;
(*mentally*) chŏngshin chang-aeja
innŭn 정신 장애가 있는; *~ by a lack
of funds* chagŭm pujogŭro pullihan
자금 부족으로 불리한
handicraft sugong-ye 수공예
handiwork sugong 수공; (*handmade
goods*) sugongp'um 수공품
handkerchief sonsugŏn 손수건
handle 1 *n* sonjabi 손잡이 **2** *v/t* taruda
다루다; *let me ~ this* chega
tarugessŭmnida 제가 다루겠습니다
handlebars chajŏn-gŏ haendŭl
자전거 핸들
hand luggage suhwamul 수화물;
handmade sugong-ŭi 수공의;
handrail nan-gan 난간; **handshake**
akssu 악수
hands-off kansŏp'aji annŭn 간섭하지
않는
handsome chal saenggin 잘 생긴
hands-on shilmurŭl chiktchŏp'anŭn
실무를 직접하는; *get some ~ ex-
perience* chiktchŏp kyŏnghŏmŭl ŏt-
tta 직접 경험을 얻다
handwriting yukp'il 육필
handwritten sonŭro ssŭn 손으로 쓴
handy *tool, device* p'yŏllihan 편리한;
it might come in ~ ama ssŭlmo
issŭl kŏshida 아마 쓸모 있을 것이다
hang 1 *v/t picture* kŏlda 걸다; *person*
mok maedalda 목 매달다 **2** *v/i* (*of
dress, hair*) nŭrŏjida 늘어지다 **3** *n:
get the ~ of* ...ŭl/rŭl ihaehage
toeda ...을/를 이해하게 되다

♦**hang around** ŏsŭllŏnggŏrida
어슬렁거리다
♦**hang on** *v/i* (*wait*) kidarida
기다리다
♦**hang on to** (*keep*) kyesok ...ŭl/rŭl
kajigo it-tta 계속 ...을/를 가지고
있다
♦**hang up** *v/i* TELEC chŏnhwarŭl
kkŭnt'a 전화를 끊다
hangar kyŏngnapkko 격납고
hanger (*for clothes*) otkkŏri 옷걸이
hang glider (*person*)
haenggŭllaidŏrŭl t'anŭn saram
행글라이더를 타는 사람; (*device*)
haenggŭllaidŏ 행글라이더; **hang
gliding** haenggŭllaidŏ pihaeng
행글라이더 비행; **hangover** sukch'wi
숙취; (*idea, attitude*) yŏp'a 여파
♦**hanker after** ... ŭl/rŭl mopsshi
katkko ship'ohada ...을/를 몹시 갖고
싶어하다
hankie, hanky F sonsugŏn 손수건
Han River Han-gang 한강
haphazard magujabiŭi 마구잡이의
happen irŏnada 일어나다; *if you ~ to
see him* manyak nega kŭrŭl uyŏnhi
mannandamyŏn 만약 네가 그를
우연히 만난다면; *what has ~ed to
you?* musŭn iri issŏssŭmnikka? 무슨
일이 있었습니까?
♦**happen across** uyŏnhi
palgyŏnhada 우연히 발견하다
happening palssaeng 발생
happily haengbok'age 행복하게;
(*gladly*) kippŭge 기쁘게; (*luckily*) un
chok'e 운 좋게
happiness haengbok 행복
happy haengbok'an 행복한
happy-go-lucky nakch'ŏnjŏgin
낙천적인
happy hour t'ŭkpyŏl yŏmkka pongsa
kigan 특별 염가 봉사 기간
harass koerop'ida 괴롭히다
harassed shidallin 시달린
harassment koerop'im 괴롭힘;
sexual ~ sŏnghŭirong 성희롱
harbor 1 *n* hanggu 항구 **2** *v/t criminal*
sumgida 숨기다; *grudge* maŭme
p'umtta 마음에 품다
hard tandanhan 단단한; (*difficult*)
ŏryŏun 어려운; *facts, evidence* hwak-

kkohan 확고한; **~ of hearing** kwiga
mŏn 귀가 먼
hardback changjŏngbon 장정본;
hard-boiled egg talgyal wansuk
달걀 완숙; **hard copy** hadŭ k'ap'i
하드 카피; **hard core** n
haeksshimch'ŭng 핵심층;
(*pornography*) nogoltchŏgin
p'orŭno 노골적인 포르노; **hard
currency** kyohwan kanŭng
t'onghwa 교환 가능 통화; **hard disk**
hadŭ tisŭk'ŭ 하드 디스크
harden 1 v/t kuch'ida 굳히다 **2** v/i (*of
glue*) kut-tta 굳다; (*of attitude*)
kanghaejida 강해지다
hardheaded naengjŏnghan 냉정한
hardliner kanggyŏngnonja 강경론자
hardly kŏŭi ...haji ant'a 거의 ...하지
않다; **he ~ ever studies** kŭnŭn kŏŭi
kongbuhaji anayo 그는 거의
공부하지 않아요; **I can ~ hear** kŏŭi
tŭlliji anayo 거의 들리지 않아요; **did
you agree? – ~!** tong-ŭihaessŏyo? –
ch'ŏnmaneyo! 동의했어요? –
천만에요!
hardness kutkki 굳기; (*difficulty*)
ŏryŏum 어려움
hard sell chŏkkŭk p'anmae 적극 판매
hardship kollan 곤란
hard shoulder toroŭi taep'isŏn
도로의 대피선; **hard up** toni
kunghan 돈이 궁한; **hardware**
ch'ŏlmul 철물; COMPUT hadŭweŏ
하드웨어; **hardware store**
ch'ŏlmultchŏm 철물점; **hard-
working** yŏlsshimhi irhanŭn 열심히
일하는
hardy kanghan 강한
hare sant'okki 산토끼
harm 1 n hae 해; **it wouldn't do any
~ to ...** ... haedo kwaench'anŭl
kŏshida ... 해도 괜찮을 것이다 **2** v/t
haech'ida 해치다
harmful haeroun 해로운
harmless muhaehan 무해한
harmonious chohwadoen 조화된
harmonize chohwashik'ida
조화시키다
harmony MUS hwasŏng 화성; (*in
relationship etc*) chohwa 조화
harp hap'ŭ 하프

♦**harp on about** F kyesok ...ŭl/rŭl
toep'uri marhada 계속 ...을/를
되풀이 말하다
harpoon n chakssal 작살
harsh *criticism, words* kahok'an
가혹한; *color, light* kŏsŭllinŭn
거슬리는
harvest n ch'usu 추수
Harvest Festival Ch'usŏk 추석
hash: make a ~ of F ...ŭl/rŭl
ŏngmang-ŭro mandŭlda ...을/를
엉망으로 만들다
hash browns kamja t'wigim 감자
튀김
hashish taemach'o 대마초
haste sŏdurŭm 서두름
hasty kŭp'an 급한
hat moja 모자
hatch n (*for serving food*) ch'anggu
창구; (*on ship*) haech'i 해치
♦**hatch out** (*of eggs*) puhwahada
부화하다
hatchback haech'ibaek 해치백
hatchet sondokki 손도끼
hate 1 n mium 미움 **2** v/t miwŏhada
미워하다
hatred chŭng-o 증오
haughty kŏmanhan 거만한
haul 1 n (*of fish*) ŏhoengnyang 어획량
2 v/t (*pull*) chabattanggida
잡아당기다
haulage unban 운반
haulage company unsong hoesa
운송 회사
haulier unsong hoesa 운송 회사
haunch tunbu 둔부
haunt 1 v/t nat'anada 나타나다; (*of
memory*) ttŏorŭda 떠오르다; **this
place is ~ed** igosŭn yuryŏng-i
nat'ananŭn koshida 이곳은 유령이
나타나는 곳이다 **2** n (*place*) chŭlgyŏ
ch'annŭn kot 즐겨 찾는 곳
haunting *tune* noerirŭl ttŏnaji annŭn
뇌리를 떠나지 않는
have ◊ kajida 가지다; **I ~ some
money** chŏn chom kajigo issŏyo
돈을 좀 가지고 있어요; **I ~ some-
thing for you** tangshinhant'e chul
kŏshi issŏyo 당신한테 줄 것이
있어요; **I ~ a headache** mŏriga
ap'ayo 머리가 아파요; **~ a cold**

kamgie köllida 감기에 걸리다; *can I ~ ...? (please give me)* ...ŭl/rŭl chushigetssŭmnikka? ...을/를 주시겠습니까?; *do you ~ ...?* ...i/ka issŭmnikka? ...이/가 있습니까?; *I ~ no family* nanŭn kajogi amudo öptta 나는 가족이 아무도 없다; *I had no choice* sönt'aegŭi yöjiga öpssöt-tta 선택의 여지가 없었다 ◊ *(own)* kajida 가지다, soyuhada 소유하다 ◊ *breakfast, lunch* möktta 먹다 ◊; *~ to (must)* ...haeya hada ...해야 하다; *I ~ to study / see him* nanŭn kongbuhaeya hamnida / kŭrŭl mannaboaya hamnida 나는 공부해야 합니다 / 그를 만나보아야 합니다; *you ~ to try* nönŭn noryök'aeya hahanda 너는 노력해야 한다 ◊ *(causative)*: *~ sth done* muösŭl haet-tta 무엇을 했다; *I had my hair cut* nanŭn mörirŭl challat-tta 나는 머리를 잘랐다; *~ sth cleaned* muösŭl set'agŭl matkkida 무엇을 세탁을 맡기다 ◊ *(auxiliary)*: *I ~ decided* nanŭn kyöltchönghaet-tta 나는 결정했다; *~ you seen her?* kŭnyörŭl pon chögi issŭmnikka? 그녀를 본 적이 있습니까?

♦ **have back** tollyöbat-tta 돌려받다; *when can I have it back?* önje kŭgösŭl tollyöbadŭl su issŭmnikka? 언제 그것을 돌려받을 수 있습니까?

♦ **have on** *(wear)* iptta 입다; *(have planned)* kyehoek'aet-tta 계획했다; *do you have anything on for tonight?* onŭl pame mwö hal il issŭmnikka? 오늘 밤에 뭐 할 일 있습니까?

haven *fig* anshikch'ö 안식처

havoc öngmangjinch'ang 엉망진창; *play ~ with* ...ŭl/rŭl öngmang-ŭro mandŭlda ...을/를 엉망으로 만들다

hawk mae 매; *fig* kanggyöngnonja 강경론자

hay könch'o 건초

hay fever könch'oyöl 건초열

hazard *n* wihöm yoso 위험 요소

hazard lights MOT pisangdŭng 비상등

hazardous wihömhan 위험한

haze ajirang-i 아지랑이

hazel *(tree)* kaeamnamu 개암나무

hazelnut kaeam 개암

hazy *view, memories* hŭrin 흐린; *I'm a bit ~ about it* nanŭn kugöse taehayö punmyönghaji ant'a 나는 그것에 대하여 분명하지 않다

he kŭ 그; *~ is American* kŭnŭn Miguk saramiyeyo 그는 미국 사람이에요 ◊ *(omission of pronoun)*: *who is ~?* - *~ is my teacher* nuguyeyo? - che sösaengnimiyeyo 누구예요? - 제 선생님이에요

head 1 *n* möri 머리; *(boss, leader)* udumöri 우두머리; *(on beer)* köp'um 거품; *(of nail)* monmöri 못머리; *(of queue, line)* söndu 선두; *$15 a ~* han saram tang 15tallö 한 사람 당 15달러; *~s or tails?* ammyön animyön twinmyön? 앞면 아니면 뒷면?; *at the ~ of the list* myöngdanŭi ch'önmörie 명단의 첫머리에; *~ over heels fall* kokkurajida 고꾸라지다; *fall in love* holttak 홀딱; *lose one's ~ (go crazy)* che chöngshinŭl ilt'a 제 정신을 잃다 **2** *v/t (lead)* ikkŭlda 이끌다; *ball* möriro pat-tta 머리로 받다

headache tut'ong 두통

header *(in soccer)* heding 헤딩; *(in document)* mörinmal 머릿말

headhunter COM injae sŭk'aut'ŭ tamdangja 인재 스카우트 담당자

heading *(in list)* p'yoje 표제

headlamp, headlight hedŭrait'ŭ 헤드라이트; **headline** mörikkisa 머릿기사; *make the ~s* mörikkisaro k'ŭge ch'wigŭpttoeda 머릿기사로 크게 취급되다; **headlong** *adv fall* köndubaktchillo 곤두박질로; **headmaster** kyojang 교장; **headmistress** yögyojang 여교장; **head office** *(of company)* ponsa 본사; **head-on 1** *adv crash* chöngmyönch'ungdoruro 정면충돌으로 **2** *adj crash* chöngmyönch'ungdorŭi 정면충돌의; **headphones** hedŭp'on 헤드폰; **headquarters** ponbu 본부; **headrest** möri patch'im 머리 받침; **headroom** *(under bridge)* wit konggöanŭi nop'i 윗 공간의 높이; *(in car)* ch'önjang-ŭi nop'i 천장의 높이;

headscarf mŏri sŭk'ap'ŭ 머리 스카프; **headstrong** wan-gohan 완고한; **head waiter** susŏk weit'ŏ 수석 웨이터; **headwind** matpparam 맞바람

heady *wine etc* ppalli ch'wihage hanŭn 빨리 취하게 하는

heal 1 *v/t* natkke hada 낫게 하다 **2** *v/i* nat-tta 낫다

health kŏn-gang 건강; *your ~!* tangshinŭi kŏn-gang-ŭl wihae! 당신의 건강을 위해!

health club helssŭ k'ullŏp 헬스 클럽; **health food** kŏn-gang shikp'um 건강 식품; **health food store** kŏn-gang shikp'umjŏm 건강 식품점; **health insurance** kŏn-gang pohŏm 건강 보험; **health resort** poyangji 보양지

healthy *person* kŏn-ganghan 건강한; *food, lifestyle* kŏn-gang-e choŭn 건강에 좋은; *economy* t'ŭnt'ŭnhan 튼튼한

heap *n* ssaa ollin tŏmi 쌓아 올린 더미
♦**heap up** ssaa ollida 쌓아 올리다

hear tŭt-tta 듣다
♦**hear about** ...e kwanhae tŭt-tta ...에 관해 듣다
♦**hear from** ...(ŭ)ro put'ŏ soshigŭl tŭt-tta ...(으)로 부터 소식을 듣다

hearing ch'ŏngnyŏk 청력; LAW shimni 심리; *within ~* tŭllinŭn pŏmwi ane(sŏ) 들리는 범위 안에(서); *out of ~* tŭllinŭn pŏmwi pakke(sŏ) 들리는 범위 밖에(서)

hearing aid poch'ŏnggi 보청기

hearsay: *by ~* p'ungmunŭro 풍문으로

hearse yŏngguch'a 영구차

heart shimjang 심장; *(emotional senses)* maŭm 마음; *(of problem)* haekssim 핵심; *(of city, organization)* haekssimbu 핵심부; *know sth by ~* muŏsŭl oeugo it-tta 무엇을 외우고 있다

heart attack shimjang mabi 심장 마비; **heartbeat** shimjang pakttong 심장 박동; **heartbreaking** aekkŭlk'e hanŭn 애끓게 하는; **heartburn** kasŭmari 가슴앓이; **heart failure** shimjang mabi 심장 마비; **heartfelt** *sympathy* chinshimesŏ urŏnan 진심에서 우러난

hearth pyŏngnallo padak 벽난로 바닥

heartless maejŏnghan 매정한

heartrending *plea, sight* pit'onghan 비통한

hearts *(in cards)* hat'ŭ 하트

heart throb F tonggyŏng-ŭi taesang 동경의 대상

heart transplant shimjang ishik 심장 이식

hearty *appetite* wangsŏnghan 왕성한; *meal* p'ungsŏnghan 풍성한; *person* tajŏngdagamhan 다정다감한

heat *n* yŏl 열
♦**heat up** teuda 데우다

heated *discussion* kyŏk'an 격한; *~ floor* ondol 온돌; *~ swimming pool* onsu suyŏngjang 온수 수영장

heater nanbang changch'i 난방 장치

heathen *n* igyodo 이교도

heating nanbang changch'i 난방 장치

heatproof, heat-resistant naeyŏlssŏng-ŭi 내열성의; **heatstroke** yŏlssabyŏng 열사병; **heatwave** yŏlp'a 열파

heave *v/t (lift)* tŭrŏollida 들어올리다

heaven ch'ŏnguk 천국; *good ~s!* chŏrŏn 저런!

heavy mugŏun 무거운; *rain* manŭn 많은; *traffic, cold, bleeding* shimhan 심한; *accent* kanghan 강한; *food* sohwaga chal andoenŭn 소화가 잘 안되는; *financial loss* shimgak'an 심각한; *loss of life* makssimhan 막심한; *~ smoker* kolch'o 골초; *~ drinker* sulgorae 술고래

heavy-duty aju t'ŭnt'ŭnhan 아주 튼튼한

heavyweight SP hebikkŭp 헤비급

heckle *v/t* yayuhada 야유하다

hectic mopsshi pappŭn 몹시 바쁜

hedge *n* ult'ari 울타리

hedgehog kosŭmdoch'i 고슴도치

heed: *pay ~ to* yunyŏmhada 유념하다

heel *(of foot)* twikkumch'i 뒤꿈치; *(of shoe)* twich'uk 뒤축

heel bar kudu susŏntchip 구두 수선집

hefty mugŏun 무거운

height nop'i 높이; *(of person)* k'i 키; *(of airplane)* kodo 고도; *(of season)* chŏltchŏng 절정

heighten *effect, tension* nop'ida 높이다

heir sangsogin 상속인

heiress yŏja sangsogin 여자 상속인

helicopter hellik'opt'ŏ 헬리콥터

hell chiok 지옥; *what the ~ are you doing / do you want?* F todaech'e muŏsŭl hanŭn / wŏnhanŭn kŏmnikka? 도대체 무엇을 하는 / 원하는 겁니까?; *go to ~!* F kkŏjyŏ pŏryŏ! 꺼져 버려!; *a ~ of a lot* F ŏmch'ŏng manŭn 엄청 많은; *one ~ of a nice guy* F koengjanghi chŏhŭn saram 굉장히 좋은 사람

hello (*polite, to older people*) annyŏnghashimnikka 안녕하십니까?; (*to friend, younger people*) annyŏng 안녕; TELEC yŏboseyo 여보세요; (*on entry phone*) nuguseyo 누구세요

helm NAUT k'i chojong changch'i 키 조종 장치

helmet helmet 헬멧

help 1 *n* toum 도움 **2** *v/t* toptta 돕다; *~ oneself* (*to food*) maŭmkkŏt tŭlda 마음껏 들다; *I can't ~ it* ŏtchŏl su ŏpssŏyo 어쩔 수 없어요; *I couldn't ~ laughing* utchi anŭl su ŏpssŏssŏyo 웃지 않을 수 없었어요

helper towajunŭn saram 도와주는 사람

help file COMPUT toummal p'ail 도움말 파일

helpful toumi toenŭn 도움이 되는

helping (*of food*) han kŭrŭt 한 그릇

helpless (*unable to cope*) honjasŏ ŏtchŏl su ŏmnŭn 혼자서 어쩔 수 없는; (*powerless*) muryŏk'an 무력한

help screen COMPUT toummal hwamyŏn 도움말 화면

hem *n* (*of dress etc*) ot-ttan 옷단

hemisphere pan-gu 반구

hemorrhage 1 *n* ch'urhyŏl 출혈 **2** *v/i* ch'urhyŏrhada 출혈하다

hemp taema 대마

hen amt'ak 암탉; (*of any bird*) amsae 암새

henchman *pej* shimbok 심복

henpecked yŏja sone chwiyŏ sanŭn 여자 손에 쥐여 사는; *~ husband* kongch'ŏga 공처가

hepatitis kannyŏm 간염

her 1 *adj* kŭnyŏŭi 그녀의; *~ ticket* kŭnyŏŭi p'yo 그녀의 표 **2** *pron* kŭnyŏrŭl 그녀; *I know ~* nanŭn kŭnyŏrŭl anda 나는 그녀를 안다; *this is for ~* igŏsŭn kŭnyŏŭi kŏshida 이것은 그녀의 것이다

herb shigyong p'ullip 식용 풀잎, hŏbŭ 허브

herb(al) tea hŏbŭ ch'a 허브 차

herd *n* tte 떼

here yŏgie(sŏ) 여기에(서); *~'s to you!* (*as toast*) kŏnbae! 건배!; *~ you are!* (*giving sth*) yŏgi issŭmnida 여기 있습니다; *~ we are!* (*finding sth*) yŏgi itkkuna! 여기 있구나!

hereditary *disease* yujŏndoenŭn 유전되는

heritage yusan 유산

hermit ŭndunja 은둔자

hernia MED t'altchang 탈장

hero yŏng-ung 영웅

heroic yŏng-ungjŏgin 영웅적인

heroin heroin 헤로인

heroine yŏjangbu 여장부

heron waegari 왜가리

herpes MED p'ojin 포진

herring ch'ŏng-ŏ 청어

hers kŭnyŏŭi kot 그녀의 것; *it's ~* igosŭn kunyŏŭi kŏshida 이것은 그녀의 것이다; *a cousin of ~* kŭnyŏŭi sach'on 그녀의 사촌

herself kŭnyŏ chashin 그녀 자신; *she hurt ~* kŭnyŏga tach'yŏt-tta 그녀가 다쳤다; *by ~* kŭnyŏ sŭsŭro 그녀 스스로

hesitate mangsŏrida 망설이다

hesitation mangsŏrim 망설임

heterosexual *adj* isŏng-aeŭi 이성애의

heyday chŏnsŏnggi 전성기

hi annyŏng 안녕

hibernate tongmyŏnhada 동면하다

hiccup *n* ttalkkuktchil 딸꾹질; (*minor problem*) yak-kkanŭi munje 약간의 문제; *have the ~s* ttalkkuktchirhada 딸꾹질하다

hick *pej* F shigolttŭgi 시골뜨기

hick town *pej* F shigol 시골

hidden *meaning, treasure* sumgyŏjin 숨겨진, kamchwŏjin 감춰진

hide[1] **1** *v/t* sumgida 숨기다, kamch'uda 감추다 **2** *v/i* sumtta 숨다

hide² n (of animal) kajuk 가죽
hide-and-seek sumbakkokchil 숨바꼭질
hideaway ŭnshinch'ŏ 은신처
hideous weather, taste kkŭmtchik'an 끔찍한; crime hyung-ak'an 흉악한; face hyunghan 흉한
hiding¹ (beating) maejil 매질
hiding²: be in ~ ŭnshinhada 은신하다; go into ~ sumtta 숨다
hiding place sumnŭn kot 숨는 곳
hierarchy kyegŭp chojik 계급 조직
hi-fi haip'ai 하이파이
high 1 adj nop'ŭn 높은; wind kanghan 강한; (on drugs) ch'wihan 취한; have a ~ opinion of s.o. nugurŭl nop'i p'yŏngkkahada 누구를 높이 평가하다; it is ~ time ... ijen kŭman ... hal ttaeda 이젠 그만 ... 할 때다 **2** n MOT koso kiŏ 고속 기어; (in statistics) nop'ŭn sujun 높은 수준; EDU kodŭnghak-kkyo 고등학교 **3** adv nopkke 높게; ~ in the sky hanŭl nopkke 하늘 높게; that's as ~ as we can go uriga hal su innŭn ch'oedaehanimnida 우리가 할 수 있는 최대한입니다
highbrow adj chishiginŭi 지식인의;
highchair yuayong nop'ŭn ŭija 유아용 높은 의자; **highclass** kogŭbŭi 고급의; **high diving** taibing 다이빙; **high-frequency** kojup'a 고주파; **high-grade** kogŭbŭi 고급의; **high-handed** koaptchŏgin 고압적인; **high-heeled** nop'ŭn kubŭi 높은 굽의; **high jump** nop'i ttwigi 높이 뛰기; **high-level** kowi kogwanŭi 고위 고관의; **high life** sangnyu sahoeŭi saenghwal 상류 사회의 생활; **highlight 1** n (main event, in hair) hailait'ŭ 하이라이트 **2** v/t (with pen) kangjohada 강조하다; COMPUT pŭllogŭl ssŭiuda 블록을 씌우다;
highlighter (pen) hyŏnggwangp'en 형광펜
highly desirable, likely k'ŭge 크게; be ~ paid nop'ŭn ponggŭbŭl pat-tta 높은 봉급을 받다; think ~ of s.o. nugurŭl nop'i p'yŏngkkahada 누구를 높이 평가하다
high-performance drill, battery

kosŏngnŭng 고성능; **high-pitched** koŭmŭi 고음의; **high point** (of life, career, program) chŏltchŏng 절정; **high-powered** engine kosŏngnŭngŭi 고성능의; intellectual t'ŭkch'urhan 특출한; salesman kkŭnjilgin 끈질긴; **high pressure 1** n (weather) kogiap 고기압 **2** adj TECH koabŭi 고압의; salesman kangnyohanŭn 강요하는; job, lifestyle kodoŭi kinjang-ŭl yohanŭn 고도의 긴장을 요하는; **high priest** taejesajang 대제사장; fig (of fashion etc) chidoja 지도자; **high school** kodŭnghak-kkyo 고등학교; **high society** sangnyu sahoe 상류 사회; **high-speed train** kosok yŏlch'a 고속 열차; **high strung** min-gamhan 민감한; **high tech 1** n ch'ŏmdan kisul 첨단 기술 **2** adj ch'ŏmdan kisurŭi 첨단 기술의; **high technology** ch'ŏmdan kisul 첨단 기술; **high-tension** cable koabŭi 고압의; **high tide** manjo 만조; **high water** ch'oego suwi 최고 수위; **highway** kosokttoro 고속도로; **high wire** (in circus) chult'agi chul 줄타기 줄
hijack 1 v/t plane kongjung napch'ihada 공중 납치하다; bus t'alch'wihada 탈취하다 **2** n (of plane) kongjung napch'i 공중 납치; (of bus) t'alch'wi 탈취
hijacker (of plane) kongjung napch'ibŏm 공중 납치범; (of bus) t'alch'wibŏm 탈취범
hike¹ 1 n toboyŏhaeng 도보여행 **2** v/i toboyŏhaenghada 도보여행하다
hike² n (in prices) insang 인상
hiker toboyŏhaengja 도보여행자
hilarious usŭmŭl chaanaenŭn 웃음을 자아내는
hill ŏndŏk 언덕; (slope) samyŏn 사면
hillbilly pej F sansaram 산사람
hillside ŏndŏgŭi samyŏn 언덕의 사면
hilltop ŏndŏk kkokttaegi 언덕 꼭대기
hilly kurŭngjidaeŭi 구릉지대의
hilt charu 자루
him kŭrŭl 그를; I know ~ nanŭn kŭrŭl anda 나는 그를 안다; this is for ~ igŏsŭn kŭŭi kŏshida 이것은 그의 것이다

himself kŭ chashin 그 자신; *he hurt ~* kŭnŭn tach'yŏt-tta 그는 다쳤다; *by ~* kŭ sŭsŭro 그 스스로

hinder panghaehada 방해하다

hindrance chang-ae 장애

hindsight twinŭjŭn kkaedarŭm 뒤늦은 깨달음; *with ~* twinŭjŭn kkaedarŭmŭro 뒤늦은 깨달음으로

hinge kyŏngch'ŏp 경첩

hint (*clue*) hint'ŭ 힌트; (*piece of advice*) choŏn 조언; (*implied suggestion*) amshi 암시; (*of red, sadness etc*) miyak'an chinghu 미약한 징후

hip kungdungi 궁둥이, ŏngdŏng-i 엉덩이

hip pocket twittchumŏni 뒷주머니

hippopotamus hama 하마

hire *v/t room, car* tonŭl chugo pillida 돈을 주고 빌리다; *person* koyonghada 고용하다

his 1 *adj* kŭŭi 그의; *~ ticket* kŭŭi p'yo 그의 표 **2** *pron* kŭŭi kŏt 그의 것; *it's ~* igosŭn kŭŭi kŏshida 이것은 그의 것이다; *a cousin of ~* kŭŭi sach'on 그의 사촌

hiss *v/i* (*of snake*) shwit sorirŭl naeda 쉿 소리를 내다; (*of audience*) yayurŭl ponaeda 야유를 보내다

historian sahaktcha 사학자

historic yŏkssasang-ŭro chungnyohan 역사상으로 중요한

historical yŏkssajŏgin 역사적인

history yŏkssa 역사

hit 1 *v/t* ch'ida 치다; (*collide with*) ch'ungdorhada 충돌하다; *he was ~ by a bullet* kŭnŭn t'anarŭl majat-tta 그는 탄알을 맞았다; *it suddenly ~ me* (*I realized*) nanŭn kaptchagi kkaedarat-tta 나는 갑자기 깨달았다; *~ town* (*arrive*) tongnee todarhada 동네에 도달하다 **2** *n* (*blow*) t'agyŏk 타격; MUS hit'ŭ 히트; (*success*) sŏnggong 성공

♦**hit back** toebadach'ida 되받아치다

♦**hit on** *idea* saenggak'aenaeda 생각해내다

♦**hit out at** (*criticize*) maengnyŏrhi pinanhada 맹렬히 비난하다

hit-and-run *adj*: *~ accident* ppaengsoni sago 뺑소니 사고; *~*

driver ppaengsoni unjŏnsu 뺑소니 운전수

hitch 1 *n* (*problem*) chang-ae 장애; *without a ~* chang-aeŏpssi 장애없이 **2** *v/t* kŏraemaeda 걸어매다; *~ X to Y* Xŭl/rŭl Ye kŏraemaeda X를/를 Y에 걸어매다; *~ a ride* p'yŏnsŭnghada 편승하다 **3** *v/i* (*hitchhike*) p'yŏnsŭnghada 편승하다

♦**hitch up** *trailer* kkŭrŏollida 끌어올리다

hitchhike p'yŏnsŭnghada 편승하다

hitchhiker p'yŏnsŭng yŏhaengja 편승 여행자

hitchhiking p'yŏnsŭnghagi 편승하기

hi-tech 1 *n* ch'ŏmdan kisul 첨단 기술 **2** *adj* ch'ŏmdan kisurŭi 첨단 기술의

hitlist taesangja myŏngdan 대상자 명단; **hitman** ch'ŏngbu sarinja 청부 살인자; **hit-or-miss** toenŭndaeroŭi 되는대로의; **hit squad** amsalttan 암살단

HIV Inch'e Myŏnyŏk Kyŏlp'ip Pairŏsŭ 인체 면역 결핍 바이러스

hive (*for bees*) pŏlt'ong 벌통

♦**hive off** *v/t* (COM: *separate off*) pullihada 분리하다

HIV-positive Eijŭ yangsŏng panŭng 에이즈 양성 반응

hoard 1 *n* pich'uk 비축 **2** *v/t* pich'uk'ada 비축하다

hoarse moksshwin 목쉰

hoax *n* sogimsu 속임수

hobble *v/i* chŏllŭmgŏrida 절름거리다

hobby ch'wimi 취미

hobo ttŭnaegi 뜨내기; (*itinerant worker*) ttŭnaegi ilkkun 뜨내기 일꾼

hockey (*ice ~*) aisŭ hak'i 아이스 하키

hog *n* (*pig*) twaeji 돼지

hoist 1 *n* kijunggi 기중기 **2** *v/t* kkŭrŏ ollida 끌어 올리다

hokum (*nonsense*) hŏt'ŭn sori 허튼 소리; (*sentimental stuff*) ssaguryŏmul 싸구려물

hold 1 *v/t* (*in hands*) chaptta 잡다, chibŏdŭlda 집어들다; (*support, keep in place*) chit'aenghada 지탱하다; *passport, job* kajida 가지다; *prisoner, suspect* puttchaptta 붙잡다; (*contain*) tamtta 담다; *course* yujihada 유지하다; *~ one's breath* sumŭl chugida 숨을 죽이다; *he can ~ his drink* kŭnŭn surŭl kyesok mashil su it-tta 그는 술을 계속 마실 수 있다; *~ s.o. responsible* nuguege ch'aegimit-ttago saenggak'ada 누구에게 책임있다고 생각하다; *~ that ...* (*believe, maintain*) ...ranŭn saenggagŭl kosuhada ...라는 생각을 고수하다; *~ the line* TELEC kkŭntchimalgo kidariseyo 끊지말고 기다리세요 **2** *n* (*in ship, plane*) hwamulsshil 화물실; *catch ~ of sth* muŏsŭl chaptta 무엇을 잡다; *lose one's ~* (*on rope*) muŏsŭl noch'ida 무엇을 놓치다

♦ **hold against**: *hold X against Y* Xttaemune Yŭl/rŭl wŏnmanghada X때문에 Y을/를 원망하다

♦ **hold back 1** *v/t crowds* maktta 막다; *facts, information* sumgida 숨기다 **2** *v/i* (*not tell all*) ta marhaji ant'a 다 말하지 않다

♦ **hold on** *v/i* (*wait*) kidarida 기다리다; TELEC kkŭntchiank'o it-tta 끊지않고 있다; *now ~ a minute!* chamkkanman kidaryŏ poseyo! 잠깐만 기다려 보세요!

♦ **hold on to** (*keep*) kyesok kajigo it-tta 계속 가지고 있다; *belief* kosuhada 고수하다

♦ **hold out 1** *v/t hand* naemilda 내밀다; *prospect* cheanhada 제안하다 **2** *v/i* (*of supplies*) kyesok namait-tta 계속 남아있다; (*survive*) pŏt'ida 버티다

♦ **hold up** *v/t hand* tŭrŏ ollida 들어 올리다; *bank etc* kangt'arhada 강탈하다; (*make late*) chich'ehage hada 지체하게 하다; *hold sth up as an example* muŏsŭl yero cheshihada 무엇을 예로 제시하다

♦ **hold with** (*approve of*) injŏnghada 인정하다

holder (*container*) kwak 곽; (*of passport, ticket etc*) soyuja 소유자; (*of record*) poyuja 보유자

holding company mohoesa 모회사

holdup (*robbery*) kangdo 강도; (*delay*) chich'e 지체

hole kumŏng 구멍

holiday (*single day*) hyuil 휴일;

(*period*) hyuga 휴가

Holland Nedŏllandŭ 네덜란드

hollow *object* sogi pin 속이 빈; *cheeks* ump'uk tŭrŏgan 움푹 들어간; *words* konghŏhan 공허한

holly horanggashinamu 호랑가시나무

holocaust Yut'aein taehaksssal 유태인 대학살

hologram hollograem 홀로그램

holster kwŏnch'ongjip 권총집

holy sŏngsŭrŏun 성스러운

Holy Spirit Sŏngnyŏng 성령

Holy Week Sŏng Chugan 성 주간

home 1 *n* kajŏng 가정, chip 집; (*native country*) koguk 고국; (*town, part of country*) kohyang 고향; (*for old people*) yangnowŏn 양로원; *at ~* (*in my house*) nae chibe nŭn 집에; (*in my country*) nae koguge 내 고국에; SP hom kyŏnggijang-esŏ 홈 경기장에서; *make oneself at ~* p'yŏnanhi hada 편안히 하다; *at ~ and abroad* kungnaeoeesŏ 국내외에서; *work from ~* chat'aek kŭnmu 자택 근무 **2** *adv* chibe 집에; (*in own country*) koguge 고국에; (*in own town, part of country*) kohyang-e 고향에; *go ~* chibe kada 집에 가다; (*in own country*) koguge kada 고국에 가다; (*to town, part of country*) kohyang-e kada 고향에 가다

home address chiptchuso 집주소; **homecoming** kwiga 귀가; **home computer** kajŏngnyong k'ŏmp'yut'ŏ 가정용 컴퓨터; **home education** kajŏng kyoyuk 가정 교육; **home game** hom kyŏnggi 홈 경기

homeless 1 *adj* chibŏmnŭn 집없는 **2** *n*: *the ~* mujut'aektcha 무주택자

homeloving kajŏngjŏgin 가정적인

homely (*homeloving*) kajŏngjŏgin 가정적인; (*not good-looking*) motssaenggin 못생긴

homemade chibesŏ mandŭn 집에서 만든; **home movie** chaga chejak yŏnghwa 자가 제작 영화; **home page** COMPUT homp'eiji 홈페이지

homeopathy tongjongnyoppŏp 동종요법

homesick: *be ~* hyangsuppyŏng-ŭl

alt'a 향수병을 앓다; **home town**
kohyang 고향; **home tutor** kajŏng
kyosa 가정 교사; **homeward** *adv* (*to
own house*) kwiga kire 귀가 길에; (*to
own country*) kwiguk kire 귀국 길에;
homework EDU suktche 숙제;
homeworking COM chat'aek
kŭnmu 자택 근무

homicide (*crime*) sarin 살인; (*police
department*) kyŏngch'al sarin
chŏndam pusŏ 경찰 살인 전담 부서

homograph tonghyŏng-iŭiŏ
동형이의어

homophobia tongsŏng-ae
hyŏmotchŭng 동성애 혐오증

homosexual 1 *adj* tongsŏng-aeŭi
동성애의 **2** *n* tongsŏng-aeja 동성애자

honest chŏngjik'an 정직한

honestly soltchik'age 솔직하게; **~!**
chŏngmalloyo! 정말로요!

honesty chŏngjik 정직

honey kkul 꿀; F (*darling*) chagi 자기;
(*to husband*) yŏbo 여보

honeycomb pŏltchip 벌집

honeymoon *n* shinhon yŏhaeng 신혼
여행

Hong Kong Hongk'ong 홍콩

honk *v/t* horn ullida 울리다

honor 1 *n* myŏng-ye 명예 **2** *v/t*
yeuhada 예우하다

honorable *person* torirŭl anŭn 도리를
아는; *thing to do* torie mannŭn
도리에 맞는

honorific kyŏng-ŏppŏbŭi 경어법의

hood (*over head*) ose tallin moja 옷에
달린 모자; (*over cooker*) tŏpkkae
덮개; MOT enjin ttukkŏng 엔진 뚜껑;
F (*gangster*) kkangp'ae 깡패

hoodlum kkangp'ae 깡패

hoof palkkup 발굽

hook kalgori 갈고리; (*to hang clothes
on*) kori 고리; (*for fishing*)
naksshippanŭl 낚시바늘; **off the ~**
TELEC suhwagirŭl pŏsŏna 수화기를
벗어나

hooked: be ~ on (*on drugs, fig*) ...e
ppajida ...에 빠지다

hooker F ch'angnyŏ 창녀

hooky: play ~ mudan kyŏlssŏk'ada
무단 결석하다

hooligan pullyangbae 불량배

hooliganism pullyangbae kijil 불량배
기질

hoop t'e 테

hoot 1 *v/t* horn uusorirŭl naeda
우우소리를 내다 **2** *v/i* (*of car*)
kyŏngjŏgŭl ullida 경적을 울리다; (*of
owl*) puŏngbuŏng ulda 부엉부엉
울다

hop[1] *n* (*plant*) hop 홉

hop[2] *v/i* kabyŏpkke twiŏ orŭda 가볍게
뛰어 오르다

hope 1 *n* hŭimang 희망; **there's no ~
of that** chŏnhyŏ kŭrŏl kamang-i
ŏptta 전혀 그럴 가망이 없다 **2** *v/i*
parada 바라다, hŭimanghada
희망하다; **~ for sth** muŏsŭl parada
무엇을 바라다; **I ~ so** kŭrŏgil
paramnida 그러길 바랍니다; **I ~ not**
kŭrŏch'i ank'irŭl paramnida 그렇지
않기를 바랍니다 **3** *v/t*: **I ~ you like it**
maŭme tŭlmyŏn chok'essŏyo 마음에
들면 좋겠어요

hopeful hŭimang-e ch'an 희망에 찬;
(*promising*) kamang-innŭn 가망있는

hopefully *say, wait* kidaehamyŏ
기대하며; (*I/we hope*) paragŏnde
바라건데

hopeless *position, propect* hŭimang-
ŭl irŭn 희망을 잃은; (*useless: person*)
kamang ŏmnŭn 가망 없는

horizon (*on land*) chip'yŏngsŏn
지평선; (*at sea*) sup'yŏngsŏn 수평선

horizontal sup'yŏng-ŭi 수평의

hormone horŭmon 호르몬

horn (*of animal*) ppul 뿔; MOT
kyŏngjŏk 경적

hornet malbŏl 말벌

horn-rimmed spectacles ppult'e
an-gyŏng 뿔테 안경

horny (*sexually*) sŏngtchŏgŭro
hŭngbunhan 성적으로 흥분한

horoscope chŏmsŏngsul 점성술

horrible chidok'an 지독한

horrify: I was horrified
ch'unggyŏktchŏgiŏssŏyo
충격적이었어요

horrifying *experience* kkŭmtchik'an
끔찍한; *idea, prices*
ch'unggyŏktchŏgin 충격적인

horror kongp'o 공포; **the ~s of war**
chŏnjaeng-ŭi ch'amsa 전쟁의 참사

horror movie kongp'o yŏnghwa 공포
영화
hors d'oeuvre chŏnch'ae 전채
horse mal 말
horseback: **on ~** marŭl t'ago 말을
타고; **horse chestnut** maronie
yŏlmae 마로니에 열매; **horsehair
hat** kat 갓; **horsepower** maryŏk
마력; **horse race** kyŏngma 경마;
horseshoe malgup 말굽
horticulture wŏnye 원예
hose hosŭ 호스
hospice yoyangso 요양소
hospitable hwandaehanŭn 환대하는
hospital pyŏng-wŏn 병원; **go into
  the ~** ibwŏnhada 입원하다
hospitality hwandae 환대
host n (at party, reception) chuin
주인; (of TV program) sahoeja
사회자
hostage injil 인질; **be taken ~** injillo
chap'ida 인질로 잡히다
hostage taker injilbŏm 인질범
hostel (inexpensive accommodations)
yŏgwan 여관; (youth ~) yusŭhŏsŭt'el
유스호스텔
hostess (at party, reception) antchuin
안주인; (on airplane) sŭt'yuŏdissŭ
스튜어디스; (in bar) yŏjong-ŏbwŏn
여종업원; (prostitute) hosŭt'essŭ
호스테스
hostile chŏkttaejŏgin 적대적인
hostility (of attitude) chŏkttaesim
적대심; **hostilities** chŏnt'u 전투
hot water, food ttŭgŏun 뜨거운;
weather tŏun 더운; (spicy) maeun
매운; F (good) maeu chal hanŭn 매우
잘 하는; **I'm ~** tŏwŏyo 더워요; **it's so
~ today** onŭl nalsshiga maeu
tŏpkkunnyo 오늘 날씨가 매우
덥군요
hot dog hattogŭ 핫도그
hotel hot'el 호텔
hotplate yoriyong ch'ŏlp'an 요리용
철판
hot spot (military, political) punjaeng
chiyŏk 분쟁 지역
hour shigan 시간
hourglass drum changgo 장고
hourly adj shiganmadaŭi 시간마다의
house n chip 집; **at your ~** nŏŭi

chibesŏ 너의 집에서
houseboat chugŏyong pae 주거용
배; **housebreaking** kat'aek ch'imip
가택 침입; **household** kajok 가족;
household name chal allyŏjin irŭm
잘 알려진 이름; **house husband**
kasarŭl tolbonŭn namp'yŏn 가사를
돌보는 남편; **housekeeper**
kajŏngbu 가정부; **housekeeping**
(activity) kasa 가사; (money) kagye
가계; **House of Representatives**
Hawŏn 하원; **housewarming**
(party) chipttüri 집들이; **housewife**
chubu 주부; **housework** chiban il
집안 일
housing chut'aek 주택; TECH t'ŭl 틀
housing conditions chut'aek sajŏng
주택 사정
hovel nuch'uhan chip 누추한 집
hover pingbing maemdolda 빙빙
맴돌다
hovercraft hobŏk'ŭrap'ŭt'ŭ
호버크라프트
how ŏttŏk'e 어떻게; **~ are you?**
annyŏnhaseyo? 안녕하세요?; **~
about ...?** ...hanŭn kŏshi
ŏttŏgessŭmnikka? ...하는 것이
어떻겠습니까?; **~ much?**
ŏlmank'ŭm? 얼마큼?; **~ much do
you want?** ŏlmank'ŭm wŏnhaseyo?
얼마큼 원하세요?; **~ much is it?**
ŏlmaimnikka? 얼마입니까?; **~
many?** ŏlmana mani? 얼마나 많이?;
~ often? ŏlmana chaju? 얼마나
자주?; **~ funny!** ŏlmana
chaemiinnŭnji! 얼마나 재미있는지!
however kŭrŏna 그러나; **~ big/rich
they are** amuri k'ŭda/puyuhada
hadŏrado 아무리 크다/부유하다
하더라도
howl v/i (of dog, person in pain)
ulbujit-tta 울부짖다; (with laughter)
sorinop'yŏ ut-tta 소리높여 웃다
hub (of wheel) pak'wiŭi chungshimbu
바퀴의 중심부
hubcap chadongch'aŭi hwilk'aep
자동차의 휠캡
♦**huddle together** tterŭl chiŏ moida
떼를 지어 모이다
huff: **be in a ~** palkkŭn hwarŭl naeda
발끈 화를 내다

hug v/t p'o-onghada 포옹하다, antta 안다

huge kŏdaehan 거대한; (in amount) makttaehan 막대한

hull n sŏnch'e 선체

hullabaloo soran 소란

hum 1 v/t song, tune k'onnoraero purŭda 콧노래로 부르다 **2** v/i (of person) k'onnoraerŭl purŭda 콧노래를 부르다; (of machine) wing-winggŏrida 윙윙거리다

human 1 n in-gan 인간, saram 사람 **2** adj species, characteristics in-ganŭi 인간의; weakness in-ganjŏgin 인간적인; ~ error saramŭi shilssu 사람의 실수

human being in-gan 인간

humane injŏng-innŭn 인정있는

humanitarian indojuŭiŭi 인도주의의

humanity (human beings) illyu 인류; (of attitude etc) saramdaum 사람다움, in-ganssŏng 인간성

human race illyu 인류

human resources insakkwa 인사과

humble attitude, person kyŏmsonhan 겸손한; origins ch'ŏnhan 천한; meal, house ch'orahan 초라한

humdrum maeu p'yŏngbŏmhan 매우 평범한

humid sŭp'an 습한

humidifier kasŭpkki 가습기

humidity sŭpkki 습기; 90% ~ kuship p'ŏsent'ŭŭi sŭpdo 구십 퍼센트의 습도

humiliate kuryogŭl chuda 굴욕을 주다

humiliating kuryoktchŏgin 굴욕적인

humiliation kuryok 굴욕

humility kyŏmson 겸손

humor haehak 해학, usŭgae sori 우스개 소리; (mood) kibun 기분; sense of ~ yumŏ kamgak 유머 감각

humorous usŭun 우스운

hump 1 n (of camel, person) hok 혹; (on road) hŏmp'ŭ 험프, sokttorŭl churige hagi wihan toro sang-ŭi changch'i 속도를 줄이게 하기 위한 도로 상의 장치 **2** v/t (carry) chilmŏjida 짊어지다

hunch (idea) yegam 예감

hundred paek 백

hundred day ceremony (after birth) paegil 백일

hundredth adj paek pŏntchaeŭi 백 번째의

hundredweight 100p'aundŭ 100파운드; Br 112p'aundŭ 112파운드

Hungarian 1 adj Hŏnggariŭi 헝가리의 **2** n (person) Hŏnggari saram 헝가리 사람 (language) Hŏnggariŏ 헝가리어

Hungary Hŏnggari 헝가리

hunger paegop'ŭm 배고픔

hung-over sukch'wiŭi 숙취의

hungry paegop'ŭn 배고픈; I'm ~ paega kop'ayo 배가 고파요

hunk: great ~ F (man) mŏtchin namja 멋진 남자

hunky-dory F mansa p'yŏnanhan 만사 편안한

hunt 1 n (for animals) sanyang 사냥; (for new leader, actor) ch'ajŭm 찾음; (for criminal, missing child) susaek 수색 **2** v/t animal sanyanghada 사냥하다

♦ **hunt for** ch'at-tta 찾다

hunter sanyangkkun 사냥꾼

hunting sanyang 사냥

hurdle SP chang-aemul 장애물; fig (obstacle) chang-ae 장애

hurdler SP chang-aemul kyŏngjuja 장애물 경주자

hurdles SP chang-aemul kyŏngju 장애물 경주

hurl himkkŏt naedŏnjida 힘껏 내던지다

hurray hwanhoŭi sori 환호의 소리; ~! manse! 만세!

hurricane t'aep'ung 태풍

hurried sŏdurŭn 서두른

hurry 1 n sŏdurŭm 서두름; be in a ~ sodullŏ hada 서둘러 하다 **2** v/i sodurŭda 서두르다

♦ **hurry up 1** v/i sŏdurŭda 서두르다; ~! sŏdurŭseyo! 서두르세요! **2** v/t chaech'ok'ada 재촉하다

hurt 1 v/i ap'ŭda 아프다; my leg ~s tariga ap'ayo 다리가 아파요; does it ~? ap'ŭmnikka? 아픕니까? **2** v/t tach'ige hada 다치게 하다; (emotionally) …ŭi maŭmŭl sanghage hada …의 마음을 상하게

하다
husband namp'yŏn 남편
hush *n* choyongham 조용함; **~!**
choyonghi! 조용히!
♦ **hush up** *scandal etc*
shwishwihaebŏrida 쉬쉬해버리다
husk (*of grain*) kkŏptchil 껍질
husky *adj* shwin mokssoriŭi 쉰
목소리의, hŏsŭk'iŭi 허스키의
hustle 1 *n*: **~ and bustle** hwalgich'an
honjap 활기찬 혼잡 **2** *v/t person*
sŏdurŭge hada 서두르게 하다
hut odumak 오두막
hyacinth hiashinsŭ 히아신스
hybrid *n* (*plant, animal*) chaptchong
잡종
hydrant kŭpssugwan 급수관; *fire ~*
sohwajŏn 소화전
hydraulic (*using water*) suabŭi
수압의; (*using oil*) yuabŭi 유압의
hydroelectric suryŏk chŏn-giŭi 수력
전기의
hydrofoil (*boat*) sujung-iksŏn
수중익선
hydrogen suso 수소
hydrogen bomb suso p'okt'an 수소
폭탄
hygiene wisaeng 위생
hygienic wisaengsang-ŭi 위생상의
hymn ch'ansongga 찬송가, sŏngga
성가
hype *n* kwadae sŏnjŏn 과대 선전
hyperactive chinach'ige sŏlch'inŭn
지나치게 설치는; **hypermarket**
taehyŏng shyup'ŏmak'et 대형

슈퍼마켓; **hypersensitive**
kwaminhan 과민한; **hypertension**
kohyŏrap 고혈압; **hypertext**
COMPUT haip'ŏt'ekssŭt'ŭ
하이퍼텍스트
hyphen iŭmp'yo 이음표
hypnosis ch'oemyŏnsul 최면술
hypnotherapy ch'oemyŏn yoppŏp
최면 요법
hypnotize ch'oemyŏnsurŭl kŏlda
최면술을 걸다
hypochondriac *n* uultchŭng hwanja
우울증 환자
hypocrisy wisŏn 위선
hypocrite wisŏnja 위선자
hypocritical wisŏnŭi 위선의
hypothermia chŏch'eontchŭng
저체온증
hypothesis kasŏl 가설
hypothetical kasŏrŭi 가설의
hysterectomy chagung chŏkch'ulssul
자궁 적출술
hysteria hisŭt'eri 히스테리
hysterical *person* pyŏngtchok
hŭngbun sangt'aeŭi 병적 흥분
상태의, hisŭt'erisŏng-ŭi
히스테리성의; *laughter*
paltchaktchŏgin 발작적인; (*very
funny*) ŏmch'ŏngnage usŭun
엄청나게 우스운; *become ~*
pyŏngtchŏk hŭngbunsangt'aega
toeda 병적 흥분상태가 되다
hysterics hisŭt'eri 히스테리;
(*laughter*) paltchaktchŏgin usŭm
발작적인 웃음

I

I ◊ na 나; H chŏ 저; **~ am American /
a student** nanŭn Migugin /
hakssaengiyeyo 나는 미국인 /
학생이에요; **can ~ buy you a
drink?** chega han chan sado
toelkkayo? 제가 한 잔 사도 될까요?
◊ *(omission of pronoun):* **~ can't
see** pol su ŏpssŏyo 볼 수 없어요; **~
don't know** mollayo 몰라요

ice ŏrŭm 얼음; **break the ~** *fig*
ŏsaek'an punwigirŭl kkaeda 어색한
분위기를 깨다
♦ **ice up** *(of engine etc)*
tonggyŏldoeda 동결되다

iceberg pingsan 빙산; **icebox** aisŭ
pakssŭ 아이스 박스; **icebreaker**
(ship) swaebingsŏn 쇄빙선; **ice
cream** aisŭ k'ŭrim 아이스 크림; **ice-
cream parlor** aisŭ k'ŭrim kage
아이스 크림 가게; **ice cube** kak
ŏrŭm 각 얼음

iced *drink* ŏrŭmŭl nŏhŭn 얼음을 넣은
iced coffee aisŭ k'ŏp'i 아이스 커피
ice hockey aisŭ hak'i 아이스 하키
ice rink sŭk'eit'ŭjang 스케이트장
icicle kodŭrŭm 고드름
icon *(cultural)* sang 상; COMPUT
aik'on 아이콘
icy *road, surface* ŏrŭmi ŏrŭn 얼음이
얼은; *welcome* ssalssarhan 쌀쌀한
idea saenggak 생각; **good ~!** choŭn
saenggagiya! 좋은 생각이야!; **I have
no ~** nan chal morŭgennŭndeyo 난
잘 모르겠는데요; **it's not a good ~
to ...** ...hanŭn kŏsŭn choŭn
saenggagi animnida ...하는 것은
좋은 생각이 아닙니다
ideal *(perfect)* isangjŏgin 이상적인
idealistic isangjuŭijŏgin 이상주의적인
identical tong-irhan 동일한; **~ twins**
illanssŏng ssangdung-i 일란성 쌍둥이
identification hwagin 확인; *(papers
etc)* chŭngmyŏngsŏ 증명서
identify hwaginhada 확인하다

identity shinwŏn 신원; **their sense of
national ~** kŭdŭrŭi kungmin
chuch'eŭishik 그들의 국민 주체의식
identity card shinbun chŭngmyŏngsŏ
신분 증명서
ideological inyŏmjŏgin 이념적인
ideology ideollogi 이데올로기
idiom *(saying)* kwanyong-ŏ 관용어
idiomatic kwanyongjŏgin 관용적인
idiosyncrasy t'ŭktchil 특질
idiot pabo 바보
idiotic ŏrisŏgŭn 어리석은
idle 1 *adj person* nat'aehan 나태한;
threat ssŭltteŏmnŭn 쓸데없는;
machinery nolgo innŭn 놀고 있는; **in
an ~ moment** hangahan ttaee
한가한 때에 **2** *v/i (of engine)*
kongjŏnhada 공전하다
♦ **idle away** *time etc* pindunggŏrida
빈둥거리다
idol usang 우상
idolize sungbaehada 숭배하다
idyllic nagwŏn-gat'ŭn 낙원같은
if manyak ...myŏn 만약 ...면; *(whether
or not)* ...inji aninji ...인지 아닌지; **~
you catch a cold** manyak kamgie
kŏllimyŏn 만약 감기에 걸리면; **ask
him ~ he will be there** kŭege kŏgi
issŭl kŏshinji aninji murŏposeyo
그에게 거기 있을 것인지 아닌지
물어보세요
igloo igŭllu 이글루
ignite *v/t* purŭl puch'ida 불을 붙이다
ignition *(in car)* chŏmhwa changch'i
점화 장치; **~ key** igŭnishyŏn k'i
이그니션 키
ignorance muji 무지
ignorant morŭnŭn 모르는; *(rude)*
muryehan 무례한
ignore mushihada 무시하다
ill ap'ŭn 아픈; **fall ~, be taken ~**
pyŏngdŭlda 병들다
illegal pulppŏbŭi 불법의
illegible ilkki ŏryŏun 읽기 어려운

illegitimate pulppŏpŭi 불법의; *an ~ child* sasaeng-a 사생아
ill-fated purunhan 불운한
illicit wibŏbŭi 위법의
illiterate munmaeng-ŭi 문맹의
ill-mannered muryehan 무례한
ill-natured sŏngmiga koyak'an 성미가 고약한
illness pyŏng 병
illogical pinollijŏgin 비논리적인
ill-tempered sŏngkkal innŭn 성깔 있는
illtreat hakttaehada 학대하다
illuminate *building etc* chomyŏnghada 조명하다
illuminating *remarks etc* punmyŏnghage hanŭn 분명하게 하는
illusion hwanyŏng 환영
illustrate *book* sap'warŭl kŭrida 삽화를 그리다; (*with examples*) yeshihada 예시하다
illustration kŭrim 그림; (*example*) shillye 실례
illustrator sap'waga 삽화가
ill will agŭi 악의
image (*picture*) imiji 이미지; (*exact likeness*) ppaedalmŭn mosŭp 빼닮은 모습; (*of politician, company*) insang 인상
image-conscious ch'emyŏnŭl ch'arinŭn 체면을 차리는
imaginable sangsanghal su innŭn 상상할 수 있는; *the biggest / smallest size* sangsanghal su innŭn ch'oedaeŭi / ch'oesoŭi k'ŭgi 상상할 수 있는 최대의/최소의 크기
imaginary kasang-ŭi 가상의
imagination sangsang 상상; *it's all in your ~* kŭgŏsŭn chŏnbu tangshinŭi sangsang-imnida 그것은 전부 당신의 상상입니다
imaginative sangsangnyŏgi p'ungbuhan 상상력이 풍부한
imagine sangsanghada 상상하다; *I can just ~ it* sangsang-i kamnida 상상이 갑니다; *you're imagining things* tangshini sangsanghanŭn kŏyeyo 당신이 상상하는 거예요
imbecile chŏngshin pagyaktcha 정신 박약자
IMF (= *International Monetary*

Fund) Kuktche T'onghwa Kigŭm 국제 통화 기금, Aiemep'ŭ 아이엠에프
imitate mobanghada 모방하다
imitation (*copying*) mobang 모방; (*something copied*) mojop'um 모조품
Imjin River Imjin-gang 임진강
immaculate t'i ŏmnŭn 티 없는
immaterial sanggwanŏmnŭn 상관없는
immature misŏngsugŭi 미성숙의
immediate chŭksshiŭi 즉시의; *the ~ family* paeuja ttonŭn pumo hyŏngje, chashik 배우자 또는 부모 형제, 자식; *in the ~ neighborhood* injŏp'an kose 인접한 곳에
immediately chŭksshiro 즉시로; *~ after the bank / church* ŭnhaeng / kyohoe paro yŏp'e 은행/교회 바로 옆에
immense ŏmch'ŏngnan 엄청난
immerse tamgŭda 담그다; *~ oneself in* molttuhada 몰두하다
immersion heater t'uip chŏnyŏlgi 투입 전열기
immigrant n ijuja 이주자
immigrate ijuhada 이주하다
immigration (*act*) iju 이주
Immigration Bureau Ch'urip Kwalliguk 출입 관리국
imminent chŏlbak'an 절박한
immobilize *factory* kadonghaji mot'age hada 가동하지 못하게 하다; *person* umjigiji mot'age hada 움직이지 못하게 하다; *car* kadongshik'iji mot'age hada 가동시키지 못하게 하다
immoderate mujŏltchehan 무절제한
immoral pudodŏk'an 부도덕한
immorality pudodŏk 부도덕
immortal pulmyŏrŭi 불멸의
immortality pulmyŏl 불멸
immune (*to illness, infection*) myŏnyŏgŭi 면역의; (*from ruling, requirement*) myŏnjedoen 면제된
immune system MED myŏnyŏk ch'egye 면역 체계
immunity (*to infection*) myŏnyŏk 면역; (*from ruling*) myŏnje 면제; *diplomatic ~* oegyomyŏnch'aek 외교면책

impact *n* (*of meteorite, vehicle*) ch'ungdol 충돌; (*of new manager etc*) yŏnghyangnyŏk 영향력; (*effect*) yŏnghyang 영향

impair haech'ida 해치다

impaired sonsangdoen 손상된

impartial kongjŏnghan 공정한

impassable *road* t'onghaenghal su ŏmnŭn 통행할 수 없는

impasse (*in negotiations etc*) kongyŏng 곤경

impassioned *speech, plea* yŏltchŏngjŏgin 열정적인

impassive naengjŏnghan 냉정한

impatience sŏnggŭp'am 성급함

impatient sŏnggŭp'an 성급한

impatiently sŏnggŭp'age 성급하게

impeccable *turnout* namural te ŏmnŭn 나무랄 데 없는; *English* wanbyŏk'an 완벽한

impeccably *dressed* namural te ŏpsshi 나무랄 데 없이; *speak Korean* wanbyŏk'age 완벽하게

impede panghaehada 방해하다

impediment (*in speech*) tŏdŭmgŏrim 더듬거림

impending imbak'an 임박한

impenetrable hearil su ŏmnŭn 헤아릴 수 없는

imperative 1 *adj* kkok haeya hal 꼭 해야 할; *it is ~ that we go now* urinŭn chigŭm kkok kaya handa 우리는 지금 꼭 가야 한다 2 *n* GRAM myŏngnyŏngppŏp 명령법

imperceptible nŏmu chaga kamjihal su ŏmnŭn 너무 작아 감지할 수 없는

imperfect 1 *adj* purwanjŏnhan 불완전한 2 *n* GRAM miwallyo 미완료

imperial chegugŭi 제국의

impersonal piin-ganjŏgin 비인간적인

impersonate (*as a joke*) hyungnaenaeda 흉내내다; (*illegally*) wijanghada 위장하다

impertinence kŏnbangjim 건방짐

impertinent kŏnbangjin 건방진

imperturbable ch'abunhan 차분한

impervious: *~ to* ...e mudŏmdŏmhan ...에 무덤덤한

impetuous ch'ungdongjŏgin 충동적인

impetus (*of campaign etc*) yŏse 여세

implement 1 *n* togu 도구 2 *v/t*

measures etc shirhaenghada 실행하다

implicate: *~ s.o. in sth* nugurŭl muŏse yŏllu shik'ida 누구를 무엇에 연루 시키다

implication hamch'uk 함축

implicit hamch'uktchŏgin 함축적인; *trust* chŏlttaejŏgin 절대적인

implore kanch'ŏnghada 간청하다

imply amshihada 암시하다

impolite pŏrŭt ŏmnŭn 버릇 없는

import 1 *n* suip 수입 2 *v/t* suip'ada 수입하다

importance chungnyosŏng 중요성

important chungnyohan 중요한

importer suiptcha 수입자

impose *tax* pugwahada 부과하다; *~ oneself on s.o.* nuguege pudamŭl chuda 누구에게 부담을 주다

imposing insangjŏgin 인상적인

impossibility pulganŭng 불가능

impossible pulganŭnghan 불가능한

impostor sagikkun 사기꾼

impotence sŏng pullŭng 성 불능

impotent muryŏk'an 무력한; MED sŏng pullŭng-ŭi 성 불능의

impoverished pin-gone tchidŭn 빈곤에 찌든

impractical *person, suggestion* pihyŏnshiltchŏgin 비현실적인

impress kammyŏng chuda 감명 주다; *be ~ed by s.o. / sth* nuguege / muŏse kammyŏng pat-tta 누구에게 / 무엇에 감명 받다; *I'm not ~ed* chŏrŭl shilmangshik'inŭn-gunyo 저를 실망시키는군요

impression nŭkkim 느낌; (*impersonation*) hyungnaenaegi 흉내내기; *make a good / bad ~ on s.o.* nuguege choŭn / nappŭn insangŭl chuda 누구에게 좋은 / 나쁜 인상을 주다; *get the ~ that ...* ...ranŭn insang-ŭl pat-tta ...라는 인상을 받다

impressionable kamsusŏng-i yeminhan 감수성이 예민한

impressive insangjŏgin 인상적인

imprint *n* (*of credit card*) nullŏ tchigŭn chaguk 눌러 찍은 자국

imprison t'uok'ada 투옥하다

imprisonment t'uok 투옥

improbable irŏnal kŏt kattchi anŭn

일어날 것 같지 않은
improper *behavior* pujŏktchŏrhan 부적절한
improve 1 *v/t* hyangsangshik'ida 향상시키다 **2** *v/i* hyangsanghada 향상하다
improvement hyangsang 향상
improvise *v/i* (*in music*) chŭk'ŭngŭro hada 즉흥으로 하다; (*in plans*) chŭkssŏgesŏ mandŭlda 즉석에서 만들다
impudent ppŏnppŏnsŭrŏun 뻔뻔스러운
impulse ch'ungdong 충동; *do sth on an* ~ ch'ungdongjŏguro muŏsŭl hada 충동적으로 무엇을 하다; ~ *buy* ch'ungdong kumae 충동 구매
impulsive ch'ungdongjŏgin 충동적인
impunity: *with* ~ pŏrŭl pat-tchi ank'o 벌을 받지 않고
impure pulssunhan 불순한
in 1 *prep* ...e(sŏ) ...에(서); ~ *Washington* / *Seoul* Wŏshingt'ŏne(sŏ) / Sŏure(sŏ) 워싱턴에(서) / 서울에(서); ~ *the street* kŏrie(sŏ) 거리에(서); *wounded* ~ *the leg* / *arm* tarie / pare pusang-ŭl ibŭn 다리에 / 팔에 부상을 입은 ◊ (*inside*) ... ane / soge ...안에 / 속에; ~ *the box* sangja ane 상자 안에; *put it* ~ *your pocket* chumŏni soge nŏŏ twŏra 주머니 속에 넣어 둬라 ◊: ~ *his novel* kŭŭi sosŏl soge(sŏ) 그의 소설 속에(서); ~ *Faulkner* P'ok'ŭnŏŭi chakp'um soge(sŏ) 포크너의 작품 속에(서) ◊ (*time*) ...e ...에; ~ *1999* 1999nyŏne 1999년에; ~ *two hours* (*from now*) tu shigan ane 두 시간 안에, tu shigan inaee 두 시간 이내에; ~ *the morning* ach'ime 아침에; ~ *the summer* yŏrŭme 여름에; ~ *August* p'arwŏre 팔월에 ◊ (*manner*) ...(ŭ)ro ...(으)로; ~ *English* / *Korean* Yŏng-ŏro / Han-gugŏro 영어로 / 한국어로; ~ *a loud voice* k'ŭn mokssoriro 큰 목소리로; ~ *yellow* noransaegŭro 노란색으로 ◊ (*while*) ~ *crossing the road* kirŭl kŏnnŏnŭn tojung-e 길을 건너는 도중에; ~ *agreeing to this* (*by virtue of*) igŏse tong-ŭihamŭrossŏ

이것에 동의함으로써 ◊: *three* ~ *all* t'ongt'ŭrŏ se kae 통틀어 세 개; *one* ~ *ten* yŏl kae chung han kae 열 개 중 한 개 **2** *adv*: *be* ~ (*at home, in the building etc*) ane it-tta 안에 있다; (*arrived: of train*) toch'ak'an 도착한; *when the diskette is* ~ tisŭk'eshi ane issŭl ttae 디스켓이 안에 있을 때; ~ *here* yŏgie 여기에 **3** *adj* (*fashionable, popular*) yuhaenghanŭn 유행하는; *pink is* ~ punhongsaegi yuhaeng-iyeyo 분홍색이 유행이에요
inability munŭng 무능
inaccessible chŏpkkŭnhagi ŏryŏun 접근하기 어려운
inaccurate pujŏnghwak'an 부정확한
inactive hwalttonghaji annŭn 활동하지 않는
inadequate pujŏkttanghan 부적당한
inadvisable kwŏnhal su ŏmnŭn 권할 수 없는
inanimate musaengmurŭi 무생물의
inapplicable chŏgyonghal su ŏmnŭn 적용할 수 없는
inappropriate pujŏkttanghan 부적당한
inarticulate marŭl ttokttok'i mot'anŭn 말을 똑똑히 못하는
inattentive pujuŭihan 부주의한
inaudible tŭlliji annŭn 들리지 않는
inaugural *speech* ch'wiimŭi 취임의
inaugurate *new building* kaegwanhada 개관하다; *new era* yŏlda 열다; *president* ...ŭi ch'wiimshigŭl kŏhaenghada ...의 취임식을 거행하다
inborn t'agonan 타고난
inbreeding tongjong pŏnshik 동종 번식
inc. (= *incorporated*) pŏbin hoesa 법인 회사
incalculable *damage* makttaehan 막대한
incapable nŭngnyŏgi ŏmnŭn 능력이 없는; *be* ~ *of doing sth* muŏsŭl hanŭn kŏse munŭnghada 무엇을 하는 것에 무능하다
incendiary device panghwajangch'i 방화장치
incense[1] *n* hyang 향

incense

incense² v/t maeu hwanage hada 매우 화나게 하다

incentive tonggi 동기

incessant kkŭnimŏmnŭn 끊임없는

incessantly kkŭnimŏpsshi 끊임없이

incest kŭnch'insanggan 근친상간

inch n inch'i 인치

incident sakkŏn 사건

incidental uyŏnhi irŏnanŭn 우연히 일어나는; **~ remark** uyŏnhi naon mal 우연히 나온 말; **~ expenses** chap-ppi 잡비

incidentally mari nan-gime 말이 난김에

incinerator sogangno 소각로

incision chŏlgae 절개

incisive mind, analysis nalk'aroun 날카로운

incite kyŏngnyŏhada 격려하다; **~ s.o. to do sth** nuguege muŏsŭl hadorok kyŏngnyŏhada 누구에게 무엇을 하도록 격려하다

inclement weather hŏmak'an 험악한

inclination (tendency, liking) sŏnghyang 성향

incline: **be ~d to do sth** muŏsŭl hanŭn kyŏnghyang-i it-tta 무엇을 하는 경향이 있다

inclose → **enclose**

include p'ohamhada 포함하다

including prep ...ŭl/rŭl p'ohamhayŏ ...을/를 포함하여

inclusive 1 adj price p'ohamhan 포함한 2 prep p'ohamhayŏ 포함하여; **~ of** ...ŭl/rŭl p'ohamhayŏ ...을/를 포함하여 3 adv ilch'erŭl p'ohamhayŏ 일체를 포함하여; **from Monday to Thursday** ~ wŏryoilbut'ŏ mogyoilkkaji 월요일부터 목요일까지

incoherent tusŏŏmnŭn 두서없는

income sodŭk 소득

income tax sodŭksse 소득세

incoming flight toch'ak'anŭn 도착하는; phone call kŏllyŏonŭn 걸려오는; president huimŭi 후임의; **~ tide** milmul 밀물

incomparable pihal te ŏmnŭn 비할 데 없는

incompatibility (of personalities) yangnip'al su ŏpssŭm 양립할 수 없음; (of systems) hohwan

pulganŭng 호환 불가능

incompatible personalities yangnip'al su ŏmnŭn 양립할 수 없는; formats, systems hohwandoeji annŭn 호환되지 않는

incompetence munŭngnyŏk 무능력

incompetent munŭngnyŏk'an 무능력한

incomplete purwanjŏnhan 불완전한

incomprehensible ihaehal su ŏmnŭn 이해할 수 없는

inconceivable saenggakhal su choch'a ŏmnŭn 생각할 수 조차 없는

inconclusive kyŏltchŏngjŏgiji anŭn 결정적이지 않은

incongruous chohwadoeji annŭn 조화되지 않는

inconsiderate saryŏŏmnŭn 사려없는

inconsistent mosundoenŭn 모순되는

inconsolable wirohal kil ŏmnŭn 위로할 길 없는

inconspicuous nune ttŭiji annŭn 눈에 띄지 않는

inconvenience n pulp'yŏn 불편

inconvenient pulp'yŏnhan 불편한

incorporate p'ohamhada 포함하다

incorporated COM pŏbin hoesa 법인 회사

incorrect t'ŭllin 틀린

incorrectly t'ŭllige 틀리게

incorrigible ŏtchŏl su ŏmnŭn 어쩔 수 없는

increase 1 v/t chŭnggashik'ida 증가시키다 2 v/i chŭnggahada 증가하다 3 n chŭngga 증가

increasing chŭnggahanŭn 증가하는

increasingly kalssurok tŏ 갈수록 더

incredible (amazing, very good) midŏjiji annŭn 믿어지지 않는

incriminate choerŭl ssŭiuda 죄를 씌우다; **~ oneself** choerŭl chainhada 죄를 자인하다

in-crowd naebu haeksshim chipttan 내부 핵심 집단

incubator ink'yubeit'ŏ 인큐베이터

incur ch'oraehada 초래하다

incurable pulch'iŭi 불치의

indebted: **be ~ to s.o.** nuguege shinserŭl chida 누구에게 신세를 지다

indecent chŏmjanch'i mot'an 점잖지

못한
indecisive kyŏlttanssŏng-i ŏmnŭn
결단성이 없는
indecisiveness uyubudan 우유부단
indeed (*in fact*) chinshillo 진실로;
(*yes, agreeing*) kŭraeyo 그래요; *very
much ~* chŏngmal kŭraeyo 정말
그래요
indefinable magyŏnhan 막연한
indefinite muhanjŏnghan 무한정한; *~
article* GRAM pujŏng kwansa 부정
관사
indefinitely mugihanŭro 무기한으로
indelicate mushin-gyŏnghan 무신경한
indent 1 *n* (*in text*) anŭro tŭryŏssŭgi
안으로 들여쓰기 **2** *v/t line* anŭro
tŭryŏsŏ ssŭda 안으로 들여서 쓰다
independence tongnip 독립
Independence Day Tongnip
Kinyŏmil 독립 기념일
independent tongniptchŏgin
독립적인
independently *deal with*
tongniptchŏgŭro 독립적으로; *~ of*
pyŏlgaero 별개로
indescribable hyŏng-ŏnhal su
ŏmnŭn 형언할 수 없는
indescribably *bad, beautiful* hyŏng-
ŏnhal su ŏpttorok 형언할 수 없도록
indestructible p'agoehal su ŏmnŭn
파괴할 수 없는
indeterminate pujŏnghwak'an
부정확한
index (*for book*) saegin 색인
index card saegin k'adŭ 색인 카드
index finger chipkke sonkkarak 집게
손가락
India Indo 인도
Indian 1 *adj* Indoŭi 인도의 **2** *n* Indoin
인도인; (*American*) Indian 인디안
Indian summer hwach'anghan nalssi
화창한 날씨
indicate 1 *v/t* karik'ida 가리키다 **2** *v/i*
(*when driving*) (tonŭn panghyang-
ŭl) p'yoshihada (도는 방향을)
표시하다
indication p'yoshi 표시
indicator (*on car*) p'yoshidŭng 표시등
indict kisohada 기소하다
indifference mugwanshim 무관심
indifferent mugwanshimhan

무관심한; (*mediocre*) pot'ong-ŭi
보통의
indigestible sowahagi ŏryŏun
소화하기 어려운
indigestion sowa pullyang 소화
불량
indignant pun-gaehan 분개한
indignation pun-gae 분개
indirect kanjŏptchŏgin 간접적인
indirectly kanjŏptchŏgŭro 간접적으로
indiscreet mubunbyŏrhan 무분별한
indiscretion (*act*) mubunbyŏl 무분별
indiscriminate much'abyŏrŭi
무차별의
indispensable p'ilssuŭi 필수의
indisposed (*not well*) momi
pulp'yŏnhan 몸이 불편한
indisputable nonŭiŭi yŏjiga ŏmnŭn
논의의 여지가 없는
indisputably ŭishimhal yŏji ŏpsshi
의심할 여지 없이
indistinct tturyŏt'aji anŭn 뚜렷하지
않은
indistinguishable pun-gan hal su
ŏmnŭn 분간 할 수 없는
individual 1 *n* kaein 개인 **2** *adj*
(*separate*) kaegaeŭi 개개의;
(*personal*) kaeinŭi 개인의
individualist kaeinjuŭija 개인주의자
individually kaebyŏltchŏgŭro
개별적으로
indivisible pulgabunŭi 불가분의
indoctrinate chuip'ada 주입하다
indolence keŭrŭm 게으름
indolent nat'aehan 나태한
Indochina Indoch'aina 인도차이나
Indochinese *adj* Indoch'ainaŭi
인도차이나의
Indonesia Indoneshia 인도네시아
Indonesian 1 *adj* Indoneshiaŭi
인도네시아의 **2** *n* (*person*)
Indoneshiain 인도네시아인
indoor shillaeŭi 실내의
indoors shillae(sŏ) 실내에(서)
induction ceremony orient'eishyŏn
오리엔테이션
indulge 1 *v/t* (*oneself, one's tastes*)
t'amnik'ada 탐닉하다 **2** *v/i*: *~ in sth*
muŏse ppajida 무엇에 빠지다
indulgence (*of tastes, appetite etc*)
t'amnik 탐닉; (*laxity*) ŭngsŏk padŭm

응석 받음
indulgent (*not strict enough*)
kwandaehan 관대한
industrial sanŏbŭi 산업의
industrial action nodong chaeng-ŭi
haeng-wi 노동 쟁의 행위
industrial dispute nosaganŭi purhwa
노사간의 불화
industrialist shirŏpkka 실업가
industrialize 1 *v/t* sanŏp'wahada
산업화하다 **2** *v/i* sanŏp'wadoeda
산업화되다
industrial park kong-ŏpttanji 공업
단지
industrial waste sanŏpp'yegimul
산업폐기물
industrious kŭnmyŏnhan 근면한
industry sanŏp 산업
ineffective *person* munŭnghan
무능한; *measures, device* hyokkwaga
ŏmnŭn 효과가 없는
ineffectual *person* munŭnghan
무능한
inefficient pinŭngnyultchŏgin
비능률적인
ineligible chagyŏgi ŏmnŭn 자격이
없는
inept nŭngnyŏgi ŏmnŭn 능력이 없는
inequality pulp'yŏngdŭng 불평등
inescapable p'ihal su ŏmnŭn 피할 수
없는
inestimable hearil su ŏmnŭn 헤아릴
수 없는
inevitable p'ihal su ŏmnŭn 피할 수
없는
inevitably p'ihal su ŏpsshi 피할 수
없이
inexcusable pyŏnmyŏnghal su
ŏmnŭn 변명할 수 없는
inexhaustible *person* chich'il tchul
morŭnŭn 지칠 줄 모르는; *supply*
mujinjanghan 무진장한
inexpensive kapsshi ssan 값이 싼
inexperienced kyŏnghŏmi ŏmnŭn
경험이 없는
inexplicable sŏlmyŏnghal su ŏmnŭn
설명할 수 없는
inexpressible *joy* hyŏngŏnhal su
ŏmnŭn 형언할 수 없는
infallible chŏlttae t'ŭllili ŏmnŭn 절대
틀릴 없는

infamous angmyŏng nop'ŭn 악명
높은
infancy yuagi 유아기; *fig* ch'ogi 초기
infant yua 유아
infantile *pej* yuch'ihan 유치한
infantry pobyŏngdae 보병대
infantry soldier pobyŏng 보병
infatuated: *be ~ with s.o.* nuguege
holttak panhada 누구에게 홀딱
반하다
infect kamyŏmshik'ida 감염시키다;
(*of person*) muldŭrida 물들이다;
food, water oyŏmshik'ida
오염시키다; *become ~ed* (*of
person*) muri tŭlda 물이 들다; (*of
wound*) kamyŏmdoeda 감염되다
infected *wound* kamyŏmdoen 감염된
infection kamyŏm 감염
infectious *disease* chŏnyŏmssŏng-ŭi
전염성의; *laughter* omgyŏjigi shwiun
옮겨지기 쉬운
infer: *~ X from Y* Yesŏ Xŭl/rŭl
ch'uronhada Y에서 X을/를 추론하다
inferior *quality* iryuŭi 이류의; (*in
rank*) hagŭbŭi 하급의; (*in company*)
hawiŭi 하위의
inferiority (*in quality*) iryu 이류
inferiority complex yŏlttŭng ŭishik
열등 의식
infertile *soil* pulmoŭi 불모의; *woman*
purimŭi 불임의
infertility (*of soil*) pulmo 불모; (*of
woman*) purim 불임
infidelity pujŏng 부정
infiltrate *v/t* ch'imip'ada 침입하다
infinite muhanhan 무한한
infinitive GRAM pujŏngsa 부정사
infinity muhan 무한
infirm hŏyak'an 허약한
infirmary (*in boarding school*)
yanghoshil 양호실; MIL chillyoso
진료소
infirmity hŏyak 허약
inflame pul t'aorŭge hada 불
타오르게 하다
inflammable inhwassŏng-ŭi 인화성의
inflammation MED yŏmtchŭng 염증
inflatable *dinghy* komu pot'ŭ 고무
보트
inflate *v/t* tire, dinghy pup'ullida
부풀리다; *economy* t'onghwa

p'aengch'angshik'ida 통화
팽창시키다
inflation inp'ŭlle(ishyŏn)
인플레(이션)
inflationary (*of inflation*)
inp'ŭlleishyŏnŭi 인플레이션의;
(*causing inflation*) inp'ŭlleishyŏnŭl
yubarhanŭn 인플레이션을 유발하는
inflection (*of voice*) ŏgyang 억양
inflexible *attitude, person* kup'il su
ŏmnŭn 굽힐 수 없는
inflict: ~ *X on Y* Xŭl / rŭl Yege
kahada X을 / 를 Y에게 가하다
in-flight pihaeng chung-ŭi 비행 중의;
~ *entertainment* kinaeorak
기내오락
influence 1 *n* yŏnghyang 영향;
(*power to influence*) yŏnghyangnyŏk
영향력; *be a good* / *bad* ~ *on s.o.*
nuguege choŭn / nappŭn yŏnghyang-
ŭl chuda 누구에게 좋은 / 나쁜 영향을
주다 **2** *v/t s.o.'s thinking* yŏnghyang
kkich'ida 영향 끼치다; *decision*
yŏnghyang chuda 영향 주다
influential yŏnghyangnyŏk innŭn
영향력 있는
influenza tok-kkam 독감
inform 1 *v/t* allida 알리다; ~ *X of Y*
Xege Yrŭl allyŏjuda X에게 Y를
알려주다; *please keep me ~ed*
kyesok'aesŏ allyŏjuseyo 계속해서
알려주세요 **2** *v/i* shin-gohada
신고하다; ~ *on s.o.* nugurŭl shin-
gohada 누구를 신고하다
informal *meeting, conversation*
pigongshigŭi 비공식의; *form of
address, agreement* yaksshigŭi
약식의; *dress* p'yŏngsangbok
ch'arimŭi 평상복 차림의
informality (*of meeting, conversation*)
pigongshik 비공식; (*of form of
address, agreement*) yaksshik 약식
informant chŏngbo chegongja 정보
제공자
information chŏngbo 정보
information science chŏngbo
kwahak 정보 과학; **information
scientist** chŏngbo kwahaktcha 정보
과학자; **information technology**
chŏngbo kisul 정보 기술
informative chŏngboga manŭn

정보가 많은
informer milgoja 밀고자
infra-red *adj* chŏgoesŏnŭi 적외선의
infrastructure (*of economy, society*)
kigan shisŏl 기간 시설; (*of
organization*) habu chojik 하부 조직
infrequent tŭmun 드문
infuriate kyŏngno shik'ida 격노
시키다; *be ~ed at* ...e
nobaldaebarhada ...에 노발대발하다
infuriating kyŏngnok'e hanŭn 격노케
하는
infuse *v/i* (*of tea*) urida 우리다
infusion (*herb tea*) uryŏnaem 우려냄
ingenious tokch'angjŏgin 독창적인
ingenuity tokch'angnyŏk 독창력
ingot (*gold*) kŭmgoe 금괴; (*silver*)
ŭn-goe 은괴
ingratiate: ~ *oneself with s.o.*
nuguŭi piwirŭl match'uda 누구의
비위를 맞추다
ingratitude paeŭnmangdŏk 배은망덕
ingredient chaeryo 재료; *fig* yoso 요소
inhabit kŏjuhada 거주하다
inhabitable sal su innŭn 살 수 있는
inhabitant kŏjuja 거주자
inhale 1 *v/t* pparadŭrida 빨아들이다
2 *v/i* (*when smoking*) hŭbip'ada
흡입하다
inhaler hŭbipkki 흡입기
inherit sangsok'ada 상속하다
inheritance sangsok 상속;
(*characteristics*) yujŏn 유전
inhibit *growth, conversation etc*
ŏktchehada 억제하다
inhibited ŏktchedoen 억제된
inhibition ŏktche 억제
inhospitable *city, people*
pulch'injŏrhan 불친절한; *climate*
hwangp'yehan 황폐한
in-house 1 *adj* sanaeŭi 사내의 **2** *adv
work* sanaee(sŏ) 사내에(서)
inhuman injŏng ŏmnŭn 인정 없는
initial 1 *adj* ch'oech'oŭi 최초의 **2** *n*
inishyŏl 이니셜 **3** *v/t* (*write initials
on*) inishyŏllo ssŭda 이니셜로 쓰다
initially ch'ŏŭmbut'ŏ 처음부터
initiate kaeshihada 개시하다
initiation kaeshi 개시
initiative chudo 주도; *do sth on
one's own* ~ muŏsŭl solssŏnhaesŏ

inject 456

hada 무엇을 솔선해서 하다
inject *medicine, drug* chusahada
주사하다; *fuel* nŏt'a 넣다; *capital*
t'uip'ada 투입하다
injection MED chusa 주사; *(of fuel)*
chuip 주입; *(of capital)* t'uip 도입
injure sangch'ŏ ip'ida 상처 입히다
injured 1 *adj leg, feelings* sangch'ŏ
ibŭn 상처 입은 **2** *n:* **the ~** pusangja
부상자
injury pusang 부상
injustice pujŏng 부정
ink ingk'ŭ 잉크
inkjet (printer) ingk'ŭ chet p'ŭrint'ŏ
잉크 젯 프린터
inland *sea* yuktchi tchogŭi 육지 쪽의;
mail, areas, trade naeryugŭi 내륙의
in-laws inch'ŏk 인척
inlay *n* samgam 상감
inlet *(of sea)* humi 후미; *(in machine)*
chuipkku 주입구
inmate *(of prison)* sugamja 수감자;
(of mental hospital) ibwŏn hwanja
입원 환자
inn yŏgwan 여관
innate t'agonan 타고난
inner naebuŭi 내부의; *thoughts*
naetchŏgin 내적인
inner city toshi chungshimŭi
(pinmin) chiyŏk 도시 중심의 (빈민)
지역
innermost kajang kippsuk'an 가장
깊숙한
inner tube (chajŏn-gŏ) t'yubŭ
(자전거) 튜브
innocence LAW kyŏlbaek 결백; *(of
child)* sunjinham 순진함
innocent LAW kyŏlbaek'an 결백한;
child sunjinhan 순진한
innovation hyŏksshin 혁신
innovative hyŏksshinjŏgin 혁신적인
innovator *(person)* hŏksshin-ga
혁신가; *(company)* hyŏksshinhanŭn
hoesa 혁신하는 회사
innumerable musuhan 무수한
inoculate yebang chŏptchonghada
예방 접종하다
inoculation yebang chŏptchong 예방
접종
inoffensive *animal* muhaehan 무해한;
person, attitude agŭiga ŏmnŭn

악의가 없는
inorganic mugiŭi 무기의
in-patient ibwŏnhwanja 입원환자
input 1 *n (into project etc)* t'uip 투입;
COMPUT imnyŏk 입력 **2** *v/t (into
project)* t'uip'ada 투입하다; COMPUT
imnyŏk'ada 입력하다
input port COMPUT imnyŏk tanja 입력
단자
inquest wŏnin kyumyŏng 원인 규명
inquire munŭihada 문의하다; **~ into**
sth muŏse taehae chosahada 무엇에
대해 조사하다
inquiry munŭi 문의
inquisitive t'amgujŏgin 탐구적인
insane mich'in 미친
insanitary piwisaengjŏgin 비위생적인
insanity chŏngshin isang 정신 이상
insatiable t'amyokssŭroun
탐욕스러운
inscription *(in book)* chemyŏng 제명
inscrutable pulgasaŭihan 불가사의한
insect konch'ung 곤충
insecticide salch'ungje 살충제
insect repellent pangch'ungje 방충제
insecure puranhan 불안한
insecurity puranjŏng 불안정
insensitive mugamgak'an 무감각한
insensitivity mugamgak 무감각
inseparable *two issues* pullihal su
ŏmnŭn 분리할 수 없는; *two people*
heŏjil su ŏmnŭn 헤어질 수 없는
insert 1 *n (in magazine etc)* sabip
kwanggo 삽입 광고 **2** *v/t* kkiwŏ
nŏt'a 끼워 넣다; **~ X into Y** Xŭl/rŭl
Ye kkiwŏ nŏt'a X을/를 Y에 끼워
넣다
insertion *(act)* sabip 삽입
inside 1 *n (of house, box)* naebu 내부;
(of road) antchok 안쪽; *somebody
on the* **~** naebuin 내부인; **~ out**
twijibŏsŏ 뒤집어서; *turn sth* **~ out**
muŏsŭl twijiptta 무엇을 뒤집다;
know sth **~ out** muŏsŭl
wanbyŏk'age alda 무엇을 완벽하게
알다 **2** *prep* ane(sŏ) 안에(서); **~ the
house** chibane(sŏ) 집안에(서); **~ of
2 hours** tushigan inae 두시간 이내
3 *adv stay, remain* naebue(sŏ)
내부에(서); *go, carry* anŭro 안으로;
we went **~** urinŭn anŭro tŭrŏgat-tta

우리는 안으로 들어갔다 4 *adj*
naebue innŭn 내부에 있는; ~ *information* naebu chŏngbo 내부 정보; ~
lane SP antchoklein 안쪽 레인; (*on
road*) antchok kil 안쪽 길; ~ *pocket*
antchumŏni 안주머니
insider naebuin 내부인
insider trading FIN insaidŏ kŏrae
인사이더 거래
insides wijang 위장
insidious *disease* chamhaengssŏng-ŭi
잠행성의
insight t'ongch'al 통찰
insignificant *amount* chagŭmahan
자그마한; *person, problem*
hach'anŭn 하찮은
insincere musŏng-ŭihan 무성의한
insincerity musŏng-ŭi 무성의
insinuate (*imply*) nŏnjishi pich'ida
넌지시 비치다
insist chujanghada 주장하다; *please
keep it, I* ~ sayangch'i mashigo
kajiseyo 사양치 마시고 가지세요
♦**insist on** kangyohada 강요하다
insistent chibyohan 집요한
insolent kŏnbangjin 건방진
insoluble *problem* haegyŏrhal su
ŏmnŭn 해결할 수 없는; *substance*
yonghaedoeji annŭn 용해되지 않는
insolvent chibul pullŭng-ŭi 지불
불능의
insomnia pulmyŏntchŭng 불면증
inspect *work, tickets, baggage*
chŏmgŏmhada 점검하다; *building,
factory, school* shich'arhada
시찰하다
inspection (*of work, tickets, baggage*)
chŏmgŏm 점검; (*of building, factory,
school*) shich'al 시찰
inspector (*in factory etc*)
kamch'altcha 감찰자
inspiration yŏnggam 영감; (*very good
idea*) kibarhan saenggak 기발한 생각
inspire *respect etc* pullŏ irŭk'ida 불러
일으키다; *be ~d by s.o. / sth*
nuguege / muŏse yŏnggamŭl pat-tta
누구에게 / 무엇에 영감을 받다
instability puranjŏng 불안정
instal(l) *equipment, software*
sŏlch'ihada 설치하다
installation (*of equipment, software*)

sŏlch'i 설치; *military* ~ kunsashisŏl
군사시설
installment (*of story, TV drama etc*)
(yŏnjaeŭi) il hoebun (연재의) 일
회분; (*payment*) punhal purip 분할
불입; *monthly ~s* wŏlbu 월부
installment plan punhal purip
pangshik 분할 불입 방식
instance (*example*) ye 예; *for ~* yerŭl
tŭrŏ 예를 들어
instant 1 *adj* chŭk-kkaktchŏgin
즉각적인 **2** *n* sun-gan 순간; *in an ~*
sunshik-kkane 순식간에
instantaneous sunshik-kkanŭi
순식간의
instant coffee insŭt'ŏnt'ŭ k'ŏp'i
인스턴트 커피
instantly chŭksshi 즉시
instead taeshine 대신에; ~ *of* ...
taeshine ... 대신에
instep palttŭng 발등
instinct ponnŭng 본능
instinctive ponnŭngjŏgin 본능적인
institute 1 *n* yŏn-guso 연구소;
(*academic*) hak'oe 학회; (*special
home*) konggong kigwan 공공 기관
2 *v/t inquiry* shijak'ada 시작하다
institution (*governmental*) kigwan
기관; (*something traditional*)
kwansŭp 관습; (*setting up*) sŏltchŏng
설정
instruct (*order*) chishihada 지시하다;
(*teach*) karŭch'ida 가르치다; ~ *X to
do Y* (*order*) Xege Y hal kŏsŭl
chishihada X에게 Y할 것을 지시하다
instruction chishi sahang 지시 사항;
~*s for use* sayongppŏp 사용법
instruction manual sayong
sŏlmyŏngsŏ 사용 설명서
instructive kyoyuktchŏgin 교육적인
instructor kangsa 강사; (*in martial
arts*) sabŏm 사범
instrument MUS ak-kki 악기; (*gadget,
tool*) togu 도구
insubordinate pulboktchonghanŭn
불복종하는
insufficient pulch'ungbunhan
불충분한
insulate ELEC chŏryŏnhada 절연하다;
(*against cold*) panghanhada 방한하다
insulation ELEC chŏryŏn 절연;

(*against cold*) panghan 방한
insulin inshyullin 인슐린
insult 1 *n* moyok 모욕 **2** *v/t* moyok'ada 모욕하다
insurance pohŏm 보험
insurance company pohŏm hoesa 보험 회사
insurance policy pohŏm chŭngsŏ 보험 증서
insure pohŏme tŭlda 보험에 들다; *be ~ed* pohŏme tŭrŏit-tta 보험에 들어있다
insurmountable kŭkppok'al su ŏmnŭn 극복할 수 없는
intact (*not damaged*) sonsangdoeji anŭn 손상되지 않은
intake (*of college etc*) suyong inwŏn 수용 인원
integrate *v/t* t'onghap'ada 통합하다
integrated circuit chiptchŏk hoero 집적 회로
integrity (*honesty*) chŏngjik 정직
intellect chisŏng 지성
intellectual 1 *adj* chitchŏgin 지적인 **2** *n* chisŏng-in 지성인
intelligence chinŭng 지능; (*news*) chŏngbo 정보
intelligence service chŏngbo kigwan 정보 기관
intelligent ttokttok'an 똑똑한
intelligible chal ihaehal su innŭn 잘 이해할 수 있는
intend ... hal chaktchŏng-ida ... 할 작정이다; *~ to do sth* (*do on purpose*) muŏsŭl ŭidohada 무엇을 의도하다; (*plan to do*) muŏsŭl hal chaktchŏng-ida 무엇을 할 작정이다; *that's not what I ~ed* kŭgŏn naega ŭidohan ke animnida 그건 내가 의도한 게 아닙니다
intense *sensation, pleasure* kangnyŏrhan 강렬한; *heat, pressure* kangnyŏk'an 강력한; *personality, concentration* kanghan 강한
intensify 1 *v/t effect, pressure* sege hada 세게 하다 **2** *v/i* (*of pain*) kanghaejida 강해지다; (*of fighting*) kyŏngnyŏrhaejida 격렬해지다
intensive *study, training, treatment* chiptchungjŏgin 집중적인
intensity (*of sensation, heat, pain*)

kangdo 강도; (*of fighting*) kyŏngnyŏl 격렬
intensive care (**unit**) chunghwanjashil 중환자실
intensive course (*of language study*) chiptchung k'osŭ 집중 코스
intent: be ~ on doing sth (*determined to do*) muŏsŭl haryŏgo chaktchŏnghada 무엇을 하려고 작정하다; (*concentrating on*) muŏsŭl hanŭnde yŏltchunghada 무엇을 하는데 열중하다
intention ŭido 의도; *I have no ~ of* (*refuse to*) nanŭn ... hal ŭidoga ŏpssŏyo 나는 ... 할 의도가 없어요
intentional ŭidojŏgin 의도적인
intentionally koŭijŏgŭro 고의적으로
interaction sangho chagyong 상호 작용
interactive sangho chagyonghanŭn 상호 작용하는
intercede chungjaehada 중재하다
intercept *ball* karoch'aeda 가로채다; *message* yŏt-tŭt-tta 엿듣다; *missile* yogyŏk'ada 요격하다
interchange *n* (*of highways*) int'ŏch'einji 인터체인지
interchangeable pakkul su innŭn 바꿀 수 있는
intercom int'ŏk'ŏm 인터컴
intercourse (*sexual*) sŏnggyo 성교
interdependent sangho ŭijonhanŭn 상호 의존하는
interest 1 *n* kwanshim 관심; (*financial*) ija 이자; *take an ~ in sth* muŏse hŭngmirŭl kajida 무엇에 흥미를 가지다 **2** *v/t* hŭngmirŭl irŭk'ige hada 흥미를 일으키게 하다; *does that offer ~ you?* kŭ cheŭiga maŭme tŭmnikka? 그 제의가 마음에 듭니까
interested kwanshimi innŭn 관심이 있는; *be ~ in sth* muŏse kwanshimŭl kajida 무엇에 관심을 가지다; *thanks, but I'm not ~* komaptchiman, chŏn kwanshimi ŏmnŭndeyo 고맙지만, 전 관심이 없는데요
interesting chaemiinnŭn 재미있는
interest rate ijayul 이자율
interface 1 *n* chŏpch'ok yŏng-yŏk

접촉 영역, int'ŏpeisŭ 인터페이스 **2** v/i chŏpssok'ada 접속하다

interfere kansŏp'ada 간섭하다

♦**interfere with** controls, plans panghaehada 방해하다

interference kansŏp 간섭; RAD honsŏn 혼선

interior 1 adj shillaeŭi 실내의 **2** n (of house) shillae 실내; (of country) naeryuk 내륙; **Department of the Interior** Naemubu 내무부

interior decorator shillae changshik-kka 실내 장식가; **interior design** int'eriŏ tijain 인테리어 디자인; **interior designer** int'eriŏ tijainŏ 인테리어 디자이너

interlude (at theater, concert) mak-kkan 막간; (period) kigan 기간

intermediary n chungjaeja 중재자

intermediate adj chungganŭi 중간의

intermission (in theater, movie theater) hyuge shigan 휴게 시간

intern v/t kusok'ada 구속하다

internal measurements anŭi 안의; trade kung-naeŭi 국내의; (within organization) naebuŭi 내부의

internal combustion engine naeyŏn kigwan 내연 기관

internally (in body) ch'enaee(sŏ) 체내에(서); (within organization) naebujuguro 내부적으로

Internal Revenue (Service) Kukssech'ŏng 국세청

international adj kuktchejŏgin 국제적인

International Court of Justice Kuktche Sabŏp Chaep'anso 국제 사법 재판소

internationally kuktchejŏguro 국제적으로

International Monetary Fund Kuktche T'onghwa Kigŭm 국제 통화 기금

Internet Int'ŏnet 인터넷; **on the ~** Int'ŏnet sangesŏ 인터넷 상에서

internist naekkwa chŏnmun ŭisa 내과 전문 의사

interpret 1 v/t (linguistically) t'ongyŏk'ada 통역하다; music, comment etc haesŏk'ada 해석하다 **2** v/i t'ongyŏk'ada 통역하다

interpretation (linguistic) t'ongyŏk 통역; (of music, of meaning) haesŏk 해석

interpreter t'ongyŏk-kka 통역가

interrelated facts sŏro kwan-gyega innŭn 서로 관계가 있는

interrogate shimmunhada 심문하다

interrogation shimmun 심문

interrogative n GRAM ŭimunsa 의문사

interrogator shimmunja 심문자

interrupt 1 v/t speaker chungdanshik'ida 중단시키다 **2** v/i chungdanhada 중단하다

interruption chungdan 중단

intersect kyoch'ahada 교차하다

intersection (crossroads) kyoch'a 교차

interstate n chugan kosok toro 주간 고속 도로

interval shigan kan-gyŏk 시간 간격; (in theater, at concert) hyuge shigan 휴게 시간

intervene (of person, police etc) chungjaehada 중재하다

intervention chungjae 중재

interview 1 n (on TV, in paper) int'ŏbyu 인터뷰; (for job) myŏnjŏp 면접 **2** v/t (on TV, for paper) int'ŏbyuhada 인터뷰하다; (for job) myŏnjŏp'ada 면접하다

interviewee (on TV) int'ŏbyu pannŭn saram 인터뷰 받는 사람; (for job) myŏnjŏp pannŭn saram 면접 받는 사람

interviewer (on TV, for paper) int'ŏbyuhanŭn saram 인터뷰하는 사람; (for job) myŏnjŏpkkwan 면접관

intestine ch'angja 창자

intimacy (of friendship) ch'insuk'am 친숙함; (sexual) kip'ŭn sai 깊은 사이

intimate friend ch'insuk'an 친숙한; (sexually) kip'ŭn saiin 깊은 사이인; thoughts kaeintchŏgin 개인적인

intimidate hyŏp-ppak'ada 협박하다

intimidation hyŏp-ppak 협박

into anŭro 안으로; (change, transition) ...(ŭ)ro ...(으)로; **he put it ~ his suitcase** kŭnŭn kŭgŏsŭl otkkabang anŭro nŏŏt-tta 그는 그것을 옷가방

안으로 넣었다; *translate ~ English*
Yŏng-ŏro pŏnyŏk'ada 영어로
번역하다; *be ~ sth* F (*like*) muŏsŭl
choahada 무엇을 좋아하다; (*be
interested in*) muŏse kwanshimi it-tta
무엇에 관심이 있다; *when you're ~
the job* nega chomdŏ kŭ ire
ikssuk'aejil ttae 네가 좀더 그 일에
익숙해질 때

intolerable ch'amŭl su ŏmnŭn 참을
수 없는

intolerant ch'amŭlssŏng ŏmnŭn
참을성 없는

intoxicated sul ch'wihan 술 취한

intransitive chadongsaŭi 자동사의

intravenous chŏngmaeng-naeŭi
정맥내의

intrepid taedamhan 대담한

intricate twiŏlk'in 뒤얽힌

intrigue 1 *n* ŭmmo 음모 **2** *v/t* hŭngmi
kkŭlda 흥미 끌다; *I would be ~d to
know ...* chŏnŭn ...ŭl/rŭl algo
shipssŭmnida 저는 ...을/를 알고
싶습니다

intriguing hogishimŭl chagŭk'anŭn
호기심을 자극하는

introduce sogaehada 소개하다; *new
technique etc* toip'ada 도입하다; *may
I ~ ...?* ...ŭl/rŭl sogaehaedo
toelkkayo? ...을/를 소개해도
될까요?

introduction (*to person, new food,
sport etc*) sogae 소개; (*in book*)
sŏron 서론; (*of new techniques etc*)
toip 도입

introvert *n* naehyangtchŏgin saram
내향적인 사람

intrude ch'imbŏmhada 침범하다

intruder ch'imiptcha 침입자

intrusion ch'imbŏm 침범

intuition chik-kkwan 직관

invade ch'imnyak'ada 침략하다

invalid[1] *adj* muhyoŭi 무효의

invalid[2] *n* MED pyŏngja 병자

invalidate *claim, theory*
muhyohwahada 무효화하다

invaluable *help* kapssŭl hearil su
ŏmnŭn 값을 헤아릴 수 없는

invariably (*always*) hangsang 항상

invasion ch'imnyak 침략

invent palmyŏnghada 발명하다

invention palmyŏng 발명

inventive ch'ang-ŭijŏgin 창의적인

inventor palmyŏngga 발명가

inventory mongnok 목록

inverse *adj order* kŏkkuro toen
거꾸로 된

invert kŏkkuro hada 거꾸로 하다

inverted commas inyong puho 인용
부호

invertebrate *n* much'ŏkch'u tongmul
무척추 동물

invest 1 *v/t* t'ujadoeda 투자되다 **2** *v/i*
t'ujahada 투자하다

investigate chosahada 조사하다

investigation chosa 조사

investigative journalism
toktchajŏgin chosa podo 독자적인
조사 보도

investment t'uja 투자

investor t'ujaja 투자자

invigorating *climate* kiuni nage
hanŭn 기운이 나게 하는

invincible mujŏgŭi 무적의

invisible nune poiji annŭn 눈에
보이지 않는

invitation ch'odae 초대

invite ch'odaehada 초대하다

invoice 1 *n* inboisŭ 인보이스 **2** *v/t
customer* kumaesŏrŭl ponaeda
구매서를 보내다

involuntary muŭishiktchŏgin
무의식적인; (*forced*) kangjejŏgin
강제적인

involve *hard work, expense*
subanhada 수반하다; (*concern*)
kwan-gyehada 관계하다; *what does
it ~?* kŭgŏsŭn muŏsŭl
subanhamnikka? 그것은 무엇을
수반합니까?; *get ~d with sth* muŏse
kwan-gyedoeda 무엇에 관계되다;
(*negative*) muŏse yŏlludoeda 무엇에
연루되다; *get ~d with s.o.* nuguwa
kwan-gyedoeda 누구와 관계되다

involved (*complex*) poktchap'an
복잡한

involvement (*in a project etc*)
kwallyŏn 관련; (*in a crime, accident*)
yŏllu 연루

invulnerable haech'il su ŏmnŭn 해칠
수 없는

inward 1 *adj* antchogŭi 안쪽의 **2** *adv*

antchŏgŭro 안쪽으로

inwardly maŭmsogŭro 마음속으로

iodine yoodŭ 요오드

IOU (= *I owe you*) yaksshik ch'ayong chŭngsŏ 약식 차용 증서

IQ (= *intelligence quotient*) aik'yu 아이큐

Iran Iran 이란

Iranian 1 *adj* Iranŭi 이란의 **2** *n* (*person*) Iranin이란인; (*language*) Iranŏ 이란어

Iraq Irak'ŭ 이라크

Iraqi 1 *adj* Irak'ŭŭi 이라크의 **2** *n* (*person*) Irak'ŭin 이라크인

Ireland Aillaendŭ 아일랜드

iris (*of eye*) hongch'ae 홍채; (*flower*) airisŭ 아이리스

Irish *adj* Aillaendŭŭi 아일랜드의

Irishman Aillaendŭ namja 아일랜드 남자

Irishwoman Aillaendŭ yŏja 아일랜드 여자

iron 1 *n* (*substance*) soe 쇠; (*for clothes*) tarimi 다리미 **2** *v/t shirts etc* tarimjirhada 다림질하다

ironic(al) panŏjŏgin 반어적인

ironing tarimjil 다림질; *do the ~* tarimjirhada 다림질하다

ironing board tarimjilttae 다림질대

ironworks ch'ŏlgongso 철공소

irony airŏni 아이러니; (*in prose style*) p'ungja 풍자

irrational purhamnihan 불합리한

irreconcilable hwahaehal su ŏmnŭn 화해할 수 없는

irrecoverable hoebok'al su ŏmnŭn 회복할 수 없는

irregular *intervals, sizes* pulgyuch'iktchŏgin 불규칙적인; *behavior* panch'igŭi 반칙의

irrelevant kwallyŏni ŏmnŭn 관련이 없는

irreparable koch'il su ŏmnŭn 고칠 수 없는

irreplaceable *object, person* taech'ehal su ŏmnŭn 대체할 수 없는

irrepressible *sense of humor* ŏngnurŭl su ŏmnŭn 억누를 수 없는; *person* mallil su ŏmnŭn 말릴 수 없는

irreproachable namural te ŏmnŭn 나무랄 데 없는

irresistible *offer* sayanghal su ŏmnŭn 사양할 수 없는; *pleasure* ŏktchehal su ŏmnŭn 억제할 수 없는

irrespective: *~ of* ...e kwan-gyeŏpsshi ...에 관계없이

irresponsible much'aegimhan 무책임한

irretrievable torik'il su ŏmnŭn 돌이킬 수 없는

irreverent pulssonhan 불손한

irrevocable ch'wisohal su ŏmnŭn 취소할 수 없는

irrigate kwan-gaehada 관개하다

irrigation kwan-gae 관개

irrigation canal kwan-gaeyong suro 관개용 수로

irritable tchajŭng-ŭl chal naenŭn 짜증을 잘 내는

irritate tchajŭngnage hada 짜증나게 하다

irritating tchajŭngnage hanŭn 짜증나게 하는

irritation ch'ajŭngnanŭn kŏt 짜증나는 것

Islam (*religion*) Isŭllamgyo 이슬람교; (*race*) Isŭllam minjok 이슬람 민족; (*Islamic state*) Isŭllam kuk-kka 이슬람 국가

Islamic Isŭllamŭi 이슬람의

island sŏm 섬

islander sŏmssaram 섬사람

isolate (*from society*) koripshik'ida 고립시키다; (*separate*) pullihada 분리시키다; (*in prison, hospital*) kyŏngnishik'ida 격리시키다; (*identify*) ppobanaeda 뽑아내다

isolated *house* oettan 외딴; *occurrence* ttaro 따로

isolation (*of a region*) korip 고립; *in ~* kyŏngnihayŏ 따로 분리해서

isolation ward kyŏngni pyŏngdong 격리 병동

Israel Isŭrael 이스라엘

Israeli 1 *adj* Isŭraerŭi 이스라엘의 **2** *n* Isŭraerin 이스라엘인

issue 1 *n* (*matter*) chaengtchŏm 쟁점; (*topic*) nontchŏm 논점; (*of magazine*) ho 호 **2** *v/t passport, visa* palgŭp'ada 발급하다; *coins* parhaenghada 발행하다; *supplies* chigŭp'ada 지급하다; *warning* kongp'yohada 공표하다; *the point at ~* nonŭi sahang 논의 사항; *take ~ with s.o. / sth* nugue / muŏse iŭirŭl chegihada 누구에 / 무엇에 이의를 제기하다

IT (= *information technology*) chŏngbo kisul 정보 기술

it ◊ (*as subject*) kŭgŏsun 그것은; (*as object*) kŭgŏsŭl 그것을 ◊ (*not translated*): *what is ~? - ~'s a novel* muŏshiyeyo? - sosŏriyeyo 무엇이예요? – 소설이예요; *~'s on the table* ch'aekssang-wie issŏyo 책상위에 있어요; *~'s me / him* chŏyeyo / kŭyeyo 저예요 / 그예요; *~'s Charlie here* TELEC chŏ, Ch'alliyeyo 저, 찰리예요; *~'s your turn* tangshin ch'aryeyeyo 당신 차례예요; *that's ~!* (*that's right*) majayo! 맞아요!; (*I've finished*) twaessŏyo! 됐어요!

Italian 1 *adj* It'alliaŭi 이탈리아의 **2** *n* (*person*) It'alliain 이탈리아인; (*language*) It'alliaŏ 이탈리아어

italic it'aellikch'eŭi 이탤릭체의

italics: *in ~* it'aellikch'aero 이탤릭체로

Italy It'allia 이탈리아

itch 1 *n* karyŏum 가려움 **2** *v/i* karyŏptta 가렵다

item hangmok 항목

itemize *invoice* myŏngserŭl palk'ida 명세를 밝히다

itinerary yŏjŏng 여정

its kŭgŏsŭi 그것의

itself kŭgŏt chach'e 그것 자체; *by ~* (*alone*) hollo 홀로; (*automatically*) chŏjŏllo 저절로

ivory (*substance*) sang-a 상아

ivy tamjaeng-i 담쟁이

J

jab v/t k'uk tchirŭda 쿡 찌르다
jack MOT chaek 잭; (in cards) chaek 잭
♦**jack up** MOT chaegŭro mirŏ ollida 잭으로 밀어 올리다
jacket chaek'it 재킷; (of book) k'ŏbŏ 커버
jacket potato kuun kamja yori 구운 감자 요리
jack-knife v/i chaengnaip'ŭch'ŏrŏm kuburŏjida 잭나이프처럼 구부러지다
jackpot kŏaegŭi sanggŭm 거액의 상금; *hit the ~* kŏaegŭi sanggŭmŭl t'ada 거액의 상금을 타다
jade n pich'wi 비취
jagged t'omni moyang-ŭi 톱니 모양의
jail kyodoso 교도소
jam¹ chaem 잼
jam² 1 n MOT kyot'ong honjap 교통 혼잡; F (difficulty) kon-gyŏng 곤경; *be in a ~* kon-gyŏng-e ch'ŏhada 곤경에 처하다 2 v/t (ram) ssushyŏ nŏt'a 쑤셔 넣다; broadcast panghaehada 방해하다; *be ~med* (of roads) kkwak ch'ait-tta 꽉 차있다; (of door, window) umjigiji ank'e toeda 움직이지 않게 되다 3 v/i (stick) umjigiji ant'a 움직이지 않다; (squeeze) ttemilgo tŭrŏgada 떼밀고 들어가다
jam-packed ppaekppaek'age kkwak ch'an 빽빽하게 꽉 찬
janitor suwi 수위
January irwŏl 일월
Japan Ilbon 일본
Japanese 1 adj Ilbonŭi 일본의 2 n (person) Ilbon saram 일본 사람; (language) Ilbonŏ 일본어
jar¹ n (container) tanji 단지
jar² v/i (of noise) ppigŏk-kkŏrida 삐걱거리다; *~ on* ...e kŏsŭllida ...에 거슬리다
jargon chŏnmun yong-ŏ 전문 용어
jaundice hwangdal 황달

jaw n t'ŏk 턱
jaywalker mudan hwoengdanhanŭn saram 무단 횡단하는 사람
jazz chaejŭ 재즈
♦**jazz up** F tach'aeropkke hada 다채롭게 하다
jealous chilt'uhanŭn 질투하는; *be ~ of* ...ŭl/rŭl chilt'uhada ...을/를 질투하다
jealousy chilt'u 질투
jeans ch'ŏngbaji 청바지
jeep chip'ŭch'a 지프차
jeer 1 n yayu 야유 2 v/i yayuhada 야유하다; *~ at* ...ŭl/rŭl usŭpkke yŏgida ...을/를 우습게 여기다
Jehovah's Witness Yŏhowaŭi Chŭng-in 여호와의 증인
jelly chaem 잼
jelly bean chelli kwaja 젤리 과자
jellyfish haep'ari 해파리
jeopardize wit'aeropkke hada 위태롭게 하다
jeopardy: *be in ~* wit'aeroptta 위태롭다
jerk¹ n kaptchagi umjigim 갑자기 움직임 2 v/t kaptchagi umjigida 갑자기 움직이다
jerk² n F (fool) mŏngch'ŏng-i 멍청이
jerky movement kaptchagi umjiginŭn 갑자기 움직이는
jest 1 n nongdam 농담; *in ~* nongdamŭro 농담으로 2 v/i nongdamhada 농담하다
Jesus Yesu(nim) 예수(님)
jet n (of water) punch'ul 분출; (nozzle) punch'ulgu 분출구; (airplane) chet'ŭgi 제트기 2 v/i (travel) chet'ŭgiro yŏhaenghada 제트기로 여행하다
jet-black saekkaman 새까만; **jet engine** chet'ŭ enjin 제트 엔진; **jet-lag** shich'aro inhan p'iro 시차로 인한 피로
jettison t'uhahada 투하하다; fig

pŏrida 버리다

jetty pudu 부두

Jew Yut'aein 유태인

jewel posŏk 보석; *fig (person)* pobae 보배

jeweler posŏkssang 보석상

jewelry posŏngnyu 보석류

Jewish *religion* Yut'aegyoŭi 유태교의; *people* Yut'aeinŭi 유태인의

jiffy: *in a* ~ F kot 곧

jigsaw (**puzzle**) chogak kŭrim match'ugi 조각 그림 맞추기

jilt ch'abŏrida 차버리다

jingle 1 *n* (*song*) kwanggoyong ŭmak 광고용 음악 **2** *v/i* (*of keys, coins*) ttallanggŏrida 딸랑거리다

jinx (*person*) chaesuŏmnŭn saram 재수없는 사람; (*bad luck*) ma 마; *there's a* ~ *on this project* i kihoegenŭn maga kkiŏt-tta 이 기획에는 마가 끼었다

jitters: *get the* ~ F anjŏlbujŏl mot'ada 안절부절 못하다

jittery F anjŏlbujŏl mot'anŭn 안절부절 못하는

job (*employment*) chigŏp 직업; (*task*) il 일; *out of a* ~ shiltchik'ayŏ 실직하여; *it's a good* ~ *you* ... nega ... hagil charhaet-tta 네가 ... 하길 잘했다; *you'll have a* ~ (*it'll be difficult*) himdŭl kŏyeyo 힘들 거예요

job description chingmu naeyong sŏlmyŏngsŏ 직무 내용 설명서

job hunt: *be job hunting* chigŏbŭl kuhago it-tta 직업을 구하고 있다

jobless shiltchik'an 실직한

job satisfaction chigŏp manjoktto 직업 만족도

Job's tears tea yulmuch'a 율무차

jockey *n* kisu 기수

jog 1 *n* choging 조깅; *go for a* ~ chogingharŏ kada 조깅하러 가다 **2** *v/i* (*as exercise*) choginghada 조깅하다 **3** *v/t elbow etc* saltchak milch'ida 살짝 밀치다; ~ *one's memory* kiŏgŭl toesallida 기억을 되살리다

jogger (*person*) choginghanŭn saram 조깅하는 사람; (*shoe*) choging shyujŭ 조깅 슈즈

jogging choging 조깅; *go* ~

chogingharŏ kada 조깅하러 가다

jogging suit chogingbok 조깅복

john F (*toilet*) hwajangshil 화장실

join 1 *n* iŭn chari 이은 자리 **2** *v/i* (*of roads, rivers*) hapch'yŏjida 합쳐지다; (*become a member*) kaip'ada 가입하다 **3** *v/t* (*connect*) yŏngyŏrhada 연결하다; *person* hamnyuhada 합류하다; *club* ip'oehada 입회하다; (*go to work for*) ipssahada 입사하다; (*of road*) mannada 만나다

♦ **join in** kach'i hada 같이 하다

joiner mokssu 목수

joint 1 *n* ANAT kwanjŏl 관절; (*in woodwork*) chŏp'ap pubun 접합 부분; (*of meat*) k'ŭn kogit-ttŏng-ŏri 큰 고깃덩어리; F (*place*) kot 곳; (*of cannabis*) marihwana 마리화나 **2** *adj* (*shared*) kongdong-ŭi 공동의

joint account kongdong kujwa 공동 구좌; **joint-stock company** haptcha hoesa 합자 회사; **joint venture** haptchak t'uja 합작 투자

joke 1 *n* (*story*) nongdam 농담; (*practical* ~) chitkkujŭn changnan 짓궂은 장난; *play a* ~ *on* ...ŭl/rŭl nollida ...을/를 놀리다; *it's no* ~ usŭl iri anida 웃을 일이 아니다 **2** *v/i* (*pretend*) ikssalburida 익살부리다; (*have a* ~) nongdamhada 농담하다

joker *pej* utkkinŭn nom 웃기는 놈; (*in cards*) chok'ŏ 조커

joking: ~ *apart* nongdam kŭmanhago 농담 그만하고

jokingly nongdamŭro 농담으로

jolly *adj* yuk'waehan 유쾌한

jolt 1 *n* (*jerk*) tŏlk'ŏk-kkŏrim 덜커거림 **2** *v/t* (*push*) sege ch'ida 세게 치다

jostle *v/t* nanp'ok'age milda 난폭하게 밀다

♦ **jot down** chŏgŏduda 적어두다

journal (*magazine*) chaptchi 잡지; (*diary*) ilgi 일기

journalism (*writing*) ŏllon 언론; (*profession* ŏllon-gye 언론계

journalist kija 기자

journey *n* yŏhaeng 여행

joy kippŭm 기쁨

jubilant hwanhohanŭn 환호하는

jubilation hwanho 환호

judge 1 *n* LAW p'ansa 판사; (*in competition*) shimsa wiwŏn 심사위원 **2** *v/t* p'andanhada 판단하다; (*competition*) shimsahada 심사하다; (*estimate*) taegang miruŏ poda 대강 미루어 보다

judgment LAW chaep'an 재판; (*opinion*) p'andan 판단; (*good sense*) p'andannyŏk 판단력

judicial sabŏbŭi 사법의

judicious punbyŏl innŭn 분별 있는

judo yudo 유도

juggle yosurŭl purida 요술을 부리다; *fig* chaejurŭl purida 재주를 부리다

juggler yosuljaeng-i 요술쟁이

juice chusŭ 쥬스

juicy chŭbi manŭn 즙이 많은; *news, gossip* hŭngmijinjinhan 흥미진진한

July ch'irwŏl 칠월

jumble *n* twibŏmbŏk 뒤범벅
♦**jumble up** twibŏmbŏgŭl mandŭlda 뒤범벅을 만들다

jump 1 *n* ttwiŏ orŭm 뛰어 오름; (*increase*) kŭpsangssŭng 급상승; *give a ~* (*of surprise*) (nollasŏ) p'ŏltchŏk ttwida (놀라서) 펄쩍 뛰다 **2** *v/i* ttwiŏ orŭda 뛰어 오르다; (*in surprise*) p'ŏltchŏk ttwida 펄쩍 뛰다; (*increase*) kŭpsangssŭnghada 급상승하다; *~ to one's feet* pŏlttŏk irŏnada 벌떡 일어나다; *~ to conclusions* kŭp'age kyŏllon chit-tta 급하게 결론 짓다 **3** *v/t fence etc* ttwiŏ nŏmtta 뛰어 넘다; F (*attack*) tŏmbyŏdŭlda 덤벼들다
♦**jump at** *opportunity* k'waehi ŭnghada 쾌히 응하다

jumper SP toyak sŏnsu 도약 선수; (*horse*) chang-aemul kyŏngjuma 장애물 경주마; COMPUT chŏmp'ŏ 점퍼

jumpy shin-gyŏng kwaminŭi 신경 과민의

junction (*of roads*) kyoch'ajŏm 교차점

June yuwŏl 유월

jungle millim 밀림

junior 1 *adj* (*subordinate*) sonaraeŭi 손아래의; (*younger*) ŏrin 어린 **2** *n* (*subordinate*) sonaraet saram 손아랫

사람; *she is ten years my ~* kŭnyŏnŭn naboda yŏl sal ŏrida 그녀는 나보다 열 살 어리다

junk (*garbage*) komul 고물

junk food chŏngk'ŭ p'udŭ 정크 푸드

junkie chungdoktcha 중독자

junk mail ssŭregi up'yŏnmul 쓰레기 우편물

junkyard komul sujipsso 고물 수집소

jurisdiction LAW sabŏpkkwŏn 사법권

juror paeshimwŏn 배심원

jury paeshimwŏndan 배심원단; (*panel*) shimsawiwŏndan 심사위원단

just 1 *adj* law kongjŏnghan 공정한; *war, cause* t'adanghan 타당한 **2** *adv* (*barely*) kyŏu 겨우; (*exactly*) mach'im 마침; (*only*) tanji 단지; *I've ~ seen her* mak kŭnyŏrŭl poassŏyo 막 그녀를 보았어요; *~ about* (*almost*) kŏŭi 거의; *I was ~ about to leave* nanŭn mak ttŏnaryŏdŏn ch'amiŏssŏyo 나는 막 떠나려던 참이었어요; *~ like that* (*abruptly*) kŭnyang kŭrŏk'e 그냥 그렇게; (*exactly like that*) paro kŭrŏk'e 바로 그렇게; *~ now* (*a few moments ago*) panggŭm 방금; (*at the moment*) paro chigŭm 바로 지금; *~ you wait!* nŏ tugo poja! 너 두고 보자!; *~ be quiet!* chom choyonghi hae! 좀 조용히 해!

justice chŏng-ŭi 정의; (*of cause*) t'adang 타당

justifiable chŏngdanghwa hal su innŭn 정당화할 수 있는

justifiably chŏngdanghage 정당하게

justification chŏngdanghwa 정당화

justify chŏngdanghwahada 정당화하다; *text* match'uda 맞추다

justly (*fairly*) chŏngdanghage 정당하게; (*deservedly*) mattanghage 마땅하게
♦**jut out** *v/i* tolch'urhada 돌출하다

juvenile 1 *adj* sonyŏnŭi 소년의; *pej* misuk'an 미숙한 **2** *n fml* sonyŏn 소년

juvenile delinquency sonyŏn pŏmjoe 소년 범죄

juvenile delinquent sonyŏn pŏmjoeja 소년 범죄자

K

k (= *kilobyte*) k'ilobait'ǔ 킬로바이트;
(= *thousand*) ch'ŏn 천
Kanghwa Island Kanghwado 강화도
karaoke karaok'e 가라오케
karaoke room noraebang 노래방
karate k'arat'e 카라테
karate chop k'arat'e ilgyŏk 카라테
일격
KBS (= *Korean Broadcasting
System*) Han-guk Pangsong
Kongsa 한국 방송 공사
keel *n* NAUT yonggol 용골
keen (*intense*) kanghan 강한
keep 1 *n*: **for ~s** F ŏnjekkajina
언제까지나 **2** *v/t* pogwanhada
보관하다; (*not give back*) chagi
kŏsŭro hada 자기 것으로 하다; (*not
lose*) yujihada 유지하다; (*detain*) put-
ttŭrŏ tuda 붙들어 두다; (*store*)
kansuhada 간수하다; *family*
puyanghada 부양하다; *animals*
kirŭda 기르다; **~ *a promise***
yakssogŭl chik'ida 약속을 지키다; **~
... *waiting*** ...ŭl/rŭl kyesok kidarige
hada ...을/를 계속 기다리게 하다; **~
... *to oneself*** ...ŭl/rŭl kyesok
alliji ant'a ...을/를 알리지 않다; **~ X
from Y** Xŭl/rŭl Yege alliji ant'a
X을/를 Y에게 알리지 않다; **~ (*on*)
*trying*** kyesok noryŏk'ada 계속
노력하다; **~ (*on*) *interrupting***
kyesok panghaehada 계속 방해하다
3 *v/i* (*remain*) ... it-tta ... 있다; (*of
food, milk*) ssŏkchi ank'o kyŏndida
썩지 않고 견디다; **~ *calm***
ch'imch'ak'age it-tta 침착하게 있다
♦ **keep away 1** *v/i* mullŏna it-tta
물러나 있다; **~ *from*** ...(ǔ)robut'ŏ
mullŏna it-tta ...(으)로부터 물러나
있다 **2** *v/t* kakkai kaji mot'age hada
가까이 가지 못하게 하다
♦ **keep back** *v/t* (*hold in check*)
maktta 막다; *information* kamch'uda
감추다

♦ **keep down** *v/t voice, noise*
natch'uda 낮추다; *costs, inflation etc*
chinjŏngshik'ida 진정시키다; *food*
padadŭrida 받아들이다
♦ **keep in** (*in hospital*) kyesok
ibwŏnhae itkke hada 계속 입원해
있게 하다; (*in school*) put-ttŭro tuda
붙들어 두다
♦ **keep off 1** *v/t* (*avoid*) p'ihada
피하다; **~ *the grass!*** chandirŭl
paltchi mashiyo! 잔디를 밟지
마시요! **2** *v/i* (*of rain*) oji ant'a 오지
않다
♦ **keep out** *v/i* tǔrogaji ant'a 들어가지
않다; **~!** (*as sign*) tǔrogaji mashiyo!
들어가지 마시요!
♦ **keep out of** *argument, trouble* ...e
kkiŏ tǔrŏgaji ant'a ...에 끼어
들어가지 않다
♦ **keep to** *path, rules* chik'ida 지키다
♦ **keep up 1** *v/i* (*when running etc*)
twijiji ank'o ttaragada 뒤지지 않고
따라가다 **2** *v/t pace, payments*
yujihada 유지하다; *bridge, pants*
chit'aenghada 지탱하다
♦ **keep up with** ...e twittŏrŏjiji ant'a
...에 뒤떨어지지 않다; (*stay in touch
with*) ...wa/kwa kyesok yŏllak'ada
...와/과 계속 연락하다
keeping: in ~ with ...wa/kwa
chohwahayŏ ...와/과 조화하여;
(*with promises*) ...wa/kwa
ilch'ihayŏ ...와/과 일치하여
kennel kaejip 개집
kennels kae sayuktchang 개 사육장
kernel haek 핵
kerosene tǔng-yu 등유
ketchup k'ech'ŏp 케첩
kettle chujŏnja 주전자
key 1 *n* (*to door, drawer*) yŏlsoe 열쇠;
COMPUT, (*on piano*) k'i 키; MUS cho
조 **2** *adj* (*vital*) maeu chungnyohan
매우 중요한 **3** *v/t* COMPUT k'irŭl
ch'ida 키를 치다

♦**key in** *data* imnyŏk'ada 입력하다
keyboard COMPUT, MUS k'ibodŭ
키보드; (*of piano*) kŏnban 건반;
keyboarder COMPUT charyorŭl
imnyŏk'anŭn saram 자료를 입력하는
사람; **keycard** k'adŭro toen yŏlsoe
카드로 된 열쇠

keyed-up kinjangdoen 긴장된
keyhole yŏlsoe kumŏng 열쇠 구멍;
keynote speech kijo yŏnsŏl 기조
연설; **keyring** yŏlsoe kori 열쇠 고리

kick 1 *n* ch'agi 차기; F (*thrill*)
hŭngbun 흥분; **get a ~ out of …**
…i/ga ssŏk chaemiit-tta …이/가 썩
재미있다; (*just*) **for ~s** chaemiro
재미로 **2** *v/t* ch'ada 차다; F *habit*
kkŭnt'a 끊다 **3** *v/i* ch'ada 차다

♦**kick around** *ball* molgo tanida 몰고
다니다; (*treat harshly*) hamburo
taruda 함부로 다루다; F (*discuss*)
yŏrŏmoro kŏmt'ohada 여러모로
검토하다

♦**kick in 1** *v/t* F (*money*) naeda 내다
2 *v/i* (*of boiler etc*) chakttonghada
작동하다

♦**kick off** *v/i* k'ik'op'ŭhada
킥오프하다; F (*start*) shijak'ada
시작하다

♦**kick out** *v/t* tchoch'anaeda
쫓아내다; **~ of the company / army**
hoesaesŏ / kundaeesŏ
tchotkkyŏnada 회사에서 / 군대에서
쫓겨나다

kickback F (*bribe*) chŏngch'i hŏn-
gŭm 정치 헌금

kickoff k'ik'op'ŭ 킥오프
kid F **1** *n* (*child*) ai 아이; **~
brother / sister** namdongsaeng /
yŏdongsaeng 남동생 / 여동생 **2** *v/t*
nollida 놀리다 **3** *v/i* nongdamhada
농담하다; *I was only ~ding* kŭnyang
nongdamiyeyo 그냥 농담이예요

kidder F nongdam chal hanŭn saram
농담 잘 하는 사람

kidnap(p)er napch'ibŏm 납치범; (*of
child*) yugoebŏm 유괴범

kidnap(p)ing napch'i 납치; (*of child*)
yugoe 유괴

kidney ANAT shinjang 신장; (*to eat*)

k'ongp'at 콩팥

kill *v/t also time* chugida 죽이다; *be
~ed in an accident* sagoro chuktta
사고로 죽다; *~ oneself* chasarhada
자살하다

killer sarinja 살인자; (*cause of death*)
sain 사인

killing sarhae 살해; *make a ~* (*lots of
money*) tte tonŭl pŏlda 떼 돈을 벌다

kiln kama 가마
kilo k'illo 킬로
kilobyte k'illobait'ŭ 킬로바이트
kilogram k'illogŭraem 킬로그램
kilometer k'illomit'ŏ 킬로미터
kimchee kimch'i 김치
kimono k'imono 키모노
kind[1] *adj* ch'injŏrhan 친절한
kind[2] *n* chongnyu 종류; *what ~ of …?*
ŏttŏn chongnyuŭi …? 어떤 종류의
…?; *what ~ of dog is that?*
chŏgŏsŭn ŏttŏn chongnyuŭi
kaeimnikka? 저것은 어떤 종류의
개입니까?; *all ~s of people* oman
chongnyuŭi saram 오만 종류의 사람;
nothing of the ~ kyŏlk'o kŭrŏn
kŏshi anida 결코 그런 것이 아니다;
~ of sad / strange F ŏnŭ chŏngdo
sŭlp'ŭda / isanghada 어느 정도
슬프다 / 이상하다

kindergarten yuch'iwŏn 유치원
kind-hearted maŭmsshi koun 마음씨
고운

kindly 1 *adj* ch'injŏrhan 친절한 **2** *adv*
ch'injŏrhage 친절하게; (*please*)
chebal 제발

kindness ch'injŏl 친절
king wang 왕
kingdom wangguk 왕국
king-size(d) F k'ing saijŭ 킹 사이즈
kink (*in hose etc*) kkoim 꼬임
kinky F pyŏnt'aejŏgin 변태적인
kiosk kani maejŏm 간이 매점
kiss 1 *n* k'isŭ 키스 **2** *v/t* k'isŭhada
키스하다 **3** *v/i* k'isŭhada 키스하다

kit (*equipment*) changbi 장비; (*for
assembly*) chorimnyongp'um
조립용품

kitchen puŏk 부엌
kite yŏn 연
kite flying yŏnnalligi 연날리기
kitten saekki koyang-i 새끼 고양이

kitty (*money*) kongdong chŏngnipkkŭm 공동 적립금

klutz F (*clumsy*) tŏllŏng-i 덜렁이

knack yoryŏng 요령

knead *dough* panjuk'ada 반죽하다

knee *n* murŭp 무릎

kneecap *n* sŭlgaegol 슬개골

kneel murŭp kkult'a 무릎 꿇다

knick-knacks chajilgurehan changshin-gu 자질구레한 장신구

knife 1 *n* k'al 칼 **2** *v/t* k'allo tchirŭda 칼로 찌르다

knit 1 *v/t* t'ŏlshillo ttŭda 털실로 뜨다 **2** *v/i* ttŭgaejirhada 뜨개질하다

♦ **knit together** (*of bone*) itta 잇다

knitting (*sth being knitted*) p'yŏnmul 편물; (*activity*) ttŭgaejil 뜨개질

knitwear nit'ŭ weŏ 니트 웨어

knob (*on door*) sonjabi 손잡이

knock 1 *n* (*on door*) mun tudŭrinŭn sori 문 두드리는 소리; (*blow*) t'agyŏk 타격 **2** *v/t* (*hit*) ch'ida 치다; F (*criticize*) kkalboda 깔보다 **3** *v/i* (*on the door*) nok'ŭhada 노크하다; ~ *at the door* munŭl nok'ŭhada 문을 노크하다

♦ **knock around 1** *v/t* (*beat*) magu tudŭlgyŏ p'aeda 마구 두들겨 패다 **2** *v/i* F (*travel*) magu toradanida 마구 돌아다니다

♦ **knock down** (*of car*) ch'iŏ nŏmŏttŭrida 치어 넘어뜨리다; *object, building etc* hŏrŏ nŏmŏttŭrida 헐어 넘어뜨리다; F (*reduce the price of*) …ŭi kapssŭl naerida …의 값을 내리다

♦ **knock out** (*make unconscious*) naga ttŏrŏjige hada 나가 떨어지게 하다; (*of medicine*) chamdŭlge hada 잠들게 하다; *power lines etc* munŏttŭrida 무너뜨리다

♦ **knock over** nŏmŏttŭrida 넘어뜨리다; (*of car*) ch'io nŏmŏttŭrida 치어 넘어뜨리다

knockout *n* SP nogaut'ŭ 녹아우트

knot 1 *n* maedŭp 매듭 **2** *v/t* maeda 매다

knotty *problem* haegyŏri kollanhan 해결이 곤란한

know 1 *v/t* alda 알다; *language* …e chŏngt'onghada …에 정통하다; (*recognize*) araboda 알아보다 **2** *v/i* algo it-tta 알고 있다; *I don't ~* mollayo 몰라요; *yes, I ~* ye, algo issŏyo 예, 알고 있어요 **3** *n: be in the ~* naebu sajŏng-ŭl chal algo it-tta 내부 사정을 잘 알고 있다

knowhow nohau 노하우

knowing alget-ttanŭn shigŭi 알겠다는 식의

knowingly (*wittingly*) algosŏdo 알고서도; *smile etc* anŭn tŭt'an 아는 듯한

know-it-all F anŭn ch'e hanŭn saram 아는 체 하는 사람

knowledge chishik 지식; *to the best of my ~* naega algo itkkironŭn 내가 알고 있기로는; *have a good ~ of* …e chŏngt'onghada …에 정통하다

knowledgeable chishigi innŭn 지식이 있는

knuckle sonkkarak madi 손가락 마디

♦ **knuckle down** chinjihage ch'akssuhada 진지하게 착수하다

♦ **knuckle under** kulbok'ada 굴복하다

KO k'ei ou 케이 오우

Koje Island Kŏjedo 거제도

Korea (*South*) Han-guk 한국; (*North*) Puk'an 북한

Korean 1 *adj* (*South*) Han-gugŭi 한국의; (*North*) Puk'anŭi 북한의 **2** *n* (*South*) Han-guk saram 한국 사람; (*North*) Puk'an saram 북한 사람; (*language*) Han-gugŏ 한국어

Korean Broadcasting System Han-guk Pangsong Kongsa 한국 방송 공사; **Korean chess** changgi 장기; **Korean costume** hanbok 한복; **Korean oboe** p'iri 피리; **Korean script** Han-gŭl 한글; **Korean Strait** Taehanhaehyŏp 대한해협, Namhae 남해; **Korean-style hotel** yŏgwan 여관; **Korean-style mattress** yo 요; **Korean War** Han-guk Chŏnjaeng 한국 전쟁; **Korean wrestling** sshirŭm 씨름

kosher REL Yut'aein yulppŏbe mannŭn 유태인 율법에 맞는; F chŏngdanghan 정당한

kudos yŏng-ye 영예

Kum River Kŭmgang 금강

L

lab shirhŏmshil 실험실
label 1 *n* kkorip'yo 꼬리표 **2** *v/t*
baggage kkorip'yorŭl puch'ida
꼬리표를 붙이다
labor *n* nodong 노동; (*giving birth*)
punman 분만; **be in ~** punman
chung-ida 분만 중이다
laboratory shirhŏmshil 실험실
laboratory technician shirhŏmshil
kisultcha 실험실 기술자
labored *style*, *speech* ŏsaek'an 어색한
laborer nodongja 노동자
laborious himdŭnŭn 힘드는
labor union nodong chohap 노동
조합
labor ward punmanshil 분만실
lace *n* leisŭ 레이스; (*for shoe*) kkŭn 끈
♦ **lace up** *shoes* kkŭnŭl maeda 끈을
매다
lack 1 *n* pujok 부족 **2** *v/t* ...i / ga ŏptta
...이/가 없다; **he ~s confidence**
kŭnŭn chashin-gami ŏptta 그는
자신감이 없다 **3** *v/i:* **be ~ing**
pujok'ada 부족하다
lacquer *n* (*for hair*) heŏsŭp'ŭrei
헤어스프레이
lacquerware ch'ilgi 칠기
lad chŏlmŭn namja 젊은 남자
ladder sadari 사다리
laden chŏktchachan 적재한
ladies' room yŏja hwajangshil 여자
화장실
ladle *n* kuktcha 국자
lady sungnyŏ 숙녀
ladybug mudangbŏlle 무당벌레
lag *v/t pipes* p'iboktchaero ssada
피복재로 싸다
♦ **lag behind** twittŏrjida 뒤떨어지다
lager lagŏ piŏ 라거 비어
lagoon sŏk'o 석호
laidback nŭgŭt'an 느긋한
lake hosu 호수
lamb saekkiyang 새끼양; (*meat*)
yanggogi 양고기

lame *person* chŏllŭmbariŭi
절름발이의; *excuse* ŏsŏlp'ŭn 어설픈
lament 1 *n* pit'an 비탄 **2** *v/t*
sŭlp'ŏhada 슬퍼하다
lamentable sŏgŭlp'ŭn 서글픈
laminated k'ot'inghan 코팅한; ~
glass yalbŭn p'anyuri 얇은 판유리
lamp tŭngppul 등불
lamppost karodŭng kidung 가로등
기둥
lampshade chŏndŭnggat 전등갓
land 1 *n* ttang 땅; (*shore*) yuktchi
육지; (*country*) nara 나라; **by ~**
yungnoro 육로로; **on ~** yuktchie(sŏ)
육지에(서); **work on the ~** (*as
farmer*) nongsa chitkko salda 농사
짓고 살다 **2** *v/t airplane*
ch'angnyukshik'ida 착륙시키다; *job*
ŏt-tta 얻다 **3** *v/i* (*of airplane*)
ch'angnyuk'ada 착륙하다; (*of ball,
sth thrown*) ttorŏjida 떨어지다
landing (*of airplane*) ch'angnyuk
착륙; (*top of staircase*)
ch'ŭnggyech'am 층계참
landing field pihaengjang 비행장;
landing gear ch'angnyuk changch'i
착륙 장치; **landing strip** kasŏl
hwaltchuro 가설 활주로
landlady (*of hostel etc*) yŏjuin 여주인;
landlord (*of hostel etc*) chuin 주인;
landmark yumyŏnghan
kŏnch'ungmul 유명한 건축물; *fig*
hoek-kkijŏgin sakkŏn 획기적인 사건;
land owner chiju 지주; **landscape
1** *n* kyŏngch'i 경치; (*painting*)
p'unggyŏnghwa 풍경화 **2** *adv print*
karo panghyang-ŭro 가로 방향으로;
landslide sansat'ae 산사태; ~ *victory* apssŭng 압승
lane (*in country*) shigolkkil 시골길;
(*alley*) chobŭn kil 좁은 길; (*on
highway*) ch'asŏn 차선
language ŏnŏ 언어
lank *hair* kirŭmgi kkin 기름기 낀

lanky *person* horihorihan 호리호리한
lantern tŭng 등
Lao (*language*) Laosŭŏ 라오스어
Laos Laosŭ 라오스
Laotian 1 *adj* Laosŭŭi 라오스의 **2** *n*
 (*person*) Laosŭin 라오스인
lap[1] *n* (*of racetrack*) han pak'wi 한
 바퀴
lap[2] *n* (*of water*) chanmulkkyŏrŭi sori
 잔물결의 소리
♦ **lap up** *milk* halt'amŏkitta 핥아먹다;
 flattery koji kot-ttaero padadŭrida
 곧이 곧대로 받아들이다
lap[3] *n* (*of person*) murŭp 무릎
lapel chŏbŭn otkkit 접은 옷깃
laptop COMPUT laept'ap 랩탑
larceny chŏlttotchoe 절도죄
large k'ŭn 큰; *at ~* (*criminal, wild
 animal*) t'alch'urhan 탈출한
largely (*mainly*) churo 주로
lark (*bird*) chongdalssae 종달새
larva yuch'ung 유충
laryngitis huduyŏm 후두염
larynx hudu 후두
laser leijyŏ 레이저
laser beam leijyŏ kwangsŏn 레이저
 광선
laser printer leijyŏ p'urint'ŏ 레이저
 프린터
lash[1] *v/t* (*with whip*)
 ch'aetchiktchirhada 채찍질하다
lash[2] *n* (*eyelash*) songnunssŏp 속눈썹
♦ **lash down** (*with rope*) tandanhi
 mukitta 단단히 묶다
last[1] *adj* (*in series*) majimak 마지막;
 (*preceding*) chŏnbŏnŭi 전번의; *~ but
 one* majimagesŏ tu pŏntchae
 마지막에서 두 번째; *~ night*
 ŏjetppam 어젯밤; *~ but not least*
 kkŭch'ijiman chungnyohage
 tŏtppuch'inŭn kŏsŭn 끝이지만
 중요하게 덧붙이는 것은; *at ~*
 mach'imnae 마침내
last[2] *v/i* chisokitoeda 지속되다
lastly majimaguro 마지막으로
latch *n* kŏlsoe 걸쇠
late (*behind time*) nŭjŭn 늦은; (*at
 night*) pam nŭjŭn 밤 늦은; *it's getting ~* nŭjŏjinda 늦어진다; *of ~*
 ch'oegŭne 최근에; *the ~ 19th/20th
 century* shipkku/iship segi mal

십구/이십 세기 말; *sleep ~*
 nŭttcham chada 늦잠자다
lately ch'oegŭne 최근에
later *adv* najung-e 나중에; *see you ~!*
 najung-e poja! 나중에 보자!; *~ on*
 najung-e 나중에
latest *news, developments* ch'oeshinŭi
 최신의; *girlfriend* ch'oegŭnŭi 최근의
lathe *n* sŏnban 선반
lather (*from soap*) kŏp'um 거품
Latin America Nammi 남미
Latin American 1 *adj* Lat'in
 Amerik'aŭi 라틴 아메리카의 **2** *n*
 Lat'in Amerik'ain 라틴 아메리카인
latitude (*geographical*) wido 위도;
 (*freedom to maneuver*) hŏyong
 pŏmwi 허용 범위
latter hujaŭi 후자의
laugh 1 *n* usŭm 웃음; *it was a ~*
 chaemiissŏt-tta 재미있었다 **2** *v/i* ut-
 tta 웃다
♦ **laugh at** (*mock*) …ŭl/rŭl piut-tta
 …을/를 비웃다
laughing stock: *make oneself a ~*
 sŭsŭrorŭl usŭmkkŏriro mandŭlda
 스스로를 웃음거리로 만들다; *be-
 come a ~* usŭmkkŏriga toeda
 웃음거리가 되다
laughter usŭm 웃음
launch 1 *n* (*boat*) chinsusŏn 진수선;
 (*of rocket*) palsa 발사; (*of ship*)
 chinsu 진수; (*of new product*)
 palmae 발매 **2** *v/t rocket* palssahada
 발사하다; *ship* chinsuhada 진수하다;
 product palmaehada 발매하다
launch(ing) ceremony (*for ship*)
 chinsushik 진수식; (*for product*)
 palmae ch'uk'ayŏn 발매 축하연
launch(ing) pad palssadae 발사대
launder set'ak'ada 세탁하다
laundromat selp'ŭ set'aksso
 셀프세탁소
laundry (*place*) set'aksso 세탁소;
 (*clothes*) set'angmul 세탁물; *get
 one's ~ done* set'ak'age hada
 세탁하게 하다
laurel wŏlgyesu 월계수
lavatory hwajangshil 화장실
lavender labendŏ 라벤더
laver (*seaweed*) kim 김
lavish *adj* p'ungbuhan 풍부한

law pŏp 법; (as subject) pŏp'ak 법학;
  against the ~ pulppŏpin 불법인;
  forbidden by ~ pŏburo kŭmjidoen
  법으로 금지된
law court pŏptchŏng 법정
lawful hap-ppŏptchŏgin 합법적인
lawless mubŏbŭi 무법의
lawn chandi 잔디
lawn mower chandi kkangnŭn kigye
  잔디 깎는 기계
lawsuit sosong 소송
lawyer pyŏnhosa 변호사
lax nŭsŭnhan 느슨한
laxative n pyŏnbiyak 변비약
lay v/t (put down) not'a 놓다; eggs
  nat'a 낳다; ∨ (sexually) sŏnggyohada
  성교하다
♦lay into (attack) konggyŏk'ada
  공격하다
♦lay off workers haegohada 해고하다
♦lay on (provide) maryŏnhada
  마련하다
♦lay out objects chinyŏrhada
  진열하다; page leiausŭl hada
  레이아웃을 하다
layer n ch'ŭng 층
layman amach'uŏ 아마추어
layout paech'i 배치
♦laze around pindŭnggŏrida
  빈둥거리다
lazy person keŭrŭn 게으른; day
  harirŏmnŭn 하릴없는
lb (= pound(s)) p'aundŭ 파운드
LCD (= liquid crystal display)
  aektchŏng p'yoshi changch'i 액정
  표시 장치
lead[1] 1 v/t procession, race sŏndue
  sŏda 선두에 서다; company, team
  ikkŭlda 이끌다; (guide, take)
  indohada 인도하다 2 v/i (in race,
  competition) sŏndue sŏda 선두에
  서다; (provide leadership)
  t'ongsorhada 통솔하다; a street
  ~ing off the square kwangjangesŏ
  ppŏdŏnaonŭn kil 광장에서
  뻗어나오는 길; where is this ~ing?
  ŏdiro hŭllŏgago innŭn kŏmnikka?
  어디로 흘러가고 있는 겁니까? 3 n
  (in race) sŏndu 선두; be in the ~
  sŏndue it-tta 선두에 있다; take the
  ~ sŏndue tŭrŏsŏda 선두에 들어서다;

  lose the ~ sŏndueso millyŏnada
  선두에서 밀려나다
♦lead on (go in front) aptchang sŏda
  앞장 서다
♦lead up to ...(ŭ)ro ikkŭlgo kada
  ...(으)로 이끌고 가다
lead[2] n (for dog) kae chul 개 줄
lead[3] n (metal) nap 납
leader chidoja 지도자
leadership (of party etc) t'ongsollyŏk
  통솔력; under his ~ kŭŭi chido ha-e
  그의 지도 하에; ~ skills chidoryŏk
  지도력
leadership contest chidoja sŏn-gŏ
  hoeŭi 지도자 선거 회의
lead-free gas muyŏnŭi 무연의
leading runner sŏnduŭi 선두의;
  company, product chudojŏgin
  주도적인
leading-edge adj company,
  technology ch'ŏmdanŭi 첨단의
leaf ip 잎
♦leaf through taech'ung pomyŏ
  nŏmgida 대충 보며 넘기다
leaflet chŏndan 전단
league yŏnmaeng 연맹
leak 1 n saeŏ naom 새어 나옴; (of
  information) nuch'ul 누출 2 v/i saeda
  새다
♦leak out (of air, gas) saeŏ naoda
  새어 나오다; (of news) nusŏldoeda
  누설되다
leaky pipe, boat saenŭn 새는
lean[1] 1 v/i (be at an angle) kidaeda
  기대다; ~ against sth muŏse
  kidaeda 무엇에 기대다 2 v/t
  kidaedorok hada 기대도록 하다; ~
  sth against sth muŏsŭl muŏse
  kidaeŏ not'a 무엇을 무엇에 기대어
  놓다
lean[2] adj meat salk'ogiŭi 살코기의;
  style, prose kundŏdŏgi ŏmnŭn
  군더더기 없는
leap 1 n toyak 도약; a great ~ forward tae chinbo 대 진보 2 v/i
  hultchŏk ttwida 훌쩍 뛰다
leap year yunnyŏn 윤년
learn paeuda 배우다; ~ how to do
  sth muŏsŭl hanŭn pangbŏbŭl
  paeuda 무엇을 하는 방법을
  배우다

learner paeunŭn saram 배우는 사람
learning n (knowledge) chishik 지식;
(act) hakssŭp 학습
learning curve hakssŭp koksson 학습
곡선; **be on the ~** shin-gisurŭl
sŭpttŭk'aeya handa 신기술을
습득해야 한다
lease 1 n imdae 임대 **2** v/t apartment,
equipment imdaehada 임대하다
♦**lease out** imdaehada 임대하다
leash n (for dog) kae chul 개 줄
least 1 adj (slightest) kajang chagŭn
가장 작은 **2** adv kajang an 가장 안;
~ difficult kajang anŏryŏun 가장
안어려운 **3** n ch'oesoryang 최소량;
**not in the ~ surprised/
disappointed** chogŭmdo
nollaji/shilmanghaji annŭn 조금도
놀라지/실망하지 않은; **at ~** chŏgŏdo
적어도
leather 1 n kajuk 가죽 **2** adj kajugŭi
가죽의
leave 1 n (vacation) hyuga 휴가; **on ~**
hyugarŭl ŏdŏ 휴가를 얻어 **2** v/t city,
place, person ttŏnada 떠나다;
husband, wife pŏrida 버리다; food on
plate namgyŏ tuda 남겨 두다; scar,
memory, message namgida 남기다;
(forget, leave behind) ijŏbŏrigo tŭgo
kada 잊어버리고 두고 가다; **let's ~
things as they are** kŭnyang
kŭdaero tugiro hapsshida 그냥
그대로 두기로 합시다; **how did you
~ things with him?** kŭ saramgwaŭi
irŭn ŏttŏk'e hagiro haessŭmnikka?
그 사람과의 일은 어떻게 하기로
했습니까?; **~ alone** (not touch)
kŭnyang kŭdaero tŭda 그냥 그대로
두다; (not interfere with) kansŏp'aji
ant'a 간섭하지 않다; (not damage)
haerŭl ip'iji ant'a 해를 입히지 않다;
be left namtta 남다; **there is nothing left** namŭn kŏshi ŏpssŭmnida
남은 것이 없습니다 **2** v/i (of person)
ttŏnada 떠나다; (of plane, train, bus)
ch'ulbarhada 출발하다
♦**leave behind** person twie namgida
뒤에 남기다; object tugo kada 두고
가다; (forget) ijŏ pŏrigo tŭgo kada
잊어 버리고 두고 가다
♦**leave on** hat ssŭn ch'aero tuda 쓴

채로 두다; coat ibŭn ch'aero tuda
입은 채로 두다; TV, computer k'yŏn
ch'aero tuda 켠 채로 두다
♦**leave out** word saengnyak'ada
생략하다; (not put away) naenoŭn
ch'ae pŏryŏduda 내놓은 채
bŏryŏduda 버려두다; **leave me out of this**
chŏnŭn i iresŏ cheoeshik'yŏ
chushipsshio 저는 이 일에서
제외시켜 주십시오
leaving party songbyŏrhoe 송별회
lecture 1 n kang-ŭi 강의 **2** v/i (at
university) kang-ŭihada 강의하다
lecture hall kang-ŭishil 강의실
lecturer kangsa 강사
LED (= light-emitting diode)
palgwang taiodŭ 발광 다이오드
ledge t'ŏk 턱
ledger COM wŏnchang 원장
leek puch'u 부추
leer n (sexual) ch'up'a 추파
left 1 adj oentchogŭi 왼쪽의; POL
chwaigŭi 좌의의 **2** n oentchok 왼쪽;
POL chwaik 좌익; **to the ~**
oentchoge(sŏ) 왼쪽에(서); **on the ~**
of sth muŏsŭi oentchoge(sŏ) 무엇의
왼쪽에(서); **to the ~** turn, look
oentchoguro 왼쪽으로 **3** adv turn,
look oentchoguro 왼쪽으로
left-hand bend oenp'yŏnŭro hanŭn
왼편으로 하는; **left-hand drive**
chwach'ŭk haendŭl unjŏn 좌측 핸들
운전; **left-handed** oensonjabi
왼손잡이; **left-overs** (food) namŭn
kŏt 남은 것; **left-wing** POL chwaik
좌익
leg tari 다리; **pull s.o.'s ~** nugurŭl
nollida 누구를 놀리다
legacy yusan 유산
legal (allowed) hap-ppŏptchŏgin
합법적인; (relating to the law)
pŏptchŏgin 법적인
legal adviser pŏptchŏk choŏnja 법적
조언자
legality hap-ppŏp 합법
legalize hap-ppŏp'wahada 합법화하다
legend chŏnsŏl 전설
legendary chŏnsŏljŏgin 전설적인
legible ilkki shwiun 읽기 쉬운
legislate chejŏnghada 제정하다
legislation (laws) pŏmyul 법률;

(*passing of laws*) ip-ppŏp 입법
legislative *powers, assembly* ip-ppŏbŭi 입법의
legislature POL ip-ppŏp-ppu 입법부
legitimate *claim* chŏkppŏbŭi 적법의; *complaint, cause* chŏngdanghan 정당한; *child* chŏkch'urŭi 적출의
leg room: *there's no* ~ tarirŭl p'yŏnhage noŭl su ŏpssŏyo 다리를 편하게 놓을 수 없어요
leisure yŏga 여가; *at your* ~ tangshini p'yŏnhan shigane 당신이 편한 시간에
leisure center lejŏ sent'ŏ 레저 센터
leisurely *pace* nŭgŭt'an 느긋한
leisure time yŏga shigan 여가 시간
lemon lemon 레몬
lemonade lemoneidŭ 레모네이드
lemon juice lemon chusŭ 레몬 주스
lemon tea lemonch'a 레몬차
lend: ~ *s.o. sth* nuguege muŏsŭl pillyŏjuda 누구에게 무엇을 빌려주다
length kiri 길이; *at* ~ *describe, explain* kilge 길게; (*eventually*) mach'imnae 마침내
lengthen nŭllida 늘리다
lengthy *speech, stay* kin 긴
lenient kwandaehan 관대한
lens lenjŭ 렌즈
lens cover lenjŭ ttukkŏng 렌즈 뚜껑
Lent sasunjŏl 사순절
lentil lenjŭ k'ong 렌즈 콩
lentil soup lenjŭ k'ong sŭp'ŭ 렌즈 콩 스프
leopard p'yobŏm 표범
leotard ch'ejobok 체조복
lesbian 1 *n* lejŭbiŏn 레즈비언 **2** *adj* lejŭbiŏnŭi 레즈비언의
less: *eat* / *talk* ~ tŏl mŏkta / marhada 덜 먹다 / 말하다; ~ *interesting* / *serious* tŏl hŭngmiroun / shimgak'an 덜 흥미로운 / 심각한; *it cost* ~ toni tŏl tŭnda 돈이 덜 든다; ~ *than $200* 200tallŏ miman 200달러 미만
lesson suŏp 수업
let *v/t* (*allow*): ~ *s.o. do sth* nuga muŏt'age haejuda 누가 무엇하게 해주다; ~ *me go!* noajwŏ! 놓아줘!; ~ *him come in* kŭrŭl tŭrŏoge haseyo

그를 들어오게 하세요; ~'*s go* / *stay* kaja / mŏmŭlja 가자 / 머물자; ~'*s not argue* ssauji malja 싸우지 말자; ~ *alone* ... kinŭn k'ŏnyŏng ...기는 커녕; *he can't read,* ~ *alone write* kŭnŭn ssŭginŭn k'ŏnyŏng iltchido mot'anda 그는 쓰기는 커녕 읽지도 못한다; ~ *go of sth* (*of rope, handle*) muŏsŭl noa pŏrida 무엇을 놓아 버리다
♦ **let down** *hair* p'urŏ naerida 풀어 내리다; *shades* naerida 내리다; (*disappoint*) shilmangshik'ida 실망시키다; (*make longer*) tanŭl naerida 단을 내리다
♦ **let in** (*to house*) tŭrŏgada 들어가다
♦ **let off** (*not punish*) yongsŏhada 용서하다; (*from car*) naeryŏ chuda 내려 주다; *let a student off homework* hakssaeng-ege suktcherŭl myŏnjehae chuda 학생에게 숙제를 면제해 주다
♦ **let out** (*of room, building*) nagage hada 나가게 하다; *jacket etc* nŭllida 늘리다; *groan, yell* ip ppakkŭro naeda 입 밖으로 내다
♦ **let up** *v/i* (*stop*) mŏt-tta 멎다
lethal ch'imyŏngjŏgin 치명적인
lethargic nogonhan 노곤한
letter (*of alphabet*) kŭltcha 글자; (*in mail*) p'yŏnji 편지
letterhead (*heading*) p'yŏnjiji wiŭi inswae munkku 편지지 위의 인쇄 문구; (*headed paper*) wit pubune inswae munkkuga innŭn p'yŏnjiji 윗부분에 인쇄 문구가 있는 편지지
letter of credit COM shinyongtchang 신용장
letter of guarantee pojŭngsŏ 보증서
lettuce sangch'u 상추
letup: *without a* ~ shwiji ank'o 쉬지 않고
leukemia paek'yŏlppyŏng 백혈병
level 1 *adj field, surface* p'yŏngp'yŏnghan 평평한; (*in competition, scores*) kat'ŭn sujunŭi 같은 수준의; *draw* ~ *with s.o.* nuguwa makssangmak'a-e irŭda 누구와 막상막하에 이르다 **2** *n* (*on scale, in hierarchy*) sujun 수준; (*amount, quantity*) yang 양; *on the*

~ (*on ~ ground*) p'yŏngp'yŏnghan kose(sŏ) 평평한 곳에(서); *be on the* ~ F (*honest*) chŏngjik'ada 정직하다

level-headed punbyŏl innŭn 분별 있는

lever 1 *n* chire 지레 2 *v/t* chirero umjigida 지레로 움직이다; ~ *sth open* muŏsŭl pijibŏ yŏlda 무엇을 비집어 열다

leverage chireŭi chagyong 지레의 작용; (*influence*) seryŏk 세력

levy *v/t taxes* chingsuhada 징수하다

lewd ch'ujap'an 추잡한

liability (*responsibility*) ch'aegim 책임

liability insurance ch'aegim pohŏm 책임 보험

liable (*answerable*) ch'aegimjyŏya hanŭn 책임져야 하는; *be ~ to* (*likely*) …hanŭn kyŏnghyang-i it-tta …하는 경향이 있다

♦ **liaise with** yŏllagŭl ch'wihada 연락을 취하다

liaison (*contacts*) yŏllak 연락

liar kŏjitmaljaeng-i 거짓말쟁이

libel 1 *n* munsŏe ŭihan myŏng-ye hweson 문서에 의한 명예 훼손 2 *v/t* myŏng-ye hwesonhada 명예 훼손하다

liberal *adj* (*broad-minded*) maŭmi nŏlbŭn 마음이 넓은; *portion etc* insaek'aji anŭn 인색하지 않은; POL chayujuŭiŭi 자유주의의

liberate haebangshik'ida 해방시키다

liberated *woman* haebangdoen 해방된

Liberation Day Kwangbokchŏl 광복절

liberty chayu 자유; *at ~* (*prisoner etc*) chayuro 자유로; *be at ~ to do sth* muŏsŭl maŭmdaero hada 마음대로 하다

librarian sasŏ 사서

library tosŏgwan 도서관

Libya Libia 리비아

Libyan 1 *adj* Libiaŭi 리비아의 2 *n* Libiain 리비아인

license 1 *n* (*for car*) myŏnhŏtchŭng 면허증; (*for imports, exports, TV, gun*) hŏgatchŭng 허가증 2 *v/t*: *be ~d* (*of car*) myŏnhŏ pat-tta 면허 받다; (*of gun, equipment*) hŏga pat-tta

허가 받다

license number tŭngnok pŏnho 등록 번호

license plate pŏnhop'an 번호판

lick 1 *n* halkki 핥기 2 *v/t* haltta 핥다; ~ *one's lips* immasŭl tashida 입맛을 다시다

licking: *get a ~* F (*defeat*) chida 지다

lid ttukkŏng 뚜껑

lie [1] 1 *n* (*untruth*) kŏjinmal 거짓말 2 *v/i* kŏjinmarhada 거짓말하다

lie [2] *v/i* (*of person*) nuptta 눕다; (*of object*) it-tta 있다; (*be situated*) wich'ihada 위치하다

♦ **lie down** nuptta 눕다

lieutenant: *first ~* chung-wi 중위; *second ~* sowi 소위

life saengmyŏng 생명; (*living*) saenghwal 생활; (*~ span*) sumyŏng 수명; *all her ~* kŭnyŏ p'yŏngsaeng-e 그녀 평생에; *that's ~!* insaeng-iran kŭrŏn kŏshimnida! 인생이란 그런 것입니다!

life belt kumyŏng tti 구명 띠; **lifeboat** kumyŏngjŏng 구명정; **life expectancy** yesang sumyŏng 예상 수명; **lifeguard** kujowŏn 구조원; **life history** saenghwalsa 생활사; **life insurance** saengmyŏng pohŏm 생명 보험; **life jacket** kumyŏng chokki 구명 조끼

lifeless saengmyŏng ŏmnŭn 생명 없는

lifelike sara innŭn tŭt'an 살아 있는 듯한; **lifelong** p'yŏngsaeng-ŭi 평생의; **life preserver** (*for swimmer*) kumyŏnggu 구명구; **life-saving** *adj equipment* kumyŏng-ŭi 구명의; *medicine, drug* saengmyŏng-ŭl kuhanŭn 생명을 구하는; **lifesized** shilmul k'ŭgiŭi 실물 크기의; **life-threatening** saengmyŏng-ŭl wihyŏp'anŭn 생명을 위협하는; **lifetime** p'yŏngsaeng 평생; *in my ~* nae p'yŏngsaeng-e 내 평생에

lift 1 *v/t* tŭrŏ ollida 들어 올리다 2 *v/i* (*of fog*) kŏch'ida 걷히다 3 *n* (*in car*) t'aeugi 태우기; Br (*elevator*) ellibeit'ŏ 엘리베이터; *give s.o. a ~* nugurŭl t'aewŏ chuda 누구를 태워 주다

♦**lift off** v/i (of rocket) sosa orŭda
솟아 오르다
liftoff (of rocket) iryuk 이륙
ligament indae 인대
light¹ 1 n pit 빛; (lamp) tŭng 등; *in the ~ of* ...e pich'uŏsŏ ...에 비추어서; *have you got a ~?* pul issŭmnikka? 불 있습니까? 2 v/t fire, cigarette pul puch'ida 불 붙이다; (illuminate) chomyŏnghada 조명하다 3 adj (not dark) palgŭn 밝은
light² 1 adj (not heavy) kabyŏun 가벼운 2 adv: *travel ~* chimŭl mani kajiji ank'o yŏhaenghada 짐을 많이 가지지 않고 여행하다
♦**light up** 1 v/t (illuminate) palkke hada 밝게 하다 2 v/i (start to smoke) puri nada 불이 나다
light bulb paegyŏl chŏn-gu 백열 전구
lighten¹ v/t color palkke hada 밝게 하다
lighten² v/t load kabyŏpkke hada 가볍게 하다
♦**lighten up** (of person) kibun p'ulda 기분 풀다
lighter (for cigarettes) lait'ŏ 라이터
light-headed (dizzy) ŏjirŏun 어지러운
light-hearted maŭm kabyŏun 마음 가벼운
lighthouse tŭngdae 등대
lighting chomyŏng 조명
lightly touch kabyŏpkke 가볍게; *get off ~* kabyŏpkke momyŏnhada 가볍게 모면하다
lightness¹ (of room) palgŭm 밝음
lightness² (in weight) kabyŏum 가벼움
lightning pŏn-gae 번개
lightning conductor p'iroech'im 피뢰침
light pen lait'ŭ p'en 라이트 펜
lightweight (in boxing) lait'ŭkkŭp sŏnsu 라이트급 선수
light year kwangnyŏn 광년
likable hogami kanŭn 호감이 가는
like¹ 1 prep kat'ŭn 같은; *be ~ s.o.* nuguwa tamtta 누구와 닮다; *be ~ sth* muŏtkkwa kat-tta 무엇과 같다; *what is she ~?* kŭ yŏjanŭn ŏttŏn saramimnikka? 그 여자는 어떤

사람입니까?; *it's not ~ him* (not his character) kŭ saramdaptchi anssŭmnida 그 사람답지 않습니다; *do it ~ this* irŏk'e haseyo 이렇게 하세요 2 conj F: *~ I said* naega marhaettŭshi 내가 말했듯이
like² v/t choahada 좋아하다; *I ~ her* nanŭn kŭnyŏrŭl choahamnida 나는 그녀를 좋아합니다; *I would ~ ...* nanŭn ...ŭl/rŭl wŏnhamnida 나는 ...을/를 원합니다; *I would ~ a bigger room* nanŭn tŏ k'ŭn pang-ŭl wŏnhaeyo 나는 더 큰 방을 원해요; *I would ~ to ...* nanŭn ...hago shipssŭmida 나는 ...하고 싶습니다; *I would ~ to leave* nanŭn ttŏnago ship'ŏyo 나는 떠나고 싶어요; *would you ~ ...?* ...ŭl wŏnhamnikka? ...을/를 원합니까?; *would you ~ to ...?* ...hago shipssŭmnikka? ...하고 싶습니까?; *~ to do sth* muŏsŭl hago shiptta 무엇을 하고 싶다; *if you ~* tangshini wŏnhamyŏn 당신이 원하면
likeable hogami kanŭn 호감이 가는
likelihood kanŭngssŏng 가능성; *in all ~* shiptchungp'algu 십중팔구
likely (probable) amado 아마도; *not ~!* maldo andoemnida! 말도 안됩니다!
likeness (resemblance) yusa 유사
liking: *to your ~* tangshin maŭme tŭnŭn 당신 마음에 드는; *take a ~ to s.o.* nuguga choajida 누구가 좋아지다
lilac (flower, color) laillak 라일락
lily paek'ap 백합
lily of the valley ŭnbang-ul kkot 은방울 꽃
limb sonbal 손발
lime¹ (fruit, tree) laim 라임
lime² (substance) sŏk'oe 석회
limegreen laim nokssaek 라임 녹색
limelight: *be in the ~* mut saramŭi chumogŭl pat-tta 뭇 사람의 주목을 받다
limit 1 n han-gye 한계; (of s.o.'s land) kyŏnggye 경계; *within ~s* chŏkttanghage 적당하게; *off ~s* ch'urip kŭmji 출입 금지; *that's the ~!* ijen tŏ isang ch'amŭl suga ŏpssŏyo! 이젠 더 이상 참을 수가

없어요! 2 v/t hanjŏnghada 한정하다
limitation han-gye 한계
limited company *Br* yuhan ch'aegim hoesa 유한 책임 회사
limo, limousine limujin 리무진
limp[1] *adj* hǔnǔjŏk-kkŏrinǔn 흐느적거리는
limp[2] *n* chŏlttuk-kkŏrim 절뚝거림; *he has a* ~ kǔnǔn parŭl chŏlttuk-kkŏrinda 그는 발을 절뚝거린다
line[1] *n* (*on paper, road, for telephone*) sŏn 선; (*of people, text, trees*) chul 줄; (*of business*) saŏp 사업; *the* ~ *is busy* t'onghwa chung imnida 통화 중 입니다; *hold the* ~ chamshiman kidariseyo 잠시만 기다리세요; *draw the* ~ *at sth* muŏsŭl handoro chŏnghada 무엇을 한도로 정하다; ~ *of inquiry* chosaŭi panghyang 조사의 방향; ~ *of reasoning* ch'uron 추론; *stand in* ~ churŭl sŏda 줄을 서다; *in* ~ *with* (*conforming with*) ...e sunŭnghayŏ ...에 순응하여
line[2] *v/t* (*with material*) ...(ŭ)ro anŭl taeda ...(으)로 안을 대다
♦**line up** *v/i* chul sŏda 줄 서다
linen (*material, sheets etc*) linen 리넨
liner (*ship*) chŏnggisŏn 정기선
linesman *SP* sŏnshim 선심
linger nama it-tta 남아 있다
lingerie lanjeri 란제리
linguist ŏnŏhaktcha 언어학자; (*good at languages*) ŏhage nŭnghan saram 어학에 능한 사람
linguistic ŏhagŭi 어학의
lining (*of clothes*) ankkam 안감; (*of pipe, brakes*) laining 라이닝
link 1 *n* (*connection*) yŏn-gwan 연관; (*in chain*) kori 고리; (*of friendship*) yudae kwan-gye 유대 관계 **2** *v/t* yŏn-gyŏrhada 연결하다
♦**link up** *v/i* mannada 만나다; TV yŏn-gyŏrhada 연결하다
lion saja 사자
lip ipssul 입술
lipread *v/t & v/i* immoyang-ŭro iltta 입모양으로 읽다
lipstick lipssŭt'ik 립스틱
liqueur lik'yurŭ 리큐르
liquid 1 *n* aekch'e 액체 **2** *adj* aekch'eŭi 액체의

liquidation ch'ŏngsan 청산; *go into* ~ ch'ŏngsanhada 청산하다
liquidity FIN yudong chasan 유동 자산
liquor sul 술
liquorice kamch'o 감초
liquor store churyu p'anmaejŏm 주류 판매점
lisp 1 *n* hyŏ tchalbŭn sori 혀 짧은 소리 **2** *v/i* hyŏ tchalbŭn soriro marhada 혀 짧은 소리로 말하다
list 1 *n* mongnok 목록 **2** *v/t* mongnoge ollida 목록에 올리다
listen tŭt-tta 듣다
♦**listen in** yŏt-ttŭt-tta 엿듣다
♦**listen to** *radio, person* ...ŭl/rŭl tŭt-tta ...을/를 듣다
listener (*to radio*) ch'ŏngch'wija 청취자; *he's a good* ~ kŭnŭn saram marŭl chal tŭrŏjumnida 그는 사람 말을 잘 들어줍니다
listings magazine pangsong p'ŭrogŭraem chaptchi 방송 프로그램 잡지
listless maŭm naek'iji annŭn 마음 내키지 않는
liter lit'ŏ 리터
literal *adj* kŭltcha kŭdaeroŭi 글자 그대로의
literary munhagŭi 문학의
literate: *be* ~ kŭrŭl ilkko ssŭl chul anda 글을 읽고 쓸 줄 안다
literature munhak 문학
litter ssŭregi 쓰레기; (*of young animals*) han pae saekki 한 배 새끼
little 1 *adj* chagŭn 작은; *the* ~ *ones* aidŭl 아이들 **2** *n* chogŭm 조금; *the* ~ *I know* naega kŏŭi morŭnŭn kŏt 내가 거의 모르는 것; *a* ~ chogŭm 조금; *a* ~ *bread/wine* ppang/p'odoju chogŭm 빵/포도주 조금; *a* ~ *is better than nothing* chogŭmirado innŭn kŏshi ŏmnŭn kŏtppoda nat-tta 조금이라도 있는 것이 없는 것보다 낫다 **3** *adv* chogŭm 조금; ~ *by* ~ chogŭmsshik 조금씩; *a* ~ *better/bigger* chogŭm tŏ choŭn/k'ŭn 조금 더 좋은/큰; *a* ~ *before 6* yŏsŏtshi chogŭm chŏne 6시 조금 전에
live[1] *v/i* salda 살다

♦ **live on 1** v/t rice, bread …ŭl/rŭl mŏk-kko salda …을/를 먹고 살다 **2** v/i (continue living) kyesok salda 계속 살다
♦ **live up**: *live it up* sach'issŭrŏpkke salda 사치스럽게 살다
♦ **live up to** …e mannŭn saenghwarŭl hada …에 맞는 생활을 하다
♦ **live with** person …wa/kwa tonggŏhada …와/과 동거하다
live² adj (living) sara innŭn 살아 있는; ELEC chŏn-giga t'onghago innŭn 전기가 통하고 있는; ~ **ammunition** shilt'an 실탄; ~ **broadcast** saengbangsong 생방송
livelihood saenggye 생계
lively hwalgi ch'an 활기 찬
liver ANAT kanjang 간장; (food) kan 간
livestock kach'uk 가축
livid (angry) nobaldaebarhan 노발대발한
living 1 adj sara innŭn 살아 있는 **2** n saenghwal 생활; (means of support) saenggye 생계; *earn one's ~* saenghwalbirŭl pŏlda 생활비를 벌다
living room kŏshil 거실
lizard tomabaem 도마뱀
load 1 n chim 짐; ELEC puha 부하; ~**s of** manŭn 많은 **2** v/t car, truck chimŭl shilt'a 짐을 싣다; camera p'illŭmŭl nŏt'a 필름을 넣다; gun changjŏnhada 장전하다; software lodŭhada 로드하다; ~ **sth onto sth** muŏsŭl muŏse shilt'a 무엇을 무엇에 싣다
loaded F (very rich) toni manŭn 돈이 많은; (drunk) ch'wihan 취한
loaf tŏng-ŏri 덩어리; *a ~ of bread* ppang han tŏng-ŏri 빵 한 덩어리
♦ **loaf around** nolgo chinaeda 놀고 지내다
loafer (shoe) kanp'yŏnhwa 간편화
loan 1 n taebu 대부; *on ~* pillin 빌린 **2** v/t: ~ *s.o. sth* nuguege muŏsŭl pillyŏjuda 누구에게 무엇을 빌려주다
loathe mopsshi shirŏhada 몹시 싫어하다
lobby (in hotel) lobi 로비; (in theater) hyugeshil 휴게실; POL amnyŏk tanch'e 압력 단체

lobster padatkkajae 바닷가재
local 1 adj chibang-ŭi 지방의; *I'm not ~* nanŭn igot sarami aniyeyo 나는 이곳 사람이 아니에요 **2** n (person) chibang saram 지방 사람
local anesthetic kukppu mach'wi 국부 마취; **local call** TELEC shinae t'onghwa 시내 통화; **local government** chibang chach'i 지방 자치
locality changso 장소
locally live, work kakkaie(sŏ) 가까이에(서)
local produce chibang t'ŭkssanmul 지방 특산물
local time hyŏnji shigan 현지 시간
locate new factory etc wich'irŭl chŏnghada 위치를 정하다; (identify position of) wich'i aranaeda 위치를 알아내다; *be ~d* wich'ihada 위치하다
location (siting) wich'i sŏnjŏng 위치 선정; (identifying position of) wich'irŭl aranaem 위치를 알아냄; *on ~ movie* yaoe ch'waryŏngjung 야외 촬영중
lock¹ (of hair) t'arae 타래
lock² 1 n (on door) chamulssoe 자물쇠 **2** v/t door chamgŭda 잠그다; ~ *sth in position* muŏsŭl chejarie kojŏngshik'ida 무엇을 제자리에 고정시키다
♦ **lock away** chamulssoerŭl ch'aewŏ nŏt'a 자물쇠를 채워 넣다
♦ **lock in** person kaduda 가두다
♦ **lock out** (of house) mot tŭrŏoge chamgŭda 못 들어오게 잠그다; *I was locked out of my office* yŏlssoega ŏpssŏsŏ samushire mot tŭrŏgassŏyo 열쇠가 없어서 사무실에 못 들어갔어요
♦ **lock up** (in prison) kamgŭmhada 감금하다
locker lok'ŏ 로커
locksmith chamulssoe chejogong 자물쇠 제조공
locust mettugi 메뚜기
lodge 1 v/t complaint chech'urhada 제출하다 **2** v/i (of bullet, ball) pak'ida 박히다
lodger hasugin 하숙인
loft tarakppang 다락방; (apartment)

könmul maen wich'ŭng-ŭi chugŏ
konggan 건물 맨 윗층의 주거 공간
lofty heights maeu nop'ŭn 매우 높은;
ideals chigohan 지고한
log (wood) t'ongnamu 통나무;
(written record) iltchi 일지
♦**log off** chongnyohada 종료하다
♦**log on** shijak'ada 시작하다
♦**log on to** ...ŭl/rŭl shijak'ada
...을/를 시작하다
logbook iltchi 일지
log cabin t'ongnamu odumaktchip
통나무 오두막집
logic nolli 논리
logical nollijŏgin 논리적인
logistics MIL pyŏngch'am ŏmmu 병참
업무; COM sangsehan kyehoek
상세한 계획
logo logo 로고
loiter pindunggŏrida 빈둥거리다
London Löndŏn 런던
loneliness oeroum 외로움; (of place)
korip 고립
lonely person oeroun 외로운; place
koripttoen 고립된
loner honja itkki choahanŭn saram
혼자 있기 좋아하는 사람
long[1] adj kin 긴; it's a ~ way
mŏroyo 멀어요; for a ~ time
oraettong-an 오랫동안 2 adv orae
오래; don't be ~ kkumulgŏriji mara
꾸물거리지 마라; 5 weeks is too ~
tasŏt chunŭn nŏmu kilda 다섯 주는
너무 길다; will it take ~? orae
köllyŏyo? 오래 걸려요?; that was ~
ago aju orae chŏniyeyo 아주 오래
전이에요; ~ before then hwŏlsshin
kŭ chŏne 훨씬 그 전에; before ~
kot 곧; we can't wait any ~er
urinŭn tŏ isang kidaril su ŏpssŏyo
우리는 더 이상 기다릴 수 없어요;
he no ~er works here kŭnŭn tŏ
isang yŏgi irhaji anayo 그는 더 이상
여기 일하지 않아요; so ~ as
(provided) ...hanŭn han ...하는 한;
so ~! annyŏng! 안녕!
long[2] v/i: ~ for sth muŏsŭl aet'age
parada 무엇을 애타게 바라다; be
~ing to do sth muŏt hanŭn kŏsŭl
aet'age parada 무엇 하는 것을
애타게 바라다

long-distance adj phonecall, race,
flight changgŏriŭi 장거리의
longing n kalmang 갈망
longitude kyŏngdo 경도
long jump nŏlbi ttwigi 넓이 뛰기;
long-range missile wŏn-gŏriŭi
원거리의; forecast changgijŏgin
장기적인; **long-sighted** sŏn-
gyŏnjimyŏng-i innŭn 선견지명이
있는; **long-sleeved** kin somaeŭi 긴
소매의; **long-standing** orae
kyesokttoenŭn 오래 계속되는; **long-
term** adj changgiŭi 장기의; **long
wave** changp'a 장파
loo Br hwajangshil 화장실
look 1 n (appearance) moyang 모양;
(glance) pom 봄; give s.o. / sth a ~
muŏsŭl / nugurŭl hult'ŏboda
무엇을 / 누구를 훑어보다; have a ~
at sth (examine) muŏsŭl
salp'yŏboda 무엇을 살펴보다; can I
have a ~? pwado toelkkayo? 봐도
될까요?; can I have a ~ around?
(in store etc) tullŏbwado toelkkayo?
둘러봐도 될까요?; ~s (beauty)
yongmo 용모 2 v/i poda 보다;
(search) ch'ajaboda 찾아보다; (seem)
poida 보이다; you ~ tired / different
nŏnŭn p'igonhae / talla poinda 너는
피곤해 / 달라보인다
♦**look after** ...ŭl / rŭl posalp'ida
...을 / 를 보살피다
♦**look around** museum, city ...ŭl / rŭl
tullŏboda ...을 / 를 둘러보다
♦**look at** ...ŭl / rŭl poda ...을 / 를
보다; (examine) ...ŭl / rŭl
salp'yŏboda ...을 / 를 살펴보다;
(consider) ...ŭl / rŭl koch'arhada
...을 / 를 고찰하다
♦**look back** twidoraboda 뒤돌아보다
♦**look down on** (despise) ...ŭl / rŭl
natch'uŏ poda ...을 / 를 낮추어 보다
♦**look for** ...ŭl / rŭl ch'at-tta ...을 / 를
찾다
♦**look forward to** ...ŭl / rŭl
kidaehada ...을 / 를 기대하다
♦**look in on** (visit) ...ŭl / rŭl
pangmunhada ...을 / 를 방문하다
♦**look into** (investigate) ...ŭl / rŭl
chosahada ...을 / 를 조사하다
♦**look on 1** v/i (watch)

panggwanhada 방관하다 2 *v/t*: ~
s.o./sth as (*consider*)
nugurŭl/muŏsŭl …(ŭ)ro kanjuhada
누구를/무엇을 …(으)로 간주하다
◆**look onto** *garden, street* …(ŭ)ro
myŏnhada …(으)로 면하다
◆**look out** (*of window etc*)
pakkach'ŭl naedaboda 바깥을
내다보다; (*pay attention*) chuŭihada
주의하다; ~! choshimhae! 조심해!
◆**look out for** …ŭl/rŭl ch'ajaboda
…을/를 찾아보다; (*be on guard
against*) …ŭl/rŭl kyŏnggyehada
…을/를 경계하다
◆**look out of** *window* pakkach'ŭl
naedaboda 바깥을 내다보다
◆**look over** *house, translation*
…ŭl/rŭl taech'ung hult'ŏboda
…을/를 대충 훑어보다
◆**look through** *magazine, notes*
…ŭl/rŭl ch'ŏltchŏhi chosahada
…을/를 철저히 조사하다
◆**look to** (*rely on*) …e ŭijihada …에
의지하다
◆**look up 1** *v/i* (*from paper etc*)
ch'ajaboda 찾아보다; (*improve*)
paltchŏnhada 발전하다; *things are
looking up* iri choajigo it-tta 일이
좋아지고 있다 2 *v/t word, phone
number* ch'ajaboda 찾아보다; (*visit*)
pangmunhada 방문하다
◆**look up to** (*respect*) chon-
gyŏnghada 존경하다
◆**lookout** (*person*) mangbogi 망보기;
be on the ~ for …ŭl/rŭl
kyŏnggyehada …을/를 경계하다
◆**loom up** ŏryŏmp'ushi nat'anada
어렴풋이 나타나다
loony F *n* mich'igwang-i 미치광이
2 *adj* mich'in 미친
loop *n* kori 고리
loophole (*in law etc*) hŏtchŏm 허점
loose *connection, button* nŭsŭnhan
느슨한; *clothes* hŏlgŏun 헐거운;
morals pangjonghan 방종한; *wording*
sanmanhan 산만한; ~ *change*
chandon pusŭrŏgi 잔돈 부스러기; *tie
up the ~ ends* kyŏlmarŭl chit-tta
결말을 짓다
loosely *tied* hŏlgŏpkke 헐겁게;
worded sanmanhage 산만하게

loosen *collar, knot* nŭsŭnhage hada
느슨하게 하다
loot 1 *n* yakt'alp'um 약탈품 2 *v/i*
yakt'arhada 약탈하다
looter yakt'alchca 약탈자
◆**lop off** sak-kkamhada 삭감하다
lop-sided hantchogŭro kiurŏjin
한쪽으로 기울어진
Lord (*God*) Chu 주; ~*'s Prayer* Chu
Kidomun 주 기도문
lorry *Br* t'ŭrŏk 트럭
lose 1 *v/t object* ilt'a 잃다; *match* chida
지다 2 *v/i* SP chida 지다; (*of clock*)
nŭjŏjida 늦어지다; *I'm lost* nanŭn
kirŭl irŏbŏryŏssŏyo 나는 길을
잃어버렸어요; *get lost!*
kkŏjyŏbŏryŏ! 꺼져버려!
◆**lose out** shilp'aehada 실패하다
loser SP p'aeja 패자; (*in life*) shilp'aeja
실패자
loss (*of object*) sonshil 손실; (*of loved
one*) sangshil 상실; (*in business*)
sonhae 손해; *make a ~* sonhaerŭl
iptta 손해를 입다; *be at a ~* ŏtchihal
parŭl morŭda 어찌할 바를 모르다
lost irŭn 잃은
lost-and-found (**office**) punshilmul
sent'ŏ 분실물 센터
lot: *a ~ of, ~s of* manŭn 많은; *a ~, ~s
eat, talk etc* mani 많이; *a ~ bet-
ter/easier* hwŏlsshin toe
choŭn/shiun 훨씬 더 좋은/쉬운
lotion loshyŏn 로션
loud shikkŭrŏun 시끄러운; *color*
yoranhan 요란한
loudspeaker hwakssŏnggi 확성기
lounge launji 라운지
◆**lounge around** pindunggŏrida
빈둥거리다
louse i 이
lousy F (*bad*) hyŏngp'yŏnŏmnŭn
형편없는
lout shigolttŭgi 시골뜨기
lovable sarangsŭrŏun 사랑스러운
love 1 *n* sarang 사랑; (*in tennis*)
mudŭktchŏm 무득점; *be in ~*
saranghago it-tta 사랑하고 있다; *fall
in ~* sarang-e ppajida 사랑에 빠지다;
make ~ sŏng kwan-gyerŭl kajida 성
관계를 가지다; *yes my ~* kŭraeyo
yŏbo 그래요 여보 2 *v/t person*,

country saranghada 사랑하다; *~ to do sth* muŏt hanŭn kŏsŭl koengjanghi choahada 무엇 하는 것을 굉장히 좋아하다

love affair yŏnae sakkŏn 연애 사건; **love life** sŏngsaenghwal 성생활; **love letter** yŏnae p'yŏnji 연애 편지

lovely *face, hair, color, tune* arŭmdaun 아름다운; *person, character* sarangsŭrŏun 사랑스러운; *holiday, weather, meal* mŏtchin 멋진; *we had a ~ time* urinŭn chŏngmal chŭlgŏpkke ponaessŏyo 우리는 정말 즐겁게 보냈어요

love marriage yŏnae kyŏrhon 연애 결혼

lover aein 애인

loving *adj* aejŏng-i innŭn 애정이 있는

low 1 *adj bridge, wall, voice, quality* najŭn 낮은; *price* ssan 싼; *salary* chagŭn 작은; *be feeling ~* ch'imurhage nŭkkida 침울하게 느끼다; *be ~ on gas/tea* kasŭga/ch'aga kŏŭi ta ttŏrŏjida 가스가/차가 거의 다 떨어지다 **2** *n* (*in weather*) chŏgiap 저기압; (*in sales, statistics*) chŏjo 저조

lowbrow *adj movie, writing* sujuni najŭn 수준이 낮은; *person* kyoyang-i ŏmnŭn 교양이 없는; **low-calorie** chŏk'alloriŭi 저칼로리의; **low-cut** *dress* kasŭmi mani p'ain 가슴이 많이 파인

lower *v/t boat, sth to the ground* naerida 내리다; *flag, hemline* natch'uda 낮추다; *pressure, price* ttŏrŏttŭrida 떨어뜨리다

low-fat chŏjibang-ŭi 저지방의; **lowkey** chajehanŭn 자제하는; **lowlands** chŏji 저지; **low-pressure area** chŏgiap chidae 저기압 지대; **low season** pisugi 비수기; **low tide** ssŏlmul 썰물

loyal ch'ungsŏngsŭrŏun 충성스러운

lozenge (*shape*) marŭmmokkol 마름모꼴; (*tablet*) marŭmmokkol chŏngje 마름모꼴 정제

Ltd (= *limited*) yuhanhoesa 유한회사

lubricant *n* yunhwaltche 윤활제

lubricate mikkŭrŏpkke hada

미끄럽게 하다

lubrication mikkŭrŏpkke ham 미끄럽게 함

lucid (*clear*) algi shwiun 알기 쉬운; (*sane*) chejŏngshinŭi 제정신의

luck un 운; *bad ~* purun 불운; *hard ~!* chaesuŏpkkun! 재수없군!; *good ~* haeng-un 행운; *good ~!* haeng-unŭl pimnida! 행운을 빕니다!

◆ **luck out** F uni chot'a 운이 좋다

luckily un chok'e 운 좋게

lucky *person* un choŭn 운 좋은; *day, number* haeng-unŭl kajyŏonŭn 행운을 가져오는; *coincidence* unttaega mannŭn 운때가 맞는; *you were ~* nŏn uni choassŏ 넌 운이 좋았어; *he's ~ to be alive* kŭnŭn un chok'edo sara namat-tta 그는 운 좋게도 살아 남았다; *that's ~!* kŭgŏ un chŏassŏyo! 그거 운 좋았어요!

ludicrous pabosŭrŏun 바보스러운

luggage suhwamul 수화물

lukewarm *water* mijigŭnhan 미지근한; *reception* naengdamhan 냉담한

lull 1 *n* (*in storm, fighting*) chinjŏng 진정; (*in conversation*) chamshi chungdandoem 잠시 중단됨 **2** *v/t: ~ s.o. into a false sense of security* nugurŭl kŏjisŭro anshimshik'ida 누구를 거짓으로 안심시키다

lullaby chajangga 자장가

lumbago yot'ong 요통

lumber *n* (*timber*) chaemok 재목

luminous pich'ŭl naenŭn 빛을 내는

lump (*of sugar*) chogak 조각; (*swelling*) hok 혹

◆ **lump together** ilgwaljŏgŭro ch'wigŭp'ada 일괄적으로 취급하다

lump sum ilsshibul 일시불

lumpy *liquid, sauce* tŏng-ŏri t'usŏng-iŭi 덩어리 투성이의; *mattress* ult'ungbult'unghan 울퉁불퉁한

lunacy mich'in chit 미친 짓

lunar tarŭi 달의

lunar calendar ŭmnyŏk 음력

Lunar New Year Sŏllal 설날

lunatic *n* mich'igwang-i 미치광이

lunch chŏmshim 점심; *have ~* chŏmshimŭl mŏktta 점심을 먹다

lunch box toshirak 도시락; **lunch**

break, lunchtime chŏmshimshigan 점심시간

lung p'ye 폐

lung cancer p'yeam 폐암

♦**lunge at** tchirŭda 찌르다

lurch *v/i* pit'ŭlgŏrida 비틀거리다

lure 1 *n* maeryŏk 매력 **2** *v/t* sogimsuro yuhok'ada 속임수로 유혹하다

lurid *color* yoranhan 요란한; *details* mushimushihan 무시무시한

lurk (*of person*) chambok'ada 잠복하다; (*of doubt*) chamjaehada 잠재하다

luscious *fruit, dessert* talk'omhan 달콤한; *woman, man* kwannŭngjŏgin 관능적인

lust *n* yongmang 욕망

luxurious sach'isŭrŏun 사치스러운

luxury 1 *n* sach'i 사치 **2** *adj* sach'isŭrŏun 사치스러운

lymph gland limp'ŭsaem 림프샘

lynch chipttan p'ok'aeng-ŭl kahada 집단 폭행을 가하다

lynx sŭrasoni 스라소니

lyricist chakssaga 작사가

lyrics kasa 가사

M

MA (= *Master of Arts*) munhak sŏkssa 문학 석사
ma'am (*to married woman*) samonim 사모님; (*to unmarried woman*) agasshi 아가씨
machine 1 *n* kigye 기계 **2** *v/t* (*on sewing machine*) chaebongt'ŭllo paktta 재봉틀로 박다; TECH kigyero saengsanhada 기계로 생산하다
machine gun *n* kigwanch'ong 기관총
machine-readable k'ŏmp'yut'ŏ ch'ŏriga kanŭnghan 컴퓨터 처리가 가능한
machinery (*machines*) kigyeryu 기계류; (*of government, organization*) kigwan 기관
machismo namjadaumŭl kangjoham 남자다움을 강조함
macho namjadaumŭl kangjohan 남자다움을 강조한
mackintosh pangsu oet'u 방수 외투
macro COMPUT maek'ŭro 매크로
mad (*insane*) mich'in 미친; F (*angry*) mich'il tŭshi hwanan 미칠 듯이 화난; **be ~ about** F (*enthusiastic*) ...ŭl/rŭl mich'idŭshi choahada ...을/를 미치듯이 좋아하다; **drive s.o. ~** nugurŭl mich'igehada 누구를 미치게 하다; **go ~** (*become insane*) mich'yŏgada 미쳐가다; (*with enthusiasm*) kippŏsŏ mich'in tŭshi nalttwida 기뻐서 미친 듯이 날뛰다; **like ~** F *run, work* mich'in tŭshi 미친 듯이
madden (*infuriate*) mich'il tŭshi hwanage hada 미칠 듯이 화나게 하다
maddening hwaga nasŏ mich'ige hanŭn 화가 나서 미치게 하는
made-to-measure match'umŭi 맞춤의
madhouse *fig* nanjangp'an 난장판
madly mich'in tŭshi 미친 듯이; **~ in love** sarang-e mich'yŏsŏ 사랑에

미쳐서
madman mich'igwang-i 미치광이
madness kwangkki 광기
Mafia: the ~ Map'ia chojik 마피아 조직
magazine (*printed*) chaptchi 잡지
maggot kudŏgi 구더기
magic 1 *n* masul 마술; (*tricks*) yosul 요술; **like ~** yosulgach'i 요술같이 **2** *adj* masurŭi 마술의
magical masuljŏgin 마술적인; *moment* shinbiroun 신비로운
magician (*performer*) masulssa 마술사
magic spell chumun 주문
magic trick yosul 요술
magnanimous kwandaehan 관대한
magnet chasŏk 자석
magnetic chagiŭi 자기의; *personality* maehoktchŏgin 매혹적인
magnetism chagi 자기; (*of person*) maehok 매혹
magnificence changnyŏham 장려함
magnificent changnyŏhan 장려한; **what a ~ day!** ŏlmana mŏtchin nariyeyo! 얼마나 멋진 날이예요!
magnify hwaktttaehada 확대하다; *difficulties* kwajanghada 과장하다
magnifying glass totppogi 돋보기
magnitude kyumo 규모
mah-jong majak 마작
maid (*servant*) hanyŏ 하녀; (*in hotel*) hot'el chong-ŏbwŏn 호텔 종업원
maiden name kyŏrhon chŏnŭi sŏng 결혼 전의 성
maiden voyage ch'ŏnyŏ hanghae 처녀 항해
mail 1 *n* up'yŏn 우편; **put sth in the ~** muŏsŭl up'yŏnŭro ponaeda 무엇을 우편으로 보내다 **2** *v/t letter* p'yŏnjihada 편지하다
mailbox (*in street*) uch'et'ong 우체통; (*of house*) up'yŏnham 우편함; COMPUT meilbakssŭ 메일박스

mailing list chusorok 주소록

mailman uch'ebu 우체부; **mail-order catalog** t'ongshin p'anmae ch'aektcha 통신 판매 책자; **mail-order firm** t'ongshin p'anmae hoesa 통신 판매 회사

maim pulguro mandŭlda 불구로 만들다

main adj chudoen 주된

mainboard COMPUT meinbodŭ 메인보드; **mainframe** n k'ŏmp'yut'ŏ ponch'e 컴퓨터 본체; **mainland** pont'o 본토; **on the ~** pont'oesŏ 본토에서; **mainland China** Chungguk pont'o 중국 본토

mainly churo 주로

main road chudoro 주도로

main street chungshimga 중심가

maintain law and order, speed, machine, house yujihada 유지하다; relationship chisok'ada 지속하다; old building pojonhada 보존하다; family puyanghada 부양하다; innocence, guilt chujanghada 주장하다; **~ that ...** ...ranŭn kosŭl chujanghada ...라는 것을 주장하다

maintenance (of machine, house, law and order) yuji 유지; (of old building) pojon 보존; (money) puyangbi 부양비

Maitreya Buddha Mirŭkppul 미륵불

majestic ungdaehan 웅대한

major 1 adj (significant) chuyohan 주요한; **in ~** MUS ta changjo 다 장조 **2** n MIL soryŏng 소령

◆**major in ...** ŭl/rŭl chŏn-gonghada ...을/를 전공하다

majority taedasu 대다수; POL kwabansu 과반수; **be in the ~** kwabansuida 과반수이다

make 1 n (brand) sangp'yo 상표 **2** v/t mandŭlda 만들다; (earn) pŏlda 벌다; MATH ida 이다; **two and two ~ four** i tŏhagi inŭn saida 이 더하기 이는 사이다; **~ a decision** kyŏltchŏng-ŭl hada 결정을 하다; **~ a telephone call** chŏnhwarŭl hada 전화를 하다; **made in Korea** Han-guksan 한국산; **~ it** (catch bus, train) che shigane t'ada 제 시간에 타다; (come) oda 오다; (succeed)

sŏnggonghada 성공하다; (survive) saranada 살아나다; **I just made it to the station** kyŏu che shigane yŏge toch'akaessŏyo 겨우 제 시간에 역에 도착했어요; **what time do you ~ it?** tangshin shigyenŭn myŏt shiimnikka? 당신 시계는 몇 시입니까?; **~ believe** ...inch'ehada ...인체 하다; **~ do with** ...(ŭ)ro manjok'ada ...(으)로 만족하다; **what do you ~ of it?** tangshinŭi saenggagŭn ŏttŏsŭmnikka? 당신의 생각은 어떻습니까? ◊: **~ s.o. do sth** (force to) nuguege muŏsŭl shik'ida 누구에게 무엇을 시키다; (cause to) nugurŭl muŏt'age hada 누구를 무엇하게 하다; **you can't ~ me do it!** tangshini nahant'e kŭgŏsŭl shik'il su ŏpssŏyo! 당신이 나한테 그것을 시킬 수 없어요! ◊: **~ s.o. happy/angry** nugurŭl haengbok'age/hwanage hada 누구를 행복하게/화나게 하다

◆**make for** (go toward) ...ro kada ...로 가다

◆**make off** taranada 달아나다

◆**make off with** (steal) humch'ida 훔치다

◆**make out** v/t list chakssŏnghada 작성하다; check ssŭda 쓰다; (see) poda 보다; (imply) nŏnjishi pich'uda 넌지시 비추다

◆**make over**: **make X over to Y** Xrŭl Yege mullyŏjuda X를 Y에게 물려주다

◆**make up 1** v/i (of woman, actor) hwajanghada 화장하다; (after quarrel) hwahaehada 화해하다 **2** v/t story, excuse kkumida 꾸미다; face hwajanghada 화장하다; (constitute) kusŏnghada 구성하다; **be made up of** ...(ŭ)ro kusŏngdoeŏ itta ...(으)로 구성되어 있다; **~ one's mind** maŭmŭl chŏnghada 마음을 정하다; **make it up** (after quarrel) hwahaehada 화해하다

◆**make up for** (compensate for) pŏlch'unghada 벌충하다

make-believe n kkumin kŏt 꾸민 것

maker saengsanja 생산자

makeshift imshi sudan 임시 수단

make-up (*cosmetics*) hwajangp'um 화장품

maladjusted chŏgŭng-ŭl mot'anŭn 적응을 못하는

Malay (*language*) Malleiŏ 말레이어; (*person*) Malleishia saram 말레이시아 사람

Malaysia Malleishia 말레이시아

Malaysian Malleishiain 말레이시아인

male 1 *adj* (*masculine*) namsŏng-ŭi 남성의; *animal, bird, fish* suk'ŏsŭi 수컷의 2 *n* (*man*) namja 남자; (*animal, bird, fish*) suk'ŏt 수컷

male chauvinist (*pig*) namsŏng uwŏltchuŭija 남성 우월주의자

male nurse namja kanhosa 남자 간호사

malevolent agŭi innŭn 악의 있는

malfunction 1 *n* chakttong pullyang 작동 불량 2 *v/i* chakttong-i chal toeji ant'a 작동이 잘 되지 않다

malice agŭi 악의

malicious agŭi innŭn 악의 있는

malignant *tumor* akssŏng-ŭi 악성의

mall (*shopping ~*) sangga 상가

malnutrition yŏngnyang shiltcho 영양 실조

malpractice kwashil 과실

maltreat hakttaehada 학대하다

maltreatment hakttae 학대

mammal p'oyu tongmul 포유 동물

mammoth *adj* (*enormous*) kŏdaehan 거대한

man *n* namja 남자; (*human being*) saram 사람; (*humanity*) illyu 인류; (*in chess, checkers*) mal 말

manage 1 *v/t business* kwallihada 관리하다; *big company* kyŏngnyŏnghada 경영하다; *money* kkuryŏgada 꾸려가다; *bags* taruda 다루다; **~ to ...** irŏktchŏrŏk ... haenaeda 이럭저럭 ... 해내다 2 *v/i* (*cope*) kyŏndida 견디다; (*financially*) kkuryŏnagada 꾸려나가다; **can you ~?** tangshini hal su issŭmnikka? 당신이 할 수 있습니까?

manageable tarugi shwiun 다루기 쉬운

management kwalli 관리; (*of big company*) kyŏngnyŏng 경영; (*managers*) kyŏngnyŏngjin 경영진; **under his ~** kuŭi kwalliha-e 그의 관리하에; (*of big company*) kuŭi kyŏngnyŏngha-e 그의 경영하에

management buyout kyŏngnyŏngkkwŏn maemae 경영권 매매; **management consultant** kyŏngnyŏng sangdamja 경영 상담자; **management studies** kyŏngnyŏnghak 경영학; **management team** kyŏngnyŏngt'im 경영팀

manager (*of department*) kwalliin 관리인; (*of factory, of people*) kwallija 관리자; (*of company*) kyŏngnyŏngja 경영자; (*executive*) kyŏngnyŏng-in 경영인; (*of shop, restaurant, hotel*) chibaein 지배인

managerial kwalliŭi 관리의

managing director pujang 부장

Mandarin (*language*) Chungguk Pukkyŏng-ŏ 중국 북경어

mandarin (*in China*) kwalli 관리

mandarin orange kyul 귤

mandate (*authority*) kwŏnhan puyŏ 권한 부여; (*task*) immu 임무

mandatory ŭimujŏgin 의무적인

mane (*of horse*) kalgi 갈기

maneuver 1 *n* umjigim 움직임; *fig* ch'aengnyak 책략 2 *v/t* kyomyohi umjigida 교묘히 움직이다

mangle *v/t* (*crush*) tchiburŏttŭrida 찌부러뜨리다

manhandle *person* kŏch'ilge taehada 거칠게 대하다; *object* illyŏgŭro umjigida 인력으로 움직이다

manhood (*maturity*) sŏngnyŏn 성년; (*virility*) namjadaum 남자다움

man-hour irindang han shiganŭi nodongnyang 일인당 한 시간의 노동량

manhunt pŏmin susaek 범인 수색

mania (*craze*): **~ for ...** ...kwang ...광

maniac mich'in saram 미친 사람

manicure *n* maenik'yuŏ 매니큐어

manifest 1 *adj* myŏngbaek'an 명백한 2 *v/t* myŏngbaek'age hada 명백하게 하다; **~ itself** nat'anada 나타나다

manipulate *person* chojonghada 조종하다; *bones* kyojŏnghada 교정하다

manipulation (*of person*) chojong

조종; (of bones) kyojŏng 교정
manipulative chojonghanŭn 조종하는
mankind illyu 인류
manly namjadaun 남자다운
man-made in-gong 인공
mannequin (for clothes) manek'ing 마네킹
manner (of doing sth) pangshik 방식; (attitude) t'aedo 태도
manners: *good / bad* ~ yeŭi parŭm / ŏpssŭm 예의 바름 / 없음; *have no* ~ yeŭiga ŏpta 예의가 없다
manpower illyŏk 인력
mansion chŏt'aek 저택
mantelpiece pyŏngnallo wiŭi sŏnban 벽난로 위의 선반
manual 1 adj sonŭro hanŭn 손으로 하는; ~ *labor* sonil 손일; *a ~ worker* yukch'e nodongja 육체 노동자 **2** n sŏlmyŏngsŏ 설명서
manufacture 1 n chejoŏp 제조업 **2** v/t equipment chejohada 제조하다
manufacturer chejoŏptcha 제조업자
manufacturing (industry) kong-ŏp 공업
manure piryo 비료
manuscript wŏn-go 원고; *original ~* wŏnbon 원본
many 1 adj manŭn 많은; ~ *times* yŏrŏ pŏn 여러 번; *not ~ people / taxis* kŭri manch'i anŭn saram / t'aeksshi 그리 많지 않은 사람 / 택시; *too ~ problems / beers* nŏmu manŭn munjedŭl / maektchu 너무 많은 문제들 / 맥주 **2** pron manŭn kŏt 많은 것; (people) manŭn saram 많은 사람; *a great ~*, *a good ~* taedanhi manŭn 대단히 많은; *how ~ do you need?* ŏlmana mani p'iryohashimnikka? 얼마나 많이 필요하십니까?
map n chido 지도
◆**map out** career etc sangsehi kyehoek'ada 상세히 계획하다
maple tanp'ungnamu 단풍나무
mar mangch'yŏnot'a 망쳐놓다
marathon (race) marat'on 마라톤
marble (material) taerisŏk 대리석
March samwŏl 삼월; *1st ~ Memorial Day* Samiltchŏl 삼일절; ~ *First Movement* Samil Undong 삼일 운동

march 1 n haengjin 행진; (demonstration) temo haengjin 데모 행진 **2** v/i haengjinhada 행진하다; (in protest) temo haengjinhada 데모 행진하다
Mardi Gras Osunjŏrŭi Hwayoil 오순절의 화요일
mare ammal 암말
margarine magarin 마가린
margin (of page) yŏbaek 여백; (profit ~) imun 이문; *by a narrow ~* kyŏu 겨우
marginal (slight) chŏgŭn 적은
marginally (slightly) chogŭm 조금
marihuana, **marijuana** taemach'o 대마초
marina yot'ŭ kyeryujang 요트 계류장
marinade n maerineidŭ 매리네이드
marinate chŏrida 절이다
marine 1 adj padaŭi 바다의 **2** n MIL haegun 해군
Marine Corps Haebyŏngdae 해병대
marital kyŏrhonŭi 결혼의
maritime haeyangŭi 해양의
mark 1 n (stain) ŏlluk 얼룩; (sign, token) p'yoshi 표시; (trace) chach'wi 자취; EDU sŏngjŏk 성적; *leave one's ~* yŏnghyang-ŭl namgida 영향을 남기다 **2** v/t (stain) chagugŭl naeda 자국을 내다; EDU sŏngjŏgŭl ŏt-tta 성적을 얻다; (indicate) p'yoshihada 표시하다; (commemorate) kinyŏmhada 기념하다 **3** v/i (of fabric) chagugnada 자국나다
◆**mark down** price kagyŏgŭl naerida 가격을 내리다
◆**mark out** (with a line etc) sŏnŭl kŭt-tta 선을 긋다; fig (set apart) karŭda 가르다
◆**mark up** price kagyŏgŭl ollida 가격을 올리다; goods p'yoshihada 표시하다
marked (definite) hwaksshirhan 확실한
marker (highlighter) hyŏnggwangp'en 형광펜
market 1 n shijang 시장; (stock ~) chushik shijang 주식 시장; *on the ~* shijang-e 시장에 **2** v/t p'anmaehada 판매하다

market economy shijang kyŏngje
시장 경제

market forces shijangnyŏk 시장력

marketing maemae 매매

market leader shijang-ŭi sŏndujuja
시장의 선두주자; **marketplace** (*in
town*) shijang 시장; (*for
commodities*) maemae changso 매매
장소; **market research** shijang
chosa 시장 조사; **market share**
shijang chŏmnyuyul 시장 점유율

mark-up kagyŏk insang 가격 인상

marmalade mamalleidŭ 마말레이드

marquee taehyŏng ch'ŏnmak 대형
천막

marriage (*institution*) kyŏrhon 결혼;
(*state of being married*) kyŏrhon
saenghwal 결혼 생활; (*event*)
kyŏrhonshik 결혼식

marriage certificate kyŏrhon
chŭngmyŏngsŏ 결혼 증명서

marriage counselor kyŏrhon
sangdamwŏn 결혼 상담원

married kihonŭi 기혼의, kyŏrhonhan
결혼한; *a ~ man* kihon namsŏng
기혼 남성, yubunam 유부남; *be ~ to
...* ...wa/kwa kyŏrhonhada ...와/과
결혼하다

marry kyŏrhonhada 결혼하다;
(*perform ceremony*) churyehada
주례하다; *get married* kyŏrhonhada
결혼하다

marsh sŭptchi 습지

marshal n (*police officer*)
kyŏngch'algwan 경찰관; (*official*)
haengsa wiwŏn 행사 위원

marshmallow mashimaello 마시맬로

marshy sŭptchiŭi 습지의

martial arts musul 무술

martial law kyeŏmnyŏng 계엄령

martyr n sun-gyoja 순교자; *fig*
hŭisaengja 희생자

marvel n nollaŭn kŏt 놀라운 것;
you're a ~ tangshinŭn
taedanhagunyo 당신은 대단하군요
♦ **marvel at** ...e nollada ...에 놀라다

marvelous koengjanghi chohŭn 굉장히
좋은

Marxism Marŭk'ŭsŭjuŭi
마르크스주의

Marxist 1 *adj* Marŭk'ŭsŭjuŭiŭi

마르크스주의의 **2** n Marŭk'ŭsŭjuŭija
마르크스주의자

mascara masŭk'ara 마스카라

mascot haeng-unŭl kajyŏonŭn kŏt
행운을 가져오는 것, masŭk'ot'ŭ
마스코트

masculine *also* GRAM namsŏngjŏgin
남성적인

masculinity namsŏngmi 남성미

mash v/t ŭkkaeda 으깨다

mashed potatoes ŭkkaen kamja
으깬 감자, maeshit'ŭ p'ot'eit'o
매시트 포테이토

mask 1 n kamyŏn 가면 **2** v/t *feelings*
kamch'uda 감추다

mask dance t'alch'um 탈춤

masochism maejŏk'ijŭm 매저키즘

masochist maejŏk'isŭt'ŭ 매저키스트

mason sŏkssu 석수

masonry tol segong 돌 세공

masquerade 1 n *fig* kajang 가장 **2** v/i:
~ as ...in ch'ŏk'ada ...인 척하다

mass¹ 1 n (*great amount*) taryang
다량; (*body*) k'ŭn tŏng-ŏri 큰 덩어리;
a solid ~ koch'e 고체; *the ~es*
taejung 대중; *~es of* aju manŭn 아주
많은 **2** v/i moida 모이다

mass² REL misa 미사

massacre 1 n taeryang hakssal 대량
학살; F (*in sport*) ch'amp'ae 참패
2 v/t hakssarhada 학살하다; F (*in
sport*) ch'ampaeshik'ida 참패시키다

massage 1 n anma 안마, masaji
마사지 **2** v/t anmahada 안마하다;
figures ŏlbŏmurida 얼버무리다

massage parlor euph maech'un-gul
매춘굴

masseur (namja) anmasa (남자)
안마사

masseuse (yŏya) anmasa (여자)
안마사

massive kŏdaehan 거대한

mass media taejung maech'e 대중
매체; **mass-produce** taeryang
saengsanhada 대량 생산하다; **mass-
production** taeryang saengsan 대량
생산

mast (*of ship*) tot-ttae 돛대; (*for
radio*) taehyŏng ant'ena 대형 안테나

master 1 n (*of dog*) chuin 주인; (*of
ship*) sŏnjang 선장; *be a ~ of* ...e

chŏngt'onghada ..에 정통하다 2 *v/t*
skill, language chŏngt'onghada
정통하다; *situation* t'ongjehada
통제하다

master bedroom anppang 안방
master key masŭt'ŏk'i 마스터키
masterly hullyunghan 훌륭한
mastermind 1 *n* ch'idoja 지도자 2 *v/t*
twiesŏ chidohada 뒤에서 지도하다;
Master of Arts munhak sŏkssa 문학
석사; **master of ceremonies**
sahoeja 사회자; **masterpiece**
myŏngjak 명작; **master's (degree)**
sŏkssa(hagwi) 석사(학위)

mastery chŏngbok 정복
masturbate chawihada 자위하다
mat *n* (*for floor*) chari 자리, maet'ŭ
매트; (*for table*) t'eibŭl po 테이블 보
match¹ (*for cigarette*) sŏngnyang 성냥
match² 1 *n* (*competition*) shihap 시합;
be no ~ for s.o. nuguŭi sandaega
andoeda 누구의 상대가 안되다;
meet one's ~ hojŏkssurŭl mannada
호적수를 만나다 2 *v/t* (*go with*)
ŏullida 어울리다; (*equal*) …e
p'iltchŏk'ada …에 필적하다 3 *v/i* (*of
colors, patterns*) ŏullida 어울리다
matchbox sŏngnyangkkap 성냥갑
matching *adj* ŏullinŭn 어울리는
mate *n* (*of animal*) tchak 짝; NAUT
hanghaesa 항해사 2 *v/i* tchaktchit-tta
짝짓다
material 1 *n* (*fabric*) otkkam 옷감;
(*substance*) chaeryo 재료 2 *adj*
multchirŭi 물질의; (*not spiritual*)
sesoktchŏgin 세속적인
materialism yumullon 유물론
materialist yumullonja 유물론자
materialistic yumullonjŏgin
유물론적인
materialize shilch'ehwahada
실체화하다
materials charyo 자료
maternal ŏmŏniŭi 어머니의; *relative*
mogyeŭi 모계의; ~ *grandfather*
oeharabŏji 외할아버지
maternity mosŏng 모성
maternity dress imsanbok 임산복;
maternity hospital sanbuinkkwa
산부인과; **maternity leave** ch'ulsan
hyuga 출산 휴가; **maternity ward**

sanbuinkkwa pyŏngdong 산부인과
병동
math suhak 수학
mathematical *calculations, formula*
suhagŭi 수학의; *mind, person* suhage
nŭnghan 수학에 능한
mathematician suhaktcha 수학자
mathematics suhak 수학
matinée (*of play*) chugan kongnyŏn
주간 공연; (*of movie*) chugan
sangnyŏng 주간 상영
matriarch yŏgajang 여가장
matrimony kyŏrhon 결혼
matt kwangt'aegi ŏmnŭn 광택이 없는
matter (*affair*) sakkŏn 사건; PHYS
multchil 물질; *as a ~ of course*
tangnyŏnhi 당연히; *as a ~ of fact*
sashirŭn 사실은; *what's the ~?*
musŭn iri issŭmnikka? 무슨 일이
있습니까?; *no - what she says*
kunyŏga muŏshirago marhadŭn
kane 그녀가 무엇이라고 말하든 간에
2 *v/i* chungnyohada 중요하다; *it
doesn't* ~ kŭgŏsŭn sanggwanŏptta
그것은 상관없다
matter-of-fact tamdamhan 담담한
mattress maet'ŭrisŭ 매트리스
mature 1 *adj* sŏngsuk'an 성숙한 2 *v/i*
(*of person*) sŏngsuk'ada 성숙하다;
(*of insurance policy etc*) man-giga
toeda 만기가 되다
maturity (*adulthood*) sŏngsuk-kki
성숙기; (*in behavior, attitude*)
sŏngsuk'am 성숙함
maximize ch'oedaehwahada
최대화하다
maximum 1 *adj* ch'oedaeŭi 최대의
2 *n* ch'oedae 최대
May owŏl 오월
may ◊ (*possibility*) …iltchido
morŭnda …일지도 모른다; *it ~ rain*
piga oltchido morŭnda 비가 올지도
모른다; *you ~ be right* nega majŭl
chido morŭnda 네가 맞을 지도
모른다; *it ~ not happen* irŏnaji
annŭl jido morŭnda 일어나지 않을
지도 모른다 ◊ (*permission*) …haedo
chot'a …해도 좋다; *you ~ go now*
inje kado chossŭmnida 인제 가도
좋습니다; ~ *I help?* towa
tŭrilkkayo? 도와 드릴까요?; ~ *I*

smoke? tambae p'iwodo toegessŭmnikka? 담배 피워도 되겠습니까?; **you ~ if you like** wŏnhashindamyŏn, hasyŏdo kwanch'ansŭmnida 원하신다면, 하셔도 괜찮습니다 ◊ (*wish, hope*) ...hagirŭl parada ...하기를 바라다; **~ you both be very happy** tubuni hamkke hangsang haengbok'ashigirŭl paramnida 두분이 함께 항상 행복하시기를 바랍니다

maybe amado 아마도

May Day Nodongjŏl 노동절

mayo, mayonnaise mayonejŭ 마요네즈

mayor shijang 시장

maze miro 미로

MB (= *megabyte*) megabait'ŭ 메가바이트

MBA (= *Master's in Business Administration*) kyŏngnyŏnghak sŏkssa 경영학 석사

MBO (= *management buyout*) kyŏngnyŏngkkwŏn maemae 경영권 매매

MD (= *Doctor of Medicine*) ŭihak paksssa 의학 박사

me na 나; chŏ 저; **it's ~** nada 나다; chŏimnida 저입니다; **he knows ~** kŭnŭn narŭl anda 그는 나를 안다; **that's for ~** naŭi kŏshida 나의 것이다

meadow ch'owŏn 초원

meager pulch'ŭngbunhan 불충분한

meal shikssa 식사

mealtime shikssa shigan 식사 시간

mean¹ (*with money*) insaek'an 인색한; (*nasty*) mot-ttoen 못된

mean² 1 *v/t* (*intend*) ŭidohada 의도하다; (*signify*) ŭimihada 의미하다; **~ to do sth** muŏsŭl haryŏgo hada 무엇을 하려고 하다; **be ~t for** ...ŭl/rŭl wihan kŏshida ...을/를 위한 것이다; (*of remark*) ...ŭl/rŭl tugo marhada ...을/를 두고 말하다; **doesn't it ~ anything to you?** (*doesn't it matter?*) tangshinege amu sanggwan ŏpssŏyo? 당신에게 아무 상관 없어요? **2** *v/i*: **~ well** choŭn ŭidorŭl

kajida 좋은 의도를 가지다

meaning (*of word*) ŭimi 의미

meaningful (*comprehensible*) ihaeganŭn 이해가는; *glance* ŭimiinnŭn 의미있는

meaningless muŭimihan 무의미한

means (*financial*) chaesan 재산; (*way*) sudan 수단; **~ of transport** kyot'ong sudan 교통 수단; **by all ~** (*certainly*) mullon 물론; **by no ~ poor** kyŏlk'o kananhaji ant'a 결코 가난하지 않다; **by ~ of** ...ŭl/rŭl ssŏsŏ ...을/를 써서

meantime: **in the ~** kŭ saie 그 사이에

measles hongnyŏk 홍역

measure 1 *n* (*step*) pangch'aek 방책; (*certain amount*) ŏnŭ chŏngdo 어느 정도 **2** *v/t* ch'issurŭl chaeda 치수를 재다 **3** *v/i* chaeŏjida 재어지다

♦**measure out** pullyang-ŭl chaeda 분량을 재다

♦**measure up to** ... mank'ŭm chal hada ... 만큼 잘 하다

measurement (*action*) ch'ŭktchŏng 측정; **~s** (*dimensions*) ch'issu 치수; **system of ~** ch'ŭktchŏngppŏp 측정법

meat kogi 고기

meatball kogi wanja 고기 완자

meatloaf mitŭ lopŭ 미트 로프, chŏmin kogiwa ppanggaru, kyeranŭl nŏk'o obŭne kuun tŏng-ŏri 저민 고기와 빵가루, 계란을 넣고 오븐에 구운 덩어리

mechanic kigyegong 기계공

mechanical *device* kigyeŭi 기계의; *gesture* kigyejŏgin 기계적인

mechanically *do sth* kigyejŏgŭro 기계적으로

mechanism kigye changch'i 기계 장치

mechanize kigyewahada 기계화하다

medal medal 메달

medalist susangja 수상자

meddle kansŏp'ada 간섭하다; **~ with** ...ŭl/rŭl manjijak-kkŏrida ...을/를 만지작거리다

media: **the ~** maesŭk'ŏm 매스컴

media hype maesŭk'ŏmŭi kwajang 매스컴의 과장

median strip chung-ang pullidae 중앙

분리대
mediate chungjaehada 중재하다
mediation chungjae 중재
mediator chungjaein 중재인
medical 1 *adj* ŭihagŭi 의학의; ~
  treatment ch'iryo 치료; ~ *insur-*
  ance ŭiryo pohŏm 의료 보험; ~
  problem kŏn-gang munje 건강 문제
  2 *n* shinch'e kŏmsa 신체 검사
medical certificate chindansŏ 진단서
Medicare noin ŭiryo pojang chedo
  노인 의료 보장 제도
medicated yagyong-ŭi 약용의
medication yak 약
medicinal yagŭi 약의
medicine (*science*) ŭihak 의학;
  (*medication*) yak 약
medieval chungseŭi 중세의; *fig*
  kushigŭi 구식의
mediocre chillajŭn 질낮은
mediocrity (*of work etc*) chillajŭm
  질낮음; (*person*) chŏjil 저질
meditate myŏngsanghada 명상하다;
  (*of Christian*) mukssanghada
  묵상하다; (*of Buddhist monk*)
  ch'amsŏnhada 참선하다
meditation myŏngsang 명상; (*in*
  Christianity) mukssang 묵상; (*in*
  Buddhism) ch'amsŏn 참선
medium 1 *adj* (*average*) chungganŭi
  중간의; *steak* pantchŭm ik'in 반쯤
  익힌 **2** *n* (*in size*) chunggan k'ŭgi
  중간 크기; (*vehicle*) maech'e 매체;
  (*spiritualist*) yŏngmae 영매
medium-sized chunggan k'ŭgiŭi 중간
  크기의
medium wave RAD chungp'a 중파
medley (*mixture*) kagyanggakssaek
  각양각색; (*of songs*) medŭlli 메들리
meek yamjŏnhan 얌전한
meet 1 *v/t* mannada 만나다; (*collect*)
  majungnagada 마중나가다; (*in*
  competition) matssŏda 맞서다; (*of*
  eyes) majuch'ida 마주치다; (*satisfy*)
  ch'ungjokshik'ida 충족시키다 **2** *v/i*
  mannada 만나다; (*in competition*)
  taejŏnhada 대전하다; (*of eyes*)
  majuch'ida 마주치다; (*of committee*
  etc) moida 모이다 **3** *n* SP kyŏnggi
  경기
  ♦ **meet with** *person* …wa / kwa

mannada …와 / 과 만나다; *approval*
pat-tta 받다; *success, failure*
majihada 맞이하다
meeting mannam 만남; (*of*
  committee, in business) hoeŭi 회의;
  he's in a ~ kŭnŭn hoeŭi chung-ida
  그는 회의 중이다
meeting place yakssok changso 약속
  장소
megabyte COMPUT megabait'ŭ
  메가바이트
melancholy *adj* ultchŏk'an 울적한
mellow 1 *adj* kammiroun 감미로운;
  fruit, wine sukssŏnghan 숙성한; *color*
  pudŭrŏun 부드러운; *person*
  wŏnsuk'an 원숙한 **2** *v/i* (*of person*)
  wŏnsuk'ada 원숙하다
melodious koktchoga arŭmdaun
  곡조가 아름다운
melodramatic melodŭramagat'ŭn
  멜로드라마같은
melody melodi 멜로디, sŏnnyul 선율
melon melon 멜론
melt 1 *v/i* noktta 녹다 **2** *v/t* nogida
  녹이다
  ♦ **melt away** *fig* sŏsŏhi sarajida
  서서히 사라지다
  ♦ **melt down** *metal* nogida 녹이다
melting pot *fig* togani 도가니
member irwŏn 일원; ~ *of Congress*
  kuk'oe ŭiwŏn 국회 의원
membership hoewŏn chagyŏk 회원
  자격; (*number of members*) hoewŏn
  su 회원 수
membership card hoewŏntchŭng
  회원증
membrane mak 막
memento kinyŏmmul 기념물
memo memo 메모, kirok 기록
memoirs hoegorok 회고록
memorable kiŏk'al manhan 기억할
  만한
memorial 1 *adj* kinyŏmŭi 기념의 **2** *n*
  kinyŏmbi 기념비
Memorial Day Hyŏnch'ung-il 현충일
memorize amgihada 암기하다
memory (*recollection*) kiŏk 기억;
  (*emotionally tinged*) ch'uŏk 추억;
  (*power of recollection*) kiŏngnyŏk
  기억력; COMPUT yongnyang 용량,
  memori 메모리; *have a good / bad*

~ kiŏngnyŏgi chot'a / nappŭda
기억력이 좋다 / 나쁘다; **in ~ of**
…ŭl / rŭl kinyŏmhamyŏ …을 / 를
기념하며

menace 1 n (*threat*) wihyŏp 위험;
(*person*) wihŏm inmul 위험 인물
2 v/t wihyŏp'ada 위협하다

menacing wihyŏp'anŭn 위협하는

mend 1 v/t koch'ida 고치다; *clothes*,
shoes susŏnhada 수선하다 **2** n: **be on**
the ~ (*after illness*) tŏ naajida 더
나아지다

menial adj ch'ŏnhan 천한

meningitis noemangnyŏm 뇌막염

menopause p'yegyŏnggi 폐경기

men's room namja hwajangshil 남자
화장실

menstruate wŏlgyŏnghada 월경하다,
saengnihada 생리하다

menstruation wŏlgyŏng 월경,
saengni 생리

mental chŏngshinŭi 정신의; *torture*,
suffering maŭmŭi 마음의; F (*crazy*)
chŏngshinppyŏng-ŭi 정신병의

mental arithmetic amsan 암산;
mental cruelty chŏngshintchŏk
hakttae 정신적 학대; **mental hos-**
pital chŏngshin pyŏng-wŏn 정신
병원; **mental illness**
chŏngshinppyŏng 정신병

mentality chŏngshin sangt'ae 정신
상태

mentally (*inwardly*) maŭm sogŭro
마음 속으로; *calculate* chitchŏgŭro
지적으로; **~ handicapped**
chŏngshintchŏk chang-aeja innŭn
정신적 장애가 있는; **~ ill**
chŏngshinppyŏng-i innŭn 정신병이
있는

mention 1 n ŏn-gŭp 언급 **2** v/t ŏn-
gŭp'ada 언급하다; **don't ~ it** (*you're*
welcome) ch'ŏnmaneyo 천만에요

mentor choryŏktcha 조력자

menu (*for food*) shikttan 식단,
menyu 메뉴; COMPUT menyu 메뉴

mercenary 1 adj tonŭl moktchŏgŭro
hanŭn 돈을 목적으로 하는 **2** n MIL
yongbyŏng 용병

merchandise sangp'um 상품

merchant sang-in 상인

merciful chabiroun 자비로운

mercifully (*thankfully*)
tahaengsŭrŏpkkedo 다행스럽게도

merciless mujabihan 무자비한

mercury suŭn 수은

mercy chabi 자비; **be at s.o.'s ~**
nuguŭi maŭmdaero toeda 누구의
마음대로 되다

mere tanji 단지

merely tanji 단지

merge v/i (*of two lines etc*) hapch'ida
합치다; (*of companies*) hap-
ppyŏnghada 합병하다

merger COM hap-ppyŏng 합병

merit 1 n (*worth*) kach'i 가치;
(*advantage*) changtchŏm 장점 **2** v/t
…hal kach'iga it-tta …할 가치가
있다

merry yuk'waehan 유쾌한; *Merry*
Christmas! chŭlgŏun Sŏngt'ani
toegirŭl paramnida! 즐거운 성탄이
되기를 바랍니다!

merry-go-round hoejŏn mongma
회전 목마

mesh n kŭmul 그물

mess n (*untidiness*) ŏngmang-in kŏt
엉망인 것; (*trouble*) kon-gyŏng 곤경;
be a ~ (*of room, desk, hair*)
ŏngmang-ida 엉망이다; (*of situation,*
s.o.'s life) hollansŭrŏpt-tta
혼란스럽다

◆**mess around 1** v/i pindanggŏrida
빈둥거리다 **2** v/t person
hollanshik'ida 혼란시키다

◆**mess around with** …ŭl / rŭl katkko
nolda …을 / 를 갖고 놀다; s.o.'s wife
…wa / kwa param p'iuda …와 / 과
바람 피우다

◆**mess up** room, papers ŏjirŭda
어지르다; plans, marriage mangch'yŏ
not'a 망쳐 놓다

message chŏnhanŭn mal 전하는 말,
mesiji 메시지; (*of movie, book*)
kyohun 교훈

messenger meshinjŏ 메신저;
(*courier*) paedalbu 배달부

messy room ŏjiroun 어지러운; person
hollanhage hanŭn 혼란하게 하는; job
chijŏbunhan 지저분한; divorce,
situation nanch'ŏhan 난처한

metabolism shinjindaesa 신진대사

metal 1 n kŭmsok 금속 **2** adj

kŭmsogŭi 금속의
metallic kŭmsokssŏng-ŭi 금속성의
meteor yusŏng 유성
meteoric *fig* yusŏnggat'ŭn 유성같은
meteorite unsŏk 운석
meteorological kisanghagŭi 기상학의
meteorologist kisanghaktcha
기상학자
meteorology kisanghak 기상학
meter[1] (*for gas etc*) kyeryanggi
계량기; (*parking ~, in cab*) yogŭm
kyesan-gi 요금 계산기
meter[2] (*unit of length*) mit'ŏ 미터
method pangbŏp 방법
methodical iltchŏnghan pangshige
ttarŭn 일정한 방식에 따른
methodically iltchŏnghan
pangshigŭro 일정한 방식으로
Methodist Church Kamni Kyohoe
감리 교회
meticulous seshimhan 세심한
metric mit'ŏppŏbŭi 미터법의
metropolis taedoshi 대도시; (*capital city*) sudo 수도
metropolitan *adj* taedoshiŭi 대도시의
mew → **miaow**
Mexican 1 *adj* Mekshik'oŭi 멕시코의
2 *n* Mekshik'oin 멕시코인
Mexico Mekshik'o 멕시코
mezzanine (**floor**) chungch'ŭng 중층
miaow 1 *n* yaong 야옹 **2** *v/i*
yaonghago ulda 야옹하고 울다
mickey mouse *adj* F *pej: course, qualification* kach'iŏmnŭn 가치없는
microchip maik'ŭroch'ip 마이크로칩;
microcosm souju 소우주; **micro-electronics** kŭksso chŏnja konghak
극소 전자 공학; **microfilm**
maik'ŭrop'illŭm 마이크로필름;
microphone maik'ŭ 마이크; **micro-processor** maik'ŭrop'ŭrosesŏ
마이크로프로세서; **microscope**
hyŏnmigyŏng 현미경; **microscopic**
kŭk'i chagŭn 극히 작은; **microwave**
(*oven*) chŏnjarenji 전자렌지
midair: *in ~* kongjung-esŏ 공중에서
midday chŏng-o 정오
middle 1 *adj* chungganŭi 중간의 **2** *n*
kaunde 가운데; *in the ~ of* (*floor, room*) ...ŭi chung-ang-esŏ ...의
중앙에서; (*period of time*) ... chung-

e ... 중에; *in the ~ of the night*
hanbam chung-e 한밤 중에; *be in the ~ of doing sth* muŏsŭl hanŭn
chung-ida 무엇을 하는 중이다
middle-aged chungnyŏnŭi 중년의;
Middle Ages Chungse 중세; **mid-dle-class** *adj* chungsanch'ŭng-ŭi
중산층의; **middle class(es)**
chungsanch'ŭng 중산층; **Middle East** Chungdong 중동; **middleman**
chunggan sang-in 중간 상인; **middle name** chunggan irŭm 중간 이름;
middleweight *n* (*boxer*)
chunggankkŭp 중간급
middling kŭjŏ kŭrŏn 그저 그런
midget *adj* ch'osohyŏng-ŭi 초소형의
midnight chajŏng 자정; *at ~* chajŏng-e 자정에; **midsummer** hannyŏrŭm
한여름; **midway** chungdo-e 중도에;
midweek *adv* chujung-e 주중에;
Midwest Chungsŏbu 중서부; **mid-wife** chosanwŏn 조산원; **midwinter**
hangyŏul 한겨울
might[1] ...iltchido morŭnda ...일지도
모른다; *I ~ be late* chŏnŭn ama
nŭjŭltchido morŭgessumnida 저는
아마 늦을지도 모르겠습니다; *it ~ rain* piga oltchido morŭgessŭmnida
비가 올지도 모르겠습니다; *it ~ never happen* kŭgŏsŭn ama
tashinŭn irŏnaji anŭl kŏshimnida
그것은 아마 다시는 일어나지 않을
것입니다; *I ~ have lost it* chŏnŭn
kŭgŏsŭl irŏporyŏnnŭnjido
morŭgessŭmnida 저는 그것을
잃어버렸는지도 모르겠습니다; *he ~ have left* hoksshi kŭga ttŏnassŭltchi
morŭgessŭmnida 혹시 그가
떠났을지 모르겠습니다; *you ~ as well spend the night here*
tanshindo yŏgisŏ pamŭl ponaeya
haltchi morŭmnida 당신도 여기서
밤을 보내야 할지 모릅니다; *you ~ have told me!* chinjak naege marŭl
haessŏyaji! 진짝 내게 말을 했어야지!
might[2] *n* (*power*) him 힘
mighty 1 *adj* himinnŭn 힘있는 **2** *adv* F
(*extremely*) maeu 매우
migraine p'yŏndŭt'ong 편두통
migrant worker iju nodongja 이주
노동자

migrate ijuhada 이주하다

migration iju 이주

mike maik'ŭ 마이크

mild *weather, climate, person* onhwahan 온화한; *taste* sunhan 순한; *voice* pudŭroun 부드러운

mildly pudŭropkke 부드럽게

mildew komp'ang-i 곰팡이

mildness (*of weather, person*) onhwaham 온화함; (*of voice*) pudŭroum 부드러움; (*of taste*) sunham 순함

mile mail 마일; *~s better / easier* F hwŏlsshin naŭn / shwiun 훨씬 나은 / 쉬운

mileage mail su 마일 수

milestone *fig* ijŏngp'yo 이정표

militant 1 *adj* t'ujaengtchŏgin 투쟁적인 **2** *n* t'usa 투사

military 1 *adj* kunŭi 군의 **2** *n: the ~* kun 군

military academy yuk-kkun sagwan hak-kkyo 육군 사관 학교

militia shimin-gun 시민군

milk 1 *n* uyu 우유 **2** *v/t* chŏjŭl tchada 젖을 짜다

milk chocolate milk'ŭ chyok'olit 밀크 쵸콜릿

milk shake milk'ŭ shweik'ŭ 밀크 쉐이크

mill *n* (*factory*) kongjang 공장; (*for grinding*) punswaegi 분쇄기

♦ **mill around** mujilssŏhage umjigida 무질서하게 움직이다

millennium ch'ŏnnyŏn 천년

milligram milligŭraem 밀리그램

millimeter millimit'ŏ 밀리미터

million paengman 백만

millionaire paengman changja 백만 장자

mime *v/t* tongjagŭro p'yohyŏnhada 동작으로 표현하다

mimic 1 *n* hyungnae 흉내 **2** *v/t* hyungnaenaeda 흉내내다

mince *v/t* chŏmida 저미다

mincemeat minsŭ p'ai sok 민스 파이 속

mince pie minsŭ p'ai 민스 파이

mind 1 *n* chŏngshin 정신; *it's all in your ~* kŭgŏsŭn ta nŏŭi sangsang-ida 그것은 다 너의 상상이다; *be out*

of one's ~ chŏngshini nagada 정신이 나가다; *bear sth in ~* muŏsŭl kiŏk'ago it-tta 무엇을 기억하고 있다; *change one's ~* maŭmŭl pakkuda 마음을 바꾸다; *it didn't enter my ~* kŭgŏsŭn na-ege sangsangdo kaji anat-tta 그것은 나에게 상상도 가지 않았다; *give s.o. a piece of one's ~* nugurŭl namurada 누구를 나무라다; *make up one's ~* maŭmŭl chŏnghada 마음을 정하다; *have sth on one's ~* (*be worried*) muŏsŭl kŭnshimhada 무엇을 근심하다; *keep one's ~ on* ...e chŏnnyŏmhada ...에 전념하다 **2** *v/t* tolboda 돌보다; (*object to*) ŏntchanahada 언짢아하다; (*heed*) maŭme tuda 마음에 두다; *I don't ~ what we do* nanŭn uriga muŏsŭl hadŭn sanggwanŏpta 나는 우리가 무엇을 하든 상관없다; *do you ~ if I smoke?* tambaerŭl p'iwŏdo kwaench'ank'essŭmnikka? 담배를 피워도 괜찮겠습니까?; *would you ~ opening the window?* ch'angmunŭl yŏrŏ chushigessŭmnikka? 창문을 열어 주시겠습니까?; *no, I don't ~* anio, kwaench'ansŭmnida 아니오, 괜찮습니다; *~ the step!* kyedanŭl choshimhaseyo! 계단을 조심하세요! **3** *v/i: ~!* (*be careful*) choshimhaseyo! 조심하세요!; *never ~!* shin-gyŏng ssŭl kŏt ŏpssŭmnida! 신경 쓸 것 없습니다!; *I don't ~* chŏnŭn sanggwanopssŭmnida 저는 상관없습니다

mind-boggling nollaun 놀라운

mindless *violence* saenggagŏmnŭn 생각없는

mine[1] *pron* naŭi kŏt 나의 것; ㅂ chŏŭi kŏt 저의 것; *a cousin of ~* naŭi sach'on 나의 사촌; ㅂ chŏŭi sach'on 저의 사촌

mine[2] **1** *n* (*for coal etc*) kwangsan 광산 **2** *v/i* (*for coal etc*) p'ada 파다; *~ for* ch'aegurhada 채굴하다

mine[3] **1** *n* (*explosive*) chiroe 지뢰 **2** *v/t* ...e chiroerŭl sŏlch'ihada ...에 지뢰를 설치하다

minefield MIL chiroepat 지뢰밭; *fig*

wihŏmjidae 위험 지대
miner kwangbu 광부
mineral *n* kwangmul 광물
mineral water kwangch'ŏnsu 광천수, saengsu 생수
minesweeper NAUT chiroe t'amsaekssŏn 지뢰 탐색선
mingle *v/i (of sounds, smells)* sŏktta 섞다; *(at party) toradanimyŏ manŭn saramdŭrege marhada* 돌아다니며 많은 사람들에게 말하다
mini → *miniskirt*
miniature *adj* sohyŏng-ŭi 소형의
minibus sohyŏng pŏsŭ 소형 버스
minimal ch'oesoŭi 최소의
minimize ch'oesohwahada 최소화하다; *(downplay)* kwaso p'yŏngkkahada 과소 평가하다
minimum 1 *adj* ch'oesohanŭi 최소한의 **2** *n* ch'oeso 최소
minimum wage ch'oejŏ ponggŭp 최저 봉급
mining kwang-ŏp 광업
miniskirt mini sŭk'ot'ŭ 미니 스커트
minister POL changgwan 장관; REL mokssa 목사
ministerial changgwan-ŭi 장관의
ministry POL pu 부; *(in US, Japan)* sŏng 성
mink *(fur)* mingk'ŭ 밍크; *(coat)* mingk'ŭ k'ot'ŭ 밍크 코트
minor 1 *adj* poda chagŭn 보다 작은; *in G ~* MUS sa tantchoŭi 사 단조의 **2** *n* LAW misŏngnyŏnja 미성년자
minority sosup'a 소수파; *be in the ~* sosup'aida 소수파이다
mint *n (herb)* pak'a 박하, mint'ŭ 민트; *(chocolate)* mint'ŭ chyok'ollit 민트 쵸콜릿; *(hard candy)* pak'a sat'ang 박하 사탕
minus 1 *n (~ sign)* ppaegi puho 빼기 부호 **2** *prep* ŭmŭi 음의; *42 ~ 18 is 24* sashibi ppaegi shipp'arŭn ishipssaida 42 빼기 18은 24이다; *temperatures of ~ 18 degrees* yŏngha shipp'alto 영하 18도
minuscule aju chagŭn 아주 작은
minute[1] *n (of time)* pun 분; *in a ~ (soon)* kot 곧; *just a ~* chamshiman kidariseyo 잠시만 기다리세요
minute[2] *adj (tiny)* aju chogŭman 아주

조그만; *(detailed)* sangsehan 상세한; *in ~ detail* sangsehi 상세히
minutely *(in detail)* sangsehage 상세하게
minutes *(of meeting)* ŭisarok 의사록
miracle kijŏk 기적
miraculous kijŏktchŏgin 기적적인
miraculously kijŏkkach'i 기적같이
mirage shin-giru 신기루
mirror 1 *n* kŏul 거울; MOT paengmirŏ 백미러 **2** *v/t* pich'uda 비추다
misanthropist saramŭl shirŏhanŭn saram 사람을 싫어하는 사람
misapprehension: *be under a ~* chalmot saenggak'ada 잘못 생각하다
misbehave nappŭge haengdonghada 나쁘게 행동하다
misbehavior nappŭn haengdong 나쁜 행동
miscalculate *v/t & v/i* chalmot kyesanhada 잘못 계산하다
miscalculation osan 오산
miscarriage MED yusan 유산; *~ of justice* oshim 오심
miscarry *(of plan)* shilp'aehada 실패하다
miscellaneous kajigakssaegŭi 가지각색의
mischief *(naughtiness)* chitkkujŭn changnan 짓궂은 장난
mischievous *child* changnankkurŏgiŭi 장난꾸러기의; *behavior* chitkkujŭn 짓궂은
misconception ohae 오해
misconduct pujŏng haeng-wi 부정 행위
misconstrue chalmot haesŏk'ada 잘못 해석하다
misdemeanor kyŏngbŏmtchoe 경범죄; *youthful ~s* ch'ŏngsonyŏn pihaeng 청소년 비행
miser kudusoe 구두쇠
miserable *(unhappy)* purhaenghan 불행한; *weather* koyak'an 고약한; *performance* hyŏngp'yŏnŏmnŭn 형편없는
miserly insaek'an 인색한
misery *(unhappiness)* purhaeng 불행; *(wretchedness)* pich'amham 비참함
misfire *(of joke, scheme)* pinnagada 빗나가다

misfit (*in society*) pujŏgŭngja 부적응자

misfortune purhaeng 불행

misgiving yŏmnyŏ 염려

misguided chalmot chidodoen 잘못 지도된

mishandle chalmot taruda 잘못 다루다

mishap sago 사고

misinterpret chalmot haesŏk'ada 잘못 해석하다

misinterpretation chalmot-ttoen haesŏk 잘못된 해석

misjudge *person, situation* chalmot p'andanhada 잘못 판단하다

mislay tun kosŭl ijŏbŏrida 둔 곳을 잊어버리다

mislead odohada 오도하다

misleading odohanŭn 오도하는

mismanage chalmot unyŏnghada 잘못 운영하다

mismanagement chalmot-ttoen unyŏng 잘못된 운영

mismatch chalmot match'uda 잘못 맞추다

misplaced *loyalty* chalmot chun 잘못 준

misprint *n* chalmot-ttoen inswae 잘못된 인쇄

mispronounce t'ŭllin parŭmŭl hada 틀린 발음을 하다

mispronunciation t'ŭllin parŭm 틀린 발음

misread *word, figures* chalmot iltta 잘못 읽다; *situation* ohaehada 오해하다

misrepresent t'ŭllige chŏnhada 틀리게 전하다

miss[1]: *Miss Smith* Sŭmisŭ yang 스미스 양; *~!* agasshi! 아가씨!

miss[2] *n* SP shiltchŏm 실점; *give sth a ~ meeting, party etc* muŏse ppajida 무엇에 빠지다 **2** *v/t* (*not hit*) noch'ida 놓치다; (*not meet*) ŏtkkallida 엇갈리다; (*emotionally*) kŭriwŏhada 그리워하다; *bus, train, plane* noch'ida 놓치다; (*not notice*) arach'aeji mot'ada 알아채지 못하다; (*not be present at*) …e ppajida …에 빠지다 **3** *v/i* noch'ida 놓치다

misshapen pijŏngsangtchŏgin

moyang-ŭi 비정상적인 모양의

missile (*rocket*) misail 미사일

missing irŏbŏrin 잃어버린; *be ~* ŏpssŏjida 없어지다

mission (*task*) samyŏng 사명; (*people*) sajŏl 사절

missionary REL sŏn-gyosa 선교사

misspell chalmot ch'ŏltchahada 잘못 철자하다

mist an-gae 안개

♦ **mist over** (*of eyes*) hŭryŏjida 흐려지다

♦ **mist up** (*of mirror, window*) kimi sŏrida 김이 서리다

mistake 1 *n* shilssu 실수; *make a ~* shilssuhada 실수하다; *by ~* shilssuro 실수로 **2** *v/t* ch'ak-kkak'ada 착각하다; *~ X for Y* Xŭl/rŭl Y(ŭ)ro chak-kkak'ada X을/를 Y(으)로 착각하다

mistaken: *be ~* t'ŭllin 틀린

mister → **Mr**

mistress (*lover*) chŏngbu 정부; (*of servant*) yŏjuin 여주인; (*of dog*) chuin 주인

mistrust 1 *n* pulsshin 불신 **2** *v/t* pulsshinhada 불신하다

misty *weather* an-gae kkin 안개 낀; *eyes* hŭryŏjin 흐려진; *color* hŭrin 흐린

misunderstand ohaehada 오해하다

misunderstanding (*mistake*) ohae 오해; (*argument*) ŭigyŏn ch'ai 의견 차이

misuse 1 *n* oyong 오용 **2** *v/t* chalmot sayonghada 잘못 사용하다

mitigating circumstances kyŏnggam sayu 경감 사유

mitt (*in baseball*) mit'ŭ 미트

mitten pŏng-ŏri changgap 벙어리 장갑

mix 1 *n* (*mixture*) sŏkkŭn kŏt 섞은 것; (*in cooking*) honhammul 혼합물; (*ready to use*) miri mandŭrŏjin yori chaeryo 미리 만들어진 요리 재료 **2** *v/t* sŏkta 섞다 **3** *v/i* (*socially*) ŏullida 어울리다

♦ **mix up** (*confuse*) hŏtkkallida 헷갈리다; (*muddle up*) sŏkkŏ not'a 섞어 놓다; *mix X up with Y* Xŭl/rŭl Ywa/kwa hondonghada X을/를

Y와 / 과 혼동하다; *be mixed up*
(*emotionally*) hollansŭrŏwŏ hada
혼란스러워 하다; (*of figures, papers*)
twisŏk-kkida 뒤섞이다; *be mixed up*
in …e kwallyŏndoeda …에 관련되다;
get mixed up with …wa / kwa
kwan-gyehada …와 / 과 관계하다
♦ **mix with** (*associate with*) …wa / kwa
ŏullida …와 / 과 어울리다

mixed *feelings* hollanhan 혼란한;
reactions, reviews sŏk-kkin 섞인

mixed marriage kuktche kyŏrhon
국제 결혼

mixer (*for food*) mikssŏ 믹서; (*drink*)
k'akt'eillyong mualk'ool ŭmnyo
칵테일용 무알코올 음료; *she's a*
good ~ kŭnyŏnŭn sagyossŏng-i
chot'a 그녀는 사교성이 좋다

mixture honhap 혼합; (*medicine*)
mulyak 물약

mix-up hollan 혼란

moan 1 *n* (*of pain*) shinŭm sori 신음
소리; (*complaint*) pulp'yŏng 불평
2 *v/i* (*in pain*) shinŭmhada 신음하다;
(*complain*) pulp'yŏnghada 불평하다

mob 1 *n* p'oktto 폭도 **2** *v/t* tterŭl chiŏ
tallyŏdŭlda 떼를 지어 달려들다

mobile[1] *adj person* umjigil su innŭn
움직일 수 있는

mobile[2] *n* (*for decoration*) mobil 모빌

mobile home idongshik chut'aek
이동식 주택

mobile phone *Br* haendŭp'on
핸드폰, idong chŏnhwa 이동 전화

mobility idong 이동

mobster p'ongnyŏk tanwŏn 폭력
단원

mock 1 *adj* hyungnaenaen 흉내낸;
exams, elections moŭiŭi 모의의 **2** *v/t*
hyungnaenaemyŏ choronghada
흉내내며 조롱하다

mockery chorong 조롱; (*travesty*)
chojak 조작

mock-up (*model*) mohyŏng 모형

mode (*form*) pangshik 방식; COMPUT
modŭ 모드

model 1 *adj employee, husband*
mobŏmŭi 모범의; *boat, plane*
mohyŏng-ŭi 모형의 **2** *n* (*miniature*)
mohyŏng 모형; (*pattern*) ponbogi
본보기; (*fashion* ~) model 모델;

male ~ namja model 남자 모델 **3** *v/t*
…ŭi modŭrŭl hada …의 모델을 하다
4 *v/i* (*for designer*) moderida
모델이다; (*for artist, photographer*)
moderŭl hada 모델을 하다

modem modem 모뎀

moderate 1 *adj* chŏkttanghan 적당한,
almajŭn 알맞은; POL on-gŏnhan
온건한 **2** *n* POL on-gŏnp'a 온건파
3 *v/t* chŏkttanghi hada 적당히 하다

moderately chŏkttanghage 적당하게

moderation (*restraint*) chungnyong
중용; *in* ~ chŏkttanghage 적당하게

modern hyŏndaeŭi 현대의

modernization hyŏndaehwa 현대화

modernize 1 *v/t* hyŏndaejŏgŭro
pakkuda 현대적으로 바꾸다 **2** *v/i* (*of*
business, country) hyŏndaehwahada
현대화하다

modest *house, apartment* susuhan
수수한; (*small*) chogŭmahan
조그마한; (*not conceited*)
kyŏmsonhan 겸손한

modesty (*of house, apartment*)
susuham 수수함; (*of wage,*
improvement) chogŭmaham
조그마함; (*lack of conceit*) kyŏmson
겸손

modification sujŏng 수정

modify sujŏnghada 수정하다

modular *furniture* choribŭi 조립의

module chorip tanwi 조립 단위;
(*space* ~) sŏn 선

moist sŭpkki innŭn 습기 있는,
ch'ukch'uk'an 축축한

moisten ch'ukch'uk'age hada
축축하게 하다

moisture sŭpkki 습기

moisturizer (*for skin*) moisch'yŏraijŏ
모이스쳐라이저

molar ŏgŭmni 어금니

molasses tangmil 당밀

mold[1] *n* (*on food*) komp'ang-i 곰팡이

mold[2] **1** *n* t'ŭl 틀 **2** *v/t clay etc* t'ŭre
nŏŏ mandŭlda 틀에 넣어 만들다;
character, person hyŏngsŏngshik'ida
형성시키다

moldy *food* komp'ang-i p'in 곰팡이
핀

mole (*on skin*) chŏm 점

molecular punjaŭi 분자의

molecule punja 분자

molest *child, woman* sŏngtchŏgŭro hŭironghada 성적으로 희롱하다

mollycoddle chinach'ige posalp'ida 지나치게 보살피다

molten nogŭn 녹은

mom F ŏmma 엄마

moment sun-gan 순간; *at the ~* chigŭmŭn 지금은; *at that ~* kŭ ttaeenŭn 그 때에는; *at the very ~* paro kŭ sun-gane 바로 그 순간에; *for the ~* tangbun-gan 당분간

momentarily (*for a moment*) chamshi tong-an 잠시 동안; (*in a moment*) kot 곧

momentary sun-ganŭi 순간의

momentous chungdaehan 중대한

momentum him 힘

monarch kunju 군주

monastery sudowŏn 수도원

monastic sudosŭng kat'ŭn 수도승 같은

Monday wŏryoil 월요일

monetary kŭmnyung-ŭi 금융의

money ton 돈

money-lender taegŭmŏptcha 대금업자; **money market** kŭmnyung shijang 금융 시장; **money order** up'yŏnhwan 우편환

Mongolia Monggo 몽고

Mongolian 1 *adj* Monggoŭi 몽고의 **2** *n* (*person*) Monggoin 몽고인

mongrel chaptchonggyŏn 잡종견

monitor 1 *n* COMPUT monit'ŏ 모니터 **2** *v/t* chik'yŏboda 지켜보다

monk sudosa 수도사

monkey wŏnsung-i 원숭이; F (*child*) ŏrin nom 어린 놈

♦**monkey around with** F ...ŭl/rŭl kajigo changnanch'ida ...을/를 가지고 장난치다

monkey wrench mŏngk'i sŭp'aenŏ 멍키 스패너

monogram *n* yaktcha 약자

monogrammed yaktchaga saegyŏjin 약자가 새겨진

monolog tokppaek 독백

monopolize toktchŏmhada 독점하다

monopoly toktchŏm 독점

monotonous tanjoroun 단조로운

monotony tanjoroum 단조로움

monsoon monsun 몬순

monsoon season monsun kyejŏl 몬순 계절

monster *n* koemul 괴물

monstrosity hyungmul 흉물

monstrous (*frightening*) koemulgat'ŭn 괴물같은; (*enormous*) kŏdaehan 거대한; (*shocking*) ch'unggyŏktchŏgin 충격적인

month tal 달, wŏl 월

monthly 1 *adj* maedarŭi 매달의 **2** *adv* maedalmada 매달마다 **3** *n* (*magazine*) wŏlganji 월간지

monument kinyŏmbi 기념비; (*sculpture*) kinyŏm tongsang 기념 동상

mood (*frame of mind*) kibun 기분; (*bad ~*) kibuni nappŭn sangt'ae 기분이 나쁜 상태; (*of meeting, country*) punwigi 분위기; *be in a good / bad ~* kibuni chot'a / nappŭda 기분이 좋다 / 나쁘다; *be in the ~ for* ... hago ship'ŭn kibunida ... 하고 싶은 기분이다

moody kibuni chaju pyŏnhanŭn 기분이 자주 변하는; (*bad-tempered*) kibuni nappŭn 기분이 나쁜

moon *n* tal 달

moonlight 1 *n* talppit 달빛 **2** *v/i* F pame puŏbŭl hada 밤에 부업을 하다

moonlit talppich'i ŏrin 달빛이 어린

moor *v/t boat* chŏngbakshik'ida 정박시키다

moorings chŏngbaktchang 정박장

moose k'ŭn sasŭm 큰 사슴

mop 1 *n* taegŏlle 대걸레 **2** *v/t floor* taegŏllero takta 대걸레로 닦다; *eyes, face* takta 닦다

♦**mop up** takta 닦다; MIL sot'anghada 소탕하다

mope uurhaehada 우울해하다

moral 1 *adj person, behavior etc* todŏktchŏgin 도덕적인 **2** *n* (*of story*) kyohun 교훈; *~s* todŏk kwannyŏm 도덕 관념

morale sagi 사기

morality todŏkssŏng 도덕성

morbid pyŏngtchŏgin 병적인

more 1 *adj* tŏ manŭn 더 많은; *some ~ tea?* ch'arŭl chom tŏ tŭshigessŭmnikka? 차를 좀 더

드시겠습니까?; *~ and ~ students* / *time* chŏmjŏm tŏ manŭn hakssaengdŭl / shigan 점점 더 많은 학생들 / 시간 **2** *adv* tŏuk 더욱; *~ important* tŏ chung-yohan 더 중요한; *~ often* tŏuk chaju 더욱 자주; *~ and ~* tŏuk tŏ 더욱 더; *~ or less* (*about*) chŏngdo 정도; (*virtually*) sashilssang 사실상; *once ~* hanbŏn tŏ 한번 더; *~ than ...* poda tŏ mani ... 보다 더 많이; *~ than 80 people were injured* 80myŏngboda tŏ manŭn sarami pusang-ŭl tanghaet-tta 80명보다 더 많은 사람이 부상을 당했다; *I don't live there any ~* nanŭn tŏ isang kŏgi salji ansŭmnida 나는 더 이상 거기 살지 않습니다 **3** *pron* tŏ 더; *do you want some ~?* tŏ wŏnhashimnikka? 더 원하십니까?; *a little ~* chogŭm tŏ 조금 더

moreover kŏgidaga 거기다가

morgue yŏng-anshil 영안실

Mormonism Molmon-gyo 몰몬교

morning ach'im 아침; *in the ~* (*early*) ach'ime 아침에; (*before noon*) ojŏne 오전에; (*tomorrow*) naeil ach'im 내일 아침; *four o'clock in the ~* ojŏn neshi 오전 네시; *this ~* onŭl ach'im 오늘 아침; *tomorrow ~* naeil ach'im 내일 아침; *good ~* annyŏnghaseyo 안녕하세요; (*on waking up*) annyŏnghi chumusyŏssŏyo 안녕히 주무셨어요

moron pabo 바보

morose uurhan 우울한

morphine morŭp'in 모르핀

morsel: *a ~ of* han chogagŭi 한 조각의

mortal 1 *adj* chugŏyahal unmyŏng-ŭi 죽어야할 운명의; *blow* ch'imyŏngjŏgin 치명적인; *~ enemy* pulgu taech'ŏnŭi wŏnsu 불구 대천의 원수 **2** *n* pot'ong saram 보통 사람

mortality chugŭl unmyŏng 죽을 운명; (*death rate*) samangnyul 사망률

mortar[1] MIL pakkyŏkp'o 박격포

mortar[2] (*cement*) hoebanjuk 회반죽

mortgage 1 *n* chŏdang 저당 **2** *v/t* chŏdang chap'ida 저당 잡히다

mortician chang-ŭisa 장의사

mortuary yŏng-anshil 영안실

mosaic mojaik'ŭ 모자이크

mosquito mogi 모기

mosquito coil mogihyang 모기향

mosquito net mogijang 모기장

moss ikki 이끼

mossy ikki kkin 이끼 낀

most 1 *adj* taebubunŭi 대부분의; *~ people would agree with you* taebubunŭi saramdŭri tangshin ŭigyŏne tong-ŭihal kŏshimnida 대부분의 사람들이 당신 의견에 동의할 것입니다 **2** *adv* kajang 가장; (*very*) maeu 매우; *the ~ beautiful* / *interesting* kajang arŭmdaun / chaemiinnŭn 가장 아름다운 / 재미있는; *that's the one I like ~* kŭgŏshi naega kajang choahanŭn kŏshida 그것이 내가 가장 좋아하는 것이다; *~ of all* muŏtppodado 무엇보다도 **3** *pron* taebubun 대부분; (*maximum*) ch'oedaehanŭi kŏt 최대한의 것; *at (the) ~* manaya 많아야; *make the ~ of* ch'oedaehan hwaryonghada 최대한 활용하다

mostly taebubunŭn 대부분은, churo 주로

motel mot'el 모텔

moth nabang 나방

mother 1 *n* ŏmŏni 어머니 **2** *v/t* ŏmŏnigach'i tolboda 어머니같이 돌보다

motherboard COMPUT madŏbodŭ 마더보드; **motherhood** ŏmŏniim 어머니임; **mother-in-law** shiŏmŏni 시어머니

motherly ŏmŏnigat'ŭn 어머니같은

mother-of-pearl chagae 자개; *~ inlay* chagae changshik 자개 장식; **Mother's Day** ŏmŏninal 어머니날; **mother tongue** mogugŏ 모국어

motif chuje 주제

motion 1 *n* umjigim 움직임; (*of the body*) tongjak 동작; (*proposal*) chean 제안; *set things in ~* ch'ujinhada 추진하다 **2** *v/t: he ~ed me forward* kŭga na-ege ap'ŭro orago sonjit'aet-tta 그가 나에게 앞으로 오라고 손짓했다

motionless umjigiji annŭn 움직이지

않는

motivate *person* tonggirŭl puyŏhada 동기를 부여하다; *I don't feel very ~d* nanŭn pyŏllo ŭiyogi annanda 나는 별로 의욕이 안난다

motivation tonggi puyŏ 동기 부여

motive tonggi 동기

motor naeyŏn-gigwan 내연기관, mot'ŏ 모터

motorbike ot'obai 오토바이; **motorboat** mot'ŏbot'ŭ 모터보트; **motorcade** chadongch'a haengnyŏl 자동차 행렬; **motorcycle** ot'obai 오토바이; **motorcyclist** ot'obairŭl t'anŭn saram 오토바이를 타는 사람; **motor home** idong chut'aekch'a 이동 주택차

motorist unjŏnja 운전자

motorscooter sŭk'ut'ŏ 스쿠터

motor vehicle chadongch'a 자동차

motto chwaumyŏng 좌우명, mot'o 모토; *school ~* kyohun 교훈

mound (*hillock*) chagŭn ŏndŏk 작은 언덕; (*in baseball*) maundŭ 마운드; (*pile*) sandŏmi 산더미

mount 1 *n* (*mountain*) san 산; (*horse*) sŭngma 승마 2 *v/t steps* orŭda 오르다; *horse, bicycle* t'ada 타다; *campaign* ch'aksuhada 착수하다; *photo etc* tandanhan tee puch'ida 단단한 데에 붙이다 3 *v/i* orŭda 오르다

♦**mount up** nŭlda 늘다

mountain san 산

mountain bike sanak chajŏn-gŏ 산악 자전거

mountaineer tŭngsan-ga 등산가, sanagin 산악인

mountaineering tŭngsan 등산

mountainous sanjiŭi 산지의

mountain spirits sanshin 산신

mourn 1 *v/t* ch'udohada 추도하다 2 *v/i*: *~ for* …ŭi chugŭmŭl sŭlp'ŏhada …의 죽음을 슬퍼하다

mourner chogaek 조객

mournful sŭlp'ŭme chamgin 슬픔에 잠긴

mourning sang 상; *be in ~* sang chung-ida 상 중이다; *wear ~* sangbogŭl ipta 상복을 입다

mouse chwi 쥐; COMPUT mausŭ 마우스

mouse mat COMPUT mausŭ maet'ŭ 마우스 매트

mouth *n* ip 입; (*of river*) ŏgwi 어귀, hagu 하구

mouthful han ip kadŭk 한 입 가득

mouthorgan hamonik'a 하모니카; **mouthpiece** (*of instrument*) ibe taego punŭn pubun 입에 대고 부는 부분; (*spokesperson*) taebyŏnin 대변인; **mouthwash** yangch'iaek 양치액; **mouthwatering** kunch'im tolge hanŭn 군침 돌게 하는

move 1 *n* (*in chess, checkers*) su 수; (*step, action*) umjigim 움직임; (*change of house*) isa 이사; *get a ~ on!* sŏdŭrŭshipsshio! 서두르십시오!; *don't make a ~!* umjigiji ma! 움직이지 마!; *it's your ~* (*in chess etc*) tangshin ch'aryeimnida 당신 차례입니다 2 *v/t object* umjigida 움직이다; (*transfer*) omgida 옮기다; (*emotionally*) kamdongshik'ida 감동시키다 3 *v/i* umjigida 움직이다; (*transfer*) omgida 옮기다; *~ house* isahada 이사하다

♦**move around** (*in room*) toradanida 돌아다니다; (*from place to place*) idonghada 이동하다

♦**move away** mullŏnada 물러나다; (*move house*) isahada 이사하다

♦**move in** isaoda 이사오다

♦**move on** (*to another town*) isahada 이사하다; (*to another job*) chŏnjinhada 전직하다; (*to another subject*) pakkuda 바꾸다

♦**move out** (*of house*) isanagada 이사나가다; (*of area*) ttŏnada 떠나다

♦**move up** (*be promoted*) sŭngjinhada 승진하다; (*make room*) charirŭl mandŭlda 자리를 만들다; *they have moved up to second position* kŭdŭrŭn che iwie ollat-tta 그들은 제 이위에 올랐다

movement umjigim 움직임; (*organization*) undong 운동; MUS aktchang 악장

movers isatchim unsong-ŏptcha 이삿짐 운송업자

movie yŏnghwa 영화; *go to a ~/the ~s* yŏnghwa porŏ kada 영화 보러 가다

moviegoer: *be a big* ~ yŏnghwa
  porŏ kanŭn kŏsŭl maeu choahada
  영화 보러 가는 것을 매우 좋아하다
movie theater yŏnghwagwan 영화관
moving (*which can move*) umjiginŭn
  움직이는; (*emotionally*)
  kamdongjŏgin 감동적인
mow *grass* peda 베다
mower p'ulbenŭn kigye 풀베는 기계
moxibustion ssukttŭm 쑥뜸
MP (= *Military Policeman*)
  hŏnbyŏng 헌병
mph (= *miles per hour*) shisok 시속;
  at 50 ~ shisok 50maillo 시속
  50마일로
Mr: ~ *Kevin Brown* K'ebin
  Pŭraunssi 케빈 브라운씨
Mrs: ~ *Margo MacDonald* Mago
  Maekttonaldŭ yŏsa 마고 맥도날드
  여사
Ms: ~ *Sunmi Lee* I Sunmissi 이
  순미씨
much 1 *adj* manŭn 많은; *I have as* ~
  time as you need shiganŭn
  ŏlmadŭnji issŏyo 시간은 얼마든지
  있어요; *there's not* ~ *difference*
  pyŏllo tarŭji anayo 별로 다르지
  않아요 **2** *adv* mani 많이; *very* ~ aju
  mani 아주 많이; *too* ~ nŏmu mani
  너무 많이; *do you like it? - not* ~
  kŭgŏsŭl choahaeyo? - pyŏlloyo
  그것을 좋아해요? - 별로요; *as* ~ *as*
  ... ...mank'ŭm mani ...만큼 많이; *I*
  thought as ~ nado kŭrŏk'e
  saenggak'aessŏyo 나도 그렇게
  생각했어요 **3** *pron* manŭn kŏt 많은
  것; *he earns as* ~ *as me* kŭnŭn
  namank'ŭm tonŭl pŏnda 그는
  나만큼 돈을 번다; *nothing* ~ pyŏllo
  별로
muck (*dirt*) tŏrŏun kŏt 더러운 것
mucus chŏmaek 점액; (*in nose*)
  k'onmul 콧물
mud chinhŭk 진흙
muddle 1 *n* (*mess*) ŏmmang-in
  sangt'ae 엉망인 상태; (*confusion*)
  hollan 혼란 **2** *v/t* hŏllanshik'ida
  혼란시키다
♦ **muddle up** ŏngmang-ŭro mandŭlda
  엉망으로 만들다; (*confuse*)
  hŏtkkallida 헷갈리다

muddy *adj* chinhŭkt'usŏng-iŭi
  진흙투성이의
muffin mŏp'in 머핀
muffle chal andŭllige hada 잘
  안들리게 하다
♦ **muffle up** *v/i* ttattŭt'age kamssada
  따뜻하게 감싸다
muffler MOT pang-ŭm changch'i 방음
  장치; (*scarf*) mokttori 목도리
mug[1] *n* (*for tea, coffee*) mŏgŭjan
  머그잔; F (*face*) ŏlgul 얼굴
mug[2] *v/t* (*attack*) nosang kangdojirŭl
  hada 노상 강도질을 하다
mugger nosang kangdo 노상 강도
mugging nosang kangdo haeng-wi
  노상 강도 행위
muggy hut'ŏptchigŭnhan 후텁지근한
mule nosae 노새; (*slipper*) myul 뮬,
  twiga t'ŭin kudu 뒤가 트인 구두
♦ **mull over** chuŭi kipkke
  saenggak'ada 주의 깊게 생각하다
multilingual tagugŏŭi 다국어의
multimedia *n* mŏlt'imidiŏ 멀티미디어,
  tajung maech'e 다중 매체
multinational 1 *adj* taguktchŏgŭi
  다국적의 **2** *n* COM taguktchŏk kiŏp
  다국적 기업
multiple *adj* tayanghan 다양한
multiplication MATH kopssem 곱셈
multiply 1 *v/t* kop'ada 곱하다 **2** *v/i*
  chŭnggahada 증가하다
mumble 1 *n* chung-ŏlgŏrim 중얼거림
  2 *v/t* & *v/i* chung-ŏlgŏrida 중얼거리다
mumps ihasŏnnyŏm 이하선염
munch *v/t* & *v/i* ujŏkujŏk sshiptta
  우적우적 씹다
municipal shiŭi 시의
mural *n* pyŏk'wa 벽화
murder 1 *n* sarin 살인 **2** *v/t person*
  sarinhada 살인하다; *song* mangch'yŏ
  not'a 망쳐 놓다
murderer sarinja 살인자
murderous *rage, look* sarinhal kŏt
  kat'ŭn 살인할 것 같은
murmur 1 *n* sokssagim 속삭임 **2** *v/t*
  sokssagida 속삭이다
muscle kŭnyuk 근육
muscular *pain, strain* kŭnyugŭi
  근육의; *person* kŭnyuktchirŭi
  근육질의
muse *v/i* saenggage chamgida 생각에

잠기다

museum pangmulgwan 박물관

mushroom 1 *n* pŏsŏt 버섯 **2** *v/i* ppalli charada 빨리 자라다

music ŭmak 음악; (*written*) akppo 악보

musical 1 *adj* ŭmagŭi 음악의; *person* ŭmaktchŏgin 음악적인; *voice* ŭmakkat'ŭn 음악같은 **2** *n* myujik'ŏl 뮤지컬

musical instrument akki 악기

musician ŭmak-kka 음악가

mussel honghap 홍합

must ◊ (*necessity*) ...haeya hada ...해야 하다; *I ~ be on time* nanŭn pandŭshi cheshigane issŏya handa 나는 반드시 제시간에 있어야 한다; *I ~ kŭraeyaman handa 그래야만 한다; I ~n't be late* nanŭn nŭjŏsŏnŭn andoenda 나는 늦어서는 안된다 ◊ (*probability*): *it ~ be about 6 o'clock* 6shi tchŭm toessŭl kŏyeyo 6시 쯤 됐을 거예요; *they ~ have arrived by now* kŭdŭrŭn chigŭmimyŏn toch'ak'aekketchyo 그들은 지금이면 도착했겠죠

mustache k'otssuyŏm 콧수염

mustard kyŏja 겨자

musty komp'angnae nanŭn 곰팡내 나는

mute *adj* muŏnŭi 무언의

muted *color* pudŭrŏun 부드러운; *opposition, criticism* yak'an 약한

mutilate *person* sanghaerŭl ip'ida 상해를 입히다; *thing* hwesonhada

훼손하다

mutiny 1 *n* pallan 반란 **2** *v/i* pallanŭl irŭk'ida 반란을 일으키다

mutter *v/t & v/i* chung-ŏlgŏrida 중얼거리다

mutual sanghoganŭi 상호간의

muzzle 1 *n* (*of animal, dog*) chudung-i 주둥이; (*device*) immagae 입마개 **2** *v/t*: *~ the press* ŏllon podorŭl maktta 언론 보도를 막다

my ◊ naŭi 나의; ㅂ chŏŭi 저의; *~ decision / money* naŭi kyŏltchŏng / ton 나의 결정 / 돈; *~ leg hurts* tariga ap'ayo 다리가 아파요 ◊ (*referring to family, groups etc, Korean usually uses the pronoun 'our'*) uriŭi 우리의; *~ house / mother* uri chip / ŏmŏni 우리 집 / 어머니; *~ family* uri kajok 우리 가족; *~ country / company* uri nara / hoesa 우리 나라 / 회사

myopic kŭnshianŭi 근시안의

myself na chashin 나 자신; *by ~* (*alone*) honja 혼자; (*without any help*) sŭsŭro 스스로

mysterious shinbihan 신비한

mysteriously shinbihage 신비하게

mystery shinbi 신비; (*fact which is mysterious*) pulgasaŭi 불가사의

mystify pulgahaehage mandŭlda 불가해하게 만들다; *I'm mystified* ihaehal su ŏpssŏyo 이해할 수 없어요

myth shinhwa 신화; *fig* mangsang 망상

mythical shinhwaŭi 신화의

mythology shinhwahak 신화학

N

nab (*take for oneself*) nakka ch'aeda 낚아 채다

nag v/t & v/i chansorihada 잔소리하다; **~ s.o. to do sth** nuguege muŏsŭl harago chansorihada 누구에게 무엇을 하라고 잔소리하다

nagging *person* chansorihanŭn 잔소리하는; *doubt* sŏnggashin 성가신; *pain* kkŭnjilgin 끈질긴

nail (*for wood*) mot 못; (*on finger, toe*) sont'op 손톱

nail clippers sont'opkkak-kki 손톱깎이; **nail file** sont'optchul 손톱줄; **nail polish** maenik'yuŏ 매니큐어; **nail polish remover** maenik'yuŏ chiunŭn yak 매니큐어 지우는 약; **nail scissors** sont'op kkangnŭn kawi 손톱 깎는 가위; **nail varnish** maenik'yuŏ 매니큐어

naive sunjinhan 순진한

naked pŏlgŏbŏsŭn 벌거벗은; *truth, aggression* chŏngnarahan 적나라한; **to the ~ eye** yuganŭronŭn 육안으로는

name 1 *n* irŭm 이름; (*on document*) sŏngmyŏng 성명; **what's your ~?** irŭmi muŏsshimnikka? 이름이 무엇입니까?; (*polite*) sŏnghami ŏttŏk'e toeshimnikka? 성함이 어떻게 되십니까?; **what's his ~?** kŭŭi irŭmŭn muŏshimnikka? 그의 이름은 무엇입니까?; **call s.o. ~s** nugurŭl yok'ada 누구를 욕하다; **make a ~ for oneself** yumyŏnghaejida 유명해지다 **2** v/t irŭmŭl chit-tta 이름을 짓다

♦ **name for:** *name X for Y* Yŭi irŭmŭl ttasŏ Xŭi irŭmŭl chit-tta Y의 이름을 따서 X의 이름을 짓다

namely chŭk 즉

namesake tongmyŏng-iin 동명이인

nametag irŭmp'yo 이름표

Namhae Island Namhaedo 남해도

nanny *n* yumo 유모

nap *n* nattcham 낮잠; **have a ~** nattchamŭl chada 낮잠을 자다

nape: **~ of the neck** mokttŏlmi 목덜미

napkin (*table ~*) naepk'in 냅킨; (*sanitary ~*) saengnidae 생리대

narcotic *n* mayak 마약

narcotics agent mayak tansokppan 마약 단속반

narrate iyagihada 이야기하다

narration (*telling*) iyagihagi 이야기하기

narrative 1 *n* (*story*) iyagi 이야기 **2** *adj poem, style* iyagishigŭi 이야기식의

narrator iyagihanŭn saram 이야기하는 사람

narrow *street, bed, views* chobŭn 좁은; *victory* kakkasŭro ŏdŭn 가까스로 얻은

narrowly *win, escape* kakkasŭro 가까스로

narrow-minded maŭmi chobŭn 마음이 좁은

nasal *voice* k'ossoriŭi 콧소리의

nasty *person, thing to say* mot-ttoen 못된; *smell, weather* pulk'waehan 불쾌한; *cut, wound, disease* shimhan 심한

nation kuk-kka 국가, nara 나라

national 1 *adj* kuk-kkaŭi 국가의, naraŭi 나라의 **2** *n* kungmin 국민

national anthem kuk-kka 국가; (*South Korean*) Aeguk-kka 애국가; **National Assembly** Kuk'oe 국회; **national debt** kukch'ae 국채; **national flag** (*South Korean*) t'aegŭk-kki 태극기; **National Foundation Day** Kaech'ŏnjŏl 개천절

nationalism minjoktchuŭi 민족주의

nationality kuktchŏk 국적

nationalize *industry etc* kugyŏnghwahada 국영화하다

national park kungnip kong-wŏn 국립 공원

native 1 *adj* ch'ulssaeng-ŭi 출생의; ~ *language* mogugŏ 모국어 **2** *n* ch'ulsshinŭi saram 출신의 사람; (*tribesman*) wŏnjumin 원주민

native country ch'ulssaengguk 출생국

native speaker wŏnŏmin 원어민

NATO (= *North Atlantic Treaty Organization*) Pukttaesŏyang Choyak Kigu 북대서양 조약 기구

natural *resources* chayŏnŭi 자연의; *flavor* sunsuhan 순수한; (*obvious*) tangnyŏnhan 당연한; ~ *blonde* t'agonan kŭmbal 타고난 금발; ~ *death* chayŏnsa 자연사

natural gas ch'ŏnyŏn kassŭ 천연 가스

naturalist saengt'aehaktcha 생태학자

naturalize: *become ~d* kwihwahada 귀화하다

naturally (*of course*) tangnyŏnhi 당연히; *behave*, *speak* chayŏnsŭrŏpkke 자연스럽게; (*by nature*) pollae 본래

natural science chayŏn kwahak 자연 과학

natural scientist chayŏn kwahaktcha 자연 과학자

nature chayŏn 자연; (*of person*) ch'ŏnsŏng 천성; (*of problem*) sŏngkkyŏk 성격

nature reserve chayŏn pohogu 자연 보호구

naughty chitkkujŭn 짓궂은; *photograph*, *word etc* yahan 야한

nausea mesŭkkŏum 메스꺼움; *fig* yŏk-kkyŏum 역겨움

nauseate *fig* (*disgust*) yŏk-kkyŏpkke hada 역겹게 하다

nauseating *fig* yŏk-kkyŏun 역겨운

nauseous: *feel ~* t'ohal kŏt kat-tta 토할 것 같다

nautical hanghaeŭi 항해의

nautical mile haeri 해리

naval haegunŭi 해군의

naval base haegun kiji 해군 기지

navel paekkop 배꼽

navigable *river* hanghaehal su innŭn 항해할 수 있는

navigate *v/i* (*in ship*, *airplane*) hanghaehada 항해하다; (*in car*) kil annaerŭl hada 길 안내를 하다; COMPUT kŏmsaek'ada 검색하다

navigation hanghaesul 항해술; (*in car*) kil annaehagi 길 안내하기

navigator (*in ship*, *airplane*) hanghaesa 항해사; (*in car*) kil annaerŭl hanŭn saram 길 안내를 하는 사람

navy haegun 해군

navy blue 1 *n* namsaek 남색 **2** *adj* namsaegŭi 남색의

near 1 *adv* kakkai 가까이 **2** *prep* kakkaie 가까이에; ~ *the bank* ŭnhaeng kakkaie 은행 가까이에; *do you go ~ the bank?* ŭnhaeng kŭnch'ŏro kamnikka? 은행 근처로 갑니까? **3** *adj* kakkaun 가까운; *the ~est bus stop* kajang kakkaun pŏssŭ chŏngnyujang 가장 가까운 버스 정류장; *in the ~ future* kakkaun mirae-e 가까운 미래에

nearby *adv live* kakkapkke 가깝게

nearly kŏŭi 거의

near-sighted kŭnshiŭi 근시의

neat *room*, *desk* kkaekkŭt'an 깨끗한; *person* tanjŏnghan 단정한; *whiskey* sunsuhan 순수한; *solution* hyŏnmyŏnghan 현명한; F (*terrific*) kŭnsahan 근사한

necessarily pandŭshi 반드시

necessary p'iryohan 필요한; *it is ~ to …* …hal p'iryoga it-tta …할 필요가 있다

necessitate p'iryoro hada 필요로 하다

necessity p'iryossŏng 필요성; (*sth necessary*) p'ilssup'um 필수품

neck mok 목

necklace mok-kkŏri 목걸이; **neck-line** (*of dress*) moksssŏn 목선; **neck-tie** nekt'ai 넥타이

née mihon ttaeŭi sŏng 미혼 때의 성

need 1 *n* p'iryo 필요; *if ~ be* p'iryohadamyŏn 필요하다면; *in ~* toumŭi p'iryohan 도움이 필요한; *be in ~ of sth* muŏshi p'iryohada 무엇이 필요하다; *there's no ~ to be upset* kibun nappahal p'iryonŭn

hanado ŏptta 기분 나빠할 필요는
하나도 없다 2 v/t p'iryohada
필요하다; **you'll ~ to buy one**
nŏnŭn hanarŭl sayahal kŏshida 너는
하나를 사야할 것이다; **you don't ~
to wait** kidaril p'iryoga ŏptta 기다릴
필요가 없다; **I ~ to talk to you**
tangshin-gwa iyagihaeyagessŏyo
당신과 이야기해야겠어요; **~ I say
more?** tŏ marhal p'iryoga
issŭmnikka? 더 말할 필요가
있습니까?

needle (*for sewing, on dial*) panŭl
바늘; (*for injection*) chusa panŭl 주사
바늘

needlework panŭjil 바느질

needy pin-gunghan 빈궁한

negative 1 *adj* GRAM pujong-ŭi
부정의; *attitude, person* pujŏngjŏgin
부정적인; ELEC ŭmgŭgŭi 음극의 2 *n*:
answer in the ~ aniragro taedap'ada
아니라고 대답하다

neglect 1 *n* pangch'i 방치 2 *v/t*
garden, one's health tolboji ant'a
돌보지 않다; **~ to do X** Xŭl/rŭl haji
ant'a X을/를 하지 않다

neglected *garden, author* pŏryŏjin
버려진; **feel ~** pŏryŏjin tŭt'an
nŭkkimi tŭlda 버려진 듯한 느낌이
들다

negligence t'aeman 태만

negligent sohorhan 소홀한

negligible *amount* mushihaedo
choŭn 무시해도 좋은

negotiable *salary, terms*
hyŏpssanghal su innŭn 협상할 수
있는

negotiate 1 *v/i* hyŏpssanghada
협상하다 2 *v/t* *deal, settlement*
hyŏpssanghada 협상하다; *obstacles*
ttulkko nagada 뚫고 나가다; *curve*
chal tolda 잘 돌다

negotiation hyŏpssang 협상

negotiator hyŏpssangga 협상가

Negro Hŭgin 흑인

neigh *v/i* hinghinggŏrida
힝힝거리다

neighbor iut saram 이웃 사람; (*at
table*) yŏp saram 옆 사람

neighborhood iut 이웃; **in the ~ of**
fig ... kakkai ... 가까이

neighboring *house, state* iushin
이웃인

neighborly iutkkach'i tajŏnghan
이웃같이 다정한

neither 1 *adj* ŏnŭ ...to anin 어느 ...도
아닌 (+ *negative verb*); **~ applicant
was any good** ŏnŭn hubojado
mattanghaji anat-tta 어느 후보자도
마땅하지 않았다 2 *pron* ŏnŭ
tchŏktto ... 어느 쪽도 ... (+ *negative
verb*); **which do you want? -~,
thanks** ŏttŏn kŏsŭl wŏnhaseyo? –
komaptchina, ŏnŭ tchŏktto
animnida 어떤 것을 원하세요? –
고맙지만, 어느 쪽도 아닙니다 3 *adv*:
~ X nor Y ... Xto Yto ... X도 Y도 ...
(+ *negative verb*); **Jane nor Sally
knew where it was** Cheindo
Saellido kŭgŏshi ŏdi innŭnji mollat-
tta 제인도 샐리도 그것이 어디
있는지 몰랐다 4 *conj*: **~ do I** nadoyo
나도요, chŏdoyo 저도요; **I don't like
it - ~ do I** nanŭn kŭgŏt choahaji
anayo – nado choahaji anayo 나는
그것 좋아하지 않아요 - 나도
좋아하지 않아요; **I can't see it - ~
can I** nanŭn anboinŭn teyo – chŏdo
anboyŏyo 나는 안보이는 데요 - 저도
안보여요

neon light neon ssain 네온 싸인

Nepal Nep'al 네팔

Nepalese 1 *adj* Nep'arŭi 네팔의 2 *n*
(*person*) Nep'arin 네팔인

nephew chok'a 조카

nerd F ŏlgani 얼간이

nerve shin-gyŏng 신경; (*courage*)
yonggi 용기; (*impudence*)
ppŏnppŏnham 뻔뻔함; **it's bad for
my ~s** shin-gyŏng ssŭige handa 신경
쓰이게 한다; **get on s.o.'s ~s**
nuguŭi shin-gyŏng-ŭl kŏndŭrida
누구의 신경을 건드리다

nerve-racking chomajomahage
hanŭn 조마조마하게 하는

nervous *person* shin-gyŏng-i
kwaminhan 신경이 과민한; **be ~
about doing sth** muŏt hanŭn kŏsŭl
puranhaehada 무엇 하는 것을
불안해하다

nervous breakdown shin-gyŏng
soeyak 신경 쇠약

nervous energy shin-gyŏng enŏji
신경 에너지

nervousness shin-gyŏngtchil 신경질

nervous wreck shin-gyŏng
soeyaktcha 신경 쇠약자

nervy (*fresh*) ppŏnppŏnhan 뻔뻔한

nest *n* tungji 둥지

♦ **nestle up to**: ~ *s.o.* nuguege
momŭl p'yŏnhi kidaeda 누구에게
몸을 편히 기대다

net[1] (*for fishing*) kŭmul 그물; (*for
tennis*) net'ŭ 네트

net[2] *adj amount* sunsuhan 순수한;
price chŏngkka 정가; *weight* p'ojang-
ŭl cheoehan 포장을 제외한

net curtain mangsa k'ŏt'ŭn 망사 커튼

net profit suniik 순이익

nettle *v/t* shin-gyŏngtchilnage hada
신경질나게 하다

network (*of contacts, cells*)
kŭmulmang 그물망; COMPUT
net'ŭwŏk'ŭ 네트워크

neurologist shin-gyŏngkkwa ŭisa
신경과 의사

neurosis shin-gyŏngtchŭng 신경증

neurotic *adj* shin-gyŏng kwaminŭi
신경 과민의

neuter *v/t animal* kŏsehada 거세하다

neutral 1 *adj country* chungnibŭi
중립의; *color* chunggansaegŭi
중간색의 **2** *n* (*gear*) chungnip wich'i
중립 위치; *in* ~ chungnibe 중립에

neutrality chungnipssŏng 중립성

neutralize muryŏk'age hada 무력하게
하다

never chŏlttae (+ *negative verb*) 절대;
you're ~ *going to believe this*
tangshinŭn chŏlttaero kŭgŏsŭl midŭl
su ŏpssŭl kŏshimnida 당신은 절대로
그것을 믿을 수 없을 것입니다; *you*
~ *promised, did you?* tangshinŭn
chŏlttaero yakssok'aji anatchyo?
당신은 절대로 약속하지 않았죠? ◊
(*past*) han pŏndo (+ *negative verb*)
한 번도; *I have* ~ *eaten kimchee*
han pŏndo kimch'irŭl mŏgŏbon
chŏgi ŏpssŏyo 한 번도 김치를
먹어본 적이 없어요

never-ending kkŭdŏmnŭn 끝없는

nevertheless kŭrŏmedo pulguhago
그럼에도 불구하고

new saeroun 새로운; *this system is
still* ~ *to me* i pangshigŭn na-ege
yŏjŏnhi saerop-tta 이 방식은 나에게
여전히 새롭다; *I'm* ~ *to the job*
nanŭn kŭ ire ikssuk'aji ant'a 나는 그
일에 익숙하지 않다; *that's nothing*
~ saeroun kŏsŭn amu kŏt-tto ŏptta
새로운 것은 아무 것도 없다

newborn *adj* kannan 갓난

newcomer saero on saram 새로 온
사람; (*to organization*) shinip 신입

newly (*recently*) ch'oegŭn 최근

newly-weds shinhon pubu 신혼 부부

new moon ch'ossŭngttal 초승달

news soshik 소식; (*on TV, radio*)
nyusŭ 뉴스; *that's* ~ *to me* kŭmshi
ch'omunida 금시 초문이다

news agency t'ongshinsa 통신사;
newscast TV nyusŭ pangsong 뉴스
방송; **newscaster** TV nyusŭ
pangsonghanŭn saram 뉴스
방송하는 사람; **news dealer**
shinmun p'anmaeso 신문 판매소;
news flash sokppo 속보; **newspaper** shinmun 신문; **newsreader** TV
etc nyusŭ pangsonghanŭn saram
뉴스 방송하는 사람; **news report**
nyusŭ podo 뉴스 보도; **newsstand**
shinmun kap'andae 신문 가판대;
newsvendor shinmun p'anmaewŏn
신문 판매원

New Year Saehae 새해; (*public
holiday*) Shinjŏng 신정; *Happy* ~!
Saehae pok mani padŭseyo! 새해 복
많이 받으세요!; **New Year's Day**
Saehae Ch'ŏnnal 새해 첫날; (*lunar*)
Sŏllal 설날; **New Year's Eve** Sŏttal
Kŭmnal 섣달 그믐날; **New York**
Nyuyok 뉴욕; **New Zealand**
Nyujillaendŭ 뉴질랜드; **New Zea-
lander** Nyujillaendŭin 뉴질랜드인

next 1 *adj* taŭmŭi 다음의; *the* ~
*week/month he came back
again* taŭm chu/tare kŭga tashi
torawat-tta 다음 주/달에 그가 다시
돌아왔다; *who's* ~? taŭm pun? 다음
분? **2** *adv* taŭme 다음에; ~ *to*
(*beside*) ...ŭi yŏp'ye ...의 옆에; (*in
comparison with*) ...e iŏsŏ ...에
이어서

next-door 1 *adj neighbor* yŏptchibŭi

옆집의 2 *adv live* yŏptchibe 옆집에
next of kin kŭnch'in 근친
nibble *v/t* kalga mŏktta 갉아 먹다;
s.o.'s ear saltchak kkaemulda 살짝
깨물다
nice mŏtchin 멋진; *be ~ to your
father* ne abŏjihant'e charhae 네
아버지한테 잘해; *that's very ~ of
you* chŏngmal ch'injŏrhagunnyo
정말 친절하군요
nicely *written, presented* chal 잘;
(*pleasantly*) kippŭge 기쁘게
niceties: *social ~* sagyoppŏp 사교법
niche (*in market*) t'ŭmsae 틈새;
(*special position*) chŏktchŏrhan
changso 적절한 장소
nick *n* (*cut*) hŭm 흠; *in the ~ of time*
paro che ttaee 바로 제 때에
nickel nik'el 니켈; (*coin*)
ossent'ŭtchari tongjŏn 오센트짜리
동전
nickname *n* pyŏlmyŏng 별명
niece yŏja chok'a 여자 조카
niggardly *adj* insaek'an 인색한
night pam 밤; (*in hotel*) pak 박; *tomorrow ~* naeil pam 내일 밤;
(*evening*) naeil chŏnyŏk 내일 저녁;
11 o'clock at ~ pam yŏrhanshi 밤
11시; *travel by ~* pam yŏhaeng 밤
여행; *during the ~* pam saie 밤
사이에; *stay the ~* pamŭl chinaeda
밤을 지내다; *a room for 3 ~s* samil
pamŭl mugŭl pang 3일 밤을 묵을
방; *work ~s* yagan kŭnmuida 야간
근무이다; *good ~* annyŏnghi
chumushipsshiyo 안녕히 주무십시요,
F chal cha 잘 자
nightcap (*drink*) chagi chŏne
mashinŭn sul 자기 전에 마시는 술;
nightclub nait'ŭ k'ŭllŏp 나이트클럽;
nightdress chamot 잠옷; **nightfall:**
at ~ ch'ojŏnyŏge 초저녁에; **night
flight** pambihaenggi 밤비행기;
nightgown chamot 잠옷
nightingale nait'inggeil 나이팅게일
nightlife pam yuhŭng 밤 유흥
nightly 1 *adj* maeil pamŭi 매일 밤의
2 *adv* maeil pame 매일 밤에
nightmare angmong 악몽; *fig*
angmonggat'ŭn kŏt 악몽같은 것
night porter yagŭn poi 야근 보이;

night school yagan hak-kkyo 야간
학교; **night shift** yagan kŭnmu 야간
근무; **nightshirt** chamot 잠옷; **nightspot** nait'ŭ k'ŭllop 나이트 클럽;
nighttime: *at ~*, *in the ~* pame 밤에
nimble chaeppparŭn 재빠른
nine ahop 아홉, ku 구
nineteen yŏrahop 열 아홉, shipkku
십구
nineteenth yŏrahop pŏntchaeŭi 열
아홉 번째의
ninetieth ahŭn pŏntchaeŭi 아흔
번째의
ninety ahŭn아흔, kuship 구십
ninth ahop pŏntchaeŭi 아홉 번째의
nip *n* (*pinch*) kkojipk-kki 꼬집기;
(*bite*) mulgi 물기
nipple chŏtkkoktchi 젖꼭지, yudu
유두
nitrogen chilso 질소
no 1 *adv* ◊ aniyo 아니오 ◊ (*using 'yes',
ie yes, that is right*): *you don't know
the answer, do you? - ~, I don't*
tabŭl morŭjyo? - ye, mollayo 답을
모르죠? - 예, 몰라요 **2** *adj*: *there's
~ coffee / tea left* namŭn
k'ŏp'i / ch'aga ŏptta 남은 커피 / 차가
없다; *I have ~ family* nanŭn kajogi
amudo ŏptta 나는 가족이 아무도
없다; *I'm ~ linguist* nanŭn
ŏnŏhaktchaga anida 나는
언어학자가 아니다; *~ smoking / ~
parking* kŭmyŏn / chuch'agŭmji
금연 / 주차금지; *~ man is perfect*
nugudo wanjŏnhaji ant'a 누구도
완전하지 않다
nobility kip'um 기품; *the ~* kwijok
귀족
noble *adj* kogwihan 고귀한
nobody amudo (+ *negative verb*)
아무도; *~ knows* amudo morŭnda
아무도 모른다; *there was ~ at
home* chibenŭn amudo ŏpssŏt-tta
집에는 아무도 없었다; *who was
there? - ~* kŏgi nuga issŏssŏyo? -
amudo ŏpssŏssŏyo 거기 누가
있었어요? - 아무도 없었어요
nod 1 *n* kkŭdŏgim 끄덕임 **2** *v/i*
kogaerŭl kkŭdŏgida 고개를 끄덕이다
♦**nod off** (*fall asleep*) kkubŏk-
kkubŏk cholda 꾸벅꾸벅 졸다

no-hoper F munŭngnyŏktcha 무능력자

noise sori 소리; (*loud, unpleasant*) soŭm 소음

noisy shikkŭrŏun 시끄러운

nominal *amount* irŭmppunin 이름뿐인

nominate (*appoint*) immyŏnghada 임명하다; **~ s.o. for a post** (*propose*) nugurŭl kongch'ŏnhada 누구를 공천하다

nomination (*appointing*) immyŏng 임명; (*proposal*) kongch'ŏn 공천; (*person proposed*) kongch'ŏnja 공천자

nominee (*person proposed*) kongch'ŏnja 공천자; (*for prize*) hubo 후보; (*person appointed*) immyŏngja 임명자

nonalcoholic alk'oori ŏmnŭn 알코올이 없는

nonaligned chungniptchŏgin 중립적인

nonchalant t'aeyŏnhan 태연한

noncommissioned officer yuk-kkun hasagwan 육군 하사관

noncommittal *response* aemaemohohan 애매모호한; **he was very ~** kŭnŭn koengjanghi aemaemohohan t'aedorŭl chihaett-tta 그는 굉장히 애매모호한 태도를 취했다

nondescript t'ŭktching-ŏmnŭn 특징없는

none amu kŏtto (+ *negative verb*) 아무 것도; (*person*) amudo (+ *negative verb*) 아무도; **~ of the students is American** hakssaengdŭl chung amudo Miguk sarami anida 학생들 중 아무도 미국 사람이 아니다; **~ of the chocolate was sold** amu ch'yok'ollitto p'alliji anatta 아무 쵸콜릿도 팔리지 않았다; **there is / are ~ left** amu kŏtto namŭn kŏshi ŏptta 아무 것도 남은 것이 없다

nonentity pojal kŏt ŏmnŭn 보잘 것 없는

nonetheless kŭrŏmedo pulguhago 그럼에도 불구하고

nonexistent chonjaehaji annŭn 존재하지 않는; **nonfiction** nonp'iksshyŏn 논픽션;

non(in)flammable puryŏnsŏng-ŭi 불연성의; **noninterference, nonintervention** pulgansŏp 불간섭; **non-iron** *shirt* tarimjiri p'iryoŏmnŭn 다림질이 필요없는

no-no F: **that's a ~** kŭgŏsŭn haesŏnŭn andoenda 그것은 해서는 안된다

no-nonsense *approach* hyŏnshiltchŏgin 현실적인

nonpayment mibul 미불; **nonpolluting** mugonghaeŭi 무공해의; **nonresident** *n* pigŏjuja 비거주자; **nonreturnable** *deposit* hwanbul pulgaŭi 환불 불가의

nonsense maldo andoenŭn kŏt 말도 안되는 것; **don't talk ~** maldo andoenŭn sori haji mara 말도 안되는 소리 하지 마라; **~, it's easy!** musŭn sori, shwiun kŏshiya! 무슨 소리. 쉬운 것이야!

nonskid *tires* mikkŭrŏjiji annŭn 미끄러지지 않는; **nonslip** *surface* mikkŭrŏjiji annŭn 미끄러지지 않는; **nonsmoker** (*person*) pihŭbyŏnja 비흡연자; **nonstandard** p'yojune mat-tchi annŭn 표준에 맞지 않는; **nonstick** *pan* nurŏputtchi annŭn 눌어붙지 않는; **nonstop 1** *adj flight, train* chik'aengŭi 직행의; *chatter* chungdan ŏmnŭn 중단 없는 **2** *adv fly, travel* chik'aeng-ŭro 직행으로; *chatter, argue* chungdan ŏpsshi 중단 없이; **nonswimmer** suyŏng-ŭl mot'anŭn saram 수영을 못하는 사람; **nonunion** *adj* chohabe kaip'aji anŭn 조합에 가입하지 않은; **nonviolence** pip'ongnyŏk 비폭력; **nonviolent** pip'ongnyŏgŭi 비폭력의

noodles kukssu 국수; (*instant*) ramyŏn 라면; (*chilled*) naengmyŏn 냉면

nook kusŏk 구석

noon chŏng-o 정오; **at ~** chŏng-o-e 정오에

noose olgami 올가미

nor ...to ttohan (+ *negative verb*) ...도 또한; **~ do I** nado anida 나도 아니다

norm chŏngsang 정상

normal chŏngsang-ŭi 정상의
normality chŏngsang sangt'ae 정상
상태
normalize *relationships*
chŏngsanghwahada 정상화하다
normally (*usually*) pot'ong-ŭro
보통으로; (*in a normal way*)
chŏngsang-ŭro 정상으로
north 1 *n* puk 북; **to the ~ of** …ŭi
puktchoge …의 북쪽에 **2** *adj*
puktchogŭi 북쪽의 **3** *adv travel*
puktchogŭro 북쪽으로; **~ of** …ŭi
pukppang-e …의 북방에
North America Pungmi 북미
North American 1 *adj* Pungmiŭi
북미의 **2** *n* Pungmiin 북미인
northeast *n* tongbuk 동북
northerly *adj* puk'yang-ŭi 북향의
northern pukppugŭi 북부의
northerner pukppu chibang saram
북부 지방 사람
North Korea Puk'an 북한
North Korean 1 *adj* Puk'anŭi 북한의
2 *n* Puk'an saram 북한 사람
North Pole Pukkŭk 북극
northward *travel* puktchogŭro
북쪽으로
northwest *n* pukssŏ 북서
Norway Norŭwei 노르웨이
Norwegian 1 *adj* Norŭweiŭi
노르웨이의 **2** *n* (*person*) Norŭweiin
노르웨이인; (*language*) Norŭweiŏ
노르웨이어
nose k'o 코; *it was right under my
~!* paro nae nun ap'esŏ irŏnat-tta!
바로 내 눈 앞에서 일어났다!
♦ **nose around** k'aeda 캐다
nosebleed k'op'i 코피
nostalgia hyangsu 향수
nostalgic hyangsuŭi 향수의
nostril k'otkkumŏng 콧구멍
nosy ch'amgyŏnhagi choahanŭn
참견하기 좋아하는
not: **~ this one, that one** igŏshi
anira chŏgŏt 이것이 아니라 저것;
igŏt malgo chŏgŏt 이것 말고 저것; **~
now** chigŭm malgo 지금 말고; **~
there** kŭgŏt malgo 그곳 말고; **~
before Tuesday / next week**
hwayoil / taŭm chu chŏnenŭn
andoego 화요일 / 다음 주 전에는

andoego; **~ for me, thanks**
komaptchiman, chŏnŭn
kwanch'anssŭmnida 고맙지만, 저는
괜찮습니다; **~ a lot** pyŏllo 별로 ◊
(*with verbs*): *it's ~ ready / allowed*
igŏsŭn chunbitoeji / hŏgadoeji anat-
tta 그것은 준비되지 / 허가되지
않았다; *I don't know* nanŭn
morŭnda 나는 모른다; *I am ~
American* nanŭn Miguk-in-i
animnida 나는 미국인이 아닙니다;
he didn't help kŭnŭn toptchi anat-
tta 그는 돕지 않았다; *don't do it
like that* kŭrŏk'e haji maseyo
그렇게 하지 마세요
notable chumok'al manhan 주목할
만한
notary kongjŭng-in 공증인
notch *n* pen chaguk 벤 자국
note *n* (*short letter*) tchalbŭn p'yŏnji
짧은 편지; MUS ŭmp'yo 음표; (*to self*)
memo 메모; (*comment on text*) chu
주; *take ~s* chŏktta 적다; *take ~ of
sth* muŏsŭl arach'aeda 무엇을
알아채다
♦ **note down** chŏgŏduda 적어두다
notebook kongch'aek 공책; COMPUT
not'ŭbuk 노트북
noted allyŏjin 알려진
notepad memojich'ŏp 메모지첩
notepaper p'yŏnjiji 편지지
nothing amu kŏt-tto (+ *negative verb*)
아무 것도; *there's ~ left* amu kŏt-
tto namtchi anat-tta 아무 것도 남지
않았다; *what did you do? - ~*
muŏsŭl mŏgŏssŏyo? - amu kŏt-tto
무엇을 먹었어요? - 아무 것도; **~ for
me thanks** chŏnŭn kwaench'anayo
저는 괜찮아요; **~ can change it**
ŏttŏn kŏt-tto kŭgŏsŭl pakkul su
ŏptta 어떤 것도 그것을 바꿀 수
없다; **~ but…** …il ppun …일 뿐; *he's
~ but trouble* kŭnŭn munjekkŏriil
ppunida 그는 문제거리일 뿐이다; **~
much** pyŏllo 별로; **for ~** (*for free*)
muryoro 무료로; (*for no reason*)
amu iyu ŏpsshi 아무 이유 없이; *I'd
like ~ better* naega cheil choahanŭn
kŏshida 내가 제일 좋아하는 것이다
notice 1 *n* (*on bulletin board, in
street*) keshi 게시; (*advance warning*)

chuŭi 주의; (*in newspaper*) konggo 공고; (*to leave job, to leave house*) t'ongji 통지; *at short ~* tchalbŭn shihanŭl namgin ch'ae 짧은 시한을 남긴 채; *until further ~* ch'uhu t'ongjiga issŭl ttaekkaji 추후 통지가 있을 때까지; *give s.o. his / her ~* (*to quit job*) nuguege haeim t'ongjirŭl hada 누구에게 해임 통지를 하다; *hand in one's ~* (*to employer*) sajik'al kŏsŭl allida 사직할 것을 알리다; *four weeks' ~* saju chŏne t'ongjihanŭn kŏt 사주 전에 통지하는 것; *take ~ of* ...e chuŭihada ...에 주의하다; *take no ~ of* ...e amurŏn chuŭirŭl haji ant'a ...에 아무런 주의를 하지 않다 2 *v/t* arach'aeda 알아채다

noticeable chumok'al manhan 주목할 만한

notify konggohada 공고하다

notion saenggak 생각

notions panŭjil yongp'um 바느질 용품

notorious angmyŏng nop'ŭn 악명 높은

nougat nuga 누가

noun myŏngsa 명사

nourishing yŏngnyang-innŭn 영양있는

nourishment yŏngnyangbun 영양분

novel *n* sosŏl 소설

novelist sosŏlga 소설가

novelty (*being novel*) chamshinham 참신함; (*sth novel*) saeroum 새로움

November shibirwŏl 십일월

novice ch'oshimja 초심자

now chigŭm 지금; *~ and again, ~ and then* ttaettaero 때때로; *by ~* chigŭmtchŭm 지금쯤; *from ~ on* chigŭmbut'ŏ 지금부터; *right ~* paro chigŭm 바로 지금; *just ~* (*at this moment*) chigŭm paro 지금 바로; (*a little while ago*) paro chŏne 바로 전에; *~, ~!* cha, cha! 자, 자!; *~, where did I put it?* ŏ, naega kŭgŏsŭl ŏdie tuŏssŭlkka? 어, 내가 그것을 어디에 두었을까?

nowadays yojŭŭm 요즈음

nowhere amu kosedo 아무 곳에도; *it's ~ near finished* hanado

kkŭnnaji anat-tta 하나도 끝나지 않았다

nozzle kkŭt 끝

nuclear haegŭi 핵의, haek 핵

nuclear energy haek enŏji 핵 에너지; **nuclear fission** haek punnyŏl 핵 분열; **nuclear-free** pihaegŭi 비핵의; **nuclear physics** haek mullihak 핵 물리학; **nuclear power** wŏnjaryŏk 원자력; **nuclear power station** wŏnjaryŏk paltchŏnso 원자력 발전소; **nuclear reactor** wŏnjaro 원자로; **nuclear waste** haek p'yegimul 핵 폐기물; **nuclear weapons** haek mugi 핵 무기

nude 1 *adj* almomŭi 알몸의 2 *n* (*painting*) nach'ehwa 나체화; *in the ~* nach'ero 나체로

nudge *v/t* p'alkkumch'iro k'ukk'uk tchirŭda 팔꿈치로 쿡쿡 찌르다

nudist *n* nach'ejuŭija 나체주의자

nuisance kwich'anŭn kŏt 귀찮은 것; *make a ~ of oneself* namege p'yerŭl kkich'ida 남에게 폐를 끼치다; *what a ~!* irŏk'e kwich'anŭl suga! 이렇게 귀찮을 수가!

nuke *v/t* haek konggyŏk'ada 핵 공격하다

null and void muhyoŭi 무효의

numb kamgagŏmnŭn 감각없는; (*emotionally*) mugamgak'an 무감각한

number 1 *n* (*figure, quantity*) su 수; (*of hotel room, house, phone - etc*) pŏnho 번호; *quite a ~ of* manŭn 많은; *a small ~ of* chŏgŭn 적은 2 *v/t* (*put a number on*) pŏnhorŭl maegida 번호를 매기다

numeral sutcha 숫자

numerate kyesanŭl hal su innŭn 계산을 할 수 있는

numeric keys COMPUT sutchap'an 숫자판

numerous manŭn 많은

nun sunyŏ 수녀

nurse kanhosa 간호사

nursery yugashil 육아실; (*for plants*) onshil 온실

nursery rhyme tongnyo 동요; **nursery school** poyugwŏn 보육원; **nursery school teacher** poyugwŏn

kyosa 보육원 교사
nursing kanho ŏmmu 간호 업무
nursing home (*for old people*)
yangnowŏn 양로원
nut kyŏn-gwa 견과; (*for bolt*) nŏt'ŭ
너트; **~s** F (*testicles*) pural 불알
nutcrackers hodu kkanŭn kigu 호두
까는 기구
nutrient yŏngnyangbun 영양분
nutrition yŏngnyang 영양
nutritious yŏngnyang-i innŭn 영양이

있는
nuts *adj* F (*crazy*) mich'in 미친; *be ~*
about s.o. nugue mich'ida 누구에
미치다
nutshell: *in a ~* aju kanttanhage 아주
간단하게
nutty *taste* kyŏn-gwa mashi nanŭn
견과 맛이 나는; F (*crazy*) mich'in
미친
nylon 1 *n* naillon 나일론 **2** *adj*
naillonŭi 나일론의

O

oak (*tree*) ok'ŭnamu 오크나무;
(*wood*) ok'ŭ 오크

oar no 노

oasis oashissŭ 오아시스; *fig*
hyushikch'ŏ 휴식처

oath LAW sŏnsŏ 선서; (*swearword*)
yokssŏl 욕설; *you are on ~*
tangshinŭn sŏnsŏrŭl haessŭmnida
당신은 선서를 했습니다

oatmeal ot'ŭmil 오트밀

oats kwiri 귀리

obedience sunjong 순종

obedient sunjonghanŭn 순종하는

obey ...e sunjonghada ...에 순종하다

obituary *n* pugo 부고

object¹ *n* (*thing*) mulch'e 물체; (*of
love, pity*) taesang 대상; (*aim*)
moktchŏk 목적; GRAM moktchŏgŏ
목적어

object² *v/i* pandaehada 반대하다
♦ **object to** ...e pandaehada ...에
반대하다

objection pandae 반대

objectionable (*unpleasant*)
pulk'waehan 불쾌한

objective 1 *adj* kaekkwanjŏgin
객관적인 2 *n* mokp'yo 목표

obligation ŭimu 의무; *be under an ~
to s.o.* nuguege ŭnhyerŭl ipkko it-
tta 누구에게 은혜를 입고 있다

obligatory ŭimuŭi 의무의

oblige: *much ~d!* chŏngmal
komawŏyo! 정말 고마워요!

obliging chal tolbwajunŭn 잘
돌봐주는

oblique 1 *adj reference* kanjŏptchŏgin
간접적인 2 *n* (*in punctuation*)
pitkkŭm 빗금

obliterate *city* wanjŏnhi p'agoehada
완전히 파괴하다; *memory* chiuda
지우다

oblivion ich'yŏjin sangt'ae 잊혀진
상태; *fall into ~* ich'yŏjida 잊혀지다

oblivious: *be ~ of* ...ŭl/rŭl arach'ariji

mot'ada ...을/를 알아차리지 못하다

oblong *adj* chikssagak'yŏng-ŭi
직사각형의

obnoxious aju pulk'waehan 아주
불쾌한

obscene ŭmnanhan 음란한; *poverty*
kkŭmtchik'an 끔찍한

obscure (*hard to see*) chal poiji
annŭn 잘 보이지 않는; (*hard to
understand*) nanhaehan 난해한;
(*little known*) mumyŏng-ŭi 무명의

observance (*of festival*) haengsa 행사

observant kwanch'allyŏgi yerihan
관찰력이 예리한

observation (*of nature*) kwanch'al
관찰; (*comment*) kwanch'al kyŏlgwa
관찰 결과

observatory kwanch'ŭksso 관측소

observe (*notice*) nunch'ich'aeda
눈치채다; *natural phenomena*
kwanch'arhada 관찰하다; *he was ~d
leaving the ...* kŭga ...ŭl/rŭl
ttŏnanŭn kŏshi mok-kkyŏkttoeŏt-tta
그가 ...을/를 떠나는 것이
목격되었다

observer kwanch'altcha 관찰자; (*at
conference, elections*) ip'oein 입회인

obsess: *be ~ed with* ...e(ge)
sarojap'ida ...에(게) 사로잡히다

obsession kangbak kwannyŏm 강박
관념

obsessive kangbak kwanyŏme
sarojap'in 강박 관념에 사로잡힌

obsolete p'yemuri toen 폐물이 된

obstacle chang-ae 장애; (*to progress
etc*) panghae 방해

obstetrician sanbuinkkwa ŭisa
산부인과 의사

obstinacy kojip 고집

obstinate kojibi sen 고집이 센

obstruct *road, passage* maktta 막다;
investigation, police panghaehada
방해하다

obstruction (*on road etc*)

panghaemul 방해물
obstructive *tactics* panghaehanŭn
방해하는
obtain hoektŭk'ada 획득하다; *advice*
ŏt-tta 얻다
obtainable *products* kuibi kanŭnghan
구입이 가능한
obvious myŏngbaek'an 명백한; (*not
subtle*) nogoltchŏgin 노골적인
obviously myŏngbaek'age 명백하게;
~! mullonijiyo! 물론이지요!
occasion ttae 때
occasional kakkŭmŭi 가끔의
occasionally ttaettaero 때때로
occult 1 *adj* mabŏbŭi 마법의 **2** *n:* the
~ mabŏp 마법
occupant (*of vehicle*) sŭnggaek 승객;
(*of house*) chugŏja 주거자
occupation (*job*) chigŏp 직업; (*of
country*) chŏmnyŏng 점령
occupy ch'ajihada 차지하다; *country*
chŏmnyŏnghada 점령하다
occur irŏnada 일어나다; *it ~red to
me that ...* na-ege ...ranŭn
saenggagi ttollat-tta 나에게 ...라는
생각이 떠올랐다
occurrence sakkŏn 사건
ocean pada 바다
o'clock: *at five/six ~* tasŏt/yŏsot
shie 다섯/여섯 시에
October shiwŏl 시월
octopus munŏ 문어; (*very small*)
naktchi 낙지
odd (*strange*) isanghan 이상한; (*not
even*) holssu 홀수; *the ~ one out*
(*person*) yubyŏlnan saram 유별난
사람; (*thing*) yubyŏlnan kŏt 유별난
것
odds: *be at ~ with* ...wa/kwa
ch'ungdorhada ...와/과 충돌하다
odds and ends chapttongsani
잡동사니; (*to do*) chapttahan kŏttŭl
잡다한 것들
odometer chuhaeng kŏrigye 주행
거리계
odor naemsae 냄새
of (*possession*) ...ŭi ...의; *the color ~
the car* kŭ ch'aŭi saek 그 차의 색;
the works ~ Dickens Tik'insŭŭi
chakp'um 디킨스의 작품; *five/ten
minutes ~ twelve* yŏldushi obun/

shippun jŏn 열두시 오분/십분 전;
die ~ cancer/pneumonia
amŭro/p'yeryŏmŭro chuktta
암으로/폐렴으로 죽다; *love ~
money/adventure* tone/mohŏme
taehan sarang 돈에/모험에 대한
사랑; ~ *the three this is ...* set
chung-e igŏshi ...ida 셋 중에 이것이
...이다
off 1 *prep* ...esŏ ttŏrŏjyŏsŏ ...에서
떨어져서; ~ *the main road* (*away
from*) chudoroesŏ ttŏrŏjyŏ
주도로에서 떨어져; (*leading off*)
chudoroesŏ pŏsŏna 주도로에서
벗어나; *$20 ~ the price* 20tallŏ
harinhayŏ 20달러 할인하여; *he's ~
his food* kŭnŭn immasŭl irŏt-tta
그는 입맛을 잃었다 **2** *adv: be ~* (*of
light, TV, machine*) kkŏjyŏ it-tta
꺼져 있다; (*of brake*) p'ullyŏ it-tta
풀려 있다; (*of lid*) yŏllyŏ it-tta 열려
있다; (*not at work*) shwida 쉬다;
(*canceled*) ch'wisodoeda 취소되다;
we're ~ tomorrow (*leaving*) urinŭn
naeil ttŏnanda 우리는 내일 떠난다;
I'm ~ to New York nanŭn Nyuyoge
kal kŏshida 나는 뉴욕에 갈 것이다;
with his pants/hat ~ pajirŭl/
mojarŭl pŏsŭnch'ae 바지를/모자를
벗은채; *take a day ~* haru shwida
하루 쉬다; *it's 3 miles ~* 3mail
ttŏrŏjyŏ it-tta 3마일 떨어져 있다; *it's
a long way ~* (*in the distance*) mŏlli
ttŏrojyŏ it-tta 멀리 떨어져 있다; (*in
the future*) mŏn amnarŭi irida 먼
앞날의 일이다; *drive/walk ~* ch'arŭl
molgo/kŏrŏsŏ ka pŏrida 차를
몰고/걸어서 가 버리다 **3** *adj: the ~
switch* chŏngji pŏt'ŭn 정지 버튼
offend *v/t* (*insult*) kibun sanghage
hada 기분 상하게 하다
offender LAW pŏmjoeja 범죄자
offense LAW wibŏp 위법
offensive 1 *adj* pulk'waehan 불쾌한
2 *n* MIL konggyŏk 공격; *go onto the
~* konggyŏk'ada 공격하다
offer 1 *n* chegong 제공 **2** *v/t*
chegonghada 제공하다; ~ *s.o. sth*
nuguege muŏsŭl kwŏnhada 누구에게
무엇을 권하다
offhand *adj attitude* amurŏk'ena

hanŭn aimurŏk'e hanŭn
office (*building*) samushillyong
kŏnmul 사무실용 건물; (*room*)
samushil 사무실; (*position*)
kwanch'ŏng 관청
office block samushillyong koch'ŭng
piltting 사무실용 고층 빌딩
office hours ŏmmu shigan 업무 시간
officer MIL changgyo 장교; (*in police*)
kyŏnggwan 경관
official 1 *adj organization, statement*
kongshigŭi 공식의; *view, theory*
kongtchŏgin 공적인; (*confirmed*)
kongshik'wadoen 공식화된 **2** *n*
kongmuwŏn 공무원
officially (*strictly speaking*)
kongshiktchŏgŭro 공식적으로
off-line *adj* chŏpssogŭl anhan
sangt'aeŭi 접속을 안한 상태의; **go ~**
chŏpssogŭl kkŭnt'a 접속을 끊다
off-peak *rates* hansanhan ttaeŭi
한산한 때의; *season* pisugiŭi
비수기의
off-season 1 *adj* pisugiŭi 비수기의
2 *n* pisugi 비수기
offset *v/t losses* sangswaehada
상쇄하다
offside 1 *adj wheel etc* ch'ado tchogŭi
차도 쪽의 **2** *adv* SP op'ŭsaidŭ
오프사이드
offspring chashik 자식
off-white *adj* misaegŭi 미색의
often chaju 자주
oil 1 *n* kirŭm 기름; (*for machine*)
sŏgyu 석유; (*for skin*) oil 오일 **2** *v/t*
hinges, bearings kirŭmch'irŭl hada
기름칠을 하다
oil company sŏgyu hoesa 석유 회사;
oil painting yuhwa 유화; **oil rig**
sŏgyu kulch'ak changch'i 석유 굴착
장치; **oil tanker** yujosŏn 유조선; **oil
well** yujŏng 유정
oily kirŭmkki manŭn 기름기 많은
ointment yŏn-go 연고
ok: **can I? - ~** haedo toelkkayo? -
kŭraeyo 해도 될까요? - 그래요; **is it
~ with you if ...?** ... haedo
kwaench'angessŭmnikka? ... 해도
괜찮겠습니까?; **that's ~ by me**
nanŭn kwaench'anayo 나는
괜찮아요; **are you ~?** (*well, not hurt*)

kwaench'anŭseyo? 괜찮으세요?; **are
you ~ for Friday?** kŭmnyoire
kwaench'anŭseyo? 금요일에
괜찮으세요?; **he's ~** (*is a good guy*)
kŭnŭn kwaench'anŭn saramida 그는
괜찮은 사람이다; **is this bus ~
...?** i pŏssŭ ...e kamnikka? 이 버스
...에 갑니까?; **the car's going ~
now** ch'aga ijenŭn chal kanda 차가
이제는 잘 간다
old *person* nŭlgŭn 늙은; *building, car
etc* oraedoen 오래된; *custom* oraen
오랜; (*previous*) yejŏnŭi 예전의; (*no
longer fresh*) nalgŭn 낡은; **how ~
are you/is he?** tangshinŭn/kŭnŭn
myŏtssarimnikka? 당신은/그는
몇살입니까?
old age nonyŏn 노년
Old Choson Kojosŏn 고조선
old-fashioned kushigŭi 구식의
olive ollibŭ 올리브
olive oil ollibŭ kirŭm 올리브 기름
Olympic Games Ollimp'ik Keim
올림픽 게임
omelet omŭllet 오믈렛
ominous pulgirhan 불길한
omission (*act*) t'aeman 태만; (*that
omitted*) ppajin kŏt 빠진 것
omit ppaeda 빼다; **~ to do sth**
muŏsŭl hagirŭl it-tta 무엇을 하기를
잊다
on 1 *prep* ... wie ... 위에; **~ the table**
t'eibŭl wie 테이블 위에; **~ the wall**
pyŏge 벽에; **~ the bus/train** pŏsŭe/
kich'a-e 버스에/기차에; **~ TV/the
radio** t'ibŭiro/radioro TV로/
라디오로; **~ Sunday** iryoire
일요일에; **~ the 1st of ...** ...ŭi
ch'ŏtchaenare ...의 첫째날에; **this is
~ me** (*I'm paying*) chega
naegessŭmnida 제가 내겠습니다; **~
his arrival/departure** kŭga
toch'ak'aja/ch'ulbarhaja kot 그가
도착하자/출발하자 곧 **2** *adv* **be ~**
(*of light, TV, computer etc*) k'yŏjyŏ
it-tta 켜져 있다; (*of brake*) kŏllyŏ it-
tta 걸려 있다; (*of lid, top*) tach'yŏ it-
tta 닫혀 있다; (*of program*)
pangsongdoeda 방송되다; (*of
meeting etc: be scheduled to happen*)
itkket-tta 있겠다; **what's ~ tonight?**

(*on TV etc*) onŭrŭn muŏsŭl hamnikka? 오늘은 무엇을 합니까?; (*what's planned?*) onŭrŭn muŏsŭl hal kŏsimnikka? 오늘은 무엇을 할 것입니까?; *with his jacket / hat ~* oet'urŭl ipkko / mojarŭl ssŭgo 외투를 입고 / 모자를 쓰고; *you're ~* (*I accept your offer etc*) chossŭmnida 좋습니다; *~ you go* (*go ahead*) kyesok'ahipsshio 계속하십시오; *walk / talk ~* kyesok kŏt-tta / iyagi hada 계속 걷다 / 이야기 하다; *and so ~* kit'adŭngdŭng 기타 등등; *~ and ~ talk etc* kkŭnimŏpsshi kyesok'aesŏ 끊임없이 계속해서 3 *adj*: *the ~ switch* shijak pŏt'ŭn 시작 버튼

once 1 *adv* (*one time*) han pŏn 한 번; (*formerly*) hanttaee 한때에; *~ again*, *~ more* tashi han pŏn 다시 한 번; *at ~* (*immediately*) chŭksshi 즉시; *at ~* (*suddenly*) kaptchagi 갑자기; (*all*) *at ~* (*together*) hankkŏbŏne 한꺼번에; *~ upon a time there was ...* yennal yettchŏge ... i issŏt-tta 옛날 옛적에 ... 이 있었다 2 *conj*: *...hal ttae ...*할 때; *~ you have finished* nega ta kkŭnnaessŭl ttae 네가 다 끝냈을 때

one 1 (*number*) hana 하나, il 일 2 *adj* hanaŭi 하나의; *~ day* ŏnŭ nal 어느 날 3 *pron* hana 하나; *which ~?* (*person*) ŏnŭ saram? 어느 사람?; (*thing*) ŏnŭ kŏt? 어느 것?; *~ by ~* enter, deal with hanasshik 하나씩; *~ another* sŏro 서로; *what can say / do?* nuga muŏsŭl marhal / hal su itkketssŭmnikka? 누가 무엇을 말할 / 할 수 있겠습니까?; *the little ~s* aidŭl 아이들

one-off *n* (*unique event, person*) yuirhan kŏt 유일한 것; (*exception*) yeoeŏpsshi han pŏn ppunin kŏt 예외없이 한 번 뿐인 것

one-parent family p'yŏnch'in kajŏng 편친 가정

oneself chagi chashin 자기 자신; *do sth by ~* muŏsŭl sŭsŭro hada 무엇을 스스로 하다

one-sided *discussion, fight* ilbangjŏgin 일방적인; **one-way street** ilbang t'onghaengno 일방

t'onghaengno 통행로; **one-way ticket** p'yŏndo sŭngch'akkwŏn 편도 승차권

onion yangp'a 양파

on-line *adj* ollainŭi 온라인의; *go ~ to* ...wa / kwa chŏpssok'ada ...와 / 과 접속하다

on-line service COMPUT ollain sŏbissŭ 온라인 서비스

onlooker kugyŏngkkun 구경꾼

only 1 *adv* tanji 단지; *not ~ X but Y also* Xppunman anira Ydo ttohan X뿐만 아니라 Y도 또한; *~ just* kanshinhi 간신히, kyŏu 겨우 2 *adj* yuirhan 유일한; *~ son* oeadŭl 외아들; *~ daughter* oedongttal 외동딸

onset shijak 시작

onside *adv* SP chŏnggyuŭi wich'ie 정규의 위치에

onto: *put X ~ Y* (*on top of*) Xŭl / rŭl Ywie not'a X을 / 를 Y위에 놓다

onward ap'ŭro 앞으로; *from ... ~* ...esŏbut'ŏ ...에서부터

ooze 1 *v/i* (*of liquid, mud*) sŭmyŏnaoda 스며나오다 2 *v/t*: *he ~s charm* kŭegenŭn nŏmch'yŏnanŭn maeryŏgi it-tta 그에게는 넘쳐나는 매력이 있다

opaque *glass* pult'umyŏnghan 불투명한

OPEC (= *Organization of Petroleum Exporting Countries*) Sŏgyu Such'ulguk Kigu 석유 수출국 기구

open 1 *adj* door, shop, window yŏllyŏ innŭn 열려 있는; *flower* p'in 핀; COMPUT *file* yŏllin 열린; (*honest, frank*) sumgimŏmnŭn 숨김없는; *market, society* kaebangdoen 개방된; *relationship* sŏro kusok'aji annŭn 서로 구속하지 않는; *countryside* hwŏnhi t'ŭin 훤히 트인; *in the ~ air* yaoeesŏ 야외에서 2 *v/t also* COMPUT *file* yŏlda 열다; *book, paper* p'ida 피다; *bank account* t'ŭda 트다; *meeting* shijak'ada 시작하다 3 *v/i* (*of door, shop*) yŏllida 열리다; (*of flower*) p'ida 피다

♦ **open up** *v/i* (*of person*) songmaŭmŭl t'ŏnot'a 속마음을 터놓다

open-air *adj* meeting, concert yaoeŭi 야외의; *pool* ogoeŭi 옥외의

open-ended *contract etc* handoga ŏmnŭn 한도가 없는

opening (*in wall etc*) t'ŭm 틈; (*of movie, novel etc*) appubun 앞부분; (*job going*) kongsŏk 공석

openly (*honestly, frankly*) sumgimŏpsshi 숨김없이

open-minded hŏshimt'anhoehan 허심탄회한; **open plan office** op'ŭn p'ŭllaen samushil 오픈 플랜 사무실, *kubunŏpsshi yŏrŏshi hamkke ssŭnŭn samushil* 구분없이 여럿이 함께 쓰는 사무실; **open ticket** op'ŭnt'ik'et 오픈티켓, *sayong-irŭl chehanhaji annŭn p'yo* 사용일을 제한하지 않은 표

opera op'era 오페라

opera glasses op'era mang-wŏn-gyŏng 오페라 망원경; **opera house** op'era haussŭ 오페라 하우스; **opera singer** op'era kasu 오페라 가수

operate 1 *v/i* (*of company*) unyŏngdoeda 운영되다; (*of airline etc*) chojongdoeda 조종되다; (*of machine*) chakttonghada 작동하다; MED susurŭl hada 수술을 하다 **2** *v/t machine* chojonghada 조종하다

♦ **operate on** MED susurhada 수술하다

operating instructions sayongppŏp 사용법; **operating room** MED susulshil 수술실; **operating system** COMPUT op'ŏreit'ing shisŭt'em 오퍼레이팅 시스템

operation MED susul 수술; (*of machine*) chojong 조종; **~s** (*of company*) unyŏng 운영; **have an ~** MED susurŭl pat-tta 수술을 받다

operator TELEC kyohwansu 교환수; (*of machine*) kisa 기사; (*tour ~*) kwan-gwang-ŏptcha 관광업자

ophthalmologist an-kkwa ŭisa 안과 의사

opinion ŭigyŏn 의견; *in my ~* naŭi ŭigyŏnŭronŭn 나의 의견으로는

opponent (*in game*) sangdae 상대; (*of tax reforms etc*) pandaeja 반대자

opportunity kihoe 기회

oppose pandaehada 반대하다; *be ~d to* ...e pandaehada ...에 반대하다; *as ~d to* ...wa/kwa pandaero

...와/과 반대로

opposite 1 *adj side, direction, meaning* pandaeŭi 반대의; *views, characters* sangbandoen 상반된; *the ~ sex* isŏng 이성 **2** *n* pandae 반대

opposition (*to plan*) pandae 반대; POL yadang 야당

oppress *the people* appak'ada 압박하다

oppressive *rule* kahok'an 가혹한; *dictator* p'oak'an 포악한; *weather* uurhagehanŭn 우울하게하는

optical illusion ch'aksshi 착시

optician an-gyŏngsang 안경상

optimism nakch'ŏnjuŭi 낙천주의

optimist nakch'ŏnjuŭija 낙천주의자

optimistic *attitude, person* nakch'ŏnjŏgin 낙천적인; *view, speech* nakkwanjŏgin 낙관적인

optimum 1 *adj* ch'oejŏgŭi 최적의 **2** *n* ch'oejŏk 최적

option sŏnt'aek-kkwŏn 선택권

optional sŏnt'aegŭi 선택의

optional extras opsshŏn sangp'um 옵션 상품

or hogŭn 혹은, ttonŭn 또는; *~ else!* kŭroch'i anŭmyŏn! 그렇지 않으면!

oral *exam* kusurŭi 구술의; *hygiene* kugang-ŭi 구강의; *~ sex* oral sekssŭ 오랄 섹스

orange 1 *adj* (*color*) chuhwangsaegŭi 주황색의 **2** *n* (*fruit*) orenji 오렌지; (*color*) chuhwangsaek 주황색

orange juice orenji chusŭ 오렌지 쥬스

orator yŏnsŏlga 연설가

orbit 1 *n* (*of earth*) kwedo 궤도; *send sth into ~* muŏsŭl kwedo-e ollida 무엇을 궤도에 올리다 **2** *v/t* kongjŏnhada 공전하다

orchard kwasuwŏn 과수원

orchestra ok'esŭt'ŭra 오케스트라

orchid nanch'o 난초

ordeal shiryŏn 시련

order 1 *n* (*command*) myŏngnyŏng 명령; (*sequence*) sunsŏ 순서; (*being well arranged*) paeyŏl 배열; (*for goods, in restaurant*) chumun 주문; *in ~ to* ... hagi wihayŏ ... 하기 위하여; *out of ~* (*not functioning*) kojangnan 고장난; (*not in sequence*)

sunsŏga pakkwin 순서가 바뀐 2 *v/t*
(*put in sequence, layout*) sunsŏdaero
chŏngnihada 순서대로 정리하다;
goods, meal chumunhada 주문하다;
~ s.o. to do sth nuguege muŏsŭl
harago myŏngnyŏnghada 누구에게
무엇을 하라고 명령하다 3 *v/i* (*in
restaurant*) chumunhada 주문하다

orderly 1 *adj lifestyle* parŭn 바른 2 *n*
(*in hospital*) pyŏng-wŏnŭi
chabyŏkppu 병원의 잡역부

ordinary pot'ong-ŭi 보통의

ore kwangsŏk 광석

organ ANAT chojik 조직; MUS orŭgan
오르간

organic *food* yugi nongppŏbŭi 유기
농법의; *fertilizer* yugiŭi 유기의

organism saengmul 생물

organization kigu 기구; (*organizing*)
chojik 조직

organize chojik'ada 조직하다

organizer (*person*) chojiktcha 조직자

orgasm orŭgajŭm 오르가즘

Orient Tongnyang 동양

orient *v/t: the teacher ~ed me
toward ...* sŏnsaengnimi naŭi
kwanshimŭl ... tchoguro ikkŭro
chuŏt-tta 선생님이 나의 관심을 ...
쪽으로 이끌어 주었다; **~ oneself**
(*get bearings*) chagi wich'irŭl
ttokpparo alda 자기 위치를 똑바로
알다

Oriental 1 *adj* tongnyang-ŭi 동양의
2 *n* Tongnyang saram 동양 사람

origin kiwŏn 기원; *person of Chinese ~* Chunggugesŏ on saram
중국에서 온 사람

original 1 *adj* (*not copied*) chintchaŭi
진짜의; (*first*) ch'och'oŭi 최초의 2 *n*
(*painting etc*) wŏnjak 원작

originality tokch'angssŏng 독창성

originally wŏllaenŭn 원래는; (*at first*)
ch'ŏŭmenŭn 처음에는

originate 1 *v/t scheme, idea* shijak'ada
시작하다 2 *v/i* (*of idea, belief*)
pirot'ada 비롯하다; (*of family*)
ch'ulshinida 출신이다

originator (*of scheme etc*) ch'angshija
창시자; *he's not an ~* kŭnŭn ch'ang-
ŭijŏgin sarami anida 그는 창의적인
사람이 아니다

ornament *n* changsshikp'um 장식품

ornamental changshingnyong-ŭi
장식용의

ornate *style, architecture* hwaryŏhage
changshik'an 화려하게 장식한

orphan *n* koa 고아

orphanage koawŏn 고아원

orthopedic chŏnghyŏng oekkwaŭi
정형 외과의

ostentatious kwashihanŭn 과시하는

other 1 *adj* tarŭn 다른; *the ~ day*
(*recently*) chinan pŏne 지난 번에;
every ~ day haru kŏnnŏ 하루 건너;
every ~ person han myŏng kŏnnŏ
한 명 건너 2 *n* (*thing*) tarŭn hanaŭi
kŏt 다른 하나의 것; (*person*) tarŭn
han myŏng 다른 한 명; *the ~s*
(*objects*) namŏji kŏt 나머지 것;
(*people*) namŏji saram 나머지 사람

otherwise kŭrŏch'i anŭmyŏn 그렇지
않으면; (*differently*) tarŭge 다르게

otter sudal 수달

ought ...haeya hada ...해야 하다;
I/you ~ to know ... nanŭn/nŏnŭn
...ŭl/rŭl araya handa 나는/너는
...을/를 알아야 한다; *you ~ to have
done it* nŏnŭn kŭgŏsŭl haessŏya
haet-tta 너는 그것을 했어야 했다

ounce onsŭ 온스

our uriŭi 우리의

ours uriŭi kŏt 우리의 것; *an idea of
~* uri saenggak 우리 생각

ourselves uri chashin 우리 자신; *by ~*
uri chashinŭro 우리 자신으로

oust (*from office*) naetchot-tta 내쫓다

out: be ~ (*of light, fire*) kkŏjyŏ it-tta
꺼져 있다; (*of flower, sun*) chyŏ it-
tta 져 있다; (*not at home, not in
building*) ŏptta 없다; (*of
calculations*) t'ŭllida 틀리다; (*be
published*) ch'ulp'andoeda 출판되다;
(*of secret*) t'allonada 탄로나다; (*no
longer in competition*) t'allak'ada
탈락하다; (*no longer in fashion*)
yuhaeng-e twijida 유행에 뒤지다; *~
here in Dallas* i kot Tallasŭesŏ 이
곳 달라스에서; *he's ~ in the garden* kŭnŭn chŏng-wŏne nagait-tta
그는 정원에 나가있다; (*get*) *~!*
nagaseyo! 나가세요!; (*get*) *~ of my
room!* naebang-esŏ nagaseyo! 내

outboard motor

방에서 나가세요!; *that's ~!* (*out of the question*) 말도 안된다! 말도 안된다!; *he's ~ to win* (*fully intending to*) 그는 이기고자 한다 그는 이기고자 한다

outboard motor sŏnoe mot'ŏ 선외 모터

outbreak (*of violence, war*) tolbal 돌발

outburst kamjŏng-ŭi p'okppal 감정의 폭발

outcast so-oeja 소외자

outcome kyŏlkkwa 결과

outcry kangnyŏrhan hang-ŭi 강렬한 항의

outdated kushigŭi 구식의

outdo poda tŏ charhada 보다 더 잘하다

outdoor *toilet, activities, life* yaoeŭi 야외의

outdoors *adv* yaoeesŏ 야외에서

outer *wall etc* oebuŭi 외부의

outer space uju 우주

outfit (*clothes*) ŭisang 의상; (*company, organization*) chojik 조직

outgoing *flight* ttŏnaganŭn 떠나가는; *personality* oehyangtchŏgin 외향적인

outgrow *old ideas* pŏsŏnada 벗어나다

outing (*trip*) sop'ung 소풍

outlet (*of pipe*) paech'ulgu 배출구; (*for sales*) maejang 매장; ELEC sok'et 소켓

outline 1 *n* (*of person, building etc*) yun-gwak 윤곽; (*of plan, novel*) kaeyo 개요 **2** *v/t plans etc* ...ŭi yun-gwagŭl chaptta ...의 윤곽을 잡다

outlive poda tŏ orae salda 보다 더 오래 살다

outlook (*prospects*) chŏnmang 전망

outlying *areas* oejin 외진

outnumber poda suga mant'a 보다 수가 많다

out of ◊ (*motion*) ...esŏ pakkŭro ...에서 밖으로; *run ~ the house* chibesŏ pakkŭro tallyŏnaoda 집에서 밖으로 달려나오다 ◊ (*position*) ...(ŭ)robut'ŏ ttŏrŏjin ...(으)로부터 떨어진; *20 miles ~ Detroit* Tit'ŭroit'ŭro put'ŏ 20mail ttŏrŏjin 디트로이트로 부터 20마일 떨어진 ◊ (*cause*) ttaemune 때문에; *~ jeal-*

~ousy / **curiosity** chilt'ushim / hogishim ttaemune 질투심 / 호기심 때문에 ◊ (*without*) ta ttŏrŏjin 다 떨어진; *we're ~ beer* urinŭn maektchuga ta ttŏrŏjyŏt-tta 우리는 맥주가 다 떨어졌다; *we're ~ gas* urinŭn hwiballyuga ta ttŏrŏjyŏt-tta 우리는 휘발유가 다 떨어졌다 ◊ (*from a group*): *5 ~ 10* yŏl chung tasŏt 10중 5

out-of-date kushigŭi 구식의

out-of-the-way oejin 외진

outperform poda ttwiŏnada 보다 뛰어나다

output 1 *n* (*of factory*) saengsan 생산; COMPUT ch'ullyŏk 출력 **2** *v/t* (*produce*) saengsanhada 생산하다; COMPUT *signal* ch'ullyŏk'ada 출력하다

outrage 1 *n* (*feeling*) pun-gae 분개; (*act*) p'ongnyŏk 폭력 **2** *v/t* maeu hwanage hada 매우 화나게 하다; *I was ~d to hear ...* nanŭn ...ŭl / rŭl tŭtkko mopsshi hwaga nat-tta 나는 ...을 / 를 듣고 몹시 화가 났다

outrageous *acts* p'ongnyŏktchŏgin 폭력적인; *prices* t'ŏmuniŏmnŭn 터무니없는

outright 1 *adj winner* wanjŏnhan 완전한 **2** *adv win* wanjŏnhi 완전히; *kill* chŭksshi 즉시

outrun poda ppalli tallida 보다 빨리 달리다

outset shijak 시작; *from the ~* shijak'al ttaebut'ŏ 시작할 때부터

outside 1 *adj surface, wall, lane* pakkach'ŭi 바깥의 **2** *adv sit* pakkat'e 바깥에; *go* pakkŭro 밖으로 **3** *prep* ...ŭi pakke ...의 밖에 (*apart from*) ... oeŭi ... 외의; *~ Seoul* Sŏul oegwage 서울 외곽에 **4** *n* (*of building, case etc*) pakkat myŏn 바깥 면; *at the ~* ch'oedaehanŭro 최대한으로

outside broadcast sŭt'yudio pakkŭi pangsong 스튜디오 밖의 방송

outsider oebusaram 외부사람

outsize *adj clothing* t'ŭkttaehyŏng-ŭi 특대형의

outskirts pyŏnduri 변두리

outspoken soltchik'an 솔직한

outstanding t'ŭkch'urhan 특출한; FIN *invoice, sums* miburŭi 미불의

outward *adj appearance* oegwanŭi 외관의; **~ journey** ttŏnanŭn yŏhaeng 떠나는 여행

outwardly kŏt'ŭronŭn 겉으로는

outweigh poda chungnyohada 보다 중요하다

outwit sŏnsuch'ida 선수치다

oval *adj* talgyarhyŏng-ŭi 달걀형의

ovary (*of animals, people*) nanso 난소

oven obŭn 오븐

over 1 *prep* (*above*) ...ŭi witchoge ...의 윗쪽에; (*across*) ...ŭi chŏtchok p'yŏne ...의 저쪽 편에; (*more than*) poda tŏ 보다 더; (*during*) tong-ane 동안에; **travel all ~ Korea** Han-guk chŏnyŏgŭl yŏhaenghada 한국 전역을 여행하다; **you find them all ~ Korea** kŭgŏsŭn Han-guk ŏdiena it-tta 그것은 한국 어디에나 있다; **let's talk ~ a drink / meal** mashimyŏnsŏ / mŏgŭmyŏnsŏ iyagihapsshida 마시면서 / 먹으면서 이야기합시다; **we're ~ the worst** urinŭn ch'oeagŭi sanghwang-ŭl nŏmgyŏt-tta 우리는 최악의 상황을 넘겼다 **2** *adv:* **be ~** (*finished*) kkŭnnada 끝나다; (*left*) namtta 남다; **~ to you** (*your turn*) nŏŭi ch'arye 너의 차례; **~ in Europe** Yurŏbesŏnŭn 유럽에서는; **~ here / there** yŏgie / chŏgie 여기에 / 저기에; **it hurts all ~** onmomi ssushida 온몸이 쑤시다; **painted white all ~** chŏnbu hayak'e p'eit'ŭ ch'irhaejin 전부 하얗게 페인트 칠해진; **it's all ~** ta kkŭnnat-tta 다 끝났다; **~ and ~ again** myŏtppŏnigo toep'urihaesŏ 몇번이고 되풀이해서; **do sth ~** (*again*) muŏsŭl tashi toep'urihada 무엇을 다시 되풀이하다

overall 1 *adj length* chŏnch'eŭi 전체의 **2** *adv modify* chŏnbanjŏgin 전반적인

overawe: **be ~d by s.o. / sth** nuguege / muŏse kŏmmŏktta 누구에게 / 무엇에 겁먹다

overboard: **man ~!** sarami ppajyŏt-tta! 사람이 빠졌다!; **go ~ for s.o. / sth** nuguege / muŏsege ppajida 누구에게 / 무엇에게 빠지다

overcast *day, sky* hŭrin 흐린

overcharge *v/t customer* pagaji ssŭiuda 바가지 씌우다

overcoat oet'u 외투

overcome *difficulties* kŭkppok'ada 극복하다; **be ~ by emotion** kamjŏng-ŭl ŏngnurŭji mot'ada 감정을 억누르지 못하다

overcrowded nŏmu honjap'an 너무 혼잡한

overdo (*exaggerate*) chinach'ige hada 지나치게 하다; (*in cooking*) nŏmu ik'ida 너무 익히다; **you're ~ing things** tangshinŭn irŭl chinach'ige hanŭn-gunnyo 당신은 일을 지나치게 하는군요

overdone *meat* chinach'ige ik'in 지나치게 익힌

overdose *n* kwaing pogyong 과잉 복용

overdraft chanaegŭl ch'ogwahanŭn inch'ul 잔액을 초과하는 인출; **have an ~** chanaekppoda tŏ inch'urhada 잔액보다 더 인출하다

overdraw *account* ...esŏ chanaekppoda tŏ inch'ulshik'ida ...에서 잔액보다 더 인출시키다; **be $800 ~n** chanaekppoda p'albaektallŏrŭl tŏ inch'ulshik'ida 잔액보다 800달러를 더 인출시키다

overdrive MOT obŏdŭraibŭ 오버드라이브

overdue *apology, change* nŭjŭn 늦은

overestimate *abilities, value* kwadae p'yŏngkkahada 과대 평가하다

overexpose *photograph* chinach'ige noch'urhada 지나치게 노출하다

overflow 1 *n* (*pipe*) nŏmch'im 넘침 **2** *v/i* (*of water*) nŏmch'ida 넘치다

overgrown *garden* musŏnghan 무성한; **he's an ~ baby** kŭnŭn aich'ŏrŏm kunda 그는 아이처럼 군다

overhaul *v/t engine* chŏngmil kŏmsahada 정밀 검사하다; *plans* chŏngmilkŏmt'ohada 정밀 검토하다

overhead 1 *adj lights* mŏri wiesŏ 머리 위에서, *railroad* kokkaŭi 고가의 **2** *n* FIN kanjŏppi 간접비

overhear uyŏnhi tŭt-tta 우연히 듣다

overjoyed taedanhi kippŭn 대단히 기쁜

overland 1 *adj route* yungnoŭi 육로의
2 *adv travel* yungnoro 육로로

overlap *v/i (of tiles etc)* pubunjŏgŭro kyŏpch'ida 부분적으로 겹치다; *(of periods, theories)* chungbokdoeda 중복되다

overload *v/t vehicle* nŏmu mani shiltta 너무 많이 싣다; ELEC kwabuhahada 과부하하다

overlook *(of building etc)* naeryŏdaboda 내려다보다; *(not see)* motppoda 못보다; *(pretend not to see)* nun-gama chuda 눈감아 주다

overly chinach'ige 지나치게; *not ~ ...* chinach'iji ank'e ... 지나치지 않게 ...

overnight *adv travel* pamsae 밤새; *stay ~* haruppamŭl chinaeda 하룻밤을 지내다

overnight bag chagŭn yŏhaeng-yong kabang 작은 여행용 가방

overpaid kwadahage chibuldoen 과다하게 지불된

overpass *(for car)* kokka toro 고가 도로; *(for people)* yukkyo 육교

overpower *v/t (physically)* muryŏk'age hada 무력하게 하다

overpowering *smell* aju kanghan 아주 강한; *sense of guilt* aju k'ŭn 아주 큰

overpriced nŏmu pissan 너무 비싼

overrated kwadae p'yŏngkkadoen 과대 평가된

overrule *decision* muhyohwahada 무효화하다

overrun *country* wanjŏnhi ch'imnyak'ada 완전히 침략하다; *time* ch'ogwahada 초과하다; *be ~ with* ...(ŭ)ro tŭlkkŭlt'a ...(으)로 들끓다

overseas 1 *adv* haeoero 해외로 **2** *adj* haeoeŭi 해외의

overseas Koreans haeoe kyop'o 해외 교포

oversee kamdok'ada 감독하다

oversight kan-gwaro inhan shilssu 간과로 인한 실수

oversleep nŭttcham chada 늦잠자다

overtake *(in work, development)* ttarajaptta 따라잡다; *Br* MOT ch'uwŏrhada 추월하다

overthrow chŏnbok 전복

overtime 1 *n* ch'ogwa kŭnmu 초과 근무; SP yŏnjangjŏn 연장전 **2** *adv work* kŭnmu shigan oero 근무 시간 외로

overture MUS sŏgok 서곡; *make ~s to* ...ege cheŭihada ...에게 제의하다

overturn 1 *v/t object* twiŏptta 뒤엎다; *government* chŏnbok'ada 전복하다 **2** *v/i (of vehicle)* twijip'ida 뒤집히다

overweight *baggage* chungnyang ch'ogwaŭi 중량 초과의; *person* ch'ejung kwadaŭi 체중 과다의

overwhelm *(with work)* apttohada 압도하다; *(with emotion)* kaptchagi tanghwanghage hada 갑자기 당황하게 하다; *be ~ed by (by response)* ...(ŭ)ro ŏtchŏl chul morŭda ...(으)로 어쩔 줄 모르다

overwork 1 *n* kwaro 과로 **2** *v/i* kwarohada 과로하다 **3** *v/t* kwaroshik'ida 과로시키다

owe *v/t* pitchida 빚지다; *~ s.o. $500* nuguege 500tallŏrŭl pitchida 누구에게 500달러를 빚지다; *~ s.o. an apology* nuguege sagwahal kŏshi it-tta 누구에게 사과할 것이 있다; *how much do I ~ you?* chega tangshinege ŏlmana tŏ tŭryŏya hamnikka? 제가 당신에게 얼마나 더 드려야 합니까?

owing to ...ttaemune ...때문에; *~ the weather* nalsshittaemune 날씨때문에

owl olppaemi 올빼미

own¹ *v/t* soyuhada 소유하다

own² **1** *adj* soyuŭi 소유의 **2** *pron: a car/an apartment of my ~* nae soyuŭi ch'a/ap'at'ŭ 내 소유의 차/아파트; *on my/his ~* honja 혼자
♦ **own up** mojori chabaek'ada 모조리 자백하다

owner chuin 주인; *(of hotel, company etc)* soyuja 소유자

ownership soyukkwŏn 소유권

ox hwangso 황소

oxide sanhwamul 산화물

oxygen sanso 산소

oyster kul 굴

ozone ojon 오존

ozone layer ojonch'ŭng 오존층

P

pace 1 *n* (*step*) kŏrŭm 걸음; (*speed*) soktto 속도 **2** *v/i:* ~ *up and down* watta katta hada 왔다 갔다 하다

pacemaker MED maekppak chojŏnggi 맥박 조정기; SP sŏndu chuja 선두 주자

Pacific: *the* ~ (*Ocean*) T'aep'yŏng-yang 태평양

Pacific Rim: *the* ~ T'aep'yŏng-yang yŏnan 태평양 연안; ~ *countries* T'aep'yŏng-yang yŏnan kuk-kka 태평양 연안 국가

pacifier komu chŏtkkoktchi 고무 젖꼭지

pacifism p'yŏnghwajuŭi 평화주의

pacifist *n* p'yŏnghwajuŭija 평화주의자

pacify chinjŏngshik'ida 진정시키다

pack 1 *n* (*back~*) paenang 배낭; (*of cereal, food*) t'ong 통; (*of cigarettes,cards*) kap 갑 **2** *v/t bag, item of clothing, groceries etc* ssada 싸다; *goods* p'ojanghada 포장하다 **3** *v/i* chim kkurida 짐 꾸리다

package 1 *n* sop'o 소포; (*of offers etc*) ilgwal 일괄 **2** *v/t* (*in packs, for promotion*) p'ojanghada 포장하다

package deal ilgwal kŏrae 일괄 거래

package tour p'aek'iji kwangwang 패키지 관광

packaging (*of product*) p'ojang 포장; (*of rock star etc*) sangp'umhwa 상품화

packed (*crowded*) honjap'an 혼잡한

packet pongji 봉지; (*of envelopes*) mukkŭm 묶음

pact kyeyak 계약

pad¹ 1 *n* (*piece of cloth etc*) ch'ŏntchogak 천조각; (*for writing*) chong-i mukkŭm 종이 묶음 **2** *v/t* (*with material*) taeda 대다; *speech, report* kilge nŭllida 길게 늘리다

pad² *v/i* (*move quietly*) soriŏpsshi kŏt-tta 소리없이 걷다

padded: ~ *jacket* nubi chaek'it 누비 재킷; ~ *shoulders* ŏkkaeshimŭl taen 어깨심을 댄

padding (*material*) p'aeding 패딩; (*in speech etc*) pulp'iryohan sabibŏgu 불필요한 삽입어구

paddle¹ 1 *n* (*for canoe*) no 노 **2** *v/i* (*in canoe*) chŏt-tta 젓다

paddle² *v/i* (*in water*) multchangnanŭl ch'ida 물장난을 치다

paddock ul ch'in chandipat 울 친 잔디밭

padlock 1 *n* chamulsoe 자물쇠 **2** *v/t* chamulsoero chamgŭda 자물쇠로 잠그다; ~ *X to Y* Xŭl/rŭl Ykkaji chamgŭda X을/를 Y까지 잠그다

page¹ *n* (*of book etc*) p'eiji 페이지; ~ *number* tchok pŏnho 쪽 번호

page² *v/t* (*call*) hoch'urhada 호출하다

pager hoch'ulgi 호출기

pagoda t'ap 탑

paid employment yugŭp koyong 유급 고용

pail yangdong-i 양동이

pain ap'ŭm 아픔; *be in* ~ ap'ahada 아파하다; *take ~s to ...* ... hagi wihae mopsshi aessŭda ... 하기 위해 몹시 애쓰다; *a ~ in the neck* F nunŭi kashi 눈의 가시

painful *arm, leg etc* ap'ŭn 아픈; (*distressing*) kot'ongsŭrŏun 고통스러운; (*laborious*) himdŭn 힘든

painfully (*extremely, acutely*) kot'ongsŭrŏpkke 고통스럽게

painkiller chint'ongje 진통제

painless mut'ong-ŭi 무통의

painstaking *work* himdŭnŭn 힘드는; *worker* sugorŭl akkiji annŭn 수고를 아끼지 않는

paint 1 *n* (*for wall, car*) p'eint'ŭ 페인트; (*for artist*) mulkkam 물감 **2** *v/t wall etc* ch'irhada 칠하다; *picture* kŭrida 그리다 **3** *v/i* (*as art form*) kŭrida 그리다

paintbrush (*for wall, ceiling etc*) p'eint'ŭ sol 페인트 솔; (*of artist*) kŭrim put 그림 붓

painter (*decorator*) changshik-kka 장식가; (*artist*) hwaga 화가

painting (*activity*) kŭrim kŭrigi 그림 그리기; (*picture*) hoehwa chakp'um 회화 작품

paintwork tojang 도장

pair (*of people, animals, objects*) ssang 쌍; (*of shoes*) k'yŏlle 켤레; *a ~ of shoes / sandals* shinbal / saendŭl han k'yŏlle 신발 / 샌들 한 켤레; *a ~ of pants* paji han pŏl 바지 한 벌

pajama jacket chamot wit-ttori 잠옷 윗도리

pajama pants chamot paji 잠옷 바지

pajamas chamot 잠옷

Pakistan P'ak'isŭt'an 파키스탄

Pakistani 1 *adj* P'ak'isŭt'anŭi 파키스탄의 **2** *n* P'ak'isŭt'anin 파키스탄인

pal F (*friend*) ch'in-gu 친구; *hey ~, got a light?* ŏi, igŏt pwa, pul chom issŏ? 어이, 이것 봐, 불 좀 있어?

palace kunggwŏl 궁궐

palate kugae 구개; *fig* migak 미각

palatial kunggwŏlgat'ŭn 궁궐같은

pale *person* ch'angbaek'an 창백한; *~ pink / blue* yŏt'ŭn punhongsaek / p'aransaek 열은 분홍색 / 파란색

pallet hwamul unbanttae 화물 운반대

pallor ch'angbaek 창백

palm[1] (*of hand*) sonppadak 손바닥

palm[2] (*tree*) yajanamu 야자나무

palpitations MED shimgyehangjin 심계항진

paltry chwikkorimanhan 쥐꼬리만한

pamper aejijungjihada 애지중지하다

pamphlet p'amp'ŭllet 팜플렛

pan 1 *n* (*for cooking*) nambi 남비 **2** *v/t* F (*criticize*) hokp'yŏnghada 혹평하다

♦ **pan out** (*develop*) chŏn-gaehada 전개하다

pancake p'aenk'eik'ŭ 팬케이크; (*Korean-style*) chŏn 전

panda p'aendŏ kom 팬더 곰

pandemonium asurajang 아수라장

pane (*of glass*) ch'ang-yuri 창유리

panel (*section*) k'an 칸; (*in TV discussion*) p'aenŏl 패널; (*investigating*) chosadan 조사단; (*committee*) wiwŏndan 위원단

paneling p'annerhagi 판넬하기

panhandle *v/i* F kugŏrhada 구걸하다

panic 1 *n* tanghwang 당황 **2** *v/i* tanghwanghada 당황하다; *don't ~* tanghwanghaji mara 당황하지 마라

panic selling FIN pisangshiŭi kŭmmae 비상시의 급매

panic-stricken kŏbe chillin 겁에 질린

panorama p'anorama 파노라마

panoramic *view* hwak t'ŭin 확 트인

pansy (*flower*) p'aenji 팬지

pant *v/i* sumi ch'ada 숨이 차다

panties p'aent'i 팬티

pantihose → *pantyhose*

pants paji 바지; *a pair of ~* paji han pŏl 바지 한 벌

pantyhose p'aent'i sŭt'ak'ing 팬티 스타킹

paper 1 *n* (*material*) chong-i 종이; (*news~*) shinmun 신문; (*wall~*) pyŏktchi 벽지; (*academic*) nonmun 논문; (*examination ~*) shihŏmji 시험지; *~s* (*documents*) sŏryu 서류; (*identity ~s*) shinbuntchŭng 신분증; *a piece of ~* chong-i han chang 종이 한 장 **2** *adj* chong-iro mandŭn 종이로 만든 **3** *v/t room, walls* tobaehada 도배하다

paperback chong-ip'yojiŭi yŏmkkap'an ch'aek 종이표지의 염가판 책; **paper bag** chong-i kabang 종이 가방; **paper clip** k'ŭllip 클립; **paper cup** chong-ik'ŏp 종이컵; **paperwork** munsŏ ŏmmu 문서 업무

par (*in golf*) p'a 파; *be on a ~ with* …wa / kwa kat-tta …와 / 과 같다; *feel below ~* k'ŏndishyŏni nappŭda 컨디션이 나쁘다

parachute 1 *n* nak'asan 낙하산 **2** *v/i* nak'asanŭro naeryŏoda 낙하산으로 내려오다 **3** *v/t troops, supplies* nak'asanŭro t'uhahada 낙하산으로 투하하다

parachutist nak'asankanghaja 낙하산강하자

parade 1 *n* (*procession*) p'ŏreidŭ 퍼레이드 **2** *v/i* haengjinhada 행진하다

3 *v/t* (*show off*) kwashihada 과시하다

paradise nagwŏn 낙원

paradox yŏkssŏl 역설

paradoxical yŏkssŏltchŏgin 역설적인

paradoxically yŏlssŏltchŏgŭro 역설적으로

paragraph mundan 문단

parallel 1 n p'yŏnghaeng 평행; (*of latitude*) wido 위도; *fig* yusattchŏm 유사점; *do two things in ~* tugaji irŭl tongshie hada 두가지 일을 동시에 하다 **2** *adj* lines p'yŏnghaenghanŭn 평행하는; *fig* tongshie irŏnanŭn 동시에 일어나는 **3** *v/t* (*match*) p'iltchok'ada 필적하다

paralysis mabi 마비

paralyze mabishik'ida 마비시키다; *fig* muryŏkk'ehada 무력케하다

paramedic chun ŭiryo hwalttong chongsaja 준 의료 활동 종사자

parameter chehan pŏmwi 제한 범위

paramilitary 1 *adj* chun kunsajŏgin 준 군사적인 **2** n chun kunsayowŏn 준 군사요원

paramount kajang chung-yohan 가장 중요한; *be ~* kajang chung-yohada 가장 중요하다

paranoia p'ihae mangsang 피해 망상

paranoid *adj* p'ihae mangsang-ŭi 피해 망상의

paraphernalia chapttongsani 잡동사니

paraphrase n pakkuŏ ssŭgi 바꾸어 쓰기

paraplegic n habanshin mabihwanja 하반신 마비환자

parasite kisaeng tongshingmul 기생 동식물; *fig* kisaengch'unggat'ŭn saram 기생충같은 사람

parasol p'arasol 파라솔

paratrooper nak'asanbyŏng 낙하산병

parcel n sop'o 소포

♦**parcel up** kkurŏmiro ssada 꾸러미로 싸다

parch *v/t*: *be ~ed* (*of person*) mogi t'ada 목이 타다

pardon 1 n LAW samyŏn 사면; *I beg your ~?* (*what did you say?*) mwŏrago hashyŏttchyo? 뭐라고 하셨죠?; *I beg your ~* (*I'm sorry*) choesonghamnida 죄송합니다 **2** *v/t*

yongsŏhada 용서하다; LAW samyŏnhada 사면하다; *~ me?* mwŏraguyo? 뭐라구요?

pare (*peel*) kkŏptchirŭl pŏtkkida 껍질을 벗기다

parent pumo 부모

parental pumo-ŭi 부모의

parent company mohoesa 모회사; **Parents' Day** Ŏbŏinal 어버이날; **parent-teacher association** sach'inhoe 사친회

park[1] (*area*) kong-wŏn 공원

park[2] *v/i & v/t* MOT chuch'ahada 주차하다

parka p'ak'a 파카

parking MOT chuch'a 주차; *no ~* chuch'agŭmji 주차금지

parking brake sudong pŭreik'ŭ 수동 브레이크; **parking garage** ch'ago 차고; **parking lot** chuch'ajang 주차장; **parking meter** chuch'a yogŭmgi 주차 요금기; **parking place** chuch'a changso 주차 장소; **parking ticket** chuch'a wiban ttaktchi 주차 위반 딱지

parliament ŭihoe 의회; (*in Korea*) Kuk'oe 국회

parliamentary ŭihoeŭi 의회의; *~ buildings* kuk'oe ŭisadang 국회 의사당

parole 1 n kasŏkppang 가석방; *be on ~* kasŏkppangdoeda 가석방되다 **2** *v/t* kasŏkppanghada 가석방하다

parrot aengmusae 앵무새

parsley p'asŭlli 파슬리

part 1 n (*portion*) pubun 부분; (*section*) p'yŏn 편; (*area*) chiyŏk 지역; (*of machine*) pup'um 부품; (*in play, movie*) yŏk 역; MUS p'at'ŭ 파트; (*in hair*) karŭma 가르마; *take ~ in* ch'amyŏhada 참여하다 **2** *adv* (*partly*) pubuntchŏgŭro 부분적으로 **3** *v/i* heŏjida 헤어지다 **4** *v/t*: *~ one's hair* karŭmarŭl t'ada 가르마를 타다

♦**part with** ch'ŏbunhada 처분하다

part exchange ton taeshin mulgŏnŭro chugo patkki 돈 대신 물건으로 주고 받기; *take sth in ~* ton taeshin mulgŏnŭl kajida 돈 대신 물건을 가지다

partial (*incomplete*) purwanjŏnhan

불완전한; **be ~ to** choahada 좋아하다
partially pubuntchŏguro 부분적으로
participant ch'amgaja 참가자
participate ch'amgahada 참가하다; **~ in sth** muŏse ch'amgahada 무엇에 참가하다
participation ch'amga 참가
particle PHYS soriptcha 소립자; (*small amount*) kŭkssoryang 극소량
particular (*specific*) t'ŭktchŏnghan 특정한; (*special*) t'ŭkppyŏrhan 특별한; (*fussy*) kkadaroun 까다로운; **in ~** t'ŭkppyŏrhi 특별히
particularly t'ŭkppyŏrhage 특별하게
parting (*of people*) ibyŏl 이별
partition 1 *n* (*screen*) k'anmagi 칸막이; (*of country*) pulli 분리 **2** *v/t* *country* pullihada 분리하다
♦ **partition off** k'anmagirŭl hada 칸막이를 하다
partly pubuntchŏguro 부분적으로
partner COM tong-ŏptcha 동업자; (*personal*) paeuja 배우자; (*professional*) tong-ŏptcha 동업자; (*in particular activity*) tchak 짝
partnership COM tong-ŏp 동업; (*in particular activity*) hyŏmnyŏk kwan-gye 협력 관계
part of speech p'umsa 품사; **part owner** kongdong soyuja 공동 소유자; **part-time 1** *adj* shiganjeŭi 시간제의 **2** *adv* *work* shiganjero 시간제로
party 1 *n* (*celebration*) p'at'i 파티; POL chŏngdang 정당; (*group of people*) muri 무리; **be a ~ to** yŏlludoeda 연루되다 **2** *v/i* F p'at'irŭl hada 파티를 하다
pass 1 *n* (*permit*) SP p'aesŭ 패스; (*in mountains*) sankkil 산길; **make a ~ at** kuaehada 구애하다 **2** *v/t* (*hand*) chŏnhaejuda 전해주다; (*go past*) chinagada 지나가다; MOT ch'uwŏrhada 추월하다; (*go beyond*) nŏmŏsŏda 넘어서다; (*approve*) sŭng-in pat-tta 승인 받다; SP p'aesŭhada 패스하다; **~ an exam** shihŏme hapkkyŏk'ada 시험에 합격하다; **~ sentence** LAW p'an-gyŏrŭl naerida 판결을 내리다; **~ the time** shiganŭl ponaeda 시간을 보내다 **3** *v/i* (*of

time) ponaeda 보내다; (*in exam*) shihŏme put-tta 시험에 붙다; SP p'aesŭhada 패스하다; (*go away*) ŏpssŏjida 없어지다
♦ **pass around** tollida 돌리다
♦ **pass away** (*die*) sesang-ŭl ttŭda 세상을 뜨다
♦ **pass by** *v/t & v/i* (*go past*) chinagada 지나가다
♦ **pass on 1** *v/t* *information, book* chŏnhada 전하다; *costs, savings* tollyŏjuda 돌려주다 **2** *v/i* (*die*) sesang-ŭl ttŭda 세상을 뜨다
♦ **pass out** (*faint*) kijŏrhada 기절하다
♦ **pass through** *town* t'onghae chinagada 통해 지나가다
♦ **pass up** *chance* noch'ida 놓치다
passable *road* chinagal su innŭn 지나갈 수 있는; (*acceptable*) kwaench'anŭn 괜찮은
passage (*corridor*) poktto 복도; (*from poem*) chŏl 절; (*from book*) tallak 단락; (*of time*) kyŏnggwa 경과
passageway t'ongno 통로
passenger sŭnggaek 승객
passenger seat sŭnggaeksŏk 승객석
passer-by t'onghaengin 통행인
passion (*emotion*) kyŏngnyŏrhan kamjŏng 격렬한 감정; (*sexual desire*) yoktchŏng 욕정; (*fervor*) yŏltchŏng 열정
passionate *lover* chŏngnyŏltchŏgin 정열적인; (*fervent*) yŏltchŏngjŏgin 열정적인
passive 1 *adj* sudongjŏgin 수동적인 **2** *n* GRAM sudongt'ae 수동태; **in the ~** sudongt'aero 수동태로
pass mark hapkkyŏktchŏm 합격점; **passport** yŏkkwŏn 여권; **passport control** yŏkkwŏn kwalli 여권 관리; **password** amho 암호
past 1 *adj* (*former*) mŏnjŏtppŏnŭi 먼젓번의; **the ~ few days** chinan myŏch'il 지난 며칠; **that's all ~ now** kŭgŏn ije ta chinagassŏyo 그건 이제 다 지나갔어요 **2** *n* kwagŏ 과거; **in the ~** kwagŏe 과거에 **3** *prep* (*in time*) nŏmŏ 넘어; (*in position*) chinasŏ 지나서; **it's ~ 7 o'clock** ilgop shiga nŏmŏssŏyo 일곱 시가 넘었어요; **it's half ~ two** tushi

paniyeyo 두시 반이에요 **4** *adv* : *run /*
walk ~ ttwiŏsŏ / kŏrŏsŏ chinagada
뛰어서 / 걸어서 지나가다
paste 1 *n* (*adhesive*) p'ul 풀 **2** *v/t*
(*stick*) puch'ida 붙이다
pastel 1 *n* (*color*) p'asŭt'el 파스텔
2 *adj* p'asŭt'erŭi 파스텔의
pastime ch'wimi 취미
pastor kyogu mokssa 교구 목사
past participle kwagŏ punsa 과거
분사
pastrami hunje soegogi 훈제 쇠고기
pastry (*for pie*) milkkaru panjuk
밀가루 반죽; (*small cake*)
p'aesŭch'yuri 패스추리
past tense kwagŏ shije 과거 시제
pasty *adj complexion* ch'angbaek'an
창백한
pat 1 *n* kabyŏpkke tudŭrigi 가볍게
두드리기; *give s.o. a ~ on the back*
fig nugurŭl ch'uk'ahada 누구를
축하하다 **2** *v/t* kabyŏpkke tudŭrida
가볍게 두드리다
patch 1 *n* (*on clothes*) hŏnggŏp 헝겊;
(*period*) kigan 기간; (*area*) kot 곳;
(*of fog*) charak 자락; *not be a ~ on*
…wa / kwa pigyodo toeji ant'a
…와 / 과 비교도 되지 않다 **2** *v/t*
clothes hŏnggŏp'ŭl taeda 헝겊을
대다
♦**patch up** (*repair*) mibongjŏgŭro
koch'ida 미봉적으로 고치다; *quarrel*
haegyŏrhada 해결하다
patchwork 1 *n* (*needlework*)
p'aech'iwŏk'ŭ 패치워크 **2** *adj quilt*
p'aech'iwŏk'ŭŭi 패치워크의
patchy *quality, work* korŭji mot'an
고르지 못한
patent 1 *adj* (*obvious*) punmyŏnghan
분명한 **2** *n* (*for invention*) t'ŭk'ŏ 특허
3 *v/t invention* t'ŭk'ŏrŭl ŏt-tta 특허를
얻다
patent leather enamel kajuk 에나멜
가죽
patently (*clearly*) punmyŏnghi 분명히
paternal *relative* pugyeŭi 부계의;
pride, love pusŏngŭi 부성의
paternalism kajoktchuŭi 가족주의
paternalistic kajotchŏgin 가족적인
paternity pusŏng 부성
path kil 길; *fig* chillo 진로

pathetic aech'ŏroun 애처로운; F
(*very bad*) hyŏngp'yŏnŏmnŭn
형편없는
pathological pyŏngtchŏgin 병적인
pathologist pyŏngnihaktcha 병리학자
pathology pyŏngnihak 병리학
patience ch'amŭlssŏng 참을성
patient 1 *n* hwanja 환자 **2** *adj*
ch'amŭlssŏng innŭn 참을성 있는;
just be ~! ch'amara! 참아라!
patiently ch'amŭlssŏng itkke 참을성
있게
patio anttŭl 안뜰
patriot aeguktcha 애국자
patriotic aeguktchŏgin 애국적인
patriotism aeguksshim 애국심
patrol 1 *n* sunch'al 순찰; *be on ~*
sunch'arhada 순찰하다 **2** *v/t streets,*
border sunch'arhada 순찰하다
patrol car sunch'alch'a 순찰차; **pa-**
trolman sunch'algwan 순찰관; **pa-**
trol wagon choesu hosongch'a 죄수
호송차
patron (*of store, movie house*)
kogaek 고객; (*of artist, charity etc*)
huwŏnja 후원자
patronize *store* tan-gollo tanida
단골로 다니다; *person* sŏnshimŭl
ssŭnŭn tŭt'ada 선심을 쓰는 듯하다
patronizing sŏnshimŭl ssŭnŭn tŭt'an
선심을 쓰는 듯한
patter 1 *n* (*of rain etc*) hududuk'anŭn
sori 후두둑하는 소리; F (*of salesman*)
ppalli chikkŏrinŭn mal 빨리
지껄이는 말 **2** *v/i* hududuk ttŏrŏjida
후두둑 떨어지다
pattern *n* (*fabric*) munŭi 무늬; (*for*
knitting, sewing) p'aet'ŏn 패턴;
(*model*) ponbogi 본보기; (*in*
behavior, events) yangshik 양식
patterned munŭi innŭn 무늬 있는
paunch ttongppae 똥배
pause 1 *n* chungdan 중단 **2** *v/i*
chungdanhada 중단하다 **3** *v/t tape*
chungdanshik'ida 중단시키다
pave kkalda 깔다; *~ the way for*
…ŭi kirŭl yŏlda …의 길을 열다
pavement (*asphalt*) asŭp'alt'ŭ
아스팔트
paving stone p'osŏk 포석
paw 1 *n* (*of animal*) pal 발; F (*hand*)

son 손 2 *v/t* F sonŭro manjida 손으로
만지다

pawn[1] *n* (*in chess*) chol 졸; *fig* iyong
tanghanŭn saram 이용 당하는 사람

pawn[2] *v/t* chŏdang-ŭl chap'ida 저당을
잡히다

pawnbroker chŏndangp'o chuin
전당포 주인

pawnshop chŏndangp'o 전당포

pay 1 *n* posu 보수; *in the* ~ *of*
koyongdoen 고용된 2 *v/t employee*
posurŭl chuda 보수를 주다; *sum*
chiburhada 지불하다; *bill* nap-
ppuhada 납부하다; ~ *attention*
chuŭirŭl kiurida 주의를 기울이다; ~
s.o. a compliment nuguege
ch'ingch'anŭl hada 누구에게 칭찬을
하다 3 *v/i* chiburhada 지불하다; (*be
profitable*) sujiga matta 수지가 맞다;
it doesn't ~ to ... ... hanŭn kŏshi
tŭgi toeji anayo ... 하는 것이 득이
되지 않아요; ~ *for purchase* sada
사다; *you'll ~ for this! fig* i ire
taehan taetkkarŭl ch'irŭge
toelkkŏyeyo! 이 일에 대한 댓가를
치르게 될꺼예요!

♦ **pay back** *person* kaptta 갚다; *loan*
pyŏnjehada 변제하다; (*get revenge
on*) anggap'ŭmŭl hada 앙갚음을
하다

♦ **pay in** (*bank*) yegŭmhada 예금하다

♦ **pay off 1** *v/t debt* kaptta 갚다;
corrupt official noemurŭl chuda
뇌물을 주다 2 *v/i* (*be profitable*)
idŭgi toeda 이득이되다

♦ **pay up** chiburhada 지불하다

payable chiburhaeya hal 지불해야 할

pay check ponggŭp 봉급

payday ponggŭmnal 봉급날

payee such'wiin 수취인

pay envelope ponggŭp pongt'u 봉급
봉투

payer chiburin 지불인

payment (*of bill*) nabip 납입;
(*money*) chibul 지불

pay phone kongjung chŏnhwa 공중
전화

payroll (*money*) chibul ponggŭp
ch'ongaek 지불 봉급 총액;
(*employees*) chongŏbwŏn ch'ongsu
종업원 총수; *be on the* ~

koyongdoeda 고용되다

PC (= *personal computer*) p'isshi
피씨; (= *politically correct*) p'yŏn-
gyŏni omnŭn 편견이 없는

pea wanduk'ong 완두콩

peace (*not war*) p'yŏnghwa 평화;
(*quietness*) koyo 고요

peaceable *person* onsunhan 온순한

Peace Corps P'yŏnghwa Pongsadan
평화 봉사단

peaceful p'yŏnghwaroun 평화로운

peacefully p'yŏnghwaropkke
평화롭게

peach pokssung-a 복숭아

peacock kongjakssae 공작새

peak 1 *n* (*of mountain*) chŏngsang
정상; (*mountain*) san 산; *fig*
ch'oegoch'i 최고치 2 *v/i* ch'oegoch'ie
tarhada 최고치에 달하다

peak consumption ch'oedae
sobiryang 최대 소비량

peak hours p'ik'ŭ shigan 피크 시간

peanut ttangk'ong 땅콩; *get paid ~s*
F chwikkorimank'ŭm tonŭl
pannŭnda 쥐꼬리만큼 돈을 받는다;
that's ~s to him F kŭ saramegen
sae parŭi p'iyeyo 그 사람에겐 새
발의 피예요

peanut butter ttangk'ong pŏt'ŏ 땅콩
버터

pear pae 배

pearl chinju 진주

peasant nongmin 농민

pebble chagal 자갈

pecan p'ik'an 피칸

peck 1 *n* (*bite*) tchogi 쪼기; (*kiss*)
ppoppo 뽀뽀 2 *v/t* (*bite*) tchoda 쪼다;
(*kiss*) ppoppohada 뽀뽀하다

peculiar (*strange*) kimyohan 기묘한;
~ *to* (*special*) ...t'ŭgŭi ...특유의

peculiarity (*strangeness*) kimyoham
기묘함; (*special feature*) tokt'ŭk'am
독특함

pedal 1 *n* p'edal 페달 2 *v/i* (*turn ~s*)
p'edarŭl paltta 페달을 밟다; (*cycle*)
chajŏn-gŏrŭl t'ada 자전거를 타다

pedantic hyŏnhaktchŏgin 현학적인

pedestal (*for statue*) (chogaŭi)
patch'imttae (조각의) 받침대

pedestrian *n* pohaengja 보행자

pedestrian precinct pohaengja

chŏnyong kuyŏk 보행자 전용 구역
pediatrician soakkwa ŭisa 소아과
의사
pediatrics soakkwa 소아과
pedicab samnyun t'aekssi 삼륜 택시
pedigree 1 n hyŏlt'ong 혈통 2 adj
hyŏlt'ong-i punmyŏnghan 혈통이
분명한
pee v/i F ojum nuda 오줌 누다
peek 1 n saltchak yŏtppogi 살짝
엿보기 2 v/i saltchak yŏtppoda 살짝
엿보다
peel 1 n kkŏptchil 껍질 2 v/t fruit,
vegetables kkŏptchirŭl pŏtkkida
껍질을 벗기다 3 v/i (of nose,
shoulders) kkŏptchiri pŏtkkyŏjida
껍질이 벗겨지다
peep → peek
peephole tŭryŏda ponŭn kumŏng
들여다 보는 구멍
peer¹ n (in status) taedŭnghan saram
대등한 사람; (in age) tongbae 동배
peer² v/i chasehi poda 자세히 보다; ~
through the mist an-gae sogŭl
tturŏjige poda 안개 속을 뚫어지게
보다; ~ **at** tturŏjige poda 뚫어지게
보다
peeved F shin-gyŏng-i kŏsŭllinŭn
신경이 거슬리는
peg n (for coat) mot 못; (for tent)
malttuk 말뚝; **off the ~** kisŏngbok
기성복
pejorative kyŏngmyŏro 경멸어
pellet chagŭn kong 작은 공; (air rifle
bullet) chagŭn ch'ong-al 작은 총알
pelt 1 v/t: ~ **X with Y** Xege Yŭl/rŭl
tŏnjida X에게 Y을/를 던지다 2 v/i:
they ~ed along the road kŭdŭrŭn
kirŭl ttarasŏ kŭp'i kat-tta 그들은
길을 따라서 급히 갔다; **it's ~ing
down** piga sech'age naeryŏch'yŏyo
비가 세차게 내려쳐요
pelvis kolbanppyŏ 골반뼈
pen¹ n (ballpoint ~) polp'en 볼펜;
(fountain ~) mannyŏnp'il 만년필
pen² (enclosure) uri 우리
pen³ → penitentiary
penalize ch'ŏbŏrhada 처벌하다
penalty ch'ŏbŏl 처벌; SP p'aenŏlt'i
패널티
penalty area SP p'aenŏlt'i kuyŏk

패널티 구역
penalty clause (kyeyakŭi) wiyak
pŏlch'ik chohang (계약의) 위약 벌칙
조항
pencil yŏnp'il 연필
pencil sharpener yŏnp'il kkak-kki
연필 깍기
pendant (necklace) mok-kkŏri 목걸이
pending 1 prep ...ŭl/rŭl ttaekkaji
...을/를 때까지 2 adj: **be ~**
(awaiting decision) kyŏltchŏngi
naogikkaji kidarinŭn 결정이
나오기까지 기다리는; (about to
happen) imbak'an 임박한
penetrate kwant'onghada 관통하다;
market chinch'urhada 진출하다
penetrating stare, sound nalk'aroun
날카로운; analysis kanp'ahanŭn
간파하는
penetration ch'imt'u 침투; (of
market) chinch'ul 진출
pen friend p'enp'al ch'in-gu 펜팔
친구
penicillin p'enishillin 페니실린
peninsula pando 반도
penis ŭmgyŏng 음경
penitence huhoe 후회
penitent adj nwiuch'inŭn 뉘우치는
penitentiary kyodoso 교도소
pen name p'ilmyŏng 필명
pennant samgak-kki 삼각기
penniless muilp'unŭi 무일푼의
penpal p'enp'al ch'in-gu 펜팔 친구
pension yŏn-gŭm 연금
♦ **pension off** myŏng-ye
t'oejiksshik'ida 명예 퇴직시키다
pension fund yŏn-gŭmchohap 연금
조합
pension scheme yŏn-gŭm chedo
연금 제도
pensive saenggage chamgin 생각에
잠긴
Pentagon: the ~ Miguk
kukppangssŏng 미국 국방성
penthouse p'aent'ŭhausŭ 팬트하우스
pent-up ŏngnullin 억눌린
penultimate ŏmiesŏ tubŏntchae
ŭmjŏrŭi 어미에서 두번째 음절의
people saram 사람; (race, tribe)
minjok 민족; **the ~** kungmin 국민;
the American ~ Miguk kungmin

미국 국민; ~ *say* ... saramdŭrŭn ...
rago marhanda 사람들은 ... 라고
말한다

pepper (*spice*) huch'u 후추; (*chilli*)
koch'u 고추; (*pimiento*) p'imang
피망

peppermint (*candy*) pak'asat'ang
박하사탕; (*flavoring*) pak'ahyang
박하향

pep talk kyŏngnyŏ yŏnsŏl 격려 연설

per tang 당; ~ *annum* illyŏne 일년에

perceive (*with senses*) kamjihada
감지하다; (*view, interpret*)
arach'arida 알아차리다

percent p'ŏsent'ŭ 퍼센트; *10/20 ~*
ship/iship p'ŏsent'ŭ 십/이십 퍼센트

percentage piyul 비율

perceptible chigak'al su innŭn 지각할
수 있는

perceptibly arach'aril su itkke
알아차릴 수 있게

perception (*through senses*) kamji
감지; (*of situation*) inji 인지; (*insight*)
chigak 지각

perceptive t'ongch'allyŏk innŭn
통찰력 있는

perch 1 *n* (*for bird*) hwaet-ttae 횃대
2 *v/i* (*of bird*) hwaet-ttaee antta
횃대에앉다; (*of person*) chamshi
antta 잠시 앉다

percolate *v/i* (*of coffee*) k'ŏp'irŭl
naerida 커피를 내리다

percolator k'ŏp'i meik'ŏ 커피 메이커

percussion t'aak-kki 타악기

percussion instrument t'aak-kki
타악기

perfect 1 *n* GRAM wallyohyŏng
완료형 **2** *adj* wanbyŏk'an 완벽한 **3** *v/t*
wanjŏnhage hada 완전하게 하다

perfection wanbyŏk 완벽; *to ~*
wanbyŏk'i 완벽히

perfectionist *n* wanbyŏkjuŭija
완벽주의자

perfectly wanbyŏk'age 완벽하게;
(*totally*) wanjŏnhage 완전하게

perforated *line* chŏmsŏni tchik'in
점선이 찍힌

perforations chŏlch'wisŏn 절취선

perform 1 *v/t* (*carry out*) tahada
다하다; (*of actor, musician*) kong-
yŏnhada 공연하다 **2** *v/i* (*of actor,*

musician, dancer) kong-yŏnhada
공연하다; (*of machine*)
chakttonghada 작동하다

performance (*by actor, musician*)
kong-yŏn 공연; (*of employee,*
company etc) ŏmmu suhaeng 업무
수행; (*by machine*) sŏngnŭng 성능

performance car sŏngnŭng-i usuhan
ch'a 성능이 우수한 차

performer kong-yŏnja 공연자

perfume hyanggi 향수; (*of flower*)
hyanggi 향기

perfunctory hyŏngshiktchŏgin
형식적인

perhaps amado 아마도

peril wihŏm 위험

perilous wihŏmhan 위험한

perimeter chubyŏn 주변; (*of circle*)
chuwi 주위

perimeter fence kyŏnggyesŏn ult'ari
경계선 울타리

period (*time*) kigan 기간;
(*menstruation*) saengni 생리;
(*punctuation mark*) mach'imp'yo
마침표; *I don't want to, ~!* tŏ isang
marhal p'iryodo ŏpsshi nan hago
shiptchi anayo! 더 이상 말할 필요도
없이 난 하고 싶지 않아요!

periodic chugijŏgin 주기적인

periodical *n* chŏnggi kanhaengmul
정기 간행물

periodically chŏnggijŏguro
정기적으로

peripheral 1 *adj* (*not crucial*)
taesuroptchi anŭn 대수롭지 않은 **2** *n*
COMPUT chubyŏn changch'i 주변
장치

periphery chuwi 주위

perish (*of rubber*) ssŏktta 썩다; (*of*
person) sesang-ŭl ttŭda 세상을 뜨다

perishable ssŏk-kki shwiun 썩기 쉬운

perjure: ~ *oneself* wijŭnghada
위증하다

perjury wijŭng 위증

perk *n* (*of job*) itchŏm 이점

♦ **perk up 1** *v/t* saenggi tolge hada
생기 돌게 하다 **2** *v/i* saenggiga nada
생기가 나다

perky (*cheerful*) kiun ch'an 기운 찬

perm 1 *n* p'ama 파마 **2** *v/t* p'ama hada
파마 하다

permanent yŏnggujŏgin 영구적인
permanently yŏngguhi 영구히
permissible hŏyongdoel su innŭn 허용될 수 있는
permission hŏrak 허락
permissive kwandaehan 관대한
permit 1 *n* hŏgaso 허가서 2 *v/t* hŏrak'ada 허락하다; ~ *X to do Y* Xi/ga Yhanŭn kŏsŭl hŏrak'ada X이/가 Y하는 것을 허락하다
perpendicular *adj* sujigŭi 수직의
perpetual kkŭnimŏmnŭn 끊임없는
perpetually kyesok'aeso 계속해서
perpetuate yŏng-wŏnhage hada 영원하게 하다
perplex tanghok'age hada 당혹하게 하다
perplexed tanghok'an 당혹한
perplexity tanghok 당혹
persecute pak'aehada 박해하다
persecution pak'ae 박해
perseverance kkŭn-gi 끈기
persevere kyesok'aeso hada 계속해서 하다
persist chisok'ada 지속하다; ~ *in* kkŭndŏktchige toep'urihada 끈덕지게 되풀이하다
persistence (*perseverance*) kkŭn-gi 끈기; (*continuation*) chisok 지속
persistent *person, questions* kkŭndŏktchige toep'urihanŭn 끈덕지게 되풀이하는; *rain, unemployment etc* chisoktchŏgin 지속적인
persistently (*continually*) kyesok'aeso 계속해서
person saram 사람; *in* ~ ponini chiktchŏp 본인이 직접
personal (*private*) kaeintchŏgin 개인적인; (*relating to a particular individual*) kaeinŭi 개인의; *don't make* ~ *remarks* satchŏgin marŭn haji maseyo 사적인 말은 하지 마세요
personal assistant kaeinbiso 개인 비서; **personal computer** kaeinnyong k'ŏmp'yut'ŏ 개인용 컴퓨터; **personal hygiene** kaein wisaeng 개인 위생
personality sŏngkkyŏk 성격; (*celebrity*) yumyŏng-in 유명인

personally (*for my part*) narossŏnŭn 나로서는; (*in person*) chiktchŏp 직접; *don't take it* ~ tangsin mariragonŭn saenggak'aji maseyo 당신 말이라고는 생각하지 마세요
personal pronoun inch'ing taemyŏngsa 인칭 대명사; **personal seal, personal stamp** tojang 도장; **personal stereo** kaeinyong sŭt'ereo 개인용 스테레오
personnel (*employees*) chigwŏn 직원; (*department*) insakkwa 인사과
personnel manager insa tamdang pujang 인사 담당 부장
perspiration ttam 땀
perspire ttamŭl hŭllida 땀을 흘리다
persuade sŏlttŭk'ada 설득하다; ~ *s.o. to do sth* nugurŭl muŏt'adorok sŏlttŭk'ada 누구를 무엇하도록 설득하다
persuasion sŏlttŭk 설득
persuasive sŏlttŭngnyŏk innŭn 설득력 있는
pertinent chŏktchŏrhan 적절한
perturb uryŏhada 우려하다
perturbing uryŏdoenŭn 우려되는
pervasive *influence, ideas* nŏlli p'ŏjyŏ innŭn 널리 퍼져 있는
perverse (*awkward*) isanghan 이상한
perversion (*sexual*) pyŏnt'ae 변태
pervert *n* (*sexual*) pyŏnt'ae sŏngnyŏktcha 변태 성욕자
pessimism pigwanjuŭi 비관주의
pessimist pigwanjuŭija 비관주의자
pessimistic pigwanjŏgin 비관적인
pest yuhaehan kŏt 유해한 것; F (*person*) koltchitkkŏri 골칫거리
pest control pyŏngch'unghae kwalli 병충해 관리
pester kwich'ank'e kulda 귀찮게 굴다; ~ *s.o. to do sth* nuguege muŏsŭl hae tallago chorŭda 누구에게 무엇을 해 달라고 조르다
pesticide salch'ungje 살충제
pet 1 *n* (*animal*) aewandongmul 애완동물; (*favorite person*) t'ŭk'i choahanŭn saram 특히 좋아하는 사람 2 *adj* (*favorite*) t'ŭk'i choahanŭn 특히 좋아하는 3 *v/t animal* ssŭdadŭmtta 쓰다듬다 4 *v/i* (*of couple*) aemuhada 애무하다

petal kkonnip 꽃잎

♦ peter out chŏmch'ajŏguro
ŏpssŏjida 점차적으로 없어지다

petite momtchibi chagŭn 몸집이 작은

petition n ch'ŏng-wŏnsŏ 청원서

petrified sosŭrach'in 소스라친

petrify sosŭrach'ige hada 소스라치게
하다

petrochemical sŏgyu hwahak
chep'um 석유 화학 제품

petroleum sŏgyu 석유

petty person, behavior piyŏrhan
비열한; details shishihan 시시한

petty cash ssamjit-tton 쌈짓돈

petulant sŏngmarŭn 성마른

pew kyohoeŭi shindosŏk 교회의
신도석

pewter paengnap 백랍

pharmaceutical cheyagŭi 제약의

pharmaceuticals cheyak 제약

pharmacist (in store) yaksa 약사

pharmacy (store) yak-kkuk 약국

phase shigi 시기

♦ phase in tan-gyejŏguro t'uip'ada
단계적으로 투입하다

♦ phase out tan-gyejŏguro
chegŏhada 단계적으로 제거하다

PhD (= Doctor of Philosophy)
paksa 박사

phenomenal koengjanghan 굉장한

phenomenally koengjanghi 굉장히

phenomenon hyŏnsang 현상

philanthropic injŏng-i manŭn 인정이
많은

philanthropist chasŏn-ga 자선가

philanthropy chasŏn 자선

Philippines: the ~ P'illip'in 필리핀

philistine n kyoyang ŏmnŭn saram
교양 없는 사람

philosopher ch'ŏrhaktcha 철학자

philosophical ch'ŏrhaktchŏgin
철학적인

philosophy ch'ŏrhak 철학

phobia kongp'otchŭng 공포증

phone 1 n chŏnhwa 전화 2 v/t
chŏnhwa kŏlda 전화 걸다 3 v/i
chŏnhwahada 전화하다

phone book chŏnhwabŏnhobu
전화번호부; phone booth kongjung
chŏnhwa pakssŭ 공중 전화 박스;
phonecall chŏnhwa 전화; phone

number chŏnhwa pŏnho 전화 번호

phon(e)y adj katchaŭi 가짜의; a ~
ten dollar bill ship tallŏ tchari wijo
chip'ye 십 달러 짜리 위조 지폐

photo n sajin 사진

photo album sajinaelbŏm 사진앨범;
photocopier pokssagi 복사기;
photocopy 1 n pokssa 복사 2 v/t
pokssahada 복사하다

photogenic sajini chal pannŭn 사진이
잘 받는

photograph 1 n sajin 사진 2 v/t sajin
tchiktta 사진 찍다

photographer sajinsa 사진사

photography sajin ch'waryŏng 사진
촬영

phrase 1 n munkku 문구 2 v/t mallo
p'yohyŏnhada 말로 표현하다

phrasebook sugŏjip 숙어집

physical 1 adj (relating to the body)
yukch'eŭi 육체의 2 MED shinch'e
kŏmsa 신체 검사

physical handicap shinch'e chang-ae
신체 장애

physically yukch'ejŏguro 육체적으로

physician naekkwa ŭisa 내과 의사

physicist mullihaktcha 물리학자

physics mullihak 물리학

physiotherapist mulli ch'iryosa 물리
치료사

physiotherapy mulli ch'iryo 물리
치료

physique mommae 몸매

pianist p'ianisŭt'ŭ 피아니스트

piano p'iano 피아노

pick 1 n: take your ~ korŭseyo
고르세요 2 v/t (choose) sŏnt'aek'ada
선택하다; flowers, fruit ttada 따다; ~
one's nose k'orŭl hubida 코를
후비다 3 v/i: ~ and choose korŭda
고르다

♦ pick at: ~ one's food saech'ŏrŏm
chogŭmsshik mŏktta 새처럼 조금씩
먹다

♦ pick on (treat unfairly)
ch'abyŏrhada 차별하다; (select)
kollanaeda 골라내다

♦ pick out (identify) araboda
알아보다

♦ pick up 1 v/t chibŏ tŭlda 집어 들다;
(from ground) chuwŏ ollida 주워

올리다; *person, the kids etc* teryŏoda
데려오다; *dry cleaning etc* kajyŏoda
가져오다; *information* ipssuhada
입수하다; (*from airport etc*) majung
naoda 마중 나오다; (*in car*) ch'a-e
t'aeuda 차에 태우다; (*sexually*)
ch'inhaejida 친해지다; *language, skill*
paeuda 배우다; *habit* sŭpttŭk'ada
습득하다; *illness* ...-e kŏllida ...에
걸리다; (*buy*) sada 사다; *criminal*
ch'ep'ohada 체포하다 **2** *v/i*
(*improve*) hojŏndoeda 호전되다; (*of
weather*) choajida 좋아지다

picket 1 *n* (*of strikers*) p'ik'et 피켓
2 *v/t* kamshihada 감시하다

picket fence malttuk ult'ari 말뚝
울타리

picket line p'ik'et lain 피켓 라인

pickle *v/t* (sogŭm / shikch'oe) chŏrida
(소금 / 식초에) 절이다

pickles p'ik'ŭl 피클

pickpocket somaech'igi 소매치기

pick-up (**truck**) t'ŭrŏk 트럭

picky F kkadaroun 까다로운

picnic 1 *n* sop'ung 소풍 **2** *v/i* sop'ung
kada 소풍 가다

picture 1 *n* (*photo*) sajin 사진;
(*painting*) hoehwa 회화;
(*illustration*) kŭrim 그림; *keep s.o.
in the ~* nuguege allyŏjuda 누구에게
알려주다 **2** *v/t* sangsanghada
상상하다

picture book kŭrimch'aek 그림책

picturesque kŭrimgwa kat'ŭn 그림과
같은

pie p'ai 파이

piece (*fragment*) chogak 조각;
(*component*) pup'um 부품; (*in board
game*) mal 말; *a ~ of pie / bread*
p'ai / ppang han chogak 파이 / 빵 한
조각; *a ~ of advice* ch'unggo han
madi 충고 한 마디; *go to ~s*
chwajŏrhada 좌절하다; *take to ~s*
punhaehada 분해하다

♦ **piece together** *broken plate*
chogagŭl moŭda 조각을 모으다;
facts, evidence tcha match'uda 짜
맞추다

piecemeal *adv* han pŏne han
kajisshik 한 번에 한 가지씩

piecework *n* sangnil 삯일

pierce (*penetrate*) kwant'onghada
관통하다; *ears* ttult'a 뚫다

piercing *noise* kwirŭl tchinnŭn tŭt'an
귀를 찢는 듯한; *eyes* nalk'aroun
날카로운; *wind* maesŏun 매서운

pig twaeji 돼지; (*unpleasant person*)
twaejigat'ŭn nom 돼지같은 놈

pigeon pidulgi 비둘기

pigheaded wan-gohan 완고한; **pigpen** twaejiuri 돼지우리; *fig*
chijŏbunhago pulgyŏrhan kot
지저분하고 불결한 곳; **pigskin**
twaeji kajuk 돼지 가죽; **pigtail** ttaŭn
mŏri 땋은 머리

pile tŏmi 더미; *a ~ of work*
santtŏmigach'i manŭn il 산더미같이
많은 일

♦ **pile up 1** *v/i* (*of work, bills*) moida
모이다 **2** *v/t* ssat'a 쌓다

piles MED ch'ijil 치질

pile-up MOT yŏnswae ch'ungdol 연쇄
충돌

pilfering chomttoduktchil 좀도둑질

pilgrim sullyeja 순례자

pilgrimage sullye 순례

pill aryak 알약; *the ~* mŏngnŭn
p'iimnyak 먹는 피임약; *be on the ~*
p'iimhada 피임하다

pillar kidung 기둥

pillion (*of motorbike*) twitjwasŏk
뒷좌석

pillow *n* pegae 베개

pillowcase pegaennit 베갯잇

pilot 1 *n* (*of airplane*) chojongsa
조종사 **2** *v/t airplane* chojonghada
조종하다

pilot plant shihŏm kongjang 시험
공장

pilot scheme yebi kyehoek 예비
계획

pimp *n* p'oju 포주

pimple yŏdŭrŭm 여드름

PIN (= *personal identification
number*) kaein hwagin pŏnho 개인
확인 번호

pin 1 *n* (*for sewing*) p'in 핀; (*in
bowling*) pollingp'in 볼링핀; (*badge*)
paetchi 배지; *a 2-~ electric plug*
p'ini tu kaein p'ŭllŏgŭ 핀이 두 개인
플러그 **2** *v/t* (*hold down*) kkomtchak
mot'age nurŭda 꼼짝 못하게 누르다;

pin

(*attach*) kkot-tta 꽂다
♦ **pin down**: *pin s.o. down to a date*
nugurŭl t'ŭktchŏng naltcha-e
tongŭihadorok mandŭlda 누구를
특정 날짜에 동의하도록 만들다
♦ **pin up** *notice* puch'ida 붙이다
pincers p'ench'i 펜치; (*of crab*)
chipkkebal 집게발
pinch 1 *n* kkojipkki 꼬집기; (*of salt,
sugar etc*) son-garagŭro chogŭm
chipkki 손가락으로 조금 집기; *at a ~*
yusashie 유사시에 **2** *v/t* kkojiptta
꼬집다 **3** *v/i* (*of shoes*) kkok kkida 꼭
끼다
pine[1] *n* (*tree, wood*) sonamu 소나무
pine[2] *v/i*: *~ for* kŭriwŏhada
그리워하다
pineapple p'ainaep'ŭl 파인애플
ping *n* p'inghanŭn sori 핑하는 소리
ping-pong t'ak-kku 탁구
pink (*color*) punhongsaegŭi 분홍색의
pinnacle *fig* chŏngsang 정상
pinpoint chŏnghwak'i aranaeda
정확히 알아내다
pins and needles chŏrim 저림
pinstripe *adj* kanŭn serojul munŭiŭi
가는 세로줄 무늬의
pint p'aint'ŭ 파인트
pin-up (**girl**) p'in ŏp(yŏja) 핀
업(여자)
pioneer 1 *n* *fig* sŏn-guja 선구자 **2** *v/t*
kaech'ŏk'ada 개척하다
pioneering *adj* sŏn-gujŏgin 선구적인
pious kyŏnggŏnhan 경건한
pip *n* (*of fruit*) sshi 씨
pipe 1 *n* (*for smoking*) p'aip'ŭ 파이프;
(*for water, gas, sewage*) kwan 관
2 *v/t* kwanŭro ponaeda 관으로
보내다
♦ **pipe down** choyonghi hada 조용히
하다
piped music shillae kyŏng-ŭmak
실내 경음악
pipeline p'aip'ŭrain 파이프라인; *in
the ~* chinhaeng chung-in 진행 중인
piping hot kimi solsol nage ttŭgŏun
김이 솔솔 나게 뜨거운
pirate *v/t* *software* p'yojŏrhada
표절하다
piss *v/i* ∨ (*urinate*) ojum nuda 오줌
누다

pissed F (*annoyed*) hwaga nan 화가
난; *Br* (*drunk*) ch'ihan 취한
pistol kwŏnch'ong 권총
piston p'isŭt'on 피스톤
pit *n* (*hole*) kumŏng 구멍; (*coal mine*)
kaeng 갱; (*in fruit*) sshi 씨
pitch[1] *n* MUS karak 가락
pitch[2] **1** *v/i* (*in baseball*) t'uguhada
투구하다 **2** *v/t* *tent* ch'ida 치다; *ball*
tŏnjida 던지다
pitch black ch'irhŭk 칠흑
pitcher[1] (*baseball player*) t'usu 투수
pitcher[2] (*container*) chujŏnja 주전자
piteous pulssanghan 불쌍한
pitfall hamjŏng 함정
pith (*of citrus fruit*) shim 심
pitiful *sight* yŏnminŭl cha-anaenŭn
연민을 자아내는; *excuse, attempt*
hanshimhan 한심한
pitiless maejŏnghan 매정한
pittance aju chŏgŭn ton 아주 적은 돈
pity 1 *n* tongjŏng 동정; *it's a ~ that
… …* hadani aesŏk'agunyo …
하다니 애석하군요; *what a ~!*
andwaetkkunyo! 안됐군요!; *take ~
on* pulssanghi yŏgida 불쌍히 여기다
2 *v/t* *person* tongjŏnghada 동정하다
pivot *v/i* hoejŏnhada 회전하다
pixel COMPUT p'iksel 픽셀
pizza p'ija 피자
placard pyŏkppo 벽보
place 1 *n* changso 장소; (*restaurant*)
shikttang 식당; (*bar*) sultchip 술집;
(*apartment, house*) chip 집; (*in
book*) ikttŏn kot 읽던 곳; (*in race,
competition*) tŭngssu 등수; (*seat*)
chari 자리; *at my / his ~* naŭi / kŭŭi
chibesŏ 나의 / 그의 집에서; *in ~ of*
taeshine 대신에; *feel out of ~*
pulp'yŏnhada 불편하다; *take ~*
yŏllida 열리다; *in the first ~* (*firstly*)
ch'ŏt-tchaero 첫째로; (*in the
beginning*) ch'ŏŭmenŭn 처음에는
2 *v/t* (*put*) not'a 놓다; (*identify*)
ŏttŏk'e algo innŭn saraminji
aranaeda 어떻게 알고 있는 사람인지
알아내다; *~ an order* chumunhada
주문하다
place mat shikt'agyong maet'ŭ
식탁용 매트
placid ch'abunhan 차분한

plague 1 *n* chŏnyŏmppyŏng 전염병
2 *v/t* (*bother*) koeropʼida 괴롭히다
plain¹ *n* pʼyŏng-ya 평야
plain² 1 *adj* (*clear, obvious*)
myŏngbaekʼan 명백한; (*not fancy*)
pʼyŏngbŏmhan 평범한; (*not pretty*)
motssaenggin 못생긴; (*not patterned*)
mujiŭi 무지의; (*blunt*) soltchikʼan
솔직한; ~ *chocolate* pʼullein
chʼokʼollit 플레인 초콜릿 **2** *adv crazy
etc* wanjŏnhi 완전히
plain clothes: *in* ~ sabogŭi 사복의
plainly (*clearly*) punmyŏnghage
분명하게; (*bluntly*) soltchikʼage
솔직하게; (*simply*) kanttanhi 간단히
plain-spoken soltchikʼi marhanŭn
솔직히 말하는
plaintiff wŏn-go 원고
plaintive kusŭlpʼŭn 구슬픈
plait 1 *n* (*in hair*) ttaŭn mŏri 땋은
머리 **2** *v/t hair* ttatʼa 땋다
plan 1 *n* (*project, intention*) kyehoek
계획; (*drawing*) sŏlgyedo 설계도 **2** *v/t*
(*prepare*) chunbihada 준비하다;
(*design*) tijainhada 디자인하다; ~ *to
do* …hal kŏsŭl kyehoekʼada …할
것을 계획하다 **3** *v/i* kyehoekʼada
계획하다
plane¹ *n* (*airplane*) pihaenggi 비행기
plane² *n* (*tool*) taepʼae 대패
planet haengsŏng 행성
plank nŏlppanji 널빤지; *fig* (*of policy*)
chŏngdang kangnyŏng hangmok
정당 강령 항목
planning chunbi 준비; *at the ~ stage*
chunbihanŭn tan-gye-esŏ 준비하는
단계에서
plant¹ 1 *n* shingmul 식물 **2** *v/t* shimtta
심다
plant² *n* (*factory*) kongjang 공장;
(*equipment*) changbi 장비
plantation pʼullaentʼeishyŏn
플랜테이션
plaque¹ (*on wall*) kinyŏm aektcha
기념 액자
plaque² (*on teeth*) chʼisŏk 치석
plaster 1 *n* (*on wall, ceiling*)
hoebanjuk 회반죽 **2** *v/t wall, ceiling*
hoebanjugŭl parŭda 회반죽을
바르다; *be ~ed with* … (ŭ)ro
ttŏkchʼiri toeda … (으)로 떡칠이

doeda
되다
plaster cast sŏk-kkosang 석고상,
kibsŭ 깁스
plastic 1 *n* pʼullasŭtʼik 플라스틱 **2** *adj*
(*made of ~*) pʼullasŭtʼigŭi 플라스틱의
plastic bag pinil pongji 비닐 봉지;
plastic money shinyong kʼadŭ 신용
카드; **plastic surgeon** sŏnghyŏng
ŭisa 성형 의사; **plastic surgery**
sŏnghyŏng susul 성형 수술
plate *n* (*for food*) chŏpssi 접시; (*sheet
of metal*) pʼan-gŭm 판금
plateau kowŏn 고원
platform (*stage*) tansang 단상; RAIL
pʼullaetpʼom 플랫폼; *fig* (*political*)
chŏngdang kangnyŏng 정당 강령
platinum 1 *n* paek-kkŭm 백금 **2** *adj*
paek-kkŭmŭi 백금의
platitude chinbuhan mal 진부한 말
platonic *relationship*
chŏngshintchŏgin 정신적인
platoon (*of soldiers*) sodae 소대
platter (*for food*) taehyŏng chŏpssi
대형 접시
plausible kŭrŏl ttŭtʼan 그럴 듯한
play 1 *n* (*in theater, on TV*) yŏn-gŭk
연극; (*of children*) nori 놀이; TECH
tongnŏk 동력; SP kyŏnggi 경기 **2** *v/i*
(*of children*) nolda 놀다; (*of
musician*) yŏnjuhada 연주하다; (SP:
perform) undonghada 운동하다; (SP:
take part) chʼamgahada 참가하다
3 *v/t musical instrument, piece of
music* yŏnjuhada 연주하다; *game*
hada 하다; *opponent* kyŏruda 겨루다;
Macbeth etc yŏn-gihada 연기하다; ~
a joke on nollida 놀리다
♦**play around** (*be unfaithful*)
paramŭl pʼiuda 바람을 피우다
♦**play down** kyŏngshihada
경시하다
♦**play up** (*of machine*) kojang-i nada
고장이 나다; (*of child*)
yadanbŏpsŏgŭl pʼiuda 야단법석을
피우다; (*of tooth etc*) sangtʼaega
nappajida 상태가 나빠지다
playact (*pretend*) chʼŏkʼada 척하다;
playback chaesaeng 재생; **playboy**
paramdung-i 바람둥이
player SP kyŏnggija 경기자; MUS
yŏnjuja 연주자; THEA yŏn-gija 연기자

playful

playful *punch etc* changnanŭi 장난의
playground norit'ŏ 놀이터
playing card k'adŭ 카드
playing field kyŏnggijang 경기장
playmate norich'in-gu 놀이친구
playwright kŭkchak-kka 극작가
plaza (*for shopping*) p'ŭllaja 플라자
plea *n* kanch'ŏng 간청
plead *v/i*: ~ **for** kanch'ŏnghada
간청하다; ~ **guilty** / **not guilty**
yujoe / mujoerŭl hangbyŏnhada
유죄 / 무죄를 항변하다; ~ **with**
kanch'ŏnghada 간청하다
pleasant yuk'waehan 유쾌한
please 1 *adv* chebal 제발; **more tea?**
- yes, ~ ch'a tŏ hashigessŏyo? - ne,
tŏ chuseyo 차 더 하시겠어요? - 네,
더 주세요 **2** *v/t* kippŭge hada 기쁘게
하다; ~ **do** mullonimnida
물론입니다 **2** *v/t* kippŭge hada 기쁘게
하다; ~ **yourself** cho-ŭshil taero
haseyo 좋으실 대로 하세요
pleased kippŏn 기쁜; (*satisfied*)
manjok'an 만족한; **be ~ with sth**
musŏse manjok'ada 무엇에
만족하다; ~ **to meet you** mannasŏ
pan-gapssŭmnida 만나서 반갑습니다
pleasing chŭlgŏun 즐거운
pleasure (*happiness, satisfaction*)
manjok 만족; (*not business*) orak
오락; (*delight*) kippŭmŭl chunŭn kŏt
기쁨을 주는 것; **it's a ~** (*you're
welcome*) ch'ŏnmaneyo 천만에요;
with ~ kikkŏi 기꺼이
pleat *n* (*in skirt*) churŭm 주름
pledge 1 *n* (*promise*) yakssok 약속;
Pledge of Allegiance kuk-kkie
taehan maengse 국기에 대한 맹세
2 *v/t* (*promise*) yakssok'ada 약속하다
plentiful nŏngnŏk'an 넉넉한
plenty (*abundance*) p'ung-yo 풍요; ~
of manŭn 많은; **that's ~** twaessŏyo
됐어요; **there's ~ for everyone**
moduege toragal mank'ŭm
ch'ungbunhamnida 모두에게 돌아갈
만큼 충분합니다
pliable hwigi shwiun 휘기 쉬운
pliers p'ench'i 펜치; **a pair of ~**
p'ench'i han pŏl 펜치 한 벌
plight kon-gyŏng 곤경
plod *v/i* (*walk*) mugŏun kŏrŭmŭro
ch'ŏnch'ŏnhi kŏt-tta 무거운

걸음으로 천천히 걷다
♦**plod along, plod on** (*with a job*)
yŏrŭi ŏpsshi kŭrŏktchŏrŏk hada
열의 없이 그럭저럭 하다
plodder (*at work, school*) kkujunhi
irhanŭn saram 꾸준히 일하는 사람
plot¹ *n* (*land*) chagŭn kuhoegŭi ttang
작은 구획의 땅
plot² **1** *n* (*conspiracy*) kyeryak 계략;
(*of novel*) kusŏng 구성 **2** *v/t*
hoekch'aek'ada 획책하다 **3** *v/i*
ŭmmohada 음모하다
plotter ŭmmoja 음모자; COMPUT
p'ŭllot'ŏ 플로터
plow 1 *n* chaenggi 쟁기 **2** *v/t* kalda
갈다 **3** *v/i* kyŏngjak'ada 경작하다
♦**plow back** *profits* chaet'ujahada
재투자하다
pluck *v/t eyebrows* ppoptta 뽑다;
chicken t'ŏrŭl chaba ppoptta 털을
잡아 뽑다
♦**pluck up**: ~ **courage** yonggirŭl
naeda 용기를 내다
plug 1 *n* (*for sink, bath*) magae 마개;
(*electrical*) p'ŭllŏgŭ 플러그; (*spark ~*)
chŏmhwa p'ŭllŏgŭ 점화 플러그; (*for
new book etc*) sŏnjŏnyong
ch'uch'ŏnsa 선전용 추천사 **2** *v/t hole*
t'ŭrŏ maktta 틀어 막다; *new book
etc* sŏnjŏnhada 선전하다
♦**plug away** F yŏlsshimhi
kkujunhage hada 열심히 꾸준하게
하다
♦**plug in** *v/t* p'ŭllŏgŭrŭl kkot-tta
플러그를 꽂다
plum 1 *n* chadu 자두 **2** *adj job* taeuga
t'ŭkppyŏrhan 대우가 특별한
plumage kitt'ŏl 깃털
plumb *adj* sujigŭi 수직의
plumber paegwangong 배관공
plumbing (*pipes*) paegwan 배관
plummet (*of airplane*) sujigŭro
ttŏrŏjida 수직으로 떨어지다; (*of
prices*) chik kangha 직 강하
plump *adj* p'odongp'odonghan
포동포동한
♦**plump for** korŭda 고르다
plunge 1 *n* ttwiŏdŭm 뛰어듦; (*in
prices*) harak 하락; **take the ~**
mohŏmŭl hada 모험을 하다 **2** *v/i*
torip'ada 돌입하다; (*of prices*)

harak'ada 하락하다 3 v/t tchirŭda
찌르다; *the city was ~d into darkness* toshiga ŏduum sogŭro ppajyŏ
tŭrŏt-tta 도시가 어둠 속으로 빠져
들었다; *the news ~d him into despair* kŭ soshigŭro, kŭnŭn
chŏlmang-e ppajyŏt-tta 그 소식으로,
그는 절망에 빠졌다

plunging *neckline* kip'i p'ajin 깊이
파진

plural 1 *adj* pokssuŭi 복수의 **2** *n*
pokssuhyŏng 복수형

plus 1 *prep* tŏhayŏ 더하여 **2** *adj* isang-
ŭi 이상의; *$500 ~ 500 tallŏ isang 오
백 달러 이상 **3** *n* (*symbol*) tŏhagi
더하기; (*advantage*) ittchŏm 이점
4 *conj* (*moreover*) tŏugi tŏugi 더욱이

plush hwaryŏhan 화려한

plywood happ'an 합판

p.m. ohu 오후

pneumatic kich'eŭi 기체의

pneumatic drill konggi tŭril 공기
드릴

pneumonia p'yeryŏm 폐렴

poach¹ *v/t* (*cook*) ttŭgŏun mure
samtta 뜨거운 물에 삶다

poach² **1** *v/i* millyŏp'ada 밀렵하다
2 *v/t* (*hunt*) *salmon etc* mollae
chaptta 몰래 잡다

poached egg suran 수란

P.O. Box sasŏham 사서함

pocket 1 *n* hojumŏni 호주머니; *line
one's own ~s* chagi hojumŏnirŭl
ch'aeuda 자기 호주머니를 채우다;
be out of ~ pint'ŏlt'ŏriga toeda
빈털터리가 되다 **2** *adj* (*miniature*)
sohyŏng-ŭi 소형의 **3** *v/t* sŭltchŏk
kajida 슬쩍 가지다

pocketbook (*purse*) chagŭn
sonkkabang 작은 손가방; (*billfold*)
chigap 지갑; (*book*) p'ok'etyong
ch'aek 포켓용 책; **pocket calculator** p'ok'etyong kyesan-gi 포켓용
계산기; **pocketknife** chumŏnik'al
주머니칼

podium yŏndan 연단

poem shi 시

poet shiin 시인

poetic shittchŏgin 시적인

poetic justice sap'ilgwijŏng 사필귀정

poetry shi 시

poignant kamdongjŏgin 감동적인

point 1 *n* (*of pencil, knife*) kkŭt 끝; (*in
competition, exam*) chŏmsu 점수;
(*purpose*) moktchŏk 목적; (*moment*)
sun-gan 순간; (*in argument,
discussion*) yotchŏm 요점; (*in
decimals*) sosutchŏm 소수점; *5~3
otchŏm sam* 오점 삼; *beside the ~*
yotchŏmŭl pŏsŏnan 요점을 벗어난;
be on the ~ of mak haryŏgo hada
막 하려고 하다; *get to the ~*
yotchŏmŭl marhada 요점을 말하다;
the ~ is ... yotchŏmŭn ... 요점은...;
there's no ~ in waiting / trying
kidaril / shidohal iyuga ŏpssŏyo
기다릴 / 시도할 이유가 없어요 **2** *v/i*
sonkkaragŭro karik'ida 손가락으로
가리키다 **3** *v/t* *gun* kyŏnuda 겨누다

♦**point at** (*with finger*) karik'ida
가리키다

♦**point out** *sights, advantages*
chijŏk'ada 지적하다

♦**point to** (*with finger*) sonkkaragŭro
karik'ida 손가락으로 가리키다; *fig*
(*indicate*) amshihada 암시하다

point-blank 1 *adj* *refusal*
nogoltchŏgin 노골적인; *at ~ range*
chikssa kŏriesŏ 직사 거리에서 **2** *adv*
refuse nogoltchŏgŭro 노골적으로

pointed *remark* nalk'aroun 날카로운

pointer (*for teacher*) kyop'yŏn 교편;
(*hint*) chŏon 조언; (*sign, indication*)
amshi 암시

pointless soyongŏmnŭn 소용없는; *it's
~ trying* noryŏk'aedo soyong-
ŏpssŏyo 노력해도 소용없어요

point of sale (*place*) maejang 매장;
(*promotional material*) sŏnjŏnyong
mulp'um 선전용 물품

point of view kwantchŏm 관점

poise ch'imch'ak 침착

poised *person* ch'imch'ak'an 침착한

poison 1 *n* tok 독 **2** *v/t* tokssarhada
독살하다; *water* togŭl t'ada 독을
타다; *fig: relationship* mangch'ida
망치다

poisonous yudok'an 유독한

poke 1 *n* tchirŭgi 찌르기 **2** *v/t* (*prod*)
ssushida 쑤시다; (*stick*) k'uk tchirŭda
쿡 찌르다; *~ fun at* nollida 놀리다; *~
one's nose into* ch'amgyŏnhada

참견하다
♦**poke around** (*in a place*) twijida 뒤지다; (*ask about a person*) kkoch'ikkoch'i k'aeda 꼬치꼬치 캐다

poker (*card game*) p'okŏ 포커

poky (*cramped*) pijobŭn 비좁은

Poland P'ollandŭ 폴란드

polar kŭktchiŭi 극지의

polar bear puk-kkŭk kom 북극 곰

polarize *v/t* yangbunhwahada 양분화하다

Pole P'ollandŭin 폴란드인

pole[1] (*of wood, metal*) kidung 기둥

pole[2] (*of earth*) kŭk 극

polevault changttae nop'i ttwigi 장대 높이 뛰기

police *n* kyŏngch'al 경찰

policeman kyŏngch'algwan 경찰관; **police state** kyŏngch'al kuk-kka 경찰 국가; **police station** kyŏngch'alsŏ 경찰서; **policewoman** yŏgyŏng 여경

policy[1] chŏngch'aek 정책

policy[2] (*insurance ~*) yak-kkwan 약관

polio soamabi 소아마비

Polish 1 *adj* P'ollandŭŭi 폴란드의 2 *n* P'ollandŭŏ 폴란드어

polish 1 *n* kwangt'aektche 광택제; (*nail ~*) maenik'yuŏ 매니큐어 2 *v/t* kwangnaeda 광내다; *speech* tadŭmtta 다듬다

♦**polish off** *food* ta mŏgŏ ch'iuda 다 먹어 치우다

♦**polish up** *skill* kalgo tadŭmtta 갈고 다듬다

polished *performance* chal tadŭmŏjin 잘 다듬어진

polite kongsonhan 공손한

politely kongsonhage 공손하게

politeness kongsonham 공손함

political chŏngch'ijŏgin 정치적인

politically correct p'yŏn-gyŏni ŏmnŭn 편견이 없는

politician chŏngch'iga 정치가

politics chŏngch'i 정치; **what are his ~?** kŭ saramŭi chŏngch'ijŏk sogyŏni mwŏn-gayo? 그 사람의 정치적 소견이 뭔가요?

poll 1 *n* (*survey*) yŏron chosa 여론 조사; **the ~s** (*election*) sŏn-gŏ 선거; **go to the ~s** t'up'yohada 투표하다

2 *v/t people* yŏronŭl mut-tta 여론을 묻다; *votes* tŭkp'yohada 득표하다

pollen hwabun 화분

pollen count hwabunnyang 화분량

polling booth kip'yoso 기표소

pollster yŏron chosawŏn 여론 조사원

pollutant oyŏmmultchil 오염물질

pollute oyŏmshik'ida 오염시키다

pollution oyŏm 오염

polo neck t'ŏt'ŭlnek 터틀넥

polo shirt p'olo shyŏch'ŭ 폴로 셔츠

polyethylene p'olliet'illen 폴리에틸렌

polyester p'olliesŭt'erŭ 폴리에스테르

polystyrene p'ollisŭt'iren 폴리스티렌

polyunsaturate kodo pulp'ohwa multchil 고도 불포화 물질

pompous kŏdŭrŭm p'iunŭn 거드름 피우는

pond yŏnmot 연못

ponder *v/i* komgomi saenggak'ada 곰곰이 생각하다

pony chorangmal 조랑말

ponytail twiro mungnŭn mŏri 뒤로 묶는 머리

poodle p'udŭl 푸들

pool[1] (*swimming ~*) suyŏngjang 수영장; (*of water, blood*) ungdŏng-i 웅덩이

pool[2] (*game*) Migukshik tanggu 미국식 당구

pool[3] 1 *n* (*fund*) kongdonggigŭm 공동기금 2 *v/t resources* kongdong ikkwŏnŭro hada 공동 이권으로 하다

pool hall tanggujang 당구장

pool table tanggudae 당구대

pooped F nokch'oga toen 녹초가 된

poor 1 *adj* (*not wealthy*) kananhan 가난한; (*not good*) sŏt'urŭn 서투른; (*unfortunate*) purhaenghan 불행한; **be in ~ health** kŏn-gang-i choch'i antta 건강이 좋지 않다; **~ old Tony!** pulssanghan T'oni! 불쌍한 토니! 2 *n:* **the ~** pinja 빈자

poorly 1 *adv* hyŏngp'yŏnŏpssi 형편없이 2 *adj* (*unwell*) momi choch'i anŭn 몸이 좋지 않은

pop[1] 1 *n* (*noise*) p'ŏng hanŭn sori 펑 하는 소리 2 *v/i* (*of balloon etc*) p'ŏng hanŭn soriga nada 펑 하는 소리가 나다 3 *v/t cork* ttada 따다; *balloon* p'ŏng hago t'ŏjida 펑 하고 터지다

pop[2] **1** *n* MUS taejunggayo 대중가요 **2** *adj* taejung-ŭi 대중의

pop[3] F (*father*) appa 아빠

pop[4] F (*put*) noa tuda 놓아 두다

♦**pop up** *v/i* (*appear suddenly*) pulssuk nat'anada 불쑥 나타나다

popcorn p'apk'on 팝콘

pope kyohwang 교황

poppy yanggwibi 양귀비

Popsicle® aisŭ k'eik'ŭ 아이스 케이크

pop song p'apssong 팝송

popular inkki innŭn 인기 있는; *belief, support* taejungtchŏgin 대중적인

popularity inkki 인기

populate kŏjuhada 거주하다

population in-gu 인구

porcelain 1 *n* tojagi 도자기 **2** *adj* tojagiŭi 도자기의

porch peranda 베란다

porcupine hojŏ 호저

pore (*of skin*) mogong 모공

♦**pore over** chasehi poda 자세히 보다

pork twaejigogi 돼지고기

porn *n* p'orŭno 포르노

porn(o) *adj* p'orŭnoŭi 포르노의

pornographic oesŏltchŏgin 외설적인

pornography p'orŭno 포르노

porous t'ugwassŏngi choŭn 투과성이 좋은

port[1] *n* (*town*) hanggu 항구; (*area*) pudu 부두

port[2] *adj* (*left-hand*) chwatch'ugŭi 좌측의

port[3] COMPUT p'ot'ŭ 포트

portable 1 *adj* hyudaeyong-ŭi 휴대용의 **2** *n* COMPUT, TV p'ot'ŏbŭl 포터블

porter unbanin 운반인; (*doorkeeper*) munjigi 문지기

porthole NAUT hyŏnch'ang 현창

portion *n* pubun 부분; (*of food*) inbun 인분

portrait 1 *n* (*painting, photograph*) ch'osanghwa 초상화; (*depiction*) myosa 묘사 **2** *adv print* seroro 세로로

portray (*of artist, photographer*) ch'osanghwarŭl kŭrida / tchiktta 초상화를 그리다 / 찍다; (*of actor*) yŏn-gihada 연기하다; (*of author*) myosahada 묘사하다

portrayal (*by actor*) yŏn-gi 연기; (*by author*) myosa 묘사

Portugal P'orŭt'ugal 포르투갈

Portuguese 1 *adj* P'orŭt'ugarŭi 포르투갈의 **2** *n* (*person*) P'orŭt'ugarin 포르투갈인; (*language*) P'orŭt'ugarŏ 포르투갈어

pose 1 *n* (*pretense*) kŏtch'ire 겉치레 **2** *v/i* (*for artist, photographer*) p'ojŭ ch'wihada 포즈 취하다; ~ *as* (*of person*) … in ch'ŏk'ada … 인 척하다 **3** *v/t*: ~ *a problem / a threat* munje / wihyŏbŭl yagihada 문제 / 위협을 야기하다

position 1 *n* (*location*) wich'i 위치; (*stance*) chase 자세; (*in race, competition*) wi 위; (*occupied by soldiers*) chinji 진지; (*point of view*) kwantchŏm 관점; (*situation*) iptchang 입장; (*job*) chigŏp 직업; (*status*) chiwi 지위 **2** *v/t* paech'ihada 배치하다

positive *attitude* chŏk-kkŭktchŏgin 적극적인; *response* kŭngjŏngjŏgin 긍정적인; *test results* yangsŏng-ŭi 양성의; GRAM wŏnkkŭbŭi 원급의; ELEC yanggŭgŭi 양극의; *be ~* (*sure*) hwaksshinhada 확신하다

positively (*decidedly*) punmyŏnghi 분명히; (*definitely*) hwaksshirhi 확실히

possess soyuhada 소유하다

possession (*ownership*) soyu 소유; (*thing owned*) soyumul 소유물; *~s* chaesan 재산

possessive *person* soyuyogi kanghan 소유욕이 강한; GRAM soyukkyŏk 소유격

possibility kanŭngssŏng 가능성

possible kanŭnghan 가능한; *the quickest ~ …* kanŭnghan kajang pparŭn … 가능한 가장 빠른 …; *the best ~ …* kanŭnghan ch'oesŏnŭi … 가능한 최선의 …

possibly (*perhaps*) amado 아마도; *how could I ~ have known that?* chega kwayŏn ŏttŏk'e kŭgŏsŭl al su issŏtkkessŭmnikka? 제가 과연 어떻게 그것을 알 수 있었겠습니까?; *that can't ~ be right* kŭgŏn chŏlttaero orŭl li ŏpssŏyo 그건

절대로 옳을 리 없어요; *could you ~ tell me ...?* ...을/를 말씀해 chushil su innŭnjiyo? ...을/를 말씀해 주실 수 있는지요?

post¹ 1 *n (of wood, metal)* kidung 기둥 2 *v/t notice* keshihada 게시하다; *profits* kongshihada 공시하다; *keep s.o. ~ed* nuguege kyesok soshigŭl chŏnhada 누구에게 계속 소식을 전하다

post² 1 *n (place of duty)* pusŏ 부서 2 *v/t soldier, employee* paesok'ada 배속하다; *guards* paech'ihada 배치하다

postage up'yŏn yogŭm 우편 요금

postal up'yŏnŭi 우편의

postcard yŏpssŏ 엽서

postdate shiltcheboda naltcharŭl nŭtch'uŏ chŏktta 실제보다 날짜를 늦추어 적다

poster p'osŭt'ŏ 포스터

posterior *n* F kungdung-i 궁둥이

posterity hudae 후대

postgraduate 1 *n* taehagwŏn hakssaeng 대학원 학생 2 *adj* taehagwŏnŭi 대학원의

posthumous sahuŭi 사후의; *a ~ child* yuboktcha 유복자

posthumously sahue 사후에

posting *(assignment)* immyŏng 임명

postmark soin 소인

postmortem kŏmshi 검시

post office uch'eguk 우체국

postpone yŏn-gihada 연기하다

postponement yŏn-gi 연기

posture chase 자세

postwar chŏnhuŭi 전후의

pot¹ *(for cooking)* naembi 냄비; *(for coffee, tea)* chujŏnja 주전자; *(for plant)* hwabun 화분

pot² F *(marijuana)* taemach'o 대마초

potato kamja 감자

potato chips kamja ch'ip 감자 칩

potent kangnyŏk'an 강력한

potential 1 *adj* chamjaejŏgin 잠재적인 2 *n* chamjaeryŏk 잠재력

potentially chamjaejŏgŭro 잠재적으로

pothole *(in road)* p'aein kumŏng 패인 구멍

potter *n* togong 도공

pottery *(activity)* toye 도예; *(items)*

togi 도기; *(place)* toyeji 도예지

potty *n (for baby)* yuayong pyŏn-gi 유아용 변기

pouch *(bag)* chagŭn chumŏni 작은 주머니

poultry *(birds)* kagŭm 가금; *(meat)* kagŭm kogi 가금 고기

pounce *v/i (of animal)* tŏmbida 덤비다; *fig* tŏpch'ida 덮치다

pound¹ *n (weight)* p'aundŭ 파운드

pound² *(for strays)* uri 우리; *(for cars)* ch'aryang kyŏninso 차량 견인소

pound³ *v/i (of heart)* ttwida 뛰다; *~ on (hammer on)* magu tudŭrida 마구 두드리다

pound sterling p'aundŭ ton 파운드 돈

pour 1 *v/t liquid* ssoda put-tta 쏟아 붓다 2 *v/i: it's ~ing (with rain)* (piga) ŏkssugach'i p'ŏbunnŭnda (비가) 억수같이 퍼붓는다

♦ **pour out** *liquid* ttarŭda 따르다; *troubles* t'ŏ not'a 터 놓다

pout *v/i* ppurut'unghada 뿌루퉁하다

poverty kanan 가난

poverty-stricken tchijŏjige kananhan 찢어지게 가난한

powder 1 *n* karu 가루; *(for face)* pun 분 2 *v/t face* pun parŭda 분 바르다

powder room hwajangshil 화장실

power 1 *n (strength)* him 힘; *(authority)* kwŏllyŏk 권력; *(energy)* enŏji 에너지; *(electricity)* chŏn-gi 전기; *in ~* POL chipkkwŏnhanŭn 집권하는; *fall from ~* POL kwŏnjwaesŏ ttŏrŏjida 권좌에서 떨어지다 2 *v/t: be ~ed by* ...(ŭ)ro umjigida ...(으)로 움직이다

power cut chŏngjŏn 정전

powerful kangnyŏk'an 강력한

powerless muryŏk'an 무력한; *be ~ to ...* tojŏhi ...hal su ŏptta 도저히 ...할 수 없다

power line chŏn-gisŏn 전기선; **power outage** chŏngjŏn 정전; **power station** paltchŏnso 발전소; **power steering** p'awŏ sŭt'iŏring 파워 스티어링; **power unit** *(of computer)* p'awŏ yunit 파워 유닛; *(motor)* enjin 엔진

PR (= *public relations*) hongbo 홍보

practical *experience* shiltchejŏgin 실제적인; *person* shillijŏgin 실리적인; (*functional*) shiryongjŏgin 실용적인

practical joke haengdong-ŭro hanŭn mot-ttoen changnan 행동으로 하는 못된 장난

Practical Learning Shirhak 실학

practically *behave, think* shillijŏguro 실리적으로; (*almost*) kŏui 거의

practice 1 *n* shiltche 실제; (*training*) yŏnsŭp 연습; (*rehearsal*) lihŏsŏl 리허설; (*custom*) sŭpkkwan 습관; *in ~* (*in reality*) hyŏnshiltchŏgŭro 현실적으로; *be out of ~* sŏt'urŭda 서투르다 2 *v/i* hullyŏnhada 훈련하다 3 *v/t* yŏnsŭp'ada 연습하다; *law, medicine* chongsahada 종사하다

pragmatic shillijŏgin 실리적인

pragmatism shiryongjuŭi 실용주의

prairie taech'owŏn 대초원

praise 1 *n* ch'ingch'an 칭찬 2 *v/t* ch'ingch'anhada 칭찬하다

praiseworthy ch'ingch'an hal manhan 칭찬 할 만한

prank changnan 장난

prattle *v/i* chaejalgŏrida 재잘거리다

pray kidohada 기도하다

prayer kido 기도

preach 1 *v/i* REL sŏlgyohada 설교하다; (*moralize*) t'airŭda 타이르다 2 *v/t* sŏlgyohada 설교하다

preacher sŏlgyoja 설교자

precarious puranjŏnghan 불안정한

precariously puranjŏnghage 불안정하게

precaution yebang 예방

precautionary *measure* yebang-ŭi 예방의

precede *v/t* (*in time*) miri haenghaejida 미리 행해지다; (*walk in front of*) apssŏ kada 앞서 가다

precedence: *take ~* usŏnhada 우선하다; *take ~ over* ...e usŏnhada ...에 우선하다

precedent sŏllye 선례

preceding *week etc* chŏn(ŭi) 전(의); *chapter* ap'ŭi 앞의

precinct (*district*) haengjŏng kuyŏk 행정 구역

precious kwijunghan 귀중한

precipitate *v/t crisis* yagishik'ida 야기시키다

précis *n* yoyak 요약

precise chŏnghwak'an 정확한

precisely chŏnghwak'age 정확하게

precision chŏnghwak 정확

precocious *child* chosuk'an 조숙한

preconceived *idea* sŏnibŭi 선입의

precondition p'ilssu chokkŏn 필수 조건

predator (*animal*) yukssik tongmul 육식 동물

predecessor (*in job*) chŏnimja 전임자; (*machine*) ijŏn model 이전 모델

predestination unmyŏng yejŏngsŏl 운명 예정설

predicament kungji 궁지

predict yegyŏnhada 예견하다

predictable yegyŏnhal su innŭn 예견 할 수 있는

prediction yegyŏn 예견

predominant chuyohan 주요한

predominantly churo 주로

predominate chuga toeŏ it-tta 주가 되어 있다

prefabricated choripsshigŭi 조립식의

preface *n* sŏmun 서문

prefer sŏnhohada 선호하다; *~ X to Y* Xŭl/rŭl Ypoda tŏ choahada X을/를 Y보다 더 좋아하다; *~ to do* ohiryŏ ...nŭn kŏshi natkket-tta 오히려 ...는 것이 낫겠다

preferable ohiryŏ naŭn 오히려 나은; *be ~ to* poda nat-tta 보다 낫다

preferably toedorok imyŏn 되도록 이면

preference sŏnho 선호

preferential udaehanŭn 우대하는

prefix *n* chŏpttusa 접두사

pregnancy imshin 임신

pregnant imshinhan 임신한

prehistoric sŏnsashidaeŭi 선사시대의; *fig* shidaee aju twittŏrŏjin 시대에 아주 뒤떨어진

prejudice 1 *n* sŏnipkkyŏn 선입견 2 *v/t person* p'yŏn-gyŏnŭl p'umkke hada 편견을 품게 하다; *chances* sonsangshik'ida 손상시키다

prejudiced p'yŏn-gyŏnŭl kajin 편견을 가진

preliminary *adj* yebiŭi 예비의

premarital honjŏnŭi 혼전의; **~ sex** honjŏn sŏnggyo 혼전 성교

premature shigisangjoŭi 시기상조의; **~ baby** misuga 미숙아; **~ death** yojŏl 요절

premeditated kyehoektchŏgin 계획적인

premier n POL susang 수상

première n ch'oyŏn 초연

premises kunae 구내

premium n (in insurance) p'ŭrimiŏm 프리미엄

premonition yegam 예감

prenatal ch'ulssaeng chŏnŭi 출생 전의

preoccupied molttuhan 몰두한

preparation (act) chunbi 준비; **in ~ for** ...ŭl/rŭl chunbihaesŏ ...을/를 준비해서; **~s** chunbi 준비

prepare 1 v/t room, meal chunbihada 준비하다; **be ~d to do sth** (willing) muŏsŭl hal chunbiga toeŏ it-tta 무엇을 할 준비가 되어 있다 **2** v/i chunbihada 준비하다

preposition chŏnch'isa 전치사

preposterous t'ŏmuni ŏmnŭn 터무니 없는

prerequisite chŏnjejokkŏn 전제조건

Presbyterian Church Changno Kyohoe 장로 교회

prescribe (of doctor) ch'ŏbanghada 처방하다

prescription MED ch'ŏbangjŏn 처방전

presence issŭm 있음; **in the ~ of** myŏnjŏnesŏ 면전에서

presence of mind ch'imch'ak'am 침착함

present[1] **1** adj (current) hyŏnjaeŭi 현재의; **be ~** ch'amsŏk'ada 참석하다 **2** n: **the ~** hyŏnjae 현재; GRAM hyŏnjaehyŏng 현재형; **at ~** chigŭm 지금

present[2] **1** n (gift) sŏnmul 선물 **2** v/t award, bouquet suyŏhada 수여하다; program sogaehada 소개하다; **~ X with Y** Yŭl/rŭl Xege chŭngjŏnghada Y을/를 X에게 증정하다

presentation (to audience) palp'yo 발표

present-day onŭlnarŭi 오늘날의

presently (now) hyŏnjaeronŭn 현재로는; (soon) kot 곧

preservation pojon 보존

preservative n pangbuje 방부제

preserve 1 n (domain) yŏngyŏk 영역 **2** v/t standards, peace etc pojonhada 보존하다; wood etc pohohada 보호하다; food chŏjanghada 저장하다

preside v/i (at meeting) sahoe poda 사회 보다; **~ over** meeting ŭijang norŭt'ada 의장 노릇하다

presidency (term) taet'ongnyŏng imgi 대통령 임기; (office) taet'ongnyŏngjik 대통령직

president POL taet'ongnyŏng 대통령; (of company) sajang 사장

presidential taet'ongnyŏngŭi 대통령의

press 1 n: **the ~** ŏllon 언론 **2** v/t button nurŭda 누르다; (urge) kangyohada 강요하다; hand kkwak chwida 꽉 쥐다; grapes tchada 짜다; clothes tarimjirhada 다림질하다 **3** v/i: **~ for** chorŭda 조르다

press conference kijahoegyŏn 기자회견

pressing adj chŏlsshirhan 절실한

pressure 1 n amnyŏk 압력; (air ~) kiap 기압; (of work, demands) amnyŏk 압력; **be under ~** sŭt'ŭresŭga it-tta 스트레스가 있다; **be under ~ to ...** ... haeya hal wigie mollyŏit-tta ... 해야 할 위기에 몰려있다 **2** v/t amnyŏgŭl kahada 압력을 가하다

prestige myŏngsŏng 명성

prestigious myŏngsŏng-i nainnŭn 명성이 나있는

presumably amado 아마도

presume ch'ujŏnghada 추정하다; **~ to ...** ... kamhi...hada 감히 ...하다

presumption (of innocence, guilt) ch'ujŏng 추정

presumptuous kŏnbangjin 건방진

pre-tax segŭmŭl p'ohamhan 세금을 포함한

pretend 1 v/t ... in ch'ŏk'ada ... 인 척하다 **2** v/i ch'ŏk'ada 척하다

pretense kŏjit 거짓

pretentious challan ch'ŏk'anŭn 잘난 척하는

pretext p'inggye 핑계
pretty 1 *adj* yeppŭn 예쁜 **2** *adv (quite)* sangdanghi 상당히
prevail igida 이기다
prevailing usehan 우세한
prevent maktta 막다; **~ X (from) doing Y** Xi/ga Yhanŭn kŏsŭl mot'age hada X이/가 Y하는 것을 못하게 하다
prevention yebang 예방
preventive yebangŭi 예방의
preview *n (of movie)* shisa 시사; *(of exhibition)* shiyŏn 시연
previous ijŏnŭi 이전의
previously chŏne 전에
prewar chŏnjaeng chŏnŭi 전쟁 전의
prey *n* mŏgi 먹이
♦ **prey on** chabamŏktta 잡아먹다; *fig (of conman etc)* tŭngch'yŏmŏktta 등쳐먹다
price 1 *n (in book, newspaper etc)* kagyŏk 가격 **2** *v/t* COM kagyŏgŭl maegida 가격을 매기다
priceless kapssŭl maegil su ŏmnŭn 값을 매길 수 없는
price war kagyŏk harin kyŏngjaeng 가격 할인 경쟁
prick[^1] 1 *n (pain)* tchirŭm 찌름 **2** *v/t (jab)* tchirŭda 찌르다
prick[^2] *n* V *(penis)* chot 좆; *(person)* yabihan nom 야비한 놈
♦ **prick up: ~ one's ears** *(of dog)* kwirŭl tchonggŭt seuda 귀를 쫑긋 세우다; *(of person)* kwi kiurida 귀 기울이다
prickle *(on plant)* kashi 가시
prickly *beard, plant* ttakkŭmgŏrinŭn 따끔거리는; *(irritable)* sŏngmarŭn 성마른
pride 1 *n (in person, achievement)* charang 자랑; *(self-respect)* chajonshim 자존심 **2** *v/t:* **~ oneself on** charangsŭrŏpkke yŏgida 자랑스럽게 여기다
priest sŏngjiktcha 성직자; *(Catholic)* shinbu 신부
primarily ponjiltchŏguro 본질적으로
primary 1 *adj* chuyohan 주요한 **2** *n* POL yebisŏn-gŏ 예비선거
prime 1 *n:* **be in one's ~** hanch'ang ttaeida 한창 때이다 **2** *adj example, reason* kajang chungnyohan 가장

중요한; *of ~ importance* aju chungdaehan 아주 중대한
prime minister kungmuch'ongni 국무총리
prime time TV hwanggŭmshiganttae 황금시간대
primitive wŏnshiŭi 원시의; *conditions* wŏnshijŏgin 원시적인
prince wangja 왕자
princess kongju 공주
principal 1 *adj* chuyohan 주요한 **2** *n (of school)* kyojang 교장
principally taegae 대개
principle *(in moral sense)* toŭi 도의; *(rule)* wŏnch'ik 원칙; **on ~** toŭisang 도의상; **in ~** wŏnch'iktchŏguro 원칙적으로
print 1 *n (in book, newspaper etc)* inswae 인쇄; *(photograph)* inhwa 인화; *out of ~* chŏlp'andoen 절판된 **2** *v/t book, newspaper* parhaenghada 발행하다; COMPUT inswaehada 인쇄하다; *(using block capitals)* taemuntcharo ssŭda 대문자로 쓰다
♦ **print out** inswaehada 인쇄하다
printed matter inswaemul 인쇄물
printer *(person)* inswaeŏptcha 인쇄업자; *(machine)* p'ŭrint'ŏ 프린터
printing press inswaegi 인쇄기
printout p'ŭrint'ŭdoen kŏt 프린트된 것
prior 1 *adj* ijŏnŭi 이전의 **2** *prep:* **~ to** chŏne 전에
prioritize *(put in order of priority)* usŏn sunwirŭl maegida 우선 순위를 매기다; *(give priority to)* usŏnkkwŏnŭl chuda 우선권을 주다
priority ch'oeusŏn sahang 최우선 사항; *have ~* usŏnkkwŏni it-tta 우선권이 있다
prison kamok 감옥
prisoner choesu 죄수; *take s.o. ~* nugurŭl p'ororo chaptta 누구를 포로로 잡다
prisoner of war chŏnjaeng p'oro 전쟁 포로
privacy sasaenghwal 사생활
private 1 *adj* satchŏgin 사적인 **2** *n* MIL sabyŏng 사병; *in ~* naemirhage 내밀하게
privately *(in private)* naemirhage

내밀하게; *funded, owned* min-gane üihae 민간에 의해; (*inwardly*) maŭm sogŭro 마음 속으로

private sector min-gan pumun 민간 부문

privilege (*special treatment*) t'ŭktchŏn 특전; (*honor*) yŏnggwang 영광

privileged t'ŭk-kwŏnŭl kajin 특권을 가진; (*honored*) yŏnggwangsŭrŏun 영광스러운

prize 1 *n* sang 상 **2** *v/t* kach'i itkke yŏgida 가치 있게 여기다

prizewinner susangja 수상자

prizewinning ipsanghan 입상한

pro¹ *n*: **the ~s and cons** ch'anban yangnon 찬반 양론

pro² → *professional*

pro³: **be ~ ...** (*in favor of*) ...e ch'ansŏnghada ...에 찬성하다

probability kamangsŏng 가망성

probable kŭrŏlttŭt'an 그럴듯한

probably ama 아마

probation (*in job*) kyŏnsŭp 견습; LAW chip'aeng yuye 집행 유예

probation officer poho kamch'algwan 보호 감찰관

probation period (*in job*) kyŏnsŭpkkigan 견습기간

probe 1 *n* (*investigation*) ch'ŏltchŏhan chosa 철저한 조사; (*scientific*) t'amsa 탐사 **2** *v/t* (*investigate*) chasehi chosahada 자세히 조사하다

problem munje 문제; *no* ~ muje ŏpssŏyo 문제 없어요

procedure chŏltch'a 절차

proceed 1 *v/i* (*of people*) kada 가다; (*of work etc*) chinhaengdoeda 진행되다; ~ **with the lesson** tashi suŏbŭl kyesok'ada 다시 수업을 계속하다 **2** *v/t*: ~ **to do sth** kŭrigonasŏ muŏsŭl hada 그리고나서 무엇을 하다

proceedings (*events*) haengsa 행사

proceeds suik 수익

process 1 *n* kwajŏng 과정; *in the* ~ (*while doing it*) kŭrŏnŭn kwajŏng-e 그러는 과정에 **2** *v/t* *food, raw materials* kagonghada 가공하다; *data, application etc* ch'ŏrihada

처리하다

procession haengjin 행진

processor COMPUT p'ŭrosesŏ 프로세서

proclaim sŏnŏnhada 선언하다

prod 1 *n* tchirŭgi 찌르기 **2** *v/t* ssushida 쑤시다

prodigy: (*child*) ~ shindong 신동

produce 1 *n* nongsanmul 농산물 **2** *v/t* *commodity* saengsanhada 생산하다; (*bring about*) yagihada 야기하다; (*bring out*) kkŏnaeda 꺼내다; *play, movie, TV program* chejak'ada 제작하다

producer (*of commodity*) saengsanja 생산자; (*of play, movie, TV program*) chejaktcha 제작자

product saengsanmul 생산물; (*result*) kyŏlgwa 결과

production saengsan 생산; (*of play, movie, TV program*) chejak 제작

production capacity saengsannyŏk 생산력

production costs saengsanbi 생산비

productive saengsanjŏgin 생산적인

productivity saengsanssŏng 생산성

profane *language* pulgyŏnghan 불경한

profess ...in ch'ŏk'ada ...인 척하다

profession chigŏp 직업

professional 1 *adj* (*not amateur*) p'ŭroŭi 프로의; *advice, help* chigŏptchŏgin 직업적인; *piece of work* chŏnmunjŏgin 전문적인; *turn* ~ p'ŭroro chŏnhyanghada 프로로 전향하다 **2** *n* (*doctor, lawyer etc*) chŏnmunjik chongsaja 전문직 종사자; (*not an amateur*) p'ŭro 프로

professionally *play sport* p'ŭro sŏnsuro 프로 선수로; (*well, skillfully*) chŏnmunjŏgŭro 전문적으로

professor kyosu 교수

proficiency nŭngsuk 능숙

proficient nŭngsuk'an 능숙한

profile (*of face*) yŏm mosŭp 옆 모습; (*description*) p'ŭrop'il 프로필

profit 1 *n* iik 이익 **2** *v/i*: ~ *from* ...(ŭ)ro iigŭl ŏt-tta ...(으)로 이익을 얻다

profitability suikssŏng 수익성

profitable suigi chŏun 수익이 좋은

profit margin sunsuik 순수익
profound *shock* kip'ŭn 깊은; *hatred* ppuri kip'ŭn 뿌리 깊은; *a ~ thinker* shimohan sasaek-kka 심오한 사색가
profoundly kipkke 깊게
prognosis yeji 예지
program 1 *n* kyehoek 계획; RAD, TV, COMPUT, THEA p'ŭrogŭraem 프로그램 **2** *v/t* COMPUT p'ŭrogŭraem tchada 프로그램 짜다
programmer COMPUT p'ŭrogŭraemŏ 프로그래머
progress 1 *n* chinhaeng 진행; *make ~* (*of patient*) ch'adorŭl poida 차도를 보이다; (*of building work*) chinch'ŏkdoeda 진척되다; *in ~* chinhaeng chung-in 진행 중인 **2** *v/i* (*in time*) chinhaengdoeda 진행되다; (*move on*) chindoga nagada 진도가 나가다; (*improve*) hyangsanghada 향상하다; *how is the work ~ing?* irŭn ŏttŏk'e toeŏ kago issŏyo? 일은 어떻게 되어 가고 있어요?
progressive *adj* (*enlightened*) chinbojŏgin 진보적인; *disease* chinhaenghanŭn 진행하는
progressively chŏmch'ajŏgŭro 점차적으로
prohibit kŭmjihada 금지하다
prohibition kŭmji 금지; *Prohibition* Kŭmjuppŏp 금주법
prohibitive *prices* koengjanghi pissan 굉장히 비싼
project[1] *n* (*plan*) kyehoek 계획; (*undertaking*) saŏp 사업; EDU kwaje 과제; (*housing area*) chut'aek tanji 주택 단지
project[2] 1 *v/t figures, sales* yesanhada 예산하다; *movie* yŏngsahada 영사하다 **2** *v/i* (*stick out*) t'wiŏnaoda 튀어나오다
projection (*forecast*) yesan 예산
projector (*for slides*) yŏngsagi 영사기
prolific *writer, artist* tajagŭi 다작의
prolong yŏnjanghada 연장하다
prom (*school dance*) hak-kkyo ch'uktche 학교 축제
prominent *nose, chin* t'uk t'wiŏ naon 툭 튀어 나온; (*significant*) t'agwŏrhan 탁월한
promiscuity hon-gyo 혼교

promiscuous nanjap'an 난잡한
promise 1 *n* yakssok 약속 **2** *v/t* yakssok'ada 약속하다; *~ to ...* hagiro yakssok'ada ... 하기로 약속하다; *~ X to Y* Xege Yŭl/rŭl yakssok'ada X에게 Y을/를 약속하다 **3** *v/i* yakssok'ada 약속하다
promising chŏndoga ch'angch'anghan 전도가 창창한
promote *employee* sŭngjinhada 승진하다; (*encourage, foster*) ch'oktchinhada 촉진하다; COM sŏnjŏnhada 선전하다
promoter (*of sports event*) p'ŭromot'ŏ 프로모터
promotion (*of employee*) sŭngjin 승진; (*of scheme, idea*) sŏnjŏn 선전; COM p'anmae ch'oktchin 판매 촉진
prompt 1 *adj* (*on time*) shiganŭl chik'inŭn 시간을 지키는; (*speedy*) chŭk-kkaktchŏgin 즉각적인 **2** *adv*: *at two o'clock ~* chŏngnyak tu shie 정각 두 시에 **3** *v/t* (*cause*) yubalshik'ida 유발시키다; *actor* taesarŭl illŏjuda 대사를 일러주다 **4** *n* COMPUT p'ŭromp'ŭt'ŭ 프롬프트
promptly (*on time*) cheshigane 제시간에; (*immediately*) chŭksshi 즉시
prone: *be ~ to do ...* ... hagi shwipta ... 하기 쉽다
pronoun taemyŏngsa 대명사
pronounce *word* parŭmhada 발음하다; (*declare*) kongp'yohada 공표하다
pronounced *accent* kanghan 강한; *views* hwak-kkohan 확고한
pronunciation parŭm 발음
proof *n* chŭnggŏ 증거; (*of book*) kyojŏngswae 교정쇄
prop 1 *v/t* kidaeŏ not'a 기대어 놓다 **2** *n* (*in theater*) sop'um 소품
♦**prop up** ollyŏ patch'ida 올려 받치다; *regime* chijihada 지지하다
propaganda sŏnjŏn hwalttong 선전 활동
propel ch'ujinhada 추진하다
propellant (*in aerosol*) koap kkassŭ 고압 가스
propeller (*of boat*) p'ŭrop'ellŏ 프로펠러

proper (*real*) chŏngshigŭi 정식의; (*correct*) parŭn 바른; (*fitting*) almajŭn 알맞은

properly (*correctly*) chedaero 제대로; (*fittingly*) chŏk'ap'age 적합하게

property soyumul 소유물; (*land*) ttang 땅

property developer t'oji kaebarŏptcha 토지 개발업자

prophecy yeŏn 예언

prophesy yeŏnhada 예언하다

proportion (*ratio*) piyul 비율; (*number, amount*) pubun 부분; **~s** (*dimensions*) yongjŏk 용적

proportional piryehanŭn 비례하는

proposal (*suggestion*) chean 제안; (*of marriage*) ch'ŏnghon 청혼

propose 1 *v/t* (*suggest*) cheanhada 제안하다; (*plan*) kyehoek'ada 계획하다 **2** *v/i* (*make offer of marriage*) ch'ŏnghonhada 청혼하다

proposition 1 *n* cheŭi 제의 **2** *v/t woman* yuhok'ada 유혹하다

proprietor kyŏngnyŏng-in 경영인

proprietress yŏsŏng kyŏngnyŏng-in 여성 경영인

prose sanmun 산문

prosecute *v/t* LAW kisohada 기소하다

prosecution LAW kiso 기소; (*lawyers*) kisojach'ŭk 기소자측

prosecutor kŏmsa 검사

prospect 1 *n* (*chance, likelihood*) kamang 가망; (*thought of something in the future*) yesang 예상; **~s** chŏnmang 전망 **2** *v/i*: **~ for** gold shigurhada 시굴하다

prospective kidaedoenŭn 기대되는

prosper (*of person*) sŏnggonghada 성공하다; (*of business, city*) pŏnch'anghada 번창하다

prosperity pŏnch'ang 번창

prosperous *person* sŏnggonghan 성공한; *businesss, city* pŏnch'anghanŭn 번창하는

prostitute *n* maech'unbu 매춘부; **male ~** namch'ang 남창

prostitution maech'un 매춘

prostrate: **be ~ with grief** sŭlp'ŭme ppajyŏ it-tta 슬픔에 빠져 있다

protect pohohada 보호하다

protection poho 보호

protection money poho pannŭn taekkaro ttŭtkkinŭn ton 보호 받는 대가로 뜯기는 돈

protective pohohanŭn 보호하는

protector suhoja 수호자

protein tanbaektchil 단백질

protest 1 *n* hang-ŭi 항의; (*demonstration*) temo 데모 **2** *v/t* hang-ŭihada 항의하다; (*object to*) iŭirŭl chegihada 이의를 제기하다 **3** *v/i* panbak'ada 반박하다; (*demonstrate*) temohada 데모하다

Protestant 1 *n* Shin-gyodo 신교도 **2** *adj* Shin-gyodoŭi 신교도의

Protestantism Kaeshin-gyo 개신교

protester temoja 데모자

protocol ŭirye 의례

prototype wŏnhyŏng 원형

protracted orae kkŭnŭn 오래 끄는

protrude *v/i* pulssuk t'wiŏ naoda 불쑥 튀어 나오다

proud charangsŭrŏun 자랑스러운; (*independent*) chajonshimi kanghan 자존심이 강한; **be ~ of** charangsŭrŏpkke yŏgida 자랑스럽게 여기다

proudly charangsŭrŏpkke 자랑스럽게

prove chŭngmyŏnghada 증명하다

provide chegonghada 제공하다; **~ Y to X, ~ X with Y** Xege Yŭl/rŭl chegonghada X에게 Y을/를 제공하다; **~d** (*that*) ... ...ranŭn chokkŏnŭro ...라는 조건으로

♦ **provide for** *family* puyanghada 부양하다; (*of law etc*) kyujŏnghada 규정하다

province chibang 지방

provincial *city* chibang-ŭi 지방의; *pej* ch'onssŭrŏun 촌스러운

provision (*supply*) konggŭp 공급; (*of law, contract*) chohang 조항

provisional imshijŏgin 임시적인

proviso tansŏ 단서

provocation hwanage hanŭn kŏt 화나게 하는 것

provocative (*intended to annoy*) chaguk'anŭn 자극하는; (*controversial*) nonjaengjŏgin 논쟁적인; (*sexually*) chagŭktchŏgin 자극적인

provoke (*cause*) yubarhada 유발하다;

(*annoy*) sŏnggashige hada 성가시게
하다
prow NAUT paenmŏri 뱃머리
prowess ttwiŏnan somsshi 뛰어난
솜씨
prowl *v/i* (*of tiger etc*) ŏsŭllŏnggŏrida
어슬렁거리다; (*of burglar*)
sŏsŏngdaeda 서성대다
prowler sŏsŏngdaenŭn saram
서성대는 사람
proximity kŭnjŏp 근접
proxy (*authority*) taerikkwŏn 대리권;
(*person*) taeriin 대리인
prude ssungmaek 쑥맥
prudence shinjung 신중
prudent punbyŏl innŭn 분별 있는
prudish ssungmaegin 쑥맥인
prune[1] *n* mallin chadu 말린 자두
prune[2] *v/t plant* (kajirŭl) ch'ida
(가지를) 치다; *expenditure, labor
force* sak-kkamhada 삭감하다; *essay*
kan-gyŏrhi hada 간결히 하다
pry k'aego tanida 캐고 다니다
♦ **pry into** kkoch'ikkoch'i
k'aemutkko tanida 꼬치꼬치 캐묻고
다니다
PS (= *postscript*) ch'ushin 추신
pseudonym ka-myŏng 가명
psychiatric chŏngshinkkwaŭi
정신과의
psychiatrist chŏngshinkkwa ŭisa
정신과 의사
psychiatry chŏngshinŭihak 정신의학
psychic *adj* shimnyŏng-ŭi 심령의
psychoanalysis chŏngshin punsŏk
정신 분석
psychoanalyst chŏngshin punsŏk
haktcha 정신 분석 학자
psychoanalyze chŏngshin
punsŏk'ada 정신 분석하다
psychological shimnijŏgin 심리적인
psychologically shimnijŏgŭro
심리적으로
psychologist shimnihaktcha
심리학자
psychology shimnihak 심리학
psychopath chŏngshinppyŏngja
정신병자
puberty sach'un-gi 사춘기
pubic hair ŭmmo 음모
public 1 *adj* (*in ~*) konggaejŏgin

공개적인; (*of the masses*) taejung-ŭi
대중의; (*open to the ~*) konggong-ŭi
공공의 **2** *n: the ~* taejung 대중; *in ~*
kongtchŏgin changso-e(sŏ) 공적인
장소에(서)
publication (*of book, report*)
ch'ulp'an 출판; (*by newspaper*)
parhaeng 발행; (*book*) ch'ulp'an
출판; (*newspaper*) parhaeng 발행
publicity sŏnjŏn 선전
publicize (*make known*) sŏnjŏnhada
선전하다; COM kwanggohada
광고하다
publicly konggaejŏgŭro 공개적으로
public prosecutor kŏmch'algwan
검찰관; **public relations** hongbo
홍보; **public school** kongnip hak-
kkyo 공립 학교; **public sector**
konggong pumun 공공 부문
publish ch'ulp'anhada 출판하다
publisher (*person*) ch'ulp'anŏptcha
출판업자; (*company*) ch'ulp'ansa
출판사
publishing ch'ulp'anŏp 출판업
publishing company ch'ulp'ansa
출판사
puddle *n* ungdŏng-i 웅덩이
puff 1 *n* (*of wind, smoke*) hanbŏn huk
pulgi 한번 훅 불기 **2** *v/i* (*pant*)
hŏlttŏk-kkŏrida 헐떡거리다
puffy *eyes, face* puŏrŭn 부어오른
pull 1 *n* (*on rope*) chaba tanggigi 잡아
당기기; F (*appeal*) hoŭng 호응; F
(*influence*) yŏnghyangnyŏk 영향력
2 *v/t* kkŭlda 끌다; *rope, hair* chaba
tanggida 잡아 당기다; *tooth* ppoptta
뽑다; *muscle* murihage ssŭda
무리하게 쓰다 **3** *v/i* tanggida 당기다
♦ **pull apart** (*separate*) tteŏnaeda
떼어내다
♦ **pull away** *v/t* chabach'aeda
잡아챘다
♦ **pull down** naerida 내리다;
(*demolish*) hŏmulda 허물다
♦ **pull in** (*of bus, train*) toch'ak'ada
도착하다
♦ **pull off** *leaves etc* tteŏnaeda
떼어내다; *coat etc* pŏt-tta 벗다; F *deal
etc* sŏnggongjŏgŭro haenaeda
성공적으로 해내다
♦ **pull out 1** *v/t* kkŏnaeda 꺼내다;

troops hut'oeshik'ida 후퇴시키다
2 *v/i* (*of an agreement*) ch'ŏrhoehada
철회하다; (*of a competition*) ppajida
빠지다; (*of troops*) hut'oehada
후퇴하다; (*of ship*) ch'urhanghada
출항하다

♦**pull through** (*from an illness*)
wank'waehada 완쾌하다

♦**pull together 1** *v/i* (*cooperate*)
hyŏpttonghada 협동하다 **2** *v/t*: **pull
oneself together** maŭmŭl
karaanch'ida 마음을 가라앉히다

♦**pull up 1** *v/t* kkŭrŏollida 끌어올리다;
plant, weeds chaba ppoptta 잡아
뽑다 **2** *v/i* (*of car etc*) sŏda 서다

pulley torŭrae 도르래

pulp kwayuk 과육; (*for paper-
making*) p'ŏlp'ŭ 펄프

pulpit sŏlgyodan 설교단

pulsate (*of heart, blood*)
kodongch'ida 고동치다; (*of rhythm*)
chindonghada 진동하다

pulse maekppak 맥박

pulverize karuro mandŭlda 가루로
만들다

pump 1 *n* p'ŏmp'ŭ 펌프 **2** *v/t water*
p'ŏmp'ŭro p'ŏ ollida 펌프로 퍼
올리다; *air* mirŏnaeda 밀어내다

♦**pump up** konggirŭl chuip'ada
공기를 주입하다

pumpkin hobak 호박

pun tong-ŭmiŭiŭi maltchangnan
동음이의의 말장난

punch 1 *n* (*blow*) chumŏktchil
주먹질; (*implement*) kumŏng ttullŭn
kigu 구멍 뚫는 기구 **2** *v/t* (*with fist*)
huryŏch'ida 후려치다; *hole* kumŏng-
ŭl ttult'a 구멍을 뚫다; *ticket*
kaech'arhada 개찰하다

punch line *nongdam chung utkkinŭn
taemok* 농담 중 웃기는 대목

punctual shiganŭl ŏmsuhanŭn 시간을
엄수하는

punctuality shigan ŏmsu 시간 엄수

punctually chŏnghwak'i 정확히

punctuate kudutchŏmŭl tchiktta
구두점을 찍다

punctuation kudutppŏp 구두법

punctuation mark kuduttchŏm
구두점

puncture 1 *n* kumŏng 구멍 **2** *v/t*

kumŏng ttult'a 구멍 뚫다

pungent chagŭk'anŭn 자극하는

punish *person* ch'ŏbŏrhada 처벌하다

punishing *pace, schedule* chich'ige
hanŭn 지치게 하는

punishment ch'ŏbŏl 처벌

puny *person* hŏyak'an 허약한

pup (*young dog*) kang-aji 강아지

pupil [1] (*of eye*) nunttongja 눈동자

pupil [2] (*student*) hakssaeng 학생

puppet kkŏkttugaksshi 꼭두각시

puppet government koeroe
chŏngbu 괴뢰 정부

puppy kang-aji 강아지

purchase [1] **1** *n* kumae 구매 **2** *v/t*
kumaehada 구매하다

purchase [2] (*grip*) sone chwida 손에
쥐다

purchaser maeiptcha 매입자

pure *silk* sunsuhan 순수한; *air, water*
kkaekkŭt'an 깨끗한; *sound* malgŭn
맑은; (*morally*) kyŏlbaek'an 결백한;
~ wool / gold / white sunmo / sun-
gŭm / sunbaek 순모 / 순금 / 순백

purely wanjŏnhi 완전히

purge 1 *n* (*of political party*)
sukch'ŏng 숙청 **2** *v/t* sukch'ŏnghada
숙청하다

purify *water* chŏnghwahada 정화하다

puritan ch'ŏnggyodo 청교도

puritanical ŏmkkyŏk'an 엄격한

purity ch'ŏnggyŏl 청결; (*moral*)
kyŏlbaek 결백

purple *adj* chajuppich'ŭi 자주빛의

Purple Heart MIL myŏng-ye sang-i
hunjang 명예 상이 훈장

purpose moktchŏk 목적; **on ~**
koŭijŏgŭro 고의적으로

purposeful tanhohan 단호한

purposely ilburŏ 일부러

purr *v/i* (*of cat*) kŭrŭrŏng-gŏrida
그르렁거리다

purse *n* (*pocketbook*) haendŭbaek
핸드백

pursue *v/t person* ch'ujŏk'ada
추적하다; *career* ch'uguhada
추구하다; *course of action*
kyesok'ada 계속하다

pursuer ch'ujŏktcha 추적자

pursuit (*chase*) ch'ujŏk 추적; (*of
happiness etc*) ch'ugu 추구; (*activity*)

il 일

pus korŭm 고름

Pusan Pusan 부산

push 1 n (shove) milgi 밀기; (of button) nurŭgi 누르기 **2** v/t (shove) milda 밀다; button nurŭda 누르다; (pressure) kaap'ada 가압하다; drugs mayak milmaehada 마약 밀매하다; be ~ed for mojarada 모자라다; be ~ing 40 kŏŭi mahŭni ta toeda 거의 마흔이 다 되다 **3** v/i milda 밀다

♦ **push along** cart etc milgo kada 밀고 가다

♦ **push away** mirŏ chech'ida 밀어 제치다

♦ **push off 1** v/t lid mirŏnaeda 밀어내다 **2** v/i F (leave) ttŏnada 떠나다; ~! chŏri ka! 저리 가!

♦ **push on** v/i (continue) kyesok'ada 계속하다

♦ **push up** prices ollida 올리다

push-button nurŭm tanch'ushigŭi 누름 단추식의

pusher (of drugs) mayak milmaeja 마약 밀매자

push-up p'al kup'yŏ p'yŏgi 팔 굽혀 펴기

pushy ppŏnppŏnsŭrŏun 뻔뻔스러운

puss, pussy (cat) koyang-i 고양이

put not'a 놓다; question mut-tta 묻다; ~ the cost at … …(ŭ)ro kagyŏgŭl ŏrimjaptta …(으)로 가격을 어림잡다

♦ **put aside** money chŏgŭmhada 저금하다; work chŏbŏduda 접어두다

♦ **put away** (in closet etc) ch'iuda 치우다; (in institution) kamgŭmhada 감금하다; drink mashida 마시다; money chŏgŭmhada 저금하다; animal allakssashik'ida 안락사시키다

♦ **put back** (replace) chejarie tollyŏnot'a 제자리에 돌려놓다

♦ **put by** money chŏgŭmhada 저금하다

♦ **put down** not'a 놓다; deposit sŏnburhada 선불하다; rebellion chinap'ada 진압하다; (belittle) nach'uda 낮추다; (in writing) ssŭda 쓰다; put one's foot down (in car) kasok'ada 가속하다; (be firm) kutkke kyŏlsshimhada 굳게 결심하다; put X down to Y

(attribute) Xŭl/rŭl Yŭi t'asŭro tollida X을/를 Y의 탓으로 돌리다

♦ **put forward** idea etc cheanhada 제안하다

♦ **put in** nŏt'a 넣다; time ponaeda 보내다; request, claim cheshihada 제시하다

♦ **put in for** yoch'ŏnghada 요청하다

♦ **put off** light, radio, TV kkŭda 끄다; (postpone) yŏn-gihada 연기하다; (deter) tannyŏmshik'ida 단념시키다; (repel) pulk'waehada 불쾌하다; put X off Y Xi/ga Yŭl/rŭl tannyŏmhage hada X이/가 Y을/를 단념하게 하다

♦ **put on** light, radio, TV k'yŏda 켜다; tape, music t'ŭlda 틀다; jacket iptta 입다; shoes shintta 신다; eyeglasses ssŭda 쓰다; make-up hada 하다; brake chakttongshik'ida 작동시키다; (perform) kongyŏnhada 공연하다; (assume) kajanghada 가장하다; ~ weight ch'ejung-ŭl nŭrida 체중을 늘이다; she's just putting it on kŭ yŏjanŭn kŭ-nyang kŭrŏn ch'ŏk'ago innŭn kŏyeyo 그 여자는 그냥 그런 척하고 있는 거에요

♦ **put out** hand naemilda 내밀다; fire sohwahada 소화하다; light kkŭda 끄다

♦ **put through** (on phone) pakkwŏ chuda 바꿔 주다

♦ **put together** (assemble) chorip'ada 조립하다; (organize) chojik'ada 조직하다

♦ **put up** hand tŭlda 들다; person chaewŏjuda 재워주다; (erect) seuda 세우다; prices ollida 올리다; poster, notice puch'ida 붙이다; money naeda 내다; ~ for sale p'allyŏgo naenot'a 팔려고 내놓다

♦ **put up with** (tolerate) ch'amtta 참다

putty yuri chŏp'aptche 유리 접합제

puzzle 1 n (mystery) susukkekki 수수께끼; (game) p'ojŭl 퍼즐 **2** v/t yŏngmunŭl morŭge hada 영문을 모르게 하다

puzzling yŏngmun morŭl 영문 모를

PVC p'i pŭi sshi 피 브이 씨

pylon koapssŏnnyong ch'ŏlt'ap 고압선용 철탑

P'yongyang P'yŏngnyang 평양

Q

quack¹ 1 *n* (*of duck*) kkwaek-kkwaek
unŭn sori 꽥꽥 우는 소리 **2** *v/i*
kkwaek-kkwaek ulda 꽥꽥 울다
quack² F (*bad doctor*) tolp'ari ŭisa
돌팔이 의사
quadrangle (*figure*) sagak'yŏng
사각형; (*courtyard*) anttŭl 안뜰
quadruped ne pal chimsŭng 네 발
짐승
quadruple *v/i* ne paero hada 네 배로
하다
quadruplets ne ssangdung-i 네
쌍둥이
quaint *cottage* yeppŭjanghan
예쁘장한; *ideas etc* kimyohan 기묘한
quake 1 *n* (*earth~*) chijin 지진 **2** *v/i*
(*of earth*) hŭndŭllida 흔들리다; (*with
fear*) tŏdŏl ttŏlda 덜덜 떨다
qualification (*from university etc*)
chagyŏk 자격; (*of remark etc*)
chehan 제한; *have the right ~s for
a job* ŏttŏn chigŏbe chŏk'ap'an
chagyŏgŭl kajida 어떤 직업에 적합한
자격을 가지다
qualified *doctor, engineer etc*
chagyŏktchŭng-i innŭn 자격증이
있는; (*restricted*) chehandoen 제한된;
I am not ~ to judge nanŭn
p'andanhal chagyŏgi ŏpssŭmnida
나는 판단할 자격이 없습니다
qualify 1 *v/t* (*of degree, course etc*)
chagyŏgŭl chuda 자격을 주다;
remark etc chehanhada 제한하다
2 *v/i* (*get degree etc*) chagyŏgŭl ŏt-tta
자격을 얻다; (*in competition*)
yesŏnŭl t'onggwahada 예선을
통과하다; *our team has qualified
for the semi-final* uri t'imŭn chun-
gyŏlssŭngjŏne chinch'urhaet-tta 우리
팀은 준결승전에 진출했다; *that
doesn't ~ as ...* kŭgŏsŭn ...(ŭ)rosŏ
chagyŏgi ŏptta 그것은 ...(으)로서
자격이 없다
quality p'umjil 품질; (*characteristic*)

sŏngjil 성질
quality control p'umjil kwalli 품질
관리
qualm yangshimŭi kach'aek 양심의
가책; *have no ~s about* ...e taehae
yangshimŭi kach'aegŭl pat-tchi ant'a
...에 대해 양심의 가책을 받지 않다
quantify yang-ŭl chaeda 양을 재다
quantity yang 양
quarantine (*for animals*) kŏmnyŏk
검역; (*for people*) kyŏngni 격리
quarrel 1 *n* tat'um 다툼 **2** *v/i* tat'uda
다투다
quarrelsome tat'ugi choahanŭn
다투기 좋아하는
quarry (*for mining*) ch'aesŏktchang
채석장
quart yak 0.95lit'ŏ 약 0.95리터
quarter 1 *n* sabunŭi il 사분의 일; (*25
cents*) ishibossent'ŭ tongjŏn
이십오센트 동전; (*part of town*)
chiyŏk 지역; *a ~ of 5* tasŏtshi
shibobun 십오분; *a ~ of 5* tasŏtsshi
shibobun chŏn 다섯시 십오분 전; *~
after 5* tashŏtsshi shibobun 다섯시
십오분 **2** *v/t* saro nanuda 사로 나누다
quarterback SP k'wŏt'ŏbaek 쿼터백;
quarterfinal chunjun-gyŏlssŭng
준준결승; **quarterfinalist** chunjun-
gyŏlssŭng chinch'ultcha 준준결승
진출자
quarterly 1 *adj* kyeganŭi 계간의 **2** *adv*
kyeganŭro 계간으로
quarter note MUS sabun ŭmp'yo 사분
음표
quarters MIL pyŏngnyŏng 병영
quartet MUS sajungju 사중주
quartz sŏgyŏng 석영
quaver 1 *n* (*in voice*) ttŏllinŭn sori
떨리는 소리 **2** *v/i* (*of voice*) ttŏllida
떨리다
queen yŏwang 여왕
queen bee yŏwangbŏl 여왕벌
queer (*peculiar*) kimyohan 기묘한

quench *thirst* kashige hada 가시게 하다; *flames* kkǔda 끄다

query 1 *n* ǔimun 의문 **2** *v/t* (*express doubt about*) ǔimunǔl chegihada 의문을 제기하다; (*check*) hwaginhada 확인하다; ~ *X with Y* Yege Xe kwanhan ǔimunǔl chegihada Y에게 X에 관한 의문을 제기하다

question 1 *n* chilmun 질문; (*matter*) munje 문제; *in ~* (*being talked about*) munjeǔi 문제의; (*in doubt*) ǔishimtchǒgǔn 의심쩍은; *it's a ~ of money / time* tonǔi / shiganǔi munjeyeyo 돈의 / 시간의 문제예요; *out of the ~* chǒnhyǒ pulganǔnghan 전혀 불가능한 **2** *v/t person* chilmunhada 질문하다; LAW shimmunhada 심문하다; (*doubt*) ǔishimhada 의심하다

questionable *honesty, figures* ǔishimsǔrǒun 의심스러운

questioning *look, tone* ǔishimtchǒgǒ hanǔn 의심쩌거 하는

question mark murǔmp'yo 물음표

questionnaire chilmunsǒ 질문서

quick pparǔn 빠른; *be ~!* ppalli hae! 빨리 해!; *let's have a ~ drink* ttak han chanman mashija 딱 한 잔만 마시자; *can I have a ~ look?* chamkkan pwado toelkkayo? 잠깐 봐도 될까요?; *that was ~!* ppalli haenneyo! 빨리 했네요!

quicksand yusa 유사; **quicksilver** suǔn 수은; **quickwitted** chaech'i innǔn 재치 있는

quiet choyonghan 조용한; *life, town* koyohan 고요한; *keep ~ about* …ǔl / rǔl pimillo haeduda …을 / 를 비밀로 해두다; *~!* choyonghi hae! 조용히 해!

♦ **quieten down 1** *v/t children, class* choyonghage hada 조용하게 하다 **2** *v/i* (*of children*) choyonghaejida 조용해지다; (*of political situation*) chinjǒngdoeda 진정되다

quilt (*on bed*) nubi ibul 누비 이불

quinine k'inine 키니네

quip 1 *n* chaech'i innǔn mal 재치 있는 말 **2** *v/i* nollida 놀리다

quirky pyǒllan 별난

quit 1 *v/t job* kǔmanduda 그만두다; *~ doing sth* muǒt hanǔn kǒsǔl kǔmanduda 무엇 하는 것을 그만두다 **2** *v/i* (*leave job*) chiktchang-ǔl kǔmanduda 직장을 그만두다; COMPUT kkǔnnaeda 끝내다; *get one's notice to ~* (*from landlord*) chip piuranǔn t'ongjirǔl pat-tta 집 피우라는 통지를 받다

quite (*fairly*) kkwae 꽤; (*completely*) wanjǒnhi 완전히; *not ~ ready* chunbiga wanjǒnhi toeji anǔn 준비가 완전히 되지 않은; *I didn't ~ understand* ta ihaehal su ǒpssǒssǒyo 다 이해할 수 없었어요; *is that right? - not ~* majayo? - kǒǔi 맞아요? - 거의; *~!* chǒngmal! 정말!; *~ a lot* kkwae manǔn 꽤 많은; *it was ~ a surprise* kkwae nollaun iriǒssǒyo / kkwae k'ǔn pyǒnhwayǒssǒyo 꽤 놀라운 일이었어요 / 꽤 큰 변화였어요

quits: *be ~ with* …wa / kwa p'ijangp'ajang-i toeda …와 / 과 피장파장이 되다

quiver *v/i* hǔndǔllida 흔들리다

quiz 1 *n* k'wijǔ 퀴즈 **2** *v/t* murǒboda 물어보다

quiz program k'wijǔ p'ǔro 퀴즈 프로

quota mok 몫

quotation (*from author*) inyong 인용; (*price*) kyǒnjǒk 견적

quotation marks inyong puho 인용 부호

quote 1 *n* (*from author*) inyongmun 인용문; (*price*) kyǒnjǒk 견적; (*quotation mark*) inyong puho 인용 부호; *give X a ~ for Y* Xege Yǔi piyong-ǔl kyǒnjǒk'ada X에게 Y의 비용을 견적하다 **2** *v/t text* inyonghada 인용하다; *price* kyǒnjǒk'ada 견적하다 **3** *v/i inyonghada 인용하다; *~ from an author* chak-kkaǔi kǔrǔl inyonghada 작가의 글을 인용하다

R

rabbit t'okki 토끼
rabies kwanggyŏnppyŏng 광견병
raccoon miguk nŏguri 미국 너구리
race[1] *n* (*of people*) injong 인종
race[2] **1** *n* SP kyŏngju 경주; *the ~s*
(*horse ~s*) kyŏngma 경마 **2** *v/i* (*run
fast*) chiltchuhada 질주하다; SP
kyŏngjuhada 경주하다; *he ~d
through his meal / work* kŭnŭn
kŭp'i shikssarŭl / irŭl haet-tta 그는
급히 식사를 / 일을 했다 **3** *v/t: I'll ~
you* kyŏngjuhaja 경주하자
racecourse kyŏngju k'osŭ 경주 코스;
racehorse kyŏngjuma 경주마;
racetrack (*for cars, athletics*)
kyŏngjujang 경주장
racial injong-ŭi 인종의; *~ equality*
injong p'yŏngdŭng 인종 평등
racing kyŏngju 경주
racing car kyŏngjuch'a 경주차
racing driver kyŏngjuja 경주자
racism injong ch'abyŏltchuŭi 인종
차별주의
racist 1 *n* injong ch'abyŏltchuŭija
인종 차별주의자 **2** *adj* injong
ch'abyŏltchŏgin 인종 차별적인
rack 1 *n* (*for parking bikes*)
chuch'adae 주차대; (*for bags on
train*) sŏnban 선반; (*for CDs*) kkoji
꽂이; (*for coats*) kŏri 걸이 **2** *v/t: ~
one's brains* mŏrirŭl tchada 머리를
짜다
racket[1] SP lak'et 라켓
racket[2] (*noise*) soŭm 소음; (*criminal
activity*) pujŏnghan tonppŏri 부정한
돈벌이
radar leida 레이다
radiant *smile, appearance* hwanhi
pinnanŭn 환히 빛나는
radiate *v/i* (*of heat, light*) pich'ŭl
parhada 빛을 발하다
radiation PHYS pangsasŏn 방사선
radiator (*in room*) nanbanggi 난방기;
(*in car*) ladiet'ŏ 라디에이터

radical 1 *adj* kŭnbonjŏgin 근본적인;
POL *views* kŭptchinjŏgin 급진적인
2 *n* POL kŭptchinjuŭija 급진주의자
radicalism POL kŭptchinjuŭi 급진주의
radically kŭnbonjŏgŭro 근본적으로
radio ladio 라디오; *on the ~*
ladioe(sŏ) 라디오에(서); *by ~*
mujŏnŭro 무전으로
radioactive pangsanŭng-i innŭn
방사능이 있는; **radioactivity**
pangsanŭng 방사능; **radio station**
ladio pangsongguk 라디오 방송국;
radiotherapy pangsanŭng yoppŏp
방사능 요법
radish mu 무
radius panjirŭm 반지름
raffle *n* chebi ppopkki 제비 뽑기
raft ttenmok 뗏목
rafter sŏkkarae 서까래
rag (*for cleaning etc*)
hŏnggŏptchogak 헝겊조각
rage 1 *n* kyŏngno 격노; *be in a ~*
kyŏngnohada 격노하다; *all the ~*
taeyuhaeng 대유행 **2** *v/i* (*of person*)
kyŏngnohada 격노하다; (*of storm*)
sanapkke morach'ida 사납게
몰아치다
ragged *edge* tŭltchungnaltchuk'an
들쭉날쭉한; *appearance* namnuhan
남루한; *clothes* tchijŏjin 찢어진
raid 1 *n* (*by troops, police*) kŭpssŭp
급습; (*by robbers*) ch'imip 침입; FIN
ilje maedo 일제 매도 **2** *v/t* (*of troops,
police*) kŭpssŭp'ada 급습하다; (*of
robbers*) ch'imip'ada 침입하다
raider (*bank robber etc*) ch'imiptcha
침입자
rail (*on track*) ch'ŏltto 철도; (*hand~*)
nan-gan 난간; (*for towel*) sugŏn kŏri
수건 걸이; *by ~* kich'aro 기차로
railings (*around park etc*) ult'ari
울타리
railroad ch'ŏltto 철도
railroad station kich'ayŏk 기차역

rain 1 n pi 비; *in the* ~ pitssoge(sŏ) 빗속에(서); *the* ~**s** changma 장마 **2** v/i piga oda 비가 오다; *it's* ~*ing* piga onda 비가 온다

rainbow mujigae 무지개; **raincheck:** *can I take a* ~ *on that?* ŏnjen-ga taŭme hamyŏn andoelkkayo? 언젠가 다음에 하면 안될까요?; **raincoat** ubi 우비; **raindrop** pitppang-ul 빗방울; **rainfall** kang-u 강우; **rain forest** urim 우림; *tropical* ~ yŏlttae urim 열대 우림; **rainstorm** p'okp'ung-u 폭풍우

rainy piga onŭn 비가 오는; *it's* ~ piga onnŭn-gunnyo 비가 오는군요

rainy season changmach'ŏl 장마철

raise 1 n (*in salary*) insang 인상 **2** v/t *shelf etc* ollida 올리다; *offer* nŭllida 늘리다; *children* k'iuda 키우다; *question* chegihada 제기하다; *money* moŭda 모으다

raisin kŏnp'odo 건포도

rake n (*for garden*) kalk'wi 갈퀴

rally n (*meeting, reunion*) taehoe 대회; MOT, (*in tennis*) laelli 랠리

♦ **rally around 1** v/i tourŏ moida 도우러 모이다 **2** v/t ...ŭl/rŭl tourŏ tallyŏoda ...을/를 도우러 달려오다

RAM (= *random access memory*) laem 램

ram 1 n sunnyang 숫양 **2** v/t *ship, car* puditch'ida 부딪히다

ramble 1 n (*walk*) sanch'aek 산책 **2** v/i (*walk*) sanch'aek'ada 산책하다; (*when speaking, talk incoherently*) tusŏŏpsshi iyagihada 두서없이 이야기하다

rambler (*walker*) sanch'aek'anŭn saram 산책하는 사람

rambling 1 n (*walking*) sanch'aek 산책; (*in speech*) hoengsŏlsusŏl 횡설수설 **2** adj *speech* tusŏŏmnŭn 두서없는

ramp hanggonggiŭi t'ŭraep 항공기의 트랩; (*for raising vehicle*) raemp'ŭ 램프]

rampage 1 v/i nalttwimyŏ toradanida 날뛰며 돌아다니다 **2** n: *go on the* ~ nalttwimyŏ toradanida 날뛰며 돌아다니다

rampart sŏngbyŏk 성벽

ramshackle *building* kŭmbang-irado munŏjil tŭt'an 금방이라도 무너질 듯한; *car* kŭmbang-irado pusŏjil tŭt'an 금방이라도 부서질 듯한

ranch moktchang 목장

rancher moktchangju 목장주

rancid ssŏgŭn 썩은

rancor wŏnhan 원한

R & D (= *research and development*) yŏn-gu kaebal 연구 개발

random 1 adj mujagwiŭi 무작위의; ~ *sample* mujagwi saemp'ŭl 무작위 샘플 **2** n: *at* ~ mujagwiro 무작위로

range 1 n (*of products*) pŏmwi 범위; (*of voice*) ŭmnyŏk 음역; (*of airplane*) hanggsok kŏri 항속 거리; (*of gun, missile*) sajŏng kŏri 사정 거리; (*of mountains*) sanmaek 산맥 **2** v/i: ~ *from X to Y* Xesŏ Ykkaji irŭda X에서 Y까지 이르다

ranger (*forest* ~) sallim kyŏngbiwŏn 산림 경비원

rank 1 n MIL kyegŭp 계급; (*in society*) shinbun 신분; *the* ~**s** MIL ilban sabyŏng 일반 사병 **2** v/t tŭnggŭbŭl maegida 등급을 매기다

♦ **rank among** ...(ŭ)ro p'yŏngkkahada ...(으)로 평가하다

ransack satssach'i twijida 샅샅이 뒤지다

ransom momkkap 몸값; *hold s.o. to* ~ nugurŭl ŏngnyuhayŏ momkkapssŭl yoguhada 누구를 억류하여 몸값을 요구하다

rant: ~ *and rave* koraegorae sorich'ida 고래고래 소리치다

rap 1 n (*at door etc*) t'ok'ok tudŭrigi 톡톡 두드리기; MUS laep 랩 **2** v/t *table etc* t'ok'ok tudŭrida 톡톡 두드리다

♦ **rap at** *window etc* t'ok'ok tudŭrida 톡톡 두드리다

rape 1 n kanggan 강간 **2** v/t kangganhada 강간하다

rape victim kanggan p'ihaeja 강간 피해자

rapid shinssok'an 신속한

rapidity shinssok 신속

rapids kŭmnyu 급류

rapist kangganbŏm 강간범

rapturous yŏlgwangtchŏgin 열광적인

rare tŭmun 드문; *antique, skills* chingihan 진기한; *steak* tŏl igŭn 덜 익은

rarely tŭmulge 드물게

rarity chinp'um 진품

rascal changnankkurŏgi 장난꾸러기

rash¹ MED paltchin 발진

rash² *action, behavior* sŏnggŭpp'an 성급한

raspberry namuttalgi 나무딸기

rat *n* chwi 쥐

rate 1 *n* (*of birth, death etc*) piyul 비율; (*of exchange*) hwannyul 환율; (*price*) yogŭm 요금; (*speed*) chindo 진도; *an hourly ~* (*of pay*) shigandang 시간당; *a weekly ~* (*of pay*) chudang 주당; *~ of interest* FIN ijayul 이자율; *at this ~* (*at this speed*) i chŏngdo sokttomyŏn 이 정도 속도면; (*carrying on like this*) kyesok irŏn sangt'aeramyŏn 계속 이런 상태라면 **2** *v/t* (*consider, rank*) p'yŏngkkahada 평가하다

rather (*somewhat*) taso 다소; (*preferably*) ohiryŏ 오히려; *I would ~ stay here* nanŭn ohiryŏ yŏgi innŭn p'yŏni natkkessŏyo 나는 오히려 여기 있는 편이 낫겠어요; *or would you ~ have coffee?* animyŏn ohiryŏ k'ŏp'iro hagessŏyo? 아니면 오히려 커피로 하겠어요?

ration 1 *n* paegŭmnyang 배급량 **2** *v/t supplies* paegŭp'ada 배급하다

rational hamnijŏgin 합리적인

rationality hamnisŏng 합리성

rationalization (*of production etc*) hyoyurhwa 효율화

rationalize 1 *v/t production* hyoyurhwahada 효율화하다; *actions etc* hamnihwahada 합리화하다 **2** *v/i* hamnihwahada 합리화하다

rat race kwada kyŏngjaeng sahoe 과다 경쟁 사회

rattle 1 *n* (*noise*) tŏlk'ŏk-kkŏrinŭn sori 덜컥거리는 소리 **2** *v/t* tŏlk'ŏk-kkŏrida 덜컥거리다 **3** *v/i* tŏlk'ŏk-kkŏrida 덜컥거리다

♦ **rattle off** *poem, list of names* kŏch'imŏpsshi chikkŏrida 거침없이 지껄이다

rattlesnake pang-ulbaem 방울뱀

ravage: *~d by war* chŏnjaeng-ŭro hwangp'yehaejin 전쟁으로 황폐해진

rave *v/i* (*talk deliriously*) hŏtssorihada 헛소리하다; (*talk wildly*) chŏngshinŏpsshi chikkŏrida 정신없이 지껄이다; *~ about sth* (*be very enthusiastic*) muŏse yŏlgwanghada 무엇에 열광하다

raven kkamagwi 까마귀

ravenous *appetite* kegŏlssŭrŏun 게걸스러운

rave review kŭkch'anŭi p'yŏng 극찬의 평

ravine chobŭn koltchagi 좁은 골짜기

raving mad wanjŏnhi mich'in 완전히 미친

ravishing maehoktchŏgin 매혹적인

raw *meat, vegetables* nalkkŏsŭi 날것의; *sugar, iron* kagonghaji anŭn 가공하지 않은

raw fish hoe 회

raw materials wŏllyo 원료

ray pit 빛; *a ~ of hope* han kadak hŭimang 한 가닥 희망

razor myŏndok'al 면도칼

razor blade myŏndonal 면도날

re COM ...e kwanhayŏ ...에 관하여

reach 1 *n*: *within ~* (*close to hand*) soni tannŭn kose 손이 닿는 곳에; (*easily accessible*) kakkaun kose 가까운 곳에; *out of ~* soni tach'i annŭn kose 손이 닿지 않는 곳에 **2** *v/t city etc* tŏch'ak'ada 도착하다; (*go as far as*) ...e tat'a ...에 닿다; *decision, agreement* ...e irŭda ...에 이르다

♦ **reach out** *v/i* sonŭl ppŏtch'ida 손을 뻗치다

react panjagyonghada 반작용하다; (*to news etc*) panŭnghada 반응하다

reaction panjagyong 반작용; (*to news etc*) panŭng 반응

reactionary 1 *n* pandongjuŭija 반동주의자 **2** *adj* pandong-ŭi 반동의

reactor (*nuclear*) wŏnjaro 원자로

read 1 *v/t* iltta 읽다; *diskette* ...ŭi chŏngborŭl iltta ...의 정보를 읽다 **2** *v/i* iltta 읽다; *~ to s.o.* nuguege ilgŏ chuda 누구에게 읽어 주다

♦ **read out** *v/t* (*aloud*) k'ŭn soriro iltta 큰 소리로 읽다

♦**read up on** ...ŭl/rŭl yŏn-guhada
...을/를 연구하다

readable ilgŭl su innŭn 읽을 수 있는

reader (*person*) tokssŏga 독서가

readily *admit, agree* sŏnttŭt 선뜻

readiness (*for action*) chunbiga toeŏ
issŭm 준비가 되어 있음;
(*willingness*) kikkŏi hanŭn maŭm
기꺼이 하는 마음

reading (*activity*) toksssŏ 독서; (*from
meter etc*) ch'ŭktchŏng 측정

reading matter ilgŭl kŏri 읽을 거리

readjust 1 *v/t equipment, controls*
chaejŏngnihada 재정리하다 **2** *v/i* (*to
conditions*) chaejŏgŭnghada
재적응하다

read-only file COMPUT p'andok
chŏnyong p'ail 판독 전용 파일

read-only memory COMPUT p'andok
chŏnyong kiŏk changch'i 판독 전용
기억 장치

ready (*prepared*) chunbidoen 준비된;
(*willing*) kikkŏi ...handa 기꺼이
...하다; *he is always ~ to listen*
kŭnŭn hangsang kikkŏi tŭnnŭnda
그는 항상 기꺼이 듣는다; *get* (*oneself*) *~* chunbihada 준비하다; *get ...
ready* ...ŭl/rŭl chunbihada ...을/를
준비하다

ready-made *meal* miri mandŭrŏjyŏ
innŭn 미리 만들어져 있는; *solution*
chinbuhan 진부한

ready-to-wear kisŏngbok 기성복

real chintcha-ŭi 진짜의

real estate pudongsan 부동산

realism hyŏnshiltchuŭi 현실주의; (*in
literature, art*) sashiltchuŭi 사실주의

realist hyŏnshiltchuŭija 현실주의자;
(*in literature, art etc*) sashiltchuŭija
사실주의자

realistic hyŏnshiltchŏgin 현실적인

reality hyŏnshil 현실

realization (*of goal*) shirhyŏn 실현;
(*understanding*) kkaedarŭm 깨달음

realize *v/t* kkaedat-tta 깨닫다; FIN
...ŭi iigŭl poda ...의 이익을 보다; *I ~
now that ...* nanŭn ijeya ...ranŭn
kŏsŭl kkaedannŭnda 나는 이제야
...라는 것을 깨닫는다

really chŏngmallo 정말로; (*very*)
taedanhi 대단히; *~?* chŏngmariyeyo?

정말이예요?; *not ~* (*not much*)
pyŏlloyeyo 별로예요

real time COMPUT shilsshigan 실시간

real-time COMPUT shilsshiganŭi
실시간의

realtor pudongsan chunggaein 부동산
중개인

reap suhwak'ada 수확하다

reappear tashi nat'anada 다시
나타나다

rear 1 *n* paehu 배후 **2** *adj* twiŭi 뒤의;
lights twittchogŭi 뒷쪽의

rearm 1 *v/t* chaemujangshik'ida
재무장시키다 **2** *v/i* chaemujanghada
재무장하다

rearmost maen twittchogŭi 맨 뒷쪽의

rearrange *flowers, chairs*
chaebaeyŏrhada 재배열하다;
schedule chaejŏngnihada 재정리하다

rear-view mirror paengmirŏ 백미러

reason 1 *n* (*faculty*) isŏng 이성;
(*cause*) iyu 이유 **2** *v/i: ~ with s.o.*
nugurŭl sŏlttŭk'ae poda 누구를
설득해 보다

reasonable *person, behavior* punbyŏl
innŭn 분별 있는; *price* chŏkttanghan
적당한; *a ~ number of people*
sangdanghi manŭn saramdŭl 상당히
많은 사람들

reasonably *act, behave* ich'ie matkke
이치에 맞게; (*quite*) sangdanghi
상당히

reassure anshimshik'ida 안심시키다

reassuring anshimhage hanŭn
안심하게 하는

rebate (*money back*) hwanbul 환불

rebel *n* panyŏktcha 반역자; *~ troops*
pallan-gun 반란군

rebellion pallan 반란

rebellious panhangjŏgin 반항적인

rebound *v/i* (*of ball etc*) toet'wida
되튀다

rebuff *n* kŏjŏl 거절

rebuild kaech'uk'ada 개축하다;
relationship hoebok'ada 회복하다

rebuke *v/t* chilch'aek'ada 질책하다

recall *v/t ambassador* sohwanhada
소환하다; (*remember*) sanggihada
상기하다

recapture *v/t* MIL t'arhwan 탈환;
criminal chaech'ep'ohada

재체포하다
receding *hair* pŏtkkyŏjinŭn 벗겨지는
receipt yŏngsujŭng 영수증; *acknowledge ~ of* ...ŭl/rŭl padassŭmŭl injŏnghada ...을/를 받았음을 인정하다; *~s* FIN suip 수입
receive pat-tta 받다
receiver (*of letter*) such'wiin 수취인; TELEC suhwagi 수화기; RAD sushin-gi 수신기
receivership: *be in ~* chaesan kwalli sangt'aee noyŏ it-tta 재산 관리 상태에 놓여 있다
recent ch'oegŭnŭi 최근의
recently ch'oegŭne 최근에
reception (*in hotel, company*) p'ŭront'ŭ 프론트; (*formal party*) lisepsshyŏn p'at'i 리셉션 파티; (*welcome*) hwanyŏng 환영; RAD sushin 수신
reception desk annae tesŭk'ŭ 안내 데스크
receptionist chŏpssuwŏn 접수원
receptive: *be ~ to* ...ŭl/rŭl chal padadŭrida ...을/를 잘 받아들이다
recess (*in wall etc*) ump'uk tŭrŏgan kot 움푹 들어간 곳; EDU shwinŭn shigan 쉬는 시간; (*of legislature*) hyuhoe 휴회
recession pulgyŏnggi 불경기
recharge *battery* ch'ungjŏnhada 충전하다
recipe choribŏp 조리법
recipient (*of parcel etc*) such'wiin 수취인; (*of payment*) suryŏng-in 수령인
reciprocal sanghoganŭi 상호간의
recital MUS lisait'ŭl 리사이틀
recite *poem* nangsonghada 낭송하다; *details, facts* yŏlgŏhada 열거하다
reckless mumohan 무모한
reckon (*think, consider*) ...rago saenggak'ada ...라고 생각하다
♦ **reckon with**: *have s.o./sth to ~* nugurŭl/muŏsŭl koryŏe nŏt'a 누구를/무엇을 고려에 넣다
reclaim *land from sea* kanch'ŏk'ada 간척하다
recline *v/i* kidaeda 기대다
recluse ŭndunja 은둔자

recognition (*of state, achievements*) injŏng 인정; (*of person*) arabom 알아봄; *change beyond ~* arabol su ŏpssŭl chŏngdoro pyŏnhada 알아볼 수 없을 정도로 변하다
recognizable arabol su innŭn 알아볼 수 있는
recognize *person, voice, tune* araboda 알아보다; (*distinguish*) punganhada 분간하다; POL state sŭng-inhada 승인하다; *it can be ~d by ...* ...(ŭ)ro pun-gandoel su it-tta ...(으)로 분간될 수 있다
recollect hoesanghada 회상하다
recollection hoesang 회상
recommend ch'uch'ŏnhada 추천하다
recommendation ch'uch'ŏn 추천
reconcile *people* hwahaeshik'ida 화해시키다; *differences* chohwashik'ida 조화시키다; *facts* ilch'ishik'ida 일치시키다; *~ oneself to ...* ...ŭl/rŭl kamsuhada ...을/를 감수하다; *be ~d* (*of two people*) hwahaehada 화해하다
reconciliation (*of people*) hwahae 화해; (*of differences*) chohwa 조화; (*of facts*) ilch'i 일치
recondition ...ŭl/rŭl surihada ...을/를 수리하다
reconnaissance MIL chŏngch'al 정찰
reconsider *v/t & v/i* chaegohada 재고하다
reconstruct *city* chaegŏnhada 재건하다; *one's life* tashi ch'usŭrida 다시 추스리다; *crime* chaehyŏnhada 재현하다
record 1 *n* MUS lek'odŭ 레코드; SP *etc* kyŏnggi kirok 경기 기록; (*written document etc*) kirok munsŏ 기록 문서; (*in database*) hanbŏrŭi teit'ŏ 한벌의 데이터; *~s* (*archives*) kirok munsŏ 기록 문서; *say sth off the ~* muŏsŭl pigongshigŭro marhada 무엇을 비공식으로 말하다; *have a criminal ~* chŏnkkwaga it-tta 전과가 있다; *have a good ~ for ...* ...i/ga chot'anŭn p'yŏngp'anŭl kajigo it-tta ...이/가 좋다는 평판을 가지고 있다 **2** *v/t* (*on tape etc*) nogŭmhada 녹음하다
record-breaking kirogŭl kkaenŭn

기록을 깨는
recorder MUS lik'odŏ 리코더
record holder kirok poyuja 기록
　보유자
recording nogŭm 녹음
recording studio nogŭmshil 녹음실
record player nogŭmgi 녹음기
recoup *losses* toech'at-tta 되찾다
recover 1 *v/t* (*get back*) toech'at-tta
　되찾다 **2** *v/i* (*from illness*)
　hoebok'ada 회복하다
recovery (*of sth lost, stolen goods*)
　toech'ajŭm 되찾음; (*from illness*)
　hoebok 회복; **he has made a good**
　~ kŭŭi hoebogŭn sunjorowat-tta
　그의 회복은 순조로왔다
recreation orak 오락
recruit 1 *n* MIL shinbyŏng 신병; (*to*
　company) shinip sawŏn 신입 사원
　2 *v/t new staff* mojip'ada 모집하다
recruitment shin-gyu mojip 신규
　모집
recruitment drive shin-gyu mojip
　k'aemp'ein 신규 모집 캠페인
rectangle chikssagak'yŏng 직사각형
rectangular chikssagak'yŏng-ŭi
　직사각형의
recuperate hoebok'ada 회복하다
recur chaebarhada 재발하다
recurrent chaebarhanŭn 재발하는
recycle chaesaeng iyonghada 재생
　이용하다
recycling chaesaeng iyong 재생 이용
red ppalgan 빨간; *hair* pulgŭn 붉은; *in*
　the ~ chŏktchaga nada 적자가 나다
Red Cross Chŏksshiptcha 적십자
redden *v/i* (*blush*) pulgŏjida 붉어지다
redecorate *v/t* sae tanjanghada 새
　단장하다
redeem *debt* sanghwanhada 상환하다;
　sinners kuwŏnhada 구원하다
redeeming: **~** *feature* kyŏltchŏmŭl
　powanhae chunŭn changtchŏm
　=결점을 보완해 주는 장점
redevelop *part of town*
　chaegaebarhada 재개발하다
red-handed: *catch* **~**
　hyŏnhaengbŏmŭro chaptta
　현행범으로 잡다; **redhead**
　mŏrik'aragi pulgŭn saram
　머리카락이 붉은 사람; **red-hot**

saeppalgak'e tan 새빨갛게 단; **red**
　light ppalgan pul 빨간 불; **red light**
　district hongdŭngga 홍등가; **red**
　meat pulgŭn saegi tonŭn kogi 붉은
　색이 도는 고기; **red tape**
　kwallyojŏk hyŏngshiktchuŭi 관료적
　형식주의
reduce churida 줄이다
reduction kamso 감소
redundant (*unnecessary*)
　pulp'iryohan 불필요한
reed BOT kalttae 갈대
reef (*in sea*) amch'o 암초
reef knot ongmaedŭp 옭매듭
reek *v/i* naemsaega nada 냄새가 나다;
　~ *of* …ŭi naemsaega nada …의
　냄새가 나다
reel *n* (*of film*) lil 릴; (*of thread*)
　shilp'ae 실패
refer *v/t*: **~** *a decision* / *problem to*
　…ege kyŏltchŏng-ŭl / mun-jerŭl
　nŏmgida …에게 결정을 / 문제를
　넘기다
♦ **refer to** (*allude to*) …ŭl / rŭl ŏn-
　gŭp'ada …을 / 를 언급하다;
　dictionary etc …e chohoehada …에
　조회하다
referee SP shimp'an 심판; (*for job*)
　shinwŏn pojŭng-in 신원 보증인
reference (*allusion*) ŏn-gŭp 언급;
　(*for job*) ch'uch'ŏnsŏ 추천서; (*~*
　number) chohoe 조회; **with ~ to** …e
　kwallyŏnhayŏ …에 관련하여
reference book ch'amgo tosŏ 참고
　도서
referendum kungmin t'up'yo 국민
　투표
refill *v/t tank, glass* tashi ch'aeuda
　다시 채우다
refine *oil, sugar* chŏngjehada
　정제하다; *technique* chŏnggyohage
　hada 정교하게 하다
refined *manners, language*
　seryŏndoen 세련된
refinery chŏngjeso 정제소
reflation t'onghwa chaep'aengch'ang
　통화 재팽창
reflect 1 *v/t light* pansahada 반사하다;
　be ~ed in … …e pich'wŏjida …에
　비춰지다 **2** *v/i* (*think*) komgomhi
　saenggak'ada 곰곰히 생각하다

reflection (*in water, glass etc*)
pansadoen kŭrimja 반사된 그림자;
(*consideration*) shimsasuk-kko
심사숙고

reflex (*in body*) pansa shin-gyŏng
반사 신경

reflex reaction pansa undong 반사
운동

reform 1 *n* kaehyŏk 개혁 **2** *v/t*
kaehyŏk'ada 개혁하다

refrain¹ *v/i* samgahada 삼가하다;
please ~ from smoking tambaerŭl
samgahae chushigi paramnida
담배를 삼가해 주시기 바랍니다

refrain² *n* (*in song etc*) huryŏm 후렴

refresh *person* kiun ch'arige hada
기운 차리게 하다; *feel ~ed*
sangk'waehage nŭkkida 상쾌하게
느끼다

refresher course chaegyoyuk
kwajŏng 재교육 과정

refreshing *experience* ch'amshinhan
참신한; *~ drink* ch'ŏngnyang ŭmnyo
청량 음료

refreshments tagwa 다과

refrigerate naengjanghada 냉장하다

refrigerator naengjanggo 냉장고

refuel 1 *v/t airplane* yŏllyorŭl
konggŭp'ada 연료를 공급하다 **2** *v/i*
(*of airplane*) yŏllyorŭl pogŭp pat-tta
연료를 보급 받다

refuge p'inanch'ŏ 피난처; *take ~*
(*from storm etc*) p'inanhada
피난하다

refugee namnin 난민

refund 1 *n* hwanbul 환불 **2** *v/t*
hwanburhada 환불하다

refusal kŏjŏl 거절

refuse kŏjŏrhada 거절하다; *~ to ...*
...hagirŭl kŏjŏrhada ...하기를
거절하다

regain *control, the lead* toech'at-tta
되찾다

regard 1 *n*: *have great ~ for*
...ŭl/rŭl chon-gyŏnghada ...을/를
존경하다; *in this ~* i chŏme
kwanhaesŏnŭn 이 점에 관해서는;
with ~ to ...e kwanhaesŏ ...에
관해서; (*kind*) ~s anbu 안부; *give
my ~s to Mina* Minaege anbu
chŏnhaejuseyo 미나에게 안부

chŏnhaejuseyo; *with no ~ for* ...ŭl/rŭl
koryŏhaji ank'o ...을/를 고려하지
않고 **2** *v/t*: *~ X as Y* Xŭl/rŭl Y(ŭ)ro
kanjuhada X을/를 Y(으)로 간주하다;
as ~s ...e kwanhaesŏnŭn ...에
관해서는

regarding ...e taehaesŏ ...에 대해서

regardless ŏtchaet-ttŭn 어쨌든; *~ of*
...e kaeŭich'i ank'o ...에 개의치
않고

regime (*government*) chŏngkkwŏn
정권

regiment *n* yŏndae 연대

region chibang 지방; *in the ~ of*
yak... 약 ...; *in the ~ of $5,000* yak
5,000tallŏ 약 5,000달러

regional chiyŏgŭi 지역의

register 1 *n* tŭngnok 등록 **2** *v/t birth,
death* shin-gohada 신고하다; *vehicle*
tŭngnok'ada 등록하다; *letter*
tŭngkkiro puch'ida 등기로 부치다;
emotion nat'anaeda 나타내다; *send
a letter ~ed* pyŏnjirŭl tŭngkkiro
ponaeda 편지를 등기로 보내다 **3** *v/i*
(*at university*) ip'ak tŭngnogŭl hada
입학 등록을 하다; (*for a course*)
tŭngnogŭl hada 등록을 하다; (*with
police*) shin-gohada 신고하다

registered letter tŭngkki up'yŏn
등기 우편

registration (*at university*) ip'ak
tŭngnok 입학 등록; (*for course*)
tŭngnok'ada 등록하다

regret 1 *v/t* huhoehada 후회하다 **2** *n*
yugam 유감

regrettable yugamsŭrŏun 유감스러운

regrettably yugamsŭrŏpkkedo
유감스럽게도

regular 1 *adj* kyuch'iktchŏgin
규칙적인; *pattern, shape* iltchŏnghan
일정한; (*normal*) pot'ong-ŭi 보통의
2 *n* (*at bar etc*) tan-gol 단골

regulate kyujehada 규제하다

regulation (*rule*) kyuch'ik 규칙

rehabilitate *ex-criminal* sahoero pok-
kkwishik'ida 사회로 복귀시키다

rehearsal lihŏsŏl 리허설

rehearse *v/t & v/i* lihŏsŏrhada
리허설하다

reign 1 *n* kullim 군림 **2** *v/i* kullimhada
군림하다

reimburse ...ŭi piyong-ŭl kaptta ...의 비용을 갚다
rein koppi 고삐
reincarnation hwansaeng 환생
reinforce *structure* poganghada 보강하다; *beliefs* kanghwahada 강화하다
reinforced concrete ch'ŏlgŭn k'onk'ŭrit'ŭ 철근 콘크리트
reinforcements MIL chŭng-wŏn-gun 증원군
reinstate *person in office* poktchiksshik'ida 복직시키다; *paragraph in text* pogwŏnhada 복원하다
reject *v/t* kŏjŏrhada 거절하다
rejection kŏjŏl 거절
relapse MED chaebal 재발; *have a ~* pyŏng-i chaebarhada 병이 재발하다
relate 1 *v/t story* iyagihada 이야기하다; *~ X to Y* Xŭl/rŭl Yege yŏn-gyŏlshik'ida X을/를 Y에게 연결시키다 2 *v/i*: *~ to ...* (*be connected with*) ...wa/kwa kwallyŏni it-tta ...와/과 관련이 있다; *he doesn't ~ to people* kŭnŭn saramdŭlgwa chal sŏk-kkijil mot'anda 그는 사람들과 잘 섞이질 못한다
related (*by family*) ch'inch'ŏgi toenŭn 친척이 되는; *events, ideas etc* kwallyŏni innŭn 관련이 있는
relation (*in family*) ch'inch'ŏk 친척; (*connection*) kwan-gye 관계; *business/diplomatic ~s* saŏp/oegyo kwan-gye 사업/외교 관계
relationship kwan-gye 관계; (*sexual*) sŏnggwan-gye 성관계
relative 1 *n* ch'inch'ŏk 친척 2 *adj* sangdaejŏgin 상대적인; *X is ~ to Y* Xŭn/nŭn Ye piryehada X은/는 Y에 비례한다
relatively sandaejŏguro 상대적으로
relax 1 *v/i* p'yŏnhi shwida 편히 쉬다; *~!, don't get angry* maŭm p'yŏnhage saenggak'ae! hwanaeji mallagu 마음 편하게 생각 해! 화내지 말라구 2 *v/t muscle* himŭl ppaeda 힘을 빼다; *pace* nŭtch'uda 늦추다; *laws* wanhwashik'ida 완화시키다

relaxation kinjang wanhwa 긴장 완화
relay 1 *v/t message* chŏnhada 전하다; *radio, TV signals* chunggyehada 중계하다 2 *n*: *~ (race)* kyeju kyŏnggi 계주 경기
release 1 *n* (*from prison*) sŏkppang 석방; (*of CD etc*) palmae 발매; (*of news, information*) palp'yo 발표 2 *v/t prisoner* sŏkppanghada 석방하다; *CD* palmaehada 발매하다; *parking brake* p'ulda 풀다; *information* konggaehada 발표하다
relent maŭmi nugŭrŏjida 마음이 누그러지다
relentless (*determined*) tanhohan 단호한; *rain etc* sajŏng-ŏmnŭn 사정없는
relevance kwallyŏnssŏng 관련성
relevant kwallyŏndoen 관련된
reliability shilloessŏng 신뢰성
reliable shilloehal su innŭn 신뢰할 수 있는
reliably hwaksshirhage 확실하게; *I am ~ informed that ...* nanŭn ...ranŭn kosŭl hwaksshirhage chŏnhae tŭrŏtta 나는 ...라는 것을 확실하게 전해 들었다
reliance ŭijon 의존; *~ on s.o./sth* nugue/muŏse taehan ŭijon 누구에/무엇에 대한 의존
relic yumul 유물
relief anshim 안심; *that's a ~* anshimi toemnida 안심이 됩니다
relieve *pressure, pain* churida 줄이다; (*take over from*) kyodaehada 교대하다; *be ~d* (*at news etc*) anshimi toeda 안심이 되다
religion chonggyo 종교
religious chonggyojŏgin 종교적인; *person* shinangshim-i kip'ŭn 신앙심이 깊은
religiously (*conscientiously*) yangshimjŏguro 양심적으로
relish 1 *n* (*sauce*) yangnyŏm 양념 2 *v/t idea, prospect* chŭlgida 즐기다
relive *the past* sanggihada 상기하다
relocate *v/i* (*of business*) ijŏnhada 이전하다; (*of employee*) chaebaech'ihada 재배치하다
reluctance naek'iji anŭm 내키지 않음
reluctant naek'iji annŭn 내키지 않는;

reluctantly 556

be ~ to do sth muŏsŭl hanŭn kŏshi naek'iji ant'a 무엇을 하는 것이 내키지 않다

reluctantly maji mot'ae 마지 못해

♦**rely on** ŭijihada 의지하다; **~ s.o. to do sth** nuguege muŏt hanŭn kŏsŭl ŭijihada 누구에게 무엇 하는 것을 의지하다

remain (*be left*) namgyŏjida 남겨지다; (*stay*) kyesok … it-tta 계속 … 있다; *they ~ed silent* kŭdŭrŭn kyesok choyonghage issŏt-tta 그들은 계속 조용하게 있었다

remainder *also* MATH namŏji 나머지

remains (*of body*) yuhae 유해

remand 1 *v/t:* **~ s.o. in custody** nugurŭl kuryushik'ida 누구를 구류시키다 **2** *n:* **be on ~** kuryu chung-ida 구류 중이다

remark 1 *n* ŏn-gŭp 언급 **2** *v/t* ŏn-gŭp'ada 언급하다

remarkable chumok'al manhan 주목할 만한

remarkably taedanhi 대단히

remarry *v/i* chaehonhada 재혼하다

remedy 1 *n* MED ch'iryo 치료; *fig* kujech'aek 구제책

remember 1 *v/t* kiŏk'ada 기억하다; **~ to lock the door** mun chamgŭnŭn kŏl, ittchi marayo 문 잠그는 걸, 잊지 말아요; **~ me to her** kŭnyŏege nae anburŭl chŏnhaejuseyo 그녀에게 내 안부를 전해주세요 **2** *v/i* kiŏk'ada 기억하다; *I don't ~* chŏnŭn kiŏgi naji anayo 저는 기억이 나지 않아요

remind: ~ s.o. of sth (*bring to their attention*) nuguege muŏsŭl ilkkaewŏjuda 누구에게 무엇을 일깨워주다; (*make remember*) nuguege muŏsŭl kiŏng nage hada 누구에게 무엇을 기억 나게 하다; **~ s.o. of s.o.** nugurŭl pomyŏn nungun-gaga saenggangnada 누구를 보면 누군가가 생각나다

reminder saenggangnage hanŭn kŏt 생각나게 하는 것; COM tokch'oktchang 독촉장

reminisce hoesang 회상

reminiscent: be ~ of sth muŏsŭl yŏnsangshik'ida 무엇을 연상시키다

remnant yumul 유물

remorse chach'aek 자책

remorseless *person* mujabihan 무자비한; *demands* kkŭnimŏmnŭn 끊임없는; *pace* mŏmch'ul su ŏmnŭn 멈출 수 없는

remote *village* oettan 외딴; *possibility, connection* hŭibak'an 희박한; (*aloof*) ch'oyŏnhan 초연한; *ancestor* mŏn 먼

remote access COMPUT wŏnkkyŏk chŏpkkŭn 원격 접근

remote control wŏnkkyŏk chojong 원격 조종

remotely *connected* mŏlli 멀리; *just ~ possible* kanŭngssŏng-i kŏŭi hŭibak'an 가능성이 거의 희박한

removal chegŏ 제거

remove ch'iuda 치우다; *top, lid* pŏtkkida 벗기다; *coat etc* pŏt-tta 벗다; *doubt, suspicion* ŏpssaeda 없애다

remuneration posu 보수

remunerative posuga ch'ungbunhan 보수가 충분한

rename kaemyŏnghada 개명하다

render haenghada 행하다; **~ a service** pongsahada 봉사하다; **~ s.o. helpless / unconscious** nugurŭl mugiryŏk'age / ŭishigŭl ilk'e hada 누구를 무기력하게 / 의식을 잃게 하다

rendering (*of music*) yŏnju 연주

rendez-vous (*romantic*) langdebu 랑데부; MIL chipkkyŏltchi 집결지

renew *contract, license* kaengshinhada 갱신하다; *discussions* chaegaehada 재개하다

renewal (*of contract etc*) kaengshin 갱신; (*of discussions*) chaegae 재개

renounce *v/t title, rights* p'ogihada 포기하다

renovate *building* kaejohada 개조하다

renovation (*of building*) kaejo 개조

renown yumyŏng 유명

renowned yumyŏnghan 유명한

rent 1 *n* imdaeryo 임대료; *for ~* imdaeyong 임대용 **2** *v/t apartment, car* imdaehada 임대하다

rental (*money*) imdae kŭmaek 임대 금액

rental agreement imdae kyeyaksŏ

임대 계약서
rental car imdae chadongch'a 임대
자동차
rent-free *adv* imdaeryoga ŏpsshi
임대료가 없이
reopen 1 *v/t store* chaegaejanghada
재개장하다; *business, negotiations,*
case chaegaehada 재개하다 2 *v/i (of*
theater etc) chaegaejanghada
재개장하다
reorganization chaep'yŏnsŏng
재편성
reorganize chaep'yŏnsŏnghada
재편성하다
rep COM seiljŭ maen 세일즈 맨
repaint tashi ch'irhada 다시 칠하다
repair 1 *v/t* koch'ida 고치다 2 *n:* **in a**
good / bad state of ~ suriga chal
toen / chal toeji anŭn 수리가 잘
된 / 잘 되지 않은
repairman surigong 수리공
repatriate songwanhada 송환하다
repay *money, person* kaptta 갚다
repayment pyŏnje 변제
repeal *v/t law* p'yejihada 폐지하다
repeat 1 *v/t something said*
panbok'ada 반복하다; *performance,*
experience toep'urihada 되풀이하다;
am I ~ing myself? chŏne marhaet-
ttŏn chŏgi innayo? 전에 말했던 적이
있나요? 2 *v/i* panbok'ada 반복하다; *I*
~, **do not touch it** tashi
marhanŭnde, kŭgŏsŭl manjiji
maseyo 다시 말하는데, 그것을
만지지 마세요 3 *n (TV program)*
chaebangsong 재방송
repeat business COM chaegŏrae
재거래
repeated panboktoenŭn 반복되는
repeat order COM chaejumun
재주문
repel *v/t invaders, attack*
kyŏkt'oehada 격퇴하다; *insects*
moranaeda 몰아내다; *(disgust)*
pulk'waegamŭl irŭk'ida 불쾌감을
일으키다
repellent 1 *n (insect ~)* pŏllee mulliji
ank'e hanŭn yak 벌레에 물리지 않게
하는 약 2 *adj* pulk'waehan 불쾌한
repent huhoehada 후회하다
repercussions p'agŭp hyokkwa 파급

효과
repetition *(of word, event etc)*
panbok 반복
repetitive toep'uridoenŭn 되풀이되는
replace *(put back)* toedollyŏnot'a
되돌려놓다; *(take the place of)*
taeshinhada 대신하다
replacement *(person)* huimja 후임자;
(thing) taech'ep'um 대체품
replacement part taech'ebup'um
대체부품
replay 1 *n (recording)* chaesaeng
재생; *(match)* chaeshihap 재시합
2 *v/t match* chaeshihap'ada
재시합하다
replica poktchep'um 복제품
reply 1 *n* taedap 대답 2 *v/t & v/i*
taedap'ada 대답하다
report 1 *n (account)* pogosŏ 보고서;
(by journalist) podo 보도 2 *v/t*
pogohada 보고하다; ~ **one's find-**
ings to s.o. nuguege chosa
kyŏlgwarŭl pogohada 누구에게 조사
결과를 보고하다; ~ **a person to the**
police saramŭl kyŏngch'are
kobarhada 사람을 경찰에 고발하다;
he is ~ed to be in Hong Kong
kŭnŭn hongk'onge innŭn kŏsŭro
pogodoeŏtta 그는 홍콩에 있는
것으로 보고되었다 3 *v/i (of*
journalist) podohada 보도하다;
(present oneself) ch'ulttuhada
출두하다
♦**report to** *(in business)* …ege
pogohada …에게 보고하다
report card sŏngjŏkp'yo 성적표
reporter kija 기자
repossess COM *miwanbuldoen*
sangp'umŭl hoesuhada 미완불된
상품을 회수하다
reprehensible pinan padŭlmanhan
비난 받을만한
represent *(act for)* taerihada
대리하다; *(stand for)* taep'yohada
대표하다; *(of images in painting etc)*
myosahada 묘사하다
representative 1 *n* taeriin 대리인;
COM taep'yoja 대표자; POL taebyŏnja
대변자 2 *adj (typical)*
chŏnhyŏngjŏgin 전형적인
repress *revolt* ŏgap'ada 억압하다;

repression

feelings, natural urges ŏngnurŭda
억누르다; *laugh* ch'amtta 참다
repression POL chinap 진압
repressive POL ŏgaptchŏgin
억압적인
reprieve 1 *n* LAW chip'aeng yuye 집행
유예; *fig* ilshijŏk yŏn-gi 일시적 연기
2 *v/t prisoner* chip'aeng-ŭl yuyehada
집행을 유예하다
reprimand *v/t* chilch'aek'ada
질책하다
reprint 1 *n* chaep'an 재판 **2** *v/t*
chaep'anhada 재판하다
reprisal pokssu 복수; *take ~s*
pokssuhada 복수하다
reproach 1 *n* pinan 비난; *be beyond*
~ pinanŭl yŏjiga ŏptta 비난의 여지가
없다 **2** *v/t* pinanhada 비난하다
reproachful pinanhanŭn 비난하는
reproduce 1 *v/t atmosphere, mood*
chaehyŏnhada 재현하다 **2** *v/i* BIO
chaesaengshik'ada 재생식하다
reproduction BIO chaesaengshik
재생식; *(of sound, images)*
chaesaeng 재생; *(piece of furniture)*
poktche 복제
reproductive BIO
chaesaengshik'anŭn 재생식하는
reptile p'ach'ungnyu 파충류
republic konghwaguk 공화국
Republic of Korea Taehanmin-guk
대한민국
republican 1 *n* konghwadangjuŭija
공화당주의자; *Republican* POL
Konghwadang-wŏn 공화당원;
(supporter) Konghwadang chijija
공화당 지지자 **2** *adj* Konghwadang-
ŭl chijihanŭn 공화당을 지지하는
repudiate *(deny)* kŏjŏrhada 거절하다
repulsive mesŭkkŏun 메스꺼운
reputable p'yŏngp'ani chŏun 평판이
좋은
reputation p'yŏngp'an 평판; *have a*
good / bad ~ p'yŏngp'ani chot'a /
nappŭda 평판이 좋다 / 나쁘 다
request 1 *n* yoch'ŏng 요청; *on ~*
yoch'ŏnge ttara 요청에 따라 **2** *v/t*
ch'ŏnghada 청하다
require *(need)* p'iryohada 필요하다; *it*
~s great care seshimhan chuŭiga
p'iryohamnida 세심한 주의가

p'iryohamnida 필요합니다; *as ~d by law* pŏbŭro
chŏnghaejyŏ it-ttŭshi 법으로 정해져
있듯이; *guests are ~d to ...*
sonnimdŭrŭn ...ŭl / rŭl haeya
hamnida 손님들은 ...을 / 를 해야
합니다
required *(necessary)* p'iryohan 필요한
requirement *(need)* yogu 요구;
(condition) chokkŏn 조건
reroute *airplane etc* k'osŭrŭl pyŏn-
gyŏnghada 코스를 변경하다
rerun *tape* chaesangyŏnghada
재상영하다
rescue 1 *n* kujo 구조; *come to s.o.'s*
~ nugurŭl kujoharŏ oda 누구를
구조하러 오다 **2** *v/t* kujohada
구조하다
rescue party kujodae 구조대
research *n* yŏn-gu 연구
♦ **research into** ...e taehan yŏn-gu
...에 대한 연구
research and development yŏn-gu
kaebal 연구 개발
research assistant yŏn-gu pojowŏn
연구 보조원
researcher yŏn-guwŏn 연구원
research project yŏn-gu kyehoek
연구 계획
resemblance yusa 유사
resemble tamtta 닮다
resent ...e pun-gaehada ...에
분개하다
resentful pun-gaehan 분개한
resentment pun-gae 분개
reservation *(of room, table)* yeyak
예약; *(mental)* ŭigushim 의구심;
(special area) t'ŭkppyŏl poryuji 특별
보류지; *I have a ~* nanŭn yeyagŭl
haet-tta 나는 예약을 했다
reserve 1 *n* *(store)* pich'uk 비축;
(aloofness) naengdam 냉담; SP hubo
sŏnsu 후보 선수; *~s* FIN poyugŭm
보유금; *keep sth in ~* muŏsŭl
pich'uk'ada 무엇을 비축하다 **2** *v/t*
seat, table yeyak'ada 예약하다;
judgment poryuhada 보류하다
reserved *person, manner* malssuga
chŏgŭn 말수가 적은; *table, seat*
yeyaktoen 예약된
reservoir *(for water)* chŏsuji 저수지
reside kŏjuhada 거주하다

residence (*house etc*) kŏjuji 거주지; (*stay*) ch'eryu 체류
residence permit kŏju hŏga 거주 허가
resident 1 *n* kŏjuja 거주자 2 *adj manager etc* sangjuhanŭn 상주하는
residential *district* chugŏŭi 주거의
residue chanyŏmul 잔여물
resign 1 *v/t position* saimhada 사임하다; ~ **oneself to** ch'enyŏmhago ...hagiro hada 체념하고 ...하기로 하다 2 *v/i* (*from job*) sagjik'ada 사직하다
resignation (*from job*) sajik 사직; (*mental*) tannyŏm 단념
resigned ch'enyŏmhanŭn 체념하는; *we have become* ~ *to the fact that* ... urinŭn ...ranŭn sashire tannyŏmhage toeŏtta 우리는 ...라는 사실에 단념하게 되었다
resilient *personality* k'waehwarhan 쾌활한; *material* naegussŏng-i kanghan 내구성이 강한
resin suji 수지
resist 1 *v/t enemy, s.o.'s advances* chŏhanghada 저항하다; *new measures* pandaehada 반대하다; *temptation* kyŏndida 견디다 2 *v/i* pŏt'ida 버티다
resistance chŏhang 저항
resistant *material* chŏhangnyŏgi innŭn 저항력이 있는
resolute ŭijiga kudŭn 의지가 굳은
resolution (*decision*) kyŏlsshim 결심; (*determination*) kyŏryŏnham 결연함
resolution (*of problem*) haegyŏl 해결; (*of image*) sŏnmyŏngdo 선명도
resolve *problem, mystery* haegyŏrhada 해결하다; ~ *to do sth* muŏsŭl hagi wihae kyŏlsshimhada 무엇을 하기 위해 결심하다
resort 1 *n* (*place*) hyuyangji 휴양지; *as a last* ~ majimak sudanŭro 마지막 수단으로
resounding *success* wanjŏnhan 완전한
resource chawŏn 자원
resourceful kiryagi p'ungbuhan 기략이 풍부한
respect 1 *n* chon-gyŏng 존경; (*consideration*) paeryŏ 배려; *show* ~

to kyŏngŭirŭl p'yohada 경의를 표하다; *with* ~ *to* ...e taehayŏ ...에 대하여; *in this / that* ~ irŏhan / chŏrŏhan kwantchŏmesŏ 이러한 / 저러한 관점에서; *in many* ~s yŏrŏ myŏnesŏ 여러 면에서; *pay one's last* ~ *s to s.o.* nuguege ch'oehuŭi kyŏng-ŭirŭl p'yohada 누구에게 최후의 경의를 표하다 2 *v/t person, opinion* chon-gyŏnghada 존경하다; *law, privacy* chonjunghada 존중하다
respectable hullyunghan 훌륭한
respectful chon-gyŏnghanŭn 존경하는
respectfully chŏngjunghage 정중하게
respective kak-kkagŭi 각각의
respectively kak-kki 각기
respiration hohŭp 호흡
respirator MED in-gong hohŭpkki 인공 호흡기
respite hyushik 휴식; *without* ~ shwim ŏpsshi 쉼 없이
respond (*answer*) taedap'ada 대답하다; (*react*) panŭnghada 반응하다
response (*answer*) taedap 대답; (*reaction*) panŭng 반응
responsibility ch'aegim 책임; (*duty*) ŭimu 의무; *accept* ~ *for* ch'aegimŭl chida 책임을 지다
responsible chaegimi innŭn 책임이 있는; (*trustworthy*) shilloehal su innŭn 신뢰할 수 있는; *job* ch'aegimi mugŏun 책임이 무거운
responsive *audience, brakes* panŭnghanŭn 반응하는
rest[1] 1 *n* hyushik 휴식 2 *v/i* shwida 쉬다; ~ *on* (*be based on*) ...e kich'ohada ...에 기초하다; (*lean against*) ...e kidaeda ...에 기대다; *it all* ~*s with him* modŭn kŏn kŭ saram sone tallyŏ issŭmnida 모든 건 그 사람 손에 달려 있습니다 3 *v/t* (*lean, balance etc*) kidaeda 기대다
rest[2]: *the* ~ namŏji 나머지
restaurant shikttang 식당
restaurant car RAIL shikttangch'a 식당차
rest cure anjŏng yoppŏp 안정 요법
rest home yoyangso 요양소
restless kamanit-tchi mot'anŭn

가만있지 못하는; **have a ~ night**
cham mot irunŭn pamŭl ponaeda 잠
못 이루는 밤을 보내다
restoration pok-kku 복구
restore *building etc* pok-kkuhada
복구하다
restrain *dog, troops* cheap'ada
제압하다; *emotions* ŏngnurŭda
억누르다; **~ oneself** chajehada
자제하다
restraint (*moderation*) ŏktche 억제
restrict chehanhada 제한하다; **I'll ~
myself to ...** chŏnŭn ...man
hagessŭmnida 저는 ...만 하겠습니다
restricted *view* hanjŏngdoen 한정된
restricted area MIL chehan-guyŏk
제한구역
restriction chehan 제한
rest room hwajangshil 화장실
result *n* kyŏlgwa 결과; **as a ~ of this**
igŏssŭi kyŏlgwaro 이것의 결과로
♦ **result from** ...e kiinhada ...에
기인하다
♦ **result in** ...(ŭ)ro kkŭnnada
...(으)로 끝나다
resume *v/t* chaegaehada 재개하다
résumé iryŏkssŏ 이력서
resurface 1 *v/t roads*
chaep'ojanghada 재포장하다 **2** *v/i*
(*reappear*) chaehyŏndoeda 재현되다
resurrection REL puhwal 부활
resuscitate sosaengshik'ida
소생시키다
retail 1 *adv* somaero 소매로 **2** *v/i:* **~ at**
...e somaero p'alda ...에 소매로
팔다
retailer somae sangin 소매 상인
retail price somae kagyŏk 소매 가격
retain kyesok yujihada 계속 유지하다;
lawyer koyonghada 고용하다
retainer FIN suimnyo 수임료
retaliate pokssuhada 복수하다
retaliation pokssu 복수
retarded (*mentally*) chŏnŭnghan
저능한
retire *v/i* (*from work*) ŭnt'oehada
은퇴하다
retired ŭnt'oehan 은퇴한
retirement ŭnt'oe 은퇴
retirement age chŏngnyŏn 정년
retiring naehyangjŏgin 내향적인

retort 1 *n* panbak 반박 **2** *v/i*
panbak'ada 반박하다
retrace *footsteps* toedoragada
되돌아가다
retract *v/t claws* omŭrida 오므리다;
undercarriage kkŭrŏdanggida
끌어당기다; *statement* ch'ŏlhoehada
철회하다
retreat 1 *v/i* MIL hut'oehada 후퇴하다;
(*in discussion etc*) mullŏsŏda
물러서다 **2** *n* MIL hut'oe 후퇴; (*place*)
p'inanch'ŏ 피난처
retrieve toech'at-tta 되찾다
retriever (*dog*) lit'ŭribŏ 리트리버
retroactive *law etc* sogŭp'anŭn
소급하는
retrograde *move* t'oebohada
퇴보하다; *decision* chŏrhoehada
철회하다
retrospect: in ~ hoegohae pomyŏn
회고해 보면
retrospective (*of movies*) hoegojŏn
회고전
return 1 *n* (*coming back, going back*)
kwihwan 귀환; (*giving back*)
panhwan 반환; COMPUT shirhaeng
실행; (*in tennis*) pan-gyŏk 반격; **by ~
(of post)** pannŭn chŭksshiro 받는
즉시로; **~s** (*profit*) iik 이익; **many
happy ~s (of the day)** saeng-irŭl
ch'uk'ahamnida 생일을 축하합니다
2 *v/t* (*give back*) tollyŏjuda 돌려주다;
(*put back*) tollyŏnot'a 돌려놓다;
favor, invitation podap'ada 보답하다
3 *v/i* (*go back*) toedoragada
되돌아가다; (*come back*) toedoraoda
되돌아오다; (*of good times, doubts
etc*) chaehyŏnhada 재현하다
return flight wangbok pihaenggi 왕복
비행기
return journey wangbok yŏhaeng
왕복 여행
reunification t'ong-il 통일
reunion chaehoe 재회
reunite *v/t country* chaet'onghap'ada
재통합하다; *old friends* chaehoehada
재회하다
reusable chaesayong-i kanŭnghan
재사용이 가능한
reuse chaesayonghada 재사용하다
rev *n* hoejŏn 회전; **~s per minute**

pun tang hoejŏn 분 당 회전
♦ **rev up** *v/t engine* sokttorŭl pparŭge hada 속도를 빠르게 하다

revaluation p'yŏngkkajŏlssang 평가절상

reveal (*make visible*) tŭrŏnaeda 드러내다; (*make known*) palk'ida 밝히다

revealing *remark* palk'yŏjunŭn 밝혀주는; *dress* noch'uldoen 노출된

revelation p'ongno 폭로

revenge *n* pobok 보복; *take one's ~* pobok'ada 보복하다

revenue seip 세입

reverberate (*of sound*) ullyŏ p'ŏjida 울려 퍼지다

Reverend sŏngjiktcha 성직자

reverent kyŏngŏnhan 경건한

reverse 1 *adj sequence* kŏkkurodoen 거꾸로된 **2** *n* (*opposite*) pandae 반대; (*back*) twittchang 뒷장; (*of envelope*) twinmyŏn 뒷면; MOT hujin 후진 **3** *v/t sequence* kŏkkuro hada 거꾸로 하다; *vehicle* hujinhada 후진하다 **4** *v/i* MOT hujinhada 후진하다

review 1 *n* (*of book, movie*) pip'yŏng 비평; (*of troops*) yŏlbyŏngshik 열병식; (*of situation etc*) chaegŏmt'o 재검토 **2** *v/t book, movie* nonp'yŏnghada 논평하다; *troops* sayŏrhada 사열하다; *situation etc* chaegŏmt'ohada 재검토하다; EDU pokssŭp'ada 복습하다

reviewer (*of movie etc*) p'yŏngnon-ga 평론가

revise *v/t opinion, text* sujŏnghada 수정하다

revision (*of opinion, text*) sujŏng 수정

revisionism POL sujŏngjuŭi 수정주의

revival (*of custom, old style etc*) puhwal 부활; (*of patient*) sosaeng 소생

revive 1 *v/t custom, old style etc* puhwarhada 부활하다; *patient* sosaengshik'ida 소생시키다 **2** *v/i* (*of business etc*) hoeboktoeda 회복되다

revoke *law, license* muhyoro hada 무효로 하다

revolt 1 *n* pallan 반란 **2** *v/i* pallanhada 반란하다

revolting (*disgusting*) hyŏmogamŭl nŭkkige hanŭn 혐오감을 느끼게 하는

revolution POL hyŏngmyŏng 혁명; (*turn*) hoejŏn 회전

revolutionary 1 *n* POL hyŏngmyŏngga 혁명가 **2** *adj spirit, forces* hyŏngmyŏng-ŭi 혁명의; *ideas* hyŏngmyŏngjŏgin 혁명적인

revolutionize hyŏngmyŏng-ŭl irŭk'ida 혁명을 일으키다

revolve *v/i* hoejŏnhada 회전하다

revolver kwŏnch'ong 권총

revolving door hoejŏnmun 회전문

revue THEA shisap'ungjagŭk 시사풍자극

revulsion kyŏkppyŏn 격변

reward 1 *n* posang 보상; (*financial*) posu 보수 **2** *v/t* (*financially*) posurŭl chuda 보수를 주다

rewarding porami innŭn 보람이 있는

rewind *v/t film, tape* tashi kamtta 다시 감다

rewrite *v/t* tashi ssŭda 다시 쓰다

rhetoric susa 수사

rheumatism lyumat'ijŭm 류마티즘

rhinoceros k'otppulsso 코뿔소

rhubarb changgunp'ul 장군풀

rhyme 1 *n* un 운 **2** *v/i* chakssihada 작시하다; *~ with* …wa/kwa uni matta …와/과 운이 맞다

rhythm lidŭm 리듬

rib *n* kalbippyŏ 갈비뼈

ribbon libon 리본

rice ssal 쌀; (*cooked*) pap 밥

rice bowl pap kŭrŭt 밥 그릇; **rice cake** ttŏk 떡; **rice cooker** chŏn-gi papssot 전기 밥솥; **ricefield, rice paddy** non 논; **rice planting** monaegi 모내기; **rice wine** makkŏlli 막걸리

rich 1 *adj* puyuhan 부유한; *food* mashi chinhan 맛이 진한 **2** *n: the ~* puja 부자

rid: *get ~ of* ŏpssaeda 없애다

riddle susukkekki 수수께끼

ride 1 *n* t'am 탐; (*journey*) yŏhaeng 여행; *do you want a ~ into town?* shinae t'aewŏ chulkkayo? 시내에 태워 줄까요? **2** *v/t horse, bike* t'ada 타다 **3** *v/i* (*on horse*) sŭngmahada

승마하다; (*on bike, in vehicle*) t'ada 타다

rider (*on horse*) kisu 기수; (*on bike*) chajŏn-gŏ t'anŭn saram 자전거 타는 사람

ridge (*raised strip*) ollagan t'ŏk 올라간 턱; (*of mountain*) santtŭngsŏng-i 산둥성이; (*of roof*) chibung kkokttaegi 지붕 꼭대기

ridicule 1 *n* choso 조소 **2** *v/t* choronghada 조롱하다

ridiculous t'ŏmuniŏmnŭn 터무니없는

ridiculously t'ŏmuniŏpsshi 터무니없이

riding (*on horseback*) sŭngma 승마

rifle *n* soch'ong 소총

rift (*in earth*) tanch'ŭng 단층; (*in party etc*) kyunyŏl 균열

rig 1 *n* (*oil ~*) kulch'ak changch'i 굴착 장치; (*truck*) t'ŭrŏk 트럭 **2** *v/t elections* chojak'ada 조작하다

right 1 *adj* (*correct*) mannŭn 맞는; (*proper, just*) olbarŭn 올바른; (*suitable*) chŏktchŏrhan 적절한; (*not left*) orŭntchogŭi 오른쪽의; **be ~** (*of answer, person*) mat-tta 맞다; (*of clock*) chŏnghwak'ada 정확하다; **that's ~!** paro kŭgŏya! 바로 그거야!; **put things ~** irŭl haegyŏrhada 일을 해결하다; **that's not ~** (*not fair*) kŭgŏsŭn andoel irida 그것은 안될 일이다; → **alright 2** *adv* (*directly*) paro 바로; (*correctly*) olbarŭge 올바르게; (*completely*) wanjŏnhi 완전히; (*not left*) orŭntchogŭro 오른쪽으로; **~ now** (*immediately*) tangjang 당장; (*at the moment*) chigŭm 지금 **3** *n* (*civil, legal etc*) kwŏlli 권리; (*not left*) orŭntchok 오른쪽; POL uik 우익; **on the ~** orŭntchoge(sŏ) 오른쪽에(서); POL uige(sŏ) 우익에(서); **turn to the ~, take a ~** orŭntchogŭro toshio 오른쪽으로 도시오; **be in the ~** torie mat-tta 도리에 맞다; **know ~ from wrong** olk'o kŭrŭmŭl kubyŏrhada 옳고 그름을 구별하다

right-angle chik-kkak 직각; **at ~s to** ...wa/kwa chik-kkagŭro ...와/과 직각으로

righteous army ŭibyŏng 의병

rightful *heir, owner etc* happ-pŏptchŏgin 합법적인

right-hand *adj* orŭntchogŭi 오른쪽의; **on the ~ side** orŭnp'yŏne 오른편에; **right-hand drive** MOT uch'ŭk haendŭl unjŏn 우측 핸들 운전; **right-handed** orŭnsonjabiŭi 오른손잡이의; **right-hand man** shimbok 심복; **right of way** (*in traffic*) t'onghaeng usŏnkkwŏn 통행 우선권; (*across land*) t'onghaengkkwŏn 통행권; **right wing** *n* POL uik 우익; SP uch'ŭk konggyŏkssu 우측 공격수; **right-wing** *adj* POL uigŭi 우익의; **right-winger** POL uik chijija 우익 지지자; **right-wing extremism** POL kŭgup'a 극우파

rigid *material* tandanhan 단단한; *principles* ŏmkkyŏk'an 엄격한; *attitude* wangohan 완고한

rigor (*of discipline*) ŏmkkyŏk 엄격; **the ~s of winter** kyŏurŭi hokttok'am 겨울의 혹독함

rigorous *discipline* ŏmkkyŏk'an 엄격한; *tests, analysis* myŏnmirhan 면밀한

rim (*of wheel*) t'eduri 테두리; (*of cup*) kajangjari 가장자리; (*of eyeglasses*) t'e 테

ring[1] (*circle*) wŏnhyŏng 원형; (*on finger*) panji 반지; (*in boxing, at circus*) ling 링

ring[2] **1** *n* (*of bell*) ullim 울림; (*of voice*) ullinŭn sori 울리는 소리 **2** *v/t bell* ullida 울리다 **3** *v/i* (*of bell*) ullida 울리다; **please ~ for attention** chong-ŭl ch'yŏsŏ pullojuseyo 종을 쳐서 불러주세요

ringleader chumoja 주모자

ring-pull chabadangginŭn kori 잡아당기는 고리

rink chang 장

rinse 1 *n* (*for hair color*) linssŭ 린스 **2** *v/t clothes, dishes* hengguda 헹구다; *hair* linssŭhada 린스하다

riot 1 *n* p'oktong 폭동 **2** *v/i* p'oktongŭl irŭk'ida 폭동을 일으키다

rioter p'oktongja 폭동자

riot police kyŏngch'al kidongdae 경찰 기동대

rip 1 *n* (*in cloth etc*) tchijŏjin kot 찢어진 곳 **2** *v/t cloth etc* tchit-tta 찢다; ~ *sth open* muŏsŭl tchijŏ yŏlda 무엇을 찢어 열다

♦ **rip off** F (*cheat*) sogida 속이다; *customers* p'ongnirŭl ch'wihada 폭리를 취하다

ripe *fruit* igŭn 익은

ripen *v/i* (*of fruit*) iktta 익다

ripeness (*of fruit*) sukssŏng 숙성

rip-off *n* F sagi 사기

ripple *n* (*on water*) mulkkyŏl 물결

rise 1 *v/i* (*from chair etc*) irŏnada 일어나다; (*of sun*) ttŏorŭda 떠오르다; (*of rocket*) sosaorŭda 솟아오르다; (*of price, temperature, water level*) orŭda 오르다 **2** *n* (*in price, salary*) insang 인상; (*in water level, temperature*) sangsŭng 상승

risk 1 *n* wihŏm 위험; *take a* ~ wihŏmŭl murŭpssŭda 위험을 무릅쓰다 **2** *v/t* wihŏme ppattŭrida 위험에 빠뜨리다; *let's* ~ *it* kamhaenghae popsshida 감행해 봅시다

risky wihŏmhan 위험한

ritual 1 *n* ŭishik 의식 **2** *adj* ŭishigŭi 의식의

rival 1 *n* kyŏngjaengja 경쟁자 **2** *v/t* …wa/kwa kyŏngjaenghada …와/과 경쟁하다; *I can't* ~ *that* i isang tŏ chal hal sunŭn ŏpssŏyo 이 이상 더 잘 할 수는 없어요

rivalry kyŏngjaeng 경쟁

river kang 강

riverbed kangppadak 강바닥

riverside kangbyŏn 강변

rivet 1 *n* taemot 대못 **2** *v/t* taemosŭro paktta 대못으로 박다

road kil 길; *it's just down the* ~ paro chŏtchoge issŏyo 바로 저쪽에 있어요

roadblock parik'eidŭ 바리케이드; **road hog** nanp'ok unjŏnja 난폭 운전자; **road holding** (*of vehicle*) chuhaeng anjŏngssŏng 주행 안정성; **road map** toro chido 도로 지도; **roadside**: *at the* ~ kilkkae 길가에; **roadsign** toro p'yojip'an 도로 표지판; **roadway** toro 도로; **road works** toro kongsa 도로 공사; **roadworthy** torochuhaeng-e

almajŭn 도로 주행에 알맞은

roam toradtanida 돌아다니다

roar 1 *n* (*of traffic, engine*) urŭrŭnggŏrinŭn sori 우르릉거리는 소리; (*of lion*) p'ohyo 포효; (*of person*) koham 고함 **2** *v/i* (*of engine*) urŭrŭnggŏrida 우르릉거리다; (*of lion*) p'ohyohada 포효하다; (*of person*) kohamch'ida 고함치다; ~ *with laughter* k'ŭge ut-tta 크게 웃다

roast 1 *n* (*of beef etc*) kuun ŭmshik 구운 음식 **2** *v/t* kuptta 굽다 **3** *v/i* (*of food*) kuwŏjida 구워지다; *we're* ~*ing* F tchidŭshi tŏptta 찌듯이 덥다

roast beef kuun soegogi 구운 쇠고기

roast pork kuun twaejigogi 구운 돼지고기

rob *person, bank* kangt'arhada 강탈하다; *I've been* ~*bed* kangdo tanghaessŏyo 강도 당했어요

robber kangdo 강도

robbery kangdojil 강도질

robe (*of judge*) pŏp-ppok 법복; (*of priest*) yebok 예복; (*bath~*) mogyok kkaun 목욕 가운

robin kaettong chippagwi sae 개똥 지빠귀 새

robot lobot 로봇

robust t'ŭnt'ŭnhan 튼튼한

rock 1 *n* tol 돌; MUS lak 락; *on the* ~*s drink* ŏrŭmŭl kyŏt-ttŭryŏ 얼음을 곁들여; *marriage* p'at'ane irŭrŏ 파탄에 이르러 **2** *v/t baby, cradle* choyonghi hŭndŭlda 조용히 흔들다; (*surprise*) nollage hada 놀라게 하다 **3** *v/i* (*on chair*) hŭndŭlgŏrida 흔들거리다; (*of boat*) chindonghada 진동하다

rock bottom: *reach* ~ mitppadagŭro ttŏrŏjida 밑바닥으로 떨어지다

rock-bottom *adj prices* ch'oejŏŭi 최저의

rocket 1 *n* (*space* ~) lok'et 로켓; (*firework*) ssoaollinŭn pulkkot 쏘아올리는 불꽃 **2** *v/i* (*of prices etc*) ch'isot-tta 치솟다

rocking chair hŭndŭl ŭija 흔들 의자

rock'n' roll lakk'ŭllol 락큰롤

rock star laksŭt'a 락스타

rocky *beach, path* pawiga manŭn

바위가 많은
rod makttae 막대; (*for fishing*)
nakkshit-ttae 낚싯대
rodent sŏlch'iryu 설치류
rogue kŏndal 건달
ROK (= *Republic of Korea*)
Taehanmin-guk 대한민국
role yŏk'al 역할
role model ponbogiga toenŭn saram
본보기가 되는 사람
roll 1 *n* (*bread*) lolppang 롤빵; (*of film*) lol 롤; (*of thunder*) ullim 울림; (*list, register*) mongnok 목록 **2** *v/i* (*of ball etc*) kuruda 구르다; (*of boat*) hŭndŭlgŏrida 흔들거리다 **3** *v/t*: **~ sth into a ball** muŏsŭl kongch'ŏrŏm kullida 무엇을 공처럼 굴리다
♦ **roll over 1** *v/i* twinggulda 뒹굴다 **2** *v/t person, object* kullyŏ nŏmŏttŭrida 굴려 넘어뜨리다; (*renew*) kiganŭl yŏnjangshik'ida 기간을 연장시키다; (*extend*) nŭllida 늘리다
♦ **roll up 1** *v/t sleeves* kŏdŏollida 걷어올리다 **2** *v/i* F (*arrive*) toch'ak'ada 도착하다
roll call chŏmho 점호
roller (*for hair*) mŏri manŭn lol 머리 마는 롤
roller blade *n* lollŏ pŭlleidŭ 롤러 블레이드; **roller coaster** lollŏ k'osŭt'ŏ 롤러 코스터; **roller skate** *n* lollŏ sŭk'eit'ŭ 롤러 스케이트
rolling pin panjugŭl minŭn pangmangi 반죽을 미는 방망이
ROM (= *read only memory*) lom 롬
Roman Catholic 1 *n* Loma K'at'ollik 로마 카톨릭 **2** *adj* Loma K'at'ollik-kkyoŭi 로마 카톨릭교의
Roman Catholicism Ch'ŏnjugyo 천주교
romance (*affair*) lomaensŭ 로맨스; (*novel, movie*) yŏnae 연애
romantic lomaent'ik'an 로맨틱한
roof chibung 지붕
roof rack MOT lup'ŭraek 루프랙
room pang 방; (*space*) changso 장소; **there's no ~ for ...** ...ŭl/rŭl wihan changsoga ŏptta ...을/를 위한 장소가 없다
room clerk kaekssil tamdangja 객실

담당자; **roommate** lum meit'ŭ 룸 메이트; **room service** lum ssŏbissŭ 룸 서비스
roomy *house etc* nŏlbŭn 넓은; *clothes* hŏllŏnghan 헐렁한
root ppuri 뿌리; (*of word*) kŭnwŏn 근원; **~s** (*of person*) kohyang 고향
♦ **root out** (*get rid of*) chegŏhada 제거하다; (*find*) ch'at-tta 찾다
root directory COMPUT ŭddŭm tirekt'ori 으뜸 디렉토리
rope pattchul 밧줄
♦ **rope off** churŭl ch'ida 줄을 치다
rose BOT changmi 장미
Rose of Sharon Mugunghwa 무궁화
rostrum yŏndan 연단
rosy *cheeks* hongjorŭl ttin 홍조를 띤; *future* yumanghan 유망한
rot 1 *n* (*in wood, teeth*) ssŏgŭm 썩음 **2** *v/i* (*of food, wood, teeth*) ssŏktta 썩다
rota tangbŏn 당번
rotate *v/i* hoejŏnhada 회전하다
rotation (*around the sun etc*) hoejŏn 회전; **do sth in ~** muŏsŭl kyodaero hada 무엇을 교대로 하다
rotten *food, wood etc* ssŏgŭn 썩은; *trick, thing to do* pup'aehan 부패한; *weather, luck* pulk'waehan 불쾌한
rough 1 *adj surface* ult'ungbult'unghan 울퉁불퉁한; *hands, skin, voice* kŏch'in 거친; (*violent*) nanp'ok'an 난폭한; *crossing, seas* sananun 사나운; (*approximate*) taegang-ŭi 대강의; **~ draft** ch'ogo 초고 **2** *adv*: *sleep* **~** nosuk'ada 노숙하다 **3** *n* (*in golf*) lŏp'ŭ 러프 **4** *v/t*: **~ it** pulp'yŏnhan saenghwarŭl hada 불편한 생활을 하다
roughage (*in food*) sŏmnyujil 섬유질
roughly (*approximately*) taeryak 대략
roulette lullet 룰렛
round 1 *adj* tunggŭn 둥근; *in ~ fig-ures* kkŭtch'ŭl charŭn sutcharo 끝을 자른 숫자로 **2** *n* (*of mailman*) paedal kuyŏk 배달 구역; (*of toast*) chok쪽; (*of drinks*) ch'a차; (*of competition*) hoe 회; (*in boxing match*) laundŭ 라운드 **3** *v/t the corner* tolda 돌다 **4** *adv, prep* → **around**

♦**round off** *edges* tunggŭlge hada 둥글게 하다; *meeting etc* mamurihada 마무리하다

♦**round up** *figure* kkŭtch'ŭl challa ollida 끝을 잘라 올리다; *suspects, criminals* kŏmgŏhada 검거하다

roundabout *adj route* uhoeŭi 우회의; *way of saying sth* kanjŏptchŏgin 간접적인; **round trip** wangbok yŏhaeng 왕복 여행; **round trip ticket** wangbok yŏhaengp'yo 왕복 여행표; **round-up** (*of cattle*) mori 몰이; (*of suspects, criminals*) kŏmgŏ 검거; (*of news*) yoyak 요약

rouse (*from sleep*) kkaeda 깨다; *interest, emotions* chagŭk'ada 자극하다

rousing *speech etc* kŭktchŏgin 극적인

route kil 길

routine 1 *adj* ilsangjŏgin 일상적인 2 *n* ilgwa 일과; *as a matter of ~* ilsangjŏgŭro 일상적으로

row (*line*) yŏl 열; *5 days in a ~* tatssae yŏniŏsŏ 닷새 연이어서

row[2] 1 *v/t boat* no chŏt-tta 노 젓다 2 *v/i* chŏŏgada 저어가다

rowboat chŏnnŭn pae 젓는 배

rowdy nanp'ok'an 난폭한

row house yollip chut'aek 연립 주택

royal *adj* wang-ŭi 왕의

royalty (*royal persons*) wangjok 왕족; (*on book, recording*) loyŏlt'i 로열티

rub *v/t* munjirŭda 문지르다; (*to polish*) yun naeda 윤 내다

♦**rub down** (*clean*) ch'ŏngsohada 청소하다

♦**rub off** 1 *v/t dirt* munjillŏ ŏpssaeda 문질러 없애다; *paint etc* pŏtkkida 벗기다 2 *v/i: it rubs off on you* tangshinege yŏnghyang-ŭl kkich'imnida 당신에게 영향을 끼칩니다

♦**rub out** (*with eraser*) chiuda 지우다

rubber 1 *n* (*material*) komu 고무 2 *adj* komuŭi 고무의

rubble chapssŏk 잡석

ruby (*jewel*) lubi 루비

rucksack paenang 배낭

rudder paeŭi k'i 배의 키

ruddy *complexion* pulgŭn 붉은

rude muryehan 무례한; *it is ~ to ...*

...hanŭn kŏsŭn muryehada ...하는 것은 무례하다; *I didn't mean to be ~* muryehage haryŏgo haet-ttŏn ke aniyeyo 무례하게 하려고 했던 게 아니예요

rudeness murye 무례

rudimentary kich'oŭi 기초의

rudiments kich'o 기초

ruffian purhandang 불한당

ruffle 1 *n* (*on dress*) ch'urŭm changshik 주름 장식 2 *v/t hair* hŏngk'ŭrŏjige hada 헝클어지게 하다; *person* sŏngnage hada sŏng-i nada; *get ~d* sŏng-i nada 성이 나다

rug kkalgae 깔개; (*blanket*) tamnyo 담요

rugged *scenery, cliffs* pawi t'usŏng-iŭi 바위 투성이의; *face* kŏch'in 거친; *resistance* wan-ganghan 완강한

ruin 1 *n* p'agoe 파괴; *~s* yujŏk 유적; *in ~s* (*of city, building*) p'agoedoen 파괴된; (*of plans, marriage*) p'amyŏrhan 파멸한 2 *v/t party, birthday, vacation* mangch'ida 망치다; *plans* manggattŭrida 망가뜨리다; *reputation* p'agoehada 파괴하다; *be ~ed* (*financially*) p'asanhada 파산하다

rule 1 *n* (*of club, game*) kyuch'ik 규칙; (*of monarch*) chibae 지배; (*for measuring*) cha 자; *as a ~* taech'ero 대체로 2 *v/t country* tasŭrida 다스리다; *the judge ~d that ...* p'ansanŭn ...rago p'an-gyŏrhaet-tta 판사는 ...라고 판결했다 3 *v/i* (*of monarch*) t'ongch'ihada 통치하다

♦**rule out** choeoehada 제외하다

ruler (*for measuring*) cha 자; (*of state*) t'ongch'ija 통치자

ruling 1 *n* p'an-gyŏl 판결 2 *adj party* chibaehanŭn 지배하는

rum (*drink*) lŏm 럼

rumble *v/i* (*of stomach*) kkorŭrŭkkŏrida 꼬르륵거리다; (*of train in tunnel*) yoranhan sorirŭl naeda 요란한 소리를 내다

♦**rummage around** twijyŏ ch'ajanaeda 뒤져 찾아내다

rummage sale chapttongsani p'anmae 잡동사니 판매

rumor 1 *n* somun 소문 2 *v/t: it is ~ed*

that ... ...rago somuni nada ...라고 소문이 나다

rump (of animal) ŏngdŏngi 엉덩이

rumple clothes, paper kugida 구기다

rumpsteak lŏmp'ŭ sŭt'eik'ŭ 럼프 스테이크

run 1 n (on foot) talligi 달리기; (in pantyhose) orŭi p'ullim 올의 풀림; (of play) yŏnsok kong-yŏn 연속 공연; *go for a* ~ choginghada 조깅하다; *make a* ~ *for it* tomangch'ida 도망치다; *a criminal on the* ~ tomang chungin pŏmjoeja 도망 중인 범죄자; *in the short / long* ~ tchalkke / kilge pomyŏn 짧게 / 길게 보면; *a* ~ *on the dollar* tallŏ kangse 달러 강세 **2** v/i (of person, animal) tallida 달리다; (of river) hŭrŭda 흐르다; (of trains etc) unhaengdoeda 운행되다; (of paint, make-up) pŏnjida 번지다; (of nose, eyes) hŭrŭda 흐르다; (of faucet) hŭrŭda 흐르다; (of play) yŏnsok kong-yŏndoeda 연속 공연되다; (of engine, machine) umjigida 움직이다; (of software) shirhaengtoeji ant'a 실행되지 않다; (in election) ch'ulmahada 출마하다; ~ *for President* taet'ongnyŏnge ch'ulmahada 대통령에 출마하다 **3** v/t race kyŏngjuhada 경주하다; *3 miles etc* tallida 달리다; business, hotel, project etc unyŏnghada 운영하다; software shirhaenghada 실행하다; *he ran his eye down the page* kŭnŭn kŭ p'eijirŭl taegang hult'ŏ poat-tta 그는 그 페이지를 대강 훑어 보았다

♦ **run across** (meet) uyŏnhi mannada 우연히 만나다; (find) ch'at-tta 찾다

♦ **run away** taranada 달아나다

♦ **run down 1** v/t (knock down) tŭribat-tta 들이받다; (criticize) hŏlttŭt-tta 헐뜯다; stocks kach'irŭl ttŏrŏttŭrida 가치를 떨어뜨리다 **2** v/i (of battery) taltta 닳다

♦ **run into** (meet) uyŏnhi mannada 우연히 만나다; difficulties ch'ŏhada 처하다; car tŭribat-tta 들이받다

♦ **run off 1** v/i tomangch'ida 도망치다 **2** v/t (print) inswaehada 인쇄하다

♦ **run out** (of contract) man-giga

toeda 만기가 되다; (of time) ta hada 다 하다; (of supplies) ttŏrŏjida 떨어지다

♦ **run out of** time, patience ta ssŏbŏrida 다 써버리다; supplies ttŏrŏjida 떨어지다; *I ran out of gas* kassŭga ttŏrŏjyŏssŏyo 가스가 떨어졌어요

♦ **run over 1** v/t (knock down) tŭribat-tta 들이받다; *can we* ~ *the details again?* tashi hanbŏn chasehan sahange taehae arabolkkayo? 다시 한번 자세한 사항에 대해 알아볼까요? **2** v/i (of water etc) nŏmch'ida 넘치다

♦ **run through** (rehearse) shiyŏnhada 시연하다; (go over, check) kŏmt'ohada 검토하다

♦ **run up** v/t debts ssat'a 쌓다; clothes mandŭlda 만들다

run-down person chich'in 지친; part of town, building hŏrŭmhan 허름한

rung (of ladder) tan 단

runner (athlete) kyŏngjuja 경주자

runner-up ch'attchŏmja 차점자

running 1 n SP talligi 달리기; (of business) kyŏngyŏng kwalli 경영 관리 **2** adj: *for two days* ~ yŏniŏ it'ŭl ttong-ane 연이어 이틀 동안에

running water (supply) yusu 유수

runny liquid, nose hŭrŭnŭn 흐르는

run-up SP toumdatkki 도움닫기; *in the* ~ *to* paro chiktchŏne 바로 직전에

runway hwaltchuro 활주로

rupture 1 n (in pipe), MED p'ayŏl 파열; (in relations) tanjŏl 단절 **2** v/i (of pipe etc) p'ayŏldoeda 파열되다

rural shigorŭi 시골의

rush 1 n mopsshi sŏdurŭm 몹시 서두름; *do sth in a* ~ sodullŏ muŏsŭl hada 서둘러 무엇을 하다; *be in a* ~ mopsshi sŏdurŭda 몹시 서두르다; *what's the big* ~? wae kŭrŏk'e kŭp'aeyo? 왜 그렇게 급해요? **2** v/t person sŏdurŭge hada 서두르게 하다; meal sŏdullŏ mŏktta 서둘러 먹다; ~ *s.o. to the hospital* nugurŭl pyŏng-wŏnŭro kŭpssonghada 누구를 병원으로 급송하다 **3** v/i sŏdurŭda 서두르다

rush hour ch'ult'oegŭn shigan 출퇴근 시간

Russia Lŏshia 러시아

Russian 1 *adj* Lŏshiaŭi 러시아의 **2** *n* Lŏshiain 러시아인; (*language*) Lŏshiaŏ 러시아어

rust 1 *n* nok 녹 **2** *v/i* nokssŭlda 녹슬다

rustle *n* (*of silk, leaves*) pasŭrak-kkŏrinŭn sori 바스락거리는 소리
♦**rustle up** F *meal* chaeppalli mandŭlda 재빨리 만들다

rust-proof *adj* nogi sŭlji annŭn 녹이 슬지 않는

rust remover nok chegŏje 녹 제거제

rusty nogi sŭn 녹이 슨; *French, math etc* sŏt'un 서툰; *I'm a little ~* chŏnŭn yakkan sŏt'umnida 저는 약간 서툽니다

rut (*in road*) hom 홈; *be in a ~* p'ane pak'in saenghwarŭl hada 판에 박힌 생활을 하다

ruthless kach'ŏmnŭn 가차없는

ruthlessness kach'aŏpssŭm 가차없음

rye homil 호밀

rye bread homil ppang 호밀 빵

S

sabbatical n (of academic)
anshingnyŏn 안식년
sabotage 1 n kyehoektchŏgin p'agoe
계획적인 파괴 **2** v/t
kyehoektchŏguro p'agoehada
계획적으로 파괴하다
saccharin n sak'arin 사카린
sachet (of shampoo etc) pongji 봉지
sack 1 n (bag) p'odae 포대 **2** v/t F
haegohada 해고하다
sacred music chonggyojŏgin
종교적인; building, place
shinsŏnghan 신성한
sacrifice 1 n chemul 제물; (act)
hŭisaeng 희생; **make ~s** fig
hŭisaenghada 희생하다 **2** v/t pach'ida
바치다; one's freedom etc
hŭisaenghada 희생하다
sad sŭlp'ŭn 슬픈
saddle n anjang 안장
sadism sadijŭm 사디즘
sadist sadisŭt'ŭ 사디스트
sadistic sadisŭt'ŭjŏgin 사디스트 적인
sadly say etc sŭlp'ŭge 슬프게;
(regrettably) huhoesŭrŏpkkedo
후회스럽게도
sadness sŭlp'ŭm 슬픔
safe 1 adj anjŏnhan 안전한;
investment, prediction anshimhal su
innŭn 안심할 수 있는 **2** n kŭmgo
금고
safeguard 1 n pohoch'aek 보호책; **as
a ~ against** …e taehan
pohoch'aegŭro …에 대한 보호책으
로 **2** v/t pohohada 보호하다
safekeeping: give sth to s.o. for ~
anjŏnhage pogwanŭl wihae muŏsŭl
nuguege chuda 안전한 보관을 위해
무엇을 누구에게 주다
safely arrive musahi 무사히; complete
tests etc munjeŏpsshi 문제없이; drive
anjŏnhage 안전하게; assume chalmot
toel kŏktchŏng ŏpsshi 잘못 될 걱정
없이

safety anjŏn 안전; (of investment)
anjŏnssŏng 안전성; **be in ~**
musahada 무사하다
safety-conscious anjŏnŭl
saenggak'anŭn 안전을 생각하는;
safety first anjŏn usŏn 안전 우선;
safety pin anjŏnp'in 안전핀
sag 1 n (in ceiling etc) nŭrŏjim 늘어짐
2 v/i (of ceiling, rope) ch'uk ch'ŏjida
축 처지다; (of output, tempo) chulda
줄다
sage (herb) saelbiŏ 샐비어
sail 1 n tot 돛; (voyage) hanghae 항해;
(in small boat) paennori 뱃놀이 **2** v/t
yacht ttŭiuda 띄우다 **3** v/i
hanghaehada 항해하다; (depart)
ch'urhanghada 출항하다
sailboard 1 n windŭ sŏp'ing podŭ
윈드 서핑 보드 **2** v/i windŭ
sŏp'inghada 윈드 서핑하다
sailboarding windŭ sŏp'ing 윈드 서핑
sailboat yot'ŭ 요트
sailing SP yot'ŭ kyŏnggi 요트 경기
sailing ship pŏmsŏn 범선
sailor (in the navy) subyŏng 수병; SP
yot'ŭ kyŏnggija 요트 경기자; **be a
good/bad ~** paenmŏlmirŭl haji
ant'a/hada 뱃멀미를 하지 않다/하다
saint sŏng-in 성인
sake: for my/your ~ narŭl/nŏrŭl
wihaesŏ 나를/너를 위해서; **for the ~
of** …ŭl/rŭl wihayŏ …을/를 위하여
salad saellŏdŭ 샐러드
salad dressing sallŏdŭ tŭreshing
샐러드 드레싱
salary wŏlgŭp 월급
salary scale ponggŭp sujun 봉급
수준
sale p'anmae 판매; (reduced prices)
harin p'anmae 할인 판매; **for ~**
(sign) maemae 매매; **is this for ~?**
igŏ p'anŭn kŏmnikka? 이거 파는
겁니까?; **be on ~** p'anmae chung-ida
판매 중이다; (at reduced prices) seil

chung-ida 세일 중이다

sales (*department*) p'anmaebusŏ 판매부서

sales clerk (*in store*) p'anmae chŏmwŏn 판매 점원; **sales figures** p'anmae kŭmaek 판매 금액; **salesman** seiljŭmaen 세일즈맨; **sales manager** p'anmae pujang 판매 부장; **sales meeting** p'anmae hoeŭi 판매 회의

saliva ch'im 침

salmon yŏnŏ 연어

saloon (*bar*) sultchip 술집

salt sogŭm 소금

saltcellar sogŭm kŭrŭt 소금 그릇

salty tchan 짠

salutary *experience* yuik'an 유익한

salute 1 *n* MIL kyŏngnye 경례; *take the ~* kyŏngnyerŭl pat-tta 경례를 받다 2 *v/t v/i* MIL kyŏngnyehada 경례하다

salvage *v/t* (*from wreck*) kujohada 구조하다

salvation REL kuwŏn 구원; *fig* kujo 구조

Salvation Army Kusegun 구세군

same 1 *adj* kat'ŭn 같은 2 *pron*: *the ~* kat'ŭn kŏt 같은 것; *Happy New Year – the ~ to you* saehae pok mani padŭseyo - saehae pok mani padŭseyo 새해 복 많이 받으세요 - 새해 복 많이 받으세요; *he's not the ~ any more* kŭ saram, yejŏn katchi anayo 그 사람, 예전 같지 않아요; *all the ~* kŭraedo 그래도; *men are all the ~* namjadŭrŭn ta ttokkat'ayo 남자들은 다 똑같아요; *it's all the ~ to me* chŏn, sanggwanŏpssŏyo 전, 상관없어요 3 *adv*: *smell / sound the ~* naemsaega / soriga ttok-kkat'ayo 냄새가 / 소리가 똑같아요

sample *n* (*for inspection*) kyŏnbon 견본; (*of behavior, work*) p'yobon 표본

sanatorium yoyangso 요양소

sanction 1 *n* (*approval*) hŏga 허가; (*penalty*) chejae 제재; *economic ~s* kyŏngje chejae 경제 제재 2 *v/t* (*approve*) hŏgahada 허가하다

sanctity shinsŏng 신성

sanctuary REL sŏngjŏn 성전; (*for animals*) poho kuyŏk 보호 구역

sand 1 *n* morae 모래 2 *v/t* (*with sandpaper*) sap'oro munjirŭda 사포로 문지르다

sandal saendŭl 샌들

sandbag morae chumŏni 모래 주머니

sand dune morae ŏndŏk 모래 언덕

sander (*tool*) sap'oro tangnŭn changch'i 사포로 닦는 장치

sandpaper 1 *n* sap'o 사포 2 *v/t* sap'oro taktta 사포로 닦다; **sandpit** moraep'an 모래판; **sandstone** saam 사암

sandwich 1 *n* saendŭwich'i 샌드위치 2 *v/t*: *be ~ed between two ... tu ...* saie kkida 두 … 사이에 끼이다

sandy *beach, soil* moraeŭi 모래의; *hair* moraesaegŭi 모래색의

sane chejŏngshinŭi 제정신의

sanitarium yoyangso 요양소

sanitary *conditions* wisaeng-ŭi 위생의; *installations* wisaengjŏgin 위생적인

sanitary napkin saengnidae 생리대

sanitation (*sanitary installations*) wisaengsŏlbi 위생설비; (*removal of waste*) wisaengch'ŏri 위생처리

sanitation department ch'ŏngsokkwa 청소과

sanity chejŏngshin 제정신

Santa Claus Sant'ak'ŭllosŭ 산타클로스

sap 1 *n* (*in tree*) suaek 수액 2 *v/t s.o.'s energy* yak'washik'ida 약화시키다

sapphire *n* (*jewel*) sap'aiŏ 사파이어

sarcasm p'ungja 풍자

sarcastic pinjŏngdaenŭn 빈정대는

sardine chŏng-ŏri 정어리

sash (*on dress, uniform*) tti 띠; (*in window*) saesshi 새시

Satan Sat'an 사탄

satellite in-gong-wisŏng 인공위성

satellite dish in-gong-wisŏng chŏpsshi 인공위성 접시

satellite TV wisŏng t'ibŭi 위성 티브이

satin kongdan 공단

satire p'ungja 풍자

satirical p'ungjajŏgin 풍자적인

satirist p'ungjaga 풍자가

satisfaction manjok 만족; *get ~ out of sth* muŏsŏ manjogŭl nŭkkida

무엇에서 만족을 느끼다; *a feeling of* ~ manjok-kkam 만족감; *is that to your* ~? maŭme tŭshimnikka? 마음에 드십니까?

satisfactory manjok'an 만족한; (*just good enough*) kŭjŏ kŭrŏn 그저 그런; *this is not* ~ igŏsŭronŭn ch'ungbunch'i anayo 이것으로는 충분치 않아요

satisfy *customers* manjoksshik'ida 만족시키다; *hunger, sexual desires, conditions* ch'ungjokshik'ida 충족시키다; *I am satisfied* (*had enough to eat*) chŏnŭn ch'ungbunhi mŏgŏssŏyo 저는 충분히 먹었어요; *I am satisfied that ...* (*convinced*) ...ranŭn-gŏshi napttŭg kamnida ...라는 것이 납득 갑니다; *I hope you're satisfied!* sogi shiwŏnhajiyo! 속이 시원하지요!

Saturday t'oyoil 토요일

sauce sossŭ 소스

saucepan naembi 냄비

saucer pach'im chŏpsshi 받침 접시

saucy *person* kŏnbangjin 건방진; *dress* mŏtchin 멋진

Saudi Arabia Saudi Arabia 사우디 아라비아

Saudi (Arabian) 1 *adj* Saudi Arabiaŭi 사우디 아라비아의 2 *n* (*person*) Saudi Arabiain 사우디 아라비아인

sauna sauna 사우나

saunter *v/i* ŏsŭllŏnggŏrida 어슬렁거리다

sausage soshiji 소시지

savage *adj animal* yasaeng-ŭi 야생의; *attack* chaninhan 잔인한; *criticism* hokttok'an 혹독한

save 1 *v/t* (*rescue*) kuhada 구하다; (*put aside: money*) moanot'a 모아놓다; (*in bank*) chŏch'uk'ada 저축하다; *time, money* chŏryak'ada 절약하다; (*collect*) moŭda 모으다; COMPUT chŏjanghada 저장하다; *goal* chŏjihada 저지하다; *you could* ~ *yourself a lot of effort* tŏl himdŭrŏssŭl sudo issŏnnŭnde 덜 힘들었을 수도 있었는데 2 *v/i* (*put money aside*) chŏgŭmhada 저금하다; SP maganaeda 막아내다 3 *n* SP

♦**save up for** ...e taebihae moŭda ...에 대비해 모으다

saving (*amount saved*) chŏryakpun 절약분; (*activity*) chŏryak 절약

savings yegŭm 예금

savings account pot'ong yegŭm 보통 예금

savings bank chŏch'uk ŭnhaeng 저축 은행

Savior REL Kuseju 구세주

savor *v/t* ŭmmihada 음미하다

savory *adj* (*not sweet*) tchaptcharhan 짭짤한

saw 1 *n* (*tool*) t'op 톱 2 *v/t* t'obŭro charŭda 톱으로 자르다

♦**saw off** t'obŭro k'yŏda 톱으로 켜다

sawdust t'op-ppap 톱밥

saxophone saekssŏp'on 색소폰

say 1 *v/t* marhada 말하다; *can I* ~ *something?* chega muŏl chom yaegihaedo toelkkayo? 제가 뭘 좀 얘기해도 될까요?; *that is to* ~ chŭk 즉; *what do you* ~ *to that?* kŭgŏse taehae ŏttŏk'e saenggak'anayo? 그것에 대해 어떻게 생각하나요? 2 *n*: *have one's* ~ hago ship'ŭn marŭl hada 하고 싶은 말을 하다

saying sokttam 속담

scab (*on wound*) ttaktchi 딱지

scaffolding palp'an 발판

scald *v/t*: *be ~ed* teda 데다

scale[1] (*on fish*) pinŭl 비늘

scale[2] 1 *n* (*size*) kyumo 규모; (*on thermometer etc*) nunkkŭm 눈금; (*of map*) ch'ukch'ŏk 축척; MUS ŭmgye 음계; *on a larger / smaller* ~ chomdŏ k'ŭn / chagŭn kyumoro 좀더 큰 / 작은 규모로 2 *v/t cliffs etc* orŭda 오르다

scale drawing ch'ukch'ŏk tomyŏn 축척 도면

scales (*for weighing*) chŏul 저울

scalp *n* mŏritkkajuk 머리가죽

scalpel oekkwayong mesŭ 외과용 메스

scalper amp'yosang 암표상

scam F sagi 사기

scan 1 *v/t horizon, page* chasehi salp'yŏboda 자세히 살펴보다; MED chŏngmil chosahada 정밀 조사하다;

COMPUT sŭk'aenhada 스캔하다 2 *n*
MED ch'enae pangsanŭng punp'o
sajin 체내 방사능 분포 사진
♦ **scan in** COMPUT sŭk'aenhada
스캔하다
scandal sŭk'aendŭl 스캔들
scandalous *affair* such'isŭrŏun
수치스러 운; *prices* t'ŏmuniŏmnŭn
터무니없는
scanner MED, COMPUT sŭk'aenŏ
스캐너
scantily *adv*: ~ *clad* osŭl chedaero
katch'wo iptchi anŭn 옷을 제대로
갖춰 입지 않은
scanty *clothes* sonppadangmanhan
손바닥만한
scapegoat hŭisaengnyang 희생양
scar 1 *n* hyungt'ŏ 흉터 2 *v/t*
hyungt'ŏrŭl namgida 흉터를 남기다
scarce (*in short supply*) mojaranŭn
모자라는; *make oneself* ~ sŭltchŏk
nagada 슬쩍 나가다
scarcely: *I had* ~ *begun to speak
when* ... nanŭn ...hajamaja marhagi
shijak'aet-tta 나는 ...하자마자
말하기 시작했다; *I* ~ *know her* chŏn,
kŭ yŏjarŭl kŏŭi mollayo 전, 그
여자를 거의 몰라요; ~ *any* kŏŭi
ŏptta 거의 없다
scarcity pujok 부족
scare 1 *v/t* kŏptchuda 겁주다; *be ~d
of* musŏwŏhada 무서워하다 2 *n*
(*panic, alarm*) puran 불안; *give s.o.
a* ~ nuguege kŏptchuda 누구에게
겁주다
♦ **scare away** kŏptchuŏ
tchoch'anaeda 겁주어 쫓아내다
scarecrow hŏsuabi 허수아비
scaremonger hŏtssomunŭl
p'ŏttŭrinŭn saram 헛소문을 퍼뜨리는
사람
scarf (*around neck*) mokttori 목도리;
(*over head*) sŭk'ap'ŭ 스카프
scarlet chuhongsaek 주홍색
scarlet fever sŏnghongnyŏl 성홍열
scary mushimushihan 무시무시한
scathing t'ongnyŏrhan 통렬한
scatter 1 *v/t leaflets, seeds* ppurida
뿌리다; *be ~ed all over the room*
pang chŏnch'e-e ppuryŏjyŏ it-tta 방
전체에 뿌려져 있다 2 *v/i* (*of crowd*

etc) hŭt'ŏjida 흩어지다
scatterbrained mŏriga sanmanhan
머리가 산만한
scattered *showers* sanbaltchŏgin
산발적인; *family, villages* hŭt'ŏjin
흩어진
scenario shinario 시나리오
scene THEA chang 장; (*view, sight*)
changmyŏn 장면; (*of accident, crime
etc*) hyŏnjang 현장; (*setting: of novel,
in a movie*) paegyŏng 배경; (*part of
movie*) changmyŏn 장면; (*argument*)
soran 소란; *make a* ~ soranŭl p'iuda
소란을 피우다; ~*s* THEA mudae
paegyŏng 무대 배경; *jazz* ~ / *drugs*
~ F chaejŭgye / mayak-kkye
재즈계 / 마약계; *behind the* ~*s fig*
nam morŭge 남 모르게
scenery p'unggyŏng 풍경; THEA
mudae paegyŏng 무대 배경
scent *n* (*smell*) hyanggi 향기;
(*perfume*) hyangsu 향수; (*of animal*)
naemsae 냄새
schedule 1 *n* (*of events*) yejŏng 예정;
(*of work*) iltchŏng 일정; (*for trains,
of lessons*) shiganp'yo 시간표; *be on
~* yejŏngdaeroida 예정대로이다; *be
behind* ~ yejŏngboda nŭt-tta
예정보다 늦다 2 *v/t* (*put on ~*)
yejŏnghada 예정하다; *it's ~d for
completion next month* taŭmttare
kkŭnmach'igiro toeŏ issŏyo 다음달에
끝마치기로 되어 있어요
scheduled flight chŏnggi
hanggongp'yŏn 정기 항공편
scheme 1 *n* (*plan*) kyehoek 계획;
(*wicked plot*) moŭi 모의 2 *v/i* (*plot*)
moŭihada 모의하다
scheming *adj* kyohwarhan 교활한
schizophrenia chŏngshin
punyŏltchŭng 정신 분열증
schizophrenic 1 *n* chŏngshin
punyŏltchŭng hwanja 정신 분열증
환자 2 *adj* chŏngshin punyŏltchŭng-
ŭi 정신 분열증의
scholar haktcha 학자
scholarship (*scholarly work*)
hangmun 학문; (*financial award*)
changhak-kkŭm 장학금
school hak-kkyo 학교; (*university*)
taehak 대학

schoolbag 572

schoolbag ch'aek-kkabang 책가방;
schoolboy namhakssaeng 남학생;
schoolchildren hakttong 학동;
school days suŏbil 수업일; **schoolgirl** yŏhakssaeng 여학생; **schoolteacher** hak-kkyo sŏnsaengnim
학교 선생님
sciatica chwagol shin-gyŏngt'ong
좌골 신경통
science kwahak 과학
science fiction kongsang kwahak
sosŏl 공상 과학 소설
scientific kwahaktchŏgin 과학적인
scientist kwahaktcha 과학자
scissors kawi 가위
scoff[1] v/t (eat fast) kegŏlsŭrŏpkke
mŏkta 게걸스럽게 먹다; (eat whole
lot) ta mŏgŏ ch'iuda 다 먹어 치우다
scoff[2] v/i nollida 놀리다
◆ **scoff at** ...ŭl/rŭl piut-tta ...을/를
비웃다
scold v/t child, husband kkujit-tta
꾸짖다
scoop 1 n (for food) kuktcha 국자;
(for mud, coal) sap 삽; (in
journalism) t'ŭktchong 특종 **2** v/t
p'uda 푸다; ice cream ttŭda 뜨다
◆ **scoop up** p'ŏ ollida 퍼 올리다; kids,
books ana ollida 안아 올리다
scooter (with motor) sŭk'ut'ŏ 스쿠터;
(child's) oe pal sŭk'eit'ŭ 외 발
스케이트
scope pŏmwi 범위; (opportunity)
kihoe 기회; (latitude) yŏji 여지
scorch v/t kŭsŭllida 그을리다
scorching hot tchinŭn tŭshi tŏun
찌는 듯이 더운
score 1 n SP tŭktchŏm 득점; (written
music) akppo 악보; (of movie etc)
ŭmak 음악; what's the ~?
chŏmsuga ŏttaeyo? 점수가 어때요?;
have a ~ to settle with s.o.
nuguege ssain wŏnhanŭl p'ulda
누구에게 쌓인 원한을 풀다 **2** v/t
goal, point chŏmsurŭl kirok'ada
점수를 기록하다; (cut: line) saegim
nunŭl naeda 새김 눈을 내다 **3** v/i
tŭktchŏmhada 득점하다; (keep the
score) chŏmsurŭl kirok'ada 점수를
기록하다; that's where he ~s kŭge
kŭ namjaŭi kangtchŏmiyeyo 그게 그

namjaŭi kangtchŏmiyeyo
남자의 강점이에요
scorer (of goal, point) tŭktchŏmja
득점자; (score-keeper) chŏmsu
kirogwŏn 점수 기록원
scorn 1 n kyŏngmyŏl 경멸; pour ~ on
sth muŏsŭl kyŏngmyŏrhada 무엇을
경멸하다 **2** v/t idea, suggestion
kyŏngmyŏrhada 경멸하다
scornful kyŏngmyŏrhanŭn 경멸하는
Scot Sŭk'ot'ŭllaendŭin 스코틀랜드인
Scotch (whiskey) sŭk'ach'i 스카치
Scotland Sŭk'ot'ŭllaendŭ 스코틀랜드
Scottish Sŭk'ot'ŭllaendŭŭi
스코틀랜드의
scot-free: get off ~ pŏrŭl
momyŏnhada 벌을 모면하다
scoundrel akttang 악당
scour[1] (search) ch'aja tanida 찾아
다니다
scour[2] pans munjillŏ taktta 문질러
닦다
scout n (boy ~) sŭk'aut'ŭ 스카우트
scowl 1 n tchinggŭrin ŏlgul 찡그린
얼굴 **2** v/i tchinggŭrida 찡그리다
scram F tomanggada 도망가다
scramble 1 n (rush) punmang 분망
2 v/t message ilburŏ twisŏktta 일부러
뒤섞다 **3** v/i (climb) chaepparŭge kiŏ
orŭda 재빠르게 기어 오르다; he ~d
to his feet kŭnŭn chaeppalli irŏnat-
tta 그는 재빨리 일어났다
scrambled eggs sŭk'ŭraembŭrhan
talgyal yori 스크램블한 달걀 요리
scrap 1 n (metal) p'yech'ŏl 페철;
(fight) ssaum 싸움; (little bit)
chogŭm 조금 **2** v/t project etc
p'yegishik'ida 폐기시키다; paragraph
etc chiuda 지우다
scrapbook sŭk'ŭraep puk 스크랩 북
scrape 1 n (on paintwork etc) kŭlk'in
chaguk 긁힌 자국 **2** v/t paintwork,
one's arm etc kŭktta 긁다; vegetables
k'allo tadŭmtta 칼로 다듬다; ~ a
living irŏktchŏrŏk saenghwarhada
이럭저럭 생활하다
◆ **scrape through** (in exam)
kanshinhi hapkkyŏk'ada 간신히
합격하다
scrap heap ssŭregi tŏmi 쓰레기 더미;
good for the ~ amu tchagedo
ssŭlmo ŏmnŭn 아무 짝에도 쓸모

없는

scrap metal p'yech'ŏl 폐철

scrappy *work* chirimyŏllŏrhan 지리멸렬한

scratch 1 *n* (*to stop itching*) kŭlkki 긁기; (*by cat etc*) halk'wigi 할퀴기; (*on paintwork*) kŭlk'in chaguk 긁힌 자국; **have a ~** (*to stop itching*) kŭktta 긁다; **start from ~** ch'ŏŭmbut'ŏ shijak'ada 처음부터 시작하다; **not up to ~** manjoksŭrŏpchi mot'an 만족스럽지 못한 **2** *v/t* (*to stop itching*) kŭktta 긁다; (*by cat etc*) halk'wida 할퀴다 **3** *v/i* (*of cat, nails*) kŭktta 긁다

scrawl 1 *n* hwigalgyŏ ssŭn kŭltcha 휘갈겨 쓴 글자 **2** *v/t* hwigalgyŏ ssŭda 휘갈겨 쓰다

scream 1 *n* oech'imsori 외침소리 **2** *v/i* sorich'ida 소리치다

screech 1 *n* (*of tires*) kkik'anŭn sori 끽하는 소리; (*scream*) pimyŏng sori 비명 소리 **2** *v/i* (*of tires*) kkik'anŭn soriga nada 끽하는 소리가 나다; (*scream*) pimyŏngŭl chirŭda 비명을 지르다

screen 1 *n* (*in room, hospital*) k'anmagi 칸막이; (*protective*) magi 막이; (*in movie theater*) sŭk'ŭrin 스크린; COMPUT hwamyŏn 화면; **on the ~** (*in movie*) ŭnmage 은막에; **on (the) ~** COMPUT hwamyŏnsang-e 화면상에 **2** *v/t* (*protect, hide*) kamch'uda 감추다; *movie* sangyŏnghada 상영하다; (*for security reasons*) sŏnbyŏrhada 선별하다

screenplay kakppon 각본; **screen saver** COMPUT hwamyŏn pohogi 화면 보호기; **screen test** sŭk'ŭrin t'esŭt'ŭ 스크린 테스트

screw 1 *n* nasamot 나사못; V (*sex*) sŏnggyo 성교 **2** *v/t* V sŏnggyorŭl hada 성교를 하다; F (*cheat*) sogida 속이다; **~ sth to sth** muŏsŭl muŏse nasamosŭro kojŏngshik'ida 무엇을 무엇에 나사못으로 고정시키다

♦ **screw up 1** *v/t* eyes tchinggŭrida 찡그리다; *piece of paper* toldol mungch'ida 돌돌 뭉치다; F (*make a mess of*) mangch'ida 망치다 **2** *v/i* F (*make a bad mistake*) k'ŭn shilssuro

ŏngmang-i toege hada 큰 실수로 엉망이 되게 하다

screwdriver tŭraibŏ 드라이버

screwed up F (*psychologically*) pitturŏjin 비뚤어진

screw top (*on bottle*) pit'ŭrŏ yŏnŭn magae 비틀어 여는 마개

scribble 1 *n* kalgyŏ ssŭgi 갈겨 쓰기 **2** *v/t* (*write quickly*) kalgyŏ ssŭda 갈겨 쓰다 **3** *v/i* kalgyŏ ssŭda 갈겨 쓰다

script (*for play etc*) taebon 대본; (*form of writing*) kŭltchach'e 글자체

Scripture: the (*Holy*) **~s** Kyŏngjŏn 경전

scriptwriter chak-kka 작가

scroll *n* (*manuscript*) turumari 두루마리

♦ **scroll down** *v/i* COMPUT araero naerida 아래로 내리다

♦ **scroll up** *v/i* COMPUT wiro ollida 위로 올리다

scrounger kŏjŏ ŏnnŭn saram 거저 얻는 사람

scrub *v/t floors, hands* munjirŭda 문지르다

scrubbing brush sol 솔

scruffy chijŏbunhan 지저분한

♦ **scrunch up** *plastic cup etc* pusŏjida 부서지다

scruples todŏk kwannyŏm 도덕 관념; **have no ~ about doing sth** muŏsŭl hanŭn te issŏ todŏktchŏk chujŏhami ŏptta 무엇을 하는 데 있어 도덕적 주저함이 없다

scrupulous (*with moral principles*) todŏktchŏgin 도덕적인; (*thorough*) pint'ŭmŏmnŭn 빈틈없는; *attention to detail* kkomkkomhan 꼼꼼한

scrutinize chasehi chosahada 자세히 조사하다

scrutiny chosa 조사; **come under ~** semirhi chosadoeda 세밀히 조사되다

scuba diving sŭk'ubŏ taibing 스쿠버 다이빙

scuffle *n* nant'u 난투

sculptor chogak-kka 조각가

sculpture *n* (*art*) chogak chogak; (*sth sculpted*) chogakp'um 조각품

scum (*on liquid*) tchikkŏgi 찌꺼기; *pej* ssŭregi 쓰레기

scythe n nat 낫
sea pada 바다; **by the ~** pada yŏp'e 바다 옆에
seafaring nation haeyang-ŭi 해양의;
  seafood haesanmul 해산물; **sea-
  front** patatkka 바닷가; **seagoing**
  vessel wŏnyang-ŭi 원양의; **seagull**
  kalmaegi 갈매기
seal¹ n (animal) mulkkae 물개
seal² 1 n (on document) pong-in 봉인;
  TECH milbong 밀봉 2 v/t container
  milbonghada 밀봉하다
♦ **seal off** area pongswaehada
  봉쇄하다
sea level: **above/below ~**
  haesumyŏn wie/araee 해수면
  위에/아래에
seam n (on garment) solgi 솔기; (of
  ore) kwangch'ŭng 광층
seaman sŏnwŏn 선원; **seaport**
  hanggudoshi 항구도시; **sea power**
  (nation) haegun-guk 해군국
search 1 n (for missing person,
  object) susaek 수색; (for solution)
  t'amsaek 탐색; COMPUT sŏch'i 서치;
  (for happiness) ch'ugu 추구 2 v/t
  forest, room ch'at-tta 찾다; COMPUT
  sŏch'ihada 서치하다
♦ **search for** sth missing ch'at-tta
  찾다; missing person susaek'ada
  수색하다; solution t'amsaek'ada
  탐색하다; COMPUT sŏch'ihada
  서치하다; happiness ch'uguhada
  추구하다
searching adj look susaek'anŭn
  수색하는; question nalk'aroun
  날카로운
searchlight t'amjodŭng 탐조등;
  search party susaekttae 수색대;
  search warrant susaek yŏngtchang
  수색 영장
seasick paemŏlmiga nan 배멀미가
  난; **get ~** paemŏlmihada 배멀미하다;
  seaside haebyŏnkka 해변가; **at the
  ~** haebyŏne 해변에; **go to the ~**
  haebyŏnŭro kada 해변으로 가다;
  seaside resort haebyŏn lijot'ŭ 해변
  리조트; **sea slug** haesam 해삼
season n (winter etc) kyejŏl 계절;
  (for tourism etc) ch'ŏl 철
seasoned wood chal kŏnjodoen 잘

건조된; traveler etc kyŏnghŏmŭl
  ssahŭn 경험을 쌓은
seasoning chomiryo 조미료
season ticket (for transportation)
  chŏnggi sŭngch'akkwŏn 정기
  승차권; (for stadium, opera) chŏnggi
  iptchangkkwŏn 정기 입장권
seat 1 n chari 자리; (of pants)
  kungdung-i 궁둥이; **please take a ~**
  ch'akssŏk'ayŏ chushipsshio 착석하여
  주십시오 2 v/t (have seating for)
  chwasŏgŭl kajigo it-tta 좌석을
  가지고 있다; **please remain ~ed**
  ch'akssŏk'ayŏ kyeshigil paramnida
  착석하여 계시길 바랍니다
seat belt chwasŏk pelt'ŭ 좌석 벨트
sea urchin sŏngge 성게
seaweed haech'o 해초; **edible ~** kim
  김
secluded mŏlli ttŏrŏjyŏ hanjŏk'an
  멀리 떨어져 한적한
seclusion mŏlli ttŏrŏjim 멀리 떨어짐
second 1 n (of time) ch'o 초; **just a
  ~** chamkkanmanyo 잠깐만요 2 adj
  tu pŏntchaeŭi 두 번째의; **~ biggest**
  tu pŏntchaero k'ŭn 두 번째로 큰
  3 adv come in tu pŏntchaero 두
  번째로 4 v/t motion ch'ansŏnghada
  찬성하다
secondary pojojŏgin 보조적인; **of ~
  importance** ich'ajŏgŭro
  chungyohan 이차적으로 중요한
secondary education chungdŭng
  kyoyuk 중등 교육
second-best adj tu pŏntchaero chal
  hanŭn 두 번째로 잘 하는; **second
  class** adj ticket idŭngsŏgŭi 이등석의;
  second gear MOT idan kiŏ 이단
  기어; **second hand** (on clock)
  ch'och'im 초침; **secondhand** 1 adj
  chunggoŭi 중고의 2 adv buy
  chunggoro 중고로
secondly tultchaero 둘째로
second-rate iryuŭi 이류의
second thoughts: **I've had ~** chŏn,
  saenggagŭl pakkwŏssŏyo 전, 생각을
  바꿨어요
secrecy kimil 기밀
secret 1 n pimil 비밀; **do sth in ~**
  muŏsŭl pimillie hada 무엇을
  비밀리에 하다 2 adj garden, passage

ŭnmirhan 은밀한; *work*, *department* pimirŭi 비밀의

secret agent kanch'ŏp 간첩

secretarial *tasks*, *job* pisŏŭi 비서의

secretary pisŏ 비서; POL changgwan 장관

Secretary of State Kungmubu Changgwan 국무부 장관

secrete (*give off*) punbihada 분비하다; (*hide*) sumgida 숨기다

secretion (*of liquid*) punbiaek 분비액; (*liquid secreted*) punbimul 분비물; (*concealment*) ŭnnik 은닉

secretive t'ŏ noch'i annŭn 터 놓지 않는

secretly ŭnmirhi 은밀히

secret police pimil kyŏngch'al 비밀 경찰

secret service pimil chŏngbo kigwan 비밀 정보 기관

sect punp'a 분파

section (*of book*, *text*) kwa 과; (*of apple*) chogak 조각; (*of building*) kuhoek 구획; (*of company*) pusŏ 부서

sector yŏngnyŏk 영역

secular sesogŭi 세속의

secure 1 *adj shelf*, *job* anjŏnhan 안전한; *feeling* anshimhanŭn 안심하는 **2** *v/t shelf etc* anjŏnhage hada 안전하게 하다; *s.o.'s help*, *funding* ŏt-tta 얻다

security (*in job*) anjŏnssŏng 안전성; (*for investment*) pojang 보장; (*at airport etc*) poan 보안; (*department responsible for ~*) poankkwa 보안과; (*of beliefs etc*) hwaksshin 확신; *se-curities* FIN yukka chŭngkkwŏn 유가 증권; *securities market* FIN yukka chŭngkkwŏn shijang 유가 증권 시장

security alert poan kyŏnggye 보안 경계; **security check** poan hwagin 보안 확인; **security-conscious** poanŭl chungshihanŭn 보안을 중시하는; **security forces** anjŏn-gun 안전군; **security guard** kyŏngbiwŏn 경비원; **security risk** (*person*) wihŏm inmul 위험 인물

sedan MOT ssallongch'a 쌀롱차

sedative *n* chinjŏngje 진정제

sediment ch'imjŏnmul 침전물

seduce (*sexually*) yuhok'ada 유혹하다

seduction (*sexual*) yuhok 유혹

seductive *dress* maeryŏktchŏgin 매력적인; *offer* yuhoktchŏgin 유혹적인

see poda 보다; (*understand*) alda 알다; *can I ~ the manager?* ch'aegimjarŭl mannal su issŭlkkayo? 책임자를 만날 수 있을까요?; *you should ~ a doctor* tangshinŭn ŭisahant'e kabwaya toemnida 당신은 의사한테 가봐야 됩니다; *~ s.o. home* nuga chibe musahi wannŭnjirŭl hwaginhada 누가 집에 무사히 왔는지를 확인하다; *I'll ~ you to the door* munkkaji paraeda chulkkeyo 문까지 바래다 줄께요; *~ you!* tto mannayo! 또 만나요!; *I ~* algessŏyo 알겠어요

♦ **see about** (*look into*) salp'yŏboda 살펴보다

♦ **see off** (*at airport etc*) paeunghada 배웅하다; (*chase away*) tchoch'a ponaeda 쫓아 보내다

♦ **see to:** *~ sth* muŏshi chal ch'ŏri toeŏnnŭnji hwaginhada 무엇이 잘 처리 되었는지 확인하다; *~ it that sth gets done* muŏsŭl kkŭnnaenŭn kŏsŭl t'ŭllimŏpsshi hada 무엇을 끝내는 것을 틀림없이 하다

seed sshi 씨; (*in tennis*) sidŭ 시드; *go to ~* (*of person*, *district*) t'oerak'ada 퇴락하다

seedling (*of tree*) myomok 묘목; (*of plant*) myojong 묘종

seedy *bar*, *district* p'yŏngp'ani nappŭn 평판이 나쁜

seeing (*that*) ...(i)gi ttaemune ...(이)기 때문에

seeing-eye dog maengdogyŏn 맹도견

seek 1 *v/t employment* ch'at-tta 찾다; *truth* ch'uguhada 추구하다 **2** *v/i* t'amsaek'ada 탐색하다

seem ...kŏt kat-tta ...것 같다; *it ~s that* ...in kŏt kat'a poida ...인 것 같아 보이다

seemingly poginŭn 보기에는

seep (*of liquid*) saeda 새다

♦ **seep out** (*of liquid*) saeŏnaoda 새어나오다

seesaw shiso 시소

see-through *dress, material* pich'inŭn 비치는

segment (*of chart, structure*) pubun 부분; (*of orange*) chogak 조각

segmented pubunchŏgin 부분적인

segregate pullihada 분리하다

segregation pulli 분리

seismology chijinhak 지진학

seize chaptta 잡다; *opportunity* p'och'ak'ada 포착하다; (*of customs, police etc*) amnyuhada 압류하다

♦ **seize up** (*of engine*) mŏmch'uda 멈추다

seizure MED paltchak 발작; (*of drugs etc*) amnyu 압류

seldom tŭmulge 드물게

select 1 *v/t* sŏnt'aek'ada 선택하다 **2** *adj* (*exclusive*) chŏngsŏnhan 정선한

selection (*choice*) sŏnt'aek 선택; (*that chosen*) sŏnt'aekttoen kŏt 선택된 것; (*people chosen*) sŏnt'aekttoen saram 선택된 사람; (*assortment*) kusaek 구색

selection process sŏnbal kwajŏng 선발 과정

selective anmogi nop'ŭn 안목이 높은

self chaa 자아

self-addressed envelope ponin chusorŭl chŏgŭn pongt'u 본인 주소를 적은 봉투; **self-assured** chashin innŭn 자신 있는; **self-catering** sŭsŭro ŭmshigŭl haemŏngnŭn 스스로 음식을 해먹는; **self-centered** chagi ponwiŭi 자기 본위의; **self-confessed** chainhanŭn 자인하는; **self-confidence** chashin 자신; **self-confident** chashin innŭn 자신 있는; **self-conscious** chaŭishigi kanghan 자의식이 강한; **self-contained** *apartment* tongnipshigŭi 독립식의; **self-control** chaje 자제; **self-defense** chagi pang-ŏ 자기 방어; **self-discipline** chagi suyang 자기 수양; **self-doubt** chagi pulshin 자기 불신; **self-employed** chayŏng-ŭi 자영의; **self-evident** chamyŏnghan 자명한; **self-**

interest sarisayok 사리사욕

selfish igijŏgin 이기적인

selfless yoksshimi ŏmnŭn 욕심이 없는

self-made man chasusŏnggahan saram 자수성가한 사람; **self-possessed** ch'imch'ak'an 침착한; **self-reliant** tongniptchŏgin 독립적인; **self-respect** chajonshim 자존심; **self-righteous** *pej* tokssŏnjŏgin 독선적인; **self-satisfied** *pej* chagi manjogŭi 자기 만족의; **self-service** *adj* selp'ŭssŏbisŭŭi 셀프서비스의; **self-service restaurant** selp'ŭssŏbisŭ shikttang 셀프서비스 식당

sell 1 *v/t* p'alda 팔다; **you have to ~ yourself** ne chashinŭl sŏnjŏnhaeya twaeyo 네 자신을 선전해야 돼요 **2** *v/i* (*of products*) p'anmaedoeda 판매되다

seller p'anmaeja 판매자

selling *n* COM p'anmae 판매

selling point COM p'anmae kangjotchŏm 판매 강조점

semen chŏng-aek 정액

semester hak-kki 학기

semi (*truck*) t'ŭrŏk 트럭

semicircle panwŏn 반원; **semicircular** panwŏnhyŏngŭi 반원형의; **semiconductor** ELEC pandoch'e 반도체; **semifinal** chun-gyŏlssŭng 준결승

seminar semina 세미나

semiskilled pan sungnyŏnŭi 반 숙련의

senate sang-wŏn 상원

senator sang-wŏnŭiwŏn 상원의원

send *v/t* ponaeda 보내다; **~ sth to s.o.** nuguege muŏsŭl ponaeda 누구에게 무엇을 보내다; **~ s.o. to s.o.** nugurŭl nuguege ponaeda 누구를 누구에게 보내다; **~ her my best wishes** kŭnyŏege anbu chŏnhae chuseyo 그녀에게 안부 전해 주세요

♦ **send back** *letter* pansonghada 반송하다; *person, food* tollyŏ ponaeda 돌려 보내다

♦ **send for** *doctor, help* purŭrŏ ponaeda 부르러 보내다

♦**send in** *troops* ponaeda 보내다; *next interviewee* tŭryŏ ponaeda 들여 보내다; *application form* chech'urhada 제출하다

♦**send off** *letter, fax etc* palssonghada 발송하다

♦**send up** (*mock*) nollida 놀리다

sender (*of letter*) palssong-in 발송인

senile nosoehan 노쇠한

senility nosoe 노쇠

senior (*older*) sonwiŭi 손위의; (*in rank*) sanggŭpŭi 상급의; **be ~ to X** (*in rank*) Xboda wittcharie innŭn X보다 윗자리에 있는

senior citizen ŏrŭshin 어르신

sensation (*feeling*) kamgak 감각; (*event*) sensseisyŏn 센세이션; (*person*) sŏnp'ungjŏgŭro inkki innŭn saram 선풍적으로 인기 있는 사람; (*thing*) sŏnp'ungjŏgŭro inkki innŭn kŏt 선풍적으로 인기 있는 것

sensational *news, discovery* sesangŭl ttŏdŭlssŏk'age hanŭn 세상을 떠들썩하게 하는; (*very good*) nunbushin 눈부신

sense 1 *n* (*meaning*) ttŭt 뜻; (*purpose, point*) ŭimi 의미; (*common ~*) sangshik 상식; (*of sight, smell etc*) kamgak 감각; (*feeling*) nŭtkkim 느낌; *in a ~* ŏttŏn ŭimiesŏnŭn 어떤 의미에서는; *talk ~, man!* ŏi, ich'ie mannŭn marŭl hae! 어이, 이치에 맞는 말을 해!; *it doesn't make ~* kŭgŏn mari andwaeyo 그건 말이 안돼요; *there's no ~ in waiting / trying* kidaril / shidohal iyuga ŏpssŏyo 기다릴 / 시도할 이유가 없어요 **2** *v/t s.o.'s presence* arach'aeda 알아채다

senseless (*pointless*) muŭimihan 무의미한

sensible *person, decision* punbyŏri innŭn 분별이 있는; *advice* hyŏnmyŏnghan 현명한

sensitive *skin* min-gamhan 민감한; *person* yeminhan 예민한

sensitivity min-gamham 민감함

sensual kwangnŭngtchŏgin 관능적인

sensuality kwangnŭng 관능

sensuous kamgaktchŏgin 감각적인

sentence 1 *n* GRAM munjang 문장;

LAW p'an-gyŏl 판결 **2** *v/t* LAW p'an-gyŏrŭl naerida 판결을 내리다

sentiment (*emotion*) kamsang 감상; (*opinion*) sogam 소감

sentimental kamsangtchŏgin 감상적인

sentimentality kamsang 감상

sentry poch'o 보초

Seoul Sŏul 서울

separate 1 *adj* pyŏlgaeŭi 별개의; *keep X ~ from Y* Xwa / kwa Yŭl / rŭl pullihada X와 / 과 Y을 / 를 분리하다 **2** *v/t* pullihada 분리하다; *~ X from Y* Xŭl / rŭl Yesŏ pullihada X을 / 를 Y에서 분리하다 **3** *v/i* (*of couple*) pyŏlgŏhada 별거하다

separated *couple* pyŏlgŏhan 별거한

separately *pay, treat, deal with* ttaro 따로

separation pulli 분리; (*of couple*) pyŏlgŏ 별거

September kuwŏl 구월

septic pup'aessŏng-ŭi 부패성의; *go ~* komtta 곪다

sequel sokp'yŏn 속편

sequence *n* sunsŏ 순서; *in ~* sunsŏdaero 순서대로; *out of ~* sunsŏe mat-tchi ank'e 순서에 맞지 않게; *the ~ of events* sakkŏnŭi sunsŏ 사건의 순서

serene *person* ch'abunhan 차분한; *lake, smile* p'yŏng-onhan 평온한

sergeant chungsa 중사

serial *n* yŏnsongmul 연속물

serialize *novel on TV* yŏnsok pangyŏnghada 연속 방영하다

serial killer yŏnsok sarhaebŏm 연속 살해범; **serial number** (*of product*) illyŏnbŏnho 일련번호; **serial port** COMPUT sshiriŏl p'ot'ŭ 씨리얼 포트

series (*of numbers, events*) yŏnsok 연속

serious *illness, situation, damage* shimgak'an 심각한; (*person: earnest*) chinjihan 진지한; *company* shinmang innŭn 신망 있는; *I'm ~* chinshimiyeyo 진심이예요; *we'd better take a ~ look at it* uri kŭgŏse taehae chinjihage ponŭn ke choŭl kŏt kat'ayo 우리 그것에 대해 진지하게 보는 게 좋을 것 같아요

seriously *injured* shimhage 심하게;
understaffed chinjŏngŭro 진정으로; ~
intend to ... chinjihage ...haryŏgo
hada 진지하게 ...하려고 하다; ~?
chŏngmallo? 정말로?; **take s.o.** ~
nugurŭl chinjihage saenggak'ada
누구를 진지하게 생각하다
sermon sŏlgyo 설교
servant koyongin 고용인
serve 1 *n* (*in tennis*) sŏbŭ 서브 **2** *v/t*
food, meal naeda 내다; *person,*
guests shijungdŭlda 시중들다;
customer in shop moshida 모시다;
one's country, the people
pongsahada 봉사하다; *it ~s*
you / him right nŏnŭn / kŭnŭn
hapttanghan taeurŭl padat-tta
너는 / 그는 합당한 대우를 받았다
3 *v/i* ch'arida 차리다; (*in post, job*)
kŭnmuhada 근무하다; (*in tennis*)
sŏbŭhada 서브하다
♦ **serve up** *meal* ch'aryŏnaeda
차려내다
server (*in tennis*) sŏbŭhanŭn saram
서브하는 사람; COMPUT sŏbŏ 서버
service 1 *n* sŏbissŭ 서비스; (*in tennis*)
sŏbŭhanŭn kkŏt 서브하는 것; *the ~s*
kundae 군대 **2** *v/t vehicle, machine*
sŏbissŭhada 서비스하다
service area hyugeso 휴게소; **service**
charge (*in restaurant, club*)
sŏbissŭryo 서비스료; **service**
industry sŏbissŭ sanŏp 서비스 산업;
serviceman MIL kunin 군인;
service provider COMPUT sŏbissŭ
chegonghoesa 서비스 제공회사;
service sector sŏbissŭ sanŏp
pubun 서비스 산업 부분; **service**
station chuyuso 주유소
session (*of parliament*) kaejŏng
chungim 개정 중임; (*with*
psychiatrist, consultant etc) mit'ing
미팅
set 1 *n* (*of tools, books etc, in tennis,*
scenery) set'ŭ 세트; (*group of*
people) chipttan 집단; MATH chip'ap
집합; (*where a movie is made*)
ch'waryŏngjangso 촬영장소; **televi-**
sion ~ t'ellebijŏn set'ŭ 텔레비전
세트 **2** *v/t* (*place*) not'a 놓다; *movie,*
novel etc ...ŭi paegyŏng-ŭl

chŏnghada ...의 배경을 정하다; *date,*
time, limit chŏnghada 정하다;
mechanism chojŏnghada 조정하다;
alarm clock match'uŏ not'a 맞추어
놓다; *broken limb* umjigiji ank'e
kojŏnghada 움직이지 않게 고정하다;
jewel paganŏt'a 박아넣다; (*type~*)
shiktchahada 식자하다; ~ **the table**
sang-ŭl ch'arida 상을 차리다; ~ **a**
task for s.o. nuguege ch'aegimŭl
pugwahada 누구에게 책임을
부과하다 **3** *v/i* (*of sun*) chida 지다; (*of*
glue) ŭnggohada 응고하다 **4** *adj*
views, ideas hwak-kkohan 확고한; **be**
dead ~ on X X hanŭn kŏsŭl
hwakssirhi maŭm mŏktta X 하는
것을 확실히 마음 먹다; **be very ~ in**
one's ways chagi pangshinmanŭl
kojip'ada 자기 방식만을 고집하다; ~
book / reading (*in course*) sojŏngŭi
ch'aek / ilgŭlkkŏri 소정의
책 / 읽을거리; ~ **meal** chŏngshik 정식
♦ **set apart**: **set X apart from Y**
Xŭl / rŭl Ywa / kwa kubyŏrhada
X을 / 를 Y와 / 과 구별하다
♦ **set aside** (*for future use*)
ch'aenggyŏduda 챙겨두다
♦ **set back** (*in plans etc*) twich'yŏjige
hada 뒤쳐지게 하다; *it set me back*
$400 nanŭn kŭgŏse 400tallŏrŭl ssŏt-
tta 나는 그것에 400달러를 썼다
♦ **set off 1** *v/i* (*on journey*)
ch'ulbarhada 출발하다 **2** *v/t*
explosion chŏmhwahada 점화하다;
chain reaction shijak'age hada
시작하게 하다
♦ **set out 1** *v/i* (*on journey*)
ch'ulbarhada 출발하다; ~ **to do X**
(*intend*) X hanŭn kŏsŭl
chaktchŏnghada X 하는 것을
작정하다 **2** *v/t ideas, proposal*
sŏlmyŏnghada 설명하다; *goods*
naenot'a 내놓다
♦ **set to** (*start on a task*) shijak'ada
시작하다
♦ **set up 1** *v/t new company* sŏllip'ada
설립하다; *system* seuda 세우다;
equipment, machine chorip'ada
조립하다; *market stall* set'inghada
세팅하다; F (*frame*) ummorŭl
kkumida 음모를 꾸미다 **2** *v/i* (*in*

business) kaeŏp'ada 개업하다

setback hut'oe 후퇴

setting (*of novel etc*) paegyŏng 배경; (*of house*) wich'i 위치

settle 1 v/i (*of bird*) antta 앉다; (*of liquid*) malgajida 맑아지다; (*of dust*) karaantta 가라앉다; (*to live*) chŏngch'ak'ada 정착하다 **2** v/t *dispute, argument* hwahaeshik'ida 화해시키다; *uncertainty* haegyŏrhada 해결하다; *s.o.'s debts* ch'ŏngsanhada 청산하다; *check* chiburhada 지불하다; *that ~s it!* kŭgŏsŭro irŭn kyŏltchŏngdwaessŏyo! 그것으로 일은 결정됐어요!

♦ **settle down** (*stop being noisy*) choyonghaejida 조용해지다; (*stop wild living*) charijaptta 자리잡다; (*in an area*) chŏngch'ak'ada 정착하다

♦ **settle for** padadŭrida 받아들이다

settlement (*of claim, debt*) ch'ŏngsan 청산; (*of dispute*) hwahae 화해; (*payment*) chibul 지불; (*of building*) ch'imha 침하

settler (*in new country*) ijuja 이주자

set-up (*structure*) kujo 구조; (*relationship*) kwan-gye 관계; F (*frame-up*) kkumyŏjin il 꾸며진 일

seven ilgop 일곱, ch'il 칠

seventeen yŏrilgop 열 일곱, shipch'il 십칠

seventeenth yŏrilgop pŏntchaeŭi 열 일곱 번째의

seventh ilgop pŏntchaeŭi 일곱 번째의

seventieth irhŭn pŏntchaeŭi 일흔 번째의

seventy irhŭn 일흔, ch'ilsship 칠십

sever v/t *arm, cable etc* chŏlttanhada 절단하다; *relations* chŏryŏnhada 절연하다

several 1 adj myŏnmyŏch'ŭi 몇몇의 **2** pron myŏt kae 몇 개

severe *illness, penalty* shimhan 심한; *teacher, face* ŏmkkyŏk'an 엄격한; *winter, weather* mojin 모진

severely shimhage 심하게; *speak, stare* ŏmhage 엄하게

severity (*of illness*) shimham 심함; (*of penalty*) kahok 가혹; (*of look*) ŏmkkyŏk 엄격; (*of winter*) mojim 모짐

sew 1 v/t kkwemaeda 꿰매다 **2** v/i panŭjirhada 바느질하다

♦ **sew on** *button* kkwemaeŏ talda 꿰매어 달다

sewage hasu 하수

sewage plant hasu ch'ŏrijang 하수 처리장

sewer hasugwan 하수관

sewing (*skill*) panŭjil 바느질; (*that being sewn*) panŭjilkkŏri 바느질거리

sewing machine chaebongt'ŭl 재봉틀

sex (*act*) sŏnggyo 성교; (*gender*) sŏng 성; *have ~ with s.o.* nuguwa sŏnggyohada 누구와 성교하다

sexual sŏngtchŏgin 성적인

sexual intercourse sŏnggyo 성교

sexually transmitted disease sŏngppyŏng 성병

sexy ssekssihan 섹시한

shabby *coat etc* nalgŭn 낡은; *treatment* piyŏrhan 비열한

shack odumaktchip 오두막집

shade 1 n ŭngdal 응달; (*for lamp*) karigae 가리개; (*of color*) saektcho 색조; (*on window*) p'ŭllaindŭ 블라인드; *in the ~* ŭngdare(sŏ) 응달에(서) **2** v/t (*from sun, light*) karida 가리다

shadow n kŭrimja 그림자

shady *spot* kŭnŭljin 그늘진; *character, dealings etc* ŭishimsŭrŏun 의심스러운

shaft (*of axle, hammer*) charu 자루; (*of mine*) sugaeng 수갱

shaggy *hair, dog* tŏpssuruk'an 덥수룩한

shake 1 n: *give X a good ~* Xŭl/rŭl toege hŭndŭlda X을/를 되게 흔들다 **2** v/t hŭndŭlda 흔들다; *~ hands* akssuhada 악수하다; *~ hands with X* Xwa/kwa akssuhada X와/과 악수하다; *~ one's head* kogaerŭl chŏt-tta 고개를 젖다 **3** v/i (*of hands, voice*) ttŏlda 떨다; (*of building*) hŭndŭllida 흔들리다

shaken (*emotionally*) hollansŭrŏun 혼란스러운

shake-up kujo chojŏng 구조 조정

shaky *table etc* hŭndŭlgŏrinŭn 흔들거리는; (*after illness, shock*) pit'ŭlgorinŭn 비틀거리는; *grasp of sth, grammar etc* puranjŏnghan 불안정한

shall (*future*) …hal kŏshida …할 것이다; *I ~ do my best* nanŭn ch'oesŏnŭl tahal kŏshida 나는 최선을 다할 것이다 ◊ (*determined*) …hagessŭmnida …하겠습니다; *I shan't see them* nanŭn kŭdŭrŭl mannaji ank'essŭmnida 나는 그들을 만나지 않겠습니다 ◊ (*suggesting*): *we go now?* uri chigŭm kalkkayo? 우리 지금 갈까요?

shallow *water* yat'ŭn 얕은; *person* ch'ŏnbak'an 천박한

shaman mudang 무당

shaman rite kut 굿

shaman song muga 무가

Shamanism Musok Shinang 무속 신앙

shamanistic music muak 무악

shame 1 *n* such'ishim 수치심; *bring ~ on* …e such'ishimŭl an-gyŏjuda …에 수치심을 안겨주다; *what a ~!* chŏngmal andwaessŏyo! 정말 안됐어요!; *~ on you!* pukkŭrŏptchido anni! 부끄럽지도 않니! **2** *v/t* mangshinshik'ida 망신시키다; *~ X into doing Y* X(ŭ)ro hayŏgŭm pukkŭrŏwŏ Yhage hada X(으)로 하여금 부끄러워 Y하게 하다

shameful such'isŭrŏun 수치스러운

shameless p'aryŏmch'ihan 파렴치한

shampoo *n* shyamp'u 샴푸

shape 1 *n* moyang 모양 **2** *v/t clay* moyang-ŭl mandŭlda 모양을 만들다; *s.o.'s life, the future* sŏlgyehada 설계하다

shapeless *dress etc* polp'umŏmnŭn 불품없는

shapely *figure* mommaega choŭn 몸매가 좋은

share 1 *n* mok 몫; FIN chushik 주식; *do one's ~ of the work* chagi mokssŭl irŭl hada 자기 몫의 일을 하다 **2** *v/t punbaehada* 분배하다; *room, bed* hamkke ssŭda 함께 쓰다; *s.o.'s feelings, opinions* hamkke hada 함께 하다 **3** *v/i* hamkke nanuda 함께 나누다

♦ **share out** kyundŭnghage nanuda 균등하게 나누다

shareholder chuju 주주

shark sangŏ 상어

sharp 1 *adj knife* nalk'aroun 날카로운; *mind* myŏngminhan 명민한; *pain* sarŭl enŭn tŭt'an 살을 에는 듯한; *taste* chaguktchŏgin 자극적인; *~ tongue* tokssŏl 독설 **2** *adv* MUS panŭm nopke 반음 높게; *at 3 o'clock ~* seshi chŏnggage 세시 정각에

sharpen *knife* kalda 갈다; *skills* yŏnmahada 연마하다; *pencil* kkaktta 깎다

shatter 1 *v/t glass* pusuda 부수다; *illusions* kkaejida 깨지다 **2** *v/i* (*of glass*) pusŏjida 부서지다

shattered F (*exhausted*) chich'in 지친; (*very upset*) tandanhi ch'unggyŏgŭl padŭn 단단히 충격을 받은

shattering *news, experience* ch'imyŏngjŏgin 치명적인; *effect* ŏmch'ŏngnan 엄청난

shave 1 *v/t & v/i* myŏndohada 면도하다 **2** *n* myŏndo 면도; *have a ~* myŏndohada 면도하다; *that was a close ~* kanshinhi myŏnhaet-tta 간신히 면했다

♦ **shave off** *beard* kkakkabŏrida 깎아버리다; *piece of wood* kkakanaeda 깍아내다

shaven *head* sakpparhan 삭발한

shaver (*electric*) myŏndogi 면도기

shaving brush myŏndoyong sol 면도용 솔

shaving soap myŏndoyong pinu 면도용 비누

shawl shyol 숄

she kŭnyŏ 그녀, kŭ yŏja 그 여자; *~ is American* kŭnyŏnŭn Miguk saramieyo 그녀는 미국 사람이에요 ◊ (*omission of pronoun*): *who is ~? - ~ is my teacher* nuguyeyo? - che sŏnsaengnimieyo 누구예요? - 제 선생님이에요

shears k'ŭn kawi 큰 가위

sheath *n* (*for knife*) k'altchip 칼집; (*contraceptive*) k'ondom 콘돔

shed[1] *v/t blood, tears* hŭllida 흘리다; *leaves* ttŏrŏttŭrida 떨어뜨리다; *~*

light on fig haemyŏnghada 해명하다

shed[2] *n* ch'anggo 창고

sheep yang 양

sheepdog yang chik'inŭn kae 양
지키는 개

sheepish tanghwanghanŭn 당황하는

sheepskin *adj lining* yanggajuk
양가죽

sheer *adj madness, luxury* wanjŏnhan
완전한; *drop* kŏŭi sujigin 거의
수직인; *cliffs* kap'arŭn 가파른

sheet (*for bed*) shit'ŭ 시트; (*of paper*)
chang 장; (*of metal, glass*) p'an 판

shelf sŏnban 선반; *shelves* yŏrŏgaeŭi
sŏnban 여러개의 선반

shell 1 *n* (*of mussel, egg etc*) kkŏptchil
껍질; (*of tortoise*) tŭngttaktchi
등딱지; MIL yut'an 유탄; *come out
of one's ~* fig maŭmŭl t'ŏnot'a
마음을 터놓다 **2** *v/t peas* pŏtkkida
벗기다; MIL p'ogyŏk'ada
포격하다

shellfire p'ohwa 포화; *come under ~*
p'ogyŏgŭl pat-tta 포격을 받다

shellfish kapkkangnyu 갑각류

shelter 1 *n* (*refuge*) p'inanch'ŏ
피난처; (*against air raids*) taep'iho
대피호; (*at bus stop*) chŏngnyujang
정류장 **2** *v/i* (*from rain, bombing etc*)
p'ihada 피하다 **3** *v/t* (*protect*)
pohohada 보호하다

sheltered *place* p'ihal su innŭn 피할
수 있는; *lead a ~ life*
ŭndunsaenghwarŭl hada 은둔생활을
하다

shepherd *n* yangch'i-gi 양치기

sherry seriju 세리주

shield 1 *n* pangp'ae 방패; (*sports
trophy*) usŭngp'ae 우승패; TECH
magi 막이 **2** *v/t* (*protect*) pohohada
보호하다

shift 1 *n* (*in attitude, thinking*)
pyŏnhwa 변화; (*switchover*) pyŏn-
gyŏng 변경; (*in direction of wind etc*)
idong 이동; (*period of work*) kyodae
교대 **2** *v/t* (*move*) omgida 옮기다;
stains etc ŏpssaeda 없애다; *~ the
emphasis onto* ...(ŭ)ro
kangjochŏmŭl idonghada ...(으)로
강조점을 이동하다 **3** *v/i* (*move*)
omgida 옮기다; (*of attitude, opinion*)

pyŏnhada 변하다; (*of wind*)
idonghada 이동하다; *that's ~ing!* F
kkwae pparŭgunyo! 꽤 빠르군요!

shift key COMPUT ship'ŭt'ŭ k'i 시프트
키

shift work kyodae kŭnmu 교대 근무

shifty *pej* kansahan 간사한

shifty-looking *pej* kansahae poinŭn
간사해 보이는

shimmer *v/i* arŭn-gŏrida 아른거리다

shin *n* chŏnggang-i 정강이

shine 1 *v/i* (*of sun, moon*) pinnada
빛나다; (*of shoes*) pantchagida
반짝이다; fig (*of student etc*)
ttwiŏnada 뛰어나다 **2** *v/t flashlight
etc* pich'uda 비추다 **3** *n* (*on shoes etc*)
pantchak-kkŏrim 반짝거림

shingle (*on beach*) chagal 자갈

shingles MED taesangp'ojin 대상포진

shiny *surface* pantchak-kkŏrinŭn
반짝거리는

ship 1 *n* pae 배 **2** *v/t* (*send*) ponaeda
보내다; (*send by sea*) sŏnjŏk'ada
선적하다

shipment (*consignment*) hwamul
화물

shipowner sŏnbak soyuja 선박
소유자

shipping (*sea traffic*) haesang
kyot'ong 해상 교통; (*sending*)
palssong 발송; (*sending by sea*)
sŏnjŏk 선적

shipping company haeunhoesa
해운회사

shipshape *adj* chŏngdondoen 정돈된;

shipwreck 1 *n* nanp'a 난파 **2** *v/t*
nanp'ashik'ida 난파시키다; *be ~ed*
nanp'adoeda 난파되다; **shipyard**
chosŏnso 조선소

shirk keŭllihada 게을리하다

shirt shyŏch'ŭ 셔츠

shirt sleeves: *in his ~* usosŭl pŏtkko
웃옷을 벗고

shit F **1** *n* ttong 똥; (*bad quality goods,
work*) ssŭregi 쓰레기; *I need a ~*
hwajangsire kayagessŏ 화장실에
가야겠어 **2** *v/i* yongbyŏnboda
용변보다 **3** *interj*: *~!* chegiral!
제기랄!

shitty F chinjŏlmŏri nanŭn 진절머리
나는

shiver

shiver v/i ttŏlda 떨다

shock 1 n ch'unggyŏk 충격; ELEC shyok'ŭ 쇼크; *be in ~* MED ch'unggyŏgesŏ pŏsŏnaji mot'ada 충격에서 벗어나지 못하다 **2** v/t nollage hada 놀라게 하다; *be ~ed by* ch'unggyŏgŭl pat-tta 충격을 받다

shock absorber MOT wanch'unggi 완충기

shocking ch'unggyŏktchŏgin 충격적인; F (*very bad*) chidok'i choch'i anŭn 지독히 좋지 않은

shoddy *goods* p'umjiri nappŭn 품질이 나쁜; *behavior* such'isŭrŏun 수치스러운

shoe shinbal 신발

shoelace shinbalkkŭn 신발끈; **shoestore** shinbalkkage 신발가게; **shoestring**; *do X on a ~* Xŭl/rŭl aju chŏgŭn yesanŭro hada X을/를 아주 적은 예산으로 하다

♦ **shoo away** shwitsori naeŏ tchoch'abŏrida 쉿소리 내어 쫓아버리다

shoot 1 n BOT ŏrin-gaji 어린가지 **2** v/t ssoda 쏘다; (*and kill*) ch'ongsarhada 총살하다; *movie* ch'waryŏnghada 촬영하다; *~ X in the leg* Xŭi tarirŭl ssoda X의 다리를 쏘다 **3** v/i ch'ongŭl ssoda 총을 쏘다

♦ **shoot down** *airplane* ssoa ttŏrŏttŭrida 쏘아 떨어뜨리다; *suggestion* kŏjŏrhada 거절하다

♦ **shoot off** (*rush off*) taranada 달아나다

♦ **shoot up** (*of prices*) ch'isot-tta 치솟다; (*of children*) ssukssuk charada 쑥쑥 자라다; (*of buildings etc*) tanshigane chiŏjida 단시간에 지어지다; (*of new suburbs*) pulssuk saenggida 불쑥 생기다

shooting star yusŏng 유성

shop 1 n sangjŏm 상점; *talk ~* il iyagiman hada 일 이야기만 하다 **2** v/i shijangbo tada 시장보다; *go ~ping* changborŏ kada 장보러 가다

shopkeeper somaesang-in 소매상인

shoplifter somaech'igi 소매치기

shopper shyop'inghanŭn saram 쇼핑하는 사람

shopping (*activity*) shyop'ing 쇼핑;

(*items*) chang pon mulgŏn 장 본 물건; *do one's ~* changboda 장보다

shopping mall shyop'ingssent'ŏ 쇼핑센터

shop steward nodongjohabŭi chiktchangwiwŏn 노동조합의 직장위원

shore mulkka 물가; *on ~* (*not at sea*) yukssang-e(sŏ) 육상에(서)

short 1 adj (*in height*) k'iga chagŭn 키가 작은; *road, distance* tchalbŭn 짧은; (*in time*) oraedoeji anŭn 오래되지 않은; *be ~ of* mojarada 모자라다 **2** adv: *cut a vacation/meeting ~* hyugarŭl/hoeŭirŭl yejŏngboda ppalli kkŭnnaeda 휴가를/회의를 예정보다 빨리 끝내다; *stop a person ~* sarami marhanŭn kŏsŭl kkŭnŏborida 사람이 말하는 것을 끊어버리다; *go ~ of* chogŭm mojarŭge chinaeda 조금 모자르게 지내다; *in ~* yoyak'amyŏn 요약하면

shortage pujok 부족

short circuit n tallak 단락; **shortcoming** kyŏltchŏm 결점; **shortcut** chirŭmkkil 지름길

shorten v/t *dress, vacation, workday etc* churida 줄이다; *hair* tchalkke hada 짧게 하다; *~ a movie* yŏnghwaŭi pullyang-ŭl churida 영화의 분량을 줄이다

shortfall pujok 부족; **shorthand** n sok-kki 속기; **shortlist** n (*of candidates*) ch'oejong myŏngdan 최종 명단; **short-lived** tanmyŏnghan 단명한

shortly (*soon*) kot 곧; *~ before that* kŭ chŏne paro 그 전에 바로

shorts panbaji 반바지; (*underwear*) sogot 속옷

shortsighted kŭnshiŭi 근시의; *fig* kŭnshianjŏgin 근시안적인; **short-sleeved** panp'arŭi 반팔의; **shortstaffed** chigwŏni mojaranŭn 직원이 모자라는; **short story** tanp'yŏnsosŏl 단편소설; **short-tempered** sŏnggŭp'an 성급한; **short-term** tangigan 단기간; **short time**: *be on ~* (*of workers*) choŏp tanch'uk'ada 조업 단축하다; **short wave** tanp'a

단파
shot (*from gun*) ch'ongssori 총소리;
(*photograph*) sajin 사진; (*injection*)
chusa 주사; *be a good / poor ~*
ch'ong-ŭl chal / mot ssonŭn saramida
총을 잘 / 못 쏘는 사람이다; *like a ~
accept, run off* ch'ong-algatchi
총알같이

shotgun yŏpch'ong 엽총

should haeya hada 해야 하다; *what ~
I do?* nanŭn musŭn irŭl haeya
hamnikka? 나는 무슨 일을 해야
합니까?; *you ~n't do that*
tangshinŭn kŭrŏk'e hamyŏn
andoemnida 당신은 그렇게 하면
안됩니다; *that ~ be enough* kŭgŏllo
ch'ungbunhagetchyo 그걸로
충분하겠죠; *you ~ have heard him!*
nŏnŭn kŭga ttŏdŭnŭn kŏl turossŏya
haessŏ! 너는 그가 떠드는 걸
들었어야 했어!

shoulder n ŏkkae 어깨
shoulder blade kyŏngapkkol 견갑골
shout 1 n pimyŏngsori 비명소리 **2** v/i
sorich'ida 소리치다 **3** v/t *order*
myŏngnyŏnghada 명령하다
♦**shout at** …e taego sorijirŭda …에
대고 소리지르다

shouting n sorijirŭm 소리지름
shove 1 n ttemilgi 떼밀기 **2** v/t
mirŏnaeda 밀어내다 **3** v/i milda 밀다
♦**shove in** v/i (*in line-up*)
saech'igihada 새치기하다
♦**shove off** v/i F (*go away*) ka pŏrida
가 버리다

shovel n sap 삽
show 1 n THEA, TV shyo 쇼; (*display*)
p'yohyŏn 표현; *on ~* (*at exhibition*)
chŏnshi chung-in 전시 중인; *it's all
done for ~* pej kŭgŏ shyohanŭn
kŏyo 그거 쇼하는 거에요 **2** v/t
passport, ticket poyŏjuda 보여주다;
interest, emotion nat'anaeda
나타내다; (*at exhibition*)
chŏnshihada 전시하다; *movie*
sangyŏnghada 상영하다; *~ X to Y*
Xrŭl Yege poyŏjuda X를 Y에게
보여주다 **3** v/i (*be visible*) poida
보이다; (*of movie*) sangyŏngdoeda
상영되다
♦**show off 1** v/t *skills* parhwihada

발휘하다 **2** v/i pej uttchuldaeda
우쭐대다
♦**show up 1** v/t *shortcomings etc*
hwagyŏnhi poyŏjuda 확연히
보여주다; *don't show me up in
public* saramdŭl ap'esŏ narŭl
tanghwanghage haji maseyo 사람들
앞에서 나를 당황하게 하지 마세요
2 v/i (*arrive*) nat'anada 나타나다; (*be
visible*) poyŏjida 보여지다

show business shyo pijinisŭ 쇼
비즈니스
showdown han p'an taegyŏl 한 판
대결
shower 1 n (*of rain*) sonagi 소나기;
(*to wash*) shyawŏ 샤워; *take a ~*
shyawŏhada 샤워하다 **2** v/i
shyawŏhada 샤워하다 **3** v/t: *~ X with
compliments / praise* Xege
ch'ansarŭl / ch'ingch'anŭl p'ŏbut-tta
X에게 찬사를 / 칭찬을 퍼붓다
shower bath shyawŏ 샤워; **shower
cap** shyawŏ k'aep 샤워 캡; **shower
curtain** shyawŏ k'ŏt'ŭn 샤워 커튼;
showerproof pangsuŭi 방수의
show jumping chang-aemul
ttwiŏnŏmkki 장애물 뛰어넘기
show-off hŏp'ungjang-i 허풍장이
showroom shyo rum 쇼 룸; *in ~
condition* hanbŏndo sayongdoeji
anŭn 한번도 사용되지 않은
showy *jacket, behavior* nŏmu nune
ttŭinŭn 너무 눈에 띄는
shred 1 n (*of paper etc*) chogak 조각;
(*of evidence etc*) tanp'yŏn 단편 **2** v/t
paper kalgari tchijŏbŏrida 갈가리
찢어버리다; (*in cooking*) chogak
naeda 조각 내다
shredder (*for documents*) sŏryu
chŏlttan-gi 서류 절단기
shrewd pint'ŭm ŏmnŭn 빈틈 없는
shriek 1 n pimyŏng 비명 **2** v/i
pimyŏngŭl chirŭda 비명을 지르다
shrimp saeu 새우
shrine sŏnggorham 성골함
shrink v/i (*of material*) churŏdŭlda
줄어들다; (*of support etc*)
kamsohada 감소하다
shrink-wrap such'uk p'ojanghada
수축 포장하다
shrink-wrapping such'uk p'ojang

수축 포장

shrivel tchugŭlgŏrige hada 쭈글거리게 하다

shrub, shrubbery kwanmok 관목

shrug 1 *n* ŏkkaerŭl ŭssŭk-kkŏrim 어깨를 으쓱거림 **2** *v/t & v/i*: ~ (**one's shoulders**) ŏkkaerŭl ŭssŭk-kkŏrida 어깨를 으쓱거리다

shudder 1 *n* (*of fear, disgust*) momsŏri ch'im 몸서리 침; (*of earth etc*) ttŏllim 떨림 **2** *v/i* (*with fear, disgust*) momsŏrich'ida 몸서리치다; (*of earth, building*) ttŏllida 떨리다

shuffle 1 *v/t cards* twisŏktta 뒤섞다 **2** *v/i* (*in walking*) chiljil kkŭlmyŏ kada 질질 끌며 가다

shun *person* p'ihada 피하다; *drugs etc* kkŏrida 꺼리다

shut 1 *v/t* tat-tta 닫다 **2** *v/i* tatch'ida 닫히다; *the shop was ~* kagega munŭl tadat-tta 가게가 문을 닫았다

♦ **shut down 1** *v/t business* p'yeŏp'ada 폐업하다; *computer* chongnyonaeda 종료내다 **2** *v/i* (*of business*) p'yeŏp'ada 폐업하다; (*of computer*) chongnyohada 종료하다

♦ **shut up** *v/i* (*be quiet*) choyonghi hada 조용히 하다; *~!* choyonghi hae! 조용히 해!

shutter (*on window*) tŏnmun 덧문; PHOT shyŏt'ŏ 셔터

shuttle *v/i* wangbok'ada 왕복하다

shuttlebus (*at airport*) shyŏt'ŭlppŏsŭ 셔틀버스; **shuttlecock** SP paedŭmint'ŏn kong 배드민턴 공; **shuttle service** shyŏt'ŭl sŏbisŭ 셔틀 서비스

shy *person* sujubŏhanŭn 수줍어하는; *animal* sunhan 순한

shyness sujubŭm 수줍음; (*of animal*) sunham 순함

Siamese twins shyam ssangdung-i 샴 쌍둥이

sick ap'ŭn 아픈; *sense of humor* pulk'waehan 불쾌한; *society* kuyŏktchil nanŭn 구역질 나는; *I'm going to be ~* (*vomit*) t'ohallaeyo 토할래요; *be ~ of* (*fed up with*) chigyŏptta 지겹다

sicken 1 *v/t* (*disgust*) yŏk-kkyŏwŏ hada 역겨워 하다 **2** *v/i*: *be ~ing for*

chŭngsangŭl poida 증상을 보이다

sickening pulk'waehan 불쾌한

sickle wŏnhyŏng nat 원형 낫

sick leave pyŏngga 병가; *be on ~* pyŏngga chung-ida 병가 중이다

sickly *person* pyŏngyak'an 병약한; *color* hyŏlssaegi nappŭn 혈색이 나쁜

sickness pyŏng 병

side *n* (*of box, house*) yŏmmyŏn 옆면; (*of room, field*) ch'ungmyŏn 측면; (*of mountain*) kyŏngsa-myŏn 경사면; (*of person*) yŏpkkuri 옆구리; SP t'im 팀; *take ~s* (*favor one side*) p'yŏnŭl tŭlda 편을 들다; *take ~s with* ...ŭi p'yŏnŭl tŭlda ...의 편을 들다; *I'm on your ~* tangshin p'yŏniyeyo 당신 편이예요; *~ by ~* naranhi 나란히; *at the ~ of the road* kilkkae(sŏ) 길가에(서); *on the big / small ~* k'ŭn / chagŭn p'yŏn 큰 / 작은 편

♦ **side with** chijihada 지지하다

sideboard ch'antchang 찬장; **side dish** panch'an 반찬; **side effect** pujagyong 부작용; **sidelight** MOT ch'ap'okttŭng 차폭등; **sideline 1** *n* puŏp 부업 **2** *v/t*: *feel ~d* panggwanjach'ŏrŏm nŭkkida 방관자처럼 느끼다; **side street** kolmok-kkil 골목길; **sidetrack** *v/t* ...ŭi chuŭirŭl tollida ...의 주의를 돌리다; *he got ~ed into talking about politics again* kŭnŭn tto tashi yŏpkkilo ppajyŏ chŏngch'ie taehae iyagihaet-tta 그는 또 다시 옆길로 빠져 정치에 대해 이야기했다; **sidewalk** indo 인도; **sidewalk café** noch'ŏn k'ap'e 노천 카페; **sideways** *adv* yŏp'ŭro 옆으로

siege p'owi konggyŏk 포위 공격; *lay ~ to* p'owi konggyŏk'ada 포위 공격하다

sieve *n* ch'e 체

sift *v/t corn, ore* ch'ero ch'ida 체로 치다; *data* kŏllŏnaeda 걸러내다

♦ **sift through** *details, data* chosahayŏ kŏllŏnaeda 조사하여 걸러내다

sigh 1 *n* hansum 한숨; *heave a ~ of relief* andoŭi hansumŭl shwida 안도의 한숨을 쉬다 **2** *v/i* hansum chit-tta 한숨 짓다

sight *n* kwanggyŏng 광경; (*power of*

seeing) shiryŏk 시력; *~s* (*of city*)
kyŏnggwan 경관; **catch ~ of**
…ŭl/rŭl ŏnttŭt poda …을/를 언뜻
보다; **know by** ~ ŏlgulloman alda
얼굴로만 알다; **within ~ of** …i/ga
poinŭn kose(sŏ) …이/가 보이는
곳에(서); **out of ~** poji annŭn 보이지
않는; **what a ~ you are!** ne kkori
pol manhaguna! 네 꼴이 볼
만하구나!; **lose ~ of** main objective
etc …ŭl/rŭl ijŏbŏrida …을/를
잊어버리다

sightseeing kwan-gwang 관광; **go ~**
kwan-gwanghada 관광하다

sightseeing tour kwan-gwang
yŏhaeng 관광 여행

sightseer kwan-gwanggaek 관광객

sign 1 n (indication) kimi 기미; (road
~) p'yojip'an 표지판; (outside shop,
on building) kanp'an 간판; **it's a ~
of the times** yojŭm shidaega
kŭrŏssŭmnida 요즘 시대가
그렇습니다 **2** v/t & v/i sŏmyŏnghada
서명하다

♦**sign up** (join the army) ipttaehada
입대하다

signal 1 n shinho 신호; **be sending
out all the right / wrong ~s**
wanjŏnhi parŭn/kŭrŭt-ttoen insangŭl chuda 완전히 바른/그릇된 인상을
주다 **2** v/i (of driver) shinhohada
신호하다

signatory sŏmyŏng-in 서명인

signature sŏmyŏng 서명

signature tune t'ema ŭmak 테마
음악

significance chungnyosŏng 중요성

significant event etc chungdaehan
중대한; (quite large) sangdanghan
상당한

signify ŭimihada 의미하다

sign language suhwa 수화

signpost kyot'ong p'yojip'an 교통
표지판

silence 1 n koyo 고요; (of person)
ch'immuk 침묵; **in ~** work, march
choyonghage 조용하게; **~!**
choyonghi! 조용히! **2** v/t
ch'immukshik'ida 침묵시키다

silencer (on gun) pang-ŭm changch'i
방음 장치

silent choyonghan 조용한; forest
koyohan 고요한; machine, suffering
sori ŏmnŭn 소리 없는; movie
musŏng-ŭi 무성의; **stay ~** (not
comment) ch'immugŭl chik'ida
침묵을 지키다

silent partner ingmyŏng tong-ŏptcha
익명 동업자

silhouette n shilluet 실루엣

silicon shillik'on 실리콘

silicon chip shillik'on ch'ip 실리콘 칩

silk 1 n pidan 비단 **2** adj shirt etc
pidanŭi 비단의

Silla Silla 신라

silly ŏrisŏgŭn 어리석은

silver 1 n ŭn 은 **2** adj ring ŭnŭi 은의;
hair ŭnppich'ŭi 은빛의

silver medal ŭnmedal 은메달

silver-plated ŭn togŭmhan 은 도금한

similar pisŭt'an 비슷한

similarity yusa 유사

simmer v/i (in cooking) sŏsŏhi
kkŭltta 서서히 끓다; (with rage)
pugŭlbugŭl hwaga kkŭlt'a 부글부글
화가 끓다

♦**simmer down** ch'imch'ak'aejida
침착해지다

simple (easy) shwiun 쉬운; (not very
bright) tansunhan 단순한

simplicity kanttanham 간단함

simplify tansunhwahada 단순화하다

simplistic chinach'ige
tansunhwadoen 지나치게 단순화된

simply (absolutely) chŏngmal 정말;
(in a simple way) kanttanhage
간단하게; **it is ~ the best** tumal hal
kŏt ŏpsshi ch'oegoimnida 두말 할
것 없이 최고입니다

simulate hyungnaenaeda 흉내내다

simultaneous tongshiŭi 동시의

simultaneously tongshie 동시에

sin 1 n choe 죄 **2** v/i choe chit-tta 죄
짓다

since 1 prep ihuro 이후로; **~ last
week** chinan chu ihuro 지난 주
이후로 **2** adv iraero 이래로; **I haven't seen him ~** chŏgi kŭrŭl pon
chŏgi ŏptta 이래로 그를 본 적이
없다 **3** conj (expressions of time)
…han hue …한 후에; (seeing that)
…hagi ttaemune …하기 때문에; ~

sincere

you left nega ttonan hue 네가 떠난 후에; ~ **you don't like it** nega kŭgŏsŭl sirŏhagi ttaemune 네가 그것을 싫어하기 때문에

sincere sŏngshirhan 성실한

sincerely chinshimŭro 진심으로; *hope* chinshillo 진실로

sincerity sŏngshil 성실

sinful choega innŭn 죄가 있는

sing v/t & v/i noraehada 노래하다

Singapore Shinggap'orŭ 싱가포르

Singaporean 1 adj Shinggap'orŭ-ŭi 싱가포르의 **2** n (person) Shinggap'orŭin 싱가포르인

singe v/t kŭullida 그을리다

singer kasu 가수

single[1] adj (sole) hana 하나; (not double) han kyŏp 한 겹; (not married) toksshinja 독신자; **there wasn't a ~ ...** tan hanaŭi ...to ŏpssŏt-tta 단 하나의 ...도 없었다; **in ~ file** chul chiŏ 줄 지어 **2** n MUS singgŭlp'an 싱글판; **~s** (in tennis) tanshik 단식

♦ **single out** (choose) sŏnbarhada 선발하다; (distinguish) kubyŏrhada 구별하다

single-breasted oejul tanch'uŭi 외줄 단추의; **single-handed 1** adj tandogŭin 단독의 **2** adv honjasŏ 혼자서; **single-minded** chŏnnyŏmhanŭn 전념하는; **single mother** p'yŏnmo 편모; **single parent family** p'yŏnbumo sŭrhaŭi kajŏng 편부모 슬하의 가정

singular GRAM **1** adj tansuŭi 단수의 **2** n tansu 단수; **in the ~** tansuro 단수로

sinister sky, look etc pulgirhae poinŭn 불길해 보이는; person saak'an 사악한

sink 1 n shingk'ŭ 싱크 **2** v/i (of ship, object) karaantta 가라앉다; (of sun) chida 지다; (of interest rates etc) churŏdŭlda 줄어들다; **he sank onto the bed** kŭnŭn ch'imdaee p'ulssŏk tŭrŏnuwŏt-tta 그는 침대에 풀썩 드러누웠다 **3** v/t ship karaanch'ida 가라앉히다; funds t'ujahada 투자하다

♦ **sink in** (of liquid) ppajida 빠지다; **it still hasn't really sunk in** yŏjŏnhi

hyŏnshillo padadŭryŏjiji anayo 여전히 현실로 받아들여지지 않아요

sinner choein 죄인

sinusitis MED ch'ungnongtch'ŭng 축농증

sip 1 n holtchak-kkŏrim 홀짝거림 **2** v/t holtchak-kkŏrida 홀짝거리다

sir sŏnsaengnim 선생님; **excuse me, ~** shillyehamnida 실례합니다

siren sairen 사이렌

sirloin soŭi hŏri witbubun kogi 소의 허리 윗부분 고기

sister yŏja hyŏngje 여자 형제

sister-in-law (elder brother's wife) hyŏngsu 형수; (wife's younger sister) ch'ŏje 처제; (husband's younger/elder sister) shinui 시누이; (younger/elder brother's wife) olk'e 올케

sit 1 v/i antta 앉다 **2** v/t exam ch'irŭda 치르다

♦ **sit down** antta 앉다

♦ **sit up** (in bed) irŏna antta 일어나 앉다; (straighten back) ttokpparo antta 똑바로 앉다; (wait up at night) chaji ank'o kkaeŏ it-tta 자지 않고 깨어 있다

sitcom shit'ŭk'om 시트콤

site 1 n changso 장소 **2** v/t new offices etc ...ŭi wich'irŭl chŏnghada ...의 위치를 정하다

sitting (of committee, court) kaejŏng 개정; (for artist) moderi toegi 모델이 되기; (for meals) shikssa shigan 식사 시간

sitting room kŏshil 거실

situated: be ~ wich'ihada 위치하다

situation sanghwang 상황; (of building etc) wich'i 위치

six yŏsŏt 여섯, yuk 육

sixteen yŏlyŏsŏt 열 여섯, shimyuk 십육

sixteenth yŏlyŏsŏt pŏntchaeŭi 열 여섯 번째의

sixtieth yesun pŏntchaeŭi 예순 번째의; **~ birthday** hwan-gap 환갑

sixth yŏsŏt pŏntchaeŭi 여섯 번째의

sixty yesun 예순, yuksship 육십

size (of room, car, company) k'ŭgi 크기; (of loan, project) kyumo 규모; (of jacket, shoes) ch'issu 치수

♦**size up** p'yŏngkkahada 평가하다

sizeable *house* sangdanghi k'ŭn 상당히 큰; *meal, order* kkwae manŭn 꽤 많은

sizzle chigŭlgŏrida 지글거리다

skate 1 *n* sŭk'eit'ŭ 스케이트 **2** *v/i* sŭk'eit'ŭ t'ada 스케이트 타다

skateboard *n* sŭk'eit'ŭbodŭ 스케이트보드

skater sŭk'eit'ŭ t'anŭn saram 스케이트 타는 사람

skating sŭk'eit'ŭ t'agi 스케이트 타기

skeleton haegol 해골

skeleton key kyŏtssoe 곁쇠

skeptic hoeŭironja 회의론자

skeptical hoeŭijŏgin 회의적인

skepticism hoeŭiron 회의론

sketch 1 *n* sŭk'ech'i 스케치; THEA ch'ongŭk 촌극 **2** *v/t* sŭk'ech'ihada 스케치하다

sketchbook sŭk'ech'ibuk 스케치북

sketchy *knowledge etc* tanp'yŏntchŏgin 단편적인

ski 1 *n* sŭk'i 스키 **2** *v/i* sŭk'i t'ada 스키 타다

skid 1 *n* mikkŭrŏm 미끄럼 **2** *v/i* mikkŭrŏjida 미끄러지다

skier sŭk'i t'anŭn saram 스키 타는 사람

skiing sŭk'i t'agi 스키 타기

ski lift sŭk'i lip'ŭt'ŭ 스키 리프트

skill kisul 기술

skilled sungnyŏndoen 숙련된

skilled worker sungnyŏn-gong 숙련공

skillful nŭngsuk'an 능숙한

skim *surface* sŭch'idŭt chinagada 스치듯 지나가다

♦**skim off** *the best* sŏnch'wihada 선취하다

♦**skim through** *text* taech'ung hult'ŏboda 대충 훑어보다

skimmed milk t'altchi uyu 탈지 우유

skimpy *account etc* pinyak'an 빈약한; *little dress* kkwak choenŭn 꽉 죄는

skin 1 *n* (*of person*) p'ibu 피부; (*of animal*) kajuk 가죽; (*of fish*) kkŏptchil 껍질 **2** *v/t* ...ŭi kkŏptchirŭl pŏtkkida ...의 껍질을 벗기다

skin diving sŭk'in taibing 스킨 다이빙

skinny kkangmarŭn 깡마른

skin-tight mome kkok mannŭn 몸에 꼭 맞는

skip 1 *n* (*little jump*) ttwiŏ orŭm 뛰어 오름 **2** *v/i* kkangch'unggŏrimyŏ ttwiŏdanida 깡충거리며 뛰어다니다 **3** *v/t* (*omit*) ppattŭrida 빠뜨리다

ski pole sŭk'i chip'ang-i 스키 지팡이

skipper NAUT sŏnjang 선장; (*of team*) chujang 주장

skirt *n* ch'ima 치마

ski run sŭk'i hwaltchuro 스키 활주로

ski tow sŭk'it'o 스키토

skull tugaegol 두개골

sky hanŭl 하늘

skylight ch'aegwangch'ang 채광창

skyline sŭk'airain 스카이라인; **sky-scraper** mach'ŏllu 마천루

slab (*of stone*) sŏkp'an 석판; (*of cake etc*) tut'umhage k'ŭn chogak 두툼하게 큰 조각

slack *discipline, rope* nŭsŭnhan 느슨한; *person, work* pujuŭihan 부주의한; *period* pulgyŏnggiŭi 불경기의

slacken *v/t rope* nŭsŭnhage hada 느슨하게 하다; *pace* nŭtch'uda 늦추다

♦**slacken off** *v/i* (*of trading*) yak'wadoeda 약화되다; (*of pace*) nŭtch'uŏjida 늦추어지다

slacks paji 바지

slam 1 *v/t door* k'wang tat-tta 쾅 닫다 **2** *v/i* (*of door etc*) k'wang tach'ida 쾅 닫히다

♦**slam down** t'ŏlssŏk naeryŏnot'a 털썩 내려놓다

slander 1 *n* chungsang 중상 **2** *v/t* chungsanghada 중상하다

slang sogŏ 속어; (*of a specific group*) ŭnŏ 은어

slant 1 *v/i* kiulda 기울다 **2** *n* kyŏngsa 경사; (*given to a story*) kwantchŏm 관점

slanting *roof* pisŭdŭmhan 비스듬한; *eyes* ch'ik'yŏ ollagan 치켜 올라간

slap 1 *n* (*blow*) ch'igi 치기 **2** *v/t* ch'alssak ttaerida 찰싹 때리다

slash 1 *n* (*cut*) pegi 베기; (*in punctuation*) süllaeshwi 슬래쉬 **2** *v/t skin etc* naeribeda 내리베다; *prices, costs* sak-kkamhada 삭감하다; ~

slate

one's wrists tongmaegŭl peda 동맥을 베다

slate *n* sülleit'ŭ 슬레이트

slaughter 1 *n (of animals)* tosal 도살; *(of people, troops)* hakssal 학살 **2** *v/t animals* tosarhada 도살하다; *people, troops* hakssarhada 학살하다

slave *n* noye 노예

slay sarhaehada 살해하다

slaying *(murder)* sarhae 살해

sleazy *bar, character* t'arak'an 타락한

sled(ge) *n* ssŏlmae 썰매

sledge hammer taehyŏng mangch'i 대형 망치

sleep 1 *n* cham 잠; *go to ~* chami tŭlda 잠이 들다; *I need a good ~* ch'ungbunhage chaya haeyo 충분하게 자야 해요; *I couldn't get to ~* chal suga ŏpssŏssŏyo 잘 수가 없었어요 **2** *v/i* chada 자다

♦ **sleep on** *v/t proposal, decision* ch'ungbunhi saenggak'ada 충분히 생각하다

♦ **sleep with** *(have sex with)* …wa/kwa kach'i chada …와/과 같이 자다

sleeping bag süllip'ing paek 슬리핑백; **sleeping car** ch'imdaech'a 침대차; **sleeping pill** sumyŏnje 수면제

sleepless *night* cham mot irunŭn 잠 못 이루는

sleepwalker mongnyuppyŏngja 몽유병자

sleepy *yawn* chollin 졸린; *town* choyonghan 조용한; *I'm ~* chollyŏyo 졸려요

sleet *n* ssaragi nun 싸라기 눈

sleeve *(of jacket etc)* somae 소매

sleeveless somaega ŏmnŭn 소매가 없는

sleight of hand kamtchok-kkat'ŭn sonnollim 감쪽같은 손놀림

slender *figure, arms* kanyalp'ŭn 가냘픈; *chance* hüibak'an 희박한; *income, margin* ŏlma andoenŭn 얼마 안되는

slice 1 *n (of bread, tart)* chogak 조각; *(of profits etc)* pubun 부분 **2** *v/t loaf etc* yalkke charŭda 얇게 자르다

sliced bread challanoŭn ppang

잘라놓은 빵

slick 1 *adj performance* nŭngsuk'an 능숙한; *pej (cunning)* kyomyohan 교묘한 **2** *n (of oil)* mak 막

slide 1 *n (for kids)* mikkŭrŏmt'ŭl 미끄럼틀; PHOT süllaidŭ 슬라이드 **2** *v/i* mikkŭrŏjida 미끄러지다; *(of exchange rate etc)* ttŏrŏjida 떨어지다 **3** *v/t* mirŏnŏt'a 밀어넣다

sliding door midaji mun 미닫이 문

slight 1 *adj person, figure* kanyalp'ŭn 가냘픈; *difference etc* yakkanŭi 약간의; *no, not in the ~est* anio, chogŭmdo animnida 아니오, 조금도 아닙니다 **2** *n (insult)* moyok 모욕

slightly yakkan 약간

slim 1 *adj* nalsshinhan 날씬한; *chance* hüibak'an 희박한 **2** *v/i* sal ppaeda 살 빼다

slime kkŭnjŏk-kkŭnjŏk'an kŏt 끈적끈적한 것

slimy *liquid* chilch'ŏk'an 질척한; *person* allanggŏrinŭn 알랑거리는

sling 1 *n (for arm)* samgak-kkŏn 삼각건 **2** *v/t (throw)* tŏnjida 던지다

slip 1 *n (on ice etc)* mikkŭrŏjim 미끄러짐; *(mistake)* shilssu 실수; *a ~ of paper* chagŭn chong-i 작은 종이; *a ~ of the tongue* shirŏn 실언; *give s.o. the ~* nugurŭl ttadollida 누구를 따돌리다 **2** *v/i (on ice etc)* mikkŭrŏjida 미끄러지다; *(of quality etc)* chŏhadoeda 저하되다; *he ~ped out of the room* künün saltchak pangŭl nagat-tta 그는 살짝 방을 나갔다 **3** *v/t (put)* saltchak not'a 살짝 놓다; *he ~ped it into his briefcase* künün sŏryugabang-e kügŏsŭl salmyŏshi nŏŏt-tta 그는 서류가방에 그것을 살며시 넣었다

♦ **slip away** *(of time)* sunshik-kkane chinagada 순식간에 지나가다; *(of opportunity)* künyang sarajida 그냥 사라지다; *(die quietly)* choyonghi sesang-ŭl ttŭda 조용히 세상을 뜨다

♦ **slip off** *v/t jacket etc* pŏt-tta 벗다

♦ **slip out** *v/i (go out)* ppajyŏ nagada 빠져 나가다

♦ **slip up** *v/i (make mistake)* shilssuhada 실수하다

slipped disc ch'uganp'an 추간판

slipper sŭllip'ŏ 슬리퍼

slippery mikkŭrŏun 미끄러운

slipshod kkomkkomhaji anŭn 꼼꼼하지 않은

slit 1 *n* (*tear*) tchijŏjin kot 찢어진 곳; (*hole*) kumŏng 구멍; (*in skirt*) kilge t'ŭn kot 길게 튼 곳 **2** *v/t* tchijŏ yŏlda 찢어 열다; *throat* peda 베다

slither *v/i* mikkŭrŏjida 미끄러지다

slobber *v/i* kunch'im hŭllida 군침 흘리다

slogan sŭllogŏn 슬로건

slop *v/t* ppurida 뿌리다

slope 1 *n* (*of roof*) kyŏngsa 경사; (*of handwriting*) kiulgi 기울기; (*of mountain*) kisŭk 기슭; *built on a ~* kisŭlge sewŏjin 기슭에 세워진 **2** *v/i* kyŏngsajida 경사지다; *the road ~s down to the sea* kiri padatchogŭro kyŏngsajyŏ it-tta 길이 바다쪽으로 경사져 있다

sloppy *work* pujuŭihan 부주의한; (*in dress*) tanjŏngch'i mot'an 단정치 못한; (*too sentimental*) chinach'ige kamsangjŏgin 지나치게 감상적인

sloshed F (*drunk*) sul ch'wihan 술 취한

slot *n* t'ŭmsae 틈새; (*in schedule*) tcham 짬, piŏinnŭn shigan 비어있는 시간

♦ **slot in 1** *v/t* kkiuda 끼우다 **2** *v/i* kkiwŏjida 끼워지다

slot machine (*for vending*) chap'an-gi 자판기; (*for gambling*) sŭllot mŏshin 슬롯 머신

slouch *v/i* momŭl kuburida 몸을 구부리다

slovenly tanjŏngch'i mot'an 단정치 못한

slow nŭrin 느린; *be ~* (*of clock*) nŭrida 느리다

♦ **slow down 1** *v/t* nŭrige hada 느리게 하다 **2** *v/i* nŭryŏjida 느려지다

slowdown (*in production*) t'aeŏp 태업

slow motion: *in* ~ nŭrin tongjagŭro 느린 동작으로

slug *n* (*animal*) mindalp'aeng-i 민달팽이

sluggish *pace* nŭrin 느린; *river* wanmanhan 완만한; *start* hwalbarhaji mot'an 활발하지 못한

slum *n* pinmin-ga 빈민가

slump 1 *n* (*in trade*) pulgyŏnggi 불경기 **2** *v/i* (*of economy*) soet'oehada 쇠퇴하다; (*collapse: of person*) ssŭrŏjida 쓰러지다

slur 1 *n* (*on s.o.'s character*) pibang 비방 **2** *v/t words* punmyŏnghaji ank'e marhada 분명하지 않게 말하다

slurred *speech* parŭmi punmyŏngch'i anŭn 발음이 분명치 않은

slush nok-kki shijak'an nun 녹기 시작한 눈; *pej* (*sentimental stuff*) nunmul tchage hanŭn kŏt 눈물 짜게 하는 것

slush fund pijagŭm 비자금

slut p'umhaeng-i nappŭn yŏja 품행이 나쁜 여자

sly kyohwarhan 교활한; *on the* ~ nam mollae saltchak 남 몰래 살짝

smack 1 *n* sonppadagŭro han tae ttaerigi 손바닥으로 한 대 때리기 **2** *v/t child, bottom* sonppadagŭro ch'alssak ttaerida 손바닥으로 찰싹 때리다

small 1 *adj* (*in size*) chagŭn 작은; (*in amount*) chŏgŭn 적은 **2** *n: the ~ of the back* hŏri tŭngtchogŭi chilluk'an pubun 허리 등쪽의 질룩한 부분

small change chandon 잔돈; **small hours** shimnya 심야; **smallpox** ch'ŏnyŏndu 천연두; **small print** (*on a contract*) sebu chohang 세부 조항; **small talk** chapttam 잡담

smart 1 *adj* (*elegant*) mŏtchin 멋진; (*intelligent*) ttokttok'an 똑똑한; *pace* sangdanghi pparŭn 상당히 빠른; *get* ~ *with* (*fresh*) ...ege kŏnbangjige kulda ...에게 건방지게 굴다 **2** *v/i* (*hurt*) ssushida 쑤시다

smart card chŏnja k'adŭ 전자 카드

♦ **smarten up** *v/t* malssuk'age hada 말쑥하게 하다

smash 1 *n* (*noise*) pusŏjinŭn sori 부서지는 소리; (*car crash*) ch'ungdol 충돌; (*in tennis*) sŭmaeshi 스매시 **2** *v/t* (*break*) pusuda 부수다; (*hit hard*) kangt'ahada 강타하다; ~ *X to pieces* Xŭl/rŭl sansanjogak naeda

smash hit

X을 / 를 산산조각 내다 **3** *v/i* (*break*) pusŏjida 부서지다; *the driver ~ed into …* e ch'ungdorhaet-tta 운전자는 …에 충돌했다

smash hit F taehit'ŭ 대히트

smashing F kkŭnnaejunŭn 끝내주는

smattering (*of a language*) ŏsŏlp'ŭn shillyŏk 어설픈 실력

smear 1 *n* (*of ink etc*) ŏlluk 얼룩; MED tomal p'yobon kŏmsa 도말 표본 검사; (*on character*) otchŏm 오점 **2** *v/t paint etc* parŭda 바르다; *character* tŏrŏp'ida 더럽히다

smear campaign chungsang moryak 중상 모략

smell 1 *n* naemsae 냄새; *sense of ~* hugak 후각 **2** *v/t* …ŭi naemsaerŭl mat-tta …의 냄새를 맡다 **3** *v/i* (*unpleasantly*) naemsaega nada 냄새가 나다; (*sniff*) naemsaerŭl mat-tta 냄새를 맡다; *what does it ~ of?* ŏttŏn naemsaega nanŭndeyo? 어떤 냄새가 나는데요?; *you ~ of beer* tangshinhant'esŏ maektchu naemsaega nayo 당신한테서 맥주 냄새가 나요

smelly naemsae nanŭn 냄새 나는

smile 1 *n* miso 미소 **2** *v/i* misojit-tta 미소짓다

♦ **smile at** …ege misojit-tta …에게 미소짓다

smirk 1 *n* nŭnggŭlmajŭn usŭm 능글맞은 웃음 **2** *v/i* nŭnggŭlmatkke ut-tta 능글맞게 웃다

smog sŭmogŭ 스모그

smoke 1 *n* yŏn-gi 연기; *have a ~* tambaerŭl p'iuda 담배를 피우다 **2** *v/t cigarettes* p'iuda 피우다; *bacon* hunjehada 훈제하다 **3** *v/i* yŏn-giga nada 연기가 나다; *I don't ~* chŏn, tambaerŭl p'iuji anayo 전, 담배를 피우지 않아요

smoker (*person*) hŭbyŏnja 흡연자

smoking hŭbyŏn 흡연; *no ~* kŭmyŏn 금연

smoky *air* yŏn-giga chauk'an 연기가 자욱한

smolder (*of fire*) yŏn-giman p'iuda 연기만 피우다; (*with anger*) sogŭro ssaida 속으로 쌓이다; (*with desire*)

tŭlkkŭlt'a 들끓다

smooth 1 *adj surface, skin, sea* maekkŭrŏun 매끄러운; *ride* pudŭrŏun 부드러운; *transition* sunjoroun 순조로운; *pej: person* chinach'ige yejŏl parŭn 지나치게 예절 바른 **2** *v/t hair* ssŭdadŭmda 쓰다듬다

♦ **smooth down** (*with sandpaper etc*) pudŭrŏpkke mandŭlda 부드럽게 만들다

♦ **smooth out** *paper, cloth* p'yŏda 펴다

♦ **smooth over**: *smooth things over* wŏnmanhage haegyŏrhada 원만하게 해결하다

smother *flames* tŏp'ŏ kkŭda 덮어 끄다; *person* chilshik shik'ida 질식 시키다; *~ X with kisses* Xege k'isŭrŭl p'ŏbut-tta X에게 키스를 퍼붓다

smudge 1 *n* ŏlluk 얼룩 **2** *v/t* tŏrŏp'ida 더럽히다

smug chal nan ch'ehanŭn 잘 난 체하는

smuggle *v/t* millsuhada 밀수하다

smuggler millsuŏptcha 밀수업자

smuggling millsu 밀수

smutty *joke* ŭmnanhan 음란한

snack *n* kanshik 간식

snack bar kani shikttang 간이 식당

snag (*problem*) ttŭt'aji anŭn chang-ae 뜻하지 않은 장애

snail talp'aeng-i 달팽이

snake *n* paem 뱀

snap 1 *n* ttak'anŭn sori 딱하는 소리; PHOT sŭnaep sajin 스냅 사진 **2** *v/t* (*break*) purŏttŭrida 부러뜨리다; (*say sharply*) ttakttak-kkŏrida 딱딱거리다 **3** *v/i* (*break*) purŏjida 부러지다 **4** *adj decision, judgment* sunshik-kkanŭi 순식간의

♦ **snap up** *bargain* ŏllŭn sada 얼른 사다

snappy *person, mood* sŏnggŭp'an 성급한; *decision, response* minch'ŏp'an 민첩한; (*elegant*) uahan 우아한

snapshot sŭnaep sajin 스냅 사진

snarl 1 *n* (*of dog*) ŭrŭrŏnggŏrim 으르렁거림 **2** *v/i* ŭrŭrŏnggŏrida

으르렁거리다

snatch 1 *v/t* chabach'aeda 잡아채다;
(*steal*) humch'ida 훔치다; (*kidnap*)
yugoehada 유괴하다 **2** *v/i*
chabach'aeda 잡아채다

snazzy seryŏndoen 세련된

sneak 1 *v/t* (*remove, steal*) sŭltchŏk
kajyŏgada 슬쩍 가져가다; **~ a
glance at** kyŏnnunjirhada
곁눈질하다 **2** *v/i*: **~ into the
room / out of the room** sŭlgŭmŏni
pang-ŭro tŭrŏgada / pang-esŏ nagada
슬그머니 방으로 들어가다 / 방에서
나가다

sneakers undonghwa 운동화

sneaking: **have a ~ suspicion that
...** ...ranŭn ŭishimŭl ŭn-gŭnhi kajida
...라는 의심을 은근히 가지다

sneaky F (*crafty*) kyomyohan 교묘한

sneer 1 *n* piusŭm 비웃음 **2** *v/i* piut-tta
비웃다

sneeze 1 *n* chaech'aegi 재채기 **2** *v/i*
chaech'aegihada 재채기하다

sniff 1 *v/i* (*to clear nose*) k'orŭl
hultchŏk-kkŏrida 코를 훌쩍거리다;
(*to catch scent*) k'orŭl
k'ŭngk'ŭnggŏrida 코를 킁킁거리다
2 *v/t* (*smell*) k'oro tŭrishwida 코로
들이쉬다

sniper chŏgyŏkppyŏng 저격병

snitch F **1** *n* (*telltale*) kojajiltchaeng-i
고자질쟁이 **2** *v/i* kojajirhada
고자질하다

snob songmul 속물

snobbish songmurŭi 속물의

snooker tanggu 당구

♦**snoop around** kiutkkŏrimyŏ
toradanida 기웃거리며 돌아다니다

snooty kŏmanhan 거만한

snooze 1 *n* cholgi 졸기; **have a ~**
cholda 졸다 **2** *v/i* cholda 졸다

snore k'o kolda 코 골다

snoring *n* k'o kolgi 코 골기

snorkel sŭnok'ŭl 스노클

snort *v/i* (*of animal*) k'otkkimŭl
naeppumtta 콧김을 내뿜다; (*of
person*: *disdainfully*) k'otppanggwi
kkwida 콧방귀 뀌다

snout (*of pig*) chudung-i 주둥이

snow 1 *n* nun 눈 **2** *v/i* nuni naerida
눈이 내리다

♦**snow under**: **be snowed under
with ...** ...(ŭ)ro apttodanghada
...(으)로 압도당하다

snowball *n* nunttong-i 눈덩이; **snowbound** nune katch'in 눈에 갇힌;
snow chains MOT sŭnou ch'ein
스노우 체인; **snowdrift** ssain
nundŏmi 쌓인 눈더미; **snowdrop**
anemone 아네모네; **snowflake**
nunsong-i 눈송이; **snowman**
nunssaram 눈사람; **snowplow**
chesŏlgi 제설기; **snowstorm**
nunbora 눈보라

snowy *weather* nuni onŭn 눈이 오는;
roads, hills nuni ssain 눈이 쌓인

snub 1 *n* naengdae 냉대 **2** *v/t*
naengdaehada 냉대하다

snub-nosed chumŏk k'oŭi 주먹코의

snug anŭk'an 아늑한; (*tight-fitting*)
kkok mannŭn 꼭 맞는

♦**snuggle down** p'ogŭnhage momŭl
mut-tta 포근하게 몸을 묻다

♦**snuggle up to** ...ŭl / rŭl kkŭrŏ antta
...을 / 를 끌어 안다

so 1 *adv* nŏmu 너무; **~ hot / cold**
nŏmu tŏun / ch'uun 너무 더운 / 추운;
not ~ much nŏmu manch'i ank'e
너무 많지 않게; **~ much bet-
ter / easier** hwŏlsshin tŏ
choŭn / shwiun 훨씬 더 좋은 / 쉬운;
eat / drink ~ much nŏmu mani
mŏktta / mashida 너무 많이
먹다 / 마시다; **I miss you ~** nega
koengjanghi pogo shiptta 네가
굉장히 보고 싶다; **~ am I / do I** nado
kŭraeyo / kŭrŏk'e haeyo 나도
그래요 / 그렇게 해요; **~ is she / does
she** kŭ yŏjado kŭraeyo / kŭrŏk'e
haeyo 그 여자도 그래요 / 그렇게
해요; **and ~ on** kit'a tŭngdŭng 기타
등등; **~ what?** kŭraesŏ ŏtchaet-
ttanŭn kŏya? 그래서 어쨌다는 거야?
2 *pron*: **I hope ~ / think ~** kŭrŏk'e
toegil paramnida / kŭrŏk'e
saenggak'amnida 그렇게 되길
바랍니다 / 그렇게 생각합니다; **you
didn't tell me - I did** ~ nahant'e
marhaji anassŏ - ani, marhaessŏ
나한테 말하지 않았어 - 아니,
말했어; **50 or ~** oship chŏngdo 오십
정도 **3** *conj* (*for that reason*)

soak

kŭgŏsŭro inhaesŏ 그것으로 인해서;
(in order that) kŭraesŏ 그래서; **and
~ I missed the train** kŭraesŏ nanŭn
kich'arŭl notch'ŏt-tta 그래서 나는
기차를 놓쳤다; ~ **(that) I could
come too** kŭrŏk'e haesŏ na yŏkssi
ol su itssŏtta 그렇게 해서 나 역시 올
수 있었다

soak *v/t (steep)* tamgŭda 담그다; *(of
water, rain)* chŏksshida 적시다

♦ **soak up** *liquid* pparadŭrida
빨아들이다

soaked hŭmppŏk chŏjŭn 흠뻑 젖은

so-and-so F *(unknown person)*
amugae 아무개; *(annoying person)*
shirŭn nom 싫은 놈

soap *n (for washing)* pinu 비누

soap (opera) yŏnsok tŭrama 연속
드라마

soapy *water* pinuŭi 비누의

soar *(of rocket etc)* sosa orŭda 솟아
오르다; *(of prices)* ch'isot-tta 치솟다

sob 1 *n* hŭnŭkkim 흐느낌 **2** *v/i*
hŭnŭkkyŏ ulda 흐느껴 울다

sober *(not drunk)* ch'wihaji anŭn
취하지 않은; *(serious)* chinjihan
진지한

♦ **sober up** suri kkaeda 술이 깨다

so-called *(referred to as)* lago hanŭn
kŏsŭn 라고 하는 것은; *pej* sowi 소위

soccer ch'uk-kku 축구

sociable sagyojŏgin 사교적인

social *adj* sahoeŭi 사회의;
(recreational) ch'inmogŭi 친목의

socialism sahoejuŭi 사회주의

socialist 1 *adj* sahoejuŭijŏgin
사회주의적인 **2** *n* sahoejuŭija
사회주의자

socialize saramgwa sagwida 사람과
사귀다

social work sahoe saŏp 사회 사업

social worker sahoe saŏpkka 사회
사업가

society sahoe 사회; *(organization)*
tanch'e 단체

sociology sahoehak 사회학

sock¹ *(for wearing)* yangmal 양말

sock² **1** *n (punch)* kangt'a 강타 **2** *v/t
(punch)* sege ch'ida 세게 치다

socket ELEC sok'et 소켓; *(of eye)*
angu 안구; *(of arm)* kwanjŏl 관절

soda *(~ water)* t'ansansu 탄산수; *(ice-
cream ~)* k'ŭrimsoda 크림소다; *(soft
drink)* ch'ŏngnyang ŭmnyo 청량
음료

sofa sop'a 소파

sofa bed sop'ashik ch'imdae 소파식
침대

soft *pillow, chair* p'uksshinhan 푹신한;
voice, music, skin, color pudŭrŏun
부드러운; *light* onhwahan 온화한;
(lenient) kwandaehan 관대한; **have
a ~ spot for** ...ŭl/rŭl koengjanghi
choahada ...을/를 굉장히 좋아하다

soft drink ch'ŏngnyang ŭmnyo 청량
음료

soften 1 *v/t* pudŭrŏpkke hada
부드럽게 하다, wanhwahada
완화하다 **2** *v/i (of butter, ice cream)*
pudŭrŏwŏjida 부드러워지다

softly pudŭrŏpkke 부드럽게

software sop'ŭt'ŭweŏ 소프트웨어

soggy chŏjŭn 젖은; *pastry* sŏlguwŏjin
설구워진

soil 1 *n (earth)* hŭk 흙 **2** *v/t* tŏrŏp'ida
더럽히다

solar energy t'aeyang enŏji 태양
에너지

solar panel t'aeyang chŏnjip'an 태양
전지판

soldier kunin 군인

sole¹ *n (of foot, shoe)* padak 바닥

sole² *adj* tan hanaŭi 단 하나의

solely ojik 오직

solemn *(serious)* ŏmssuk'an 엄숙한

solid *adj (hard)* tandanhan 단단한;
(without holes) kyŏn-gohan 견고한;
gold, silver sun 순; *(sturdy)*
t'ŭnt'ŭnhan 튼튼한; *evidence* hwak-
kkohan 확고한; *support*
kangnyŏk'an 강력한

solidarity tan-gyŏl 단결

solidify *v/i* kudŏjida 굳어지다

solitaire *(card game)* sollit'erŭ
솔리테르

solitary *life, activity* kodok'an 고독한;
(single) tan hanaŭi 단 하나의

solitude kodok 고독

solo 1 *n* MUS *(of vocalist)* tokch'ang
독창; *(of instrumentalist)* toktchu
독주 **2** *adj* honjaŭi 혼자의

soloist *(vocalist)* tokch'angja 독창자;

(*instrumentalist*) toktchuja 독주자
soluble *substance* kayongssŏng-ŭi 가용성의; *problem* haegyŏrhal su innŭn 해결할 수 있는
solution haedap 해답; (*mixture*) honhap 혼합
solve p'ulda 풀다
solvent *adj* (*financially*) chibul nŭngnyŏgi innŭn 지불 능력이 있는
somber (*dark*) kŏmusŭrŭmhan 거무스름한; (*serious*) ch'imurhan 침울한
some 1 *adj* ŏttŏn 어떤, ŏlmaganŭi 얼마간의; ~ *people say that ...* ŏttŏ saramdŭrŭn ... rago malhanda 어떤 사람들은 ... 라고 말한다; *would you like ~ water / cookies?* mul / kwaja chom tŭshigessŏyo? 물 / 과자 좀 드시겠어요? **2** *pron* (*people*) ŏttŏn saramdŭl 어떤 사람들; (*things*) ŏttŏn kŏt 어떤 것; ~ *of the group* kŭrubŭi ŏttŏn idŭl 그룹의 어떤 이들; *would you like ~?* chom hashigessŏyo? 좀 하시겠어요?; *give me ~* chogŭm chuseyo 조금 주세요 **3** *adv* (*a bit*) chogŭm 조금; *we'll have to wait ~* urin chogŭm kidaryŏya hae 우린 조금 기다려야 해
somebody nugun-ga 누군가
someday ŏnjen-ga 언젠가
somehow (*by one means or another*) ŏttŏk'edŭnji 어떻게든지; (*for some unknown reason*) ŏtchŏnji 어쩐지
someone → **somebody**
someplace → **somewhere**
somersault 1 *n* chaeju nŏmkki 재주 넘기 **2** *v/i* chaeju nŏmtta 재주 넘다
something muŏtin-ga 무엇인가; *would you like ~ to drink / eat?* mashil / ŏgŭl kŏt chom hashigessŏyo? 마실 / 먹을 것 좀 하시겠어요?; *is ~ wrong?* muŏshi chalmot toeŏssŭmnikka? 무엇이 잘못 되었습니까?
sometime ŏnjen-ga 언젠가; ~ *last year* changnyŏn ŏnjen-ga 작년 언젠가
sometimes ttaettaero 때때로
somewhere 1 *adv* ŏdin-gae 어딘가에 **2** *pron*: *let's go ~ quiet* ŏdi choyonghan kosŭro kapsshida 어디

choyonghan kosŭro kapsshida 조용한 곳으로 갑시다; *is there ~ to park?* ŏdie chuch'ahal koshi issŏyo? 어디 주차할 곳이 있어요?
son adŭl 아들
song norae 노래
songwriter chakssa chak-kkok-kka 작사 작곡가
son-in-law sawi 사위
son of a bitch F kaesaekki 개새끼
soon kot 곧; *as ~ as* ...haja maja ...하자 마자; *as ~ as possible* kanŭnghan han ppalli 가능한 한 빨리; ~ *er or later* choman-gan 조만간; *the ~er the better* pparŭmyŏn pparŭlssurok choayo 빠르면 빠를수록 좋아요
soot kŭŭrŭm 그을음
soothe chinjŏngshik'ida 진정시키다
sophisticated *person, tastes* seryŏndoen 세련된; *machine* chŏnggyohan 정교한
sophomore ihangnyŏn 이학년
soprano *n* sop'ŭrano 소프라노
sordid *affair, business* tŏrŏun 더러운
sore 1 *adj* (*painful*) ap'ŭn 아픈; F (*angry*) hwaga nan 화가 난; *is it ~?* ap'ayo? 아파요? **2** *n* sangch'ŏ 상처
sorrow *n* sŭlp'ŭm 슬픔
sorry (*sad*) *day* sŭlp'ŭn 슬픈; *sight* pulssanghan 불쌍한; (*I'm*) ~ (*apologizing*) mianhae 미안해; (*polite*) mianhamnida 미안합니다; (*I'm*) ~ *but I can't help* (*regretting*) mianhajiman, chega toul suga ŏmneyo 미안하지만, 제가 도울 수가 없네요; *I will be ~ to leave Seoul* Sŏurŭl ttŏnani yugamimnida 서울을 떠나니 유감입니다; *I won't be ~ to go home* chŏnŭn chibe kanŭn ke natkkessŏyo 저는 집에 가는 게 낫겠어요; *I feel ~ for her* kŭ yŏjaga andwaetkkunyo 그 여자가 안됐군요
sort 1 *n* chongnyu 종류; ~ *of ...* F taso ... 다소 ...; *is it finished? - ~ of* F kkŭnnassŏyo? - kŭrŏndaeroyo 끝났어요? - 그런대로요 **2** *v/t* pulluyhada 분류하다; COMPUT kubunhada 구분하다
♦ **sort out** *papers* karyŏnaeda 가려내다; *problem* haegyŏrhada 해결하다

so-so adv kŭjŏ kŭrŏn 그저 그런
soul REL yŏnghon 영혼; *fig (of a
nation etc)* chŏngshin 정신;
(character) t'ukssŏng 특성; *(person)*
saram 사람
sound¹ adj *(sensible)* punbyŏl innŭn
분별 있는; *(healthy)* kŏn-ganghan
건강한; ~ *sleep* sungmyŏn 숙면
sound² 1 n so.ı 소리 2 v/t
(pronounce) parŭmhada 발음하다;
MED ch'ŏngjinhada 청진하다; ~
one's horn kyŏngjŏgŭl ullida 경적을
울리다 3 v/i: *that ~s interesting*
chaemiissŭl kŏt kat'ayo 재미있을 것
같아요; *that ~s like a good idea*
choŭn saenggak kat'ayo 좋은 생각
같아요; *she ~ed unhappy* kŭ
yŏjanŭn purhaenghage tŭllyŏtta 그
여자는 불행하게 들렸다
sound card COMPUT saundŭ k'adŭ
사운드 카드
soundly *sleep* kip'i 깊이; *beaten*
wanbyŏk'age 완벽하게
soundproof adj pang-ŭmŭi 방음의
soundtrack paegyŏng ŭmak 배경
음악
soup *(western)* sup'ŭ 수프; *(Korean)*
kuk 국
soup bowl *(western)* sup'ŭ chŏpsshi
수프 접시; *(Korean)* kuk kŭrŭt 국
그릇
sour adj *apple* shin 신; *milk* sanghan
상한; *comment* shimsulgujŭn
심술궂은
source n wŏnch'ŏn 원천; *(of river)*
suwŏnji 수원지; *(person)* chŏngbo
chegongja 정보 제공자
south 1 adj namtchogŭi 남쪽의 2 n
namtchok 남쪽; *(of country)*
namtchok chibang 남쪽 지방; *to the
~ of* ...ŭi namtchoge ...의 남쪽에
3 adv namtchogŭro 남쪽으로
South Africa Namap'ŭrik'a
남아프리카; **South African** 1 adj
Namap'ŭrik'aŭi 남아프리카의 2 n
Namap'ŭrik'ain 남아프리카인; **South
America** Nammi 남미; **South
American** 1 adj Nammiŭi 남미의 2 n
Nammiin 남미인; **southeast** 1 n
namdongtchok 남동쪽 2 adj
namdongtchogŭi 남동쪽의 3 adv

namdongtchogŭro 남동쪽으로; *it's ~
of* ...ŭi namdongtchoge it-tta ...의
남동쪽에 있다; **Southeast Asia**
Tongnam Ashia 동남 아시아;
Southeast Asian adj Tongnam
Ashiaŭi 동남 아시아의; **southeastern** namdongtchogŭi 남동쪽의
southerly adj namhyang-ŭi 남향의
southern nambuŭi 남부의
South Korea Namhan 남한
South Korean 1 adj Namhanŭi
남한의 2 n *(person)* Namhanin
남한인
southward adv namtchogŭro
남쪽으로
southwest 1 n namsŏtchok 남서쪽
2 adj namsŏtchogŭi 남서쪽의 3 adv
namsŏtchogŭro 남서쪽으로; *it's ~ of*
...ŭi namsŏtchoge it-tta ...의
남서쪽에 있다
southwestern namsŏtchogŭi
남서쪽의
souvenir kinyŏmp'um 기념품
sovereign adj *state* tongnibŭi 독립의
sovereignty *(of state)* tongnipkkuk
독립국
Soviet Union Soryŏn 소련
sow¹ n *(female pig)* amt'waeji 암퇘지
sow² v/t *seeds* ppurida 뿌리다
soy bean k'ong 콩; **soy milk** tuyu
두유; **soy sauce** kanjang 간장
spa onch'ŏn 온천
space n *(atmosphere)* uju 우주; *(area)*
pin k'an 빈 칸; *(room)* konggan 공간
♦**space out** iltchŏnghan kan-gyŏgŭl
tuda 일정한 간격을 두다
spacebar COMPUT sŭp'eisŭ pa
스페이스 바; **spacecraft**, **spaceship** ujusŏn 우주선; **space shuttle**
uju wangbokssŏn 우주 왕복선;
space station uju chŏnggŏjang 우주
정거장; **spacesuit** ujubok 우주복
spacious tŭnŏlbŭn 드넓은
spade sap 삽; *~s (in card game)*
sŭp'eidŭ 스페이드
Spain Sŭp'ein 스페인
span v/t *(in time, of bridge)* kŏlch'ida
걸치다
Spaniard Sŭp'ein saram 스페인 사람
Spanish 1 adj Sŭp'einŭi 스페인의 2 n
(language) Sŭp'einŏ 스페인어

spank sonppadaguro ttaerida 손바닥으로 때리다

spare 1 v/t *money* pillida 빌리다; *time* naeda 내다; (*do without*) ŏpsshi chinaeda 없이 지내다; *can you ~ the time?* shiganŭl nael su issŏyo? 시간을 낼 수 있어요?; *there were 5 to ~* 5kaega nama issŏssŏyo 5개가 남아 있었어요 **2** adj yebiŭi 예비의 **3** n (*part*) yebip'um 예비품

spare ribs kalbi 갈비; **spare room** yebi pang 예비 방; **spare time** namnŭn shigan 남는 시간; **spare tire** MOT yebi t'aiŏ 예비 타이어; **spare wheel** yebi pak'wi 예비 바퀴

spark n pulkkot 불꽃

sparkle v/i pinnada 빛나다

sparkling wine shyamp'ein 샴페인

spark plug chŏmhwajŏn 점화전

sparrow ch'amsae 참새

sparse *vegetation* sanjaehanŭn 산재하는

sparsely: *~ populated* in-guga hŭibak'an 인구가 희박한

spatter v/t *mud, paint* t'wigida 튀기다

speak 1 v/i marhada 말하다; (*make a speech*) yŏnsŏrhada 연설하다; *we're not ~ing* (*to each other*) urinŭn sŏro maldo anhaeyo 우리는 서로 말도 안해요; *~ing* TELEC chŏndeyo 전데요 **2** v/t *foreign language* marhada 말하다; *~ one's mind* songmaŭmŭl t'ŏnot'a 속마음을 터놓다

♦ **speak for** ...ŭl/rŭl taep'yohada ...을/를 대표하다

♦ **speak out** kŏrikkimŏpsshi marhada 거리낌없이 말하다

♦ **speak up** (*speak louder*) k'ŭn soriro marhada 큰 소리로 말하다

speaker (*at conference*) yŏnsŏltcha 연설자; (*orator*) ungbyŏn-ga 웅변가; (*of sound system*) sŭp'ik'ŏ 스피커

spearmint sŭp'iamint'ŭ 스피아민트

special t'ŭkpyŏrhan 특별한; (*particular*) t'ŭktchŏnghan 특정한

specialist chŏnmun-ga 전문가

specialize (*of company*) chŏnmunŭro hada 전문으로 하다; (*of student*) chŏn-gonghada 전공하다; *~ in* (*of company*)

chŏnmunŭro hada 전문으로 하다; (*of student*) ...ŭl/rŭl chŏn-gonghada ...을/를 전공하다

specially → especially

specialty chŏnmun 전문

species chong 종

specific t'ŭktchŏnghan 특정한

specifically t'ŭk'i 특히

specifications (*of machine etc*) myŏngseosŏ 명세서

specify myŏnggihada 명기하다

specimen (*of work*) kyŏnbon 견본; MED p'yobon 표본

speck (*of dust, soot*) chagŭn ŏlluk 작은 얼룩

spectacle (*impressive sight*) changgwan 장관

spectacular adj nunbushin 눈부신 *profit* kwalmok'al manhan 괄목할 만한

spectator kwan-gaek 관객

spectrum fig pŏmwi 범위

speculate v/i ch'uch'ŭk'ada 추측하다; FIN t'ugihada 투기하다

speculation ch'uch'ŭk 추측; FIN t'ugi 투기

speculator FIN t'ugiŏptcha 투기업자

speech (*address*) yŏnsŏl 연설; (*in play*) taesa 대사; (*ability to speak*) marhanŭn nŭngnyŏk 말하는 능력; (*way of speaking*) malt'u 말투

speechless hal marŭl irŭn 할 말을 잃은

speech defect ŏnŏ chang-ae 언어 장애; **speech therapist** ŏnŏ ch'iryo chŏnmun-ga 언어 치료 전문가; **speech writer** yŏnsŏlmun chakssŏngja 연설문 작성자

speed 1 n soktto 속도; *at a ~ of 150 mph* shisok 150mairŭi sokttoro 시속 150마일의 속도로 **2** v/i ppalli kada 빨리 가다; (*drive too quickly*) kwasok'ada 과속하다

♦ **speed by** ppalli chinagada 빨리 지나가다

♦ **speed up 1** v/i ppalli hada 빨리 하다 **2** v/t ppalli hage hada 빨리 하게 하다

speedboat k'waesoktchŏng 쾌속정

speedily pparŭge 빠르게

speeding n (*when driving*) kwasok 과속

speeding fine kwasok pŏlgŭm 과속 벌금

speed limit soktto chehan 속도 제한

speedometer sokttogye 속도계

speedy pparŭn 빠른

spell[1] v/t & v/i ch'ŏltchahada 철자하다

spell[2] n (period of time) kigan 기간

spellbound mabŏbe kŏllin 마법에 걸린; **spellcheck** COMPUT ch'ŏltcha hwagin 철자 확인; **do a ~ on** ...ŭi ch'ŏltcharŭl hwaginhada ...의 철자를 확인하다; **spellchecker** COMPUT ch'ŏltcha hwagin togu 철자 확인 도구

spelling ch'ŏltcha 철자

spend money ssŭda 쓰다; time ponaeda 보내다

spendthrift adj nangbibyŏgi shimhan 낭비벽이 심한

sperm chŏngja 정자; (semen) chŏngaek 정액

sperm bank chŏngja ŭnhaeng 정자 은행

sphere ku 구; fig punya 분야; **~ of influence** seryok-kkwŏn 세력권

spice n (seasoning) yangnyŏm 양념

spicy food maeun 매운

spider kŏmi 거미

spiderweb kŏmijul 거미줄

spike n ppyojuk'an kkŭt 뾰죽한 끝; (on railings) taemot 대못

spill 1 v/t ŏptchirŭda 엎지르다 2 v/i ŏptchillŏjida 엎질러지다

spin[1] 1 n (turn) hoejŏn 회전 2 v/t hoejŏnshik'ida 회전시키다 3 v/i (of wheel) hoejŏnhada 회전하다; **my head is ~ning** moriga tol chigyŏng-iyeyo 머리가 둘 지경이에요

spin[2] v/t wool, cotton pangjŏk'ada 방적하다; web tchada 짜다

♦ **spin around** (of person, car) chaepparŭge tolda 재빠르게 돌다

♦ **spin out** kkŭlda 끌다

spinach shigŭmch'i 시금치

spinal ch'ŏkch'uŭi 척추의; problem, defect chungch'ujŏgin 중추적인

spinal column ch'ŏkch'u 척추

spin doctor taebyŏnin 대변인; **spin-dry** v/t t'alssuhada 탈수하다; **spin-dryer** t'alssugi 탈수기

spine ch'ŏkch'u 척추; (of book) tŭng;

(on plant, hedgehog) kashi 가시

spineless (cowardly) kŏbi manŭn 겁이 많은

spin-off pusanmul 부산물

spiral 1 n nasŏnhyŏng-ŭi 나선형의 2 v/i (rise quickly) kŭpssok'i orŭda 급속히 오르다

spiral staircase nasŏnhyŏng-ŭi ch'ŭnggye 나선형의 층계

spire ppyojokt'ap 뾰족탑

spirit n (attitude) chŏngshin 정신; (soul) yŏnghon 영혼; (energy) hwalgi 활기; (courage) yonggi 용기

spirited performance hwalbarhan 활발한

spirit level kip'o sujun-gi 기포 수준기

spirits[1] (alcohol) chŭngnyuhayŏ mandŭn sul 증류하여 만든 술

spirits[2] (morale) sagi 사기; **be in good/poor ~** kibuni chot'a/p'uri chugŏit-tta 기분이 좋다/풀이 죽어있다

spiritual adj chŏngshintchŏgin 정신적이

spiritualism shimnyŏngjuŭi 심령주의

spiritualist n shimnyŏngjuŭija 심령주의자

spit v/i (of person) ch'imŭl paet-tta 침을 뱉다; **it's ~ting with rain** posŭlbiga ogo it-tta 보슬비가 오고 있다

♦ **spit out** food, liquid naebaet-tta 내뱉다

spite n agŭi 악의; **in ~ of** pulguhago 불구하고

spiteful agŭi innŭn 악의 있는

spitting image: **be the ~ of s.o.** nuguwa ttok-kkat-tta 누구와 똑같다

splash 1 n (noise) mul t'winŭn sori 물 튀는 소리; (small amount of liquid) soryang 소량; **a ~ of red/blue** ppalgan/p'aran taejo saekssang 빨간/파란 대조 색상 2 v/t t'wigida 튀기다 3 v/i murŭl t'wigida 물을 튀기다; (of water) t'wida 튀다

♦ **splash down** (of spacecraft) susang ch'angnyuk'ada 수상 착륙하다

♦ **splash out** 1 v/t money ssŭda 쓰다 2 v/i: **I splashed out on a round the world trip** nanŭn segye iltchu hanŭnde tonŭl mani ssŏssŏyo 나는

세계 일주 하는데 돈을 많이 썼어요

splendid mŏtchin 멋진

splendor hwaryŏham 화려함

splint n MED pumok 부목

splinter 1 n kashi 가시 **2** v/i chogangnada 조각나다

splinter group punp'a 분파

split 1 n (in wood) tchogaejim 쪼개짐; (in leather) tchijŏjim 찢어짐; (disagreement) purhwa 불화; (division, share) mok 몫 **2** v/t logs tchogaeda 쪼개다; leather tchit-tta 찢다; (cause disagreement in) punyŏlsshik'ida 분열시키다; (divide) nanuda 나누다 **3** v/i (of wood) tchogaejida 쪼개지다; (of leather) tchijŏjida 찢어지다; (disagree) punyŏldoeda 분열되다

♦ **split up** v/i (of couple) heŏjida 헤어지다

split personality PSYCH ijung inkkyŏk 이중 인격

splitting: ~ *headache* ppagaejinŭn tŭt'an tut'ong 빠개지는 듯한 두통

spoil v/t mangch'ida 망치다; child pŏrŭdŏpsshi mandŭlda 버릇없이 만들다

spoilsport F punwigi kkaenŭn saram 분위기 깨는 사람

spoilt adj child pŏrŭtŏmnŭn 버릇없는; **be ~ for choice** nŏmu manasŏ korŭl suga ŏptta 너무 많아서 고를 수가 없다

spoke (of wheel) sal 살

spokesman, spokesperson, spokeswoman taebyŏnin 대변인

sponge n sŭp'onji 스폰지

♦ **sponge off** F pilbut'ŏ salda 빌붙어 살다

sponger F pilbut'ŏ sanŭn saram 빌붙어 사는 사람

sponsor 1 n (for membership etc) pojŭngin 보증인; (for sports, cultural event) huwŏnja 후원자 **2** v/t (for membership etc) pojŭnghada 보증하다; (for sports, cultural event) huwŏnhada 후원하다

sponsorship huwŏn 후원

spontaneous chabaltchŏgin 자발적인

spooky F mushimushihan 무시무시한

spool n (for film) ril 릴; (for thread)

---

shilp'ae 실패

spoon n sutkarak 숟가락; ~ *and chopsticks* sujŏ 수저

spoonfeed fig chinach'ige pohohada 지나치게 보호하다

spoonful han sutkarak 한 숟가락

sporadic sanbaltchŏgin 산발적인

sport n sŭp'och'ŭ 스포츠

sporting event undong-ŭi 운동의; (fair, generous) kwandaehan 관대한

sportscar sŭp'och'ŭ k'a 스포츠 카: **sportscoat** undong-yong chaek'it 운동용 재킷; **sports journalist** sŭp'och'ŭ kija 스포츠 기자; **sportsman** namja undongga 남자 운동가; **sports news** sŭp'och'ŭ nyusŭ 스포츠 뉴스; **sports page** sŭp'och'ŭran 스포츠란; **sportswoman** yŏja undongga 여자 운동가

sporty person sŭp'och'ŭrŭl choahanŭn 스포츠를 좋아하는; clothes sŭp'ot'ihan 스포티한

spot[1] (pimple) yŏdŭrŭm 여드름; (from measles etc) panjŏm 반점; (part of pattern) mulppang-ul munŭi 물방울 무늬

spot[2] (place) changso 장소; **on the ~** (in the place in question) hyŏnjang-esŏ 현장에서; (immediately) chŭkssi 즉시; **put s.o. on the ~** nugurŭl kollanhan ch'ŏjie not'a 누구를 곤란한 처지에 놓다

spot[3] v/t (notice) arach'aeda 알아채다; (identify) shikppyŏrhada 식별하다

spot check mujagwi ch'uch'ul kŏmsa 무작위 추출 검사; **carry out spot checks** mujagwiro kŏmsahada 무작위로 검사하다

spotless mŏnji han chŏm ŏmnŭn 먼지 한 점 없는

spotlight n sŭp'ot'ŭrait'ŭ 스포트라이트

spotted fabric mulppang-ul munŭiŭi 물방울 무늬의

spotty (with pimples) yŏdŭrŭmi nan 여드름이 난

spouse fml paeuja 배우자

spout 1 n chudung-i 주둥이 **2** v/i (of liquid) punch'uldoeda 분출되다

sprain 1 n ppim 삠 **2** v/t ppida 삐다

sprawl v/i k'ŭn taetcharo ppŏt-tta 큰

대자로 뻗다; (*of city*) sabang-ŭro ppŏt-tta 사방으로 뻗다; **send s.o. ~ing** nugurŭl ttaeryŏ nup'ida 누구를 때려 눕히다

sprawling *city, suburbs* ppŏdŏnagago innŭn 뻗어나가고 있는

spray 1 *n* (*of sea water, from fountain*) mulbora 물보라; (*paint, for hair*) sŭp'ŭrei 스프레이 **2** *v/t* ppurida 뿌리다; **~ X with Y** Xe Yŭl/rŭl ppurida X에 Y을/를 뿌리다

spraygun punmugi 분무기

spread 1 *n* (*of disease, etc*) manyŏn 만연; (*of religion*) pogŭp 보급; F (*big meal*) chanch'itssang 잔칫상 **2** *v/t* (*lay*) p'yŏlch'ida 펼치다; *butter, jam* parŭda 바르다; *news, rumor, disease* p'ŏttŭrida 퍼뜨리다; *arms, legs* pŏllida 벌리다 **3** *v/i* p'ŏjida 퍼지다; (*of butter*) pallajida 발라지다

spreadsheet COMPUT sŭp'ŭredŭshit'ŭ 스프레드시트

spree: go on a ~ F shinnage surŭl mashimyŏ nolda 신나게 술을 마시며 놀다; **go on a shopping ~** hŭngch'ŏngmangch'ŏng shyop'ing-ŭl hada 흥청망청 쇼핑을 하다

sprightly wŏn-giwangsŏnghan 원기왕성한

spring¹ *n* (*season*) pom 봄

spring² *n* (*device*) yongsuch'ŏl 용수철

spring³ 1 *n* (*jump*) ttwigi 뛰기; (*stream*) saem 샘 **2** *v/i* irŏsŏda 일어서다; **~ from** ...esŏ pirot-ttoeda ...에서 비롯되다

springboard taibing tae 다이빙 대; **spring chicken: she's no ~** (*hum*) kŭnyŏnŭn kŭrŏk'e chŏmtchi anayo 그녀는 그렇게 젊지 않아요; **spring-cleaning** pommaji taech'ŏngso 봄맞이 대청소; **springtime** pomch'ŏl 봄철

springy *ground* t'ansŏng-i innŭn 탄성이 있는; *walk, mattress* t'allyŏgi innŭn 탄력이 있는

sprinkle *v/t* ppurida 뿌리다; **~ X with Y** Xe Yŭl/rŭl ppurida X에 Y을/를 뿌리다

sprinkler (*for garden*) salssugi 살수기; (*in ceiling*) chadong sohwa changch'i 자동 소화 장치

sprint 1 *n* SP tan-gŏri yukssang kyŏnggi 단거리 육상 경기; (*for the bus etc*) chiltchu 질주 **2** *v/i* chiltchuhada 질주하다

sprinter SP tan-gŏri yukssang sŏnsu 단거리 육상 선수

sprout 1 *v/i* (*of seed*) t'ŭda 트다 **2** *n*: (*Brussels*) **~s** ssagyangbaech'u 싹양배추

spruce *adj* maepsshi innŭn 맵시 있는

spur *n* fig chaguk 자극; **on the ~ of the moment** ch'ungdongtchŏgŭro 충동적으로

♦ **spur on** (*encourage*) chagŭk'ada 자극하다

spurt 1 *n* (*in race*) punbal 분발; **put on a ~** sokto naeda 속도 내다 **2** *v/i* (*of liquid*) ppumŏjyŏ naoda 뿜어져 나오다

spy 1 *n* kanch'ŏp 간첩 **2** *v/i* kanch'ŏp norŭsŭl hada 간첩 노릇을 하다 **3** *v/t* yŏtpoda 엿보다

♦ **spy on** kamshihada 감시하다

squabble 1 *n* maldat'um 말다툼 **2** *v/i* maldat'umhada 말다툼하다

squalid chijŏbunhan 지저분한

squalor nuch'uham 누추함

squander *money* nangbihada 낭비하다

square 1 *adj* (*in shape*) sagak'yŏng-ŭi 사각형의; **~ mile/yard** p'yŏngbang mail/yadŭ 평방 마일/야드 **2** *n* (*shape*) sagak'yŏng 사각형; (*in town*) kwangjang 광장; (*in board game*) k'an 칸; MATH chegop 제곱; **we're back to ~ one** urinŭn wŏntchŏmŭro torawat-tta 우리는 원점으로 돌아왔다

square root chegopkkŭn 제곱근

squash¹ *n* (*vegetable*) hobak 호박

squash² *n* (*game*) sŭk'wŏshi 스쿼시

squash³ *v/t* (*crush*) nullŏ tchigŭrŏttŭrida 눌러 찌그러뜨리다

squat 1 *adj* (*in shape*) ttangttalmak'an 땅딸막한 **2** *v/i* (*sit*) ungk'ŭrigo antta 웅크리고 앉다; (*illegally*) mudan kŏjuhada 무단 거주하다

squatter mudan kŏjuja 무단 거주자

squeak 1 *n* (*of mouse*) tchiktchk-kkŏrinŭn sori 찍찍거리는 소리; (*of* *hinge*) ppigŏk-kkŏrinŭn sori 삐걱거리는 소리 **2** *v/i* (*of mouse*) tchiktchk-kkŏrida 찍찍거리다; (*of hinge, shoes*) ppigŏk-kkŏrida 삐걱거리다

squeal 1 *n* kkaek-kkaek-kkŏrinŭn sori 꽥꽥거리는 소리 **2** *v/i* kkaek-kkaek-kkŏrida 꽥꽥거리다

squeamish mŏlmiga chal nanŭn 멀미가 잘 나는

squeeze 1 *n* (*of hand, shoulder*) kkwak chwim 꽉 쥠 **2** *v/t* (*press*) kkwak chwida 꽉 쥐다; (*remove juice from*) tchada 짜다

♦ **squeeze in 1** *v/i* (*to a car etc*) kkwak kkiida 꽉 끼이다 **2** *v/t* kkiŏ nŏt'a 끼어 넣다

♦ **squeeze up** *v/i* (*to make space*) mirŏ puch'ida 밀어 붙이다

squid ojing-ŏ 오징어

squint *n* sap'alnun 사팔눈

squirm (*wriggle*) pŏdunggŏrida 버둥거리다; (*in embarrassment*) pibi kkoda 비비 꼬다

squirrel *n* taramjwi 다람쥐

squirt 1 *v/t* ppumŏnaeda 뿜어내다 **2** *n pej* F p'unnaegi 풋내기

stab 1 *n* F shido 시도 **2** *v/t person* tchirŭda 찌르다

stability anjŏngssŏng 안정성

stabilize 1 *v/t prices, currency* anjŏngshik'ida 안정시키다; *boat* kojŏngshik'ida 고정시키다 **2** *v/i* (*of prices etc*) anjŏngdoeda 안정되다

stable¹ *n* (*for horses*) magutkkan 마구간

stable² *adj* anjŏngdoen 안정된

stack 1 *n* (*pile*) tŏmi 더미; (*smoke~*) kulttuk 굴뚝 **2** *v/t* ssaaollida 쌓아올리다

stadium kyŏnggijang 경기장

staff *n* (*employees*) chigwŏn 직원; (*teachers*) kyosa 교사

staffroom (*in school*) kyomushil 교무실

stage¹ *n* (*in life, project etc*) tan-gye 단계; (*of journey*) yŏjŏng 여정

stage² *n* THEA mudae 무대; *go on the ~* paeuga toeda 배우가 되다 **2** *v/t play* kong-yŏnhada 공연하다; *demonstration, strike* pŏrida 벌이다

stage door punjangshil ipkku 분장실 입구

stagger 1 *v/i* hwich'ŏnggŏrida 휘청거리다 **2** *v/t* (*amaze*) kkamtchak nollage hada 깜짝 놀라게 하다; *coffee breaks etc* sŏro ŏtkkallige hada 서로 엇갈리게 하다

staggering kiga mak'inŭn 기가 막히는

stagnant *water* koeŏ innŭn 괴어 있는; *economy* ch'imch'ehan 침체한

stagnate (*of person, mind*) ch'imch'ehada 침체하다

stag party ch'onggak p'at'i 총각 파티

stain 1 *n* (*dirty mark*) ŏlluk 얼룩; (*for wood*) ch'aksaek 착색 **2** *v/t* (*dirty*) tŏrŏp'ida 더럽히다; *wood* ch'aksaek'ada 착색하다 **3** *v/i* (*of wine etc*) ŏllugi saenggida 얼룩이 생기다; (*of fabric*) tŏrŏwŏjida 더러워지다

stained glass sŭt'eindŭ kŭllasŭ 스테인드 글라스

stainless steel 1 *n* sŭt'einlesŭ 스테인레스 **2** *adj* sŭt'einlesŭŭi 스테인레스의

stain remover ŏlluk chegŏje 얼룩 제거제

stair kyedan 계단; *the ~s* ch'ŭnggye 층계

staircase ch'ŭnggye 층계

stake 1 *n* (*of wood*) malttuk 말뚝; (*when gambling*) p'antton 판돈; (*investment*) t'uja 투자; *be at ~* wigie ch'ŏhada 위기에 처하다 **2** *v/t tree* malttugŭro chijihada 말뚝으로 지지하다; *money* kŏlda 걸다; *person* kyŏngjejŏgŭro wŏnjohada 경제적으로 원조하다

stale *bread* shinsŏnhaji anŭn 신선하지 않은; *air* k'wik'wihan 퀴퀴한; *news* chinbuhan 진부한

stalemate (*in chess*) suga modu mak'im 수가 모두 막힘; *fig* chint'oeyangnan 진퇴양난

stalk¹ *n* (*of fruit, plant*) chulgi 줄기

stalk² *v/t animal* ch'ujŏk'ada 추적하다; *person* twirŭl paltta 뒤를 밟다

stalker (*of person*) sŭt'ok'ŏ 스토커

stall¹ *n* (*at market*) chinyŏllttae 진열대;

stall 600

(for cow, horse) han k'an 한 칸
stall² 1 *v/i (of vehicle, plane, engine)*
mŏmch'uda 멈추다; *(play for time)*
kyomyohage shiganŭl kkŭlda
교묘하게 시간을 끌다 **2** *v/t engine*
kkŭda 끄다; *people* chiyŏnshik'ida
지연시키다
stallion chongma 종마
stalwart *adj* tŭndŭnhan 든든한
stamina ch'eryŏk 체력
stammer 1 *n* maldŏdŭm 말더듬 **2** *v/i*
marŭl tŏdŭmtta 말을 더듬다
stamp¹ 1 *n (for letter)* up'yo 우표;
(device) tojang 도장; *(mark made with device)* tojang chaguk 도장 자국
2 *v/t letter* up'yo puch'ida 우표
붙이다; *document, passport* tojang
tchiktta 도장 찍다
stamp² *v/t*: ~ one's feet parŭl
kurŭda 발을 구르다
♦ **stamp out** *(eradicate)* kŭnjŏrhada
근절하다
stampede *n (of cattle etc)* ururu
taranam 우루루 달아남; *(of people)*
swaedo 쇄도
stance *(position)* iptchang 입장
stand 1 *n (at exhibition)* kwallamsŏk
관람석; *(witness ~)* chŭng-insŏk
증인석; *(support, base)* patch'imttae
받침대; **take the ~** LAW chŭnggŏrŭl
chech'urhada 증거를 제출하다 **2** *v/i*
(be situated of person) sŏda 서다;
(of object, building) wich'ihada
위치하다; *(as opposed to sit)* sŏda
서다; *(rise)* irŏsŏda 일어서다; **~ still**
umjigiji ank'o sŏ it-tta 움직이지 않고
서 있다; **where do I ~ with you?**
urinŭn ŏttŏn kwan-gyein-gayo?
우리는 어떤 관계인가요? **3** *v/t*
(tolerate) ch'amtta 참다; *(put)* not'a
놓다; **you don't ~ a chance**
tangshinhant'enŭn kamang ŏpssŏyo
당신한테는 가망 없어요; **~ one's
ground** mullŏsŏji ant'a 물러서지
않다
♦ **stand back** mullŏna it-tta 물러나
있다
♦ **stand by 1** *v/i (not take action)*
panggwanhada 방관하다; *(be ready)*
taegihada 대기하다 **2** *v/t person*
chijihada 지지하다; *decision*

kojip'ada 고집하다
♦ **stand down** *(withdraw)* mullŏnada
물러나다
♦ **stand for** *(tolerate)* ch'amtta 참다;
(represent) p'yoshihada 표시하다
♦ **stand in for** taeshinhada 대신하다
♦ **stand out** nune ttŭida 눈에 띄다
♦ **stand up 1** *v/i* irŏsŏda 일어서다 **2** *v/t*
F param mach'ida 바람 맞히다
♦ **stand up for** pang-ŏhada 방어하다
♦ **stand up to** matssŏda 맞서다
standard 1 *adj (usual)* pot'ong-ŭi
보통의 **2** *n (level of excellence)* kijun
기준; *(expectation)* kidae 기대; TECH
p'yojun 표준; **be up to ~** p'yojune
tarhada 표준에 달하다; **not be up to
~** p'yojune midarhada 표준에
미달하다
standardize *v/t* kyugyŏk'wahada
규격화하다
standard of living saenghwal sujun
생활 수준
standby: on ~ *(for flight)* taegihago
innŭn 대기하고 있는
standby passenger t'apssŭng taegija
탑승 대기자
standing *n (in society etc)* chiwi 지위;
(repute) myŏngsŏng 명성; ***a musician of some ~*** p'yŏngp'ani choŭn
ŭmak-kka 평판이 좋은 음악가
standing room ipssŏk 입석
standoffish ssalssarhan 쌀쌀한;
standpoint kwantchŏm 관점;
standstill: be at a ~ mŏmch'un
멈춘; **bring to a ~** mŏmch'uge hada
멈추게 하다
staple¹ *n (foodstuff)* chuyo shikp'um
주요 식품
staple² 1 *n (fastener)* hoch'ik'isŭ al
호치키스 알 **2** *v/t* hoch'ik'isŭro
tchiktta 호치키스로 찍다
staple diet chuyoshikttan 주요식단
staple gun sŭt'eip'ŭl kŏn 스테이플 건
stapler hoch'ik'isŭ 호치키스
star 1 *n* pyŏl 별; *fig* sŭt'a 스타 **2** *v/t (of movie)* chuyŏnŭro hada 주연으로
하다 **3** *v/i (in movie)* chuyŏnhada
주연하다
starboard *adj* uch'ŭgŭi 우측의
stare 1 *n* ppanhi ch'yŏdabom 빤히
쳐다봄 **2** *v/i* ppanhi ch'yŏdaboda

빤히 쳐다본다; ~ *at* ...ül/rül ppanhi ch'yŏdaboda ...을/를 빤히 쳐다보다

starfish pulgasari 불가사리

stark 1 *adj landscape* sangmak'an 삭막한; *reminder, contrast etc* chŏngnarahan 적나라한 **2** *adv:* ~ *naked* holttak pŏsŭn 홀딱 벗은

starling tchirŭregi 찌르레기

Stars and Stripes sŏngjogi 성조기

start 1 *n* shijak 시작; *get off to a good/bad ~* (*in race*) choŭn/nappŭn ch'ulbarŭl hada 좋은/나쁜 출발을 하다; (*in marriage, career*) choŭn/nappŭn shijagŭl hada 좋은/나쁜 시작을 하다; *from the ~* ch'ŏŭmbut'ŏ 처음부터; *well, it's a ~!* kŭraedo shijagŭn han semijiyo! 그래도 시작은 한 셈이지요! **2** *v/i* shijakdoeda 시작되다; (*set off*) ch'ulbarahada 출발하다; (*of engine, car*) shidongdoeda 시동되다; *~ing from tomorrow* naeilbut'ŏ shijak'aesŏ 내일부터 시작해서 **3** *v/t* shijak'ada 시작하다; *engine, car* shidongshik'ida 시동시키다; *business* seuda 세우다; *~ to do X* Xhagi shijak'ada X하기 시작하다

starter (*part of meal*) ep'it'aijyŏ 에피타이져; (*of car*) shidongjangch'i 시동장치

starting point (*for walk*) ch'ulbaltchŏm 출발점; (*for discussion, thesis*) kitchŏm 기점

starting salary ch'ŏtwŏlgŭp 첫 월급

startle kkamtchak nollage hada 깜짝 놀라게 하다

startling kkamtchak nollage hanŭn 깜짝 놀라게 하는

starvation kia 기아

starve *v/i* kumjurida 굶주리다; *~ to death* kulmŏchuktta 굶어 죽다; *I'm starving* I' pae kop'a chukkessŏyo 배 고파 죽겠어요

state¹ 1 *n* (*of car, house etc*) sangt'ae 상태; (*part of country*) chu 주; (*country*) kuk-kka 국가; *the States* Miguk 미국 **2** *adj capital etc* chu(rib)ŭi 주(립)의; *banquet etc* kongshiktchŏgin 공식적인

state² *v/t* kongshiktchŏguro

parŏnhada 공식적으로 발언하다

State Department (Mi)Kungmusŏng (미)국무성

statement (*to police*) chinsul 진술; (*announcement*) palp'yo 발표; (*bank ~*) (ŭnhaeng) t'ongjang (은행) 통장

state of emergency pisangsat'ae 비상사태

state-of-the-art *adj* ch'oech'ŏmdanŭi 최첨단의

statesman chŏngch'iga 정치가

state trooper churip kyŏngch'al 주립 경찰

state visit kongsshik pangmun 공식 방문

static (electricity) chŏngjŏn-gi 정전기

station 1 *n* RAIL yŏk 역; RAD, TV pangsongguk 방송국 **2** *v/t guard etc* paech'ihada 배치하다; *be ~ed at* (*of soldier*) ...e paech'idoeda ...에 배치되다

stationary chŏngjihan 정지한

stationery munbanggu 문방구

stationery store munbanggujŏm 문방구점

station wagon waegŏn 왜건

statistical t'onggyeŭi 통계의

statistically t'onggyejŏguro 통계적으로

statistics (*science*) t'onggyehak 통계학; (*figures*) t'onggye 통계

statue sang 상

Statue of Liberty chayuŭi yŏshinsang 자유의 여신상

status chiwi 지위

status symbol shinbunŭi sangjing 신분의 상징

statute pŏmnyŏng 법령

staunch *adj* ch'ungshirhan 충실한

stay 1 *n* ch'eryu 체류 **2** *v/i* (*in a place*) mŏmurŭda 머무르다; (*in a condition*) yujihada 유지하다; *~ in a hotel* hot'ere muktta 호텔에 묵다; *~ right there!* kŏgisŏ kkomtchaktto hajima! 거기서 꼼짝도 하지마!; *~ put* ŏdiro ka pŏriji ant'a 어디로 가 버리지 않다

♦ **stay away** ttŏrŏjyŏ it-tta 떨어져 있다

♦ **stay away from** ...put'ŏ ttŏrŏjyŏ it-tta …부터 떨어져 있다

♦**stay behind** twie namtta 뒤에 남다

♦**stay up** (*not go to bed*) (chaji ank'o) irŏna it-tta (자지 않고) 일어나 있다

steadily *improve etc* chŏmch'ajŏgŭro 점차적으로

steady 1 *adj* (*not shaking*) ttŏlliji annŭn 떨리지 않는; (*regular*) iltchŏnghan 일정한; (*continuous*) kkŭnimŏmnŭn 끊임없는 **2** *adv*: *be going* ~ iltchŏnghage sagwida 일정하게 사귀다; ~ *on!* ch'imch'ak'age hae! 침착하게 해! **3** *v/t* anjŏngshik'ida 안정시키다

steak sŭt'eik'ŭ 스테이크

steal 1 *v/t money etc* humch'ida 훔치다 **2** *v/i* (*be a thief*) toduktchirhada 도둑질하다; ~ *into* / *out of* (*move quietly*) salgŭmŏni tŭrŏgada / ppajyŏnagada 살그머니 들어가다 / 빠져나가다

stealthy mollae hanŭn 몰래 하는

steam 1 *n* kim 김 **2** *v/t food* tchida 찌다

♦**steam up 1** *v/i* (*of window*) kimi sŏrida 김이 서리다 **2** *v/t*: *be steamed up* F yŏl pat-tta 열 받다

steamer (*for cooking*) tchimt'ong 찜통

steam iron sŭt'im tarimi 스팀 다리미

steel 1 *n* kangch'ŏl 강철 **2** *adj* kangch'ŏllo mandŭn 강철로 만든

steep[1] *adj hill etc* kap'arŭn 가파른; F *prices* pissan 비싼

steep[2] *v/t* (*soak*) tamgŭda 담그다

steeplechase (*in athletics*) chang-aemul kyŏnggi 장애물 경기

steer[1] *n* (*animal*) kŏsehan hwangso 거세한 황소

steer[2] *v/t car, boat* chojonghada 조종하다; *person, conversation* ikkŭlda 이끌다

steering (*of motor vehicle*) sŭt'ŏring 스터링

steering wheel haendŭl 핸들

stem[1] *n* (*of plant*) chulgi 줄기; (*of glass*) sonjabi 손잡이; (*of pipe*) tae 대; (*of word*) ŏgan 어간

♦**stem from** …esŏ yuraehada …에서 유래하다

stem[2] *v/t* (*block*) ŏktchehada 억제하다

stemware sultchan 술잔

stench akch'wi 악취

step 1 *n* (*pace*) kŏrŭm 걸음; (*stair*) kyedan 계단; (*measure*) choch'i 조치; ~ *by* ~ ch'arye ch'aryero 차례 차례로 **2** *v/i* han-gŏrŭm naedidida 한걸음 내디디다; *don't* ~ *on it* paltchi mara 밟지 마라

♦**step down** (*from post etc*) mullŏnada 물러나다

♦**step out** *v/i* (*go out for a short time*) chamkkan nagada 잠깐 나가다

♦**step up** *v/t* (*increase*) chŭnggashik'ida 증가시키다

stepbrother ŭibut'yŏngje 의붓형제; **stepdaughter** ŭibut-ttal 의붓딸; **stepfather** kyebu 계부; **stepladder** palp'an tallin sadari 발판 달린 사다리; **stepmother** kyemo 계모

stepping stone tidimttol 디딤돌; *fig* palp'an 발판

stepsister (*in marriage*) ŭibut-chamae 의붓자매

stepson ŭibudadŭl 의붓아들

stereo *n* (*sound system*) sŭt'ereo 스테레오

stereotype *n* chŏnhyŏng 전형

sterile *woman, man* purimŭi 불임의; *equipment* salgyundoen 살균된

sterilize *woman* purimk'ehada 불임케 하다; *equipment* sodok'ada 소독하다

sterling *n* FIN p'aundŭ 파운드

stern *adj* ŏmkkyŏk'an 엄격한

steroids sŭt'eroidŭ 스테로이드

stethoscope ch'ŏngjin-gi 청진기

Stetson® k'auboi moja 카우보이 모자

stevedore pudu nodongja 부두 노동자

stew *n* sŭt'yu 스튜

steward (*on plane, ship*) samujang 사무장

stewardess (*on plane, ship*) sŭt'yuŏdisŭ 스튜어디스

stick[1] *n* (*wood*) makttaegi 막대기; (*of policeman*) konbong 곤봉; (*walking* ~) chip'ang-i 지팡이; *the* ~*s* F tumesankkol 두메산골

stick[2] 1 *v/t* (*with adhesive*) puch'ida 붙이다; F (*put*) nŏt'a 넣다 **2** *v/i* (*jam*) tallabut-tta 달라붙다; (*adhere*) put-tta 붙다

♦**stick around** F mŏmullŏ it-tta 머물러 있다

♦**stick by** F ...ege ch'ungshirhada ...에게 충실하다

♦**stick out** *v/i* (*protrude*) pulssuk naoda 불쑥 나오다; (*be noticeable*) nune ttŭida 눈에 띄다

♦**stick to** (*adhere to*) ...e tallabut-tta ...에 달라붙다; *plan etc* ...e ch'ungshirhada ...에 충실하다; *path* chal ttaragada 잘 따라가다; *story* kosuhada 고수하다; F (*follow*) ttarŭda 따르다

♦**stick together** F kach'i put'ŏit-tta 같이 붙어있다

♦**stick up** *poster* puch'ida 붙이다

♦**stick up for** onghohada 옹호하다

sticker sŭt'ik'ŏ 스티커

sticking plaster panch'anggo 반창고

stick-in-the-mud kut'ae-ŭiyŏnhan saram 구태의연한 사람

sticky *hands, surface* kkŭnjŏk-kkŏrinŭn 끈적거리는; *label* punnŭn 붙는

sticky rice ch'apssal 찹쌀

stiff **1** *adj brush, leather* ppŏtppŏt'an 뻣뻣한; *muscle, body* ppŏgŭnhan 뻐근한; *mixture, paste* toen toen 된; (*in manner*) ttakttak'an 딱딱한; *drink* tok'an 독한; *competition* shimhan 심한; *penalty* kwajunghan 과중한 **2** *adv*: **be scared ~** F koengjanghi kŏbe chillida 굉장히 겁에 질리다; **be bored ~** F koengjanghi chiruhaejida 굉장히 지루해지다

stiffen *v/i* ttattak'aejida 딱딱해지다

♦**stiffen up** (*of muscle*) ppŏtppŏt'age hada 뻣뻣하게 하다

stifle *v/t yawn, laugh* kkuk ch'amtta 꾹 참다; *criticism, debate* ŏktchehada 억제하다

stifling tapttap'an 답답한

stigma omyŏng 오명

stilettos ppyojok kudu 뾰족 구두

still[1] **1** *adj* koyohan 고요한 **2** *adv* kamanhi 가만히; **keep ~!** kamanhi issŏ! 가만히 있어!; **stand ~!** kamanhi sŏ issŏ 가만히 서 있어!

still[2] *adv* (*yet*) ajikkto 아직도;

(*nevertheless*) kŭraedo 그래도; *do you ~ want it?* ajiktto kŭgŏsŭl kajigo ship'ŏyo? 아직도 그것을 가지고 싶어요?; *she ~ hasn't finished* kŭnyŏnŭn ajiktto kkŭnnaeji anassŏyo 그녀는 아직도 끝내지 않았어요; *she might ~ come* kŭnyŏnŭn kŭraedo oltchi morŭmnida 그녀는 그래도 올지 모릅니다; *they are ~ my parents* kŭdŭrŭn kŭraedo na-ŭi pumonimimnida 그들은 그래도 나의 부모님입니다; *~ more* tŏ-uk tŏ 더욱 더

stillborn: *be ~* sasandoeda 사산되다

stilted ttakttak'an 딱딱한

stilts (*under house*) kidung 기둥

stimulant chakŭktche 자극제

stimulate *person, growth, demand* chagŭk'ada 자극하다

stimulating chagŭktchŏgin 자극적인

stimulation hŭngbun 흥분

stimulus (*incentive*) chagŭk 자극

sting **1** *n* (*from bee, jellyfish*) ssoin sangch'ŏ 쏘인 상처 **2** *v/t* (*of bee, jellyfish*) ssoda 쏘다 **3** *v/i* (*of eyes, scratch*) ttakkŭmgŏrida 따끔거리다

stinging *remark, criticism* shillarhan 신랄한

stingy F insaek'an 인색한

stink **1** *n* akch'wi 악취; F (*fuss*) malssŏng 말썽; *make a ~* F malssŏng-ŭl purida 말썽을 부리다 **2** *v/i* koyak'an naemsaega nada 고약한 냄새가 나다; F (*be very bad*) hyŏngp'yŏnŏpsshi nappŭda 형편없이 나쁘다

stint *n* (*period*) iltchŏng kigan 일정 기간

♦**stint on** ...ŭl/rŭl akkida ...을/를 아끼다

stipulate kyujŏnghada 규정하다

stipulation kyujŏng 규정

stir **1** *n*: **give the soup a ~** kugŭl hwijŏt-tta 국을 휘젓다; **cause a ~** *fig* sodong-ŭl irŭk'ida 소동을 일으키다 **2** *v/t* hwijŏt-tta 휘젓다 **3** *v/i* (*of sleeping person*) twich'ŏgida 뒤척이다

♦**stir up** *crowd* sŏndonghada 선동하다; *bad memories* irŭk'ida

일으키다

stir-crazy: be ~ F mŏriga saltchak ton 머리가 살짝 돈

stir-fry v/t poktta 볶다

stirring music, speech changk'waehan 장쾌한

stitch 1 n (in sewing) panŭlttam 바늘땀; (in knitting) k'o 코; ~es MED panŭl 바늘; **take the ~es out** MED shirŭl ppoptta 실을 뽑다; **have a ~** ssushida 쑤시다 **2** v/t sew kkwemaeda 꿰매다
♦ **stitch up** wound kkwemaeda 꿰매다

stitching (stitches) panŭjil 바느질

stock 1 n (reserves) chŏjang 저장; (COM: of store) sangp'um 상품; (animals) kach'uk 가축; FIN chushik 주식; (ingredient) sup'ŭ chaeryo 수프 재료; **in ~** maejang-e innŭn 매장에 있는; **out of ~** (of products) maejindoen 매진된; **we are out of ~** ta p'allyŏnnŭndeyo 다 팔렸는데요 **take ~** kŏmt'ohada 검토하다 **2** v/t COM katch'uda 갖추다
♦ **stock up on** tŭryŏnot'a 들여놓다

stockbroker chushik chungmae-in 주식 중매인; **stock exchange** chŭngkkwŏn kŏraeso 증권 거래소; **stockholder** chuju 주주

stocking sŭt'ak'ing 스타킹

stock market chŭngkkwŏn shijang 증권 시장; **stockmarket crash** chŭngkkwŏn shijang punggoe 증권 시장 붕괴; **stockpile 1** n (of food, weapons) pich'uk 비축 **2** v/t pich'uk'ada 비축하다; **stockroom** ch'anggo 창고; **stock-still**: stand ~ kkomtchagank'o innŭn 꼼짝않고 있는; **stocktaking** chaego josa 재고 조사

stocky ttangttalmak'an 땅딸막한

stodgy food sohwaga chal andoenŭn 소화가 잘 안되는

stomach 1 n (organ) wi 위; (abdomen) pae 배 **2** v/t (tolerate) ch'amtta 참다

stomach-ache pokt'ong 복통

stone n (material) sŏktcho 석조; (pebble) tol 돌; **precious ~** posŏk 보석

stoned F (on drugs) ch'wihan 취한

stone-deaf aju kwiga mŏgŭn 아주 귀가 먹은

stonewall v/i F ŏlbŏmurida 얼버무리다

stony ground, path tori manŭn 돌이 많은

stool (seat) (tŭng-i ŏmnŭn) kŏlssang (등이 없는) 걸상

stoop[1] **1** n: he has a ~ kŭnŭn tŭng-i kuburŏjyŏssŏyo 그는 등이 구부러졌어요 **2** v/i (bend down) ungk'ŭrida 웅크리다; (have bent back) tŭng-i kuptta 등이 굽다

stoop[2] n (porch) hyŏn-gwan ipkku-ŭi ch'ŭngch'ŭngdae 현관 입구의 층층대

stop 1 n (for train) yŏk 역; (for bus) chŏngnyujang 정류장; **come to a ~** mŏmch'uda 멈추다; **put a ~ to** ...ŭl/rŭl mŏmch'uda ...을/를 멈추다 **2** v/t (put an end to) mŏmch'uda 멈추다; (prevent) mot'age hada 못하게 하다; (cease) kŭmanduda 그만두다; person in street seuda 세우다; car, bus, train, etc: of driver mŏmch'uge hada 멈추게 하다; ~ talking immediately! yaegirŭl chŭksshi kŭmanduseyo! 얘기를 즉시 그만두세요!; I ~ped her from leaving nanŭn kŭnyŏrŭl mot-ttŏnage haet-tta 나는 그녀를 못떠나게 했다; it has ~ped raining piga kŭch'yŏt-tta 비가 그쳤다; ~ a check chiburŭl chŏngjishik'ida 지불을 정지시키다 **3** v/i (come to a halt) mŏmch'uda 멈추다; (of snow, rain) kŭch'ida 그치다; (in a particular place: of bus, train) sŏda 서다
♦ **stop by** (visit) tŭllŭda 들리다
♦ **stop off** tojung-e tŭllŭda 도중에 들리다
♦ **stop over** chamshi mŏmurŭda 잠시 머무르다
♦ **stop up** sink maktta 막다

stopgap imshi pyŏnt'ong 임시 변통; **stoplight** (traffic light) ppalgan pul 빨간 불; (brake light) sŭt'op lait'ŭ 스톱 라이트; **stopover** chamshi mŏmum 잠시 머뭄

stopper (for bath, basin) kumŏng magae 구멍 마개; (for bottle) pyŏng magae 병 마개

stopping: *no ~ (sign)* mŏmch'um chŏngji 멈춤 정지

stop sign mŏmch'um shinho 멈춤 신호

stopwatch sŭt'op wŏch'i 스톱 워치

storage pogwan 보관; *put in ~* …ŭl/rŭl ch'anggo-e nŏ-ŏ pogwanhada …을/를 창고에 넣어 보관하다; *be in ~* pogwan chung-ida 보관 중이다

storage capacity COMPUT kiŏk yongnyang 기억 용량; **storage jar** hang-ari 항아리; **storage space** pogwan changso 보관 장소

store 1 *n* kage 가게; *(stock)* chŏjang 저장; *(storehouse)* ch'anggo 창고 **2** *v/t* chŏjanghada 저장하다; COMPUT kiŏk'ada 기억하다

storefront sangjŏmŭi chŏngmyŏn 상점의 정면; **storehouse** ch'anggo 창고; **storekeeper** kage chuin 가게 주인; **storeroom** ch'anggo 창고; **store window** shyowindo 쇼윈도

storm *n* p'okp'ung 폭풍; *(with rain)* p'okp'ung-u 폭풍우

storm drain paesuro 배수로; **storm window** tŏt-ch'angmun 덧창문; **storm warning** p'okp'ungju-ŭibo 폭풍주의보

stormy *weather* p'okp'ung-u-ga ch'inŭn 폭풍우가 치는; *relationship* kyŏngnyŏrhan 격렬한

story¹ *(tale, account)* iyagi 이야기; *(newspaper article)* kisa 기사; F *(lie)* chiŏnaen iyagi 지어낸 이야기

story² *(of building)* ch'ŭng 층

stout *adj person* ttungttunghan 뚱뚱한; *boots* chilgin 질긴

stove *(for cooking)* yoriyong konno 요리용 곤로; *(for heating)* sŭt'obŭ 스토브

stow chibŏnŏt'a 집어넣다

♦ **stow away** *v/i* mirhanghada 밀항하다

stowaway mirhangja 밀항자

straight 1 *adj line, hair* kodŭn 곧은; *back* kkotkkot'an 꼿꼿한; *(honest, direct)* soltchik'an 솔직한; *(not criminal)* chŏnkkwaga ŏmnŭn 전과가 없는; *whiskey etc* sŭt'ŭreit'ŭ

스트레이트; *(tidy)* chŏngdondoen 정돈된; *(conservative)* kojishik'an 고지식한; *(not homosexual)* tongsŏng-yŏnaejaga anin 동성연애자가 아닌; *be a ~A student* sŏngjŏgi maeu usuhan hakssaeng 성적이 매우 우수한 학생 **2** *adv (in a straight line)* ttokpparo 똑바로; *(directly, immediately)* kotch'ang 곧장; *stand up ~!* paro sŏ! 바로 서!; *look … ~ in the eye* …ŭi nunŭl ttokpparo ch'yŏdaboda …의 눈을 똑바로 쳐다보다; *go ~* F *(of criminal)* ch'aksshirhan saenghwarŭl hada 착실한 생활을 하다; *give it to me ~* F naege ttokpparo yaegihaejuseyo! 내게 똑바로 얘기해주세요!; *~ ahead* be situated paro ap'e 바로 앞에; *walk, drive* ttokpparo 똑바로; *look* ttokpparŭn 똑바른; *carry ~ on (of driver etc)* ttokpparo kada 똑바로 가다; *~away*, *~ off* chŭksshi 즉시; *~ out* soltchik'age 솔직하게; *~ up (without ice)* sŭt'ŭreit'ŭ 스트레이트

straighten *v/t* ttokpparŭge hada 똑바르게 하다

♦ **straighten out 1** *v/t situation* haegyŏrhada 해결하다 **2** *v/i (of road)* pallajida 발라지다

♦ **straighten up** hŏrirŭl p'yŏda 허리를 펴다

straightforward *(honest, direct)* soltchik'an 솔직한; *(simple)* kanttanhan 간단한

strain¹ 1 *n (on rope)* p'aengp'aengham 팽팽함; *(on engine, heart)* muri 무리; *(on person)* kinjang 긴장 **2** *v/t (injure)* murirŭl hada 무리를 하다; *finances, budget* pudamŭl chuda 부담을 주다

strain² *v/t vegetables* murŭl kŏrŭda 물을 거르다; *oil, fat etc* kŏllŏnaeda 걸러내다

strainer *(for vegetables etc)* ch'e 체

strait haehyŏp 해협

straitlaced ŏmkkyŏk'an 엄격한

strand¹ *n (of hair, wool, thread)* kadak 가닥

strand² *v/t* odogado mot'age hada 오도가도 못하게 하다; *be ~ed* odogado mot'ada 오도가도 못하다

strange (*odd, curious*) isanghan
이상한; (*unknown, foreign*) morŭnŭn
모르는

strangely (*oddly*) isanghage
이상하게; ~ *enough* isanghagedo
이상하게도

stranger (*person you don't know*)
natssŏn saram 낯선 사람; *I'm a ~
here myself* yŏginŭn nado chal
morŭnŭn koshimnida 여기는 나도
잘 모르는 곳입니다

strangle *person* kyosarhada 교살하다

strap *n* (*of purse*) kajuk-kkŭn 가죽끈;
(*of bra, dress, shoe*) kkŭn 끈; (*of
watch*) chul 줄

♦ **strap in** kojŏngshik'ida 고정시키다

strapless ŏkkaekkŭni ŏmnŭn
어깨끈이 없는

strategic chŏllyaktchŏgin 전략적인

strategy MIL chŏllyak 전략; (*plan*)
kyehoek 계획

straw[1] miltchip 밀짚; *that's the last
~!* innaeŭi han-gyerŭl nŏmkke
hanŭn kŏshida! 인내의 한계를 넘게
하는 것이다!

straw[2] (*for drink*) sŭt'ŏro 스트로

strawberry ttalgi 딸기

stray 1 *adj animal* chuin ŏmnŭn 주인
없는; *bullet* pinnagan 빗나간 2 *n*
(*dog, cat*) ttŏdori chimsŭng 떠돌이
짐승 3 *v/i* (*of animal*) kirŭl ilt'a 길을
잃다; (*of child*) yŏp killo pinnagada
옆 길로 빗나가다; (*of eyes, thoughts*)
hemaeda 헤매다

streak *n* (*of dirt, paint*) chulmunŭi
ŏlluk 줄무늬 얼룩; (*of nastiness etc*)
kimi 기미 2 *v/i* (*move quickly*) pŏn-
gaech'ŏrŏm tallida 번개처럼 달리다
3 *v/t*: *be ~ed with* ...(ŭ)ro churi
chida ...(으)로 줄이 지다

stream 1 *n* kaeul 개울; (*of people*)
mulkkyŏl 물결; *come on ~*
saengsanŭl kadonghada 생산을
가동하다 2 *v/i* hŭrŭda 흐르다; *~ out
of* ...esŏ nŏmch'yŏ hŭrŭda ...에서
넘쳐 흐르다; *sunlight ~ed into the
room* haetppich'i pang-anŭro
nŏmch'yŏ tŭrŏwat-tta 햇빛이
방안으로 넘쳐 들어왔다

streamer ch'uktcheyong chong-i

t'eip'ŭ 축제용 종이 테이프

streamline *v/t fig* nŭngnyultchŏguro
hada 능률적으로 하다

streamlined *car, plane* yusŏnhyŏng-
ŭi 유선형의; *fig: organization*
nŭngnyultchŏgin 능률적인

street kŏri 거리

streetcar chŏnch'a 전차; **streetlight**
karodŭng 가로등; **streetpeople**
puranja 부랑자; **streetwalker**
ch'angnyŏ 창녀; **streetwise** *adj*
sesang multchŏng-e palgŭn 세상
물정에 밝은

strength him 힘; *fig* (*strong point*)
changtchŏm 장점; (*of wind, current*)
kangdo 강도; (*of emotion, friendship
etc*) kangham 강함; (*of currency*)
kangse 강세

strengthen 1 *v/t* kanghage hada
강하게 하다 2 *v/i* kanghaejida
강해지다

strenuous himdŭn 힘든

stress 1 *n* (*emphasis*) akssent'ŭ
악센트; (*tension*) sŭt'ŭresŭ 스트레스;
be under ~ sŭt'ŭresŭrŭl pat-tta
스트레스를 받다 2 *v/t syllable*
akssent'ŭrŭl chuda 악센트를 주다;
importance etc kangjohada 강조하다;
I must ~ that ... nanŭn ...ranŭn
kŏsŭl kangjohaeyagessŭmnida 나는
...라는 것을 강조해야겠습니다

stressed out F sŭt'ŭresŭrŭl shimhage
pannŭn 스트레스를 심하게 받는

stressful sŭt'ŭresŭga shimhan
스트레스가 심한

stretch 1 *n* (*of land, water, road*)
p'yŏlch'yŏjim 펼쳐짐; *at a ~* (*non-
stop*) tansume 단숨에 2 *adj fabric*
shinch'ukssŏng innŭn 신축성 있는
3 *v/t material* nŭrida 늘이다; *small
income* akkyŏ ssŭda 아껴 쓰다; F
rules hwakttae chŏgyonghada 확대
적용하다; *he ~ed out his hand*
kŭnŭn sonŭl naemirŏt-tta 그는 손을
내밀었다; *a job that ~es me* nae
nŭngnyŏgŭl hankkŏt parhwihage
hanŭn chigŏp 내 능력을 한껏
발휘하게 하는 직업 4 *v/i* (*to relax
muscles*) tchuk ppŏt-tta 쭉 뻗다; (*to
reach sth*) naemilda 내밀다; (*extend*)
ppŏtch'ida 뻗치다; (*of fabric: give*)

nŭrŏnada 늘어나다; (*of fabric: sag*)
nŭröjida 늘어지다; ~ *from X to Y*
(*extend*) Xesŏ Ykkaji ppŏdŏ it-tta
X에서 Y까지 뻗어 있다
stretcher tŭlkkŏt 들것
strict *person* ŏmhan 엄한;
instructions, *rules* ŏmkkyŏk'an
엄격한
strictly ŏmkkyŏk'age 엄격하게; *it is ~
forbidden* kŭgŏsŭn ŏmkkyŏk'age
kŭmjidoeŏ it-tta 그것은 엄격하게
금지되어 있다
stride 1 *n* k'ŭn kŏrŭm 큰 걸음;
lengthen one's ~ songnyŏgŭl
naeda 속력을 내다; *take sth in
one's ~* muŏsŭl shwipke
ttwiŏnŏmtta 무엇을 쉽게 뛰어넘다
2 *v/i* sŏngk'ŭmsŏngk'ŭm kŏt-tta
성큼성큼 걷다
strident kwie kŏsŭllinŭn 귀에
거슬리는; *demands* soranhan 소란한
strike 1 *n* (*of workers*) p'aŏp 파업; (*in
baseball*) sŭt'ŭraik'ŭ 스트라이크; (*of
oil*) palgyŏn 발견; *be on ~*
tongmaeng p'aŏp chung-ida 동맹
파업 중이다; *go on ~* tongmaeng
p'aŏbŭl kyŏrhaenghada 동맹 파업을
결행하다 **2** *v/i* (*of workers*)
tongmaeng p'aŏp'ada 동맹 파업하다; (*attack*) konggyŏk'ada 공격하다; (*of
disaster*) ttŏrŏjida 떨어지다; (*of
clock*) ch'ida 치다 **3** *v/t person*
ttaerida 때리다; *object* pudich'ida
부딪히다; *fig* (*of disaster, illness*)
kaptchagi tŏpch'ida 갑자기 덮치다;
match kŭt-tta 긋다; (*of idea, thought*)
ttŏ-orŭda 떠오르다; *oil* palgyŏnhada
발견하다; *she struck me as being
... kŭnyŏnŭn naege ...(ŭ)ro poyŏt-
tta 그녀는 내게 ...(으)로 보였다
♦**strike out** *v/t* (*delete*) saktchehada
삭제하다
strikebreaker p'aŏp panghaeja 파업
방해자
striker (*person on strike*) p'aŏptcha
파업자
striking (*marked*) tudŭrŏjinŭn
두드러지는; (*eye-catching*)
insangjŏgin 인상적인
string *n* (*cord*) kkŭn 끈; (*of violin,
tennis racket etc*) chul 줄; *~s*

(*musicians*) hyŏnak-kki yŏnjuja
현악기 연주자; *pull ~s* paehu-esŏ
chojonghada 배후에서 조종하다; *a ~
of* (*series*) illyŏnŭi 일련의
♦**string along 1** *v/i* ttaragada
따라가다 **2** *v/t: string X along*
(*deceive*) Xŭl/rŭl sogida X을/를
속이다
♦**string up** F kyosuhyŏng-e ch'ŏhada
교수형에 처하다
stringed instrument hyŏnak-kki
현악기
stringent ŏmjunghan 엄중한
string player hyŏnak-kki yŏnjuja
현악기 연주자
strip 1 *n* kanŭlgo kin chogak 가늘고
긴 조각; (*comic ~*) manhwaran
만화란 **2** *v/t* (*remove*) pŏtkkida
벗기다; *leaves from tree* ttŏrŏttŭrida
떨어뜨리다; (*undress*) osŭl pŏtkkida
옷을 벗기다; *~ X of Y* Xegesŏ
Yŭl/rŭl ppaeat-tta X에게서 Y을/를
빼앗다 **3** *v/i* (*undress*) osŭl pŏt-tta
옷을 벗다; (*of stripper*)
sŭt'ŭripsshorŭl hada 스트립쇼를
하다
strip club sŭt'ŭripsshorŭl hanŭn kot
스트립쇼를 하는 곳
stripe chulmunŭi 줄무늬; (*indicating
rank*) kyegŭp 계급
striped chulmunŭi-ŭi 줄무늬의
stripper sŭt'ŭrip'ŏ 스트리퍼
strip show sŭt'ŭripssho 스트립쇼
striptease sŭt'ŭripssho 스트립쇼
strive 1 *v/t: ~ to do ... ...*ŭl/rŭl
haryŏgo noryŏk'ada ...을/를 하려고
노력하다 **2** *v/i: ~ for ...*ŭl/rŭl
ŏdŭryŏgo noryŏk'ada ...을/를
얻으려고 노력하다
stroke 1 *n* MED noejol 뇌졸; (*in
writing, painting*) hoek 획; (*style of
swimming*) suyŏngppŏp 수영법; *~ of
luck* ttŭtppakkŭi haeng-un 뜻밖의
행운; *she never does a ~* (*of
work*) kŭnyŏnŭn sonkkaraktto
kkadak'aji annŭnda 그녀는 손가락도
까닥하지 않는다 **2** *v/t* ssŭdadŭmtta
쓰다듬다
stroll 1 *n* sanch'aek 산책 **2** *v/i*
sanch'aek'ada 산책하다; *she ~ed
over to the radio* kŭnyŏnŭn ladio

innŭn tchogŭro ŏsullŏnggŏrimyŏ
kŏrŏgat-tta 그녀는 라디오 있는
쪽으로 어슬렁거리며 걸어갔다
stroller (*for baby*) yumoch'a 유모차
strong *person* himssen 힘센; *feeling*
kanghan 강한; *structure* kyŏn-gohan
견고한; *candidate* yuryŏk'an 유력한;
support, supporter kangnyŏk'an
강력한; *wind* ssen 센; *tea, coffee*
chinhan 진한; *alcoholic drink* tok'an
독한; *taste, perfume* kangnyŏrhan
강렬한; *smell* chidok'an 지독한;
views, objections kanggyŏnghan
강경한; *currency* kangseŭi 강세의
stronghold *fig* kŭn-gŏji 근거지
strongly *object, feel* kanghage 강하게
strong-minded shimjiga kujŭn
심지가 굳은
strong-willed ŭijiga kanghan 의지가
강한
structural kujosang-ŭi 구조상의
structure 1 *n* (*sth built*)
kŏnch'ungmul 건축물; (*mode of
construction*) kujo 구조 **2** *v/t* tchada
짜다
struggle 1 *n* (*fight*) ssa-um 싸움; (*for
power*) t'ujaeng 투쟁; (*hard time*)
aktchŏn kot'u 악전 고투 **2** *v/i* (*with a
person*) momburimch'ida
몸부림치다; (*have a hard time*)
aktchŏn kot'uhada 악전 고투하다;
(*mentally*) aessŭda 애쓰다 **3** *v/t*: ~ **to
do** ...ŭl/rŭl haryŏgo
momburimch'ida ...을/를 하려고
몸부림치다; **she was struggling to
understand** kŭnyŏnŭn ihaeharyŏgo
aessŏt-tta 그녀는 이해하려고 애썼다
strum kabyŏpkke ch'ida 가볍게 치다
strut *v/i* kŏdŭlmŏk-kkŏrimyŏ kŏt-tta
거들먹거리며 걷다
stub 1 *n* (*of cigarette*) kkongch'o 꽁초;
(*of check, ticket*) tteŏjugo namŭn
tchok 떼어주고 남은 쪽 **2** *v/t*: ~
one's toe palkkŭch'ŭl ch'ae-ida
발끝을 채이다
♦ **stub out** pibyŏ kkŭda 비벼 끄다
stubble (*on man's face*)
kkach'irhaejin suyŏm 까칠해진 수염
stubborn kojibi ssen 고집이 센;
refusal, defense wan-ganghan 완강한
stubby mungttuk'an 뭉뚝한

stuck: **be ~ on** ... F (*romantically*)
...ege panhae it-tta ...에게 반해
있다
stuck-up F kŏmanhan 거만한
student hakssaeng 학생
student movement hakssaeng
undong 학생 운동; **student nurse**
kanho shilssŭpssaeng 간호 실습생;
student teacher kyoyuk
shilssŭpssaeng 교육 실습생,
kyosaeng 교생
studio (*of artist, sculptor*) chagŏpsshil
작업실; (*recording ~*) nogŭmshil
녹음실; (*film ~*) yŏnghwa
ch'waryŏngso 영화 촬영소; (*TV ~*)
pangsongshil 방송실
studious yŏlsshimhi kongbuhanŭn
열심히 공부하는
study 1 *n* (*room*) sŏjae 서재;
(*learning*) kongbu 공부; (*research*)
yŏn-gu 연구 **2** *v/t* (*at school,
university*) kongbuhada 공부하다;
(*examine*) chal salp'yŏboda 잘
살펴보다 **3** *v/i* kongbuhada 공부하다
stuff 1 *n* (*things*) mulgŏn 물건;
(*belongings*) chim 짐 **2** *v/t turkey*
sogŭl ch'ae-uda 속을 채우다; ~ **X
into Y** Xŭl/rŭl Ye ch'aewŏ nŏt'a
X을/를 Y에 채워 넣다
stuffed toy inhyŏng 인형
stuffing (*for turkey*) sok 속; (*in chair,
teddy bear*) sogŭl ch'aeunŭn chaeryo
속을 채우는 재료
stuffy *room* t'ongp'ung-i chal
andoenŭn 통풍이 잘 안되는; *person*
ttattak'an 딱딱한
stumble hŏt-ttidida 헛디디다
♦ **stumble across** uyŏnhi majuch'ida
우연히 마주치다
♦ **stumble over** ...e kŏllyŏ nŏmŏjida
...에 걸려 넘어지다; *words* tŏdŭmtta
더듬다
stumbling block chang-aemul 장애물
stump 1 *n* (*of tree*) kŭrut'ŏgi 그루터기
2 *v/t* (*of question, questioner*)
nanch'ŏhage hada 난처하게 하다
♦ **stump up** F tonŭl naeda 돈을 내다
stun (*with a blow*) kijŏlsshik'ida
기절시키다; (*by news*)
ŏribŏngbŏnghage hada 어리벙벙하게
하다

stunning (*amazing*) koengjanghan 굉장한; (*very beautiful*) maeu mŏshinnŭn 매우 멋있는

stunt *n* (*for publicity*) imogŭl kkŭlgi wihan haengdong 이목을 끌기 위한 행동; (*in movie*) wihŏmhan changmyŏn 위험한 장면

stuntman sŭt'ŏnt'ŭmaen 스턴트맨

stupefy mŏnghage hada 멍하게 하다

stupendous koengjanghan 굉장한; (*very large*) ŏmch'ŏngnan 엄청난

stupid ŏrisŏgŭn 어리석은; *book*, *movie* shishihan 시시한

stupidity ŏrisŏgŭm 어리석음

stupor (*drunken*) insa pulssŏng 인사 불성

sturdy ŏkssen 억센; *object* t'ŭnt'ŭnhan 튼튼한

stutter *v/i* marŭl tŏdŭmtta 말을 더듬다

style *n* (*method, manner*) pangbŏp 방법; (*of writing*) munch'e 문체; (*of architecture*) yangshik 양식; (*fashion*) yuhaeng 유행; (*elegance*) p'umkkyŏk 품격; *go out of* ~ yuhaeng-i chinada 유행이 지나다

stylish mŏshinnŭn 멋있는

stylist (*hair* ~) sŭt'aillisŭt'ŭ 스타일리스트

subcommittee punkkwa wiwŏnhoe 분과 위원회

subcompact (*car*) sohyŏng chadongch'a 소형 자동차

subconscious: *the* ~ (*mind*) mu-ŭishik 무의식

subcontract *v/t* hach'ŏnghada 하청하다

subcontractor hach'ŏng-ŏptcha 하청업자

subdirectory COMPUT ttallin tirekt'ori 딸린 디렉토리

subdivide *v/t* sebunhada 세분하다

subdued kara-anjŭn 가라앉은; *lighting* natch'un 낮춘

subheading chagŭn chemok 작은 제목

subject 1 *n* (*of country*) kungmin 국민; (*topic*) chuje 주제; (*branch of learning*) kwamok 과목; GRAM chuŏ 주어; *change the* ~ hwajerŭl pakkŭda 화제를 바꾸다 **2** *adj*: *be* ~

to ...hagi shwiun ...하기 쉬운; ~ *to availability* yŏbuni namainnŭn hando naeesŏ 여분이 남아 있는 한도 내에서 **3** *v/t*: ~ *s.o. to* nuguege ...ŭl/rŭl kyŏk-kke hada 누구에게 ...을/를 겪게 하다

subjective chugwanjŏgin 주관적인

sublet *v/t* chŏndaehada 전대하다

submachine gun kigwan tanch'ong 기관 단총

submarine chamsuham 잠수함

submerge 1 *v/t* chamgige hada 잠기게 하다 **2** *v/i* (*of submarine*) chamsuhada 잠수하다

submission (*surrender*) hangbok 항복; (*to committee etc*) chech'uran 제출안

submissive sunjongjŏgin 순종적인

submit *v/t plan, proposal* chech'urhada 제출하다

subordinate 1 *adj* arae-ŭi 아래의 **2** *n* araet saram 아랫 사람

subpoena 1 *n* sohwantchang 소환장 **2** *v/t person* sohwanhada 소환하다

♦**subscribe to** *magazine etc* chŏnggi kudok'ada 정기 구독하다; *theory* ...e tong-ŭihada ...에 동의하다

subscriber (*to magazine*) chŏnggi kudoktcha 정기 구독자

subscription chŏnggi kudok 정기 구독

subsequent ttarasŏ irŏnan 따라서 일어난

subsequently kŭ hu-e 그 후에

subside (*of flood waters*) ppajida 빠지다; (*of winds, fears*) karaantta 가라앉다; (*of building*) naeryŏantta 내려앉다

subsidiary *n* chahoesa 자회사

subsidize pojogŭmŭl chigŭp'ada 보조금을 지급하다

subsidy pojogŭm 보조금

♦**subsist on** ... (ŭ)ro sara nagada ...(으)로 살아 나가다

subsistence farmer chagŭmnong 자급농

subsistence level ch'oejŏ saenghwal sujun 최저 생활 수준

substance (*matter*) multchil 물질

substandard p'yojun midarŭi 표준 미달의

substantial sangdanghan 상당한
substantially (*considerably*) sangdanghage 상당하게; (*in essence*) shiltchiltchŏgŭro 실질적으로
substantiate chŭnggŏrŭl taeda 증거를 대다
substantive *adj* shiltchiltchŏgin 실질적인
substitute 1 *n* (*for person*) taeriin 대리인; (*for commodity*) taeyongp'um 대용품; SP pogyŏl sŏnsu 보결 선수 **2** *v/t* taeshinŭro ssŭda 대신으로 쓰다; ~ *X for Y* X(ŭ)ro Yŭl/rŭl taeshinhada X(으)로 Y을/를 대신하다 **3** *v/i*: ~ *for s.o.* nugurŭl taeshinhada 누구를 대신하다
substitution (*act*) taeyong 대용; *make a* ~ SP taeshin kiyonghada 대신 기용하다
subtitle 1 *n* chamak 자막 **2** *v/t movie* chamagŭl talda 자막을 달다
subtle mimyohan 미묘한
subtract *v/t number* ppaeda 빼다; ~ *X from Y* Yesŏ Xŭl/rŭl ppaeda Y에서 X을/를 빼다
suburb kyo-oe 교외; *the* ~*s* kŭn-gyo 근교
suburban kŭn-gyo-ŭi 근교의
subversive 1 *adj* chŏnbokshik'inŭn 전복시키는 **2** *n* chŏnbok 전복
subway chihach'ŏl 지하철
subzero *adj* yŏnghaŭi 영하의
succeed 1 *v/i* (*be successful*) sŏnggonghada 성공하다; (*to the throne*) kyesŭnghada 계승하다; (*in office*) in-gyehada 인계하다; ~ *in doing* ...ŭl/rŭl hanŭn te sŏnggonghada ...을/를 하는 데 성공하다 **2** *v/t* (*come after*) huimjaga toeda 후임자가 되다; *monarch* kyesŭnghada 계승하다
succeeding twiŭn 뒤이은
success sŏnggong 성공; *be a* ~ taesŏnggong-ida 대성공이다
successful sŏnggongtchŏgin 성공적인
successfully sŏnggongtchŏgŭro 성공적으로
succession (*sequence*) yŏnsok 연속; (*to the throne*) kyesŭng 계승; (*to office*) in-gye 인계; *in* ~ kyesok'aesŏ 계속해서
successive it-ttarŭn 잇따른
successor huimja 후임자
succinct kan-gyŏrhan 간결한
succulent *meat, fruit* chŭbi manŭn 즙이 많은
succumb (*give in*) kulbok'ada 굴복하다; ~ *to temptation* yuhoge kulbok'ada 유혹에 굴복하다
such 1 *adj* (*of that kind*) kŭrŏn 그런; ~ *a* (*to that extent*) kŭ chŏngdo-ŭi 그 정도의; ~ *as* ...wa/kwa kat'ŭn ...와/과 같은; *there is no* ~ *word as* ... ...wa/kwa kat'ŭn marŭn ŏptta ...와/과 같은 말은 없다 **2** *adv* kŭrŏk'e 그렇게; *as* ~ kŭrosŏ 그로서; *it was* ~ *a hot day* kŭrŏk'e tŏun nariŏssŏyo 그렇게 더운 날이었어요
suck *candy* ppara mŏktta 빨아 먹다; ~ *one's thumb* sonkkaragŭl ppalda 손가락을 빨다; ~ *X from Y* Yesŏ Xŭl/rŭl ppalda Y에서 X을/를 빨다
♦**suck up 1** *v/t* ppparadŭrida 빨아들이다 **2** *v/i*: ~ *to s.o.* nuguege ach'ŏmhada 누구에게 아첨하다
sucker F (*person*) chal songnŭn saram 잘 속는 사람; (*lollipop*) makttaegi sat'ang 막대기 사탕
sucking pig chŏnmŏgi twaeji 젖먹이 돼지
suction hŭbip 흡입
sudden kaptchaksssŭrŏn 갑작스런; *all of a* ~ kaptchagi 갑자기
suddenly kaptchagi 갑자기
suds (*soap* ~) kŏp'um 거품
sue *v/t* kosohada 고소하다
suede *n* süweidŭ 스웨이드
suffer 1 *v/i* (*be in pain*) kosaenghada 고생하다; (*deteriorate*) nappajida 나빠지다; (*of school work etc*) chijang-ŭl pat-tta 지장을 받다; *be* ~*ing from* ...ranŭn pyŏng-ŭl kajigo it-tta ...라는 병을 가지고 있다 **2** *v/t*: ~ *a loss* sonhaerŭl iptta 손해를 입다; ~ *a setback* panghaerŭl pat-tta 방해를 받다
suffering *n* kot'ong 고통
sufficient ch'ungbunhan 충분한
sufficiently ch'ungbunhage 충분하게

suffocate 1 *v/i* chilsshikssahada 질식사하다 **2** *v/t* chilsshiksshik'ida 질식시키다

suffocation chilsshik 질식

sugar 1 *n* sŏlt'ang 설탕 **2** *v/t* sŏlt'ang-ŭl nŏt'a 설탕을 넣다

sugar bowl sŏlt'ang-t'ong 설탕통

sugar cane sat'ang susu 사탕 수수

suggest *v/t* cheanhada 제안하다; *I ~ that we stop now* nanŭn uriga chigŭm kŭmandul kŏsŭl cheanhamnida 나는 우리가 지금 그만둘 것을 제안합니다

suggestion chean 제안

suicide chasal 자살; *commit ~* chasarhada 자살하다

suit 1 *n* yangbok han pŏl 양복 한 벌; *(in cards)* tchakp'ae han pŏl 짝패 한 벌 **2** *v/t (of clothes, color)* ŏullida 어울리다; *~ yourself!* maŭmdaero haseyo! 마음대로 하세요!; *be ~ed for* ...e chŏk'ap'ada ...에 적합하다

suitable ŏullinŭn 어울리는; *choice of words, time* chŏkttanghan 적당한

suitcase yŏhaeng kabang 여행 가방

suite *(of rooms)* sŭwit'ŭ 스위트; *(furniture)* sop'a sett'ŭ 소파 셋트; MUS chogok 조곡

sulfur yuhwang 유황

sulk *v/i* purut'unghaejida 부루퉁해지다

sulky purut'unghan 부루퉁한

sullen ch'imurhan 침울한

sultry *climate* hut'ŏptchigŭnhan 후텁지근한; *(sexually)* kwannŭngjŏgin 관능적인

sum *(total)* ch'onggye 총계; *(amount)* kŭmaek 금액; *(in arithmetic)* kyesan 계산; *a large ~ of money* manŭn ton 많은 돈; *the ~ insured* hwaktchŏng kŭmaek 확정 금액; *the ~ total of his efforts* kŭŭi noryŏgŭi ch'ongch'e 그의 노력의 총체

♦ **sum up 1** *v/t (summarize)* yoyak'ada 요약하다; *(assess)* p'yŏnggkahada 평가하다 **2** *v/i* LAW p'ansaga kaegwarhayŏ marhada 판사가 개괄하여 말하다

summarize *v/t* yoyak'ada 요약하다

summary *n* yoyak 요약

summer yŏrŭm 여름

summit *(of mountain)* chŏngsang 정상; *fig* chŏltchŏng 절정; POL sunoe hoedam 수뇌 회담

summon sojip'ada 소집하다

♦ **summon up** *strength* pullŏ irŭk'ida 불러 일으키다

summons LAW sohwantchang 소환장

sump *(for oil)* kirŭmt'ong 기름통

sun t'aeyang 태양; *in the ~* haetppyŏch'e(sŏ) 햇볕에(서); *out of the ~* kŭnŭre(sŏ) 그늘에(서); *he has had too much ~* kŭnŭn haetppyŏch'ŭl nŏmu tchoe-ŏt-tta 그는 햇볕을 너무 쬐었다

sunbathe ilgwangnyogŭl hada 일광욕을 하다; **sunblock** haetppyŏt ch'adannyong k'ŭrim 햇볕 차단용 크림; **sunburn** haetppyŏch'e t'am 햇볕에 탐; **sunburnt** haetppyŏch'e t'an 햇볕에 탄

Sunday iryoil 일요일

sundial haeshigye 해시계

sundries chap-ppi 잡비

sunglasses saegan-gyŏng 색안경

sunken *cheeks* holtchuk'an 홀쭉한

sunny *day* hwach'anghan 화창한; *disposition* myŏngnanghan 명랑한; *it's ~* hwach'anghan narimnida 화창한 날입니다

sunrise ilch'ul 일출; **sunset** ilmol 일몰; **sunshade** p'arasol 파라솔; **sunshine** haetppit 햇빛; **sunstroke** ilssappyŏng 일사병; **suntan** haetppyŏch'e t'am 햇볕에 탐; *get a ~* haetppyŏch'e t'aeuda 햇볕에 태우다

super 1 *adj* F ch'oegoŭi 최고의 **2** *n (of apartment block)* kwalliin 관리인

superb koengjanghi ttwiŏnan 굉장히 뛰어난

superficial *analysis* p'yomyŏnjŏgin 표면적인; *person* ch'ŏnbak'an 천박한; *wounds* yat'ŭn 얕은

superfluous pulp'iryohan 불필요한

superhuman *efforts* ch'oinjŏgin 초인적인

superintendent *(of apartment block)* kwalliin 관리인

superior 1 *adj (better)* poda ttwiŏnan 보다 뛰어난; *pej: attitude* kŏmanhan

거만한 2 n (in organization, society) witssaram 윗사람

supermarket sup'ŏmak'et 수퍼마켓;

supernatural 1 adj powers ch'ojayŏnjŏgin 초자연적인 2 n: the ~ ch'ojayŏnjŏgin hyŏnsang 초자연적인 현상; **superpower** POL ch'ogangdaeguk 초강대국; **super-sonic** ch'ŭmsogŭi 초음속의

superstition mishin 미신

superstitious person mishinŭl minnŭn 미신을 믿는

supervise kamdok'ada 감독하다

supervisor (at work) kamdoktcha 감독자

supper chŏnyŏk shikssa 저녁 식사

supple yuyŏnhan 유연한

supplement (extra payment) ch'uga-aek 추가액

supplier COM konggŭbwŏn 공급원

supply 1 n konggŭp 공급; ~ and demand konggŭpkkwa suyo 공급과 수요; supplies konggŭpp'um 공급품 2 v/t goods konggŭp'ada 공급하다; ~ X with Y Xege Yŭl/rŭl konggŭp'ada X에게 Y을/를 공급하다; be supplied with ...i/ga naejangdoeŏ it-tta ...이/가 내장되어 있다

support 1 n (structural) t'odae 토대; (backing) chiji 지지 2 v/t building, structure chit'aenghada 지탱하다; (financially) puyanghada 부양하다; (back) chijihada 지지하다

supporter chijija 지지자; (of football team etc) huwŏnja 후원자

supportive chal towajunŭn 잘 도와주는

suppose (imagine) kajŏnghada 가정하다; I ~ so ama kŭrŏk'etchi 아마 그렇겠지; be ~d to ... (be meant to) ...hagiro toeŏit-tta ...하기로 되어있다; (be said to be) ...(ŭ)ro allyŏjyŏ it-tta ...(으)로 알려져 있다; you are not ~d to ... (not allowed to) ...haji ank'iro toeŏit-tta ...하지 않기로 되어있다

suppository MED chwayak 좌약

suppress rebellion etc chinap'ada 진압하다

suppression chinap 진압

supremacy chudokkwŏn 주도권

supreme being, commander ch'oegowiŭi 최고위의; effort, courage, delight kŭkttoŭi 극도의

Supreme Court Kodŭng Pŏbwŏn 고등 법원

surcharge n puga yogŭm 부가 요금

sure 1 adj hwaksshinhanŭn 확신하는; I'm ~ hwaksshinhamnida 확신합니다; I'm not ~ kŭlsseyo 글쎄요; be ~ about ...e taehae hwaksshinhada ...에 대해 확신하다; make ~ that ...ranŭn kŏsŭl hwaksshirhage hada ...라는 것을 확실하게 하다 2 adv: ~ enough chŏngmallo 정말로; it ~ is hot to-day F onŭrŭn hwaksshirhi tŏpkkunnyo 오늘은 확실히 덥군요; ~! mullon! 물론!

surely (certainly) pandŭshi 반드시; (gladly) kikkŏi 기꺼이; (slight doubt) sŏlma 설마; (strong doubt) kyŏlk'o 결코; you don't mean that sŏlma chinjŏnguro kŭrŏk'e marhanŭn kŏsŭn anigetchiyo 설마 진정으로 그렇게 말하는 건 아니겠지요; ~ that can't be right kyŏlk'o majŭl li ŏpssŏyo 결코 맞을 리 없어요

surf 1 n (on sea) millyŏdŭnŭn p'ado 밀려드는 파도 2 v/t: ~ the Net int'ŏnesŭl tullŏboda 인터넷을 둘러보다

surface 1 n (of table, object) p'yomyŏn 표면; (of water) sumyŏn 수면; on the ~ fig kŏt'ŭronŭn 겉으로는 2 v/i (of swimmer, submarine) ttŏorŭda 떠오르다; (appear) nat'anada 나타나다

surface mail yukssang up'yŏnmul 육상 우편물

surfboard sŏp'ing podŭ 서핑 보드

surfer (on sea) sŏp'inghanŭn saram 서핑하는 사람

surfing sŏp'ing 서핑; go ~ sŏp'ingharŏ kada 서핑하러 가다

surge n ELEC chŏllyuŭi tongnyo 전류의 동요; (in demand etc) kŭpssangssŭng 급상승

♦ **surge forward** (of crowd) millyŏnagada 밀려나가다

surgeon oekkwa ŭisa 외과 의사

surgery susul 수술; *undergo ~*
susurŭl pat-tta 수술을 받다
surgical susurŭi 수술의
surly muttukttuk'an 무뚝뚝한
surmount *difficulties* kŭkppok'ada
극복하다
surname sŏng 성
surpass nŭnggahada 능가하다
surplus 1 *n* ing-yŏ 잉여 **2** *adj*
namŏjiŭi 나머지의
surprise 1 *n* nollaum 놀라움; *it'll*
come as no ~ nollaptchi anŭn iri
toel kŏshida 놀랍지 않은 일이 될
것이다 **2** *v/t* nollage hada 놀라게
하다; *be* / *look ~d* nollada / nolla
poida 놀라다 / 놀라 보이다
surprising nollaun 놀라운
surprisingly nollapkke 놀랍게
surrender 1 *v/i* MIL hangbok'ada
항복하다 **2** *v/t* (*hand in: weapons etc*)
nŏmgyŏjuda 넘겨주다 **3** *n* hangbok
항복; (*handing in*) indo 인도
surrogate mother taerimo 대리모
surround *v/t* tullŏ ssada 둘러 싸다; *be*
~ed by … (ŭ)ro tullŏssaida …(으)로
둘러싸이다
surrounding *adj* chuwiŭi 주위의
surroundings hwan-gyŏng 환경
survey 1 *n* (*of modern literature etc*)
kaekwan 개관; (*of building*) chosa
조사 **2** *v/t* (*look at*) tullŏboda
둘러보다; *building* chosahada
조사하다
surveyor kŏnmul chosawŏn 건물
조사원
survival saranamŭm 살아남음; *strug-*
gle for ~ saengjon kyŏngjaeng 생존
경쟁; *~ of the fittest* chŏktcha
saengjon 적자 생존
survive 1 *v/i* (*of species, patient*)
saranamtta 살아남다; *how are you?*
– surviving ŏttŏseyo? – kŭjŏ
kŭraeyo 어떠세요? - 그저 그래요;
his two surviving daughters kŭga
namgin tu ttal 그가 남긴 두 딸 **2** *v/t*
accident, operation saranamtta
살아남다; (*outlive*) poda orae salda
보다 오래 살다
survivor saengjonja 생존자; *he's a ~*
fig kŭnŭn saengjonnyŏgi kanghada
그는 생존력이 강하다

susceptible (*emotionally*)
kamsusŏng-i kanghan 감수성이 강한;
be ~ to the cold / *heat*
ch'uwie / yŏre min-gamhada
추위에 / 열에 민감하다
suspect 1 *n* hyŏmŭija 혐의자 **2** *v/t*
person ŭishimhada 의심하다;
(*suppose*) chimjak'ada 짐작하다
suspected *murderer* hyŏmŭirŭl
pannŭn 혐의를 받는; *cause, heart*
attack etc chimjakttoenŭn 짐작되는
suspend (*hang*) maedalda 매달다;
(*from office, duties*) chŏngjishik'ida
정지시키다
suspenders (*for pants*) melppang
멜빵
suspense sŏsŭp'ensŭ 서스펜스
suspension (*in vehicle*)
sŏsŭp'enshyŏn 서스펜션; (*from duty*)
chŏngji 정지
suspension bridge hyŏnsugyo
현수교
suspicion ŭishim 의심
suspicious (*causing suspicion*)
susanghan 수상한; (*feeling*
suspicion) ŭishimsŭrŏun 의심스러운;
be ~ of ~ …ŭl / rŭl ŭishimhada
…을 / 를 의심하다
sustain *pressure etc* chit'aenghada
지탱하다; *injuries* pat-tta 받다
swab *v/t* kŏllejirhada 걸레질하다
swagger *n* ppomnaenŭn kŏrŭm
뽐내는 걸음
swallow[1] *v/t & v/i* samk'ida 삼키다
swallow[2] *n* (*bird*) chebi 제비
swamp 1 *n* nŭp 늪 **2** *v/t: be ~ed with*
…(ŭ)ro mirŏdakch'yŏ it-tta …(으)로
밀어닥쳐 있다
swampy *ground* nŭp kat'ŭn 늪 같은
swan paektcho 백조
swap *v/t: ~ X for Y* Xŭl / rŭl
Ywa / kwa pakkuda X을 / 를 Y와 / 과
바꾸다 **2** *v/i* pakkuda 바꾸다
swarm 1 *n* (*of bees*) tte 떼 **2** *v/i* (*of*
ants, tourists etc) tterŭl chit-tta 떼를
짓다; *the town was ~ing with*
tourists toshinŭn kwan-
gwanggaeguro ttejiŏ issŏt-tta 도시는
관광객으로 떼지어 있었다
swarthy kŏmusŭrehan 거무스레한
swat *v/t insect, fly* ch'alssak ch'ida

찰싹 치다

sway 1 n (influence, power) seryŏk 세력 **2** v/i hŭndŭlgŏrida 흔들리다

swear v/i (use swearword) yogŭl hada 욕을 하다; (promise) maengsehada 맹세하다; LAW sŏnsŏhada 선서하다; ~ **at** ...ege yogŭl hada ...에게 욕을 하다

♦ **swear in**: ~ **as a witness** chŭnginŭro sŏnsŏhada 증인으로 선서하다

swearword yok 욕

sweat 1 n ttam 땀; covered in ~ ttamt'usŏng-iin 땀투성이인 **2** v/i ttamŭl hŭllida 땀을 흘리다

sweater sŭwet'ŏ 스웨터

sweatshirt sŭwet'ŭ shyŏch'ŭ 스웨트 셔츠

sweaty hands ttami paen 땀이 밴; smell ttamnae nanŭn 땀내 나는

Swede Sŭweden saram 스웨덴 사람

Sweden Sŭweden 스웨덴

Swedish 1 adj Sŭwedenŭi 스웨덴의 **2** n Sŭweden mal 스웨덴 말

sweep 1 v/t floor, leaves ssŭlda 쓸다 **2** n (long curve) man-gok 만곡

♦ **sweep up** v/t mess, crumbs ssŭrŏ moŭda 쓸어 모으다

sweeping adj generalization, statement taegang-ŭi 대강의; changes chŏnmyŏnjŏgin 전면적인

sweet adj taste, tea tan 단; F (kind) ch'injŏrhan 친절한; F (cute) kwiyŏun 귀여운

sweet and sour adj saek'omdalk'omhan 새콤달콤한

sweetcorn okssusu 옥수수

sweeten v/t drink, food talgehada 달게 하다

sweetener (for drink) kammiryo 감미료

sweetheart aein 애인

swell 1 v/i (of limb) put-tta 붓다 **2** adj F (good) mŏtchin 멋진 **3** n (of the sea) kubich'im 굽이침

swelling n MED pugi 부기

sweltering tchinŭn tŭt'an 찌는 듯한

swerve v/i (of driver, car) pinnagada 빗나가다

swift adj pparŭn 빠른

swim 1 v/i suyŏnghada 수영하다; go ~ming suyŏngharŏ kada 수영하러

가다; my head is ~ming hyŏngijŭng-i nanda 현기증이 난다 **2** n suyŏng 수영; go for a ~ suyŏngharŏ kada 수영하러 가다

swimmer suyŏnghanŭn saram 수영하는 사람

swimming suyŏng 수영

swimming pool suyŏngjang 수영장

swimsuit suyŏngbok 수영복

swindle 1 n sagi 사기 **2** v/t sagirŭl ch'ida 사기를 치다; ~ **X out of Y** Xegesŏ Yŭl/rŭl sach'wihada X에게서 Y을/를 사취하다

swine F (person) saekki 새끼

swing 1 n (of pendulum) hŭndŭllim 흔들림; (for child) kŭne 그네; there has been a ~ to the Democrats yŏroni Minjudang tchogŭro kiulgo it-tta 여론이 민주당 쪽으로 기울고 있다 **2** v/t hŭndŭlda 흔들다 **3** v/i hŭndŭlgŏrida 흔들거리다; (turn) hoejŏnshik'ida 회전시키다; (of public opinion etc) kiulda 기울다

swing-door hoejŏnmu 회전문

Swiss adj Sŭwisŭŭi 스위스의

switch 1 n (for light) sŭwich'i 스위치; (change) chŏnhwan 전환 **2** v/t (change) pakkuda 바꾸다 **3** v/i (change) pakkwida 바뀌다

♦ **switch off** v/t lights, engine, PC kkŭda 끄다

♦ **switch on** v/t lights, engine, PC k'yŏda 켜다

switchboard paejŏnban 배전반

switchover (to new system) chŏnhwan 전환

Switzerland Sŭwisŭ 스위스

swivel v/i hoejŏnhada 회전하다

swollen puŭn 부은

swoop v/i (of bird) naeri tŏpch'ida 내리 덮치다

♦ **swoop down on** prey ...ŭl/rŭl hyanghae naeri tŏpch'ida ...을/를 향해 내리 덮치다

♦ **swoop on** (of police etc) tŏpch'ida 덮치다

sword kŏm 검

sycamore k'ŭn tanp'ungnamu 큰 단풍나무

syllable ŭmjŏl 음절

syllabus kaeyo 개요

symbol (*character*) kiho 기호; (*in poetry etc*) sangjing 상징

symbolic sangjingjŏgin 상징적인

symbolism sangjingjuŭi 상징주의

symbolize sangjinghada 상징하다

symmetric(al) taech'ingjŏgin 대칭적인

symmetry taech'ing 대칭

sympathetic (*showing pity*) tongjŏnghanŭn 동정하는; (*understanding*) chal arajunŭn 잘 알아주는; *be ~ toward a person / an idea* nugurŭl / saenggagŭl chal ihaehada 누구를 / 생각을 잘 이해하다

♦**sympathize with** *person*, *views* chal ihaehada 잘 이해하다

sympathizer POL tongjoja 동조자

sympathy (*pity*) tongjŏngshim 동정심; (*understanding*) ihae 이해; *don't expect any ~ from me!* naege ihaebadŭl saenggagŭn ilch'e haji mara 내게 이해받을 생각은 일체 하지 마라

symphony kyohyanggok 교향곡

symptom MED, *fig* chŭnghu 증후

symptomatic: *be ~ of* …ŭi chŭnghurŭl poida …의 증후를 보이다

synchronize shiganŭl match'uda 시간을 맞추다

synonym tong-ŭiŏ 동의어

syntax munjangnon 문장론

synthetic hapssŏng-ŭi 합성의

syphilis maedok 매독

syringe chusagi 주사기

syrup shirŏp 시럽

system ch'egye 체계; (*structure: political etc*) chojik 조직; (*method*) pangshik 방식; (*orderliness*) sunsŏ 순서; (*computer*) shisŭt'em 시스템; *the braking / fuel injection ~* pŭreik'ŭ changch'i / yŏllyo konggŭp changch'i 브레이크 장치 / 연료 공급 장치; *digestive ~* sohwa kyet'ong 소화 계통

systematic *approach* chojiktchŏgin 조직적인

systematically *study* ch'egejŏgŭro 체계적으로; *destroy* kyehoektchŏgŭro 계획적으로

systems analyst COMPUT shisŭt'em punsŏk-kka 시스템 분석가

T

tab n ttagae 따개; (in text) t'aep 탭;
  pick up the ~ hant'ŏk naeda 한턱
  내다
table n sang 상; (of figures) p'yo 표
tablecloth shikt'akppo 식탁보
tablespoon k'ŭn sutkkarak 큰 숟가락
tablet MED allyak 알약, chŏngje 정제
table tennis t'ak-kku 탁구
tabloid n (newspaper) t'abŭlloidŭp'an
  shinmun 타블로이드판 신문
taboo adj kŭmgiŭi 금기의
tacit muŏnŭi 무언의
tack 1 n (nail) aptchŏng 압정 2 v/t
  (sew) shich'imjirhada 시침질하다
  3 v/i (of yacht) kaltchitchahyŏng-ŭro
  naagada 갈짓자형으로 나아가다
tackle 1 n (gear) togu 도구; SP t'aek'ŭl
  태클 2 v/t SP t'aek'ŭrhada 태클하다;
  problem ...wa/kwa sshirŭmhada
  ...와/과 씨름하다; intruder ...e
  tallyŏdŭlda ...에 달려들다
tacky paint, glue kkŭnjŏk-kkŭnjŏk'an
  끈적끈적한; (cheap, poor quality)
  polp'um ŏmnŭn 볼품 없는; behavior
  ch'ŏnbak'an 천박한
tact chaech'i 재치
tactful chaech'i innŭn 재치 있는
tactical chŏnsultchŏgin 전술적인
tactics chŏnsul 전술
tactless chaech'i ŏmnŭn 재치 없는
Taedong River Taedonggang 대동강
T'aekwondo T'aekkwŏndo 태권도
tag (label) kkorip'yo 꼬리표
tail n kkori 꼬리
tail light midŭng 미등
tailor chaebongsa 재봉사
tailor-made suit match'umŭi 맞춤의;
  solution ansŏng match'umŭi 안성
  맞춤의
tail wind sunp'ung 순풍
tainted food ssŏgŭn 썩은; reputation,
  atmosphere tŏrŏp'yŏjin 더럽혀진
Taiwan Taeman 대만

Taiwanese 1 adj Taemanŭi 대만의
  2 n Taemanin 대만인; (dialect)
  Taemanŏ 대만어
take v/t (remove) kajigo kada 가지고
  가다; (steal) humch'ida 훔치다;
  (transport) t'aewŏ chuda 태워 주다;
  (accompany) terigo kada 데리고
  가다; (accept: money, gift, credit
  cards) pat-tta 받다; (study: math,
  French) suganghada 수강하다; exam
  ch'ida 치다; degree ch'widŭk'ada
  취득하다; s.o.'s temperature chaeda
  재다; (endure) ch'amtta 참다;
  (require) p'iryoro hada 필요로 하다;
  this bus will ~ you to the center i
  pŏsŭrŭl t'amyŏn sent'ŏkkaji kal su
  issŭmnida 이 버스를 타면 센터까지
  갈 수 있습니다; **~ a photograph of
  s.o.** nuguŭi sajinŭl tchiktta 누구의
  사진을 찍다; **~ a photocopy**
  pokssahada 복사하다; **~ a stroll**
  sanch'aek'ada 산책하다; **it ~s 2
  hours** 2shigani kŏllida 2시간이
  걸리다; **how long does it ~?**
  ŏlmana kŏllimnikka? 얼마나
  걸립니까? **I'll ~ it** (when shopping)
  igŏsŭro hagessŭmnida 이것으로
  하겠습니다
  ♦ **take after** ...wa/kwa tamtta
    ...와/과 닮다
  ♦ **take away** pain ŏpssaeda 없애다;
    object kajigo kada 가지고 가다;
    MATH ppaeda 빼다; **take sth away
    from s.o.** (by force) nugurobut'ŏ
    muŏsŭl ppaeasakada 누구로부터
    무엇을 빼앗아가다
  ♦ **take back** (return: object)
    toedollyŏjuda 되돌려주다; person
    teryŏdajuda 데려다주다; (accept
    back: husband etc) tashi padadŭrida
    다시 받아들이다; **that takes me
    back** yennal saenggagi nage handa
    옛날 생각이 나게 한다
  ♦ **take down** (from shelf) naerida

내리다; *scaffolding* haech'ehada 해체하다; *pants* pŏt-tta 벗다; (*lengthen*) nŭrida 늘이다; (*write down*) pada chŏktta 받아 적다

♦ **take in** (*take indoors*) chibanŭro tŭrida 집안으로 들이다; (*give accommodation*) mukke hada 묵게 하다; (*make narrower*) churida 줄이다; (*deceive*) sogida 속이다; (*include*) p'ohamhada 포함하다

♦ **take off** 1 *v/t clothes, hat* pŏt-tta 벗다; *10% etc* kkaktta 깎다; (*mimic*) hyungnaenaeda 흉내내다; *can you take a bit off here?* (*to barber*) yŏgirŭl chogŭmman challa chushigessŭmnikka? 여기를 조금만 잘라 주시겠습니까?; *take a day/week off* harurŭl/iltchuirŭl shwida 하루를/일주일을 쉬다 2 *v/i* (*of airplane*) iryuk'ada 이륙하다; (*become popular*) inkkirŭl ŏt-tta 인기를 얻다

♦ **take on** *job* mat-tta 맡다; *staff* koyonghada 고용하다

♦ **take out** (*from bag, pocket*) kkŏnaeda 꺼내다; *stain* chiuda 지우다; *appendix, tooth* ppoptta 뽑다; *word from text* ppaenaeda 빼내다; *money from bank* inch'urhada 인출하다; (*to dinner etc*) terigo nagada 데리고 나가다; *insurance policy* ...e tŭlda ...에 들다; *take it out on s.o.* nuguege hwap'urihada 누구에게 화풀이하다

♦ **take over** 1 *v/t company etc* insuhada 인수하다; *tourists ~ the town* kwan-gwanggaekttŭri toshirŭl kadŭk ch'aeuda 관광객들이 도시를 가득 채우다 2 *v/i* (*of new management etc*) chang-ak'ada 장악하다; (*do sth in s.o.'s place*) taeshinhada 대신하다

♦ **take to** (*like*) choahage toeda 좋아하게 되다; (*form habit of*) ...hanŭn sŭpkkwani tŭlda ...하는 습관이 들다

♦ **take up** *carpet etc* turŏ ollida 들어 올리다; (*carry up*) wiro unbanhada 위로 운반하다; (*shorten*) churida 줄이다; *hobby, new job* shijak'ada 시작하다; *judo, new language* paeugi

shijak'ada 배우기 시작하다; *offer* surak'ada 수락하다; *space, time* ch'ajihada 차지하다; *I'll take you up on your offer* tangshinŭi cheŭirŭl padadŭrigessŭmnida 당신의 제의를 받아들이겠습니다

take-home pay shilssuip 실수입; **takeoff** (*of airplane*) iryuk 이륙; (*impersonation*) hyungnae 흉내; **takeover** COM insu 인수; **takeover bid** konggae maeip 공개 매입

takings maesanggo 매상고

talcum powder ttamtti karu 땀띠 가루

tale iyagi 이야기

talent chaenŭng 재능

talented chaenŭng-i innŭn 재능이 있는

talk 1 *v/i* marhada 말하다; *can I ~ to ...?* ...wa/kwa marhal su issŭmnikka? ...와/과 말할 수 있습니까?; *I'll ~ to him about it* chega kŭege kŭgŏse kwanhae iyagi hagessŏyo 제가 그에게 그것에 관해 이야기 하겠어요 2 *v/t English* marhada 말하다; *business* ŭinonhada 의논하다; *~ s.o. into sth* nugurŭl sŏlttŭk'ayŏ muŏsŭl shik'ida 누구를 설득하여 무엇을 시키다 3 *n* (*conversation*) taehwa 대화; (*lecture*) kangnyŏn 강연; *he's all ~* kŭnŭn hŏp'ungjang-iyeyo 그는 허풍장이예요

♦ **talk over** ŭinonhada 의논하다

talkative mari manŭn 말이 많은

talk show chwadamhoe 좌담회

tall k'iga k'ŭn 키가 큰

tall order murihan yogu 무리한 요구

tall story hŏp'ung 허풍

tame *adj animal* kildŭryŏjin 길들여진; *joke etc* shishihan 시시한

♦ **tamper with** manjijak-kkŏrida 만지작거리다; (*deliberately interfere with*) hamburo manjida 함부로 만지다

tampon t'amp'on 탐폰

tan 1 *n* (*from sun*) ssŏnt'en 썬텐; (*color*) hwanggalssaek 황갈색 2 *v/i* (*in sun*) haetppyŏch'e t'ada 햇볕에 타다 3 *v/t leather* mudujirhada 무두질하다

tandem (*bike*) 2insŭng chajŏn-gŏ 2인승 자전거

tangerine milgam 밀감, kyul 귤

tangle *n* ŏngk'im 엉킴

♦ **tangle up**: *get tangled up* (*of string etc*) ŏngk'ida 엉키다

tango *n* t'aenggo 탱고

tank chŏjang t'aengk'ŭ 저장 탱크; MOT, MIL, (*for skin diver*) t'aengk'ŭ 탱크

tanker (*ship*) yujosŏn 유조선; (*truck*) yujoch'a 유조차

tanned (*sun-~*) haetppyŏch'e t'an 햇볕에 탄

tantalizing kamjilnage hanŭn 감질나게 하는

tantamount: *be ~ to* …wa/kwa tongdŭnghada …와/과 동등하다

tantrum tchatchŭng 짜증

Taoism Togyo 도교

tap 1 *n* kkoktchi 꼭지 **2** *v/t* (*knock*) kabyŏpkke tudŭrida 가볍게 두드리다; *phone* toch'ŏnghada 도청하다

♦ **tap into** *resources* iyonghagi shijak'ada 이용하기 시작하다

tap dance *n* t'aepttaensŭ 탭댄스

tape 1 *n* (*for recording, sticky*) t'eip'ŭ 테이프 **2** *v/t* *conversation etc* nogŭmhada 녹음하다; (*video*) nok'wahada 녹화하다; (*with sticky tape*) t'eip'ŭro puch'ida 테이프로 붙이다

tape deck k'aset'ŭ p'ŭlleiŏ 카셋트 플레이어; **tape drive** COMPUT paegŏp tŭraibŭ 백업 드라이브; **tape measure** chulja 줄자

taper *v/i* chŏmjŏm kanŭrŏjida 점점 가늘어지다

♦ **taper off** (*of production, figures*) chŏmjŏm churŏdŭlda 점점 줄어들다

tape recorder nogŭmgi 녹음기

tape recording t'eip'ŭ nogŭm 테이프 녹음

tapestry t'aep'isŭt'ŭri 태피스트리

tar *n* t'arŭ 타르

tardy nŭjŭn 늦은

target 1 *n* (*in shooting*) kwanyŏk 과녁, p'yojŏk 표적; (*for sales, production*) mokp'yo 목표 **2** *v/t* *market* mokp'yoro hada 목표로 하다

target date mokp'yo magamil 목표 마감일; **target group** COM mokp'yo kŭrup 목표 그룹; **target market** p'yojŏk shijang 표적 시장

tariff (*price*) yogŭmp'yo 요금표; (*tax*) kwanse 관세

tarmac (*at airport*) hwaltchuro 활주로

tarnish *v/t* *metal* pyŏnsaeksshik'ida 변색시키다; *reputation* sonsangshik'ida 손상시키다

tarpaulin pangsup'o 방수포

tart *n* kwail p'ai 과일 파이

task immu 임무

task force t'ŭkppyŏl chosadan 특별 조사단; MIL t'ŭkssu kidongdae 특수 기동대

tassel sul 술

taste 1 *n* (*sense*) migak 미각; (*of food etc*) mat 맛; (*in clothes, art etc*) ch'wihyang 취향; *he has no ~ in clothes* kŭnŭn amurŏn p'aeshyŏn kamgagi ŏptta 그는 아무런 패션 감각이 없다 **2** *v/t also fig* matppoda 맛보다

tasteful kamgaginnŭn 감각있는

tasteless *food* ammu mat ŏmnŭn 아무 맛 없는; *remark, person* mŏdŏmnŭn 멋없는

tasty mashinnŭn 맛있는

tattered *clothes, book* tchijŏjin 찢어진

tatters: *in ~ also fig* nudŏgiga toeŏ 누더기가 되어

tattoo munshin 문신

taunt 1 *n* chorong 조롱 **2** *v/t* choronghada 조롱하다

taut p'aengp'aenghan 팽팽한

tax 1 *n* segŭm 세금; *before/after ~* segŭmŭl p'ohamhan/kongjehan 세금을 포함한/공제한 **2** *v/t* *people* …ege segŭmŭl pugwahada …에게 세금을 부과하다; *product* …e segŭmŭl pugwahada …에 세금을 부과하다

taxation kwase 과세; (*collection of taxes*) chingse 징세

tax code segŭm kiho 세금 기호; **tax-deductible** segŭm kongjega kanŭnghan 세금 공제가 가능한; **tax evasion** t'alsse 탈세; **tax-free** myŏnseŭi 면세의

taxi t'aeksshi 택시

taxidriver t'aeksshi unjŏnsa 택시 운전사

tax inspector semu chosagwan 세무 조사관

taxi rank t'aeksshi sŭngch'ajang 택시 승차장

tax payer napsseja 납세자

tax return (*form*) napsse shin-gosŏ 납세 신고서

tea (*drink*) ch'a 차; (*meal*) tagwa 다과; **green ~** nokch'a 녹차; **black ~** hongch'a 홍차

teabag ch'a pongji 차 봉지

teach 1 *v/t person, subject* karŭch'ida 가르치다; **~ s.o. to do sth** nuguege muŏt hanŭn kŏsŭl karŭch'ida 누구에게 무엇 하는 것을 가르치다 **2** *v/i* karŭch'ida 가르치다

teacher sŏnsaeng 선생; (*form of address*) sŏnsaengnim 선생님; (*describing profession*) kyosa 교사

Teachers' Day Sŭsŭng-ŭi nal 스승의 날

teacher training kyosa hullyŏn 교사 훈련

teaching (*profession*) kyojik 교직

teaching aid pojo kyojae 보조 교재

teaching assistant kangsa 강사

tea cloth marŭn haengju 마른 행주; **teacup** ch'atchan 찻잔; **tea drinker** ch'a aehoga 차 애호가

teak t'ik'ŭ namu 티크 나무

tea leaves ch'annip 찻잎

team t'im 팀

team spirit tanch'e chŏngshin 단체 정신

teamster t'ŭrŏk unjŏnsa 트럭 운전사

teamwork hyŏpttong chagŏp 협동 작업

teapot chattchujŏnja 찻주전자

tear¹ 1 *n* (*in cloth etc*) tchijŏjin t'ŭm 찢어진 틈 **2** *v/t paper, cloth* tchit-tta 찢다; **be torn between two alternatives** tu taean saiesŏ mangsŏrida 두 대안 사이에서 망설이다 **3** *v/i* (*go fast*) chiltchuhada 질주하다

♦ **tear up** *paper* kalgigalgi tchit-tta 갈기갈기 찢다; *agreement* ch'wisohada 취소하다

tear² (*in eye*) nunmul 눈물; **burst into ~s** urŭmŭl t'ŏttŭrida 울음을

be in ~s nunmurŭl hŭllida 눈물을 흘리다

teardrop nunmul pang-ŭl 눈물 방울

tearful nunmul ŏrin 눈물 어린

tear gas ch'oerugasŭ 최루가스

tearoom chattchip 찻집

tease *v/t* (*maliciously*) koerop'ida 괴롭히다; (*for fun*) nollida 놀리다

tea service, tea set ch'attchan set'ŭ 찻잔 세트; **teaspoon** ch'atssutkkarak 찻숟가락

teat chŏtkkoktchi 젖꼭지

technical kisultchŏgin 기술적인; (*relating to particular field*) chŏnmunŭi 전문의

technicality (*technical nature*) chŏnmunsŏng 전문성; LAW sasohan sahang 사소한 사항; **that's just a ~** kŭgŏsŭn kŭnyang sasohan iril ppunida 그것은 그냥 사소한 일일 뿐이다

technically kisultchŏgŭro 기술적으로; (*strictly speaking*) ŏmmirhi marhamyŏn 엄밀히 말하면

technician kisultcha 기술자

technique kisul 기술; (*of performer*) kigyo 기교

technological kwahak kisulsang-ŭi 과학 기술상의

technology kwahak kisul 과학 기술

technophobia kwahak kisul kongp'otchŭng 과학 기술 공포증

tedious chiruhan 지루한

tee *n* (*in golf*) t'i 티

teem: be ~ing with rain p'oguga ssodajigo it-tta 폭우가 쏟아지고 있다; **be ~ing with tourists**/**ants** kwan-gwanggaekttŭllo/kaemidŭllo nŏmch'ida 관광객들로 / 개미들로 넘치다

teenage *fashions* ship taeŭi 십 대의

teenager t'ineijŏ 틴에이저

teens: be in one's ~ ship taeida 십 대이다; **reach one's ~** ship taega toeda 십 대가 되다

telecommunications t'ongshin 통신

telegram chŏnbo 전보

telegraph pole chŏnshinju 전신주

telepathic chŏngshin kamŭng-ŭi 정신 감응의; **you must be ~!** maŭmi t'onghaetkkunyo! 마음이 통했군요!

telepathy chŏngshin kamŭng 정신 감응

telephone 1 *n* chŏnhwa 전화; *be on the ~* (*be speaking*) t'onghwa chung-ida 통화 중이다; (*possess a phone*) chŏnhwaga it-tta 전화가 있다 **2** *v/t person* ...ege chŏnhwarŭl kŏlda ...에게 전화를 걸다 **3** *v/i* chŏnhwahada 전화하다

telephone booth kongjung chŏnhwa pakssŭ 공중 전화 박스; **telephone call** chŏnhwa 전화; **telephone directory** chŏnhwa pŏnhobu 전화 번호부; **telephone exchange** chŏnhwa kyohwan-guk 전화 교환국; **telephone number** chŏnhwa pŏnho 전화 번호

telephoto lens mang-wŏn lenjŭ 망원 렌즈

telesales chŏnhwa p'anmae 전화 판매

telescope mang-wŏn-gyŏng 망원경

televise pang-wŏnghada 방영하다

television t'ellebijŏn 텔레비전; (*set*) t'ellebijŏn susanggi 텔레비전 수상기; *on ~* t'ellebijŏne(sŏ) 텔레비전에(서); *watch ~* t'ellebijŏnŭl poda 텔레비전을 보다

television program t'ellebijŏn p'ŭrogŭraem 텔레비전 프로그램; **television set** t'ellebijŏn susanggi 텔레비전 수상기; **television studio** t'ellebijŏn nok'washil 텔레비전 녹화실

tell 1 *v/t story* marhada 말하다; *lie* kŏjinmarhada 거짓말하다; *the difference* kubyŏrhada 구별하다; *~ s.o. sth* nuguege muŏsŭl marhada 누구에게 무엇을 말하다; *don't ~ Mom* ŏmmahant'e marhajima 엄마한테 말하지마; *could you ~ me the way to ...?* ...(ŭ)ro kanŭn kirŭl karŭch'yŏ chushigessŏyo? ...(으)로 가는 길을 가르쳐 주시겠어요?; *~ s.o. to do sth* nuguege muŏsŭl harago marhada 누구에게 무엇을 하라고 말하다; *you're ~ing me!* chŏngmal kŭraeyo! 정말 그래요! **2** *v/i* (*have effect*) yŏnghyang-ŭl mich'ida 영향을 미치다; *the heat is ~ing on him* kŭnŭn tŏwirŭl mŏk-

kko it-tta 그는 더위를 먹고 있다; *time will ~* shigani chinamyŏn kkaedatkke toel kŏshida 시간이 지나면 깨닫게 될 것이다

♦ **tell off** (*reprimand*) kkujit-tta 꾸짖다

teller ŭnhaeng ch'ullabwŏn 은행 출납원

telltale 1 *adj signs* sashirŭl tŭrŏnaenŭn 사실을 드러내는 **2** *n* kojajiljaeng-i 고자질쟁이

temp 1 *n* (*employee*) imshi chigwŏn 임시 직원 **2** *v/i* imshijiguŏro irhada 임시직으로 일하다

temper (*bad ~*) sŏngjil 성질, kibun 기분; *be in a ~* hwarŭl naego it-tta 화를 내고 있다; *keep one's ~* hwarŭl ch'amtta 화를 참다; *lose one's ~* hwarŭl naeda 화를 내다

temperament kijil 기질

temperamental (*moody*) pyŏndŏkssŭrŏun 변덕스러운

temperature ondo 온도; (*fever*) yŏl 열; *have a ~* yŏri it-tta 열이 있다

temple[1] REL sawŏn 사원

temple[2] ANAT kwanjanori 관자놀이

tempo MUS paktcha 박자; (*of work*) soktto 속도

temporarily ilsshijŏguŏro 일시적으로

temporary ilsshijŏgin 일시적인

tempt yuhok'ada 유혹하다

temptation yuhok 유혹

tempting yuhoktchŏgin 유혹적인

ten yŏl 열, ship 십

tenacious wan-ganghan 완강한

tenant ch'ayongja 차용자

tend[1] *v/t* (*look after*) tolboda 돌보다

tend[2]: *~ to do sth* muŏt hanŭn p'yŏnida 무엇 하는 편이다; *~ toward sth* muŏsŭi kyŏnghyang-i it-tta 무엇의 경향이 있다

tendency kyŏnghyang 경향

tender[1] *adj* (*sore*) manjimyŏn ap'ŭn 만지면 아픈; (*affectionate*) tajŏnghan 다정한; *steak* yŏnhan 연한

tender[2] *n* COM ipch'al 입찰

tenderness (*soreness*) manjimyŏn ap'ŭm 만지면 아픔; (*of kiss etc*) tajŏngham 다정함; (*of steak*) yŏnham 연함

tendon himtchul 힘줄

tennis t'enissŭ 테니스
tennis ball t'enissŭ kong 테니스 공;
 tennis court t'enissŭ chang 테니스
 장; **tennis player** t'enissŭ sŏnsu
 테니스 선수; **tennis racket** t'enissŭ
 lak'et 테니스 라켓
tenor n MUS t'enŏ 테너
tense¹ n GRAM shije 시제
tense² adj muscle kinjangdoen
 긴장된; voice, person kinjanghan
 긴장한; moment kinjangdoenŭn
 긴장되는
♦ **tense up** kinjangdoeda 긴장되다
tension (of rope) p'aengp'aengham
 팽팽함; (in atmosphere, voice)
 kinjang 긴장; (in movie, novel)
 kinbak-kkam 긴박감
tent ch'ŏnmak 천막
tentacle ch'oksu 촉수
tentative chujŏhanŭn 주저하는
tenterhooks: be on ~
 chobashimhada 조바심하다
tenth yŏl pŏntchaeŭi 열 번째의
tepid water, reaction mijigŭnhan
 미지근한
term (period of time) kigan 기간;
 (condition) kiil 기일; (word) yong-ŏ
 용어; be on good / bad ~s with s.o.
 nuguwa chohŭn / nappŭn kwan-
 gyeida 누구와 좋은 / 나쁜 관계이다;
 in the long / short ~
 changgijŏgŭro / tan-gijŏgŭro
 장기적으로 / 단기적으로; come to ~s
 with sth muŏsŭl padadŭrida 무엇을
 받아들이다
terminal 1 n (at airport, for buses)
 t'ŏminŏl 터미널; (for containers)
 chip'atchang 집하장; ELEC tanja
 단자; COMPUT tanmal changch'i 단말
 장치 2 adj illness pulch'iŭi 불치의
terminally adv: ~ ill pulch'ippyŏng-ŭi
 불치병의
terminate 1 v/t contract wanjŏnhi
 kkŭnnaeda 완전히 끝내다; ~ a
 pregnancy nakt'aeshik'ida
 낙태시키다 2 v/i kkŭnnada
 끝나다
termination (of contract) man-gi
 만기; (of pregnancy) nakt'ae 낙태
terminology chŏnmun yong-ŏ 전문
 용어

terminus (for buses, trains)
 chongtchŏm 종점
terrace (on hillside) kyedanshik pat
 계단식 밭; (patio) t'erasŭ 테라스
terra cotta t'erak'ot'a 테라코타
terrain chihyŏng 지형
terrestrial 1 n chiguin 지구인 2 adj
 television chisang-ŭi 지상의
terrible kkŭmtchik'an 끔찍한
terribly (very) mopsshi 몹시
terrific koengjanghan 굉장한
terrifically (very) koengjanghage
 굉장하게
terrify kŏmnage hada 겁나게 하다; be
 terrified kŏbe chillida 겁에 질리다
terrifying kŏmnage hanŭn 겁나게
 하는
territorial yŏngt'oŭi 영토의
territorial waters yŏnghae 영해
territory yŏngt'o 영토; fig kuyŏk 구역
terror kongp'o 공포
terrorism t'erŏrijŭm 테러리즘
terrorist t'erŏbŏm 테러범
terrorist organization t'erŏ chojik
 테러 조직
terrorize wihyŏp'ada 위협하다
test 1 n shihŏm 시험 2 v/t shihŏmhada
 시험하다; new product, drug etc
 shirhŏmhada 실험하다
testament (to a person, life etc)
 kinyŏmmul 기념물; Old / New Testament REL Kuyak / Shinyak Sŏngsŏ
 구약 / 신약 성서
testicle kohwan 고환
testify v/i LAW chŭng-ŏnhada
 증언하다
testimonial ch'uch'ŏntchang 추천장
test tube shihŏmgwan 시험관
test-tube baby shihŏmgwan agi
 시험관 아기
testy sŏngmi kŭp'an 성미 급한
tetanus p'asangp'ung 파상풍
tether 1 v/t horse maeda 매다 2 n: be
 at the end of one's ~ han-gyee
 irŭda 한계에 이르다
text ponmun 본문
textbook kyokkwasŏ 교과서
text file COMPUT t'eksŭt'ŭ p'ail 텍스트
 파일
textile chingmul 직물
texture (of skin, material) kyŏl 결; (of

food) sship'inŭn nŭkkim 씹히는 느낌

Thai 1 *adj* T'aegugŭi 태국의 **2** *n* *(person)* T'aegugin 태국인; *(language)* T'aegugŏ 태국어

Thailand T'aiguk 태국

than …poda …보다; *bigger / faster ~ me* naboda tŏ k'ŭn / pparŭn 나보다 더 큰 / 빠른

thank *v/t* kamsahada 감사하다; *~ you (polite)* kamsahamnida 감사합니다, komapssŭmnida 고맙습니다; F komawŏ 고마워; *no ~ you* komaptchiman, kwaench'ansŭmnida 고맙지만, 괜찮습니다

thanks kamsa 감사, komaum 고마움; *~!* komapssŭmnida! 고맙습니다!; *(to friend, to younger people)* komawŏ! 고마워!; *~ to* …tŏkt'aege …덕택에

thankful kamsahanŭn 감사하는

thankfully kamsahagedo 감사하게도, komapkkedo 고맙게도; *(luckily)* tahaenghido 다행히도

thankless *task* poram ŏmnŭn 보람 없는

Thanksgiving (Day) Ch'usu Kamsajŏl 추수 감사절

that 1 *adj* chŏ 저; *~ one (thing)* chŏgŏt 저것; *(person)* chŏ saram 저 사람 **2** *pron (thing)* chŏgŏt 저것; 사람; *what is ~?* chŏgŏsŭn muŏshimnikka? 저것은 무엇입니까?; *who is ~?* chŏ saramŭn nuguimnikka? 저 사람은 누구입니까?; *~'s mine* kŭgŏsŭn che kŏshimnida 그것은 제 것입니다; *~'s tea* kŭgŏsŭn ch'aimnida 그것은 차입니다; *~'s very kind* kŭgŏsŭn chŏngmal ch'injŏrhan irimnida 그것은 정말 친절한 일입니다 ◊ *(relative)* …hanŭn …하는; *the person / car ~ you see* tangshini pogo innŭn saram / ch'a 당신이 보고 있는 사람 / 차 **3** *conj*: *I think ~ …* jŏnŭn …rago saenggak'amnida 저는 …라고 생각합니다 **4** *adv (so)* kŭrŏk'e 그렇게; *~ big* kŭrŏk'e k'ŭn 그렇게 큰

thaw *v/i (of snow, frozen food)* noktta 녹다

the ◊ *(no equivalent in Korean)*: *~ border* kuk-kkyŏng 국경 ◊

(identifying or with previous reference) kŭ 그; *~ doctor who treated me* narŭl ch'iryohan kŭ ŭisa 나를 치료한 그 의사; *is that ~ ring he gave you?* igŏshi kŭga tangshinege chun kŭi panjiyeyo? 이것이 그가 당신에게 준 그 반지예요?; *~ blue bag is mine* kŭ p'aran kabang-i che kŏshiyeyo 그 파란 가방이 제 것이에요 ◊: *~ sooner ~ better* pparŭmyŏn pparŭlsurok chot'a 빠르면 빠를수록 좋다

theater yŏn-gŭk 연극; *(building)* kŭktchang 극장

theatrical yŏn-gŭgŭi 연극의; *(overdone)* kwajangdoen 과장된

theft toduktchil 도둑질

their kŭdŭrŭi 그들의; *(his or her)*: *somebody has left ~ coat behind* nugun-ga k'ot'ŭrŭl nwadugo kassŏyo 누군가 코트를 놔두고 갔어요

theirs kŭdŭrŭi kŏt 그들의 것; *a friend of ~* kŭdŭrŭi ch'in-gu 그들의 친구

them kŭdŭl 그들; *that's for ~* kŭdŭrŭi kŏshimnida 그들의 것입니다; *who's that? - it's ~ again* nuguyeyo? - tto kŭdŭriyeyo 누구예요? - 또 그들이에요 ◊ *(him or her)*: *nobody had a car with ~* amudo ch'arŭl kajigo oji anassŏyo 아무도 차를 가지고 오지 않았어요

theme t'ema 테마

theme park t'ema kong-wŏn 테마 공원

theme song chujega 주제가

themselves kŭdŭl chashin 그들 자신; *by ~ (alone)* kŭdŭl sŭsŭro 그들 스스로

then *(at that time)* kŭ ttae 그 때; *(after that)* kŭrigo nasŏ 그리고 나서; *(deducing)* kŭrŏt'amyŏn 그렇다면; *by ~* kŭ ttaeenŭn 그 때에는

theology shinhak 신학

theoretical ironŭi 이론의; *~ physics* iron mullihak 이론 물리학

theory iron 이론; *in ~* ironsang-ŭro 이론상으로

therapeutic ch'iryoŭi 치료의

therapist ch'iryo chŏnmun-ga 치료
전문가
therapy ch'iryo 치료
there kŭ kose 그 곳에; *over ~ / down
~* chŏ wie / araee 저 위에 / 아래에; *~
is* ...i it-tta ...이 있다; *~ are* ...tŭri it-
tta ...들이 있다; *is / are ~ ...?* ...i / tŭri
issŭmnikka? ...이 / 들이 있습니까?;
isn't / aren't ~ ...? ...i / tŭri
ŏpssŭmnikka? ...이 / 들이 없습니까?;
~ you are (*giving sth*) yogi
issŭmnida 여기 있습니다; (*finding
sth*) yŏgi issŏkkunyo 여기 있었군요;
(*completing sth*) twaessŭmnida
됐습니다; *$50 ~ and back* wangbok
50tallŏimnida 왕복 50달러입니다; *~
he is!* kŭga chŏgi itkkunyo 그가
저기 있군요!; *~, ~!* cha, cha! 자, 자!
thereabouts kŭ chŏngdo 그 정도
therefore ttarasŏ 따라서, kŭrŏmŭro
그러므로
thermometer ondogye 온도계
thermos flask poonbyŏng 보온병
thermostat chadong ondo chojŏl
changch'i 자동 온도 조절 장치
these 1 *adj* igŏttŭrŭi 이것들의, i ...dŭl
이 ...들 **2** *pron* igŏttŭl 이것들
thesis nonmun 논문
they kŭdŭl 그들; (*things*) kŭgŏttŭl
그것들 ◊ (*he or she*): *if anyone
knows ~ should say so* manyak
nugurado andamyŏn, kŭrŏk'e
yegihaeya hamnida 만약 누구라도
안다면, 그렇게 얘기해야 합니다 ◊
(*impersonal*): *~ say that ...* kŭdŭri
...rago marhada 그들이 ...라고
말하다; *~ are going to change the
law* kŭdŭrŭn pŏbŭl pakkul kŏshida
그들은 법을 바꿀 것이다
thick tukkŏun 두꺼운; F (*stupid*)
tunhan 둔한; *fog* chit'ŭn 짙은; *soup*
kŏltchuk'an 걸쭉한; *~ hair* such'i
manŭn mŏri 숱이 많은 머리
thicken *sauce* kŏltchuk'age hada
걸쭉하게 하다
thickset ttangttalmak'an 땅딸막한
thickskinned *fig* ppŏnppŏnsŭrŏun
뻔뻔스러운
thief totuk 도둑
thigh nŏptchŏkttari 넓적다리
thimble kolmu 골무

thin *material* yalbŭn 얇은; *hair, line*
kanŭn 가는; *person* marŭn 마른;
soup mulgŭn 묽은
thing samul 사물; *~s* (*belongings*)
soyumul 소유물; *how are ~s?*
ŏttŏk'e chinaeseyo? 어떻게
지내세요?; *good ~ you told me*
naege marŭl chal haet-tta 내게 말을
잘 했다; *what a ~ to do / say!*
musŭn chishiya / mariya! 무슨
짓이야 / 말이야!
thingumajig F kŭ mwŏrago hanŭn
kŏt 그 뭐라고 하는 것; (*person*) kŭ
mwŏrago hanŭn saram 그 뭐라고
하는 사람
think saenggak'ada 생각하다; *I ~ so*
kŭrŏn kŏt kat'ayo 그런 것 같아요; *I
don't ~ so* kŭroch'i anŭn kŏt
kat'ayo 그렇지 않은 것 같아요; *I ~
so too* chŏdo kŭrŏk'e
saenggak'aeyo 저도 그렇게
생각해요; *what do you ~?* ŏttŏk'e
saenggak'aseyo? 어떻게
생각하세요?; *what do you ~ of it?*
kŭgŏsŭl ŏttŏk'e saenggak'aeyo?
그것을 어떻게 생각해요?; *I can't ~
of anything more* kŭ isang-ŭn
saenggangnaji anayo 그 이상은
생각나지 않아요; *~ hard!* chal
saenggak'ae pwa! 잘 생각해 봐!; *I'm
~ing about emigrating* nanŭn
imin-ganŭn kŏsŭl saenggak chung-
ida 나는 이민가는 것을 생각 중이다
♦ **think over** suk-kkohada 숙고하다
♦ **think through** yomojomo
saenggak'ae poda 요모조모 생각해
보다
♦ **think up** *plan* saenggak'aenaeda
생각해내다
third 1 *adj* chesamŭi 제3의, se
pŏntchaeŭi 세 번째의 **2** *n* (*in
sequence*) chesam 제3, se pŏntchae
세 번째; (*fraction*) sambunŭi il
삼분의 일
thirdly se pŏntchaeronŭn 세 번째로는
third-party insurance ch'aegim
pohŏm 책임 보험; **third-rate**
samnyuŭi 삼류의; **Third World**
Chesam Segye 제3 세계
thirst kaltchŭng 갈증
thirsty mongmarŭn 목마른; *be ~*

mongmarŭda 목마르다

thirteen yŏlsset 열 셋, shipssam 십삼

thirteenth yŏlsse pŏntchaeŭi 열 세 번째의

thirtieth sŏrŭn pŏntchaeŭi 서른 번째의

thirty sŏrŭn 서른, samship 삼십

Thirty-Eighth Parallel Samp'alssŏn 삼팔선

this 1 adj i 이; ~ **one** igŏt 이것 **2** pron igŏt 이것; ~ **is good** igŏsŭn chota 이것은 좋다; ~ **is** (introducing) i saramŭn ...imnida 이 사람은 ...입니다; TELEC chŏnŭn ...imnida 저는 ...입니다 **3** adv: ~ **big / high** i chŏngdoro k'ŭda / noptta 이 정도로 크다 / 높다

thorn kashi 가시

thorough search, person ch'ŏltchŏhan 철저한; knowledge wanjŏnhan 완전한

thoroughbred sunjong 순종

those 1 adj people kŭdŭrŭi 그들의; things, animals kŭgŏttŭrŭi 그것들의; **in ~ days** kŭ tangshienŭn 그 당시에는 **2** pron (people) kŭdŭl 그들; (things, animals) kŭgŏttŭl 그것들

though 1 conj (although) ...ijiman ...이지만; **even ~ ...** ...handa hadŏrado ...한다 하더라도; ~ **it might fail** shilp'aehagetchiman 실패하겠지만; **as ~** mach'i ...ch'ŏrŏm 마치 ...처럼 **2** adv kŭrŏt'ŏrado 그럴더라도; **it's not finished ~** kŭrŏt'arado ajik kkŭnnan kŏsŭn anida 그럴더라도 아직 끝난 것은 아니다

thought (single) sago 사고, saenggak 생각; (collective) sasang 사상

thoughtful saenggagi kip'ŭn 생각이 깊은; book shimsasuk-kkohan 심사숙고한; (considerate) saryŏ kip'ŭn 사려 깊은

thoughtless namŭl koryŏhaji annŭn 남을 고려하지 않는

thousand ch'ŏn 천; ~**s of** su ch'ŏnŭi 수 천의; **ten ~** man 만; **hundred ~** shim man 십만

thousandth adj ch'ŏn pŏntchaeŭi 천 번째의

thrash v/t magu ttaerida 마구 때리다;

SP ch'amp'aeshik'ida 참패시키다

♦ **thrash around** (with arms etc) momburimch'ida 몸부림치다

♦ **thrash out** solution nonŭihaesŏ haegyŏrhada 논의해서 해결하다

thrashing ch'aetchiktchil 채찍질; SP ch'amp'ae 참패

thread 1 n shil 실; (of screw) nasasan 나사산 **2** v/t needle, beads ...e shirŭl kkweda ...에 실을 꿰다

threadbare tarŭn 닳은

threat wihyŏp 위협

threaten wihyŏp'ada 위협하다

threatening gesture, tone wihyŏp'anŭn 위협하는; sky tchip'urin 찌푸린; **a ~ letter** hyŏppak p'yŏnji 협박 편지

three set 셋, sam 삼

Three Han Samhan 삼한; **Three Kingdoms** Samguk 삼국; **three-quarters** n sabunŭi sam 사분의 삼

thresh v/t corn t'algok'ada 탈곡하다

threshold (of house) muntchibang 문지방; (of new age) ch'ulbaltchŏm 출발점; **on the ~ of** ...ŭi ch'ulbaltchŏme ...의 출발점에

thrift chŏryak 절약

thrifty chŏryak'anŭn 절약하는

thrill 1 n chŏnyul 전율 **2** v/t: **be ~ed** kamgyŏk'ada 감격하다

thriller sŭrillŏmul 스릴러물

thrilling kamgyŏk'age hanŭn 감격하게 하는

thrive (of plant) ulch'anghage charada 울창하게 자라다; (of economy) pŏnch'anghada 번창하다

throat mokkumŏng 목구멍

throat lozenges mok sat'ang 목 사탕

throb 1 n (of heart) maekppak 맥박; (of music) ttŏllimŭm 떨림음 **2** v/i (of heart) ttwida 뛰다; (of music) ttŏllida 떨리다

thrombosis hyŏltchŏntchŭng 혈전증

throne wangjwa 왕좌

throttle 1 n (on motorbike, boat) soktto chojŏl changch'i 속도 조절 장치 **2** v/t (strangle) moktchorŭda 목조르다

♦ **throttle back** v/i kamsok'ada 감속하다

through 1 prep ◊ (across) ...ŭl

t'onghayŏ …을 통하여; **go ~ the
city** toshirŭl chinagada 도시를
지나가다 ◊ (during) …ŭi tong-an
naenae …의 동안 내내; **~ the win-
ter/summer** kyŏul/yŏrŭm tong-an
naenae 겨울/여름 동안 내내; **Monday ~ Friday** wŏryoilbut'ŏ
kŭmnyoil tong-an naenae 내내 ◊
(thanks to) … tŏkppune … 덕분에;
arranged ~ him kŭ tŏkppune 그
덕분에 **2** adv: **wet ~** mongttang
chŏjŏt-tta 몽땅 젖었다; **watch a
movie** ~ yŏnghwarŭl kkŭtkkaji
poda 영화를 끝까지 보다; **read a
book** ~ ch'aegŭl kkŭtkkaji iltta 책을
끝까지 읽다 **3** adj: **be ~** (of couple)
kwan-gyega kkŭnnada 관계가
끝나다; (have arrived: of news etc)
toch'ak'ada 도착하다; **you're ~**
TELEC yŏn-gyŏldwaessŭmnida
연결됐습니다; **I'm ~ with** person
nanŭn …wa/kwa kwan-gyerŭl
kkŭnnaet-tta 나는 …와/과의 관계를
끝냈다; (no longer need) nanŭn
…ŭl/rŭl ta ssŏt-tta 나는 …을/를 다
썼다
through flight chik'aeng pihaenggi
직행 비행기
throughout 1 prep journey, night
…tong-an naenae …동안 내내;
novel …ŭi toch'ŏe …의 도처에
2 adv (in all parts) chŏnch'ejŏgŭro
전체적으로
through train chik'aeng yŏlch'a 직행
열차
throw 1 v/t tŏnjida 던지다; (of horse)
naep'aenggaech'ida 내팽개치다;
(disconnect) tanghwanghage hada
당황하게 하다; party yŏlda 열다 **2** n
tŏnjigi 던지기
♦**throw away** pŏrida 버리다
♦**throw out** old things naebŏrida
내버리다; person naetchot-tta 내쫓다;
plan pugyŏrhada 부결하다
♦**throw up 1** v/t ball wiro tŏnjida
위로 던지다; **~ one's hands** tu son
tŭlda 두 손 들다 **2** v/i (vomit)
t'ohada 토하다
throw-away remark amurŏch'i ank'e
han 아무렇지 않게 한; (disposable)

irhoeyong 일회용
throw-in SP sŭroin 스로인
thru → **through**
thrush (bird) kaettongjippagwi
개똥지빠귀
thrust v/t (push hard) sege tchirŭda
세게 찌르다; **~ sth into s.o.'s
hands** muŏsŭl nuguŭi sone ŏktchiro
ttŏmatkkida 무엇을 누구의 손에
억지로 떠맡기다; **~ one's way
through the crowd** kunjung sogŭl
hech'igo naagada 군중 속을 헤치고
나아가다
thud n k'unghanŭn sori 쿵하는 소리
thug hyung-akppŏm 흉악범
thumb 1 n ŏmji sonkkarak 엄지
손가락 **2** v/t: **~ a ride**
p'yŏnsŭnghada 편승하다
thumbtack app'in 압핀
thump 1 n (blow) chumŏktchil
주먹질; (noise) k'unghanŭn sori
쿵하는 소리 **2** v/t person ch'ida 치다;
~ one's fist on the table t'eibŭrŭl
chumŏgŭro tudŭrida 테이블을
주먹으로 두드리다 **3** v/i (of heart)
tugŭndugŭn ttwida 두근두근 뛰다; **~
on the door** mune k'unghago
puditch'ida 문에 쿵하고 부딪치다
thunder n ch'ŏndung 천둥
thunderstorm noeu 뇌우
thundery weather ch'ŏndung-i
morach'il ttŭt'an 천둥이 몰아칠 듯한
Thursday mogyoil 목요일
thus ttarasŏ 따라서
thwart person, plans panghaehada
방해하다
thyroid (gland) kapssangsŏn 갑상선
Tibet T'ibet'ŭ 티베트
Tibetan 1 adj T'ibet'ŭŭi 티베트의 **2** n
(person) T'ibet'ŭin 티베트인;
(language) T'ibet'ŏ 티베트어
tick 1 n (of clock) ttokttak sori 똑딱
소리; (checkmark) chŏmgŏm p'yoshi
점검 표시 **2** v/i (of clock) ttokttak-
kkŏrida 똑딱거리다
♦**tick off** (reprimand) chuŭi chuda
주의 주다
ticket p'yo 표
ticket collector kaech'arwŏn 개찰원;
ticket inspector p'yo kŏmsawŏn 표
검사원; **ticket machine** p'yo

chadong p'anmaegi 표 자동 판매기;
ticket office (*at station*) maep'yoso 매표소

tickle 1 *v/t person* kanjirŏp'ida 간지럽히다 **2** *v/i* (*of material*) kanjilkanjirhada 간질간질하다; (*of person*) kanjirida 간질이다

ticklish *person* kanjirŏumŭl chal t'anŭn 간지러움을 잘 타는

tidal wave chosŏkp'a 조석파

tide chosu 조수; *high* ~ manjo 만조; *low* ~ kanjo 간조; *the* ~ *is in/out* milmurida/ssŏlmurida 밀물이다/썰물이다

tidy *person, habits* tanjŏnghan 단정한; *room, house* chŏngdondoen 정돈된
♦ **tidy up 1** *v/t room, shelves* chŏngdonhada 정돈하다; *tidy oneself up* tanjŏnghi hada 단정히 하다 **2** *v/i* chŏngdonhada 정돈하다

tie 1 *n* (*necktie*) nekt'ai 넥타이; (SP: *even result*) tongtchŏm 동점; *he doesn't have any* ~s kŭnŭn amu yŏn-gojado ŏptta 그는 아무 연고자도 없다 **2** *v/t knot* choida 조이다; *hands* muktta 묶다; ~ *two ropes together* tu kaeŭi kkŭnŭl hamkke muktta 두 개의 끈을 함께 묶다 **3** *v/i* SP tongtchŏmi toeda 동점이 되다
♦ **tie down** (*with rope*) mukkŏ not'a 묶어 놓다; (*restrict*) kusok'ada 구속하다
♦ **tie up** muktta 묶다; *boat* maeda 매다; *I'm tied up tomorrow* nanŭn naeil yakssogi it-tta 나는 내일 약속이 있다

tier ch'ŭng 층

tiger horang-i 호랑이

tight 1 *adj clothes* kkok kkinŭn 꼭 끼는; *security* tandanhan 단단한; (*hard to move*) kkok kkiin 꼭 끼인; (*properly shut*) kkok tach'in 꼭 닫힌; (*not leaving much time*) ch'okppak'an 촉박한; F (*drunk*) ch'wihan 취한 **2** *adv hold* tandanhi 단단히; *shut* kkok kkok

tighten *screw* tandanhi choida 단단히 조이다; *control, security* kanghwahada 강화하다; ~ *one's grip on sth* muŏsŭl chang-ak'ada

무엇을 장악하다
♦ **tighten up** *v/i* (*in discipline, security*) ŏmhage hada 엄하게 하다

tight-fisted insaek'an 인색한

tightrope p'aengp'aenghan chul 팽팽한 줄

tile t'ail 타일

till[1] → *until*

till[2] (*cash register*) ton sŏrap 돈 서랍

till[3] *v/t soil* kyŏngjak'ada 경작하다

tilt 1 *v/t* kiurida 기울이다 **2** *v/i* kiulda 기울다

timber moktchae 목재

time shigan 시간; (*occasion*) pŏn 번; ~ *is up* ije shigani ta twaet-tta 이제 시간이 다 됐다; *for the* ~ *being* tangbun-gan 당분간; *have a good* ~ chŏun shiganŭl ponaeda 좋은 시간을 보내다; *have a good* ~! chŏun shiganŭl ponaeseyo! 좋은 시간을 보내세요!; *what's the* ~? myŏt shiimnikka? 몇 시입니까?; *the first* ~ ch'oŭmŭro 처음으로; *four* ~s ne pŏn 네 번; ~ *and again* myŏt pŏnina kyesok 몇 번이나 계속; *all the* ~ nŭl 늘; *three at a* ~ han pŏne set 한 번에 셋; *at the same* ~ *speak, reply etc* tongshie 동시에; (*however*) kŭrŏmyŏnsŏdo 그러면서도; *in* ~ shiganŭl match'uŏ 시간을 맞추어; *on* ~ chŏnggage 정각에; *in no* ~ kot 곧

time bomb shihan p'okt'an 시한 폭탄; **time clock** (*in factory*) ch'ult'oegŭn shigan kirok-kkye 출퇴근 시간 기록계; **time-consuming** manŭn shigani kŏllinŭn 많은 시간이 걸리는; **time lag** shich'a 시차; **time limit** chehan shigan 제한 시간

timely chŏksshiŭi 적시의

time out SP t'aim aut 타임 아웃

timer t'aimŏ 타이머

timesaving *n* shigan chŏryak 시간 절약; **timescale** (*of project*) shigi 시기; **time switch** t'aim sŭwich'i 타임 스위치; **timetable** shiganp'yo 시간표; **timewarp** waegoktoen shigandae 왜곡된 시간대; **time zone** p'yojun shiganttae 표준 시간대

timid *person, animal* kŏmmanŭn

겁많은; *smile* kŏmmŏgŭn 겁먹은

timing (*choosing a time*) shigirŭl match'ugi 시기를 맞추기; (*of actor, dancer*) t'aiming 타이밍

tin (*metal*) chusŏk 주석

tinfoil ŭnjong-i 은종이

tinge *n* (*of color*) yŏt'ŭn saektcho 옅은 색조; (*of sadness*) kisaek 기색

tingle *v/i* ttakkŭmgŏrida 따끔거리다

♦ **tinker with** manjijak-kkŏrida 만지작거리다

tinkle *n* (*of bell*) ttallangttallang 딸랑딸랑

tinsel pantchak-kkŏrinŭn kŭmsok changshik 반짝거리는 금속 장식

tint 1 *n* (*of color*) yŏnhan saektcho 연한 색조; (*in hair*) yŏmsaek 염색 2 *v/t hair* yŏmsaek'ada 염색하다

tinted *glasses* saek-kkal innŭn 색깔 있는

tiny chogŭmahan 조그마한

tip[1] *n* (*of stick, finger*) kkŭt 끝; (*of mountain*) chŏngsang 정상; (*of cigarette*) p'ilt'ŏ 필터

tip[2] 1 *n* (*piece of advice*) pigyŏl 비결; (*money*) t'ip 팁 2 *v/t waiter etc* ...ege t'ibŭl chuda ...에게 팁을 주다

♦ **tip off** pimil chŏngborŭl chuda 비밀 정보를 주다

♦ **tip over** *jug, liquid* twiŏptta 뒤엎다; **he tipped water all over me** kŭnŭn na-ege murŭl ont'ong twijibŏ ssŭiwŏt-tta 그는 나에게 물을 온통 뒤집어 씌웠다

tipped *cigarettes* p'ilt'ŏ innŭn tambae 필터 있는 담배

tippy-toe: on ~ palkkŭt'ŭro 발끝으로

tipsy ŏlk'ŭnhage ch'wihan 얼큰하게 취한

tire[1] *n* t'aiŏ 타이어

tire[2] 1 *v/t* chich'ige hada 지치게 하다 2 *v/i* chich'ida 지치다; **he never ~s of it** kŭnŭn kŭgŏsŭl kyŏlk'o shiltchŭng naeji annŭnda 그는 그것을 결코 싫증 내지 않는다

tired p'igonhan 피곤한; **be ~ of s.o. / sth** nugue / muŏse shiltchŭng nada 누구에 / 무엇에 싫증 나다

tireless *efforts* chich'il chul morŭnŭn 지칠 줄 모르는

tiresome kwich'anŭn 귀찮은,

sŏnggashin 성가신

tiring chich'ige hanŭn 지치게 하는

tissue ANAT chojik 조직; (*handkerchief*) hwajangji 화장지

tissue paper p'ojangji 포장지

tit[1] (*bird*) pakssae 박새

tit[2]: **~ for tat** matppadach'igi 맞받아치기

tit[3] ∨ (*breast*) chŏtkkasŭm 젖가슴

title (*of novel etc*) chemok 제목; (*of person*) chik'am 직함; LAW kwŏlli 권리

titter *v/i* k'ikk'ik-kkŏrida 킥킥거리다

to 1 *prep* ...(ŭ)ro ...(으)로; **~ Korea** Han-guguro 한국으로; **~ Chicago** Shik'agoro 시카고로; **go ~ my place** uri chiburo kada 우리 집으로 가다; **walk ~ the station** yŏguro kŏrŏgada 역으로 걸어가다; **~ the north / south of ...** ...ŭi puktchoguro / namtchoguro ...의 북쪽으로 / 남쪽으로; **give sth ~ s.o.** muŏsŭl nuguege chuda 무엇을 누구에게 주다; **from Monday ~ Wednesday** wŏryoilbut'ŏ suyoilkkaji 월요일부터 수요일까지; **from 10 ~ 15 people** 10myŏng-esŏ 15myŏng-ŭi saramdŭl 10명에서 15명의 사람들 2 (*with verbs*) ...hagi wihae ...하기 위해, ...hanŭn kŏt ...하는 것; **~ speak** marhanŭn kŏt 말하는 것; **learn ~ drive** unjŏnhanŭn kŏsŭl paeuda 운전하는 것을 배우다; **nice ~ eat** mŏk-kkie chŏun 먹기에 좋은; **too heavy ~ carry** unbanhagie nŏmu mugŏun 운반하기에 너무 무거운; **~ be honest with you** nŏhant'e soltchik'i marhajamyŏn 너한테 솔직히 말하자면 3 *adv*: **~ and fro** apttwiro 앞뒤로

toad tukkŏbi 두꺼비

toadstool tokppŏsŏt 독버섯

toast 1 *n* t'osŭt'ŭ 토스트; (*when drinking*) kŏnbae 건배; **propose a ~ to s.o.** nugurŭl wihae kŏnbaehajago hada 누구를 위해 건배하자고 하다 2 *v/t person* kŏnbaehada 건배하다

tobacco tambae 담배

toboggan *n* ssŏlmae 썰매

today onŭl 오늘

toddle (*of child*) ajang-ajang kŏt-tta 아장아장 걷다

toddler ajang-ajang kŏnnŭn ai 아장아장 걷는 아이

toe 1 *n* palkkarak 발가락; (*of shoe*) palkkŭt pubun 발끝 부분 **2** *v/t*: ~ *the line* kyuch'igŭl ttarŭda 규칙을 따르다

toffee t'op'i 토피

tofu tubu 두부

together hamkke 함께; (*at the same time*) tongshie 동시에

toil *n* nogo 노고

toilet hwajangshil 화장실; *go to the ~* hwajangshire kada 화장실에 가다

toilet paper hwajangji 화장지, hyuji 휴지

toiletries semyŏn yongp'um 세면 용품

Tok Island Toktto 독도

token (*sign*) p'yoshi 표시; (*gift ~*) sangp'umkkwŏn 상품권; (*for slot machine*) t'ok'ŭn 토큰

Tokyo Tonggyŏng 동경

tolerable *pain etc* ch'amŭl su innŭn 참을 수 있는; (*quite good*) kkwae kwaench'anŭn 꽤 괜찮은

tolerance kwanyong 관용

tolerant kwanyong innŭn 관용 있는

tolerate *noise, person* ch'amtta 참다; *I won't ~ it!* igŏsŭn ch'amŭl suga ŏpssŏyo! 이것은 참을 수가 없어요!

toll[1] *v/i* (*of bell*) ch'ŏnch'ŏnhi kyesok'aesŏ ullida 천천히 계속해서 울리다

toll[2] (*deaths*) hŭisaeng 희생

toll[3] (*for bridge, road*) t'onghaengnyo 통행료; TELEC t'onghwaryo 통화료

toll booth yogŭm chingsuso 요금 징수소; **toll-free** TELEC muryo t'onghwa 무료 통화; **toll road** yuryo toro 유료 도로

tomato t'omat'o 토마토

tomato ketchup t'omat'o k'ech'ap 토마토 케찹

tomb mudŏm 무덤

tomboy malgwallyang-i 말괄량이

tombstone pisŏk 비석

tomcat suk'oyang-i 수코양이

tomorrow naeil 내일; *the day after ~* more 모레; *~ morning* naeil ach'im 내일 아침

ton t'on 톤

tone (*of color*) saektcho 색조; (*of musical instrument*) ŭmsaek 음색; (*of conversation etc*) ŏjo 어조; (*of neighborhood*) punwigi 분위기; *~ of voice* mokssori 목소리

♦ **tone down** *demands, criticism* pudŭrŏpkke hada 부드럽게 하다

toner t'onŏ 토너

tongs chipkke 집게; (*for hair*) mŏri indu 머리 인두

tongue *n* hyŏ 혀

tonic MED kangjangje 강장제

tonic (**water**) t'onik wŏt'ŏ 토닉 워터

tonight onŭl pam 오늘 밤

tonsillitis p'yŏndosŏnnyŏm 편도선염

tonsils p'yŏndosŏn 편도선

too (*also*) ttohan 또한, to 도; (*excessively*) nŏmu 너무; *me ~* chŏdoyo 저도요; *~ big / hot* nŏmu k'ŭn / ttŭgŏun 너무 큰 / 뜨거운; *~ much food* nŏmu manŭn ŭmshik 너무 많은 음식; *eat ~ much* nŏmuna mani mŏktta 너무 많이 먹다

tool togu 도구

tooth i 이

toothache ch'it'ong 치통; **toothbrush** ch'itssol 칫솔; **toothless** iga ŏmnŭn 이가 없는; **toothpaste** ch'iyak 치약; **toothpick** issushigae 이쑤시개

top 1 *n* (*upper part*) witppubun 윗부분; (*of mountain, tree*) kkokttaegi 꼭대기; (*lid: of bottle etc, pen*) ttukkŏng 뚜껑; (*of class, league*) sangnyu 상류; (*clothing*) sang-ŭi 상의; (MOT: *gear*) t'opkki ŏ 톱기어; *on ~ of* …ŭi wie …의 위에; *at the ~ of* …ŭi witchoge …의 위쪽에; *get to the ~* (*of company etc*) chŏngsang-e orŭda 정상에 오르다; *be over the ~* (*exaggerated*) kwajangdoeda 과장되다 **2** *adj branches* kkokttaegiŭi 꼭대기의; *floor* maenwiŭi 맨위의; *management, official* sangbuŭi 상부의; *player* ch'oesang-ŭi 최상의; *speed, note* ch'oegoŭi 최고의 **3** *v/t*: *~ped with cream* k'ŭrimŭro tŏp'in 크림으로 덮힌

◆**top up** *glass, tank* kadŭk ch'aeuda
가득 채우다
top hat chungsanmo 중산모
topheavy puranjŏnghan 불안정한
topic hwaje 화제
topical hwajeŭi 화제의
topless *adj* kasŭmŭl tŭrŏnaen 가슴을
드러낸, t'op'ŭllisŭ 토플리스
topmost *branches, floor* ch'oesang-ŭi
최상의
topping (*on pizza*) t'op'ing 토핑
topple 1 *v/i* ssŭrŏjida 쓰러지다 **2** *v/t*
government ssŭrŏttŭrida 쓰러뜨리다
top secret kŭkppi 극비
topsy-turvy *adj* (*in disorder*)
twijukppaktchugin 뒤죽박죽인;
world hollansŭrŏun 혼란스러운
torch (*with flame*) hwaetppul 횃불
torment 1 *n* kot'ong 고통 **2** *v/t person,
animal* koerop'ida 괴롭히다; *~ed by
doubt* ŭishimŭro koerowahanŭn
의심으로 괴로와하는
tornado hoeori param 회오리 바람
torrent kŭmnyu 급류; (*of lava*)
punch'ul 분출; (*of abuse, words*)
yŏnbal 연발
torrential *rain* ŏkssugat'ŭn 억수같은
tortoise kŏbuk 거북
torture 1 *n* komun 고문 **2** *v/t*
komunhada 고문하다
toss 1 *v/t ball* kabyŏpkke tŏnjida
가볍게 던지다; *rider* ttŏrŏttŭrida
떨어뜨리다; *salad* pŏmurida
버무리다; *~ a coin* tongjŏnŭl tŏnjyŏ
chŏnghada 동전을 던져 정하다 **2** *v/i:*
~ and turn twich'ŏk-kkŏrida
뒤척거리다
total 1 *n* hapkkye 합계 **2** *adj sum,
amount* chŏnch'eŭi 전체의; *disaster,
idiot, stranger* wanjŏnhan 완전한; *~
amount of money* ch'ong-aek 총액
3 *v/t* F (*car*) wanjŏnhi pusuda 완전히
부수다
totalitarian chŏnch'ejuŭiŭi
전체주의의
totally wanjŏnhi 완전히
tote bag taehyŏng haendŭbaek 대형
핸드백
totter (*of person*) pit'ŭlgŏrida
비틀거리다
touch 1 *n* (*act of touching*) chŏpch'ok

접촉; (*sense*) ch'ok-kkam 촉감; (*little
bit*) yakkan 약간; SP t'ŏch'i 터치;
lose ~ with s.o. nuguwa yŏllagi
kkŭnkkida 누구와 연락이 끊기다;
keep in ~ with s.o. nuguwa kyesok
yŏllak'ada 누구와 계속 연락하다; *be
out of ~* chopch'ok'aji ank'o
chinaeda 접촉하지 않고 지내다 **2** *v/t*
manjida 만지다; (*emotionally*)
kamdongshik'ida 감동시키다 **3** *v/i*
manjida 만지다; (*of two lines etc*)
chŏpch'ok'ada 접촉하다
◆**touch down** (*of airplane*)
ch'angnyuk'ada 착륙하다; SP
tŭktchŏmhada 득점하다
◆**touch on** (*mention*) kandanhi ŏn-
gŭp'ada 간단히 언급하다
◆**touch up** *photo* sonjirhada 손질하다
touchdown (*of airplane*) ch'angnyuk
착륙; SP t'ŏch'idaun 터치다운
touching *adj* kamdongshik'inŭn
감동시키는
touchline SP t'ŏch'irain 터치라인
touchy *person* chinach'ige yeminhan
지나치게 예민한
tough *person* ŏkssen 억센; *meat*
chilgin 질긴; *question, exam* ŏryŏun
어려운; *material* kŏch'in 거친;
punishment ŏmhan 엄한
tough guy ŏkssen sanai 억센 사나이
tour 1 *n* kwan-gwang 관광 **2** *v/t area*
kwan-gwanghada 관광하다
tourism kwan-gwang-ŏp 관광업
tourist kwan-gwanggaek 관광객
tourist (**information**) **office** kwan-
gwang annaeso 관광 안내소
tournament shihap 시합
tour operator kwan-gwang-ŏptcha
관광업자
tousled *hair* hŏngk'ŭrŏjin 헝클어진
tow 1 *v/t car, boat* kkŭlda 끌다 **2** *n*
kkŭlgi 끌기; *give s.o. a ~* nugurŭl
kkŭrŏjuda 누구를 끌어주다
◆**tow away** *car* kyŏninhada 견인하다
toward *prep* ...ŭl/rŭl hyanghayŏ
...을/를 향하여; (*in behavior,
attitude*) ...ege 에게
towel sugŏn 수건
tower *n* t'ap 탑
town toshi 도시
town council shi ŭihoe 시 의회

town hall shich'ŏng 시청
township myŏn 면
towrope kyŏninnyong patchul 견인용
밧줄
toxic toksSŏng-ŭi 독성의
toy changnankkam 장난감
♦**toy with** *object* kajigo nolda 가지고
놀다; *idea* halkkamalkka
saenggak'ada 할까말까 생각하다
trace 1 *n* (*of substance*) hŭnjŏk 흔적
2 *v/t* (*find*) susaek'ada 수색하다;
(*follow: footsteps*) ch'ujŏk'ada
추적하다; (*draw*) kŭrida 그리다
track *n* (*path*) kil 길; (*on race course*)
t'ŭraek 트랙; (*race course*) k'osŭ
코스; RAIL ch'ŏltto 철도; ~ **10** RAIL
10ppŏn sŏllo 10번 선로; *keep ~ of*
sth muŏshi kirogŭl namgida 무엇의
기록을 남기다
♦**track down** twitchoch'a
ch'ajanaeda 뒤쫓아 찾아내다
tracksuit poon undongbok 보온
운동복
tractor t'ŭraekt'ŏ 트랙터
trade 1 *n* (*commerce*) sang-ŏp 상업;
(*between countries*) muyŏk 무역;
(*profession, craft*) chigŏp 직업 **2** *v/i*
(*do business*) changsahada 장사하다;
~ *in sth* musŭn changsarŭl hada
무슨 장사를 하다 **3** *v/t* (*exchange*)
kyohwanhada 교환하다; ~ *sth for*
sth muŏtkkwa muŏsŭl
kyohwanhada 무엇과 무엇을
교환하다
♦**trade in** *v/t* (*when buying*) uttonŭl
naego shinp'umgwa kyohwanhada
웃돈을 내고 신품과 교환하다
trade fair muyŏk chŏnshihoe 무역
전시회; **trademark** tŭngnok
sangp'yo tŭngnok 상표; **trade mission**
muyŏk-kkwan 무역관
trader sang-in 상인
trade secret kiŏp pimil 기업 비밀
tradesman (*plumber etc*) surigong
수리공; (*deliveryman etc*) paedarwŏn
배달원
trade(s) union nodong chohap 노동
조합
tradition chŏnt'ong 전통
traditional chŏnt'ongjŏgin
전통적인

traditionally chŏnt'ongjŏgŭro
전통적으로
traffic *n* kyot'ong 교통; (*in drugs*)
milssu 밀수
♦**traffic in** *drugs* milssuhada 밀수하다
traffic circle lot'ŏri 로터리; **traffic**
cop F kyot'ong sun-gyŏng 교통
순경; **traffic jam** kyot'ong ch'ejŭng
교통 체증; **traffic light** shinhodŭng
신호등; **traffic police** kyot'ong sun-
gyŏng 교통 순경; **traffic sign**
kyot'ong shinho 교통 신호; **traffic**
violation kyot'ong wiban 교통 위반
tragedy pigŭk 비극
tragic pigŭktchŏgin 비극적인
trail 1 *n* (*path*) kil 길; (*of blood*)
hŭnjŏk 흔적 **2** *v/t* (*follow*) ttaragada
따라가다; (*tow*) kkŭlda 끌다 **3** *v/i* (*lag*
behind) kkŭllida 끌리다
trailer (*pulled by vehicle*) t'ŭreillŏ
트레일러; (*mobile home*) idong
chut'aek 이동 주택; (*of movie*)
yegop'yŏn 예고편
train[1] *n* kich'a 기차; *go by ~* kich'aro
kada 기차로 가다
train[2] **1** *v/t team, athlete, dog*
hullyŏnshik'ida 훈련시키다;
employee kyoyukshik'ida 교육시키다
2 *v/i* (*of team, athlete*) yŏnssŭp'ada
연습하다; (*of teacher etc*) kyoyukpat-
tta 교육받다
trainee kyŏnsŭpssaeng 견습생
trainer SP k'och'i 코치; (*of dog*)
hullyŏnsa 훈련사
trainers *Br* (*shoes*) undonghwa
운동화
training (*of new staff*) kyoyuk 교육;
SP hullyŏn 훈련; *be in ~* SP hullyŏn
chung-ida 훈련 중이다; *be out of ~*
SP hullyŏn chung-i anida 훈련 중이
아니다
training course kyŏnsŭp kwajŏng
견습 과정
training scheme hullyŏn kyehoek
훈련 계획
train station kich'ayŏk 기차역
trait t'ŭkssŏng 특성
traitor paebanja 배반자
tramp 1 *n pej* (*woman*) kŏlle 걸레; *Br*
(*hobo*) ttŏdori 떠돌이 **2** *v/i*
k'ungk'ung kŏt-tta 쿵쿵 걷다

trample *v/t*: *be ~d to death* palp'yŏ chuktta 밟혀 죽다; *be ~d underfoot* magu chitppalp'ida 마구 짓밟히다
♦ **trample on** *person, object* palba munggaeda 밟아 뭉개다
trampoline t'ŭraemp'ollin 트램폴린
trance honsu sangt'ae 혼수 상태; *go into a ~* honsu sangt'aee ppajida 혼수 상태에 빠지다
tranquil p'yŏng-onhan 평온한
tranquility p'yŏng-on 평온
tranquilizer chinjŏngje 진정제
transact *deal, business* ch'ŏrihada 처리하다
transaction kŏrae 거래
transatlantic Taesŏyang hoengdanŭi 대서양 횡단의
transcendental ch'owŏltchŏgin 초월적인
transcript (*of meeting, trial*) sabon 사본
transfer 1 *v/t* omgida 옮기다; *money* songgŭmhada 송금하다; *player* ijŏk'ada 이적하다 2 *v/i* (*switch*) pakkuda 바꾸다 (*when traveling*) omgyŏt'ada 옮겨타다 3 *n* idong 이동; (*in travel*) karat'agi 갈아타기; (*of money*) songgŭmhwan 송금환
transferable *ticket* yangdohal su innŭn 양도할 수 있는
transform *v/t* pyŏnhyŏngshik'ida 변형시키다
transformation pyŏnhyŏng 변형
transformer ELEC pyŏnapkki 변압기
transfusion chuip 주입
transistor t'ŭraenjisŭt'ŏ 트랜지스터; (*radio*) t'ŭraenjisŭt'ŏ ladio 트랜지스터 라디오
transit: *in ~ goods* susong chung-in 수송 중인; *~ passenger* t'onggwa yŏgaek 통과 여객
transition pyŏnhwa 변화
transitional kwadojŏgin 과도적인; *~ period* kwadogi 과도기
transit lounge (*at airport*) t'onggwa yŏgaek taehapsshil 통과 여객 대합실
translate pŏnyŏk'ada 번역하다
translation pŏnyŏk 번역
translator pŏnyŏkka 번역가
transliterate ŭmnyŏk'ada 음역하다
transmission (*of news, program*)

pangsong 방송; (*of disease*) chŏnyŏm 전염; MOT pyŏnsokki 변속기
transmit *program* pangsonghada 방송하다; *disease* chŏnyŏmshik'ida 전염시키다
transmitter RAD, TV songshin-gi 송신기
transpacific T'aep'yŏngyang hoengdanŭi 태평양 횡단의
transparency PHOT sŭllaidŭ 슬라이드
transparent t'umyŏnghan 투명한; *blouse* sogi pich'inŭn 속이 비치는; (*obvious*) myŏngbaek'an 명백한
transplant MED 1 *v/t* ishik'ada 이식하다 2 *n* ishik susul 이식 수술
transport 1 *v/t* goods, people susonghada 수송하다 2 *n* (*of goods, people*) susong 수송
transportation (*of goods, people*) susong 수송; *means of ~* kyot'ong sudan 교통 수단; *public ~* taejung kyot'ong 대중 교통; *Department of Transportation* Kyot'ongbu 교통부
transvestite isŏng-ŭi osŭl ipkki choahanŭn saram 이성의 옷을 입기 좋아하는 사람
trap 1 *n* (*for animal*) tŏt 덫; (*question, set-up etc*) hamjŏng 함정; *set a ~ for s.o.* nugurŭl hamjŏnge ppattŭrida 누구를 함정에 빠뜨리다 2 *v/t* animal tŏch'ŭro chaptta 덫으로 잡다; *person* hamjŏng-e ppattŭrida 함정에 빠뜨리다; *be ~ped* hamjŏng-e ppajida 함정에 빠지다; (*in marriage, bad job etc*) tŏch'e kŏllida 덫에 걸리다
trapdoor tŭlch'angmun 들창문
trapeze kogyeyong kŭne 곡예용 그네
trappings (*of power*) pugamul 부가물
trash (*garbage*) ssŭregi 쓰레기; (*poor product*) pullyangp'um 불량품; (*book, movie etc*) choltchak 졸작; (*despicable person*) in-gan ssŭregi 인간 쓰레기
trashcan ssŭregi t'ong 쓰레기 통
trashy *goods, novel* ssŭlmoŏmnŭn 쓸모없는
traumatic chŏngshinjŏgŭro k'ŭn ch'unggyŏgŭl chunŭn 정신적으로 큰 충격을 주는

travel 1 *n* yŏhaeng 여행; ~s yŏhaeng
여행 **2** *v/i* yŏhaenghada 여행하다
3 *v/t miles* yŏhaenghayŏ chinagada
여행하여 지나가다
travel agency yŏhaengsa 여행사
travel bag yŏhaeng kabang 여행 가방
traveler yŏhaenggaek 여행객
traveler's check yŏhaengja sup'yo
여행자 수표; **travel expenses**
yŏhaeng piyong 여행 비용; **travel
insurance** yŏhaeng pohŏm 여행
보험
trawler t'ŭrol ŏsŏn 트롤 어선
tray (*for food etc*) chaengban 쟁반;
(*to go in oven*) p'an 판; (*in printer,
copier*) holdŏ 홀더
treacherous paebanhanŭn 배반하는;
currents, roads wihŏmhan 위험한
treachery paeban 배반
tread 1 *n* palkkŏrŭm 발걸음; (*of
staircase*) tidimp'an 디딤판; (*of tire*)
t'ŭredŭ 트레드 **2** *v/i* paltta 밟다
♦ **tread on** paltta 밟다
treason panyŏk 반역
treasure 1 *n* pomul 보물; (*person*)
sojunghan saram 소중한 사람 **2** *v/t
gift etc* sojunghi hada 소중히 하다
treasurer hoegye tamdangja 회계
담당자
Treasury Department Chaemusŏng
재무성
treat 1 *n* (*pleasure*) k'ŭn kippŭm 큰
기쁨; *it was a real* ~ chŏngmal
kippŏssŏ 정말 기뻤어; *I have a ~ for
you* tangshinŭl nollage hae tŭril iri
issŭmnida 당신을 놀라게 해 드릴
일이 있습니다; *it's my* ~ (*I'm
paying*) chega hant'ŏk
naegessŭmnida 제가 한턱
내겠습니다 **2** *v/t materials* taruda
다루다; *illness* ch'iryohada 치료하다;
(*behave toward*) taeuhada 대우하다;
~ *s.o. to sth* nuguege muŏsŭl
taejŏp'ada 누구에게 무엇을 대접하다
treatment (*of materials*) ch'wigŭp
취급; (*of illness*) ch'iryo 치료; (*of
people*) taeu 대우
treaty choyak 조약
treble[1] MUS ch'oegoŭmbuŭi
최고음부의
treble[2] **1** *adv*: ~ *the price* sebaero

ttwin kagyŏk 세배로 뛴 가격 **2** *v/i*
sebaero chŭnggahada 세배로
증가하다
tree namu 나무
tremble (*of person*) ttŏlda 떨다; (*of
hand, voice*) ttŏllida 떨리다; (*of
building*) hŭndŭllida 흔들리다
tremendous (*very good*)
koengjanghan 굉장한; (*enormous*)
aju kŏdaehan 아주 거대한
tremendously (*very*) koengjanghi
굉장히; (*a lot*) maeu 매우
tremor (*of earth*) yaktchin 약진
trench ch'amho 참호
trend kyŏnghyang 경향; (*fashion*)
yuhaeng-ŭi kyŏnghyang 유행의 경향
trendy ch'oeshin yuhaeng-ŭi 최신
유행의; *person* yuhaeng-ŭl ttarŭnŭn
유행을 따르는
trespass ch'imip'ada 침입하다; *no
~ing* ch'urip kŭmji 출입 금지
♦ **trespass on** *land* ...e ch'imip'ada
...에 침입하다; *privacy* ...ŭl/rŭl
ch'imhaehada ...을/를 침해하다;
s.o.'s time ...ŭl/rŭl ppaeat-tta
...을/를 빼앗다
trespasser pulppŏp ch'imiptcha 불법
침입자
trial LAW kongp'an 공판; (*of
equipment*) shihŏm 시험; *on* ~ LAW
kongp'an chung 공판 중; *have sth
on* ~ *equipment* muŏsŭl shihŏmhae
poda 무엇을 시험해 보다
trial period (*for employee*) kyŏnsŭp
kigan 견습 기간; (*for equipment*)
shihŏm kigan 시험 기간
triangle samgak'yŏng 삼각형; MUS
t'ŭraiaenggŭl 트라이앵글
triangular samgak'yŏng-ŭi 삼각형의
tribe pujok 부족
tribunal shimp'an wiwŏnhoe 심판
위원회
tributary (*river*) chiryu 지류
trick 1 *n* (*to deceive*) sogimsu 속임수;
(*knack*) kigyo 기교; *play a* ~ *on s.o.*
nuguege changnanjirŭl hada
누구에게 장난질을 하다 **2** *v/t* sogida
속이다; ~ *s.o. into doing sth*
nugurŭl sogyŏsŏ muŏsŭl shik'ida
누구를 속여서 무엇을 시키다
trickery sagi 사기

trickle *v/i* ttokttok ttŏrŏjida 똑똑 떨어지다

trickster sagikkun 사기꾼

tricky (*difficult*) tarugi himdŭn 다루기 힘든; *person* kyohwarhan 교활한

tricycle sebal chajŏn-gŏ 세발 자전거

trifle (*triviality*) hach'anŭn kŏt 하찮은 것

trifling hach'anŭn 하찮은

trigger *n* pang-asoe 방아쇠; (*on camcorder*) shijak pŏt'ŭn 시작 버튼; (*cause*) yubal yoin 유발 요인

♦ **trigger off** yubarhada 유발하다

trim 1 *adj* (*neat*) malkkŭmhan 말끔한; *figure* nŭlsshinhan 늘씬한 **2** *v/t hair, hedge* sonjirhada 손질하다; *budget, costs* sak-kkamhada 삭감하다; (*decorate: dress*) changshik'ada 장식하다 **3** *n* (*cut*) saltchak charŭm 살짝 자름; *just a ~, please* (*to hairdresser*) kŭnyang saltchak tadŭmŏ chuseyo 그냥 살짝 다듬어 주세요; *in good ~ car, machine, boxer* chal chŏngbidoen 잘 정비된; *house* chal kakkuŏjin 잘 가꾸어진

trimming (*on clothes*) tŏtppuch'in changshik 덧붙인 장식; *with all the ~s* modŭn pugaŭi kŏttŭlgwa 모든 부가의 것들과

trinket chajilgurehan changshin-gu 자질구레한 장신구

trio MUS samjungju 삼중주

trip 1 *n* (*journey*) yŏhaeng 여행 **2** *v/i* (*stumble*) kŏllyŏ nŏmŏjida 걸려 넘어지다 **3** *v/t person* kŏrŏ nŏmŏttŭrida 걸어 넘어뜨리다

♦ **trip up 1** *v/t* (*cause to fall*) kŏrŏ nŏmŏttŭrida 걸어 넘어뜨리다; (*cause to go wrong*) shilp'aehage hada 실패하게 하다 **2** *v/i* (*fall*) nŏmŏjida 넘어지다; (*make a mistake*) shilssuhada 실수하다

tripe (*food*) yang 양

Tripitaka Koreana REL P'almandaejanggyŏng 팔만대장경

triple → **treble**²

triplets se ssangdung-i 세 쌍둥이

tripod PHOT samgakttae 삼각대

trite chinbuhan 진부한

triumph *n* sŭngni 승리

trivial sasohan 사소한

triviality sasohan kŏt 사소한 것

trombone t'ŭrŏmbon 트럼본

troops kundae 군대

trophy usŭngk'ŏp 우승컵

tropic hoegwisŏn 회귀선

tropical yŏlttaeŭi 열대의

tropics yŏlttae chibang 열대 지방

trot *v/i* ch'ongch'ong kŏrŭmŭro kada 총총 걸음으로 가다

trouble 1 *n* (*difficulties*) munje 문제; (*inconvenience*) pulp'yŏn 불편; (*disturbance*) malssong 말썽; *go to a lot of ~ to do sth* muŏsŭl hagi wihae manŭn sugorŭl hada 무엇을 하기 위해 많은 수고를 하다; *no ~* munje ŏpssŭmnida 문제 없습니다; *get into ~* malssong-i nada 말썽이 나다 **2** *v/t* (*worry*) kŏktchŏngshik'ida 걱정시키다; (*bother, disturb*) kwich'ank'e hada 귀찮게 하다; (*of back, liver etc*) koerop'ida 괴롭히다

trouble-free kojang-i ŏmnŭn 고장이 없는; **troublemaker** malssongkkun 말썽꾼; **troubleshooter** (*problem solver*) munje haegyŏlssa 문제 해결사; (*mediator*) punjaeng chojŏngja 분쟁 조정자; **troubleshooting** (*problem solving*) munje haegyŏl 문제 해결; (*for faulty equipment*) kojang suri 고장 수리

troublesome kolch'i ap'ŭn 골치 아픈

trousers *Br* paji 바지

trout song-ŏ 송어

truce hyujŏn 휴전

truck hwamulch'a 화물차

truck driver t'ŭrŏk unjŏnsa 트럭 운전사; **truck farm** ship'anyong nongsanmul chaebae nongga 시판용 농산물 재배 농가; **truck farmer** ship'anyong nongsanmul chaebae nongbu 시판용 농산물 재배 농부; **truck stop** t'ŭrŏk unjŏnsa shikttang 트럭 운전사 식당

trudge 1 *v/i* mŏlgo ŏryŏpkke kada 멀고 어렵게 가다 **2** *n* mŏlgo ŏryŏun kil 멀고 어려운 길

true chŏngmaruŭi 정말의; *friend, American* chintchaŭi 진짜의; *come ~* (*of hopes, dream*) shirhyŏndoeda 실현되다

truly 634

truly chŏngmallo 정말로; *Yours ~*
...ollim ...올림

trumpet *n* t'ŭrŏmp'et 트럼펫

trunk (*of tree*) chulgi 줄기; (*of body*)
momttung-i 몸뚱이; (*of elephant*) k'o
코; (*container, of car*) t'ŭrŏngk'ŭ
트렁크

trust 1 *n* (*in person, car etc*) shilloe
신뢰; (*in an organization*) shinyong
신용; FIN witak 위탁 2 *v/t* shilloehada
신뢰하다; *I ~ you* tangshinŭl
shilloehamnida 당신을 신뢰합니다

trusted shilloehal su innŭn 신뢰할 수
있는

trustee p'ishint'agin 피신탁인

trustful, trusting shilloehanŭn
신뢰하는

trustworthy shilloehal su innŭn
신뢰할 수 있는

truth chinshil 진실; (*fact*) sashil 사실

truthful chinshirhan 진실한; *account*
chintchaŭi 진짜의

try 1 *v/t* noryŏk'ada 노력하다; *food*
mŏgŏboda 먹어보다; *plan, route*
shidohada 시도하다; LAW
chaep'anhada 재판하다; *~ to do sth*
muŏsŭl haryŏgo hada 무엇을 하려고
하다 2 *v/i* haeboda 해보다; *you must
~ harder* tangshinŭn tŏ yŏlshimhi
noryŏk'aeya hamnida 당신은 더
열심히 노력해야 합니다 3 *n* shido
시도; *can I have a ~?* (*of food*)
hanbŏn matppwado toelkkayo? 한번
맛봐도 될까요?; (*at doing sth*)
hanbŏn haebwado toelkkayo? 한번
해봐도 될까요?

♦ try on *clothes* ibŏboda 입어보다

♦ try out *machine, method* shihŏmhae
poda 시험해 보다

trying (*annoying*) tchajŭngnanŭn
짜증나는

T-shirt t'ishyŏch'ŭ 티셔츠

tub (*bath*) yoktcho 욕조; (*of liquid*)
t'ong 통; (*for yoghurt, ice cream*)
kwak 곽

tubby *adj* t'ongt'onghan 통통한

tube (*pipe*) kwan 관; (*of toothpaste,
ointment*) t'yubŭ 튜브

tubeless *tire* t'yubŭga ŏmnŭn 튜브가
없는

tuberculosis kyŏrhaek 결핵

tuck 1 *n* (*in dress*) tan 단 2 *v/t* (*put*)
kkiwŏ nŏt'a 끼워 넣다

♦ tuck away (*put away*) ch'iuda
치우다; (*eat quickly*) sunshik-kkane
mŏgŏch'iuda 순식간에 먹어치우다

♦ tuck in *v/t children* iburŭl
tŏp'ŏjuda 이불을 덮어주다; *sheets*
...ŭi kkŭch'ŭl chŏbŏ nŏt'a ...의 끝을
접어 넣다 2 *v/i* (*start eating*) mŏk-
kki shijak'ada 먹기 시작하다

♦ tuck up *sleeves etc* kŏdŏ ollida 걷어
올리다; *tuck s.o. up in bed* nugurŭl
ch'imdaee nŏk'o iburŭl tŏp'ŏjuda
누구를 침대에 넣고 이불을 덮어주다

Tuesday hwayoil 화요일

tuft sul 술; (*of grass*) sup'ul 수풀

tug 1 *n* (*pull*) chaba tanggim 잡아
당김; NAUT yeinsŏn 예인선 2 *v/t*
(*pull*) chaba tanggida 잡아 당기다

tuition suŏp 수업; *private ~* kaein
kyosŭp 개인 교습

tulip t'yullip 튤립

tumble *v/i* kullŏ ttŏrŏjida 굴러
떨어지다; (*of wall*) munŏjida
무너지다

tumbledown munŏjilttŭt'an 무너질
듯한

tumbler (*for drink*) chan 잔; (*in
circus*) kogyesa 곡예사

Tumen River Tuman-gang 두만강

tummy pae 배

tummy ache pokt'ong 복통

tumor chongnyang 종양

tumult soran 소란

tumultuous soransŭrŏun 소란스러운

tuna ch'amch'i 참치

tune 1 *n* koktcho 곡조; *in ~* ŭmjŏng-i
mannŭn 음정이 맞는; *out of ~*
ŭmjŏng-i t'ŭllin 음정이 틀린 2 *v/t*
instrument choyurhada 조율하다

♦ tune in *v/i* RAD, TV ch'aenŏrŭl
match'uda 채널을 맞추다

♦ tune in to (*on radio*)
ch'ŏngch'wihada 청취하다; (*on TV*)
shich'ŏnghada 시청하다

♦ tune up 1 *v/i* (*of orchestra, players*)
ak-kkiŭi ŭmŭl match'uda 악기의
음을 맞추다 2 *v/t engine* chojŏrhada
조절하다

tuneful arŭmdaun sŏnyurŭi 아름다운
선율의

tuner (*hi-fi*) t'yunŏ 튜너

tunic EDU kyobok sang-ŭi 교복 상의

tunnel *n* t'ŏnŏl 터널

turbine t'ŏbin 터빈

turbot kajami 가자미

turbulence (*in air travel*) nan-giryu 난기류

turbulent *love affair* kyŏngnyŏrhan 격렬한; *meeting, life* tongnyohanŭn 동요하는; *weather* kŏch'in 거친

turf chandibat 잔디밭; (*piece*) chandi 잔디

Turk T'ŏk'iin 터키인

Turkey T'ŏk'i 터키

turkey ch'ilmyŏnjo 칠면조

Turkish 1 *adj* T'ŏk'iŭi 터키의 **2** *n* (*language*) T'ŏk'iŏ 터키어

turmoil hollan 혼란

turn 1 *n* (*rotation*) hoejŏn 회전; (*in road*) mot'ung-i 모퉁이; (*in vaudeville*) ch'arye 차례; *take ~s doing sth* muŏsŭl kyodaero hada 무엇을 교대로 하다; *it's my ~* che ch'aryeimnida 제 차례입니다; *it's not your ~ yet* ajik tangshin sunsŏga animnida 아직 당신 순서가 아닙니다; *take a ~ at the wheel* ch'arŭl kyodaero unjŏnhada 차를 교대로 운전하다; *do s.o. a good ~* nuguege ch'injŏrhage hada 누구에게 친절하게 하다 **2** *v/t key, screw etc* tollida 돌리다; *wheel* hoejŏnshik'ida 회전시키다; *corner* tolda 돌다; *food, sheets* twijiptta 뒤집다; *pages of book* nŏmgida 넘기다; *~ one's back on s.o.* nuguege tŭng-ŭl tollida 누구에게 등을 돌리다 **3** *v/i* (*of driver, car*) tolda 돌다; (*of wheel*) hoejŏnhada 회전하다; *~ right / left here* yŏgisŏ orŭntchoguro / oentchoguro toseyo 여기서 오른쪽으로 / 왼쪽으로 도세요; *it has ~ed sour / cold* shiŏjyŏt-tta / ch'uwŏjyŏt-tta 시어졌다 / 추워졌다; *he has ~ed 40* kŭnŭn sashibi nŏmŏt-tta 그는 40이 넘었다

♦ **turn around 1** *v/t object* tollida 돌리다; *company* hojŏnshik'ida 호전시키다; (COM: *deal with*) chumune match'uda 주문에 맞추다 **2** *v/i* (*of person, driver*) tolda 돌다

♦ **turn away 1** *v/t* (*send away*) tchoch'abŏrida 쫓아버리다 **2** *v/i* (*walk away*) chinach'yŏ kada 지나쳐 가다; (*look away*) oemyŏnhada 외면하다

♦ **turn back 1** *v/t edges, sheets* twijiptta 뒤집다 **2** *v/i* (*of walkers etc*) toedoragada 되돌아가다; (*in course of action*) mullŏsŏda 물러서다

♦ **turn down** *v/t offer, invitation* kŏjŏrhada 거절하다; *volume, TV, heating* churida 줄이다; *edge, collar* chŏptta 접다

♦ **turn in 1** *v/i* (*go to bed*) chamjarie tŭlda 잠자리에 들다 **2** *v/t* (*to police*) shin-gohada 신고하다

♦ **turn off 1** *v/t TV, heater, engine* kkŭda 끄다; *water* chamgŭda 잠그다; F (*sexually*) sŏngtchŏk hŭngmirŭl ilk'e hada 성적 흥미를 잃게 하다 **2** *v/i* (*in driving etc*) tarŭn killo tŭrŏsŏda 다른 길로 들어서다; (*of machine*) kkŏjida 꺼지다

♦ **turn on 1** *v/t TV, heater, engine* k'yŏda 켜다; *water* t'ŭlda 틀다; F (*sexually*) sŏngtchŏguro hŭngbunshik'ida 성적으로 흥분시키다 **2** *v/i* (*of machine*) k'yŏjida 켜지다

♦ **turn out 1** *v/t lights* kkŭda 끄다 **2** *v/i*: *as it turned out* kyŏlguk 결국

♦ **turn over 1** *v/i* (*in bed*) twich'ŏk-kkŏrida 뒤척거리다; (*of vehicle*) twijibŏjida 뒤집어지다 **2** *v/t* (*put upside down*) twijiptta 뒤집다; *page* nŏmgida 넘기다; FIN ...ŭi maesang-ŭl ollida ...의 매상을 올리다

♦ **turn up 1** *v/t collar* seuda 세우다; *volume, heating* nop'ida 높이다 **2** *v/i* (*arrive*) nat'anada 나타나다

turning mot'ung-i 모퉁이

turning point chŏnhwanjŏm 전환점

turnip sunmu 순무

turnout (*people*) ch'amsŏktcha 참석자; **turnover** FIN maesanggo 매상고; **turnpike** yuryo kosokttoro 유료 고속도로; **turnstile** shiptchahyŏng hoejŏnshik mun 십자형 회전식 문; **turntable** (*of record player*) t'ŏnt'eibŭl 턴테이블

turquoise *adj* ch'ŏngnoksssaegŭi

청록색의
turret (*of castle*) t'ap 탑; (*of tank*)
p'ot'ap 포탑
turtle kŏbuk 거북
turtleneck (**sweater**) t'ŏt'ŭllek
sŭwet'ŏ 터틀넥 스웨터
turtle ship kŏbukssŏn 거북선
tusk ŏmni 엄니
tutor: (*private*) ~ kaein kyosa 개인
교사
tutorial *n* kaebyŏl chido shigan 개별
지도 시간
tuxedo t'ŏksshido 턱시도
TV t'ibi 티비, t'ellebi 텔레비; **on** ~
t'ibie 티비에
TV program t'ibi p'ŭrogŭraem 티비
프로그램
twang 1 *n* (*in voice*) k'otssori 콧소리
2 *v/t guitar string* t'winggida 튕기다
tweezers choktchipkke 족집게
twelfth *adj* yŏldu pŏntchaeŭi 열 두
번째의
twelve yŏldul 열 둘, shibi 십이
twentieth *adj* sŭmu pŏntchaeŭi 스무
번째의
twenty sŭmul 스물, iship 이십
twice tu pŏn 두 번; ~ **as much** tu
paeŭi yang-ŭro 두 배의 양으로
twiddle manjijak-kkŏrida
만지작거리다; ~ **one's thumbs**
pindunggŏrida 빈둥거리다
twig *n* kaji 가지
twilight noŭl 노을
twin (*of pain*) ssushinŭn tŭt'an
ap'ŭm 쑤시는 듯한 아픔
twin han ssang-ŭi hantchok 한 쌍의
한쪽; ~**s** ssangdung-i 쌍둥이
twin beds t'ŭwin pedŭ 트윈 베드
twinge (*of pain*) ssushinŭn tŭt'an
ap'ŭm 쑤시는 듯한 아픔
twinkle *v/i* (*of stars*) pantchagida
반짝이다; (*of eyes*) pinnada 빛나다
twin town chamae toshi 자매 도시
twirl 1 *v/t* pingbing tollida 빙빙 돌리다
2 *n* (*of cream etc*) soyongdori kkorŭi
changshik 소용돌이 꼴의 장식
twist 1 *v/t* kkoda 꼬다; ~ **one's ankle**

palmogŭl ppida 발목을 삐다 **2** *v/i* (*of
road, river*) kuburŏjida 구부러지다
3 *n* (*in rope*) kkoim 꼬임; (*in road*)
kulgok 굴곡; (*in plot, story*) ttŭt
pakkŭi chŏn-gae 뜻 밖의 전개
twisty *road* kkubulkkuburhan
꾸불꾸불한
twit F pabo 바보
twitch 1 *n* (*nervous*) kyŏngnyŏn 경련
2 *v/i* (*jerk*) kyŏngnyŏni ilda 경련이
일다
twitter *v/i* (*of birds*) chijŏgwida
지저귀다
two tul 둘, i 이; **the** ~ **of them** kŭdŭl
tul 그들 둘
two-faced ijung in-gyŏgŭi 이중
인격의; **two-stroke** *adj engine*
ihaengjŏng ssaik'ŭrŭi 이행정
싸이클의; **two-way traffic**
yangbanghyang t'onghaengno
양방향 통행로
tycoon kŏmul 거물
type 1 *n* (*sort*) yuhyŏng 유형; **what** ~
of ...? ŏttŏn yuhyŏng-ŭi ...? 어떤
유형의 ...? **2** *v/i* (*use a keyboard*)
t'aja ch'ida 타자 치다 **3** *v/t* (*with a
typewriter*) t'ajagiro ch'ida 타자기로
치다
typewriter t'ajagi 타자기
typhoid (**fever**) changt'ip'usŭ
장티푸스
typhoon t'aep'ung 태풍
typhus paltchint'ip'usŭ 발진티푸스
typical chŏnhyŏngjŏgin 전형적인;
that's ~ **of him!** kŭnŭn hangsang
kŭrŏch'anayo! 그는 항상
그렇잖아요!
typically ilbanjŏgŭro 일반적으로; ~
American chŏnhyŏngjŏgin Migugin
전형적인 미국인
typist t'aip'isŭt'ŭ 타이피스트
tyrannical p'okkunjŏgin 폭군적인
tyrannize aptchehada 압제하다
tyranny chŏnje chŏngch'i 전제 정치
tyrant p'ok-kkun 폭군

U

ugly hyunghan 흉한; *situation* kkŭmtchik'an 끔찍한

UK (= *United Kingdom*) Yŏngguk 영국

ulcer kweyang 궤양

Ullung Island Ullŭngdo 울릉도

ultimate (*best, definitive*) ch'oesang-ŭi 최상의; (*final*) kunggŭktchŏgin 궁극적인; (*fundamental*) kibonjŏgin 기본적인

ultimately (*in the end*) kyŏlguk 결국

ultimatum ch'oehu t'ongch'ŏp 최후 통첩

ultrasound MED ch'oŭmp'a 초음파

ultraviolet *adj* chaoeŭi 자외의; ~ *rays* chaoesŏn 자외선

umbilical cord t'aetchul 탯줄

umbrella usan 우산

umpire *n* shimp'an 심판

umpteen F musuhan 무수한

UN (= *United Nations*) Kuktche Yŏnhap 국제 연합

unable: *be ~ to do X* (*not know how to*) Xŭl/rŭl hal churŭl morŭnda X을/를 할 줄을 모른다; (*not be in a position to*) Xŭl/rŭl hal su ŏptta X을/를 할 수 없다

unacceptable padadŭril su ŏmnŭn 받아들일 수 없는; *poverty* issŭl su ŏmnŭn 있을 수 없는; *it is ~ that...* ...ranŭn kŏsŭn padadŭril su ŏptta ...라는 것은 받아들일 수 없다

unaccountable sŏlmyŏnghal su ŏmnŭn 설명할 수 없는

unaccustomed: *be ~ to X* Xe ikssuk'aji ant'a X에 익숙하지 않다

unadulterated *fig* (*absolute*) sunjŏnhan 순전한

un-American panmiguktchŏgin 반미국적인

unanimous *verdict* manjang-ilch'iŭi 만장일치의; *be ~ on* ...e manjang-ilch'ihada ...에 만장일치하다

unanimously *vote, decide* manjang-

ilch'iro 만장일치로

unapproachable *person* kakkaihagi ŏryŏun 가까이하기 어려운

unarmed *person* pimujang-ŭi 비무장의; ~ *combat* yukt'anjŏn 육탄전

unassuming kyŏmsonhan 겸손한

unattached (*without a partner*) toksshinin 독신인

unattended naebŏryŏdun 내버려둔; *leave X ~* Xŭl/rŭl naebŏryŏduda X을/를 내버려두다

unauthorized muhŏgaŭi 무허가의

unavoidable p'ihal su ŏmnŭn 피할 수 없는

unavoidably: *be ~ detained* pulgap'ihage nŭjŏjida 불가피하게 늦어지다

unaware: *be ~ of* ...ŭl/rŭl kkaedatchi mot'ada ...을/를 깨닫지 못하다

unawares: *catch X ~* Xŭl/rŭl pulsshie sŭpkkyŏk'ada X을/를 불시에 습격하다

unbalanced kyunhyŏng-ŭl irŭn 균형을 잃은; PSYCH puranjŏnghan 불안정한

unbearable kyŏndil su ŏmnŭn 견딜 수 없는; *he's ~* kŭnŭn kyŏndil su ŏmnŭn saramiyeyo 그는 견딜 수 없는 사람이에요

unbeatable *team, quality* amudo ttaraol su ŏmnŭn 아무도 따라올 수 없는

unbeaten *team* ch'ŏnhamujŏgŭi 천하무적의

unbeknown(st): ~ *to his parents* kŭŭi pumonim mollae 그의 부모님 몰래

unbelievable midŭl su ŏmnŭn 믿을 수 없는; F (*heat, value*) ŏmch'ŏngnan 엄청난; *he's ~* F (*very good/bad*) kŭnŭn koengjanghi choŭn/mot-ttoen saramimnida 그는

굉장히 좋은 / 못된 사람입니다
unbias(s)ed p'yŏn-gyŏnŏmnŭn
편견없는
unblock *pipe* ttult'a 뚫다
unborn ajik t'aeŏnaji anŭn 아직
태어나지 않은; *an ~ baby* t'aea 태아
unbreakable *plate*, *world's record*
kkaejiji annŭn 깨지지 않는
unbutton p'ulda 풀다
uncalled-for chujenŏmŭn 주제넘은
uncanny *skill*, *feeling* myohan 묘한;
  have an ~ resemblance to
  ...ŭl / rŭl myohage tamtta ...을 / 를
  묘하게 닮다
unceasing kkŭnimŏmnŭn 끊임없는
uncertain *future*, *weather*
  purhwakssirhan 불확실한; *origins*
  pulmyŏnghwak'an 불명확한; *be ~
  about X* Xŭl / rŭl hwaksshinhaji
  mot'ada X을 / 를 확신하지 못하다;
  it's ~ hwakssirhaji anssŭmnida
  확실하지 않습니다
uncertainty (*of the future*)
  purhwakssilssŏng 불확실성; *there
  is still ~ about ...* ...ŭn / nŭn ajik
  purhwakssirhamnida ...은 / 는 아직
  불확실합니다
unchecked: *go ~* chŏjidoeji ant'a
  저지되지 않다
uncle (*in general*) ajŏsshi 아저씨;
  (*father's brother, single*) samch'on
  삼촌; (*mother's brother, single*)
  oesamch'on 외삼촌; (*father's sister's
  husband*) komobu 고모부; (*mother's
  sister's husband*) imobu 이모부
uncomfortable pulp'yŏnhan 불편한:
  feel ~ about X (*about decision etc*)
  Xi / ga kkŏrimchik'ada X이 / 가
  꺼림칙하다; *I feel ~ with him* nanŭn
  kŭga pulp'yŏnhada 나는 그가
  불편하다
uncommon hŭnhaji anŭn 흔하지
  않은; *it's not ~* kŭgŏsŭn hŭnhaji
  anŭn irida 그것은 흔하지 않은
  일이다
uncompromising t'ahyŏp'aji annŭn
  타협하지 않는
unconcerned shin-gyŏngssŭji annŭn
  신경쓰지 않는; *be ~ about X* Xe
  shin-gyŏngssŭji annŭnda X에
  신경 쓰지 않는다

unconditional mujokkŏnŭi 무조건의
unconscious MED muŭishik
  sangt'aeŭi 무의식 상태의; PSYCH
  muŭishiktchŏgin 무의식적인; *knock
  ~ ch'yŏsŏ kijŏlshik'ida 쳐서
  기절시키다; *be ~ of X* (*not aware*)
  Xŭl / rŭl kkaedatchi mot'ada X을 / 를
  깨닫지 못하다
uncontrollable *anger*, *desire* chajehal
  su ŏmnŭn 자제할 수 없는; *children*
  kamdanghal su ŏmnŭn 감당할 수
  없는
unconventional pigwansŭptchŏgin
  비관습적인
uncooperative pihyŏptchojŏgin
  비협조적인
uncork *bottle* magaerŭl ppoptta
  마개를 뽑다
uncover (*remove covering from*)
  tŏpkkaerŭl pŏtkkida 덮개를 벗기다;
  (*discover*) palgurhada 발굴하다; *plot*
  palk'yŏnaeda 밝혀내다
undamaged sonsangdoeji anŭn
  손상되지 않은
undaunted: *carry on ~* kurhaji ank'o
  haenaeda 굴하지 않고 해내다
undecided *matter* chŏnghaji anŭn
  정하지 않은; *be ~ about X* Xŭl / rŭl
  kyŏltchŏnghaji mot'ada X을 / 를
  결정하지 못하다
undelete COMPUT twesalligi 되살리기
undeniable pujŏnghal su ŏmnŭn
  부정할 수 없는
undeniably pujŏnghal su ŏpsshi
  부정할 수 없이
under 1 *prep* (*beneath*) ...ŭi arae ...의
  아래에; (*less than*) ... miman ... 미만;
  ~ $500 500tallŏ miman 500달러
  미만; *~ the water* mul mit'e 물
  밑에; *it is ~ review / investigation*
  kŭgŏsŭn kŏmt'o / chosa chung-ida
  그것은 검토 / 조사 중이다 **2** *adv*
  (*anesthetized*) *the patient is still ~*
  hwanjanŭn ajik mach'iesŏ kkaeŏnaji
  anassŭmnida 환자는 아직 마취에서
  깨어나지 않았습니다
underage *drinking etc* misŏngnyŏnŭi
  미성년의; *be ~* misŏngnyŏnjaida
  미성년자이다
underarm *adv throw* mit'ŭro tŏnjyŏ
  밑으로 던져

undercarriage ch'angnyuk changch'i
착륙 장치

undercover adj agent pimillie
sumgyŏjin 비밀리에 숨겨진

undercut v/t COM poda tŏ kkakka
chegonghada 보다 더 깎아 제공하다

underdog yaktcha 약자

underdone meat tŏl ik'in 덜 익힌; **I
prefer my steak** ~ chŏnŭn tŏl ik'in
sŭt'eik'ŭga chossŭmnida 저는 덜
익힌 스테이크가 좋습니다

underestimate v/t person, skills, task
kwasop'yŏngkkahada 과소평가하다

underexposed PHOT noch'uri
pujok'an 노출이 부족한

underfed yŏngnyangbujogŭi
영양부족의

undergo surgery, treatment pat-tta
받다; experiences kyŏktta 겪다

underground 1 adj passages etc
chihaŭi 지하의; POL resistance,
newpaper etc pimirŭi 비밀의; ~ **activities** POL chiha undong 지하 운동
2 adv work chiha-esŏ 지하에서; **go ~**
POL chiharo ŭnnik'ada 지하로
은닉하다

undergrowth tŏmbul 덤불

underhand adj (devious) ŭmhŏmhan
음험한

underlie v/t ...ŭi kŭn-gŏga toeda ...의
근거가 되다

underline v/t text mitchul kŭt-tta 밑줄
긋다

underlying causes, problems
kŭnwŏnjŏgin 근원적인

undermine v/t s.o.'s position mollae
hwesonhada 몰래 훼손하다; theory
hŭndŭlda 흔들다

underneath 1 prep ...ŭi mit'e ...의
밑에 **2** adv mit'e 밑에

underpants p'aench'ŭ 팬츠

underpass (for pedestrians) chihado
지하도

underprivileged hyet'aekpat-tchi
mot'an 혜택받지 못한

underrate v/t kwasop'yŏngkkahada
과소평가하다

undershirt rŏning shyŏch'ŭ 러닝 셔츠

undersized pot'ongboda chagŭn
보통보다 작은

underskirt sokch'ima 속치마

understaffed chŏgŭn suŭi chigwŏnŭl
kajin 적은 수의 직원을 가진

understand 1 v/t ihaehada 이해하다; **I
~ that you ...** naega algienŭn
tangshini ... 내가 알기에는 당신이
...; **they are understood to be in
Canada** kŭdŭrŭn K'aenadae innŭn
kŏsŭro allyŏjyŏit-tta 그들은
캐나다에 있는 것으로 알려져있다
2 v/i ihaehada 이해하다

understandable ihaehal su innŭn
이해할 수 있는

understandably ihaehal su itkke
이해할 수 있게

understanding 1 adj person
ihaeshiminnŭn 이해심있는 **2** n (of
problem, situation) ihae 이해;
(agreement) tong-ŭi 동의; **on the ~
that** ...ranŭn chokkŏn ha-e ...라는
조건 하에

understatement ŏktchedoen
p'yohyŏn 억제된 표현

undertake task surak'ada 수락하다; ~
to do X (agree to) Xŭl/rŭl hal kŏsŭl
surak'ada X을/를 할 것을 수락하다

undertaking (enterprise) saŏp 사업;
(promise) yakssok 약속

undervalue v/t kwaso p'yŏngkkahada
과소 평가하다

underwear sogot 속옷, naeŭi 내의

underweight adj person ch'ejung
midarŭi 체중 미달의

underworld (criminal) amhŭk-kka
암흑가; (in mythology) chosŭng 저승

underwrite v/t FIN pojŭnghada
보증하다

undeserved padŭl kach'iga ŏmnŭn
받을 가치가 없는

undesirable features, changes
paramjik'aji annŭn 바람직하지 않은;
person pulk'waehan 불쾌한; ~ **element** nune kashi 눈에 가시

undisputed champion, leader amudo
nŏmboji mot'al 아무도 넘보지 못할

undo parcel, wrapping, buttons p'ulda
풀다; s.o. else's work soyong-ŏpkke
hada 소용없게 하다

undoubtedly ŭishimhal yŏji ŏpsshi
의심할 여지 없이

undreamt-of riches kkumdo mot
kkul chŏngdoŭi 꿈도 못 꿀 정도의

undress 1 v/t pŏtkkida 벗기다; *get ~ed* osŭl pŏt-tta 옷을 벗다 **2** v/i ot pŏtkkida 옷 벗기다

undue (*excessive*) chinach'in 지나친

unduly chinach'ige 지나치게

unearth *ancient remains* palgurhada 발굴하다; *fig* (*find*) palgyŏnhada 발견하다; *secret* p'ahech'ida 파헤치다

unearthly: *at this ~ hour* ŏngttunghan shigane 엉뚱한 시간에

uneasy *relationship*, *peace* puranhan 불안한; *feel ~ about* ...ŭl/rŭl puranhae hada ...을/를 불안해 하다

uneatable mŏgŭl su ŏmnŭn 먹을 수 없는

uneconomic iigi andoenŭn 이익이 안되는

uneducated kyoyukppat-tchi mot'an 교육받지 못한

unemployed shiltchik'an 실직한; *the ~* shirŏptcha 실업자

unemployment shirŏp 실업

unending kkŭdŏmnŭn 끝없는

unequal ttokkatchi anŭn 똑같지 않은; *pay* pulgongp'yŏnghan 불공평한; *be ~ to the task* kŭ irŭl hal nŭngnyŏgi ŏptta 그 일을 할 능력이 없다

unerring *judgment*, *instinct* t'ŭllimŏmnŭn 틀림없는

uneven *quality* kyunirhaji anŭn 균일하지 않은; *surface*, *ground* korŭji anŭn 고르지 않은

unevenly *distributed*, *applied* korŭji ank'e 고르지 않게; *~ matched* sangdaega andoenŭn 상대가 안되는

uneventful *day*, *journey* pyŏril ŏmnŭn 별일 없는

unexpected yesanghaji mot'an 예상하지 못한

unexpectedly yesang pakke 예상 밖에

unfair pulgongjŏnghan 불공정한

unfaithful *husband*, *wife* pujŏnghan 부정한; *be ~ to X* X morŭge paramŭl p'iuda X 모르게 바람을 피우다

unfamiliar ikssuk'aji anŭn 익숙하지 않은; *be ~ with X* Xe ikssuk'aji ant'a X에 익숙하지 않다

unfasten *belt* p'ulda 풀다

unfavorable *weather conditions*

hogami an-ganŭn 호감이 안가는; *report*, *review* hoŭijŏgi anin 호의적이 아닌

unfeeling *person* mujŏnghan 무정한

unfinished kkŭnnaeji anŭn 끝내지 않은; *leave X ~* Xŭl/rŭl kkŭnnaeji anŭn ch'aero tuda X을/를 끝내지 않은 채로 두다

unfit (*physically*) undong pujogin 운동 부족인; (*not morally suited*) pujŏkkyŏgin 부적격인; *be ~ to eat/drink* mŏk-kkie/mashigie pujŏkttanghada 먹기에/마시기에 부적당하다

unfix *part* pullihada 분리하다; *screw* ppaenaeda 빼내다

unflappable ch'imch'ak'an 침착한

unfold 1 v/t *sheets*, *letter*, *one's arms* p'yŏda 펴다 **2** v/i (*of story*, *view etc*) p'yŏlch'ŏjida 펼쳐지다

unforeseen yesanghaji mot'an 예상하지 못한

unforgettable ijŭl su ŏmnŭn 잊을 수 없는

unforgivable yongsŏhal su ŏmnŭn 용서할 수 없는; *that was ~ of you* kŭgŏsŭn yongsŏpat-tchi mot'al irida 그것은 용서받지 못할 일이다

unfortunate *people* un ŏmnŭn 운 없는; *choice of words*, *event* chalmot-ttoen 잘못된; *that's ~ for you* kŭgŏt chŏngmal andwaetkkunyo 그것 정말 안됐군요

unfortunately purhaenghi 불행히

unfounded kŭn-gŏŏmnŭn 근거없는

unfriendly pulch'injŏrhan 불친절한; *software* tarugi ŏryŏun 다루기 어려운

unfurnished kaguga ŏmnŭn 가구가 없는

ungodly: *at this ~ hour* ŏngttunghan shigane 엉뚱한 시간에

ungrateful kamsahal chul morŭnŭn 감사할 줄 모르는

unhappiness purhaeng 불행

unhappy purhaenghan 불행한; (*not satisfied*) pulmansŭrŏun 불만스러운; *be ~ with the service* sŏbissŭe pulmanida 서비스에 불만이다

unharmed musahan 무사한

unhealthy *person* kŏn-ganghaji

mot'an 건강하지 못한; *conditions*
choch'i anŭn 좋지 않은; *food,
atmosphere* kŏn-gang-e choch'i anŭn
건강에 좋지 않은; *economy, balance
sheet* choch'i mot'an 좋지 못한
unheard-of chŏllye ŏmnŭn 전례 없는
unhurt tach'iji anŭn 다치지 않은
unhygienic piwisaengjŏgin
비위생적인
unification t'ong-il 통일
uniform 1 *n* MIL chebok 제복; (*of
school pupil*) kyobok 교복; (*of
sportsman, air hostess*) yunip'om
유니폼 **2** *adj* iltchŏnghan 일정한
unify t'ong-irhada 통일하다
unilateral ilbangjŏgin 일방적인
unimaginable sangsanghal su ŏmnŭn
상상할 수 없는
unimaginative sangsangnyŏgi ŏmnŭn
상상력이 없는
unimportant chungnyohaji anŭn
중요하지 않은
uninhabitable sal su ŏmnŭn 살 수
없는
uninhabited sarami salji annŭn
사람이 살지 않는
uninjured sangch'ŏ ŏmnŭn 상처 없는
unintelligible ihaehal su ŏmnŭn
이해할 수 없는
unintentional koŭiga anin 고의가
아닌
unintentionally ŭidoch'i ank'e 의도치
않게
uninteresting chaemi ŏmnŭn 재미
없는
uninterrupted *sleep, two hours' work*
kkŭnimŏmnŭn 끊임없는
union POL yŏnhap 연합; (*labor ~*)
nojo 노조
unique tokt'ŭk'an 독특한; *with his
own ~ humor / style* kŭ t'ŭgyuŭi
yumŏro / sŭt'aillo 그 특유의 유머로 /
스타일로
unit (*of measurement*) tanwi 단위;
(*section: of machine, structure*)
pup'um 부품; (*department*) pusŏ
부서; MIL pudae 부대
unit cost COM tanwi wŏnkka 단위
원가
unite 1 *v/t* kyŏrhap'ada 결합하다;
company hap-ppyŏnghada 합병하다

2 *v/i* hanaga toeda 하나가 되다
united hanaga toen 하나가 된; *group,
organization, country* yŏnhapttoen
연합된
United Kingdom Yŏngguk 영국
United Nations Kuktche Yŏnhap
국제 연합 ~ *troops* Yuen-gun
유엔군
United People's Party T'ong-il
Kungmindang 통일 국민당
United States (of America) Miguk
미국, Mihaptchungguk 미국미합중국
fml
unity t'ong-il 통일; (*of all being*)
tanilssŏng 단일성
universal (*general*) pop'yŏnjŏgin
보편적인; *language* kongt'ong-ŭi
공통의
universally pop'yŏnjŏgŭro
보편적으로
universe uju 우주
university taehak-kkyo 대학교; *he is
at ~* kŭnŭn taehakssaeng-ida 그는
대학생이다
unjust pulgongjŏnghan 불공정한
unkempt tanjŏnghaji mot'an
단정하지 못한
unkind pulch'injŏrhan 불친절한
unknown 1 *adj* allyŏjiji anŭn 알려지지
않은 **2** *n*: *a journey into the ~*
mijiroŭi yŏhaeng 미지로의 여행
unleaded (**gasoline**) muyŏn
hwibaryu 무연 휘발유
unless …haji anŭmyŏn …하지
않으면; ~ *he pays us tomorrow*
kŭga naeilkkaji tonŭl chuji anŭmyŏn
그가 내일까지 돈을 주지 않으면
unlike *prep* kach'i anŭn 같지 않은;
it's ~ him to drink so much
kŭrŏk'e mani mashidani kŭdaptchi
ant'a 그렇게 많이 마시다니 그답지
않다; *the photograph was completely ~ her* kŭ sajinŭn
kŭnyŏgach'i anboinda 그 사진은
그녀같이 안보인다
unlikely issŭl kŏt kach'i anŭn 있을 것
같지 않은; *he is ~ to win* kŭnŭn igil
kŏt kach'i ant'a 그는 이길 것 같지
않다; *it is ~ that* …hal kŏt kach'i
ant'a …할 것 같지 않다
unlimited hanŏmnŭn 한없는

unload (*baggage etc*) naerida 내리다

unlock chamulsoerŭl yŏlda 자물쇠를 열다

unluckily unŏpkke 운없게

unlucky *day, choice, person* unŏmnŭn 운없는; *that was so ~ for you!* chŏngmal uni ŏpssŏtkunyo! 정말 운이 없었군요!

unmade-up *face* hwajanghaji anŭn 화장하지 않은

unmanned *spacecraft* muinŭi 무인의

unmarried mihonŭi 미혼의

unmistakable t'ŭllimŏmnŭn 틀림없는

unmoved (*emotionally*) tongnyo ŏmnŭn 동요 없는

unmusical *person* ŭmaktchŏk sojiri ŏmnŭn 음악적 소질이 없는; *sounds* kwie kŏsŭllinŭn 귀에 거슬리는

unnatural pujayŏnsŭrŏun 부자연스러운; *it's not ~ to be annoyed* hwanaenŭn kŏt-tto tangnyŏnhamnida 화내는 것도 당연합니다

unnecessary pulp'iryohan 불필요한

unnerving kŏmnage hanŭn 겁나게 하는

unnoticed: *it went ~* nune ttŭiji anassŏyo 눈에 띄지 않았어요

unobtainable *goods* ŏdŭl su ŏmnŭn 얻을 수 없는; TELEC yŏn-gyŏri andoenŭn 연결이 안되는

unobtrusive nune ttŭiji annŭn 눈에 띄지 않는

unoccupied *building, house, post* piŏinnŭn 비어있는; *room* amudo ŏmnŭn 아무도 없는; *person* hal il ŏmnŭn 할 일 없는

unofficial pigongshiktchŏgin 비공식적인

unofficially pigongshiktchŏgŭro 비공식적으로

unpack *v/t & v/i* p'ulda 풀다

unpaid *work* mugŭbŭi 무급의

unpleasant pulk'waehan 불쾌한; *he was very ~ to her* kŭnŭn kŭnyŏŭi kibunŭl sanghage haet-tta 그는 그녀의 기분을 상하게 했다

unplug *v/t TV, computer* ...ŭi p'ŭllŏgŭrŭl ppoptta ...의 플러그를 뽑다

unpopular *person* inkkiŏmnŭn 인기없는; *decision* chijipat-tchi mot'anŭn 지지받지 못하는

unprecedented chŏllye ŏmnŭn 전례 없는; *it was ~ for a woman to ...* yojaga ...hanŭn kŏsŭn ijŏnenŭn ŏptttŏn iriŏt-tta 여자가 ...하는 것은 이전에는 없던 일이었다

unpredictable *person, weather* yech'ŭk'al su ŏmnŭn 예측할 수 없는

unprincipled *pej* pidodŏktchŏgin 비도덕적인

unpretentious hŏshigŏmnŭn 허식없는

unproductive *meeting, discussion* pisaengsanjŏgin 비생산적인

unprofessional *person, behavior* chŏnmunindaptchi anŭn 전문인답지 않은; *workmanship* pip'ŭrojŏgin 비프로적인

unprofitable iigi ŏmnŭn 이익이 없는

unpronounceable parŭmhal su ŏmnŭn, parŭmi pulganŭnghan 발음할 수 없는, 발음이 불가능한

unprotected *borders* mubangbiŭi 무방비의; *machine* pohodoeji anŭn 보호되지 않은; *~ sex* k'ondomŭl sayonghaji ank'o hanŭn sŏnggyo 콘돔을 사용하지 않고 하는 성교

unprovoked *attack* tobaldoeji anŭn 도발되지 않은

unqualified *worker, doctor etc* chagyŏgi ŏmnŭn 자격이 없는

unquestionably (*without doubt*) murŏ pol p'iryodo ŏpsshi 물어 볼 필요도 없이

unquestioning ŭishimŏmnŭn 의심없는

unravel *v/t string, mystery* p'ulda 풀다

unreadable *book* ilkki ŏryŏun 읽기 어려운

unreal *creature* shiltchaehaji annŭn 실재하지 않는; (*unrealistic*) pihyŏnsshiltchŏgin 비현실적인; *this is ~!* F midŭl su ŏpssŏyo! 믿을 수 없어요!

unrealistic pihyŏnsshiltchŏgin 비현실적인

unreasonable pihamnijŏgin 비합리적인

unrelated kwan-gyŏmnŭn 관계없는

unrelenting kkujunhan 꾸준한
unreliable midŭl su ŏmnŭn 믿을 수
없는
unrest puran 불안
unrestrained *emotions* ŏktchedoeji
anŭn 억제되지 않은
unroadworthy wihŏmhal chŏngdoro
kojangna innŭn 위험할 정도로
고장나 있는
unroll *v/t carpet, scroll* p'ida 피다
unruly tarugi himdŭn 다루기 힘든
unsafe anjŏnhaji anŭn 안전하지 않은;
~ to drink / eat mashigie / mŏk-kkie
anjŏnhaji anŭn 마시기에 / 먹기에
안전하지 않은
unsanitary piwisaengjŏgin 비위생적인
unsatisfactory manjokssŭrŏptchi
mot'an 만족스럽지 못한
unsavory *person, reputation*
pulk'waehan 불쾌한; *district*
hŏmak'an 험악한
unscathed tach'in te ŏmnŭn 다친 데
없는; (*not damaged*)
hŭmtchibŏmnŭn 흠집없는
unscrew nasarŭl p'ulda 나사를 풀다;
top magaerŭl yŏlda 마개를 열다
unscrupulous pudodŏk'an 부도덕한
unselfish it'ajŏgin 이타적인
unsettled *issue* kyŏltchŏngdoeji anŭn
결정되지 않은; *weather, stock market*
pyŏnhagi shwiun 변하기 쉬운;
lifestyle iltchŏngch'i anŭn 일정치
않은; *bills* migyŏltcheŭi 미결제의; *of
stomach* paet'allan 배탈난
unshaven myŏndohaji anŭn 면도하지
않은
unsightly pogi hyunghan 보기 흉한
unskilled misuk'an 미숙한; **~ labor**
misungnyŏn nodongja 미숙련 노동자
unsociable pisagyojŏgin 비사교적인
unsophisticated tansunhan 단순한
unstable *person, structure*
puranjŏnghan 불안정한; *area,
economy* puranhan 불안한
unsteady (*on one's feet*)
pit'ŭlgŏrinŭn 비틀거리는; *ladder*
hŭndŭlgŏrinŭn 흔들거리는
unstinting: **be ~ in one's efforts**
noryŏgŭl akkiji ant'a 노력을 아끼지
않다
unstuck: **come ~** (*of notice etc*)

ttŏrŏjida 떨어지다; (*of plan etc*)
manghada 망하다
unsuccessful *writer, party etc*
shilp'aehan 실패한; *candidate*
nakssŏndoen 낙선된; *attempt*
sŏngonghaji mot'an 성공하지 못한;
he tried but was ~ kŭnŭn
noryŏk'aet-tchiman shilp'aehaet-tta
그는 노력했지만 실패했다
unsuccessfully *try, apply*
sŏngongjŏgiji mot'age 성공적이지
못하게
unsuitable pujŏkttanghan 부적당한
unsuspecting ŭichimhaji annŭn
의심하지 않는
unswerving *loyalty, devotion*
hwakkobudonghan 확고부동한
unthinkable saenggak'al su choch'a
ŏmnŭn 생각할 수 조차 없는
untidy chijŏbunhan 지저분한
untie *knot, laces* p'ulda 풀다; *prisoner*
p'urŏjuda 풀어주다
until 1 *prep* kkaji 까지; **from Monday
~ Friday** wŏryoilbut'ŏ
kŭmnyoilkkaji 월요일부터
금요일까지; **I can wait ~ tomorrow**
naeilkkaji kidaril su issŭmnida
내일까지 기다릴 수 있습니다; **not ~
Friday** kŭmnyoil chŏnenŭn malgo
금요일 전에는 말고; **it won't be
finished ~ July** ch'irwŏlkkajinŭn
mot kkŭnnael kŏt kassŭmnida
칠월까지는 못 끝낼 것 같습니다
2 *conj* hal ttaekkaji 할 때까지; **can
you wait ~ I'm ready?** chega
chunbidoel ttaekkaji kidaril su
itkkessŭmnikka? 제가 준비될 때까지
기다릴 수 있겠습니까?; **they won't
do anything ~ you say so**
tangshini kŭrŏrago hal ttaekkaji
kŭdŭrŭn amu kŏtto haji anŭl
kŏshimnida 당신이 그러라고 할
때까지 그들은 아무 것도 하지 않을
것입니다
untimely *death* ttae anin 때 아닌
untiring *efforts* chich'iji annŭn 지치지
않는
untold *riches, suffering* makttaehan
막대한; *story* palk'yŏjiji anŭn
밝혀지지 않은
untranslatable pŏnyŏk'al su ŏmnŭn

번역할 수 없는

untrue sashiri anin 사실이 아닌

unused[1] *goods* sayonghaji anŭn 사용하지 않은

unused[2]: *be ~ to sth* muŏse ikssŭk'aji ant'a 무엇에 익숙하지 않다; *be ~ to doing sth* muŏsŭl hanŭn kŏshi ikssŭk'aji ant'a 무엇을 하는 것이 익숙하지 않다

unusual tŭmun 드문

unusually tŭmulge 드물게

unveil *memorial, statue etc* pŏtkkida 벗기다; *plans* konggaehada 공개하다

unwell (*physically*) momi choch'i anŭn 몸이 좋지 않은; (*mentally*) kibuni choch'i anŭn 기분이 좋지 않은

unwilling: *be ~ to do sth* muŏsŭl hanŭn kŏsŭl naek'yŏhaji ant'a 무엇을 하는 것을 내켜하지 않다

unwritten *rule* kwansŭptchŏgin 관습적인; *~ law* kwansŭppŏp 관습법

unzip *v/t dress etc* chip'ŏrŭl yŏlda 지퍼를 열다; COMPUT apch'ugŭl p'ulda 압축을 풀다

up 1 *adv* wie 위에; *~ in the sky/on the roof* hanŭl/chibung wie 하늘/지붕 위에; *~ here/there* yŏgi/chŏgi wie 여기/저기 위에; *be ~* (*out of bed*) irŏna it-tta 일어나 있다; (*of sun*) ttŏolla it-tta 떠올라 있다; (*be built*) sewŏjyŏ it-tta 세워져 있다; (*of shelves*) sŏlch'idoeŏ it-tta 설치되어 있다; (*of prices, temperature*) olla it-tta 올라 있다; (*have expired*) kkŭnnada 끝나다; *what's ~?* musŭn il issŭmnikka? 무슨 일 있습니까?; *~ to the year 1989* 1989nyŏnkkaji 1989년까지; *he came ~ to me* kŭnŭn na-ege tagawat-tta 그는 나에게 다가왔다; *what are you ~ to these days?* yojŭm musŭn irŭl hamyŏ chinaeshimnikka? 요즘 무슨 일을 하며 지내십니까?; *what are those*

kids ~ to? aidŭri musŭn chisŭl hago it-tchi? 아이들이 무슨 짓을 하고 있지?; *be ~ to something* (*bad*) mot-ttoen chisŭl hago it-tta 못된 짓을 하고 있다; *I don't feel ~ to it* nanŭn kŭrŏl kibuni tŭlji anssŭmnida 나는 그럴 기분이 들지 않습니다; *it's ~ to you* tangshinhant'e tallyŏssŏyo 당신한테 달렸어요; *it's ~ to them to solve it* kŭdŭri haegyoerhaeyajiyo 그들이 해결해야지요; *be ~ and about* (*after illness*) hoebok'ayŏ toradanida 회복하여 돌아다니다

2 *prep*: *further ~ the mountain* sanŭi tŏ nop'ŭn tchoge 산의 더 높은 쪽에; *he climbed ~ a tree* kŭnŭn namurŭl t'ago ŏllagat-tta 그는 나무를 타고 올라갔다; *they ran ~ the street* kŭdŭrŭn kirŭl ttara tallyŏt-tta 그들은 길을 따라 달렸다; *the water goes ~ this pipe* murŭl i kwanŭl ttara hŭrŭmnida 물은 이 관을 따라 흐릅니다; *we traveled ~ to Kang-wondo* urinŭn Kang-wŏndokkaji yŏhaenghae ollagat-tta 우리는 강원도까지 여행해 올라갔다

3 *n*: *~s and downs* kibok 기복

upbringing kajŏng kyoyuk 가정 교육

upcoming *adj* tagaonŭn 다가오는

update 1 *v/t file, records* ch'oeshinŭi kŏsŭro pakkuda 최신의 것으로 바꾸다; *~ s.o. on sth* nuguege muŏse kwanhan ch'oeshin chŏngborŭl chuda 누구에게 무엇에 관한 최신 정보를 주다 **2** *n* (*of files, records*) ch'oeshin kŏsŭrŏŭi kyoch'e 최신 것으로의 교체; *can you give me an ~ on the situation?* kajang ch'oegŭnŭi sanghwang-ŭl allyŏjushigessŭmnikka? 가장 최근의 상황을 알려주시겠습니까?

upgrade 1 *v/t computers, ticket etc* ŏpkkŭreidŭhada 업그레이드하다; (*replace with new version*) saeroun kŏsŭrŏ kyoch'ehada 새로운 것으로 교체하다; *product* hyangsangshik'ida 향상시키다 **2** *n* (*software version*) ŏpkkŭreidŭ 업그레이드

upheaval (*emotional, physical*) k'ŭn pyŏnhwa 큰 변화; (*political, social*) kyŏkppyŏn 격변

uphill 1 *adv walk* ŏndŏk wiro 언덕 위로; *the road goes* ~ orŭmak kirida 오르막 길이다 **2** *adj struggle* himdŭnŭn 힘드는

uphold *traditions, rights* yujihada 유지하다; (*vindicate*) hwaginhada 확인하다

upholstery (*fabric*) kagu changshik 가구 장식; (*padding*) kaguŭi sok 가구의 속

upkeep *n* (*of buildings, parks etc*) yuji 유지

upload *v/t* COMPUT ŏprodŭhada 업로드하다

upmarket *adj restaurant, hotel* kop'umkkyŏgŭi 고품격의

upon → **on**

upper *part of sth* wi tchogŭi 위 쪽의; *stretches of a river* sangnyuŭi 상류의; *atmosphere* wiŭi 위의; ~ *deck* sanggapp'an 상갑판

upper-class sangnyuch'ŭng-ŭi 상류층의

upper classes sangnyuch'ŭng 상류층

UPP (= *United People's Party*) T'ongil Kungmindang 통일국민당

upright 1 *adj citizen* parŭn 바른 **2** *adv sit* ttokpparo 똑바로

upright (**piano**) ŏmnait'ŭ p'iano 업라이트 피아노

uprising p'okttong 폭동

uproar (*loud noise*) soran 소란; (*protest*) hang-ŭi 항의

upset 1 *v/t drink, glass* twijiptta 뒤집다; (*emotionally*) kibun sanghagehada 기분 상하게 하다 **2** *adj* (*emotionally*) kibun sanghan 기분 상한; *get* ~ *about sth* muŏse kibun sanghada 무엇에 기분 상하다; *have an* ~ *stomach* paet'allada 배탈나다

upsetting sokssanghan 속상한

upshot (*result, outcome*) kyŏlgwa 결과

upside down *adv* kŏkkuro 거꾸로; *turn sth* ~ *box etc* muŏsŭl kŏkkuro twijiptta 무엇을 거꾸로 뒤집다

upstairs 1 *adv* wich'ŭng-e 위층에 **2** *adj room* wich'ŭng-ŭi 위층의

upstart pyŏrak ch'ulssehan nom 벼락 출세한 놈

upstream *adv* sangnyuro 상류로

uptight F (*nervous*) anjŏlbujŏl mot'anŭn 안절부절 못하는; (*inhibited*) kinjang-ŭro ttakttak'aejin 긴장으로 딱딱해진

up-to-date *fashions, data* ch'oeshinŭi 최신의

upturn (*in economy*) hojŏn 호전

upward *adv fly, move* wiro 위로; ~ *of 10,000* man isang-ŭro 만 이상으로

uranium uranyum 우라늄

urban toshiŭi 도시의

urbanization toshihwa 도시화

urchin kkoma 꼬마

urge 1 *n* ch'ungdong 충동; *I felt an* ~ *to hit him* nanŭn kŭrŭl ttaerigo ship'ŭn ch'ungdong-ŭl nŭkkyŏt-tta 나는 그를 때리고 싶은 충동을 느꼈다 **2** *v/t*: ~ *X to do Y* Xege Y(ŭ)rago puch'ugida X에게 Y(으)라고 부추기다

♦ **urge on** kyŏngnyŏhada 격려하다

urgency (*of situation*) kin-gŭp 긴급

urgent *job, letter* kŭp'an 급한; *be in* ~ *need of* …i/ga kŭp'age p'iryohada …이/가 급하게 필요하다; *is it* ~? kŭp'an kŏshimnikka? 급한 것입니까?

urinate sobyŏnŭl poda 소변을 보다

urine sobyŏn 소변

urn tanji 단지

us uri 우리; *that's for* ~ uri kŏshimnida 우리 것입니다; *who's that? - it's* ~ nuguseyo? - uriyeyo 누구세요? - 우리예요

US(A) (= *United States* (*of America*)) Miguk 미국, Mihaptchungguk 미국미합중국 *fml*

usable ssŭl su innŭn 쓸 수 있는

usage (*linguistic*) ŏppŏp 어법

use 1 *v/t* ssŭda 쓰다, sayonghada 사용하다; *pej: person* iyonghada 이용하다; *I could* ~ *a drink* F mwŏ chom mashyŏyagessŏyo 뭐 좀 마셔야겠어요 **2** *n* sayong 사용, ssŭgi 쓰기, iyong 이용; *be of great* ~ *to s.o.* nuguege k'ŭge ssŭlmo it-tta 누구에게 크게 쓸모 있다; *be of no* ~ *to s.o.* nuguege ssŭlmo ŏptta 누구에게 쓸모 없다; *is that of any* ~? ssŭlmo issŭmnikka? 쓸모

있습니까?; *it's no* ~ soyong ŏmnŭn irimnida 소용 없는 일입니다; *it's no ~ trying* / *waiting* haebwaya / kidaryŏbwaya soyong ŏpssŭmnida 해봐야 / 기다려봐야 소용 없습니다

♦ **use up** ta ssŏbŏrida 다 써버리다

used[1] *car etc* ch'unggo 중고

used[2]: *be ~ to s.o.* / *sth* nugue / muŏse ikssuk'aejyŏ it-tta 누구에 / 무엇에 익숙해져 있다; *get ~ to s.o.* / *sth* nugue / muŏse ikssuk'aejida 누구에 / 무엇에 익숙해지다; *be ~ to doing sth* muŏsŭl hanŭn kŏse ikssuk'aejyŏ it-tta 무엇을 하는 것에 익숙해져 있다; *get ~ to doing sth* muŏsŭl hanŭn kŏse ikssuk'aejida 무엇을 하는 것에 익숙해지다

used[3]: *I ~ to like* / *know him* hanttae nanŭn kŭrŭl choahaessŏt-tta / arassŏt-tta 한때 나는 그를 좋아했었다 / 알았었다; *I don't work there now, but I ~ to* chigŭmŭn anijiman, yejŏnenŭn kŭ gosesŏ irhaessŏssŏyo 지금은 아니지만, 예전에는 그 곳에서 일했었어요; *I ~ to work with him* nanŭn kŭwa kach'i irhaessŏssŭmnida 나는 그와 같이 일했었습니다

useful ssŭlmoinnŭn 쓸모있는

usefulness ssŭlmo 쓸모

useless ssŭlmoŏmnŭn 쓸모없는; F

person mojaran 모자란; *it's ~ trying* noryŏk'aebwattcha ssŭlmoŏmnŭn chishida 노력해봤자 쓸모없는 짓이다

user (*of product*) sayongja 사용자

user-friendly sayonghagi shwiun 사용하기 쉬운

usher *n* (*at wedding*) annaeja 안내자

♦ **usher in** *new era* ...(ŭ)ro indohada ...(으)로 인도하다

usual pot'ong-ŭi 보통의; *as ~* pot'ong ttaech'ŏrŏm 보통 때처럼; *the ~, please* nŭl hanŭn kŏsŭro chushipsshio 늘 하는 것으로 주십시오

usually pot'ong 보통

utensil yonggu 용구

uterus chagung 자궁

utility (*usefulness*) yuyongssŏng 유용성; (*software*) yut'illit'i 유틸리티; *public utilities* kong-ik saŏp 공익 사업

utilize yuyonghage hada 유용하게 하다

utmost 1 *adj* ch'oedaehanŭi 최대한의 **2** *n*: *do one's ~* ch'oesŏnŭl tahada 최선을 다하다

utter 1 *adj* wanjŏnhan 완전한 **2** *v/t* *sound* parhada 발하다

utterly wanjŏnhi 완전히

U-turn yut'ŏn U턴; *fig* (*in policy*) wanjŏnhan t'albakkum 완전한 탈바꿈

V

vacant *building* piŏ innŭn 비어 있는; *position* kongsŏgin 공석인; *look* mŏnghan 멍한

vacate *room* piuda 비우다

vacation *n* hyuga 휴가; *be on ~* hyuga chung-ida 휴가 중이다; *go to ... on ~* hyugaro ...e kada 휴가로 ...에 가다; *take a ~* hyugarŭl katta 휴가를 갖다

vacationer hyuga yŏhaenggaek 휴가 여행객

vaccinate yebang chŏptchonghada 예방 접종하다; *be ~d against ...* yebang chŏptchong chusarŭl mat-tta ... 예방 접종 주사를 맞다

vaccination yebang chŏptchong 예방 접종

vaccine paeksshin 백신

vacuum 1 *n* PHYS chin-gong 진공; *fig (in one's life)* konghŏ 공허 2 *v/t floors* chin-gong ch'ŏngsogiro ch'ŏngsohada 진공 청소기로 청소하다

vacuum cleaner chin-gong ch'ŏngsogi 진공 청소기; **vacuum flask** chin-gonggwan 진공관; **vacuum-packed** chin-gongp'ojang-ŭi 진공포장의

vagina chil 질

vaginal chirŭi 질의

vague mohohan 모호한; *feeling* ŏryŏmp'ut'an 어렴풋한; *taste of sth, resemblance* hŭrit'an 흐릿한; *he was very ~ about it* kŭnŭn kŭ ire taehae mohohan t'aedorŭl ch'wihaet-tta 그는 그 일에 대해 모호한 태도를 취했다

vaguely *answer* mohohage 모호하게; *(slightly)* yakkan 약간

vain 1 *adj person* hŏyŏngshimi manŭn 허영심이 많은; *hope* hŏt-ttoen 헛된 2 *n: in ~* hŏt-ttoege 헛되게; *their efforts were in ~* kŭdŭrŭi noryŏgŭn hŏtssugoro torakat-tta 그들의

노력은 헛수고로 돌아갔다

valet *(person)* shijung tŭnŭn saram 시중 드는 사람

valet service *(for clothes)* se'tak sŏbissŭ 세탁 서비스; *(for cars)* sech'a sŏbissŭ 세차 서비스

valiant yonggamhan 용감한

valid *passport, document* yuhyohan 유효한; *reason, argument* t'adanghan 타당한

validate *(with official stamp)* yuhyohage hada 유효하게 하다; *(back up)* chŭngmyŏnghada 증명하다

validity t'adangsŏng 타당성

valley koltchagi 골짜기

valuable 1 *adj* kwijunghan 귀중한 2 *n: ~s* kwijungp'um 귀중품

valuation kamjŏng 감정; *at his ~* kŭga kamjŏnghan paronŭn 그가 감정한 바로는

value 1 *n* kach'i 가치; *be good ~* kŭmanhan kach'iga it-tta 그만한 가치가 있다; *get ~ for money* ton mank'ŭmŭi kach'irŭl ŏt-tta 돈 만큼의 가치를 얻다; *rise/fall in ~* kach'iga orŭda/ttŏrŏjida 가치가 오르다/떨어지다 2 *v/t s.o.'s friendship, one's freedom* sojunghi yŏgida 소중히 여기다; *I ~ your advice* tangshiŭi ch'unggorŭl sojunghi saenggak'aeyo 당신의 충고를 소중히 생각해요; *have an object ~d* ŏttŏn mulgŏnŭi kapssŭl p'yŏngkkabat-tta 어떤 물건의 값을 평가받다

valve paelbŭ 밸브

van ponggoch'a 봉고차

vandal koŭijŏgŭro konggongmurŭl pusunŭn saram 고의적으로 공공물을 부수는 사람

vandalism koŭijŏk p'agoe 고의적 파괴

vandalize koŭijŏgŭro p'agoehada 고의적으로 파괴하다

vanilla 1 *n* panilla 바닐라 **2** *adj* panillaŭi 바닐라의

vanish sarajida 사라지다

vanity chamanshim 자만심; *(of hopes)* konghŏham 공허함

vanity case hwajangp'um kabang 화장품 가방

vantage point *(on hill etc)* chŏnmang-i choŭn chijŏm 전망이 좋은 지점

vapor chŭnggi 증기

vaporize *v/t (of bomb)* chŭngbalshik'ida 증발시키다

vapor trail pihaeng-un 비행운

variable 1 *adj amount* kabyŏnŭi 가변의; *moods, weather* pyŏndŏkssŭrŏun 변덕스러운 **2** *n* MATH, COMPUT pyŏnsu 변수

variation pyŏndong 변동

varicose vein nojang chŏngmaek 노장 정맥

varied *range, diet* tayanghan 다양한

variety pyŏnhwa 변화; *(type)* tayangssŏng 다양성; *a ~ of things to do* yŏrŏ kaji hal il 여러 가지 할 일

various *(several)* yŏrŏ 여러; *(different)* kaji kakssaegŭi 가지 각색의

varnish 1 *n* nisŭ 니스 **2** *v/t* nisŭrŭl ch'irhada 니스를 칠하다

vary 1 *v/i* pakkwida 바뀌다; *it varies* ch'ŏnch'amanbyŏrijiyo 천차만별이지요 **2** *v/t* pakkuda 바꾸다

vase kkotppyŏng 꽃병

vast *desert, city* kwanghwarhan 광활한; *collection, knowledge* pangdaehan 방대한

vaudeville shyo 쇼

vault[1] *n (in roof)* tunggŭn ch'ŏnjang 둥근 천장; *~s (cellar)* chiha ch'anggo 지하 창고

vault[2] **1** SP toyak 도약 **2** *v/t beam etc* ttwiŏnŏmtta 뛰어넘다

VCR (= *video cassette recorder*) pŭi ssi al 브이 시이 알

veal songaji kogi 송아지 고기

vegan 1 *n* ch'ŏltchŏhan ch'aeshiktchuŭija 철저한 채식주의자 **2** *adj* ch'ŏltchŏhan ch'aeshigŭi 철저한 채식의

vegetable yach'ae 야채

vegetarian 1 *n* ch'aeshiktchuŭija 채식주의자 **2** *adj* ch'aeshigŭi 채식의

vehicle unban sudan 운반 수단; *(for information etc)* chŏndal sudan 전달 수단

veil 1 *n* peil 베일 **2** *v/t* karida 가리다

vein *(in leg etc)* chŏngmaek 정맥

Velcro® *n* tchiktchigi 찍찍이

velocity soktto 속도

velvet pelbet 벨벳

vending machine chadong p'anmaegi 자동 판매기

vendor LAW maegagin 매각인

veneer *(on wood)* peniŏ hap'an 베니어 합판; *(of politeness etc)* hŏshik 허식

venereal disease sŏngppyŏng 성병

venetian blind penishyŏn pŭllaidŭ 베니션 블라인드

vengeance pokssu 복수; *with a ~* kyŏngnyŏrhage 격렬하게

venison sasŭm kogi 사슴 고기

venom *(of snake)* tok 독

vent *n (for air)* t'onggi kumŏng 통기 구멍; *give ~ to feelings* t'ŏttŭrida 터뜨리다

ventilate *room* hwan-gihada 환기하다

ventilation t'onggi 통기

ventilation shaft hwan-gigaeng 환기갱

ventilator hwan-gi changch'i 환기 장치

ventriloquist pok'wasulssa 복화술사

venture 1 *n (undertaking)* mohŏm 모험; COM t'ugijŏk saŏp 투기적 사업 **2** *v/i* kwagamhi haeboda 과감히 해보다

venue *(for meeting etc)* changso 장소

veranda peranda 베란다

verb tongsa 동사

verdict LAW p'yŏnggyŏl 평결; *(opinion, judgment)* p'andan 판단

verge *n (of road)* kajangjari 가장자리; kyŏnggye 경계; *be on the ~ of ruin, collapse, tears ...* ilbo chiktchŏne itta ... 일보 직전에 있다

♦**verge on** kŏŭi kat-tta 거의 같다

verification iptchŭng 입증; *(confirmation)* hwagin 확인

verify *(check out)* chŭngmyŏnghada 증명하다

증명하다; (*confirm*) hwaginhada 확인하다

vermicelli perümich'elli 베르미첼리

vermin haech'ung 해충

vermouth perümut'üju 베르무트주

vernacular *n* ilssang-yong-ö 일상용어

versatile *person* tajaedanünghan 다재다능한; *equipment, mind* mannüng-üi 만능의

versatility (*of person*) tajaedanüng 다재다능; (*of equipment, mind*) mannüng 만능

verse (*poetry*) shi 시; (*part of poem, song*) chöl 절

versed: *be well ~ in a subject* han chujee chöng'onghada 한 주제에 정통하다

version (*of song, book*) p'an 판; *what is your ~ of what happened?* kü sakköne taehae öttök'e saenggak'aeyo? 그 사건에 대해 어떻게 생각해요?

versus SP, LAW tae 대

vertebra ch'ökch'ugol 척추골

vertebrate *n* ch'ökch'udongmul 척추동물

vertical sujigüi 수직의

vertigo hyön-gitchüng 현기증

very 1 *adv* taedanhi 대단히; *was it cold? – not ~* ch'uwössöyo? - maninün aniössöyo 추웠어요? - 많이는 아니었어요; *the ~ best* kajang choün 가장 좋은 **2** *adj* paro 바로; *in the ~ act* hyönhaengbömüro 현행범으로; *that's the ~ thing I need* chögöshi paro naega p'iryoro hanün kü mulgöniyeyo 저것이 바로 내가 필요로 하는 그 물건이예요; *the ~ thought* paro kü saenggak 바로 그 생각; *right at the ~ top / bottom* kkokttaegi / padag-üi paro kögie 꼭대기 / 바닥의 바로 거기에

vessel NAUT pae 배

vest chokki 조끼

vestige (*of previous civilization etc*) yujök 유적; (*of truth*) hünjök 흔적

vet¹ *n* (*for animals*) suüisa 수의사

vet² *v/t applicants etc* chömgömhada 점검하다

vet³ *n* MIL koch'ambyöng

veteran 1 *n* pet'erang 베테랑 **2** *adj* (*old*) orae sayonghan 오래 사용한; (*experienced*) pet'erang-üi 베테랑의

veterinarian suüisa 수의사

veto 1 *n* köbukkwön 거부권 **2** *v/t* köbuhada 거부하다

vexed (*worried*) komindoenün 고민되는; *the ~ question of ...* nollanüi yöjiga manün ... munje 논란의 여지가 많은 ... 문제

via kyöngnyuhayö 경유하여

viable *life form, company* saengjonhal su innün 생존할 수 있는; *alternative, plan* hyoryögi innün 효력이 있는

vibrate *v/i* hündüllida 흔들리다

vibration chindong 진동

vice ak 악; *the problem of ~* sahoeagüi munje 사회악의 문제

vice president (*of company*) pusajang 부사장; (*of state*) put'ongnyöng 부통령

vice squad p'unggi saböm tansokppan 풍기 사범 단속반

vice versa pandaero 반대로

vicinity künch'ö 근처; *in the ~ of* ...üi künch'öe(sö) ...의 근처에(서); (*with figures*) taeryak ... 대략 ...

vicious *dog* söngjiri koyak'an 성질이 고약한; *attack, temper, criticism* chidok'an 지독한

victim hüisaeng 희생

victimize hüisaengshikida 희생시키다

victor süngnija 승리자

victorious süngnihan 승리한

victory süngni 승리; *win a ~ over* ...e taehae süngnihada ...에 대해 승리하다

video 1 *n* pidio 비디오; *have X on ~* Xül / rül pidioe tamtta X을 / 를 비디오에 담다 **2** *v/t* pidioro ch'waryönghada 비디오로 촬영하다

video camera pidio k'amera 비디오 카메라; **video cassette** pidio k'aset'ü 비디오 카세트; **video cassete recorder** pidio k'aset'ü nok'wagi 비디오 카세트 녹화기; **video conference** TELEC hwasang hoeüi 화상 회의; **video game** chönja orak 전자 오락; **videophone** pidio chönhwa 비디오 전화; **video**

recorder pidio nok'wagi 비디오
녹화기; **video recording** pidio
nok'wa 비디오 녹화; **videotape**
pidio t'eip'ŭ 비디오 테이프
Vietnam Pet'ŭnam 베트남, Wŏlnam
월남
Vietnamese 1 *adj* Pet'ŭnamŭi
베트남의, Wŏlnamŭi 월남의 **2** *n*
Pet'ŭnamin 베트남인, Wŏlnamin
월남인; (*language*) Pet'ŭnamŏ
베트남어, Wŏlnamŏ 월남어
view 1 *n* kyŏngch'i 경치; (*of situation*)
kyŏnhae 견해; **in ~ of**…ŭl/rŭl
salp'yŏbomyŏn …을/를 살펴보면;
be on ~ (*of paintings*) chŏnshi
chung-ida 전시 중이다; **with a ~ to**
…hal moktchŏgŭro …할 목적으로
2 *v/t* events, situation paraboda
바라보다; *TV program*
shich'ŏnghada 시청하다; *house for
sale* tullŏboda 둘러보다 **3** *v/i* (*watch
TV*) shich'ŏnghada 시청하다
viewer TV shich'ŏngja 시청자
viewfinder PHOT p'aindŏ 파인더
viewpoint kwantchŏm 관점
vigor (*energy*) hwalgi 활기
vigorous person hwalbarhan 활발한;
shake kyŏksshimhan 격심한; denial
kangnyŏk'an 강력한
vile smell mopsshi yŏk-kkyŏun 몹시
역겨운; thing to do piyŏrhan 비열한
village maŭl 마을
villager maŭl saram 마을 사람
villain akttang 악당
vindicate …ŭi chinshirŭlip-
tchŭnghada …의 진실을 입증하다;
I feel ~d kyŏlbaek'aejin
nŭkkimiyeyo 결백해진 느낌이에요
vindictive poboktchŏgin 보복적인
vine p'odonamu 포도나무
vinegar shikch'o 식초
vineyard p'odowŏn 포도원
vintage 1 *n* (*of wine*) ch'oegogŭp
p'odoju 최고급 포도주 **2** *adj* (*classic*)
oraedoeŏ kabŏch'iga innŭn 오래되어
값어치가 있는
violate rules, treaty wibanhada
위반하다; sanctity of place
modok'ada 모독하다
violation (*of rules, treaty, traffic*)
wiban 위반; (*of sanctity*) modok 모독

violence (*of person, movie*)
p'ongnyŏk 폭력; (*of emotion,
reaction*) kyŏngnyŏrham 격렬함; (*of
gale*) kangnyŏrham 강렬함; **outbreak of ~** p'ongnyŏk sat'aeŭi
palssaeng 폭력 사태의 발생
violent person, movie nanp'okhan
난폭한; emotion, reaction
kyŏngnyŏrhan 격렬한; gale
kangnyŏrhan 강렬한; **have a ~
temper** sŏngkkyŏgi nanp'ok'ada
성격이 난폭하다
violently react nanp'ok'age 난폭하게;
object kangnyŏk'age 강력하게; **fall ~
in love with s.o.** nuguwa
kyŏktchŏngjŏgŭro sarange ppajida
누구와 격정적으로 사랑에 빠지다
violet (*color*) poratppit 보라빛;
(*plant*) chebikkot 제비꽃
violin paiollin 바이올린
violinist paiollin yŏnjuja 바이올린
연주자
VIP pŭi ai p'i 브이 아이 피이
viral infection pairŏsŭŭi 바이러스의
virgin (*female*) ch'ŏnyŏ 처녀; (*male*)
sutch'onggak 숫총각
virginity tongjŏng 동정; **lose one's ~**
sun-gyŏrŭl ilt'a 순결을 잃다
virile man namjadaun 남자다운; prose
kanggŏnhan 강건한
virility namsŏngdaum 남성다움;
(*sexual*) saengshik nŭngnyŏk 생식
능력
virtual sashilssang-ŭi 사실상의
virtual reality kasang hyŏnshil 가상
현실
virtually kŏŭi 거의
virtue tŏk 덕; **in ~ of** ttaemune 때문에
virtuoso MUS kŏjang 거장
virtuous kogyŏrhan 고결한
virulent disease yudok'an 유독한
virus MED, COMPUT pairŏsŭ 바이러스
visa pija 비자
visibility nune poim 눈에 보임; (*range
of vision*) shiya 시야
visible object poinŭn 보이는;
difference nune ttŭinŭn 눈에 띄는;
anger myŏngbaek'an 명백한; **not ~
to the naked eye** yuganŭronŭn
poiji annŭn 육안으로는 보이지 않는
visibly different nune ttŭige 눈에

띄게; *he was ~ moved* kŭnŭn kamdong padŭn kŏshi yŏngnyŏk'aet-tta 그는 감동 받은 것이 역력했다

vision (*eyesight*) shiryŏk 시력; REL *etc* hwanyŏng 환영

visit 1 *n* pangmun 방문; *pay a ~ to the doctor / dentist* ŭisa / ch'ikkwaŭisarŭl ch'ajagada 의사 / 치과의사를 찾아가다; *pay s.o. a ~* nugurŭl pangmunhada 누구를 방문하다 **2** *v/t* pangmunhada 방문하다

visiting card myŏngham 명함

visiting hours (*at hospital*) myŏnhoe shigan 면회 시간

visitor (*guest*) sonnim 손님; (*to museum etc*) kwallamgaek 관람객; (*tourist*) kwan-gwanggaek 관광객

visor ch'aeng 챙

visual shigaktchŏgin 시각적인

visual aid shigak kyojae 시각 교재

visual display unit yŏngsang p'yoshi changch'i 영상 표시 장치

visualize maŭm soge ttŏollida 마음 속에 떠올리다; (*foresee*) yegyŏnhada 예견하다

visually shigaktchŏguro 시각적으로

visually impaired shigaktchŏguro sonsangdoen 시각적으로 손상된

vital (*essential*) p'ilssujŏgin 필수적인; *it is ~ that* …ranŭn kŏsŭn kŭk'i chungdaehamnida …라는 것은 극히 중대합니다

vitality (*of person, city etc*) hwallyŏk 활력

vitally: *~ important* kŭk'i chungdaehan 극히 중대한

vital organs chungyo shinch'e kigwan 중요 신체 기관

vital statistics (*of woman*) mommae ch'itssu 몸매 치수

vitamin pit'amin 비타민

vitamin pill pit'amin chŏngje 비타민 정제

vivacious k'waehwarhan 쾌활한

vivacity k'waehwal 쾌활

vivid *color* kangnyŏrhan 강렬한; *memory* sŏnmyŏnghan 선명한; *imagination* saengsaenghan 생생한

V-neck Vchahyŏng mokssŏn V자형

목선

vocabulary ŏhwi 어휘

vocal mokssoriŭi 목소리의; (*expressing opinions*) sori nop'yŏ chujanghanŭn 소리 높여 주장하는

vocal cords sŏngdae 성대

vocal group MUS pok'ŏl kŭrup 보컬 그룹

vocalist MUS pok'ŏllisŭt'ŭ 보컬리스트

vocation (*calling*) samyŏng 사명; (*profession*) chigŏp 직업

vocational *guidance* chigŏpssang-ŭi 직업상의

vodka podŭk'a 보드카

vogue yuhaeng 유행; *be in ~* yuhaeng chung-ida 유행 중이다

voice 1 *n* mokssori 목소리 **2** *v/t* *opinions* p'yomyŏnghada 표명하다

voicemail ŭmsŏng up'yŏn 음성 우편

void 1 *n* pin konggan 빈 공간 **2** *adj*: *~ of* …i / ga ŏmnŭn …이 / 가 없는

volatile *personality, moods* pyŏndŏkssŭrŏun 변덕스러운

volcano hwasan 화산

volley *n* (*of shots*) iltchesagyŏk 일제사격; (*in tennis*) palli 발리

volleyball paegu 배구

volt polt'ŭ 볼트

voltage chŏnap 전압

volume (*of container*) ip-ppang yongjŏk 입방 용적; (*of work, business, liquid etc*) yang 양; (*of book*) han kwŏn 한 권; (*of radio etc*) ŭmnyang 음량

volume control ŭmnyang chojŏlgi 음량 조절기

voluntary *adj* chabaltchŏgin 자발적인

volunteer 1 *n* chawŏnja 자원자 **2** *v/i* chajinhaesŏ hada 자진해서 하다

voluptuous yuk-kkamjŏgin 육감적인

vomit 1 *n* kut'o 구토 **2** *v/i* t'ohada 토하다

♦ **vomit up** t'ohada 토하다

vomiting t'oham 토함

voracious *appetite* wangsŏnghan 왕성한

vote 1 *n* t'up'yo 투표; *have the ~* t'up'yokkwŏnŭl kajida 투표권을 가지다 **2** *v/i* POL t'up'yohada 투표하다; *~ for / against* …e ch'ansŏng / pandae t'up'yohada …에

찬성/반대 투표하다 3 *v/t*: *they ~d him President* kŭdŭrŭn kŭrŭl taet'ongnyŏng-ŭro t'up'yohaet-tta 그들은 그를 대통령으로 투표했다; *they ~d to stay behind* kŭdŭrŭn twiro mullŏsŏ itkkirŭl t'up'yohaet-tta 그들은 뒤로 물러서 있기를 투표했다

♦ **vote in** *new member* sŏnch'urhada 선출하다

♦ **vote on** *issue* p'yogyŏrhada 표결하다

♦ **vote out** (*of office*) t'up'yoe ŭihae ch'ubanghada 투표에 의해 추방하다

voter yukkwŏnja 유권자

voting t'up'yo 투표

voting booth kip'yoso 기표소

vouch for *person*, *truth* pojŭnghada 보증하다

voucher harinkkwŏn 할인권

vow 1 *n* sŏyak 서약 **2** *v/t*: *~ to do sth* muŏt hal kŏsŭl maengsehada 무엇 할 것을 맹세하다

vowel moŭm 모음

voyage (*by sea*) hanghae 항해; (*in space*) ujuyŏhaeng 우주여행

vulgar *person*, *language* chŏsok'an 저속한

vulnerable (*to attack*) konggyŏk tanghagi shwiun 공격 당하기 쉬운; (*to criticism etc*) sangch'ŏ patkki shwiun 상처 받기 쉬운

vulture tokssuri 독수리

W

wad n (of paper) tabal 다발; (of absorbent cotton etc) mungch'i 뭉치; **a ~ of $100 bills** paek talla chip'ye han tabal 백 달라 지폐 한 다발

waddle v/i twittunggörimyö köt-tta 뒤뚱거리며 걷다

wade körösö könnöda 걸어서 건너다

◆ **wade through** book, documents himdŭlge haenagada 힘들게 해나가다

wafer (cookie) weip'ö 웨이퍼; REL chebyöng 제병

waffle[1] n (to eat) wap'ŭl 와플

waffle[2] v/i pujirömnŭn marŭl hada 부질없는 말을 하다

wag 1 v/t tail, finger hŭndŭlda 흔들다 **2** v/i (of tail) hŭndŭlgörida 흔들거리다

wage[1] v/t war ch'irŭda 치르다

wage[2] n wölgŭp 월급

wage earner kajang 가장

wage freeze imgŭm tonggyöl 임금 동결

wage packet wölgŭp pongt'u 월급 봉투

wager n naegi 내기

waggle v/t hips, ears hŭndŭlda 흔들다; loose screw, tooth etc hŭndŭlgörida 흔들거리다

wagon: be on the ~ F surŭl kkŭnt'a 술을 끊다

wail 1 n (of person, baby) ulbujijŭm 울부짖음; (of siren) kusŭlp'ŭn sori 구슬픈 소리 **2** v/i (of person, baby) ulbujit-tta 울부짖다; (of siren) kusŭlp'ŭn sorirŭl naeda 구슬픈 소리를 내다

waist höri 허리

waistline hörisön 허리선

wait 1 n kidarim 기다림 **2** v/i kidarida 기다리다; **we'll ~ until he's ready** urinŭn kŭga chunbidoel ttaekkaji kidaril köshimnida 우리는 그가 준비될 때까지 기다릴 것입니다 **2** v/t

meal miruda 미루다; **~ table** shikttang kŭpssa norŭsŭl hada 식당 급사 노릇을 하다

◆ **wait for** …ŭl/rŭl kidarida …을/를 기다리다; **~ me!** narŭl kidaryö chuseyo! 나를 기다려 주세요!

◆ **wait on** person …ŭi shijung-ŭl tŭlda …의 시중을 들다

◆ **wait up** chaji ank'o kidarida 자지 않고 기다리다

waiter weit'ö 웨이터; **~!** weit'ö! 웨이터!

waiting n kidarinŭn köt 기다리는 것; **no ~ sign** kidariji mashio 기다리지 마시오

waiting list taegija myöngdan 대기자 명단

waiting room taegishil 대기실

waitress weit'ŭrisŭ 웨이트리스

waive (relinquish) p'ogihada 포기하다; (dispense with) ch'örhoehada 철회하다

wake (of ship) paega chinagan chari 배가 지나간 자리; **in the ~ of** fig …ŭl/rŭl it-ttara …을/를 잇따라; **follow in the ~ of** …ŭl/rŭl it-ttarŭda …을/를 잇따르다

◆ **wake up 1** v/i chami kkaeda 잠이 깨다 **2** v/t kkaeuda 깨우다

wake-up call moning k'ol 모닝 콜

Wales Weiljŭ 웨일즈

walk 1 n kötkki kötki 걷기; (in front of house) toroesö chipkkajiŭi kil 도로에서 집까지의 길; **it's a five-minute ~ from the station** yögesö körö o pun köriida 역에서 걸어 오 분 거리이다; **it's a long/short ~ to the office** samushilkkajinŭn körösö mön/kakkaun köriida 사무실까지는 걸어서 먼/가까운 거리이다; **go for a ~** sanch'aekhada 산책하다 **2** v/i köt-tta 걷다; (as opposed to taking the car/bus etc) körösö kada 걸어서 가다; (hike) tobo yöhaenghada 도보

여행하다; ~ *up to* tagagada 다가가다
3 *v/t dog* sanch'aekshik'ida
산책시키다; ~ *the streets* (*walk around*) kŏrirŭl toradanida 거리를
돌아다니다

♦**walk out** (*on spouse, of room etc*)
kaptchagi ttŏnada 갑자기 떠나다;
(*go on strike*) tongmaeng p'aŏp'ada
동맹 파업하다

♦**walk out on** *spouse, family*
...ŭl/rŭl pŏrida ...을/를 버리다

walker (*hiker*) pohaengja 보행자; (*for baby, old person*) pohaenggi 보행기;
be a slow/fast ~ kŏrŭmi nŭrida /
pparŭda 걸음이 느리다 /빠르다

walkie-talkie mujŏn-gi 무전기

walk-in closet taehyŏng ot-tchang
대형 옷장

walking (*as opposed to driving*)
kŏnnŭn kŏt 걷는 것; (*hiking*) tobo
yŏhaeng 도보 여행; *be within ~ distance* kŏrŏsŏ kal su innŭn
kŏriida 걸어서 갈 수 있는 거리이다

walking stick chip'ang-i 지팡이

walking tour tobo yŏhaeng 도보 여행

Walkman® wŏk'ŭmaen 워크맨;

walkout (*strike*) tongmaeng p'aŏp
동맹 파업; **walkover** (*easy win*)
nakssŭng 낙승; **walk-up** *n*
ellibeit'ŏga ŏmnŭn ap'at'ŭ
엘리베이터가 없는 아파트

wall (*of room, house*) pyŏk 벽;
(*around garden*) tam 담; *fig* (*of silence etc*) pyŏk 벽; *go to the* ~ (*of company*) p'asanhada 파산하다;
drive ... up the ~ F ...ŭl/rŭl
mich'ige hada ...을/를 미치게
하다

wallet chigap 지갑

wallop F **1** *n* (*to ball*) kangt'a 강타;
get a ~ shimhage mat-tta 심하게
맞다 **2** *v/t* ttaerida 때리다; *ball* ch'ida
치다; (*defeat*) ch'amp'aeshik'ida
참패시키다

wallpaper 1 *n* pyŏktchi 벽지 **2** *v/t*
pyŏktchirŭl parŭda 벽지를 바르다

Wall Street Wŏl Sŭt'ŭrit'ŭ (*Miguk kŭmyunggye*) 월 스트리트 (미국
금융계)

wall-to-wall carpet match'um
k'ap'et 맞춤 카펫

walnut hodu 호두

waltz *n* walch'ŭ 왈츠

wan *face* ch'angbaek'an 창백한

wander *v/i* (*roam*) ttŏdoradanida
떠돌아다니다; (*of tourist*) toradanida
돌아다니다; (*stray*) hemaeda 헤매다;
(*of attention*) sanmanhaejida
산만해지다

♦**wander around** yŏgijŏgi
toradanida 여기저기 돌아다니다

wane (*of interest, enthusiasm*)
chŏmjŏm churŏdŭlda 점점 줄어들다

wangle *v/t* F yongk'e kuhada 용케
구하다

want 1 *n*: *for* ~ *of* ...i/ga ŏpssŏsŏ
...이/가 없어서 **2** *v/t* (*desire*)
wŏnhada 원하다; (*need*) p'iryohada
필요하다; ~ *to do sth* muŏsŭl hago
shiptta 무엇을 하고 싶다; *I* ~ *to stay here* nanŭn yŏgi mŏmulgo
shipssŭmnida 나는 여기 머물고
싶습니다; *do you* ~ *to go too? - no,
I don't* ~ *to* tangshindo kago
ship'ŏyo?- aniyo, nanŭn kago
shiptchi anayo 당신도 가고 싶어요?
- 아니요, 나는 가고 싶지 않아요;
you can have whatever you ~
tangshini wŏnhanŭn kŏsŭn
muŏshidŭn kajil su issŏyo 당신이
원하는 것은 무엇이든 가질 수
있어요; *it's not what I* ~*ed* kŭgŏn
naega wŏnhaet-ttŏn kŏshi aniyeyo
그건 내가 원했던 것이 아니에요;
she ~*s you to go back* kŭnyŏnŭn
tangshini toragagil wŏnhaeyo 그녀는
당신이 돌아가길 원해요; *he* ~*s a
haircut* kŭnŭn mŏrirŭl
challayagessŏyo 그는 머리를
잘라야겠어요 **3** *v/i*: ~ *for nothing*
pujok'ami ŏptta 부족함이 없다

want ad saenghwal kwanggo 생활
광고

wanted *adj* (*by police*) chimyŏng
subaedoen 지명 수배된

wanting: *be* ~ *in* ...i/ga mojarada
...이/가 모자라다

wanton *adj* chemŏt-ttaeroin
제멋대로인

war *n* chŏnjaeng 전쟁; *be at* ~ kyojŏn
chung-ida 교전 중이다

warble *v/i* (*of bird*) chijŏgwida

지저귀다

ward (*in hospital*) pyŏngdong 병동; (*child*) p'ihugyŏnin 피후견인

♦ **ward off** *blow, attacker* p'ihada 피하다; *cold, illness* yebanghada 예방하다

warden (*of prison*) kyodosojang 교도소장

wardrobe (*for clothes*) ot-tchang 옷장; (*clothes*) otkkaji 옷가지

warehouse ch'anggo 창고

warfare chŏnjaeng 전쟁

warhead t'andu 탄두

warily choshimhaesŏ 조심해서

warm *adj welcome, smile etc* ttattŭt'an 따뜻한; *summer* tŏun 더운

♦ **warm up 1** *v/t person, room* ttattŭt'age hada 따뜻하게 하다; *soup, plates* teuda 데우다 **2** *v/i* (*of person, room*) ttattŭt'aejida 따뜻해지다; (*of soup*) tewŏjida 데워지다; (*of athlete etc*) chunbi undong-ŭl hada 준비 운동을 하다

warmhearted ch'injŏrhan 친절한

warmly *dressed, welcome, smile* ttattŭt'age 따뜻하게

warmth on-gi 온기; (*of welcome, smile*) onjŏng 온정

warn kyŏnggohada 경고하다

warning *n* kyŏnggo 경고; *without ~* kaptchagi 갑자기

warp 1 *v/t wood* hwigehada 휘게 하다; *character* pitturŏjige hada 비뚤어지게 하다 **2** *v/i* (*of wood*) hwida 휘다

warped *fig* pitturŏjin 비뚤어진

warplane kunyonggi 군용기

warrant 1 *n* yŏngtchang 영장 **2** *v/t* (*deserve, call for*) chŏngdanghwahada 정당화하다

warranty pojŭng 보증; *be under ~* pojŭng kigan chung-ida 보증 기간 중이다

warrior chŏnsa 전사

warship kunham 군함

wart samagwi 사마귀

wartime chŏnshi 전시

wary *look, response* shinjunghan 신중한; *keep a ~ eye on* ...ŭl/rŭl seshimhage poda ...을/를 세심하게 보다; *be ~ of* ...ŭl/rŭl ŭishimhada

...ŭl/rŭl ŭishimhada

wash 1 *n: have a ~* sshit-tta 씻다; *that jacket / shirt needs a ~* chŏ chaek'isŭn / shyŏch'ŭnŭn pparaya handa 저 재킷은 / 셔츠는 빨아야 한다 **2** *v/t clothes* ppalda 빨다; *dishes* taktta 닦다; *one's hands* sshit-tta 씻다 **3** *v/i* sshit-tta 씻다

♦ **wash up** (*wash one's hands and face*) sshit-tta 씻다

washable ppal su innŭn 빨 수 있는

washbasin, washbowl semyŏn-gi 세면기

washcloth sugŏn 수건

washed out kiuni ŏmnŭn 기운이 없는

washer (*for faucet etc*) washyŏ 와셔; → **washing machine**

washing ppallae 빨래; *do the ~* ppallaerŭl hada 빨래를 하다

washing machine set'ak-kki 세탁기

Washington (*city*) Wŏshingt'ŏn 워싱턴

washroom hwajangshil 화장실

wasp (*insect*) malbŏl 말벌

waste 1 *n* nangbi 낭비; (*from industrial process*) p'yegimul 폐기물; *it's a ~ of time / money* kŭgŏsŭn shiganŭi / tonŭi nangbiyeyo 그것은 시간의 / 돈의 낭비예요 **2** *adj* ssŭlmoŏmnŭn 쓸모없는 **3** *v/t* nangbihada 낭비하다

♦ **waste away** yawida 야위다

wasteful nangbiga shimhan 낭비가 심한

wasteland hwangp'ye chiyŏk 황폐 지역; **wastepaper** hyuji 휴지; **wastepaper basket** hyujit'ong 휴지통; **waste pipe** (*for water*) paesugwan 배수관; **waste product** p'yegimul 폐기물

watch 1 *n* (*timepiece*) shigye 시계; *keep ~* mangboda 망보다 **2** *v/t movie, TV* poda 보다; (*observe*) chal poda 잘 보다; (*spy on*) kamshihada 감시하다; (*look after*) tolbwajuda 돌봐주다 **3** *v/i* chik'yŏboda 지켜보다

♦ **watch for**: *he is watching for his father* kŭnŭn abŏjiga onŭnji chik'yŏbogo it-tta 그는 아버지가 오는지 지켜보고 있다

♦**watch out** choshimhada 조심하다;
~! choshimhae! 조심해!

♦**watch out for** (*be careful of*)
...ŭl/rŭl choshimhada ...을/를
조심하다

watchful chu-ŭigip'ŭn 주의깊은

watchmaker shigye chejoin 시계
제조인

water 1 *n* mul 물; **~s** NAUT yŏnghae
영해 **2** *v/t plant* murŭl chuda 물을
주다 **3** *v/i* (*of eyes*) nunmuri nada
눈물이 나다; *my mouth is ~ing*
ch'imŭl hŭllida 침을 흘리다

♦**water down** *drink* murŭl t'ada 물을
타다

watercolor (*paint*) such'aehwa
mulkkam 수채화 물감; (*painting*)
such'aehwa 수채화; **watercress**
mulnaeng-i 물냉이; **waterfall**
p'okp'o 폭포

watering can mulppurigae 물뿌리개

watering hole (*hum*) sultchip 술집

water level suwi 수위; **water lily**
suryŏn 수련; **waterline** (*at shore*)
hae-ansŏn 해안선; (*of ship*)
holssusŏn 흘수선; **waterlogged**
mure chamgin 물에 잠긴; **water-
mark** chip'yeŭi naebich'inŭn munŭi
지폐의 내비치는 무늬; **watermelon**
subak 수박; **water polo** sugu 수구;
waterproof *adj* pangsudoenŭn
방수되는; **watershed** punsuryŏng
분수령; **waterside** *n* mulka 물가; *at
the* **~** mulkkae(sŏ) 물가에(서); **waterskiing** susangsŭk'i 수상스키;
watertight *compartment* pangsuŭi
방수의; **waterway** suro 수로; **wa-
terwings** suyŏng yŏnsŭmnyong
t'yubŭ 수영 연습용 튜브

watery mulgŭn 묽은

watt wat'ŭ 와트

wave¹ *n* (*in sea*) p'ado 파도

wave² **1** *n* (*of hand*) sonŭl hŭndŭnŭn
shinho 손을 흔드는 신호 **2** *v/i* (*with
hand*) sonŭl hŭndŭlda 손을 흔들다;
(*of flag*) p'ŏllŏgida 펄럭이다; **~ to
s.o.** nuguege sonŭl hŭndŭlda
누구에게 손을 흔들다 **3** *v/t flag etc*
hŭndŭlda 흔들다

wavelength RAD p'ajang 파장; *be on
the same* **~** *fig* chal t'onghada 잘

통하다

waver chujŏhada 주저하다

wavy *hair, line* kupssŭlgŏrinŭn
굽슬거리는

wax *n* (*for floor, furniture*) wakssŭ
왁스; (*in ear*) kwiji 귀지

way 1 *n* (*method*) pangbŏp 방법; (*~ of
doing sth*) pangshik 방식; (*route*) kil
길; *this* **~** irŏk'e 이렇게; (*in this direction*) itchoguro
이쪽으로; *by the* **~** (*incidentally*)
kŭrŏnde 그런데; *by* **~** *of* (*via*)
...ŭl/rŭl kŏch'yŏsŏ ...을/를 거쳐서;
(*in the form of*) ...ŭl/rŭl ha semŭro
...을/를 할 셈으로; *in a* **~** (*in certain
respects*) ŏttŏn myŏnesŏnŭn 어떤
면에서는; *be under* **~** chinhaeng
chung-ida 진행 중이다; *give* **~** MOT
yangbohada 양보하다; (*collapse*)
munŏjida 무너지다; *give* **~** *to* (*be
replaced by*) ...(ŭ)ro pakkwida
...(으)로 바뀌다; *have one's* (*own*)
~ chagi maŭmdaero hada 자기
마음대로 하다; *OK, we'll do it your*
~ choayo, tangshin pangshiguro
hagessŏyo 좋아요, 당신 방식으로
하겠어요; *lead the* **~** (*go first*) apssŏ
kada 앞서 가다; (*be the leader,
pioneer*) sŏlssŏnhada 솔선하다; *lose
one's* **~** kirŭl ilt'a 길을 잃다; *make*
~ kirŭl pik'yŏjuda 길을 비켜주다; *be
in the* **~** panghaega toeda 방해가
되다; *it's on the* **~** *to the station*
yŏguro kanŭn kire issŏyo 역으로
가는 길에 있어요; *I was on my* **~** *to
the station* nanŭn yŏguro kanŭn
chung-iŏssŏyo 나는 역으로 가는
중이었어요; *no* **~!** ŏrimdo ŏpssŏ!
어림도 없어!; *there's no* **~** *he can
do it* kŭnŭn kŭgosŭl kyŏlk'o hal su
ŏpssŏyo 그는 그것을 결코 할 수
없어요 **2** *adv* F (*far*) nŏmu 너무; *it's*
~ *too soon to decide*
kyŏltchŏnghagienŭn nŏmu illŏyo
결정하기에는 너무 일러요; *they are*
~ *behind with their work* kŭdŭrŭn
iri nŏmu millyŏ issŏyo 그들은 일이
너무 밀려 있어요

way back yejŏne 예전에; **way in**
ippku 입구; **way of life** saenghwal
pangshik 생활 방식; **way out**

ch'ulgu 출구; *fig (from situation)* haegyŏlch'aek 해결책

we uri 우리; *~ are American* urinŭn Miguk saramieyo 우리는 미국 사람이에요

weak yak'an 약한; *tea, coffee* yŏnhan 연한

weaken 1 *v/t* yak'agehada 약하게 하다 **2** *v/i* yak'aejida 약해지다

weakling yaktcha 약자

weakness yaktchŏm 약점; *have a ~ for (liking)* …ege yak'ada …에게 약하다

wealth pu 부; *a ~ of* p'ungbuhan 풍부한

wealthy puyuhan 부유한

wean *v/t* chŏjŭl tteda 젖을 떼다

weapon mugi 무기

wear 1 *n*: ~ *(and tear)* tarŭm 닳음; *clothes for everyday ~ / evening ~* ilssangbok / p'at'ibok 일상복 / 파티복 **2** *v/t (have on)* iptta 입다; *(damage)* talk'e hada 닳게 하다 **3** *v/i (of carpet, fabric:* ~ *out)* tarhajida 닳아지다; *(last)* kyŏndida 견디다

♦ **wear away 1** *v/i* tarhajida 닳아지다 **2** *v/t* talk'e hada 닳게 하다

♦ **wear off** *(of effect, feeling)* chŏmjŏm ŏpssŏjida 점점 없어지다

♦ **wear out 1** *v/t (tire)* chich'ige hada 지치게 하다; *shoes* tara ttŏrŏjige hada 닳아 떨어지게 하다 **2** *v/i (of shoes, carpet)* tara ttŏrŏjida 닳아 떨어지다

wearily chich'yŏsŏ 지쳐서

wearing *(tiring)* chich'ige hanŭn 지치게 하는

weary chich'in 지친

weasel choktchebi 족제비

weather 1 *n* nalsshi 날씨; *be feeling under the ~* momi tchibudŭdŭhada 몸이 찌부드드하다 **2** *v/t crisis* ttulk'o nagada 뚫고 나가다

weather-beaten pibarame shidallin 비바람에 시달린; **weather chart** ilgido 일기도; **weather forecast** ilgi yebo 일기 예보; **weatherman** kisang yebowŏn 기상 예보원

weave 1 *v/t* tchada 짜다 **2** *v/i (move)* nubida 누비다

web tchasŏ mandŭn kŏt 짜서 만든 것;

spider's ~ kŏmijip 거미집; *the Web* Wep 웹

webbed feet mulgalk'wiga tallin pal 물갈퀴가 달린 발

web browser wep pŭraujŏ 웹 브라우저; **web page** wep p'eiji 웹 페이지; **website** wep sa-it'ŭ 웹 사이트

wedding kyŏrhonshik 결혼식

wedding anniversary kyŏrhon kinyŏmil 결혼 기념일; **wedding cake** weding k'eik'ŭ 웨딩 케이크; **wedding day** kyŏrhonshingnal 결혼식날; **wedding dress** weding tŭresŭ 웨딩 드레스; **wedding hall** yeshiktchang 예식장; **wedding ring** kyŏrhon panji 결혼 반지

wedge *n (to hold sth in place)* sswaegi 쐐기; *(of cheese etc)* sswaegi moyang 쐐기 모양

Wednesday suyoil 수요일

weed 1 *n* chapch'o 잡초 **2** *v/t* chapch'orŭl ppoptta 잡초를 뽑다

♦ **weed out** ch'uryŏnaeda 추려내다

weedkiller chech'oje 제초제

week chu 주; *a ~ tomorrow* p'aril twie 팔일 뒤에

weekday p'yŏng-il 평일

weekend chumal 주말; *on the ~* chumare 주말에

weekly 1 *adj* maeju-ŭi 매주의; ~ *payment* chugŭp 주급 **2** *n (magazine)* chugan 주간 **3** *adv* maejumada 매주마다

weep ulda 울다

weeping willow suyang pŏdŭl 수양 버들

weigh 1 *v/t* mugerŭl talda 무게를 달다; ~ *anchor* tach'ŭl ollida 닻을 올리다 **2** *v/i* mugega nagada 무게가 나가다

♦ **weigh down**: *be weighed down with* …ŭi mugero nullyŏjida …의 무게로 눌려지다; *with worries* kibuni karaantta 기분이 가라앉다

♦ **weigh up** *(assess)* p'yŏngkkahada 평가하다

weight *(of person, object)* muge 무게

weightless mujungnyŏgŭi 무중력의

weightlessness mujungnyŏk 무중력

weightlifter yŏktto sŏnsu 역도 선수

weightlifting yŏktto 역도
weir tuk 둑
weird isanghan 이상한
weirdo n F isanghan saram 이상한
사람
welcome 1 adj hwanyŏng pannŭn
환영 받는; **you're ~** ch'ŏnmaneyo
천만에요; **you're ~ to try some**
ŏlmadŭnji haseyo 얼마든지 하세요
2 n (for guests etc) hwanyŏng 환영;
(to news, proposal) kikkŏi
padadŭrim 기꺼이 받아들임 **3** v/t
guests etc hwanyŏnghada 환영하다;
decision etc kikkŏi padadŭrida
기꺼이 받아들이다
weld v/t yongjŏp'ada 용접하다
welder yongjŏpkkong 용접공
welfare poktchi 복지; (financial
assistance) saenghwal pojo 생활
보조; **be on ~** saenghwal pojorŭl
pat-tta 생활 보조를 받다
welfare check saenghwal pojogŭm
생활 보조금; **welfare state** poktchi
kuk-kka 복지 국가; **welfare work**
poktchi saŏp 복지 사업; **welfare
worker** poktchi saŏpkka 복지
사업가
well[1] n (for water) umul 우물; oil ~
yujŏn 유전
well[2] **1** adv chal 잘; **as ~** (too) ...do
...도; **as ~ as** (in addition to)
...ppunmananira ...do ...뿐만아니라
...도; **he came as ~** kŭdo wat-tta
그도 왔다; **he has a motorbike as
~ as a car** kŭnŭn ch'appunman
anira ot'obaido kajigo it-tta 그는
차뿐만 아니라 오토바이도 가지고
있다; **I can't swim as ~ as you**
nanŭn tangshinmank'ŭm suyŏng-ŭl
chal hal su ŏpssŏyo 나는 당신만큼
수영을 잘 할 수 없어요; **it's just as
~ you told me** tangshini naege
yaegihaessŏ mach'im chal toe-
ŏssŭmnida 당신이 내게 얘기해서
마침 잘 되었습니다; **very ~**
(acknowledging an order) chal
algessŭmnida 잘 알겠습니다;
(reluctant agreement) ŏtchaet-ttŭn
chossŭmnida 어쨋든 좋습니다; ~, ~!
(surprise) irŏn, irŏn! 이런, 이런!; ~
... (uncertainty, thinking) kŭlsse ...

글쎄 ... **2** adj: **be ~** chal it-tta 잘
있다; **feel ~** momi chot'a 몸이 좋다;
get ~ soon! ppalli na-ŭseyo! 빨리
나으세요!
well-balanced person, meal, diet
kyunhyŏng chap'in 균형 잡힌; **well-
behaved** p'umhaeng-i tanjŏnghan
품행이 단정한; **well-being** pongni
복리; (feeling) haengbok 행복; **well-
done** meat chal igŭn 잘 익은; **well-
dressed** chŏun osŭl ibŭn 좋은 옷을
입은; **well-earned** che himŭro ŏdŭn
제 힘으로 얻은; **well-heeled**
puyuhan 부유한; **well-known** chal
allyŏjin 잘 알려진; **well-made** chal
mandŭrŏjin 잘 만들어진; **well-
mannered** yeŭi parŭn 예의 바른;
well-meaning sŏnŭiŭi 선의의; **well-
off** puyuhan 부유한; **well-read**
paksshik'an 박식한; **well-timed**
ttaerŭl chal match'un 때를 잘 맞춘;
well-to-do puyuhan 부유한; **well-
worn** tarappajin 닳아빠진
west 1 n sŏtchok 서쪽; (western part
of a country) sŏbu 서부; **the West**
(western nations) Sŏyang 서양 **2** adj
sŏ 서; **~ wind** sŏp'ung 서풍 **3** adv
sŏtchoguro 서쪽으로; **~ of** ...ŭi
sŏtchoge ...의 서쪽에
West Coast (of USA) (Migugŭi)
T'aep'yŏng-yang Yŏnan (미국의)
태평양 연안
westerly direction sŏtchogŭi 서쪽의;
wind sŏtchogesŏ punŭn 서쪽에서
부는
western 1 adj sŏtchogŭi 서쪽의;
Western Sŏyang-ŭi 서양의 **2** n
(movie) sŏbugŭk 서부극
Westerner Sŏyang saram 서양 사람
westernized sŏyanghwadoen
서양화된
westward sŏtchoguro 서쪽으로
wet adj chŏjŭn 젖은; (rainy) piga
onŭn 비가 오는; **"~ paint"** ch'il chuŭi 칠 주의; **be ~ through** hamppak
chŏt-tta 함빡 젖다
whack F **1** n (blow) ch'ŏlssŏk ttaerim
철썩 때림 **2** v/t ch'ŏlssŏk ttaerida
철썩 때리다
whale korae 고래
whaling koraejabi 고래잡이

wharf *n* pudu 부두

what 1 *pron* ◊ muŏt 무엇; **~ is that?** chŏgŏsŭn muŏshimnikka? 저것은 무엇입니까?; **~ is it?** (*what do you want?*) wae? 왜?; (*what did you say?*) mwŏrago? 뭐라고?; (*astonishment*) musŭn soriya? 무슨 소리야?; **~ about some dinner?** chŏnyŏgŭl mŏngnŭn kŏshi ŏttŏk'essŏyo? 저녁을 먹는 것이 어떻겠어요?; **~ about heading home?** chiburo kanŭn kŏshi ŏttŏk'essŏyo? 집으로 가는 것이 어떻겠어요?; **~ for?** (*why?*) wae? 왜?; **so ~?** kŭraesŏ? 그래서? ◊ (*relative*) ...hanŭn kŏt ...하는 것; **that's not ~ I meant** kŭgŏn naega ŭimihanŭn kŏshi aniyeyo 그건 내가 의미하는 것이 아니에요; **that's ~ I like** kŭgŏshi chega choahanŭn kŏshiyeyo 그것이 제가 좋아하는 것이에요 **2** *adj* ◊ (*what kind of*) ŏttŏn 어떤; **~ color is the car?** kŭ ch'anŭn ŏttŏn saek-kkarimnikka? 그 차는 어떤 색깔입니까? ◊ (*which*) ŏnŭ 어느; **~ university are you at?** tangshinŭn ŏnŭ taehage tanigo issumnikka? 당신은 어느 대학에 다니고 있습니까? **3** *adv:* **~ a lovely day!** ŏlmana nalsshiga choŭn narinjiyŏ! 얼마나 날씨가 좋은 날인지요!

whatever 1 *pron* ...hanŭn kŏsŭn muŏshidŭnji ...하는 것은 무엇이든지; (*regardless of*) ...i/ga ...hal chirado ...이/가 ...할 지라도; **~ people say, I believe her** saramdŭri musŭn marŭl hal chirado, nanŭn kŭnyŏrŭl minnŭnda 사람들이 무슨 말을 할 지라도, 나는 그녀를 믿는다 **2** *adj* ŏttŏn ...(i)rado 어떤 ...(이)라도; **you have no reason ~ to worry** tangshinŭn hanado kŏktchŏnghal iyuga ŏpssŏyo 당신은 하나도 걱정할 이유가 없어요

wheat mil 밀

wheedle: **~ X out of Y** Yŭl/rŭl kkoshyŏsŏ Xŭl/rŭl ŏdŏnaeda Y을/를 꼬셔서 X을/를 얻어내다

wheel 1 *n* pak'wi 바퀴; (*steering ~*) haendŭl 핸들 **2** *v/t bicycle* mirŏ

umjigida 밀어 움직이다 **3** *v/i* (*of birds*) pingbing tolda 빙빙 돌다

♦ **wheel around** panghyang-ŭl hwik pakkuda 방향을 휙 바꾸다

wheelbarrow illyunch'a 일륜차;
wheelchair hwilch'eŏ 휠체어;
wheel clamp *n* ch'aryang chomsoe 차량 죔쇠

wheeze *v/i* sshigŭn-gŏrida 씨근거리다

when 1 *adv* ŏnje 언제; **~ is the baby due?** ainŭn ŏnje t'aeŏnal yejŏng-ingayo? 아이는 언제 태어날 예정인가요? **2** *conj* ...hal ttae ...할 때; **~ I was a child** naega ŏryŏssŭl ttae 내가 어렸을 때

whenever (*each time*) ...hal ttaemada ...할 때마다; (*regardless of when*) ...hal ttaenŭn ŏnjedŭnji ...할 때는 언제든지; **call me ~ you like** hago ship'ŭl ttaenŭn ŏnjedŭnji naege chŏnhwahaseyo 하고 싶을 때는 언제든지 내게 전화하세요

where 1 *adv* ŏdi 어디; **~ were you born?** kohyang-i ŏdiimnikka? 고향이 어디입니까?; **~ from?** ŏdisŏ wassŭmnikka? 어디에서 왔습니까?; **~ to?** ŏdiro kamnikka? 어디로 갑니까? **2** *conj* ...hanŭn kot ...하는 곳; **this is ~ I used to live** yŏgiga naega sarat-ttŏn koshimnida 여기가 내가 살았던 곳입니다

whereabouts *adv* ŏditchŭme(sŏ) 어디쯤에(서)

wherever 1 *conj* (*anywhere*) ...hanŭn kosŭn ŏdidŭnji ...하는 곳은 어디든지; (*regardless of where*) ŏdirŭl ...(ha)dŏrado 어디를 ...(하)더라도; **~ you go, don't forget it** ŏdirŭl kadŏrado kŭgŏsŭl ittchi maseyo 어디를 가더라도 그것을 잊지 마세요 **2** *adv* taech'e ŏdi-e 대체 어디에

whet appetite shigyogŭl totkkunŭn kŏt 식욕을 돋구는 것

whether ...inji ...인지; **he asked ~ I knew you** kŭnŭn naega tangshinŭl anŭnji murŏbwassŏyo 그는 내가 당신을 아는지 물어봤어요; **~ or not** ...inji aninji ...인지 아닌지; **I don't know ~ to tell him or not** kŭege marŭl haeya haltchi anhaeya haltchi

morŭgessŏyo 그에게 말을 해야 할지 안해야 할지 모르겠어요; **~ ... or ...** ...inji ...inji ...인지 ...인지; *I don't know* **~** *he is a student or a teacher* kŭga hakssaenginji sŏnsaengniminji morŭgessŏyo 그가 학생인지 선생님인지 모르겠어요; **~ ... or not** (*regardless*) ...inji anidŭnji kane ...인지 아니든지 간에
which 1 *adj* ŏnŭ 어느; **~ one is yours?** ŏnŭ kŏshi tangshin kŏshimnikka? 어느 것이 당신 것입니까? **2** *pron* (*interrogative*) ŏnŭ kŏt ŏnŭs 어느 것 어느스 ...하는; *the subject* **~** *I'm studying* naega kongbuhanŭn kwamok 내가 공부하는 과목; *take one, it doesn't matter* **~** ŏnŭ kŏsŭl kajyŏdo sanggwanŏpssŭmnida 어느 것을 가져도 상관없습니다
whichever 1 *adj* ŏnŭ ...irado 어느 ...이라도 **2** *pron* ...hanŭn kŏsŭn ŏnŭ kŏshidŭn ...하는 것은 어느 것이든
whiff (*smell*) huk p'unggim 훅 풍김
while 1 *conj* ...hanŭn tong-an ...하는 동안; (*although*) ...hal chirado ...할 지라도 **2** *n*: *a long* **~** orae 오래; *for a* **~** chamshi tong-an 잠시 동안; *I'll wait a* **~** *longer* nanŭn chomdŏ kidarigessŭmnida 나는 좀더 기다리겠습니다
♦ **while away** pindungbindung chinaeda 빈둥빈둥 지내다
whim pyŏndŏk 변덕; *on a* **~** kŭnyang kaptchagi 그냥 갑자기
whimper *v/i* hultchŏk-kkŏrida 훌쩍거리다; (*of animal*) kkingkkinggŏrida 낑낑거리다
whine *v/i* (*of dog*) kkingkking-gŏrida 낑낑거리다; F (*complain*) ch'ingŏlgŏrida 칭얼거리다
whip 1 *n* ch'aetchiktchil 채찍질 **2** *v/t* (*beat*) ch'aetchiktchirhada 채찍질하다; *cream* hwijŏŏ kŏp'umŭl naeda 휘저어 거품을 내다; F (*defeat*) kyŏkp'ahada 격파하다
♦ **whip out** F (*take out*) hwik kkŭjibŏnaeda 휙 끄집어내다
♦ **whip up** (*arouse*) tobalshik'ida 도발시키다
whipped cream saeng k'ŭrim 생 크림

whipping (*beating*) ch'aektchiktchil 채찍질; F (*defeat*) p'aebae 패배
whirl 1 *n*: *my mind is in a* **~** nae maŭmi kalp'irŭl mot-tchamnŭnda 내 마음이 갈피를 못잡는다 **2** *v/i* p'ing tolda 핑 돌다
whirlpool (*in river*) soyongdori 소용돌이; (*for relaxation*) chak'uji 자쿠지
whirlwind hoe-oribaram 회오리바람
whir(r) *v/i* wingwing tolda 윙윙 돌다
whisk 1 *n* (*kitchen utensil*) hwijŏnnŭn kigu 휘젓는 기구 **2** *v/t eggs* hwijŏt-tta 휘젓다
♦ **whisk away** ssak kajyŏgabŏrida 싹 가져가버리다
whiskers (*of man*) kurenarut 구레나룻; (*of animal*) suyŏm 수염
whiskey wisŭk'i 위스키
whisper 1 *n* sokssagim 속삭임 **2** *v/t & v/i* sokssagida 속삭이다
whistle 1 *n* (*sound*) hwip'aram 휘파람; (*device*) hogak 호각 **2** *v/i* hwip'aramŭl pulda 휘파람을 불다; (*of wind*) sshing pulda 씽 불다 **3** *v/t* hwip'aramŭro noraehada 휘파람으로 노래하다
white 1 *n* (*color*) hayan saek 하얀 색; (*of egg*) hŭinja 흰자; (*person*) paegin 백인 **2** *adj* hayan 하얀; *person* paegin 백인
white-collar worker samujik sawŏn 사무직 사원; **White House** Paegak-kkwan 백악관; **white lie** agŭi-ŏmnŭn kŏjinmal 악의없는 거짓말; **white meat** hŭin kogi 흰 고기; **whiteout** (*for text*) sujŏng-aek 수정액; **whitewash 1** *n* paekssaek toryo 백색 도료; *fig* tullŏdaenŭn kŏjinmal 둘러대는 거짓말 **2** *v/t* paekssaek toryorŭl ch'irhada 백색 도료를 칠하다; *fig* hodohada 호도하다; **white wine** paekp'odoju 백포도주
whittle *wood* kkakka tadŭmtta 깎아 다듬다
♦ **whittle down** churida 줄이다
whizz *n*: *be a* **~** *at* F koengjanghi chal hada 굉장히 잘 하다
♦ **whizz by** (*of time, car*) sshing chinagada 씽 지나가다

크림

whizzkid F shindong 신동
who (*interrogative*) nugu 누구; (*relative*) ...hanǔn ...하는; ~ *is that over there?* chǒ sarami nuguimnikka? 저 사람이 누구입니까?; *the woman ~ saved the boy* kǔsonyǒnǔl kuhan yǒja 그소년을 구한 여자
whodun(n)it ch'urimul 추리물
whoever ...hanǔn nugudǔnji ...하는 누구든지
whole 1 *adj* modǔn 모든; *a ~ chicken* t'ongdak han mari 통닭 한 마리; *two ~ hours* kkobak tu shigan 꼬박 두 시간; *the ~ town / country* maǔl / kuk-kka chǒnch'e 마을 / 국가 전체; *it's a ~ lot easier / better* kǔgosǔn hwolsshin shwiptta / nat-tta 그것은 훨씬 쉽다 / 낫다 **2** *n* chǒnch'e 전체; *the ~ of the United States* Miguk chǒnch'e 미국 전체; *on the ~* taech'ero 대체로
whole food chayǒn shikp'um 자연 식품; **whole-hearted** chinshimǔi 진심의; **wholemeal bread** t'ongmilppang 통밀빵; **wholesale 1** *adj* tomae-ǔi 도매의; *fig* taeryang-ǔi 대량의 **2** *adv* tomaekkapssǔro 도매값으로; **wholesaler** tomae-ǒptcha 도매업자; **wholesome** (*healthy*) kǒn-gang-e choǔn 건강에 좋은; *attitude etc* kǒnjǒnhan 건전한
wholly wanjǒnhi 완전히
wholly owned subsidiary chahoesa 자회사
whom *fml* nugurǔl 누구를
whooping cough paegirhae 백일해
whore *n* ch'angnyǒ 창녀
whose 1 *pron* (*interrogative*) nuguǔi kǒt 누구의 것; (*relative*) ...hanǔn ...하는; ~ *is this?* igǒsǔn nuguǔi kǒshimnikka? 이것은 누구의 것입니까?; *a country ~ economy is booming* kyǒngje-ǔi pumi irǒnago innǔn nara 경제의 붐이 일어나고 있는 나라 **2** *adj* nuguǔi 누구의; ~ *bike is that?* chǒgǒsǔn nuguǔi chajǒn-gǒ-imnikka? 저것은 누구의 자전거입니까?
why (*interrogative*) wae 왜; (*relative*) wae ...hanǔnji 왜 ...하는지; *that's ~*

kǔraesǒ-ida 그래서이다; ~ *not?* wae andwae? 왜 안돼?; (*agreeing to suggestion*) kǔrojyo 그러죠; *I don't know ~ he left* kǔga wae ttǒnannǔnji mollayo 그가 왜 떠났는지 몰라요
wick shimji 심지
wicked saak'an 사악한
wicker pǒdǔlgaji 버들가지
wicker chair pǒdǔllo mandǔn ǔija 버들로 만든 의자
wicket (*in station, bank etc*) ch'anggu 창구
wide *adj* nǒlbǔn 넓은; *experience* p'ong-nǒlbǔn 폭넓은; *range* kwangbǒmwihan 광범위한; *be 12 foot ~* p'ogi shibip'it'ǔ-ida 폭이 12피트이다
wide-awake wanjǒnhi chami kkaen 완전히 잠이 깬
widely *used, known* nǒlkke 넓게
widen 1 *v/t* nǒlp'ida 넓히다 **2** *v/i* nǒlbǒjida 넓어지다
wide-open *window* nǒlkke yǒllin 넓게 열린; *eyes* k'ǔge ttǔn 크게 뜬
widespread manyǒndoen 만연된
widow kwabu 과부
widower horabi 홀아비
width p'ok 폭
wield *weapon, power* hwidurǔda 휘두르다
wife anae 아내
wig kabal 가발
wiggle *v/t hips, loose screw* hǔndǔlda 흔들다
wild 1 *adj animal, flowers* yasaeng 야생; *teenager, party* kǒch'in 거친; *scheme* mich'in tǔt'an 미친 듯한; *applause* yǒlgwangtchǒgin 열광적인; *be ~ about* (*enthusiastic*) ...e yǒltchunghada ...에 열중하다; *go ~* yǒlgwanghada 열광하다; (*become angry*) mopsshi hǔngbunhada 몹시 흥분하다; *run ~* (*of children*) chemot-ttaero nolda 제멋대로 놀다; (*of plants*) magu charada 마구 자라다 **2** *n: the ~s* migaeji 미개지
wildcard character COMPUT amugaemunja 아무개문자
wilderness hwangmuji 황무지
wildfire: spread like ~ sapsshigane

p'ŏjida 삼시간에 퍼지다; **wildgoose
chase** ttŭn-gurŭm chapkki 뜬구름
잡기; **wildlife** yasaeng tongmul 야생
동물

will[1] *n* LAW yusŏ 유서

will[2] *n* (*willpower*) ŭiji 의지

will[3]: *I ~ let you know tomorrow*
naeil allyŏdŭrigessŭmnida 내일
알려드리겠습니다; *~ you be there?*
kŏgi issŭl kkŏyeyo? 거기 있을
꺼예요?; *I won't be back until late*
nanŭn nŭtkkekkaji toraoji anŭl
kkŏyeyo 나는 늦게까지 돌아오지
않을 꺼예요; *you ~ call me, won't
you?* chege chŏnhwahashilkkŏjyo?
제게 전화하실꺼죠?; *I'll pay for this
- no you won't* chega
naegessŭmnida - ani, kŭrŏji maseyo
제가 내겠습니다 - 아니, 그러지
마세요; *the car won't start* ch'a-e
shidong-i an-gŏllyŏ 차에 시동이
안걸려; *~ you tell her that ...?*
tangshini kŭnyŏege ...rago marhae
chushigessŭmnikka? 당신이
그녀에게 ...라고 말해 주시겠습니까?;
~ you have some more tea?
ch'arŭl tŏ tŭshigessŏyo? 차를 더
드시겠어요?; *~ you stop that!*
kŭmandwŏ! 그만둬!

willfull *person* kojibi sen 고집이 센;
action ilburŏ-ŭi 일부러의

willing: *be ~ to do ...* kikkŏi ...hada
기꺼이 ...하다

willingly kikkŏi 기꺼이

willingness kikkŏi hanŭn maŭm
기꺼이 하는 마음

willow pŏdŭnamu 버드나무

willpower ŭijiryŏk 의지력

willy-nilly (*at random*) mujagwiro
무작위로

wilt (*of plant*) shidŭlda 시들다

wily kkoega manŭn 꾀가 많은

wimp F mugiryŏk'an saram 무기력한
사람

win 1 *n* sŭng-ni 승리 **2** *v/t* igida 이기다;
lottery tangch'ŏmdoeda 당첨되다;
money ttada 따다; *~ a prize*
susanghada 수상하다 **3** *v/i* igida
이기다

wince *v/i* ŏlgurŭl tchip'urida 얼굴을
찌푸리다

winch *n* kwŏnyanggi 권양기

wind[1] **1** *n* param 바람; (*flatulence*)
hŏtppae purŭm 헛배 부름; *get ~ of
...* ...ŭi somunŭl tŭt-tta ...의 소문을
듣다 **2** *v/t*: *be ~ed* hŏlttŏgida
헐떡이다

wind[2] **1** *v/i* kubijida 굽이지다 **2** *v/t*
kamtta 감다

♦ **wind down 1** *v/i* (*of party etc*)
sŏsŏhi kkŭnnada 서서히 끝나다 **2** *v/t*
car window naerida 내리다; *business*
p'ye-ŏp'aryŏgo hada 폐업하려고
하다

♦ **wind up 1** *v/t clock* kamtta 감다; *car
window* ollida 올리다; *speech,
presentation* kkŭch'ŭl maet-tta 끝을
맺다; *affairs* kyŏlmarŭl chit-tta
결말을 짓다; *company* p'ye-ŏp'ada
폐업하다 **2** *v/i* (*finish*) kkŭnnada
끝나다; *~ in the hospital* kyŏlguk
pyŏng-wŏn shinserŭl chida 결국
병원 신세를 지다

windfall hoengjae 횡재

winding *adj* kkubulkkuburhan
꾸불꾸불한

wind instrument kwanak-kki 관악기

windmill p'ungch'a 풍차

window ch'angmun 창문; COMPUT
windou 윈도우; *in the ~* (*of store*)
chinyŏldoen 진열된

windowpane ch'ang-yuri 창유리;
window-shop: *go ~ping*
aishyop'inghada 아이쇼핑하다; **windowsill** ch'angt'ŏk 창턱

windpipe sumt'ong 숨통; **windshield**
(chadongch'a) amnyuri (자동차)
앞유리; **windshield wiper** waip'ŏ
와이퍼

windsurfer (*person*)
windŭsŏp'inghanŭn saram
윈드서핑하는 사람; (*board*)
windŭsŏp'ing podŭ 윈드서핑 보드

windsurfing windŭsŏp'ing 윈드서핑

windy *weather, day* param punŭn
바람 부는; *it's getting ~* parami
pulgi shijak'anda 바람이 불기
시작한다

wine p'odoju 포도주

wine list p'odoju menyu 포도주 메뉴

wing *n* nalgae 날개; *right ~/left ~* SP,
politics uik/chwaik 우익/좌익

wink 1 *n* wingk'ŭ 윙크 **2** *v/i* (*of person*) wingk'ŭhada 윙크하다; **~ at** …ege wingk'ŭhada …에게 윙크하다

winner usŭngja 우승자; (*in election*) tangsŏnja 당선자; (*in lottery*) tangch'ŏmja 당첨자; (*of prize*) susangja 수상자

winning *adj* igin 이긴; *lottery ticket* tangch'ŏmdoen 당첨된

winning post kyŏlssŭngjŏm 결승점

winnings sanggŭm 상금

winter *n* kyŏul 겨울

winter sports kyŏul sŭp'och'ŭ 겨울 스포츠

wintry kyŏul kat'ŭn 겨울같은

wipe *v/t* taktta 닦다; *tape* chiuda 지우다

♦ **wipe off** *dirty mark* takkanaeda 닦아내다; (*from tape*) chiuda 지우다

♦ **wipe out** (*kill, destroy*) chŏnmyŏlshik'ida 전멸시키다; *debt* wanje 완제

wire ch'ŏlssa 철사; ELEC chŏngit-tchul 전깃줄

wireless musŏnŭi 무선의

wire netting ch'ŏlmang 철망

wiring ELEC paesŏn 배선

wiry *person* tandanhan 단단한

wisdom chihye 지혜

wisdom tooth sarang-ni 사랑니

wise hyŏnmyŏng-han 현명한

wisecrack *n* ppyŏga innŭn nongdam 뼈가 있는 농담

wise guy *pej* anŭn ch'ŏk'anŭn nom 아는 척하는 놈

wisely *act* hyŏnmyŏng-hage 현명하게

wish 1 *n* sowŏn 소원; *best* **~es** modŭn iri chal toegirŭl paramnida 모든 일이 잘 되기를 바랍니다 **2** *v/t* …igirŭl parada …이기를 바랍니다; *I* **~** *that* … nanŭn …hagirŭl paramnida 나는 …하기를 바랍니다; **~ s.o. well** nuga chal toegirŭl parada 누가 잘 되기를 바라다; *I* **~ed him good luck** nanŭn kŭŭi haeng-unŭl pirŏt-tta 나는 그의 행운을 빌었다

♦ **wish for** parada 바라다

wishful thinking anihage nakkkwanjŏgin saenggak 안이하게 낙관적인 생각

wishy-washy *person* shishihan

wistful tamnaenŭn tŭt'an 탐내는 듯한; *color* hŭi-yŏmŏlgŏn 희여멀건

wisp (*of hair*) tabal 다발; (*of smoke*) chulgi 줄기

wistful tamnaenŭn tŭt'an 탐내는 듯한

wit (*humor*) chaech'i 재치; (*person*) chaech'i-innŭn saram 재치있는 사람; *be at one's* **~***'s end* ŏtchihal parŭl morŭda 어찌할 바를 모르다; *keep one's* **~***s about one* ch'imch'ak'age it-tta 침착하게 있다

witch manyŏ 마녀

witchcraft mabŏp 마법

with ◊ (*accompanied by, proximity*) …wa / kwa hamkke …와 / 과 함께; *I live ~ my aunt* nanŭn nae ajumŏniwa hamkke samnida 나는 내 아주머니와 함께 삽니다; *compare X* **~** *Y* Xŭl / rŭl Ywa / gwa pigyohada X을 / 를 Y와 / 과 비교하다; *be connected ~* …wa / kwa kwallyŏndoeda …와 / 과 관련되다; *are you ~ me?* (*do you understand?*) che marŭl aradŭrŭl su issŭmnikka? 제 말을 알아들을 수 있습니까?; **~** *no money* ton ŏpssi 돈 없이 ◊ (*instrument*) …(ŭ)ro …(으)로; *stabbed ~ a knife* k'allo tchillin 칼로 찔린 ◊ (*cause*) …(ŭ)ro …(으)로; *shivering ~ fear* turyŏumŭro ttŏnŭn 두려움으로 떠는 ◊ (*possession*) …i / ga innŭn …이 / 가 있는; *the house ~ the red door* ppalgan muni innŭn kŭ chip 빨간 문이 있는 그 집 ◊: *a smile /* **~** *a wave* usŭmyŏnsŏ / sontchit'amyŏnsŏ 웃으면서 / 손짓하면서 ◊: *be angry ~ s.o.* nuguege hwaga nada 누구에게 화가 나다; *be satisfied ~ sth* musŏse manjok'ada 무엇에 만족하다

withdraw 1 *v/t complaint, application* ch'wisohada 취소하다; *money from bank* ppaenaeda 빼내다; *troops* ch'ŏlssushik'ida 철수시키다 **2** *v/i* (*of competitor*) mullŏnada 물러나다; (*of troops*) ch'ŏlssuhada 철수하다

withdrawal (*of complaint, application*) ch'wiso 취소; (*of money*) inch'ul 인출; (*of troops*) ch'ŏlssu 철수; (*from drugs*) kkŭnŭm 끊음

withdrawal symptoms kŭmdan hyŏnsang 금단 현상

withdrawn 664

withdrawn *adj* person naesŏngjŏgin 내성적인

wither shidŭlda 시들다

withhold poryuhada 보류하다

within *prep* (*inside*) ...ane(sŏ) ...안에(서); (*time*) ...inae-e ...이내에; (*distance*) ...ane ...안에; *is it ~ walking distance?* kŏrŏsŏ kal su innŭn kŏri-imnikka? 걸어서 갈 수 있는 거리입니까?; *we kept ~ the budget* urinŭn yesanŭl nŏmtchi anat-tta 우리는 예산을 넘지 않았다; *~ my power / my capabilities* nae him / nŭngnyŏgŭro hal su innŭn 내 힘/능력으로 할 수 있는; *~ reach* kakkaun kose 가까운 곳에

without ...ŏpsshi ...없이; *~ looking / ~ asking* poji ank'o / murŏboji ank'o 보지 않고 / 물어보지 않고

withstand kyŏndiŏnaeda 견디어내다

witness 1 *n* (*at trial*) chŭng-in 증인; (*of accident, crime*) mok-kkyŏktcha 목격자; (*to signature*) chŭng-in sŏmyŏngham 증인으로 서명함 **2** *v/t* accident, crime mok-kkyŏk'ada 목격하다; signature chŭng-inŭro sŏmyŏnghada 증인으로 서명하다

witness stand chŭng-insŏk 증인석

witticism chaech'i 재치

witty chaech'i-innŭn 재치있는

wobble *v/i* hŭndŭlgŏrida 흔들거리다

wobbly hŭndŭlgŏrinŭn 흔들거리는; *voice* ttŏllinŭn 떨리는

wolf 1 *n* (*animal*) nŭkttae 늑대; *fig* (*womanizer*) paramdung-i 바람둥이 **2** *v/t: ~* (*down*) kyegŏlssŭre mŏkta 게걸스레 먹다

wolf whistle *n* maeryŏktchŏgin yŏjarŭl pogo punŭn hwip'aram 매력적인 여자를 보고 부는 휘파람

woman yŏja 여자

woman doctor yŏŭisa 여의사

womanizer paramdung-i 바람둥이

womanly yŏjadaun 여자다운

woman priest yŏja mokssa 여자 목사

womb chagung 자궁

women's lib yŏsŏng haebang undong 여성 해방 운동

women's libber yŏsŏng haebang undongga 여성 해방 운동가

won FIN wŏn 원

wonder 1 *n* (*amazement*) nollaum 놀라움; *no ~!* tang-yŏnhae! 당연해!; *it's a ~ that* ...ranŭn kŏsŭn nollaun irida ...라는 것은 놀라운 일이다 **2** *v/i* ŭi-ahage yŏgida 의아하게 여기다 **3** *v/t* kunggŭmhada 궁금하다; *I ~ if you could help* tangshini towajul su innŭnji kunggŭmhamnida 당신이 도와줄 수 있는지 궁금합니다

wonderful nollaun 놀라운

wood namu 나무; (*forest*) sup 숲

wooded namuga ugŏjin 나무가 우거진

wooden namuro toen 나무로 된

woodpecker ttakttaguri 딱따구리

woodwind MUS mok-kkwanak-kki 목관악기

woodwork (*wooden parts*) moktcho pubun 목조 부분; (*activity*) mok-kkong 목공

wool yangmo 양모

woolen 1 *adj* mojik 모직 **2** *n* mojingmul 모직물

word 1 *n* tanŏ 단어; (*in Bible*) pogŭm 복음; (*news*) soshik 소식; (*promise*) yakssok 약속; *I couldn't understand a ~ of what he said* kŭga hanŭn marŭn hanado ihaehal su ŏpssŏssŏyo 그가 하는 말은 하나도 이해할 수 없었어요; *is there any ~ from ...?* ...(ŭ)robut'ŏ soshigi issŏyo? ...(으)로부터 소식이 있어요?; *you have my ~* naega yakssok'agessŭmnida 내가 약속하겠습니다; *~s* (*of song*) kasa 가사; *have ~s* (*argue*) maldat'umhada 말다툼하다; *have a ~ with* ...wa / kwa handu madi marhada ...와/과 한두 마디 말하다 **2** *v/t* article, letter marŭl kollasŏ ssŭda 말을 골라서 쓰다

wording p'yohyŏn 표현

word processing wŏdŭ p'ŭrosesŭrŭl sayong 워드 프로세스를 사용

word processor (*software*) wŏdŭ p'ŭrosesŏ 워드 프로세서

work 1 *n* il 일; *out of ~* shiltchik'an 실직한; *be at ~* irhago it-tta 일하고 있다; (*at office*) chiktchang-e it-tta 직장에 있다; *I go to ~ by bus* nanŭn

pŏsŭro ch'ulgŭnhamnida 나는
버스로 출근합니다 2 v/i (of person)
irhada 일하다; (of student)
kongbuhada 공부하다; (of machine)
umjigida 움직이다; (succeed) chal
toeda 잘 되다; **how does it ~?** (of
device) ŏttŏk'e sayonghamnikka?
어떻게 사용합니까? 3 v/t employee
irŭl shik'ida 일을 시키다; machine
sayonghada 사용하다

♦ **work off** bad mood, anger ttan irŭl
haesŏ ijŏbŏrige hada 딴 일을 해서
잊어버리게 하다; flab undong-ŭro
sarŭl ppaeda 운동으로 살을 빼다

♦ **work out 1** v/t problem p'ulda 풀다;
solution haegyŏrhada 해결하다 2 v/i
(at gym) undonghada 운동하다; (of
relationship etc) chal toeda 잘 되다

♦ **work out to** (add up to) naoda
나오다

♦ **work up** enthusiasm pullŏ irŭk'ida
불러 일으키다; appetite totkkuda
돋구다; **get worked up** (angry)
hwaga nada 화가 나다; (nervous)
puranhaejida 불안해지다

workable solution shirhaeng
kanŭnghan 실행 가능한

workaholic n ilppŏlle 일벌레

workday (hours of work) kŭnmu
shigan 근무 시간; (not a holiday)
p'yŏng-il 평일

worker nodongja 노동자; **she's a
good ~** (of student) kŭnyŏnŭn
kongburŭl yŏlsshimi handa 그녀는
공부를 열심히 한다

workforce (of company) chŏn
chong-ŏbwŏn 전 종업원; (of
country) nodong in-gu 노동 인구

work hours kŭnmu shigan 근무 시간

working class nodongja kyegŭp
노동자 계급; **working-class**
nodongja kyegŭbŭi 노동자 계급의;
working knowledge kibonjŏgin
chishik 기본적인 지식

workload ŏmmuryang 업무량;
workman chagŏp inbu 작업 인부;
workmanlike somsshi innŭn 솜씨
있는; **workmanship** somsshi 솜씨;
work of art yesulp'um 예술품;
workout yŏnsŭp 연습; **work permit**
nodong hŏga 노동 허가; **workshop**

chagŏptchang 작업장; (seminar)
wŏk'ŭshyop 워크숍; **work station**
tongnip chagŏp konggan 독립 작업
공간

world segye 세계; (social) sesang 세상;
**the ~ of computers / the ~ of the
theater** k'ŏmpyut'ŏgye / yŏngŭk-
kkye 컴퓨터계 / 연극계; **out of this ~**
Ƒ tŏ hal nawiŏmnŭn 더 할 나위없는

worldly sesoktchŏgin 세속적인;
person sesang multchŏng-e palgŭn
세상 물정에 밝은; **~ goods** chaemul
재물

world power segyejŏk kangdaeguk
세계적 강대국; **world war** segye
taejŏn 세계 대전; **worldwide 1** adj
segyejŏgin 세계적인 **2** adv
segyejŏgŭro 세계적으로

worm n pŏlle 벌레

worn-out shoes, carpet, part
tarhappajin 닳아빠진; person
chich'in 지친

worried kŏktchŏngsŭrŏn 걱정스런

worry 1 n kŏktchŏng 걱정 **2** v/t
kŏktchŏngshik'ida 걱정시키다;
(upset) puranhage hada 불안하게
하다 **3** v/i kŏktchŏnghada 걱정하다;
it will be alright, don't ~!
kwaench'anŭl kŏshimnida,
kŏktchonghaji maseyo! 괜찮을
것입니다. 걱정하지 마세요!

worrying kŏktchŏngdoenŭn 걱정되는

worse 1 adj tŏ nappŭn 더 나쁜 **2** adv
tŏ nappŭge 더 나쁘게

worsen v/i tŏ nappajida 더 나빠지다

worship 1 n sungbae 숭배 **2** v/t
sungbaehada 숭배하다; fig maeu
saranghada 매우 사랑하다

worst 1 adj kajang nappŭn 가장 나쁜
2 adv kajang nappŭge 가장 나쁘게
3 n: **the ~** ch'oe-ak 최악; **if the ~
comes to ~** ch'oe-agŭi sangt'ae-
enŭn 최악의 상태에는

worth adj: **$20 ~ of gas** iship tallŏ
ŏch'iŭi kasŭ 이십 달러 어치의 가스;
be ~ ... ŭi kach'iga it-tta ...의 가치가
있다; **how much is it ~?** kŭgŏsŭn
ŏlmaimnikka? 그것은 얼마입니까?;
be ~ reading / seeing ilgŭl / pol
manhada 읽을 / 볼 만하다; **be ~ it** hal
manhada 할 만하다

worthless *object* kach'iga ŏmnŭn 가치가 없는; *person* ssŭlmo ŏmnŭn 쓸모없는

worthwhile *cause* porami innŭn 보람이 있는; **be ~** *(beneficial, useful)* ssŭlmoit-tta 쓸모있다; *(worth the effort)* hal manhada 할 만하다

worthy chon-gyŏnghal manhan 존경할 만한; *cause* chijihal manhan 지지할 만한; **be ~ of** *(deserve)* …ŭl/rŭl padŭl manhan …을/를 받을 만한

would: I ~ help if I could towadŭril su issŭmyŏn towadŭrigettchiyo 도와드릴 수 있으면 도와드리겠지요; **I said that I ~ go** nanŭn kaget-ttago maraessŭmnida 나는 가겠다고 말했습니다; **I told him I ~ not leave unless ...** nanŭn kŭege ...haji annŭn han ttŏnaji ank'et-ttago maraessŭmnida 나는 그에게 ...하지 않는 한 떠나지 않겠다고 말했습니다; **~ you like to go to the movies?** yŏnghwa porŏ kalkkayo? 영화 보러 갈까요?; **~ you mind if I smoked?** tambaerŭl p'iwŏdo kwaench'anayo? 담배를 피워도 괜찮아요?; **~ you tell her that ...?** kŭnyŏege ...rago marhaejushigessŭmnikka? 그녀에게 ...라고 말해주시겠습니까?; **~ you close the door?** munŭl tadajushigessŭmnikka? 문을 닫아주시겠습니까?; **I ~ have told you but ...** tangshinege yaegihaessŏya haetchiman... 당신에게 얘기했어야 했지만...; **I ~ not have been so angry if ...** ...myŏn nanŭn kŭrŏk'e hwarŭl naeji anassŭl kŏshimnida ...면 나는 그렇게 화를 내지 않았을 것입니다

wound 1 *n* sangch'ŏ 상처; *(in war)* pusang 부상 **2** *v/t* *(with weapon)* sangch'ŏrŭl ip'ida 상처를 입히다; *(with remark)* sanghage hada 상하게 하다

wow *interj* wa 와

wrap *v/t* *parcel, gift* ssada 싸다; *(cover, wind)* kamtta 감다

♦ **wrap up** *v/i* *(against the cold)* ttattŭt'age iptta 따뜻하게 입다

wrapper *(for product, candy)* p'ojangji 포장지

wrapping p'ojang chaeryo 포장 재료

wrapping paper p'ojangji 포장지

wrath punno 분노

wreath hwahwan 화환

wreck 1 *n* chanhae 잔해; **be a nervous ~** shin-gyŏng soeyagida 신경 쇠약이다 **2** *v/t* ŏngmang-ŭro p'agoehada 엉망으로 파괴하다; *plans, career, marriage* ŏngmang-ŭro mandŭlda 엉망으로 만들다

wreckage *(of car, plane)* chanhae 잔해; **~ of marriage / career** mangch'yŏjin kyŏrhon / kyŏngnyŏk 망쳐진 결혼 / 경력

wrecker kujoch'a 구조차

wrecking company ch'aryang kujo hoesa 차량 구조 회사

wrench 1 *n* *(tool)* lench'i 렌치; *(injury)* pp'im 삠 **2** *v/t* *(injure)* pit'ŭlda 비틀다; *(pull)* ŏktchiro ppaeda 억지로 빼다

wrestle sshirŭmhada 씨름하다

♦ **wrestle with** *problems* ...wa / kwa sshirŭmhada ...와 / 과 씨름하다

wrestler *(Korean)* sshirŭm sŏnsu 씨름 선수; *(western)* lesŭlling sŏnsu 레슬링 선수

wrestling *(Korean)* sshirŭm 씨름; *(western)* lesŭlling 레슬링

wrestling contest *(Korean)* sshirŭm kyŏnggi 씨름 경기; *(western)* lesŭlling kyŏnggi 레슬링 경기

wriggle *v/i* *(squirm)* momburimch'ida 몸부림치다; *(along the ground)* kkumt'ŭlgŏrimyŏ naagada 꿈틀거리며 나아가다

♦ **wriggle out of** hech'yŏnagada 헤쳐나가다

♦ **wring out** *cloth* tchada 짜다

wrinkle 1 *n* churŭm 주름 **2** *v/t* *clothes* churŭmjige hada 주름지게 하다 **3** *v/i* *(of clothes)* churŭmjida 주름지다

wrist sonmok 손목

wristwatch sonmok shigye 손목 시계

writ LAW yŏngtchang 영장

write 1 *v/t* ssŭda 쓰다; *music* chakkkok'ada 작곡하다 **2** *v/i* *(of author)* kŭrŭl ssŭda 글을 쓰다; *(send a letter)* p'yŏnjirŭl ssŭda

편지를 쓰다
♦ **write down** padajŏktta 받아적다
♦ **write off** *debt* ch'ŏngsanhada
청산하다; *car* pakssallaeda 박살내다
writer chak-kka 작가; (*of song*) chak-kkok-kka 작곡가
write-up p'yŏngnon 평론
writhe momburimch'ida 몸부림치다
writing (*as career*) kŭl ssŭgi 글 쓰기; (*hand-~*) kŭlsshi 글씨; (*words*) ssŭgi 쓰기; (*script*) kirok 기록; *in ~* sŏmyŏnŭro 서면으로
writing desk ch'aekssang 책상
writing paper p'ilgi yongji 필기 용지
wrong 1 *adj* t'ŭllin 틀린; *decision, choice* chalmot-ttoen 잘못된; *be ~*

(*of person*) t'ŭllida 틀리다; (*morally*) nappŭda 나쁘다; *what's ~?* musŭn iriyeyo? 무슨 일이에요?; *there is something ~ with the car* ch'a-e muŏshin-ga isang-i it-tta 차에 무엇인가 이상이 있다 **2** *adv* chalmot 잘못; *go ~* (*of person*) t'ŭllida 틀리다; (*of marriage, plan etc*) chalmot-ttoeda 잘못되다 **3** *n* chalmot 잘못; *right and ~* chaljalmot 잘잘못; *be in the ~* chalmoshida 잘못이다
wrongful pudanghan 부당한
wrongly pudanghage 부당하게
wrong number chalmot kŏllin chŏnhwa 잘못 걸린 전화
wry pikkonŭn 비꼬는

XY

xenophobia oegugin hyŏmo 외국인 혐오
X-ray 1 *n* Xsŏn X선 **2** *v/t* Xsŏn ch'waryŏng-ŭl hada X선 촬영을 하다

yacht yot'ŭ 요트
yachting yot'ŭ t'agi 요트 타기
yachtsman yot'ŭ chojongja 요트 조종자
Yalu River Amnok-kkang 압록강
Yank *n* F Miguk saram 미국 사람
yank *v/t* hwaek tanggida 홱 당기다
yap *v/i* (*of dog*) k'aengk'aeng chit-tta 캥캥 짖다; F (*talk a lot*) chaejalgŏrida 재잘거리다
yard[1] (*of prison, institution etc*) kunae 구내; (*behind house*) twinmadang 뒷마당; (*for storage*) mulgŏn tunŭn kot 물건 두는 곳
yard[2] (*measurement*) yadŭ 야드
yardstick *fig* ch'ŏktto 척도
yarn *n* (*thread*) shil 실; F (*story*) kkumyŏnaen iyagi 꾸며낸 이야기
yawn 1 *n* hap'um 하품 **2** *v/i* hap'umhada 하품하다
year nyŏn 년; *for ~s* F yŏrŏ hae tong-an 여러 해 동안
yearly 1 *adj* maenyŏnŭi 매년의 **2** *adv* maenyŏn 매년
yearn *v/i* kalmanghada 갈망하다
♦ **yearn for** …ŭl/rŭl mopsshi parada …을/를 몹시 바라다
yearning *n* kalmang 갈망
yeast hyomo 효모
yell 1 *n* koham 고함 **2** *v/i* koham chirŭda 고함 지르다 **3** *v/t* kohamch'yŏ purŭda 고함쳐 부르다
yellow 1 *n* norang 노랑 **2** *adj* noran 노란
yellow pages ŏptchongbyŏl chŏnhwa pŏnhobu 업종별 전화 번호부
Yellow Sea Hwanghae 황해, Sŏhae 서해
yelp 1 *n* kkaengkkaenggŏrinŭn sori

깽깽거리는 소리 **2** *v/i* kkaengkkaenggŏrida 깽깽거리다
yen FIN en 엔
yes ye 예 ◊ (*using 'no', ie no, that is not right*): *you don't know the answer, do you? – oh ~, I do* tabŭl morŭjyo? - aniyo, arayo 답을 모르죠? - 아니요, 알아요
yesman *pej* ach'ŏmkkun 아첨꾼
yesterday ŏje 어제; *the day before ~* kŭjŏkke 그저께
yet 1 *adv* ajik 아직; (*so far*) chigŭmkkaji 지금까지; *as ~* ajik-kkaji 아직까지; *have you finished ~?* inje ta kkŭnnaessŏyo? 인제 다 끝냈어요?; *he hasn't arrived ~* kŭnŭn ajik toch'ak'aji anat-tta 그는 아직 도착하지 않았다; *is he here? – not ~* kŭnŭn yŏgi wassŏyo? – ajik anwassŏyo 그는 여기 왔어요? - 아직 안왔어요; *~ bigger/longer* tŏuk tŏ k'ŭn/kin 더욱 더 큰/긴 **2** *conj* (*all the same, still*) yŏjŏnhi 여전히; *I'm not sure ~* yŏjŏnhi hwaksshinhal su ŏpssŏyo 여전히 확신할 수 없어요
yield 1 *n* (*from fields etc*) sanch'ul 산출; (*from investment*) iik 이익 **2** *v/t fruit, good harvest* sanch'urhada 산출하다; *interest* iigŭl naeda 이익을 내다 **3** *v/i* (*give way*) yangbohada 양보하다
yin and yang ŭmyang 음양
YMCA (= *Young Men's Christian Association*) Kidok-kkyo Ch'ŏngnyŏnhoe 기독교 청년회
yoghurt yogurŭt'ŭ 요구르트
yolk norŭnja 노른자
you ◊ nŏ 너; (*polite*) tangshin 당신; (*plural*) nŏhŭidŭl 너희들; (*plural polite*) yŏrŏbundŭl 여러분들; *he knows ~* kŭnŭn tangshinŭl arayo 그는 당신을 알아요; *that's for ~* naŭi kŏshida 나의 것이다 ◊ (*omission of pronoun*): *when are*

669

youth hostel

~ coming back? ŏnje toraol
kŏmnikka? 언제 돌아올 겁니까? ◊:
~ never know kyŏlk'o al su ŏmnŭn
iriyeyo 결코 알 수 없는 일이에요; *~
can't trust him* kŭnŭn midŭl su
ŏpssŏyo 그는 믿을 수 없어요
young chŏlmŭn 젊은; *wine*
sukssŏngdoeji anŭn 숙성되지 않은
youngster chŏlmŭni 젊은이
your nŏŭi 너의; (*polite*) tangshinŭi
당신의
yours nŏŭi kŏt 너의 것; (*polite*)
tangshinŭi kŏt 당신의 것; *a friend
of ~* nŏŭi / tangshinŭi ch'in-gu
너의 / 당신의 친구; *Yours ...* (*at end*

of letter) ...ollim ...올림
yourself ne chashin 네 자신; (*polite*)
tangshin chashin 당신 자신; *by ~*
honjasŏ 혼자서
yourselves nŏhŭidŭl chashin 너희들
자신; (*polite*) tangshindŭl chashin
당신들 자신; *by ~* nŏhŭidŭl sŭsŭro
너희들 스스로
youth (*age*) ch'ŏngch'un-gi 청춘기;
(*young man*) chŏlmŭni 젊은이;
(*young people*) chŏlmŭn saram 젊은
사람
youthful chŏlmŭn 젊은
youth hostel yusŭ hosŭt'el 유스
호스텔

Z

zap v/t (*delete*) saktchehada 삭제하다;
F (*kill*) haech'iuda 해치우다; F (*hit*)
ch'ida 치다
♦zap along F (*move fast*) chaepssage
umjigida 잽싸게 움직이다
zapped F (*exhausted*) chich'in 지친
zappy F *car, pace* pparün 빠른; (*lively,
energetic*) wŏn-giwangsŏnghan
원기왕성한
zeal yŏlsshim 열심
zebra ŏllungmal 얼룩말
Zen sŏn 선
Zen Buddhism sŏnbulgyo 선불교
zero kong 공, yŏng 영; *10 below ~*
yŏngha 10to 영하 10도
♦zero in on (*identify*) aranaeda
알아내다
zero growth chero sŏngjang 제로
성장
zest yŏltchŏng 열정
zigzag 1 *n* chigŭjaegŭhyŏng
지그재그형 2 *v/i* chigŭjaegŭro
umjigida 지그재그로 움직이다
zilch F amu kŏt-tto opssŭm 아무 것도
없음

zinc ayŏn 아연
♦zip up v/t chip'ŏrŭl chamgŭda
지퍼를 잠그다; COMPUT apch'uk'ada
하다
zip code up'yŏn pŏnho 우편 번호
zipper chip'ŏ 지퍼
zither (*with seven strings*) ajaeng
아쟁; (*plucked*) kŏmun-go 거문고
zodiac hwangdodae 황도대; *signs of
the ~* hwangdodaeŭi shibi kung
황도대의 십이 궁
zombie F (*barely human person*)
nŏng nagan saram 넋 나간 사람;
feel like a ~ (*exhausted*)
kijinmaektchinhan 기진맥진한
zone chidae 지대
zoo tongmurwŏn 동물원
zoological tongmurhakssang-ŭi
동물학상의
zoology tongmurhak 동물학
zoom F (*move fast*) kŭp'i kada 급히
가다
♦zoom in on PHOT chumnenjŭro
match'uda 줌렌즈로 맞추다
zoom lens chumnenjŭ 줌렌즈

Numbers

	Korean		**Sino-Korean**	
0	kong	공	yŏng	영
1	hana	하나	il	일
2	tul	둘	i	이
3	set	셋	sam	삼
4	net	넷	sa	사
5	tasŏt	다섯	o	오
6	yŏsŏt	여섯	yuk	육
7	ilgop	일곱	ch'il	칠
8	yŏdŏl	여덟	p'al	팔
9	ahop	아홉	ku	구
10	yŏl	열	ship	십
11	yŏrhana	열 하나	shibil	십일
12	yŏldul	열 둘	shibi	십이
13	yŏlsset	열 셋	shipssam	십삼
14	yŏllet	열 넷	shipssa	십사
15	yŏldasŏt	열 다섯	shibo	십오
16	yŏlyŏsŏt	열 여섯	shimyuk	십육
17	yŏrilgop	열 일곱	shipch'il	십칠
18	yŏlyŏdŏl	열 여덟	shipp'al	십팔
19	yŏrahop	열 아홉	shipkku	십구
20	sŭmul	스물	iship	이십
21	sŭmul hana	스물 하나	ishibil	이십일
30	sŏrŭn	서른	samship	삼십
35	sŏrŭn tasŏt	서른 다섯	samshibo	삼십오
40	mahŭn	마흔	saship	사십
50	shwin	쉰	oship	오십
60	yesun	예순	yukssip	육십
70	irhŭn	일흔	ch'ilssip	칠십
80	yŏdŭn	여든	p'alssip	팔십
90	ahŭn	아흔	kuship	구십
100	*no native Korean*		paek	백
101	*numbers above 99*		paegil	백일
200			ibaek	이백
1,000			ch'ŏn	천
2,000			ich'ŏn	이천
10,000			man	만
20,000			iman	이만
100,000			shimman	십만
1,000,000			paengman	백만
2,000,000			ibaengman	이백만
10,000,000			ch'ŏnman	천만
100,000,000			ŏk	억
1,000,000,000			ship ŏk	십억
8,655			p'alch'ŏnyuk-paegoshibo	팔천육백오십오

	Korean	Sino-Korean
1st	ch'ŏt pŏntchaeŭi 첫 번째의	che irŭi 제 1의
2nd	tu pŏntchaeŭi 두 번째의	che iŭi 제 2의
3rd	se pŏntchaeŭi 세 번째의	che samŭi 제 3의
4th	ne pŏntchaeŭi 네 번째의	che saŭi 제 4의
5th	tasŏt pŏntchaeŭi 다섯 번째의	che oŭi 제 5의
6th	yŏsŏt pŏntchaeŭi 여섯 번째의	che yugŭi 제 6의
7th	ilgop pŏntchaeŭi 일곱 번째의	che ch'irŭi 제 7의
8th	yŏdŏl pŏntchaeŭi 여덟 번째의	che p'arŭi 제 8의
9th	ahop pŏntchaeŭi 아홉 번째의	che kuŭi 제 9의
10th	yŏl pŏntchaeŭi 열 번째의	che shipŭi 제 10의
11th	yŏrhan pŏntchaeŭi 열 한 번째의	che shibirŭi 제 11의
12th	yŏldu pŏntchaeŭi 열 두 번째의	che shibiŭi 제 12의
13th	yŏlsse pŏntchaeŭi 열 세 번째의	che shipsamŭi 제 13의
14th	yŏlne pŏntchaeŭi 열 네 번째의	che shipsaŭi 제 14의
15th	yŏldasŏt pŏntchaeŭi 열 다섯 번째의	che shiboŭi 제 15의
16th	yŏl yŏsŏt pŏntchaeŭi 열 여섯 번째의	che shimyugŭi 제 16의
17th	yŏrilgop pŏntchaeŭi 열 일곱 번째의	che shipch'irŭi 제 17의
18th	yŏlyŏdŏl pŏntchaeŭi 열 여덟 번째의	che shipp'arŭi 제 18의
19th	yŏrahop pŏntchaeŭi 열 아홉 번째의	che shipguŭi 제 19의
20th	sŭmu pŏntchaeŭi 스무 번째의	che ishibŭi 제 20의
21st	sŭmul han pŏntchaeŭi 스물 한 번째의	che ishibirŭi 제 21의
30th	sŏrŭn pŏntchaeŭi 서른 번째의	che samshibŭi 제 30의
40th	mahŭn pŏntchaeŭi 마흔 번째의	che sashibŭi 제 40의
50th	shwin pŏntchaeŭi 쉰 번째의	che oshibŭi 제 50의
60th	yesun pŏntchaeŭi 예순 번째의	che yukshibŭi 제 60의
70th	irhŭn pŏntchaeŭi 일흔 번째의	che ch'ilsshibŭi 제 70의
80th	yŏdŭn pŏntchaeŭi 여든 번째의	che p'alsshibŭi 제 80의
90th	ahŭn pŏntchaeŭi 아흔 번째의	che kushibŭi 제 90의
100th	paek pŏntchaeŭi 백 번째의	che paekŭi 제 100의

Korean numbers are usually used with countwords such as **chan** 잔 (cup), **myŏng** 명 (person), **k'yŏlle** 컬레 (pair), **pŏn** 번 (time). When used in this way **hana**, **tul**, **set**, and **net** contract to **han**, **tu**, **se**, **ne**:

k'ŏp'i han chan
커피 한 잔
a cup of coffee

kyosu se myŏng
교수 세 명
three professors

Sino-Korean cardinal numbers are used with (amongst other things) dates, money and foreign loanwords. To tell the time, Korean numbers are used for hours and Sino-Korean for minutes and seconds:

ich'ŏnillyŏn irwŏl iril
이천일년 일월 일일
1st January 2001

samship k'illomit'ŏ
삼십 킬로미터
30 kilometers

ohu seshi samship-ppun
오후 세시 삼십분
3.30pm

han shigan shippun och'o
한 시간 십분 오초
1 hour, 10 minutes and 5 seconds